May 25, 1973: White House issues statement on San Clemente financing.

June 12, 1973: Sirica grants Dean, Magruder immunity for Senate testimony. Stans denies involvement in Senate testimony.

June 21, 1973: GSA reports U.S. spent $1.9 million on Nixon homes.

June 25–29, 1973: Dean implicates Nixon in cover-up during Senate testimony; submits list of "enemies."

July 10–12, 1973: Mitchell tells Ervin panel he withheld Watergate information from Nixon.

July 16, 1973: President's secret tape recording system revealed by former aide during Senate testimony.

July 16–17, 1973: Kalmbach testifies he raised money for payoffs to Watergate defendants.

July 17, 1973: Nixon bars Secret Service testimony on tapes; Ervin requests tapes.

July 20, 23, 1973: Strachan testifies Haldeman ordered him to clean files after break-in.

July 23, 26, 1973: Nixon defies Ervin and Cox subpoenas on tapes.

July 24–27, 30, 1973: Ehrlichman testifies at Senate hearings: disputes Dean; defends Nixon and Ellsberg break-in.

July 30–August 1, 1973: Haldeman denies cover-up role at Senate hearings; admits refreshing memory by listening to secret tapes.

August 1, 1973: Colson memo linking ITT antitrust deal to White House revealed at Senate hearings.

August 2–7, 1973: Helms, Cushman, Walters, Gray, Kleindienst, Petersen testify at Senate hearings.

August 6, 1973: Agnew reported under criminal investigation.

August 7, 1973: Nixon rejects courts' right to demand tapes.

August 8, 1973: Agnew denounces charges; says he won't resign.

August 9, 1973: Ervin committee sues for Watergate tapes.

August 22, 1973: Nixon accepts Watergate 'responsibility'; vows not to resign.

August 29, 1973: Sirica orders Nixon to turn over tapes; Nixon refuses.

September 4, 1973: Ehrlichman, 3 others indicted in Ellsberg break-in.

September 6–7, 1973: Nixon, Cox appeal Sirica's ruling on tapes.

September 26, 1973: House Speaker Albert denies Agnew's request for impeachment inquiry.

September 29, 1973: Agnew attacks Justice Department and defends innocence. Richardson backs Petersen.

October 3, 1973: Agnew gets subpoena power to probe leaks. Nixon backs Agnew, but defends Petersen.

October 10, 1973: Agnew resigns and pleads 'no contest' to tax evasion charge.

October 12, 1973: Appeals court orders Nixon to surrender tapes.

October 19, 1973: Nixon proposes 'Stennis compromise' on tapes. Cox rejects Nixon order forbidding an appeal.

October 20, 1973: Nixon fires Cox; Richardson quits; Ruckelshaus fired.

October 21–24, 1973: Protest telegrams flood Congress demanding impeachment action.

October 23, 1973: Nixon reverses position, promises tapes to Sirica.

October 29, 1973: Nixon's order to drop ITT case leaked after Cox informs senators.

October 30, 1973: House begins impeachment inquiry.

October 31, 1973: White House lawyers tell court two key tapes never existed.

November 1, 1973: Saxbe named attorney general; Jaworski appointed as new special prosecutor.

November 7, 1973: Nixon insists he will not resign.

November 9–20, 1973: Nixon launches Watergate counteroffensive.

November 12, 1973: Nixon memo of conversation with Dean reported missing.

November 20, 1973: Jaworski promises full-scale probe.

November 21, 1973: Erasure of subpoenaed tape of Nixon-Haldeman conversation disclosed. Rose Mary Woods takes responsibility for 'accident' during transcription.

December 7, 1973: Bahamas denies extradition of Vesco to U.S.

December 8, 1973: Nixon discloses data on personal finances.

December 19, 1973: Sirica upholds Nixon claims of executive privilege on 3 subpoenaed tapes.

WATERGATE

AND THE WHITE HOUSE
July–December 1973

Volume 2

WATERGATE
AND THE WHITE HOUSE
July-December 1973

Editors: Evan Drossman and Edward W. Knappman

Contributing Editors: Mary Elizabeth Clifford, Joseph
Fickes, Stephen Orlofsky, Gerald Satterwhite,
Joseph Sciarrino, Henry H. Schulte, Jr.

Volume 2

FACTS ON FILE ■ 119 WEST 57TH STREET ■ NEW YORK, NEW YORK

WATERGATE
AND THE WHITE HOUSE
July-December 1973

Volume 2

Library of Congress Catalog Card No. 73-83049

ISBN 0-87196-353-1

9 8 7 6 5 4 3 2

PRINTED IN THE UNITED STATES OF AMERICA

Preface

The first volume in this series (published in September 1973) recorded the lengthening list of charges against the Nixon Administration, culminating in John Dean's testimony accusing the President of full knowledge of and participation in the Watergate cover-up. Volume Two covers the period from July to December 1973, when attempts to prove or disprove these grave accusations raised questions about fundamental Constitutional issues, the rights and privileges of the Presidency. The first section of Volume Two traces developments in the Watergate affair and its related scandals from John Mitchell's testimony before the Ervin committee through the preparations of the House Judiciary Committee for its study of impeachment. Written by the editors of the Facts On File Weekly News Digest, this section reports every important event, statement and court decision—clearly, concisely and objectively.

The second half of Watergate and the White House consists of full-text editorials from some 120 major newspapers commenting on the principal Watergate developments between July and December. Carefully selected by the editors of Editorials On File, these 300 editorials represent a true cross-section of American opinion on every important aspect of the Watergate Affair.

As this volume goes to press, the focus of public attention is shifting toward the House of Representatives whose members must make the crucial decision on impeachment. But the courts are far from finished with Watergate. Grand jury indictments of many of President Nixon's former aides and advisors are assumed to be imminent. These and other developments are likely to bring the Watergate Affair to a climax within the next few months. We anticipate the third volume of Watergate and the White House will record that climax.

Evan Drossman
Edward W. Knappman
January 28, 1974

Contents:

EDITORIAL REACTION TO THE WATERGATE AFFAIR

Biographical Sketches

AGNEW, Spiro T.: Resigned vice presidency after pleading 'no contest' to charge of income tax evasion in connection with alleged acceptance of kickbacks while Maryland governor.

BAKER Jr., Sen. Howard H.: Vice-chairman of Senate Watergate committee.

BARKER, Bernard L.: Former CIA agent arrested at Watergate break-in, pled guilty at trial, sentenced, later changed plea, testified before Senate Watergate panel.

BORK, Robert H.: U.S. solicitor general, dismissed Cox as Watergate prosecutor following resignation of Richardson as attorney general and firing of Deputy Attorney General Ruckelshaus, named Jaworski new Watergate prosecutor.

BUCHANAN, Patrick J.: Nixon speechwriter, testified at Senate Watergate hearings that Democrats were guilty of similar campaign activities as those allegedly committed by GOP.

BUTTERFIELD, Alexander P.: FAA chief, former Nixon aide, revealed existence of secret tape recording setup to monitor White House conversations during Senate testimony.

BUZHARDT, J. Fred.: Special counsel to the President on Watergate matters, testified before Sirica about two non-existent subpoenaed Watergate tapes and a third partially-erased tape.

CHAPIN, Dwight L.: Haldeman's former chief aide and appointments secretary to President Nixon, implicated in CRP espionage activities and Watergate cover-up, indicted for perjury before Watergate grand jury.

COLSON, Charles W.: Former special counsel to the President, implicated in alleged CRP espionage plot, memo to Haldeman warning of possible revelation of Administration links to ITT anti-trust settlement revealed at Senate Watergate hearings, refused to testify before Senate panel after immunity from prosecution denied.

COX, Archibald: Former Harvard Law professor, appointed special Watergate prosecutor by Attorney General Richardson, fired at President Nixon's order following disagreement over Watergate tapes.

CUSHMAN Jr., Robert E.: Marine Corps commandant, testified that as deputy CIA director he gave assistance to plumbers' operation.

DASH, Samuel: Chief counsel and staff director for Senate Select Committee investigating Watergate.

DEAN 3rd, John W.: Former counsel to the President, forced to resign, admitted helping to coordinate Watergate cover-up and implicated President Nixon in Senate testimony, pled guilty to one count of conspiracy while agreeing to be a witness for federal prosecution.

EHRLICHMAN, John D.: Former adviser to the President on domestic affairs, implicated in Watergate cover-up, resigned from office, defended Nixon and denied wrongdoing at Senate Watergate hearings, indicted for alleged role in break-in at office of Ellsberg's psychiatrist.

ELLSBERG, Daniel: Defendant in Pentagon Papers trial, freed when the case was dismissed following disclosure of the White House 'plumbers' group's break-in at his psychiatrist's office.

ERVIN Jr., Sen. Sam J.: Chairman of Senate Watergate committee.

FORD, Gerald R.: Former house minority leader, nominated and confirmed to succeed Agnew as vice president.

GARMENT, Leonard: Replaced Dean as counsel to the President.

GESELL, Judge Gerhard A.: U.S. District Court judge, sentenced Segretti, ruled Cox firing illegal.

GONZALEZ, Virgilio R.: Associate of Bernard Barker, arrested at Watergate break-in, pled guilty, changed plea, sentenced.

GRAY 3rd, L. Patrick: Asked nomination as FBI director be withdrawn after admission he destroyed sensitive portion of Hunt's files, testified before Watergate panel on FBI's Watergate investigation.

GURNEY, Sen. Edward J.: Republican member of Senate Watergate committee, admitted benefiting from secret political fund.

HAIG Jr., Gen. Alexander M.: Former Army vice chief of staff, named permanent chief of White House staff to replace Haldeman.

HALDEMAN, H.R.: Former White House chief of staff, implicated in Watergate cover-up, accused of organizing GOP espionage operations, resigned from office, defended Nixon, denied any personal guilt in Watergate affair, and admitted listening to Watergate tapes during Senate testimony.

HELMS, Richard M.: Former CIA director, testified at Senate Watergate hearings on agency aid given to Hunt in support of 'plumbers' operations and use of CIA to block FBI investigation of Watergate.

HUGHES, Howard R.: Billionaire industrialist, gave campaign gift given to Nixon friend Rebozo, which was returned 3 years afterwards.

HUNT Jr., E. Howard: Former White House consultant, pled guilty to role in Watergate conspiracy, appealed, sentenced, later linked to cover-up and 'plumbers,' testified at Senate hearings on GOP dirty tricks. His wife Dorothy was channel for money from CRP to defendants.

JAWORSKI, Leon: Houston lawyer named by then Acting Attorney General Bork to replace Cox as Watergate special prosecutor.

KALMBACH, Herbert W.: Former personal attorney to President Nixon and GOP fund raiser, testified before Ervin panel on role in payments made to Watergate defendants.

KISSINGER, Henry A.: Former national security adviser to the President, nominated and confirmed as secretary of state after investigation of authorization of wiretaps on National Security Council personnel.

KLEINDIENST, Richard G.: Former U.S. attorney general, resigned from office, testified at Senate Watergate hearings.

KROGH Jr., Egil: Former White House aide, transportation undersecretary, member of 'plumbers' group, indicted for break-in at office of Ellsberg psychiatrist, pled guilty, indicted for perjury.

LAIRD, Melvin R.: Former secretary of defense, named chief domestic adviser to the President replacing Ehrlichman, resigned December 1973.

LaRUE, Frederick C.: Former Mitchell campaign aide, testified before Ervin panel on payments made to Watergate defendants, intelligence plan vs. Democrats.

LIDDY, G. Gordon: Former presidential assistant and counsel to Finance Committee to Re-Elect the President and member of 'plumbers' group, tried and convicted for involvement in Watergate conspiracy, indicted for break-in at Ellsberg's psychiatrist's office.

MacGREGOR, Clark: Successor to Mitchell as director of CRP, testified before Senate Watergate panel on contacts with Gray.

MAGRUDER, Jeb Stuart: Former deputy director of Committee to Re-Elect the President, admitted involvement in Watergate break-in and cover-up, implicated Mitchell at Senate Watergate hearings, pled guilty to Watergate conspiracy charges.

MARDIAN, Robert C.: Former assistant attorney general, denied in Senate testimony role in cover-up of Watergate facts, disputing testimony of LaRue and Magruder.

MARTINEZ, Eugenio: Associate of Bernard Barker, arrested at Watergate break-in, pled guilty, changed plea, sentenced.

McCORD Jr., James W.: Former CIA agent and, at time of arrest at Watergate break-in, security coordinator for Committee to Re-Elect the President, tried and convicted for Watergate role, sentenced, named Mitchell, Magruder and Dean in Senate testimony.

MITCHELL, John N.: Former U.S. attorney general, director of the Committee to Re-Elect the President, originally denied, later admitted to having some knowledge of Watergate cover-up, testified before Ervin panel that Nixon had no knowledge of break-in or cover-up and that he shielded the President from the truth about Watergate, indicted for dealings with financier Vesco.

MOORE, Richard A.: Former special counsel to the President, disputed Dean's testimony before Ervin committee.

PETERSEN, Henry E.: Former assistant attorney general, assigned interim Watergate prosecutor in April, testified before Ervin panel on investigation of Watergate break-in. Denounced by Agnew for Justice Department leaks concerning his case.

REBOZO, Charles G. (Bebe): Personal friend of President Nixon, reported to have kept $100,000 political contribution from Howard Hughes to Nixon fund for three years before returning it, alleged to have been financial backer in Nixon purchase of San Clemente estate.

RICHARDSON, Elliot L.: Named attorney general to replace Kleindienst, resigned from office rather than dismiss Cox as Watergate prosecutor.

RUCKELSHAUS, William D.: Appointed deputy attorney general, fired following refusal to discharge prosecutor Cox.

SAXBE, Sen. William B.: Nominated successor to Richardson as attorney general, confirmed following enactment of law lowering salary of office.

SEGRETTI, Donald H.: Former California lawyer and GOP operative, pled guilty to political sabotage in Florida Democratic primary, testified at Senate Watergate hearings on dirty tricks employed by Nixon re-election aides.

SIRICA, Judge John J.: Watergate conspiracy trial judge, charged that prosecution had failed to develop all the facts behind break-in, handed down long prison terms credited with forcing conspirators to talk, ruled in favor of grand jury access to secret White House tapes.

STANS, Maurice H.: Former chief GOP fund raiser and chairman of Finance Committee to Re-Elect the President, testified before Ervin panel he had no prior knowledge of Watergate affair, alleged to have had role in Watergate cover-up, indicted in Vesco affair.

STRACHAN, Gordon C.: General counsel to USIA, former aide to Haldeman, linked to Watergate cover-up, implicated Magruder, Haldeman in Senate testimony.

STURGIS, Frank A.: Arrested at Watergate break-in, pled guilty, later changed plea, sentenced.

THOMPSON, Fred D.: Chief minority counsel on Senate Watergate committee.

ULASEWICZ, Anthony T.: Retired New York City detective, conducted investigations for the White House, testified at Watergate hearings on role in payoffs to Watergate defendants.

VESCO, Robert L.: Financier indicted with Mitchell, Stans for illegal contributions to GOP and for mutual fund violations, extradition from Bahamas denied.

WALTERS, Vernon A.: Deputy CIA director, disclosed in Senate testimony that White House aides had attempted to enlist agency's aid for 'plumbers' operations.

WEICKER Jr., Sen. Lowell P.: Republican member of Senate Watergate committee, outspoken in criticism of Nixon Watergate positions.

WILSON, John J.: Defense counsel for Ehrlichman, Haldeman, debated with Ervin over Presidential powers of executive privilege.

WOODS, Rose Mary: President Nixon's personal secretary, testified before Judge Sirica she may have been responsible for 18 minute erasure on Watergate tape.

WRIGHT, Charles Alan: Former law professor at University of Texas, appointed White House counsel, argued Administration tapes position before courts.

YOUNG Jr., David R.: Former National Security Council member, member of 'plumbers' group, indicted for break-in at Ellsberg' psychiatrist's office.

ZIEGLER, Ronald L.: Presidential press secretary, communications director, repeatedly denied White House Watergate involvement, declaring denials 'inoperative' following Nixon's April 17 speech.

John Mitchell Testifies at Senate Hearings

Nixon bars testimony, refuses access to files. President Nixon formally notified the Senate Watergate committee July 7 that he would not testify before the committee or permit it access to presidential papers. His press office had previously drawn the line against presidential testimony. The President stated his own position in a letter to the committee chairman, Sen. Ervin.

Nixon emphasized in his letter that his action was "based on my constitutional obligation to preserve intact the powers and prerogatives of the presidency and not upon any desire to withhold information relevant to your inquiry."

"At an appropriate time during your hearings," he wrote, "I intend to address publicly the subjects you are considering." He also said his staff was under instructions to cooperate fully with the committee in furnishing "information pertinent to your inquiry."

Elsewhere in the President's statement, however, he said "the White House will continue to cooperate fully with the committee in furnishing information relevant to its investigation except in those instances where I determine that meeting the committee's demands would violate my constitutional responsibility to defend the office of the presidency against encroachment by other branches."

The President described his "acts of cooperation with the committee" as "genuine, extensive and, in the history of such matters, extraordinary."

As for his refusal to provide presidential papers, Nixon said: "No president could function if the private papers of his office, prepared by his personal staff, were open to public scrutiny. Formulation of sound public policy requires that the president and his personal staff be able to communicate among themselves in complete candor, and that their tentative judgments, their exploration of alternatives, and their frank comments on issues and personalities at home and abroad remain confidential."

He concluded "that if I were to testify before the committee irreparable damage would be done to the constitutional principle of separation of powers."

Nixon said there were "ample precedents" supporting his action. He cited President Harry S. Truman's refusal in 1953 to comply with a subpoena of a House committee after he had left office. Truman had said he would be happy to testify about anything that happened before or after he was president but he could not be compelled to testify about anything that happened while he was in office because of the separation of powers doctrine.

Among the papers requested by the Watergate committee were copies of news summaries prepared for the President and other papers involving the tax status of charitable foundations. Former Nixon counsel John W. Dean 3rd had mentioned in his testimony that his White House files contained requests from White House aides about the possibility of removing tax shelters for such institutions that were "hostile" to the Administration.

Ervin critical of decision—Ervin's reaction to the Nixon letter was critical. He said later July 7 he believed that the committee had authority to subpoena presidential testimony and papers but that he opposed such action.

"If a president wants to withhold information from the committee and the American people," he said, "I would just let him take the consequences of that."

Ervin cited precedents going back to an 1807 Supreme Court ruling requiring that presidential documents relating to a treason trial be produced.

Other committee reaction—Committee vice chairman Howard H. Baker Jr. (R, Tenn.) said July 8 the separation of powers doctrine barred the committee from subpoenaing the President, but he expressed hope "some other means can be worked out" to obtain Nixon's account of events.

Sen. Daniel K. Inouye (D, Hawaii) said testimony from Nixon was "vital to his future." While "silence does not necessarily indicate guilt," he said, "unfortunately many people do interpret silence in that manner."

Committee members Edward J. Gurney (R, Fla.) and Herman E. Talmadge (D, Ga.) appeared on the ABC "Issues and Answers" broadcast July 8. Gurney agreed with Nixon that confidential communications between a president and his staff "ought to be protected." But he also thought "we probably ought to be able to get any documents that have a direct bearing on this Watergate affair and who is involved and what happened, and I think we ought to have that for our committee deliberations."

Talmadge thought that "public records belong to the American public" and that a Senate committee "would have a right to see those records and to subpoena them if necessary."

Talmadge urged voluntary testimony by the President. "If he has nothing to hide, why does he refuse to appear?"

Nixon OKs 'courtesy' meeting with Ervin. While steadfastly refusing to testify or provide White House documents to the Senate Watergate committee, President Nixon consented July 12 to meet privately with committee chairman Ervin.

The President called Ervin during the committee's lunchtime break after receiving an urgent appeal by the panel for a conference to avert "the very grave possibility of a fundamental constitutional confrontation" over documents sought by the committee.

A White House spokesman later emphasized that Nixon's acquiescence to a meeting was merely a "courtesy" to Ervin and did not constitute any retreat from the President's position regarding presidential testimony or executive privilege.

The committee had met privately during the morning to consider subpoenaing White House documents, thus initiating a formal challenge to the doctrine of executive privilege. At the behest of Sen. Howard H. Baker (R, Tenn.), the committee agreed to one more attempt to persuade the President to voluntarily provide the documents.

Baker drafted the letter to Nixon and Ervin signed it. It said in part: "The committee feels that your position, . . . measured against the committee's responsibility to ascertain the facts, . . . presents the very grave possibility of a fundamental constitutional confrontation between the

Congress and the Presidency. We wish to avoid that, if possible."

Mitchell feared exposure of 'horror stories.' After a holiday recess, the Senate Watergate committee resumed its hearings July 10 hearing testimony from former Attorney General and Nixon campaign director John N. Mitchell. The key points of his testimony emerged in the opening interrogation by chief counsel Samuel Dash

Mitchell told Dash he was aware of the 1970 White House plan for a secret intelligence operation, some of it illegal. He had "joined" then FBI Director J. Edgar Hoover in "opposing its implementation," Mitchell said. He had talked to President Nixon and his aide H. R. Haldeman about it, and the plan was reconsidered and dropped. He did not recall receiving any formal notice of its demise; Mitchell said he was "just told verbally that it was nil." He said he opposed the plan because it dealt with surreptitious entry, mail covers and the like.

Regarding his relationship with the Nixon campaign committee while he was still attorney general, Mitchell said he "played a role" because Nixon had asked him "to keep my eye on their activities over there to make sure they did not get out of line." This included personnel and budget approval and proposed projects and involved "a substantial number" of conferences.

The Liddy plans—Mitchell described the plan presented in his office Jan. 27, 1972 by G. Gordon Liddy, later convicted as a Watergate conspirator, as "a complete horror story that involved a mish-mash of code names and lines of authority, electronic surveillance, the ability to intercept aircraft communications, the call girl bit and all the rest of it." It was "just beyond the pale." His reaction: "I told him to go burn the charts and that this was not what we were interested in. What we were interested in was a matter of information gathering and protection against the demonstrators."

"Why didn't you throw Mr. Liddy out of your office?" Dash asked.

"Well, I think, Mr. Dash, in hindsight I not only should have thrown him out of the office, I should have thrown him out of the window." Mitchell recalled that the plan's price tag was, "Oh, just a million dollars."

Mitchell contended there were "faulty recollections" about the discussion during the second meeting Feb. 4, 1972 on the Liddy operation. "I violently disagree with Mr. [Jeb Stuart] Magruder's testimony to the point that the Democratic National Committee was discussed as a target for electronic surveillance for the reasons that he gave, number one with respect to the Democratic kickback story. . . . These targets were not discussed." To the best of Mitchell's recollection, no targets were discussed.

What about previous testimony before the committee that Mitchell himself had volunteered a target, a Las Vegas newspaper office? To the best of his recollection, Mitchell said, "there was no such discussion."

What was the reaction to this plan? "Dean, just like myself, was again aghast" and "was quite strong to the point that these things could not be discussed in the attorney general's office. I have a clear recollection of that and that was one of the bases upon which the meeting was broken up." Mitchell's observation at the meeting was "that this was not going to be accepted. It was entirely out of the concept of what we needed."

Dash asked if Mitchell took any action against Liddy.

A. Other than to cut off the proposals, no.

Q. Why not? Here is a man talking to you as attorney general about illegal wiretapping and perhaps break-ins. Why not at least if you do not have him ordered arrested for trying to conspire to do things like this, why not have him fired?

A. In hindsight, I would think that would have been a very viable thing to do. And probably should have been done.

Mitchell presumed Liddy would go back to his regular duties "without engaging in such activities."

Q. Did you report to anybody the Jan. 27 meeting or the Feb. 4 meeting?

A. To the best of my recollection, no.

Q. Did you ever take it up with Mr. Haldeman or anybody in the White House?

A. No, sir.

Q. Were you aware that Mr. Liddy left the Feb. 4 meeting believing that his plan was not objectionable in itself but only that the price tag was too high and that he reported that to Mr. McCord and Mr. Hunt?

A. I cannot conceive of anybody leaving that meeting with such an understanding.

Dash questioned Mitchell about the third Liddy plan presented by Magruder in Florida March 30, 1972.

Q. What would have given Mr. Magruder the idea that you would even consider this proposal again if you had indeed, as you stated, rejected it so categorically twice before?

A. Well, I would have presumed that you would ask Mr. Magruder that question when he was here, Mr. Dash. But in hindsight I presume there were other people interested in the implementation of some type of activity in this area. Because I believe that Mr. Magruder was very clearly aware of the position that I had taken in connection with it.

Q. So that it is at least your present feeling that he was acting under some pressure for somebody to represent this plan to you?

A. This has been continued to be my feeling but I have no basis for knowing that.

Q. Now, what is your recollection of what decision you made in Key Biscayne on the so-called Liddy plan?

A. Well, it was very simple. This, again, We don't need this. I am tired of hearing it. Out. Let's not discuss it any further. This sort of a concept.

What about previous testimony by three witnesses that Mitchell had approved the third Liddy plan? "If there is a problem there, it is a problem of misunderstanding or contravention of my orders."

What about the funding of the operation? Who authorized it? Mitchell responded: "There could very well have been pressure that came from collateral areas in which they decided that this was the thing to do. I can't speculate on who they might be. I am sure that there could be such pressures." He was "not aware" of the dollar amount of the initial Liddy request for funds. "It was a question of did Magruder have continuing authorization to authorize expenditures, and of course the answer was yes."

What about previous testimony by Maurice H. Stans that he asked Mitchell about Liddy's request for "a substantial amount of money" and whether Magruder had authority to approve payments to Liddy?

A. Well, I would respectfully disagree with Mr. Stans on the fact of substantial amounts or that the discussions had to do with respect to the authorization by Magruder in the continuity of the way he had been acting.

Never saw bugging data—Mitchell was unaware at the time of the early break-in at the Democratic offices at Watergate in May 1972. He said he did not know of the "Gemstone" file of wiretap information generated from it "until a great deal later," "much after" June 17, 1972, the second break-in date.

Did he recall Magruder testifying that he had shown these documents to him.

A. I recall it very vividly because it happens to be a palpable, damnable lie.

Among other things, he had a White House appointment at the time period he was said to have been shown the files. And he never saw or talked to Liddy from Feb. 4, 1972 until June 15, 1972 so he could not have berated Liddy about the inadequate results of the first break-in, as Magruder also testified.

Mitchell said the June 15 meeting with Liddy involved a letter being sent to a newspaper about campaign financing charges.

Mitchell related "there was considerable concern" about the June 17 break-in when he learned about it while he was in California. The name of James L. McCord Jr., the campaign committee security aide, "had surfaced" and "obviously, there was an involvement" in the campaign committee.

Q. At that time, . . . did it ever cross your mind when you read about this that perhaps the Liddy plan had been put in operation?

A. Well, that had crossed my mind but the players were different and, of course, there was a lot of discussion about CIA, and because of the Cuban Americans who were involved in it. It wasn't until actually later on that it struck home to me that this could have been the same operation that

had a genesis back in the earlier conversation.

White House 'horror stories'— Following the break-in, Liddy was debriefed and Mitchell learned for the first time of what he repeatedly referred afterwards to as "the White House horrors"— the surveillance of McGovern headquarters, the "plumbers" group and Liddy's extensive activity while at the White House in connection with "the Ellsberg matter, in the Dita Beard matter and a few of the other little gems." Mitchell recalled the Beard matter involved Liddy "assisting in spiriting her out, or wherever they spirited her out of, either New York or Washington."

Other items cited by Mitchell as "horror stories" were a false cable purporting to link President Kennedy to the death of South Vietnamese President Ngo Dinh Diem, the proposal to firebomb the Brookings Institution and what he termed other "extracurricular" eavesdropping.

There was a Watergate discussion at his Washington apartment June 19, 1972, but he was unaware at that time of the Gemstone file and nobody at the meeting "knew of the wiretapping aspects" or had any connection with that. He did not recall any discussion at that time of destruction of documents, either.

Did he become aware during that June and July of Magruder's involvement in the break-in? He was aware that Magruder had provided the money, and the focus seemed to be at that time on how much money had been given Liddy.

Mitchell said Magruder was shifting his story and, facing grand jury testimony, was asked to put his statement in writing. "It got to the point where I had a very, very strong suspicion as to what the involvement was," Mitchell said, but he did not know at the time Magruder's story was not a true one. He learned later, "sometime" before Magruder went to the grand jury.

Mitchell said he "had no specific knowledge" that Haldeman and Ehrlichman were being kept informed about Magruder's testimony. He had never discussed the subject with them, to the best of his recollection. But he had discussions with Haldeman or Ehrlichman, prior to Magruder's grand jury appearance, about "the so-called White House horror stories," or the actions revealed in Liddy's debriefing.

Had Mitchell expressed concern to Haldeman or Ehrlichman that the stories would be revealed during the campaign? He thought "we all had an innate fear" that would happen.

What was his personal position on revealing the material?

A. I did not believe that it was fair to the President to have these stories come out during his political campaign.

Was he aware of a program, involving Dean, Haldeman, Ehrlichman, perhaps others, to prevent these stories from coming out? The question was very broad, Mitchell said, "I may answer it, perhaps,

by saying that we sure in hell were not volunteering anything."

The 'lid' goes on—Mitchell said he came to "a pretty strong feeling" that Magruder's imminent testimony "was not going to be entirely accurate." Magruder "would seek an audience to review his story."

Prior to Magruder's third appearance before the grand jury, Magruder, Dean and Mitchell met, not primarily to discuss the question of how to handle Magruder's testimony, but to discuss "what the recollection was" of the planning meeting and "what could be said about it to limit the impact."

Q. And did Mr. Magruder indicate that he was going to not testify concerning any intelligence plans, but would testify that he was there to discuss the election laws.

A. Well, the election laws were discussed and I think the result was that he would limit it to the election laws.

Q. And you were aware, then, in December that he would testify not completely, if not falsely, concerning the meetings on Jan. 27 and Feb. 4?

A. Well, that is generally correct. As I say again, this is something that Dean and I were listening to, as to his story as to how he was going to present it.

Q. Well, wasn't it the result of your effort or program to keep the lid on? You were interested in the grand jury not getting the full story. Isn't that true?

A. Maybe we can get the record straight so you won't have to ask me after each of these questions: Yes, we wanted to keep the lid on. We were not volunteering anything.

Mitchell said he became aware "in the fall sometime" that payments were being made to the defendants. He also learned of the involvement in the payoffs of Nixon's personal lawyer, Herbert W. Kalmbach, and Mitchell's aide Frederick C. LaRue.

He said he realized, by the time he was leaving his campaign post, that Magruder faced potential indictment.

Dash explored Mitchell's opinion about Nixon's awareness of the Watergate events and aftermath.

Did he believe the President was aware of the events prior to or after the break-in, the actual bugging or the cover-up?

A. I am not aware of it and I have every reason to believe, because of my discussions and encounters with him up through the 22nd of March, I have very strong opinions that he was not.

Asked to explain, Mitchell said of Nixon, "I think I know the individual, I know his reactions to things, and I have a very strong feeling that during the period of time in which I was in association with him . . . that I just do not believe that he had that information or had that knowledge; otherwise, I think the type of conversations we had would have brought it out."

Had he told Nixon what he discovered from Liddy's debriefing? "No, sir. I did not." Why not?

A. Because I did not believe that it was appropriate for him to have that type of knowledge, because I knew the actions that he would take and it would be most detrimental to his political campaign.

Q. Could it have been actually helpful or healthy, do you think?

A. That was not my opinion at the particular time. He was not involved; it wasn't a question of deceiving the public as far as Richard Nixon was concerned, and it was the other people that were involved in connection with these activities, both in the White House horrors and the Watergate. I believed at that particular time, and maybe in retrospect, I was wrong, but it occurred to me that the best thing to do was just to keep the lid on through the election.

Money for the defendants—Mitchell told the committee that sometime in the fall of 1972 one of the Watergate defendants, E. Howard Hunt Jr., called White House aide Charles W. Colson to demand money. Mitchell heard in March about oral communications from Hunt or his attorney "relating to requests for legal fees and so forth, which were communicated to the White House." Mitchell said his informant was probably LaRue, who told him "in this context: I have got this request, I have talked to John Dean over at the White House, they are not in the money business any more, what would you do if you were in my shoes and knowing that he had made prior payments? I said, if I were you, I would continue and I would make the payment."

Eventually, the source of the funds being paid to the defendants ran out, and Mitchell suggested seeing if the $350,000 fund "sitting" in the White House since April "was available for the purpose." Dash asked if he recalled a January meeting with Kalmbach and Dean on the subject. Mitchell could not.

On the subject of executive clemency, Mitchell thought the only conversations he had on that had to do with Colson and Hunt, that in early 1973 Hunt approached Colson about it and Colson's word "was the only word" Hunt would take on the clemency, "whatever that meant."

It had occurred to Mitchell "the possibility that the so-called lid would become uncovered." But he "always hoped that it didn't for the very simple reason that there was no necessity of scarring the President, who was not involved." Did it occur to him to tell the President the true situation after the election?

A. Well, I am sure it occurred to me and probably on hindsight I probably should have. I do not think there is any doubt about it.

Q. Did you not think it was the President's prerogative to know what to do about these matters?

A. The decision had to be made, and it is a tough one, whether or not he is not involved in it but he does not know about them, will this go away? I knew they were going to change the personnel in the White House and hopefully they would be gone and he would not have to deal with it . . . [in] his second term.

A

B

C

D

E

F

G

When Mitchell talked with Nixon June 20, 1972, shortly after the break-in, "I apologized to him for not knowing what the hell had happened and I should have kept a stronger hand on what the people in the committee were doing."

Later there were political meetings and discussions about appointing a special investigating commission and prosecutors "and things like that."

Mitchell had "never promised" executive clemency to anybody. "Obviously, there is no basis upon which I could." When Magruder came to see him in March, he told him "I thought he was a very outstanding young man and I liked and I worked with him and to the extent that I could help him in any conceivable way, I would be delighted to do so."

"And this was exactly the same conversation that we had the next day down at Haldeman's office," Mitchell added. Haldeman made no promises to Magruder "other than the fact to help him as a friend."

Mitchell had met March 22 with Nixon and Dean. Was there any discussion of the Watergate, the cover-up or possible indictments? "None whatsoever. The total discussion had to do with the White House's r onse to this committee."

Thompson questions Mitchell—Thompson asked Mitchell about the Liddy debriefing and whether Liddy had indicated the budget for his Watergate bugging plan had been approved by the White House. Mitchell was inclined to think he had. Did Mitchell ever verify any of this with Nixon? No, he never discussed it with Nixon. Had he verified it with Haldeman or Ehrlichman? Never until a later date, possibly before the end of 1972, "certainly in 1973."

Thompson asked Mitchell if he had called Dean late in 1972 about use of some of the $350,000 at the White House to pay the defendants. Mitchell said no, he had no official capacity then and no control over the money. Asked if there was a similar call before the Watergate trial, Mitchell gave the same answer.

Mitchell also denied any role in assurances of executive clemency to McCord or anyone else.

What about Dean's testimony that he had assured Ehrlichman "Hunt had been taken care of" in the payoff matter? It was "absolutely false," he had never discussed such payments with Ehrlichman.

Talmadge questions early role—Talmadge asked Mitchell about his role in campaign affairs while he was attorney general. Mitchell insisted it was a "consulting" role. Talmadge asked if he had not testified to the contrary before the Senate Judiciary Committee March 14, 1972, when he stated he had no "party responsibilities" while at the Justice Department. He drew a distinction between "party" activities and activities for the re-election campaign committee, Mitchell said.

"Let's read a little further," Talmadge said, referring to a transcript of the 1972 hearing, at a point where Mitchell was being questioned by Sen. Edward M. Kennedy (D, Mass.).

"Next question," Talmadge said, "Sen. Kennedy—'No re-election campaign responsibilities?' Mr. Mitchell—'Not as yet. I hope to.'"

Mitchell insisted the reply related back "to the same subject matter," that is, in the context of "party" responsibilities.

"'No re-election campaign responsibilities?'" Talmadge quoted incredulously. "I ask you, who was running? Mr. Nixon? And is he a Republican?"

Talmadge put in the record memorandums dating back to Dec. 3, 1971 indicating Mitchell was exercising campaign responsibility. "The public can draw their own conclusions" on the issue, he said.

Ervin interrupted with a question. "It is your position that working for a Republican candidate for president gave you no responsibilities in respect to the Republican party?"

A. That is it entirely, Mr. Chairman.

Talmadge again took up the questioning, wondering "why on earth" Mitchell had not walked into the President's office and told the truth about the crimes and conspiracies and cover-ups.

A. It wasn't a question of telling him the truth. It was a question of not involving him at all so that he could go through his campaign without being involved in this type of activity, and I am talking about the White House horrors particularly. . . . I was sure that, knowing Richard Nixon, the President, as I do, he would just lower the boom on all of this matter and it would come back to hurt him and it would affect him in his re-election.

Q. Am I to understand from your response that you placed the expediency of the next election above your responsibilities as an intimate to advise the President of the peril that surrounded him? Here was the deputy campaign director involved, here were his two closest associates in his office involved, all around him were people involved in crime, perjury, accessory after the fact, and you deliberately refused to tell him that. Would you state that the expediency of the election was more important than that?

A. Senator, I think you have put it exactly correct. In my mind, the re-election of Richard Nixon, compared with what was available on the other side, was so much more important that I put it in just that context.

July 11: Why was Nixon not told? Mitchell's second day of testimony was marked by persistent questioning from the senators on his testimony that he had protected the President by not divulging to him his knowledge of the Watergate cover-up activities and White House "horror" stories.

Sen. Daniel K. Inouye (D, Hawaii) opened the interrogation by asking if Mitchell had advised the participants of the first Liddy plan meeting "that they were essentially participating in conspiracy to commit a crime?" Not at that time, Mitchell replied.

Q. I ask this because just about that time your office, with much publicity and great vigor, had pursued the indictment of American citizens who had allegedly discussed the kidnapping of Dr. [Henry A.] Kissinger. Is there any difference between the discussion of a kidnapping and a discussion of these criminal activities in your office?

A. Senator, I think you have stopped very far short in connection with the activities of the indictment that you referred to. There were overt actions in connection with that as well as discussions.

Q. Mr. Mitchell, if the re-election of President Nixon was so important that you were willing to engage in activities which have been well described as being irregular to insure his re-election . . . to what length are you now willing to go to deceive in an effort to avoid further implication of the President in the activities under investigation by this panel? More specifically, are you willing to lie to protect the President?

A. Senator, . . . I do not have to make that choice, because to my knowledge, the President was not knowledgeable, certainly about the Watergate or certainly knowledgeable about anything that had to do with the cover-up.

Q. . . . You have suggested that it would not be fair . . . to the President if the facts relating to Watergate and the White House horrors had been brought to his attention and to the attention of the American people during the election campaign. Have you ever considered whether it was fair to the members of the opposition party or fair to the American people to conspire to keep them from the true facts of this matter?

A. Yes, I am sure that that subject matter has crossed my mind many, many times. But I do not believe now, I did not believe then that the President should be charged with the transgressions of others.

Q. Did you feel that the President was above the laws of the land?

A. The President is never above the laws of the land. To my knowledge, he has faithfully executed the laws of the land.

Inouye noted that Mitchell's assertion of Nixon's innocence was based upon his knowledge of the man. Then he noted that Mitchell had hired or was involved in the hiring of six Administration or campaign officials who had "one thing in common"—involvement "in the commission of a crime." "Would you say that you are a good judge of character, sir?" he asked. Mitchell said "they all had impeccable records" when "they came into the picture."

Baker: What is the presidency? Sen. Howard H. Baker Jr. (R, Tenn.) focused on Mitchell's "perception of the institution of the presidency." Was the presidency "so shrouded in mystique," he asked, "is there such an aura of magnificence about the presidency, is there such an awesome responsibility for a multitude of problems and undertakings of this nation that the presidency in some instances must be spared the detail, must be spared the difficulty of situations which in more ordinary circumstances might be considered by some at least to be frank, open, declarations of criminal offense? Is the presidency to be protected in that way? Is the splendor of the isolation so great that the President must be protected . . . ?

"Obviously," Mitchell replied, "the President cannot deal with all of the mundane problems that go on from day to day. He has to deal with the greater problems in the area." His concern in this instance, Mitchell said, was that the President "should not have been involved in connection with these matters that bore directly upon his election."

Q. Why?

A. In the interest of his re-election.

Q. Why is that not a presidential grade decision? . . . What is it that arrogates that authority to someone else other than the President, to take a material step that will significantly affect not only his election prospects and changes but his presidency, if he is re-elected?

A. Because of the consequence that would obviously flow from it. If he were to make the decision there would be no alternative. He would have a choice of being involved in . . . a cover-up or he would be involved in the disclosures which would affect his re-election.

Q. Mr. Mitchell, does that or not imply distrust of the decision-making ability of the man who occupied the office at the time—that is, that you spare him the responsibility to make such a fantastically important decision?

A. Quite the contrary, and I do not refer to it as a fantastically important decision. Of course, in retrospect, it has been, and perhaps the best thing maybe would have been to do that. But it is not a question of distrust of the President, it is a question of a recognition that if he were advised of the situation, that he would take these actions which would be deleterious to his campaign.

Q. Was Mitchell saying "that in certain cases, in order to preserve a range of political options, that the President should be denied access to the information on which to make a legal and valid judgment as to the propriety of those actions? And if you say yes to that, is it not true that that theorem has a significant diminishing effect on the powers of the presidency as described in the Constitution?

Do you not in fact, by that, arrogate unto yourself a presidential decision?

A. Senator, I think the answer is yes in all of those particular areas.

Q. What is the constitutional basis for arrogating unto yourself or anyone else a . . . presidential-level decision?

A. I have not found one in the Constitution, senator.

Q. Aren't you dead sure in your mind that that was a mistake, not telling the President?

A. Senator, I am not certain because we were talking about . . . June in 1972, where I still believe that the most important thing to this country was the re-election of Richard Nixon. And I was not about to countenance anything that would stand in the way of that re-election.

"Anything at all?" Baker asked. Mitchell retreated, saying if it came to "treason and other high crimes and misdemeanors" he would draw the line.

Baker persisted. Wouldn't the country and the President have been better served by calling everybody involved to account, to have informed the President and then "line up everybody on the south lawn of the White House" to ask them what happened?

If he could have been assured at that time that the President would be re-elected, Mitchell said, "I would agree with you wholeheartedly." Later, he returned to Baker's phrase and asserted, given the aftermath, "it might even have been better, senator, as you say, to take them out on the White House lawn; it would have been simpler to have shot them all and that would have been less of a problem than has developed in the meantime."

Baker spoke of the unfairness to the President that he was undergoing "the hostility and the suspicion of a nation in this respect with the allegations of cover-up, with the lingering suspicion about what he knew." Would not "it have been infinitely better," he asked, to expose the situation to "a presidential decision?"

A. In the Monday morning quarterback field in what has developed into the circumstances that exist today, I don't doubt for a moment that you are probably absolutely correct, and I believe so.

Montoya's turn—Sen. Joseph M. Montoya (D, N.M.) asked Mitchell if he had ever discussed what was discovered about the Watergate involvement shortly after the break-in with Ehrlichman or Haldeman. Mitchell was "sure that somewhere, sometime along the way, that these discussions were held. I can't pinpoint any particular meeting."

Did Ehrlichman or Haldeman know anything about the cover-up? Mitchell said he did not know "as there has been any testimony to the effect that the people in the White House were involved in the Watergate."

Q. Well, with respect to the cover-up?

A. Well, eventually along the road, there was discussion in connection with the fact that there was no volunteering or coming forward and that there was a design not to have the stories come out that had to do with the White House horror activities. There is no question about that.

Q. Well, if your interest was so profound in trying to trigger off any presidential action that might endanger his chances of re-election, why did you not go to people close to the President to make sure that they would not tell the President about the details involving Watergate?

A. I believe that they are capable of making their decisions on their own. I ob-

viously made mine and I presume that they made theirs independently.

Ervin questions dual role—Chairman Ervin elicited from Mitchell the comment that it was "rather inexpedient" for an attorney general to be engaged in managing political activities. He recalled Mitchell's testimony to him in January 1969, when the incoming attorney general had assured him that his "duties and functions will be related to the Justice Department and as the legal and not the political adviser of the President."

"I am very sorry that you didn't carry out the purpose you announced on that occasion," Ervin observed.

That "would have been my fondest wish," Mitchell said. "Unfortunately, it is very very difficult to turn down a request by the President."

Ervin wondered whether serious consideration should be given "to divorcing" the Justice Department from political matters.

Mitchell said he "would perhaps even go further and suggest that you divorce all of the departments from political matters."

Ervin then questioned Mitchell about his June 20, 1972 telephone call with Nixon, three days after the break-in, when Mitchell said he had apologized to the President for not keeping track of the committee personnel. Didn't the President ask you what you meant by your apologizing? Ervin asked. Mitchell said he told Nixon what he knew at that time, "which was very very little."

Later, Ervin asked Mitchell if the President "at any time" asked him what he knew about Watergate. Not after the June 20 phone call, Mitchell said. "Well," Ervin commented, "if the cat hadn't any more curiosity than that it would still be enjoying its nine lives, all of them." Mitchell said he hoped "the President enjoys eight more of them."

Ervin offered other observations in the course of his questioning: that anyone, whether he was president or hod carrier, who withheld evidence was subject to the inference that the evidence was unfavorable to him; that executive privilege did not cover "any political activities whatsoever" and did not "entitle a president to have kept secret information concerning criminal activities of his aides or anybody else"; that there was nothing in the Constitution "requiring the President to run for re-election" or made it "the official duty of a president to have anything to do with criminal activities" or said "the powers of the presidency should be separated from truth."

Ervin went over Mitchell's testimony he had not told the President about the conspiracy "because you didn't want the President to do what you called lowering the boom." "And it might have affected the votes of the American people?" Ervin continued. Mitchell responded that was "quite conceivable."

"Well, I have a higher opinion of the American people than that," Ervin said. If the President had been told and he had "lowered the boom and come out in the performance of his constitutional duties to take care that the laws be faithfully executed, I think he would have made his, the election more sure than ever."

Weicker confrontation hostile—Sen. Lowell P. Weicker Jr. (R, Conn.) opened by questioning whether Mitchell would lie to protect the President at the present time. Mitchell said if that were a hypothetical question "the answer would be no, that I would not here under oath, and I am answering a hypothetical question so far as any knowledge is concerned." Their confrontation was hostile.

Weicker asked about a September 1972 deposition in which Mitchell, while campaign director, denied discussing or hearing of any surveillance of the Democratic National Committee headquarters. Weicker asked about the apparent contradiction in this to Mitchell's testimony to the committee about sitting in on the Liddy plans. Mitchell defended his deposition as limited in the context of the question to the activities of the campaign committee security group.

"You felt that you answered the question truthfully?" Weicker asked. "I did," Mitchell asserted.

Referring to Nixon's March 21 statement that intensive new inquiries were being made as a result of serious charges which came to his attention, Weicker noted that Mitchell met with Nixon March 22 with Dean, Haldeman and Ehrlichman. He asked if the subject of Watergate was discussed. Mitchell said no, aside from the Senate probe, which was discussed. Weicker asked if Mitchell found this surprising since a new probe was under way. Mitchell said he did not.

Weicker wondered if the reason Watergate was not discussed at the meeting "was because they already had that knowledge." Mitchell said he did not believe that was the case.

Weicker then pointed out that Mitchell's failure to inform the court of his information on the Ellsberg case break-in, information obtained in the debriefing of Liddy, was a violation of his legal canon as a lawyer and officer of the court.

Weicker asked him if there was anything in the country aside from the President that put him "in awe." Many things, Mitchell responded.

Q. Do the courts put you in awe?

A. Very much so.

Q. Does your oath as attorney, does that put you into awe?

A. Very much so.

Q. Do you feel as an officer of the court you did the right thing?

A. In connection with the Ellsberg matter?

Q. When you did not notify the prosecution or you did not notify rather [Ellsberg trial] Judge [William M.] Byrne of the information you had in your possession?

A. I think in retrospect, it probably would have been the right thing to do.

July 12: *Inouye on Nixon reaction; Dash questions credibility*—In his final day of testimony, Mitchell was first challenged

by Sen. Inouye on the rationale of withholding information from Nixon; that is, Mitchell's fear that the President would dismiss aides guilty of wrongdoing and provoke harmful publicity.

Later, the committee's chief counsel, Samuel Dash, sharply questioned Mitchell's credibility before the committee, leading Mitchell to acknowledge that some of his testimony during the hearings differed from earlier statements to the FBI and in a deposition in the civil suit filed by the Democratic party.

Did Nixon 'lower the boom?'—Asked by Inouye for examples of Nixon's "lowering the boom" after learning of the Watergate cover-up, Mitchell cited the appointment of a special prosecutor and the "removing" of Haldeman and Ehrlichman.

Inouye was not satisfied:

Q. Was not the appointment of the special prosecutor brought about because of intensive pressure initiated by the Congress of the United States? Does not the record indicate the the White House and the President resisted this?

A. It was the President's determination. He was the one who made that determination. What were the causes of it, I think we can all have different opinions upon but it was his action that did provide for the special prosecutor.

And, concerning Haldeman and Ehrlichman:

Q. If you read the public statement, they submitted their resignations and the President reluctantly accepted this, and in so accepting the resignations praised them to the highest.

A. Senator, I have an entirely different interpretation of that.

Inouye concluded by observing that the "lid was not blown off" by the removal of Haldeman and Ehrlichman but by "two men in the Washington Post."

Dash challenges credibility—In a verbal duel with Dash, Mitchell attributed the discrepancies between his committee testimony and earlier statements to faulty recollection and the fact that he was not then "volunteering information."

In an exchange concerning Mitchell's sworn deposition in the Democratic party's action on Watergate, Dash noted that Mitchell had said earlier in the week he had been "debriefed" by Robert C. Mardian on June 21 or 22, 1972 on G. Gordon Liddy's explanation of his own role in Watergate and other espionage operations.

Q. Now, have you ever denied at any time that Mr. Mardian told you about his conversation with Mr. Liddy?

A. I have no recollection of having done so, Mr. Dash.

Dash then read Mitchell's statement from the deposition which denied any conversation with Mardian or Frederick C. LaRue about Liddy except on matters relating to the "termination" of Liddy's employment at the re-election committee. Mitchell contended that his response in the deposition had been "equivocal be-

cause of my recollection at the particular time."

Dash responded: "Well, it certainly was equivocal because you have testified three days here that the important part of that conversation that Mr. Mardian was talking to you about was the White House horrors and the Watergate break-in and since this was Sept. 5, 1972, before the election, didn't you answer no in that case as part of your willingness to keep the lid on so that if you had answered yes and had to tell about that conversation you would have been opening the lid?"

Mitchell replied "in preparation for the testimony for this committee" he had "more specific knowledge" or better recollection of what had happened in 1972.

Dash also brought out that Mitchell had denied in the deposition having any knowledge of the circumstances surrounding the hiring of Liddy as counsel to the campaign committee. But, Dash noted, Mitchell had given the Ervin committee considerable detail on the background of the hiring.

Mitchell again cited "further reflection" and a "rechecking of the records."

FBI probe—Dash then pressed Mitchell on the FBI investigation of Watergate, noting that Mitchell had told the FBI July 5, 1972 that the only knowledge he had of the incident was what he had "read in the newspapers."

Q. As a matter of fact, by July 5th, and that is pretty close to June 21 or 22, you had been given information by Mr. Mardian on what Mr. Liddy told him about the break-in.

A. Mr. Dash, at that particular time, I was not sure whether that information was correct or otherwise.

Q. Whether it was correct or not, the FBI was making an investigation and would not you want to give whatever leads or information they wanted, having been the former Attorney General and knowing how the FBI investigates, so they could check that out?

A. Mr. Dash, at that particular time, we weren't volunteering any information for the reason that I have discussed here.

Dash later asked "since you may have given false testimony under oath on prior occasions, is there really any reason for this committee to believe your testimony . . . ?

A. . . . As for the determinations of this committee, I think they can judge . . . my testimony after my appearance here . . .

Richard Moore testifies. Richard A. Moore, a special counsel to the President, followed former Attorney General John N. Mitchell to the Senate committee's witness table July 12. Moore, 59, who joined the White House staff in 1971, described himself as an "extra hand —as a source of white-haired advice and experience—whenever the President or the younger men with line responsibility seek my help."

Called at the request of Leonard Garment, counsel to the President, Moore read a 20-page statement centering on his "deep conviction that the critical facts about Watergate did not reach the President" until White House counsel John W. Dean 3rd supplied them March 21.

Moore gave his version of the California meetings Feb. 10–11 attended by H. R. Haldeman, then White House chief of staff, John D. Ehrlichman, former domestic affairs adviser to the President, Dean and himself. Moore said that the aides, concerned about the coming Watergate hearings, were meeting to devise an Administration statement on executive privilege.

According to Moore, Dean said casually Feb. 11 that "he had been told by the lawyers [for the Watergate defendants] that they may be needing some more money and did we have any ideas?" When Mitchell's name was mentioned, Moore, a former aide to Mitchell, was asked to enlist his help. Moore said that Mitchell turned him down Feb. 15; "I believe he said something like, 'Tell them to get lost.'"

Moore said, "Mr. Dean has testified we left the meeting together and that . . . he cautioned me against conveying this fundraising request when I saw Mr. Mitchell. I have absolutely no recollection of any such conversation and I am convinced it never took place."

During the ensuing month, Moore said he worked on the executive privilege question and helped prepare objections cited by the President to the press March 15 to Dean's testifying before the Senate Judiciary Committee on the confirmation of L. Patrick Gray 3rd as director of the Federal Bureau of Investigation.

A series of meetings, attended only by Nixon, Dean and Moore, were held March 15, 19 and 20 to discuss executive privilege, Moore said. Another meeting had occurred March 14, with presidential press secretary Ronald L. Ziegler present. "At no time during this meeting [March 14] or during succeeding meetings . . . did anyone say anything in my presence which related to or suggested the existence of any cover-up or any knowledge of involvement by anyone in the White House, then or now, in the Watergate affair," Moore stated.

In the interval between the March 19–20 meetings, Moore said Dean told him that convicted Watergate conspirator E. Howard Hunt Jr. was threatening to "say things that would be very serious for the White House" if he were not given a large sum of money. Moore said this was blackmail and he urged Dean to have nothing to do with it.

Moore related that Dean had told him earlier of being present at the two meetings in which Watergate conspirator G. Gordon Liddy had presented intelligence plans that were rejected. But Moore disputed Dean had advance knowledge of the Watergate breakins.

"This," Moore said, "brings me to the afternoon of March 20, when Mr. Dean and I met with the President in the Oval Office. . . . As I sat through the meeting .

. I came to the conclusion in my own mind that the President could not be aware of the things that Dean was worried about or had been hinting at to me, let alone [Watergate defendant] Howard Hunt's blackmail demand. Indeed, as the President talked about getting the whole story out— as he had done repeatedly in the recent meetings—it seemed crystal clear to me that he knew of nothing that was inconsistent with the previously stated conclusion that the White House was uninvolved in the Watergate affair, before or after the event.

"As we closed the door of the Oval Office and turned into the hall, I decided to raise the issue directly with Mr. Dean. I said that I had the feeling that the President had no knowledge of the things that were worrying Dean. I asked Dean whether he had ever told the President about them. Dean replied that he had not, and I asked whether anyone else had. Dean said he didn't think so."

That evening Moore received a call from Dean, who said he had arranged a private meeting the next day with the President. Meeting Moore after seeing the President, Dean said he had told Nixon "everything." "I asked if the President had been surprised and he said yes," Moore testified.

After delivering his statement, Moore was subjected to sharp questioning by Terry F. Lenzner, assistant to majority counsel Samuel Dash. Moore was asked in detail about meetings he had attended in 1972 and early 1973, but was unable to respond with details and became flustered. Caught by Lenzner in one apparent contradiction between what he had told the Watergate committee in private and what he had just said, Moore replied, "I'll let my answer stand—whatever it was."

July 13: *Nixon voiced regret*—In his second day of testimony, Moore reported on a private meeting he had with the President May 8, quoting him as saying, "'I have racked my brain, I have searched my mind. Were there any clues I should have seen that should have tipped me off.'"

Moore also testified that the President April 17 had related to him his reaction to Dean's March 21 revelation of Hunt's blackmail and clemency demands. When told by Dean that the cost would be $1 million and that the demands would go on, Nixon said he had replied: "'That isn't the point. Money isn't the point. You could raise money, money is not the point. It's wrong, we could not, shouldn't consider it and it's stupid because the truth comes out anyway.'"

At one point a question asked Moore by Sen. Edward J. Gurney (R, Fla.) provoked an angry objection from the committee chairman, Sen. Sam J. Ervin Jr. (D, N.C.). Gurney had asked whether, if Dean had discussed blackmail money and clemency with Nixon March 13, would he not have told Moore about it because he had confided in Moore about other aspects of the cover-up. Ervin objected but finally consented to the question.

Moore replied, "I kind of go along with the notion."

(In his testimony to the committee June 20, Dean said he "did not discuss with Moore the fact that I had discussed money and clemency with the President earlier, but I told him I really didn't think the President understood all the facts involved in the Watergate and the implication of the facts.")

Butterfield reveals tape recording setup. Following the completion of Moore's interrogation at its morning session July 16, the committee called its surprise witness—former White House aide Alexander Butterfield—to testify on the recording system President Nixon had installed to secretly tape his meetings and telephone conversations.

Butterfield's testimony made it clear that the President's conversations with key figures in the Watergate affair, including the meetings described by John Dean in his appearance before the committee, would have been routinely recorded by the system. The testimony brought immediate committee efforts to question Secret Service officials responsible for the recording equipment and to obtain the tapes of the President's conversations relating to the Watergate affair.

Butterfield, who had served as a deputy assistant to the President from the beginning of Nixon's first term until March 14, said that the secret recording system had been installed to make tapes for "historical purposes" and had been in operation since the summer of 1970. Butterfield said that the system's existence was known only to himself, his immediate superior, H. R. Haldeman, Lawrence M. Higby of Haldeman's staff, the President and the Secret Service, which maintained the system. (After being informed that presidential counsel J. Fred Buzhardt Jr. had confirmed to the committee the system's existence since spring 1971, Butterfield said he accepted that date.)

Butterfield described the operation of a White House network of "presidential locator boxes," which, in following Nixon's movements, "triggered" recording devices in the Oval Office in the White House and in Nixon's office in the Executive Office Building (EOB). The recorders in these offices were automatically activated by the sound of a voice when the locators indicated that the President was in the room. A manually-operated recorder was concealed in the White House Cabinet room.

There also were tape devices on four of Nixon's telephones: in the two offices, the Lincoln Room of the White House and in Nixon's private quarters at Camp David, Md.

Butterfield was questioned by minority counsel Fred D. Thompson:

Q. So far as the Oval Office and the EOB Office is concerned, would it be your testimony that the device would pick up any and all conversations no matter where the conversations took place in the room and no matter how soft the conversations might have been?

A. Yes, sir.

The tapes were stored and periodically checked by the Secret Service, Butterfield said. He was responsible for seeing that the system remained in working order.

"Were any of these tapes ever transcribed as far as you know?"

A. To my recollection, no.

The questioning of committee chief counsel Dash centered on the potential usefulness of the tapes to the Watergate investigation.

Q. To your knowledge, did the President ever ask while he was in the Oval Office to have the system not operate, the locator light not show in that office so as to trigger the device?

A. No sir. As matter of fact, the President seemed to be totally, really oblivious, or certainly uninhibited by this fact. . . .

Q. And so that if either Mr. Dean, Mr. Haldeman, Mr. Ehrlichman, or Mr. Colson had particular meetings in the Oval Office with the President on any particular dates that have been testified before this committee, there would be a tape recording with the President of that full conversation, would there not?

A. Yes sir.

Dash later asked the best way to "reconstruct the conversations at any particular date."

A. Well, in the obvious manner, Mr. Dash—to obtain the tape and play it.

Responding to questions by Sen. Herman E. Talmadge (D, Ga.), Butterfield said none of Nixon's visitors were informed that their conversations were being taped. Nor were there audible signals to indicate telephone taping.

Sen. Gurney raised the possibility that others had access to the tapes.

Q. Did anybody else [other than Secret Service agents] handle those, to your knowledge?

A. I am as sure as I know I am sitting here that no one else handled the tapes other than this individual I mentioned, the chief of the Technical Security Division, and the two or three people designated by him. .

Controversy Develops
over White House Tapes

Hearings uncover 'bugging' system. The existence of a recording system installed to secretly tape President Nixon's White House conversations was revealed July 16 at the continued Watergate hearings of the Senate Select Committee on Presidential Campaign Activities. [See p. 17]

Ervin requests tapes; testimony barred. The Ervin committee appealed to President Nixon July 17 to release all documents and tapes of conversations relevant to the committee's investigation of Watergate. The request—in a letter from Sen. Ervin—followed Nixon's blocking of a committee attempt to interrogate Secret Service agents on the White House recording operations.

Nixon's order preventing the interrogation came in a letter July 17 to Treasury Secretary George P. Shultz, the Cabinet official supervising the Secret Service. His letter said, "I hereby direct that no officer or agent of the Secret Service shall give testimony to Congressional committees concerning matters observed or learned while performing protective functions for the President or in their duties at the White House."

The letter said, however, that "requests for information on procedures in the White House" would be given "prompt consideration."

The letter was delivered to Ervin and committee vice chairman Howard H. Baker Jr. (R, Tenn.) as they were attempting to question Secret Service agent Alfred Wong privately during a recess in the hearings. The committee shortly afterward sent the President its request for access to the tapes and documents.

Baker, noting that the committee request was sent "in a spirit of reconciliation," said the committee sought answers to the following questions:

"1. Who is the custodian of the tapes?

2. Who has had access to the tapes?

3. How do we go about receiving that information and the tapes as they relate to the lawful inquiry of this committee, not to a general fishing expedition . . . ?"

The Washington Post July 18 quoted committee sources as having doubts about the authenticity of whatever tapes might be obtained by the committee.

White House press secretary Ronald L. Ziegler—while trying to defer official comment on the tapes—acknowledged July 17 that the White House would consider them presidential papers.

FCC asks phone probe. The Federal Communications Commission (FCC) July 17 asked the American Telephone and Telegraph Co. (AT&T) to investigate the violation of company rules by the White House's telephone recording operations. A company regulation required telephone recording equipment to emit audible tones at 15-second intervals. Butterfield had testified that the White House system emitted no such signals.

The penalty for violation of the tariff was removal of telephone service, and FCC regulations required the company to enforce the rule or be subject to fines.

A spokesman for AT&T's Washington affiliate said a letter had been sent to the White House emphasizing "the great importance to the company that its tariffs be adhered to."

The Washington Post July 17 quoted legal authorities as feeling that Nixon's recording of his meetings was legal under a 1971 Supreme Court decision allowing one party to record a conversation without the consent of the other parties. (The recordings also apparently were sanctioned by Section 2511, Title 18 of the U.S. Code under language similar to the Supreme Court decision.)

Jackson to probe wiretaps. Sen. Henry M. Jackson said July 18 his Permanent Subcommittee on Investigations would inquire, probably in September, into the possibility of restrictive legislation on both governmental and industrial wiretapping.

Calling Butterfield's testimony on the White House recordings "astonishing," Jackson said the practice "obviously inhibits the kind of frank and honest advice a President must have . . . The fact that certain people in high government positions do this does not make it right or wise."

Jackson said he would consult with Ervin before deciding whether to ask the White House for tapes.

Jackson also said he was "amazed" at the lack of strong protest from foreign

sources over the secret taping system. He asserted the Butterfield disclosures could have an adverse effect on the conduct of foreign policy.

(The New York Times reported July 18 that a check of foreign embassies had revealed little concern over the taping procedures. According to a spokesman for a Communist mission, "every statesman is aware that if conversations are not recorded as they happen, they will be recorded later from notes. Maybe they could have been more cautious.")

(The reaction of U.S. public figures whose conversations may have been recorded by the system was generally restrained, although many objected to the secrecy involved. Senate Democratic Leader Mike Mansfield [Mont.] said July 16 he "wouldn't have minded if they told me." Sen. Barry Goldwater [R, Ariz.] said he did not feel it was "inappropriate to record for historical purposes."

(House Speaker Carl Albert [D, Okla.], however, called the practice "an outrage, almost beyond belief," a position echoed by AFL-CIO president George Meany, who thanked "the blunderers at the Watergate" for bringing about the disclosure of the system. Sen. George McGovern [D, S.D.] called the practice an "invasion of privacy.")

Other Presidents' tapes. The White House's confirmation of the system's existence came during Butterfield's testimony July 16. The committee received a letter from special presidential counsel J. Fred Buzhardt Jr. confirming that "the President's meetings and conversations in the White House" had been recorded. Buzhardt asserted that "this system, which is still in use, is similar to that employed by the last Administration and which had been discontinued from 1969 until the spring of 1971."

Joseph A. Califano Jr., one of the late Lyndon B. Johnson's top advisers, called the Buzhardt statement "an outrageous smear" and asserted there "was absolutely no secret wiring in the place" during the Johnson Administration. Califano said there had been open recordings of some cabinet meetings. He also noted that Johnson had occasionally told his secretary to make notes of

C

D

E

F

G

telephone conversations while listening on an extension.

A Secret Service spokesman acknowledged July 16 that the agency had installed Nixon's recording system but said the agency had never done similar work for any other administration.

The Associated Press reported July 18, however, that the Nixon Administration had obtained affidavits from two former Johnson aides alleging the installation of manually-operated, hidden recording devices in several of Johnson's offices.

The director of the John F. Kennedy Library in Waltham, Mass. said July 17 that the library had 193 dictaphone belts and tapes of telephone conversations and meetings involving Kennedy. Dan H. Fenn Jr., the library director, said a "cursory check" showed the tapes dealt with "highly sensitive foreign policy and national defense matters." Fenn did not say whether the tapes had been made secretly.

The General Services Administration, which operated the Dwight D. Eisenhower Library in Abilene, Kan., said July 17 that there were stenographic transcriptions of presidential conversations in the library. On some transcriptions, the agency said, it was clear all parties knew the conversation was being recorded; on others it was not.

Nixon rejects committee plea—In a July 23 letter to Committee Chairman Sam J. Ervin Jr. (D, N.C.), Nixon cited his earlier refusal to allow committee access to confidential presidential papers. [See p. 11; for texts of letters, see below]

In the case of the tapes on Watergate, Nixon said, the principle of confidentiality applied "with even greater force" because the tapes could be "understood or interpreted only by reference to an enormous number of other documents and tapes." Accordingly, Nixon said, the tapes would remain under his "sole personal control."

Nixon said he had listened to "a number" of the tapes before their existence became publicly known. He maintained the tapes were "entirely consistent with what I know to be the truth and what I have stated to be the truth." He conceded, however, that they contained "comments that persons with different perspectives and motivations would inevitably interpret in different ways."

(Later July 23, Deputy White House Press Secretary Gerald L. Warren said Nixon had reviewed some of the tapes in June when Dean's pre-hearing testimony was leaked to newsmen.

Subpoenas sent—After receiving the Nixon letter, the committee voted unanimously in executive session to issue the two subpoenas, which called for a response by July 26.

Announcing the subpoenas July 23 at the televised hearings, Ervin said he deeply regretted the action but stressed that he had "very different ideas of separation of powers from those expressed by the President." Ervin asserted that if "such a thing as executive privilege is created by the doctrine of separation of powers," it exists "only in connection with official duties." He said it could not be invoked for "either alleged illegal activities or political campaign activities."

The committee action marked the first time a congressional committee had issued a subpoena to a President, and the first time since the Aaron Burr treason trial in 1807—when a document held by President Thomas Jefferson was sought— that a subpoena had been served on a President.

In a separate letter July 23, Nixon said "no useful purpose" would be served by a previously-agreed meeting with Ervin. Ervin said he agreed and would not ask for "the privilege of visiting the White House."

Cox request rejected—The White House July 23 also rejected a request from special prosecutor Archibald Cox for tapes relating to Watergate. In a letter to presidential counsel J. Fred Buzhardt Jr. July 18 (not made public until July 23), Cox had asked for tapes of eight conversations, specifying dates and times of day.

Cox pointed out in his letter that his request for tapes "in aid of an investigation of charges of criminal conspiracy plainly raises none of the separation-of-powers issues you believe to be involved in furnishing so-called 'presidential papers' to the select committee." He also said it would "set no damaging precedents."

In reply, White House consultant Charles Alan Wright, professor of law at the University of Texas, told Cox that "if you are an ordinary prosecutor and thus part of the Executive Branch ... you are subject to the instructions of your superiors, up to and including the President, and can have access to presidential papers only as and if the President sees fit to make them available to you."

Further, Wright said, the separation-of-powers argument did apply, since the tapes sought by Cox were to be used before grand juries and in criminal trials, thus creating a conflict with the Judicial Branch.

In a statement released after receipt of the Wright letter, Cox said he remained convinced "that any blanket claim of privilege to withhold this evidence from a grand jury is without legal foundation." It was his duty, Cox said, to subpoena the tapes because they were "evidence bearing directly upon whether there were criminal conspiracies ... among high government officials."

Cox later July 23 issued a subpoena for the material he had requested.

Nixon bars compliance with subpoenas—In a letter to Ervin July 26, Nixon said he "must respectfully refuse" to produce the tapes called for in the subpoena. As for the other documents, Nixon said it was "quite possible that there are other records in my custody that would be within the ambit of that subpoena" and could be released. He cautioned, however, that he would require "specific requests" and that it would "not be feasible

TEXTS OF WHITE HOUSE REPLIES TO REQUESTS & SUBPOENAS FOR PRESIDENT'S RECORDINGS

Nixon to Ervin, July 23

Dear Mr. Chairman:

I have considered your request that I permit the committee to have access to tapes of my private conversations with a number of my closest aides. I have concluded that the principles stated in my letter to you of July 6* preclude me from complying with that request, and I shall not do so. Indeed the special nature of tape recordings of private conversations is such that these principles apply with even greater force to tapes of private presidential conversations than to presidential papers.

If release of the tapes would settle the central questions at issue in the Watergate inquiries, then their disclosure might serve a substantial public interest that would have to be weighed very heavily against the negatives of disclosure.

The fact is that the tapes would not finally settle the central issues before your committee. Before their existence became publicly known, I personally listened to a number of them. The tapes are entirely consistent with what I know to be the truth and what I have stated to be the truth. However, as in any verbatim recording of informal conversations, they contain comments that persons with different perspectives and motivations would inevitably interpret in different ways. Furthermore, there are inseparably interspersed

*Received by the committee July 7 and generally referred to as "the President's July 7 letter."

in them a great many very frank and very private comments, on a wide range of issues and individuals, wholly extraneous to the committee's inquiry.

Even more important, the tapes could be accurately understood or interpreted only by reference to an enormous number of other documents and tapes, so that to open them at all would begin an endless process of disclosure and explanation of private presidential records totally unrelated to Watergate, and highly confidential in nature. They are the clearest possible example of why presidential documents must be kept confidential.

Accordingly, the tapes, which have been under my sole personal control, will remain so. None has been transcribed or made public and none will be.

On May 22 I described my knowledge of the Watergate matter and its aftermath in categorical and unambiguous terms that I know to be true. In my letter of July 6, I informed you that at an appropriate time during the hearings I intend to address publicly the subjects you are considering. I still intend to do so and in a way that preserves the constitutional principle of separation of powers, and thus serves the interest not just of the Congress or of the President, but of the people.

Sincerely,

RICHARD NIXON

Wright to Cox, July 23

Dear Mr. Cox:

Mr. Buzhardt has asked that I respond to your letters to him of June 20, July 18, and July 20† in which you made certain requests with regard to tape recording of or about conversations between the President and various members of the White House staff and others.

The President is today refusing to make available to the Senate committee material of a similar nature. Enclosed is a copy of his letter of this date to Senator Ervin stating his position about the tapes. I am instructed by the President to inform you that it will not be possible to make available to you the recordings that you have requested.

In general the reasons for the President's decision are the same as those that underlay his response to the Senate committee. But in your letter of July 18 you state that furnishing the tapes in aid of an investigation into charges of criminal conspiracy raises none of the separation-of-powers issues that are raised by the request from the Senate committee. You indicated a similar position when we met on June 6. At that time you suggested that questions of separation of powers did not arise since you were within the Executive Branch, though, as I recall, you then added that your position is a little hard to describe since, in

†The June 20 and July 20 letters had not been released or reported.

your view, you are not subject to direction by the President or the attorney general.

I note that in your subsequent letters, and particularly that of July 18 in which you argue that the separation-of-powers argument is inapplicable, there is no suggestion that you are a part of the Executive Branch. Indeed, if you are an ordinary prosecutor and thus part of the Executive Branch as well as an officer of the court, you are subject to the instructions of your superiors, up to and including the President, and can have access to presidential papers only as and if the President sees fit to make them available to you.

But quite aside from the consideration just stated, there is an even more fundamental reason why separation-of-powers considerations are fully as applicable to a request from you as to one from the Senate committee. It is clear, and your letter of July 18 specifically states, that the reason you are seeking these tapes is to use some or all of them before grand juries or in criminal trials. Production of them to you would lead to their use in the courts, and questions of separation of powers are in the forefront when the most confidential documents of the presidency are sought for use in the Judicial Branch.

Indeed most of the limited case law on executive privilege has arisen in the contest of attempts to obtain executive documents for use in the courts.

The successful prosecution of those who have broken the laws is a very important national interest, but it has long been recognized that there are other national interests that, in specific cases, may override this. When Congress provided in the Jencks Act, 18 U.S.C. [U.S. Code], Section 3500 (d), that the United States may choose to refuse to disclose material that the court has ordered produced, even though in some instances this will lead to a mistrial and to termination of the prosecution, it was merely recognizing that, as the courts had repeatedly held, there are circumstances in which other legitimate national interests requiring that documents be kept confidential outweigh the interest in punishing a particular malefactor.

Similarly in civil litigation the United States may feel obliged to withhold relevant information, because of more compelling governmental interests, even though this may cause it to lose a suit it might otherwise have won. The power of the President to withhold confidential documents that would otherwise be material in the courts comes from "an inherent executive power which is protected in the constitutional system of separation of power." *United States* v. *Reynolds,* 345 U.S. 1, 6n.9 (1953).

In your letter to Mr. Buzhardt of July 10 you quoted Mr. [Elliot L.] Richardson's statement to the Senate Judiciary Committee in which he concluded that it was the President's intention "that whatever should be made public in terms of the public interest in these investigations should be disclosed . . ."

That is, of course, the President's view, but it is for the President, and only for the President, to weigh whether the incremental advantage that these tapes would give you in criminal proceedings justifies the serious and lasting hurt that disclosure of them would do to the confidentiality that is imperative to the effective functioning of the presidency. In this instance

the president has concluded that it would not serve the public interest to make the tapes available.

Sincerely,

CHARLES ALAN WRIGHT.

Nixon to Ervin, July 26

Dear Mr. Chairman:

White House counsel have received on my behalf the two subpoenas issued by you, on behalf of the select committee on July 23.

One of these calls on me to furnish to the select committee recordings of five meetings between Mr. John Dean and myself. For the reasons stated to you in my letters of July 6 and July 23, I must respectfully refuse to produce those recordings.

The other subpoena calls on me to furnish all records of any kind relating directly or indirectly to the "activities, participation, responsibilities or involvement" of 25 named individuals "in any alleged criminal acts related to the Presidential election of 1972." Some of the records that might arguably fit within that subpoena are Presidential papers that must be kept confidential for reasons stated in my letter of July 6.

It is quite possible that there are other records in my custody that would be within the ambit of that subpoena and that I could, consistent with the public interest and my constitutional responsibilities, provide to the select committee. All specific requests from the select committee will be carefully considered and my staff and I, as we have done in the past, will cooperate with the select committee by making available any information and documents that can appropriately be produced.

You will understand, however, I am sure, that it would simply not be feasible for my staff and me to review thousands of documents to decide which do and which do not fit within the sweeping but vague terms of the subpoena.

It continues to be true, as it was when I wrote you on July 6, that my staff is under instructions to cooperate fully with yours in furnishing information pertinent to your inquiry. I have directed that executive privilege not be invoked with regard to testimony by present and former members of my staff concerning possible criminal conduct or discussions of possible criminal conduct. I have waived the attorney-client privilege with regard to my former counsel. In my July 6 letter I described these acts of cooperation with the select committee as 'genuine, extensive and, in the history of such matters, extra-ordinary.' That cooperation has continued and it will continue. Executive privilege is being invoked only with regard to documents and recordings that cannot be made public consistent with the confidentiality essential to the functioning of the office of the President.

I cannot and will not consent to giving any investigatory body private presidential papers. To the extent that I have custody of other documents or information relevant to the work of the select committee and that can properly be made public, I will be glad to make these available in response to specific requests.

Sincerely,

RICHARD NIXON.

Nixon to Sirica, July 25

Dear Judge Sirica:

White House counsel have received on my behalf a subpoena duces tecum issued out of the United States District Court for the District of Columbia on July 23 at the request of Archibald Cox. The subpoena calls on me to produce for a grand jury certain tape recordings as well as certain specified documents. With the utmost respect for the court of which you are chief judge, and for the branch of government of which it is a part, I must decline to obey the command of that subpoena. In doing so I follow the example of a long line of my predecessors as President of the United States who have consistently adhered to the position that the President is not subject to compulsory process from the courts.

The independence of the three branches of our government is at the very heart of our constitutional system. It would be wholly inadmissible for the President to seek to compel some particular action by the courts. It is equally inadmissible for the courts to seek to compel some particular action from the President.

That the President is not subject to compulsory process from the other branches of government does not mean, of course, that all information in the custody of the President must forever remain unavailable to the courts. Like all of my predecessors I have always made relevant material available to the courts except in those rare instances when to do so would be inconsistent with the public interest. The principle that guides my actions in this regard was well stated by Attorney General Speed in 1865:

"Upon principles of public policy there are some kinds of evidence which the law excludes or dispenses with. . . . the official transactions between the heads of departments of the government and their subordinate officers are, in general, treated as 'privileged communications.' The President of the United States, the heads of the great departments of the government, and the governors of the several states, it has been decided, are not bound to produce papers or disclose information communicated to them where, in their own judgment, the disclosure would, on public considerations, be inexpedient. These are familiar rules laid down by every author on the law of evidence."

A similar principle has been stated by many other attorneys general, it has been recognized by the courts, and it has been acted upon by many Presidents.

In the light of that principle, I am voluntarily transmitting for the use of the grand jury the memorandum from W. Richard Howard to Bruce Kehrli in which they are interested as well as the described memoranda from Gordon Strachan to H. R. Haldeman. I have concluded, however, that it would be inconsistent with the public interest and with the constitutional position of the Presidency to make available recordings of meetings and telephone conversations in which I was a participant and I must respectfully decline to do so.

Sincerely,

RICHARD NIXON.

for my staff and me to review thousands of documents" to decide which records would comply with the "sweeping but vague terms of the subpoena."

In reply to Cox' subpoena, Nixon said in a letter to U.S. District Court Judge John J. Sirica, dated July 25, that the "independence of the three branches of our government" was at issue and that the President was "not subject to compulsory process from the courts." Nixon agreed, however, to release several memoranda sent among his aides.

Committee votes court action—At a public session of the hearings July 26, the Ervin committee voted unanimously— on a motion by Vice Chairman Howard H. Baker Jr. (R, Tenn.)—to take the issue of Nixon's refusal to comply with the tapes subpoena to the courts.

Sen. Ervin contended the litigation was essential "if we are to determine whether

the President is above the law" and "immune from all of the duties and responsibilities" of other citizens.

The committee did not specify what form of action it would take, and Baker's motion to "present a justiciable issue to the appropriate court" was considered broad enough to allow several options. Chief committee counsel Samuel Dash said later, however, that a contempt of Congress citation would not be sought.

Sen. Ervin called Nixon's offer to consider "specific requests" for other documents almost meaningless. "Since we have never seen the documents, and since even those of the White House aides who are willing to identify the documents are not allowed to copy them," Ervin said, Nixon had put upon the committee "a manifest impossibility" to receive the records.

Cox gets court order—After notification of Nixon's refusal to comply with his

subpoena, special prosecutor Cox petitioned Judge Sirica July 26 for an order to release the tapes. Cox contended that Nixon had already at least partially waived executive privilege by allowing present and former aides to testify before the Ervin committee and the grand jury. After a 28-minute hearing, Sirica directed the White House to show cause by Aug. 7 why the tapes should not be produced.

Nixon would comply with Supreme Court order—Acknowledging that the issue would probably reach the U.S. Supreme Court, White House spokesman Gerald L. Warren said July 26 that Nixon "would abide by a definitive decision of the highest court."

White House consultant Wright had said after the Cox hearing that Nixon would withhold only papers that were clearly "presidential." Documents which had lost their confidentiality or dealt exclusively with political matters did not fall into that category, Wright said.

Hoax call on tapes. A person identifying himself as Treasury Secretary George P. Shultz telephoned Sen. Ervin July 19 to say that "the President had decided to make available" the contested tapes.

When the televised hearings resumed in the afternoon, Ervin jubilantly announced the news. But minutes later, Ervin announced that "a right dirty trick" had been played on the committee. The White House and "the real Secretary Shultz" had informed him they had not made the call, Ervin said.

Use of tapes discontinued. President Nixon had discontinued use of the taping system because of the "embarrassment" generated by its disclosure, unidentified White House officials told reporters July 20.

Press spokesman Gerald L. Warren confirmed July 24 that the system had been discontinued, but he refused to say when.

Haldeman admits listening to tapes. Former White House chief of staff H. R. Haldeman testified before the Senate Watergate committee July 30 that on two occasions and at Nixon's request he had listened to tape recordings of two meetings between the President and John Dean. [See p. 57]

White House firm on tapes. After Haldeman's testimony July 30 that he had listened to some of the tapes involved in the dispute between Nixon and the committee, the White House reaffirmed that Nixon alone would decide who could be given access to recordings of his conversations about the Watergate case.

Refusing to comment further on the implications of Haldeman's use of the tapes, Deputy White House Press Secretary Gerald L. Warren said Nixon would make his decisions based on his "judgment of who could best assist him in determining the facts of the Watergate matter without jeopardizing the confidentiality of the tapes."

Samuel Dash, chief counsel to the Ervin committee, suggested July 31 that in allowing Haldeman to review the tapes Nixon might have damaged the claim of confidentiality and undermined his legal position in the dispute with the committee and Archibald Cox.

In an earlier development, Sen. Ervin and committee Vice Chairman Howard H. Baker Jr. (R, Tenn.) proposed in a television interview July 29 that they and Cox be allowed to hear the tapes privately and screen out statements unrelated to their investigations. Reacting to the proposal July 30, Warren said Nixon had already "made his position clear on this matter."

Nixon rejects court power over tapes. Lawyers for President Nixon filed a brief in U.S. district court in Washington Aug. 7 claiming that the courts had no power to compel release of presidential documents if the President believed such a disclosure was "contrary to the public interest." The White House was responding to a show cause order obtained July 26 by special prosecutor Archibald Cox in the

dispute over tape recordings of Nixon's conversations with figures in the Watergate case.

The White House argument centered on the assertion that the courts were a "co-equal but not a superior branch of government" and, accordingly, "not free to probe...the private confidence of the President and his advisers." The Nixon brief conceded the courts' power to subpoena presidential information but argued that the power did not extend to imposing "any concurrent obligation to disclose that information."

Nixon rejected Cox's contention that a special situation had been created by the possibility of criminal prosecutions and the Watergate grand jury's need to have all relevant information. Even if the conversations in question contained details of criminal plans, the brief argued, the President had the right to withhold them to protect the confidentiality of his communications.

Executive privilege was being claimed, the brief stated, by the President himself and "not by those who may be indicted." Nixon was doing so "not to protect those others," but to preserve the rights of the presidency.

While repeating Nixon's denial of involvement in criminal acts, the brief confronted the question of possible prosecution of the President by adopting the 1867 argument of Attorney General Henry Stanbery that the President "is above the process of any court or the jurisdiction of any court to bring him to account" for any dereliction of duty or for "doing anything which is contrary to law...." Rather, as Stanbery argued, the President is subject only to one "quasi court"— Congress and the process of impeachment. Only after removal from office, the White House brief continued, could he be "liable to prosecution and punishment in the ordinary course of law."

The brief also rejected Cox's contention that Nixon had already waived executive privilege by allowing his aides to testify before the grand jury and the Senate committee. Nor was there any waiver, the brief continued, because Nixon had permitted some of the tapes to be heard "by a very few people. "Whenever the President has confidential information, he is free to disclose it to those persons, in and out of government, in whom he has confidence and from whom he seeks advice."

Nixon's brief conceded that there had been "uncertainty" about the limits of executive privilege but argued that the doctrine should include "any information that the President determines cannot be disclosed consistent with the public interest and the proper performance of his constitutional duties."

If the courts did not accept the President's determination of public interest as a criterion of executive privilege, the brief argued that the doctrine should at least apply to the tapes, which "by their very nature contain spontaneous, informal, tentative, and frequently pungent com-

ments on a variety of subjects inextricably intertwined into one conversation."

Disclosure of the tapes, the brief stated, would render any President "helpless" in office if "he and his advisers could not talk freely, if they were required always to guard their words against the possibility that ... those words might be made public."

The issue, the brief concluded, was "nothing less than the continued existence of the presidency as a functioning institution."

Judge John J. Sirica gave Cox until Aug. 13 to respond to the brief and scheduled oral arguments for Aug. 22.

Committee sues for tapes. The Senate Watergate committee filed suit in U.S. district court Aug. 9 to compel President Nixon to release tapes and other documents related to Watergate. The suit contended that Nixon's refusal to comply with the committee's subpoenas for the material was "unlawful, unwarranted and in breach of his legal duty."

The committee's complaint stated that even if the President had the authority to withhold certain confidential material, the authority did "not extend to the protection of materials relating to alleged criminal acts."

The committee also argued that Nixon had already waived executive privilege, especially regarding possible criminal matters, in his statement of May 22, by allowing present and former aides to testify before the committee, and by allowing H. R. Haldeman to listen to some of the tapes after leaving the White House staff.

Attached to the complaint was an affidavit by committee minority counsel Fred D. Thompson relating a telephone conversation in June with special presidential counsel J. Fred Buzhardt Jr. in which Buzhardt reconstructed conversations between Nixon and former White House counsel John W. Dean 3rd. Thus, the complaint argued, Nixon—acting through his special counsel—had already "revealed alleged facts demonstrating that the subject matter of these conversations is within the select committee's jurisdiction."

The committee asked the court for three forms of response to its suit: a declaratory judgment that the President must honor the subpoenas, a writ of mandamus compelling him to perform his official duty to release the materials and a mandatory injunction prohibiting Nixon from withholding the tapes and documents "in his personal capacity."

Reflecting earlier predictions that the court might decline jurisdiction in the case, the committee cited sections of the U.S. Code giving the district court jurisdiction in civil actions arising from constitutional questions and in actions taken "to remedy any 'legal wrong' suffered by the plaintiffs as the result of presidential action for which no adequate review proceeding is otherwise available."

The committee also submitted a motion asking the court to reduce the period for the President to respond from the usual 60 days to 20. The motion cited a text on federal procedure co-authored by White House legal consultant Charles Alan Wright, which said the court "probably has the inherent power" to shorten the response period "in the face of special circumstances."

Cox rebuts Nixon on tapes. In a brief filed Aug. 13 in U.S. district court, special Watergate prosecutor Archibald Cox argued that President Nixon had "no constitutional power to withhold the evidence" in the tape recordings of presidential conversations "merely by his own declaration of the public interest."

Responding to a White House brief rejecting his request for the tapes, Cox said Nixon was not "a proper judge" of the public interest in the case because Nixon would, in effect, be violating "the ancient precept that no man shall be the judge of his own cause."

Cox cited a 1971 decision by the Circuit Court of Appeals for the District of Columbia in which that court had rejected the claim that absolute executive privilege was justified by the constitutional doctrine of separation of powers. Rather, Cox said in a summary of his brief, the court had ruled "that it is for the judiciary—not the executive—to determine what materials may be held confidential."

Cox noted that the White House had "wisely" emphasized the secrecy of presidential conversations rather than absolute privilege over all material. But, Cox said, the preservation of secrecy was "unwarranted in the present case" because "the interest in confidentiality is never sufficient to support an official privilege where there is reason to believe that the deliberations may have involved criminal misconduct." Cox added that the need of the grand jury for the "critically important evidence" in the tapes outweighed the "slight risk to the freedom of executive discussions."

Cox emphasized that the President was not above the law but was bound by the same legal duties as other citizens. He said the issue was Nixon's refusal "to respond to the demand from the people, speaking through their organ, the grand jury. Unlike a monarch, the President is not the sovereign." Cox said the White House assertion that the President had "the power and thus the privilege to withhold information" ran against "our entire constitutional tradition" by equating physical power with legal privilege.

Rejecting the Nixon brief's reliance on an 1867 argument by Attorney General Henry Stanbery that a President was immune from court processes, Cox noted that the Supreme Court in that case "had no occasion to decide that *no* federal court could ever issue *any* order to the President, and it did not do so." Rather, said Cox, the court "emphatically refused to accept the claim of royal immunity for the President."

Cox reaffirmed his argument that Nixon had already waived privilege on the tapes by his selective disclosures of some

of the material. "Not even a President," Cox said, "can be allowed to select" certain accounts for public release and then "frustrate further grand jury inquiries by withholding the best evidence of what actually took place."

Cox asked for "early resolution" of the issue, contending that any indictments dealing with the Watergate cover-up "would be of questionable propriety" without the evidence contained in the tapes.

Nixon addresses nation on Watergate. President Nixon told the nation in a televised address Aug. 15 it should give up its "backward-looking obsession" with Watergate, turn the case over to the courts and start attending to "matters of far greater importance. Nixon repeated his claim that release of the tapes would destroy the confidentiality necessary for the conduct of the presidency. [See p. 38]

Nixon reaffirms power over tapes. The battle of briefs between the White House and special Watergate prosecutor Archibald Cox over the tapes of presidential conversations continued Aug. 17 as lawyers for President Nixon contended he had "absolute power to decide what may be disclosed to others."

In the final brief before oral argument, the White House argued that while Nixon had not been trying to place himself "above the law," there were "unique attributes" to the presidency which required that the office be "treated differently under the law." Perhaps the most important of these, the brief said, was "presidential privacy—the right, indeed the absolute need, to be able to speak freely, to encourage others to speak freely. . . ."

The White House dismissed Cox's argument that the court had special power over the tapes because of the criminal investigations involved. The brief stated there was "no power in the judicial branch" to decide whether a criminal investigation or prosecution should continue if the executive branch had determined that "other governmental interests dictated the contrary."

Cox had been "unduly gloomy," the brief said, in suggesting that failure to obtain the tapes might require termination of the grand jury probe. The investigation had been in progress long before the existence of the tapes was publicly known, the brief continued, and Nixon felt that his refusal to release the tapes would not "defeat prosecution" of those who might have "betrayed his confidence" by committing crimes.

Oral argument—In a two-hour hearing before U.S. District Court Judge John J. Sirica Aug. 22, special prosecutor Cox and White House legal consulant Charles Alan Wright engaged in their first courtroom clash on the issue of the presidential tapes. They repeated, for the most part, the arguments advanced in their series of briefs.

Wright rejected Cox's earlier suggestion that the White House release the

tapes to Sirica for a private determination of relevant evidence. Wright maintained that Nixon was the sole judge of what records should be made available, especially when there was a risk of revealing important national security information. Wright said Nixon had told him that one of the tapes contained "national security information so highly sensitive" that even Wright could not be told its nature.

Wright told a packed courtroom that before the Watergate scandal, no court would have considered asserting "the clout to overrule the President" and order compliance with a subpoena.

Wright said "getting to the truth of Watergate is a goal of great worth," but "there may well be times when there are other national interests more important than the fullest administration of criminal justice." Compulsory production of the tapes, Wright argued, would "impair very markedly" the ability of a president to "perform the constitutional duties vested in him."

Judge Sirica asked Wright whether withholding the tapes might "thwart further prosecutions in the case." Wright replied he did not think that would happen, since the tapes would not be given to either the prosecution or the defense, and the issue of exculpatory evidence would not arise.

Sirica also asked whether the President's claim of authority to withhold evidence might lead to "potentially grave abuse" of the system of checks and balances provided in the Constitution. Wright replied that the Constitution also provided the remedy for such an abuse: impeachment.

Cox argued that the White House was practicing "almost a deceit" in urging that the Watergate case be left to the courts while withholding material potentially crucial to its prosecution. Cox said Nixon should heed the implications of his own argument and let the matter be decided "in accordance with rules of law. If he wants to dismiss the case, if he has the power, he should exercise it, and the people will know where the responsibility lies."

Cox criticized Nixon for allowing White House aides to testify about conversations—evidence "open to the defects of human recollection"—but withholding "evidence not subject to that defect." Cox said the grand jury needed relevant sections of the tapes because there was "strong reason to believe that the integrity of the executive office has been corrupted, although the extent of the rot is not yet clear."

Cox concluded by disavowing any personal antagonism toward Nixon, saying "no one would feel more relieved than I" if the tapes showed the falsity of the accusations against him.

Sirica said he hoped to hand down a decision within a week.

McGovern urges full accounting. Sen. George McGovern (D, S.D.), the unsuccessful Democratic Presidential candidate, contended Aug. 19 that President Nixon's legal stand against release of the taped White House conversations was "an invention that the President has advanced that I find [has] no basis in constitutional law." Appearing on the CBS "Face the Nation" broadcast, McGovern said, "If the President remains steadfast in his refusal to turn over the tapes, even if the courts hold that he has an obligation to do so, then the Congress will have no other recourse except to give serious consideration to impeachment."

The President was "more than a lawyer," he said, "he is also the leader of the American people." McGovern said, "Without reference to the legal aspects of this point, I would strongly recommend to President Nixon that he not only release the tapes but that he make a full accounting of everything that he knows about this Watergate tragedy."

Nixon discusses tapes at news conference. President Nixon fielded an intense barrage of questions on Watergate during most of a 50-minute news conference Aug. 22 on the lawn of his San Clemente, Calif. home.

The President was asked why he tape recorded White House conversations and "what is your reaction to surveys that show three out of four American believe you were wrong to make the tapes?"

Nixon replied that the survey findings were "not particularly surprising." Most Americans, he said, "do not like the idea of the taping of conversations and, frankly, it is not something that particularly appeals to me."

When he became President, there was a "rather complex" taping "capacity" set up in the White House. He had "the entire system dismantled," but it was put in place again in June 1970 because "my advisers felt it was important in terms particularly of national security affairs to have a record" for the future that "would only be disclosed at the discretion of the President." "This kind of capability" existed in the Johnson and Kennedy Administrations, he asserted.

As far as he was concerned, Nixon said, "we now do not have that capability and I am just as happy that we don't." He now dictated his recollections each day, when he had time.

He was asked why he permitted his former aide H.R. Haldeman, "a man who you knew might be indicted," to hear tapes which were being withheld from the prosecutors and the public.

Nixon said Haldeman, at his request, had listened only to one tape, that of a Sept. 15, 1972 discussion at which Haldeman was present. "I asked him to listen to it in order to be sure that as far as any allegations that had been made by [his former counsel] Mr. [John W.] Dean with regard to that conversation is concerned, I wanted to be sure that we were absolutely correct in our response."

Nixon was asked whether it was possible some group could listen to the tapes "and give a report so that that might satisfy the public mind."

He did not believe that such an arrangement "would satisfy the public mind," Nixon said, "and it shouldn't." To have the tapes listened to "either by a prosecutor or by a judge or in camera or in any way would violate the principle of confidentiality." "We will oppose . . . any compromise of the principle of confidentiality. . . . The principle of confidentiality either exists or it doesn't exist." The principle covered presidential papers as well as tapes.

Nixon asserted that if confidentiality were violated, individuals who came to talk to the President "will always be speaking in a eunuch-like way, rather than laying it on the line. It has to be laid on the line if you're going to have the creative kind of discussions that we have often had and have been responsible for some of our successes in the foreign policy period, particularly in the past few years."

He was asked where was "the check on authoritarianism by the executive" if the President was "the sole judge of what the executive branch makes available and suppresses," whether he would obey a Supreme Court order to produce such tapes or other documents, and whether there was any limitation on the President, "short of impeachment, to compel the production of evidence of a criminal nature."

Nixon said there was a limitation on the President—"the limitation of public opinion" and "Congressional and other pressures that may arise."

He thought his Administration had "gone further in terms of waiving executive privilege than any Administration in my memory."

He reaffirmed his spokesman's previous statement "with regard to the President's position of complying with a definitive order of the Supreme Court."

Nixon Homes, GOP Finances Probed

GOP fund 'laundering' described. An accountant for the Nixon re-election committee described in a sworn deposition May 1 the "laundering" of about $11,000 from a secret bank account which he had returned to the committee to secretly supplement a campaign employe's income.

The deposition, by Henry M. Buchanan, brother of President Nixon's speechwriter Patrick J. Buchanan, was released June 27 in connection with a civil lawsuit by the public interest lobby Common Cause against Maurice Stans, chairman of the Finance Committee to Re-elect the President. Buchanan said in the deposition that he had set up an outside bank account in 1971 at the direction of Hugh W. Sloan, former treasurer of the finance committee. He said funds were deposited in the special bank account, and that he signed checks and took cash out of the account at the direction of Jeb Stuart Magruder, deputy director of the re-election committee.

Buchanan testified that the account was used to pay five checks to an unidentified committee employe who felt he was not earning what he deserved because of jealousies within the campaign organization.

GSA spent $1.9 million on Nixon homes. The General Services Administration (GSA) announced June 21 that it had spent almost $1.9 million on President Nixon's homes in Key Biscayne, Fla. and San Clemente, Calif. The White House attributed all of the costs to security.

The total included $1,180,522.64 for improvements and maintenance at Key Biscayne—$579,907.24 for improvements, $554,321 for operation and maintenance and $46,294.40 for equipment.

At San Clemente, the figures were $698,552.70 for improvements and $4,834.60 for equipment.

The $703,367.20 San Clemente total was an upward revision of a $460,312 estimate released by the GSA and White House aides June 14 as the amount spent on security at the California estate. The figure also contrasted sharply with the $39,525 figure listed by the White House May 26 as the amount for the same purpose.

A breakdown of the costs released by the GSA June 22 showed, among other items, expenditures at San Clemente of $184,174 for electrical work, $13,850 for landscaping, $12,315 for roof tile and repairing walls and a gazebo, $13,500 for a heating system, $2,800 for a swimming pool heater, $11,561 for a redwood fence, $3,800 for a sewer line, $4,834 for furniture in the President's den, $1,853 for installation of a flagpole and $476 for painting the flagpole.

Among the items at Key Biscayne were $122,708 for bullet-resistant glass doors and windows, $122,714 for constructing a Secret Service command post, $995 for a septic tank and lid, $587 for a flagpole, $3,030 for golf carts for Secret Service patrol, $6,321 for an ice maker for Secret Service men and $475 for swimming pool cleaner.

Funds were also spent to clean the beach at San Clemente and to correct beach erosion at Key Biscayne.

At a hearing by a House Appropriations Committee subcommittee, headed by Rep. Tom Steed (D, Okla.), Secret Service Director James J. Rowley said June 27 most of the public funds spent on the two Nixon homes had been requested by his agency for security reasons. Among the items not requested were the expenditures for a swimming pool cleaner, the flagpoles, the den furniture and the ice maker. Other items not requested by the Secret Service but paid by federal expense were surveys of the San Clemente property, one made prior to Nixon's purchase.

GSA Administrator Arthur F. Sampson also testified and said all of the funds were expended in relation to presidential business or to save additional federal expense.

Both men were of the opinion that the word "improvements" as applied to the costs was misleading in that the items were really "installations" installed for security reasons.

Both officials also told the subcommittee the spending was done by the GSA at the request of the Secret Service and not on orders of the President. Sampson said the GSA had consulted with the White House staff, particularly then Nixon chief of staff H. R. Haldeman, in preparing for the work.

Steed defended the federal expenditures as "not excessive." He said his panel, which approved the overall budget for the projects, had urged that decisions on presidential security "always be made on the side of too much rather than too little."

Ziegler denounces press—White House Press Secretary Ronald L. Ziegler July 3 angrily denounced newspaper articles that he said suggested wrongdoing in the purchase of the San Clemente estate. The outburst was sparked by a Los Angeles Times story that day saying special Watergate prosecutor Archibald Cox had begun a preliminary inquiry into the San Clemente purchase and improvements. Ziegler's denial was described as vehement.

"Statements that suggest any use of campaign funds, statements which suggest any impropriety are malicious, ill-founded and scurrilous in nature and are categorically and flatly untrue," he said. Asked if Nixon shared his view, Ziegler said, "Absolutely."

"I would say the President is appalled," he continued, "by the consistent effort, the malicious—I do not know that libelous is the word in connection with the President—but I would say by the consistent effort to suggest any wrongdoing with the purchase of this property."

A denial that Cox was opening a formal probe concerning the Nixon homes in California and Florida also was issued by Cox's office July 3, but the office acknowledged it was collecting press reports on the matter.

GOP aided Peace & Freedom party. The New York Times reported July 1 that the Peace and Freedom party, a leftist splinter group, had received secret Republican contributions in California in 1972. The funds were allegedly given to the radical group to drain votes from Democratic Congressional and state assembly candidates.

John Haag, Peace and Freedom party leader, said July 3 that Frank DeLong, an employe of the State Assembly Republican caucus, had telephoned him in the spring of 1972 with an offer to finance a party registration drive. According to

Peace and Freedom party leaders, Republicans paid the party $2,000 for filing fees in at least five assembly districts and two Congressional districts and an additional $1,500 for expenses.

The Times reported that the GOP also had provided financial aid to La Raza Unida, a militant Mexican-American party.

House probe ordered. A House probe of federal funds spent on the Nixon homes and similar spending for Vice President Spiro T. Agnew was ordered July 12 to be undertaken by the House Government Operations Subcommittee headed by Rep. Jack Brooks (D, Tex.).

"Any expenditures that are essentially for improvements that any homeowner might routinely have to undertake should not be paid for out of taxpayer's funds under the guise of security protection," Brooks said. Expenditure of large sums of public money for "improvements on private property is a matter of grave concern to the American people," he said.

Brooks sought to obtain data from the GSA on federal spending on the Nixon homes to make them "safe, secure and palatial," as he put it July 31, but a commitment from Sampson to supply the data was later rescinded pending the comprehensive GSA statement. The committee received written assurance from the White House Aug. 2 that it would have access to the data. The committee voted later Aug. 2 unanimously to use subpoena power if necessary to obtain the federal records.

American Airlines admits illegal gift. George A. Spater, chairman of American Airlines, revealed July 6 that he arranged for the illegal contribution of $55,000 in corporate funds to the Finance Committee to Re-elect the President in early 1972.

Spater said the money, with another $20,000 from individual contributors, had been given after he was approached in late 1971 by Herbert W. Kalmbach, former personal counsel to President Nixon.

"I knew Mr. Kalmbach to be both the President's personal counsel and counsel for our major competitor. I concluded that a substantial response was called for," Spater said in a statement issued by the airline.

At the time of the contribution, Kalmbach was attorney for United Airlines, the largest U.S. carrier. Further, the Civil Aeronautics Board (CAB) then had before it a plan for American's merger with Western Airlines, a move strongly opposed by United. (The CAB rejected the merger July 28, 1972.)

American acknowledged July 9 it had asked the Nixon re-election committee to return the $55,000. The finance committee said July 11 it had sent American a check for $55,000. In an accompanying cover letter, the finance committee denied being aware of the illegal nature of the gift.

Federal laws prohibited corporate campaign contributions and stated that corporations and their officers, as well as campaign committees and their officials, were liable to criminal prosecution. Fines up to $5,000 for corporations and up to $10,000, along with two-year jail terms, for individuals whose actions were judged "willfull," could be assessed.

The American Airlines contribution was initially revealed by special Watergate prosecutor Archibald Cox. Cox said if other corporate officers came forward with admissions of illegal gifts, "their voluntary acknowledgement will be considered as a mitigating circumstance in deciding what charges to bring." Cox praised Spater's forthrightness, but declined to rule out action against American and its officials.

In his statement, Spater said his admission had been made to mitigate possible penalties against those involved and to "focus attention on the evils of the present political fund-raising system."

"Under existing laws a large part of the money raised from the business community for political purposes is given in fear of what would happen if it were not given. A fair and honest law is one that would remove the need of any candidate to exert such pressures, as well as the need for any businessman to respond," Spater said.

The total of $75,000, given in five cash installments, did not have to be reported if given by individuals while the campaign fund disclosure act of 1926 remained in effect. The most recent federal campaign contribution reporting law—effective April 7, 1972—ruled out all secret cash contributions.

The Washington Post reported July 7 that some of the corporate money had been "laundered" through a broker in Lebanon. The $55,000 was raised through phony invoices for which payments were reflected on the airline's books, the Post said.

James H. O'Connor, attorney for Kalmbach, said in Phoenix his client had asked Spater for $100,000 but no mention of cash was made. Kalmbach denied that he knew American planned to make an illegal contribution, O'Connor said.

Eastern Airlines said July 6 that Kalmbach had approached the company for a contribution but had been turned down.

California quota system confirmed. Nixon campaign fund raisers in California confirmed reports July 7 that a quota system had been applied to prospective donors.

The California Finance Committee to Re-elect the President, operating independently of the Finance Committee to Re-elect the President, assessed wealthy donors 1% of their net worth. For corporate executives the assessment amounted to 1% of their firms' gross annual sales.

The system's existence was confirmed by Henry Salvatori, oilman and Nixon contributor, and by Thomas Bauer, executive director of the California Finance Committee.

Vesco verdict reaffirmed. Judge George L. Hart of the U.S. District Court in Washington reaffirmed July 9 a guilty verdict he had handed down June 20 against the Finance Committee to Re-elect the President for failing to report a $200,000 contribution from financier Robert L. Vesco.

Committee attorneys had asked for a rehearing on the ground it was legal not to have reported the contribution if it were included in a cash-on-hand report after the new campaign fund reporting law went into effect April 7, 1972.

Judge Hart rejected the request because the promised contribution had to be in writing and the Vesco pledge was made orally.

New Vesco indictment. Financier Robert L. Vesco was secretly indicted by a federal grand jury in New York on charges of wire fraud and attempting to defraud one of his companies, International Controls Corp. (ICC), and its stockholders of $250,000, it was announced June 13.

The money had been donated to President Nixon's re-election campaign in 1972 while Vesco was under investigation by the Securities and Exchange Commission (SEC). Later that year the SEC brought a civil suit against Vesco, charging him with masterminding a $224 million swindle of four mutual funds.

There were further repercussions when Vesco was indicted May 10 by a federal grand jury on criminal charges of obstructing justice. The allegations stemmed from his 1972 political contribution, of which $200,000 was a secret cash donation. Participants in that transaction, former Attorney General John N. Mitchell, Nixon finance committee chairman Maurice Stans and New Jersey politician Harry L. Sears, also were accused of attempting to block the SEC investigation as part of a quid pro quo settlement.

The secret indictment against Vesco, accusing him of illegal use of the telegraph, was the basis of U.S. ambassador Viron P. Vaky's request that Costa Rica order Vesco's extradition. He had fled to Costa Rica to avoid prosecution in the SEC suit and had evaded three bench warrants ordering his arrest.

Extradition denied—The Costa Rican Supreme Court July 24 upheld a lower court's refusal to turn Vesco over to U.S. authorities. The lower court had ruled June 22 that a 1922 extradition treaty did not cover attempted fraud. The treaty also did not cite obstruction of justice charges as a basis for extradition.

Vesco's business associate and apparent patron, Costa Rican President Jose Figueres, admitted July 9 that he had helped draft a speech Vesco had delivered over national television defending his presence in Costa Rica.

Figueres was responding to charges by a prominent San Jose lawyer, Fernandez Duran, that he had served as Vesco's "adviser and intellectual collaborator" in writing "substantial parts" of speech. Figueres congratulated Duran for "discovering that I am helping investors transfer their capital to Costa Rica."

Vesco's Bahamas activities—Vesco's investments in the Bahamas reportedly were extensive. He was believed to be living in seclusion in Nassau.

The New York Times reported June 2 that Vesco had made major cash contributions and loans to politicians in the Bahamas. Prime Minister Lynden O. Pindling July 8 confirmed reports that Vesco had contributed a "good sum" to his 1972 campaign, but he declined to reveal the amounts.

Vesco's banking interests in the Bahamas were closely linked to the U.S. charges of criminal and civil wrongdoing. In its secret indictment, the government charged that Vesco had arranged the transfer of $250,000 in cash from the Bahamas Commonwealth Bank, which he controlled, to Barclays Bank in New York April 6, 1972. Vesco intended to repay the Bahamas bank with money fraudulently obtained from International Controls Corp., it was alleged.

According to the Times, Bahamas Commonwealth Bank acquired another Nassau bank, Butler's Bank, which held a $500,000 note on a building owned by Prime Minister Pindling. (Pindling claimed to have sold the property.) Other Butler interests absorbed into Vesco's investment network included pharmacies, car dealerships, liquor stores, a hotel and a daily newspaper.

Nixon claims privilege on milk fund data. Presidential counsel Leonard Garment, acting "at the direction of the President," filed an affidavit in U.S. District Court in Washington July 11 invoking the principles of executive privilege and the lawyer-client relationship in response to a subpoena of official documents. The documents were sought by consumer advocate Ralph Nader in his lawsuit seeking to overturn the 1971 increase in the federal support price for milk. Nader contended that the increase had been granted "improperly and unlawfully" in return for large contributions by the dairy industry to Nixon's campaign.

The disclosures sought by Nader involved memoranda and supporting data on the merits of the industry's price demands and the arrangements for a meeting between Nixon and industry leaders.

In his affidavit, Garment argued that the release of the material "would be injurious to the public interest and to the constitutional doctrine of the separation of powers." Garment said he was seeking to protect Nixon's relationship with his legal staff as well as the President's "frank recommendations, opinions and considerations." Nader's lawyer William A. Dobrovir had contended that the concept of executive privilege was "not absolute."

Garment said he would also oppose Dobrovir's proposal to compel delivery of the documents under seal to Judge William Jones. Under the proposal, Jones would have ruled on the assertion of immunity for some or all of the material after a private study of the documents.

Weicker concedes White House aid. Sen. Lowell P. Weicker Jr. (R, Conn.), a member of the Senate Watergate committee, acknowledged July 11 that he had received substantial contributions from a secret White House political fund for his 1970 senatorial campaign. However, he denied a Washington Star-News report that he had not disclosed the funds as legally required.

The Star-News reported July 11 that Weicker was one of more than 20 recipients of $1.5 million in cashiers checks distributed to Senate campaigns in 1970 through the "Public Institute," a White House funding operation reportedly headed by former White House aide Jack A. Gleason.

Weicker denied that the receipt of the funds, reportedly totalling $65,000, was improper, adding that he had fully reported the contributions to the Connecticut secretary of state. The Washington paper attributed the charge against Weicker to unidentified "Nixon re-election sources."

Another member of the Senate committee, Sen. Edward J. Gurney (R, Fla.) discounted July 2 a report in the Miami Herald that he had received $20,800 from a May 23, 1973 cocktail party reception sponsored by "Friends of Ed Gurney," a group that included President Nixon's close friend G. C. (Bebe) Rebozo and former presidential adviser Murray Chotiner. The Herald had said that both Rebozo and Chotiner had purchased $100 tickets to the reception.

Gurney charged that the report was the first in a "long expected series of attempted hatchet jobs by The Miami Herald concerning my upcoming 1974 Senate campaign."

Corporations disclose pressures for gifts. The Chrysler Corporation disclosed July 12 that President Nixon's personal attorney, Herbert W. Kalmbach, had asked Chrysler board chairman Lynn A. Townsend for a major gift to the President's campaign. The admission followed the disclosure July 6 of an illegal American Airlines contribution to the Nixon campaign.

The New York Times reported July 13 that Kalmbach's request came at a time when Chrysler was preparing to seek a delay in implementation of federal standards for automobile emission controls. A Chrysler spokesman denied a report in the Detroit Free Press July 12 that Kalmbach had asked Townsend for an illegal corporate contribution, stating that the request was for contributions from Chrysler executives as individuals. The Times also reported that leaders of all the auto companies except the Ford Motor Company were asked by Kalmbach or other Nixon campaigners for $100,000 "company" contributions.

(The Washington Post reported July 13 that Henry Ford II had contributed $50,000 to the Nixon campaign in mid-March, 1972, three weeks before the law requiring disclosure of contributions became effective. A Ford spokesman said the donation was made in untraceable securities and came from Ford's "own pocketbook." Ford did not contribute to the Nixon campaign after April 7, 1972 when the new disclosure law became effective.

A General Motors spokesman said, in a July 13 report, that both Kalmbach and Nixon campaign finance chief Maurice Stans "contacted various GM executives" in the fall of 1971 and that many had made voluntary contributions.

The American Motors Corporation said its Washington representative had been asked for a $100,000 donation in March, 1972. Quoted by the Wall St. Journal July 13, a company spokesman said the request was rejected even when the amount was reduced to $50,000.

Charles Thornton, board chairman of Litton Industries, said July 12 that Stans had requested an aggregate contribution of $100,000 in February 1972. The company was having problems with a large shipbuilding contract at the time. While Thornton reportedly told Stans he would not ask his executives to make personal contributions, he added that donations made by himself and Roy Ash, then president of Litton and presently director of the Office of Management and Budget, might have brought the total Litton contribution to $100,000.

The Washington Post reported July 14 that Leonard Firestone, top Nixon campaign fund raiser in California, set a $100,000 contribution quota for the Lockheed Corporation, which had benefited by 1971 legislation guaranteeing the company a $250 million loan. Lockheed chairman Daniel Haughton said some funds had been raised, but the total "did not approach $100,000."

Union Oil Company president Fred G. Hartley said July 12 that he was asked in 1972 by Stans to donate $100,000 to the Nixon campaign, but refused to make a "contribution of such magnitude," although he donated $3,000 in personal funds.

John T. Connor, chairman of Allied Chemicals, said in a July 14 report he had declined Stans' request for $50,000 from company executives, although he personally gave $2,225 to the campaign.

The New York Times reported July 15 that investigators from both the Senate Watergate committee and the special Watergate prosecution team headed by Archibald Cox were finding a pattern of high pressure solicitations for contributions to the Nixon campaign. A Times survey of a list of corporate contributors found that campaign requests by Stans and Kalmbach were usually for $100,000 and that they centered on prime defense contractors and companies awaiting rulings from government agencies.

Maryland GOP violations charged. Maryland's state Republican chairman, Alexander M. Lankler, announced July 13 that he would resign in September because he had become a "symbol of divisiveness" in the state's party. He called for a meeting of the Republican State Central Committee in September to elect a successor.

Lankler's announcement came after the General Accounting Office (GAO) had reported July 5 that it had asked the Justice Department to investigate eight violations of the federal campaign spending law it said it had uncovered in the transfer of $50,000 from the Finance Committee to Re-elect the President to the Maryland Salute to Ted Agnew Night Committee. The money was allegedly used to inflate the proceedings from a 1972 testimonial dinner on behalf of Vice President Spiro T. Agnew.

The violations uncovered by the GAO could result in jail terms or fines for about 20 prominent Maryland Republicans, including Lankler and Blagdon H. Wharton, chairman of the Agnew committee.

The GAO charged Maryland GOP officials with "knowingly and willfully making false, fictitious and fraudulent statements" in campaign reports to conceal the $50,000 transfer. The GAO said the funds had been disguised as coming from 31 individual contributors. The GOP leaders had said they were worried the event would look like a failure without the extra funds. The money was later returned to the Nixon committee and an apparently false report was filed with both GAO and state officials.

The Maryland Republicans were also accused of failing to report to the GAO $47,000 in corporate contributions received by the Agnew committee.

Vice President Agnew said July 5 that he "took no part, direct or indirect, in the solicitation, collection or reporting of the funds used by the state committee." He added that he had "no knowledge" of the fund transfer "until the matter was reported in the press."

Beall campaign violations probed. A Maryland election official charged July 14 that the 1970 campaign of Sen. J. Glenn Beall (R, Md.) might have violated the state's election law by accepting unreported funds raised by President Nixon's former lawyer, Herbert W. Kalmbach.

In a statement released July 13, Beall acknowledged he had received the money in cash from the "National Republican Administration." Beall said that the funds were handled in the District of Columbia "in accordance with the laws that existed at the time." Maryland election supervisor Willard Morris had said the Beall campaign would have violated state law if money from the White House funding operation were spent in Maryland and not reported to Morris.

2nd grand jury called. Acting at Cox's request, U.S. District Court Judge John J. Sirica July 19 ordered the empaneling of a second grand jury to investigate irregularities in the 1972 campaign.

Spokesmen for Cox said the new panel would begin hearing testimony Aug. 13 on campaign violations apart from the Watergate break-in and the subsequent cover-up. The spokesmen said new areas for investigation would include conspiracy to defraud the government, obstruction of justice, extortion by federal officials, campaign contributions by corporations, and other violations of federal campaign financing laws.

The original Watergate grand jury was scheduled to continue through January 1974.

Ashland Oil admits illegal gift. Orin E. Atkins, chairman of the Ashland Oil Co. of Kentucky, revealed July 20 that he had illegally contributed $100,000 in corporate funds to the Finance Committee to Re-elect the President in April 1972. The admission followed the disclosure July 6 of an illegal American Airlines contribution and other pressures on large corporations for contributions to the Nixon campaign.

Atkins released a statement saying he had voluntarily informed special Watergate prosecutor Archibald Cox of the contribution and intended to "fully cooperate" with Cox in any investigation.

Cox said the contribution "was solicited by and delivered to Maurice H. Stans," former chairman of the finance committee.

Atkins said the Nixon committee "was not told that corporate funds were involved. When advised of this fact, the finance committee returned the contribution to the company." Atkins said the contribution was given by "a subsidiary" identified as the Ashland Petroleum Gabon Corp.

Cox had said earlier that voluntary disclosure of illegal contributions might be considered as a "mitigating circumstance" in deciding further action against corporations. However, in Ashland's case, Cox said, he was "in no position to make any disposition of the matter until the details of the contribution and surrounding circumstances have been fully investigated."

Nixon committee told to disclose funds. The Finance Committee to Re-elect the President was ordered July 24 to make public "a complete and accurate" account of campaign expenses and contributions between Jan. 1, 1971 and April 6, 1972, after which a new election-campaign financing law become effective. During that time, the reelection committee reportedly raised an estimated $19.6 million.

Federal District Court Judge Joseph C. Waddy issued the order, in a lawsuit filed Sept. 6, 1972 by the public interest lobby Common Cause, directing the committee to file its report within 60 days, by Sept. 28. He reserved action on dismissing the case until Common Cause could examine the documents to see if they were complete.

Common Cause Chairman John Gardner said July 24 that the decision was "just what we've been seeking since we filed the suit." He added that "now, at long last, the public will be able to learn who gave how much for the President's re-election in the crucial period when [Finance Chairman] Maurice Stans and other fund-raisers were seeking huge contributions under the promise of secrecy."

Senate approves campaign fund reform. A campaign fund reform bill that would set the strictest controls yet on political campaign funding was approved by the Senate July 30 by an 82–8 vote.

The bill would impose ceilings on the amount of single contributions and on the spending by candidates. It also would establish a new federal agency to monitor and enforce the bill's provisions.

Among those provisions:

■ Individual contributions to candidates for president or Congress would be limited to $3,000 per election, applying separately to a primary election, a general election or a runoff. The same limit would apply to gifts from special interest fund-raising organizations.

■ Donations of more than $50 would have to be made by a traceable check.

■ The total annual contributions by an individual, including his or her spouse and children, would be limited to $25,000 for all federal candidates and fund-raising committees.

■ Donor identification, as in the current law, would be required by occupation and place of business as well as by name and address.

■ Total campaign expenses for a seat in Congress would be limited to an equivalent of 10¢ a voter in the district or state represented in the primary contest and 15¢ a voter in the general election. A presidential candidate's limit would be the same as a senator's in each state.

■ The Congressional franking privilege for free mailing would be suspended for mass mailings 30 days prior to elections.

■ The current law's provision requiring equal broadcast time for all candidates for president and Congress would be repealed.

■ Another current restriction against contributions by fund-raising groups organized by corporations or unions with government contracts would be repealed, on the ground that it was discriminatory in permitting contributions by non-contractors.

During debate on the bill, a proposal for public financing of federal elections was tabled by a 53–40 vote July 26 after assurance was given the issue would be taken up later in the year in separate legislation.

GAO cites campaign violations. The General Accounting office (GAO) announced July 28 that apparent campaign fund violations in Indiana had been referred to the Justice Department for possible prosecution. At issue was a long standing patronage system used by both political parties which required kickbacks amounting to 2% of annual earnings from persons whose employment had been obtained as a result of their political connections.

In 1972 when 60% of the state's 12,000 employes were appointed by the Republican state administration, the kickbacks totaled $375,000, or 46% of all contributions collected by the GOP that year.

The GAO reported another apparent campaign law violation Aug. 13. The Wisconsin McGovern for President Committee failed to keep adequate accounting records, according to the GAO.

Tax on political parties planned. The Internal Revenue Service (IRS) announced Aug. 1 that it planned to tax political parties and fund raising committees for income derived from stocks given as political contributions.

Donors giving the properties would not pay capital gains taxes but fund raising groups would be required to pay taxes ranging from 7%–35% on stocks which had increased in value between the time the contributor acquired the property and the time it was donated to the political group. Taxes also would be levied on income derived from interest or dividends on investments and on "any ancillary commercial activities" unrelated to a candidate's campaign.

IRS Commissioner Donald C. Alexander said that unless Congress or the courts objected to the proposal, the new ruling would apply to any property given to political groups after Oct. 3, 1972, the day when the IRS had first indicated its "concern" about tax loopholes enjoyed by political groups.

The selection of the retroactive starting date was regarded by observers as a compromise gesture by the IRS permitting the bulk of the stock transfers made during the presidential campaign to escape taxation. Alexander said both political parties already had declared their opposition to the proposal. Political parties had not been required to file income tax returns in the past.

Colson sought IRS aid. Charles W. Colson, then President Nixon's special counsel, directed other White House aides to ask the Internal Revenue Service (IRS) for the names of contributors to the National Council of Senior Citizens, a Washington lobbying group which Colson described as an "outfit giving us trouble," according to a court document filed Aug. 2.

According to Roy Kinsey, a former aide to White House Counsel John W. Dean 3rd, Colson also ordered inquiries into the possibility of withdrawing tax exempt status from two other organizations regarded by the Nixon Administration as "political enemies"—Common Cause and Vietnam Veterans Against the War.

Kinsey's statements were contained in a deposition in connection with a lawsuit brought by the Center for Corporate Responsibility. The center claimed that it had been the target of political reprisals by the IRS, which had revoked its tax exempt status.

Colson's instructions to Dean were passed to him, Kinsey said. His contact at the IRS on "sensitive" matters was Roger V. Barth, deputy chief counsel, according to Kinsey.

He was unable to obtain information on the senior citizens group, Kinsey reported. He did not reveal what action was taken against the Vietnam veterans but he said the Common Cause issue was not pursued because the group had obtained only a limited tax exempt status.

IRS to disband activists study unit—The IRS announced Aug. 9 that it was dismantling a special division that had studied liberal and radical organizations for possible violations of tax laws. The group was created in August 1969 as a result of Senate investigations of extremist groups, according to Donald C. Alexander, IRS commissioner.

Testimony before the Senate Watergate committee had linked the IRS unit to planned White House reprisals against political enemies.

Alexander said that since 1972 the IRS unit had been limited to investigations of "tax rebels," which he defined as those "tax-resistance organizations and those individuals who publicly advocate noncompliance with the tax laws."

$10 million spent on Nixon homes. The Nixon Administration disclosed Aug. 6 that about $10 million of federal funds was spent for security at President Nixon's homes at San Clemente, Calif. and Key Biscayne, Fla., at Grand Cay, an island resort in the Bahamas frequented by the President and owned by his friend, industrialist Robert H. Abplanalp, and at places where the Nixon daughters lived.

Previous estimates of federal money spent on security at the Nixon homes were much lower.

Arthur F. Sampson, administrator of the General Services Administration, said the earlier estimates were announced in line with a "basic decision" taken in 1969 by White House staff members, GSA officials and members of the Secret Service to "minimize" the figures in order not to jeopardize the President's security. The latest accounting, he said, was made at the direction of the President because of "the atmosphere that exists today." Sampson said about $100,000 had been spent by the government to "satisfy press inquiries" on the matter.

The majority of the federal funding—$6 million—was spent for military facilities, mostly communications installations, at the homes in San Clemente and Key Biscayne and at Grand Cay.

Total GSA spending on presidential homes and adjacent offices was put at $3.7 million.

The Secret Service said Aug. 6 it had spent about $300,000 since 1969 for detection devices for the homes of the President and his two daughters.

Military expenditures at San Clemente totaled $3.7 million, including $1 million for communications systems and annual recurring costs of $677,000. At Key Biscayne, the one-time military cost totaled $730,000, including $418,000 for a helicopter pad, $14,000 for a shark net and about $300,000 for communications equipment. The annual recurrent cost of communications was put at about $330,000 for each of four years.

Military spending at Grand Cay and a nearby cay for installing communications equipment totaled $160,000.

The largest item in the GSA spending was $1.7 million for an office complex at San Clemente, about two-thirds of which covered maintenance and operation over a four-year period. GSA expenditures for security installations and improvements on the grounds at San Clemente (walls, lighting, alarm systems) totaled $635,000. GSA spending on the main house at San Clemente was $68,148. Some of this, $13,500, was to replace a gas furnace the Secret Service considered inherently unsafe. Electric heating was installed.

GSA spent $137,482 at Key Biscayne on Nixon's two homes, $130,000 of that on bulletproof windows and doors. Another $152,000 went for security lights and alarms at Key Biscayne, $131,000 for a command post and $75,000 for walls, fences and screening.

The GSA spent $16,000 at Grand Cay, most of it for a bunkhouse and a trailer outpost for security agents and for exterior lighting.

About $50,000 was expended by the GSA at five privately-owned residences occupied at various times by Nixon's daughters, much of it for communications systems and security command centers.

All of the installations at San Clemente and Key Biscayne were to be removed eventually, Sampson said, "provided that the cost of removal is not prohibitive." However, a major cost at San Clemente was for landscaping necessitated by installing power lines and cables underground and subsequent restoration of the property.

(A mini-golf course built on the San Clemente estate used by Nixon was the

Spending by Agency		
Location	GSA	Military
San Clemente	$2,444,447	$3,700,000
Key Biscayne	1,180,522	2,050,000
Grand Cay	16,000	160,000
Nixon Daughters	50,000	....
Totals*	$3,690,969	$5,910,000

*The Secret Service also spent a total of $300,000, which was not broken down by location.

gift of 76 Nixon friends, who valued it at $85,000 to $100,000 and contributed annual dues [$250 each] for its maintenance. "Golfing Friends of the President," disclosed the gift July 14.)

ITT memo disclosed. The Senate Watergate Committee Aug. 1 made public an internal White House memo written March 30, 1972 by then special counsel Charles Colson warning that Richard G. Kleindienst's confirmation hearings, which were delayed in the Senate Judiciary Committee, could directly link the President and other high Administration officials to a controversial government antitrust ruling involving the International Telephone and Telegraph Corp. [See p. 61]

Gulf, Goodyear disclose campaign gifts. Gulf Oil Corp. and Goodyear Tire and Rubber Co. acknowledged Aug. 10 that they had made large campaign contributions to President Nixon's re-election committee. Gulf and Goodyear were the third and fourth major corporations to admit giving illegal political donations. Both companies had notified the office of special Watergate prosecutor Archibald Cox of their actions and the subsequent refund of their money by the Finance Committee to Re-elect the President.

Gulf's $100,000 had been given in response to "intense" and "irresistible" requests for money by unidentified representatives of the Nixon finance committee, according to B. R. Dorsey, chairman of Gulf's board. Two separate contributions of $50,000 were made in 1971 and early 1972 before the federal election law requiring disclosure of all campaign funds became law April 7, 1972.

Goodyear revealed that it had made two cash contributions of $20,000 each in March 1972.

Both companies said the finance committee had not been informed that the money derived from corporate funds.

A total of $900,000 had been refunded to individual and corporate campaign donors, according to a spokesman for the finance committee

George Bush, chairman of the Republican National Committee, told reporters Aug. 12 that the GOP committee had paid a "substantial amount of money" to the Nixon finance committee in 1972 "as a kind of donation to get it [the campaign] started." The money was given under the assumption that the Nixon committee had ended the 1968 presidential race with a deficit, Bush said.

Herbert Kalmbach had admitted before the Senate Watergate Committee July 17 that a surplus of over $2 million remained from the 1968 campaign.

Other corporations approached. Gulf and Western Industries Inc. was approached on two separate occasions by representatives of President Nixon seeking campaign contributions in the form of "services," it was reported Aug. 1.

William L. Safire, then a Nixon speechwriter and currently a columnist for the New York Times, confirmed that he had met with Martin S. Davis, a Gulf and Western official in February 1972 to discuss a political contribution. Safire said he had been asked to intercede with Davis by Nixon fund raiser Herbert W. Kalmbach.

Kalmbach had met previously with Gulf and Western Chairman Charles G. Bluhdorn, who said he had rejected the request for a personal donation. Company officials said Kalmbach also had asked them to contribute 1% of their net worth or a total of $100,000. When refused, Kalmbach turned to the subject of services. Safire confirmed that he had discussed a possible campaign film with Davis. Gulf and Western owned Paramount Pictures.

Safire said he had not wanted to pursue the matter and Kalmbach had told him to "forget it."

Currier Holman, chairman of Iowa Beef Processors Inc. of Nebraska, was approached by a Nixon campaign aide who discussed quid pro quo arrangements for large contributors, the New York Times reported July 19.

Holman and his company were under federal investigation in 1971 and 1972. In March 1973, Holman was indicted by federal and state grand juries in New York, charged with conspiring to bribe union and supermarket officials to sell company products in New York. The company also was party to the state charges.

Holman donated $2,000 to the Nixon campaign in October 1972.

Holman said Clayton Yeutter, who had resigned from the Agriculture Department to work for the campaign, had solicited the money in March or April 1972. Yeutter currently was assistant secretary of agriculture. Yeutter recalled the discussion but said the rewards he promised potential contributors were "purely a public relations kind of thing," such as invitations to White House functions or luncheons with Cabinet officials.

According to Holman, Yeutter told him:

"If you gave $25,000, if you had a problem, you could talk to someone in the White House. I think I said, 'What if I gave more?' And he said maybe the yardstick would be for $25,000 you get to talk to somebody in the White House, a Cabinet officer or someone like that. For $50,000 you get to talk to the President. I can't remember the exact amounts, really, but I remember something to the effect that with a very large contribution you can talk to the President—if you had a serious problem."

Dean named in Mitchell-Stans suit. Former White House Counsel John W. Dean 3rd was named one of three co-conspirators in the federal case against financier Robert L. Vesco and former Attorney General John N. Mitchell, Maurice Stans, formerly Commerce secretary and currently chairman of the Nixon finance committee, and New Jersey politician Harry L. Sears, the Justice Department announced Aug. 13.

The bill of particulars provided by the prosecution also named as co-conspirators, but not as co-defendants, Laurence B. Richardson Jr. and Howard F. Cerny. Richardson was a former president of International Controls Corp. (ICC), which was controlled and allegedly defrauded by Vesco. According to pretrial testimony given by Sears, he and Richardson had delivered Vesco's $200,000 secret contribution to Stans in April 1972.

Sears also testified that Cerny, a Vesco attorney and reported friend of President Nixon's brothers, had solicited the aid of Edward Nixon in expediting the transfer of money from Vesco's New Jersey headquarters to the Washington offices of the Nixon finance committee.

Dean's role in the alleged conspiracy to obstruct justice related to the Securities and Exchange Commission's (SEC) investigation of Vesco's financial operations. It was alleged that Dean acted on the request of Mitchell to call SEC chairman William J. Casey, asking that subpoenas issued to ICC employes be delayed in order not to uncover Vesco's secret campaign contribution.

Casey had admitted receiving the request from Dean but said he had ignored it. The government charged that five subpoenas had been delayed up to eight days. Casey and his successor at the SEC, G. Bradford Cook, who had resigned as a result of his role in the Vesco inquiry, were not named as co-conspirators.

The bill of particulars also indicated that the secret campaign funds transaction may have been used to finance the Watergate conspirators.

Mitchell, Stans dismissal plea rejected— Federal Judge Lee P. Gagliardi Aug. 15 rejected a defense motion seeking dismissal of charges against Mitchell and Stans, or an indefinite delay or change of venue in their trial.

The defendants, who had been subpoenaed to testify before the Senate Watergate Committee, contended that the televised hearings had resulted in "massive, pervasive and prejudicial publicity." The "carnival atmosphere of Watergate, precipitated as it has been by the Senate hearings and the grand jury leaks," precluded their rights to a fair trial, the defense argued.

The prosecution agreed July 30 to separate the trial of Sears from that of his co-defendants. Sears' trial was scheduled to follow the Mitchell-Stans trial, which would begin Sept. 11.

Phillips, 3M reveal illegal gifts. Two more companies notified the office of special Watergate prosecutor Archibald Cox that they had made illegal contributions to President Nixon's re-election campaign, it was announced Aug. 17. Four other corporations had acknowledged giving political donations which were prohibited by federal campaign spending laws.

Phillips Petroleum Co. announced Aug. 17 that its former chairman, W. W. Keller, had donated $100,000 in corporate funds to the Finance Committee to Re-elect the President without permission of the company's directors. Keeler, who resigned Jan. 1, had given the money before April 7, 1972, when public disclosure of campaign donors was required by law, according to the company statement. The Nixon finance committee said Aug. 17 that the contribution had been returned to Phillips earlier that day.

Minnesota Mining and Manufacturing Co. also disclosed Aug. 17 that it had donated $30,000 in cash to the Nixon campaign. The company was seeking a return of its money.

White House releases ITT files. White House files on the International Telephone and Telegraph Corp. (ITT) were made available to the office of special Watergate prosecutor Archibald Cox Aug. 21.

Cox's request for the documents was based on authorization he had received from Attorney General Elliot L. Richardson June 8 to investigate the controversial antitrust settlement arranged for ITT by the Justice Department as it related to Watergate developments.

Cox had told a news conference July 27 that he had received no reply to his request for access to the files, which he said were of "utmost importance" in investigating possible perjury and obstruction of justice charges. A grand jury was convened in Washington Aug. 13 to study allegations of criminal actions by government and ITT officials.

Some of the White House files on the ITT case already had been made public at the Senate Watergate hearings.

Other "politically sensitive" documents relating to the antitrust settlement, in possession of ITT, had been made public by the investigation subcommittee of the House Commerce Committee.

In testimony before the subcommittee June 27, former Securities and Exchange Commission (SEC) Chairman William J. Casey said John D. Ehrlichman, the President's domestic affairs adviser, had called him March 6, 1972 to complain that SEC lawyers were harassing ITT in an effort to obtain additional documents unrelated to the SEC's investigation of the company. Under questioning, Casey admitted that Ehrlichman's call had been "clearly improper." The ITT documents were provided to the SEC later that month.

(Casey also testified that Sen. Edward Kennedy [D, Mass.] had also telephoned him about a different but unrelated aspect of the ITT case in 1972. Casey said he thought it also was an improper call to a regulatory agency.)

Casey testified he had given copies of the papers to Attorney General Richard G. Kleindienst in August 1972. According to Casey, Attorney General John N. Mitchell had obtained copies of the documents in March 1972 and had given White House Counsel John W. Dean 3rd a set of the documents just before leaving the Jus-

tice Department to become chairman of the President's re-election campaign.

When several Congressional committees also asked to examine the SEC's file, Casey turned the documents over to the Justice Department's Criminal Division. As a result of this transfer, the committees were denied access to the "politically sensitive" papers.

Braniff contribution revealed. Braniff Airways announced Aug. 23 that it had made a "voluntary disclosure" to the office of special Watergate prosecutor Archibald Cox of two contributions made in 1972 to the Nixon re-election committee.

The first donation, totaling $10,000, was made by the firm's chairman, Harding L. Lawrence, and another unidentified officer out of their personal funds. When Maurice Stans, chairman of the Nixon finance committee, solicited a "substantial further contribution," another $40,000 donation was made out of corporate funds by Braniff officers and other individuals. The company claimed that the donors subsequently had reimbursed Braniff for the $40,000 gift.

GAO details 1972 campaign spending. More than $79 million was collected for the 1972 presidential campaign, according to a comprehensive report prepared by the General Accounting Office (GAO) and released Aug. 23.

The four-volume report listed every political donation, loan, ticket sale or other payment of $100 or more which was received by major campaign contenders between April 7, 1972 and Dec. 31, 1972. (Totals for contributions and other financial transactions of less than $100 had not yet been completed.)

According to GAO figures:

71,575 individual contributors and committees gave $63.6 million in donations; there were 1,750 loans amounting to $15.5 million. President Nixon's campaign reported receipts of $37,624,279; loans of $1,-683,734. Sen. George McGovern's campaign reported receipts of $13,041,661; loans of $8,284,547.

Other contenders: Gov. George C. Wallace (D, Ala.)—receipts of $187,170, loans of $16,250; Sen. Hubert H. Humphrey (D, Minn.)—receipts of $1,745,-383, loans of $2,038,675; Sen. Edmund S. Muskie (D, Me.)—receipts of $977,200, loans of $233,500; Sen. Henry M. Jackson (D, Wash.)—receipts of $216,800, loans of $10,200; Rep. Wilbur D. Mills (D, Ark.)—receipts of $277,000, loans of $17,000; Rep. Shirley Chisholm (D, N.Y.)—receipts of $42,000, loans of $10,800; former Los Angeles Mayor Sam Yorty (D)—receipts of $83,250, loans of $25,000.

Other presidential candidates: John G. Schmitz (American party)—receipts of $195,153, loans of $8,-900; Gus Hall (Communist party)—receipts of $15,-585, loans of $4,580; Louis Fisher (Socialist Labor party)—receipts of $42,341, no loans; Earle Harold Nunn Jr. (Prohibition party)—receipts of $6,313, no loans.

The figures were believed to represent only about 80% of the total campaign spending because contributions received before April 7, 1972 did not require public disclosure under the 1971 Federal Election Campaign Act.

Audit on Nixon homes issued. An audit of the financing of President Nixon's homes revealed Aug. 27 that his close

friend C. G. (Bebe) Rebozo was one of the financial backers in the purchase of Nixon's property in San Clemente, Calif. The second financial backer, Nixon's close friend Robert Abplanalp, had been disclosed previously.

The disclosure of Rebozo's role came in an audit, said to have been paid for by the President, issued by the White House to "put to rest once and for all the questions" about the purchase of the San Clemente property, according to White House Deputy Press Secretary Gerald L. Warren. The audit was done by Coopers & Lybrand,* an accounting firm in New York, which had been recommended by attorneys H. Chapman Rose of Cleveland and Kenneth Gemmell of Philadelphia, who were consulted by the President on the matter.

A second disclosure of the audit was that Nixon had spent more of his own money on San Clemente improvements and furnishings—$217,270—than the previously announced figure of $123,514.

The total of $811,728 spent by Nixon in payments, taxes, improvements and furnishings on San Clemente and on his two properties in Key Biscayne, Fla. was approximately equivalent to his presidential salary received in the past four years.

According to the audit, which covered to May 31, Nixon owed as of that date a balance of $264,440 on the San Clemente property, at 7.5% interest, and he owed $160,000 on the Key Biscayne property, at 6% and 7.5% interest for the two mortgage holders, both Miami banks. Nixon paid $228,198 in payments and interest on his Key Biscayne sites, the original down payment coming from a $65,000 loan from a Miami bank, since paid off.

In the San Clemente real estate transaction, Nixon's indebtedness to Abplanalp at one point totaled $625,000, plus interest. The Nixon holdings were in a hidden trust administered by a title insurance and trust company. In December 1970, Nixon sold all but 5.9 acres, the part including his home, of the 28.9 acres he had acquired to the B & C Investment Co., of which Abplanalp and Rebozo were co-partners. The transfer from the title and insurance firm was in the form of an undivided interest in the trust to Abplanalp and Rebozo as co-partners of the B & C firm. The division of the property between the Nixon and B & C ownings would be made according to "a certain map entitled boundary survey map" drawn by a civil engineer.

Abplanalp subsequently acquired, "recently" according to the White House statement Aug. 27, the Rebozo interest in the B & C.

*Coopers & Lybrand evolved from Lybrand, Ross Brothers & Montgomery after 1968 when a general partner, a partner and a senior associate were convicted of distributing false financial statements and of mail fraud involving a 1962 financial statement of a vending machine firm. All three men were granted unconditional pardons by President Nixon in 1972. The White House said, in response to questions, that all three men had withdrawn from the accounting firm.

The audit did not cover any capital gains aspect of the dealings.

Mitchell, Stans seek access to tapes. Lawyers for former Attorney General John Mitchell and his co-defendant in a New York criminal case, Maurice Stans, chairman of the Finance Committee to Re-elect the President, issued a subpoena Aug. 31 in Washington in an effort to obtain any Presidential tapes and other White House documents which might relate to their trial on obstruction of justice and perjury charges.

The defense sought unspecified material from the White House covering the period November 1971–January 1973. In a related development, a new date for the Mitchell-Stans trial was set for Oct. 23.

Nixon defends San Clemente audit. President Nixon Sept. 5 defended his recently-released audit of the financing of his San Clemente, Calif. home.

He said the audit refuted reports of irregularities "that were carried usually in eight-column heads in most of the papers of this country." The "retractions ended back up with the corset ads, for the most part," he added.

In response to a question at his news conference, Nixon said the audit "gave the lie" to charges that he had used a million dollars from campaign funds to acquire the property and that, as far as his acquisitions in Florida and California were concerned, "there was any money there except my own."

Nixon said he borrowed the money to acquire the property, "and I still owe it. I own no stocks and no bonds—I think I am the first President in this office since Harry Truman—I don't own a stock or a bond. I sold everything before I came into office."

He only owned, he said, the two pieces of adjoining property in Florida, the San Clemente property and a house on Whittier Boulevard "in which my mother once lived. I have no other property, and I owe money on all of them."

The President had been asked about the "many conflicting reports" about his own and the federal expenses involved in financing the Key Biscayne and San Clemente properties. He was asked whether he had paid taxes on "the gain realized" in the sale of land at San Clemente to two close friends.

Nixon said he did not "resent at all" questions about his property but he did resent implications that his private property "was enriched because of what the government did." Citing gazebos and fences erected by the Secret Service, he said "what the government did at San Clemente reduced the value of the property."

As for the capital gain matter, Nixon said the Internal Revenue Service had conducted "a full field review," or audit, of his income tax returns for 1971 and 1972 and this covered the land sale that was queried. "Some argue there

was a capital gain," he said, "and some argue that there was not. It's a matter of difference between accountants. The IRS, after its audit, did not order any change. If it had, I would have paid the tax. It did not order a change."

As for the audit itself, he said, "the results of that audit, insofar as the acquisition of the property, have been put out. That is all that is going to be put out, because I think that is a full disclosure." There were reports that only a partial audit by the accounting firm had been disclosed and that the full audit had covered Nixon's entire financial condition.

Date altered in home sale data— Rep. Jack Brooks (D, Tex.) Aug. 31 questioned a date alteration in documents released by the White House pertaining to President Nixon's San Clemente property.

Brooks, chairman of a House subcommittee probing the public expense on Nixon's private homes, said dates had been erased and changed on documents containing a legal description of the acreage sold by Nixon to the two friends.

The documents were dated Dec. 15, 1970, and Brooks said the alterations had been made Jan. 8, 1971 by a surveying firm on orders from a private attorney for Nixon.

Brooks said his committee wanted to know the date of transfer to ascertain who owned the property when the federal improvements were made on it for presidential security. Brooks said he did not know the reason for altering dates but shifting the transaction to a different tax year was a possible reason.

White House spokesman Gerald L. Warren denied there was any significance to the matter Aug. 31. He released a letter from Presidential counselor Bryce N. Harlow attributing the date revision to an error in the original description of property. The date of the descriptions was "irrelevant to the effective date of the sales agreement," Harlow contended, and, in fact, the sales agreement had been prepared and executed before the Dec. 15 date. As for the date of the actual transaction, "there was no significance to the date or even the year," the letter said.

Brooks said the letter contradicted certain facts in his subcommittee's files. He said the panel had data indicating that the property descriptions had not been prepared until about Dec. 28 and 29, 1970 and that some information contained in the sales agreement was not in existence as of the Dec. 15 date.

Nixon's brother wiretapped. On direct orders from President Nixon, the Secret Service wiretapped the telephone of F. Donald Nixon, the President's brother, the Washington Post reported Sept. 6.

According to what the Post called "four highly reliable sources," the President feared that Donald Nixon's financial activities could result in embarrassment to the Administration.

One Post source indicated that the President was concerned in part over his brother's "involvement with the financial empire of billionaire Howard Hughes."

A White House spokesman said Sept. 7, "If there was any monitoring of the President's immediate family by the Secret Service, it would have been related to the protective function of the Secret Service." He declined to elaborate.

A Secret Service official, asked to define the President's "immediate family," listed Nixon, his wife and two daughters.

Sen. Joseph Montoya (D, N.M.), chairman of the Senate Appropriation Committee's Subcommittee on Treasury and Post Office and General Government, sent a letter to Secret Service head James J. Rowley Sept. 6 requesting complete details of the wiretap.

Nixon re-election committee reports. An estimated $4 million in cash remained in possession of President Nixon's re-election committee after almost $1 million was spent on legal fees during a period from June through August, the Finance Committee to Re-elect the President reported Sept. 10.

In its quarterly report to the General Accounting Office, the committee said $76,000 in legal expenses had been paid in connection with a lawsuit brought by Common Cause, and that $48,000 was paid to attorneys for Maurice Stans. Stans, chairman of the finance committee, was a defendant in a criminal case related to a secret campaign contribution.

Mitchell, Stans win trial delay. Former Attorney General John N. Mitchell and Maurice Stans, chairman of the Finance Committee to Re-elect the President, Sept. 11 won an indefinite delay in their trial. They had been charged with obstructing a major fraud investigation by the government in return for obtaining a secret $200,000 campaign contribution from financier Robert Vesco, whose activities had been the target of Securities and Exchange Commission scrutiny. Vesco was a co-defendant in the Mitchell-Stans trial, but he had fled the country before grand jury proceedings had begun.

A three-judge panel of the U.S. Court of Appeals for the Second Circuit met during the morning of Sept. 11, the day the trial was scheduled to begin, and urged District Court Judge Lee P. Gagliardi to grant a postponement. Attorneys for Mitchell and Stans claimed they lacked sufficient time to prepare a defense because their clients were also embroiled in other legal matters related to the Watergate case.

The appeals court acknowledged that it lacked jurisdiction to order a delay, but added, "had we been in the position of the trial judge, we would have granted at least the three-week extension to Oct. 4 that was requested." (Gagliardi had resisted past efforts to postpone the trial.)

Gagliardi acceded to the appeals court suggestion in an afternoon meeting with attorneys. No new trial date was announced.

1972 Congressional campaign spending. Common Cause, the public interest lobby in Washington, Sept. 13 released the first comprehensive survey on campaign spending by House and Senate candidates.

According to the report, expenditures by the 780 losers in primary races and by the 1,116 candidates in general elections totaled $77 million. Incumbents outspent opponents by a 2-1 margin. Large contributors—those giving donations of more than $100—accounted for 61% of funds raised.

Average spending in House races: Democratic incumbent—$56,364; GOP challenger—$32,709; GOP incumbent—$60,842; Democratic challenger—$29,657. Average spending in races without incumbents: Democrats—$89,430; Republicans—$88,375.

Average spending in Senate races: Democratic incumbent—$381,080; GOP challenger—$312,403; GOP incumbent—$559,742; Democratic challenger—$205,720. Average spending in races without incumbents: Democrats—$481,156; Republicans—$458,484.

Top spenders in House races: Rep. Paul McCloskey (R, Calif.)—$321,558; Jack Brown (defeated) (D, Ariz.)—$318,254; Allard Lowenstein (defeated) (Liberal, N.Y.)—$285,475.

Top spenders in Senate races: Sen. John Tower (R, Tex.)—$2,301,870; Sen. Charles Percy (R, Ill.)—1,408,822; Sen. Robert Griffin (R, Mich.)—$1,394,927.

Mitchells separate. In a telephone call to United Press International Sept. 16, Martha Mitchell disclosed that her husband had left their home and was living in a New York hotel.

According to Mitchell's attorney, the move was made to facilitate preparation of his defense in Mitchell's trial.

In another telephone call Aug. 25 to UPI reporter Helen Thomas, Mrs. Mitchell claimed that she had read a 1972 campaign book which she said had been written by the President and H. R. Haldeman, then White House chief of staff. Mrs. Mitchell also disputed President Nixon's claims not to have discussed the Watergate break-in with Mitchell.

Milk suit decision postponed. Federal district court in Washington July 27 ordered President Nixon to produce for court inspection 67 memos related to the Administration's 1971 decision to increase federal price supports for milk.

The order, involving Nixon's claims of executive privilege, was stayed Aug. 20 at the request of the Justice Department, which argued the case for the White House, and Archibald Cox, special Watergate prosecutor. They argued that the pending court test involving release of the White House tapes would better resolve the issue of executive privilege. According to the ruling, an appeals court in Washington would consider the milk suit at the same time that arguments concerning release of the White House tapes were being heard.

The interrelationship between Nixon's two assertions of executive privilege was compounded Sept. 18 when the White House acknowledged that tape recordings had been made of conversations held March 23, 1971 between the President and dairy industry representatives just prior to the Administration's announcement of milk price hikes; however, in the affidavit which revealed the tapes' existence, White House special counsel J. Fred Buzhardt also reiterated President Nixon's refusal to release the tapes.

An Aug. 12, 1970 memo between two unnamed presidential assistants and a Sept. 2, 1970 memo proposing 15 brief meetings for dairy industry representatives with the President also would be withheld from the court on grounds of executive privilege and separation of powers, Buzhardt said. The documents dealt with the "mechanics" and "advisability" of the presidential meetings and concerned "only the First Amendment protected activities of the President and his staff," he said.

Two other documents—a February 1972 memo dealing with "political contributions" and the milk fund lawsuit, and a list of pre-April 7, 1972 contributors to Nixon's re-election campaign—would be provided the court, according to Buzhardt.

Court action on the milk price support issue had originated with consumer advocate Ralph Nader's lawsuit, which charged that a decision by Clifford Hardin, then agriculture secretary, not to raise milk price supports had been reversed by the White House because of the promise of massive campaign contributions by the dairy industry.

The Washington Post reported June 27 that a memo supplied the Senate Watergate Committee by ousted White House counsel John W. Dean 3rd showed that he and H. R. Haldeman, then White House chief of staff, were discussing the disposition of dairy industry contributions on May 18, 1971 before most of the money was received. (Gifts to the presidential campaign from major dairy industry groups totaled $422,500.)

According to the memo, written by Gordon Strachan, then a Haldeman aide, Haldeman suggested that "the milk money can pay for the 1701 activities of the campaign." (The Committee to Re-elect the President was located at 1701 Pennsylvania Ave., near the White House.) The memo also said that Dean and Haldeman decided not to report "large expenditures and the activities of the milk money" to the General Accounting Office, which maintained public records of campaign funds received and disbursed after April 7, 1972.

The money eventually was earmarked for dummy campaign committees in Washington and concealed as numerous small contributions.

George E. Mehren, an official of one of the largest dairy cooperatives and trade associations, Associated Milk Producers, Inc. (AMPI), said July 24 that the Nixon campaign had sought additional contributions from the group two days after an antitrust suit was brought against them by the Justice Department.

The federal suit, filed in February 1972, remained pending. Herbert Kalmbach, one of President Nixon's chief fund raisers, reportedly asked Mehren for another campaign gift of $750,000. Previous donations from AMPI had totaled an estimated $200,000. (Archibald Cox' office was investigating the possible use of extortion tactics by Nixon campaign officials involved in fundraising.)

Nixon tax audit asked. An audit of President Nixon's tax returns for the past three years was requested July 29 by Tax Analysts and Advocates, a public interest law organization. The group challenged a possible deduction during those years for a donation by Nixon of his vice presidential papers to the National Archives. The papers were valued at $570,000 and, under a law in effect until July 25, 1969, an income tax deduction could have been obtained as a charitable contribution of the gift to the government.

The tax group was not challenging the legality of such a deduction but whether in fact the gift was made before the cutoff date of July 25.

The donation was said to have occurred in March 1969, when the law would have permitted Nixon to count its value against 30% of his income in 1969 and 50% in subsequent years. Such tax write-offs were barred after July 25, 1969. The tax group contended that there was neither a signed deed nor a signed receipt for the gift and that certain restrictions, such as access to the papers, were attached to the turnover, signifying some retention of ownership rights.

In a letter to the Internal Revenue Service, the tax group called for appointment of an independent auditor to review the Nixon tax returns.

A White House statement later July 29 said: "The matter has been previously raised and considered. The allegations are unfounded. The suggested procedure would be inappropriate."

The White House also declined comment Sept. 11 on New York Times and Baltimore Sun reports that Nixon might have been among the 111 persons in 1970 and 72 in 1971 who earned more than $200,000 but paid no federal income taxes. The reports were premised on the possibility that the President claimed deductions for the vice presidential papers and for loan-interest payments and real estate taxes paid on his California and Florida properties, which, taken together, could have offset his tax liabilities for 1970 and perhaps 1971.

Although White House Deputy Press Secretary Gerald L. Warren refused to comment Sept. 12 on "a personal matter," sources in the White House let it be known, without attribution, that it would be incorrect to assume that Nixon paid no taxes for those years.

The White House refused to confirm or deny an Oct. 3 report in the Providence (R.I.) Journal-Bulletin that President and Mrs. Nixon paid only $792.81 in federal income taxes for 1970 and $878.03 in 1971 despite the annual income in excess of

$200,000. The totals were equivalent to the amount of tax paid by a family of three with a maximum income of $7,550 in 1970 or $8,500 in 1971.

Nixon campaign received $60.2 million. The Finance Committee to Re-elect the President revealed Sept. 28 that the Nixon campaign had collected $60.2 million, with $1.5 million of that in cash. The report, the first complete disclosure of money raised by the finance committee, was filed under court order with the Clerk of the House after more than a year of legal battles. (The figures did not reflect funds solicited by the Republican National Committee or Democrats for Nixon.)

Common Cause, the public interest lobby in Washington, had filed suit against the finance committee in September 1972 to force disclosure of secret campaign contributions. Public reporting of donations received before April 7, 1972 had not been required under terms of the 1971 Federal Election Campaign Act; however, federal district court in Washington had upheld the Common Cause argument that the 1925 Federal Corrupt Practices Act, which was superseded by the 1971 law, also required disclosure of donors. The finance committee had argued that its pledges of confidentiality to contributors in the pre-April 7, 1972 period should continue to be honored.

In its only previous public report of contributions, the finance committee had acknowledged receiving $37.6 million in the post-April 7, 1972 period. Under pressure from the Senate Watergate Committee, finance committee chairman Maurice Stans had admitted that the campaign collected a total of $52 million.

An analysis of the report, prepared by Common Cause, showed that in the four weeks preceding April 7, 1972, Nixon aides solicited $11.4 million in secret money (nearly 20% of the total campaign contributions). Of that amount, $2.2 million was collected on April 5, 1972 and $2.9 million was raised on April 6, 1972.

It was reported Sept. 29 that the finance committee also made secret expenditures, totaling $5 million on the two days preceding April 7, 1972. (An estimated $3.8 million was spent on April 6, 1972.) The figure represented more than half of the total campaign expenses of $9.7 million which were reported for the Jan. 1, 1971–April 7, 1972 period. (Total campaign expenditures were put at $56.1 million.

The campaign fund law also required public reporting of campaign disbursements. Most of the $5 million in expenses was for "prepayments" for services performed after April 7, 1972. Prepayment was prohibited under the new law.

The secret expenditures included $2.5 million paid to the Reuben Donnelly Corp. April 6 for "direct mail"; $1 million to Walter Weintz & Co. for "mailing"; $925,000 to the November Group, the Republican advertising agency set up for the campaign, and $120,000 to Market Opinion Research for "polling."

Other campaign expenses were paid to dirty trickster Donald Segretti—$40,000 admitted participants in the Watergate coverup, John Caulfield and Tony Ulasewicz—$30,000 and $57,000 and to France Raine, a brother-in-law of former White House chief of staff H. R. Haldeman—$50,000.

President Nixon received nearly $6 million or 10% of the total collected from 10 superdonors. Eighteen other major contributors gave at least $200,000 each for a total of $4,276,500. The 28 accounted for $10,276,367 in contributions, or more than one-sixth of the final sum.

Major contributors (pre- and post-April 7, 1972):

W. Clement Stone, chairman of Combined Insurance Co. of America, Chicago—$2.1 million; Richard M. Scaife, Pittsburgh, heir to the Mellon oil, banking and industrial fortune—$1 million; John A. Mulcahy, New York, industrialist—$599,559; three dairy industry groups, ADEPT, SPACE and TAPE—$422,500; five members of the Rockefeller family—$310,310; executives of several trucking firms—$308,000; Walter T. Duncan, Texas industrialist—$305,000; John J. Louis Jr., chairman Combined Communications Corp., and family—$303,760; Arthur K. Watson, heir to International Business Machines Corp. fortune—$303,000; George and Ruth Farkas, New York, retail chain store owners—$300,000.

Total contributions from various categories in the pre-April 7, 1972 period:

Financial (banking, securities, insurance)—$4,470,000; oil and gas—$1,410,000; pharmaceutical and health—$1,120,000; U.S. government officials—$1,011,000; real estate—$1,005,000; chemicals—$950,000; entertainment—$580,000; government contractors in defense and aerospace—$501,000; transportation (airlines, railroads & shipping)—$425,000; construction, engineering and architects—$370,000; textiles—$312,000; auto and tire—$307,000; food and food processing—$295,000; dairy—$232,000, and mining—$125,000.

Other secret campaign gifts were received from Calvin Kovens, who had been convicted of mail fraud with former labor leader Jimmy Hoffa. He was granted an early parole by the President. Eight days before his January 1972 release, former Sen. George Smathers (D, Fla.) had telephoned Charles W. Colson, then White House special counsel, asking for Koven's release and suggesting that such a decision would win political support of the Jewish vote in Miami for President Nixon, according to testimony before the Senate Watergate Committee.

Armand Hammer of the Occidental Petroleum Corp. gave $46,000. Officials of Texas Eastern Transmission Corp. contributed $30,000. Both firms, whose gifts were in cash, recently acquired natural gas rights from the Soviet Union.

Cornelius V. Whitney, a Kentucky horse breeder and heir to a communications fortune, donated $250,000 but his money was refunded without explanation, according to the report. The $200,000 gift of California industrialist C. Arnholt Smith also was refunded. Several illegal contributions from corporate funds also had been returned.

Common Cause continued to seek the release of a master list of contributors in possession of Nixon's personal secretary, Rose Mary Woods.

Nixon holds news conference. President Nixon held his third news conference in six weeks Oct. 3.

A question was raised about President Nixon's earlier statement that work done at his San Clemente, Calif. residence by the government at taxpayers' expense "diminished the value of the property." He was asked: "Do you think that the $13,500 electrical heating system that was installed diminished its value? And second, do you think that when the GSA [General Services Administration] hired a local landscape architect to redesign the flower beds on the west side of the residence four times a year, that they were spending the taxpayers' money wisely?"

Nixon replied that he had preferred to install a gas heating system, which would have been cheaper than an electric one, but was overruled by the Secret Service because of fire hazard considerations. He refused to answer the second part of the question, adding that "full statements" already had been made.

Vice President Agnew resigns after pleading 'no contest' to tax evasion charge. Spiro T. Agnew, for months the target of a federal investigation of his own financial dealings, resigned the vice presidency Oct. 10 and pleaded no contest (nolo contendere) to one count of income tax evasion. In return, the Justice Department agreed to drop all pending charges against Agnew and request leniency on the tax evasion charge.

In a dramatic courtroom hearing in Baltimore shortly after he submitted his letter of resignation, Agnew avoided imprisonment by pleading no contest to a federal charge that he had failed to report $29,500 of income he received in 1967, when he was governor of Maryland. Such a plea, while not an admission of guilt, was tantamount to a plea of guilty on the charge. Agnew had faced federal indictment for violation of bribery, conspiracy and tax laws. [For the full Agnew story, see p. 74]

Rebozo returned Hughes campaign gift. Charles G. (Bebe) Rebozo, a personal friend of President Nixon, returned a $100,000 cash political contribution he had received from agents of billionaire recluse Howard Hughes, the Washington Post reported Oct. 10.

Rebozo, the Post said, kept the money in safe deposit boxes in Florida for nearly three years before deciding a few months ago to refund the money to avoid potential embarrassment.

The information reported by the Post had been obtained from Rebozo by investigators for the Senate Watergate Committee.

A White House spokesman declined comment on the report, other than that the President "personally" had received none of the money.

Post sources said Rebozo was unable to explain why he had kept the money rather than turning it over to the Republican campaign committee.

Former Hughes aide, Robert A. Maheu, said in a sworn deposition, given in his $17.3 million libel suit against Hughes, that Rebozo had received the money in two equal installments in 1969 and 1970. Maheu claimed that Rebozo had been "chosen by Mr. Nixon" to receive the cash, the Post said.

Agnew arranged Hughes gift—Hughes, at the request of Vice President Agnew, contributed $10,000 to the unsuccessful Republican gubernatorial campaign of C. Stanley Blair in 1970, the Long Island, N.Y., newspaper Newsday reported Oct. 6.

Blair was appointed a U.S. district court judge in July 1971 on the recommendation of Agnew.

Maryland Attorney General Francis B. Burch said the gift, although made secretly, was legal under Maryland law.

A

Nixon Faces Decline in Public Confidence

Nixon bars testimony, refuses access to files. President Nixon formally notified the Senate Watergate committee July 7 that he would not testify before the committee or permit it access to presidential papers. His press office had previously drawn the line against presidential testimony. The President stated his own position in a letter to the committee chairman, Ervin. [See p. 11]

GOP senators affirm support for Nixon. A delegation of 10 conservative Republican senators led by Carl T. Curtis (Neb.) called on President Nixon in the White House July 11 to affirm their support for him.

A spokesman for Curtis said those accompanying him had been asked after they had complimented him for a June 14 Senate speech criticizing those "out to get" the President.

Those invited by Curtis:

Wallace F. Bennett (Utah), Dewey F. Bartlett (Okla.), Norris Cotton (N.H.), Clifford P. Hansen (Wyo.), Jesse A. Helms (N.C.), Milton R. Young (N.D.), John G. Tower (Tex.), Paul J. Fannin (Ariz.) and Strom Thurmond (S.C.).

Nixon leaves hospital, dismisses talk of quitting. President Nixon left Bethesda (Md.) Naval Hospital July 20 after recovering from viral pneumonia.

On arrival at the White House, Nixon was welcomed in the rose garden by a group of about 200 staff members. He addressed the group briefly, saying that he would spend the weekend at Camp David and when he returned to the White House Monday "it is going to be full tilt all the way, and we want all of you to work that way, too."

He said he was amused by suggestions that he resign because of his health or the burdens of office; the idea, he said, "is just plain poppycock." Referring to the Watergate affair, he said, "Let others wallow in Watergate; we are going to do our job."

Polls show Nixon support down. A Gallup poll taken shortly after the Senate testimony of former presidential counsel John W. Dean 3rd showed Nixon's public support at the lowest level since he took office, it was reported July 22.

Asked whether they approved of the way Nixon was handling his job, 40% of those polled expressed approval, while 49% showed disapproval. The 40% figure was down from a high of 68% in January.

The Gallup analysis cited the Watergate scandal as a key factor in Nixon's popularity decline. Inflation was noted as another major factor.

A Harris survey taken July 18–22 asked several questions specifically related to Watergate. By a margin of 51%–37%, those polled believed that Nixon had been "wrong to refuse to testify personally" before the Ervin committee. A majority of 60%–30% said Nixon had been "more wrong than right" in refusing to turn over White House documents to the committee.

The Harris poll found a 50%–30% majority believing Dean's testimony that Nixon knew of the Watergate cover-up (with the remainder undecided). By 47%–28%, however, those polled did not believe that Nixon had "personally ordered the cover-up."

More White House probes. Senior White House aides ordered 16 private investigations into the private lives of such individuals as House Speaker Carl Albert (D, Okla.), former Rep. Richard H. Poff (R, Va.), the Smothers brothers comedy team and the producers of the movie Millhouse, the Washington Post reported Aug. 1.

Among the schemes was one involving the use of a New York City apartment to seduce and subsequently blackmail female friends of Mary Jo Kopechne, who drowned in July 1969 in an accident involving Sen. Edward M. Kennedy (D, Mass.), the Post reported. The apartment was rented in 1971 by Anthony T. Ulasewicz, a secret investigator for the White House. Ulasewicz allegedly hoped to extort from the women details about the party that occurred just before the accident.

Attorney William O. Bittman said July 31 that his client, Watergate conspirator E. Howard Hunt Jr., informed government attorneys in private about what he had been told of the plan, the Post reported. Ulasewicz denied the allegations.

According to the Post, Ulasewicz investigated Albert in 1972 following rumors that Albert had been drunk at the time of an automobile accident in Washington, the Post reported.

Ulasewicz looked into the background of Poff when he was being considered for an appointment to the Supreme Court in 1971, Post sources said. Fearful of a long confirmation fight in the Senate, Poff removed himself from the running.

Tom and Dick Smothers were investigated after their network television program was dropped because of disputes with the network in 1969. The Columbia Broadcasting System (CBS) said some of their comedy material was in questionable taste.

The probe of the producers of Millhouse, an anti-Nixon film, was ordered by White House Chief of Staff H. R. Haldeman, the Post said.

Nixon remains aloof. President Nixon remarked at a diplomatic event Aug. 1 that the nation should not let itself "be remembered only for the petty, little, indecent things that seem to obsess us at a time when the world is going by."

"Let others spend their time dealing with the murky, small, unimportant, vicious little things," he said. "We have spent our time and will spend our time building a better world."

His remarks, interpreted as references to the Watergate scandal, were interpolated into a toast he was offering to his visitor, Japanese Premier Kakuei Tanaka.

Another indication of the President's stance on Watergate came July 30 from Senate Republican Leader Hugh Scott (Pa.). He predicted Nixon would "come out fighting" soon after the Senate Watergate hearings recessed for the summer and he would "reply very, very strongly" to the allegations heard against him during the hearings.

Other Administration spokesmen buttressed the President's position that he was immersed in non-Watergate presidential duties. The "government is proceeding here in Washington and new initiatives for peace are going forward," Vice President Spiro T. Agnew said July 31. Nixon's chief of staff, Gen. Alexander M. Haig Jr., pointed out the same day that by the end of the week Nixon would have met with 10 heads of government since May, held eight Cabinet meetings and met 27 times with Cabinet officers, 14 times with major congressional groups and conducted numerous economic meetings.

Denying reports that a White House group was planning a counterattack against Nixon critics in Congress, Haig was optimistic that "a relatively dramatic difference" from the past few months could be established in getting legislation moving through Congress again.

Impeachment resolution proposed—An impeachment resolution against Nixon for "high crimes and misdemeanors" was presented in the House July 31 by Rep. Robert F. Drinan (D, Mass.). Drinan, a Jesuit priest, said the House should inquire not only into the Watergate scandal but also the secret bombing of Cambodia in 1969–70, Nixon's taping of White House conversations, impoundment of legislated funds and establishment of "a super-secret security force within the White House." Before going to the floor for consideration, the resolution would have to be considered either by the House Judiciary Committee or a specially-appointed House panel.

Bar unit announces probe. The California Bar Association announced Aug. 1 that it had begun an inquiry in May into the conduct of President Nixon and five other members of the state bar mentioned in the Watergate case.

The five other lawyers were: John D. Ehrlichman, Nixon's former domestic affairs counselor; Herbert W. Kalmbach, Nixon's former personal attorney; Robert C. Mardian, an official in Nixon's re-election campaign and a former assistant U.S. attorney general; Gordon C. Strachan, a former White House aide; and Donald H. Segretti, who allegedly directed sabotage efforts against Democratic candidates in the 1972 campaign.

Leonard S. Janofsky, president of the state bar, said the investigation was preliminary but could lead to more formal proceedings and possible disciplinary action such as disbarment or suspension.

Janofsky said Nixon would be treated "with respect because of the nature of the office," but the association had a duty to act if any members committed "any act of moral turpitude, dishonesty or corruption," whether or not any crime was involved.

Kissinger urges national unity. Henry A. Kissinger warned in a speech Aug. 2 that "the consensus that sustained our international participation is in danger of being exhausted." Citing the past decade of "tragedy and trauma"—from a presidential assassination in 1963 to the Watergate scandal—Kissinger said "the once-apparent reservoir of faith in our ability to do, and of confidence that the future would be better than the past, has been seriously taxed."

President Nixon's national security adviser indicated his concern about the impact of Watergate on foreign policy. "Foreign policy must not become an alibi or a distraction from domestic ills," he asserted. "But, equally, domestic problems must not be used as an excuse for abandoning our international responsibilities. There can be no moratorium in the quest for a peaceful world."

"Our foreign policy will mean little," he observed, "if other nations see our actions as sporadic initiatives of a small group reflecting no coherent national purpose or consensus."

"No foreign policy—no matter how ingenious—has any chance of success if it is born in the minds of a few and carried in the hearts of none."

Meany affirms alienation. AFL-CIO President George Meany indicated his alienation from the Nixon Administration Aug. 2. After noting that the evidence of corruption in the federal government continued to mount, Meany told newsmen that President Nixon would not be invited to address the federation's fall convention, a traditional invitation.

Meany extended the exclusion as convention guests to Labor Secretary Peter J. Brennan and Agriculture Secretary Earl L. Butz. Brennan, he specified, had taken "anti-labor positions" on a number of issues and made it clear he represented both union and nonunion workers.

Meany's remarks were made at a news conference in Oak Brook, Ill. following a quarterly meeting of the federation's executive council. The council issued a statement the same day deploring what it termed unilateral concessions to the Soviet Union made in the recent summit talks between President Nixon and Soviet leader Leonid I. Brezhnev.

Blackmun deplores 'pall' of Watergate. Supreme Court Justice Harry A. Blackmun told an American Bar Association convention Aug. 5 that the "very glue of our ship of state seems about to become unstuck" by the "pall" of the Watergate scandal.

Asserting that a general decline in American values was occurring, Blackmun said, "One senses a laxness in public life that 20 years ago, if indulged in, could not be politically surmounted."

"The pall of the Watergate, with all its revelations of misplaced loyalties, of strange measures of the unethical, of unusual doings in high places, . . . is upon us. It is something that necessarily touches us all, irrespective of political inclination," Blackmun said.

Blackmun offered a Biblical story of the prophet Nehemiah's rebuilding of the ruins of Jerusalem in 446 B.C. as a parallel to Watergate.

"Perhaps we need to make our own solitary inspection of the walls," Justice Blackmun said, "to plan; to cooperate; to resolve that it is worth doing; to provide leadership; to engage, if necessary, in activity that simultaneously is both defensive and constructive; to rededicate—or should I say dedicate—ourselves to what this bar association and this nation stand for."

Richardson tightens rules. Attorney General Elliot L. Richardson announced several steps Aug. 8 to insulate the Justice Department from outside political influence. In an appearance before the American Bar Association convention in Washington, Richardson reported a new requirement for department employes to report any work-related conversation with outside parties, including members of Congress, their staffs or other government officials. The only persons exempted from the regulation were representatives of the news media.

Richardson also announced elimination of another political association—announcement by members of Congress of Justice Department grants to their home areas. This practice would be discontinued, he said, since it created "the public impression that the senator or congressman had some sort of influence on the results when, in fact, he had nothing to do with it."

Richardson also said he was forswearing politics. He said he expected his "principal colleagues" at the department to do likewise and he hoped his successors followed suit.

Richardson said the department was studying the idea of creating an inspector general's office to overlook the fair and consistent application of the law to every person, regardless of status.

ABA urges Watergate disciplining. The American Bar Association's (ABA) House of Delegates overwhelmingly passed a resolution Aug. 8 condemning unethical action by lawyers involved in the Watergate scandal. The 318 member assembly, composed of representatives of various state and local bar groups, urged that "prompt and vigorous disciplinary investigation and appropriate action" be taken.

The resolution came as the ABA drew to a close its 96th annual convention in Washington.

The resolution followed creation by the National Organization of Bar Counsel (NOBC) Aug. 2 of a special committee to coordinate disciplinary proceedings against attorneys implicated in Watergate. The NOBC, meeting in conjunction with the ABA, consisted of lawyers involved in disciplinary actions in state and local bar associations.

Nixon's popularity declines to 31%. According to a Gallup poll released Aug. 15, 31% of those contacted approved the way President Nixon was handling his job. It was the lowest popularity rating for a president since January 1953, the final month of Harry S. Truman's term of office. The Gallup poll was conducted Aug. 3–6.

In August 1968, the month rioting broke out at the Democratic National Convention in Chicago, 35% of those polled approved President Johnson's handling of his job.

An Oliver Quayle poll, made public Aug. 14, revealed that Sen. George McGovern (D, S.D.) would receive 51% of the vote and Nixon 49% if the 1972 Presidential election were held again in August.

A Louis Harris survey, reported July 30, indicated that 22% of those questioned felt Nixon should resign because of Watergate, and 69% felt he was doing only a fair to poor job of personally inspiring confidence in the White House. The Harris poll also found that 65% of the respondents said Nixon had not been frank and honest about Watergate.

On the matter of culpability, 63% of the Quayle poll participants concluded that Nixon should bear the blame for Watergate—no matter when he knew—since his aides and advisers had been implicated.

The New York Times conducted a poll (reported Aug. 6) among the presidents of the 1,453 corporations listed on the New York Stock Exchange. While 67% of the 760 executives—as opposed to 90% in 1972—who replied said they would still vote for Nixon, 31% of those who gave campaign contributions in 1972 would not do so again. By a margin of 460–289, the executives said Watergate had had a negative impact on their confidence in government.

Nixon addresses nation on Watergate. President Nixon told the nation in a televised address Aug. 15 it should give up its "backward-looking obsession" with Watergate, turn the case over to the courts and start attending to "matters of far greater importance."

The speech, and an accompanying written statement, [texts begin on Page 40] comprised the President's fifth major statement on the Watergate scandal affecting his Administration.

In his speech, the President said it was clear that the Senate Watergate hearings and some of the commentary on them were directed toward implicating him personally in the illegalities that occurred. He accepted full responsibility for the abuses that occurred during his Administration and his re-election campaign and asserted it was his duty to defend the office of the presidency against false charges.

He declined to offer a point-by-point rebuttal of charges in the case and restated his previous denials of complicity.

Nixon explained his actions after the Watergate break-in occurred, much of it again a restatement of his previous stand that he pressed repeatedly for information and was repeatedly misled until mid-April of 1973. Then, he said, it became clear that the situation was "far more serious" than he had believed and that the investigation should be given to the Criminal Division of the Justice Department. At that time, Nixon said, he turned over all the information he had to that department with the instruction it should "pursue the matter thoroughly," and he ordered all members of his Administration "to testify fully before the grand jury." He pointed out that the case was now before a grand jury in the hands of a special prosecutor appointed with his concurrence.

"Far from trying to hide the facts," the President emphasized, "my effort throughout has been to discover the facts—and to lay those facts before the appropriate law-enforcement authorities so that justice could be done and the guilty dealt with."

Nixon dealt at length with his refusal to turn over to the special prosecutor or the Senate committee his recordings of conversations he held in his office or on his telephone. There was "a much more important principle" involved in this, he said, "than what the tapes might prove about Watergate." That principle was the confidentiality of presidential discussions. He related this confidentiality to that required in conversations between members of Congress and their aides, a lawyer and a client, a priest and a penitent and a husband and a wife.

It was "even more important that the confidentiality of conversations between a President and his advisers be protected," he said. It was "absolutely essential to the conduct of the presidency, in this and in all future Administrations."

If he released the tapes, Nixon said, the confidentiality of the presidency "would always be suspect from now on."

He said he would continue to "oppose efforts which would set a precedent that would cripple all future Presidents by inhibiting conversations between them and those they look to for advice."

Turning to "the basic issues" raised by Watergate, Nixon said he recognized "that merely answering the charges that have been made against the President is not enough. The word 'Watergate' has come to represent a much broader set of concerns."

"To most of us," he said, Watergate had come to mean "a whole series of acts that either represent or appear to represent an abuse of trust. It has come to stand for excessive partisanship, for 'enemy lists,' for efforts to use the great institutions of government for partisan political purposes." For many Americans, he continued, the term also had come to include a number of national security matters.

"No political campaign ever justifies obstructing justice, or harassing individuals, or compromising those great agencies of government that should and must be above politics," he said. "To the extent that these things were done in the 1972 campaign, they were serious abuses. And I deplore them. . . . And in the future, my Administration will be more vigilant in insuring that such abuses do not take place."

Nixon rejected "the cynical view that politics is inevitably or even usually a dirty business" and pledged "that I will do all that I can to insure that one of the results of Watergate is a new level of political decency and integrity in America."

As for the national security aspect, the President said he would continue to meet his constitutional responsibility to protect the security of the nation and only "by constitutional means."

Nixon linked the Watergate abuses to an attitude arising during the 1960s "as individuals and groups increasingly asserted the right to take the law into their own hands, insisting that their purposes represented a higher morality." He said their attitude "was praised in the press and even from some of our pulpits as evidence of a new idealism. Those of us who insisted on the old restraints, who warned of the overriding importance of operating within the law and by the rules, were accused of being reactionaries."

This new attitude, he said, "brought a rising spiral of violence and fear, of riots and arson and bombings," all in the name of peace and justice. Political discussion turned into "savage debate," he said. "Free speech was brutally suppressed, as hecklers shouted down or even physically assaulted those with whom they disagreed."

"The notion that the end justifies the means proved contagious," the President said, and it was not surprising that some persons adopted the same morality in 1972.

But, he said, "those acts cannot be defended. Those who were guilty of abuses must be punished." And ultimately, "the answer does not lie merely in the jailing of a few overzealous persons who mistakenly thought their cause justified their violations of the law. Rather, it lies in a commitment by all of us to show a renewed respect for the mutual restraints that are the mark of a free and civilized society. It requires that we learn once again to work together, if not united in all of our purposes, then at least united in respect for the system by which our conflicts are peacefully resolved and our liberties maintained."

The "extremes of violence and discord in the 1960s," he said, "contributed to the extremes of Watergate" and "both are wrong. Both should be condemned. No individual, no group and no political party has a corner on the market on morality in America."

"If we learn the important lessons of Watergate, if we do what is necessary to prevent such abuses in the future—on both sides—we can emerge from this experience a better and a stronger nation," he continued.

Speaking of the Senate hearings, Nixon said "we have reached a point at which a continued, backward-looking obsession with Watergate is causing this nation to neglect matters of far greater importance."

"We must not stay so mired in Watergate," he said, that the nation failed to respond to its national and world challenges. "We cannot let an obsession with the past destroy our hopes for the future."

Vital legislation "sits unattended" before Congress, Nixon said. "Confidence at home and abroad in our economy, our currency and our foreign policy is being sapped by uncertainty." Critical negotiations were taking place on strategic weapons, troop levels in Europe, and vital events were taking place in Southeast Asia. These were "matters that cannot wait. They cry out for action now. And either we, your elected representatives here in Washington ought to get on with the jobs that need to be done—for you—or every one of you ought to be demanding to know why."

The time had come, he said "to turn Watergate over to the courts, where the questions of guilt or innocence belong. The time has come for the rest of us to get on with the urgent business of our nation."

Nixon recited the "great goals" for which his Administration was elected—the issues of inflation, reduction of the power and size of government, preservation of America's fundamental values and its No. 1 military position, the attainment of peace with honor in Southeast Asia and the return of the prisoners of war, the building of a new prosperity and an enduring world peace.

"If you share my belief in these goals, if you want the mandate you gave this Administration to be carried out," he said, "then I ask for your help to insure that those who would exploit Watergate in order to keep us from doing what we were elected to do will not succeed."

The President appealed to the nation for "understanding" so that "we can learn the lessons of Watergate and gain from that experience."

Nixon's written statement—The President's written statement, released just prior to his speech Aug. 15, covered much the same ground as the speech and contained sections of identical text.

The statement asserted it would be "neither fair nor appropriate" for the President" to assess the evidence or comment on specific witnesses or their credibility" of the Senate Watergate hearings since that was the function of the Senate committee and the courts. It was not his intention to attempt "comprehensive and detailed response" to "the questions and contentions raised" during the hearings nor "attempt a definitive account of all that took place." He did not believe he "could enter upon an endless course of explaining and rebutting a complex of point-by-point claims and charges arising out of that conflicting testimony which may engage committees and courts for months or years to come, and still be able to carry out my duties as President."

While the judicial and legislative branches "resolve these matters," Nixon stated, he would continue his duty as President.

The statement again repeated Nixon's denials of complicity in the break-in or cover-up, his assertions that he ordered vigorous pursuit of the federal investigation of the break-in and his repeated demands for reports on Watergate developments.

When the indictments were returned against only the seven original defendants, he stated, it seemed to confirm the reports he was getting that no one then employed at the White House was involved. "It was in that context," Nixon stated, that he met with his counsel John W. Dean 3rd Sept. 15, 1972, and Dean gave him "no reason at that meeting to believe any others were involved."

"Not only was I unaware of any cover-up," Nixon continued, "but at that time, and until March 21, I was unaware that there was anything to cover up."

Nixon said his frequent meetings with Dean occurred in February and March "when my interest in Watergate rose" because of the organization of the Senate investigating committee and the hearings on L. Patrick Gray 3rd's nomination as FBI director. He was urging his staff at the time "to get all the facts out," he stated, because he was confident that full disclosure would show that persons in the White House and at his campaign committee "were the victims of unjustified innuendoes in the press."

He was also "searching for a way to disclose all of the facts without disturbing the confidentiality of communications with and among my personal staff," he stated, since that confidentiality was "essential to the functioning of any President."

Nixon cited the March 21 date on which he said he learned for the first time that the planning for the break-in "went beyond" those who had been tried and "that at least one, and possibly more, persons at the re-election committee were involved." He also learned that funds had been raised for payment to the defendants, but "not that it had been paid to procure silence," only that it was for lawyers' fees and family support. He learned "that a member of my staff had talked to one of the defendants about clemency, but not that offers of clemency had been made." And he learned that one of the defendants (E. Howard Hunt Jr.) was trying "to blackmail the White House by demanding payment of $125,000 as the price of not talking about other activities, unrelated to Watergate, in which he had engaged." "These allegations were made in general terms," Nixon stated, as "being based in part on supposition."

The allegations were "troubling," Nixon stated, they gave "a new dimension" to the Watergate matter. They also reinforced his determination, he stated, to have the full facts made available to the grand jury or the Senate committee and to have any illegalities "dealt with appropriately according to the law." If there was White House involvement, or involvement by high campaign committee personnel, he said, "I wanted the White House to take the lead in making that known."

This was the time Nixon began new inquiries into the case, the statement asserted. By April 15, based on reports from his aide John D. Ehrlichman and from then-Attorney General Richard G. Kleindienst and Watergate prosecutor Henry Petersen, and based on "independent inquiries" of his own, Nixon said, he realized he "would not be able personally to find out all of the facts and make them public" and he decided "that the matter was best handled by the Justice Department and the grand jury."

In his statement, Nixon corrected an inaccurate date in his May 22 Watergate statement that it was not until the time of his own investigation, March 21, that he learned of the break-in at the office of Daniel Ellsberg's psychiatrist. He had since determined that he first learned of that break-in March 17, he stated.

Acting on Kleindienst's advice at a meeting April 25, Nixon said, he authorized reporting the break-in to the Ellsberg case judge, "despite the fact that since no evidence had been obtained [in the break-in], the law did not clearly require it."

Concerning the special investigations unit in the White House, Nixon stated many of its activities should not be disclosed because that "would unquestionably damage the national security." He added that the Senate Watergate committee had learned of some of these matters and to date "wisely declined to make them public." At no time had he authorized "the use of illegal means by the special investigations unit," Nixon stated.

Reaction to speech—The most-quoted initial reaction to President Nixon's latest Watergate statement was Sen. Barry Goldwater's (R, Ariz) comment Aug. 15 that, "in my opinion the President did not add anything to his other speeches that would tend to divert suspicion from him."

A similar comment, that the Nixon speech "added nothing, and probably subtracted nothing, from what we knew," came Aug. 15 from Robert E. Strauss, Democratic national chairman.

Joseph L. Rauh, spokesman for the liberal Americans for Democratic Action (ADA), said Aug. 15 the speech "wholly failed to answer the charges against him and his Administration. ADA reaffirms its call for his resignation."

Sen. Edward W. Brooke (R, Mass.) said Aug. 16 "the American people want the facts. The President gave us rhetoric. He did not tell the American people what he knows."

Consumer advocate Ralph Nader considered it "a cowardly and wholly evasive performance." Commenting Aug. 15, Nader said the President "even blamed his present inability to govern on the Watergate controversy, which he has increased by rising above the law and not responding to the courts or the Congress."

However, Frank Fitzsimmons, president of the International Brotherhood of Teamsters, thought Aug. 15 the speech was "wonderful, to the extent that he is still the President of the United States, and he knows it."

Gov. Ronald Reagan (R, Calif.) described the speech Aug. 15 as "the voice of reason" and agreed with Nixon the Watergate case now belonged "in courts."

Sen. Edmund S. Muskie (D, Me.) Aug. 15 said he found it "difficult to understand how a President could be so totally ignorant of events involving the high officials in his Administration."

Sen. Edward J. Gurney (R, Fla.), a member of the Senate Watergate committee, said Aug. 16 "the committee hearings have dragged on far too long and are seriously affecting the ability of the government to function."

Another Watergate committee member, Sen. Daniel K. Inouye (D, Hawaii), said Aug. 16 of the Nixon speech: "There are ways of clearing himself—and for some reason he doesn't want to take that opportunity."

Sen. George McGovern (S.D.), 1972 Democratic presidential candidate, strongly endorsed Aug. 15 Nixon's call for decency and dignity in politics. He rejected Nixon's view that the issues involved in Watergate should be relegated to the courts. "We must recognize," McGovern said, "how dangerous it is to place political expediency, materialism and militarism above the claims of law and conscience."

Vice President Agnew said in Denver, Colo. Aug. 15 public figures must expect to draw criticism and the President "has a right to defend his reputation as well as a right to do it in the way he considers best for himself and the public he serves."

At the White House Aug. 16, where the telegram and telephone response was said to be running 6–1 in support of the President, Mrs. Nixon conveyed to her press secretary, Helen McCain Smith, "the feeling that Watergate is behind all of us now."

At the daily White House press briefing Aug. 16, Deputy Press Secretary Gerald L. Warren indicated that the President's refusal to go into details on the unresolved questions concerning the Watergate allegations against him would be maintained during the President's next news conference, tentatively scheduled during a two-week stay at San Clemente, Calif. beginning Aug. 20.

The President, Warren said, had "addressed the Watergate matter" in his speech and given "his perception of the entire matter." While the President would permit unrestricted questioning, he said, he had already spoken "forthrightly" about the matter.

The first question put to Warren at the briefing was, "When is the President going to make his Watergate statement?"

An official was quoted Aug. 16 as saying a "point-by-point rebuttal" had been considered for the President's latest statement "but the conclusion was that it wouldn't be politically productive. I wouldn't look for any retreat from that position, either at the news conference or any time in the future."

Text of President's Aug. 15 Speech on Watergate Charges

Good evening. Now that most of the major witnesses in the Watergate phase of the Senate committee hearings on campaign practices have been heard, the time has come for me to speak out about the charges made and to provide a perspective on the issue for the American people.

For over four months Watergate has dominated the news media. During the past three months the three major networks have devoted an average of over 22 hours of television time each week to this subject. The Senate committee has heard over two million words of testimony.

This investigation began as an effort to discover the facts about the break-in and bugging at the Democratic national headquarters and other campaign abuses.

But, as the weeks have gone by, it has become clear that both the hearings themselves and some of the commentaries on them have become increasingly absorbed in an effort to implicate the President personally in the illegal activities that took place.

Because the abuses occurred during my Administration, and in the campaign for my re-election I accept full responsibility for them. I regret that these events took place. And I do not question the right of a Senate committee to investigate charges made against the President to the extent that this is relevant to legislative duties.

However, it is my constitutional responsibility to defend the integrity of this great office against false charges. I also believe that it is important to address the overriding question of what we as a nation can learn from this experience, and what we should now do. I intend to discuss both of these subjects tonight.

The record of the Senate hearings is lengthy. The facts are complicated, the evidence conflicting. It would not be right for me to try to sort out the evidence, to rebut specific witnesses, or to pronounce my own judgments about their credibility. That is for the committee and for the courts.

I shall not attempt to deal tonight with the various charges in detail. Rather, I shall attempt to put the events in perspective from the standpoint of the presidency. On May 22nd, before the major witnesses had testified, I issued a detailed statement addressing the charges that had been made against the President.

I have today issued another written statement, which addresses the charges that have been made since then as they relate to my own conduct, and which describes the efforts that I made to discover the facts about the matter.

On May 22, I stated in very specific terms—and I state again to every one of you listening tonight—these facts: I had no prior knowledge of the Watergate break-in; I neither took part in nor knew about any of the subsequent cover-up activities; I neither authorized nor encouraged subordinates to engage in illegal or improper campaign tactics. That was and that is the simple truth.

In all of the millions of words of testimony, there is not the slightest suggestion that I had any knowledge of the planning for the Watergate break-in. As for the cover-up, my statement has been challenged by only one of the 35 witnesses who appeared—a witness who offered no evidence beyond his own impressions, and whose testimony has been contradicted by every other witness in a position to know the facts.

Tonight, let me explain to you what I did about Watergate after the break-in occurred, so that you can better understand the fact that I also had no knowledge of the so-called cover-up.

From the time when the break-in occurred, I pressed repeatedly to know the facts, and particularly whether there was any involvement of anyone at the White House. I considered two things essential:

First, that the investigation should be thorough and above-board; and second, that if there were any higher involvement, we should get the facts out first. As I said at my Aug. 29 press conference last year, "What really hurts in matters of this sort is not the fact that they occur, because overzealous people in campaigns do things that are wrong. What really hurts is if you try to cover it up." I believed that then, and certainly the experience of this last year has proved that to be true.

I knew that the Justice Department and the FBI were conducting intensive investigations—as I had insisted that they should. The White House counsel, John Dean, was assigned to monitor those investigations, and particularly to check into any possible White House involvement. Throughout the summer of 1972, I continued to press the question, and I continued to get the same answer: I was told again and again that there was no indication that any persons were involved other than the seven who were known to have planned and carried out the operation, and who were subsequently indicted and convicted.

On Sept. 12 at a meeting that I held with the Cabinet, the senior White House staff and a number of legislative leaders, Attorney General Kleindienst reported on the investigation. He told us it had been the most extensive investigation since the assassination of President Kennedy, and that it had established that only those seven were involved.

On Sept. 15, the day the seven were indicted, I met with John Dean, the White House counsel. He gave me no reason whatever to believe that any others were guilty; I assumed that the indictments of only the seven by the grand jury confirmed the reports he had been giving to that effect throughout the summer.

On Feb. 16, I met with Acting Director Gray prior to submitting his name to the Senate for confirmation as permanent director of the FBI. I stressed to him that he would be questioned closely about the FBI's conduct of the Watergate investigation. I asked him if he still had full confidence in it. He replied that he did; that he was proud of its thoroughness and that he could defend it with enthusiasm before the committee.

Because I trusted the agencies conducting the investigations, because I believed the reports I was getting, I did not believe the newspaper accounts that suggested a cover-up. I was convinced there was no cover-up, because I was convinced that no one had anything to cover up.

It was not until March 21 of this year that I received new information from the White House counsel that led me to conclude that the reports I had been getting for over nine months were not true. On that day, I launched an intensive effort of my own to get the facts and to get the facts out. Whatever the facts might be, I wanted the White House to be the first to make them public.

At first I entrusted the task of getting me the facts to Mr. Dean. When, after spending a week at Camp David, he failed to produce the written report I had asked for, I turned to John Ehrlichman and to the attorney general—while also making independent inquiries of my own. By mid-April I had received Mr. Ehrlichman's report, and also one from the attorney general based on new information uncovered by the Justice Department.

These reports made it clear to me that the situation was far more serious than I had imagined. It at once became evident to me that the responsibility for the investigation in the case should be given to the criminal division of the Justice Department. I turned over all the information I had to the head of that department, Assistant Attorney General Henry Petersen, a career government employe with an impeccable nonpartisan record, and I instructed him to pursue the matter thoroughly. I ordered all members of the Administration to testify fully before the grand jury.

And with my concurrence, on May 18 Attorney General Richardson appointed a special prosecutor to handle the matter, and the case is now before the grand jury.

Far from trying to hide the facts, my effort throughout has been to discover the facts—and to lay those facts before the appropriate law enforcement authorities so that justice could be done and the guilty dealt with.

I relied on the best law-enforcement agencies in the country to find and report the truth. I believed they had done so—just as they believed they had done so.

Many have urged that in order to help prove the truth of what I have said, I should turn over to the special prosecutor and the Senate committee recordings of conversations that I held in my office or my telephone.

However, a much more important principle is involved in this question than what the tapes might prove about Watergate.

Each day a President of the United States is required to make difficult decisions on grave issues. It is absolutely necessary, if the President is to be able to do his job as the country expects, that he be able to talk openly and candidly with his advisers about issues and individuals. This kind of frank discussion is only possible when those who take part in it know that what they say is in strictest confidence.

The Presidency is not the only office that requires confidentiality. A member of Congress must be able to talk in confidence with his assistants. Judges must be able to confer in confidence with their law clerks and with each other. For very good reasons, no branch of government has ever compelled disclosure of confidential conversations between officers of other branches of government and their advisers about government business.

This need for confidence is not confined to government officials. The law has long recognized that there are kinds of conversations that are entitled to be kept confidential, even at the cost of doing without critical evidence in a legal proceeding. This rule applies, for example, to conversations between a lawyer and a client, between a priest and a penitent, and between a husband and a wife. In each case it is thought so important that the parties be able to talk freely to each other that for hundreds of years the law has said that these conversations are "privileged" and that their disclosure cannot be compelled in a court.

It is even more important that the confidentiality of conversations between a President and his advisers be protected. This is no mere luxury, to be dispensed with whenever a particular issue raises sufficient uproar. It is absolutely essential to the conduct of the presidency, in this and in all future Administrations.

If I were to make public these tapes, containing as they do blunt and candid remarks on many different subjects, the confidentiality of the office of the President would always be suspect from now on. It would make no difference whether it was to serve the interests of a court, of a Senate committee or the President himself—the same damage would be done to the principle, and that damage would be irreparable. Persons talking with the President would never again be sure that recordings or notes of what they said would not suddenly be made public. No one would want to advance tentative ideas that might later seem unsound. No diplomat would want to speak candidly in those sensitive negotiations which could bring peace or avoid war. No senator or congressman would want to talk frankly about the Congressional horse-trading that might get a vital bill passed. No one would want to speak bluntly about public figures, here and abroad.

That is why I shall continue to oppose efforts which would set a precedent that would cripple all future Presidents by inhibiting conversations between them and those they look to for advice. This principle of confidentiality of presidential conversations is at stake in the question of these tapes. I must, and I shall, oppose any efforts to destroy this principle, which is so vital to the conduct of this great office.

Turning now to the basic issues which have been raised by Watergate, I recognize that merely answering the charges that have been made against the President is not enough. The word "Watergate" has come to represent a much broader set of concerns.

To most of us, "Watergate" has come to mean not just a burglary and bugging of party headquarters, but a whole series of acts that either represent or appear to represent an abuse of trust. It has come to stand for excessive partisanship, for "enemy lists," for efforts to use the great institutions of government for partisan political purposes.

For many Americans, the term "Watergate" also has come to include a number of national security matters that have been brought into the investigation, such as those involved in my efforts to stop massive leaks of vital diplomatic and military secrets, and to counter the wave of bombings and burnings and other violent assaults of just a few years ago.

Let me speak first of the political abuses. I know from long experience that a political campaign is always a hard and a tough contest. A candidate for high office has an obligation to his party, to his supporters, and to the cause he represents. He must always put forth his best efforts to win. But he also has an obligation to the country to conduct that contest within the law and within the limits of decency.

No political campaign ever justifies obstructing justice, or harassing individuals, or compromising those great agencies of government that should and must be above politics. To the extent that these things were done in the 1972 campaign, they were serious abuses. And I deplore them. Practices of that kind do not represent what I believe government should be, or what I believe politics should be. In a free society, the institutions of government belong to the people. They must never be used against the people.

And in the future, my Administration will be more vigilant in insuring that such abuses do not take place, and that officials at every level understand that they are not to take place.

And I reject the cynical view that politics is inevitably or even usually a dirty business. Let us not allow what a few overzealous people did in Watergate to tar the reputation of the millions of dedicated Americans of both parties who fought hard but clean for the candidates of their choice in 1972. By their unselfish efforts, these people make our system work and they keep America free. I pledge to you tonight

that I will do all that I can to insure that one of the results of Watergate is a new level of political decency and integrity in America—in which what has been wrong in our politics no longer corrupts or demeans what is right in our politics.

Let me turn now to the difficult questions that arise in protecting the national security. It is important to recognize that these are difficult questions and that reasonable and patriotic men and women may differ on how they should be answered.

Only last year, the Supreme Court said that implicit in the President's constitutional duty is "the power to protect our government against those who would subvert or overthrow it by unlawful means." How to carry out this duty is often a delicate question to which there is no easy answer.

For example, every President since World War II has believed that in internal security matters the President has the power to authorize wiretaps without first obtaining a search warrant. An act of Congress in 1968 had seemed to recognize such power. Last year the Supreme Court held to the contrary. And my Administration is of course now complying with that Supreme Court decision. But until the Supreme Court spoke, I had been acting, as did my predecessors—President Truman, President Eisenhower, President Kennedy, President Johnson—in a reasonable belief that in certain circumstances the Constitution permitted and sometimes even required such measures to protect the national security in the public interest.

Although it is the President's duty to protect the security of the country, we of course must be extremely careful in the way we go about this—for if we lose our liberties we will have little use for security. Instances have now come to light in which a zeal for security did go too far and did interfere impermissibly with individual liberty.

It is essential that such mistakes not be repeated. But it is also essential that we do not overreact to particular mistakes by tying the President's hands in a way that would risk sacrificing our security, and with it all our liberties. I shall continue to meet my constitutional responsibility to protect the security of this nation so that Americans may enjoy their freedom. But I shall and can do so by constitutional means, in ways that will not threaten that freedom.

As we look at Watergate in a longer perspective, we can see that its abuses resulted from the assumption by those involved that their cause placed them beyond the reach of those rules that apply to other persons and that hold a free society together. That attitude can never be tolerated in our country.

However, it did not suddenly develop in the year 1972. It became fashionable in the 1960s, as individuals and groups increasingly asserted the right to take the law into their own hands, insisting that their purposes represented a higher morality. Then, their attitude was praised in the press and even from some of our pulpits as evidence of a new idealism. Those of us who insisted on the old restraints, who warned of the overriding importance of operating within the law and by the rules, were accused of being reactionaries.

That same attitude brought a rising spiral of violence and fear, of riots and arson and bombings, all in the name of peace and in the name of justice. Political discussion turned into savage debate. Free speech was brutally suppressed as hecklers shouted down or even physically assaulted those with whom they disagreed. Serious people raised serious questions about whether we could survive as a free democracy.

The notion that the end justifies the means proved contagious. Thus it is not surprising, even though it is deplorable, that some persons in 1972 adopted the morality that they themselves had rightly condemned and committed acts that have no place in our political system.

Those acts cannot be defended. Those who were guilty of abuses must be punished. But ultimately the answer does not lie merely in the jailing of a few overzealous persons who mistakenly thought their cause justified their violations of the law. Rather, it lies in a commitment by all of us to show a renewed respect for the mutual restraints that are the mark of a free and civilized society. It requires that we learn once again to work together, if not united in all of our

purposes, then at least united in respect for the system by which our conflicts are peacefully resolved and our liberties maintained.

If there are laws we disagree with, let us work to change them—but let us obey them until they are changed. If we have disagreements over government policies, let us work those out in a decent and civilized way, within the law, and with respect for our differences.

We must recognize that one excess begets another, and that the extremes of violence and discord in the 1960s contributed to the extremes of Watergate. Both are wrong. Both should be condemned. No individual, no group and no political party has a corner on the market on morality in America.

If we learn the important lessons of Watergate, if we do what is necessary to prevent such abuses in the future—on both sides—we can emerge from this experience a better and a stronger nation.

Let me turn now to an issue that is important above all else, and that is critically affecting your life today and will affect your life and your children's in the years to come. After 12 weeks and 2 million words of televised testimony, we have reached a point at which a continued, backward-looking obsession with Watergate is causing this nation to neglect matters of far greater importance to all of the American people.

We must not stay so mired in Watergate that we fail to respond to challenges of surpassing importance to America and the world. We cannot let an obsession with the past destroy our hopes for the future.

Legislation vital to your health and well-being sits unattended on the Congressional calendar. Confidence at home and abroad in our economy, our currency and our foreign policy is being sapped by uncertainty. Critical negotiations are taking place on strategic weapons, on troop levels in Europe that can affect the security of this nation and the peace of the world long after Watergate is forgotten. Vital events are taking place in Southeast Asia which could lead to a tragedy for the cause of peace.

These are matters that cannot wait. They cry out for action now. And either we, your elected representatives here in Washington ought to get on with the jobs that need to be done—for you—or every one of you ought to be demanding to know why. The time has come to turn Watergate over to the courts, where the questions of guilt or innocence belong. The time has come for the rest of us to get on with the urgent business of our nation.

Last November, the American people were given the clearest choice of this century. Your votes were a mandate, which I accepted, to complete the initiatives we began in my first term and to fulfill the promises I made for my second term.

This Administration was elected to control inflation, to reduce the power and size of government, to cut the cost of government so that you can cut the cost of living, to preserve and defend those fundamental values that have made America great, to keep the nation's military strength second to none, to achieve peace with honor in Southeast Asia and to bring home our prisoners of war, and to build a new prosperity, without inflation and without war, to create a structure of peace in the world that would endure long after we are gone.

These are great goals. They are worthy of a great people. And I would not be true to your trust if I let myself be turned aside from achieving those goals. If you share my belief in these goals—if you want the mandate you gave this Administration to be carried out—then I ask for your help to insure that those who would exploit Watergate in order to keep us from doing what we were elected to do will not succeed.

I ask tonight for your understanding, so that as a nation we can learn the lessons of Watergate, and gain from that experience.

I ask for your help in reaffirming our dedication to the principles of decency, honor and respect for the institutions that have sustained our progress through these past two centuries. And I ask for your support, in getting on once again with meeting your problems, improving your life and building your future.

With your help, with God's help, we will achieve these great goals for America. Thank you and good evening.

Text of Nixon Statement Released Aug. 15

On May 17 the Senate Select Committee began its hearings on Watergate. Five days later, on May 22, I issued a detailed statement discussing my relationship to the matter. I stated categorically that I had no prior knowledge of the Watergate operation and that I neither knew of nor took part in any subsequent efforts to cover it up.

I also stated that I would not invoke executive privilege as to testimony by present and former members

of my White House staff with respect to possible criminal acts then under investigation.

Thirty-five witnesses have testified so far. The record is more than 7,500 pages and some two million words long. The allegations are many, the facts are complicated, and the evidence is not only extensive but very much in conflict.

It would be neither fair nor appropriate for me to assess the evidence or comment on specific witnesses

or their credibility. That is the function of the Senate committee and the courts. What I intend to do here is to cover the principal issues relating to my own conduct which have been raised since my statement of May 22, and thereby to place the testimony on those issues in perspective.

I said on May 22 that I had no prior knowledge of the Watergate operation. In all the testimony, there is not the slightest evidence to the contrary. Not a single witness has testified that I had any knowledge of the planning for the Watergate break-in.

It is also true, as I said on May 22, that I took no part in, and was not aware of, any subsequent efforts to cover up the illegal acts associated with the Watergate break-in.

In the summer of 1972 I had given orders for the Justice Department and the FBI to conduct a thorough and aggressive investigation of the Watergate break-in, and I relied on their investigation to disclose the facts. My only concern about the scope of the investigation was that it might lead into CIA or other national security operations of a sensitive nature. Mr. Gray, the acting director of the FBI, told me by telephone on July 6 that he had met with General Walters, that General Walters had told him the CIA was not involved, and that CIA activities would not be compromised by the FBI investigation. As a result, any problems that Mr. Gray may have had in coordinating with the CIA were moot. I concluded by instructing him to press forward vigorously with his own investigation.

During the summer of 1972, I repeatedly asked for reports on the progress of the investigation. Every report I received was that no persons, other than the seven who were subsequently indicted, were involved in the Watergate operation. On Sept. 12, at a meeting attended by me, and by the Cabinet, senior members of the White House staff and a number of legislative leaders, Attorney General Kleindienst reported on the investigation. He informed us that it had been the most intensive investigation since the assassination of President Kennedy, and that it had been established that no one at the White House, and no higher-ups in the campaign committee, were involved. His report seemed to be confirmed by the action of the grand jury on Sept. 15, when it indicted only the five persons arrested at the Watergate, plus Messrs. Liddy and Hunt.

Those indictments also seemed to me to confirm the validity of the reports that Mr. Dean had been providing to me through other members of the White House staff—and on which I had based my Aug. 29 statement that no one then employed at the White House was involved. It was in that context that I met with Mr. Dean on Sept. 15, and he gave me no reason at that meeting to believe any others were involved.

Not only was I unaware of any coverup, but at that time, and until March 21, I was unaware that there was anything to cover up.

Then and later, I continued to have full faith in the investigations that had been conducted and in the reports I had received based on those investigations. On Feb. 16, I met with Mr. Gray prior to submitting his name to the Senate for confirmation as permanent director of the FBI. I stressed to him that he would be questioned closely about the FBI's conduct of the Watergate investigation, and asked him if he still had full confidence in it. He replied that he did; that he was proud of its thoroughness, and that he could defend it with enthusiasm.

My interest in Watergate rose in February and March as the Senate committee was organized and the hearings were held on the Gray nomination. I began meeting frequently with my counsel, Mr. Dean, in connection with those matters. At that time, on a number of occasions, I urged my staff to get all the facts out, because I was confident that full disclosure of the facts would show that persons in the White House and at the Committee for the Re-election of the President were the victims of unjustified innuendoes in the press. I was searching for a way to disclose all of the facts without disturbing the confidentiality of communications with and among my personal staff, since that confidentiality is essential to the functioning of any President.

It was on March 21 that I was given new information that indicated that the reports I had been getting were not true. I was told then for the first time that the planning of the Watergate break-in went beyond those who had been tried and convicted, and that at least one, and possibly more, persons at the re-election committee were involved.

It was on that day also that I learned of some of the activities upon which charges of cover-up are now based. I was told that funds had been raised for payments to the defendants, with the knowledge and approval of persons both on the White House staff and at the re-election committee. But I was only told that the money had been used for attorneys' fees and family support, not that it had been paid to procure silence from the recipients. I was also told that a member of my staff had talked to one of the defendants about clemency, but not that offers of clemency had been made. I was told that one of the defendants was currently attempting to blackmail the White House by demanding payment of $120,000 as the price of not talking about other activities, unrelated to Watergate, in which he had engaged. These allegations were made in general terms, they were portrayed to me as being based in part on supposition, and they were largely unsupported by details or evidence.

These allegations were very troubling, and they gave a new dimension to the Watergate matter. They also reinforced my determination that the full facts must be made available to the grand jury or to the Senate committee. If anything illegal had happened, I wanted it to be dealt with appropriately according to the law. If anyone at the White House or high up in my campaign had been involved in wrongdoing of any kind, I wanted the White House to take the lead in making that known.

When I received this distressing information on March 21, I immediately began new inquiries into the case and an examination of the best means to give to the grand jury or Senate committee what we then knew and what we might later learn. On March 21, I arranged to meet the following day with Messrs. Haldeman, Ehrlichman, Dean and Mitchell to discuss the appropriate method to get the facts out. On March 23, I sent Mr. Dean to Camp David, where he was instructed to write a complete report on all that he knew of the entire Watergate matter. On March 28, I had Mr. Ehrlichman call the attorney general to find out if he had additional information about Watergate generally or White House involvement. The attorney general was told that I wanted to hear directly from him, and not through any staff people, if he had any information on White House involvement or if information of that kind should come to him.

The attorney general indicated to Mr. Ehrlichman that he had no such information. When I learned on March 30 that Mr. Dean had been unable to complete his report, I instructed Mr. Ehrlichman to conduct an independent inquiry and bring all the facts to me. On April 14, Mr. Ehrlichman gave me his findings, and I directed that he report them to the attorney general immediately on April 15, Attorney General Kleindienst and Assistant Attorney General Petersen told me of new information that had been received by the prosecutors.

By that time the fragmentary information I had been given on March 21 had been supplemented in important ways, particularly by Mr. Ehrlichman's report to me on April 14, by the information Mr. Kleindienst and Mr. Petersen gave me on April 15, and by independent inquiries I had been making on my own. At that point, I realized that I would not be able personally to find out all of the facts and make them public, and I concluded that the matter was best handled by the Justice Department and the grand jury. On April 17, I announced that new inquiries were under way, as a result of what I had learned on March 21 and in my own investigation since that time. I instructed all government employes to cooperate with the judicial process as it moved ahead on this matter and expressed my personal view that no immunity should be given to any individual who had held a position of major importance in this Administration.

My consistent position from the beginning has been to get out the facts about Watergate, not to cover them up.

On May 22 I said that at no time did I authorize any offer of executive clemency for the Watergate defendants, not did I know of any such offer. I reaffirm that statement. Indeed, I made my view clear to Mr. Ehrlichman in July, 1972, that under no circumstances could executive clemency be considered for those who participated in the Watergate break-in. I maintained that position throughout.

On May 22 I said that "it was not until the time of my own investigation that I learned of the break-in at the office of Mr. Ellsberg's psychiatrist, and I specifically authorized the furnishing of this information to Judge Byrne." After a very careful review, I have determined that this statement of mine is not precisely accurate. It was on March 17 that I first learned of the break-in at the office of Dr. Fielding, and that was four days before the beginning of my own investgiation on March 21. I was told then that nothing by way of evidence have been obtained in the break-in. On April 18 I learned that the Justice Department had interrogated or was going to interrogate Mr. Hunt about this break-in. I was gravely concerned that other activities of the special investigations unit might be disclosed, because I knew this could seriously injure the national security. Consequently, I directed Mr. Petersen to stick to the Watergate investigation and stay out of national security matters. On April 25 Attorney General Kleindienst came to me and urged that the fact of the break-in should be disclosed to the court, despite the fact that, since no evidence had been obtained, the law did not clearly require it. I concurred and authorized him to report the break-in to Judge Byrne.

In view of the incident of Dr. Fielding's office, let me emphasize two things.

First, it was and is important that many of the matters worked on by the special investigations unit not be publicly disclosed because disclosure would unquestionably damage the national security. This is why I have exercised executive privilege on some of these matters in connection with the testimony of Mr. Ehrlichman and others. The Senate committee has learned through its investigation the general facts of some of these security matters, and has to date wisely declined to make them public or to contest in these respects my claim of executive privilege.

Second, I at no time authorized the use of illegal means by the special investigations unit, and I was not aware of the break-in of Dr. Fielding's office until March 17, 1973.

Many persons will ask why, when the facts are as I have stated them, I do not make public the tape recordings of my meetings and conversations with members of the White House staff during this period.

I am aware that such terms as "separation of powers" and "executive privilege" are lawyers' terms, and that those doctrines have been called "abstruse" and "esoteric." Let me state the common sense of the matter. Every day a President of the United States is required to make difficult decisions on grave issues. It is absolutely essential, if the President is to be able to do his job as the country expects, that he be able to talk openly and candidly with his advisers about issues and individuals and that they be able to talk in the same fashion with him. Indeed, on occasion, they must be able to "blow off steam" about important public figures. This kind of frank discussion is only possible when those who take part in it can feel assured that what they say is in the strictest confidence.

The presidency is not the only office that requires confidentiality if it is to function effectively. A member of Congress must be able to talk in confidence with his assistants. Judges must be able to confer in confidence with their law clerks and with each other. Throughout our entire history the need for this kind of confidentiality has been recognized. No branch of government has ever compelled disclosure of confidential conversations between officers of other branches of government and their advisers about government business.

The argument is often raised that these tapes are somehow different because the conversations may bear on illegal acts, and because the commission of illegal acts is not an official duty. This misses the point entirely. Even if others, from their own standpoint, may have been thinking about how to cover up an illegal act, from my standpoint I was concerned with how to uncover the illegal acts. It is my responsibility under the Constitution to see that the laws are faithfully executed, and in pursuing the facts about Watergate I was doing precisely that. Therefore, the precedent would not be one concerning illegal actions only; it would be one that would risk exposing private presidential conversations involving the whole range of official duties.

The need for confidence is not something confined to the government officials. The law has long recognized that there are many relations sufficiently important that things said in that relation are entitled to be kept confidential, even at the cost of doing without what might be critical evidence in a legal proceeding. Among these are, for example, the relations between a lawyer and his client, between a priest and a penitent, and between a husband and wife. In each case it is thought to be so important that the parties be able to talk freely with each other, that they need not feel restrained in their conversation by fear that what they say may someday come out in court, that the law recognizes that these conversations are "privileged" and that their disclosure cannot be compelled.

If I were to make public these tapes, containing as they do blunt and candid remarks on many subjects that have nothing to do with Watergate, the confidentiality of the office of the President would always be suspect. Persons talking with a President would never again be sure that recordings or notes of what they said would not at some future time be made public, and they would guard their words against that possibility. No one would want to risk being known as the person who recommended a policy that ultimately did not work. No one would want to advance tentative ideas, not fully thought through, that might have possible merit but that might, on further examination, prove unsound. No one would want to speak bluntly about public figures here and abroad. I shall therefore vigorously oppose any actions which would set a precedent that would cripple all future Presidents by inhibiting conversations between them and the persons they look to for advice.

This principle of confidentiality in presidential communications is what is at stake in the question of the tapes. I shall continue to oppose any efforts to destroy that principle, which is indispensable to the conduct of the presidency.

I recognize that this statement does not answer many of the questions and contentions raised during the Watergate hearings. It has not been my intention to attempt any such comprehensive and detailed response, nor has it been my intention to address myself to all matters covered in my May 22 statement. With the Senate hearings and the grand jury investigations still proceeding, with much of the testimony in conflict, it would be neither possible to provide nor appropriate to attempt a definitive account of all that took place. Neither do I believe I could enter upon an endless course of explaining and rebutting a complex of point-by-point claims and charges arising out of that conflicting testimony which may engage committees and courts for months or years to come, and still be able to carry out my duties as President. While the judicial and legislative branches resolve these matters, I will continue to discharge to the best of my ability my constitutional responsibilities as President of the United States.

Ruckelshaus comment. Acting Deputy Attorney General William D. Ruckelshaus called President Nixon's Aug. 15 Watergate speech a "strong" one but said "it won't satisfy his critics because it was not specific enough." Ruckelshaus supported the President's plea that the Watergate case be relegated to the courts. But he said some questions about the break-in and cover-up "should be addressed with more specificity" by the President although, given the conflicting testimony, Ruckelshaus was not certain it was possible "to satisfy a bare majority of the American people," he said Aug. 17.

Nixon popularity rises after speech. According to a Gallup Poll taken after President Nixon's Aug. 15 speech on Watergate, 38% of those surveyed approved of the job he was doing as President. This compared with 31% registered in the Aug. 3-6 Gallup survey.

However, the President's speech did not dispel widespread doubts about Watergate. By a margin of 58%-34%, the respondents to the poll, reported Aug. 21, said they were dissatisfied with Nixon's explanation.

A Louis Harris survey made public Aug. 20 indicated that 67% of the public felt the President had failed to give "convincing proof" that he was not part of the Watergate cover-up. Of those polled by Harris, 71% believed Nixon had withheld "important information" about Watergate.

Nixon assails war foes at VFW meet. President Nixon Aug. 20 defended his order for the secret bombing of Cambodia in 1969 and denounced his war policy critics and the "unilateral disarmers" who would have the country "cop out from our responsibilities in the world." The President's remarks, made in an address to the 74th national convention of the Veterans of Foreign Wars (VFW) in New Orleans, were viewed by some political commentators as a counterattack to press criticism of his handling of Watergate.

President holds lengthy news conference. President Nixon fielded an intense barrage of questions on Watergate during most of a 50-minute news conference Aug. 22 on the lawn of his San Clemente, Calif. home. It was Nixon's first news conference in five months and his first televised news conference in 14 months.

Agnew's status—"My confidence in his integrity has not been shaken," Nixon said of Agnew, "and in fact it has been strengthened by his courageous conduct and his ability." Nixon said the charges against Agnew were "made about activities that occurred before he became vice president." It would be "improper" to comment on the charges, but not upon "the outrageous leak in information from either the grand jury or the prosecutors or the Department of Justice or all three." He said he had requested a full investigation by the department.

Not only "trying" an individual but "convicting him in the headlines and on television before he's had a chance to present his case in court is completely contrary to the American tradition. Even a vice president has a right to some . . . consideration in this respect, let alone the ordinary individual," the President said, and added, any federal employe who had leaked such information "will be summarily dismissed."

If Agnew were indicted, would Nixon "expect him to resign or somehow otherwise stand down temporarily until cleared?"

It would be inappropriate to comment on that, Nixon said. Agnew had not been indicted. "Charges have been thrown out by innuendo and otherwise," which Agnew "has denied to me personally and which he has denied publicly."

Taping of White House conversations— The President was asked why he tape recorded White House conversations and "what is your reaction to surveys that show three out of four American believe you were wrong to make the tapes?"

Nixon replied that the survey findings were "not particularly surprising." Most Americans, he said, "do not like the idea of the taping of conversations and, frankly, it is not something that particularly appeals to me."

When he became President, there was a "rather complex" taping "capacity" set up in the White House. He had "the entire system dismantled," but it was put in place again in June 1970 because "my advisers felt it was important in terms particularly of national security affairs to have a record" for the future that "would only be disclosed at the discretion of the President." "This kind of capability" existed in the Johnson and Kennedy Administrations, he asserted.

As far as he was concerned, Nixon said, "we now do not have that capability and I am just as happy that we don't." He now dictated his recollections each day, when he had time.

He was asked why he permitted his former aide H.R. Haldeman, "a man who you knew might be indicted," to hear tapes which were being withheld from the prosecutors and the public.

Nixon said Haldeman, at his request, had listened only to one tape, that of a Sept. 15, 1972 discussion at which Haldeman was present. "I asked him to listen to it in order to be sure that as far as any allegations that had been made by [his former counsel] Mr. [John W.] Dean with regard to that conversation is concerned, I wanted to be sure that we were absolutely correct in our response."

Nixon was asked whether it was possible some group could listen to the tapes "and give a report so that that might satisfy the public mind."

He did not believe that such an arrangement "would satisfy the public mind," Nixon said, "and it shouldn't." To have the tapes listened to "either by a prosecutor or by a judge or in camera or in any way would violate the principle of confidentiality." "We will oppose . . . any compromise of the principle of confidentiality. . . . The principle of confidentiality either exists or it doesn't exist." The principle covered presidential papers as well as tapes.

Nixon asserted that if confidentiality were violated, individuals who came to talk to the President "will always be speaking in a eunuch-like way, rather than laying it on the line. It has to be laid on the line if you're going to have the creative kind of discussions that we have often had and have been responsible for some of our successes in the foreign policy period, particularly in the past few years."

He was asked where was "the check on authoritarianism by the executive" if the President was "the sole judge of what the executive branch makes available and suppresses," whether he would obey a Supreme Court order to produce such tapes or other documents, and whether there was any limitation on the President, "short of impeachment, to compel the production of evidence of a criminal nature."

Nixon said there was a limitation on the President—"the limitation of public opinion" and "Congressional and other pressures that may arise."

He thought his Administration had "gone further in terms of waiving executive privilege than any Administration in my memory."

He reaffirmed his spokesman's previous statement "with regard to the President's position of complying with a definitive order of the Supreme Court."

Gray's warning he was 'wounded'—The President was asked about the reported July 6, 1972 warning by acting FBI director L. Patrick Gray that he was "being mortally wounded" by senior White House aides and why he did not inquire "who they were, and why, what was going on?"

Nixon replied that Gray had told him some of his top aides "were not cooperating" with the FBI's Watergate probe. "Whether the term used was 'mortally wounded' or not, I do not know. Some believe that it was. Some believe that it wasn't. That is irrelevant. He could have said that."

Nixon said the main point was that he had asked Gray if he had discussed the matter with Lt. Gen. Vernon A. Walters, then deputy director of the Central Intelligence Agency (CIA) "because I knew that there had been meetings between Gen. Walters representing the CIA to be sure that the CIA did not become involved in the investigation and between the director of the FBI." Gray "said that he had. He told me that Gen. Walters agreed that the investigation should be pursued and I told him to go forward with a full press on the investigation. . . . As far as the individuals were concerned I assume that the individuals that he was referring to involved this operation with the CIA. That's why I asked him the Walters question."

Mitchell's veracity—Nixon was asked about his contention that he had tried to get all the facts about the case in the light of former Attorney General John Mitchell's statement "that if you had ever asked him at any time about the Watergate matter he would have told you the whole story chapter and verse." Was Mitchell "not speaking the truth?"

"I'm not going to question Mr. Mitchell's veracity," Nixon replied. He said he had had confidence in Mitchell and was expecting him "to tell me, in the event that he was involved or that anybody else was. He did not tell me. I don't blame him for not telling me. He's given his reasons for not telling me. I regret that he did not; because he's exactly right—had he told me I would have blown my stack."

Ehrlichman and Haldeman supported—Nixon was asked if he still considered his former aides H.R. Haldeman and John D. Ehrlichman "two of the finest public servants" he had ever known. "I certainly do," he responded. They had served with great distinction he said, "and, like everybody in this deplorable Watergate business, at great personal sacrifice and with no personal gain."

"We admit the scandalous conduct," Nixon continued. "Thank God, there's been no personal gain involved. That would be going much too far, I suppose."

When all the facts came out and when Haldeman and Ehrlichman had an opportunity to have their case heard in court, "not simply to be tried before a committee, and tried in the press and tried in television—they will be exonerated," Nixon said.

Asked if he, Haldeman and Ehrlichman were "coordinating their and your defense and if so why," Nixon said no. "As far as my defense is concerned, I make it myself. As far as their defense is concerned, their lawyer demonstrated very well before the committee that he can handle it very well without any assistance from me."

The March 21 meeting with Dean—The President was asked his recollection of his March 21, 1972 meeting with his counsel, John W. Dean 3rd, on the subject of raising funds for the Watergate defendants. He replied:

Certainly. Mr. Haldeman has testified to that, and his statement is accurate.

Basically, what Mr. Dean was concerned about on March 21 was not so much the raising of money for the defendants but the raising of money for the defendants for the purpose of keeping them still. In other words so-called hush money.

The one would be legal, in other words raising the defense funds for any group, any individual, as you know is perfectly legal and is done all the time. But you raise funds for the purpose of keeping an individual from talking, that's obstruction of justice.

Mr. Dean said also, on March 21, that there was an attempt to, as he put it, to blackmail the White House, to blackmail the White House by one of the defendants; incidentally, that defendant has denied it, but at least this is what Mr. Dean had claimed and that unless certain amounts of money were paid, I think it was $120,000 for attorneys' fees and other support, that this particular defendant would make a statement, not with regard to Watergate but with regard to some national security matters in which Mr. Ehrlichman had particular responsibility.

My reaction very briefly was this: I said as you look at this, I said isn't it quite obvious, first, that if it is going to have any chance to succeed, that these individuals aren't going to sit there in jail for four years, they're going to have clemency. Isn't that correct?"

He said yes.

I said we can't given clemency.

He agreed.

Then I went to another point. The second point is that isn't it also quite obvious, as far as this is concerned, that while we could raise the money, and he indicated in answer to my question that it would probably take a million dollars over four years to take care of this defendant and others on this kind of a basis, the problem was, how do you get the money to them? And also, how do you get around the problem of clemency because they're not going to stay in jail simply because their families are being taken care of.

And so that was why I concluded, as Mr. Haldeman recalls, perhaps, and did testify very effectively, when I said John, it's wrong, it won't work, we can't give clemency, and we've got to get this story out. . . ."

Nixon's Watergate informants—Nixon was asked who had been his principal informants on the case after he had ordered Watergate investigations in June of 1972 and March 21, 1973.

In June I of course talked to Mr. MacGregor first of all who was the new chairman of the committee. He told me that he would conduct a thorough investigation as far as his entire committee staff was concerned. Apparently that investigation was very effective except for Mr. [Jeb Stuart] Magruder who stayed on, but Mr. MacGregor does not have to assume responsibility for that, . . . he believed Mr. Magruder, and many others had believed him, too. He proved, however, to be wrong.

In the White House, the investigation's responsibility were given to Mr. Ehrlichman at the highest level and, in turn, he delegated them to Mr. Dean, . . . something of which I was aware and of which I approved. Mr. Dean, as White House counsel, therefore sat in on the F.B.I. interrogations of the members of the White House staff because what I wanted to know was whether any member of the White House staff was in any way involved. If he was involved, he would be fired.

And when we met on Sept. 15 and again throughout our discussions in the month of March, Mr. Dean insisted there was not—and I use his words—a scintilla of evidence indicating that anyone on the White House staff was involved in the planning of the Watergate break-in.

Now in terms of after March 21st, Mr. Dean first was given the responsibility to write his own report but I did not rest it there—I also had a contact made with the Attorney General himself, and Attorney General Kleindienst told him—this was on the 27th of March—to report to me directly anything that he found in this particular area, and I gave the responsibility for Mr. Ehrlichman on the 29th of March to

continue the investigation that Mr. Dean was unable to conclude, having spent a week at Camp David and unable to finish the report."

I met at great length with Mr. Ehrlichman, Mr. Haldeman, Mr. Dean, Mr. Mitchell on the 22d. I discussed the whole matter with them. I kept pressing for the view that I had had throughout, that we must get this story out, get the truth out, whatever and whoever it's going to hurt, and it was there that Mr. Mitchell suggested that all the individuals involved in th∙ White House appear in an executive session before the Ervin committee.

We never got that far. But at least that was, that's an indication of the extent of my own investigation."

The President was asked why he had not turned over to the prosecutors data he received in March and April about criminal wrongdoing "and some indication that members of your staff might have been involved."

Nixon said Dean had been making contacts with the prosecutors in March and "I assumed that anything he was telling me, he was telling the prosecutors." Ehrlichman had that role in April, he said. "The President doesn't pick up the phone and call the attorney general every time something comes up on a matter. He depends on his counsel, or whoever" was assigned the task.

Approach to Ellsberg judge—Nixon was questioned about his and Ehrlichman's contacts with U.S. District Judge W. Matthew Byrne Jr. while he was presiding at the Pentagon papers trial of Dr. Daniel Ellsberg. "Could you give us some reason why the American people shouldn't believe that that was at least a subtle attempt to bribe the judge in that case and it gave at least the appearance of a lack of moral leadership?" he was asked.

Nixon said he met Byrne "for perhaps one minute outside my door here in full view of the whole White House staff and everybody who wanted to see. I asked him how he liked his job. We did not discuss the case."

The meetings occurred because the attorney general had recommended Byrne as "the best man" to succeed Gray as FBI director.

"Under those circumstances," Ehrlichman called Byrne. "He said under no circumstances will we talk to you, he, Ehrlichman will talk to you, unless if he felt that it would in any way compromise his handling of the Ellsberg case. Judge Byrne made the decision that he would talk to Mr. Ehrlichman. . . . The case was not discussed at all. Only the question of whether or not at the conclusion of this case Mr. Byrne would like to be considered as director of the FBI.

"I understand, incidentally, that he told Mr. Ehrlichman that he would be interested."

In response to questioning about the break-in at the offices of Ellsberg's former psychiatrist, Nixon said he considered the break-in "illegal, unauthorized as far as I was concerned, and completely deplorable." But he said since it "was a dry hole" and no evidence had been developed from it, "there was no requirement" that the break-in be reported to the grand jury examining the Ellsberg case.

Later, he recalled, Attorney General Kleindienst recommended "that we bend over backwards" and report the break-in to the court. Nixon said when the recommendation was made "I directed that it be done instantly."

Views on impeachment, wiretaps—The President was asked whether his authorization of a 1970 intelligence plan permitting illegal acts was a violation of his oath to execute the law. He was asked,

If you were serving in Congress, would you not be considering impeachment proceedings and discussing impeachment possibility against an elected public official who had violated his oath of office?

He replied:

I would if I had violated the oath of office. I would also, however, refer you to the recent decision of the Supreme Court or at least an opinion that even last year which indicates inherent power in the Presidency to protect the national security in cases like this. I should also point to you that in the three Kennedy years and the three Johnson years through 1966 when burglarizing of this type did take place, when it was authorized, on a very large scale basis there was no talk of impeachment and it was quite well known.

I should also like to point out that when you ladies and gentlemen indicate your great interest in wiretaps and I understand that the height of the wiretaps was when Robert Kennedy was Attorney General in 1963. I don't criticize him, however. He had over 250 in 1963 and of course the average in the Eisenhower Administration and the Nixon Administration is about 110.

The President later commented that in 1961-63 "there were wiretaps on news organizations, on news people, on civil rights leaders and on other people."

No thought of resigning—Nixon was asked "at any time during the Watergate crisis have you ever considered resigning? Would you consider resigning if you felt that your capacity to govern had been seriously weakened? And in that connection, how much do you think your capacity to govern has been weakened? He replied:

The answer to the first two questions is no. The answer to the third question is that it is true that as far as the capacity to govern is concerned, that to be under a constant barrage—12 to 15 minutes a night on each of the three major networks for four months—tends to raise some questions in the people's minds with regard to the President; and it may raise some questions with regard to the capacity to govern.

But I also know this: I was elected to do a job. Watergate is an episode that I deeply deplore; and, had I been running the campaign—other than trying to run the country, and particularly the foreign policy of this country at this time—it would never have happened. But that's water under the bridge. Let's go on now.

The point that I make now is, that we are proceeding as best we know how to get all those guilty brought to justice in Watergate. But now we must move on from Watergate to the business of the people—the business of the people is continuing with initiatives we began in the first Administration."

He added later: "And when you say, have I—do I consider resigning: the answer is no. I shall not resign."

He had almost three and a half years left in his second term, Nixon said, "and I'm going to use every day" of it "trying to get the people of the United States to recognize that whatever mistakes we have made, that in the long run this Administration, by making this world safer for their children, and this Administration, by making their lives better at home for themselves and their children, deserves high marks rather than low marks."

Blame for Watergate climate—Still another question was, "How much blame, what degree of personal blame do you accept for the climate in the White House

and . . . [the campaign committee] for the abuses of Watergate?" "I accept it all," Nixon replied.

Political opponents scored—Nixon was asked who he was referring to in his recent remark about "those who would exploit Watergate to keep you from doing your job?" He replied:

I would suggest that where the shoe fits, people should wear it. I would think that some political figures, some members of the press perhaps, some members of the television, perhaps, would exploit it. I don't impute, interestingly enough, motives, however, that are improper interests, because here's what is involved.

There are a great number of people in this country that would prefer that I do resign. There are a great number of people in this country that didn't accept the mandate of 1972. After all, I know that most of the members of the press corps were not enthusiastic. And I understand that about either my election in '68 or '72. That's not unusual. Frankly, if I had always followed what the press predicted or the polls predicted, I would have never been elected President.

But what I am saying is this. People who did not accept the mandate of '72, who do not want the strong America that I want to build, who do not want the foreign policy leadership that I want to give, who do not want to cut down the size of this Government bureaucracy that burdens us so greatly and to give more of our Government back to the people, people who do not want these things naturally would exploit any issues. If it weren't Watergate, anything else in order to keep the President from doing his job.

FBI burglaries called 'a fact.' A White House spokesman declined to elaborate Aug. 23 on President Nixon's assertion that "burglarizing" authorized by the two previous Administrations had been practiced on "a very large scale" and was "quite well known." Deputy White House Press Secretary Gerald L. Warren told newsmen who questioned the assertion that "the President said it because it was a fact." Nixon made the statement at his news conference Aug. 22.

Two former attorneys general said Aug. 23 they were unaware of any such practice during their government service. Nicholas deB. Katzenbach, who succeeded the late Robert F. Kennedy as attorney general in 1964, denied knowledge of such "official" burglaries. His successor, Ramsey Clark, in the post until 1969, said he "never heard of it" and "never authorized any burglaries." Clark said he had been approached by late FBI Director J. Edgar Hoover with a request to authorize the burglary of a foreign mission in New York City. He believed it was a "North African country," but had rejected it as "unthinkable" for an attorney general to authorize such activity.

There were reports that the FBI had engaged in burglarizing over a 30-year period ending in 1966, that the practice generally was targeted against foreign embassies and missions in the U.S. to discover cryptographic, or code, materials or against organized crime figures, that the practice was a well-kept secret within the FBI and that approval of the practice came from no higher authority than Hoover. He ordered the practice ended in 1966 because of the risk to his agency's reputation from such an activity, which benefitted another agency, the National Security Agency, it was reported.

Nixon's news conference statements about wiretaps also were at variance with

statistics released in June by Senate Republican Leader Hugh Scott (Pa.). Nixon said "the height of the wiretaps was when Robert Kennedy was attorney general in 1963" and that the average annual number of taps in his and Eisenhower's Administration had been "about 110." According to the June data, the largest number of wiretaps, 519, were in place between 1945 and 1954, and the average for each of the Eisenhower years of 1953-1960 was about 200.

George Christian, a former press secretary to President Johnson, Aug. 23 disputed another Nixon news conference statement that he found a "rather complex situation set up" in the White House when he took office, designed to record conversations in the President's office, the Cabinet room and at Camp David, a presidential retreat.

Christian said "what recording equipment there was at the White House was taken out before Mr. Nixon took office" and he "never heard of any" such equipment at Camp David.

Rogers hits security 'obsession.' Secretary of State William P. Rogers cautioned the nation Aug. 20 not to become "so obsessed with security matters that laws are freely violated." At his first press conference since Feb. 15, Rogers expressed his view that "great care should be shown before any extralegal action is undertaken." "I think one of the things that provides security for Americans," he said, "is the fact that we are a law-abiding nation" and that in particular included "protection for all individuals and a protection for individual rights."

Rogers specifically directed his concern to a 1971 break-in perpetrated by the White House "plumbers" group set up to stop leaks of government secrets. "If you were asking me," he said to the newsmen, "do I think that the security considerations were sufficiently grave and serious to justify the burglary of [Pentagon Papers defendant Daniel] Ellsberg's psychiatrist's office, the answer is no, I don't think so."

Rogers said it was discouraging when leaks that could adversely affect security interests occurred in the middle of sensitive negotiations, and the question of where to draw the line was "very difficult" to answer. "But generally speaking," he said, "I lean toward strict observance of legal requirements and only support a variance from that in very unusual circumstances."

Rogers scores wiretaps on aides. Secretary of State William P. Rogers repudiated the White House-approved wiretapping of three top foreign service officers during a 1969-71 program acknowledged by the Administration as authorized to find and plug security leaks. Acting State Department spokesman Paul J. Hare said Aug. 24 that Rogers had told him he was never informed by the White House about the wiretaps and he "would not have approved them.

A

Seventeen persons had reportedly been subjected to the wiretapping, with all but three government officials having been identified. Those identified included 10 government officials and four newsmen.

2nd news conference in two weeks. President Nixon, holding his second news conference in two weeks Sept. 5, said he would send Congress a supplementary State of the Union message focusing on measures currently before Congress "which have not been acted upon and which I consider urgent to be acted upon before the end of this year."

B

President Nixon was asked about his statement that he had ordered a new Watergate investigation March 21, which contrasted with testimony from the attorney general and FBI director at the time that "they didn't know anything about this investigation."

C

The President said he had ordered the probe "from within the White House itself," and had given the assignment to his former aide John D. Ehrlichman after his former counsel John W. Dean 3rd, who had had the task, had been unable to write a report. He said Ehrlichman had talked to the attorney general and in addition had "questioned all of the major figures involved," reported to Nixon on April 14 and turned over his report to the attorney general on April 15. "An investigation was conducted in the most thorough way," Nixon said.

D

Nixon admitted that he had a problem of rebuilding confidence in his leadership. He said it was "rather difficult" to have the President "attacked in every way" on television for four months "without having some of that confidence being worn away." He described the attack as "by innuendo, by leak, by, frankly, leers and sneers of commentators," adding that was "their perfect right."

E

As for the problem of restoring this confidence in his leadership, Nixon said "it's restored by the President not allowing his own confidence to be destroyed. That's the beginning." He added:

Second, it's restored by doing something. We have tried to do things. The country hasn't paid a great deal of attention to it. And I may say the media hasn't paid a great deal of attention to it; because your attention, quite understandably, is in the more fascinating area of Watergate. But perhaps that will now change. Perhaps as we move in the foreign policy initiative now, having ended one war, to build the structure of peace. Moving not only with the Soviet Union and with the P.R.C. [China], where Dr. Kissinger, incidentally, will go after he is confirmed by the Senate, which I hope will be soon. But as we move in those areas, and as we move on the domestic front, the people will be concerned about what the President does. And I think that will restore the confidence. What the President says will not restore it. And what you ladies and gentlemen say will certainly not restore it.

G

Agnew scores Watergate preoccupation. Echoing the President's contention that the federal government in Washington had allowed Watergate to distract it from vital tasks that lay before it, Vice President Agnew Sept. 8 urged those with a "morbid preoccupation" with Watergate to stop thwarting the will of the American people.

Speaking at a Republican fund raising dinner Sept. 8 in suburban Chicago, Agnew said: "We have reached the watershed of Watergate. In spite of that, it is obvious that some in this country are going to continue to attempt to milk this issue dry. Those embittered critics of this Administration and this party who could not discredit us at the polls in November will make every effort—no matter how reckless—to discredit us now."

Harris Poll on media's Watergate coverage. A Louis Harris poll published Sept. 8 found a substantial majority, 66%–24%, did not believe the "press is just out to get President Nixon on Watergate" but a majority, 50%–44%, thought "the press and television have given Watergate more attention than it deserves." The latter represented a turnaround from a 46%–40% plurality found in July which felt that media attention to Watergate was "not excessive."

Kissinger confirmation hearings. Henry A. Kissinger's role in the 1969–71 wiretapping of government officials and newsmen* became the major question before the Senate Foreign Relations Committee as it opened public confirmation hearings Sept. 7 on Kissinger's nomination as secretary of state.

Kissinger defended the wiretapping as necessary to stop leaks to the press. He said he had consented to the practice in 1969 on the advice of then Attorney General John N. Mitchell and the late director of the Federal Bureau of Investigation (FBI), J. Edgar Hoover. He disclaimed deep involvement in the operation and said his office's involvement ended by the summer of 1970. Kissinger urged the committee to deal directly with Attorney General Elliot L. Richardson in further pursuit of the matter. In response to a question, he said "there were cases in which the sources of some leaks were discovered and corrective action taken."

Wiretapping report requested—The panel had requested from the Justice Department the FBI report on the wiretap operation. Committee access to the report became a central factor. Committee member Clifford P. Case (R, N.J.) told Kissinger it was "very clear that the committee will not be in the position to act on the nomination until that report has been received." Committee Chairman J. W. Fulbright (D, Ark.) agreed with Case.

———————
*Disclosure of the identities of the 13 government officials and four newsmen subjected to the wiretapping was completed Aug. 31 when the New York Times identified three more officials on the list. They were James W. McLane, then on the White House Domestic Council staff, currently deputy director of the Cost of Living Council; John P. Sears, then deputy White House counsel and a former law partner of President Nixon; and Lt. Gen. Robert E. Pursley, then a colonel and military aide to the defense secretary, currently commander of American forces in Japan. Among those identified previously were Richard Moose, then on the National Security Council, currently a consultant to the Senate Foreign Relations Committee; and William Safire, then a presidential speechwriter, currently a columnist for the New York Times.

Richardson met in closed session with the committee Sept. 10 and provided a memorandum on Kissinger's role in the wiretapping. The panel released the memo, which was based on FBI records. The memo said Kissinger's role "included expressing concern over leaks of sensitive material and when this concern was coupled with that of the President and transmitted to the director of the FBI it led to efforts to stem the leaks, which efforts included some wiretaps of government employes and newsmen." The memo continued, "His role further involved the supplying to the FBI of names of individuals in the government who had access to sensitive information and occasional review of information generated by the program to determine its usefulness."

The committee voted later Sept. 10 14–0 to authorize two of its members, Case and Sen. John J. Sparkman (D, Ala.), to meet with Richardson "to obtain information on Dr. Kissinger's role respecting his initiative, or concurrence in wiretap surveillance."

At the committee's public session later Sept. 10, Kissinger was asked by Sen. Edmund S. Muskie (D, Me.) whether he would continue to approve wiretapping as secretary of state.

"The issue of wiretapping raises the balance between human liberty and the requirements of national security," Kissinger replied, "and I would say that the weight should be on the side of human liberty and that if human liberty is infringed, the demonstration of national security must be overwhelming and that would be my general attitude."

Richardson complied with the committee's action and made the FBI report available to Case and Sparkman Sept. 11. Later, the two senators met with Kissinger and Richardson to discuss it. Sparkman told newsmen there was no data in the report to jeopardize Kissinger's confirmation. Case said the committee's access to the report seemed to remove a major threat to the confirmation.

At the opening session Sept. 7, Kissinger had stressed his intention to operate in "a climate of mutual trust" with Congress. He wanted Congress to "share more fully in the design of our foreign policy."

In a letter requested by Fulbright on the current policy on wiretapping, Richardson said Sept. 12 that wiretaps without court warrant would be used only "in a limited number of cautiously and meticulously reviewed instances" that involved "a genuine national security interest." He listed three criteria to be applied to determine such instances, that the surveillance would be ordered only if it met one of these conditions: "1. To protect the nation against actual or potential attack or other hostile acts of a foreign power; 2. To obtain foreign intelligence information deemed essential to the security of the United States; or 3. To protect national security information against foreign intelligence activities."

Watergate & foreign policy. Kissinger noted the impact of Watergate on the national scene. Its "traumatic events" had shadowed the nation's "traditional optimism and self-esteem," and there was a danger that "a shrinking spirit could lead us to attempt too little. Such an attitude—and the foreign policy it would produce—would deal a savage blow to global stability."

Kissinger confirmed. Henry A. Kissinger was confirmed as the 56th secretary of state by a 78–7 Senate vote Sept. 21. The following day he was sworn in by U.S. Chief Justice Warren E. Burger at a White House ceremony.

The Senate Foreign Relations Committee had recommended to the full Senate Kissinger's confirmation by a 15–1 vote Sept. 18.

In its formal report on the nomination, the committee said Sept. 20 that "very little, if any, justification was presented in most instances" for the wiretapping of 17 government officials and newsmen during 1969–71. However, the committee accepted the findings of the special two-man subcommittee composed of Sens. John J. Sparkman (D, Ala.) and Clifford P. Case (R, N.J.) that Kissinger's role in the wiretappings "was not sufficient to bar him from confirmation."

"At the time of the surveillance in question, adequate standards of probable cause were not applied and adequate procedural safeguards with respect to authorizing and termination of taps were not observed," the report said.

A resolution calling for "a full examination of the use of electronic and other means of surveillance" in foreign policy and intelligence gathering areas was approved by the committee 15–0.

Nixon to campaign in '74 and '76. President Nixon told members of the Republican National Committee Sept. 10 that he planned to personally campaign for Republican candidates in 1974 and 1976. At a White House reception for delegates to the semiannual meeting of the committee, Nixon said he would campaign for GOP candidates for Congress in 1974 and the Presidential nominee in 1976.

Republican National Chairman George Bush was applauded Sept. 10 when he told the state delegates that the Republican party had survived the Watergate scandal and had been winning special elections across the country because the Democratic party was "too far left for the American people." He received a similar response the following day when he declared his opposition to the use of a quota system for determining composition of delegations to the 1976 Republican national convention.

State of Union message. President Nixon sent Congress Sept. 10 his seventh State of the Union message in 1973 to "refocus attention" on more than 50 legislative measures he had proposed previously in the year.

In the area of campaign reform, Nixon said "no subject over the last few months has so stirred public comment and reflection as the question of campaign practices." He urged enactment of his proposal to establish a nonpartisan commission on federal election reform.

Mondale asks presidency study. Sen. Walter F. Mondale (D, Minn.) proposed Sept. 16 creation of a national commission to prepare recommendations for reducing the presidency to "life size," insuring that its operation was "open and accountable to the American people and the Congress" and its "interaction" with Congress and the courts was "one of mutual respect."

In a speech released prior to delivery in the Senate, Mondale linked the Watergate case to a 36-year trend toward a presidency "larger than life and larger than the law."

Mondale said the proposed commission should seek a "working concept of the presidency which is strong yet legal, capable of leading but without dictating."

He suggested immediate reform through enactment of legislation to bar political wiretapping, require Senate confirmation of important White House aides and periodic questioning of Cabinet members on the Senate floor, delimit presidential authority over spending and

international conflict and provide Congress with its own law firm to challenge the executive in court.

Mondale cautioned against a Watergate-inspired temptation to "emasculate" the presidency. "While we need reform, we do not need retribution," he said. There was a danger, he said, that the public, unhappy with politics in general, would seize "on the overblown sense of presidential self-importance" and condemn "not only the excesses but also the essence of the presidential office."

He criticized President Nixon for substituting "efficiency" for accountability and for producing a Watergate "crisis of confidence" because "there has never existed the sense of mutual trust and respect between this President and the Congress and between this President and the people."

Mondale said Nixon had "misread the will of the people and misrepresented the actions of the Congress" in urging Congress to get on with other business and leave Watergate to the courts.

Nixon holds news conference. President Nixon held his third news conference in six weeks Oct. 3.

A question was raised about President Nixon's earlier statement that work done at his San Clemente, Calif. residence by the government at taxpayers' expense "diminished the value of the property."

He was asked: "Do you think that the $13,500 electrical heating system that was installed diminished its value? And second, do you think that when the GSA [General Services Administration] hired a local landscape architect to redesign the flower beds on the west side of the residence four times a year, that they were spending the taxpayers' money wisely?"

Nixon replied that he had preferred to install a gas heating system, which would have been cheaper than an electric one, but was overruled by the Secret Service because of fire hazard considerations. He refused to answer the second part of the question, adding that "full statements" already had been made.

A

B

C

D

E

F

Phase One
of Senate Investigation
Ends

Nixon cooperation urged. In separate television interviews July 15, two members of the Senate committee investigating Watergate urged President Nixon to meet voluntarily with the committee to discuss the Watergate charges and to make relevant documents available.

Asserting that Nixon was "in trouble" with the public, Sen. Daniel K. Inouye (D, Hawaii) said he would favor a subpoena of White House papers, especially those that might aid in the examination of former presidential advisers H. R. Haldeman and John D. Ehrlichman. Inouye conceded, however, that it would be "fruitless" to take the issue to court if Nixon resisted a Congressional subpoena.

Sen. Lowell. P. Weicker Jr. (R, Conn.) said he was opposed to a subpoena as a violation of the separation of powers doctrine, but he suggested that Nixon "choose his own forum" to respond to the Watergate allegations—perhaps a private meeting with the whole committee without a requirement for sworn testimony.

Committee chairman Ervin had suggested July 13 that "some representative of the White House and some representative of the committee go through" the presidential documents and separate those pertinent to the panel's investigation.

"I see no great difficulty with a little cooperation," Ervin said.

Javits, Scott urge response—Republican Senators Jacob K. Javits (N.Y.) and Hugh Scott (Pa.) called on Nixon July 16 to cooperate with the Watergate committee. Scott urged the voluntary submission of any documents which might indicate "a commission of a crime."

Copying of papers barred—Deputy White House Press Secretary Gerald L. Warren announced July 11 that former presidential aides involved in the Watergate investigation were not being allowed to photocopy documents or make notes from them in their former offices. Warren said the policy became effective May 23 without public announcement. Warren contended the ruling was based on a "desire to maintain confidentiality of presidential papers."

Another Administration source acknowledged that an exception to the policy had been made for former presidential counsel John W. Dean 3rd before his appearance at the Senate hearings, the Washington Post reported July 12.

Herbert Kalmbach testifies on payoffs. Herbert W. Kalmbach, former personal attorney and fund raiser for the President, began testimony later July 16 on his role in the payments made to the Watergate defendants for legal fees and support of their families. Kalmbach maintained throughout the questioning that he had acted with the approval of John Ehrlichman and under the specific instructions of John Dean. He testified that Ehrlichman stressed the payoffs must be kept secret to prevent "misinterpretation" of White House motives in paying the Watergate defendants.

Kalmbach described his activities on Nixon's behalf since 1969. "First," he said, "it has been the source of great pride and personal satisfaction to me" to handle the Nixon family's personal legal matters, with Ehrlichman and Dean providing instructions and contact on these matters. Under questioning by Sam Dash, Kalmbach claimed he was still working on legal matters for the President, despite White House Press Secretary Ronald L. Ziegler's remark to reporters May 1 that Nixon no longer employed Kalmbach.

(Despite the nature of his work for Nixon, Kalmbach testified that he had met with the President only four or five times since 1969 and had talked on the phone with him only a few times.)

From January 1969 to February 1972, Kalmbach said he served at the request of Maurice Stans, Nixon's chief fund raiser during the 1968 and 1972 elections, as the "trustee" for "certain surplus funds" accruing from the 1968 presidential primary elections. He disbursed these funds "only" at the direction of Haldeman "or others clearly having the authority," Kalmbach said.

In later questioning, Kalmbach identified Ehrlichman, Mitchell, Mitchell's aide Frederick C. LaRue and

Haldeman's aide Gordon Strachan as the others able to authorize disbursements.

Kalmbach said his third major task, undertaken from November 1970 to early 1972, was to solicit campaign contributions for the 1972 election. Kalmbach admitted destroying his records of those transactions after providing the Finance Committee to Re-elect the President with his files. He said he acted to preserve the "confidentiality of the contacts" with contributors, whose donations were received before public disclosure of the donors' identities was absolutely required under federal law.

In his statement, Kalmbach denied having any prior knowledge of the Watergate break-in or of participating in a conspiracy to cover-up the burglary or other acts of campaign sabotage.

Throughout the questioning by Dash and minority counsel Thompson, Kalmbach maintained that by collecting payoff money for the Watergate defendants, he was discharging a "moral obligation" to raise funds for their legal defense and family support. "The fact that I had been directed to undertake these actions by the Number 2 and Number 3 men on the White House staff [Ehrlichman and Dean] made it absolutely incomprehensible to me that my actions in this regard could have been regarded in any way as improper or unethical," he said.

Questioned about his fund raising role for Nixon's 1972 presidential campaign, Kalmbach testified that in February 1972 he closed out all campaign accounts and transferred $915,000—approximately $233,000 in cash and $670,000 in checks—to finance committee treasurer Hugh W. Sloan Jr. At the request of finance committee chairman Stans in February 1972, Kalmbach also advanced $50,000, for which he received no receipt.

He described the transfer of $350,000 in cash from the finance committee to the White House in the "last week of March or very early in April." The request was made by Haldeman's aide Lawrence Higby. Kalmbach testified that he assumed the money was targeted for polling projects planned by the White House.

Kalmbach testified that on June 28, 1972 Dean made an urgent request for a meeting in Washington to discuss raising $50,000–$100,000 "for the legal defense of these [Watergate] defendants and for the support of their families." Kalmbach said he and Dean met June 29, 1972 in Lafayette Park, across from the White House. According to Kalmbach, he urged Dean to establish a public committee for the purpose of raising the funds.

Dean rejected the idea, Kalmbach said, because a "public committee might be misinterpreted." According to Dean, the project required "absolute secrecy" in order not to jeopardize Nixon's re-election chances. Anthony J. Ulasewicz, identified in previous testimony as the White House contact with convicted Watergate conspirator James W. McCord Jr., should distribute the money Kalmbach collected, Dean told him. Dean said further instructions on the distribution of funds would come from LaRue.

Kalmbach testified that his meetings and conversations with Ulasewicz were secretive, utilizing codewords and clandestine meetings in hotel rooms and cars to exchange money. According to Kalmbach, Mrs. E. Howard Hunt Jr., wife of one of the convicted Watergate conspirators, received the money from Ulasewicz. A total of $220,000 was collected for payoff purposes. Stans and LaRue contributed funds they held.

Some of the cash—$75,000—was solicited from Thomas V. Jones of the Northrop Corp. of California. According to Kalmbach's testimony, he told Jones only that "it was for a special assignment that I would not reveal the name of, and that I had been given the assignment by one in authority at the White House."

Kalmbach said his doubts about the project prompted him to request a meeting with Ehrlichman. Kalmbach recalled the meeting July 26, 1972 in Ehrlichman's office:

"I said, John, I want you to tell me, and you know, I can remember it very vividly because I looked at him, and I said, John, I am looking right into your eyes: I said, I know that my family and my reputation mean everything to me, and it is just absolutely necessary, John, that you tell me, first, that John Dean has the authority to direct me in this assignment, that it is a proper assignment and that I am to go forward on it.

"He said, Herb, John Dean does have the authority. It is proper, and you are to go forward.

"Now, he said, in commenting on the secrecy, . . . this . . . could get into the press and be misinterpreted. And then I remember he used the figure of speech, he said, they would have our heads in their laps, which again would indicate to me that it would jeopardize the campaign."

In mid-August 1972, Kalmbach was asked to collect more money for the Watergate defendants but he refused to comply with the request because "this whole degree of concern had come back to me to the level that I knew that I did not want to participate any longer in this assignment." The fund raising request

was repeated at a meeting Jan. 19, 1973 in Mitchell's Washington office, with Mitchell, Dean and LaRue present. Kalmbach said he again rejected the bid.

July 17: *Kalmbach admits "illegal act"*—Kalmbach conceded in testimony July 17 that he, now realized his fund raising efforts for Watergate defendants represented an "improper, illegal act."

In retrospect, Kalmbach told the committee, he felt "used" by Nixon's chief aides: Haldeman, Ehrlichman, Mitchell and Dean. "It is just as if I have been kicked in the stomach," he said.

Kalmbach's role as paymaster for the cover-up attempt was examined in detail. Senators Montoya and Weicker appeared incredulous that Kalmbach would risk his legal career to act as an accomplice in silencing the Watergate defendants.

Kalmbach cited his "implicit trust" in Dean and Ehrlichman as justification for his actions. "It is incomprehensible to me, and was at that time, I just didn't think about it that these men would ask me to do an illegal act," he said.

Sen. Talmadge tried to establish that Kalmbach undertook the assignment because "the President himself might have approved it," but Kalmbach rejected that explanation.

Despite his belief that Dean "was standing, really standing in the shoes of the President" when discussing Nixon's legal affairs with Kalmbach and his law partner, Kalmbach refused to concede that Dean issued the cover-up orders with similar presidential authority.

What was there about the "nature of the White House or the presidency or the aura that surrounds it" that would cause Kalmbach to have such enormous faith and trust in the propriety of the cover-up requests, Sen. Baker inquired.

Kalmbach replied, "It was a composite of all those factors"—reverence for the institution of the presidency, personal friendship for Nixon and long acquaintanceship with Dean. It never occurred to him to talk to Nixon about his doubts, Kalmbach testified, because he knew that Ehrlichman, and Dean "had the absolute trust" of Nixon.

Ehrlichman taped phone call—Much of the session was devoted to the transcript of a recorded phone conversation between Ehrlichman and Kalmbach, taped by Ehrlichman without Kalmbach's knowledge on April 19—one day before Kalmbach's scheduled appearance before the federal grand jury investigating the Watergate scandal.

Kalmbach characterized the taping by Ehrlichman as "self-serving," adding again he felt that "it was just as if I had been kicked in the stomach."

According to the transcript, Ehrlichman told Kalmbach that Dean, who was, "cooperating with the U.S. attorney in the hopes of getting immunity," was "throwing off on Bob [Haldeman] and me [Ehrlichman] heavily."

Sen. Ervin advanced the proposition, and Kalmbach agreed, that Ehrlichman's

taping of this "conversation represented an effort on his part to advance the theory that John Dean should be made a scapegoat and sent out into some wilderness, legal wilderness, bearing the full responsibility for any impropriety or unethical aspects of the disuse of the money."

(On April 19 Dean had told reporters that he was not going to be made the "scapegoat" for the Watergate coverup.)

In the transcript, Kalmbach said he had phoned Ehrlichman to express concern "that there is a massive campaign underway to indict all the lawyers . . . and I was a little shocked and I guess what I need to get from you, John, is assurance that this is not true."

Ehrlichman told him, "I would never knowingly have put you in any kind of spot." Ehrlichman said he knew of no attempt to "target" Kalmbach, but added that through Dean, the prosecutors were "trying to get at me."

During the conversation, Ehrlichman appeared to be laying the groundwork for a cover story that would protect himself, and secondarily, Kalmbach. Dean was "taking the position [with federal investigators] that he was a mere agent," Ehrlichman said. He told Kalmbach that "as far as propriety [of the coverup project] is concerned, I think we both were relying entirely on Dean."

Ehrlichman warned Kalmbach, according to the transcript, "They'll ask you to whom you've spoken about your testimony and I would appreciate it if you would say you've talked to me in California because at that time I was investigating this thing for the President."

Kalmbach agreed with Ervin that the inference in this request was that Kalmbach not reveal to the prosecutors anything about the phone conversation.

The conversation concluded:

E. "They're out to get me and they're out to get Bob.

K. "My God. All right, well, John, it'll be absolutely clear that there was nothing looking towards any cover-up or anything. It was strictly for the humanitarian and I just want . . . when I talked to you I just wanted you to advise me that it was all right on that basis.

E. "On that basis.

K. "To go forward.

E. "That it was necessary.

K. "And that'll be precisely the way it is.

E. "Yeah, Ok. Thanks, Herb. Bye."

Surplus funds & use vs. Wallace—Other testimony by Kalmbach revealed that in 1970 he had delivered a total of $400,000 in cash to persons not known to him under instructions from Lawrence Higby, Haldeman's aide. Kalmbach said that at the time he was unaware of the money's purpose, but acknowledged that he now knew the money was used—unsuccessfully—in an effort to defeat Gov. George C. Wallace (D, Ala.).

The three deliveries were made secretly: twice in New York City hotels and once in a Los Angeles bank lobby. The cash was surplus money from the 1968 presidential campaign.

Kalmbach also testified that he had informed Mitchell that $1.9 million in cash and $570,000 in checks remained in excess funds from the 1968 campaign. Mitchell had denied knowing any surplus money existed. Sen. Inouye noted that the Nixon re-election committee had reported it ended the 1968 campaign in debt. Kalmbach acknowledged the discrepancies and suggested that federal campaign fund laws be amended to prohibit the use of cash.

Kalmbach confirmed previous reports that his orders to provide funds to Donald Segretti, identified by other Administration officials as responsible for the Nixon re-election campaign's "dirty tricks," came from Dwight Chapin, "one of Haldeman's senior deputies." Kalmbach emphasized that Chapin was "standing, clearly standing in the shoes of Haldeman" and issuing directives on Haldeman's behalf.

Kalmbach also revealed that he had loaned Ehrlichman $20,000 out of personal funds during 1972 and at Ehrlichman's request, had kept the transaction secret.

Directly contradicting statements of several board chairmen of major companies, Kalmbach denied soliciting 1972 campaign contributions from corporations. Corporate political gifts were barred by federal law.

Ulasewicz testifies on payoffs. Offering testimony complementing that of previous witness Herbert W. Kalmbach, Anthony W. Ulasewicz, the first witness to retake the stand before the Senate Watergate committee, described July 18 how he clandestinely disbursed $219,000—sometimes unsuccessfully—to Watergate conspirator G. Gordon Liddy; Dorothy Hunt, the late wife of conspirator E. Howard Hunt Jr.; Hunt himself; lawyers for the conspirators; and Frederick C. LaRue, former campaign strategist for Nixon.

Under examination by the committee's assistant majority counsel, Terry Lenzner, Ulasewicz related the details of a June 30, 1972 meeting he had with Kalmbach in a Washington hotel room. Ulasewicz, assured by Kalmbach on the question of legality, agreed to provide funds to the lawyers of the Watergate defendants and "payment to assist their families during some troublesome period." Kalmbach insisted on confidentiality, ordering Ulasewicz to use pay phones for communication and the name Novak as an alias, or Rivers if the need arose.

His first contact, M. Douglas Caddy, the original attorney for the five men caught in the Watergate, failed to keep an afternoon rendezvous in a Washington restaurant. A call by Caddy to the waiting Ulasewicz revealed that the lawyer preferred a meeting at his law office; Ulasewicz, instructed not to negotiate, demurred and said he would call back. A call to Kalmbach resulted in instructions to drop the "Caddy business."

Ulasewicz next called Paul L. O'Brien, attorney for the Committee to Re-elect the President. O'Brien, too, "showed no interest in any script, players or any type of message I would give," Ulasewicz said.

Ulasewicz finally met success when William O. Bittman, attorney for Hunt, agreed to accept an advance legal fee of $25,000.

Another recipient of funds from Ulasewicz was Dorothy Hunt, killed in a plane crash Dec. 8, 1972. On three separate occasions—the last Sept. 19, 1972—Mrs. Hunt picked up a locker key taped to the underside of a phone in Washington's National Airport, allowing her to collect a total of $136,500; in a like manner her husband accepted another $18,000.

Ulasewicz testified that Mrs. Hunt was his main contact to channel funds to the Watergate defendants. He said that each time he talked to her, she increased her demands. In the end, Ulasewicz calculated she wanted $450,000.

In a series of phone conversations in July, 1972, Mrs. Hunt suggested $3,000 per month per person for the main Watergate defendants—her husband, Liddy, and James W. McCord Jr. Moreover, she requested the payments in multiple amounts so as to avoid monthly meetings. She asked a total of $23,000 for conspirator Bernard L. Barker, as well as smaller sums for the other three Watergate defendants: Eugenio R. Martinez $2,000, Frank A. Sturgis $4,000 and Virgilio R. Gonzalez $2,000. For attorneys' fees, Mrs. Hunt requested $105,000, including $25,000 for Bittman. Ulasewicz doubted she knew that Bittman had already been paid.

Ulasewicz testified that he made two other payments. In July 1972 he left $8,000 in a National Airport locker for Liddy. Two months later he gave LaRue an envelope containing $29,900.

Ulasewicz said Mrs. Hunt's demands caused him concern over the role he was playing and eventually led to his resignation. He said he had told Kalmbach, at a California meeting in August 1972, that "something here is not kosher" and then informed Kalmbach of his plans to quit.

LaRue testifies. Frederick C. LaRue, a former Nixon re-election campaign official, succeeded Ulasewicz on the witness stand July 18. While much of his testimony concerned payments he made as part of the Watergate cover-up, LaRue also offered a third version of the March 30, 1972 meeting at which former Attorney General John Mitchell was alleged to have approved a $250,000 intelligence plan against the Democrats.

According to LaRue, Mitchell neither approved the bugging plan, as former deputy campaign director Jeb Stuart Magruder testified June 14; nor did he flatly reject the project, as Mitchell himself claimed July 10. LaRue recollected that Mitchell said of the plan, "Well, this is not something that will have to be decided at this meeting."

The bulk of LaRue's testimony, which extended to July 19, related to $230,000

he distributed after Ulasewicz quit. [See above] LaRue indicated he funneled $210,000 to William O. Bittman, attorney for E. Howard Hunt Jr. LaRue testified he used the code name "Baker" to contact Bittman and then dispatched messengers to the lawyer's home or office with bundles of bills totaling $25,000 in Sept. 1972, $50,000 in Dec. 1972, $60,000 in Jan., and $75,000 in March.

LaRue said he also sent $20,000 to Peter Maroulis, Liddy's attorney.

LaRue said he had obtained the funds from a secret $350,000 kitty of surplus 1968 campaign funds kept in the White House. While acknowledging his role as a conduit for the payoffs, LaRue expressed mystification as to how or who had made arrangements. Pressed by the committee, LaRue said he had been told that participants in the arrangements included Paul L. O'Brien and Kenneth Wills Parkinson, both lawyers for the Nixon re-election committee.

In other testimony, LaRue said that before he made the final payment of $75,000 to Bittman, he became concerned over his own criminal liability. He said he had voiced his apprehension to Mitchell and asked if he should make the payment. Informed by LaRue the money was for legal fees, Mitchell counseled him to make the payment, LaRue said.

LaRue further testified that Mitchell advised Magruder to burn documents relating to the Watergate bugging scheme.

Mardian denies role in cover-up attempt. Robert C. Mardian, a former assistant attorney general and official of the Committee to Re-Elect the President, testified July 19. Mardian disputed earlier witnesses, denying he played an illegal role in trying to conceal the events surrounding the Watergate case, while admitting he had knowledge of many of the facts.

In his opening statement, Mardian said that immediately after the Watergate burglars' arrests June 17, 1972, in the Democratic National Committee's headquarters, he was relieved of his political duties at the re-election committee and was named the committee's attorney on matters related to the Watergate case. He cited this role at several points as his justification—under the canon of attorney-client confidentiality—for not revealing the information he gained as the scandal unfolded. He acknowledged he had hoped not to be implicated in the case.

Questioned by James Hamilton, an assistant committee counsel, Mardian related how, after the arrests, he was asked by Jeb Stuart Magruder, then the re-election committee's deputy director, to help with the "slight problem" of the arrested burglars.

Hamilton asked if Magruder had described events leading to the break-in:

Q. Did Mr. Magruder inform you who had approved the budget for dirty tricks . . . ?

A. Yes.

Q. Whom did he say?

A. He told me that the budget had been approved by Mitchell.

Q. Did Mr. Mitchell later that afternoon confirm that he had approved such a budget?

A. I would like to put it this way: It is my best recollection that I think the subject was discussed and he didn't deny it. And again, it may have come up when Mr. Mitchell wasn't in the room. I want to be fair on that point.

Mardian disputed the testimony of Magruder and Frederick C. LaRue, another campaign aide, that Mardian had been present at a June 19, 1972 meeting when Mitchell suggested that Magruder destroy documents on the Watergate plans. Mardian said "no such discussion took place in my presence."

Hamilton pressed Mardian on the meetings held in the few days after the break-in. Mardian replied, describing a June 21, 1972 interview of conspirator G. Gordon Liddy at LaRue's apartment.

Liddy, who had been portrayed to Mardian as "some kind of nut," entered the apartment, turned on a radio and asked LaRue and Mardian to sit beside it—so that "this conversation can't be recorded," as Mardian quoted Liddy. Liddy then told of the break-in and assured LaRue and Mardian there was no need to worry because the job had been done by "real pros" who would divulge nothing. Mardian said he told Liddy "his best bet was to give himself up," but Liddy rejected the suggestion.

According to Mardian, Liddy told the details of his involvement in other operations by the White House "plumbers" unit—the burglary of the office of Daniel Ellsberg's psychiatrist and the removal of Dita Beard, a lobbyist for International Telephone & Telegraph Corp., to a Denver hospital to keep her away from Congressional investigators.

Mardian said he asked Liddy on whose authority he carried out the burglary of Ellsberg's psychiatrist, and, Mardian said, ". . . I don't know that he used the name of the President, but the words he did use were clearly meant to imply that he was acting on the express authority of the President of the United States, with the assistance of the Central Intelligence Agency."

Mardian testified that former presidential counsel John Dean had been "dead wrong" in telling the Ervin committee that Mardian had access to confidential FBI files on the Watergate investigation and had tried to involve the CIA in the cover-up.

Mardian also denied participating in discussions of Magruder's plans to maintain the cover-up by giving perjured testimony to the Watergate grand jury.

July 20: *Nixon asked for wiretap files—* Under questioning by Sen. Lowell P. Weicker Jr. (R, Conn.), Mardian testified that in 1971 Nixon had personally asked him to transfer from FBI files to John D. Ehrlichman the logs of wiretaps au-

thorized by the White House on National Security Council employes and newsmen.

The logs, found May 11 in a safe in Ehrlichman's office, included one of Ellsberg's conversations. A White House spokesman had said May 15 that Nixon had not known the logs were in Ehrlichman's safe.

Mardian acknowledged that while he was director of the Justice Department's Internal Security Division (from November 1970 to May 1972) there was an "extreme concern" in the Administration over news leaks, but he said his division "never ordered a single wiretap." Mardian rejected Weicker's suggestion that the division had been used "to stifle political dissent."

On another matter, Mardian denied the testimony of convicted Watergate conspirator James W. McCord Jr. that Mardian had furnished McCord with confidential Justice Department files suggesting that information on anti-Republican activist groups might be found in the Democratic Party's Watergate headquarters.

Strachan: Haldeman knew of spy plan.
Gordon C. Strachan, 29, an aide to White House chief of staff H. R. Haldeman, testified under a grant of immunity from the committee July 20. In his opening statement, Strachan declared that much of the information he would disclose "is politically embarassing to me and the Administration," adding that he was told little about the Watergate break-in by the people "at the White House . . . who have confessed to criminal wrongdoing."

Strachan, who served as liaison between the White House and the Committee to Re-elect the President, said he had told Haldeman two months before the Watergate break-in about a "sophisticated political intelligence gathering system" set up by the re-election committee. Strachan said he had destroyed documents that might link the burglars to the White House. Strachan also said he was the courier who transmitted $350,000 in White House "polling" funds to others who used the money to pay off the Watergate defendants.

Strachan testified that neither Haldeman nor John Dean had informed him of "the series of meetings with Mr. Mitchell, Dean, Liddy and Magruder" in which the Watergate operation was discussed. Strachan said that after the March 30, 1972 meeting at Key Biscayne, Magruder had called him and reported on "about 30 major campaign decisions" that included "a sophisticated political intelligence gathering system [that] has been approved with a budget of 300 [$300,000]." Strachan said that soon after the conversation, he wrote a "political matters" memo for Haldeman that included the matter along with a sample of a political intelligence report, entitled "Sedan Chair II," dealing with the Pennsylvania campaign organization of Sen. Hubert Humphrey (D, Minn.).

Strachan described a meeting with Haldeman on June 19 or 20, two or three days after the break-in, during which he showed Haldeman the political matters memo. Strachan said that "after speaking to [Haldeman], I destroyed that memo and Sedan Chair II, as well as several other documents I have told this committee and prosecutors about. I also told Mr. Dean that I had destroyed [the memo] . . . and three confidential source memos which I said could possibly have been wiretap reports."

Strachan's statement placed major responsibility for the Watergate operation on Jeb Magruder. Strachan disputed Magruder's testimony that Strachan had been informed of the three meetings in early 1972 at which the intelligence schemes were discussed. Strachan also said that John Dean, and not he, had been responsible for keeping Haldeman informed of political intelligence matters.

Strachan rejected Magruder's testimony that he "automatically sent all memos, including Watergate documents, to Strachan." Strachan told the committee that, although Magruder was supposed to report to Haldeman through him, he "frequently tried to avoid the reporting system" by giving a "full report" directly to Haldeman or to his aide, Lawrence M. Higby. Strachan said that Magruder might withhold information from the White House "on ineffective or failing projects" in order to "protect himself from later criticism."

Describing his role in turning over $350,000 in White House funds to Fred LaRue after the election, money subsequently paid to the Watergate defendants, Strachan said that he "was not told by anyone, nor did I know what use was being made of this money." He said that he "became more than a little suspicious" when he delivered about $10,000 to LaRue who "donned a pair of gloves" before touching the money, "and then said, 'I never saw you'."

July 23: *Haldeman asked files be destroyed—* Strachan said in testimony July 23 that Haldeman had told him three days after the Watergate break-in to "make sure our files are clean."

In response to a question by majority counsel Samuel Dash, Strachan said "I believe I was following his orders" in destroying the papers. Strachan testified that he had no doubt that the papers showed Haldeman had knowledge of the intelligence plan. Among the papers shredded were the memo Strachan had sent to Haldeman describing the Liddy plan and its budget and a "talking paper" Haldeman had used in an April 1972 meeting with John Mitchell that mentioned the plan.

Strachan said he believed Haldeman was aware of Liddy's intelligence activities before the break-in because Haldeman had told him in April 1972 "to contact Mr. Liddy and tell him to transfer whatever capability he had from Muskie to McGovern with particular interest in discovering what the connection between

McGovern and Sen. [Edward] Kennedy was." Strachan told the committee that Haldeman had held a series of meetings with John Mitchell in 1971–72 to discuss intelligence gathering. He testified that Haldeman had proposed putting a "24-hour tail" on Sen. Kennedy because he was "particularly interested in the area of political intelligence and information" on the Senator.

Dean testimony believed—Strachan told the committee that John Dean "had a remarkable facility . . . to remember facts." In response to a question by Dash asking him if he believed Dean's testimony that Dean had told Haldeman about the Jan. 27 and Feb. 4 meetings, Strachan replied, "I have confidence in John Dean's ability to state the facts as he recalls them."

When Sen. Joseph Montoya (D, N.M.) asked him if he believed Dean was telling the truth when he testified that he told the President about Watergate and the cover-up, Strachan answered, "This is my opinion based on my experience with John Dean, and my opinion would be that John Dean would be telling the truth."

In response to interrogation, Strachan said that Magruder did not report to him about the Feb. 4 meeting, as he had testified. Strachan denied that Magruder had showed him the Gemstone papers—transcripts of the wiretap at the Democratic National Committee headquarters. Strachan also testified that Magruder had unsuccessfully attempted to persuade him to commit perjury before the Watergate grand jury.

Questioned by Sen. Weicker, Strachan testified that a list existed of about 100 Democratic senators and congressmen, primarily from the south, who had supported the President's Vietnam position or were backed by labor unions that had endorsed the President. Strachan testified that Haldeman had ordered campaign funds withheld from their Republican opponents. Commenting, Weicker told Sen. Ervin, "It's not only your party that is aggrieved at this stage of the game but also my Republican party that has been aggrieved by the actions of these individuals."

John Ehrlichman defends actions. One of the two men closest to President Nixon, John D. Ehrlichman, until April 30 Nixon's assistant for domestic affairs, appeared before the committee July 24. The other former senior presidential aide, H. R. Haldeman, was scheduled to follow him to the witness table.

In testimony that was described as confident and aggressive and at times quarrelsome, Ehrlichman defended every aspect of his and the President's actions before, during and after the Watergate break-in and wiretapping. Declaring that his testimony would "refute every charge of illegal conduct on my part, he singled out former White House counsel John Dean as the principal source of information implicating him and the Presi-

dent in the case and he rejected it as false.

He challenged Dean's contention that the Watergate issue was a major preoccupation of the Nixon Administration during the three months following the June 17 break-in. Under questioning, Ehrlichman explained his role in the Labor Day 1971 burglary of the office of Daniel Ellsberg's psychiatrist and in the events surrounding it. Despite the committee's disbelief, Ehrlichman insisted that the President had statutory authority to order the break-in in the name of national security.

Ehrlichman's 30-page opening statement began with a rejection of charges by Dean that the White House was neurotic in its fear of demonstrators. He asserted that events in 1969 and 1970—described as bombings of public buildings, radicals' harassment of political candidates, violent street demonstrations that endangered life and property—had to be taken as "more than a garden variety exercise of the 1st Amendment." The President felt that these events affected his ability to conduct foreign policy and he gave them "balanced attention along with other events and factors."

"In 1969, when he first came into office, the President took this nation into a new international era in which the stakes were extremely high. From close observation I can testify that the President is not paranoid, weird, psychotic on the subject of demonstrators or hypersensitive to criticism. He is an able, tough, international politician, practical, complex, able to integrate many diverse elements and to see the interrelationships of minute and apparently disassociated particles of information and events," Ehrlichman said.

Ehrlichman was forceful in his denial that Watergate was the main interest of the White House in the period June 17–Sept. 15, 1972. "I do not suggest that we were all just too busy to have noticed. We did notice and we kept informed through John Dean and other sources on the assumption that he was giving us complete and accurate information," he stated. "A chain of delegation" of authority was "only as strong as its weakest link," Ehrlichman added with reference to Dean.

Countering Dean's statement that the White House was engaged by the events of the campaign, Ehrlichman said, "in 1972 with the foreign situation as it was, the President decided quite early that he simply could not and would not involve himself in the day-to-day details of the presidential primaries, the convention and the campaign. He made a very deliberate effort to detach himself from the day-to-day strategic and tactical problems."

"In 1972, the President had to delegate most of his political role and it went to people not otherwise burdened with governmental duties. As a result, I personally saw very little of the campaign activity during the spring and early summer of 1972."

Ehrlichman rejected Dean's contention that he and Haldeman blocked access to the President. Dean, like others, had only to submit a memorandum to get the President's attention, Ehrlichman testified.

Ehrlichman said sarcastically that the summer of 1972 was "a very busy time. John Dean, on the other hand, never found things so quiet and he planned the most expensive honeymoon in the history of the White House staff. . . ."

Ehrlichman distinguished his White House role from that of Haldeman. He was not inseparable from Haldeman, as Dean had implied. He was not "anyone's Siamese twin."

Ehrlichman admitted discussing the Watergate affair with Dean, but he said this was only to keep posted on campaign issues. He said he devoted only half of 1% of his time to the campaign and Watergate.

Ehrlichman's interrogation began with questioning by Samuel Dash on the 1971 break-in at the office of Ellsberg's psychiatrist.

After being assured by Ehrlichman that he played no role in the stillborn 1970 interagency intelligence plan, Dash asked if he had been requested to develop a White House capability for intelligence gathering. Ehrlichman said Egil Krogh Jr., a White House aide, had been ordered to form a special unit, and he was designated at the person Krogh should see in connection with the unit.

Q. So there came a time when you were administering an investigative unit?
A. Yes. In a literal sense, that is true.
Q. Literal sense?
A. Yes, Sir.
Q. Not in an actual sense?
A. Well, here I am dueling with a professor.
Q. I am not dueling with you. I am just trying—
A. Professor, if you say actual, it is actual.

Ehrlichman recalled how the special unit became operational in 1971. A copy of the Pentagon Papers had been turned over to the Soviet Embassy in Washington. According to then-Assistant Attorney General Mardian's report to the President, the theft was the work of a conspiracy, some of whose members had ties to domestic Communist activities.

Soon afterward, Krogh came to him, Ehrlichman said, with the complaint that the FBI was not pressing its investigation into the matter. Ehrlichman said a call to Attorney General Mitchell revealed that FBI Director J. Edgar Hoover was blocking the investigation because of friendship with Ellsberg's father-in-law, Louis Marx.

"So it was this set of facts, and the real strong feeling of the President that there was a legitimate and vital national security aspect to this, that it was decided, first on Mr. Krogh's recommendation, with my concurrence, that the two men in this special unit who had had considerable investigative experience, be assigned to follow up on the then leads." (The two men were E. Howard Hunt Jr. and G. Gordon Liddy; the special unit was the group later known as the White House "plumbers.")

Ehrlichman said the break-in at the psychiatrist's office "was totally unanticipated. Unauthorized by me." He said he thought Krogh had authorized the break-in, but this was not based on any personal knowledge.

Dash then read part of an August 11, 1971 memorandum from Krogh and David R. Young Jr., his associate in the unit, to Ehrlichman which referred to a planned meeting with a CIA psychiatrist who was doing a personality profile of Ellsberg: "In this connection," the memo said, "we would recommend that a covert operation be undertaken to examine all the medical files still held by Ellsberg's psychoanalyst covering the two year period in which he was undergoing analysis." At the bottom, Dash pointed out, was Ehrlichman's approval and a short note in his handwriting, "If done under your assurance that it is not traceable."

Under probing by Dash, Ehrlichman argued that "covert" as used in the memo meant a "covered operation" in which the investigators were not to identify themselves as being from the White House. Ehrlichman denied he had agreed to a break-in and added "there are a lot of perfectly legal ways that medical information is leaked."

Noting the trip made to Los Angeles by Liddy and Hunt to study the feasibility of a covert operation to obtain Ellsberg's medical records, Dash then asked Ehrlichman:

Q. Well, those who read it [the memo] undertook to also interpret what you thought you were approving. Did Mr. Young and Mr. Krogh call you while you were in Cape Cod after Mr. Hunt and Mr. Liddy came back, and tell you that they had established that it was feasible that they could get access and that you said, "Okay, go ahead and let them do it. . . ."

A. I don't recall any business calls while I was up there at all.

Q. Would you be surprised if I told you that Mr. Young would so testify?

A. Yes, I would.

Dash asked Ehrlichman if it would have been embarrassing if it had been revealed that the same two men who were connected to the Watergate break-in had been linked to the Los Angeles burglary. Ehrlichman's response was that Liddy and Hunt would never have revealed the Ellsberg burglary.

Ehrlichman strongly disagreed with John Mitchell's view, as cited by Dash, that revelation to the President of the Ellsberg break-in and other "White House horrors"—Mitchell's epithet for Liddy's activities—would have forced Nixon to pursue publicly the matters and that this might have cost him the presidency in 1972. Ehrlichman replied, with reference to the Ellsberg break-in, that the President had been protected by the fact that it involved national security.

". . . At that time, I considered the special unit's activities to be well within the President's inherent constitutional powers, and this particular episode, the break-in in California, likewise to have been within the President's inherent constitutional powers as spelled out in 18 U.S. Code 2511."

"I think if it is clearly understood that the President has the constitutional power to prevent the betrayal of national security secrets, as I understood he does, and that is well understood by the American people, and an episode like that is seen in that context, there shouldn't be any problem."

"In point of fact, on the first occasion when I did discuss this with the President, which was in March of this year, he expressed essentially the view that I have just stated, that this was an important, a vital national security inquiry, and that he considered it to be well within the constitutional, both obligation and function of the presidency."

Ervin on payoffs, President's powers— Sen. Ervin began his questioning by skeptically asking if the Committee to Re-elect the President were such an "eleemosynary institution" that it would give the Watergate defendants $450,000 simply because it felt sorry for them. When Ehrlichman pointed out that black militant Angela Davis and Pentagon Paper trial defendant Ellsberg had had defense funds, Ervin responded that these were public funds, publicly subscribed.

Ervin asked Ehrlichman if the contributors to radical defense funds believed in the causes involved. A "yes" from Ehrlichman brought from Ervin, "Well, certainly, the Committee to Re-elect the President and the White House aides like yourself did not believe in the cause of burglars and wiretappers, did you?" Ehrlichman said no, adding he hadn't "contributed a nickel."

Referring to Ehrlichman's claim that U.S. Code Section 2511 Title 18 was legal justification for the break-in at Ellsberg's psychiatrist's office, Ervin said the statute provided the President with the power to do anything necessary to protect the country against potential attacks or hostile acts of a foreign power, but he denied it sanctioned the break-in. Ervin said he failed to see how Ellsberg's psychiatrist was a threat to the U.S. He asserted that the CIA "had no business" doing a profile on Ellsberg because it was prohibited from engaging in domestic intelligence.

Their exchange on the matter:

Ehrlichman: I think that basically you have to take this in context. We had here an unknown quantity in terms of a conspiracy. We had an overt act in the turning over of these secret documents to the Russian embassy, and moreover we have a technique here in the development of a psychiatric profile which apparently, in the opinion of the experts, is so valuable that the CIA maintains an entire psychiatric section for that purpose.

Now, putting those all together, I submit that certainly there is in 2511

ample constitutional recognition of the President's inherent constitutional powers to form a foundation for what I said to this committee.

Ervin: Well, Mr. Ehrlichman, the Constitution specifies the President's powers to me in the 4th Amendment. It says: "The right of the people to be secure in their persons, houses, papers, and effects, against unreasonable searches and seizures, shall not be violated, and no warrant shall issue, but upon probable abuse, supported by oath or affirmation, and particularly describing the place to be searched and the person or things to be seized."

Nowhere in this does it say the President has the right to suspend the 4th Amendment.

Ehrlichman: No, I think the Supreme Court has said the search or seizure or whatever it is has to be reasonable and they have said that a national security undertaking can be reasonable and can very nicely comply with the 4th Amendment.

But, Mr. Chairman, the Congress in 1968 has said this: "Nothing contained in this chapter or in Section 605 of the Communications Act and so forth, "shall limit the constitutional power of the President to take such measures as he deems necessary to protect the nation against," and then it goes on, "to protect national security information against foreign intelligence activities."

Now, that is precisely what the President was undertaking. He was not undertaking under this statute. He was undertaking it under that constitutional over which you gentlemen and the other members of the Congress recognized in this section.

Ervin: Yes, I have studied that statute. I have committed that statute. And there is not a syllable in there that says the President can suspend the 4th Amendment or authorize burglary. It has no reference to burglary. It has reference only or interception and disclosure of—interception of wire or oral communications.

Under questioning by minority counsel Fred Thompson, Ehrlichman partially contradicted testimony given by Herbert W. Kalmbach. Ehrlichman denied he had told Kalmbach July 26, 1972 that payments to the Watergate defendants were legal and proper. He said he did not recollect telling Kalmbach the payments were being kept secret to avoid embarrassment to the President. Ehrlichman said he had not tried to determine what was being done with the money Kalmbach was raising and he was "morally certain" that Kalmbach had not asked for reassurance.

Asked later about his having taped his July 26 conversation with Kalmbach, Ehrlichman replied that this was no different than having his secretary listen in on another line and take it down in shorthand.

In other testimony, Ehrlichman reiterated his denial that he had sought CIA aid for the E. Howard Hunt Jr. He dis-

A

B

C

D

E

F

G

claimed any part in asking the CIA to formulate an excuse to block FBI investigation of financial links between the Watergate conspirators and the Committee to Re-elect the President.

July 25: *Ervin, Wilson debate President's powers*—Prior to the resumption of questioning of Ehrlichman, Sen. Ervin and the witness's attorney, John J. Wilson, engaged in a colloquy about the President's power to authorize illegal acts, among them burglary, in the name of national security.

Wilson cited a 1972 ruling in which the Supreme Court unanimously held that the government could not conduct electronic surveillance of domestic radicals without first obtaining a court order. He acknowledged that limits had been set regarding domestic surveillance, but he argued that the court had purposely not ruled on government surveillance powers with respect to foreign subversion.

Wilson quoted Justice Lewis F. Powell's opinion: "... this case involves only the domestic aspects of national security. We have not addressed and express no opinion as to the issues which may be involved with respect to the activities of foreign powers or their agents."

Moreover, Wilson pointed out, Powell argued that the Constitution (Article 2, Section 4) gave the President a source of power in his oath of office. We note "that the President ... has the fundamental duty under Article 2 Section 1 of the Constitution 'to preserve, protect and defend the Constitution of the United States.' Implicit in that duty is the power to protect our government against those who would subvert or overthrow it by unlawful means," Powell wrote.

Wilson further contended that Section 2511 Title 18 U.S. Code indicated that there existed "a reservoir of power ... for the purpose of permitting the President ... to protect the nation against foreign intelligence and for the purpose of obtaining foreign intelligence." He added that Ervin had issued no dissent when the Judiciary Committee had reported 2511.

Ervin said he recalled the paragraph and he added: "they put that in there because there was a controversy between some members of the committee having an opinion that the President almost has powers that would make an Eastern potentate turn green with envy."

Ervin did not question the interpretation of the Supreme Court ruling; he told Wilson he differed on the facts. Ervin said he failed to see how the psychiatric records of Daniel Ellsberg were related to foreign subversion.

Ervin cited the 1952 Supreme Court decision that voided President Truman's seizure of the steel industry, a case in which Wilson had successfully represented the industry.

"Now, I think your steel case, which I think is one of the remarkable cases, they held in that case, and I am sure largely on the basis of a very persuasive argument that you made, that the President, even though the U.S. was engaged in war in Korea and needed steel in order that the men fighting that war might have weapons and munitions, and even though industrial disputes were about to close down the source of that steel, namely, the steel plants, they held that the President of the U.S. did not have any inherent power under the Constitution to seize steel mills for the purpose of securing a flow of munitions and weapons to American soldiers locked in battle with a foreign force.

"If the President does not have any inherent power under the Constitution to seize steel mills in order that he might carry on a war and furnish the weapons and munitions that will enable the soldiers to fight and prevent the destruction of themselves at the hands of the enemy, I think that is authority that he has no inherent power to steal a document from a psychiatrist's office in time of peace."

Wilson replied that the case did not apply to the burglary of the psychiatrist's office. Regardless, Wilson said, the decision was superseded by 2511.

Wilson concluded by reading what the Judiciary Committee had said on national security:

"It is obvious that whatever means are necessary should and must be taken to protect the national security interest. Wiretapping and electronic surveillance techniques are proper means for the acquisition of counter-intelligence against the hostile action of foreign powers. Nothing in the proposed legislation seeks to disturb the power of the President to act in this area. Limitations that may be deemed proper in the field of domestic affairs of a nation become artificial when international relations and internal security are at stake."

The interrogation of Ehrlichman resumed with Sen. Herman Talmadge (D, Ga.) asking the witness at what point he thought there were limits on the President's power. When Ehrlichman said he did not know, Talmadge asked,

"Do you remember when we were in law school we studied a famous principle of law that came from England and also is well known in this country, that no matter how humble a man's cottage is that even the King of England cannot enter without his consent?"

Ehrlichman replied, "I am afraid that has been considerably eroded over the years, has it not?"

Asked by Talmadge if the President could authorize a murder, Ehrlichman replied that he did not know.

Talmadge elicited from Ehrlichman that the President had not "in express terms" authorized the break-in at Ellsberg's psychiatrist's office. The President had told Egil Krogh, at the time he chartered the special unit, that he wanted Krogh to take whatever steps were necessary to perform his assignment, Ehrlichman testified.

Ehrlichman asserted that the break-in had occurred more than 60 days after the Pentagon Papers had been published in the press because FBI Director Hoover had declined to fully cooperate in the investigation of Ellsberg. Ehrlichman added that the White House feared the documents acquired by the Soviets were not the same as those printed by the newspapers.

Ehrlichman denies clemency offer—Sen. Edward J. Gurney (R, Fla.) turned the questioning to the allegation that the Watergate defendants had been offered executive clemency to secure their silence about others connected with the case. Gurney asked: had Ehrlichman, as John Dean testified, told Charles Colson Jan. 3 that he had checked with the President and he could assure attorney William O. Bittman that his client, E. Howard Hunt Jr., would receive clemency?

Ehrlichman denied the allegation. He said he had been told by the President in July 1972 that it was a closed subject "and we must never get near it, and that it would be the surest way of having the actions of these [Watergate] burglars imputed to the President." All Colson told Bittman, Ehrlichman claimed, was that he had not forgotten his [Colson's] friendship with Hunt. Ehrlichman said he felt Dean had concocted this story as a cover for his own offer of executive clemency to Watergate burglar James W. McCord Jr.

Under further questioning by Gurney, Ehrlichman challenged Dean's testimony that Ehrlichman ordered him to throw into the Potomac River politically sensitive documents found in Hunt's White House safe. Ehrlichman noted that he had helped arrange the opening of Hunt's safe in the presence of witnesses and it "would have been folly for me at some time later ... to suggest that the briefcase be thrown into the flood tide of the Potomac." Ehrlichman said that if he wished, the documents could easily have been put in a burn bag, sealed, and thrown in the White House furnace.

Ehrlichman similarly took issue with statement made by former Acting FBI Director L. Patrick Gray 3rd. Gray had told government investigators that at a June 28, 1972 meeting with Ehrlichman and Dean, Ehrlichman had told him the Hunt documents should "never see the light of day." Consequently he burned them, Gray said.

Ehrlichman contended that before the meeting Dean had suggested splitting the Hunt documents into two parcels: one for the FBI's Washington field office, the other, containing politically sensitive papers, for Gray. (Ehrlichman and Dean feared news leaks from the FBI field office.) At the June 28, 1972 meeting, Dean handed Gray the parcel, and Ehrlichman warned it was to be kept secret, Ehrlichman testified.

Not only had he not ordered Gray to destroy the documents, Ehrlichman testified, but he was "nonplussed" when informed of their destruction.

In a phone conversation April 15, Gray told Ehrlichman of his intention to deny that Dean had given him the documents, Ehrlichman claimed. Ehrlichman said he called Gray back to make clear that if asked he would have no choice but to say that he had been present when Dean gave Gray the documents.

Sen. Daniel Inouye's (D, Hawaii) interrogation dealt mainly with the propriety of the offer of appointment as FBI director made by Ehrlichman April 5 to the judge presiding at Ellsberg's trial, William M. Byrne Jr. Ehrlichman said he had been willing to delay their discussion, but Byrne had failed to see why the Ellsberg case was an obstacle to it. Ehrlichman said he met Byrne twice and nothing improper was said. The second meeting had come at the request of Byrne, Ehrlichman said. Ehrlichman denied the offer was an effort to compromise Byrne. It was an effort to find the best man for the FBI job, he argued.

Why had Ehrlichman not told Byrne of the burglary of Ellsberg's psychiatrist's office? Inouye asked. Ehrlichman replied: he was enjoined from doing so for reasons of national security, and it was properly the province of the attorney general.

In another exchange with Inouye, Ehrlichman flatly denied that he or H.R. Haldeman had been fired by the President April 30. The President had been "content" to give them a leave of absence until Watergate was resolved, but they had insisted on a clean break, Ehrlichman said.

In other testimony before the committee, Ehrlichman said that contrary to John Mitchell's testimony, he had briefed the former attorney general in 1971 on the activities of the plumbers.

During Ehrlichman's second day of testimony, members of the committee admonished the public in the Senate Caucus Room not to demonstrate their feelings. The senators had been disturbed because the audience was breaking into applause each time Sen. Ervin entered the hearing room. On the other hand, several of Ehrlichman's responses to committee questions elicited derisive laughter and even hisses from the audience.

Inouye's 'liar' comment—When Sen. Inouye finished his questioning of Ehrlichman, he was overhead to say, "What a liar." Inouye apparently thought his microphone was turned off when he made his barely audible remark. Questioned by reporters afterwards, Inouye said, "I guess I must have been speaking of myself."

Weicker asks about Hoover—Sen. Weicker took issue with Ehrlichman's contention that J. Edgar Hoover's lack of cooperation with the White House in the Ellsberg matter was the primary reason for creation of the plumbers unit. Weicker read into the record a letter written by Hoover to Krogh Aug. 3, 1971. The letter told of the FBI's efforts to gather information relating to the Pentagon Papers and its readiness to pursue the inquiry.

Ehrlichman responded that the letter was a "bureaucratic device" to give the appearance of action on the part of the FBI.

July 26: *FBI role discussed*—Resuming his interrogation of Ehrlichman, Weicker asked if he were aware that the FBI had in fact interviewed Louis Marx in June 1971. Ehrlichman replied, 'no,' and requested a copy of the FBI report on the interview. However, the committee was unable to produce the data because Attorneys General Richard Kleindienst and Elliot Richardson had restricted its access to raw FBI files.

Ehrlichman maintained that the intervention of the plumbers in the Ellsberg matter was justified because the FBI investigation was marked by "lassitude," a fact borne out, he said, by the Bureau's waiting 60–90 days to designate the case "class A" priority.

Weicker, in doubt about the motive for the plumber's investigation of Ellsberg, read into the record part of an Aug. 26, 1971 memo from Krogh to Ehrlichman: "It is important to point out that with the recent article on Ellsberg's lawyer, [Leonard B.] Boudin, we have already started on a negative press image for Ellsberg. If the present Hunt/Liddy project number 1 is successful, it will be absolutely essential to have an over-all game plan developed for its use in conjunction with the congressional investigation. In this connection, I believe that the point of [White House aide Patrick J.] Buchanan's memorandum on attacking Ellsberg through the press should be borne in mind; namely, that the situation being attacked is too big to be undermined by planted leaks among the friendly press."

Ehrlichman denied there was any intent to "persecute" Ellsberg. Rather, the White House wanted to air the matter once the facts were known and hoped a Congressional committee would call witnesses and expose how such "treachery" could happen in the government, he said.

Secrecy upheld—In other testimony before the committee, Ehrlichman said the plumbers had undertaken in 1971 a mission so important to the nation's security that it justified Nixon's efforts to kept the plumbers' existence secret. He said he was under White House orders not to disclose the mission, but added he would be willing to discuss the matter privately with the committee if he received White House approval. The committee would have to pledge absolute secrecy, Ehrlichman said.

Sen. Ervin assailed Ehrlichman for statements he felt denigrated J. Edgar Hoover. Ervin asserted that at the time Tom Charles Huston was promoting his partially illegal 1970 interagency intelligence plan, Hoover was encouraging Ervin in his fight against government incursions on civil liberties. Ervin read a letter from the FBI director in 1970 that praised Ervin as "one of the guardians of our liberties and promoters of our freedom. All Americans owe you [Ervin] a debt of gratitude."

Ehrlichman reiterated he had been ordered by the President, through Haldeman, to seek assurances from the CIA that an FBI investigation of Nixon campaign funds found in the possession of the Watergate burglars would not impinge on

CIA operations in Mexico. Ehrlichman insisted Nixon had given Acting FBI Director Gray authority to determine the scope of the Bureau's investigation.

Ervin expressed skepticism that the President had in the summer of 1972 sought a vigorous inquiry into the Watergate scandal. Ehrlichman replied that Dean and Kleindienst told the President that the "most vigorous" FBI investigation since the assassination of John F. Kennedy had shown that the break-in had been perpetrated only by the seven men already implicated.

In later questioning by Sen. Gurney, Ehrlichman stated he had felt in August 1972 that the President could "take the shock" of the disclosure that campaign officials had been involved in the bugging. However, his proposal to "lay out the whole story" was rejected at a meeting that month, attended by John Mitchell, Charles Colson, then-campaign director Clark MacGregor, and former White House official Bryce N. Harlow. Thus, on the basis of information given him, Nixon made his Aug. 29, 1972 statement that no one at the White House was involved in Watergate, Ehrlichman stated.

Under questioning by Sen. Joseph M. Montoya (D, N.M.), Ehrlichman denied that 915 White House requests for tax checks by the Internal Revenue System in 1972 had been for any other purpose than to insure that potential appointees did not have income tax problems. When asked by Montoya if he agreed that the President should produce the documents subpoenaed by the Watergate committee, Ehrlichman declined to answer.

At another point, Weicker drew from the witness the fact that the President abandoned L. Patrick Gray 3rd when his nomination as FBI director ran into trouble in the Senate. Ehrlichman admitted saying that the White House "ought to let him [Gray] hang there, let him twist slowly, slowly in the wind."

July 27: *Ehrlichman testimony in conflict*—In his fourth day of testimony before the Senate Watergate committee, former Presidential Domestic Affairs Adviser John D. Ehrlichman said Nixon did not receive a thorough report on the Watergate affair until April 14.

Ehrlichman's sworn testimony was at variance with the official White House account and with testimony of ousted White House counsel John W. Dean 3rd. Those versions indicated that Dean March 21 gave the President "his theory of what happened" in the Watergate affair. White House special counsel Richard A. Moore had corroborated the White House and Dean in this respect July 12.

Ehrlichman's testimony also conflicted with Dean concerning a Feb. 27 meeting Dean had with the President, in which Nixon ordered Dean to assume full responsibility for matters relating to Watergate.

According to Ehrlichman, who was being interrogated by Sen. Gurney, the President at the Feb. 27 meeting told him and H. R. Haldeman, former White

House chief of staff, that they were to divorce themselves from Watergate. Nixon, Ehrlichman testified, wanted them to "press on" entirely different projects. In their stead Nixon ordered Dean to concentrate on executive privilege, the Senate Watergate committee, the Watergate grand jury and collateral questions.

Asked by Gurney why Nixon Feb. 27 had referred to him and Haldeman as "principals" in the Watergate matter, Ehrlichman replied that Nixon meant principals in question of the availability of presidential assistants to testify before Congress. Nixon feared that if Haldeman and Ehrlichman appeared before Congressional panels, his foreign affairs adviser Henry A. Kissinger would be next. The net result would be a breakdown in the White House staff system, since everyone, such as Cabinet secretaries, would be testifying each day and unable to find time for work, Ehrlichman said.

Asserting that nothing important transpired in the ensuing three weeks, Ehrlichman then gave his own story of the events of March 21. Ehrlichman denied that Dean that afternoon reported to him or Haldeman what he had revealed in his morning meeting with Nixon. Ehrlichman's version held that Dean in the afternoon had focused on the "question of testimonial availability of White House staff people."

According to Ehrlichman, Dean advanced a theory that the President should obtain from the attorney general blanket immunity for the entire White House staff, thus allowing the staff to testify freely. Dean explained that immunity was the kind of "lubricant" needed to clear the air, Ehrlichman said.

Ehrlichman said he told Dean he was wrong on two counts: wrongdoers ought to be subject to penalties and the move "would just be terribly misunderstood by the American people."

At the request of the President, another meeting was called for the next day, with former Attorney General John N. Mitchell also in attendance. Mitchell was invited because his views on executive privilege were at considerable variance with the White House staff, Ehrlichman said.

Like the previous one, Ehrlichman said, this meeting centered on executive privilege. It ended when the President told Dean to go to Camp David, Md. to formulate a complete statement on the matter.

Q. Now, this really puzzled me. Did not the President say at any of these meetings, "Now, listen fellows, here I have heard all about this from John Dean, what gives here, what are we going to do now, what plans do you have, who is going to get this out? We have got to do it." No discussion of that?

A. Senator, I have great difficulty in believing that the President was told what Mr. Dean says he was told because of the President's approach to this, which I saw in these two meetings.

Now, I do not know what Mr. Dean told him. I guess Mr. Haldeman was in one of those meetings or part of it and maybe he is in a position to tell you.

Q. He never told you anything about what transpired in the meeting between the President, Haldeman and Dean.

A. Well, he told me what Mr. Dean has testified to is not true. I am forced to the assumption by the President's conduct afterward that one of two things was taking place. Either he still confidently believed that the White House was without blame, and that Mr. Mitchell was without blame and was acting accordingly, or he was involved in setting a few snares on the trail and was playing it cool, because he did not get into any of the January, February, March planning meeting business or the involvement of January, of John Mitchell of any of those kinds of subjects which presumably Mr. Dean had laid all out for him, if you are to believe Mr. Dean.

Under further questioning by Gurney, Ehrlichman said he was brought into the Watergate matter by the President March 30, when Nixon concluded that Dean was so heavily involved that he could no longer have anything to do with it.

In an April 5 interview with Paul O'Brien, an attorney for the Committee to Re-elect the President, Ehrlichman said he first learned of Watergate conspirator G. Gordon Liddy's plans against the Democrats. Among the information Ehrlichman claimed to have gleaned in the O'Brien interview:

■ Deputy Nixon campaign director Jeb Stuart Magruder named Mitchell as the person who approved plans to bug the Democratic National Committee headquarters.

■ Watergate conspirator E. Howard Hunt Jr. supervised undercover agents planted in the headquarters of Democratic Presidential contenders.

■ A Magruder statement to O'Brien that "the President wants this project [the bugging] to go on" was based on a statement White House aide Gordon C. Strachan allegedly made to Haldeman, his superior.

■ The President's former personal lawyer Herbert W. Kalmbach arranged a $70,000 blackmail payment to Hunt through Hunt's attorney, William O. Bittman.

■ Dwight L. Chapin, Nixon's former appointments secretary, "will take a bath" for his role in campaign sabotage directed against the Democratic presidential contenders, and that the sabotage included a letter accusing Sen. Edmund S. Muskie (D, Me.) of casting a slur on French Canadians living in New Hampshire.

When he had finished his own investigation, Ehrlichman said, he brought what he had learned to the President April 14–15. The President immediately instructed him to contact the attorney general, which Ehrlichman said he did.

In other testimony, Ehrlichman alluded to an April 8 meeting he and Haldeman had with Dean. While Dean said neither

was indictable, each would have an awkward time explaining his connection with money that ended in the hands of the Watergate defendants, Ehrlichman testified.

Ehrlichman also suggested that the Watergate cover-up was intended to mask the role played by Mitchell in the intelligence plan that culminated in the Watergate burglary. He said Haldeman had asked if it were possible "we are taking all this anguish just to protect John Mitchell?" Ehrlichman denied that he and Haldeman tried to set up Mitchell to take the blame for Watergate.

Among the effects given to the Watergate committee by Ehrlichman was a set of scribbled, cryptic notes. They contained a suggestion from former White House counsel Charles W. Colson that Nixon disclose "damaging evidence" so as to blunt the effect of an upcoming grand jury appearance by Hunt. (Ehrlichman did not confirm this to the committee but to a reporter, the New York Times reported July 28.)

Debate with Weicker—Ehrlichman and Sen. Weicker debated the White House's use of Anthony T. Ulasewicz to dig up "political dirt" on opponents.

Ehrlichman: "I think that each candidate who contests the candidacy of an incumbent has the obligation to come forward and contest the fitness of that incumbent for office both in terms of his voting record and in terms of his probity, and in terms of his morals, if you please, and any other facts that is important or germane to the voters of his district or state or the country, for that matter. I think a candidate for office assumes that burden of proof. He assumes the burden of proof of showing the unfitness of the incumbent and I don't think in our political system that is limited to his voting record or his absenteeism. If it were, we would countenance the perpetuation of scoundrels in office who were thieves or who were fraudulent or who were profligate or who were otherwise unfit for office so I think it's perfectly competent for a challenger to meet head-on the issue of the fitness of an incumbent."

Weicker: "Do you mean to tell me and this committee that you consider private investigators going into sexual habits, drinking habits, domestic problems and personal social activities as a proper subject for investigation during the course of a political campaign?"

Ehrlichman: "Senator, I know of my own knowledge of incumbents in office who are not discharging their obligation to their constituents because of their drinking habits, and it distresses me very much, and there is a kind of unwritten law in the media that it is not discussed, and so the constituents at home have no way of knowing that you can go over here in the gallery and watch a member totter onto the floor in a condition which, of at least partial inebriation, which would preclude him from making any sort of a sober judgment on the issues that confront this country."

July 30: *Loyalty is defended*—Ehrlichman ended his testimony July 30 with an assertion of loyalty to the President and to the country. In his closing statement to the committee, Ehrlichman took exception to a statement made to the committee by Gordon Strachan, that young Americans should "stay away" from Washington politics.

"You will encounter a local culture which scoffs at patriotism and family life and morality just as it adulates the opposite, and you will find some people who have fallen for that line. But you will also find in politics and government many great people who know that a pearl of great price is not had for the asking and who feel that this country and its heritage are worth the work, the abuse, the struggle, and the sacrifices. Don't stay away. Come and join them and do it better."

In their final day of interrogation, the senators elicited from the witness little new information.

Ehrlichman revealed that during the period September 1972 to the end of March 1973, Nixon asked one or another of his aides eight times to prepare a definitive statement on Watergate, but none was ever written. Ehrlichman said he was not asked to prepare a statement.

Asked why he had not told Nixon about the burglary of Daniel Ellsberg's psychiatrist's office, Ehrlichman replied, "There was nothing the President could do about it. I just made the judgment it would unnecessarily tax his attention."

In his closing statement, Ehrlichman said: "I do not apologize for my loyalty to the President any more than I apologize for my love of this country. I only hope that my testimony here has somehow served then both."

White House limits aides' testimony. The Washington Post, quoting "reliable government sources," reported July 21 that the White House had ordered presidential aides to claim executive privilege and refuse to answer certain questions at the private, pre-hearing interviews of the Senate Watergate committee. Nixon had said in a July 7 letter to Ervin that the White House staff was under instructions to cooperate in providing information "pertinent to your inquiry."

The Post said Rose Mary Woods, Nixon's personal secretary and executive assistant, was instructed not to heed a committee request to appear for an interview. The Post's source said chief committee counsel Samuel Dash had agreed it would be inappropriate to subpoena Miss Woods, and the interview request was dropped.

Aides were also instructed not to answer questions on events after April 30, when Nixon's top advisers, H. R. Haldeman and John D. Ehrlichman resigned.

Edward C. Schmults, general counsel at the Treasury Department, confirmed to the Post July 20 that he had received oral instructions from special presidential counsel J. Fred Buzhardt Jr. expanding Nixon's earlier order restricting testimony by Secret Service agents. Under Buzhardt's order, the Secret Service was to invoke executive privilege on questions about any person protected by the agency.

Byrne offers his version. William M. Byrne Jr., presiding judge at the trial of Pentagon Papers defendant Daniel Ellsberg, gave his version of two meetings he had with Presidential adviser John D. Ehrlichman April 5 and 7, concerning a White House offer of the post of director of the Federal Bureau of Investigation (FBI).

Byrne told newsmen July 26 he had no foreknowledge of the offer. He only knew the meeting did not concern the Pentagon Papers trial itself.

Byrne said he informed Ehrlichman April 5 he "could not consider such a proposal but would reflect upon the matter." The second meeting occurred, he said, because he felt he owed a representative of the President the courtesy of a face to face meeting, although his answer would be "no."

In testimony before the Senate Watergate committee July 25, Ehrlichman said Byrne had left him with the impression that he had a "very clear interest" in the FBI post.

Haldeman testifies. H. R. Haldeman read an opening statement containing a vigorous defense of the President and a general denial of their guilt in the Watergate affair. In addition to the declaration of innocence, his statement contained a startling admission that on two occasions and at Nixon's request, Haldeman had listened to tapes of two controversial meetings between the President and John Dean. (Haldeman had been present during all of one meeting and part of another. Dean had based his testimony that the President was involved in the Watergate cover-up on recollections of those meetings held Sept. 15, 1972 and March 21, 1973.)

Haldeman's remarks renewed the public confrontation between Nixon and the committee over access to the confidential tapes, which the President had declared to be presidential papers protected from public scrutiny by the constitutional doctrine of separation of powers and the less explicitly defined thesis of executive privilege.

Haldeman's testimony that he had listened to the tapes came toward the end of his two-hour opening statement. He admitted hearing the taped conversations but told the committee that "the President has directed that I not testify as to any facts which I learned solely by listening to the tape of the meetings."

John Wilson, Haldeman's lawyer, submitted a brief letter from White House special counsel J. Fred Buzhardt regarding Haldeman's orders not to testify. Buzhardt asked Wilson to tell the committee that Nixon based his instructions to Haldeman on the separation of powers doctrine.

Following a brief recess to consider the matter, Sen. Ervin overruled the White House claim and ordered Haldeman to testify. He readily complied, providing an "addendum" to his previous testimony.

Before reading the addendum, Haldeman was questioned briefly by the committee members. He revealed that Nixon had asked him to listen to the tapes and provide him with a report on the conversations. Haldeman added that the notes he had taken while listening to the recordings had been returned to the White House with the tapes. The notes were filed with other presidential papers and were unavailable to the Senate committee.

Haldeman said he listened to the March 21, 1973 tape at his White House office in April. The Sept. 15, 1972 tape had been delivered to his office in the Executive Office Building (EOB) in early July, taken home and kept "overnight," he testified. No one had been present when he listened to the tape, according to Haldeman. (He had resigned as White House chief of staff April 30, but had been provided with an EOB office to aid in the preparation of his Watergate defense, Haldeman said.)

His remarks prompted Sen. Ervin to observe: "If a private citizen of the U.S. can get permission to listen to the tapes in private at home, the Senate select committee should be able to hear them." Sen. Inouye added that "in the eyes of the American people," the President had waived his right to claim executive privilege regarding the tapes by allowing Haldeman sole access to the recordings.

A refutation of Dean's charges was at the heart of Haldeman's defense. He denied that he or the President had "knowledge of or involvement in" either the Watergate break-in or the subsequent cover-up.

He declared they were unaware of the cover-up attempt until March 1973, when the President "intensified his personal investigation into the facts of the Watergate."

Haldeman said:

The question is asked: "How could the President not have known?" Very easily. Reverse the question. How could the President have known?

Only if he were directly involved himself or if he were told by someone who was either directly involved or had knowledge. The fact is that the President was not directly involved himself and he was not told by anyone until March, when he intensified his own investigation. Even then, he was given conflicting and unverified reports that made it impossible to determine the precise truth regarding Watergate or the cover-up and, at the outset at least, he was relying primarily on one man, John Dean, who has admitted that he was a major participant in the illegal and improper cover-up, a fact unknown to the President until March 1973.

"There is absolutely no question in my mind," Haldeman said, "that John Dean was in fact conducting an investigation for the White House regarding the Watergate as it might involve the White House."

Dean "apparently did not keep us [Ehrlichman and Haldeman] fully posted and it now appears he did not keep us accurately posted," Haldeman declared.

"As it now appears, we were badly misled by one or more of the principals and even more so by our own man [Dean], for reasons which are still not completely clear."

Haldeman's version of the post-break-in events closely resembled Ehrlichman's. Both insisted that they and the President had been too busy with other matters to investigate the Watergate affair.

"The view of all three of us through the whole period was that the truth must be told, and quickly; although we did not know what the truth was. Every time we pushed for action in this direction we were told by Dean that it could not be done," he testified.

Haldeman denied he had ordered Dean "to cover up anything," although he admitted it was "obvious that some people at the [re-election] committee were involved." Not knowing who to believe, Haldeman said he remained uncertain as to which campaign officials were involved.

He admitted there had been a White House effort during the 1972 election year "to contain the Watergate case in several perfectly legal and proper aspects."

One effort was made "to avoid the Watergate investigation possibly going beyond the facts of the Watergate affair itself and into national security activities totally unrelated to Watergate." Haldeman cited discussions with Central Intelligence Agency officials June 23, 1972 as part of this effort to limit the Watergate probe.

We discussed the White House concern regarding possible disclosure of non-Watergate-related covert CIA operations or other nonrelated national security activities that had been undertaken previously by some of the Watergate participants, and we requested Deputy Director [Vernon A.] Walters to meet with Director Gray of the FBI to express these concerns and to coordinate with the FBI so that the FBI's area of investigation of the Watergate participants not be expanded into unrelated matters which could lead to disclosures of earlier national security or CIA activities.

Other steps were taken to "reduce adverse political and publicity fallout" arising from the many lawsuits and investigations related to the actual Watergate break-in. There was a third concern about "distortion or fabrication of facts in the heat of a political campaign that would unjustly condemn the innocent or prevent discovery of the guilty."

Haldeman insisted that underlying this "containment effort" and "counterattack" strategy was a "concurrent effort" to obtain facts about the Watergate and make that information public.

Payoff money—Haldeman testified he did not recall authorizing Dean to have Herbert Kalmbach raise money for the Watergate defendants. (Like Kalmbach and Ehrlichman, Haldeman insisted that the money was intended for the defendants' legal fees and family support.) All his information about the fund came from Dean and John Mitchell, according to Haldeman. He also claimed to have "no knowledge" of the use made of the cash delivered to the defendants.

Haldeman echoed a theme familiar in past Senate testimony about the payoff money: "The rest of us relied on Dean and

all thought that what was being done was legal and proper." They remained convinced of that, Haldeman said, until March 1973 when Dean said the payoff money could prove to be a "political embarrassment."

Sept. 15, 1972 meeting—Haldeman said Dean never advised Nixon of a Watergate cover-up during that meeting and said he "totally disagreed" with Dean's conclusion that the President was aware of any cover-up.

According to Haldeman's statement:

Turning to the Sept. 15 [1972] meeting, I was in meetings with the President all afternoon on Sept. 15, 1972. At the end of the afternoon, the President had John Dean come in. This was the day that the indictments had been brought down in the Watergate case, and the President knew John Dean had been concentrating for a three-month period on the investigation for the White House. I am sure therefore that the President thought it would be a good time to give Dean a pat on the back.

There was no mood of exuberance or excitement on the President's part at the time the indictments were brought down. He does not take joy from the misfortunes of other people, and I don't think he found it very pleasant that the people had been indicted. Naturally, however, it was good news as far as the White House and the Administration were concerned that when the indictments were brought down, after a thorough investigation, it had been established there was not any involvement by anyone in the White House. This confirmed what Mr. Dean had been telling us, and we had been reporting to the President over the period of the past three months.

As was the case with all meetings in the Oval Office when the President was there, this meeting with Mr. Dean was recorded. At the President's request, I recently reviewed the recording of that meeting (at which I was present throughout) in order to report on its contents to the President. I should interject here that I also reviewed the recording of the March 21st (1973) meeting of the President, Mr. Dean and myself for the same purpose, and I have made reports to the President on both of those meetings. I have not at any time listened to any other recordings of the meetings in the President's office or of the President's phone calls.

The President did not open the meeting of Sept. 15th with the statement that "Bob has kept me posted on your handling of the Watergate" or anything even remotely resembling that. He said, "Hi, this is quite a day, you've got Watergate on the way" or something to that effect. Dean responded that it had been quite a three months and then reported to the President on how the press was handling the indictments and, apparently, a Clark MacGregor press conference.

The discussion then covered the matter of the new bug that had recently been discovered in the Democratic National Committee and the question of whether it had been planted by the D.N.C. [Democratic National Committee] and the matter of Mr. Nixon's campaign being bugged in 1968 and some discussion of whether to try to get out evidence of that. There was some discussion about Judge Charles R. J. Richey hearing the civil case and a comment that he would keep Roemer McPhee abreast of what was happening. I don't recall any comment about the judge trying to accommodate Dean's hopes of slowing down the suit, but there was some discussion about the problem of the civil case depositions interfering with the criminal prosecution—apparently as a result of a conversation between Judge Richey and Assistant U.S. Attorney Earl J. Silbert.

Dean indicated that the indictments meant the end of the investigation by the grand jury and now there would be the GAO audit and some Congressional inquiries, such as the Patman [Banking and Currency] committee. But he assured the President that nothing would come out to surprise us. In other words, there was apparently no information that would be harmful that had not been uncovered already.

The President did at that point commend Dean for his handling of the whole Watergate matter, which was a perfectly natural thing for him to do. Dean reported that he was keeping a close eye on possible campaign law violations by the opposition; said there were some problems of bitterness at the re-election committee between the finance committee and the political group; and said he was trying to keep notes on people who were emerging out of all this that were clearly not our friends.

There was, as Mr. Dean has indicated, quite a lengthy discussion of the Patman hearings and the various factors involved in that. There was some discussion of the reluctance of the IRS to follow up on complaints of possible violations against people who were supporting our opponents because there are so many Democrats in the IRS bureaucracy that they won't take any action.

There was a discussion of cleaning house after the election, moving quickly to replace people at all levels of the government. The meeting closed, as I recall, with a fairly long philosophical discussion.

La Costa meeting—Haldeman said he concurred with Richard Moore's testimony regarding the February meeting in California, but he objected to Dean's statement about the strategy session.

Dean "overlooked one of the principal purposes of the meeting, which was a discussion at great length of how to develop some way to learn the entire Watergate story—including the other activities that were by then bunched together as Watergate—and get it out in its totality and accurately."

Haldeman said the group also considered a Nixon objective—to establish ways in which information could be provided to the Senate committee without encountering the problem of separation of powers or executive privilege.

Dean's investigation—Dean and Nixon held numerous meetings between Feb. 27 and March 21 that were "primarily concerned with executive privilege," according to Haldeman, but Nixon was also "intensifying pressure on Dean to find out a way to get the full story out."

"Dean at this time point was clearly in charge of any matters relating to the Watergate. He was meeting frequently with the President and he still indicated that he was positive there was no White House involvement," Haldeman said.

Haldeman testified he had no notes on his brief participation at a March 13 meeting between Nixon and Dean. He added, "I have no recollection of that meeting at all. I seriously doubt that the conversation John Dean has described actually took place on March 13."

March 21, 1973 meeting—Haldeman insisted that Dean's "erroneous conclusions" about the President's involvement in a cover-up attempt were based partially on a confusion of dates. Several events which Dean testified took place on March 13 actually occured on March 21, according to Haldeman.

Haldeman's version of the March 21 meeting depicted a President thwarted in efforts to obtain information from Dean about the Watergate but continuing to press for the facts. His addendum stated:

I was present for the final 40 minutes of the President's meeting with John Dean on the morning of March 21. While I was not present for the first hour of the meeting, I did listen to the tape of the entire meeting. Following is the substance of that meeting to the best of my recollection.

Dean reported some facts regarding the planning and the break-in of the DNC and said again there were no White House personnel involved. He felt Magruder was fully aware of the operation, but he was not sure about Mitchell. He said that Liddy had given him a full rundown right after Watergate and that no one in the White House was involved. He said that his only concerns regarding the White House were in relation to the Colson phone call to Magruder which might indicate White House pressure and the possibility that Haldeman got some of the fruits of the bugging via Strachan since he had been told the fruits had been supplied to Strachan.

He outlined his role in the January planning meetings and recounted a report he said he made to me regarding the second of those meetings.

Regarding the post-June 17th situation, he indicated concern about two problems, money and clemency. He said that Colson had said something to Hunt about clemency. He did not report any other offers of clemency although he felt the defendants expected it. The President confirmed that he could not offer clemency and Dean agreed.

Regarding money, Dean said he and Haldeman were involved. There was a bad appearance which could be developed into a circumstantial chain of evidence regarding obstruction of justice. He said that Kalmbach had raised money for the defendants; that Haldeman had okayed the return of the $350,000 to the committee, and that Dean had handled the dealings between the parties in doing this. He said that the money was for lawyers' fees.

He also reported on a current Hunt blackmail threat. He said Hunt was demanding $120,000 or else he would tell about the seamy things he had done for Ehrlichman. The President pursued this in considerable detail, obviously trying to smoke out what was really going on. He led Dean on regarding the process and what he would recommend doing. He asked such things as—well, this is the thing you want recommend? We ought to do this? Is that right? And he asked where the money would come from? How it would be delivered? And so on.

He asked how much money would be involved over the years and Dean said probably a million dollars—but the problem is that it is hard to raise. The President said there is no problem in raising a million dollars, we can do that, but it would be wrong. I have the clear impression that he was trying to find out what it was Dean was saying and what Dean was recommending. He was trying to get Dean's view and he was asking him leading questions in order to do that. This is the method the President often used when he was moving toward a determination.

Dean also mentioned his concern about other activities getting out, such as the Ellsberg break-in, something regarding Brookings [Institution], the other Hunt activities for Colson on Chappaquiddick, the Segretti matter, use of Kalmbach funds, etc.

When I entered the meeting, there was another discussion regarding the Hunt threat and the President again explored in considerable depth the various options and tried to draw Dean out on his recommendation.

The meeting then turned to the question of how to deal with the situation and the President mentioned Ehrlichman's recommendation that everybody should go to the grand jury. The President told Dean to explore all of this with Haldeman, Ehrlichman and Mitchell.

There was no discussion while I was in the room, nor do I recall any discussion on the tape on the question of clemency in the context of the President saying that he had discussed this with Ehrlichman and with Colson. The only mention of clemency was Dean's report that Colson discussed clemency with Hunt and the President's statement that he could not offer clemency and Dean's agreement—plus a comment that Dean thought the others expected it.

Dean mentioned several times during this meeting his awareness that he was telling the President things the President had known nothing about.

I have to surmise that there is a genuine confusion in Mr. Dean's mind as to what happened on March 13th vs. what happened on March 21, because some of what he describes in quite vivid detail as happening on March 13 did, in fact, happen on March 21. The point about my laughing at his being more knowledgeable next time, and the question that he says he raised on March 13 regarding the million dollars are so accurately described, up to a point, as to what really happened on March 21 that I believe he is confused between the two dates.

Mr. Dean's recollection that the President had told him on March 13 that Ehrlichman had discussed an offer of clemency to Hunt with him and he had also discussed Hunt's clemency with Colson is at total variance with everything that I have ever heard from the President, Ehrlichman or Colson. I don't recall such a discussion in either the March 13 or the March 21 meeting.

Now, to the question of impression. Mr. Dean drew the erroneous conclusion that the President was fully knowledgeable of a cover-up at the time of the March 13 meeting in the sense (1) of being aware that money had been paid for silence and that (2) the money demands could reach a million dollars and that the President said that was no problem. He drew his con-

clusion from a hypothetical discussion of questions since the President told me later that he had no intention to do anything whatever about money and had no knowledge of the so-called cover-up.

I had no difficulty accepting the President's version, based on years of very close association with President Nixon and on hundreds of hours meetings with him. Having observed the President all those years, in many different situations, it was very clear to me on March 21 that the President was exploring and probing; that he was surprised; that he was trying to find out what in the world was going on; he didn't understand how this all fit together and he was trying to find out. He was pushing hard for that kind of information about Mr. Dean.

The President further was concerned about how this ought to be dealt with and he was interested in getting views from Ehrlichman, Dean, Haldeman and Mitchell because he felt that those views might be enlightening as to what the true situation was. For that reason he asked that a meeting be held with the four of us in the immediate future and such a meeting was scheduled for the next day.

Segretti activities—Haldeman acknowledged "having agreed to the suggestion" that the White House hire Donald Segretti and that Kalmbach arrange to pay his salary and expenses.

He said Segretti's role was to be that of a Republican "Dick Tuck, who has been widely praised by political writers as a political prankster, whose basic stock in trade is embarrassing Republican candidates by activities that have been regarded as clever and acceptable parts of our political tradition."

According to Haldeman, there was nothing "wrong with the Segretti activity as it was conceived." It was his "clear understanding" he said, "that [Segretti] was to engage in no illegal acts." But, on behalf of the entire Nixon campaign, Haldeman apologized to Sens. Edmund Muskie (D, Me.) and Hubert H. Humphrey (D, Minn.) for defamatory letters attributed to Segretti.

In disavowing Segretti's excesses, Haldeman leveled new charges against the Democrats. He claimed that during the 1972 campaign they had engaged in: "violent demonstrations and disruption, heckling or shouting down speakers, burning or bombing campaign headquarters, physical damage or trashing of headquarters and other buildings, harassment of candidates' wives and families by obscenities, disruption of the national convention by splattering dinner guests with eggs and tomatoes, indecent exposure, rock throwing, assaults on delegates, slashing bus tires, smashing windows, setting trash fires under the gas tank of a bus, knocking policemen from their motorcycles. Some of them took place with the clear knowledge and consent of agents of the opposing candidate in the last election; others were acts of people who were clearly unsympathetic to the President but may not have had direct orders from the opposing camp."

Haldeman declared that there had "been no investigation of these activities and very little publicity of them."

In other testimony, Haldeman recounted White House efforts to deal with national security leaks. In mid-1971, he said, Nixon dubbed him "lord high executioner" directing a program to uncover leaks throughout the government and to

report them to the department head involved.

Haldeman testified that he was "unfamiliar" with the "specifics of sources, amounts or disbursements" of surplus funds from the 1968 campaign which were held by Kalmbach, although he admitted authorizing expenditures of 1968 money for "continuing polling," support of an Alabama opponent of Gov. George C. Wallace in 1970 and funding Segretti.

Haldeman said 1972 presidential considerations justified use of the secret money against Wallace in 1970. It was hoped that by defeating his bid for governor, Wallace would be unable to launch a third party candidacy in 1972 and pose a "potential problem of an indecisive election in the House of Representatives," Haldeman said.

Haldeman also testified that although he had authorized the transfer of $350,000 in cash from the White House to the re-election committee, his subsequent involvement in the money matter "was entirely through John Dean."

Haldeman said he had "no recollection" of seeing Gemstone material or other intelligence reports related to the Watergate break-in and had "no recollection" of ordering Gordon Strachan to destroy intelligence files.

Haldeman testified that to the best of his recollection, he had not talked about Watergate to Jeb Stuart Magruder after a June 18, 1972 phone conversation. A February meeting with Magruder was devoted to a discussion about a job, he said.

July 31: *Tape controversy flares*—The controversy over Haldeman's access to tapes of presidential meetings heightened July 31 during his second day of testimony.

Sen. Weicker was the first committee member to express anger at special privileges accorded Haldeman by Nixon, charging that it was "grossly unfair" to other witnesses whose testimony had been prepared without hearing tapes that might corroborate their statements. Weicker asked the chair to rule that Haldeman's testimony on the subject of the March 21, 1973 and Sept. 15, 1972 meetings was inadmissible.

Sen. Ervin allowed Haldeman to proceed but later voiced anger at the White House strategy of making calculated "leaks" of the "counterfeit evidence." Under questioning about the extent of his "collaboration" with White House lawyers regarding preparation of his statement, Haldeman first denied that there had been communication with the White House. Then he acknowledged that his lawyers had discussed his testimony regarding the tapes with attorneys for the President on June 29.

Ervin denounced the White House tactic of raising "feeble" and "powder puff objections" to Haldeman's testimony in an effort to outflank the committee. "I would say that the clear indication is that the White House counsels wanted Mr. Haldeman to reveal his interpretation of the tapes to the public," Ervin declared.

A

B

C

D

E

F

G

"If they had really meant the objection to be sustained," he said, "they would have been right here raising cain about it themselves."

Sens. Baker and Gurney, who expressed less alarm and indignation about Haldeman's admission than did other committee members, nonetheless appeared unsettled by the issue. Baker termed it a "strange situation," and Gurney asked why Haldeman had not listened to tapes of the March 13, 1973 meeting between Nixon and Dean.

Haldeman maintained that "any reasonable person" listening to the tapes would agree with the conclusion he and Nixon had reached absolving the President of any complicity in the Watergate cover-up. Release of the tapes to the committee would confirm his belief and on that basis, he said, he would welcome the committee's examination of the recorded conversations.

Haldeman said Nixon had made several other tapes available to him during the July 9–11 period when he listened to tapes of the Sept. 15, 1972 meeting. He testified, however, that he decided not to listen to them because they were recordings of meetings at which he had not been present.

Could the tapes have been "doctored" while in his possession? Sen. Inouye asked. Haldeman thought not, although he acknowledged that several tapes had remained unguarded in a closet at his home for 48 hours.

While Haldeman was able to provide specific answers to questions about the taped conversations, he was unable to remember whether he or Nixon had initiated the request to hear the recordings.

Haldeman was also "unsure" about a number of other incidents and events in which he had participated, principally, when he first learned of the Watergate break-in. Haldeman replied: "I have to give, I guess, the most incredible answer. I don't know. I simply don't remember how I learned about it or precisely when or from whom."

He claimed to be unaware of specifics of the 1970 interagency intelligence gathering plan drawn up by Tom Charles Huston, despite the fact that Huston reported to Haldeman and Haldeman had conveyed Nixon's approval of the plan to Huston.

Haldeman contended he was unaware that the plan included illegal activities, or that Federal Bureau of Investigation (FBI) Director J. Edgar Hoover and Attorney General John N. Mitchell opposed the plan. He said he was unsure whether he had read the plan's recommendations for expanded domestic intelligence operations—recommendations he had presented to the President.

Haldeman testified he did not know the identities of those who had transmitted secret cash to Gov. George C. Wallace's opponent in a 1970 gubernatorial race. Regarding the $350,000 cash fund held in the White House at his request and transferred to the re-election committee

with his approval, Haldeman admitted that the cash had never been used by his office for "polling purposes" as previously described. The eventual use of the money, identified in earlier testimony as payoff money for the Watergate defendants, remained unknown to him, Haldeman insisted.

Haldeman claimed that his authority over budget matters involving the re-election committee was very general, but he admitted authorizing an allocation of $90,000 for "black" campaign projects conducted by White House counsel Charles Colson's office. When asked what "black" projects referred to, Haldeman said he was "not sure," but added that he doubted the reference was to "black advance" projects described by previous witnesses.

Ervin challenged Haldeman's prior testimony that acts of violence had been committed by President Nixon's opponents during the 1972 campaign. Ervin produced a letter to committee counsel Samuel Dash, dated June 8, from the Justice Department's Internal Security Division stating that its files and those of the FBI revealed "no information" about criminal acts allegedly committed by Democrats during the campaign.

Inouye recalled the testimony of a former chief of the Internal Security Division, Robert C. Mardian, who had said he knew of no acts of political sabotage or espionage by Democrats in the 1972 campaign.

Haldeman responded that there are "lots of things that aren't in their files." "If you had traveled with us," he added, "you would have the impression we were in a state of insurrection" during the presidential race.

When pressed for specific allegations, Haldeman could only recall a "very large demonstration" in California, but he said a list of violent or disruptive incidents had been provided the committee. An investigation of the charges was under way, Dash said.

Haldeman's low-key demeanor as a witness was in sharp contrast to Ehrlichman's aggressive manner before the committee.

Haldeman repeatedly minimized his own importance within the White House, insisting that his role was not one of policy making, but, rather, was related to matters of procedure. Acknowledging that he "ran a tight ship" as White House chief of staff, Haldeman testified that his operations were based on a "zero defect system."

His generally amiable presentation was interrupted only when Sen. Weicker questioned Haldeman's assertion that the President emphasized qualities of "intelligence, integrity and initiative" in his personal staff. In light of the Watergate scandal, Weicker remarked, "everything that was touched was corroded."

Haldeman refuted the charge immediately, adding, "It's a tragedy that anyone might think it might be true."

Aug. 1: *Haldeman confronted with memos*—Committee members challenged White House political practices during a session devoted almost entirely to an examination of several memos involving the former White House chief of staff.

Attention was focused on a 1972 memo to Haldeman from then White House special counsel Charles Colson dealing with the controversial nomination of Richard G. Kleindienst as attorney general. The memo's disclosure severely tested White House claims that Kleindienst and other high Administration officials had exerted no pressure on the Justice Department to drop antitrust charges against the International Telephone and Telegraph Corp. (ITT).

The White House had continued to insist that there had been no quid pro quo arrangement related to the government's settlement of the lawsuits and ITT's offer of financial support for the 1972 GOP convention, then scheduled for San Diego.

Haldeman testified that he was "not familiar" with the Colson memo, which committee counsel Dash said had been obtained from an unidentified White House secretary under the committee's general subpoena powers.

Campaign tactic memos—Sen. Weicker accused Haldeman of having "given the impression" in previous testimony that Sen. George McGovern and the Democratic party had been responsible for violent and disruptive campaign tactics in the 1972 presidential election. Based on several documents he introduced, Weicker charged that illegal acts occurring during the campaign "did not serve" McGovern's interests, but "did on occasion serve" President Nixon's re-election interests.

Weicker documented his assertion with a memo from White House aide Ronald H. Walker to Haldeman, dated Oct. 14, 1971, regarding expected demonstrations in Charlotte, N. C.

The memo predicted that "violent" demonstrators carrying "extremely obscene signs" would be present Oct. 15, 1971 at a Presidential ceremony honoring the Rev. Billy Graham. Haldeman had penciled "good" next to his underlinings of "violent" and "obscene." "Great" was penciled next to a remark that Graham would be a target of the demonstrations.

Haldeman also wrote "good" next to a report that "the Charlotte police department is extremely tough and will probably use force" to prevent disruptions at the event.

At the bottom of the memo, Haldeman indicated approval of the plan "to prevent demonstrators from entering" the site of the ceremony, but he added as a warning—"as long as it is local police and local volunteers doing it [demonstration control], not our people."

Haldeman explained his annotations to the committee. He said the Nixon campaign was convinced that the disruptions were staged and also believed that the media was portraying the incidents as spontaneous.

"The reason for reacting to the indication that they would be violent, obscene and directed toward Billy Graham as good was that if, in fact, they were going to do this in this way it would be seen that they were doing so clearly. Sometimes they weren't that ineffective. They did a better job of disguising their true intents and their true method of operation, and the reaction of 'good' to those indications was very much in that sense," Haldeman said.

Sen. Ervin commented that he had been present at the Charlotte ceremony. It was a "most orderly meeting" with "no disturbance inside the hall," he remarked. Ervin noted, however, that a federal district judge in Charlotte had ruled July 31 that demonstrators who had been barred from the hall had been denied their constitutional rights.

The court held that the Secret Service could not prevent dissenters from attending Presidential functions unless it could be proven that they endangered the President's personal safety. The judge ordered that a damage suit, brought by 14 persons excluded from the ceremony, be sent to trial.

Weicker introduced a second memo written by Haldeman to John Dean Feb. 10, 1973.

Haldeman testified that he "accepted responsibility" for the memo which read:

"We need to get our people to put out the story on the foreign or Communist money that was used in support of demonstrations against the President in 1972. We should tie all 1972 demonstrations to McGovern and, thus, to the Democrats as part of the peace movement."

The "counteroffensive" should lead "directly" to McGovern and Sen. Edward M. Kennedy (D, Mass.), Haldeman wrote. Dean was asked to "order [Federal Bureau of Investigation Acting Director L. Patrick] Gray to go ahead on the FBI investigation against those who tapped Nixon and Agnew in 1968." Another strategy included leaking "the Fort Wayne story now—[to prove] that we ran a clean campaign compared to theirs, libel and slander such as against [Charles G.] Rebozo, et cetera.

"We could let [columnists Rowland] Evans and [Robert] Novak put it out and then be asked about it to make the point that we knew and the President said it was not to be used under any circumstances."

Under questioning, Haldeman admitted he did not know the facts which might establish a link between the Democrats and foreign support for anti-Nixon demonstrations.

On another memo dealing with a routine political proposal, Weicker noted Haldeman had written, "I'll approve whatever will work and I'm concerned with results—not methods." Haldeman said he saw no connection between that "psychology" and what Weicker termed the "excesses" epitomized in the Watergate affair.

Sen. Inouye also questioned the "attitude of people at the White House." He cited a Jan. 20, 1972 memo to Haldeman from his aide Alexander Butterfield relating to Ernest Fitzgerald. (Fitzgerald had been dismissed from his Pentagon job after criticizing cost overruns in Air Force contracts.)

Butterfield wrote:

"Fitzgerald is no doubt a top notch cost expert but he must be given very low marks in loyalty, and after all, loyalty is the name of the game."

Inouye's effort to elicit testimony about a 1962 incident which had occurred during Nixon's gubernatorial race in California was thwarted by Sen. Ervin. He ruled that the incident had occurred too "far back."

(A San Francisco judge had ruled Oct. 30, 1964 that a deliberately misleading postcard poll aimed at Nixon's opponent had been "reviewed, amended and finally approved by Nixon personally." Haldeman, who had worked in the campaign in 1962, also had "approved the plan," the court declared.)

During a recess in the hearings, John Wilson, Haldeman's attorney, referred to Inouye as "that little Jap." (Inouye, a native of Hawaii, was a much decorated World War II veteran who had fought in Europe.) Wilson later refused to apologize for the remark, adding, "I wouldn't mind being called a little American."

In other testimony related to alleged acts of intelligence gathering by the White House:

■ Haldeman admitted requesting a "background report" on Columbia Broadcasting System correspondent Daniel Schorr. "I don't know why, but the check was made," Haldeman said. Contrary to previous White House statements, Haldeman said, Schorr was not being considered for an Administration appointment. He also revealed that similar checks had been made on Frank Sinatra, Helen Hayes and others.

■ Haldeman testified that the political enemies list represented "an exclusion list" to White House social functions. "They did not have a right to be extended the courtesy of the President's hospitality in order to express their opposition," Haldeman said.

■ Haldeman could "not recall" authorizing 24-hour surveillance of Sen. Kennedy, a charge made in earlier Senate testimony. He also professed ignorance about reports Aug. 1 that other White House projects were planned to obtain information about the Chappaquiddick incident.

■ Haldeman conceded "it was quite possible" that tax audits had been made of Administration foes, but he could not recall whether efforts had been made to quash tax audits of Administration friends.

Regarding the tape controversy, Haldeman revealed that he had taken home, but had not listened to, three tapes from the Feb. 27–March 21 period. He also testified that he had discussed the tapes with his successor Alexander M. Haig Jr., Nixon's special Watergate counselor J. Fred Buzhardt and White House aide Stephen B. Bull.

Based on his memory of hearing the March 21 tape, Haldeman confirmed John Dean's testimony that the President had been warned that Watergate represented a "cancer" growing on the presidency.

Warned of Nixon link. The Senate Watergate Committee Aug. 1 made public an internal White House memo written March 30, 1972 by then special counsel Charles Colson warning that Richard G. Kleindienst's confirmation hearings, which were delayed in the Senate Judiciary Committee, could directly link the President and other high Administration officials to a controversial government antitrust ruling involving the International Telephone and Telegraph Corp. (ITT).

In the memo, Colson argued that Kleindienst's nomination as attorney general should be withdrawn in order to prevent disclosure of other White House memos which could "lay this case on the President's doorstep."

It was Colson's concern that this incriminating evidence would provide the Democrats with additional ammunition against the President. Nixon, Colson contended, was the Senate's real target in the confirmation fight.

In addition to the President, the Colson memo also named the following officials as having taken an active interest in the ITT case:

Vice President Spiro T. Agnew; Attorney General John N. Mitchell; White House chief of staff H. R. Haldeman; White House domestic affairs adviser John D. Ehrlichman; Communications Director Herbert Klein; White House aide Peter Peterson; Treasury Secretary John B. Connally Jr.; Solicitor General Erwin Griswold; Assistant Attorney General Richard McLaren; and Deputy Attorney General Richard Kleindienst.

The Colson memo appeared to provide new evidence to support charges that political considerations had influenced prosecution of a major antitrust case, as well as allegations that perjury had been committed during the Senate's investigation of the case.

Kleindienst had testified before the Judiciary Committee that the ITT case had been handled "exclusively" by McLaren, who was chief of the Justice Department's antitrust division. The White House also had made repeated claims that the Justice Department's decision not to pursue antitrust charges was unrelated to ITT's financial backing of the 1972 GOP convention to be held in San Diego.

Colson's memo, addressed to Haldeman, included a summary of those additional documents posing a political risk to the Administration if they were made public during the confirmation hearings:

■ Colson mentioned ITT files "which were not shredded" and had been turned over to the Securities and Exchange Commission (SEC). One of those documents

Text of Colson Memo to Haldeman on Kleindienst Nomination

Memorandum For: H. R. Haldeman March 30, 1972

From: Charles Colson   Subject: I.T.T.

There are four points in the analysis you outlined to [President Nixon's Congressional liaison Clark] MacGregor and me this morning with which MacGregor, Wally Johnson and I disagree:

[1]

Mitchell, Kleindienst or [Robert] Mardian dealing with [Sen. James O.] Eastland and MacGregor presumably dealing with the other members of the committee guarantees a dividend approach. One or the other has to call the shots. Kleindienst has already this morning told MacGregor that he, MacGregor, should not deal with any of the other Republican senators (Scott, Cook, etc.) but rather should deal only through [Sen. Roman] Hruska. In the kind of day-to-day operation this is, that is simply an untenable arrangement.

I know you and the President are concerned that all of us are taken away from other more important matters. You should be, however, equally concerned that Mitchell in the last 30 days has done little with respect to the campaign and that may be a more serious loss than MacGregor's time and mine.

[2]

On the one hand, you have the assessment of Kleindienst, Mardian and Mitchell as to what will happen in the committee and on the floor. On the other hand, you have the legislative assessment of MacGregor, Colson and Johnson which is very different. (Johnson spent from 1968–1970 as minority counsel of this same committee and has been involved in all of the confirmation battles of this Administration either from the committee end or from the Justice Department end. He left the committee to go to Justice in 1970. MacGregor spent 10 years in Congress. I spent 5 years as a senior Senate assistant and 9 years in law practice, involving very considerable contact with the Hill. The Justice team simply has not had the same experience.)

Admittedly it is all opinion at this point, but Johnson, MacGregor and I unanimously do not believe that Kleindienst can be confirmed by June 1. Johnson does not feel he can be confirmed at all and on this point I am at least doubtful. I emphasize that this is an opinion and a judgment call. Lots of things could happen. We could get a big break in the case; the media could turn around and become sympathetic to Kleindienst; the Democrats could decide that they are better having him in the job than beating him. Obviously, there are many unforeseen possibilities, but as of now that is our best assessment. I would think that whatever decision we make now should be based on the most knowledgeable—and I would add the most detached—assessment of our legislative prospects.

Wally Johnson has done a detailed analysis of the various procedural moves that are likely to be made in committee or on the floor. He is not shooting from the hip. He has analyzed it, and a Senate vote, in his judgement, cannot be achieved by June 1; the Democrats will only let it come to a vote if they have votes to reject Kleindienst, which is the least desirable outcome. Neither Johnson, MacGregor or Colson are prepared to predict whether we can hold the votes necessary to confirm him should the nomination in fact get to a vote.

[3]

Assuming MacGregor, Johnson and Colson are correct, then setting June 1 as our deadline date merely puts the hard decision off to a time when it will be considerably more volatile politically than it is today. Kleindienst's withdrawal will then be an admission of defeat but it will come two months closer to the election. In June Kleindienst will be a hot issue for the Democratic convention. Confirmation of Kleindienst's replacement will also be vastly more difficult in June than it would be now. Obviously this again is opinion.

[4]

The most serious risk for us is being ignored in the analysis you gave us this morning—there is the possibility of serious additional exposure by the continuation of this controversy. Kleindienst is not the target, the President is, but Kleindienst is the best available vehicle for the Democrats to get to the President. Make no mistake, the Democrats want to keep this case alive—whatever happens to Kleindienst—but the battle over Kleindienst elevates the visibility of the I.T.T. matter and, indeed, guarantees that the case will stay alive. It may stay alive in any event and, hence, the key question not addressed in your analysis is whether pendency or withdrawal of the Kleindienst nomination serves to increase the Democrats' desire to continue. That is the hardest call to make but for the following reasons it may be the most important point to make.

Neither Kleindienst, Mitchell nor Mardian know of the potential dangers. I have deliberately not told Kleindienst or Mitchell since both may be recalled as witnesses and Mardian does not understand the problem. Only Fred Fielding, myself and Ehrlichman have fully examined all the documents and/or information that could yet come out. A summary of some of these is attached.

[1]

Certain I.T.T. files which were not shredded have been turned over to the S.E.C., there was talk yesterday in the committee of subpoenaing these from I.T.T. These files would undermine Griswold's testimony that he made the decision not to take the appeal to the Supreme Court. Correspondence to Connally and Peterson credits the delay in Justice's filing of the appeal to the Supreme Court in the Grinell case to direct intervention by Peterson and Connally. A memo sent to the Vice President, addressed, "Dear Ted," from Ned Gerrity tends to contradict John Mitchell's testimony because it outlines Mitchell's agreement to talk to McLaren following Mitchell's meeting with [I.T.T. President Harold S.] Geneen in August 1970.

It would carry some weight in that the memo was written contemporaneous with the meeting. Both Mitchell and Geneen have testified discussed policy only, not this case, and that Mitchell talked to no one else. The memo further states that Ehrlichman assured Geneen that the President had "instructed" the Justice Department with respect to the bigness policy. (It is, of course, appropriate for the President to instruct the Justice Department on policy, but in the context of these hearings, that revelation would lay this case on the President's doorstep.) There is another internal [I.T.T. employe John F.] Ryan to

[William] Merriam [I.T.T. representative in Washington] memo, which is not in the hands of the S.E.C.; it follows the 1970 Agnew meeting and suggests that Kleindienst is the key man to pressure McLaren, implying that the vice president would implement this action. We believe that all copies of this have been destroyed.

[2]

There is a Klein to Haldeman memo, date June 30, 1971, which of course precedes the date of the I.T.T. settlement, setting forth the $400,000 arrangement with I.T.T. Copies were addressed to Magruder, Mitchell and [White House aide William] Timmons. This memo put the A.G. [attorney general] on constructive notice at least of the I.T.T. commitment at that time and before the settlement, facts which he has denied under oath. We don't know whether we have recovered all the copies. If known, this would be considerably more damaging than [California Lt. Gov. Ed] Reinecke's statement. Magruder believes it is possible, the A.G. transmitted his copy to Magruder. Magruder doesn't have the copy he received, he only has a Xerox of the copy. In short, despite a search this memo could be lying around anything at 1701.

[3]

Q. The Justice Department has thus far resisted a request for their files, although their files were opened to Robert Hammond, one of Turner's deputies and a holdover who is now a practicing Democratic lawyer in Washington. Hammond had access to several memos that could be embarrassing. Whether he kept them or not is unknown, but it is probable that he recalls them. One is a memo of April 1969, from Kleindienst and McLaren to Ehrlichman responding to an Ehrlichman request with respect to the rationale for bringing the case against I.T.T. in the first place. There is a subsequent April 1970, memo from [White House aide Tod] Hullin to McLaren stating that Ehrlichman had discussed his meeting with Geneen with the A.G., and suggesting to McLaren that Mitchell could give McLaren "more specified guidance."

There is another memo of September 1970, from Ehrlichman to the A.G. referring to an "understanding" with Geneen and complaining of McLaren's actions. There is a May 5, 1971, memo from Ehrlichman to the A.G. alluding to discussions between the President and the A.G. as to the "agreed upon ends" in the resolution of the I.T.T. case and asking the A.G. whether Ehrlichman would work directly with McLaren or through Mitchell. There is also a memo to the President in the same time period. We know we have control of all the copies of this, but we don't have control of the original Ehrlichman memo to the A.G. This memo would once again contradict Mitchell's testimony and more importantly directly involve the President. We believe we have absolute security on this file within Justice, provided no copies were made within Justice and provided there are no leaks. We have no idea of the distribution that took place within Justice.

[4]

Merriam's testimony will of necessity involve direct contact with Jack Gleason. I can't believe that after Merriam's testimony, Gleason will not be called as a witness.

referred to Nixon's "instructions" to the Justice Department. Another internal ITT memo, not in possession of the SEC and believed by Colson to have been destroyed, linked Agnew and Kleindienst to the pressure on McClaren.

■ An unknown number of copies existed of a June 30, 1971 memo describing ITT's $400,000 offer to defray costs of the Republican convention. The copies were unaccounted for and could be in the files of the Nixon re-election committee, Colson said.

■ Several "embarrasing" memos were in Justice Department files and may have been leaked, Colson reported.

■ Another memo, which would contradict Mitchell's testimony and directly involve the President," Colson said, was unaccounted for.

Reaction—The White House had no comment on the allegations in Colson's memo.

Contacted by reporters Aug. 1, Colson verified the memo and said Mitchell would have committed perjury at the Senate hearings "if he had read his mail." But in a subsequent interview, Colson contended he had written the memo as a "good staff guy" in the "devil's advocate role" of presenting facts and problems of appearance "in their worst context."

The memo did not substantiate charges of a "quid pro quo" arrangement with ITT, Colson contended.

ITT spokesmen reaffirmed earlier statements that there had been "no connection" between the contribution pledge and the settlement of antitrust lawsuits. The spokesmen insisted that the promised

donation amounted to an initial $100,000 and another $100,000 if matched by local contributors. They claimed that the pledge was not made until July 21, 1971.

CIA heads Helms, Cushman testify. The Senate Watergate committee heard testimony from former Central Intelligence Agency (CIA) Director Richard Helms Aug. 2 in an effort to shed light on the role of the CIA in the Watergate break-in. The question that most concerned the committee was: had the White House attempted to use the CIA to block a Federal Bureau of Investigation (FBI) probe of the Mexican aspects of the Watergate burglary?

Testimony by Helms and the two succeeding witnesses—former Deputy CIA Director Robert E. Cushman and present

Deputy CIA Director Vernon A. Walters—had previously been given privately before other Congressional committees investigating the CIA.

Former White House aides H. R. Haldeman and John D. Ehrlichman had contended in their own testimony before the Watergate committee that the White House had wanted the FBI to limit its investigation of the use of a Mexico City bank to "launder" money used by the Watergate burglars. Both had maintained they were fearful that the FBI might impinge on CIA operations in Mexico, a point that was confirmed, they said, in a June 23, 1972 meeting when Helms was unable to assure them that this would not happe.

Helms gave the committee his version of the June 23 meeting attended by Helms, his deputy Walters, Haldeman and Ehrlichman.

According to Helms, Haldeman, after making an "incoherent reference to an investigation in Mexico, or an FBI investigation running into the Bay of Pigs," turned to Walters and asked him to talk to Acting FBI Director L. Patrick Gray 3rd and indicate that the FBI probe might run into CIA operations in Mexico. Haldeman wanted the FBI to taper off its Mexican investigation.

Helms said Haldeman's references to Mexico were unclear but he acceded because the President often possessed information no one else had.

After the meeting, Helms said he advised Walters not to follow Haldeman's order but to confine himself to reminding Gray of a long-standing agreement between the FBI and the CIA that if either agency ran into operations of the other it would notify that agency immediately.

Helms said he learned later that funds used by the Watergate burglars had been channeled through a Mexico City bank.

Helms admitted that Watergate burglar Eugenio Martinez had been on a $100 a month retainer from the CIA. The CIA severed its ties with Martinez immediately after the break-in, Helms said.

This admission, plus the fact that at least four other Watergate conspirators had CIA ties, prompted Sen. Howard H. Baker (R, Tenn.) and Minority Counsel Fred D. Thompson to suggest that this information alone was sufficient to cause the White House to show concern about CIA involvement in Watergate.

Baker pressed Helms: why didn't Helms launch an investigation to see if the equipment the CIA had supplied Watergate conspirator E. Howard Hunt in 1971 had been used in the Watergate bugging? Helms replied that once the burglars were arrested, it was the FBI's job.

Helms also admitted that he had authorized a CIA personality profile on Pentagon Papers defendant Daniel Ellsberg after White House aide David R. Young Jr. "pled" with him that the assessment was necessary to stop leaks of classified government information.

Helms testified about meetings that Walters held June 26–28, 1972 with White House counsel John W. Dean 3rd. Helms said Dean put out "feelers" in the hope that he could get the CIA to offer support for the Watergate burglars. Helms stated that he told Walters, "to be absolutely certain that he permitted nothing to happen using the agency's name, facilities or anything else in connection with this business."

Cushman affirms Ehrlichman request— Cushman followed Helms on the stand. Cushman, current Marine Corps commandant, had given Hunt technical assistance that was utilized in the 1971 burglary of Ellsberg's psychiatrist's office.

The committee's attention focused on whether Ehrlichman had asked Cushman to assist Hunt. In testimony before the Watergate committee and other Congressional panels, Ehrlichman consistently maintained that he could not recollect calling Cushman in July 1971 on the matter. The issue had been clouded when Cushman had first asserted that Ehrlichman had asked for assistance. Cushman then had said he could not remember who had asked for aid for Hunt. Cushman May 31 recanted and announced that after an intensive search, CIA documents had been found establishing that Ehrlichman had made the call to request CIA aid. Official minutes of a July 8, 1971 CIA staff meeting confirmed that Ehrlichman had made a request for CIA assistance the day before.

Cushman also produced for the Senate committee the transcript of the conversation he had with Hunt in his CIA office July 22, 1971. The conversation, tape recorded by Cushman, confirmed that Ehrlichman had made the call to Cushman.

Throughout their testimony, Cushman and Helms insisted they had not known that Hunt intended to use the CIA equipment to burglarize Ellsberg's psychiatrist's office. Both witnesses contended they had not learned of the break-in until it was made public during the Ellsberg trial April 27.

Walters testifies. Succeeding Cushman at the witness table Aug. 3 was Deputy CIA Director Vernon A. Walters.

Offering a version of the June 23, 1972 meeting similar to that of Helms, Walters emphasized that Haldeman had directed him to see Gray even after Helms had repeatedly assured Haldeman that no CIA operations in Mexico would be compromised by an FBI investigation.

Walters' testimony differed with his former superior in one respect. At no time, Walters said, did Helms say that Haldeman's message was not to be delivered to Gray.

The remainder of Walters' testimony was a reiteration of his statements before other Congressional subcommittees.

Gray testifies. Before the committee recessed for the weekend Aug. 3, former Acting FBI Director L. Patrick Gray 3rd read an opening statement into the record. The statement was in two sections: the first dealt with the question of CIA involvement in some aspects of the Watergate burglary, the second with Gray's handling of E. Howard Hunt's White House files which he later destroyed.

Gray told the committee of a meeting with White House counsel John Dean June 22, 1972. Dean told him that he [Dean] was to be the liaison between the White House and the FBI in the Watergate matter and, as the President's counsel, he would sit in on FBI interviews of White House staff members. During the meeting, Gray said, he indicated to Dean that the FBI had evidence linking the Watergate burglars to the Committee to Re-elect the President.

In a second meeting that day, Gray said he discussed with Dean some of the bureau's early theories about Watergate, one of which was that the burglary might somehow have been part of a CIA operation.

During the meeting, Gray said he probably informed Dean of a conversation he had with Helms, also that day, in which Helms had stated that the CIA was not involved in Watergate. When Dean raised the possibility that the FBI would uncover a CIA operation in Mexico if it pushed its investigation, Gray said he responded "that the FBI was going to pursue all leads aggressively unless we were told by the CIA that there was a CIA interest or involvement."

Gray next spoke of a meeting he had with Deputy CIA Director Walters June 23, 1972, in which Walters "informed me that we were likely to uncover some CIA assets or resources if we continued our investigation into the Mexican money chain." Gray's statement conflicted with Walters' testimony about the meeting. Gray insisted that Walters did not say that he had just come from the White House. Gray contended, "I understood him to be stating a CIA position, not a White House message." Walters had asserted in his testimony that he had told Gray he was on a White House-ordered mission.

After his meeting with Walters, Gray received a call from Dean who asked the FBI to hold up its investigation of Manuel Ogarrio, who was a go-between in the Mexican money transactions. Four days later Dean called to ask the FBI not to interview Kenneth Dahlberg, another middle man in the Mexican money chain, because of alleged CIA interest in him. A call to Helms the next day revealed that the CIA had no interest in Ogarrio, Gray said.

Gray testified that he was ordered by John Ehrlichman to cancel a meeting he had scheduled with Helms and Walters for June 28, 1972. Gray had returned an earlier phone call from Ehrlichman. Ehrlichman's "first words, issued abruptly, were, 'cancel your meeting with Helms and Walters today; it isn't necessary.' I asked him for his reasons and he simply said that such a meeting is not necessary. I then asked him point blank who was going to make the decisions as to who was going to be interviewed. He responded, 'You do.'" Gray added that he canceled his meeting with Helms and Walters.

Gray also testified about another meeting with Walters July 6, 1972, in which Walters delivered a letter to him saying that the CIA had no interest in either Dahlberg or Ogarrio.

During the meeting, Gray said, he and Walters concluded that the President should be informed of efforts to confuse the FBI investigation into the Mexican aspects of Watergate. However, they were unable to decide who would be the person to talk to the President.

Later in the day, Gray said, he received a phone call from Nixon, who congratulated him on the way FBI agents had handled an attempted airplane hijacking.

Gray thanked Nixon and said:

Mr. President, there is something I want to speak to you about. Dick Walters and I feel that people on your staff are trying to mortally wound you by using the CIA and FBI and by confusing the question of CIA interest in, or not in, people the FBI wishes to interview. I have just talked to [campaign director] Clark MacGregor and asked him to speak to you about this.

There was a slight pause and the President said, "Pat, you just continue to conduct your aggressive and thorough investigation."

Following this conversation I experienced no further concerns of this kind. I believed that if there was anything to the concerns I expressed to the President or to Mr. MacGregor that I would hear further in the matter. I did not. Frankly, I came to the conclusion that Gen. Walters and I had been alarmists, a belief I held for many months. . . .

Gray receives Hunt files—At a White House meeting with Ehrlichman and Dean June 28, 1972, Gray testified that Dean gave him two legal size file folders, which Dean said contained papers of a sensitive political nature that Hunt had been working on. Dean warned that the papers had national security implications, and while they were not related to Watergate itself, they could not be allowed to confuse the Watergate issue, Gray said.

I asked whether these files should become a part of our FBI Watergate file. Mr. Dean said these should not become a part of our FBI Watergate file but that he wanted to be able to say if called upon later, that he had turned all of Howard Hunt's files over to the FBI.

I distinctly recall Mr. Dean saying that these files were "political dynamite," and clearly should not see the light of day.

It is true that neither Mr. Ehrlichman nor Mr. Dean expressly instructed me to destroy the files. But there was, and is, no doubt in my mind that destruction was intended. Neither Mr. Dean nor Mr. Ehrlichman said or implied that I was being given the documents personally merely to safeguard against leaks . . . The clear implication of the substance and tone of their remarks was that these two files were to be destroyed and I interpreted this to be an order from the counsel to the President of the United States issued in the presence of one of the two top assistants to the President of the United States.

Gray testified that he held the files until shortly after Christmas 1972, when he burned them at his home in Connecticut with trash that had been accumulated during the holiday. Before destroying the files, Gray opened one which contained what appeared to him to be a top-secret State Department cable.

I read the first cable. I do not recall the exact language but the text of the cable implicated officials of the Kennedy Administration in the assassination of President [Ngo Dinh] Diem of South Vietnam. I had no reason then to doubt the authenticity of the "cable" and was shaken at what I read. I thumbed through the other "cables" in this file. They appeared to be duplicates of the first "cable." I merely thumbed through the second of the two files and noted that it contained onionskin copies of correspondence. I did not absorb the subject matter of the correspondence and do not today, of my own knowledge, know what it was.

Gray added parenthetically that Dean called him at his Connecticut home in late October or early November, 1972 to inquire about the files. Gray said he told Dean that he still had the files but had not read them.

Gray denied that he lied about his possession of the files to the Senate Judiciary Committee during his abortive confirmation hearings for the post of FBI director. Gray did admit that he had not volunteered information with regard to the files.

Gray contested Ehrlichman's version of two phone calls that took place between them April 15. Gray said he did not remember ever telling Ehrlichman that he would deny having received the Hunt files from Dean.

At the time I accepted the two files from Dean and Ehrlichman, at the time I destroyed them, and on the several occasions, prior to my denial to [Watergate prosecution supervisor] Henry Petersen on April 16, in which I resisted disclosure of the fact that I had received and destroyed the documents, I believed that I was acting faithfully, loyally, properly and legally pursuant to instructions given me by top assistants to the President of the United States.

I have come to believe, however, what I should have realized then, that my acceptance of the documents in the first place, and my keeping them out of the normal FBI files, was a grievous misjudgment. My destroying them and resistance of disclosure only compounded the error.

That the documents were not in fact Watergate evidence, while legally significant, does not lessen my present belief that I permitted myself to be used to perform a mere political chore. I shall carry the burden of that act with me always.

Aug. 6: *Committee examines Gray*— Under questioning by Sen. Herman Talmadge (D, Ga.), Gray agreed that the warning he gave President Nixon during their July 6, 1972 phone conversation should have been sufficient to make Nixon aware of possible obstruction of justice by top Presidential aides.

Q. Let me ask you something that I think is very important. The only evidence that this committee has had to date implicating the President of the United States is that of John Dean and you and General Walters. Did you think that your conversation with the President on July 6, 1972, was sufficient to adequately put him on notice that the White House staff was engaged in obstructing justice?

A. I don't know that I thought in terms of obstruction of justice but I certainly think there was. It was adequate to put him on the notice that the members of the White House staff were using the FBI and the CIA.

Q. Do you think an adequate, do you think a reasonable and prudent man on the basis of the warning that you gave him at that time, would have been alerted to the fact that his staff was engaged in something improper, unlawful, and illegal?

A. I do because I frankly expected the President to ask me some questions. . . .

Part of the questioning of Gray by Sen. Lowell P. Weicker Jr. (R, Conn.) dealt with President Nixon's statement April 30 that he (Nixon), as of March 21, "ordered all those conducting investigations [with regard to Watergate] to get all the facts and report them directly to me. . . ." Weicker wanted to know if Nixon had

contacted Gray and issued such instructions between March 21 and April 27, the date Gray resigned his FBI post.

Gray replied that he had received a call from Nixon March 23, the day after he told the Senate Judiciary Committee that he suspected that John Dean had lied to FBI agents. Gray related that the President "called me on March 23 and it was in the nature of a buck-up call to say, and I cannot remember his precise words, but to say I know the beating that you are taking up there and it is very unfair and there will be another day to get back at our enemies and there will always be a place for you in the Nixon Administration, and I thanked the President and then I remembered distinctly him saying, 'you will recall, Pat, that I told you to conduct a thorough and aggressive investigation,' and I remembered that so distinctly because I had the eerie feeling that this was being said to me but why, and I related it immediately to the July 6 telephone conversation I had had with the President in the previous year . . ."

In other testimony, Gray admitted that he had acceded to a request by Dean around July 2, 1972 that he give Dean FBI files on the Watergate investigation. Asked why he had failed to clear this decision with Attorney General Richard Kleindienst, Gray responded that the President was ultimately his superior and when the counsel for the President levied the request, he saw no reason not to comply. Gray added that Dean on at least two occasions claimed to be reporting directly to the President.

Gray also explained his failure to immediately destroy the Howard Hunt files. He hadn't known that the two waste baskets beneath his desk in his FBI office were "burn baskets," whose contents were always incinerated. As for not looking at the contents of the files until he burned them (six months after Dean gave them to him), Gray said, "I didn't have the curiosity of a cat or of a female."

When Sen. Joseph Montoya (D, N.M.) asked Gray why the "tentacles of Watergate touch so many people so adversely," Gray answered in Spanish: "Yo tengo mucho dolor en mi corazon ahora." Montoya supplied the translation: "I have a lot of hurt in my heart at this time."

At another point Gray, a submarine commander in World War II, said, ". . . in the service of my country I withstood hours and hours of depth charging, shelling, bombing, but I never expected to run into a Watergate in the service of a President of the U.S. and I ran into a buzzsaw, obviously."

Richard Kleindienst testifies. Former Attorney General Richard G. Kleindienst appeared before the committee Aug. 7. He testified that while he ordered a thorough investigation of Watergate immediately on learning of the break-in June 17, 1972, he did not have "credible evidence" implicating high Administration officials until April 15.

Early in the morning of April 15, he heard Watergate prosecutors Seymour

Glanzer, Donald Campbell, and Earl J. Silbert summarize in detail testimony they had taken from John Dean and Jeb Stuart Magruder. Among those implicated in the cover-up were two of Kleindienst's closest friends, former Attorney General John Mitchell and Robert C. Mardian, an official of the Committee to Re-elect the President. "I think that one of the things I did that night was—I wept," he said.

Hours later, Kleindienst said, he and Henry Petersen met with Nixon and laid before him what they had learned from the Watergate prosecutors. Kleindienst said Nixon was "dumbfounded" at the news. In the discussion that followed, Kleindienst agreed that he must remove himself from the Watergate investigation because of his links to those who were implicated. But, he added, it had been "unfortunate" that the announcement of his resignation April 30 had come at the same time as Dean's, Haldeman's and Ehrlichman's resignations.

Kleindienst recounted for the Senate committee that on the morning of June 17, 1972—three hours after Kleindienst had learned of the Watergate break-in—he was visited at the Burning Tree golf club outside Washington by Watergate conspirator G. Gordon Liddy and Powell Moore, a campaign aide to John Mitchell. Kleindienst said Liddy had come at the suggestion of Mitchell to talk about those arrested in the break-in. Kleindienst said he responded by immediately calling Henry E. Petersen, assistant attorney general in charge of the Justice Department's Criminal Division. While Liddy and Moore listened, Kleindienst instructed Petersen not to treat the Watergate defendants any differently from anyone else. Kleindienst said he also asked the two men to leave.

Several days later, Kleindienst suggested to John Dean that he convey to Nixon that the FBI would be compelled to conduct an intensive investigation. He urged Nixon to issue a statement on Watergate "setting forth his attitude in respect to this fantastic event," Kleindienst testified. The witness added that he had denied Dean access to raw FBI data on Watergate and had not been aware that Gray had opened his files to Dean.

Kleindienst told of a call he received from John Ehrlichman Aug. 8 or 9, 1972. Ehrlichman was agitated because Petersen had refused to follow his instructions, which were not to "harass" Maurice Stans, chairman of the Finance Committee to Re-elect the President. Kleindienst said he told Ehrlichman he was lucky that Petersen was someone who "does not blow off the handle." Kleindienst said he told Ehrlichman that Petersen could resign, call a press conference, repeat what Ehrlichman had said, and Ehrlichman would then be open to a charge of obstruction of justice. Kleindienst took responsibility for letting Stans give grand jury testimony in private, thus allowing him to avoid the newsmen at the federal courthouse.

Ehrlichman still was not placated, Kleindienst stated, and backed down only after Kleindienst himself threatened to resign if Ehrlichman did not stop interfering, Kleindienst testified.

Kleindienst was asked about a luncheon with Ehrlichman in the interval between the conviction and sentencing of the Watergate burglars (Jan. 30–March 23). Kleindienst said that during the meeting "the question came up as to the procedures of sentencing, what happens, and Mr. Ehrlichman did not have much of a knowledge of the criminal justice system and I think they were talking about what happens when somebody is convicted of a crime, how the sentence is meted out, what is the probation report, what happens when you go to jail, when are you eligible for a pardon, when do the circumstances arise for executive pardon, and it was a technical procedural discussion that I had. No individual name was mentioned at that time."

In his testimony, Kleindienst praised Petersen and the Watergate prosecutors. He said the case had been broken only after the prosecutors elicited important testimony from Dean and Magruder.

Panel recesses after hearing Petersen. Henry E. Petersen, assistant attorney general in charge of the Watergate prosecution, offered direct and outspoken testimony in his appearance before the committee Aug. 7. Petersen detailed how the U.S. prosecutors had proceeded in the Watergate investigations.

Petersen took credit for informing the President April 18 that the Watergate prosecution team had learned of the 1971 burglary of Daniel Ellsberg's psychiatrist's office. "The President said when I told him, 'I know about that. This is a national security matter. You stay out of that. Your mandate is to investigate Watergate.' Now he didn't say he knew about the burglary. He said he knew about it—about the [prosecutor's] report. I think that is a vital distinction to be made."

Petersen said he was dissatisfied with Nixon's instructions and conveyed his feelings to Kleindienst April 25. Kleindienst, Petersen said, agreed that the judge in the Pentagon Papers trial, William M. Byrne Jr., should be told. Prepared to resign, Petersen said, if Nixon did not agree with their suggested course of action, the two men met with Nixon. However, the President endorsed "without hesitation" their intention to pass information about the burglary to Byrne.

Petersen was asked by Sen. Gurney if at any time he had suspected there was a cover-up of Watergate taking place. Petersen responded that he had a "visceral reaction. The word I used to the prosecutors and Kleindienst, nobody acts innocent. You couldn't translate that. There was an overriding concern. There were no records. Things were destroyed. They didn't act like innocent people. Innocent people come in and say, 'Fine, what do you want to know?' It was not like that, it was a visceral reaction. Yes, that is the reason we were so insistent to get this thing, get them tied down to sentence and immunize

them [the seven original Watergate defendants]."

Petersen's testimony—like that of Gray and Kleindienst—conflicted with part of Nixon's April 30 statement on Watergate. Petersen denied that the President directed him March 21 or any time before April 15 "to get all the facts" about Watergate. Petersen's statement prompted Sen. Weicker to ask, "Exactly who was it in the city of Washington who received [Nixon's] orders?"

Petersen, who accompanied Kleindienst April 15 to tell Nixon what the Watergate prosecutors had learned from Dean and Magruder, told the Senate panel that he advised the President to dismiss Haldeman and Ehrlichman.

Q. Now, did you make any recommendation with regard to Mr. Dean?

A. Yes, I did. The President said, "You know, Haldeman and Ehrlichman deny this and I have to go to find this out. Dean in effect has admitted it. Should I request his resignation?" And I said, "My goodness, no. Now, here is the first man who has come in to cooperate with us and certainly we don't want to give the impression that he is being subjected to reprisal because of his cooperation. So please don't ask for his resignation at this point."

Later that month, Petersen said he informed Nixon that the prosecutor's negotiations with Dean had reached an impasse and Dean should not be retained on the White House staff.

Nixon had another conversation with Petersen about Dean April 18. Dean had told Nixon that he had been given immunity from prosecution; Petersen said he told the President no such offer had been made. The President then responded that he had Dean's statement on tape. Petersen testified that he declined Nixon's offer to listen to the tape.

Petersen added at another point that no one in Washington had been more surprised than he when Dean implicated himself in the Watergate cover-up.

Petersen was asked by Majority Counsel Samuel Dash about a phone call he received from the President April 30. Petersen answered:

He called up and said "You can tell your wife that the President has done what needed to be done, and I want to thank you for what you have done."

To the extent that requires some explanation in the course of our conversations, I was impressing upon the President the situation so far as I was concerned was degenerating and it was vitally affecting the people's confidence in the White House and I relate to him a conversation that I had with my wife at the breakfast table in which she had said, "Do you think the President is involved?" And I related that to the President and I said, "If I reach the point where I think you are involved I have got to resign. If I come up with evidence of you I am just going to waltz it over to the House of Representatives" but I said, "What is important is that my wife, who is no left wing kook, is raising these questions of me and that indicates to me that you have got a most serious problem."

And that affected the President quite strongly and when he called me on April 30 he made that point.

Petersen expressed anger that a special prosecutor had been appointed for the Watergate case. "That case was snatched out from under us when it was 90% complete," he said.

Petersen defended his decision not to extend his investigation of Watergate to the activities of political trickster Donald

A

B

C

D

E

F

G

Segretti. Neither he nor Silbert thought Segretti's actions were violations of the law. Moreover, they were guarding against making the Watergate probe a wide-open, political fishing expedition, Petersen testified.

In other testimony, Petersen related a conversation with Kleindienst after Kleindienst had discussed sentencing procedure and clemency for the Watergate burglars with Ehrlichman.

Petersen told Kleindienst he intended to ask for jail sentences for the conspirators and of his intention after sentencing to use immunization from further prosecution to compel testimony.

After more discussion, Petersen related, Kleindienst said, "Do me a favor,... tell those crazy guys over there [at the White House] what you just told me before they do something they will be sorry for."

Hearings recess until September. The Senate Select Committee on Presidential Campaign Activities recessed its televised Watergate hearings Aug. 7. It planned to resume Sept. 10. Since May 17, the panel had taken sworn testimony from 33 witnesses and compiled 7,573 pages of testimony in 37 daily sessions.

Since that time the committee, under the chairmanship of Sen. Sam J. Ervin Jr. (D, N.C.), had focused primarily on the first phase of its Watergate investigation, the origin and aftermath of the break-in at the Democratic headquarters in the Watergate building in Washington June 17, 1972.

A second phase was planned to probe alleged political sabotage during the 1972 presidential campaign as well as a third phase dealing with campaign funding irregularities. Further inquiry on the first phase was expected to spill over into the resumption of hearings in September.

Senate investigators, previewing the second phase, portrayed the Watergate break-in as only "one small part" of an extensive and prolonged White House effort to prevent the nomination of a strong Democratic presidential contender in 1972.

Ehrlichman sees 'destructive' probe. Former presidential assistant John D. Ehrlichman told newsmen Aug. 13 he thought the Senate Watergate probe was "destructive" and being conducted in a "sort of circus atmosphere." He said the Senate probers "weighed what they see as the national interest versus the rights of individuals" and decided to pursue the inquiry despite possible violation of individual rights.

Haldeman amends Senate testimony. White House chief of staff H. R. Haldeman provided the Senate Watergate Committee with an amended version of earlier testimony given at committee hearings about the controversial White House tapes, it was reported Aug. 28.

In an Aug. 10 letter, Haldeman's attorney, Frank Strickler, told the committee that his client "believes" that on July 10 he received the Sept. 15, 1972 tape "plus phone call tapes for that day" from a White House aide, Stephen Bull, who delivered the material to Haldeman at the home of another White House aide, Lawrence Higby. Strickler said Haldeman did not listen to the phone call tapes.

Polls on hearings. In a Gallup Poll published Sept. 2, 52% of the respondents thought the Ervin committee hearings were a "good thing for the country," 41% thought they were a "bad thing for the country." In response to another question, 57% thought the Watergate committee was more interested in getting at the facts than in trying to discredit the Nixon Administration, 28% believed the committee was not.

Senate hearings delayed. The Senate Select Committee on Presidential Campaign Activities decided Sept. 12 to resume its Watergate hearings Sept. 24, to hold three public sessions a week and to try to conclude the sessions by Nov. 1. When the committee had recessed its televised hearings Aug. 7, it had tentatively set a resumption date for earlier in September.

The need for more investigation on the panel's final two phases of its probe—campaign sabotage and contributions—was given as the cause of the later resumption date. The first phase dealt with the Watergate break-in and aftermath. There was also uncertainty about the availability of the next scheduled witness, Charles W. Colson, former White House special counsel, considered a possible target of a federal grand jury investigating the 1971 burglary of the office of a psychiatrist who had treated Daniel Ellsberg.

Committee Chairman Sam J. Ervin Jr. (D, N.C.) said committee members hoped to expedite the hearings by concentrating on "salient points" from "key witnesses" and abstaining from "such detail that we won't be able to see the forest for the bushes and the trees."

Vice Chairman Howard H. Baker Jr. (R, Tenn.) said the committee in its deliberation that day had not considered the political pressures of the investigation, generated largely by President Nixon's public appeal for the Watergate matter to be left to the courts.

The committee was determined "to finish this thing promptly and thoroughly," Baker said, adding that "that happens to coincide with what I think the public wants, that is, to continue but to continue with as much dispatch as possible."

Committee renews pleas for tapes—The Senate committee investigating Watergate said in court papers filed Sept. 18 that its need for Nixon's Watergate tapes was greater than that of special prosecutor Cox because the committee was focusing "on the President's own possible criminality." The filing was part of the committee's suit in federal district court for the release of the tapes. [See p. 88]

Colson refuses to give testimony. Former White House special counsel Charles W. Colson invoked his constitutional protection against self-incrimination under the Fifth Amendment in refusing to answer questions from the Senate Watergate committee Sept. 19. He appeared at a closed session of the committee, which voted unanimously not to grant Colson immunity from prosecution for his testimony.

A request for limited immunity had been presented by his lawyer, David Shapiro, who also asked the committee to delay calling Colson until after the second federal Watergate grand jury had returned indictments. Shapiro said Colson would refuse to answer the committee's questions at this time because he was a "target" of the grand jury probing the burglary at the office of the psychiatrist who had treated Pentagon Papers defendant Daniel Ellsberg and other matters, including the relationship between the Nixon Administration and the International Telephone and Telegraph Corp.

Colson had repeatedly asserted his innocence of illegality and, prior to the grand jury development, made clear his willingness to testify. He had been linked by various witnesses to presidential discussions of executive clemency for a Watergate defendant, pressure for approval of the espionage plan leading to the Watergate break-in, fund-raising associated with the psychiatrist's office break-in, awareness of Administration activity concerning settlement of ITT antitrust suits and promotion of "dirty tricks" against Democratic candidates.

After the closed session, Committee Chairman Sam J. Ervin Jr. (D, N.C.) told reporters Colson had affirmed his innocence of wrongdoing. "As a lawyer," Ervin commented, "I must note that a man is entitled to plead the Fifth Amendment even if he is not guilty of any offense." He said Colson would not be called to testify when the open hearings resumed Sept. 24.

Committee Vice Chairman Howard H. Baker Jr. (R, Tenn.) said Colson had indicated that he would be "not only willing but eager" to testify if he ceased being a "target" for indictment.

Hunt concludes first phase of inquiry. The Senate Watergate committee resumed its televised hearings Sept. 24 with convicted Watergate conspirator E. Howard Hunt Jr. in the witness chair.

Sept. 24: *Hunt tells Colson role*—E. Howard Hunt Jr. testified about his activity in the Watergate break-in and, before that, as a member of the White House "plumbers" group. The latter activity, which he described as "seamy activities for the White House," included the break-in at the office of a psychiatrist who had treated Pentagon Papers defendant Daniel Ellsberg.

Hunt also related his personal plight in the aftermath of Watergate, that he had been physically attacked and robbed and had suffered a stroke in his six months in jail, that he was "isolated from my four motherless children," that he had an "enormous financial burden" from legal fees and that he was "crushed by the failure of my government to protect me and my family, as in the past it has always done for its clandestine agents." Hunt had been a CIA agent for 21 years before his retirement in 1970.

When he became involved in the Watergate break-in, Hunt told the committee, "I considered my participation as a duty to my country." After a career as a spy, "following orders without question," he said, he had never thought to question the propriety or legality of the Watergate break-in. He regretted lacking "the wisdom to withdraw," he said, but "at the same time I cannot escape feeling that the country I have served for my entire life and which directed me to carry out the Watergate entry is punishing me for the very thing it trained and directed me to do."

He frequently cited his working relationship with Charles W. Colson, then a special counsel to the President.

Hunt said he had been offered his White House job as a consultant by Colson and had worked under Colson's direction. His original work involved probing the origins of the Vietnam war and leaks of classified information, specifically the Pentagon papers. He began collecting derogatory information about Ellsberg, Hunt said, and assumed it was to be made available by Colson to selected members of the media.

The faked Diem cables—Hunt related similar activity regarding the Kennedy family. Following Colson's suggestion he "might be able to improve upon the record," Hunt said, he forged cables purporting a link between President John F. Kennedy and the assassination of South Vietnamese President Ngo Dinh Diem. He said the faked cables were shown to a reporter, but the reporter never wrote about them. It was Colson's intention, Hunt said, "to demonstrate that a Catholic U.S. Administration had, in fact, conspired in the assassination of a Catholic chief of state of another country."

This line of questioning by committee chief counsel Samuel Dash was interrupted by Sens. Edward J. Gurney (R, Fla.) and Howard H. Baker Jr. (R, Tenn.). Gurney doubted the relevance of the questioning to the 1972 election. When Dash cited the activity as an attempt to discredit the Kennedy Administration and the Democratic party during the election and to alienate the Catholic vote from the Democrats, Baker insisted that Dash refrain from reaching conclusions in his effort to elicit the facts. Dash continued his questioning after Committee Chairman Sam Ervin (D, N.C.) observed that the best way to determine the witness's knowledge of the facts was to question him.

Hunt also acknowledged attempts to obtain derogatory information on Sen. Edward M. Kennedy (D, Mass.) and Sen. Edmund S. Muskie (D, Me.). The move against Kennedy, in which he employed a disguise and false credentials supplied by the CIA in making a contact in Hyannis Port, Mass., was unsuccessful. The attempt against Muskie, involving a burglary of a newspaper office in Las Vegas, was aborted.

The Ellsberg break-in—The break-in at the psychiatrist's office also was attributed in Hunt's testimony to an attempt to uncover derogatory information against Ellsberg. One of his assignments, he said, was to collect data on Ellsberg and some of this was released to a reporter who incorporated it in an article.

The committee put in the record a July 28, 1971 memorandum from Hunt to Colson suggesting a plan to destroy Ellsberg's public image and credibility. One suggestion was, "Obtain Ellsberg's files from his psychiatric analyst." The committee also produced an Aug. 27, 1971 memo from then-Presidential adviser John Ehrlichman to Colson saying, "On the assumption that the proposed undertaking by Hunt and [G. Gordon] Liddy would be carried out, and would be successful, I would appreciate receiving from you by next Wednesday a game plan as to how and when you believe the materials should be used." Hunt told the committee the reference in the memo was to "covert entry" of the psychiatrist's office.

Hunt also said the break-in, over the Labor Day weekend in 1971, had produced no files and when he tried to inform Colson about the incident Colson told him " 'I don't want to hear anything about it.' "

The Watergate break-in—Hunt said he believed the Watergate break-ins May 27 and June 17, 1972 were "unwise" but "lawful" and undertaken to obtain information to back up a reported contribution of campaign funds to the Democratic party from the Cuban government.

He had advised Colson beforehand, Hunt said, that he was working with Liddy on an extensive political intelligence plan for the Nixon re-election committee. Colson's reaction was that he "indicated that he was aware of the overall intelligence plan and his only problem with it was that he would much prefer me, [to] see me heading it rather than Mr. Liddy," Hunt said. Later, in February of 1972, he introduced Liddy to Colson, he said, relating Liddy's impression that the meeting "may have done us some good" in getting the plan effected.

Hunt disclosed to the committee that he had proposed to "junk" the June 17 Watergate break-in after discovering the tape put on the door locks had been removed, but Liddy and another convicted conspirator, James W. McCord Jr., overruled him.

After the burglars were caught that night, Hunt, who was not apprehended, said he went to the White House and deposited in his safe some of McCord's electronic equipment and removed $10,000 of "contingency" funds that were used for bail bonds for those arrested. Hunt said Liddy advised him to leave town, which he did, going to California after informing Colson's secretary that his (Hunt's) safe was "loaded."

The committee documented two subsequent contacts between Hunt and Colson. The first was an Aug. 9, 1972 letter from Hunt to Colson expressing regret at "your being dragged into the case through association with me, superficial and occasional though the association was."

The second was a Nov. 24, 1972 telephone conversation, taped by Colson, in which Colson repeatedly advised Hunt not to give him details of his involvement in Watergate, that his value to him would be tainted unless he remained "as unknowing as I am." The "less specifics I know," Colson insisted, "the better off I am, we are, you are."

The thrust of Hunt's conversation was for financial assistance for the Watergate defendants. "We're protecting the guys who are really responsible," Hunt told Colson, "but now that's that—and of course that's a continuing requirement, but at the same time, this is a two-way street and as I said before, we think that now is the time when a move should be made and surely the cheapest commodity available is money."

"I'm reading you," Colson assured him. "You don't need to be more specific."

Hunt told the committee he was unaware that the conversation was taped. In retrospect, he said, he felt that he "was set up on this one."

Hunt admitted receiving funds for his legal fees and family assistance after his indictment and conviction but denied he made threats in order to get the money. William O. Bittman, who withdrew as his attorney in August, received $156,000 in legal fees. The payments were clandestine, Hunt said.

When the anonymous packets of money stopped coming, Hunt said, he called Colson about it but eventually went to the Nixon re-election committee to see Paul O'Brien. He told O'Brien he would like his family to have the equivalent of two years' subsistence before he was jailed. And he told him of his "other activities, which I believe I described as 'seamy activities,' for the White House." Hunt denied that this was a threat to extract the funds in return for his silence about the "seamy activities." Rather, he said, he was citing his long and loyal service as grounds for receiving the subsistence.

O'Brien advised him, he said, to contact Colson, who by now had left the White House to practice law. Hunt tried but was rebuffed. He did see Colson's law partner, David Shapiro, who approached him "rather aggressively," Hunt said, "and subjected me to a lengthy monologue which I considered to be highly self-serving."

After these events, Hunt related, he received a final payment of cash on March 20 or 21, totaling $75,000, but he said he put it in a safe deposit box and eventually paid Bittman $80,000 collected from his late wife's insurance.

Sept. 25: *Hunt concludes testimony*—In his concluding testimony, Hunt acknowledged that he felt "let down" by individuals in the White House and the Nixon re-election committee. Responding to a question by Sen. Joseph M. Montoya (D, N.M.), Hunt specified that the feeling stemmed from "their failure" to exert "every reasonable effort" on behalf of the Watergate defendants. He reiterated his belief the Watergate break-in was sanctioned by high government officials for legitimate national security purposes and, therefore, was legal. "I regret my participation," he declared, "but I do not think it justifies my conviction or the punishment which has been imposed upon me."

Hunt also said he had never been offered nor sought executive clemency and denied directing or encouraging other defendants to follow his example and plead guilty. He repeated his denial that the payments he had received were in exchange for his silence or that of the other defendants.

The committee further explored Hunt's effort to obtain psychiatric data on Ellsberg. In this and other areas, Hunt's testimony seemed to parallel in substance the more than 40 spy novels he had written during his career. He proposed that the Watergate break-in had been subverted by a "double agent." He identified the "Fat Jack" intermediary of another "double agent" deal against Sen. Muskie's campaign, and told of an assignment to assess admitted GOP saboteur Donald H. Segretti. He identified some of the material taken from his White House safe after the unsuccessful burglary at Watergate as notebooks that would have uncovered the whole "Gemstone" operation. And he detailed his bedside interview in disguise with lobbyist Dita Beard in a Denver hospital at midnight.

Kissinger linked to Ellsberg profile—The committee released an affidavit obtained from the Central Intelligence Agency (CIA) linking Secretary of State Henry A. Kissinger to a 1971 request for a psychiatric profile on Ellsberg. The affadavit, dated May 9, was from a CIA staff psychiatrist, Dr. Bernard M. Malloy, who quoted former White House aide David M. Young Jr. as having told him the request for an agency profile on Ellsberg had come from Kissinger and Nixon aide John D. Ehrlichman. Kissinger was then national security adviser to President Nixon.

(Kissinger Sept. 26 again denied that he had any part in the 1971 request for the profile. At a news conference, Kissinger said, "I did not know of any request for a profile. I never saw this profile, and I never discussed the subject with David Young.")

Hunt was quoted in the document as saying he regarded the requested profile as a tool to "render Dr. Ellsberg ineffective or to make him the object of pity as a broken man." It also quoted him as stating "he wished to 'try Dr. Ellsberg in public.'"

Hunt told the committee the affidavit was "a question of salt mixed with pepper" and denied he had sought to evoke pity for Ellsberg.

The "double agent" theory—Hunt suggested that the Watergate conspirators were "trapped" by a "double agent" and named the possible informer as Alfred Baldwin 3rd, a lookout during the break-in and one of those who monitored the telephone taps. Developing his theory in response to a question from Gurney whether a double agent was involved, Hunt cited Baldwin who, among other things, he said, "had rather intimate ties" to the Democratic party in Connecticut, being a nephew of a Democratic judge.

The theory was disputed by Sen. Lowell P. Weicker Jr., Republican from Connecticut, who identified Baldwin's judicial relative as Raymond Baldwin, a former senator and governor, who was a Republican.

'Fat Jack' identified—The previous day Hunt had mentioned "Fat Jack" as a contact in 1972 who provided material obtained from a penetration of Muskie campaign headquarters. "Fat Jack" was in charge of an agent planted in the opposition camp. With the help of a photograph submitted by Weicker, "Fat Jack" was identified as John R. Buckley, who retired June 30 as chief of the inspection division of the Office of Economic Opportunity.

Segretti rated 'sophomoric'—Hunt testified that he and Liddy had been assigned to meet with Segretti in the spring of 1972 to assess Segretti's undercover effort to sabotage Democratic contenders. Their finding was that it was "sophomoric" and should be terminated. But their recommendation was overruled and they were instructed to monitor Segretti's endeavors.

The Dita Beard assignment—Hunt said his assignment to interview Dita Beard came from White House aide Wallace Johnson. He said he had been sent to Johnson by Colson. The purpose was to determine whether a controversial memo attributed to Mrs. Beard, a lobbyist for the International Telephone & Telegraph Corp. (ITT), was fraudulent. The memo appeared to link a favorable antitrust settlement for ITT to a $400,000 pledge to help underwrite the 1972 Republican national convention.

Hunt related that he visited Mrs. Beard, hospitalized in Denver, sometime in March 1972, wearing a brown wig and using an assumed name. During the course of the interview, occurring between 11 p.m. and 3 a.m. one night, Hunt said he repeatedly was interrupted by Mrs. Beard's physician and took those occasions to call Colson in Washington for advice on the course of his questioning. Hunt said he was unable to make a determination whether she had written the memorandum, which she later disavowed.

The missing 'Gemstone' notebook—Hunt told the committee that among the material taken from his White House safe after the arrest of the Watergate burglars was a notebook containing "names, addresses, pseudonyms and phone numbers of every person that I dealt with" in the "Gemstone" operation that evolved into the Watergate break-in. He said the notebook would have been "a ready handbook by which any investigator with any resources at all could quickly determine the parameters" of the intelligence operation conducted for the Nixon re-election committee.

Hunt's claim for a dismissal of charges against him was based in part on deprival of evidence that could have assisted him in his original defense.

List of Defendants Grows

Witnesses thwart CIA investigation. The House Armed Services Committee's Subcommittee on Intelligence Operations failed to obtain a single substantive response from four witnesses it hoped would shed light on the role of the Central Intelligence Agency in the Watergate affair.

Egil Krogh Jr. and David R. Young Jr., who headed the White House plumbers unit, invoked 5th Amendment rights against self-incrimination. Neither Krogh, who appeared July 17, nor Young, who took the oath July 18, had been granted immunity against prosecution.

Ousted White House counsel John W. Dean 3rd, who also appeared without immunity, invoked the 5th Amendment July 18.

Watergate conspirator G. Gordon Liddy appeared July 19 and refused even to be sworn in as a witness. The panel voted unanimously July 19 to recommend Liddy be cited for contempt of Congress.

Plot to discredit Ellsberg. Documents supplied to the Senate Watergate committee by former White House aide David R. Young Jr. indicated that the 1971 burglary of Daniel Ellsberg's psychiatrist's office was part of a larger plot to discredit the former government official who made public the Pentagon Papers, the Washington Post reported July 25.

One memo, sent Aug. 26, 1971 by Young to Nixon adviser John D. Ehrlichman, described a meeting held a month earlier and attended by J. Fred Buzhardt, then general counsel to the Defense Department; Robert C. Mardian, then an assistant attorney general in charge of the Justice Department's Internal Security Division; William B. Macomber Jr., then undersecretary of state for administration; Rep. Edward Hebert (D, La.), chairman of the House Armed Services Committee; and Rep. Leslie C. Arends (Ill.), then ranking Republican member on the committee.

According to the memo, Hebert and Arends agreed to begin a Congressional investigation of the Pentagon Papers affair, with Buzhardt, Mardian and Macomber setting its format, supplying its substantive data and developing its scenario.

"The plan," Young wrote, "was to slowly develop a very negative picture around the whole Pentagon study affair ... and then to identify Ellsberg's associates and supporters on the new left with this negative image."

Ultimately the investigation, the Young memo said, was to show that Ellsberg and his associates had undermined the policy of the government they were supposedly serving and how they had put themselves above the law.

The memo also spoke of "planting" negative information about Ellsberg in the press, perhaps including material gleaned from Ellsberg's psychiatrist's records, the Post said.

(Hebert and Arends denied any knowledge of the proposed investigation. Hebert labeled the memo "sheer fantasy.")

Another Young document showed that Buzhardt planned an "all-out adversary interrogation" of Defense Department officials involved in the preparation of the Pentagon Papers, and officials of the Rand Corp., where Ellsberg was employed at the time of the Pentagon Papers' disclosure.

CIA profile of Ellsberg released. The first of two psychological profiles produced by the Central Intelligence Agency (CIA) on Pentagon Papers trial defendant Daniel Ellsberg was published by the New York Times Aug. 3. The Times said it was unable to obtain the second.

The assessment, prepared August 1971, described Ellsberg as an "extremely intelligent and talented individual" with a "knack for drawing attention to himself." A man who saw himself destined for a brilliant career, Ellsberg found himself at mid-life not achieving the prominence and success he had expected, the study said. (The profile defined mid-life as 35–45 years of age and said of the period that it was "a time when many men come to doubt their earlier commitments and are impelled to strike out in new directions.")

Regarding Ellsberg's release of the Pentagon Papers, the study stated:

There is no suggestion that subject thought anything treasonous in his act. Rather, he seemed to be responding to what he deemed a higher order of patriotism. His exclusion of the three volumes of the papers concerned with the secret negotiations would support this.

Many of subject's own words would confirm the impression that he saw himself as having a special mission, and indeed as bearing a special responsibility. On several occasions he castigated himself for not releasing the papers earlier.

After publication of the documents, Ellsberg experienced "jubilation, an apparent enjoyment of the limelight," the profile said. This was followed by "quiet satisfaction," which was succeeded by bitterness because the press and Congress had not wholeheartedly supported him, the assessment said.

The study pointed out that the data base had been fragmentary and no direct clinical evaluation had been available. "This indirect assessment should be considered highly speculative and in no way definitive," the study warned.

Ellsberg denies Hoover-Marx link — Ellsberg said July 25 that his father-in-law, Louis Marx, was not a friend of J. Edgar Hoover, the late director of the Federal Bureau of Investigation (FBI).

Former White House domestic affairs adviser John D. Ehrlichman had told the Senate Watergate committee July 24 that the FBI had curtailed its probe of the Pentagon Papers affair because of the Marx-Hoover friendship.

Ellsberg said Marx recalled that it was "possible" that 30 years earlier he had met Hoover in a large group.

Ellsberg also said Marx, a wealthy industrialist, had been interviewed by the FBI in 1971, a fact also in conflict with Ehrlichman's testimony.

Ellsberg FBI probe defended—W. Mark Felt, former associate director of the FBI, said July 27 that the bureau's investigation of Ellsberg in 1971 was "extensive and exhaustive." At no time, Felt said, did the White House tell the FBI it was dissatisfied with the probe.

MacGregor critical of Ehrlichman. Clark MacGregor, director of the 1972 Nixon re-election campaign, said he was "misled, deceived and . . . lied to repeatedly" by his own campaign staff and White House aides about Watergate.

MacGregor's statement was part of a 113-page deposition, released July 28, that was given in connection with civil suits stemming from the Watergate break-in.

MacGregor pictured himself as being pressed by White House aides to act as campaign spokesman on Watergate, when in fact it was they who had information and had no intention of passing it to him.

In this context, MacGregor was critical of John D. Ehrlichman, former domestic affairs adviser to Nixon. "It is utterly ridiculous for John Ehrlichman, who had a great deal of information I didn't have, to be calling on me to disclose information that I didn't possess but which was known to him," MacGregor said. "I don't recall that Ehrlichman was a champion of disclosure...," he added.

MacGregor testified that he asked his predecessor, John N. Mitchell, if he had been involved in Watergate and was assured by Mitchell he had not. A similar question put to Mitchell's campaign aide, Jeb Stuart Magruder, brought a like denial, MacGregor said.

Magruder enters guilty plea. Jeb Stuart Magruder, former deputy director of the Committee to Re-elect the President, pleaded guilty in Washington Aug. 16 to a one-count indictment charging him with plotting the electronic bugging of the Democratic national headquarters at the Watergate and with the subsequent cover-up of the crime.

Chief U.S. District Court Judge John J. Sirica delayed sentencing until after U.S. prosecutors had produced more indictments. In return for his guilty plea on reduced charges, Magruder agreed to waive a jury trial and to cooperate fully with the prosecution. Sirica indicated that the severity of Magruder's sentence would depend on the degree of his cooperation. He faced a maximum of five years in prison and a $10,000 fine.

Magruder pleaded guilty to the following charges: plotting the Watergate break-in; obstructing a Department of Justice investigation into Watergate; perjuring himself and suborning the perjury of other unnamed co-conspirators; conspiring to misrepresent the Central Intelligence Agency as having an interest in limiting the investigation; giving false testimony to the Federal Bureau of Investigation; and secretly raising funds to buy the silence of the original Watergate conspirators.

McGovern camp spy unmasked. A freelance journalist admitted Aug. 18 she was paid $1,000 a week, plus expenses, by former White House aide Murray M. Chotiner to travel with and spy on the Presidential campaign of Sen. George McGovern from Labor Day to election day, 1972.

Lucianne C. Goldberg, who said she took the assignment only after Chotiner agreed to let her write a book on her experiences, indicated that she transmitted her intelligence to Washington by telephone under the codename "Chapman's Friend."

Denying that he had asked Goldberg to dig up "dirt" on the McGovern campaign, Chotiner conceded Aug. 20 that he paid her from his own funds and then was reimbursed by the Committee to Re-elect the President.

Freidin preceded Goldberg—Chotiner confirmed Aug. 28 that he had hired journalist Seymour K. Freidin, also at $1,000 a week, to supply intelligence on Democratic candidates to the Nixon campaign.

Freidin preceded Goldberg as an intelligence source. Freidin quit his job with the Republicans in September 1972 to take a position as chief of the London bureau for the Hearst newspaper group.

Freidin denied he had spied on the Democrats and said he took the job to write a book about his experiences.

Chotiner commented on the use of Goldberg and Freidin: "We didn't get anything we couldn't have gotten in the public press. . . . I guess it was worth the $1,000 just to know the stuff the newspapers were reporting was quite accurate."

Secret Service agent passed data. The Secret Service Aug. 16 announced the resignation of one of its agents, James C. Bolton Jr., who had divulged confidential information about the Presidential campaign of Sen. George McGovern (D, S.D.) that eventually found its way to the White House.

While at a family dinner, Bolton allegedly told his father of a McGovern meeting with a subversive—a later memo showed no such meeting had occurred. Bolton Sr., an assistant to Rep. Glenn R. Davis (R, Wis.), passed the item to the White House.

Bolton Sr. denied he had given any other information to the White House, but a White House memo obtained by the Washington Post said Bolton Jr. had "promised to keep his dad informed" on the McGovern campaign.

The Secret Service said it had determined the incident was an "isolated" one occurring through a family relationship.

Four indicted in Ellsberg break-in. Four former Nixon Administration officials were indicted Sept. 4 by a Los Angeles County grand jury on charges stemming from the 1971 break-in at the office of Daniel Ellsberg's psychiatrist.

Named in the four-count indictment were John D. Ehrlichman, domestic affairs adviser to Nixon until April 30; Egil Krogh Jr., and David R. Young Jr., who supervised the White House "plumbers unit;" and G. Gordon Liddy, convicted Watergate conspirator. The "plumbers unit" was formed in 1971 to plug security leaks.

The indictment detailed 16 overt acts in connection with the planning and execution of the burglary. Ehrlichman was also charged with perjury for his denial July 8 before the grand jury of prior knowledge of the break-in.

Listed in the charges as unindicted co-conspirators were convicted Watergate conspirators E. Howard Hunt Jr., Bernard L. Barker, and Eugenio Martinez; and Felipe DeDiego, a Cuban national from Miami.

Sirica halts Watergate lectures. James W. McCord Jr. and Jeb Stuart Magruder were ordered by Chief U.S. District Court Judge John J. Sirica Sept. 5 to refrain from offering public lectures or interviews. Both were free pending sentencing for their roles in the Watergate burglary.

Asserting that criminals should not "profit by their wrongdoing," Sirica warned McCord and Magruder that such speeches might have an adverse effect on future trials growing out of the Watergate affair.

The action by Sirica came after McCord received $2,000 for a lecture at an Illinois college.

However, Sirica placed no restrictions on their right to travel within the U.S. for the purpose of conducting business.

House cites Liddy for contempt. The House voted 334–11 Sept. 10 to cite convicted Watergate conspirator G. Gordon Liddy for contempt of Congress for refusing to testify before a House Armed Services Committee panel investigating Watergate. Liddy had refused to take the oath as a witness.

The panel's recommendation for contempt had been upheld by a unanimous vote of the full committee July 31. The next legal step would be presentation of the House citation to a grand jury for consideration of indictment.

Segretti cooperating with Cox. Donald H. Segretti agreed Sept. 17 to plead guilty to a four-count indictment involving charges of political sabotage and was cooperating with the office of Watergate special prosecutor Archibald Cox in its investigation of "dirty tricks" employed by re-election aides to President Nixon.

The charges against Segretti stemmed from a two-count Florida indictment in which he was accused of preparing fraudulent campaign material. The spurious documents, ostensibly distributed by Sen. Edmund S. Muskie (D, Me.), suggested that there had been sexual misconduct on the part of Sen. Hubert H. Humphrey (D, Minn.) and Sen. Henry M. Jackson (D, Wash.), rival contenders for the 1972 Democratic primary in Florida. Segretti had pleaded innocent to those charges.

A Tampa grand jury had broadened the case Aug. 24, handing down a four-count indictment which included the previous charges. Segretti also was accused of distributing cards at a rally for Gov. George C. Wallace (D, Ala.), another candidate for the presidential nomination, reading: "If you like Hitler, you'll love Wallace . . . Vote for Muskie."

According to the indictment, Segretti also circulated posters during the Florida primary reading "Help Muskie Support Busing our Children." Another Muskie letter, prepared by Segretti, claimed that Florida Rep. Sam M. Gibbons' (D) staff and equipment were being used in Muskie's Tampa office.

Legal proceedings under the new indictment, made public Sept. 17, were transferred to Washington. Each of the four counts was a misdemeanor, punishable by up to $1,000 in fines and a year in jail each.

Robert M. Benz and George A. Hearing were named co-conspirators, but not co-defendants, in the case.

Defendants seek plea change. Five of the original defendants in the Watergate case filed petitions with the federal court in the District of Columbia Sept. 14 and 17 seeking to have their pleas of guilty withdrawn.

Four of the defendants—Bernard L. Barker, Frank A. Sturgis, Virgilio R. Gonzalez and Eugenio R. Martinez—filed a petition with the court Sept. 14 so they could be tried before a jury. A petition for E. Howard Hunt Jr., the fifth defendant, was filed Sept. 17 for dismissal of the charges against him.

All five had been sentenced provisionally March 23 to prison terms for conspiracy, burglary and wiretapping.

The four told the court they were victims of "a cruel fraud initially perpetrated on them to obtain their participation in the Watergate activities" and their guilty pleas had been "false and involuntarily entered under the force and compulsion of a belief that the necessity to protect national security interests precluded them from asserting the defenses they had to the charges against them."

They also contended that they had been directed to plead guilty "to avoid the exposure of secret, confidential and sensitive national security operations of which they were a part." Such pleas "were premised on false assumptions which had been fostered on them by others, including co-defendant E. Howard Hunt Jr. and, ultimately, high officials in the executive branch of the government," they said. Two other defendants, James W. McCord Jr. and G. Gordon Liddy, had been convicted by a jury.

McCord, citing newly uncovered evidence, possible perjury and selective prosecution, had filed an appeal for a new trial June 8.

Hunt's petition contended that he thought he had been acting lawfully, "pursuant to the President's power to protect the national security," that Liddy was his supporting witness but refused to talk, that new evidence had since been exposed and that the case against Hunt should be dismissed because of "outrageous government conduct."

The appeal claimed that Hunt was "coerced into abandoning" his defense because the government "unconstitutionally deprived him of evidence" to support his defense and, further, that "the investigation and prosecution of this case were contaminated by misconduct by many responsible White House and law enforcement officials."

Even assuming that Hunt's acts were illegal, the petition said, Hunt "cannot be convicted for acts committed within the scope of his employment at the direction of high government officials."

At the time of Hunt's indictment and plea, it said, "responsible government officials had engaged in a deliberate clandestine and successful campaign to obstruct justice." The petition also stated: "In the White House and down through the Executive Office of the President and the Department of Justice, there had been destruction and withholding of evidence, and perjury and subornation of perjury"; "whether or not the evidence, unexposed because of now known notorious corruption by government officials, would have established defendant's innocence, such misconduct so gravely violated his constitutional rights as to require dismissal of the proceedings."

Sirica rules out maximum sentences. John J. Sirica, chief judge of U.S. district court in the District of Columbia, told five of the Watergate burglars Oct. 1 it was not his intention to impose maximum sentences in their cases. He said "such a disposition would not only be unwarranted but unjust."

The five men—E. Howard Hunt Jr., Virgilio Gonzales, Eugenio Martinez, Frank Sturgis and Bernard Barker—had received provisional maximum sentences from Sirica in March. But Sirica, calling them into court, explained that a maximum term was mandatory under the law in any provisional sentencing announced while awaiting more information for final sentencing. The final sentence would be based on presentencing reports, on the law and on "fairness, compassion, understanding and justice," Sirica emphasized. He reminded the defendants that the degree of their cooperation with investigatory panels was one of his evaluating factors.

Sirica took the unusual step because of an apparent "widespread misunderstanding" about the provisional sentences, which he wanted to clarify out of "fairness" to the defendants.

Segretti pleads guilty. Donald H. Segretti pleaded guilty Oct. 1 to three misdemeanor charges arising from his activities in the 1972 Florida presidential primary campaign. He pleaded guilty to a conspiracy charge and to two charges of distributing fake campaign literature.

A fourth charge against him—a fake campaign letter alleging one of the Democratic contenders used a Florida Democratic congressman's equipment and personnel in his campaign—was dropped. When Judge Gerhard A. Gesell asked if any promises were made involving the guilty plea, assistant Watergate special prosecutor Richard Davis turned over a letter of understanding and asked that it be sealed. Segretti's cooperation with the prosecution had been made known Sept. 17, when it was expected he would plead guilty to a four-count indictment.

Krogh indicted again. Former White House aide Egil Krogh Jr. was indicted Oct. 11 on two counts of making false declarations to a federal prosecutor in connection with trips in 1971 by convicted Watergate conspirators G. Gordon Liddy and E. Howard Hunt Jr. concerning "declassification of the Pentagon Papers"

by Daniel Ellsberg. A Los Angeles County grand jury had indicted Krogh and three others Sept. 4 on charges stemming from the Labor Day 1971 break-in at the office of Ellsberg's psychiatrist.

The indictment was the first obtained by Watergate special prosecutor Archibald Cox since his appointment in May. It was returned in U.S. district court in Washington by the federal grand jury impaneled Aug. 13 to investigate campaign activities other than the Watergate break-in.

According to the U.S. Code, making false declarations was essentially the same as perjury and carried similar penalties. Perjury was willful lying under oath; making a false declaration was the giving of "irreconcilably contradictory declarations" under oath.

Krogh, who told the federal prosecutor he had no knowledge of trips by Liddy or Hunt concerning the Pentagon Papers, submitted a sworn affidavit to Pentagon Papers trial Judge William M. Byrne Jr. May 7, in which he acknowledged authorizing Hunt and Liddy "to engage in covert activity to obtain a psychological history" of Ellsberg.

John Dean pleads guilty. John W. Dean 3rd, former counsel to the President, pleaded guilty Oct. 19 to a single count of conspiring to cover up the truth about the Watergate break-in.

The plea was part of a bargain Dean made with Watergate prosecutor Archibald Cox: Dean agreed to be a witness for the prosecution in return for Cox's promise not to bring other charges against him.

Dean entered his plea before U.S. District Court Judge John J. Sirica, who delayed sentencing until after Dean had kept his part of the bargain. Dean was subject to a prison sentence of five years and a fine of $10,000.

In pleading guilty, Dean admitted the following: asking Watergate conspirator G. Gordon Liddy to tell fellow conspirator E. Howard Hunt Jr. to leave the U.S.; asking Deputy Central Intelligence Agency (CIA) Director Vernon Walters if the CIA would use covert funds to pay the salaries and bail of the men arrested in the Watergate break-in; asking the President's former private attorney, Herbert W. Kalmbach, to raise money to pay the Watergate defendants; suborning perjured testimony by former deputy Nixon reelection campaign director Jeb Stuart Magruder; asking former Treasury Department official John J. Caulfield to offer executive clemency to Watergate burglar James W. McCord Jr.; and asking former Acting Director of the Federal Bureau of Investigation L. Patrick Gray 3rd for reports of information acquired in the investigation of the Watergate break-in.

Sirica refuses bail to Watergate 5— Judge Sirica Oct. 16 refused to release on bail five of the original Watergate defendants, pending their final sentencing. Sirica said that the guilty plea each had entered was a "conviction of the highest order" and as a result caused each defendant to forfeit his automatic right of appeal.

The five defendants were E. Howard Hunt Jr., Frank Sturgis, Eugenio Martinez, Bernard L. Barker and Virgilio Gonzalez.

House panel says CIA duped. In the first formal Congressional report on a Watergate-related investigation, the House Armed Services Special Subcommittee on Intelligence said Oct. 30 that Central Intelligence Agency (CIA) officials had been "unwitting dupes for purely domestic White House staff endeavors that were beyond the realm of CIA authority."

The subcommittee, under the chairmanship of Rep. Lucien N. Nedzi (D, Mich.), concluded that the CIA and the Federal Bureau of Investigation (FBI) had been subjected to "tremendous pressure" from key White House aides to curtail the FBI's probe of the "laundering" of funds for the Watergate burglars through a Mexican bank. The White House, the report said, had invoked "nonexisting conflicts" with CIA operations.

Citing testimony by former White House domestic adviser John D. Ehrlichman, the subcommittee suggested that President Nixon had publicly misrepresented the reason for his July 6, 1972 phone call to former Acting FBI Director L. Patrick Gray 3rd. In a statement May 22, Nixon said the purpose of the call was to congratulate Gray on FBI handling of an airplane hijacking. During the conversation, Nixon said, the "progress of the Watergate investigation" had been discussed. According to Ehrlichman, however, the real purpose of the call was to sound out Gray on Gray's "concern over the FBI role" in the probe and to put pressure on him and Deputy CIA Director Vernon A. Walters to deflect the investigation.

The subcommittee said that as early as June 22, 1972 former CIA Director Richard Helms had assured Gray there was no danger the FBI would conflict with covert CIA operations. Helms repeated that position in a June 23, 1972 meeting with Walters, Ehrlichman and former White House chief of staff H. R. Haldeman. Nonetheless, Haldeman the same day instructed Walters to tell Gray that the FBI investigation might be harmful to national security. Walters was then pressured by former presidential counsel John W. Dean 3rd to delay the probe.

The subcommittee report criticized Walters for not telling Gray that the alleged White House security concern was unfounded. According to the report, Walters had testified that he assumed Dean would tell Gray there was "no CIA problem." The report called Walters' explanation "rather strange."

Another portion of the Ehrlichman testimony released by the subcommittee conflicted with Nixon's earlier explanation of the formation of the special White House investigation unit (the "plumbers"). Nixon had said in his May 22 state-ment that the unit had been formed in the week after the publication of the Pentagon papers in June 1971. Ehrlichman told the subcommittee that Nixon's statement was "not accurate" and implied that the unit had been created much earlier. Ehrlichman blamed the "drafter of the statement" for having "stumbled in a few places."

The subcommittee also concluded that the CIA had operated illegally in providing E. Howard Hunt Jr. with equipment and disguises for domestic intelligence operations, including the burglary of the office of former Pentagon papers defendant Daniel Ellsberg's psychiatrist. The report said it had been "an abuse of CIA facilities" for the agency to prepare, at the request of White House officials, a psychological profile of Ellsberg.

The Nedzi panel issued an overall criticism of the CIA for taking requests from high White House aides, "almost without exception," as "orders from people who were speaking for the President."

The subcommittee said it would prepare legislation to tighten the provisions of the National Security Act which barred the CIA from domestic operations. The panel said it would also seek to prohibit the CIA from taking any actions not explicitly covered by the National Security Act without personal authorization from the President.

Segretti given 6 months in jail. Confessed political saboteur Donald H. Segretti was ordered by U.S. District Court Judge Gerhard A. Gesell Nov. 5 to begin serving a six-month prison term. Gesell, who also placed Segretti on probation for three years after his sentence had been served, rejected an arrangement between government and Segretti's lawyers, under which Segretti would have remained free pending further prosecutions arising from Watergate.

Dean destroyed evidence. A special assistant Watergate prosecutor disclosed Nov. 5 that John W. Dean 3rd destroyed two notebooks and an address book belonging to Watergate conspirator E. Howard Hunt Jr. during the January trial of the original Watergate defendants. Dean was then counsel to the President.

Richard Ben-Veniste told Chief U.S. District Court Judge John J. Sirica that Dean found the material in the personal estate file of President Nixon. Thinking that it was potential evidence against the Watergate defendants, Dean shredded the notebooks and threw the address book into a waste basket for destruction, Ben-Veniste said.

Dean, who said he recognized the material as coming from Hunt's White House safe, told prosecutors that he believed the notebooks contained information concerning the Labor Day 1971 break-in at the office of the psychiatrist who had treated Pentagon Papers defen-dant Daniel Ellsberg. (Hunt had claimed that the notebooks contained names and addresses of persons involved in the Watergate scandal.)

Ben-Veniste did not explain how the material appeared in Nixon's estate file. A White House spokesman denied Nov. 5 that Nixon was aware the notebooks were in the file.

Watergate defendants sentenced. Six of the seven original Watergate defendants were given final prison sentences Nov. 9 by U.S. Chief District Court Judge John J. Sirica.

Eugenio Martinez, Virgilio Gonzalez and Frank Sturgis, Cuban residents of Miami, apprehended in the headquarters of the Democratic National Committee June 17, 1972, were sentenced to terms of one–four years in jail. Since the men had been in jail 11 months prior to sentencing, each would be eligible for parole in December.

Bernard L. Barker, a Miamian of Cuban extraction who recruited Martinez, Gonzalez and Sturgis, was sentenced to 18 months–six years in jail. Barker, who had also served 11 months, would be eligible for parole in mid-1974.

James W. McCord Jr., whose sentencing had been postponed March 23 after he told Sirica that others had perjured themselves during the trial, was given a prison term of one–five years.

E. Howard Hunt Jr., a member of the White House "plumbers" and the recruiter of Barker, was sentenced to 30 months–eight years in prison and fined $10,000. Hunt would be eligible for parole in the fall of 1975.

Jaworski to get access to documents. Special Watergate prosecutor Leon Jaworski informed U.S. District Court Judge Gerhard A. Gesell Nov. 14 that the White House had assured him he would have access to tapes and other documents relating to the work of the White House "plumbers" squad.

Stephen N. Shulman, attorney for former White House aide Egil Krogh Jr., had filed a motion with Gesell seeking access to a series of tapes of President Nixon's conversations concerning the work of the plumbers squad, which Krogh had headed. Krogh was indicted Oct. 11 on two counts of making false declarations to a federal prosecutor in connection with the 1971 break-in at the office of the psychiatrist treating Pentagon Papers defendant Daniel Ellsberg.

The affidavit from Jaworski to Gesell indicated that the special prosecutor's office would have access to the material in question and would give Krogh any information of an exculpatory nature.

Bars national security defense—In his first act as special prosecutor, Jaworski Nov. 12 filed a legal brief in U.S. district court in Washington, rejecting arguments that Krogh's action was justified by reason of national security when he lied under oath.

In seeking to have charges of making false declarations under oath dismissed against his client, Shulman, Krogh's lawyer, told Gesell that President Nixon had personally ordered Krogh to maintain the secrecy surrounding the activities of the plumbers squad, even if that meant lying under oath.

In opposing Krogh's motion, Jaworski said, "While the claim of national security gives these claims of legalized burglary and perjury a deceptively compelling ring, ultimately they rest on a wholesale rejection of the rule of law and espouse a doctrine that government officials may ignore the requirements of positive criminal statutes when they feel the circumstances dictate. No government office, not even the highest office in the land, carries the right to ignore the law's command, any more than orders of a superior can be used by government officers to justify illegal behavior."

Chapin indicted on perjury counts. Dwight L. Chapin, 32, President Nixon's former appointments secretary, was indicted by the special Watergate grand jury Nov. 29 on four counts of perjury.

The charges concerned statements Chapin made before the Watergate grand jury in April on his dealings with Donald H. Segretti, who was serving a six-month sentence at a federal correctional institution after pleading guilty to three misdemeanor charges citing his Nixon campaign activity in 1972.

Chapin, who left the White House in January, had worked there under former Nixon chief of staff H. R. Haldeman. Chapin had accompanied Nixon on his visits to China and the Soviet Union in 1972. He had not been called for public testimony before the Senate Watergate committee after it was told he would invoke his constitutional rights against self-incrimination. His indictment brought to 26 the number of individuals, as well as seven corporations, involved in court action arising from the Watergate scandal and related issues.

United Air Lines, which employed Chapin as director of market planning, said Nov. 29 it had granted him a leave of absence without pay to allow him to devote all his time to prepare his defense.

Grand jury extended. President Nixon Nov. 30 signed a bill providing for extension of the original Watergate grand jury six months to June 4, 1974. The bill also provided that a further six-month extension could be granted by the U.S. District Court for the District of Columbia if the grand jury requested. [See p. 134]

Krogh pleads guilty in Ellsberg break-in. Egil Krogh Jr., former head of the special White House investigations unit dubbed "the plumbers," pleaded guilty Nov. 30 to a civil rights charge stemming from the Labor Day 1971 break-in at the Los Angeles office of the psychiatrist who had treated Pentagon Papers defendant Daniel Ellsberg.

Krogh, who admitted seven overt acts that constituted a conspiracy to violate the rights of Dr. Lewis J. Fielding, faced a maximum of 10 years in prison and a $10,-000 fine.

In return for Krogh's guilty plea, the special U.S. prosecutor's office agreed to dismiss charges of making false declarations in connection with the break-in. Krogh told U.S. District Court Judge Gerhard Gesell he would cooperate with the special Watergate prosecutors after he had been sentenced.

In Los Angeles where Krogh faced state charges arising from the break-in, Superior Court Judge Gordon Ringer Dec. 3 accepted a recommendation by the Los Angeles County district attorney's office that charges against Krogh be dropped. Ringer said he had taken into account Krogh's guilty plea on the federal charges.

Prior to entering his plea before Gesell, Krogh read a short statement, which said in part, "I now feel that the sincerity of my motivation cannot justify what was done, and I cannot in conscience assert national security as a defense. . . . I simply feel that what was done in the Ellsberg operation was in violation of what I perceive to be a fundamental idea in this country—the paramount importance of the rights of the individual. I don't want to be associated with that violation any longer by attempting to defend it."

Chapin pleads innocent. Dwight Chapin, President Nixon's former appointments secretary and aide to former Nixon chief of staff H. R. Haldeman, pleaded not guilty Dec. 7 to charges he had lied to a federal grand jury investigating the Watergate case.

Chapin was accused of "making false declarations" when he said that he knew nothing about distribution of campaign material by Donald Segretti; that he had told Segretti to cooperate with the Federal Bureau of Investigation; that he could not recall instructing Segretti about tactics to pursue against Democratic candidates for the presidential nomination; and that he learned only from newspaper accounts about arrangements made to finance Segretti's campaign to discredit Democratic contenders.

Hunt, Barker freed for appeals. The U.S. Court of Appeals for the District of Columbia Dec. 28 ordered convicted Watergate defendants E. Howard Hunt Jr. and Bernard L. Barker released from prison without bail pending appeals. Both men had pleaded guilty but later requested permission to have the pleas withdrawn.

Agnew Resigns
after Plea Bargain

Agnew target of criminal probe. Vice President Spiro T. Agnew announced Aug. 6 he had been informed he was under investigation for possible violations of criminal law. The investigation was being conducted by George Beall, U.S. attorney for Maryland, concerning allegations of kickbacks by contractors, architects and engineers to officials of Baltimore County. Agnew was Baltimore County executive from 1962 to 1967 before his election as governor of Maryland.

Agnew held a televised press conference Aug. 8 to deny wrongdoing. He called reports that he took kickbacks "damned lies."

In his brief statement Aug. 6, Agnew had said he would make no further comment on the investigation until it was completed, "other than to say that I am innocent of any wrongdoing, that I have confidence in the criminal justice system of the United States and that I am equally confident my innocence will be affirmed."

Agnew's statement was issued late Aug. 6 after the Aug. 7 issue of the Wall Street Journal went to press with a story of the investigation of Agnew concerning allegations of bribery, extortion and tax fraud. The Journal had advised Agnew's office of its story. After Agnew's statement of innocence was published, Knight Newspapers carried a report that the government was investigating allegations that Agnew received $1,000 a week from contractors while county executive and governor and a lump sum payment of $50,000 after he became vice president.

There were further reports Aug. 8 that Agnew had retained the New York City law firm of Paul, Weiss, Rifkind, Wharton and Garrison and had met with President Nixon and that the probe was focusing on state contracts awarded during Agnew's tenure as governor in 1967–68 and on federal contracts by the General Services Administration in Maryland since Agnew became vice president in 1969.

Another target of the Baltimore probe, William E. Fornoff, administrative officer of Baltimore County under four executives (including Agnew and his Democratic successor, incumbent Dale Anderson), was reported to have pleaded guilty to a minor tax charge in exchange for testimony against other targets—politicians and businessmen.

Agnew: 'Nothing to hide'—At his news conference Aug. 8 in the Executive Office Building, adjacent to the White House, Agnew said he had "nothing to hide." He had "no expectation of being indicted," he said, and no intention of resigning.

Agnew said reports that he received payoffs from contractors were "false, scurrilous and malicious." He denounced as "damned lies" reports he took kickbacks of $1,000 a week from contractors.

Asked if ever had "a political slush fund financed by Baltimore County contractors," Agnew said "never." Had he ever received money from contractors or businessmen for his personal use? "Absolutely not." Had anyone "threatened to drag you into this unless you helped to kill the Baltimore County investigation?" "I'm not going to foreclose the possibility that such things may have happened," he said. "Neither am I going to assert at this moment that they did." But no one had directly asked him to kill the probe, Agnew said.

"Defamatory" statements were "being leaked to the news media," he said, and he could not "remain silent." Whatever their source, he asserted, "I have no intention to be skewered in this fashion."

Agnew suggested that the allegations against him be "looked at as accusations that are coming from those who have found themselves in very deep trouble and are looking to extricate themselves from this trouble and are flirting with the idea that they can obtain immunity or reduced charges, perhaps, by doing so."

Agnew said he first heard rumors of the Baltimore probe in February. He said he had retained Washington attorney Judah Best in April to assure U.S. attorney Beall "I would in no way attempt to impede the investigation."

He said he believed he discussed the matter in April with Nixon's chief of staff, Gen. Alexander Haig. He had not discussed the matter directly with Nixon until Aug. 7, he said, when he had a "far-reaching" conversation of an hour and three-quarters, during which Nixon' had "unequivocally" expressed his support. However, Agnew said, "I'm not spending my time looking around to see who's supporting me. I'm defending myself."

Agnew released the text of the letter from Beall notifying him of the investigation of allegations concerning possible violations by him and others of federal criminal statutes, including but not limited to conspiracy, extortion, extortion and bribery and certain tax provisions.

Agnew was invited in the letter to furnish the investigators with his financial records. Agnew said he had turned over the records to his attorneys but a final decision on their further disposition had not yet been made.

Nixon statement—President Nixon issued a statement through a spokesman Aug. 8 saying that the fact Agnew was under investigation was "no reason for the President to change his attitude about the vice president or his confidence in the vice president."

Agnew cooperates in inquiry. Vice President Spiro T. Agnew made his personal finance records available Aug. 14 to the U.S. attorney's office in Baltimore, Md. He also volunteered to answer questions in the investigation being conducted by that office into allegations of possible violations of criminal statutes involving bribery, tax fraud, extortion and conspiracy.

"I wish in no way to impede your investigation," Agnew said in a letter delivered by his counsel to the U.S. attorney, George Beall. "I have done nothing wrong. I have nothing to hide. And I have no desire save that justice be done speedily and efficiently."

In volunteering to open his records for inspection, which Beall had invited him to do, Agnew made several constitutional reservations. "I do not acknowledge that you or any grand jury have any right to the records of the vice president," he said. "Nor do I acknowledge the propriety of any grand jury investigation of possible wrongdoing on the part of the vice president so long as he occupies that office."

There were "difficult constitutional questions," Agnew said, "which need not at this moment be confronted."

Agnew said his "desire to cooperate" in the inquiry went beyond his consent to open his records. "I am eager to be of any help I can. Specifically, should you wish, I shall be glad to meet with you and your colleagues for a personal interview so that I may answer any questions you may have."

A personal interview had not been requested by Beall in his letter about the records.

Agnew said the records requested had been assembled and he was prepared to make them available to Beall "immediately."

The records of Agnew's two-year administration as governor of Maryland and "any and all" financial records of his campaign for the governorship were subpoenaed by federal investigators Aug. 10.

After his televised news conference Aug. 8 to deny wrongdoing and denounce charges against him as "scurrilous," Agnew flew the next day to the home of entertainer Frank Sinatra, in Palm Springs, Calif. for a vacation. He returned to Washington Aug. 13.

Nixon urges full federal probe—President Nixon was "interested in making sure that all appropriate steps" were taken by federal investigators in the Agnew case, Deputy White House Press Secretary Gerald L. Warren said Aug. 14. Warren stressed that the President was not intervening in the case and had not sought reports on it from the Justice Department.

Warren denied news reports that the President had urged Agnew not to turn personal papers over to the probers because of the possible adverse precedent concerning the President's own stand against producing certain presidential documents in the Watergate case.

Vice president denounces leaks. Vice President Spiro T. Agnew Aug. 21 denounced leaks to the press on the federal investigation in Baltimore concerning possible violations by him of certain criminal statutes.

In a nationally televised statement, Agnew said he could only assume from such press accounts "that some Justice Department officials have decided to indict me in the press whether or not the evidence supports their position."

This was "a clear and outrageous effort to influence the outcome of possible grand jury deliberations," Agnew charged.

He specifically referred to an article in the Aug. 27 issue of Time magazine, published Aug. 20, reporting the view of unidentified Justice Department officials that the case against Agnew was "growing steadily stronger and that an indictment appears inevitable."

Referring to his press conference Aug. 8 to rebut press allegations against him "coming from people who were actually participating in the investigation," Agnew said "since then the leaks have continued unabated." It had become clear, he said, "that sources so frequently quoted—were

indeed that—persons involved in the investigatory process." Agnew deplored "the impact which this smear publicity may have on the rights of others, particularly private citizens who have been swept into this highly publicized investigation."

Agnew said he had asked Attorney General Elliot L. Richardson to fulfill his promise and "vigorously" pursue an investigation of the possibility that his department was the source of such leaks. Agnew referred to a denial by Richardson Aug. 19 that any of the leaks came from his department.

In a reference to his earlier offer to meet with the U.S. Attorney George Beall conducting the investigation in Baltimore, Agnew was critical of Beall's handling of the case. Beall said "that he's not sure whether he even wishes to question me," Agnew said. "I suppose that if he only wants to hear one side of the story that's up to him. I will say only that it seems to me a very strange way to run an investigation."

Richardson statement—In his Aug. 19 statement, made on the ABC-TV "Issues and Answers" broadcast, Richardson said leaks about the Agnew case had caused him "considerable distress" but an investigation had satisfied him that Beall and his staff were not responsible for them. Richardson said he would discipline any department employe found culpable in the matter.

Richardson said he personally would decide whether the evidence found by the federal prosecutors would be presented to a grand jury, and that the decision involved another decision whether a vice president could be indicted for a crime while in office. He also assumed personal responsibility for the "ultimate resolution" of that constitutional issue.

Richardson defended his Aug. 6 meeting with Agnew about the Maryland probe to outline the substance of the evidence gathered against him. The meeting had been reported and confirmed. The reports had carried, as did the Time magazine account, allegations that at least three Agnew associates had informed prosecutors that they had delivered cash payments to Agnew. The Richardson meeting was said to have supplemented information Agnew received the week before in the letter informing him of the investigation.

After Agnew's Aug. 21 statement demanding a probe of departmental leaks, Richardson himself read a brief statement later Aug. 21 reaffirming his stand "that every reasonable step is being taken to assure" that the department "has not been and will not be the source of such publicity." While he "fully shared Agnew's "concern about unfair and inaccurate publicity," Richardson said, there was no "firm basis for the assumption that the information which has appeared in the press has come from law enforcement officials."

In any case, Richardson continued, "any plausible lead implicating" the department "will be pursued vigorously and appropriate disciplinary action will be taken against any department employe found to be responsible."

Beall also denied Aug. 21 that his prosecutors were "in any way" the source of the leaks.

Other developments in the Agnew probe. All nine federal judges in Maryland, six Republicans and three Democrats, disqualified themselves Aug. 15 from handling the grand jury probe involving Agnew because of Agnew's "unique position" and "his relationship to the state of Maryland." A Virginia federal judge, Walter E. Hoffman, was appointed to oversee the probe Aug. 18. The appointment was made by Chief Judge Clement F. Haynsworth of the 4th U.S. Circuit Court of Appeals encompassing Maryland.

■ There were press reports that some key Republican members of Congress were being cautioned from the White House to refrain from public comments on the Agnew case, presumably in his defense. Rep. John B. Anderson (Ill.), chairman of the House Republican Conference, admitted receiving advice from Melvin R. Laird, President Nixon's domestic adviser. Anderson said Aug. 20 the advice was to avoid "premature comments pending further investigation." Laird said the same day his advice was to "stay loose" in commenting. He denied Aug. 21 the advice was an attempt to undercut Agnew but said it was to "keep an open mind" on the probe. He said the call was made prior to Agnew's Aug. 8 news conference and he had talked to Agnew about the advice and "he understood."

■ Agnew attended a political rally in Maryland Aug. 18 on behalf of State Sen. Robert E. Bauman's bid for Congress. Speaking of the leaks from "informed sources close to the investigation," Agnew said "they don't have any hesitancy about violating my civil rights."

Nixon discusses Agnew at news meet. President Nixon fielded an intense barrage of questions on Watergate during most of a 50-minute news conference Aug. 22 on the lawn of his San Clemente home.

"My confidence in his integrity has not been shaken," Nixon said of the vice president, "and in fact it has been strengthened by his courageous conduct and his ability." Nixon said the charges against Agnew were "made about activities that occurred before he became vice president." It would be "improper" to comment on the charges, but not upon "the outrageous leak in information from either the grand jury or the prosecutors or the Department of Justice or all three." He said he had requested a full investigation by the department.

Not only "trying" an individual but "convicting him in the headlines and on television before he's had a chance to present his case in court is completely contrary to the American tradition. Even a vice president has a right to some . . . consideration in this respect, let alone the ordinary individual," the President said, and added, any federal employe who had leaked such information "will be summarily dismissed."

If Agnew were indicted, would Nixon "expect him to resign or somehow otherwise stand down temporarily until cleared?"

It would be inappropriate to comment on that, Nixon said. Agnew had not been indicted. "Charges have been thrown out by innuendo and otherwise," which Agnew "has denied to me personally and which he has denied publicly."

Baltimore successor indicted. Baltimore County Executive N. Dale Anderson was indicted Aug. 23 on 39 counts involving bribery, extortion and conspiracy. The indictment was returned by the federal grand jury investigating possible corruption of a number of leading Maryland businessmen and politicians, including Vice President Spiro T. Agnew.

Anderson, a Democrat, succeeded Agnew as county executive in 1966 and was re-elected in 1970. In a statement on the indictment, Agnew said he knew Anderson personally and found the charges against him "totally at variance with my impressions of him and everything I know about him." In his own associations with him, Agnew said, Anderson "exhibited unusual candor and integrity."

Anderson was charged with having received $46,420 in cash and $1,375 in checks in some 33 payments from 1968 to 1972 from eight companies doing business with the county on sewer, water, road and courthouse projects.

Named as a co-conspirator but not a defendant in the indictment was William E. Fornoff, former top aide in Baltimore County under both Agnew and Anderson. Fornoff resigned in June, pleading guilty to a tax violation and admitting he had acted as a conduit for cash payments between architects and engineers and an unnamed county official.

Agnew GOP committee indicted. In a separate investigation, an Anne Arundel County grand jury indicted on an election law violation a Maryland Republican committee that sponsored a 1972 testimonial dinner for Agnew. The indictment, announced Aug. 22, alleged a conspiracy to conceal a $49,900 contribution to the dinner, actually coming from Nixon re-election funds, as proceeds from ticket sales listed to 31 persons. [See p. 28]

Seven persons, including Maryland Republican friends or supporters of Agnew, were named in the indictment as unindicted co-conspirators (not charged with a crime). These included J. Walter Jones, a long-time Agnew fund-raiser and friend,

and Maryland Republican chairman Alexander Lankler.

Lankler entered a plea of not guilty on behalf of the committee Aug. 29, but in later statements, both he and the committee's lawyer, indicated that the innocent plea was procedural and that it would be changed to guilty.

Nixon, Agnew confer privately. President Nixon and Vice President Spiro T. Agnew conferred at the White House Sept. 1 on the federal investigation of possible criminal violations involving Agnew. No aides were present at the meeting.

Deputy White House Press Secretary Gerald L. Warren said afterward that "the vice president brought the President up to date on the matters concerning himself." Warren, who was briefed by the President after the two-hour meeting, told newsmen "a good discussion" was held. Agnew's press secretary, J. Marsh Thomson, called it "a relaxed discussion."

According to both spokesmen, Nixon and Agnew did not discuss the possible resignation of Agnew if he were indicted, the question of immunity against prosecution or selection of a replacement.

Nixon returned to Washington for the meeting after an 11-day stay at San Clemente, Calif. The meeting was announced the day before from San Clemente. Warren said it had been requested by Agnew.

At his news conference Sept. 5, Nixon was asked the topic of their discussion, whether he would take part in any future legal moves against Agnew and if he had called former Treasury Secretary John Connally Jr. afterward as reported.

Nixon said he had not talked to Connally for several weeks but "may be talking to him in the future about energy or about a trip that he is going to be making abroad."

As for the Agnew discussion, Nixon said he did not consider it appropriate to discuss its topic with newsmen. He said he would not dignify with an answer any questions about Agnew "with regard to the charges that have been made by innuendo and otherwise. . . . It would be an infringement on his rights."

Agnew poll rating drops—A Gallup Poll conducted after the disclosure of the probe against Agnew found Republican support for him as a possible 1976 presidential candidate declining to 22% and a tie with Gov. Ronald Reagan of California. The findings were released Aug. 29. In the previous such sampling in April, Agnew had a dominant lead over Reagan, 35% to 20%.

Agnew resignation rumors mount. Speculation that Vice President Spiro T. Agnew was considering resignation from office mounted as the federal investigation of possible criminal violations involving the vice president continued.

According to a report published by the New York Times Sept. 19, some high White House officials had been saying privately that it might be best for Agnew to resign and allow President Nixon to choose a new vice president.

According to a Washington Post report Sept. 20, a principal White House official had predicted Agnew's resignation in the "next few weeks." That report was said to have come from an "Eastern Republican" who was told by the official that Agnew's resignation "would give the President an opportunity to set a whole new tone for the Administration."

However, Gerald L. Warren, deputy White House press secretary, denied the Post report Sept. 20 and said Nixon was not seeking to apply any pressure on Agnew to leave office.

At a White House briefing Sept. 19, Warren had reaffirmed the President's Sept. 5 statement that he had "confidence in the vice president's integrity during the period that he had served as vice president." The investigation involving Agnew covered the period prior to his election as vice president in 1968.

A report by David S. Broder in the Post Sept. 18 had said Agnew held lengthy discussions recently on the "advisability of resigning voluntarily." It quoted "a senior Republican figure, strongly in Agnew's corner" as saying he was "99½% certain" Agnew would resign, "and probably this week." The source was reported to have attempted to dissuade Agnew but to have left a subsequent conversation with Agnew convinced he had failed.

Agnew was intent on such a course, according to the report, first because of the pressure on his family from his current position, facing, as he was, grand jury investigation of possible criminal wrongdoing, and secondly because of "the plain indication that the White House—and apparently the President himself—wants Agnew out." The source was reported to have expressed Agnew's determination to clear himself.

The Broder report stressed that Agnew staff members and his political supporters "expressed strong and uniform skepticism" that Agnew would, in fact, resign.

Reports identifying Sen. Barry Goldwater (R, Ariz.), a friend of Agnew, as the source of the Broder article were denied by Goldwater. "I don't think he's going to quit," Goldwater told reporters Sept. 18. "My hunch is that he's going to stay. I would advise him to fight it out."

But Goldwater's press spokesman, Anthony Smith, told reporters the same day reports that Goldwater was the source for the resignation speculation "appear to have come from somewhere in the White House." Smith said several persons had called the office on the source question and many of the callers indicated that Goldwater's name had been suggested by someone on the White House staff. Smith said "someone in the White House seems intent on convincing people that the source of that speculation was Sen. Goldwater."

At a news conference in New York Sept. 19, Goldwater expressed belief Agnew would consider resigning if he were indicted rather than have the country and himself go through the ordeal of a long impeachment process.

House Dems would seek caretaker— The New York Times reported Sept. 21 that House Democratic leaders assured a group of freshmen Democratic congressmen Sept. 19 that a caretaker vice president would be sought by them if Agnew were to resign.

"The will of the [House Democratic] leadership . . . was to strive for a stand-in vice president who would be committed to bypass the 1976 [presidential] election," the Times quoted one of the meeting's participants.

Democratic National Chairman Robert Strauss Sept. 20 echoed the concern of the House Democrats when he commented that President Nixon should avoid a "tricky, treacherous situation" by choosing a "nonpresidential person."

Agnew, Nixon hold 2 private meetings. The federal grand jury in Baltimore investigating political corruption began hearing evidence against Vice President Spiro T. Agnew Sept. 27 after Agnew had failed, at least temporarily, in an attempt to have the House investigate charges of violation of bribery, conspiracy and tax laws.

In an atmosphere of rumors and denials involving his possible resignation and reports of "plea bargaining" with the Justice Department, Agnew Sept. 25 attempted to block the grand jury proceeding by requesting the House to begin an inquiry into the case, arguing that any criminal proceeding against a vice president holding office was unconstitutional and that the House was the only proper forum for the case. After a meeting with House Democratic leaders Sept. 26, Speaker Carl Albert (D, Okla.) said he would take no action "at this time" on Agnew's request.

Agnew's approach to the House came after two private meetings with President Nixon, on Sept. 20 at Agnew's request and on Sept. 25 at Nixon's request.

Plea to House follows Nixon meetings— Before calling in Agnew Sept. 25, Nixon had conferred with Attorney General Elliot L. Richardson and Assistant Attorney General Henry E. Petersen for "an assessment of the investigation under way involving the vice president," according to deputy White House Press Secretary Gerald L. Warren. Nixon's meeting with Agnew was disclosed by Warren, who denied that Nixon had asked Agnew to resign or that anyone in the White House had been pressing Agnew to resign. Asked whether Agnew had offered to resign, Warren said Nixon and Agnew had agreed there would be no comment on the substance of their meeting.

Rumors of a resignation offer were strengthened later in the day when the

Dow Jones news service, citing unnamed sources, reported that Agnew had offered to resign and that the Justice Department had tentatively agreed to allow him to plead guilty to one minor charge. The report was denied by an Agnew spokesman.

Reportedly unaware that Agnew intended to approach the House regarding the charges, Richardson issued a statement late in the afternoon saying that the Baltimore grand jury would be presented with evidence involving the vice president. Although Agnew had informed Nixon of his intentions, the Washington Post reported Sept. 26 that the information had not been relayed to Richardson.

In his statement, the attorney general said he, Petersen and U.S. Attorney George Beall had been meeting with Agnew's attorneys since Sept. 12 "to discuss procedural aspects of the case and options available to the vice president" in an attempt to avoid a "constitutional dilemma of potentially serious consequence to the nation." But, said Richardson, a "satisfactory resolution" had not been reached.

Nixon and Agnew had met privately Sept. 20. Spokesmen for both refused to comment on the conversations, nor would they comment on reports that Agnew had been bargaining with the Justice Department on a possible guilty plea to minor charges.

House probe asked; Albert declines— Within half an hour after the Richardson statement was issued Sept. 25, Agnew met with Speaker Carl Albert and other House leaders of both parties to transmit a letter asking that the House, because of its "sole power of impeachment," investigate the charges against him.

Citing what he believed to be his constitutional immunity to ordinary court proceedings, Agnew said he "cannot acquiesce in any criminal proceeding being lodged against me in Maryland or elsewhere."

As a precedent for his request, Agnew relied on the 1826–27 case of Vice President John C. Calhoun, who had asked the House to inquire into newspaper allegations of profiteering on military contracts while Calhoun was secretary of war. A report by a select House committee had exonerated Calhoun.*

*The Calhoun case did not supply a complete parallel to the Agnew situation, since Calhoun was not the subject of a criminal investigation by a judicial body.

Calhoun had requested a House probe immediately after the Alexandria (Va.) Gazette, on Dec. 28, 1826, published—with editorial comment—a letter alleging that Calhoun had profited from an 1818 contract for a military fort.

The contract had been investigated in 1822 by a House committee, which had found no "facts which clearly stamp the transaction with a fraudulent character." The committee, however, expressed its "disapprobation of the conduct" of the War Department's engineering section.

As requested by Calhoun, the speaker appointed a seven-man committee to re-investigate the charges, and Calhoun temporarily relinquished his duties as presiding officer of the Senate. The committee issued its report Feb. 13, 1827, stating that Calhoun was innocent of the charge of having participated in War Department contracts. Calhoun resumed his duties the next day.

Noting that he had been the subject of "public attacks" that might "assume the character of impeachable offenses," Agnew called on the House to "discharge its constitutional obligation" and follow the Calhoun precedent.

After conferring with House Democratic leaders Sept. 26, Albert—without further comment—issued a statement which said in its entirety: "The vice president's letter relates to matters before the courts. In view of that fact, I, as speaker, will not take any action on the letter at this time."

House Republican Leader Gerald R. Ford Jr. (Mich.) called Albert's decision "unfortunate" and political but conceded that there would be little chance of a vote overturning it. Nevertheless, two Republican-sponsored resolutions were introduced Sept. 26 seeking some form of House inquiry. The first, by Rep. Paul Findley (Ill.), called for a select committee to determine whether the House should begin impeachment proceedings. The second, by John B. Anderson (Ill.) and William S. Cohen (Me.), called on Albert to appoint an "appropriate committee" to investigate whether any of Agnew's alleged improper activities occurred after he became vice president. (Anderson had said after Albert's statement that the speaker should have asked the Justice Department for such information before making his decision.)**

Fourteen Republican members of the Judiciary Committee Sept. 27 introduced a resolution directing the committee to investigate the charges and report to the House within three months. The resolution was sent to the Rules Committee.

Majority Whip John J. McFall (D, Calif.) said Sept. 26 that part of the reasoning behind a quick decision on the Agnew request was the fear that Agnew's lawyers might attempt to block the grand jury not only on broad constitutional grounds but with the procedural argument that an inquiry was pending in the House. But the basic reasoning, according to Judiciary Committee Chairman Peter W. Rodino Jr. (D, N.J.), was that the

**Lawyers for Agnew and House leaders concerned with impeachment precedents were reportedly studying the 1872–73 case of Vice President Schuyler Colfax, who had been charged with illegal activities, all of which took place before he became vice president in 1869.

A House committee began hearings in December 1872 into charges that Colfax, while speaker of the House, had been given shares in Credit Mobilier, the company formed to build, with government subsidies, the Union Pacific railroad. During its probe, the committee discovered other incidents of possible bribery. Despite the evidence of misconduct, the committee concluded that impeachment was intended to remove a person from an office he had abused while occupying it. The committee decided not to impeach.

On the question of whether a vice president could be indicted while in office, some legal historians cited the 1804 indictment of Vice President Aaron Burr on state charges of murder in connection with the slaying of Alexander Hamilton in a duel in New Jersey. Both the crime and the indictment occurred while Burr was vice president. Burr was never arrested or prosecuted on the charge.

question of the validity of Agnew's "broad claim of immunity from criminal prosecution" while holding office could not be resolved by Congress "but must be dealt with by the courts."

Nixon urges fairness; role denied—In a statement issued Sept. 25, Nixon said that during their meeting earlier in the day Agnew had, as in previous meetings, denied the charges made against him. [See text] Nixon urged that Agnew be accorded "the same presumption of innocence which is the right of any citizen." Nixon again gave Agnew a measure of support, noting that "during these past four and a half years, the vice president has served his country with dedication and distinction."

Responding to questions Sept. 26, Deputy Press Secretary Warren said Nixon had taken a neutral position on Agnew's decision to take his case to the House. And, said Warren, Nixon had neither approved nor disapproved Richardson's move to send the evidence to the grand jury.

Warren said that during the Nixon-Agnew meeting the "options available" to the vice president had been discussed, including the possibility of Agnew's resignation. Agnew told newsmen later that "the President and I have not discussed that possibility. I want to make it very clear that I am not resigning." (Agnew also denied that he or his attorneys had "initiated any plea bargaining" with the Justice Department. [See above])

Informed later of Agnew's statement on resignation, Warren attempted to clarify his earlier comment, saying that "in the broad context of options open to the vice president, resignation did come up. There was no detailed discussion of resignation. No resignation was asked for and none was offered."

Grand jury meets—The federal grand jury in Baltimore held its first session on the Agnew evidence Sept. 27 under strict conditions of secrecy. Several witnesses were reportedly heard, but only one, William J. Muth, commented publicly afterwards.

Muth, a public relations man and former Agnew fund raiser, denounced the proceedings and said he had declined to answer questions on 5th Amendment grounds. He acknowledged that he was also a target of the grand jury investigation.

Judah Best, one of Agnew's attorneys, said Sept. 27 that a motion would be filed to block the investigation.

Agnew tells friends he will fight—Agnew had been telling friends he would not resign, even if indicted, and that he would continue his efforts to have the House investigate the charges against him, the

New York Times reported Sept. 28. But, the Times said, Agnew had abandoned any hope of a Presidential nomination in 1976.

According to the Times, Agnew had decided to appeal to the House after Assistant Attorney General Petersen was quoted by a television reporter Sept. 22 as saying "We've got the evidence [on Agnew]. We've got it cold."

The incident increased Agnew's anger over Justice Department leaks in the case. The Times said Agnew had become convinced that the leaks were coming from high officials in the department and that the grand jury proceedings would be "utterly poisoned."

Agnew was not critical of Nixon's handling of the affair, the Times reported, but he was "less sure" about some members of Nixon's staff.

Lawyers launch 2-pronged attack. Lawyers for Vice President Spiro T. Agnew filed suit in federal district court in Baltimore Sept. 28 in an attempt to halt the grand jury investigation of possible criminal violations by Agnew.

In a formal motion and accompanying affidavit, Agnew's lawyers launched a two-pronged attack on the investigation, citing constitutional restraints on the prosecution of a vice president in office, and charging the Justice Department with conducting "a deliberate campaign" of news leaks "calculated and intended to deprive [Agnew] of his basic rights to due process and fair hearing."

The suit asked the court to prohibit the grand jury "from conducting any investigation looking to possible indictment" of Agnew and from "issuing any indictment, presentment or other charge or statement" pertaining to the vice president. The suit also petitioned the court "to enjoin the attorney general of the United States, the United States attorney for the District of Maryland and all officials of the United States Department of Justice from presenting to the grand jury any testimony, documents or other materials" that might be used to indict Agnew. It asked the court to bar the department from "discussing with or disclosing to any person any such testimony, documents or materials."

Citing the "awesome responsibility" of Agnew's office, the suit said the nation should "not be deprived of his services while he defends himself against an indictment voted by perhaps 12 of 23 grand jurors, or an information filed at the whim of a prosecutor."

The suit asked further that if the Justice Department "asserts its innocence of wrongdoing" regarding news leaks, the court should hold a separate hearing on that issue.

In a statement issued later Sept. 28, the Justice Department said it was "patently ridiculous" for Agnew to assert that the

investigation was a plot to drive him from office. The statement contended that the alleged leaks would in fact defeat the purpose of the probe.

After meeting with representatives of both sides, U.S. District Court Judge Walter E. Hoffman of Norfolk, Va.—who had been assigned to oversee the investigation after Maryland judges had disqualified themselves—ruled that the grand jury could continue to hear evidence pending his final decision on the suit. Final arguments were set for Oct. 12.

Subpoena power on leaks granted—In an unusual action Oct. 3, Judge Hoffman authorized Agnew's attorneys to investigate—with full powers of subpoena—the alleged news leaks by Justice Department officials. Under Hoffman's order, the lawyers could privately question under oath and take sworn depositions from any persons they deemed "appropriate and necessary."

Hoffman ordered that transcripts of the depositions be sealed and kept from public court records, and all lawyers involved in the case were directed to withhold comment on the depositions. Hoffman also required that Agnew's attorneys notify the Justice Department 48 hours before witnesses were questioned.

Some lawyers were quoted Oct. 4 as believing that Hoffman's order was unprecedented in that a person under criminal investigation but not yet under indictment was granted such broad authority to question prosecutors and others involved.

The order was also seen as a potential source of further constitutional issues in the Agnew case if reporters questioned by his attorneys refused to reveal their sources.

In another action Oct. 3, Judge Hoffman summoned the grand jurors to an open session and delivered a special charge cautioning them to "disregard totally any comments you might have seen or heard from any source, save and except what you have heard or seen in your grand jury room while in official session."

Hoffman called the press "integral and necessary," but added that "unfortunately, in the present-day grab for priority in getting news items, the news media frequently overlook the rights of others, especially where criminal matters are involved."

Hoffman also cautioned the jurors to disregard one of the major constitutional issues raised by Agnew's attorneys, saying they were not to be "concerned with whether a person is immune from indictment or trial."

Agnew attacks prosecution. In a speech delivered in Los Angeles Sept. 29, Vice President Agnew reasserted his innocence of criminal charges and issued a bitter denunciation of the Justice Department's handling of his case.

Speaking to a cheering, sympathetic audience at the convention of the National Federation of Republican Women, Agnew said that because of "these tactics which have been employed against me, . . . I will not resign if indicted."

Agnew first delivered a prepared text devoted to a general discussion of the need for secrecy in grand jury proceedings, the violation of which, he said, had led "during the past few months" to a "cruel form of trial in the media."

In the informal remarks which followed, Agnew said—without naming Assistant Attorney General Henry E. Petersen directly—that "conduct of high individuals in the Department of Justice, particularly the conduct of the chief of the criminal investigation division, is unprofessional and malicious and outrageous, if I am to believe what has been printed in the news magazines and said on the television networks. . . ."

Agnew said he intended to use the courts in an attempt "to examine under oath those people who are trying to destroy me politically through the abuse of the criminal justice system. . . ." If department employes were found to "have abused their sacred trust and forsaken their professional standards," Agnew added, he would ask President Nixon to "summarily discharge" them.

Referring to the apparent inconsistency of a Republican vice president being the target of a Republican Justice Department, Agnew said "individuals in the upper professional echelons" had been "severely stung by their ineptness in the prosecution of the Watergate case" and the necessity of appointing a special prosecutor. "They are trying to recoup their reputation at my expense," Agnew said. "I'm a big trophy." And "one of those individuals," Agnew said, had not only "failed to get any of the information out about the true dimensions of the Watergate matter," but had through "ineptness and blunder" hampered the prosecution of "high crime figures" because of wiretapping errors.

Agnew criticized the use of immunity in the Maryland probe, saying that "small and fearful men have been frightened into furnishing evidence against me." He added that it was his "understanding" that in many cases they had perjured themselves.

Agnew also rebutted press criticism of his attempt to have the House consider his case as, in his words, "attempting to hide behind a constitutional shield and suppress the facts." Rather, Agnew said, he was seeking the "fullest possible hearing [of the charges], widely publicized . . . I'm not trying to hide anything."

In a statement released later Sept. 29, Attorney General Elliot L. Richardson defended Petersen as a "distinguished

government lawyer" who was "constrained from defending himself" against Agnew's attack "by the ethical standards governing a criminal investigation." Final responsibility for the department's conduct of the Agnew investigation, Richardson added, rested with the attorney general.

Deputy White House Press Secretary Gerald L. Warren said Oct. 1 that Richardson had assured Nixon that Petersen was not the source of the "we've got the evidence. We've got it cold" quote which had reportedly angered Agnew.

Further clarification was offered by Fred P. Graham, the Columbia Broadcasting System reporter who had cited Petersen's remarks. In a letter to the New York Times Oct. 1, Graham said Petersen "has never discussed the merits" of the Agnew case with him. Graham said he had made it clear in his broadcast that an unnamed "source close to the negotiations" had told him Petersen had made the comment during a meeting with Agnew's lawyers.

Deputy Attorney General William D. Ruckelshaus said later that Petersen did not recall making the comment, nor did Richardson remember hearing it. And, asked Ruckelshaus, "who stands to lose the most" from the incident? He added that the Justice Department would suffer if the case were harmed by prejudicial publicity.

In a letter to the Washington Post Oct. 3, Agnew criticized newspaper misuse of Graham's television report, saying it did not "make a great deal of difference who in the Justice Department dropped this little morsel in the hands of Mr. Graham. The fact remains that four newspapers of considerable circulation left the distinct impression . . . that Mr. Petersen made this improper, unprofessional and highly prejudicial comment."

Agnew said he had since become concerned over the Justice Department implications that the leak of Petersen's remark had come from Agnew's own attorneys. He said his attorneys were "willing to sign affidavits that they did not discuss anything concerning the meeting with the news media."

Nixon backs Agnew, Petersen. President Nixon told a news conference Oct. 3 that Agnew's determination not to resign even if indicted was "altogether proper," but took issue with Agnew's criticism of Assistant Attorney General Petersen's handling of the investigation.

Nixon said he had never requested Agnew's resignation and that Agnew's decision to remain in office "should be respected." The President drew a distinction between Agnew, who was "elected by all the people," and Nixon's appointed aides, who he had said would be suspended if indicted in relation to the Watergate case.

As for the charges against Agnew, Nixon noted they had been denied publicly and "to me privately on three occasions." Other aspects of his conversations with Agnew on the case were "privileged," Nixon said.

Asked whether there was substance to Agnew's assertion that the investigation was a "frame-up" and a "smear," Nixon said he had been briefed "on what it is believed the witnesses might testify to," and that the charges were "serious and not frivolous." Agnew's concern, which Nixon said he shared, was rather that leaks "had convicted him in advance."

Nixon then said he accepted Richardson's assurances that neither Petersen nor members of his office in the Justice Department had acted improperly. Nixon added "if I did not support Mr. Petersen's handling of the investigation, he would have been removed at this time."

Responding to another question, Nixon said there had "certainly not" been any "contingency planning" for a possible replacement for Agnew should he leave office. Nixon again urged that Agnew be presumed innocent until his case was heard, adding that this presumption of innocence "should be underlined in view of his years of distinguished service as vice president; having in mind, too, the fact that the charges that have been made against him do not relate in any way to his activities as vice president of the United States."

Defense fund formed. W. Clement Stone of Chicago, a major contributor to Nixon's presidential campaigns, Sept. 28 announced formation of a "defense fund" to assure that Agnew would have "the best possible legal counsel to defend himself." Stone said two other trustees of the fund would be Sen. Barry M. Goldwater (R, Ariz.) and Warren E. Hearnes, a former Democratic governor of Missouri.

Stone said there was "no reason why the names [of contributors] should not be disclosed" and that Agnew had insisted that the fund not accept contributions offered on condition of secrecy. Stone added that he had not discussed the fund or other aspects of Agnew's case with President Nixon.

Anderson indicted on taxes. N. Dale Anderson, the Democrat who succeeded Agnew as Baltimore County executive in 1966, was indicted Oct. 4 on four counts of failing to pay federal income taxes. The indictment was returned by the same grand jury investigating Agnew. Anderson had been indicted earlier on charges of bribery, extortion and conspiracy.

The indictment charged that Anderson had avoided paying taxes of $67,834 on unreported income totaling $131,189 during the years 1969-72. According to the indictment, $122,208 of the unreported income was received in the election years 1970 and 1972.

The latest indictment superseded the earlier one and included all of its 39 counts. Anderson had pleaded not guilty to the previous charges Sept. 14.

Vice President resigns, pleads no contest to tax evasion. Spiro T. Agnew, twice elected vice president of the U.S., resigned his office Oct. 10 and pleaded no contest (nolo contendere) to one count of income tax evasion. In return, the Justice Department agreed to drop all pending charges against Agnew and request leniency on the tax evasion charge.

In a dramatic courtroom hearing in Baltimore shortly after he submitted his letter of resignation, Agnew avoided imprisonment by pleading no contest to a federal charge that he had failed to report $29,500 of income he received in 1967, when he was governor of Maryland. Such a plea, while not an admission of guilt, war tantamount to a plea of guilty on the charge. Agnew had faced federal indictment for violation of bribery, conspiracy and tax laws.

Agnew's action touched off an immediate search by President Nixon for a successor. Nixon began meeting with Congressional leaders of both parties and with George Bush, chairman of the Republican National Committee, in an effort to set up procedures to be followed in selecting a new vice president.

As required by law, Agnew's formal instrument of resignation was a statement transmitted to Secretary of State Henry A. Kissinger. The statement, delivered at 2:05 p.m., said in its entirety: "I hereby resign the Office of Vice President of the United States, effective immediately." Agnew became only the second vice president in U.S. history to resign.*

House Speaker Carl Albert (D, Okla.) became next in line for the presidency until the office of vice president was filled, for the first time, under the provisions of the 25th Amendment to the Constitution, ratified in 1967.

Agnew also formally notified President Nixon by letter, saying "the accusations against me cannot be resolved without a long, divisive and debilitating struggle in the Congress and in the courts." Agnew had concluded that it was "in the best interest of the nation" that he relinquish the office.

Nixon said in his letter of acceptance that Agnew's resignation "leaves me with a great sense of personal loss." He praised Agnew's "strong patriotism" and "all that you have contributed to the nation by your years of service as vice president." But, said Nixon, "I respect your decision, and I also respect the concern for the national interest" which led to the conclusion that resignation "was advisable in order to prevent a protracted period of national division and uncertainty."

*After a series of policy disputes with President Andrew Jackson, Vice President John C. Calhoun resigned Dec. 28, 1832 to take a Senate seat to which he had been appointed by the South Carolina legislature.

The letters were exchanged amid indications of a persistent conflict between Nixon and Agnew on the issue of resignation. According to the New York Times Oct. 11, "close and authoritative associates" of Agnew said that contrary to Nixon's public denials, he had at least twice asked Agnew to resign after the Aug. 6 disclosure of the Maryland investigation. White House Press Secretary Ronald L. Ziegler said Oct. 10 that Nixon had played "no direct role" in the "personal decision only the vice president could make."

Ziegler said Agnew had informed Nixon of his decision in a private meeting the evening of Oct. 9, after Agnew's attorneys had reached agreement with the Justice Department earlier in the day.

Almost simultaneously with the delivery of his resignation letter to Kissinger, Agnew appeared before U.S. District Court Judge Walter E. Hoffman in Baltimore to plead no contest to the charge of filing a "false and fraudulent" income tax return for the year 1967 and attempting to evade payment of $13,551.47 in federal taxes. According to the charge, Agnew had understated his and Mrs. Agnew's joint income by $29,500.

Hoffman asked Agnew if he understood the implications of waiving indictment and entering a plea of no contest, which, Hoffman noted, was "the full equivalent of a plea of guilty" and would protect Agnew only in that it could not be used in a civil suit as evidence that Agnew had actually committed the offense. As Hoffman pointed out in a formal statement, a no contest plea used in tax evasion cases "merely permits the parties to further litigate the amount due without regard to the conviction following such a plea."

Hoffman cited the provisions of Agnew's agreement with the Justice Department: that Agnew resign; that the department would not prosecute on other charges while reserving the right to use Agnew's name in proceedings against others; and that Agnew might still be subject to action by the State of Maryland "or some private organization."

"Do you understand and ratify the agreement as I have stated it?" Hoffman asked.

"I do so understand it," Agnew said.

Agnew was sentenced to a fine of $10,000 and three years' unsupervised probation. Hoffman said that without the recommendation for leniency by Attorney General Elliot L. Richardson, he would have been inclined to follow his usual procedure in tax evasion cases of imposing a fine and prison sentence of two to five months. But, Hoffman added, "I am persuaded that the national interests in the present case are so great and so compelling . . . that the ends of justice would be better served by making an exception to the general rule."

In a statement read to the court, Richardson said no agreement could have been reached without a provision that he appeal for leniency. Mindful of the "historic magnitude of the penalties inherent in the vice president's resignation from his high office and his acceptance of a judgment of conviction of a felony," Richardson said that a prison sentence was more than he could "recommend or wish."

Richardson emphasized that a central element of the agreement was that the department be allowed to present the details of its other evidence against Agnew while agreeing to waive prosecution based on it.

Richardson said that for the people to "fairly judge the outcome" of the Agnew case, he would offer "for the permanent record" an "exposition of evidence" which "establishes a pattern of substantial cash payments to the defendant during the period when he served as governor of Maryland in return for engineering contracts with the State of Maryland." Richardson added that none of the government's major witnesses had been promised immunity from prosecution and that each who would have testified to making direct payments to Agnew had signed a sworn statement "subject to the penalties of perjury."

According to the "exposition of evidence," Agnew—shortly after becoming governor in 1967—established a system of taking payments from engineering firms. I.H. Hammerman 2d, a Baltimore investment banker, acted as "collector" from companies designated by Jerome B. Wolff, then chairman of the Maryland State Roads Commission. After initial disagreements about division of the payments, the three agreed—on Agnew's order—that the payments would be divided 50% for Agnew and 25% each for Hammerman and Wolff. The three would then discuss which firms should be awarded contracts, but "the governor always exercised the final decision-making authority."

The evidence also detailed the relationship between Agnew and the presidents of two engineering firms who made direct cash payments. Agnew allegedly complained to Allen Green of Green Associates, Inc. about the "financial burdens" of the office of governor, and Green began making payments which continued until the beginning of the Maryland grand jury investigation in January 1973.

A similar relationship existed with Lester Matz of Matz, Childs and Associates who also continued making "corrupt payments" to Agnew after he became vice president. In addition to payments "still owed" for contracts awarded to Matz while Agnew was Maryland governor, Matz allegedly paid $2,500 in April 1971 in return for the awarding of a federal contract to a Matz company.

According to the evidence, Agnew received payments totaling about $100,000.

Green and Hammerman had agreed to plead guilty to single tax charges and to cooperate with the prosecution. Matz and Wolff had agreed to cooperate with the prosecution with assurances that their testimony before the grand jury would not be used against them in subsequent criminal trials.

In acknowledging to the court that he had received taxable payments in 1967, Agnew conceded that such payments had been made by companies receiving state contract awards in 1967 "and other years," but he denied that the payments had "in any way" influenced his official actions. He stressed that no contracts were awarded to "contractors who were not competent to perform the work and in most instances state contracts were awarded without any arrangement for the payment of money by the contractor."

Judge Hoffman said it would have been his "preference" to omit the evidence presented by Richardson, which Hoffman said was "totally unrelated to the charge of income tax evasion." He added that all parties agreed that he must disregard the other charges in considering sentence.

Settlement voids other issues—Agnew's plea of no contest to the tax evasion charge and the Justice Department's agreement not to pursue prosecution rendered moot the litigation on two constitutional issues which had become central to the Agnew case: whether a vice president could be indicted while in office and the confidentiality of newsmen's sources. At the end of the Agnew hearing Oct. 10, Judge Hoffman said the questions had no further legal standing in the Agnew case.

Agnew's attorneys, acting on Hoffman's authority, had issued subpoenas Oct. 5 to reporters and news organizations allegedly involved in receiving leaks on the Agnew case from the Justice Department. Subpoenas for "all writings and other forms of record (including drafts)" reflecting on sources were served on Richard M. Cohen, Washington Post; Nicholas Gage, New York Times; Ronald Sarro and Robert Walters, Washington Star-News; William Sherman, New York Daily News; Stephan Lesher, Newsweek magazine; Ronald Nessen, National Broadcasting Company; and Fred P. Graham, Columbia Broadcasting System.

Newsweek and Time magazines were subpoenaed for the testimony of all staff members who had written or contributed to certain stories on Agnew. Justice Department officials were also subpoenaed, and all were scheduled to appear for questioning Oct. 11, in Hoffman's presence.

Spokesmen for the news organizations were unanimous in their determination to fight the subpoenas on First Amendment grounds. They noted that in the 1972 Supreme Court decision subjecting newsmen to subpoena on confidential information, Associate Justice Lewis F. Powell Jr. had said the courts were "available to newsmen in instances where legitimate First Amendment interests are in question and require protection." Lawyers also noted that the 1972 case involved newsmen who were allegedly direct witnesses to criminal acts, while the current subpoenas were a part of Agnew's civil

action to halt the grand jury investigation by proving potentially prejudicial news leaks.

The Justice Department filed its first reply Oct. 5 to Agnew's suit to stop the probe, arguing that a vice president could be indicted and tried on criminal charges while in office, but offering to submit the evidence to the House for possible impeachment proceedings before trial if Agnew were indicted.

In its memorandum to the court, the department contended that a president should not be made to answer criminal charges while in office, since such an action would "incapacitate" the government. In contrast, the department said, the office of vice president—while a "high one"—was not "indispensible to the orderly operation of government."

A department spokesman later Oct. 5 dismissed the suggestion that the argument on presidential immunity could be related to the issue of Nixon's refusal to surrender the tapes of Watergate conversations. The spokesman noted that in the Agnew case the issues were indictment and trial, whereas the controversy over the Watergate tapes centered on the President's compliance with a subpoena.

In a second reply to the Agnew suit Oct. 8, the department branded as "frivolous" Agnew's charges of a deliberate campaign of news leaks and accused the Agnew defense of a "fishing expedition" in subpoenaing newsmen.

The department also submitted the results of its internal investigation of Agnew's charges, which, the department said, indicated that Justice officials were not necessarily the source of leaks. "There appears to be," the document stated, "a high correlation between the facts transmitted by the Department of Justice to the White House and/or the vice president and the disclosures which have appeared in the press."

The department urged a speedy decision on whether the grand jury could proceed with its investigation, since the federal statute of limitations would expire on some of the charges against Agnew as early as Oct. 26.

Newsmen and lawyers were in Baltimore Oct. 10, prepared to argue motions which had been filed to quash their subpoenas. The issue was almost forgotten as Agnew and Richardson appeared for their historic day in court.

Richardson defends agreement. Urging "consideration and compassion" for Agnew, Attorney General Elliot L. Richardson Oct. 11 called the agreement culminating in Agnew's resignation "just and honorable" to the parties involved, "but above all to the American people."

Speaking at a joint news conference with Maryland U.S. Attorney George Beall, Richardson reiterated his feeling that leniency for Agnew had been justified. While commending Beall and his assistants for their "tenacious pursuit of justice and wise counsel" in the case, Richardson acknowledged that "they did

not always agree with me, particularly with regard to the painful issue of sentencing."

Asked whether acceptance of a plea to a single count of tax evasion might have been too lenient in view of the weight of the evidence accumulated against Agnew, Richardson replied that "the very essence of a negotiated plea" was the yielding by both sides to achieve agreement.

Richardson added that the Justice Department had not initiated the plea bargaining. He said the first period of negotiations—which had failed—had begun in early September after a call from "the President's counsel" asking if Richardson would be willing to meet with Agnew's attorneys. Responding to a later question, Richardson said the call had come from White House counsel J. Fred Buzhardt Jr., who, Richardson said, "did not indicate that he was acting at the President's behest." Richardson said Buzhardt had "at various stages" of the negotiations served in a capacity of "facilitating communications."

Referring to Nixon's personal role in the negotiations, Richardson said the President had been kept "fully informed at all times" and had "fully approved each of the major steps." But, Richardson added, Nixon had not participated "in the negotiations as such," nor had he suggested any of the elements of the agreement. According to Richardson, the President also felt "it was not appropriate for him to be informed of the details of the case."

Richardson said he had first discussed the case with Nixon in early August after informing White House chief of staff Alexander M. Haig Jr. in July. He had "no reason" to believe that Nixon knew of Agnew's misconduct before then.

Beall was asked about his disagreements with Richardson on the degree of leniency to be extended to Agnew. Beall sought to play them down as "honest" and understandable differences, noting that "our vantage point in Baltimore was entirely different than the attorney general's vantage point in Washington." Beall added that the federal investigation in Maryland would continue.

Asked about possible further prosecution of Agnew, Richardson pointed out that the agreement did not preclude action by state prosecutors. Asked whether his department would aid such an action, Richardson said he would "consider what steps to take," adding that the lengthy criminal information filed with Judge Hoffman was now a matter of record. He also noted that Agnew remained subject to civil tax action by the Internal Revenue Service.

Richardson rejected a suggestion that the agreement with Agnew had reflected "permissiveness" on the part of the Justice Department and was a political rather than a prosecutorial judgment. He said, however, that "in the fundamental sense" of the word, the agreement was indeed seriously "political" since a lengthy and divisive prosecution of the person second in line to the presidency would not have been in the national interest.

Buzhardt role detailed—Contrary to Richardson's assertion that the role in the Agnew case of presidential counsel J. Fred Buzhardt Jr. had been one of "facilitating communications" during the negotiations, Agnew's attorneys and Administration sources portrayed a more important role.

Judah Best, one of Agnew's lawyers, said Oct. 11 that the key meeting to work out the final details of the agreement was between him and Buzhardt in a Miami hotel Oct. 5–6. According to the Agnew defense team, the core of the Best-Buzhardt accord was that Agnew would be free to deny in court the charges in the criminal information submitted by the Justice Department and would retain the right to review the summary of the government's evidence against him.

According to the New York Times Oct. 12, a "source close to Agnew's lawyers" said the document detailing the Agnew payoff system was about "10%" of the evidence developed by the prosecution.

The Times also cited Administration sources as saying that Buzhardt had assumed the role of middleman at Nixon's behest. According to one official, Buzhardt "couldn't do that without the full cognizance, support and direction of the President."

Sources "close to Agnew" told the Times that Agnew had been prepared to resign in exchange for a halt to the prosecution as early as Sept. 13, the occasion of the first negotiating session with the Justice Department. The most troublesome point in the talks was the extent to which the department would be allowed to reveal evidence against Agnew. According to the sources, the talks dragged on without agreement because Agnew felt that his bargaining position was worsening because of the news leaks on the evidence. Then, as a tactical move to strengthen his position with the Justice Department, Agnew tried to have the House consider his case and issued the declaration that he would not resign.

Leaders shocked by action. Agnew's surprise resignation stunned Congressional and other political leaders of both parties.

House Speaker Carl Albert (D, Okla.), who became next in line in succession to the presidency, and whose security guard was increased within minutes of the announcement of Agnew's resignation, said he learned of the resignation "with surprise and shock." Agnew had advised him by letter, he said, and "under the Constitution the matter is now in the hands of the President and I have no further comment."

House Republican Leader Gerald R. Ford (Mich.) reacted with disbelief, then "great sadness." Senate Democratic Leader Mike Mansfield's (Mont.) reaction was, "I just don't know what to say."

Senate Republican Leader Hugh Scott (Pa.) issued a statement: "I admire him as a man. I admired and respected him as a

vice president. I recognize his courage and dedication to his country in making his decision."

Former Missouri Gov. Warren E. Hearnes, a Democrat but trustee of a legal defense fund being organized for Agnew, described the tone of Agnew's call informing him of the resignation: "It was like someone in the family had died." (W. Clement Stone, head of the Agnew defense fund, said Oct. 11 that all contributions to the fund would be returned at Agnew's request.

Republican National Chairman George Bush, said, "for myself and the entire Republican party, I deeply regret but thoroughly understand why Mr. Agnew found it necessary to take this action." "The action took great personal courage," Bush said, but "in the circumstances it clearly was in the best interest of the country."

Sen. Robert Dole (Kan.), former GOP national chairman, thought it would hurt the party. The party "has been temporarily hurt by Watergate and this would be another blow," he said

Gov. Nelson A. Rockefeller (R, N.Y.), considered a possible nominee for the vacant vice presidency, disagreed. He said it was "a personal tragedy, not a party tragedy."

Rep. John J. Rhodes (R, Ariz.), chairman of the House Republican Policy Committee, raised the question of succession. He hoped the President would promptly select a replacement "of unquestionable credentials so that his confirmation will be carried out swiftly." "We must do everything necessary," Rhodes said, "to restore the confidence of the American people in their government."

Another potential nominee for the vacancy, Gov. Ronald Reagan (R, Calif.), said, "Ted Agnew was and is a friend of mine. I am shocked and saddened as I am sure all Americans are."

Sen. Barry M. Goldwater (R, Ariz.) criticized the Administration for its handling of the Agnew case. Agnew had been "threatened shamefully by persons in responsible government positions," Goldwater said, and "in effect was tried and judged in a manner completely foreign to the proper pursuit of justice in the United States, a manner which convicted him by headlines and newscasts based on leaks of official information but before a single legal charge had been filed."

Search for a successor. The question of a successor to the vice president quickly became the dominant issue at the White House and in Congress. A planned Oct. 12–29 Senate recess was canceled, and Congressional leaders began discussing procedures to handle confirmation of a vice presidential nominee, a situation unprecedented in the nation's history.

According to the 25th Amendment to the Constitution, which went into effect in February 1967, Section 2, relating to a vacancy in office of Vice President, stated: "Whenever there is a vacancy in the office

of the Vice President, the President shall nominate a Vice President who shall take the office upon confirmation by a majority vote of both houses of Congress."

Among other questions, the Congressional discussions covered whether the confirmation vote should be taken in joint session or separately by each house of Congress, and, if the latter, in what order; and whether there should be confirmation hearings and if so by what committee, a special "select" committee or a standing committee.

The political question brought up previously by the Democrats, the majority party in both houses, was also raised: concern over a nominee whose stature could carry him from the vice presidency into the Republican presidential candidacy for 1976.

Meanwhile, the White House promised prompt action on a successor. "President Nixon intends to move expeditiously in selecting a nominee and he trusts the Congress will then act promptly to consider the nomination," White House Press Secretary Ronald L. Ziegler announced Oct. 10 after word of Agnew's resignation became public.

Nixon met that day with Republican Congressional leaders. He talked with GOP National Chairman George Bush and Sen. James O. Eastland (D, Miss.), chairman of the Senate Judiciary Committee. Later he consulted with House Speaker Carl Albert (D, Okla.) and Senate Democratic Leader Mike Mansfield (Mont.).

The President asked for suggestions— up to three names each—from the Republican members of the House and Senate, the 19 Republican governors, members of the Republican National Committee and the GOP state chairmen. The suggested nominations were to be received in sealed letters, signed or unsigned.

Mansfield, who along with Albert also had been invited to present recommendations, offered his choices at a news conference Oct. 10: Former Secretary of State William P. Rogers and former Sen. John Sherman Cooper (R, Ky.).

Other speculation on possible choices centered on former Treasury Secretary John B. Connally Jr., who became a Republican in 1973, Chief Justice Warren E. Burger, White House counselor Melvin R. Laird, New York Gov. Nelson Rockefeller (R), former Gov. William W. Scranton (R, Pa.) and Gov. Ronald Reagan (R, Calif.).

Senate GOP Leader Hugh Scott (Pa.) stressed after meeting with Nixon that the President was keeping an "open mind" on the selection. He also reported a qualification the President was applying to the selection, that the nominee should share his foreign policy views. House GOP Leader Gerald R. Ford (Mich.) revealed two other Nixon criteria Oct. 11: the nominee should have the ability to be president and stand a reasonable chance to gain confirmation. Ford was mentioned as another possible choice.

After further consultations with his staff and other political leaders Oct. 11, Nixon flew to the presidential retreat at Camp David, Md. accompanied only by a military aide and Secret Service guards.

Further IRS action possible. An official spokesman for the Internal Revenue Service (IRS) said Oct. 10 that despite Vice President Agnew's no contest plea to one charge of tax evasion, there was nothing in the Justice Department's agreement with Agnew that would prevent the agency from bringing civil action against him on other charges of tax evasion.

According to the evidence presented by the government and detailed in the bill of particulars, Agnew was said to have received an estimated $100,000 in illegal payments. The IRS could seek to recover any money that was not reported to the agency. There was no statute of limitations on civil fraud charges.

After the Baltimore court determined that criminal fraud had been committed in 1967, the IRS automatically undertook to recover the unpaid money, a penalty of 50% of that sum and 6% interest a year. Since Agnew's offense involved the failure to report $13,551 six years ago, he would be assessed more than $25,000, according to the New York Times Oct. 10.

According to IRS figures, Agnew's failure to receive a prison sentence was not unprecedented. During fiscal 1973, only 44% of all persons convicted of criminal tax evasion charges served jail terms; in 1972, the figure had been 38%. (The maximum sentence for one count of criminal tax fraud was a $10,000 fine and up to five years in prison.)

Former IRS Commissioner Johnnie M. Walters had been critical of the lenient treatment afforded convicted felons. He had told a Michigan lawyer's group in September 1972: "It is indeed strange that the theft of a used car worth $500 rates a three-year prison sentence, whereas the theft of $50,000 of taxes rates only a small fine and no prison time. Yes, theft; what else is tax evasion?"

Agnew office urged GSA contract awards. Arthur F. Sampson, administrator of the General Services Administration (GSA), said Oct. 10 that Vice President Agnew's office had urged the GSA on numerous occasions to select certain companies for government contracts.

Among the three companies cited by Sampson was the Baltimore architectural firm of Gaudreau, Inc., which had been named in a federal indictment returned against Baltimore County Executive N. Dale Anderson Aug. 23. Neither the firm, which allegedly paid $24,000 to Anderson in connection with a contract award, nor the firm's head Paul L. Gaudreau, who was granted immunity from prosecution in return for his testimony, was named a defendant.

Sampson's disclosure came at a press conference he had called to announce the termination of Gaudreau, Inc.'s services for the second phase of a design project concerning the nearly $200 million expansion of the Social Security Administration's headquarters in suburban Baltimore. Dropped because of the adverse publicity stemming from the Anderson case, Gaudreau, Inc. had received $318,000 of an estimated $5.1 million total fee for initial design work. The fee was to be split with two other companies.

According to Sampson, a member of Agnew's staff had telephoned his agency in 1969 or 1970 on behalf of Gaudreau in connection with a contract for modernization plans for the Justice Department. The GSA awarded Gaudreau the contract in December 1971 and paid a $16,000 fee for renovation plans that were never used because of high cost estimates. Sampson said a check of GSA records had failed to reveal the identity of the Agnew staff member or the GSA employe who received the call.

The Social Security Administration contract had been awarded to Gaudreau by Sampson over the recommendations of the Social Security Administration and a GSA advisory panel of architects and engineers in private practice, the New York Times reported Oct. 10.

The other two firms that Sampson said had been recommended to the GSA by Agnew's office were Greiner Environmental Systems, Inc., a Baltimore engineering consulting firm, and Planner, Inc., a Washington urban planning firm. Both had been linked to the federal investigation of Agnew.

Agnew denies enriching himself. Former Vice President Spiro T. Agnew delivered a nationally televised farewell address Oct. 15 to correct "misconceptions" relating to his resignation and acceptance of conviction for income tax evasion.

Agnew denied he had ever "enriched" himself in betrayal of public trust. He said he had resigned "to still the raging storm" of controversy swirling around his family and nation. He attacked the news media for "scurrilous and inaccurate reports" of leaks from a grand jury investigation and denounced his accusers as "self-confessed bribe-brokers, extortionists and conspirators."

He praised Nixon as "a great president," and Rep. Ford as "clearly qualified" to assume the presidency if necessary. [See p. 84]

And Agnew suggested reform of the system in which he became enmeshed:

■ Campaign financing, where "the opportunity for evil or the appearance of evil" should be removed by public funding, and state and local governments should "close the loopholes in their laws which invite abuse or suspicion of abuse in letting lucrative contracts to private business."

■ Grants of immunity, where control should be exercised over prosecutors trying "to coax from frightened defendants accusations against higher targets."

"As things now stand," Agnew said, "immunity is an open invitation to perjury. In the hands of an ambitious prosecutor it can amount to legalized extortion and bribery."

"If these beneficial changes do flow from our current national trauma," he said, "then the suffering and sacrifice that I've had to undergo in the course of all this will be worthwhile."

Agnew did not offer a point-by-point rebuttal of the charges in the Justice Department's case against him submitted to the court in Baltimore. Excepting his "decision not to contest the 1967 tax charge," he repeated his denial of wrongdoing. His plea to the court, he said, was "not an admission of guilt but a plea of no contest, done to still the raging storm, delivering myself for conviction in one court on one count, the filing of a false income tax return for 1967." The "prosecution's assertion that I was the initiator and the gray eminence in an unprecedented and complex scheme of extortion is just not realistic," he said.

"For trained prosecution's witnesses," he continued, "who have long been experienced and aggressive in Maryland politics to masquerade as innocent victims of illegal enticements from me is enough to provoke incredulous laughter from any experienced political observer. All knowledgeable politicians and contractors know better than that. They know where the questionable propositions originate. They know how many shoddy schemes a political man must reject in the course of carrying out his office."

Agnew said "at every level of government in this country, local, state and national, public officials in high executive positions must make choices in the course of carrying out engineering and architectural projects undertaken for the public good."

He continued: "Public officials who do not possess large personal fortunes face the unpleasant but unavoidable necessity of raising substantial sums of money to pay their campaign and election expenses. In the forefront of those eager to contribute always have been the contractors seeking non-bid state awards.

"Beyond the insinuation that I pocketed large sums of money, which has never been proven, and which I emphatically deny, the intricate tangle of criminal charges leveled at me which you've been reading and hearing about during these past months boils down to the accusation that I permitted my fund-raising activities and my contract-dispensing activities to overlap in an unethical and unlawful manner. Perhaps, judged by the new post-Watergate political morality, I did."

His current net worth, Agnew declared, "less than $200,000, is modest for a person of my age and position. Every penny of it can be accounted for from lawful sources."

He spoke of "this technological age," where "image becomes dominant, appearance supersedes reality," where an appearance of wrongdoing whether true or false in fact is damaging to any man" and "fatal to a man who must be ready at any moment to step into the presidency."

"The American people," he said, "deserve to have a vice president who commands their unimpaired confidence and implicit trust. For more than two months now you have not had such a vice president. Had I remained in office and fought to vindicate myself through the courts and the Congress, it would have meant subjecting the country to a further agonizing period of months without an unclouded successor for the presidency.

"This I could not do despite my tormented verbal assertion in Los Angeles. To put his country through the ordeal of division and uncertainty that that entailed would be a selfish and unpatriotic action for any man in the best of times. But at this especially critical time, with a dangerous war raging in the Mideast and with the nation still torn by the wrenching experiences of the past year, it would have been intolerable."

By taking the course of action he did, Agnew said, he spared his family "great anguish" and gave the President and Congress the opportunity to select a new vice president "who can fill that office unencumbered by controversy."

He paid tribute to Nixon "for the restraint and the compassion" in his dealings with him on the case and expressed regret "for any interference which the controversy surrounding me may have caused in the country's pursuit of the great goals of peace, prosperity and progress which the Nixon Administration last year was overwhelmingly re-elected to pursue."

In closing, Agnew said, "Thank you. Goodnight and farewell."

Agnew cites 'highest level' pressure—The Nashville (Tenn.) Banner reported Oct. 14, on the basis of an interview with Agnew, that Agnew did not wish to resign and that "terrific pressure" from the highest levels of the Nixon Administration forced him to take that course.

The report coincided with other press reports that the White House was not only the initiator of the plea-bargaining negotiations in the case, which had been reported previously, but also had been instrumental in resumption of plea-bargaining sessions where the final settlement was reached.

During the suspension in the negotiations, Agnew made the Los Angeles speech vowing not to resign if indicted and instituted diversionary actions against indictment of a sitting vice president and prejudicial news stories. A protracted legal battle involving constitutional issues threatened on these points before resolution of the criminal case.

Newsweek magazine, in its Oct. 22 issue, reported that the White House "evidently got the message" on the prospect of protracted preoccupation with the Agnew problem and "quickly reopened private contacts." With this development, and apparently bereft of White House support, Agnew was said to have forsaken his position and signaled approval for his attorney to reopen plea bargaining. The attorney was said to have contacted presidential counsel J. Fred Buzhardt, and it was arranged.

One last sticking point was the insistence of the prosecutors that Agnew be jailed, according to Newsweek, and "the persuader in the end was the President himself. Mr. Nixon, according to one high Administration source, cleared that one last concession to his veep" and Attorney General Elliot L. Richardson, emphasizing the trauma of an arduous trial or impeachment, finally prevailed upon the prosecutors to relent on the jailing. Time magazine's Oct. 22 issue reported that Richardson promised his aides, as a mollifier, the privilege of public dissent.

One of the attorneys brought in by the department to defend its officials on the press leaks issue—James Thompson Jr., U.S. attorney for Northern Illinois—was widely quoted after his return to Chicago Oct. 10 as saying that he had "never seen a stronger extortion case," that "the man [Agnew] is a crook" and the country "well rid of him."

Maryland officials report finances—Maryland state officials filed public financial disclosure statements Oct. 15 under a new state law and a directive from the governor. The directive asked for the filings six months in advance of the deadline to generate public confidence in the state government.

Marvin Mandel (D), who succeeded Agnew as governor, and J. Millard Tawes, Agnew's predecessor as governor, refuted Agnew's contention that political payoffs were an established and accepted part of the state government operation.

U.S. weighed Agnew obstruction charge. George Beall, U.S. attorney for Maryland, disclosed Nov. 1 that federal prosecutors considered filing obstruction of justice charges against former Vice President Spiro Agnew. Beall said the idea was dropped when his staff concluded it lacked sufficient proof.

Beall said Agnew tried to influence the testimony of three key witnesses against him. Except for adding that Agnew had used an intermediary in attempting to influence the witnesses, Beall declined to elaborate. However, the Washington Post, citing "other sources," reported Nov. 2 that an Agnew associate, I. H. Hammerman, tried to dissuade Lester Matz and Jerome Wolff from cooperating with federal investigators. (Eventually, all three cooperated with prosecutors.)

Beall also said that Agnew had called then Attorney General Richard Kleindienst in February to complain that the federal investigation of political corruption in Baltimore was designed as an effort to embarrass him.

Agnew pays fine—Beall announced Oct. 31 that he had received in the mail a $10,000 certified check from Agnew in payment for the fine levied against Agnew Oct. 10 when he pleaded no contest to a charge of tax evasion.

(Maryland Gov. Marvin Mandel [D] said Oct. 31 that he had returned $53,950 in contributions for his 1974 re-election campaign from consulting engineers and architects eligible for nonbid contracts from the state. Federal prosecutors in the Agnew case had described such contributions as a "long-standing system of kickbacks."

Agnew pleads against disbarment. Former Vice President Spiro T. Agnew pleaded before a panel of Maryland judges in Annapolis Dec. 18 against being disbarred. Seeking a temporary suspension rather than a disbarment, Agnew told the court "I would conduct myself in a way that would not bring discredit upon the bar . . . and attempt to bring credit on my state and on the legal profession." The disbarment had been requested by the Maryland Bar Association because of Agnew's conviction for tax evasion. Conviction of a felony was grounds for disbarment under state law.

GAO reports Agnew office costs—The General Accounting Office (GAO) said Dec. 17 that at least $100,000 in federal funds had been spent to provide aides and offices for Agnew since his resignation.

Gerald Ford designated successor. Rep. Gerald R. Ford (Mich.), Republican Leader in the House of Representatives, was named by President Nixon Oct. 12 as his choice to replace Vice President Spiro T. Agnew.

Nixon submitted to Congress Oct. 13 the nomination of Ford to be the 40th vice president of the U.S.

Ford bars '76 candidacy—Meeting with reporters in the House press gallery Oct. 13, Ford stated "as emphatically and as strongly as I can, I have no intention of being a candidate for any office—president, vice president or anything else—in 1976."

Senate panel OKs Ford. The nine members of the Senate Rules Committee Nov. 20 unanimously approved the nomination of Rep. Gerald R. Ford as vice president, after what Chairman Howard W. Cannon (D, Nev.) called "the most exhaustive examination of a nominee ever undertaken by a Senate committee."

Senate confirms Ford as vice president. The Senate by a 92–3 vote Nov. 27 approved the nomination of Rep. Gerald Ford (R, Mich.) as vice president.

In the House, the Judiciary Committee, after completing six days of hearings Nov. 26, voted by a 29–8 margin Nov. 29 to report Ford's nomination to the floor for action.

Gerald Ford sworn in. Gerald R. Ford was sworn in as the 40th vice president of the U.S. Dec. 6.

Ford became the first non-elected vice president to take office through the 25th Amendment to the Constitution. The office, vacant 17 times in the country's history, had been vacant since Oct. 10 when Spiro T. Agnew resigned before pleading no contest to a charge of income tax evasion.

The confirmation process was completed an hour earlier Dec. 6 when the House voted its approval of the nomination by a 387–35 vote.

Judge Sirica Orders Nixon to Hand over Tapes

Haldeman amends testimony. Former White House chief of staff H. R. Haldeman provided the Senate Watergate Committee with an amended version of earlier testimony given at committee hearings about the controversial White House tapes, it was reported Aug. 28. [See p. 57]

In an Aug. 10 letter, Haldeman's attorney, Frank Strickler, told the committee that his client "believes" that on July 10 he received the Sept. 15, 1972 tape "plus phone call tapes for that day" from a White House aide, Stephen Bull, who delivered the material to Haldeman at the home of another White House aide, Lawrence Higby. Strickler said Haldeman did not listen to the phone call tapes.

On July 11, Bull delivered tapes from three other days to Haldeman, although Haldeman "is not sure what the other dates were," Strickler told the committee. (Haldeman had testified that he had not listened to those tapes.)

Haldeman returned all the tapes to Bull July 12, but was uncertain whether Bull picked them up at the Executive Office Building or elsewhere, according to Strickler.

Committee member Daniel K. Inouye, (D, Hawaii) criticized the handling of the tapes, which had been reported to be in the custody of the Secret Service. "Now we find that they [the tapes] were handed over at somebody else's house, left in a closet for 48 hours and dropped off at the Executive Office Building for someone to pick up," he observed.

The added disclosures supported his doubts, Inouye said, that the tapes could be introduced in evidence in a criminal trial.

Sirica orders tapes released. U.S. District Court Judge John J. Sirica Aug. 29 ordered President Nixon to turn over to him for private examination the tape recordings of presidential conversations involving the Watergate case. The disputed tapes had been subpoenaed by special prosecutor Archibald Cox.

A statement from the Western White House in San Clemente, Calif. Aug. 30 said Nixon would appeal the order.

While rejecting Nixon's claim of immunity from court processes, Sirica said

in an opinion accompanying his order that he had "attempted to walk the middle ground between a failure to decide the question of privilege at one extreme, and a wholesale delivery of tapes to the grand jury at the other."

Sirica said he was willing to recognize the validity of a privilege "based on the need to protect presidential privacy," but the courts must decide whether such a privilege had been properly claimed. He said he was "simply unable to decide the question of privilege without inspecting the tapes."

Sirica said he had found it necessary to decide only two questions "for the present": (1) whether the court had jurisdiction on the issue of executive privilege, and (2) whether the court had the authority to enforce the subpoena by ordering production of the material for private inspection. Both questions, he said, "must be answered in the affirmative."

Sirica rejected as "unpersuasive" the White House argument that constitutional separation of powers barred compulsory court process from the President. Such a contention, Sirica said, "overlooks history."

The framers of the Constitution, Sirica noted, had shown a "general disfavor of government privileges, or at least uncontrolled privileges." Nor had they intended to create a "watertight" division of functions among the branches of government. Nixon's arguments, Sirica said, tended "to set the White House apart as a fourth branch of government."

On the issue of privilege, Sirica relied heavily on the rulings of Supreme Court Chief Justice John Marshall in the 1807 treason trial of Aaron Burr, in which President Thomas Jefferson had been ordered to comply with a subpoena.* Sirica equated the rights of Burr with those of the Watergate grand jury and cited

_____
*In the Burr case, Marshall—while chief justice of the Supreme Court—was presiding in a lower federal court. Burr asked that a letter held by President Jefferson be subpoenaed. Over the objections of the prosecution, which claimed the letter was confidential, Marshall ruled that the President could be subpoenaed to provide essential information in a trial, while expressing doubt as to how the President might be compelled to comply. That issue became moot when Jefferson declined to appear in court but agreed to release the letter and offered to testify by deposition.

Marshall's ruling that "there is no exception whatever" in the right of the accused (or the grand jury) to the compulsory process of the court.

Sirica said a central issue was the need of the grand jury for the "best evidence" from all citizens. This need, he ruled, was "well documented and imposing." There was no reason, Sirica said, "for suspending the power of courts to get evidence and rule on questions of privilege in criminal matters simply because it is the President of the U.S. who holds the evidence."

Although Sirica decided that the proper procedure would be his examination of the tapes and a determination of portions not subject to privilege and thus available to the grand jury, he said he was "extremely reluctant to finally stand against a declaration of the President" that the taped conversations had occurred in the exercise of official duties and were subject to privilege in their entirety. He conceded that his inspection might indeed constitute a "compromise of privilege," but said it would be an "extremely limited infraction and in this case an unavoidable one."

Sirica's compromise would be to excise portions he might deem privileged and send only the unprivileged parts to the grand jury. This procedure, he had said earlier in his opinion, would be "tantamount to fully enforcing the subpoena as to any unprivileged matter." But, if the evidence was so "inextricably intertwined" that separation became impossible, "the whole must be privileged and no disclosure made to the grand jury."

Sirica stayed enforcement of his order to allow Nixon to appeal and ruled that if the President appealed, the stay would be extended indefinitely pending completion of appeals.

Nixon will appeal—In a statement released at San Clemente Aug. 30, the White House said Nixon would seek review of Judge Sirica's order to release the tapes in the U.S. Court of Appeals for the District of Columbia. Nixon had said Aug. 22 that he would abide by a "definitive" Supreme Court decision.

A statement released Aug. 29 had said Nixon would not comply with the order. That statement said in its entirety:

As Mr. [Charles Alan] Wright [White House legal consultant] pointed out in his oral argument before the court, in camera inspection of these tapes is inconsistent with the President's position relating to the question of separation of powers as provided by the Constitution and the necessity of maintaining the precedent of confidentiality of private Presidential conversations for this President and for Presidents in the future.

The President consequently will not comply with this order.

White House counsel are now considering the possibility of obtaining appellate review or how otherwise to sustain the President's position.

A spokesman for special prosecutor Cox had said Aug. 29 that Cox was "very pleased" by Sirica's decision and would do everything possible" to expedite appeals proceedings.

Ervin, Baker laud ruling—Sen. Sam J. Ervin Jr. (D, N.C.), chairman of the committee investigating Watergate, called Sirica's decision "a great victory for the search for truth." Ervin added he felt his committee was "entitled to the tapes just as much as the courts because we have the constitutional power to conduct the investigation."

Ervin said he did not interpret the White House announcement barring compliance with the order as implying Nixon would not heed an order by the Supreme Court.

Sen. Howard H. Baker Jr. (R, Tenn.), vice chairman of the Watergate committee, said Sirica's ruling had placed "adequate safeguards on the national security and separation of powers issues" raised by the conflict.

Nixon responds to Ervin committee suit. Lawyers for President Nixon Aug. 29 rejected the demand by the Senate Watergate committee for tapes of presidential conversations on the grounds that neither the committee nor the federal district court had jurisdiction over Nixon as President or as an individual. The White House was responding to a suit filed Aug. 9 by the committee.

The White House argued that the committee had exceeded its mandate and was illegally attempting to determine whether "criminal acts have been committed and the guilt or innocence of individuals." Nixon "owes no duty," the White House brief stated, to provide the committee with confidential recordings or other documents. The suit, according to the brief, was an "unconstitutional attempt to interfere with the confidentiality" of the presidency.

Among other arguments advanced by the White House:

■ The committee did not have sufficient authorization from the Senate to file the suit, and the original subpoenas were void because they had not been authorized by a full Senate vote.

■ The committee members had not "suffered any legal wrong," nor had they been "adversely affected or aggrieved" by Nixon's rejection of the subpoenas.

■ The subpoena for White House papers relating to alleged criminal acts was "so unreasonably broad and oppressive as to make compliance impossible."

The Senate committee filed additional papers in the suit Aug. 29, including a motion that the committee's subpoenas be enforced with a minimum of further proceedings.

In a memorandum supporting the motion, the committee said it was not seeking a "wholesale invasion of the President's files," nor was it requesting a broad ruling that might "serve as a dangerous precedent for the conduct of presidential business." Rather, the committee said, it sought only tapes and material relating to possible criminal activity in the 1972 campaign.

The committee said it had a mandate to "ferret out all the facts regarding the Watergate affair," both to aid in the Senate's legislative function, and to inform the public. "So long as key evidence is withheld," the committee said, "public confidence in the self-corrective processes of government will remain at low ebb."

Federal District Court Judge John J. Sirica Aug. 30 rejected the committee's petition to consolidate its suit with that of special prosecutor Archibald Cox. [See above] Both the White House and Cox had opposed consolidation.

Nixon and aide differ on tapes heard. President Nixon's statement in a Sept. 5 news conference that he had listened to two Watergate tapes June 4—neither of which, he said, contained anything inconsistent with his other statements on Watergate—did not coincide with presidential aide Stephen B. Bull's account of the events of June 4, Time magazine reported Sept. 17.

According to Time, Bull had told investigators for the Senate Watergate committee that he had taken eight or ten tapes, loaded onto at least five playback machines, to Nixon's office in the Executive Office Building. Bull said Nixon kept the tapes for 12 hours, and when Bull retrieved them, all had been fully unwound.

Nixon gets delay in committee suit. The suit by the Senate Watergate committee for presidential tapes relevant to its investigation was dealt a potentially damaging blow Sept. 6. U.S. District Court Judge John J. Sirica granted the White House a two-week delay—until Sept. 24—for responding to the committee's motion to force compliance with its subpoenas.

Because of appeals which would follow Sirica's decision on the suit, the latest delay was seen as pushing a final resolution past the committee's projected adjournment date of Nov. 1.

Sirica rejected committee counsel Samuel Dash's argument that the delay would in effect rule the Senate "really out of court." Sirica said he was "determined not to be pushed into a half-baked job."

Sirica also said the jurisdictional issue was central to the case and that the courts might not have the power to rule in the committee's civil suit.

Nixon appeals Sirica decision—Lawyers for President Nixon Sept. 6 asked the U.S. Court of Appeals for the District of Columbia to overturn Sirica's order to Nixon to surrender tapes of his conversations on Watergate for Sirica's private inspection.

The White House action was technically not a routine appeal of Sirica's decision but a separate suit, naming Sirica as defendant and special prosecutor Archibald Cox as an interested party, asking the court to nullify Sirica's ruling.

Calling the case a matter of "exceptional importance," the White House requested that the challenge be considered by all nine judges of the court.

The court agreed to hear the case *en banc* and confirmed its speeded up schedule, announced Sept. 4, under which filing of briefs and oral arguments were to be completed by Sept. 14.

Nixon deflects questions on tapes—President Nixon Sept. 5 declined to elaborate on what he would consider a "definitive decision" by the Supreme Court on the issue of the Watergate tapes. He had said earlier that he would heed such a decision.

At his Sept. 5 news conference, Nixon said the matter would be discussed in court during the appeal procedure and comment before then would be "inappropriate."

Responding to a question as to whether he might be placing himself above the law by determining on his own what form of decision he would abide by, Nixon reiterated his position that absolute confidentiality of presidential conversations was essential to the "proper conduct" of the office. This principle, he said, was the justification for the "hard line" he had taken in regard to compliance with Judge Sirica's order.

Asked whether he could assure that the content of the tapes did not "reflect unfavorably" on his Watergate position, Nixon replied that in the two tapes he had listened to June 4 there was "nothing whatever" inconsistent with his statements on Watergate. He maintained, however, that the content of the tapes was not his concern; the issue was the principle of confidentiality.

Tape conflict in appeals court. The conflict between President Nixon and special prosecutor Archibald Cox over tapes of Nixon's Watergate conversations moved further into the appeals process Sept. 7–13. Cox appealed U.S. District Court Judge John J. Sirica's decision ordering Nixon to surrender the tapes for Sirica's private inspection, and the Court of Appeals for the District of Columbia, after hearing arguments from Sirica, Cox and lawyers for Nixon, issued a memorandum suggesting an out-of-court compromise.

In his response Sept. 7 to Sirica's order, Cox took an approach similar to that of the White House in its appeal: rather than appealing directly, Cox filed a separate action naming Sirica as respondent and asking that the court amend Sirica's order.

Cox asked first that Nixon be ordered to surrender the tapes directly to the grand jury without judicial screening. If the court were to decide that Sirica's inspection of the tapes was proper, Cox asked the court to set standards for the screening. Cox added that he should be allowed to assist Sirica in the determination of relevant evidence, since Sirica, unlike the prosecutors, was "not in a position" to have complete knowledge of the possible relevance of all portions of the tapes.

The "core" of Sirica's decision was "entirely correct," but some parts needed clarification, Cox argued.

The three parties filed briefs with the appeals court Sept. 10. Sirica defended his ruling that he had the power to enforce a subpoena on the President, and said his decision had been based on "mature deliberation and consideration of the authorities." He did not respond to Cox's suggestion that the prosecution be allowed to assist in screening the tapes but said he would "welcome" standards and guidelines from the court.

The White House brief asserted that Sirica's decision sanctioned "breaching the wall of confidentiality" of presidential communications. "The heat and excitement of an unprecedented political scandal," the brief stated, were twisting the Constitution and subverting the President's rightful powers. Any discussions of Watergate crimes Nixon might have held with his aides were part of his "constitutional duty to see that the laws are faithfully executed" and exempt from grand jury scrutiny.

Cox's brief rejected as "intolerable" Nixon's claim of executive privilege to keep the tapes from the grand jury while allowing his aides to testify on their own potentially faulty recollections of the same conversations. Cox emphasized that the grand jury needed the tapes not only to resolve conflicting accounts of the conversations in question, but to show the "initiation, duration and thrust of any conspiracy on the part of the alleged participants." Cox said he had already shown in Sirica's court that the tapes contained evidence of "some fraud or criminal misconduct" by presidential aides. Because of "the predominant public interest," Cox said, law enforcement was more important than presidential privacy.

Oral arguments were heard Sept. 11 by seven of the nine appeals judges; Roger Robb and Edward A. Tamm—considered part of the conservative wing of the court—disqualified themselves. No reason was given for Tamm's action, but Robb said a former law partner, Kenneth W. Parkinson, was an attorney for the Committee to Re-elect the President.

Charles Alan Wright, representing Nixon, argued that if the court upheld Sirica's decision there would be "no limit on the extent to which presidential privacy can be invaded." Under a 1969 Supreme Court decision on exculpatory evidence, Wright said, Watergate defendants would

have access to sensitive national security discussions on the tapes.

Cox replied that if any defendants demanded the full tapes, he would seek some showing that the withheld portions would aid in their defense. The White House could have "state secrets" deleted at the outset, Cox said, by submitting affidavits supporting such editing.

Wright asserted that although the tradition was "very strong that judges should have the last word" in determining what evidence should be available, there were times "when that simply cannot be true." He suggested that the court might avoid an "aura of confrontation" by entering a declaratory judgment rather than a direct order on the President and rely on Nixon's "good judgment" to act voluntarily. Wright said it was "conceivable" that Nixon might give a deposition on the conversations.

Cox agreed that the court did not have to make a "black and white choice" between full access to the tapes and absolute executive privilege. But, he said, the need for the truth dictated that relevant portions be made available.

In final papers filed Sept. 12, Cox said Nixon's lawyers had raised a "bogus fear" in arguing that upholding Sirica's decision would lead to unlimited invasion of presidential privacy. He noted that in the 1969 Supreme Court decision cited by Wright, the court had ruled that defendants would not have the "unlimited right to rummage in the files of the Department of Justice," and that other decisions had established the right of a trial judge to delete national security material. Cox urged the court to issue a direct order on Nixon to release the subpoenaed tapes.

The White House was granted a delay to Sept. 19 to file its final reply.

In a surprise move Sept. 13, the appeals court issued a unanimous memorandum urging an out-of-court settlement under which Nixon (or his delegate), along with Wright and Cox, would examine the tapes to determine what material might be privileged and what could go to the grand jury.

The court said a resolution of the issue without a constitutional ruling was "enhanced by the stature and character" of Wright and Cox and the fact that both had been selected for their positions, "directly or indirectly," by Nixon himself. A compromise, the court said, would serve the national interest, and neither side would have "surrendered or subverted the principles for which they have contended."

The court noted that the settlement would require voluntary submission of the tapes by Nixon, but beyond that the court would not "presume to prescribe the details" of how Nixon should work with the two counsel.

"If, after the most diligent efforts of all three concerned," the memo stated, "there appear to be matters the President deems privileged and the special prosecutor believes necessary and not privileged, then this court will discharge its duty of determining the controversy

with the knowledge that it has not hesitated to explore the possibility of avoiding constitutional adjudication."

Even if that were necessary, the issues remaining "might be substantially narrowed and clarified." The court asked to be told by Sept. 20 whether a settlement had been reached.

Cox said later he would be "more than glad" to meet with Nixon or a representative to discuss the court's proposal. A White House spokesman said Nixon's lawyers were "studying the memo."

Connally comments on tape controversy. As part of a nationwide tour aimed at building contacts within the Republican party, former Treasury Secretary John B. Connally Jr. attended a Washington reception in his honor Sept. 10 by the Texas Republican party. Connally told newsmen that it was wrong to assume that the Supreme Court was the ultimate arbiter in all disputes. Connally said there were instances in which the President might be justified in not obeying a Supreme Court ruling on the disposition of the Watergate tapes.

Goldwater urges Watergate resolution. Sen. Barry Goldwater (R, Ariz.), writing for the New York Times Sept. 11-13, urged those involved in Watergate to resolve their differences to allow the nation to attack the other serious problems facing it.

Acknowledging that extraordinary measures might be necessary, Goldwater suggested that President Nixon make available to the Senate relevant portions of select Watergate tapes. He also suggested "that we call a halt to the daily television spectacle that, by its very nature, holds the United States government up to criticism and ridicule."

As an extreme solution, Goldwater proposed a nationally televised debate—with stringent ground rules worked out in advance—between Nixon and Watergate committee chairman Sen. Sam J. Ervin Jr. (D, N.C.).

Goldwater cautioned the press against equating the actions of those involved in Watergate with conservatism: "It was the lack of ideology and the lack of experience and the lack of deeply rooted philosophy of life which brought the unfortunate and unforgivable activity" of Watergate. No "sincere conservative" would have adopted the ends-justify-the-means philosophy that seemed present in Watergate, he said.

Tape accord try fails. Special prosecutor Archibald Cox and attorneys for President Nixon told the U.S. Court of Appeals for the District of Columbia Sept. 20 that they had failed in their efforts to reach an out-of-court compromise on access to tapes of Nixon's Watergate conversations.

The court's Sept. 13 memorandum suggesting the compromise attempt had said that if the effort failed, the court would rule on the issue.

In similar letters to the court, Cox and Nixon's legal consultant Charles Alan Wright said they and other staff members, in three meetings, had made "sincere efforts" to reach an accord. The letters did not say whether Cox had listened to any tapes. Cox and Wright told the court they had agreed not to make public comment on the content of their conversations.

White House brief filed—Nixon's firm position against release of the tapes had been reiterated in his final reply brief filed with the court Sept. 19. Nixon's lawyers said any order compelling release of the tapes would "tear down the office" of the presidency—"too high a price to pay, even for Watergate."

Repeating Nixon's contention that any conversations he might have had on Watergate were part of his constitutional responsibilities, the brief stated these "duties and prerogatives" could not be delegated to Cox; such an action "would move beyond accommodation to irresponsibility."

Permitting Judge John J. Sirica to screen the tapes or otherwise rule on Nixon's claim of privilege would, the brief argued, amount to giving the judge the power to judge Nixon's guilt or innocence. This "wholly intolerable" precedent "presupposes the possibility that in some future case a judge might conclude that some future president has been party to a crime and that his claim to privilege must be overruled." Such a conclusion, "merely as an incident to an evidentiary ruling," would leave a president "condemned in the eyes of the nation without any of the safeguards that even the humblest citizen enjoys before he may be branded as a criminal."

Committee renews plea for tapes—The Senate committee investigating Watergate said in court papers filed Sept. 18 that its need for Nixon's Watergate tapes was greater than that of special prosecutor Cox because the committee was focusing "on the President's own possible criminality." The filing was part of the committee's suit in federal district court for release of the tapes.

The committee asserted that if the testimony of former White House counsel John W. Dean 3rd was "sustained in all particulars, the continuance of [Nixon's] presidency may be in jeopardy and he may be subjected to criminal penalties."

Emphasizing its special position with regard to the subpoenaed tapes and documents, the committee said "the public interest in determining the extent of malfeasance in the executive branch and the need for corrective legislation" was more important than the indictment and conviction of a few individuals.

Chairman Sen. Sam J. Ervin Jr. (D, N.C.) added in an affidavit that the committee's hearings might be prolonged without the tapes because of the need to question many persons who might have had access to the tapes or who might have other knowledge about Dean's allegations.

Mitchell, Stans seek access to tapes—Lawyers for former Attorney General John Mitchell and his co-defendant in a New York criminal case, Maurice Stans, chairman of the Finance Committee to Re-elect the President, issued a subpoena Aug. 31 in Washington in an effort to obtain any Presidential tapes and other White House documents which might relate to their trial on obstruction of justice and perjury charges.

The defense sought unspecified material from the White House covering the period November 1971–January 1973. In a related development, a new date for the Mitchell-Stans trial was set for Oct. 23.

'More than 2' tapes heard, says Ziegler—White House Press Secretary Ronald L. Ziegler said Sept. 20 that President Nixon had listened to "more than two" of the Watergate tapes, contrary to some versions of Nixon's statement in his Sept. 5 news conference.

The confusion in wording lay in different transcripts of the news conference. According to the New York Times transcript, Nixon said: ". . . the only time I listened to the tapes, two certain tapes . . . was June 4." According to the Washington Post and the official transcript, the wording was: ". . . listened to the tapes—to certain tapes."

Kennedy suggests impeachment if tape order defied—Sen. Edward M. Kennedy (D, Mass.) said Sept. 13 that if President Nixon defied a Supreme Court order to release the Watergate tapes, "a responsible Congress would be left with no recourse but to exercise its power of impeachment."

In a Senate speech, Kennedy said Nixon would have no basis in history for such defiance; Nixon's only "argument from law," Kennedy added, would be "the law of the jungle, the law of raw and naked power, which the country will never tolerate."

Sen. Edward W. Brooke (R, Mass.) said later that defiance of the Supreme Court would be sufficient ground to begin impeachment proceedings, but Sen. John G. Tower (R, Tex.) contended that in the "shadowy area of separation of powers" there was no precedent to rely upon.

Court orders Nixon to give up tapes. The U.S. Circuit Court of Appeals for the District of Columbia, in a 5–2 decision Oct. 12, held that President Nixon must turn over his Watergate tape recordings to the U.S. district court and declared that the President was "not above the law's commands." The decision upheld in substance U.S. District Court Judge John J. Sirica's decision Aug. 29 for the President to turn over the tapes so the court could determine whether they contained evidence that should be presented to the grand jury.

The appeals court ordered the President to turn over the complete tapes in question, specifying which parts should and should not be disclosed. The final decision to send any or all of the material to the grand jury would then be made by the district court. The judge would hold a closed hearing on the issue if either disputant desired. Then he could "order disclosure of all portions of the tapes relevant to matters within the proper scope of the grand jury's investigation," the appeals court held, unless it found in "particular" statements or information "that the public interest served by nondisclosure outweighed the grand jury's need for the information."

The appeals court did not give up its earlier bid for an out-of-court compromise. "Perhaps," it suggested, "the President will find it possible to reach some agreement with the special prosecutor as to what portions of the subpoenaed evidence are necessary to the grand jury." But, it continued, "should our hope provide unavailing, we think that *in camera* inspection is a necessary and appropriate method protecting the grand jury's interest in securing evidence directly relevant to its decisions.

In a statement issued later Oct. 12 special Watergate prosecutor Archibald Cox expressed "complete willingness" to again try for the out-of-court compromise.

Nixon's deputy press secretary, Gerald L. Warren, said the White House was "studying" the opinion. The court granted a five-day stay of its order to give the President time for an appeal to the Supreme Court.

The majority opinion was rendered by David L. Bazelon, chief judge, J. Skelly Wright. Carl McGowan, Harold Levanthal and Spottswood W. Robinson 3rd. George E. MacKinnon and Malcolm R. Wilkey were in the minority.

All seven participating judges in the appeals court decision agreed that the courts had jurisdiction to consider the President's claim of privilege.

As for the question of presidential immunity, the court said: "The Constitution makes no mention of special presidential immunities. Indeed, the executive branch generally is afforded none. This silence cannot be ascribed to oversight."

"Lacking textual support," it continued, the President's counsel "nonetheless would have us infer immunity from the President's political mandate, or from his vulnerability to impeachment, or from his discretionary powers. These are invitations to refashion the Constitution and we reject them.

"Though the President is elected by nationwide ballot, and is often said to represent all the people, he does not embody the nation's sovereignty. He is not above the law's commands. . . . Sovereignty remains at all times with the people and they do not forfeit through elections the right to have the law construed against and applied to every citizen.

"Nor does the impeachment clause imply immunity from routine court process. While the President argues that the clause means that impeachability precludes criminal prosecution of an incumbent, we see no need to explore this question except to note its irrelevance to the case before us. . . . By contemplating the possibility of post-impeachment trials for violations committed in office, the impeachment clause itself reveals that incumbency does not relieve the President of the routine legal applications that confine all citizens."

On the issue of executive privilege, the court said "the Constitution mentions no executive privilege, much less any absolute executive privilege." While there had been "longstanding judicial recognition" of executive privilege, it noted, it was the longstanding corollary opinion of the courts that "the applicability of the privilege is in the end for them and not the executive to decide."

"Throughout our history," the court said, "there have frequently been conflicts between independent organs of the federal government, as well as between the state and federal governments. . . . Our constitutional system provides a means for resolving them—one Supreme Court. To leave the proper scope and application of executive privilege to the president's sole discretion would represent a mixing, rather than a separation, of executive and judicial functions."

As for the application of executive privilege to this case, the court said the presumption in favor of utilizing privilege "must fall in the face of the uniquely powerful showing made by the special prosecutor." The court referred to the President's decision not to assert a privilege for oral testimony by his aides, which diluted his claim of privilege for the tapes.

It also referred to the prosecutor's showing from testimony by the aides that there was a "significant likelihood" of a broad criminal conspiracy, that important evidence about it was contained in conversations that were taped, and that there were "significant inconsistencies" relating to the taped conversations that raised a "distinct possibility" that perjury had been committed before a Congressional committee and perhaps a grand jury.

In conclusion, the court cautioned that its order "represents an unusual and limited requirement that the President produce material evidence. We think this required by law, and by the rule that even the chief executive is subject to the mandate of law when he has no valid claim of privilege." It also pointed out that "the courts in this country always assume that their orders will be obeyed, especially when addressed to responsible government officials."

In dissent, Judge MacKinnon expressed concern about the effect the majority's decision would have "upon the constitutional independence of our president for all time." Judge Wilkey stated that "the practical capacity of the three independent branches to adjust to each other their sensitivity to the approval or disapproval of the American people have been sufficient guides to responsible action, without imposing the authority of one co-equal branch over another."

Nixon wins Senate tapes ruling—Judge Sirica Oct. 17 dismissed the Senate Watergate committee's lawsuit to obtain the disputed presidential tapes. The judge held that his court lacked jurisdiction in the civil case in contrast to the special prosecutor's case, which involved a subpoena issued for a criminal investigation by a grand jury.

Jurisdiction in a civil complaint of this nature, he said, was a threshold issue and the committee had failed to demonstrate statutory basis for jurisdiction.

The committee had brought the suit in the name of the U.S., but Sirica said this could only be done by the attorney general or authorized by Congress, which had not acted. It had sought to "compel an officer of the U.S. to perform his duty," but Sirica denied official duty was involved, noting that "there is nothing in the Constitution, for example, that makes it an official duty of Presidents to comply with Congressional subpoenas."

He also found: the committee suit failed to meet the rule that a minimum of $10,-000 must be involved for district courts to assume jurisdiction; and a federal agency was not involved and thus the issue did not fall under the Administrative Procedure Act, which could not be used in any case in his circuit as an independent basis of jurisdiction.

A White House statement later Oct. 17 expressed pleasure with the decision, the first major legal victory for the President on the issue of the tapes.

Ervin Panel Investigates
Political Sabotage

Buchanan opens second phase. Presidential speechwriter Patrick J. Buchanan was the lead-off witness Sept. 26 as the committee opened the second phase of its hearings into alleged political sabotage of the 1972 presidential campaign. Buchanan was a special consultant to President Nixon on political strategy.

Committee counsel Samuel Dash began aggressive questioning to establish to what limits Buchanan would go to insure a Republican victory in 1972. He referred to a Buchanan memo which indicated that "knocking out the front-runner" of the opposition would be one of the strategies. But Buchanan handled the questions deftly.

"What tactics would I be willing to use?" he answered Dash. "Anything that was not immoral, unethical, illegal or unprecedented in previous Democratic campaigns."

Buchanan drew a line against illegality, and exhibited an independence rarely demonstrated by previous witnesses. He told the committee he had refused an assignment—a 1971 White House investigation of Daniel Ellsberg—because he considered it "a waste of my time and abilities" and "did not see the value" of anyone doing it. He said he was unaware of the secret Ellsberg probe that resulted in a break-in in California.

He admitted that the Watergate incident and other aspects of the 1972 campaign might have constituted improper actions, but also affirmed that the individuals responsible for them would have to answer to them and that there was no "connection" in such incidents to the President or himself. He declared loyalty to President Nixon, quoting a Colson remark "I would do anything the President of the United States would ask me to do, period." Buchanan said he subscribed to that statement "for this reason: The President of the United States would not ask me to do anything unethical, improper or wrong or illegal ... I am loyal to the President of the United States, that is correct. I have been loyal to him for eight years."

The witness castigated the committee for failing to prevent leaks to the news media about his expected testimony. He had been the victim, Buchanan said, of a "convert campaign of vilification" to "malign" his reputation. "I did not recommend or authorize nor was I aware of," he said, "any ongoing campaign of political sabotage against Sen. Muskie or any other Democratic candidate. I did not recommend, either verbally or in memoranda, that the re-election committee infiltrate the campaigns of our opposition."

While some of the President's supporters may have committed "errors, mistakes, misjudgments and wrongdoing" in the 1972 campaign, Buchanan said, the election "was not stolen."

"The President of the United States did not achieve the greatest landslide of any minority party candidate in history because of Watergate and dirty tricks—but in spite of them," he said.

The committee was interested in a series of memos Buchanan had written in the early stages of the 1972 campaign. They favored activity to help eliminate Muskie from contention on the ground he would be the strongest competitor against Nixon and subsequent action to aid the Democratic cause of Sen. George S. McGovern (S.D.) on the ground that he would be the easiest to "inundate" in the final stretch of the campaign. One memo said "we should elevate and assist McGovern in every way conceivable." In another, entitled "Assault Strategy," Buchanan advocated taking advantage of an apparent negative stock market reaction to McGovern by having prominent Administration spokesmen predict that McGovern's election "would mean a depression or panic on Wall Street."

Buchanan denied any illegal or unethical intention from such an approach, specifying that traditional techniques had been contemplated, such as planting unfriendly pickets at Muskie rallies or simply withholding criticism of McGovern prior to the nomination.

In his view, there were "four gradations" of campaign activities. "There are things that are certainly outrageous," Buchanan specified as his first gradation, citing a situation when a Democrat had been prevented by demonstrations from speaking. "Then, there is dirty tricks," he continued. "Then there is political hard-ball, then there is pranks. I think you will almost have to leave it to the individual and his own sense of ethics as to what is permissible. There is no question but what the line was probably breached in both campaigns in 1972, and perhaps previous ones."

While he had been unaware of the alleged activities of the Segretti group, Buchanan said, if it were true that Nixon backers had distributed false campaign literature making "salacious" charges against Democratic contenders, such activity was beyond the pale of acceptable political operation. However, he said, ghost-written ads for "citizen" groups, humorous pranks or even some forms of "clandestine activities" did not fall in this category, having the acceptability of standard political procedure.

The committee probed Buchanan's views on foundations, as exhibited in some of his memos. One such 1970 memo to the President addressed a request for suggestions to "combat the institutionalized power of the Left concentrated in the foundations that succor the Democratic party." In the memo, Buchanan suggested creation of a conservative foundation funded by Nixon supporters and federal contracts for studies then being undertaken by liberal-oriented foundations. The contracts would be shifted to the favored foundations, leaving the unfavored ones "without a dime" of federal money. Another recommendation was for installing a "friendly" staff in the Internal Revenue Service to oversee the exempt status of private organizations.

Buchanan told the committee he believed the Ford Foundation's influence on political thought had created a "distortion" of the political process on the liberal side. He said he had prepared speeches on the subject, advocating "something analogous to antitrust action" to split up the Ford Foundation, but none had been delivered.

Committee releases other memos— Other memos released by the committee Sept. 26 disclosed an extensive operation by the White House to draft letters and telegrams of support for the President to be sent to "opinion leaders" throughout the country over other persons' signatures. The "opinion leaders" included editors, publishers and business leaders. Under the system, the news media was denounced following a presidential press conference.

A Dec. 11, 1970 memo from Jeb Stuart Magruder, then White House aide, to H. R. Haldeman, then White House chief of staff, listed action taken following the press conference. Among the actions: "Ten telegrams have been drafted by Buchanan. They will be sent to Time and Newsweek by 20 names around the country from our letter-writing system"; an op-ed page statement for the New York Times was being drafted by two aides and Herbert Klein, then the President's director of communications, was recommended as the "best signatory" for the article.

According to another memo, Nixon tried to influence the public interpretation of New York Mayor John V. Lindsay's re-election in 1969. In a memo to Haldeman, Nixon wrote that "the press, of course, will try to interpret this as a referendum on Vietnam" and "it is vitally important that this be nailed prior to the election and, of course, be nailed immediately afterwards as strongly as possible." He suggested "it would be helpful" if conservative columnists could "hit" the issue "and better still if some more in the center were to do so."

Senate committee hears Segretti. The Senate Watergate committee took testimony Oct. 3 from Donald H. Segretti on the "dirty tricks" he played on Democratic candidates seeking the presidential nomination in 1972.

Segretti appeared at the televised public hearing under a court grant of limited immunity from prosecution. Segretti, 32, had pleaded guilty Oct. 1 to three charges of conspiracy and illegal campaign activities, the case being handled by the special federal Watergate prosecution. [See below]

Segretti, a lawyer, told the committee he had been recruited by and reported to a White House aide, Dwight L. Chapin, Nixon's appointments secretary until January when he resigned. He said he was told his work was secretive and was not to be traced to the White House. He related his "dirty tricks"—fake letters, posters, pamphlets, press releases, all false, planting fake demonstrators and placards and questions in news conferences, even surveillance on a candidate.

Looking back, Segretti said he realized his activities were wrong and regretted any harm caused by them. He apologized for one "scurrilous letter" he faked purporting sexual misconduct to two Democratic candidates. But he said his activities had been exaggerated "out of all proportion" by the news media and he had suffered abuse by "rumor, character assassination, innuendo" and invasion of privacy.

Among highlights of his testimony:

Oct. 3: *Segretti's 'dirty tricks'*—Segretti testified that his original contact for his campaign role of "dirty tricks" was

Dwight Chapin, Nixon's appointments secretary, and Gordon Strachan, at the time an aide to H. R. Haldeman, then White House chief of staff. Chapin, who became his 'boss" for the operation and gave him some strategies to be used, stressed the need for secrecy so that his activity could not be traced to the White House, Segretti testified. His activity was to consist of "political tricks" to confuse the Democratic contender involved and his campaign.

His salary was arranged with Nixon's personal attorney, Herbert W. Kalmbach, Segretti said, and he was to receive $16,000 a year plus expenses. Kalmbach was unaware of the nature of his work, he testified. Eventually, he received a total of about $45,000 in salary and expenses for his activities during 1971 and 1972, Segretti said. From September until June of those years, he said, he traveled from state to state where important primaries were being conducted, devising ways to carry out his assignment "to foster a split between the various Democratic hopefuls." At first, he focused on Sen. Edmund S. Muskie's (D, Me.) campaign, considered the front runner at the time. The focus was later shifted somewhat, after Muskie's campaign faded, to an attempt to sow dissension between Muskie and the other Democratic contenders. Segretti said he sent regular reports of his activities, and copies of the false campaign literature he was disseminating, to Chapin.

Asked Chapin's reaction to false press releases he had received from Segretti, as examples of his handiwork, Segretti replied, "There was a comment that he laughed for a period of time regarding the press releases."

Q. He thought it was funny that you sent a press release saying that [Rep.] Shirley Chisholm [D, N.Y., and one of the presidential contenders] was at one time confined to a mental institution in Virginia? [A false charge Segretti admitted he concocted himself]

A. Yes.

Segretti was especially penitent about a phony letter on Muskie's stationery he had distributed during the Florida primary election accusing two other Democratic contenders, Sens. Hubert H. Humphrey (Minn.) and Henry M. Jackson (Wash.), of sexual and drinking misconduct. "It was a scurrilous letter," he said, and he wished to "apologize publicly for this stupid act." He testified that Chapin's reaction to the letter, which cost about $20 to reproduce, was mixed. Chapin told him afterward, he said, "for your $20, you received $10,000 to $20,000 worth of free publicity, but be careful next time."

Segretti told the committee of some of his other tricks:

■ Posters distributed in Florida reading "Help Muskie in Busing More Children Now," signed "Mothers Backing Muskie Committee," a fictitious group.

■ An ad placed in a Miami newspaper asking, "Sen. Muskie, Would You Accept a Jewish Running Mate?"

■ Arranging for pickets at various Democratic rallies and for a private detective to trail Muskie in California.

■ Hiring accomplices, one of whom broke into Muskie headquarters in Florida and planted a "stink bomb." At the most, he testified, he had 11 persons working with him, but he changed the figure later to 28 to conform with expense accounts he had filed.

■ Distributing a false letter on the stationery of former Sen. Eugene J. McCarthy (D, Minn.) urging his supporters to switch to Humphrey, and a similar letter sent to Chisholm supporters.

Segretti also identified for the committee a written directive from Chapin urging him to "prove" Muskie could not keep his temper.

Segretti testified that he was not involved in the Watergate break-in in June 1972 and that he stopped his campaign disruption activity afterwards.

In October 1972 when press reports of his activity appeared, Segretti said, he was summoned to Washington by White House counsel John W. Dean 3rd to discuss his activity and prepare a response. It was indicated he should stay out of sight—"There was a social discussion regarding how nice the Greek islands were at that time of year"—but what he did was take a cross-country train ride to California.

During this period Chapin was identified as his contact and the White House press office denounced the report as "hearsay, innuendo and guilt by association" and "fundamentally inaccurate."

Dean's advice to him, Segretti said, was to refrain from comment, that "the media people decided that things will die on their own volition." Regarding any FBI probe, Dean advised him to tell the truth but not to volunteer information. Segretti told the committee the federal Watergate prosecutors had not pressed him for details of his campaign role. After testifying before the grand jury in 1972, Segretti said, he "believed then that there was something going on behind the scenes" and he recalled to the committee Dean's comment that Dean "might be able to put parameters" on the federal probe of the break-in.

Among the factors that entered into his decision to engage in such activity in the first place, Segretti told the committee, was the opportunity to work for the White House. During his testimony he volunteered that he "had no knowledge whether Mr. Nixon or President Nixon knew anything that I did."

Segretti said his activities "have been blown out of all proportion by the news media. I accept the fact that most of my present problems are the direct result of my own conduct. However, I cannot help but feel that I have been abused by rumor, character assassination, innuendo and a complete disregard for the privacy of myself, my friends and my family."

He added: "This in no way lessens my sincere belief that my activities were

A

wrong and have no place in the American political system. To the extent my activities have harmed other persons and the political process, I have the deepest regrets."

Sergretti aides testify Oct. 4. Two witnesses detailed the "dirty tricks" they played on Democratic presidential candidates in an effort to disrupt their campaigns in 1972. The witnesses, Martin Kelly, 24, and Robert M. Benz, 24, said they had been hired by Donald H. Segretti, who had testified before the committee Oct. 3.

They were paid $150 a month, plus expenses. For this, they performed, mostly in the Florida primary, the "dirty tricks," such as hiring pickets, distributing false campaign literature and letters, placing false advertisements and planting stink bombs.

Kelly was contrite and cooperative before the committee; Benz, while expressing regret for his activity and acknowledging its illegality, was laconic in his answers and sparred with the committee, even challenging Chairman Sam J. Evrin Jr. (D, N.C.) at one point.

Benz, who had received limited immunity from prosecution, had been named as an unindicted co-conspirator by the Florida grand jury that had indicted Segretti. Benz had recruited George Hearing to assist in the campaign of sabotage.

Benz said he committed the political sabotage and espionage to give the Democrats "a little bit of a dose of their own type of activities." He contended that the Democrats had performed similar activities against a Republican senatorial candidate in Florida whom Benz had unsuccessfully worked to elect in 1970. As for the fake letter sent by accomplice Hearing accusing two Democratic contenders of sexual misconduct, Benz said he knew it was an illegal act and he was not proud of it, but he said he "felt like I did what I should do." "If my actions in any way would have cleaned up politics," he said, "they would have contributed something."

Ervin questioned Benz about this.

Q. Do you believe the fact that somebody did evil yesterday justified you to do evil today?

A.   No, I do not believe that.

Q. That is what you said you did in this. You said Democrats had done this. Can you tell me any time in the history of the United States that aides in the White House and the President's personal attorney made money available to people to spread lies and libel on candidates of the opposition party?

A.   I do not know if that has been proven or not, senator.

Q. I have been engaged in and concerned with politics for a long time and I have been interested in the political history of the United States and I challenge you or anybody else to point out a single instance in the history of this nation where money donated to advance the political fortunes of a President was used with the

consent of the President's assistants in the White House to spread libels against the candidates of the opposition political party?

A.   Are you asking me that question?

Q. Yes, there was a question mark after that.

A.   I think the first thing to answer that, can you tell me whenever a President has been investigated by the news media and by a committee as much as this one? Second, where were you in 1960 when it was accused that an election was stolen out in Chicago? We are talking now about a campaign being influenced and I believe you were a member of the Senate when it was accused that a campaign was stolen. Where were you then? Where were you in 1964 and 1968?

Q. I was right here in the United States Senate and I never heard of a campaign being stolen on the credible testimony of any individual. And this is the first time in the history of the United States that the Senate of the United States, by a unanimous vote, has been moved by reports of rascality on a national scale to set up a committee to conduct an investigation.

Kelly, on the other hand, told the committee he "felt guilty" for his campaign activities and that "any shame or abuse that is heaped on me is certainly well deserved." He attributed his acts "to being politically immature. I guess I was overly ambitious," he said, "and frankly, I was expecting to have high contact. I was not sure exactly who I was working with, but I had an idea it was maybe the White House or the re-election committee and my ideas of short-term success, I am afraid, were very unfortunate."

"It began with pranks," he told the committee, then got "more and more intense. . . . I kind of . . . was weaving my own spiderweb. I could not get out of it."

He said the goal of his activity was "to get the candidates to start back-biting each other." "Almost the complete purpose" of the effort, Kelly said, was not to influence voters directly but to "have the [Democratic] candidates get upset and maybe do something back to the other candidates."

He told the panel about some of his "pranks," all against the candidacy of Sen. Edmund S. Muskie (D, Me.):

Releasing white mice and a bird at a news conference; placing radio ads to alienate Cubans in Florida against Muskie; inviting African diplomats to attend a Washington dinner for Muskie, arriving by limousine, all costs charged to Muskie headquarters; and hiring a young woman to run naked in front of a hotel where Muskie was staying, shouting, "Muskie, I love you."

Sen. Edward J. Gurney (R, Fla.) commented that most of the tricks were "rinky-dink" and that politicians were inured to them. "I loathe it but it is part of politics," he said.

Kelly said, "I'm not here to defend my position; I don't have a position to defend."

Oct. 9: 'Fat Jack' affirms spy role— Testimony was taken from John R. Buckley, 53, who admitted engaging in campaign espionage activity against Sen. Muskie while an employe of the federal government. Buckley, who retired from federal service in June, had been director of the inspection division at the Office of Economic Opportunity (OEO). He did not admit any illegality or immorality in such activity, which he viewed as "a matter of course" in most political campaigns.

Buckley related that he was paid $1,000 a month from late 1971 until sometime in April 1972 for inside information on the Muskie campaign. He had planted a messenger in Muskie headquarters, Buckley explained, who called him at the OEO whenever he obtained Muskie documents. Buckley would leave his office at lunch time, he said, pick up the documents and photograph the ones he wanted in an office he rented for that purpose.

In turn, Buckley continued, he would deliver the copied documents, during lunch hour on street corners near the White House, to Nixon campaign officials. He identified the latter as Kenneth S. Reitz, who had first given him the assignment, and later E. Howard Hunt Jr., subsequently a Watergate conspirator. Reitz then was youth director of the Nixon re-election campaign.

Buckley, known as "Fat Jack" to his campaign contacts, told the committee much of the material was worthless, although he had obtained some Muskie itineraries and position papers.

Buckley said he did not know what was done with the material, but one item appeared in the nationally-syndicated column of Rowland Evans and Robert Novak. When his spy informed him of the concern at Muskie headquarters about the information leak, Buckley related, he in turn complained to Reitz that "it was not our purpose to be furnishing any internal memoranda of Sen. Muskie to the newspapers or to anybody else and if they were doing that we would discontinue also." Buckley said Reitz denied that the memo had been leaked by the Nixon committee but subsequently acknowledged that the denial was not the truth.

Buckley considered his activity "a normal transaction for an election year." "My theory is," he told the committee, "that a candidate has a right and it is proper for him to gather intelligence on the opposition, and I expect it is done in most, if not all, campaigns." Sen. Herman E. Talmadge (D, Ga.) asked him if he did not think "taking someone else's personal documents and photographing them and delivering them elsewhere" was theft. "No, sir, I do not," Buckley responded. Sen. Daniel K. Inouye (D, Hawaii) asked him if his activity had been "absolutely proper as far as you are concerned?" "As far as I am concerned, it was," Buckley said.

"I think political espionage goes on all the time," Buckley replied to a question whether this was "an acceptable practice." "It has gone on for many, many years. I do not feel that I invented it."

Oct. 10: 'Sedan Chair'; non-GOP tricks—Michael W. McMinoway testified that he infiltrated three different Democratic campaigns for the Nixon re-election committee, and Frederick J. Taugher testified that, as a Democrat, he became an ally in arranging for a protest demonstration against a Nixon rally. Taugher was southern California campaign coordinator for Sen. George McGovern (S.D.), the Democratic presidential nominee. His testimony, plus McMinoway's that McGovern workers planned and carried out a disruptive anti-Muskie demonstration in the Wisconsin primary, were the first public evidence presented to the committee of questionable campaign tactics by Democrats in the 1972 campaign.

Taugher told the committee he permitted persons planning an antiwar protest against Nixon's appearance in Los Angeles Sept. 27, 1972 to use McGovern telephones for two days to organize support for the protest. The protest took place but, according to news accounts at the time, had a minimal effect on the rally. A Los Angeles policeman told the committee that the protest had been basically "peaceful" and that only three arrests had been made, one for interfering with a police officer, two for possession of narcotics.

McMinoway, the fifth Nixon re-election committee spy to testify before the Senate panel, said he had been hired by the Nixon re-election committee at $1,500 a month to infiltrate Democratic campaigns. His contact was a man identifying himself as Jason Rainier, later identified as Roger Stone, a Nixon re-election committee employe. He was paid a total of about $6,000 for his work, he said, which he carried out from February–July 1972.

During this period, when he made daily reports to Stone, he enlisted as a Muskie campaign worker in Wisconsin, as a campaign worker for Sen. Hubert H. Humphrey (D, Minn.) in Pennsylvania and California and as a McGovern worker at the Democratic National Convention in Miami Beach. Part of his job was to collect scheduling data of the Democratic candidates and send it to a post office box in Washington. The information was circulated eventually, under the code name Sedan Chair II, within the re-election committee and the White House.

In addition to such espionage, McMinoway testified that he occasionally did minor sabotage, such as scrambling card files and dismissing volunteers who were actually needed.

McMinoway, a Louisville, Ky. resident, said he was recalled to Washington after the Watergate break-in, given assurance by Stone that his activity was not illegal and assigned one last task to infiltrate the McGovern camp at Miami Beach. He was appointed a security man for McGovern's hotel suite, he testified, and even gained entry one night to watch the convention proceedings on television with McGovern.

McMinoway contended that there were prostitutes, or "at least people with low moral standards," in the same hotel and that McGovern's staff was aware that "these people existed in the building." He related an assignment by the McGovern staff—to transport a convention delegate who had conferred with McGovern's campaign manager to the Playboy Plaza Hotel accompanied by two women who "exhibited," according to McMinoway, "some, what I considered immoral activities" during the car ride. Under questioning, McMinoway later admitted that he did not know whether the women were, in fact, prostitutes or whether the delegate's visit to the campaign manager had any relationship to his departure with the women.

McMinoway maintained before the committee that his activity was not illegal or unethical and that he had not misrepresented himself in his work for the Democrats, even while working in the Humphrey camp under an assumed name.

Oct. 11: *Democrats say tricks worked*—Frank Mankiewicz, national political director of the McGovern campaign, testified that the Republican "dirty tricks" in the 1972 campaign were successful in causing discord among the Democratic candidates and that this quite possibly changed the course of the campaign.

He said the campaign sabotage and espionage conducted by the GOP agents were not "politics as usual." The apparent concerted testimony of previous GOP witnesses that it was normal political practice might be the latest and most dangerous "dirty trick" of all, Mankiewicz said.

Both he and a later witness, Richard Stearns, McGovern's Western states campaign leader, affirmed that the Democrats had not engaged in any "dirty tricks" during the campaign.

Stearns, who was linked by Taugher to approval of the decision to let the antiwar group man the McGovern telephones to promote the anti-Nixon protest, denied knowledge of such a decision. Stearns said he passed over the incident without remonstrance or objection to higher authority because the protest mounted by the antiwar people had been peaceful and was, actually, an activity protected by the Constitution.

Stearns took offense at what he viewed as an attempt at the hearing to equate the incident with the serious "dirty tricks" played by the Republicans. "The attempt to find fault where there is none, to lay blame where it does not belong, to whitewash the guilty by blackening the innocent is a pathetic piece of political gamesmanship," he said.

He was challenged in his attitude by the committee chief Republican counsel Fred D. Thompson and Republican members Howard H. Baker Jr. (Tenn.) and Edward J. Gurney (Fla.). But Stearns insisted upon the ethical nature of the McGovern effort. While mistakes were made, he said, "we did not commit crimes."

Sen. Lowell P. Weicker (R, Conn.) cautioned the committee that pursuit of this line of questioning, which seemingly put a constitutionally protected activity in the same category as criminal activities, was itself a dangerous practice.

Mankiewicz told the committee "an unparalleled atmosphere of rancor and discord within the Democratic party" had been created by the GOP sabotage effort in the 1972 presidential campaign, and had it not been for this divisiveness "the course of the campaign might have been different." He said the rancor might have influenced Muskie's decision not to endorse McGovern when Muskie withdrew his candidacy, and might have influenced Humphrey to decide to enter the California primary, a bitter contest carried over into the Democratic convention. Humphrey, he said, might not have contested the California delegation composition "had he not become convinced—because of the Nixon campaign's planned sabotage—that Sen. McGovern's campaign had attacked him unfairly in May."

Both McGovern and Humphrey "were led to believe that the other was involved in a vicious campaign of distortion and vilification," he said, "and any re-uniting of factions—normally the course in a Democratic campaign after the primaries—became far more difficult."

"The purpose of it all, the slimy letters, the forged press releases, the fake leaflets," Mankiewicz said, "seems to have been not to influence the result of any single primary election, but to create within the Democratic party such a strong sense of resentment among the candidates and their followers as to make unity of the party impossible once a nominee was selected. At that the effort seems to have been most successful."

"I think it is important for someone to state, clearly and firmly," Mankiewicz said, "that these 'dirty tricks' are not politics as usual, that American politics does not include any history of or tolerance for sabotage, espionage, perjury, forgery or burglary." That kind of activity, he said, "may well be politics as usual for Nixon campaigns, but not for any other Democratic or Republican presidential campaign of which I have any knowledge. And I believe it to be the gravest disservice to the Republic to suggest that it is."

Mankiewicz specifically refuted testimony by former Nixon aide H. R. Haldeman that McGovern agents were responsible for violent demonstrations, disruptions, heckling, burning, bombing, attacks upon police and other incidents.

Nixon wins Senate tapes ruling. Judge Sirica Oct. 17 dismissed the Senate Watergate committee's lawsuit to obtain the disputed presidential tapes. The judge held that his court lacked jurisdiction in the civil case in contrast to the special prosecutor's case, which involved a subpoena issued for a criminal investigation by a grand jury. [See p. 89]

Nixon presents tapes proposal; crisis results. President Nixon Oct. 19 announced a "compromise" plan to provide the federal court and Senate Watergate investigators with a personally prepared summary of Watergate-related material on the secret tapes. The objection of special prosecutor Archibald Cox to the plan led to the President's firing of Cox, his dissolution of the office of special prosecutor, the resignation of Attorney General Elliot Richardson and the firing of Deputy Attorney General William Ruckelshaus. [See p. 97]

Senate panel hears MacGregor. Clark MacGregor, the successor to John N. Mitchell as director of the Committee to Re-elect the President, testified before the Senate Watergate Committee Nov. 1. Most of what MacGregor told the committee was already contained in a sworn deposition he gave in connection with civil suits stemming from the Watergate break-in.

MacGregor was questioned about a July 6, 1972 phone conversation between President Nixon and L. Patrick Gray 3rd, the former acting director of the Federal Bureau of Investigation (FBI). Gray had told the Watergate Committee Aug. 3 that he had called MacGregor in California at 10:51 a.m. (7:51 a.m. California time) to tell him people around the President were trying to "mortally wound" the President by obstructing the investigation into the Watergate break-in. Gray said he asked MacGregor to ask the President to call him back in Washington. Nixon returned the call 37 minutes later, Gray said.

MacGregor testified that he received the call from Gray at 11 p.m. California time July 5 (2 a.m. July 6, Washington time). While agreeing that Gray had expressed concern about obstruction of the Watergate investigation, MacGregor denied that Gray had asked him to tell Nixon. MacGregor added that while going through a White House reception line Oct. 11, President Nixon said to him: "Clark, you did not mention the Pat Gray matter to me on July 6." Under further questioning, MacGregor was unable to explain what had prompted Nixon's remark Oct. 11.

MacGregor's testimony about the call also differed with that of John D. Ehrlichman, the former domestic affairs adviser to the President. Ehrlichman told

the House Armed Services Special Subcommittee on Intelligence that the call from Nixon to Gray resulted from "MacGregor's conveying a request from Gray to the President."

Berl I. Bernhard, Presidential campaign manager for Sen. Edmund S. Muskie (D, Me.), appeared before the Watergate committee Oct. 31 to testify about the effect Republican dirty tricks had on Muskie's unsuccessful bid for the Democratic presidential nomination.

Bernhard conceded to the panel that the Republicans had been successful in their attempts to create confusion among the Democratic presidential contenders and to cause division that made it difficult for the party to unite behind one candidate.

"In my judgment," Bernhard said, the efforts directed against Muskie "took a toll." He cited theft by Republican infiltrators of a campaign scheduling proposal for use during the fall and winter of 1971-72, when the presidential primaries were getting under way. "It was the most vital document we had put together," he said.

Bernhard also testified that fraudulent advertising during the Presidential primary campaign in Florida cost Muskie potential backers and forced him to divert scarce campaign funds to answer attacks against him.

In addition, the Watergate committee heard testimony from one of its own investigators, Mark Lackritz, who said that at least $110,000 was spent by the Committee to Re-elect the President in the 1972 campaign to hire 22 political saboteurs to infiltrate and disrupt the Democratic presidential campaigns.

2nd phase of Watergate hearings ends. The 'dirty tricks' phase of the Senate Watergate hearings was concluded Nov. 6.

Among highlights of the testimony:

Michael Heller, a 19-year-old Oregon college student and a Democrats for Nixon committee worker in Los Angeles during 1972, testified that he saw McGovern workers distributing a leaflet during the campaign in Jewish areas of Los Angeles saying, "Nixon is Treyf " and "Nixon brings the ovens to the people rather than the people to the ovens." Heller implied the word "treyf," generally connoting non-kosher food, held a "hard core" meaning in the area where it was being distributed and represented a "slimy

tactic." The "ovens" phrase apparently was an attempt to link Nixon's Vietnam war policy to the Nazi slaughter of Jews during World War II.

Paul Brindze, California law school student, testified that the leaflet originated with a Jewish antiwar group and he had helped mimeograph copies without having absorbed its contents, which he now described as "unfortunate," and without permission from anyone in the McGovern campaign.

Truman Campbell, a Republican lawyer from California, testified that an Oct. 30, 1972 GOP rally had to be canceled after disruption by heckling and jostling from persons appearing to be members of the United Farm Workers (UFW). He said funds—about $52,000—had been allotted by the McGovern campaign to the UFW for voter registration, but, under questioning, admitted he had no evidence the funds were used for the disruption or any purpose other than voter registration.

Rep. Tim Lee Carter (R, Ky.) testified that the 1972 GOP Convention in Miami had been marred by various demonstrations he attributed to "revolutionaries," part of a "maniacal mob" and "fanatics."

Jeremiah Sullivan, a Boston police superintendent, testified about a demonstration Oct. 31, 1972 at a fund raising dinner in Boston attended by the President's wife, when some 20 arrests were made, nine policemen injured and property damaged. Under questioning, he said no evidence had been found by the Boston police of any "conspiracy."

All of the witnesses except Brindze, who was called by the committee's Democratic majority, were presented by the panel's Republican minority. At the end of the session, committee vice chairman Howard H. Baker Jr. (R, Tenn.), said "it is not our purpose to imply a connection between these activities and any candidate or campaign worker if the facts do not merit such a conclusion."

Baker put in the committee record about 40 affidavits which he said concerned violence, property damage, heckling and disruption perpetrated primarily against Republicans and Nixon campaign offices during the 1972 campaign, one being a previously reported break-in at the Long Beach, Calif. office of Nixon's personal physician.

Nixon Fires Cox, Richardson Resigns; Tapes to be Surrendered

ACLU urges impeachment of Nixon. The American Civil Liberties Union called Oct. 4 for the impeachment of President Nixon.

In a resolution adopted "overwhelmingly" by its board of directors, the organization said "there is now substantial public evidence of President Nixon's participation in high crimes and misdemeanors, and these acts have violated the civil liberties of the people of the United States and the rule by law."

ACLU Chairman Edward J. Ennis said the impeachment was being sought on six grounds: "specific proved violations of the rights of political dissent; usurpation of Congressional war-making powers; establishment of a personal secret police which committed crimes; attempted interference in the trial of Daniel Ellsberg, distortion of the system of justice; and perversion of other federal agencies."

ACLU Executive Director Aryeh Neier said pursuit of the impeachment goal would be "a major purpose" of the organization, which would push a lobbying effort through its 250,000 members and three lobbyists in Washington.

Nixon's popularity dips. A Gallup Poll made public Oct. 4 indicated that 32% of a polling sample group of 1,505 persons approved of the way President Nixon was conducting his office. The figure was a 16% decline from the 38% approval registered in a Gallup Poll released Aug. 21. The most recent Gallup survey was made Sept. 21–24.

According to another Gallup survey reported Sept. 23, the sample group by a 61%–32% margin felt President Nixon should release the White House tapes to U.S. District Court Judge John J. Sirica.

A Louis Harris survey, released Oct. 4, indicated that a national sample group by

a 54%–34% margin concluded that Congress would be justified in beginning impeachment proceedings against Nixon if he refused to obey a court order directing him to turn over the tapes.

Laird cautions Nixon on impeachment. White House domestic adviser Melvin R. Laird said Oct. 16 he had advised President Nixon to expect an impeachment move in Congress if he rejected a Supreme Court order to relinquish the tapes. Laird said he also told the President he thought the vote on impeachment "would be negative." The President had declared his willingness to abide by a "definitive" Supreme Court ruling on the issue.

Nixon presents tapes proposal. A crisis was touched off Oct. 19 when President Nixon announced his "compromise" plan to provide the federal court and Senate Watergate investigators with a personally-prepared summary of Watergate-related material on the tapes. The "authenticity" of the summary was to "be assured by giving unlimited access to the tapes" to someone "highly respected by all elements of American life for his integrity, his fairness and his patriotism." Nixon selected Sen. John C. Stennis (D, Miss.) to listen to the tapes in question and "verify" that Nixon's summary was "full and accurate." Another part of the compromise plan, according to Nixon, "so that the constitutional tensions of Watergate would not be continued," was an understanding that "there would be no further attempt by the special prosecutor to subpoena still more tapes or other presidential papers of a similar nature."

The President said the compromise plan had been drawn up by Richardson and

---

Taped Conversations Requested July 23 by Special Watergate Prosecutor Cox

Meeting of June 20, 1972 in the President's office in the Executive Office Building (EOB) between Nixon and aides John Ehrlichman and H. R. Haldeman from 10:30 a.m. to 1 p.m.

Telephone conversation of June 20, 1972 between the President and former Attorney General John N. Mitchell from 6:08 p.m. to 6:12 p.m.

Meeting of June 30, 1972 in Nixon's EOB office between the President and Haldeman and Mitchell from 12:55 p.m. to 2:10 p.m.

Meeting of Sept. 15, 1972 in the President's oval office between Nixon and his aide John Dean from 5:15 p.m. to 6:17

p.m. Haldeman joined the meeting at 5:27 p.m.

Meeting of March 13, 1973 in Nixon's oval office between the President and Dean from 12:42 p.m. to 2 p.m. Haldeman was present from 12:43 to 12:55.

Meetings of March 21, 1973 in the oval office between Nixon and Dean and Haldeman from 10:12 a.m. to 11:55 a.m.

Meeting of March 22, 1973 in Nixon's EOB office between Nixon and Dean from 1:57 p.m. to 3:43 p.m. Ehrlichman joined the meeting at 2 p.m., and Haldeman and Mitchell joined at 2:01 p.m.

Meeting of April 15, 1973 in the EOB office between the President and Dean from 9:17 p.m. to 10:12 p.m.

A

agreed to by Senate Watergate committee Chairman Sam J. Ervin Jr. (D, N.C.) and Vice Chairman Howard H. Baker Jr. (R, Tenn.). Nixon said Stennis had consented to his verification role.

Special Prosecutor Cox had rejected his compromise plan, Nixon said, but he had decided to take "decisive actions" anyway in order to avert a "constitutional crisis" and "lay the groundwork upon which we can assure unity of purpose at home and end the temptation abroad to test our resolve." Nixon felt that the Watergate issue at home had "taken on overtones of a partisan political contest" and that there were "those in the international community who may be tempted by our Watergate-related difficulties at home to misread America's unity and resolve" in meeting its challenges abroad.

B

He had decided, therefore, Nixon said, not to seek Supreme Court review of the appeals court decision Oct. 12 ordering him to surrender the tapes to the U.S. district court supervising the Watergate probe.

C

It was not in the national interest, the President contended, "to leave this matter unresolved for the period that might be required for a review by the highest court" although he was "confident that the dissenting opinions, which are in accord with what until now has always been regarded as the law, would be sustained upon review by the Supreme Court."

Instead, Nixon said, he would adopt the compromise plan to provide a summary of the tapes to the court and the Senate committee. The President said he took this step "with greatest reluctance" since it was "a breach in the confidentiality that is so necessary to the conduct of the presidency." But he also felt it was necessary "to bring the issue of the Watergate tapes to an end and to assure our full attention to more pressing business affecting the very security of the nation."

D

"Accordingly," he continued, "though I have not wished to intrude upon the independence of the special prosecutor, I have felt it necessary to direct him, as employe of the executive branch, to make no further attempts by judicial process to obtain tapes, notes or memoranda of presidential conversations. I believe that with the statement that will be provided to the court, any legitimate need of the special prosecutor is fully satisfied and that he can proceed to obtain indictments against those who may have committed any crimes."

E

The President expressed his opinion that the compromise tapes plan would resolve "any lingering thought that the President himself might have been in a Watergate cover-up."

F

Cox rejects Nixon plan—Special prosecutor Cox rejected Nixon's "compromise" tapes plan later Oct. 19 and said he would take his objections to it before the court. In his judgment, Cox said, "the President is refusing to comply with the court decrees."

G

Cox said the proposed summary would lack "the evidentiary value of the tapes

themselves" and "no steps are being taken to turn over the important notes, memoranda and other documents that the court orders require."

The President's order to cease the legal attempt to obtain the presidential tapes and other papers violated the attorney general's word given at his confirmation, Cox said, and compliance with such an order would violate his own pledge to the Senate and the country "to invoke judicial process to challenge exaggerated claims of executive privilege."

Acceptance of the President's directions, Cox said, would "defeat the fair administration of criminal justice. It would deprive prosecutors of admissible evidence in prosecuting wrongdoers who abuse high government office. It would also enable defendants to go free, by withholding material a judge rules necessary to a fair trial. The President's action already threatens this result in the New York prosecution of [former Attorney General] John Mitchell and [former Commerce Secretary] Maurice Stans. I cannot be a party to such an arrangement."

Cox cites 'insuperable difficulties'—Cox reasserted his position at a televised news conference at the National Press Club Oct. 20. He considered it his "duty as the special prosecutor, as an officer of the court and as the representative of the grand jury," he said, "to bring to the court's attention what seems to be noncompliance with the court's order." He said he could seek to initiate contempt proceedings against the President but it "might be preferable" to seek to have the situation arising from the President's new position clarified in court.

Cox said he found four "insuperable difficulties" with the President's plan to provide a summary of the tapes:

(1) In a criminal case, especially one involving "a cover-up," it was "simply not enough to make a compromise in which the real evidence is available only to two or three men operating in secrecy, all but one of them aides to the President and men who have been associated with those who are the subject of the investigation."

(2) No one would know what standards were applied to decide what to exclude from the summary. If the criteria were national defense or foreign policy items, for example, Cox said, he was "very troubled by the lack of precision on those standards." He noted that such criteria had been applied in the "Ellsberg-Fielding break-in" and certain telephone taps.

(3) It was "most unlikely" that a summary of the tapes would be admissible as court evidence and "I would be left without the evidence with which to prosecute people whom I had used the summaries, perhaps, to indict."

(4) The withholding of the tapes, and probable legal insufficiency of a summary, would jeopardize prosecution of cases in which the defendants were claiming the tapes were vital to their defenses.

Cox also cited his dealings with the White House. His efforts to get information from it, beginning in May,

"have been the subject of repeated frustration," he said. Many papers of presidential aides, Cox said, were "taken out of the usual files and put in something special called presidential files." He had requested an inventory of the files in June, as well as logs of White House meetings, and still had received neither, he said, and there were "many pending letter requests." "The delays have been extraordinary," Cox said.

In his current negotiations on Nixon's plan to present a summary of the tapes, conducted with Nixon's legal consultant Charles Alan Wright, Cox said "it was my impression that I was being confronted with things that were drawn in such a way that I could not accept them." At one point, Cox recalled, Wright referred to certain stipulations the White House deemed essential to any agreement "and, as I understood him, he said, 'You won't agree to these.'" In their final exchange of letters on the subject, Cox related, there was about a 7½-hour interval between his own letter and "one final letter" from the White House "which suggested that I had misunderstood the scope of some of the things." "There was ample time to explain if I had misunderstood anything of critical importance," Cox said, in that interval before announcement by the White House of Nixon's plan and Cox's rejection of it.

Cox said there was a question whether anyone could dismiss him except the attorney general, who had appointed him. But "eventually, a president can always work his will," he noted.

Cox stressed that "I'm not looking for a confrontation" and "I'm certainly not out to get the President of the United States."

Ervin, Baker meet with Nixon. President Nixon announced Oct. 19 that Senate Watergate committee leaders Ervin and Baker had agreed to his tapes summary plan and that Sen. Stennis had agreed to be the verifier of the summary. But these agreements later became clouded.

Baker called the plan "a good proposal" Oct. 19. Stennis said Oct. 19 while he was willing to perform his role, he could not give "a full answer" until he learned "what all of the facts" were and got "a full outline of the service" he was expected to render.

The next day Stennis said he had conditioned his role on Ervin's and Baker's acceptance of the President's plan. He said Nixon had telephoned him Oct. 19 and implied consent by Ervin and Baker. Stennis said he was unaware at the time that Cox had rejected the plan. Nixon had "assured" him, he said, that the tapes had not been doctored.

Ervin renounced Nixon's plan Oct. 20 but later reaccepted it. Ervin, who had met with Nixon along with Baker at the White House Oct. 19, said he left the President believing the committee would get partial, verbatim transcripts of the tapes, but it appeared the committee would obtain only a summary, which he considered unacceptable. "I would not accept anybody's interpretation of what the tapes contain," he said.

Later, Ervin told reporters he had "just been in communication with the White House" and had been advised "my interpretation of the agreement is identical with that of the White House."

Baker Oct. 20 downgraded the apparent misunderstanding as a "battle of semantics."

Both Ervin and Baker said Oct. 20 they had not been fully informed of the details of the Nixon tapes plan; neither was aware Nixon was planning to order Cox to end his court pursuit of the tapes.

After announcing Nixon's decision to provide the court with the contested tapes [See p. 99], the White House dropped its plan to give the Ervin committee a verified summary of the tapes. Ervin sent a telegram to the President Oct. 23 requesting "a verbatim copy of the exact words as recorded on the tapes," but Nixon's chief of staff Alexander M. Haig said Nixon had withdrawn the offer.

He said the President did not want "to impose" on Stennis who had undergone a long recuperation period from a gunshot wound, "when the information is now being divulged" in the court, and he referred to the committee's own court action on the issue. The committee filed that day a motion with the appeals court to expedite its bid for a reversal from the district court's dismissal of its case.

Liberals attack Nixon tapes plan— There had been some support in Congress, mostly from liberals, for Cox's initial rejection of Nixon's tapes summary plan.

Four Democrats on the Senate Judiciary Committee—Edward M. Kennedy (Mass.), Birch Bayh (Ind.), John V. Tunney (Calif.) and Philip A. Hart (Mich.)—signed a statement Oct. 20 backing Cox and urging Nixon "to pull back from this new and dangerous constitutional brink."

The same day, Sen. Edmund S. Muskie (D, Me.) considered the President's action "an unacceptable" defiance of the court. Sen. Walter F. Mondale (D, Minn.) thought it "brazen and arrogant." Rep. Donald M. Fraser (D, Minn.) suggested an impeachment proceeding should be initiated if the President's defiance of the court persisted.

Expressions of support for Nixon's plan came from the GOP Congressional leaders. Rep. Gerald R. Ford (Mich.), Nixon's nominee for vice president, said Oct 20 the plan was "sensible." Sen. Hugh Scott (Pa.) Oct. 19 thought it "a wise solution" to the constitutional impasse.

Cox fired, Richardson resigns. The White House announced at 8:24 p.m. Oct. 20 that President Nixon had discharged special prosecutor Cox and Deputy Attorney General Ruckelshaus for refusing to obey his orders on the handling of the Watergate tapes. Nixon also accepted the resignation of Attorney General Richardson.

White House Press Secretary Ronald L. Ziegler said Richardson had resigned rather than discharge Cox, who had appeared at a news conference earlier in the day [See above] to explain his refusal to comply with Nixon's order not to take further court action in attempts to obtain the tapes and other White House correspondence and memorandums relating to the Watergate case.

Ruckelshaus was then asked to carry out the President's order to discharge Cox. When he refused, according to Ziegler, Ruckelshaus was fired.

Cox's dismissal was finally carried out by Solicitor General Bork, who was appointed acting attorney general.

The President also announced through Ziegler that he had abolished the special Watergate prosecutor's office as of 8 p.m. and transferred its duties back to the Justice Department where they would "be carried out with thoroughness and vigor."

Ziegler said Cox had been discharged because he had "pressed for a confrontation at a time of serious world crisis." The press secretary said the President's tape plan would have provided the Watergate grand jury with "what it needs with the least possible intrusion into presidential privacy."

FBI agents were sent later that evening to seal off the special prosecutor's offices. The next day, they were replaced by U.S. marshals. Nixon aide Alexander Haig conceded Oct. 23 he was "guilty" of ordering the FBI to seal off the offices. He said he acted, after hearing reports that staffers were leaving with "huge bundles under their arms," to preserve the files.

Acting Attorney General Bork announced Oct. 22 that he had placed Henry E. Petersen in direct charge of the Watergate case "and all related matters previously being directed by the special prosecutor." Petersen would use the evidence and staff already assembled, as well as other department personnel, Bork said, "to see that these cases are pressed to a conclusion and that justice is done." Bork, who said he would have "ultimate authority and responsibility in these matters," said he planned "to adhere exactly to President Nixon's directive" to pursue the cases "with full vigor." Petersen, an assistant attorney general in charge of the criminal division, had been in charge of the Watergate investigation for 16 months prior to the appointment of the special prosecutor.

At a news conference Oct. 24, Bork pledged to take any steps necessary to obtain evidence from the White House if it was vital to prosecution of the Watergate cases. "If the law entitles us to any item of evidence, I will go after it," he said. Bork said he was not going to be the person "who in any way compromised any investigation." He said the President had told him "I want you to carry out these investigations and prosecutions fully." On the basis of his talk with the President, Bork said, he believed he was free to conduct the Watergate probes "the way I think they ought to be done."

In explaining how he could have performed the firing his predecessors could not, Bork said he was "not in the special position" Richardson and Ruckelshaus "found themselves," and the departure of Cox, he felt, had become "inevitable—it was going to be done."

Cox's reaction—Later Oct. 20, Cox issued a one-sentence statement on his firing: "Whether ours shall continue to be a government of laws and not of men is now for Congress and ultimately the American people [to decide]."

Walter Cronkite asked him during a CBS interview broadcast Oct. 24 about the state of his Watergate investigations at the time of his ouster. Cox indicated that "inquiries were being pushed into the raising of campaign funds, especially very large funds raised in conjunction with the White House staff in 1970—raised, I think, chiefly in cash." He also indicated that the probers were looking into "possible abuses" of national security and certain government agencies, including the Internal Revenue Service.

Richardson explains—Richardson explained his position in the controversy at a televised news conference Oct. 23. The conference was held prior to the announcement of President Nixon's decision to surrender the tapes to the court.

He began by asserting he still "strongly" believed "in the general purposes and priorities" of the Nixon Administration. He resigned, Richardson said, "because to continue would have forced me to refuse to carry out a direct order of the President" to dismiss Cox and because "I did not agree with the decisions which brought about the necessity for the issuance of that order." Cox's dismissal was based on his refusal to accept the President's directive to make no further attempt by judicial process to obtain tape, notes or memoranda of presidential conversations.

Richardson's position at the time Nixon directed Cox to end his quest for presidential documents was that the Nixon plan to give the court a summary of requested tapes should be carried through, "for the court's determination of its adequacy to satisfy the subpoenas." "Other questions" such as access to other documents, should be dealt with as they arose, Richardson said.

Because of his "role in guaranteeing the independence of the special prosecutor, as well as my beliefs in the public interest embodied in that role," Richardson said, he felt he could not discharge Cox, "so I resigned."

Richardson said he considered the tapes-summary plan "reasonable" but he did not think "it should be tied to the foreclosure of the right of the special prosecutor to invoke judicial process in future situations." But he supported the President's right to "revise the terms on which he has appointed somebody to his Administration." He also considered it advisable to have an independent prosecutor, advocating appointment of a replacement for Cox. At the same time, he was confident the Justice Department would "pick up where Mr. Cox left off."

Richardson attested to Cox's impartiality, and denied Cox had been out to "get the President." If he had been in Cox's position, Richardson said, "I would have done what he has done." As for impeachment, Richardson declined comment, saying it was "a question for the American people."

Richardson denied that he had been directed to dismiss Cox early the previous week or that Cox's ouster to end his investigation was the true aim of the White House in the tapes dispute. He said Cox's dismissal had come up in discussions with Nixon aides but as "one way of mooting the case" and "resolving the constitutional impasse." He also remarked that there had been "continuing concerns on the part of the President's counsel" about the scope of the Cox investigation and "continuing arguments" between Cox and the White House "over the issue of jurisdiction and access to particular notes, memoranda, documents and so on."

Ruckelshaus: 'easy' decision—Ruckelshaus said Oct. 23 his refusal to obey the President's order to fire Cox was a "very easy" decision and "not an heroic act." Public figures always had "the option to resign," he observed when "a fundamental disagreement" with a superior arose.

Cox had been promised a free hand for "a vigorous, thorough and fair" probe, Ruckelshaus said, and "what I was requested to do was to violate" that promise. He had been and still was convinced of the need for an independent investigation because of the "crisis of confidence in our institutions."

Asked if he would take another job in the Nixon Administration, Ruckelshaus replied, "No."

A flood of protests over firings—A flood of protest erupted over the abrupt ouster of Cox and resultant departures of Richardson and Ruckelshaus Oct. 20. The call for impeachment became insistent, inside Congress and out.

Telegrams and letters of protest began arriving at the White House and at the Capitol. By Oct. 23, Western Union in Washington had been "inundated" with messages, according to a company official—more than 150,000 telegrams, "the heaviest concentrated volume on record." Some 10,000 were directed to the White House, the rest to Congress, which normally received about 6,000 weekly. By Oct. 24, the volume was up to 220,000.

Even conservative members of Congress reported the preponderant tone of the messages was "negative" advocating impeachment. At the White House, "no tally" was being taken on the tenor of the messages.

In front of the White House, there was a steady response to protesters' signs, "Honk for Impeachment."

Nixon was denounced by the American Bar Association (ABA) and the Bar of the City of New York.

ABA President Chesterfield Smith warned Oct. 22 that Nixon was attempting to "abort the established processes of justice." He urged the courts and Congress to take "appropriate action" to "repel" the "attacks" by the President. Orville Schell, head of the New York bar group, mounted a lobbying effort for establishment of a special prosecution office to handle the Watergate cases. "They've got to consider impeachment," he commented Oct. 22.

Consumer advocate Ralph Nader warned Oct. 22 that "every citizen in this land must strive to reclaim the rule of law which this tyrant [Nixon] has been destroying month by month, strand by strand." Nader planned court action challenging Cox's ouster.

Historian Henry Steele Commager said Oct. 22 Nixon should be impeached "not merely for the most recent developments but for a long, unparalleled record of corruption and illegal actions."

A joint statement Oct. 22 from Robert S. Strauss, Democratic national chairman, and Gov. Wendell Ford (Ky.), chairman of the Democratic Governors Caucus, said Nixon had "abandoned the principle of law" and "his oath of office" and expressed "legitimate doubt as to whether he can continue to serve."

Melvin R. Laird, counselor to the President, defended the ouster of Cox on NBC's "Meet the Press" broadcast Oct. 21. Cox won "a tremendous victory" in the "compromise" offered him on the tapes, Laird said, and he did not believe "anyone should be in a position where they demand total surrender." He thought Congress would "wait to see the product of this compromise" and then would "take a negative position as far as the question . . . on impeachment proceedings" was concerned.

AFL-CIO asks Nixon to resign—Delegates to the 10th biennial convention of the American Federation of Labor and Congress of Industrial Organizations (AFL-CIO), meeting in Bal Harbour, Fla. Oct. 18–23, passed a resolution by acclamation Oct. 22 calling on President Nixon to resign and the House to impeach him "forthwith" if he did not.

"Clearly a President who has placed himself on the brink of impeachment," the resolution added with reference to Nixon's nomination of Rep. Gerald Ford (R, Mich.) to succeed Spiro Agnew as vice president, "should not be allowed to name his successor until charges against him have been disposed of satisfactorily."

The resolution, which was a statement drafted by and presented to the delegates by the AFL-CIO executive council, blamed Nixon for precipitating a "constitutional crisis" by trying to "prevent judicial examination" of the Watergate tapes "no matter what the cost to our constitutional system."

AFL-CIO President George Meany, 79, opened the convention Oct. 18 with a condemnation on the Nixon Administration, whose policies, he charged, were geared to "making a fast buck" for big corporations, the banks and other "fat cats" at the expense of the working man. "In the final analysis, let us keep in mind that Watergate and the cover-up itself were paid for by the great corporations of America—members of the National Association for Manufacturers and the [U.S.] Chamber of Commerce," Meany said.

After Meany spoke, delegates approved a resolution calling for an early end to the Administration's wage stabilization programs.

In a break with AFL-CIO tradition, neither President Nixon nor Secretary of Labor Peter J. Brennan was invited to address the convention.

Among the speakers addressing the convention were Sens. Henry M. Jackson (D, Wash.), Edward M. Kennedy (D, Mass.), Daniel Inouye (D, Hawaii) and Hubert H. Humphrey (D, Minn.).

The Nixon Administration "makes the Harding Administration look like boy scouts and the Hoover Administration look like economic geniuses," Jackson said Oct. 19. Inouye, a member of the Senate Watergate committee, called on the President to resign Oct. 22. Kennedy Oct. 19 and Humphrey Oct. 23 strongly attacked the policies of the Nixon Administration.

Meany charges Nixon instability—AFL-CIO President Meany said in Washington Oct. 24 that President Nixon appeared to be suffering from "dangerous emotional instability." The remark was made when Meany renewed his call for Nixon's resignation.

The White House labeled Meany's charge "incredible, inexcusable and irresponsible" and declared Nixon's health "excellent."

House airs impeachment resolutions. The threat of impeachment began to take shape in Congress Oct. 23. Eight impeachment resolutions, co-sponsored by a total of 31 Democrats, were offered in the House, where impeachment charges could be brought by majority vote.

Also introduced were 13 resolutions, with a total of 76 co-sponsors, proposing inquiries into possible impeachment or studies of possible presidential misconduct.

A total of 88 co-sponsors introduced six resolutions and two bills dealing with appointment of a Watergate prosecutor.

One of the impeachment resolutions was from Rep. Thomas L. Ashley (D, Ohio), who told the House the original resolution for impeachment of President Andrew Johnson had been introduced by his great-grandfather.

Rep. Dan Kuykendall (R, Tenn.), urging the House Oct. 23 "to go slow and don't be part of a legislative lynch mob," was hissed from the aisle and the gallery when he held up a noose as "a symbol of your action."

Comments from members of Congress ranged Oct. 21 from Sen. Harrison A. Williams Jr.'s (D, N.J.) that Nixon's actions were "all too reminiscent of a beleaguered man in a bunker destroying himself" to Sen. John G. Tower's (R,

Tex.) that Nixon had acted properly "to forestall a constitutional crisis."

House Democratic leaders agreed unanimously Oct. 23 to have the Judiciary Committee begin an inquiry into possible impeachment. House Republican leaders, facing the Democratic move, endorsed the inquiry.

The Washington Post reported Oct. 24 that House Republican leaders had warned Nixon, through his counselor Bryce N. Harlow, that they would not "go to the wall" with him in blocking impeachment proceedings unless he made the Watergate tapes available to the courts. The warning was said to have been delivered prior to the President's decision to turn the tapes over to the court.

Nixon reverses on tapes. The President's reversal of position and consent to turn over the tapes to the court was revealed in a dramatic and brief announcement before U.S. District Court Judge John J. Sirica in the District of Columbia Oct. 23. At that time, the administration had been expected to present the response of the President to the court's decision, upheld by the appeals court, to surrender the tapes; a response incorporating the President's plan to deliver the Nixon-edited summary of the contents of the tapes had been delivered informally to the court.

Earlier Oct. 23, Sirica had summoned the two Watergate grand juries before him to assure the jurors their probes were still "operative and intact" and he himself would "safeguard" their rights and "preserve the integrity of your proceedings."

At a later hearing, Sirica asked the President's attorneys if they were prepared to file "the response of the President" to his Aug. 29 order as modified by the appeals court.

Charles Alan Wright, chief of the President's Watergate legal defense team, stepped forward and said "the President of the United States would comply in all respects" with Sirica's order as modified by the higher court. The announcement was totally unexpected. Wright explained that the President still maintained that his previous posture was correct and the "summary" would satisfy the court's needs, but the problem was that even if the court agreed with him "there would have been those who would have said the President is defying the law."

"This President does not defy the law," Wright declared, "and he has authorized me to say he will comply in full with the orders of the court."

At a news conference later Oct. 23 with Nixon's chief of staff Alexander M. Haig, Wright said "we all miscalculated" the reaction to the President's recent course. "My own mood was one of euphoria," Wright said, that Nixon had made such an "extraordinarily generous proposal" to yield a "summary."

Haig said there had been a great deal of "misunderstanding and misinformation" regarding the President's position, and "the President concluded after very painful and anguished discussions that

the circumstances were sufficiently grave that he should abandon his very strongly held and long held right to protect the prerogatives of his office not only for himself but for future presidents." He denied the President's decision stemmed solely from the threat of impeachment. It arose from the "whole milieu of national concern" over recent events, Haig said.

The President scheduled a national broadcast for Oct. 24 to explain his position, but this was canceled because of the President's preoccupation with the Middle East crisis, according to Deputy Press Secretary Gerald Warren. He said the President would hold a news conference instead on Oct. 25. This was later rescheduled, for the same reason, for Oct. 26.

Action in Congress. The President's decision to yield the tapes to the court did not deter the move in Congress toward an opening of the impeachment process. House Judiciary Committee chairman Peter W. Rodino Jr. (D, N.J.) said Oct. 24, after conferring with 19 other Democrats on the panel, that its impeachment investigation would "proceed full steam ahead."

Rodino also said the committee would investigate any allegations of "impeachable offenses." Other committee members reported these would include the secret bombing of Cambodia in 1970, the 1970 Administration plan for wiretapping and burglary of suspected subversives, and the President's refusal to spend funds appropriated by Congress.

Vice President-designate Gerald Ford said Oct. 25 he thought the investigation "should carry on." He also said he would support an independent Watergate investigation, outside the Justice Department, if that was the will of a majority of the Congress.

Strong statements against Nixon continued. The Congressional Black Caucus Oct. 24 urged a Congressional probe of what it called a "cascade" of "executive crimes." Rep. Robert L. Leggett (D, Calif.) accused Nixon Oct. 25 of violating at least seven criminal laws in the Watergate case and other matters. "Just at a glance," he said, "I can see a prima facie case of commission of sufficient felonies in Mr. Nixon's record to imprison him for 173 years."

House Speaker Carl Albert (D, Okla.) said Oct. 24 that the impeachment inquiry would continue until it "lays this thing to rest one way or the other."

GOP urges new special prosecutor. Nixon aides were advised by the House Republican Conference Oct. 25 that the President should appoint a new special prosecutor and should make public the contents of the White House tapes.

John B. Anderson (R, Ill.), chairman of the conference, reported a "frank and forthright" exchange between the House Republicans and three White House officials—Bryce Harlow, Leonard Garment and Charles Alan Wright.

There were also suggestions from several sources, including Sen. Edward J. Gurney (R, Fla.) Oct. 25, that Nixon should appoint Elliot Richardson special prosecutor.

The Senate Republican leadership had also suggested Oct. 24 that Nixon name a new special prosecutor. Senate Majority Leader Hugh Scott (Pa.) gave the message to Harlow in a telephone call after conferring with GOP whip Robert P. Griffin (Mich.), GOP Policy Committee Chairman John G. Tower (Tex.), GOP Conference Chairman Norris Cotton (N.H.) and Conference Secretary Wallace F. Bennett (Utah).

The Scott message also communicated the GOP leaders' feeling that if Nixon did not appoint a new prosecutor, the court should do so, and that Petersen should act to bring indictments in the Watergate cases as soon as possible. The message recommended the procedures as moves to allay public concern.

Later Oct. 24, Scott and other members of the Senate Judiciary Committee met and unanimously approved a recommendation for appointment of a special prosecutor. The committee also planned to request the Justice Department to limit access to and preserve the evidence gathered by the Cox probe.

(Petersen and the remaining Cox special prosecution staff asked Judge Sirica Oct. 25 to take custody of the Cox force's records in light of the prevailing "uncertain" conditions.)

Alert questioned in U.S. Several major American newspapers and news magazines reported public suspicion that the U.S. military alert ordered in response to the reported threat of the movement of Soviet troops to the Middle East to enforce the ceasefire these had been influenced by the political "fire storm" of reaction resulting from the widening Watergate scandal.

This view was rejected by Congressional leaders Oct. 25, immediately after the alert was ordered, although many were reported to have expressed reservations privately. Among those supporting Nixon's action were House Speaker Carl Albert (D, Okla.) and several of Nixon's political opponents, Senators Edward Kennedy (D, Mass.), Edmund Muskie (D, Me.) and Charles Percy (R, Ill.). The strongest expression of doubt in Congress Oct. 25 was that of Rep. John E. Moss (D, Calif.), who said "this is an effort to divert attention from the more damaging disclosures the President feared [Watergate prosecutor] Archibald Cox was about to make when he fired him."

Newsweek, in its Nov. 5 issue, suggested that the President's "flourish of crisis diplomacy" was a device to divert attention from his domestic political troubles. According to Newsweek, an unnamed Administration aide said that "we had a problem and we decided to make the most of it."

Time's Nov. 5 issue questioned "whether the alert scare [was] necessary." After citing the doubts of "some military experts" that Soviet actions toward the Middle East warranted the military response ordered by the President, Time concluded that "perhaps some less dramatic action might have ended the crisis."

The Wall Street Journal concluded Oct. 26 that the crisis was "real," but it noted that a "few Nixon foes—grown so cynical about presidential actions because of past White House duplicity—may claim that yesterday's exercise was merely a calculated ploy by a man in deep political trouble."

The Washington Post reported Oct. 26 that there was bipartisan support for the President's warning to the Soviets "despite" privately expressed reservations and an "undercurrent of suspicion that the President might have escalated the crisis. . . . to . . . take people's minds off his domestic problems."

Kissinger explains U.S. action—Secretary of State Henry Kissinger, asked at an Oct. 25 news conference whether the military alert might have been designed with domestic political considerations in mind, said the suggestion was "a symptom of what is happening to our country" and denied the charge. He implied that "crises of authority" in the U.S. "for a period of months" may have influenced the Soviet Union to gamble on a unilateral Mideast intervention. He insisted that the alert decision had been made unanimously by the National Security Council in response to a reporter who questioned the rationality of Nixon's order.

Stock market plummets. Fears over possibility of a recession and other aspects of the widening domestic energy crisis, paired with continued uncertainty over the Middle East cease-fire, were reflected in a dramatic decline in investors' confidence and a plummeting stock market. President Nixon's entanglement in the Watergate affair and evidence of his steep decline in public esteem and confidence also contributed to the volatile market conditions.

The New York Stock Exchange staged a recovery Oct. 26 following several days of abruptly declining prices in the wake of Nixon's firing of special Watergate prosecutor Archibald Cox, but record lows were posted one week later. The Dow Jones industrial average closed at 987.06, up 12.57 points on its recovery, the best showing since Feb. 13, but the index was down 13.55 points to close at 935.28 Nov. 2. The week's decline of 51.78 points was the largest single week drop since 1965.

In other key Dow Jones closings:

Nov. 5—919.4, down 15.88 points, following publication of editorials calling for Nixon's resignation.

Nov. 8—932.65, up 12.57, following broadcast of Nixon's energy message.

Nov. 9—908.41, down 24.24 points, the largest single day loss since May 28, 1962. (A belated reaction to fears of widespread fuel shortages.)

Nov. 12—897.65, down 10.76 points.

Nov. 14—869.88, down 21.15 points.

Nov. 16—891.33, up 16.78 points following Nixon's statement that the Arab oil embargo might soon be relaxed.

Nov. 19—862.66, down 28.67 points, another 11-year low and its fifth largest decline in history. The Arabs' reaffirmation of the U.S. oil cutoff was blamed for the plunge in stock prices.

Nov. 20—844.9, down 17.76 points, its lowest level since Nov. 30, 1971.

Nixon discusses firings at news conference. President Nixon held a 40-minute televised news conference Oct. 26 and discussed the most recent Watergate developments.

Nixon tended to disagree that Watergate may have led the Soviet Union to miscalculate. Brezhnev understood the power of the U.S., he said, and he knew "the President of the United States," that the President, "when he was under unmerciful assault" at the time of the U.S. invasion of Cambodia in 1970 and the bombing of North Vietnam in 1972, "still went ahead and did what he thought was right. The fact that Mr. Brezhnev knew that regardless of the pressures at home, regardless of what people see and hear on television night after night, he would do what was right. That's what made Mr. Brezhnev act as he did."

The President had referred to the Indochina war criticism earlier in the conference, in response to a question about "what goes through your mind when you hear of people who love this country and people who believe in you say, reluctantly, that perhaps you should resign or be impeached."

"I'm glad we don't take the vote of this room," Nixon began, then referred to "the most difficult decision of my first term"—the bombing of North Vietnam in December 1972. At that time, he said, "exactly the same words were used on the networks . . . that were used now—tyrant, dictator, he's lost his senses, he should resign, he should be impeached. But I stuck it out and as a result of that we not only got our prisoners of war home . . . on their feet rather than on their knees, but we brought peace to Vietnam, something we haven't had and didn't for over 12 years."

Nixon realized some persons felt there were grounds for impeachment concerning the Cox dismissal. He suggested that Cox and Elliot L. Richardson, who resigned as attorney general rather than discharge Cox, agreed that the President had the right to dismiss anyone in the federal government, and he pointed out that he was in compliance with the law with regard to the presidential tapes that evoked the dispute.

"As far as what goes through my mind," he said, "I will simply say that I intend to continue to carry out to the best of my ability the responsibilities I was elected to carry out last November. The events of this past week I know, for example, in your head office in New York [CBS-TV] some thought it was simply a blown-up exercise, there wasn't a real [Middle East] crisis. I wish it had been that. It was a real crisis. It was the most

difficult crisis we've had since the Cuban confrontation of 1962.

"But because we had had our initiative with the Soviet Union, because I had a basis of communication with Mr. Brezhnev, we not only avoided a confrontation but we moved a great step forward toward real peace in the Mideast. Now as long as I can carry out that kind of responsibility, I'm going to continue to do this job."

Nixon said the new special Watergate prosecutor he would appoint "next week" within the Justice Department would have "independence" and "total cooperation from the executive branch." His primary responsibility would be to bring "this matter" to "an expeditious conclusion." "It's time for those who are guilty to be prosecuted and for those who are innocent to be cleared," Nixon said, and he had "no greater interest" than to see that the new prosecutor had the cooperation from the executive branch and the independence necessary "to bring about that conclusion."

Asked if the new prosecutor would "have your go-ahead to go to court if necessary to obtain evidence from your files if he felt it was vital," Nixon said he did not expect that to be necessary, that the events that led to Cox's dismissal were "matters that can be worked out and should be worked out in cooperation and not by having a suit filed by a special prosecutor within the executive branch against the President."

Referring to his plan to release a summary of the tapes, Nixon said, despite approval of the plan by himself, the attorney general and the two major senators on the Watergate committee, Cox had rejected the proposal and "I had no choice but to dismiss him." As for the new prosecutor, "we will cooperate with him," he insisted, "and I do not anticipate that we will come to the time when he would consider it necessary to take the President to court. I think our cooperation will be adequate."

Nixon stated firmly that "we will not provide presidential documents to a special prosecutor. We will provide, as we have in great numbers, all kinds of documents from the White House. But if it is a document involving a conversation with the President I would have to stand on the principle of confidentiality. However, information that is needed from such documents would be provided."

A reporter pointed out that there was "a great deal of suspicion" in Congress over any arrangement that would permit the executive branch to investigate itself or would establish a prosecutor the President could fire again. But Nixon thought his decision to appoint a new prosecutor would be satisfactory to Congress. As far as he was concerned, "we had cooperated" with Cox but Cox "seemed to be more interested in the issue than he was in the settlement."

'Vicious reporting' cited—The American people "can ride through the shocks that they have," Nixon said. But he observed a "difference" between now and earlier days—"the electronic media."

"I have never heard or seen," he continued, "such outrageous, vicious, distorted reporting in 27 years of public life. I'm not blaming anybody for that. Perhaps what happened is that what we did brought it about, and therefore the media decided that they would have to take that particular line. But when people are pounded night after night with that kind of frantic, hysterical reporting, it naturally shakes their confidence.

"And yet I should point out that even in this week when many thought that the President was shellshocked, unable to act, the President acted decisively in the interests of peace and the interests of the country, and I can assure you that whatever shocks gentlemen of the press may have, or others—political people—these shocks will not affect me and my doing my job."

As to how he was "bearing up emotionally under the stress of recent events," Nixon replied:

"Well, those who saw me during the Middle East crisis thought I bore up rather well. . . . I have a quality which is, I guess I must have inherited it from my Midwestern mother and father, which is that the tougher it gets the cooler I get. Of course it isn't pleasant to get criticism; some of it is justified, of course. It isn't pleasant to find your honesty questioned, it isn't pleasant to find for example that, speaking of my friend, Mr. Rebozo, that despite the fact that those who printed it and those who said it knew it was untrue—said that he had a million-dollar trust fund for me that he was handling—it was nevertheless put on one of the networks, knowing it was untrue. It isn't pleasant, for example, to hear, or read, that a million dollars in campaign funds went into my San Clemente property, and even after we have a complete audit, to have it repeated.

"Those are things which of course do tend to get under the skin of the man who holds this office. But as far as I'm concerned, I have learned to expect it. It has been my lot throughout my political life, and I suppose because I've been through so much, that maybe one of the reasons is when I have to face an international crisis, I have what it takes."

A reporter questioned him about his criticism of television reporting.

Q. Mr. President, you've lambasted the television networks pretty well. Could I ask you, at the risk of reopening an obvious wound—you say, after you've put on a lot of heat, that you don't blame anyone. I find that a little puzzling. What is it about the television coverage of you in these past weeks and months that has so aroused your anger? **A. Don't get the impression that you arouse my anger.** Q. I have that impression. **A. You see, one can only be angry with those he respects.**

Later in the conference, Nixon returned to the subject. He did not want to leave an impression with his "good friends from CBS," he said, "that I don't respect the reporters. What I was simply saying was this: That when a commentator takes a bit of news and then with knowledge of what the facts are distorts it viciously, I have no respect for that individual."

As for regaining the peoples' confidence, Nixon expected "to move forward in building a structure of peace in the world." His European initiative and continued initiatives with the Soviet Union and China, he said, "will be the major legacy of this Administration." He also spoke of "moving forward at home" in the battle against the high cost of living and the "deplorable" campaign abuses uncovered in the Watergate matter.

Nixon attempted to banter with one of his former aides, Clark Mollenhoff, who said he had to be loud to gain recognition "because you happen to dodge my questions all the time." He was asked for an explanation of "the rationale of a law and order Administration covering up evidence, primafacie evidence, of high crimes and misdemeanors."

Nixon responded: "Well, I should point out that perhaps all the other reporters in the room are aware of the fact we have waived executive privilege on all individuals within the Administration—it's been the greatest waiver of executive privilege in the whole history of this nation—and as far as any other matters are concerned, the matters of the tapes, the matters of Presidential conversations, those are matters in which the President has the responsibility to defend this office, which I shall continue to do."

Media officials rebut attack. Network executives rebutted President Nixon's news conference criticism of television reporting Oct. 27.

NBC News President Richard C. Wald said he felt the President was "making a mistake—the old mistake of blaming the messenger for the message."

CBS News President Richard Salant said "we are professionally obligated to try not to be directly involved in a dispute with the President" and "we are convinced that none of the network reporting justifies the adjectives" used by Nixon.

Elmer Lower, the president of ABC News, said "we have never knowingly broadcast anything false" and he stood by his network's record "for fairness and balance."

Bos Johnson, president of the Radio-Television News Director's Association, said Oct. 30 in Huntington, W.Va. that the news media did not create the issues but reported them.

Other reactions—Vice President-designate Gerald R. Ford commented Oct. 27 he believed the President, "on second thought, probably wished he hadn't" made the remark that "one can only be angry with those he respects." He said he thought Nixon was "totally on top of the job."

Assistant Senate GOP Leader Robert P. Griffin (Mich.) said Oct.26 that Nixon had given "a cool, reassuring performance in a very tense and hostile atmosphere [that] demolished myths about his ability to govern under fire."

Sen. Edmund S. Muskie (D, Me.) said Oct. 26 that Nixon had tried to "divert our attention" from his political and legal problems by overstating developments in the Middle East and by attacking the media.

On the Watergate issue, Senate assistant Democratic leader Robert C. Byrd (W. Va.) said Oct. 26 that the press conference augmented "the suspicion—rightly or wrongly—that the White House is trying to hide something."

Senate Watergate Committee Chairman Sam J. Ervin Jr.'s (D, N.C.) comment Oct. 26: "We had a special prosecutor before and he got fired. We want one they can't fire."

Rep. John B. Anderson (Ill.), the third-ranking Republican in the House, agreed. The President, he said, "wholly failed to comprehend that the Cox experience showed that cooperation was not possible."

Former Treasury Secretary John B. Connally said Oct. 28 that Nixon "owed the country a better explanation for his actions than we got" on the tapes issue and ouster of Cox. In a speech in Houston that day, and in another in New York Oct. 30, Connally said the attacks on Nixon had "the smell of a vendetta, and if wiser and cooler heads in both political parties don't take control we are in for a much greater national trauma" than before.

White House presses media attack—President Nixon's attack on the news media was elaborated by spokesmen Oct. 29 and 30.

Deputy Press Secretary Gerald L. Warren lectured White House correspondents Oct. 29 on the President's insistence on "perspective" in their reports. He indicated his displeasure with specific television broadcasts. Warren again assailed TV networks Oct. 30.

Nixon speechwriter Patrick Buchanan appeared on the CBS morning news program Oct. 29. He likened the mood at the Nixon press conference to that in a bull ring and gave his "personal" recommendation that the Administration make a legislative effort "to break the power of the networks."

Nixon's son-in-law, David Eisenhower, appeared on a morning NBC-TV interview Oct. 30 to assert there was too much "reporting without applying any perspective to it at all." In his view, the "irresponsibility" of the media had been "matched by the irresponsibility of the people they may quote."

(An official of the Veterans of Foreign Wars disclosed Oct. 25 that a White House aide had approached him to solicit statements of support for Nixon following the President's news conference, originally scheduled for that day. A spokesman for the National Association of Manufacturers said the organization's lobbyist had been contacted by "a lower echelon" White House official who suggested "we might want to make a comment" after the Nixon press session.)

A

B

C

D

E

F

G

House begins impeachment inquiry. The House Judiciary Committee met Oct. 30 to consider impeachment proceedings against President Nixon. It was the first official step toward possible impeachment of a president in 105 years and only the second in U.S. history.

The committee approved a grant of broad subpoena power to its chairman, Rep. Peter W. Rodino Jr. (D, N.J.), after rejecting two Republican proposals to permit the panel's Republican minority to share in the subpoena authority or exercise its own separate subpoena authority. All three votes were on straight party lines. 21 D. vs. 17 R.

Rodino was authorized to issue subpoenas without the consent of the full committee. He also was authorized by the committee to issue subpoenas covering its hearings on the nomination of House GOP Leader Gerald R. Ford (Mich.) to be vice president.

The impeachment inquiry was launched on a partisan note despite Rodino's assurances that he would not engage in any "wholesale issuing of subpoenas," that he would consult with the committee's ranking Republican, Rep. Edward Hutchinson (Mich.), on each subpoena and that he would "respect" Republican requests for subpoenas.

In an interview Oct. 29, Rodino had said "this cannot be a partisan effort" but "has to be something that all of our members understand—an attempt to clear the air. If we find there are impeachable offenses, then we've got to move ahead. If not, fine."

The panel's Republicans, however, considered the committee action Oct. 30 as test votes on whether the inquiry would be bipartisan or not.

Rodino pledged Oct. 30 not to conduct a "witch hunt" and not to hold Ford's nomination "hostage" until the impeachment inquiry was completed. Neither should "this crisis in authority" be permitted to continue for a long time, he said, because of the "high level of intensity and urgency" surrounding the issue.

Plans against news media revealed. A Senate Watergate Committee member, Sen. Lowell P. Weicker Jr. (R, Conn.), released Oct. 31 and Nov. 1 a series of White House memoranda that suggested means to counter what the President viewed as unfavorable coverage by the news media.

One memorandum, from former White House aide Jeb Stuart Magruder to the President's Chief of Staff, H. R. Haldeman, said that efforts "to get" the media on a case by case basis were "very unfruitful and wasteful of our time." Instead, Magruder said in the memo, dated Oct. 17, 1969, "a major impact" could be made if the Administration: had the Federal Communications Commission (FCC) monitor the networks to prove bias on their part; threatened antitrust action against major news organizations; threatened an Internal Revenue Service (IRS) investigation of "the various organizations that we are most concerned about"; gave exclusive information to favorable newsmen; conducted major letter writing campaigns through the Republican National Committee.

Attached to the memorandum was a log of 21 requests made by President Nixon between mid-September and mid-October, 1969. Among Nixon's requests, White House Communications Director Herbert G. Klein was asked "to take appropriate action to counter biased TV coverage over the summer."

Peter M. Flanigan, a top White House aide, was asked by Nixon to "take action to counter" a report by Dan Rather, a reporter for the Columbia Broadcasting System (CBS), that Gen. Lewis B. Hershey had been fired as head of the Selective Service System because of student protests. In another memo to Klein, Nixon asked "to have the Chicago Tribune hit Senator [Charles H.] Percy (R, Ill.) hard on his ties with the peace group."

Commenting on the Magruder memorandum and others he had released, Weicker said there "was no way to know" if White House officials had acted on any of the proposals, but "it shows the type of thinking that was going on at the White House."

Weicker also made public a memorandum from former White House Counsel Charles W. Colson to Haldeman that was dated Sept. 25, 1970. Colson wrote that officials of the major television networks were "very much afraid of us and are trying hard to prove they are good guys." Colson had met with network executives to urge them to resist requests by Democrats for free air time to counter televised statements made by Nixon.

Colson added that he would ask FCC Chairman Dean Burch to consider issuing "an interpretive ruling" on the fairness doctrine after the Republicans had obtained a majority on the FCC.

Two key recordings 'nonexistent.' White House counsel J. Fred Buzhardt asserted Oct. 31 that two key tape recordings of Presidential conversations about the Watergate affair sought by the prosecution did not exist. The disclosure was made in an appearance before Chief Judge John J. Sirica of the U.S. District Court in Washington. The tapes were among nine pledged to be turned over to the court in the Administration's surprise compliance Oct. 23 with court orders to do so.

Judge Sirica disclosed that the matter had come up the day before, during discussion of procedures for turning over the tapes, when Buzhardt informed him two of the tapes had "never been made." Sirica then set the public hearing Oct. 31 to make the facts "a matter of public record."

The tapes said to be nonexistent involved a telephone conversation on June 20, 1972, three days after the Watergate burglary, between President Nixon and his then campaign manager, John N. Mitchell, and an April 15, 1973 conversation Nixon had with his former counsel, John W. Dean 3rd.

Buzhardt said the Mitchell call had not been recorded because Nixon had made the call from the residential part of the White House on a phone that was not plugged into the White House recording system. The Dean conversation was not recorded, Buzhardt said, because of an apparent malfunction of a tape recorder in the Executive Office Building.

The Mitchell conversation was considered important in light of Mitchell's testimony before the Senate Watergate committee that he talked to Nixon only about the burglary without mentioning involvement of Administration officials. In the April discussion, according to Dean, the President had remarked that it had probably been foolish of him to have discussed executive clemency for a Watergate defendant with his aide Charles Colson and that he had been joking in an earlier conversation about raising a $1 million fund for the defendants.

Sirica requested the White House logs listing persons who had access to the tapes and which tapes had been withdrawn and by whom.

In a statement Oct. 30, Sirica said he would "hear argument in closed session on the various claims of privilege" before listening to the tapes. He said he would then "examine the tapes and written material and make individual decisions on each claim of privilege."

According to White House deputy press secretary Gerald Warren Oct. 31, Buzhardt had discovered that the two tapes did not exist on Oct. 27. Warren had said Oct. 29 the tapes were under the "personal physical control" of Nixon.

Cox recalls comment—Former special Watergate prosecutor Archibald Cox said Oct. 31 he was unaware that the two tapes did not exist and had been assured by Buzhardt all the tapes were safe. He said he would be "awfully surprised" if Buzhardt knew that the two were missing. He recalled being told, a few days prior to his dismissal Oct. 20, that Buzhardt had remarked to a New York prosecutor seeking other tapes that "sometimes there are mechanical problems."

Cox's comments were made to the Senate Judiciary Committee after the disclosure the tapes were missing.

Congressional reaction harsh—The immediate reaction of members of Congress was unfavorable to the President.

Sen. James B. Pearson (R, Kan.)—"I'm shocked, I'm surprised—I thought all the surprises were out of me. I think it will weaken his position very much, not only with the Senate but with the country, and we were getting to the point where we desperately needed something to strengthen it."

Sen. Barry M. Goldwater (R, Ariz.) issued a statement Nov. 1 saying that in the wake of the latest tapes episode Nixon's credibility "has reached an all-time low from which he may not be able to recover." Reiterating his suggestion Nixon testify before the Senate Watergate committee, Goldwater said "I feel now more than ever that this may offer the only way out."

Other senators were quoted as follows Oct. 31:

Sen. Richard S. Schweiker (R, Pa.)—The disclosure was "another tragedy of credibility in the long crisis of credibility that has engulfed this Administration."

Sen. James L. Buckley (Conservative-Republican, N.Y.)—The burden of proof had "dramatically shifted." "As of this moment, President Nixon has the clear burden of satisfying the American people that he has been speaking the truth. If he fails in this then we are faced with a political crisis of the most profoundly disturbing proportions."

Sen. Mark O. Hatfield (R, Ore.)—The "startling revelation" about "certain key tapes" that were "fought over to the brink of a constitutional crisis dramatically escalates the problems of the Administration's credibility."

Senate GOP Leader Hugh Scott (Pa.)—"This machine age isn't always perfect."

Sen. Sam J. Ervin Jr. (D, N.C.)—"Everything about this has been curious from the first day." (Ervin, chairman of the Senate Watergate committee, told reporters Oct. 31 he had been assured by the White House as late as Oct. 19 that all nine tapes being sought by his panel were intact.)

Sen. Hubert H. Humphrey (D, Minn.)—"This doesn't have the characteristic of a recent discovery. The public is fed up with this sort of business."

Recorder ran out of tape—At a fact-finding session Nov. 1, Buzhardt told the U.S. District Court that the Nixon-Dean discussion had occurred on a Sunday, and the recording was missing because the recorder had run out of tape. Testimony also was heard indicating that the security on access to the White House tapes had been haphazard.

Technical testimony was offered to show that a six-hour tape reel had nearly been used up on Saturday, April 14, after long Nixon meetings in the same office, and that the tape ran out without replacement before the Nixon-Dean conversation the following day.

One witness was John Nesbitt, who was assigned by the National Archives to keep a daily log of the President's movements at the White House for the benefit of his-

torians. Nesbitt's record showed that Nixon had met in that room for more than five hours that April 14, but Nesbitt testified that the log had been revised on July 26 after members of his staff had found some inaccuracies. Nesbitt said he believed it was coincidental that July 26 was the day the Watergate prosecution served its subpoena on the White House for the tapes and related documents. His log also provided verification for the non-existence of a tape recording of the Mitchell phone call; it indicated that Nixon at the time was on the second floor of the White House residence where the phone was not attached to the recording system.

Two White House Secret Service agents, Raymond C. Zumwalt and James Baker, who supervised the tapings, testified that the cardboard box in which the April 15 tape was stored was marked, "Part I." Both agents said they did not know who had marked that on the box nor could they explain it.

Their testimony showed that some of the check-out records for the tapes were kept on scraps torn from paper bags and that the lack of a return check on tapes checked out was not unusual. According to the logs, Nixon aide Stephen V. Bull took 26 tapes on June 4, 1973, the day Nixon was said to have listened to some of them, but there was no listing on their return. Questioned about the practice, Zumwalt said, "That's normal." Zumwalt said Bull also took out on July 11 the tapes marked as covering the room in question during the April 11–16 period.

Buzhardt contended that an inventory of the tapes had not actually been conducted prior to the previous weekend because "we thought we were going to win the suit" denying the prosecution's request for them.

New attorney general, prosecutor named. In a brief appearance at the White House Nov. 1, President Nixon announced he would appoint Sen. William B. Saxbe (R, Ohio) to succeed Elliot L. Richardson as attorney general. Nixon then left the room without answering questions, and Acting Attorney General Robert H. Bork announced that with Nixon's approval he had appointed Houston lawyer Leon Jaworski, a Democrat, to succeed Archibald Cox as special Watergate prosecutor.

Saxbe, a freshman senator who had announced he would not seek re-election in 1974, was described by Nixon as "eminently qualified" and "an individual who wants this position and will do everything that he possibly can to serve the nation as the first lawyer in the nation."

Saxbe had often been at odds with the Administration on issues ranging from Watergate to the Indochina War.

After Nixon's announcement, Saxbe spoke briefly, saying he was "happy to tackle" the job, understanding that the country was in "difficult times" and undergoing a "crisis of leadership."

In announcing Jaworski's appointment, Bork said Jaworski would have the same charter as Cox, with the additional commitment that Nixon would not exercise "his constitutional powers" to fire him without the consent of a "substantial majority" of eight Congressional leaders from both parties.

Bork said Jaworski would have the "full cooperation of the executive branch" and, in the event of a disagreement with the Administration "with regard to the release of presidential documents, there will be no restrictions placed on his freedom of action." The assurance signaled a retreat from the conditions Nixon outlined in his Oct. 26 news conference.

Asked about the staff of Watergate prosecutors whose status had been left uncertain by Cox's dismissal, Bork said he had told Jaworski that he thought the staff was "indispensable to the rapid investigation and prosecution of these cases, and Mr. Jaworski fully agrees."

Jaworski, 68, an associate of the late Lyndon B. Johnson and 1971–72 president of the American Bar Association, told a news conference in Houston later Nov. 1 that an investigation into the two "missing" presidential Watergate tapes would receive top priority in his operation. He said he would begin work Nov. 5, adding that "the American people are entitled to have some answers without waiting forever, and I intend to get those answers."

Jaworski also revealed that he had been approached in May for the post of Watergate prosecutor but had declined because there had been no guarantee of independence.

Congress presses for independent prober—Sen. John G. Tower (R, Tex.) said Nov. 1 the Jaworski appointment "should forestall any action that Congress might take to create an independent prosecutor." But Sen. Walter F. Mondale (D, Minn.) said the need for "a truly independent prosecutor" still existed.

The Democratic push for an independent prosecutor was broad-based. Senate Democratic Leader Mike Mansfield's comment Oct. 27 on President Nixon's plan to name a special prosecutor within the Administration; "No soap." Mansfield supported a bill with 53 co-sponsors calling for a court-appointed prosecutor.

A resolution calling for an independent special prosecutor was overwhelmingly approved by Senate Democrats in caucus Oct. 30. The resolution was sponsored by Sen. Sam J. Ervin Jr. (N.C.), chairman of the Senate Watergate committee. Mansfield told the caucus it was no longer possible "to contemplate the shutdown of the Ervin committee" and he hoped the committee would be continued and its mandate enlarged to include all of the probes under way by the special prosecutor's office at the time of Cox's dismissal. He was given a standing ovation after he spoke.

Sen. Adlai E. Stevenson 3rd (D, Ill.), appearing before the Judiciary Committee

Nov. 1, said that as long as the terms on which the special prosecutor was appointed "consist of promises by the President, they are irrelevant. There is only one way now—that is by law of this Congress."

Similar sentiment was expressed in the House Nov. 1.

Rep. John C. Culver (D, Iowa), sponsor of a bill for a court-appointed prosecutor, said "the special prosecutor's independence must be guaranteed by law." "The truth is we cannot have any faith in the President on this matter," said Rep. Robert Kastenmeier (D, Wis.).

Rep. Wiley Mayne (R, Iowa) said the legislation "should have very strong language assuring the independence of the special prosecutor." Rep. Henry P. Smith (R, N.Y.) said, "We still have the problem of control of the prosecutor and the right to discharge him."

Cox on new prosecutor—Ousted Watergate prosecutor Archibald Cox told the Senate Judiciary Committee Oct. 29 that "total independence" for a new special Watergate prosecutor was "crucial." Cox was the lead-off witness in hearings on bills proposing the establishment of a special prosecutor independent of the executive branch.

Cox testified to the "repeated frustration" of his attempts to obtain necessary documents from the White House. He asserted that some requests had not been acted upon two months after they were made.

However, Cox asserted that the favorable rulings in the White House tapes case had set a precedent, and he would now "expect a large number of requests [for documents] and a large number of subpoenas" by his successor.

To back his contention that the White House had not cooperated in making available evidence, Cox listed a number of items he had been unable to obtain: logs and diaries of communications between President Nixon and former Administration officials; records, notes and logs belonging to members of the White House plumbers team; records on the electronic surveillance of columnist Joseph Kraft; information concerning campaign gifts by the Milk Producers Fund.

In his second day of testimony Oct. 30, Cox said that continued White House efforts to withhold papers and recordings would place "a substantial number" of prosecutions connected with Watergate in "jeopardy." Cox said he felt that "nearly all" the potential defendants would claim that the documents withheld contained evidence that would tend to exonerate them. Withholding of evidence made dismissal of the cases likely.

Judiciary Committee member Sen. Hugh Scott (R, Pa.) questioned the legality of a bill, drawn up by Sens. Birch Bayh (D, Ind.) and Phillip A. Hart (D, Mich.) and co-sponsored by 53 other senators, that would give U.S. District Court Judge John J. Sirica the power to appoint an independent special Watergate prose-

cutor to replace Cox. Scott cited a federal court rule requiring the executive branch to sign any indictment before it became legally binding. Scott said that indictments not signed by the Justice Department might be thrown out of court.

During his last day of testimony Oct. 31, Cox, a former solicitor general, responded to Republican charges that because his staff had been stacked with Democrats, it was incapable of conducting an impartial investigation. Nine of his senior staff lawyers also had worked for Republican attorneys general, Cox said.

White House compiles press 'sins'. The New York Times reported Nov. 5 that the White House had been compiling a list of alleged "sins" committed by the press, especially television, against President Nixon. The Times suggested that the list had been the basis for Nixon's attack on the press Oct. 26.

Among the items on the list was an analysis of news coverage by the three television networks Oct. 22, the first weekday subsequent to the firing of Archibald Cox, the special Watergate prosecutor. The programs contained 19 spots the White House considered unfavorable to Nixon, two spots it considered favorable and one spot it judged neutral, the Times reported.

Ken W. Clawson, director of the White House Office of Communications, said: "Were those 19 television spots reporting, or were they creating an impeachment atmosphere? That day on television was probably the last straw for the President— the outcries for impeachment on television in the wake of the Cox firing."

In a related development, the Washington Post reported Nov. 5 it had obtained a White House memorandum that called for a campaign of "pestering" the Post and its publisher, Katharine Graham.

In the May 6, 1970 memo to former White House Chief of Staff H.R. Haldeman, Jeb Stuart Magruder, then a White House aide, said a letter writing team was calling and writing the Post every day to complain about the paper's "childish, ridiculous and overboard" critical attitude toward President Nixon. As a second measure against the Post, Magruder suggested that White House aide Lyn Nofziger "work out with someone in the House a round robin letter to the Post that says we live in Washington D.C. and read the D.C. papers, but fortunately we also have the opportunity to read the papers from our home districts and are appalled by the biased coverage the people of Washington receive of the news, compared to that in the rest of the country."

Continued confusion on tapes. Presidential aide Stephen B. Bull said in a federal district court hearing Nov. 2 that President Nixon knew Sept. 29 that tapes of two of his subpoenaed Watergate conversations did not exist. The White House had said earlier that the problem was discovered Oct. 27.

The tapes involved a June 20, 1972 telephone conversation between Nixon and his campaign manager John N. Mitchell, and an April 15 meeting between Nixon and his counsel John W. Dean 3rd.

Testifying before Judge John J. Sirica, Bull said he had arranged on Sept. 29 for Nixon to listen to a series of tapes, when it became apparent that two of the conversations "were not on the tapes provided to me." Bull added that "ultimately, the President" had told him the tapes were not there.

Bull said he had written "Part 1" on the box containing the April 15 tape, which—according to the White House— ran out before the Nixon-Dean meeting took place. He had done this, Bull said, on the assumption that "there had to be another reel"—which the White House had said never existed.

Bull acknowledged he earlier told investigators for the Senate Watergate Committee that he had, on June 25, played a tape dated "around April 15" for White House counsel J. Fred Buzhardt Jr. so that Buzhardt could telephone a summary to Nixon in San Clemente, Calif. Bull said he had since "refreshed his recollection" and had been "educated" that the tape was dated March 20.

After Bull told the court Nixon had spent 10–12 hours June 4 reviewing parts of 20 tapes, the prosecution asked that the tape for that date be made available, in the hope the recording system might have picked up Nixon listening to his own tapes. There were conflicting reports, however, as to whether Nixon listened to the tapes with earphones. Sirica denied the request on the ground that the date was not covered in the original subpoena, and prosecution sources said later they planned to issue a new subpoena.

Bull testified Nov. 6 that during the late September examination of the tapes a second reel marked April 15 had been found but that its beginning did not match with the first reel, which he said ended in mid-sentence during a conversation before the Dean meeting. Bull assumed that the "second" tape began late April 15 or early the next day. Bull said he had originally thought that Rose Mary Woods, Nixon's personal secretary and executive assistant, had made full or partial transcripts of all the subpoenaed tapes in late September. Later events indicated differently, he said, but "there's no chicanery involved in this."

John C. Bennett, an aide to White House chief of staff Alexander M. Haig Jr., said Nov. 6 that Miss Woods currently had custody of 14 tapes, some of which related to an April 16 meeting with Dean. Bennett said Nixon wanted a transcript of the meeting, which was not covered by the prosecution's subpoena.

Bennett, who took custody of the tape collection after recordings were discontinued, was asked by assistant prosecutor Richard Ben-Veniste if he could be "certain that the tapes you received on the 18th of July were all the tapes that have been made."

"Nope. No way," Bennett replied.

Regarding the disputed April 14–16 period, Ben-Veniste contended that Bennett's own notes and Secret Service logs indicated the existence of a third tape. Bennett insisted there were only two, saying he used different notations at different times to describe the same reel.

Bennett testified Nov. 7 that Miss Woods told him earlier in the day she had discovered a "gap" in one of the recordings—presumably of a meeting with Dean. He said, however, that the April 15 meeting could not have been involved, since the tape from that date was locked in his office safe. He also quoted her as saying she had not been making verbatim transcripts of the tapes.

Under questioning by Ben-Veniste, Bennett said Miss Woods was playing the tapes on a machine without a device to prevent accidental erasures or mutilations. In case of damage, he said, there would be no chance of retrieving the lost conversations, since to his knowledge there were no copies. (A White House lawyer disclosed Nov. 8 that because of concern over "fragility" of the tapes, copies were now being made of the subpoenaed material.)

Miss Woods appeared in court Nov. 8 and denied there had been any "gap" in a tape sent her by Bennett. Nixon's April 16 meeting with Dean, she said, had been found on another tape, and she was "perfectly satisfied" that no gaps existed.

The main problem with the tapes, Miss Woods said, was the poor quality, which made some conversations almost inaudible. Extraneous noises had been a persistent hindrance: Nixon's putting his foot on the desk ("like a bomb hitting you right in the ears"), Nixon's whistling, or the clinking of dishes. Nonetheless, she said she had been able to make a rough transcript for Nixon, without making extra copies. She then destroyed her typewriter ribbons.

(Former White House aide Alexander P. Butterfield, who had revealed the existence of the taping system July 16, said then that conversations, even soft ones, were picked up "very clearly."

Asked whether she had taken special precautions to avoid erasures of the tapes, Miss Woods said she was not "so stupid" as to let such a thing happen. "I used every possible precaution."

"What precaution?" she was asked.

"I used my head, the only one I have to use," she replied.

Under questioning by a White House lawyer, Miss Woods denied that she had edited the tapes or added words during her typing.

Former presidential chief of staff H. R. Haldeman, appearing under prosecution subpoena Nov. 8, called the quality of the tapes "fair," and "quite adequate for a report of a conversation" despite some bad intervals.

Haldeman said he could not recall why he had been given 22 tapes April 25 (while he was still on the White House staff), since he had listened to only one. He said he thought he had returned the tapes the next day, although Secret Ser-

vice logs showed the tapes being returned May 2. (Haldeman resigned April 30 and, according to his testimony before the Senate Watergate committee, listened to other tapes in July.

Technical testimony sought—Concerning future testimony in the hearings, Judge Sirica announced Nov. 7 that he wanted analysis and testimony from electronics experts to explore "the reasons that might exist for the nonexistence of these conversations." This phase, he said might be "the most important and conclusive" of the hearings.

April 15 memo offered—Deputy White House Press Secretary Gerald L. Warren had announced Nov. 2 that Nixon would give Judge Sirica a personal memorandum he dictated after the April 15 meeting with Dean.

Warren said the memo would be released "if it's relevant" and if all parties agreed to respect its confidentiality. He did not say when Nixon had dictated the memo.

Wright unaware tapes 'nonexistent'—White House legal consultant Charles Alan Wright said in Austin, Tex. Nov. 6 that he had not been told until the day of the public announcement that two of Nixon's disputed Watergate conversations were not recorded.

Wright, who had been a central figure in earlier court proceedings involving Nixon's tapes and documents, said his White House secretary had called him from Austin Oct. 31, telling him "You won't believe this, but two of the tapes don't exist. You should hear it from us before hearing it on the radio." Presidential counsel Buzhardt made his announcement in Judge Sirica's court shortly afterwards.

Wright said he did not resent his dealings with the White House, but added he "would be happier" if he had been told of the nonexistent tapes earlier.

Wright had returned to his duties at the University of Texas Law School but said he remained on call for further consultation with Nixon on constitutional issues. While asserting that he believed the White House statement that the tapes had never existed, he said if it later turned out that the conversations had been recorded and the tapes destroyed, he would withdraw from participation in the White House case.

Nixon says he won't resign. Demands for President Nixon's resignation increased in the first week of November but White House spokesmen repeatedly insisted that the President intended to remain on the job. Nixon himself said he had no intention of "walking away from the job" he was elected to do, in a national address Nov. 7 on the energy crisis. [See p. 125]

The President's chief of staff, Alexander M. Haig Jr., had admitted Oct. 23 that a "firestorm" of protest had been leveled against the President over his firing of special Watergate prosecutor Archibald Cox Oct. 20, prompting the decision to turn the presidential tapes of Watergate dis-

cussions over to the court for inspection. This reversal of policy came after a three-month dispute with the Watergate prosecution and the courts to retain the tapes, waged at the brink of a constitutional crisis over separation of powers. The abrupt reversal of policy, and the subsequent disclosure that two key tapes did not exist, fueled the controversy and demands for resignation of the President.

"He must leave office for the common good," Sen. John V. Tunney (D, Calif.) said Oct. 30. "The people do not believe him and he has shamed them." He was the second senator to call for Nixon's resignation. Sen. Daniel K. Inouye (D, H.) had spoken out Oct. 22.

The Democratic National Committee, meeting in Louisville, Ky. Oct. 26, had called on Congress to "take all necessary action, including impeachment . . . if warranted" against the President. "The political process has been sullied and the high calling of public service has been subjected to cynical manipulation and criminal behavior which has reached into the highest office of the land," the resolution stated. The Democrats urged appointment of an independent special prosecutor to continue the federal Watergate investigation.

Helen Wise, president of the National Education Association representing 2.2 million teachers, wrote Nixon Oct. 21 saying teachers shared the "groundswell of public outrage" at the Administration's handling of Watergate. Teachers were asking, she told him, "how they can fulfill their responsibilities in teaching young people the moral, ethical and spiritual values required in a free society while the President . . . disregards the nation's traditionally high standards of morality."

Some 350 law students and lawyers met Oct. 30 to lobby for appointment of an independent Watergate prosecutor and continuation of the probe of charges against the President that could lead to impeachment.

More than 200 political scientists, led by Professors James MacGregor Burns and Robert Dahl, announced formation Oct. 31 of "Political Scientists for Impeachment."

Individual expressions of protest continued to flood Congress and the White House. More than 350,000 telegrams had been received by Oct. 29 in response to the Cox firing. More than 45,000 telegrams were handled in Washington by Oct. 30 following the President's news conference Oct. 26.

The White House reported its telephone lines were "flaming" with support for the President after the press conference. But the Congressional mail was heavy with support of impeachment: Tunney reported Oct. 30 a 16–1 ratio for impeachment in his office mail, Sen. Alan Cranston (D, Calif.) a 22–1 ratio, Sen. Jacob Javits (R, N.Y.) a 40–1 ratio. Sen. James Buckley (Conservative-Republican, N.Y.) said 95% of his telegrams backed impeachment.

'No intention of resigning'—White House deputy press secretary Gerald L. Warren assured reporters Nov. 2 that Nixon was "not giving any thought to resigning" and "has no intention of resigning." The question came up at the daily news briefing in Florida after the President had left Washington so abruptly Nov. 1 for his home in Key Biscayne that the customary accompanying pool of reporters and photographers was left behind. The President, Warren told them Nov. 2 after they arrived by other means, was putting in a routine day of work, dealing with the energy problem. Queried about Watergate and the tapes situation, Warren voiced confidence that "the American people will understand after all the facts are brought out and will view this matter in its totality as it should be." The President, he said, was "vitally interested" in having "this whole matter cleared up."

Poll rating drops 11 points—A Gallup Poll issued Nov. 3 showed that only 27% of the respondents approved of the way the President was handling his job, 60% disapproved (13% undecided), the lowest popularity rating in Nixon's presidency. The interviewing was conducted Oct. 19–22 and was three-quarters completed before announcement of the Cox dismissal. The rating contrasted with the 38% approval, 54% disapproval recorded in the Aug. 17–19 Gallup survey.

On the question of impeachment, Gallup reported a 33% yes, 52% no (15% no opinion) reaction in its Oct. 19–22 polling. The finding Aug. 3–6 had been 26% yes, 61% no.

Editorials urge resignation—The Detroit News, which supported Nixon for re-election in 1972, called for his resignation in an editorial Nov. 4. Another newspaper which also supported Nixon's re-election, the Denver Post, also called upon the President to resign.

Editorials calling for Nixon's resignation appeared in the New York Times Nov. 4 and the Nov. 12 issue of Time magazine (published Nov. 4), the first editorial in Time's 50-year history.

Resignation also was advocated Nov. 2 by syndicated columnist Joseph Alsop, long a Nixon supporter on defense and Vietnam policies, and the same week by ABC-TV anchor man Howard K. Smith. Conservative spokesman William F. Buckley Jr. told a Kansas State University audience Nov. 2 he believed Nixon would resign upon the urging of Republicans and friends.

Congressional 'discussion'—"A lot of discussion" of resignation was heard in the cloakrooms of Congress, according to Rep. Robert H. Michel (Ill.) Nov. 3. Michel was chairman of the GOP Congressional Campaign Committee. Rep. John H. Rousselot (R, Calif.) said "discussion of how effective he can be as a President is very much evident."

Sen. Edward W. Brooke (Mass.) became the first Republican senator to publicly call for Nixon's resignation. On the ABC "Issues and Answers" broadcast Nov. 4, Brooke said "there is no question that President Nixon has lost his effectiveness as the leader of this country, primarily because he has lost the confidence of the people of the country, and I think, therefore, that in the interests of this nation that he loves that he should step down, should tender his resignation." Nixon could remain in office to "sort of limp along," Brooke said, but he had "reluctantly" come to the conclusion he should resign. "The lack of confidence is so deep," he said, he did not know "of anything that the President could do now to turn it around."

Sen. Henry M. Jackson (D, Wash.), said on NBC's "Meet the Press" program Nov. 4 that "the real issue is whether or not there is enough confidence left for the President to govern this nation." He urged Nixon to appear before the Senate Watergate committee to "lay his cards on the table." If Nixon did not do this, Jackson felt he would face "an unchallengable demand on impeachment or the possibility of a direct request for resignation, and I think the push will come from the Republican leadership, not just from Democrats."

Sen. Howard W. Cannon (D, Nev.), on CBS's "Face the Nation" program Nov. 4, said his mail reflected "a strong urging" to delay action on the confirmation of Rep. Gerald R. Ford (R, Mich.) to be vice president, which was before his Rules Committee, because of a belief that Nixon might resign. Cannon said he opposed holding the Ford nomination "hostage to anything else." He said he did not believe that Nixon had any intention of resigning.

White House Deputy Press Secretary Warren echoed those comments in Florida Nov. 4—that Nixon had "absolutely no intention of resigning." "The President intends to pursue his objectives," he said, "in foreign policy, national policy and in clearing up the Watergate matter." The President himself remained in seclusion. He met separately with Haig and Press Secretary Ronald L. Ziegler, according to Warren, but did not meet with his counsels J. Fred Buzhardt or Leonard Garment, who had arrived from Washington the day before to "review the proceedings" on the tapes. Instead, they met with Haig and presidential assistant Bryce N. Harlow. Warren expressed confidence that the proceedings "will show there are no missing tapes," that, in fact, they had never been made. Ziegler, interviewed on a special CBS television program that day, "The Embattled President," said Nixon had "a good story to tell" about the two tapes in question but was finding it difficult to tell in "the environment of the confusion" caused by the "rush of events" in the Middle East, the economy and other issues.

On the President's return to Washington Nov. 5, Ziegler told reporters that most of the President's time in Florida had been taken up with the Middle East situation. As for Watergate, "The President is not going to walk away from the problem," Ziegler said. "He intends to see this thing out. He is not a quitter and never has been in his entire political career. He has been devoting his energies not only to this Watergate foolishness . . ."

"Foolishness, Ron?" a reporter interrupted.

"Foolishness and tragedy," he continued. "He knows his energies have been devoted to building foreign policy in which we move from confrontation to negotiation and carry through with what he stands for domestically."

The White House continued the theme Nov. 6. Warren emphasized that Nixon had a "complete and full understanding" of the credibility problem, intended "to meet this matter head on" and would "deal with it in a forthright way and see that it is cleared up." The President would "speak out on these matters," he said.

The President did so during a televised speech to the nation Nov. 7 on the energy crisis, which he concluded "on a personal note" by declaring he had "no intention whatever of walking away from the job I was elected to do."

But discussion continued in Congress on the issue of impeachment or resignation.

Sen. Peter H. Dominick (R, Colo.), normally an Administration supporter, said in Denver Nov. 5 he was "reluctant to talk about impeachment" but "the genie was already out of the bottle and it cannot be put back in. The confidence of the American people cannot be restored until the impeachment question is disposed of and this must be done as quickly as possible." Dominick urged Nixon to divulge everything he knew about Watergate and permit complete access to the data requested by the Senate and federal probers. "There can be no more deals and no more technical arguments about evidence," he said. Dominick said the Republican party "would be well advised to follow a more independent course" from the Administration.

Sen George D. Aiken (Vt.), 81, dean of Congressional Republicans, told the Senate Nov. 7 Congress should move to impeach Nixon or "get off his back." He said it was the President's duty "not to resign" and Congress' duty to make a decision on the impeachment question. He said the House should set a deadline for a charge of impeachment or not, and, if the latter, make public an explanation. The White House had shown "relentless incompetence" in dealing with its domestic troubles and had been "astonishingly inept" in its Watergate explanations, he said, but these were not sufficient grounds for impeachment.

Sen. Barry Goldwater (R, Ariz.) opposed Nixon's resignation. He told reporters Nov. 5 the only way out for Nixon now "would be to show up some morning at the Ervin committee . . . and say, 'Here I am, Sam. What do you want to know?'" Senate GOP Leader Hugh Scott (Pa.) supported Goldwater, expressing hope Nov. 5 "a forum" could be found, possibly through the Ervin committee or by the White House, for "all relevant information" about the tapes to be made public. (Ervin said Nov. 6 there was a "general consensus" among committee members at a meeting that morning that the panel should explore with the White House the possibility of some kind of meeting with Nixon.)

Scott opposed resignation, as did House Speaker Carl Albert (D, Okla.), who was next in line at the moment to succeed the President. "Based on anything I know at this time," Albert said Nov. 5, "I would not join the group that thinks the President should resign."

But statements for Nixon's resignation continued. Sen. George McGovern (D, S.D.) Nov. 7 noted that the day was the anniversary of his landslide defeat by Nixon in the 1972 presidential election. "I think President Nixon has lost the capacity to govern the country," McGovern said.

Rep. George E. Danielson (D, Calif.) predicted Nov. 7 Nixon would resign within four months. Democratic Reps. Clarence D. Long (Md.) and Charles B. Rangel (N.Y.) introduced separate resolutions Nov. 7 calling on Nixon to submit his resignation. "I am calling upon the House," Rangel said, "to offer the President its honorable means of averting a total collapse of national leadership."

More Republicans expressed concern about the fate of the party Nov. 7. Sen. Richard S. Schweiker (R, Pa.) referring to the "dismal" Republican results in several state and municipal elections the previous day, said "the Watergate scandals have become a devastating burden on the Republican party." Sen. Jacob Javits (R, N.Y.) said it was time to "spell out clearly the relationship of the party to the President," that it had become evident that the nation had a "three-party system—the Democrats and Republicans and those political zealots operating under the banner of the Committee for the Re-election of the President. . . ."

The Ripon Society, a group of liberal and moderate Republicans, said Nov. 7 the Nixon Administration had become so "debilitated" that it was "unable to act as a source of coherent national policy."

Jaworski independence affirmed. Acting Attorney General Robert H. Bork Nov. 5 promised the independence of the new special Watergate prosecutor, Leon Jaworski, appointed within the Justice Department.

Testifying before the House Judiciary Committee, Bork said "it is clear and understood on all sides that he [Jaworski] has the power to use judicial processes to pursue evidence if a disagreement should develop." Bork told the committee President Nixon "will not exercise his constitutional power to discharge the special prosecutor or to limit his independence in any way without first consulting" the majority and minority leaders of the House and Senate and the chairman and ranking members of the Judiciary Committees of both houses of Congress.

On the matter of a special court-appointed prosecutor as proposed in many bills before Congress, Bork said he thought "such a course would almost certainly not be valid and would, in any event, pose more problems than it would solve."

Jaworski, who was sworn in Nov. 5, testified before the House Judiciary Committee Nov. 8. Jaworski said he had taken the assignment only after receiving "what I consider the most solemn and substantial assurances of my absolute independence" in the post. The assurances, he said, were made by White House chief of staff Alexander M. Haig Jr. Jaworski considered the assurance "unqualified" and containing "absolutely no constraints on my freedom" to seek evidence, including presidential files and use of the courts to obtain documents. "Maybe I'm naive," Jaworski remarked, "but I accepted those assurances in good faith."

Nixon irritation with Cox related— Former Attorney General Elliot L. Richardson told the Senate Judiciary Committee Nov. 6 and 8 of repeated protests from the White House about Cox's conduct of the Watergate probe. At one point, Richardson said Nov. 6, the President telephoned him from Key Biscayne, Fla. requesting a public statement from Cox (later issued) denying that the Nixons' property acquisition in San Clemente, Calif. was under investigation.

Richardson said sometime in September or early October Nixon spoke to him, at the end of a meeting on another topic, and "it had something to do with getting rid of Cox." Richardson said he "didn't take it seriously." "I thought it was an expression of irritation."

In response to a question, Richardson told the committee Nov. 6 "there was a period from around early July in which I thought the President showed a considerable sense of strain."

Richardson said he believed the President should drop all claims of executive privilege to withhold information on Watergate. "I see no other way at this juncture," he said, "of providing the reassurance necessary to the Congress and the American people that the special prosecutor can get to the bottom of all these matters. We have reached the point where it seems to me, any further conversation about privilege ought to be eliminated." He even thought it would be a "good idea" to delay confirmation of his successor as attorney general until Nixon gave a firm agreement on executive privilege.

Richardson preferred to leave the prosecutor's post under the presidency but subject to Senate confirmation.

Returning before the committee Nov. 8, Richardson related other instances when he had been informed of Nixon's displeasure at the Cox probe. In a telephone call June 19, less than a month after Cox's appointment, Richardson said, Haig informed him Nixon was upset by Cox's

news conference remarks about possible subpoena of the President. Haig told him the "whole thing is blatantly partisan," Richardson said.

Haig informed him July 23, Richardson said, that Nixon was "very uptight about Cox" and "wants a tight line drawn. There can be no further mistakes." Richardson said he was told if Cox could not stay within the guidelines they would have to "get rid of Cox." The particular incident involved letters sent to agencies requesting wiretapping policies and procedures. Richardson said both times he talked with Cox about the matters.

Richardson also told of a discussion with Nixon's counselor J. Fred Buzhardt Jr. about restricting the range of the Cox probe. He quoted Buzhardt as saying, "If he can't agree to that, we'll have to get rid of him."

Both the House and Senate Judiciary Committees took expert testimony Nov. 7 on the constitutional issue of a court-appointed prosecutor. Four of the five experts, all from law schools, upheld the legality of the court appointment method. The fifth, Dean Roger C. Crampton of Cornell University Law School, the only one to appear before both committees, said it was important to avoid putting such strain on the Constitution "at a time when the President has acted with doubtful legality and little wisdom." Nixon's actions in firing Cox and releasing the tapes, he said, were "irrational" and he said Nixon should seriously consider resigning.

Democrats gain in off-year elections. Elections were held across the U.S. Nov. 6, and with few exceptions Democratic candidates emerged victorious in the major off-year contests.

Despite the one-sided results, neither national party chairman was willing to ascribe great significance to the returns. Democratic National Chairman Robert S. Strauss said, "Of course we're pleased, . . . but these results are not earthshaking. I don't read any national significance into this, but I think it shows we're on the right track in trying to put the party back together." Republican National Chairman George Bush called the results a "kind of mixed bag."

Both said they believed Watergate had been a minor factor in GOP defeats.

However, GOP Rep. Charles W. Sandman Jr., defeated in the New Jersey gubernatorial race, said, "The national scene did not help." In Minneapolis, Gladys Brooks, a Republican who ran third in the mayoral contest there, commented that "a great deal of Watergate has carried over here."

Campaign against Senate critics. H. R. Haldeman ordered White House aides in October 1969 to organize campaigns—

A
B
C
D
E
F
G

letters, telegrams and telephone calls—aimed at "blasting" three Republican senators for "their consistent opposition to the President," the New York Times reported Nov. 7.

At the same time, Haldeman, then White House chief of staff, ordered aides to have sent telegrams of praise to Sen. Hubert H. Humphrey (D, Minn.) for his Oct. 11, 1969 statement to the press that Nixon "was proceeding along the right lines" in Vietnam.

A series of four memoranda concerning a White House effort against Sens. Charles H. Percy (Ill.) and Charles Mathias (Md.) as well as former Sen. Charles Goodell (N.Y.) was made available by what the Times called "Watergate investigative sources."

More Financial Disclosures; Senate Looks into Campaign Practices

U.S. costs at Nixon homes probed. A subcommittee of the House Government Operations Committee held hearings Oct. 10–15 on the issue of federal spending on private homes of presidents.

The federal cost of security and office space for the late President Lyndon B. Johnson when he was in Texas amounted to $5.1 million, the panel was told Oct. 10 by Rep. John Buchanan Jr. (Ala.), its ranking Republican member. The figure was comparable to the $10.2 million spent for similar service for President Nixon, since the latter involved two residences at San Clemente, Calif. and Key Biscayne, Fla. But the Johnson total covered a 10-year period from 1964 to 1973, compared to the five-year Nixon span, and, except for $3.5 million spent on communications at the Johnson ranch, the bulk of the spending was on office space for Johnson at a federal building in Austin and at the Johnson Library, both public property then and now.

Much of the testimony at the hearings, however, focused on spending at the Nixon homes. The panel was told Oct. 10 that the annual cost to the government for guards and security agents at these homes was approximately $500,000. It also was told of an incident when a fence was redesigned at Key Biscayne, adding $20,000 to the cost, at the instigation of a Nixon friend acting on Nixon's behalf who informed the Secret Service that Nixon preferred "a more conventional fence, like the one around the White House." Subcommittee Chairman Jack Brooks (D, Tex.) observed that after the fence was installed costing $65,000, a "security" hedge to obscure it was planted.

Arthur P. Sampson, administrator of the General Services Administration, Oct. 11 defended his agency's spending at the Nixon homes. He said the GSA work had not improved the appearance at the homes, increased the comfort or helped pay living expenses. In fact, he testified, federal spending at Nixon homes had detracted from the value of the properties.

Brooks disputed the testimony, accusing the GSA of "a deliberate attempt to obscure the facts."

Sampson conceded "mistakes" had been made, such as supplying a full-time gardener for Key Biscayne, since "terminated." But he insisted the mistakes were not significant.

The panel heard testimony Oct. 12 that public funds had been expended at San Clemente for work ordered by Nixon's personal attorney and private architect. The work included surveys of the boundary and structure of the house done before the GSA had entered the picture. It paid the bills sent to it later.

According to the New York Times Oct. 15, Brooks said "serious questions of propriety" had been raised relevant to the use of public funds at Nixon's private homes, that there were indications that some funds expended had augmented the property value without security justification.

Republicans on the panel had brought out during the hearings, which were marked by partisanship, that federal spending at the Johnson property also covered some nonsecurity areas such as flower beds and an ice chest. The sums involved generally were small.

Vesco indicted again. Robert Vesco was secretly indicted by a federal grand jury in New York, it was reported Oct. 16. The charges, the second instance of sealed indictments being handed up against Vesco, accused him of using $50,000 in International Controls Corp. funds as part payment for stock in Investors Overseas Services, Ltd. (IOS) in January 1972.

Vesco, whose financial empire had included control of both companies, had been accused by the Securities and Exchange Commission of masterminding a massive swindle of four mutual funds in the IOS network.

Despite three bench warrants issued for his arrest in connection with the civil suit and a criminal suit involving former Nixon Administration Cabinet officials, Vesco had eluded investigators by fleeing to Costa Rica and the Bahamas. Efforts at extradition had proven fruitless. According to the prosecution, the second secret indictment would be used in a renewed attempt to win his extradition.

Court voids Vesco suit—Federal district court in Newark, N.J. Sept. 30 dismissed a $20 million defamation suit brought by Vesco against four business associates who had accused him of "deliberately looting" IOS. Vesco had failed to meet a deadline for filing depositions in the case, the court said.

Corporations fined for gifts. Special Watergate prosecutor Archibald Cox announced Oct. 17 that criminal charges had been brought against Goodyear Tire & Rubber Co. and its chairman, Russell DeYoung; Minnesota Mining and Manufacturing Co. (3M) and its chairman, Harry Heltzer; and American Airlines. They were accused of making illegal contributions to President Nixon's re-election campaign.

After entering guilty pleas the same day, the defendants were fined but received no prison sentences. (The maximum penalty for corporations was a $5,000 fine. Individuals faced a $1,000 penalty and one year in jail.) Goodyear and DeYoung were fined $5,000 and $1,000 each by federal district court in Cleveland. 3M and Heltzer paid $3,000 and $500 each in Minneapolis federal court decision. American was fined $5,000 by federal district court in Washington.

All three companies had voluntarily admitted donating a total of $125,000 to the Finance Committee to Re-elect the President, which later returned the money.

Cox's office had urged corporations to make public disclosures of their wrongdoing after investigations uncovered evidence that a large amount of campaign funds had originated with corporate contributors. George A. Spater, former chairman of American Airlines, had been the first business official to reveal an illegal contribution, a factor which Cox said caused him to seek more lenient treatment for Spater.

"I believe that the example of American Airlines had something to do with prompting others to come forward with voluntary disclosures of corporate contributions," he said.

Cox predicted that other charges would be filed against violators of the federal fund law. (Four other firms had also admitted making illegal donations to the Nixon campaign.) An estimated two dozen corporations and labor unions were under investigation by Cox's office, according to a staff member.

"The general policy of this office," Cox said, "will be to charge the primarily responsible corporate officer with [a] misdemeanor violation." Legal action against the corporation alone would have "little deterrent effect," he added.

Cox also warned that felony charges could be brought under certain circumstances: if investigations showed evidence of criminal actions but violators refused to make a voluntary confession; if evidence showed that the contribution was offered to influence government action; and if there was an effort to conceal or withhold evidence of other federal crimes by persons under investigation.

According to Cox, all three companies charged had used "secret and clandestine" methods to hide their contributions. Goodyear and American had employed overseas channels to conceal the source of the money.

The defendants also had made "much smaller" contributions to other Democratic and Republican political campaigns but no charges were filed for these violations, he said.

Cox said the investigation showed no evidence that the firms sought a tangible return for their contributions in government actions, but merely wished to "be known as supportive" of the Nixon Administration.

Further legal action could result from the misdemeanor convictions. Cox said he was turning the evidence over to the Internal Revenue Service, which could prosecute on tax evasion charges if the campaign gifts had been deducted as business expenses.

Cox clears Abplanalp—Cox said Oct. 18 that he had found "no evidence of improper conduct" in the Justice Department's 1971 decision not to file antitrust charges against Robert H. Abplanalp, owner of the nation's largest manufacturer of aerosol valves, Precision Valve Corp., which was accused of pricing violations.

Rep. Bertram L. Podell (D, N.Y.) had asked Cox to investigate the circumstances of the government's action when it was revealed that Abplanalp, a close friend of President Nixon, had financed the purchase of Nixon's California home.

Nixon supports Rebozo on Hughes gift. Deputy White House Press Secretary Gerald L. Warren said Oct. 17 that President Nixon felt that his friend Charles G. Rebozo acted properly when he received a $100,000 gift from billionaire recluse Howard Hughes.

Warren had said Oct. 16 that Nixon earlier in 1973 learned of the gift before Rebozo returned it to Hughes. Nixon was also informed when the money was returned to Hughes, Warren said. He declined to elaborate.

In a related development, syndicated columnist Jack Anderson reported Oct. 17 that the Internal Revenue Service was investigating a report that Sen. Hubert H.

Humphrey (D, Minn.) received a $50,000 campaign contribution from Hughes when he ran for President in 1968. The alleged gift was revealed in a deposition given by former Hughes aide Robert Maheu in his $17.3 million libel suit against Hughes. According to Anderson, Humphrey said he had heard about the contribution from Maheu but had no record that the money had ever been received.

Maheu also testified in his deposition that $25,000 was delivered to former Democratic National Committee Chairman Lawrence F. O'Brien soon after the burial of Robert F. Kennedy. The money, used to pay Kennedy's campaign debts, had been promised before his assassination.

McGovern unit cited. The Office of Federal Elections in the General Accounting Office said Oct. 17 that it was referring the Massachusetts McGovern for President Committee's "apparent violations" of the federal campaign fund law to the Justice Department for "appropriate action."

It was the first McGovern committee inquiry sent to the Justice Department for possible prosecution, although several had been investigated by the government watchdog agency overseeing political gifts.

The alleged violations included failure to report $50,000 as part payment for a $75,000 loan, failure to itemize some receipts, failure to file reporting statements since the beginning of 1973 and inadequate identification of contributors.

Illegal gift to Humphrey. The office of special Watergate prosecutor Archibald Cox filed a criminal information Oct. 19 in federal district court in Minneapolis charging that Dwayne O. Andreas had "consented to" the illegal donation of $100,000 in corporate funds to the presidential campaign of Sen. Hubert H. Humphrey (D, Minn.) in 1968.

The money, made in four contributions of $25,000 each in October 1968 to Humphrey committees in Illinois, originated with the First Interoceanic Corp., of which Andreas was chairman, according to the four-count charge. (The firm's name later was changed to Independent Bancorporation.)

Andreas faced maximum penalties of $1,000 in fines and one year in jail on each misdemeanor count. The company, which also was charged with four violations of the federal campaign spending law, could be fined up to $5,000 on each charge. Three other corporations and two business executives had been convicted of similar violations.

Andreas, a Minneapolis resident who was chief executive officer of one of the nation's largest soybean processing firms, had been a supporter of Humphrey until 1972, when he backed President Nixon after Humphrey's loss in the Democratic presidential primaries. Andreas' secret $25,000 contributions to the Nixon re-election committee in 1972 had partially financed the Watergate break-in.

It also had been alleged that Andreas had been rewarded for his sizable campaign gift with a Minneapolis area bank charter. William B. Camp, comptroller of the currency, who was responsible for the final decision, denied that any impropriety was associated with the award of the charter.

Milk fund case widens. Before his firing, special Watergate prosecutor Archibald Cox had obtained a copy of a December 1970 letter to President Nixon from a representative of a large dairy cooperative, Associated Milk Producers Inc. (AMPI), it was reported Oct. 23. The letter suggested that if the Administration imposed import quotas on certain dairy products, Nixon could expect up to $2 million in campaign contributions from the group.

Fifteen days after the White House received the letter, dated Dec. 16, 1970, from Patrick J. Hillings, a California attorney, former GOP congressman, long time friend of Nixon and the Washington counsel, with Marion E. Harrison, for AMPI, Nixon ordered quotas set on four specific dairy products, although at a lower level than desired by the dairy industry.

In his presidential proclamation of Dec. 31, 1970, Nixon sharply curtailed the import of cheese and its substitutes, chocolate containing butterfat, animal feeds containing milk or its derivatives and ice cream from 25%–90% for the different exporting nations. In comparison with the previous import levels set in January 1969 in the last days of the Johnson Administration, Nixon fixed an annual import quota of 431,000 gallons of ice cream, down from unrestricted imports of eight million gallons in 1970; 4.7 million pounds of chocolate products, down from 1970 imports of 16 million pounds; 16.2 million pounds of animal feed, down from 27.5 million pounds in 1970, and 8.9 million pounds of low-fat cheese, down from 11 million pounds in 1970. The dairy lobby had sought to ban all imports of those products.

Campaign contributions from AMPI and other major dairy cooperatives began to flow to the White House soon after another Administration decision, also sought by the industry, was announced in March 1971.

Hillings' letter complained that a favorable Tariff Commission ruling had been buried in the federal bureaucracy. "This problem is bogged down within the White House. We write you both as advocates and supporters. The time is ripe politically and economically to impose the recommended quotas," Hillings wrote.

"AMPI contributed about $135,000 to Republican candidates in the 1970 election," he continued. "We are . . . working with Tom Evans and Herb Kalmbach in setting up appropriate channels for AMPI to contribute $2 million for your re-election. AMPI is also funding a special project."

(Thomas W. Evans, a partner in Nixon's former law firm—Mudge Rose Guthrie & Alexander, drafted charters in early 1971 for 50 secret, dummy campaign committees. Kalmbach was Nixon's personal attorney, the principal fund raiser in the pre-1972 period, and an admitted courier for Watergate coverup money.

Other information related to the dairy industry's ties to the Administration corroborated portions of the 1970 letter: one of the White House memos that had been sought by attorneys for Ralph Nader in connection with his court test of the Administration's increase of federal milk price supports was filed in the court record and published by the Washington Post Oct. 21.

The memo, written for then White House chief of staff H. R. Haldeman by his aide, Gordon Strachan, indicated that the dairy industry's original campaign "commitment" had been reduced to $1 million.

According to the Feb. 1, 1972 memo, "Kalmbach is very concerned about his involvement in the milk producers situation," a statement which prompted Strachan to recommend Kalmbach's dissociation with the milk project "because of the risk of disclosure."

A notation at the end of the document, apparently by Haldeman, added: "I'll dis. w/ AG [Attorney General John N. Mitchell]." Mitchell had testified before the Senate Judiciary committee in March 1972 that he had no party or re-election responsibilities before his selection as President Nixon's campaign manager and would have none until he formally left the Administration.

Cox sought a court order Oct. 16 to compel testimony from another AMPI attorney, Joseph Rose. According to the court records, Rose had already given information to the Federal Bureau of Investigation in August about possible violations of the federal law banning corporate campaign gifts "or other federal crimes."

Dairy funds linked to Ellsberg break-in—The Cox investigation had established a link between the White House plumbers' activities and secret contributions from dairy farmers, according to the Washington Post Oct. 11.

Joseph Baroody, a Washington businessman who had been a Nixon campaign fund raiser and organizer, said he had received a telephone call in the "last day or two" of August 1971 from White House special counsel Charles W. Colson. He sought an immediate temporary loan of $5,000 from Baroody, who said he had not asked what the money would be used for.

Colson also called Marion Harrison, who was collecting dairy money for distribution to secret committees, and asked him to deliver $5,000 to one of those committees headed by another Washington attorney, George D. Webster. Colson had alerted him to receive the money, Webster said. (He added that in 1971 he had or-

ganized several of the paper committees for the purpose of receiving secret campaign donations at the request of Colson.)

Harrison obtained $5,000 from AMPI and turned it over to Webster Sept. 7, 1971. Colson telephoned again and instructed Webster to convert the money to cash and give it to a messenger whom Colson would send. Baroody retrieved the money shortly after Sept. 21, 1971.

Baroody, Harrison and Webster said lawyers from Cox's office had determined that the transaction had financed the break-in at the office of Dr. Lewis Fielding, a psychiatrist who had treated Pentagon Papers defendant Daniel Ellsberg. The burglary had occurred Sept. 3, 1971.

Mitchell, Stans trial delayed. Federal Judge Lee P. Gagliardi Oct. 23 postponed the criminal trial of President Nixon's former Cabinet members, John N. Mitchell and Maurice H. Stans, until Jan. 6, 1974 at the request of the prosecution.

The delay hinged on John Dean's expected testimony against Mitchell and Stans, and the defense's right to test Dean's credibility as a witness, under provision of the Jencks Act. (The Jencks Act required the government to turn over evidence pertaining to a witness after the witness had testified, so the defense could attempt to discredit the testimony under cross-examination. In a 1959 decision of the Supreme Court upholding the Jencks Act, Justice Felix Frankfurter said the legislation was "designed to eliminate the danger of distortion and misrepresentation inherent in a report which merely selects portions, albeit accurately, from a lengthy oral report.")

The issue of Dean's testimony, and the defense's right to test it by subpoenaing presidential tapes and other records of Nixon's communication with Dean, arose as a consequence of a deal arranged for him by the Watergate special prosecutor's office. Dean had pleaded guilty to one count of conspiracy in the Watergate case in return for a pledge of immunity from other prosecution after promising to testify against other Nixon officials.

Dean's promise to appear as a witness had a direct bearing on the trial of Mitchell and Stans. Dean had been named an unindicted co-conspirator in their alleged scheme to hinder a Securities and Exchange Commission (SEC) investigation of Robert Vesco, a financier and major contributor to Nixon's re-election campaign. As a Mitchell protege and White House counsel, Dean had been privy to Administration discussions about Vesco's controversial campaign contribution and the alleged related efforts to thwart the SEC's investigation of Vesco's financial affairs

Gagliardi Oct. 18 had quashed the first subpoena seeking President Nixon's tapes and other documents related to his communications with Dean Feb. 28–April 15, but the judge warned federal attorneys that he would have to review the tapes if they contained evidence relating to prosecution witnesses.

Because Dean's testimony was considered vital to the trial of Mitchell and Stans, the entire case against them appeared jeopardized when the prosecution told Gagliardi Oct. 19 that the White House would not relinquish the tapes "at this stage."

During the morning of Oct. 22, before it was known that President Nixon would turn over other disputed tapes relating to the Watergate investigation for inspection by federal court in Washington, federal prosecutors informed the judge that the controversy appeared to be nearing a solution. White House officials had agreed to "give us something" and would "let us know within two weeks . . . what they can give us," according to prosecuting attorneys. Gagliardi then ordered a 2½ month delay, during which time he would review the material and determine its use by the defense.

Attorneys for Mitchell and Stans had filed a second subpoena on President Nixon Oct. 19 for release of the relevant material; another on former SEC chairman G. Bradford Cook, who had known of Mitchell and Stans' involvement in the SEC investigation; and Frederick T. Engman, chairman of the Federal Trade Commission and a former White House aide. Cook had discussed the Vesco case with Engman.

Butz role in FTC study examined. The federal Watergate prosecution staff assembled by ousted special prosecutor Archibald Cox was investigating charges that Agriculture Secretary Earl L. Butz had tried to use political pressure in 1972 to influence the disposition of a Federal Trade Commission (FTC) case, the Washington Star-News reported Oct. 26.

Despite Cox's firing, investigators were examining Butz's meeting in the spring of 1972 with FTC Chairman Miles J. Kirkpatrick. Kirkpatrick confirmed details of the incident, which had been brought to the attention of Cox's office in August by his legal adviser, Michelle Corash, who had been present at the meeting.

The discussion centered on the 1969 acquisition of United Vintners Inc., a California wine growers' cooperative and the second largest producer of wine in the state, by Heublein Inc., one of the nation's largest wine and liquor distributors.

The FTC's Bureau of Competition had recommended that the full commission formally challenge the acquisition on the basis of violations of restraint of trade. The Agriculture Department reportedly had tried to dissuade the bureau from seeking a challenge for several months before the recommendation was filed, but Butz's role in the department's effort was not clear.

At his meeting with Kirkpatrick, Butz indicated his concern that FTC opposition would be detrimental to the wine growers' need for a large marketing outlet such as Heublein. There was nothing improper about the talks at that point, Kirkpatrick said.

But at the end of the meeting, when he appeared unpersuaded, Kirkpatrick said that in an "almost offhand remark," Butz observed that "this was an election year and California was a critical state." According to an affidavit given by Corash, Butz asked Kirkpatrick to delay issuing the challenge until after the election because an unfavorable ruling could damage President Nixon's chances in California.

Kirkpatrick was reported to be "furious" at Butz's suggestions, and after verifying the bureau's evidence, voted with a majority of the commissioners in July 1972 to challenge the acquisition.

Kirkpatrick said he considered Butz's effort to place the discussion in a political context "foolish," but added he did not believe Butz thought the suggestion would "influence me or impede the case."

Butz denied that his remarks were improper. He termed his political comment "incidental."

Nixon role in ITT case disclosed. Former Attorney General Richard G. Kleindienst told Watergate special prosecutor Archibald Cox two weeks before Cox was fired by President Nixon that the President had personally intervened in the Justice Department's antitrust case against International Telephone & Telegraph Corp. (ITT). Nixon had ordered him not to appeal a lawsuit against ITT to the Supreme Court, Kleindienst said.

The New York Times, which broke the story Oct. 29, based its report on the incident on "sources close to the case," but Kleindienst issued the report Oct. 31 after controversy arose about the source of the leak of his "confidential" disclosure to Cox.

Nixon intervention detailed—The political aspects of the ITT issue originated with the Justice Department's challenge of three acquisitions made by the ITT conglomerate in the late 1960s: Canteen Corp., a large food vending firm; Grinnell Corp., a plumbing and fire equipment maker, and Hartford Fire Insurance Co., a large and highly lucrative insurance company.

Lower courts had ruled against the government on the Grinnell and Canteen cases, but an appeal to the Supreme Court was expected in 1971 because the high court had not ruled against the Justice Department on a major merger case during the 1960s. (Charges of antitrust violations arising from the Hartford Fire purchase were then in pre-trial stages.)

Solicitor General Erwin N. Griswold and Richard W. McLaren, chief of the Justice Department's antitrust division, had testified before Congress in March 1972 that they had urged Kleindienst, then deputy attorney general, to appeal the Grinnell case. Both officials wanted the Supreme Court to rule on the Clayton Act's applicability to conglomerate mergers. (The final decision rested with Kleindienst because then-Attorney General John N. Mitchell, who had repre-

sented ITT as a private attorney, had disqualified himself from the case.)

In his statement Oct. 31, Kleindienst said:

"On Monday afternoon, April 19th, 1971 [presidential domestic affairs advisor John] Ehrlichman abruptly called and stated that the President directed me not to file the appeal in the Grinnell case. That was the last day in whch that appeal could be taken. I informed him that we had determined to take that appeal, and that he should so inform the President. Minutes later the President called me and, without any discussion, ordered me to drop the appeal."

"Immediately" after receiving Nixon's phone call, Kleindienst said, "I sent word to the President that if he persisted in this direction I would be compelled to submit my resignation. Because that was the last day in which the appeal could be perfected, I obtained an extension of time from the Supreme Court to enable the President to consider my position.

"The President changed his mind and the appeal was filed 30 days later in the exact form it would have been filed one month earlier." Kleindienst added that his firm stand had forced a White House turnaround on the matter and led to an eventually favorable settlement of the case.

The issue of an appeal to the Supreme Court became moot when the Justice Department announced July 31, 1971 that an out of court settlement had been reached with ITT. The government agreed to drop its three lawsuits against the corporation and ITT was allowed to retain Hartford Fire if, among other provisions, it began divestiture proceedings for Canteen, a division of Grinnell and four other firms.

The Times report Oct. 29 said that negotiations leading to the settlement began immediately after Kleindienst ordered the appeal delayed. Kleindienst met with Felix Rohatyn, an ITT director, and Peter M. Flanigan, a White House aide, to discuss the terms of the agreement. (In earlier sworn testimony, Kleindienst had said that the settlement was "handled and negotiated exclusively" by McLaren.)

According to a Times report Oct. 31, based on information published during recent ITT investigations, the delay of a Justice Department appeal was a vital part of ITT's defense strategy. ITT officials believed the government had a "high probability" of winning an appeal and they argued that a new interpretation of the antitrust laws should not be undertaken without legislation, or at the least, without interagency review of the Justice Department's case before it went to the Supreme Court. (Other high Administration officials were known to oppose McLaren's conglomerate opinions.)

On April 16, 1971, ITT officials and lawyers sought appointments with Kleindienst and other Administration officials to seek a delay. On April 19, Kleindienst was reported to have said that a delay was impossible because of McLaren's op-

position. The presidential phone call to Kleindienst was made that afternoon.

Former Solicitor General Griswold said Aug. 1, "I knew someone wanted a delay but I never figured out who."

The ITT settlement became a matter of public political dispute in early 1972 when syndicated columnist Jack Anderson published an internal ITT memo indicating that the settlement had been arranged by the Administration in return for the promise of a large campaign contribution from ITT.

The Senate Judiciary Committee, which then was considering Kleindienst's nomination to succeed Mitchell as attorney general, held hearings on the ITT question and examined Kleindienst's role in the controversy.

In his statement Oct. 31, Kleindienst denied that he had committed perjury before the Senate committee:

"At the time of my testimony before the Senate Judiciary Committee, I was not asked whether I had had any contacts with the White House at the time of this decision, and I did not deny any such contacts.

"The focus of the hearings dealing with the I.T.T. affair was the negotiations in May, June and July of 1971 leading to settlement of the pending cases on July 31. I was questioned at length concerning these negotiations and particularly with reference to any conversations or meetings I might have had with Mr. Peter Flanigan of the White House staff. It was in the context of those questions that I made the statement quoted on C.B.S. news last evening, as follows:

"'In the discharge of my responsibilities as the acting attorney general in these cases, I was not interfered with by anybody at the White House. I was not importuned; I was not pressured; I was not directed.'"

According to the Times, Kleindienst made the disclosures to Cox and two prosecution assistants because of fears that he would be charged with perjury in connection with his testimony before the Senate. He also had informed the White House of his "irrevocable" decision to give Cox the information, the Times reported.

White House denounces leak—The White House issued a statement Oct. 29 that did not deny but sought to explain President Nixon's order to halt the Justice Department's suit against ITT. The statement condemned the leak of the "confidential" information and blamed Cox's staff for making the disclosures public.

"This is an inexcusable breach of confidence on the part of the staff of the former special prosecutor. This information comes from a highly confidential conversation between Archibald Cox and former Attorney General Kleindienst and from documents furnished voluntarily and also in absolute confidence by the White House to Mr. Cox.

"The information furnished by the White House and Mr. Kleindienst put the matter into fair and accurate perspective. However, the information provided to The New York Times by Mr. Cox's staff is distorted and unfair in its implication insofar as both the President and Mr. Kleindienst are concerned.

"The President's direction to Mr. Kleindienst was based on his belief that the Canteen [Grinnell case, error admitted Oct. 30] case represented a policy of the Justice Department with which he strongly disagreed, namely, that bigness per se was unlawful. When the specific facts of the appeal were subsequently explained in greater detail, the President withdrew his objection and the appeal was prosecuted in exactly the form originally proposed."

Cox admitted Oct. 30 that he may have been an indirect source of the leak. Appearing before the Senate Judiciary Committee which was investigating the circumstances of his dismissal, Cox said he had told committee members Sen. Edward M. Kennedy (D, Mass.) and Sen. Philip A. Hart (D, Mich.) and two of their aides about Kleindienst's conversation with him. "It is quite clear I broke the attorney general's confidence," Cox said, but he blamed the "inexcusable" incident on "carelessness, not malice."

The White House and Senate Republican leaders cited Cox's admission as evidence of the "partisan" investigation his office had been conducting against the President for the past several months.

Kennedy and Hart denied that they or their staff had been the source of the leak. Kennedy said Cox had not discussed the matter as part of a criminal case, but as a "single shocking example" of how Administration officials had lied to the Judiciary Committee during Kleindienst's confirmation hearings.

(Cox also told the committee that he regarded the Justice Department's settlement with ITT as a "fairly good bargain from the government's point of view and that's what I get from most antitrust lawyers.")

When he appeared before the committee Oct. 31, Cox broadened the list of persons familiar with the Kleindienst information. Members of his staff had briefed Justice Department officials, including Assistant Attorney General Henry Petersen, Oct. 26, Cox said. (Petersen issued a denial through another committee member, Sen. Edward Gurney [R, Fla.], that he had been responsible for the leak.)

The trail of news leaks also led to the White House, Cox said: "Witnesses and witnesses' attorneys get wind of these things and sometimes the White House counsels get wind of them."

FDIC probes Rebozo stock sale. The Federal Deposit Insurance Corp. (FDIC) said Oct. 30 it would postpone a request by Sen. William Proxmire (D, Wis.) that it suspend Charles G. Rebozo, president of the Key Biscayne (Fla.) Bank & Trust Co., while it investigated reports that

Rebozo sold $91,500 worth of stock he knew to be stolen.

Proxmire, a member of the Senate Banking, Housing and Urban Affairs Committee, asked for the suspension following a report by the Washington Post Oct. 25 that Rebozo, a friend of President Nixon, sold 300 shares of International Business Machines Corp. (IBM) stock more than a week after being told by an insurance investigator that the stock had been stolen from the New York City brokerage firm of E. F. Hutton & Co. by the Mafia in 1968.

The stock, 900 shares in all, had come into Rebozo's possession July 30, 1968, when he accepted it as collateral on a $195,000 loan he granted to Charles L. Lewis, who, Rebozo said, wanted money to set up a business in Miami. Lewis did not establish a business.

The Federal Bureau of Investigation (FBI) traced the stolen securities to Rebozo's bank in October 1968 and sent an agent to talk to Rebozo, the Post said. Immediately afterward, Rebozo canceled the loan and gave Lewis two days to repay the outstanding balance. When Lewis said he could not raise the money, Rebozo sold 600 shares of the stock. Although the sale of 600 shares was sufficient to cover the loan, Lewis subsequently ordered the sale of the remaining 300 shares, the Post reported.

In a sworn deposition in a civil suit filed by Hutton against Rebozo's bank, George H. Riley Jr., an insurance investigator for Continental Insurance Cos., stated that he twice tried to tell Rebozo the stock had been stolen, but Rebozo canceled both appointments. When he did see Rebozo, Riley said, Rebozo said all the IBM stock had been sold.

According to court records, the Post reported, Rebozo sold 600 shares of IBM during the same period he canceled the appointments with Riley. The court records also indicated that Rebozo sold the last 300 shares after Riley told him the stock had been purloined, the Post said.

In deferring action on Proxmire's request, the FDIC said it would probe Rebozo's conduct after completing an investigation of Franklin S. DeBoer, head of the trust department of Rebozo's bank. DeBoer was barred from being a stock broker by the Securities and Exchange Commission (SEC) in 1972. The SEC charged DeBoer with falsifying records, selling unregistered securities and appropriating $300,000—which he later repaid—from a public company. DeBoer neither admitted nor denied the charges. Rebozo hired DeBoer six months after the SEC order was issued.

In a related development, the Miami criminal strike force of the Justice Department said Oct. 25 it would open an investigation into Rebozo's role in the sale of the stock. In 1970, the strike force indicted eight persons in connection with the theft of the stock from Hutton. A strike force spokesman said that in 1970 there was no evidence linking Rebozo to anything illegal.

Nixon affirms Rebozo's honesty. In his Oct. 26 press conference, President Nixon asserted that his friend Charles Rebozo had shown "very good judgment" in holding a $100,000 contribution from billionaire Howard Hughes in a safe-deposit box for three years. Nixon said Rebozo returned the money "intact," when Rebozo concluded that the gift would be politically embarrassing because of internal disputes in the Hughes industrial empire. Nixon characterized Rebozo as a "totally honest man."

The Washington Post reported Oct. 31 that Rebozo, on the advice of his lawyer, returned the money after Internal Revenue Service (IRS) began a probe of Rebozo's handling of the money.

Due to standing White House policy, Nixon told the press, he did not learn of the $100,000 until after the 1972 presidential election when he sent notes of appreciation to contributors.

Nixon also denied a report by American Broadcasting Co. (ABC) News Oct. 23 that Rebozo had administered a $1 million trust on Nixon's behalf. According to ABC, unreported political gifts constituted the fund.

In a related development, the Senate Watergate Committee issued a subpoena to Rebozo, asking access to the three bank accounts maintained by Nixon in Rebozo's bank, the Wall Street Journal reported Oct. 30.

Other tough questions—Nixon was asked other tough questions: whether he thought America was at the point of rebellion over "too many shocks"; how he was bearing up emotionally "under the stress"; how he could regain the confidence of the people; if he could explain the rationale of a law and order Administration covering up "primafacie evidence" of high crimes and misdemeanors. He was asked if the Administration's story was "credible" that a close friend had not told him for three years that he had a $100,000 cash contribution from billionaire Howard Hughes. "Well, it's obviously not credible to you," Nixon began his answer to the newsman.

GAO cites Wallace, Humphrey campaigns. An allegedly illegal contribution to the presidential campaign of Gov. George C. Wallace (D, Ala.) was referred to the Justice Department Oct. 30 for possible prosecution by the General Accounting Office (GAO), the federal agency overseeing campaign spending laws.

A $100 gift in corporate funds was said to have been donated by a West Memphis, Ark. roadside restaurant and gasoline station, Mid-Continent Truck Stop, Inc., but later was returned. The Wallace campaign also was guilty of numerous technical violations in the federal reporting law, according to the GAO, but action was taken on the illegal corporate gift because major corporations had been penalized recently for making big donations to the Nixon re-election committee.

A
B
C
D
E
F
G

The GAO Oct. 12 referred an "apparent violation" by the Committee for the Nomination of [Sen. Hubert H.] Humphrey [D, Minn.]. The committee's failure to disclose $456,732 in contributions was cited as a "serious frustration" of election laws. The GAO also accused the Humphrey committee of failing to document properly $200,000–$300,000 in expenditures for 1972 and receiving $1,000 in illegal contributions from six corporations.

U.S. probing Gurney's finances. Sen. Edward J. Gurney (R, Fla.), a member of the Senate Watergate Committee, Oct. 31 confirmed reports that the Justice Department was investigating charges that Florida builders contributed more than $300,000 to a secret "boosters" fund in 1971.

The money allegedly was used to pay office and travel expenses.

The Federal Bureau of Investigation (FBI) had investigated charges brought in November 1971 by a Gainesville, Fla. builder, Philip I. Emmer. He said he had been "shaken down" in February 1971 by a Gurney aide who demanded a $5,000 "contribution" in exchange for winning federal approval of two Federal Housing Administration (FHA) funded apartment projects.

The aide, Larry E. Williams, also was said to have set up the boosters fund and accepted contributions seven months after the FBI investigation began.

Gurney denied knowledge of the Emmer incident when questioned by the FBI, which took no further action on the complaint. The Justice Department and the Department of Housing and Urban Development reopened the case after the Miami Herald published details of Emmer's allegations in July.

Gurney said Oct. 31 that federal investigators had asked him not to comment until the government concluded its investigation of the builders' fund charges.

Gurney had said in July that he was "unfamiliar" with any fund raising activities Williams "may have done on behalf of the state Republican party," but he insisted, "On no occasion have I ever discussed fund raising on my behalf with" Williams.

New ITT inquiry sought. There was Congressional reaction to former Attorney General Richard G. Kleindienst's charge that President Nixon had personally intervened in the International Telephone & Telegraph Corp. (ITT) antitrust dispute.

Sen. Robert Byrd (D, W. Va.), a member of the Senate Judiciary Committee, called on the committee Oct. 31 to reopen its 1972 hearings which had examined then Attorney General-designate Kleindienst's role in the government's settlement of the ITT lawsuits. Byrd asked the committee to consider: "Did the government lie about the ITT case and also did high government witnesses commit perjury?"

Another committee member, Sen. Birch Bayh (D, Ind.), demanded an answer from the Justice Department on the committee's long-standing request for a perjury investigation into testimony given at the hearings. The request for an investigation had been filed in June 1972.

Archibald Cox, who appeared before the committee Oct. 30 to testify about the circumstances leading to his dismissal by President Nixon as special Watergate prosecutor, refuted Justice Department claims that by July 1972 the ITT perjury investigation had been given priority treatment. (Kleindienst had made his disclosures to Cox, it was reported Oct. 29, out of fears that he might be indicted for perjury regarding ITT.)

According to L. Patrick Gray, then Federal Bureau of Investigation (FBI) director, the FBI did not enter the case until December 1972. In March 1973, he had said the FBI probe was "virtually complete," but in May, major figures in the case had not been interviewed. At his confirmation hearings, Attorney General-designate Elliot Richardson promised the Judiciary Committee a full report on the investigation but none was filed before his resignation. Cox said Oct. 30 that when Richardson turned the ITT probe over to the Watergate prosecution office in June, there had not been "any significant investigation before it was referred" to his office.

Richardson Sept. 12 had rejected Sen. John V. Tunney's request that the antitrust division re-examine the ITT settlement in light of disclosures made before the Senate Watergate Committee that internal White House memos would "lay this [ITT] case on the President's doorstep."

The investigations subcommittee of the House Commerce Committee Oct. 11 referred to the Justice Department the subcommittee's record of hearings conducted on the sudden transfer of ITT-related documents by the Securities and Exchange Commission (SEC) in late 1972. The effect of the SEC's decision to place the documents in the Justice Department's care was to remove the papers from the scrutiny of Congressional committees investigating the ITT affair. The record "indicates that violations of law, including obstruction of justice and perjury, may have taken place," according to subcommittee chairman Rep. Harley O. Staggers (D, W. Va.).

Consumer activist Ralph Nader Oct. 19 asked federal district court in Bridgeport, Conn. to reopen his case challenging the controversial ITT-Hartford Fire merger. There was a "prima facie case of malfeasance or fraud in the procurement of the settlement and in a subsequent coverup," Nader charged.

Maryland ends inquiry of Sen. Beall. Warren B. Duckett Jr., state's attorney for Anne Arundel County in Maryland, announced Nov. 1 that no charges of campaign finance violations would be filed against Sen. J. Glenn Beall Jr. although Beall admitted receiving $185,000 in contributions for his 1970 campaign from President Nixon's chief fund raiser, Herbert W. Kalmbach.

The money was channeled through a Washington finance committee and not reported to Maryland officials. (Maryland did not change its laws and require candidates to file financial statements for out-of-state campaign committees until 1972.) Certain expenditures of the secret money did require reporting under Maryland election laws, but no action was taken against Beall because the statute of limitation had expired.

Rebozo stock sale ruled legal. The Justice Department said Nov. 1 it had no evidence that Charles G. Rebozo, President Nixon's friend, had engaged in criminal conduct when he sold 900 shares of International Business Machines Corp. (IBM) stock that was later discovered to have been stolen. "The stock [Rebozo] had possession of was not, in fact, stolen stock," Edward T. Joyce, deputy chief of the department's organized crime section, said.

Joyce said that after Rebozo received the stock as collateral for a loan he granted Charles Lewis, Rebozo forwarded the stock certificates to the bank acting as transfer agent for IBM stock. The transfer agent, after checking with E. F. Hutton and Co.—whose name appeared on the stock—issued new certificates in Lewis' name to Rebozo and destroyed the old certificates. Joyce said Hutton "obviously didn't check" closely to see if the stock had been stolen. Hence, Joyce stated, the actual certificates that Rebozo sold were not stolen.

Even if Rebozo had been told by insurance investigator George H. Riley Jr. that the stock was stolen, Rebozo did not violate any laws, Joyce said. The stock had to be considered stolen for a crime to have been committed, he added.

Rebozo sues Washington Post—Rebozo filed a $10.5 million suit against the Washington Post Nov. 7, claiming that the Post libeled him Oct. 25 when it reported that he had cashed 300 shares of IBM stock he knew to be stolen.

Rebozo, in a suit filed in federal district court in Miami, asserted that the Post printed the story although it knew the information was contrary to court records concerning the sale.

He said insurance investigator George H. Riley Jr. could not have told him Oct. 22, 1968 that the stock had been stolen from the New York brokerage firm of E. F. Hutton & Co. because neither Hutton nor Riley's employer, the Fidelity and Casualty Co. of New York (Hutton's insurer), knew the stock had been stolen until Dec. 22, 1968.

Rebozo bank aide quits—The directors of the Federal Deposit Insurance Corp. (FDIC) voted to remove Franklin S. DeBoer from his position as vice president of the trust department of the Key Biscayne (Fla.) Bank & Trust Co., an FDIC spokesman said Nov. 9.

However, the FDIC delayed its action when it was notified that DeBoer had submitted his resignation. Rebozo was president of the bank.

States pass campaign fund laws. The Wall Street Journal reported Nov. 6 that seven states—Maryland, New Jersey, Hawaii, Florida, Texas, California and Nevada—had enacted stringent campaign finance laws in 1973 in reaction to the federal level abuses epitomized in the Watergate scandal, the high cost of electioneering and the increasing prominence of millionaire politicians.

Local issues also contributed to public awareness of the need for new reporting laws. In Nevada, the fear of candidates' dependence on contributions from the gambling industry prompted a law limiting legislative contestants to a $15,-000 spending limit or 50¢ per vote tallied by the winner in the previous election, whichever was higher.

In New Jersey, where scandals about the financing of his 1969 race for the gubernatorial post had caused Gov. William J. Cahill (R) to lose his bid for renomination in 1973, legislators specified criminal penalties for willful violations of state election laws.

Texas voters reacted to the recent conviction of several high state officials on stock manipulation charges. A newspaper expose of a pattern of campaign contributions and preferential legislative treatment caused Hawaiians to act. Another newspaper, the Miami Herald, was instrumental in the passage of Florida's spending limit and disclosure bill. The paper revealed that in 1972, lobbyists had donated half the $2.7 million received by candidates for the state legislature.

Pennsylvania, Michigan, Ohio and Massachusetts were debating similar proposals to close loopholes in present laws, but nine states remained without any laws governing campaign finances.

Vesco arrested in the Bahamas. Financier Robert L. Vesco, who had sought self-imposed exile in Costa Rica and the Bahamas to avoid arrest in connection with criminal charges of conspiracy and obstruction of justice, was arrested Nov. 6 in the Bahamas on a warrant seeking his extradition to the U.S.

Vesco's arrest was based on an indictment unrelated to the criminal trial, which also involved two former Cabinet officials of the Nixon Administration, John N. Mitchell and Maurice H. Stans. The extradition request, which would require approval of a Bahamian court, stemmed from an indictment accusing Vesco of defrauding International Controls Corp. (ICC), which he formerly controlled. Vesco had evaded extradition earlier when a Costa Rican court ruled that two other indictments, alleging conspiracy and obstruction of justice and attempted wire fraud, were not extraditable offenses.

Bahamian officials had accused the U.S. of delaying extradition proceedings against Vesco. Foreign Minister and Attorney General Paul Adderley said Sept. 14 that the U.S. had not responded to a request from a Bahamian magistrate for additional information to supplement the ICC fraud indictment. The New York Times Nov. 3 quoted a high Cabinet officer in the Bahamian government, otherwise unidentified, saying that the U.S. had made little effort to speed Vesco's extradition. Ronald Spiers, U.S. ambassador to the Bahamas, Nov. 3 confirmed reports that no action was taken on the Bahamian request made in June for submission of a Justice Department affidavit justifying the issuance of an arrest warrant under terms of the extradition treaty between the U.S. and the Bahamas.

"I guess someone in Washington preferred not to do anything more at that time," Spiers said.

The Justice Department denied the charges of inaction, noting that Spiers had presented the request for extradition Nov. 1, one day after the secret fraud indictment was unsealed by a New York Court.

Truckers' donations to Nixon. The Nixon re-election committee received its largest single industry gift—more than $600,000—from the trucking industry, according to Senate Watergate Committee investigators. The contributions were offered while the industry was opposing an Administration-sponsored bill in Congress that would have lowered trucking rates and increased shipping competition, the New York Times reported Nov. 6.

John Ruan, an official of the Washington-based lobbying group, the American Trucking Association, was identified as the organizer of the fundraising drive. He denied that truckers, whose rates and routes were regulated by the government, had contributed the money in order to obtain favorable Administration rulings.

The Nixon re-election committee made public disclosures of the truckers' donations in the fall of 1972, but did not identify the funds as comprising an industry-wide money package. The bill which was opposed by the truckers died in Congress during the same period.

Watergate committee opens 3rd phase. The Senate Watergate Committee concluded the second phase of its inquiry Nov. 6—into alleged "dirty tricks" of the 1972 presidential campaign—and took two days testimony Nov. 7 and 8 in its third and final phase of inquiry into campaign finance practices.

Among highlights of the testimony:

Nov. 7—The committee's 3rd phase opened with testimony from John J. Priestes, 36, a Miami homebuilder who had pleaded guilty earlier in 1973 to receipt of cash kickbacks from subcontractors and filing a false tax return. He testified that in March, 1972 he had been called by Ben Fernandez, then chairman of the National Hispanic Finance Committee for the Re-election of the President, and in a series of meetings was told by Fernandez that Nixon's campaign finance chairman Maurice H. Stans would get an FHA suspension against Priestes revoked if he would contribute $100,000 to the Nixon campaign. Priestes said he brought the first payment, $25,000, to Washington as instructed by Fernandez, and gave it to Stans, who promised to call then HUD Secretary George Romney. "I thought I was paying $25,000 for a political favor," Priestes said. "I thought it was the way things were done."

Priestes said his uncashed check was returned two weeks later with the message that his problem was "more serious than previously expected" and that he would have to give the money in cash. Priestes said he refused to do this, called Fernandez, who made a "complete turnabout" and denied any promise had been made for the contribution.

A statement from Stans filed with the committee denied any promise of favors in return for the contribution. Stans said he had met Priestes without being aware of his circumstances, accepted the check but found after consulting with HUD and the Justice Department that Priestes was "unreliable," whereupon he ordered Priestes to be "totally and permanently rebuffed" and his check returned.

Former White House official William H. Marumoto testified that political considerations entered into determination of government contract awards for Spanish-speaking Americans, that grants to aid the Spanish-Americans were not given to unqualified persons but where a choice was necessary the aid would go to those most politically favorable to the Nixon Administration.

Nov. 8—Fernandez, calling Priestes a "liar," testified that Priestes had made the first contact with him, that he had not heard of Priestes until a Priestes associate made the contact, that he had not promised any favors in exchange for the contribution, that the $100,000 figure had never been requested, that the $25,000 had been volunteered, that there was never any discussion of a cash contribution, that Priestes never asked Stans to call anyone and that Stans never promised to call anyone.

Three more corporations fined. Three more firms and their corporate officials were penalized for giving illegal contributions to the Nixon re-election committee. Braniff International Airways Inc. and its board chairman, Harding L. Lawrence, pleaded guilty Nov. 12 in federal district court in Washington to violations of the federal campaign finance law.

Braniff had made a $40,000 cash donation from corporate funds immediately prior to the April 7, 1972 deadline requiring public disclosure of the source and expenditure of campaign funds.

Maximum fines were imposed on Braniff, which was assessed $5,000 and Lawrence, who was penalized $1,000. Defense attorneys told the court that although Lawrence had made a substantial personal contribution, estimated at $10,000, to the Nixon committee, he had been "under some pressure to make this [illegal corporate] contribution" because Nixon campaign officials had expressed dissatisfaction with the original amount.

Ashland Petroleum Gabon Corp., a unit of Ashland Oil Inc., pleaded guilty Nov. 13 in federal district court in Catlettsburg, Ky. to charges of donating $100,000 in corporate funds to Nixon's re-election committee. Ashland Oil's chairman, Orin E. Atkins, pleaded no contest and was fined $1,000. The corporation was fined $5,000.

Gulf Oil Corp. and its vice president, Claude C. Wild Jr., entered guilty pleas the same day in federal district court in Washington. The court fined Gulf $5,000 and Wild $1,000 for contributing $100,000 to President Nixon's campaign committee, $15,000 to the presidential campaign of Rep. Wilbur D. Mills (D, Ark.) and $10,000 to Sen. Henry M. Jackson (D, Wash.), another unsuccessful contender for the Democratic presidential nomination.

The Mills and Jackson donations were the first known evidence that Democratic contenders for the presidency had accepted illegal contributions. Neither had joined in the voluntary disclosures of campaign funds made in early 1972 by their rivals in the Democratic race.

Jackson, who denied knowledge that Gulf's contribution had come from corporate funds, said he was "preparing to return the money." Mills was "seeking information from the company as to whether the company feels a refund is in order," a spokesman said.

Braniff, Ashland and Gulf had made voluntary disclosures recently to the special Watergate prosecutor's office after investigations had begun which could have led to felony charges against the firms and individuals involved. Because voluntary admissions of guilt had been made, only criminal misdemeanor charges were filed.

The charges against Braniff, Gulf and Ashland were brought by Leon Jaworski, President Nixon's newly appointed Watergate special prosecutor. Three other firms had also been convicted of campaign fund violations involving the Nixon re-election committee.

Testimony on corporate gifts. The Senate Watergate Committee heard testimony Nov. 13–15 from officers of six major U.S. corporations, who admitted engaging in schemes to circumvent federal campaign laws barring corporate gifts to political campaigns.

Among highlights of the testimony:

Nov. 13—Two officials of the American Ship Building Co. told the committee that they and six other "loyal" employes had been used as conduits through which the company's president, George M. Steinbrenner 3rd, had channeled $25,000 in contributions to the President's re-election fund.

The two witnesses, Robert E. Bartlome, company secretary, and Matthew E. Clark Jr., director of purchasing, also said Steinbrenner had induced them to lie to agents of the Federal Bureau of Investigation (FBI) when questioned about the contributions.

The two witnesses testified that in 1972 Steinbrenner arranged to have bonuses paid to the eight employes, totaling $26,000 after taxes. Each recipient of a bonus then wrote personal checks totaling the amount of his bonus, and the checks were forwarded to Herbert W. Kalmbach, the President's personal attorney, at the Washington headquarters of the Committee to Re-elect the President. According to Clark, the transactions occurred April 6, 1972, the day before a new campaign contribution law took effect.

While the witnesses indicated that they had received other bonuses in 1970 and 1971, their testimony failed to make clear the amounts or the disposition of the money.

"I knew from those conversations" with Bartlome in 1970, Clark testified, "that the bonuses I was to receive were for political contributions and weren't bonuses at all."

Bartlome testified that the company began a cover-up of the contributions in January 1973. The company granted real bonuses to legitimize the bogus ones, Bartlome said. In April, a false memo, backdated a year, was placed in the files for "cosmetic" purposes. However, the cover-up lasted only until August, when the eight employes, subpoenaed to testify before a grand jury, decided against perjuring themselves, Bartlome said.

When informed of the decision by his employes to tell the truth, Steinbrenner, Bartlome testified, "laid his head on his desk" and cried that both he and the company would be "ruined."

The Wall Street Journal reported Nov. 15 that records of the Committee to Re-elect the President showed that Steinbrenner, who in 1970 received company bonuses totaling $75,000, had made his own $75,000 contribution to the 1972 Nixon re-election campaign. Committee sources, the Journal said, indicated they had no evidence showing Steinbrenner had been reimbursed for his contribution, merely implications of a pattern.

Nov. 14—Two oil company executives testified that they had both been approached for $100,000 contributions to the 1972 Nixon re-election campaign.

Orin E. Atkins, chairman of Ashland Oil Inc., and Claude C. Wild Jr., vice president for governmental affairs for Gulf Oil Corp., said they had arranged for the contributions to be paid to Maurice Stans, director of the Finance Committee to Re-elect the President.

Atkins said he obtained the money from an Ashland subsidiary in Gabon, Africa. Wild said he chose to withdraw cash from a Gulf subsidiary in the Bahamas.

In neither case, both witnesses testified, did Stans or Lee Nunn, a re-election committee official who helped solicit Gulf, ask for contributions directly from the corporations. But both men used company funds because, as Atkins put it, "in my mind it could have only come from one place, the corporation ... because $100,000 is an awful lot of money."

Atkins also testified that Stans, afraid the Nixon re-election committee would be forced to make its campaign contribution lists public, called him sometime in 1973 and asked him to reconstruct a list of individual contributors. Atkins said he refused.

Nov. 15—The Watergate committee took testimony from the chairman of the Goodyear Tire & Rubber Co., the former chairman of American Airlines and two officials from Braniff International Airways, Inc.

Russell DeYoung of Goodyear admitted that his company had used a Swiss bank account as a secret source of funds for the Nixon re-election committee. The money, which for accounting purposes was disguised as rebates given by Goodyear to European suppliers, was given to Stans in two $20,000 payments, and DeYoung claimed that he added $5,000 of his own money. Unlike other executives who claimed to have been pressured into contributing, DeYoung said he agreed to the gift "solely because we thought the re-election of the President was in the best interest of the country." When Watergate committee member Sen. Lowell P. Weicker Jr. (R, Conn.) said that it was a "sorry day" for Goodyear when the $40,000 in corporate money was given to the campaign, DeYoung interrupted with the comment, "not necessarily."

George A. Spater, formerly of American Airlines, related information he had divulged in July, when he became the first corporate executive to voluntarily admit illegal corporate gifts to the Nixon campaign.

Spater reiterated that it had been his "fear" that his company would suffer competitively if a contribution were not made.

He told the committee that such abuses could be discouraged by a law barring certain persons with obvious control over government decisions from soliciting campaign gifts.

Camilio Fazrega, an official for Braniff, said he had been asked by a company vice president to raise $40,000 and did so through a family-owned company in his native Panama. The cash was forwarded to Braniff and then to the Committee to Re-elect the President, Fazrega testified.

Braniff and its board chairman Harding H. Lawrence pleaded guilty to making illegal contributions Nov. 12.

Chisholm fund violations alleged. The General Accounting Office (GAO) Nov. 16 recommended that the Justice Department take legal action against Rep. Shirley Chisholm (D, N.Y.) for her "apparent violations" of federal campaign finance laws during the 1972 race for the Democratic presidential nomination.

The GAO's charges involved failure to keep accurate records of contributions and expenditures (a $6,000 final deficit actually concealed an $18,000–$23,000 surplus); failure to report an estimated $30,000 in receipts and $51,000 in expenditures received after April 7, 1972; acceptance of three illegal corporate donations totaling $686 and failure to name a campaign committee chairman. The alleged violations all were misdemeanors punishable upon each conviction by up to one year in jail and fines up to $1,000.

Chisholm admitted there were "bookkeeping irregularities" in her campaign, but she attributed them to errors committed by a small, inexperienced staff. She had been "singled out" for "harassment" and "investigation" by the Nixon Administration, Chisholm charged, because of her opposition to Administration policies. (The GAO was the auditing and investigative agency for Congress.)

Nixon discusses finances. President Nixon discussed his personal finances in an appearance Nov. 17 before the Associated Press Managing Editors Association at the Disney World Hotel near Orlando, Fla.

Nixon said: "I've made my mistakes, but in all of my years of public life I have never profited, never profited from public service. I've earned every cent. And in all of my years in public life I have never obstructed justice. . . . People have got to know whether or not their President is a crook. Well I'm not a crook. I've earned everything I've got."

The President made the declaration in discussing his personal finances. When he had left office as vice president in 1961, he said, his net worth was $47,000, but he "made a lot of money" in the next eight years: $250,000 from his book, Six Crises; between $100,000 and $250,000 a year practicing law; selling all his stock in 1968 for about $300,000; his New York apartment for $300,000; and another $100,000 due him from his law firm.

The President was asked about a press report he paid $792 in federal income tax in 1970 and $878 in 1971 and whether public officials should disclose their personal finances. Nixon said he had disclosed his personal finances and would make another report available "because, obviously, you're all so busy that when these things come across your desk maybe you don't see them."

In reply to the query, he said he paid $79,000 in income tax in 1969 and "nominal amounts" in the next two years. Why

the nominal amounts? he asked. "It wasn't because of the deductions for shall we say a cattle ranch or interest or you know all these gimmicks that you've got where you can deduct from." But because his predecessor Lyndon Johnson "came in to see me shortly after I became President" and suggested he take the legal deduction from his income tax for his vice presidential papers, as Johnson had with most of his Presidential papers. He did this, Nixon said, his papers being appraised at $500,000, "many believe conservatively, at that amount," he added. He would be glad to have the papers back, he said, and pay the tax "because I think they're worth more than that."

Raising the milk prices—Nixon himself raised the issue of the 1971 increase in federal milk price supports.

"I want the fact out because the facts will prove that the President is telling the truth," he told the editors. Charges that his Administration raised the price support for milk in 1971 "as a quid pro quo" for a promise by milk producers of substantial contributions, he said, was "just not true." He said "Democrats in Congress put a gun to our head" by demanding a price-support increase, so his Administration put a lower increase into effect.

Agnew committee fined. A Maryland county court judge Nov. 19 fined the "Salute to Ted Agnew Committee" $2,000 after the committee entered guilty pleas to four counts of violating state election laws.

The charges stemmed from a report filed by the committee in which $49,900 from Nixon re-election funds had been falsely described as contributions from individual donors to a 1972 testimonial dinner for former Vice President Spiro Agnew.

Still to be tried was committee treasurer Blagdon H. Wharton, who had been indicted separately on a charge of signing false contribution reports.

Andreas pleads not guilty. Dwayne O. Andreas, a Minneapolis businessman and contributor to the Nixon re-election campaign in 1972, entered a not guilty plea Nov. 23 in federal district court in Minneapolis. He was accused of authorizing an illegal $100,000 donation to Sen. Hubert H. Humphrey's (D, Minn.) 1968 presidential campaign.

Teamsters' donations disputed. Former Teamsters President James R. Hoffa claimed that the union had given the Nixon re-election campaign far more than the $18,000 reported, according to Newsweek magazine in its Nov. 26 issue. Total Teamsters contributions were "$60,000–$70,000," Hoffa said.

According to a deposition filed during the summer in a libel suit against the

Manchester (N.H.) Union Leader, Hoffa testified that the union contributions reached an estimated $175,000.

Hoffa told Newsweek that Teamster business agents were assessed $1,000. Donations also were solicited from "friends" in Las Vegas who borrowed from the union pension funds.

The union contributions were related to Hoffa's release from prison. Teamster President Frank Fitzsimmons urged the President to commute Hoffa's 13-year sentence for jury tampering and pension fund fraud, Hoffa said, but he added that he was double crossed by Fitzsimmons and White House Counsel Charles W. Colson who had a clause added to the commutation decree barring Hoffa from holding union office (and challenging Fitzsimmons) until 1980. (When Colson left the White House, his Washington law firm was retained to represent the union.)

Fitzsimmons replied Nov. 22, calling Hoffa a "damned liar." "Every quarter" of the union contributions had been reported, Fitzsimmons declared. (According to the Washington Post Nov. 22, Teamster donations that were reported to the General Accounting Office by the Finance Committee to Re-elect the President had totaled more than $40,000.)

Financial data pledged. President Nixon's intention to disclose his income tax returns was reported by Sen. J. Bennett Johnston (D, La.) Nov. 26 as he emerged from a meeting the President held with a group of Senators from both parties. The meeting was a continuation of what the White House had dubbed Nixon's "Operation Candor" counteroffensive against the Watergate disclosures and other problems.

His spokesman, Gerald L. Warren, said Nov. 27 the President planned to make public "complete information" on his personal finances to put to rest "erroneous charges and allegations" about them. No decision had been made on release of the income tax returns, he said. The next day Warren disclosed plans to provide the information in packets of documents to be sent to all members of Congress and governors.

Panel probes SBA, White House pressure. The House Banking and Currency Committee's Subcommittee on Small Business began public hearings Nov. 27 on charges of corruption and mismanagement in the Small Business Administration (SBA) and allegations that the White House had pressured the agency both to grant loans to Nixon supporters and halt investigations of some loan recipients.

While testimony focused on charges of misconduct in the Richmond, Va. district office of the SBA, chief subcommittee investigator Curtis Prins said he had evidence of political pressure, bribery and kickbacks and faulty loan practices in 21 other offices.

In appearances Nov. 27 and Nov. 29, Prins said the Richmond office had granted $11.7 million in direct and indirect loans to Joseph C. Palumbo, brother-in-law of Thomas F. Regan, who had been suspended as director of the Richmond office earlier in November.

Regan appeared Nov. 29 to defend his loan policies, denying conflict of interest. Nor was there any conflict, he maintained, in his incurring almost $500,000 in personal financial obligations from banks doing business with the SBA.

Prins also told the panel that the SBA's Office of Minority Business Enterprise was heavily politicized and had been misused in many parts of the country.

A prime example, Prins said in testimony Nov. 29 and Dec. 10, was the case of Dr. Thomas W. Matthew, an advocate of black capitalism and strong Nixon supporter. Prins said Nixon had once personally ordered that "all assistance be given to Matthew." When Matthew later began defaulting on SBA loans and other federal assistance, the White House attempted to thwart investigations of Matthew by the SBA and local authorities in New York City. The SBA had continued to make loans to Matthew, Prins charged, even after Matthew had defaulted on some loans and had come under criminal investigation

Asked Dec. 10 why the assistance to Matthew had continued, SBA Administrator Thomas S. Kleppe said "aside from the pressure that existed," Matthew was "trying to help reach people having trouble—drug addicts, prostitutes and criminals. This appealed to me."

(It was reported Dec. 4 that the minority business program was also currently the subject of investigations by the Federal Bureau of Investigation, the General Accounting Office and the Senate Watergate Committee.)

Kleppe had first appeared before the subcommittee Dec. 4, reading a statement defending his agency and accusing Prins of "innuendo and smear." He denied that the minority aid program was politicized but said that it was inherently "controversial and difficult to manage." He defended the quality of the loan guarantee program and argued that the proportion of defaults was relatively small.

The subcommittee's hearings had been conducted as part of its consideration of an increase in the SBA's lending authority. The panel voted Dec. 12 to authorize an increase in the ceiling to $4.875 billion from $4.3 billion, but recommended that the authority be limited to six months to allow further investigation of the agency.

Ervin committee suspends hearings. The Senate Watergate Committee Nov. 27 suspended further public hearings until early 1974. It said the action was taken to allow more time for preliminary investigation of the two remaining items on its agenda—a

contribution by milk producers to the Nixon re-election campaign and a cash payment of $100,000 accepted by Nixon's friend, Charles G. Rebozo, from aides of industrialist Howard R. Hughes. The money, purportedly intended for Nixon campaign use, was later returned.

The committee's chief counsel, Samuel Dash, told reporters Nov. 26 the investigation had encountered difficulties in obtaining White House documents on the milk case and in serving subpoenas in the Hughes case.

In other action Nov. 27, the committee voted to subpoena additional presidential tapes and documents relating to its campaign fund-raising probe. The committee received a report from a three-member subcommittee clearing the panel's chief investigator, Carmine Bellino, of charges he engaged in electronic surveillance of Republican officials during the 1960 presidential campaign. The charges were made by GOP national chairman George Bush. The two Democrats on the subcommittee, Sens. Herman E. Talmadge (Ga.) and Daniel K. Inouye (Hawaii), said there was "no direct, competent or credible evidence" to sustain the charges; the Republican member, Sen. Edward J. Gurney (Fla.), said the evidence was contradictory and inconclusive.

Seafarers' donation probed. Time magazine reported Nov. 25 that the Watergate special prosecutor was investigating the SIU's $100,000 contribution to Nixon's 1972 campaign. The article, published in Time's Dec. 3 edition, said that the contribution was made on the same day the union borrowed $100,000 from a New York bank but that "no loan should have been necessary if the money had come from voluntary contributions by members as required by law." It charged that the Nixon campaign committee had waited three months to report the contribution although the law required reporting of donations within 48 hours of receipt. A federal indictment against the Seafarer's union and eight of its officers in 1970 on charges of illegal campaign donations had been dropped.

Prosecution 'leaks' deplored—Time's report that the Seafarers' donation was under investigation was deplored Nov. 26 by deputy White House press secretary Gerald L. Warren as what "might be called" a news leak by the office of Watergate special prosecutor Leon Jaworski.

Warren linked another press report to a leak from Jaworski's office—an account Nov. 26 by columnists Rowland Evans and Robert Novak of a meeting between Jaworski and two White House lawyers who, the account said, attempted to persuade the prosecutor to refrain from immediate disclosure that an 18-minute section of one of the court-sought Watergate conversations taped by the White House had been obliterated. Jaworski refused the request and the disclosure was made in the court the same day.

Committee hears Hughes aides. The Senate Watergate Committee Dec. 3 began hearing testimony from the first of a dozen aides to billionaire Howard Hughes. They had been subpoenaed to give evidence on the $100,000 gift made by Hughes to Charles G. Rebozo, a personal friend of President Nixon.

The Hughes aides had been faced with possible contempt citations when they, on advice of Hughes' attorney Chester C. Davis, initially balked at appearing before the committee behind closed doors. Davis, acting as counsel for the Hughes aides, had said his clients would give public testimony but they would not submit to questioning in private because they would become victims "of partial and distorted" leaks in the press. Davis had sought an injunction against the private hearings, but U.S. District Court Judge Aubrey E. Robinson Jr. Dec. 5 expressed reluctance to interfere in Congressional matters. However, Robinson set Dec. 10 for a full hearing on the issue.

Davis appeared before the committee Dec. 4, bringing with him 1,000 one-hundred dollar bills that he said he had received from Rebozo in June. Davis reportedly slammed down on the table before committee chairman Sen. Sam J. Ervin (D, N.C.) two manila envelopes containing the money and shouted at Ervin, "Here's the goddamn money. Do what you want with it."

On Ervin's orders, the money was removed to committee offices where it was photocopied. Committee investigators subsequently indicated they hoped to determine when the bills had been printed and test the truth of Rebozo's statement that in June he had given to Davis the same bills he had received in two $50,000 installments in 1969 and 1970.

Public funding effort beaten. A Senate effort to enact public funding for presidential election campaigns collapsed Dec. 3 after repeated failure to break a filibuster. The funding effort was riding on an amendment to raise the federal debt limit, which expired in the interim, and carried the Senate into an unusual Sunday session. There had been a previously unsuccessful effort in the House to make the debt ceiling bill a vehicle for tax reform and higher Social Security benefits.

During the impasse, the temporary debt ceiling of $465 billion expired at midnight Nov. 30 and the ceiling automatically reverted to its permanent statutory level of $400 billion, $64.9 billion less than the government's outstanding debt. After the expiration, the Treasury Department announced plans to halt the sale of savings bonds and Treasury bills and issuance of special obligations to federal trust funds, since the legal borrowing authority had already been exceeded.

After collapse of the effort to break the filibuster, the Senate voted 48–36 Dec. 3 to drop the campaign finance amendment and approve the House version of the debt ceiling increase. This cleared it for President Nixon's desk. He signed it later

Dec. 3, increasing the debt ceiling to $475.7 billion through June 30, 1974.

Filibuster by Allen—The filibuster against the campaign funding plan was launched by Sen. James B. Allen (D, Ala.) Nov. 30, charging it was a "raid on the federal treasury for the politicians of the country."

The plan had emerged in the Senate Nov. 27 under sponsorship of 34 senators, 28 of them Democrats. However, they included Senate Republican Leader Hugh Scott (Pa.), one of the chief drafters with Sen. Edward M. Kennedy (D, Mass.). As a way to gain House consideration, in a Senate-House conference committee, the provisions were attached to the House-passed debt ceiling bill. (A less drastic campaign funding bill passed by the Senate had not been granted consideration by the House Administration Committee since the summer. The Senate plan, adopted by a 57–34 vote Nov. 27, called for public financing of campaigns for the presidency and Congress.

But public funding of Congressional campaigns had generated opposition in the House. Members were reluctant to provide an election opponent with equal financing, some $90,000 in the general election or 15¢ a voter, whichever was greater, according to the Senate plan. Senate nominees would receive $175,000 or 15¢ a voter.

The House Democratic leaders decided Nov. 28 to support the plan for public financing of the presidential campaigns and defer the plan for Congressional campaign financing for further study. On Nov. 29, the House approved 347–54 a resolution to delete all of the campaign funding provisions from the debt limit and return the bill in that form to the Senate.

White House opposition to the campaign financing plan also became known Nov. 29 through Sen. Wallace F. Bennett (R, Utah). He reported that Treasury Secretary George P. Shultz and Melvin R. Laird, presidential domestic affairs adviser, would recommend a veto if the bill reached the President.

When the plan reached the Senate floor Nov. 30, it had been revised by its sponsors to include only presidential campaign funding. It would allow a major party candidate in the general election campaign to spend only 15¢ for each eligible voter, or about $21 million. The funds would come from the current $1 federal income tax checkoff fund. Private contributions would be allowed only if the checkoff did not produce enough money. Minor candidates would have federal funds available in proportion to their voting strength. In primaries, the presidential candidates would be entitled to matching funds from the Treasury for each $100 contribution after raising $100,000 privately, the latter to discourage "nuisance candidates" without popular backing.

The total subsidy for primaries would be limited to 5¢ per voter or about $7 million; total spending in all primaries by any one candidate would be limited to $15 million.

Individual contributions would be limited to $3,000 a candidate in a general election or primary campaign.

The plan, attached to the debt ceiling bill, led to Allen's filibuster. It led to Saturday and Sunday sessions Dec. 1 and 2, the latter the first Sunday Senate meeting since March 3, 1929.

With the opposing sides unable to muster either enough votes to cut off the debate or kill the campaign fund plan, the impasse lasted until Dec. 3. Two cloture votes failed—one Dec. 2 by a 47–33 vote (40 D & 7 R vs 23 R & 10 D), seven less than the required two-thirds majority for adoption; the second on Dec. 3 by a 49–39 vote, 10 votes short of the required two-thirds. Two moves by Allen to kill the campaign financing plan also were rejected—45–36 Dec. 2 and 43–42 Dec. 3. Confronted by the declining vote for cloture and near defeat by simple majority vote, the campaign reformers retreated. But assurance was obtained from the Senate Rules Committee that a campaign financing bill would be sent to the floor in early 1974.

Supporters of the campaign funding plan accused the White House of abetting the filibuster. Sen. Walter F. Mondale (D, Minn.) said Dec. 2 the filibuster "is the work of President Richard Nixon far more than it is the work of Sen. James Allen." The floor manager of the campaign fund bill, Sen. Russell B. Long (D, La.), agreed. It was clear "on the face of it," he said Dec. 2, "that the Administration does not want the measure to reach the President's desk. From a political point of view they'd rather have it die by filibuster in the Senate than have the President veto it."

Phillips pleads guilty. Phillips Petroleum Co. and its retired chairman, William W. Keeler, pleaded guilty Dec. 4 in federal district court in Washington to charges of making an illegal $100,000 cash contribution to President Nixon's re-election campaign.

The firm, one of the nation's 10 largest oil companies, was fined the maximum $5,000 for the misdemeanor. Phillips was the last of seven corporations, which had made voluntary disclosures of illegal donations, to be convicted. The special Watergate prosecutor's office warned that other companies liable for the same offense but not offering public disclosure of their crimes would be charged with felony violations and their corporate officials would be subject to jail terms.

Keeler was fined $1,000 for authorizing the gift. (He had invoked Fifth Amendment rights and refused to testify before the Senate Watergate Committee Nov. 22 regarding the Phillips contribution to the Nixon campaign and those of other oil companies. Keeler was believed to have coordinated President Nixon's fund-raising efforts within the oil industry.)

The prosecutor's office also revealed that Phillips had admitted making other gifts to the campaigns of House and Senate candidates in 1970 and 1972. The

contributions, totaling $50,000–$60,000, were "still under investigation," according to a spokesman for the prosecutor's staff.

Gurney concedes 'wrongdoing.' Sen. Edward J. Gurney (R, Fla.), a member of the Senate Watergate Committee, answered charges in a televised news conference Dec. 6 that he had benefited from a secret fund totaling $300,000.

Gurney conceded that there had been "wrongdoing" in campaign fund-raising activities conducted on his behalf, but he added, "I have not engaged in any wrongdoing. I did not know it was going on." He also denied receiving any of the $300,000 collected for him by a former aide, Larry E. Williams. Gurney had said previously that Williams had never worked for him, but at his news conference, Gurney said Williams had served as his chauffeur and traveling companion.

The Miami Herald reported Dec. 6 that Williams and Jim Groot, Gurney's former administrative assistant, had given sworn statements to federal investigators that Gurney had been aware of an estimated $50,000 cash contribution delivered to his Washington office in July 1972. (The money, which was not reported as required by law, was received four months after the deadline had passed for making public disclosures of all campaign contributions.) Gurney was not present when the money was delivered, but knew that it was expected and knew of its arrival, Williams testified.

Groot testified that he had received the money from Winter Park, Fla. banker George Anderson, who had been accompanied to Washington by Williams. The money was turned over to Groot and put in Gurney's inner office safe, to which only Gurney, Groot and a secretary had access.

Williams testified that the secret money was collected from Florida builders who were dependent upon Gurney's appointees to the Federal Housing Administration (FHA) for approval of their FHA construction projects.

The Herald reported Nov. 8 that Williams had agreed to plead guilty to two felony charges—filing a false income tax return and offering a gratuity to a federal employe—in return for a grant of immunity from further federal prosecution.

Vesco extradition to U.S. denied. A Bahamian magistrate Dec. 7 refused to order the extradition of Robert L. Vesco, a U.S. citizen sought in connection with separate but inter-related securities fraud and obstruction of justice charges.

Emmanuel Osadebay granted a defense motion to dismiss the case without hearing evidence presented on Vesco's behalf.

The U.S. had based its case against Vesco on affidavits from Laurence Richardson, a former ICC president, Robert Ost, a former ICC accountant, and C. Henry Buhl 3rd, a former director of Investors Overseas Services Ltd., an ICC unit. According to Buhl's testimony, he agreed in December 1971 to sell Vesco 375,000 IOS shares for $140,000. Buhl claimed that he had received a $50,000 deposit by wire for the sale Jan. 4, 1972.

Osadebay ruled that the U.S. had not proven that Vesco had ordered $50,000 in ICC funds transferred from a U.S. bank to Buhl's account in Switzerland for the private stock sale. Ost testified that he had received orders to make the transfer from an ICC vice president and not from Vesco. The court rejected the U.S. contention that orders for the disbursal originated with Vesco. Richardson had testified that Vesco gave four contradictory explanations to the ICC board when asked about the $50,000 withdrawal. (ICC records showed that the payments had been made to Buhl.)

The defense produced another affidavit from Buhl denying his earlier statement.

The court ruled that the U.S.' 1931 extradition treaty with Great Britain which was in effect before the Bahamas won independence, continued to have the force of law. But lacking a wire fraud precedent in the Bahamian treaty, Osadebay cited a precedent in another U.S. request for extradition from Canada. U.S. officials had conceded at that time that wire fraud was not an extraditable offense, Osadebay said.

Vesco denied Argentine haven—Prior to his arrest in Nassau, Vesco began negotiating another escape route to Argentina. His efforts failed just as the Bahamian court ruled in his favor.

Vesco linked to heroin smuggling— Frank Peroff, an undercover narcotics agent, told Congressional investigators and a New York federal grand jury that Robert Vesco had backed a scheme to smuggle 100 kilograms of heroin into the U.S., the New York Times reported Nov. 24.

When Peroff's government contacts notified the White House of the information, Peroff said the investigation was ended abruptly and his undercover identity was revealed, forcing him into hiding to protect his life.

Mitchell-Stans judge to get tape. The White House agreed to provide the Feb. 28 tape of a conversation between ousted White House Counsel John W. Dean and President Nixon for private examination by the judge at the trial of John Mitchell and Maurice Stans, federal prosecutors revealed Dec. 6.

Presiding Judge Lee P. Gagliardi had demanded the entire tape after rejecting as "not sufficient" a partial transcript provided by the White House. Federal prosecutors, who had been asked by Gagliardi to obtain the recording, said White House Special Counsel J. Fred Buzhardt Jr. agreed to furnish the "entire conversation" not later than Dec. 14.

(Dean had said he discussed the Vesco matter with the President in the Feb. 28 meeting.)

The Feb. 28 tape was not among those subpoenaed by the Watergate special

prosecutor's office but it was one of five subpoenaed by the Senate Watergate Committee. Another tape sought by Gagliardi was an April 15 recording of another Nixon-Dean meeting, in which Dean said he would seek immunity in return for testimony against top Administration officials.

When he informed the parties to the case of his displeasure with receiving only the partial transcript, Gagliardi said he also received two affidavits, one vouching for the authenticity of the transcript and another declaring that the April 15 conversation had not been recorded.

Gagliardi also announced he had advanced the trial date from Jan. 7 to Jan. 9, 1974.

Nixon discloses finance data. President Nixon disclosed data on his personal finances Dec. 8 to "remove doubts" that had arisen and "correct misinformation" about "what I have earned and what I own." The data included his income tax returns for 1969–72 and an audit of his private financial affairs since Jan. 1, 1969 conducted by the New York accounting firm of Coopers & Lybrand.

According to the data, Nixon had become a millionaire during his presidency, his net worth having more than tripled (from $307,141 to $988,522). It also revealed that he had paid unusually low federal income tax payments for one with his income and no state income tax, although he maintained a residence and voted in California.

It was also disclosed that a wealthy friend, head of a pharmaceutical firm, had set up a trust fund for Nixon's daughter, Tricia, in 1958 at the time a drug-price probe was being undertaken.

The President acknowledged the controversial nature of two major tax decisions which substantially reduced his federal income tax obligations. One involved his gift to the U.S. of his vice presidential papers, which enabled him to list huge continuing deductions. The other involved the sale of some California property in 1970 for which no capital gain was reported and no capital gain tax paid.

The President offered to submit both matters for re-evaluation to a Congressional tax committee and to abide by its decision. This could amount to an additional claim of nearly $300,000 in taxes. The committee selected, which consented to Nixon's request, was the Congressional Joint Committee on Internal Revenue Taxation, composed of the five senior members of the House Ways and Means Committee and the five senior members of the Senate Finance Committee.

The committee met Dec. 12 and chairman Wilbur D. Mills (D, Ark.) told reporters afterwards its members agreed to proceed as it customarily did in other cases with a full inspection of all aspects of the Nixon tax returns. A review of part of a tax return was impossible, it was felt, and the committee would not confine itself to the two controversial items as specifically requested by the President.

In his statement on his financial affairs, Nixon declared his intention to make a gift to the American people of his home at San Clemente, Calif. at the time of his death or the death of Mrs. Nixon, whichever was later. He had requested the legal action to accomplish this, he said, "so that future Administrations and future generations can take advantage of this beautiful Western setting to help maintain a truly national perspective for the presidency."

Nixon's statement—In his statement, Nixon said he was making "a full disclosure" of his financial affairs as President and that "no previous President, to my knowledge, has ever made so comprehensive and exhaustive a disclosure" of assets and liabilities, expenses and income during his tenure of office.

"To the open-minded," he said, the data "will lay to rest such false rumors as that campaign contributions were converted to my personal use, that campaign funds were used in the purchase of my home in San Clemente, that I have hidden away a secret $1 million investment portfolio, that I sheltered the income on which my daughter, Tricia, should have paid taxes, and that $10 million in federal funds was spent on my homes in Key Biscayne and San Clemente."

His private affairs had been conducted "in a manner I thought both prudent and in the best interests of my family," Nixon stated, and even though both law and tradition protected the privacy of such matters, he was releasing the data "because the confidentiality of my private finances is far less important to me than the confidence of the American people in the integrity of the President."

Nixon was aware that "questions and controversies may continue as a consequence of these disclosures." Even his financial advisers and those who prepared his financial records, he said, "have disagreements of professional opinion among themselves." But the tax lawyers and accountants who assisted him in preparing his federal income tax returns, Nixon said, advised him that the two controversial tax items—the California land sale and gift of vice presidential papers—"were correctly reported" to the Internal Revenue Service (IRS). "My tax attorneys today are giving me similar advice," he said, and the IRS advised him that the items were correctly reported when it conducted an examination of his tax returns for 1971 and 1972.

The President also raised "another concern" of his—"the degree of public misunderstanding about government expenditures at my home in San Clemente."

"The perception is now widespread," he said, "that the government spent anywhere from $6 million to $10 million on improvements at my home. One myth breeds another, so many observers also believe that the government improvements have vastly enriched me personally. Those views are grossly inaccurate."

The facts, the President stated, were that the General Services Administration

(GSA) spent $68,000 on his San Clemente home and $635,000 on the grounds surrounding the home, all for protection, security and safety reasons. By comparison, he said, almost $6 million was spent by the military services on the Western White House office complex on government property adjacent to San Clemente. "Unfortunately," Nixon contended, "the American people have been misled into believing that the funds for the office complex were spent on my home. The fact that the total spent on my home was $68,000 has been ignored; the fact that my wife and I spent ourselves three times as much as that, $187,977 out of our own funds, for real improvements to our homes, has been lost altogether."

Data on income—According to the data released by the President, he and Mrs. Nixon had a total adjusted gross income of $1,122,264 for the four years 1969-72, or an average of $280,556 a year. The total federal income tax paid on that income was $78,650, an annual average of $19,662, which was the level paid by a family with an income of $67,000.

In the years 1970-72, the Nixons paid an income tax for each respective year at the level of families' with incomes of $7,500, $8,500 and $25,000; the average for the three years was at the level of a family with $15,000 income a year. For 1970, the Nixons listed no taxable income, but paid a $793 tax because of the "minimum tax" clause of the 1969 tax act.

The year-by-year breakdown:

	Income	Tax
1969	328,161	$72,682
1970	262,942	793
1971	262,384	878
1972	268,777	4,298

Of the $200,000 Nixon received in expense allowances—$50,000 a year—he used about $108,000, which was deducted from his income tax; $92,000 went into his bank accounts and was taxable.

The President's paycheck was sent monthly to California to his personal attorney, Herbert W. Kalmbach, who deposited it in the Nixon account at a Key Biscayne, Fla. bank headed by Nixon's friend C. G. Rebozo.

Nixon's net worth when he entered the presidency was $307,141. This rose to $988,522 as of May 31.

Major deductions—The President's deductions for his federal income tax returns for 1969-72 totaled $988,964. The breakdown by year: 1969—$178,535; 1970—$307,182; 1971—$255,677; and 1972—$247,570.

The four-year total included deductions of $482,019 for the donation of the vice presidential papers to the government. It also included total deductions of $257,376 over the four-year period for interest payments on his properties, $81,255 for property taxes, $142,700 for the miscellaneous category. The latter included unreimbursed official expenses ($56,956) for use of his properties at San Clemente and Key Biscayne. A deduction was claimed for $1.24 in interest payments to a Washington department store, another

for $3,332 in "depreciation of personally owned White House furniture."

The President's taxes were so low—in 1970 his deductions actually exceeded his income and the minimum tax provision of the tax code was applied—that his returns in 1971 and 1972 were automatically targeted by the IRS for closer inspection.

Deductions for charity—Deductible charitable contributions from the Nixons in four years ranged from $7,512 in 1970 to $295 in 1972. In 1969, the total was $3,150, in 1971 $2,524. The largest item was $4,500 given to the Billy Graham Evangelistic Association. Four church donations were listed: $250 in 1969 and $1,000 in 1971 to the E. Whittier Friends Church and $50 to the Marble Collegiate Church and $20 to the Holy Rosary Church in 1972.

Tricia's trust fund—According to the data released by the White House, a Nixon friend, Elmer H. Bobst, established a trust fund of more than $25,000 for Nixon's older daughter Tricia in 1958 when he was chairman of the Warner-Lambert Pharmaceutical Co. The fund consisted primarily of Warner-Lambert stock. After Tricia received the proceeds

from the fund when she reached 21 in 1967, Nixon borrowed $20,000 from her for a $38,080 purchase of two undeveloped lots in Key Biscayne. Under an "oral agreement," Tricia was to get 40% of any profit from the real estate. The lots were sold for $150,000 in December 1972. The data showed that Tricia paid $11,617 in capital gains in 1972.

The vice presidential papers—Nixon donated his vice presidential papers to the national archives after they were appraised by rare books expert Ralph Newman of Chicago at $576,000. The Nixons deducted $482,019 from their income taxes for the years 1969-72 because of the donation, which would leave them $93,981 more for deduction on their 1973 tax return. The law permitting such deductions was repealed by Congress with a July 25, 1969 cutoff date. Nixon attorneys said the gift was made on March 27, 1969.

But questions had been raised about the procedures for the deductions: whether Nixon himself should have signed the deed for transferring the papers to the government; whether Edward L. Morgan, the White House lawyer who signed it, had the legal authority to do so; whether the no-

---

Nixons' Income and Disbursement

A summary of cash received and spent by President and Mrs. Nixon from Jan. 1, 1969 to May 31, 1973:

SOURCE OF CASH

Salary and allowances	$1,090,635
Sale of New York residence	311,023
Redemption of Fisher's Island, Inc., stock	371,782
Sale of interest in two unimproved lots on Key Biscayne	134,350
Payment of share of undivided profits from Mudge, Rose, Guthrie & Alexander for period prior to Jan. 1, 1969, and repayment of capital	128,611
Interest on bank accounts, rents from Whittier property, book royalties and interest on capital with law firm	65,240
Principal from estate of Hannah Nixon	13,577
Borrowings	725,000
Refund from Balustrol Golf Club	1,500
Collection of miscellaneous accounts	1,218
Reimbursement of expenses for maintenance of Golf Club by Golfing Friends of the President	4,800
Collection of insurance claim for fire loss damage	11,954
	$2,859,690

APPLICATION OF CASH

Payments for residence operating expenses		$172,835
Personal expenses		300,206
Official expenses		63,029
Rental and investment property expenses		24,382
Interest paid		271,350
Income taxes:		
Income taxes 1969 through 1972, inclusive	$78,651	
Federal income tax paid in 1969 and 1970 on 1968 income	38,646	
New York State income tax paid in 1969 on 1968 income	7,351	
1973 withholding of Federal income tax	30,816	155,464
Payments for improvements, furnishings, and other capital costs at residences		293,691
Repayment of debt incurred to acquire residences		385,592
Payments for purchase of residences		419,663
Repayment to Mrs. P. N. [Tricia Nixon Cox] Cox		65,000
Repayment of other debt		296,396
Deposit C. G. Rebozo		10,000
Acquisition of savings bonds		3,975
Purchase of furniture—Wash., D.C.		7,186
Payment of accounts payable owing at Jan. 1, 1969		5,845
Payments to contractors, vendors and Treasurer of U.S. for fire damage		11,954
		$2,486,568

INCREASE IN CASH

Cash received	$2,859,690
Cash disbursed	2,486,568
Increase	**$373,122**

Cash on hand, Jan. 1, 1969	$59,752
Cash on hand, May 31, 1973	$432,874

tarization of the date of the deed was valid since the corroborating record required by California law had not been located; whether the transfer was made before the deadline since the deed was not transmitted to the GSA until April 1970.

If the deductions were disallowed, the Nixons could owe some $235,000 in federal income taxes for 1969–72.

California land sale—Another $32,000 in additional taxes could be owed if it were decided that the Nixons should have declared a taxable capital gain for the California land sale, which involved land from a larger parcel bought by the Nixons for the San Clemente estate. Nixon's tax accountant, Arthur Blech, concluded that the sale did not constitute a capital gain. The data released by the White House revealed that Coopers & Lybrand in its audit of Nixon's finances concluded that a capital gain of $117,370 should have been reported on the 1970 tax return.

1968 deduction reported—The White House reported Dec. 9 that Nixon received a substantial deduction on his 1968 income tax return for a previous gift of pre-presidential papers to the government appraised at $80,000. The donation was listed as having been made Dec. 30, 1968 after the appraiser, Newman, had examined them Dec. 29, 1968 and reported his estimate the next day. His accompanying affidavit was dated April 1969.

Apartment sale question—Another tax question arising from the data released

Dec. 8 concerned a $142,912 gain realized by the Nixons from the sale of their New York City cooperative apartment, which, if reinvested within a year in another "primary residence" was exempt from the capital gains tax. If the money went into the purchase at San Clemente, avoiding the capital gain status, it would put the California home in the primary residence category. But the Nixon residence for tax purposes was at Washington, D.C., where elected federal officials were exempt from local income taxes. The question of residence thus also arose. If the Nixons did not pay the potential capital gain tax from the sale of the New York apartment on the grounds he was a California resident, could they claim exemption from California state income taxes on the grounds they were residents of the District of Columbia?

Response to disclosures—Nixon's financial disclosures, according to newly sworn Vice President Gerald Ford Dec. 9, should satisfy "any reasonable member of Congress" and the American people. Appearing on the ABC "Issues and Answers" broadcast, Ford said Nixon had "followed the law" as far as his tax payments were concerned and, in any event, the promise to donate the San Clemente home to the nation would "wipe out" any alleged impropriety.

Ford had strongly supported Nixon after meeting with the President Dec. 7. "I can assure you that the President has no intention whatever of resigning," Ford

told reporters. "It was reiterated to me this morning."

He added: "There is no evidence that would justify impeachment" and "I don't think the President is a political liability to any candidate [and] in his five years he has done a super job in foreign policy. He has many more pluses in the political scene than minuses."

Senate Democratic Leader Mike Mansfield (Mont.) suggested Dec. 10 that the President's financial activity was legal but "it still raises questions of appearances."

Sen. Lowell P. Weicker Jr. (R, Conn.), a member of the Senate Watergate committee, questioned the tax deduction for the vice presidential papers. "There was no gift" of the papers before the cutoff date, Weicker said Dec. 11. He sent the IRS a legal brief seeking "a fresh look" at the matter.

Nixon and his attorneys gave eight Republican Congressional leaders and GOP National Chairman George Bush a private preview of the Nixon financial data Dec. 3. The reaction to the disclosures was "mixed," according to Sen. John Tower (Tex.), one of the participants. He and Sens. Hugh Scott and Robert P. Griffin (Mich.) were satisfied, Tower said, but "there were still some doubters." Others attending included Ford, Sen. Norris Cotton (N.H.) and Reps. Leslie Arends (Ill.), John Anderson (Ill.) and John Rhodes (Ariz.).

In a talk prepared for his constituents in Pennsylvania, Scott had said Nov. 29 that Nixon owed the public "a complete all-out disclosure" and "answer to all of the charges." Scott said he himself was in "a very, very difficult position" and had "never been more uncomfortable." "I've had a terribly difficult job," he said, "trying to strike a balance as a party leader and at the same time trying to hold the confidence of people that I'm telling the truth and that I'm being just and fair about it."

Sen. Jacob K. Javits (R, N.Y.) said Dec. 5 that when Ford was sworn into office as vice president "there will exist a new situation concerning any call on the President to resign in the interest of the country." "I and others will have to give every thoughtful consideration to that possibility," he said.

White House criticized on tax ruling. Judge Charles R. Richey of federal district court in Washington Dec. 11 ordered the Internal Revenue Service (IRS) to grant tax-exempt status to the Center for Corporate Responsibility. Richey said the IRS had acted improperly in delaying for more than two years action on the group's request for determination of its status and eventually denying tax-free standing to the nonprofit organization.

Because the White House had failed to comply with court orders regarding evidence in the case, Richey said he regarded this as an admission that the White House had acted improperly in causing the center's request to be denied.

Nixons' Statement of Assets and Liabilities
Jan. 1, 1969

ASSETS		
Cash in banks		$ 59,752
Due from Mudge, Rose, Guthrie & Alexander		128,611
Due from estate of Hannah Nixon		13,577
Cash value of life insurance and civil service pension fund deposit		44,593
Investment in stock of Fisher's Island, Inc.		199,891*
Investment in real estate		539,367*
Miscellaneous accounts receivable		2,718
Total Assets		**$988,509**
LIABILITIES		
Mortgages, notes and loans payable		$629,869**
Federal income tax payable		37,987
State income tax payable		7,351
Accounts payable and accrued liabilities		6,161
Total Liabilities		**$681,368**
Net Assets		**$307,141**

May 31, 1973†

ASSETS		
Cash in Banks		
Key Biscayne Bank, Key Biscayne, including $250,000 of certificates of deposit, due June 21, 1973	$426,313	
Other banks	6,561	$432,874
Accounts and notes receivable		28,609
Income tax withheld in excess of estimated taxes		19,816
U.S. Savings Bonds, Series E, at cost (face amount $5,300)		3,975
Cash value of life insurance and Civil Service Pension Fund deposit		63,519
Land, buildings and furnishings, at cost, less accumulated depreciation:		
Residential properties: Casa Pacifica, San Clemente, Calif.	$571,162	
Key Biscayne, Fla.	311,929	
Improved real estate, Whittier, Calif.	77,515	
Office furniture, Washington, D.C.	3,553	$964,164
Total Assets		**$1,512,957**
LIABILITIES		
Withholding tax payable		335
Accrued interest and real estate taxes		20,399
Deferred income tax accrued		33,000
Mortgages payable		206,241
Obligation for note payable issued by Trust for San Clemente property		264,440
Total Liabilities		**$524,435**
Net Assets		**$988,522**

* carried at cost
**includes $20,000 due to Tricia Nixon
† From Coopers & Lybrand audit report

Richey agreed with the center's charge that it had been "denied a favorable ruling because it was singled out for selective treatment for political, ideological and other improper reasons which have no basis in the statute and regulations."

Richey found no specific instances of political pressure being used against the organization. But attorneys for the center had "discovered seven pages of hand-written notes [on the request for exemption] by Mr. Richard Cox [assistant director of the IRS' interpretive division] with the notation 'perhaps White House pressure,'" Richey said. He also noted that the "usual review panels" decided to issue a favorable ruling in August 1972. The decision was unchanged "until the personal intervention of the chief counsel and his deputy, both political appointees," in May 1973, two weeks after the center filed suit to force final action.

During the trial, searches of White House files by White House aide Bruce A. Kerhli and J. Fred Buzhardt Jr., President Nixon's special counsel in charge of Watergate matters, were too limited and failed to comply with the court order for a thorough search of the White House files. The search had been made after it was alleged by ousted White House aide John W. Dean 3rd that the IRS had been used to thwart the Administration's "enemies."

Richey also said the White House had improperly claimed executive privilege on four documents and one tape recorded conversation. The documents eventually were submitted to him privately. They "demonstrate that the White House staff did in fact consider using the IRS against their 'enemies.' This conduct is at best reprehensible," Richey ruled. He asked the U.S. Court of Appeals to decide whether he could make the papers public.

Richey concluded that during the trial the White House "delayed and hindered the discovery of information solely in their possession and crucial to a key issue in the case."

In another controversial IRS ruling, the Washington Post reported Nov. 19 that the IRS had revoked the tax-exempt status of the Fair Campaign Practices Committee, a 19-year-old nonprofit, nonpartisan group.

The committee lost its tax-free status by issuing information about a candidate's unfair campaign practices, which were, according to the IRS, actually statements on behalf of the candidate's opponent. The ruling was made retroactive to 1966.

Committee Chairman Charles P. Taft said he believed the IRS ruling was in reprisal for the committee's criticism of the Nixon re-election campaign's tactics and the committee's disclosure that Republicans had financed a series of newspaper advertisements during the 1970 Congressional campaign, labeling Democratic senatorial candidates as "extremists" and "radicals."

GAO reports on Nixon homes' costs. A General Accounting Office (GAO) report Dec. 18 on federal spending for President Nixon's private residences said almost all of the spending was for protective purposes but was critical of the "casual attitude" of the authorization procedure. The report questioned some of the spending and found it "disturbing" that some work had been verbally authorized by Nixon aides.

The GAO recommended that Congress consider legislation to revise the authorization procedure for such work and to limit the number of private residences of a president protected at public expense. It recommended that all security appropriations be requested directly from the Secret Service and that the service make an annual public report to Congress on the requests. Any non-security appropriations on the matter, it said, should be made to the White House with the President giving an annual accounting to Congress.

The report confirmed previous announcements that the federal spending at Nixon's two homes at San Clemente and Key Biscayne totaled $1.4 million, not counting federal expenditures at both sites for office complexes and military communications and other support systems which raised the federal costs to about $10 million

The GAO indicated that some of the spending was inappropriate, citing landscape work, driveway paving and house heating. On the "casual" authorization issue, it cited five full-time gardeners paid at government expense at San Clemente after a meeting between a Nixon aide and General Services Administration officials. "It appears that the government did some landscape maintenance at both residences which should have been done at the President's expense," the report said.

Other items criticized by the agency as possibly inappropriate government expense were expenditures for a bullet-resistant swimming pool screen, a private railroad crossing, a cabana, property surveys, and fencing redesigned to match the White House fence. Some items, such as sewer and heating system work and repaving, the GAO found, were replacement work that presumably would have been done by the owner.

Kalmbach got $100,000 in 1969. William Dobrovir took a deposition Nov. 7 from Jake Jacobsen, a former AMPI lawyer, who said the dairy co-op had paid Herbert Kalmbach, President Nixon's personal attorney and chief fund raiser, $100,000 in cash in August 1969, a year before Kalmbach had testified he began soliciting contributions for Nixon.

Jacobsen, who was chairman of the bank from which AMPI withdrew the money, testified that before its delivery he was consulted about the payment by Herbert Nelson, AMPI's general manager, and David Parr. "I said it was a good idea," Jacobsen testified. "I thought it might produce a more sympathetic understanding in this Administration to the problems of the dairy industry."

The cash was delivered by Jacobsen's Washington law partner, Milton P. Semer, who was then the chief fund raiser for Sen. Edmund S. Muskie, a Democratic presidential contender.

Semer testified that he offered Kalmbach checks but was asked for a cash payment. According to other court testimony, Attorney General Mitchell had directed AMPI to Kalmbach, and H. R. Haldeman, then White House chief of staff, had cleared the money for receipt when Kalmbach accepted it.

Jacobsen also testified that he had discussed the price support question with John B. Connally Jr., then Treasury secretary, "and he said he would do all he could to help us." Jacobsen said he met Connally twice—just before Clifford Hardin rejected the milk price increase and "shortly before" the Administration reversed the decision.

Connally told Senate Watergate Committee investigators Nov. 15 that he had favored higher price supports for the dairy industry but that he had refused to discuss their campaign contributions.

Campaign violations alleged. Two more apparent violations of the federal campaign law by officials of the Nixon re-election campaign were uncovered by the General Accounting Office (GAO), which announced Dec. 11 that the Nixon-Agnew Committee had reported payment of a $5,220 bill to the Columbia Advertising Agency "when, in fact, no check had been written for this amount."

The matter was referred to the Justice Department for investigation. Three other apparent violations also were sent to the Justice Department Dec. 19 by the GAO. The allegations concerned the funding of two reporters to spy on Sen. George McGovern (D, S.D.) during the presidential race.

Payments of $35,000 were made to Murray Chotiner to finance the spying plan but the Committee to Re-elect the President reported the transaction as reimbursement to Chotiner for travel expenses.

Lawyer plays White House tape. William A. Dobrovir, an attorney for Ralph Nader in the milk fund lawsuit, admitted Dec. 18 that he had played a White House tape recording of a conversation between President Nixon and dairy industry leaders at a Washington cocktail party the night before.

The tape of the March 23, 1971 meeting had been turned over to Dobrovir Dec. 15 after the White House had first denied that any recording existed.

Dobrovir said he was "extremely sorry. I've made a terrible mistake." He had made a copy of the White House tape, Dobrovir said, because the recording was "practically inaudible" and he planned to listen to it on his stereo equipment at home.

The disclosure prompted federal District Court Judge William B. Jones Dec. 19 to order all subpoenaed documents sealed at the Justice Department's request. However, he refused another Justice Department request to order Dobrovir and other lawyers to refrain from making public statements on the case.

Judge Jones had also been provided with a copy of a second tape of a meeting later March 23, 1971 between Nixon and several Cabinet officers. The White House, which had claimed executive privilege on the taped conversation, submitted the tape to the court for secret inspection. Dobrovir had not received a copy of that tape.

The milk fund dispute, which involved charges that the White House had reversed an Agriculture Department decision and allowed an increase in the federal support price of milk in return for large campaign contributions from the dairy industry, also was the subject of investigations by the Senate Watergate Committee and the office of Watergate special prosecutor Leon Jaworski.

In a meeting with Senate Watergate Committee investigators Oct. 16, the White House claimed executive privilege and refused to allow former Agriculture Secretary Clifford D. Hardin to testify on his role in the milk price decision.

The Justice Department Nov. 29 had provided Jaworski's office with data on the milk fund case, information which had been denied his predecessor, Archibald Cox. The documents were not believed to include tape recordings.

GSA concedes political hiring. The General Services Administration (GSA) conceded that it had sometimes given preferential treatment to politically-referred applicants for civil service jobs in violation of Civil Service Commission personnel regulations, it was reported Nov. 24. [See p. 133]

2nd 'enemies' list revealed. The Joint Committee on Internal Revenue Taxation disclosed in a report Dec. 20 that the White House gave the Internal Revenue Service (IRS) in September 1972 a list of 575 persons "to see what type of information could be developed concerning the people on the list." [See p. 136]

Mrs. Beard out as witness. The Watergate special prosecutor's office decided not to call Dita D. Beard as a witness before the Watergate grand jury after two psychiatrists, one selected by Mrs. Beard and one appointed by the court, administered psychiatric examinations, the New York Times reported Dec. 19.

Although the results of the tests were not made public, it was believed they supported her contention that she would not prove to be a valuable witness in the controversial International Telephone & Telegraph Corp. (ITT) case.

A subpoena requiring her to appear before the grand jury was withdrawn and she was interviewed privately by members of the prosecutor's staff.

Carnation convicted of gift-giving. Carnation Co. and its chairman, H. Everett Olson, pleaded guilty Dec. 19 in federal district court in Washington to charges that $7,900 had been contributed to President Nixon's re-election campaign and $1,000 to a fund for Senate Republican candidates. The donations, made from corporate funds, violated the federal campaign spending law.

The firm was fined $5,000 and Olson $1,000 (for authorizing a $5,000 contribution to Nixon officials).

Mid-America Dairymen sued. The Justice Department filed a civil antitrust suit Dec. 27 against Mid-America Dairymen Inc., a dairy cooperative that already was under investigation for its role in the disputed Administration pricing decision. Two other suits were pending against Associated Milk Producers Inc. and Dairymen Inc., which had also made large contributions to the Nixon re-election campaign.

The Mid-America suit, filed in federal district court in Kansas City, Mo., charged the group with attempting to monopolize milk sales in a 10-state area.

The civil antitrust suit filed in February 1972 against Associated Milk Producers (AMPI) itself was a source of controversy. The Justice Department acknowledged Dec. 26 that John Mitchell, then attorney general, had rejected two recommendations from the department's antitrust division that criminal proceedings be instituted against AMPI.

According to Richard McLaren, then head of the antitrust division, he authorized a civil suit against the dairy cooperative because of Mitchell's urging.

McLaren's testimony was filed as part of a government brief in the AMPI case, asking the court to reject a motion by the defense to obtain access to all government documents and tapes relating to a possible quid pro quo in the relationship between the price support increase and campaign contributions.

The defense contended that the Administration had used extortion in extracting campaign donations from the industry and that the antitrust case had been initiated after AMPI refused a second request from Nixon fund raisers for a subsequent contribution.

According to McLaren, he had favored criminal proceedings be launched in recommendations made Sept. 9, 1971 and Oct. 29, 1971, and that the decision to file a civil suit was made Jan. 22, 1972.

AMPI documents that could have shed light on the current investigations were destroyed in the spring of 1971 by employes in the Arkansas division office, according to the Chicago Tribune Nov. 28. David Parr of the Arkansas office had been instrumental in arranging meetings with President Nixon for dairy leaders, AMPI officials said.

Nixon's Counter-Offensive; Tape Erasure Disclosed

Nixon's energy message: 'I won't resign.' In a nationally televised address Nov. 7, President Nixon presented the Administration's wide-ranging energy conservation proposals designed to meet the current oil crisis precipitated by the Middle East war.

He put aside his prepared text to conclude the 25-minute energy message "on a personal note."

"I would be less than candid if I were not to admit that this has not been an easy year . . . as all of you are quite aware.

"As a result of the deplorable Watergate matter, great numbers of Americans have had doubts raised as to the integrity of the President of the United States. I've even noted that some publications have called on me to resign the office of President of the United States.

"Tonight I would like to give my answer to those who have suggested that I resign.

"I have no intention whatever of walking away from the job I was elected to do.

Nixon seeks GOP support. President Nixon undertook a series of meetings with Republican members of Congress Nov. 9–15 to counteract the serious decline in public confidence in his leadership in the wake of the Watergate scandal. In his only public appearance (his first in public in nearly three months), before a friendly convention in Washington Nov. 15, Nixon again vowed he would not resign.

The White House sessions were given a mixed review from those members of Congress who commented to reporters afterwards. Some said they were convinced of the President's good intentions, others remained unconvinced without further public demonstration of the President's cooperation on Watergate and disentanglement from charges of wrongdoing.

By the end of the week, a partisan dispute broke out in the House. Democratic Leader Thomas P. O'Neill Jr. (Mass.) accused Nixon Nov. 15 of trying to "curry favor with his prospective grand jurors" by his White House sessions. O'Neill said the meetings represented an "unbecoming, if not improper" attempt to influence the outcome of the

impeachment investigation. His remarks drew hisses from Republicans, who retorted with charges that the impeachment effort was being run by the House Democratic leadership.

The dispute erupted in debate over a resolution authorizing the House Judiciary Committee to spend $1 million on its inquiry into possible impeachment of the President. The resolution was adopted 367–51. Rep. David Dennis (R, Ind.) considered the action "improvident" and "premature." O'Neill cautioned the House to "preserve a cool impartiality" because "ultimately the entire House may be called upon to sit as a grand jury on charges against the President."

The key vote during the session was on a Republican move to recommit the resolution for revision to give the GOP minority one-third of the committee staffing funds and stipulate that none of the inquiry funds be spent until·the nature and scope of the probe were defined. It was rejected by an almost straight party line vote of 227–190.

The White House meetings—Nixon's meetings with members of Congress began Nov. 9 when he summoned seven Republican leaders of the Senate and House to the White House for a two-hour discussion. Afterwards, Rep. John B. Anderson (Ill.), chairman of the House Republican Conference, told reporters that he felt "very much encouraged," that White House advisers had communicated a "full understanding" of the President's credibility problem and a determination "to take steps to restore confidence." The President "was very open, he seemed to be accessible," Anderson reported, and "it was not a presidential monologue." Nixon "indicated," Anderson said, "he is going to be totally cooperative with [Watergate Judge John J.] Sirica, the court and the special prosecutor and that he will devote a good deal of time to assuring the American people he was not involved in the Watergate burglary or coverup."

The President went to the presidential retreat at Camp David, Md. Nov. 9, returning to the White House Nov. 11. The White House announced that day, after Sen. Charles Percy (R, Ill.) disclosed it on a television program, that the President intended to meet with every Republican

member of Congress in the coming week, and expected to meet with at least some Democratic leaders, for full discussion of the Watergate case and related matters. White House Press Secretary Ronald L. Ziegler said Nov. 12 the meetings would show Nixon's determination "to meet the Watergate matter head on."

Meets with committee—A Republican Coordinating Committee assembled at the White House Nov. 12 and heard a 40-minute speech from Nixon promising full cooperation and several specific pieces of evidence to the Watergate probers. The committee, consisting of party leaders from Congress, governors, the national committee and regional officers, had been created in the party's crisis after the 1964 presidential landslide defeat. GOP National Chairman George Bush said Nov. 9 he had been authorized to reconvene the group at a Sept. 10 meeting of the national committee.

After meeting with Nixon Nov. 12, the 28-member committee issued a resolution welcoming Nixon's pledges of "full disclosure" and asserting its own intention to "develop positions" on national policy matters, cater to the interests of local party workers, study election reforms and "actively involve itself in assessing and developing issues of major importance in future campaigns."

Comments of some of the participants were restrained about the President's attempt to regain credibility. Anderson, one of the participants, reported he had stressed at the meeting that "time is not on [Mr. Nixon's] side" and that the new offensive would be a "futile gesture" if it was only an exercise in public relations. Asked about the future of impeachment proceedings, he said, "This is a time when mere words will not suffice. But this will give him an opportunity to make his case before we rush headlong into action."

(Anderson revealed Nov. 14 he was forsaking a race for the Senate in 1974 largely because of the "specter of Watergate." He said a private poll showed 46% of Illinois' voters felt Watergate the most important issue, the cost of living a distant second at 15%. "My advisers tell me it is unprecedented for one issue to be so all pervasive on the minds of voters," he said.)

Another member of the GOP committee, Gov. Francis W. Sargent (Mass.), said the President was starting "a campaign to attempt to reveal everything that's occurred" but "it will be awfully difficult to restore the trust of the people of this country in his Administration." "The vast majority of people in my state," he said, "don't know whether to believe [Mr. Nixon] or not." Asked if he believed the President's statement that day, Sargent said, "I'm trying very hard to."

Gov. Robert Ray (Iowa) indicated the attempt at disclosure might be too late. "This is something we hoped he might have done a long long time ago," he said.

Rep. Barber B. Conable Jr. (N.Y.), chairman of the House Republicans' Research Committee, said it was "embarrassing" to see the President "standing up and trying to defend himself to people who presumably are his supporters." He analyzed Nixon's problem as "insensitivity to the position he is in" although he believed "if the information comes out fully, the President will get the exoneration he's looking for."

Meeting with Democrats—Later Nov. 12, Nixon held a Watergate session in his family quarters in the White House with six southern Democratic senators and Sen. Harry F. Byrd Jr. (Va.), an independent. The others were James O. Eastland and John C. Stennis of Mississippi, John J. Sparkman and James B. Allen of Alabama, Russell B. Long of Louisiana and John L. McClellan of Arkansas.

Key GOP senators hear comments—The President held a 2 hour 20 minute meeting at the White House Nov. 13 with 15 Republican senators. "Everyone in the room—everyone—agreed on the need for full disclosure," Senate Republican leader Hugh Scott (Pa.) said afterwards.

"It was more comments than questions," observed Sen. William E. Brock (Tenn.). "The emphasis was primarily on the more fundamental question of how do we get this information to the courts, the Congress and especially the American people."

Sen. Edward W. Brooke (Mass.), who had called for Nixon's resignation said he reiterated his view to the President, whose response was gracious but negative, that resignation "would be the easy way out and he was not going to take it."

He said Nixon also rejected another suggestion from another senator to voluntarily submit to an impeachment inquiry to clear the air.

Asked if he thought Nixon could recoup his political stature, Brooke replied, "It would take almost a miracle to do so but he's done miracles before. Maybe he can do so again."

The President reportedly told the group he had not decided whether to accept a Senate Watergate committee request for a private meeting with immediate public release of a transcript of the proceedings. The resolution requesting the meeting, approved earlier Nov. 13 with only Sen. Edward J. Gurney (R, Fla.) in dissent, asserted the panel's belief that "such a procedure must take precedence over other nonpublic opportunities for discussion afforded by the President to individual members of the committee." Two Republican members of the committee, Gurney and Sen. Howard H. Baker Jr. (Tenn.), attended the White House session Nov. 13. Another Republican committee member, Sen. Lowell P. Weicker Jr. (Conn.), who had drafted the resolution, renounced meeting with the President as part of a larger group. "If we go as individuals," he said, "it detracts from our [committee] mandate."

Watergate meeting ruled out—After more White House sessions Nov. 14—with 75 House Republicans in the morning and 14 Republican senators in late afternoon—the President was reported to have ruled out a meeting, even an informal one, with the Senate Watergate committee because of the "predisposition" of some of its members to disbelieve him. He was reported to have held out the possibility of meeting with the committee's chairman—Sen. Sam J. Ervin Jr. (D, N.C.)—and vice chairman—Baker. Ervin reportedly opposed such an audience without the full committee.

The President also was reported to have rejected a suggestion at the morning session to offer his Watergate defense to a joint session of Congress. According to Reps. Alphonzo Bell (Calif.) and Marvin L. Esch (Mich.), Nixon jokingly explained his position: "The Democrats would probably say, 'The son of a bitch is lying,' and the Republicans would probably say, 'Well, he's lying, but he's our son of a bitch.'"

Bell reported another Nixon response, concerning allegations of improper financing of his Florida and California estates and a secret $1 million fund: "If I wanted to make money, I would not be in this business. If I wanted to cheat, I wouldn't do it here."

Concerning the climate for impeachment or resignation, Nixon was reported to have cautioned that "if you cut the legs off the President, America is going to lose" and that U.S. allies of the U.S. might consider "leaning toward" the Soviet Union if domestic issues weakened presidential authority.

Nixon was reported to have disputed charges that antitrust action had been dropped against the International Telephone and Telegraph Corp. or milk price supports raised in exchange for 1972 campaign contributions. And he renounced action to block any court move to obtain Watergate evidence, while predicting court action would be unlikely because the prosecutor "should have everything, and when he asks for it, he will get it."

Nixon also was reported to have given assurance that his Watergate tapes had not been altered and would prove that his former counsel John W. Dean 3rd had erred in testifying under oath the President was cognizant of the Watergate coverup well before March 21. "I'm not saying John Dean is a liar," the quote was, "I'm just saying he's mistaken."

Among the comments after the Nixon meetings Nov. 14: Rep. John M. Ashbrook (Ohio)—"The content of the meeting boiled down to 'Believe us or believe them.' Some of us don't believe that's a good posture to go to the public with."

Rep. Silvio O. Conte (Mass.)—"The President said he was going to make chapter and verse public. I'm reserving judgment until I find out what the chapter and verse are."

Rep. Albert H. Quie (Minn.) said Nixon's answers were "satisfactory" and Rep. John Dellenback (Ore.) said the session had "heightened" his impression there was a "clear conflict" between the charges against the President and the explanations.

Further reports on the meeting with the senators that day were revealed Nov. 15. One of them was that the President did not dispute stories that he paid only $1,670 in income taxes for the years 1970 and 1971, because of large allowable deductions, but did reveal he paid $50,000 to $100,000 in taxes for 1969.

According to another report, Nixon had accused former Attorney General Elliot Richardson of misleading (of having "lied," according to some sources) in testifying about his role in the dismissal of Watergate prosecutor Archibald Cox. Another source said the President had not used the word "lied" but implied it. Sen. Roman L. Hruska (Neb.) said the word used had been "inaccurate," in relation to Richardson's recollection. Others recalled a point made at the meeting by Nixon's chief of staff Alexander M. Haig Jr. that Richardson had in fact been an originator of the plan to restrict Cox's try for White House materials.

A White House statement later Nov. 15 from Kenneth W. Clawson, deputy director of communications, said it was "simply not true" that Nixon had either accused Richardson of lying or suggested the possibility of a perjury charge against Richardson.

More Republicans, Democrats—On Nov. 15, Nixon met in the morning at a breakfast session with 78 House Republicans, in the late afternoon with more Republican senators and in the evening with 50 to 60 Democratic House members.

Among the comments afterwards: Rep. Dan Kuykendall (R, Tenn.)—"No fairminded person could fail to believe [Mr. Nixon] was telling the truth."

Rep. Peter A. Peyser (R, N.Y.)—The meetings were an "opening step" but there was "still a great deal unanswered."

Nixon describing his personal plight, said, "It's been seven months of pure hell over Watergate."

Rep. Earl F. Landgrebe (R, Ind.)—Nixon spoke sympathetically of former Vice President Spiro T. Agnew, commenting, "Let's not pour any more coals on his head." Nixon advised everyone to run their own campaigns personally to "be sure to keep the jackasses from taking over."

Rep. Ralph S. Regula (R, Ohio)—Nixon said he had sent a birthday greeting to former Vice President Spiro Agnew's wife and that he did not "give a damn who knows it."

Sen Robert W. Packwood (R, Ore.)—He suggested to Nixon his Administration had given the impression to the public that it cared only that it be "above criminal guilt" but not suspicion and told the President "Watergate has destroyed your ability to inspire and lead the country."

Rep. Paul N. McCloskey (R, Calif.)—There was "an air of unreality" about the session because Nixon was "adopting the posture that the opposition to him is politically and partisanly motivated rather than motivated by a search for truth."

A similar comment came from Sen. Charles Mathias (R, Md.) during an interview on the NBC "Today" program Nov. 15, that there was "an air of fantasy" about the meetings. They were sort of get-acquainted" sessions, he observed, "after we've been doing business for five years."

Public debate continues—Public comment continued on the status of the Nixon presidency.

Vice President-designate Gerald R. Ford urged Nixon supporters Nov. 13 to "speak up and speak now" to offset the impeachment and resignation demands.

Labor Secretary Peter J. Brennan cited gains under the Administration's economic policies in a New York speech Nov. 13.

Former Treasury Secretary John B. Connally Jr., in a San Antonio speech Nov. 14, urged patience during what he described as "a great period of political stress unequaled certainly in our lifetime and perhaps in the history of the republic." Impeachment was "a very drastic step," he cautioned.

Former Attorney General Elliot L. Richardson expressed his belief Nov. 9 Nixon was telling the truth in denying prior knowledge of Watergate or the alleged coverup. But he suggested that Nixon should answer questions under oath before a "responsible and informed" group to restore public confidence in his innocence.

Former Deputy Attorney General William Ruckelshaus agreed, saying Nov. 8 that the only way Nixon could inspire public confidence would be to turn over "all documents relevant" to the Watergate case.

Sen. Barry Goldwater (R, Ariz.) told reporters Nov. 14 there was "no way" Nixon could be impeached and "no sensible reason for him to resign." Nixon was "not guilty of anything," he said, and "we're going to have to live with him."

Sen. Philip A. Hart (D, Mich.) said Nov. 14 "if the President should resign with grace it might be the best way to bring us out of the situation." He was the fourth senator to call for Nixon's resignation.

Another senator, William D. Hathaway (D, Me.), presented legislation Nov. 9 for a new national election if both the presidency and vice presidency became vacant. The bill, based on a precedent in the Succession Act of 1792, would designate the senior House member from the presi-

dent's party to serve as acting president until the election was held. Hathaway told the Senate there was "something troubling about a President who is under threat of impeachment or forced resignation having the power to name his successor."

An editorial in the Long Island, N.Y. newspaper Newsday Nov. 9 called for Nixon's impeachment "as soon as possible."

A nationwide campaign for Nixon's impeachment was launched Nov. 8 by the AFL-CIO, which was distributing 500,000 copies of a statement listing 19 charges against Nixon, including that he used his office "for personal enrichment" and had "consistently lied to the American people."

Student newspapers at 84 colleges and universities endorsed an editorial calling for Nixon's impeachment that was being sent Nov. 11 to Congress by its originators at Amherst College.

Polls also reflected a continued downturn in public confidence in Nixon.

The Gallup Poll reported Nov. 10 that public support for Congressional Republicans was at the lowest point in 38 years of measurement, that if national Congressional elections had been held on election day Nov. 6 the likely split would have been 58% Democratic, 30% Republican.

The ABC network reported Nov. 10 the results of a public opinion survey conducted for it by Lieberman Research, Inc. (Nov. 4): 59% of respondents did not believe the President's statements "these days," 30% did; two-thirds did not believe Nixon's assertion that two Watergate tapes sought by the prosecution never existed, 17% did believe it; 49% thought Nixon should resign, 41% thought he should not.

A Gallup survey issued Nov. 12 (conducted Nov. 2–5) said three of four respondents believed Nixon was involved to some extent in the Watergate scandal but a majority, 54%–37%, opposed removing him from office.

Memo on Dean unavailable; other data offered. The issue of nonexistent White House Watergate evidence became further clouded Nov. 12 as President Nixon revealed that a previously-mentioned memorandum on his April 15 conversation with his counsel John W. Dean 3rd was not among his files for that date. A dictation belt of the memo was to have been released to U.S. District Court Judge John J. Sirica.

The White House had already asserted that the subpoenaed recording of the Dean meeting and a tape of a June 20, 1972 telephone conversation between Nixon and his campaign manager John N. Mitchell were never made.

In a statement released to "clear up this aspect of the Watergate matter once and for all," Nixon related the chronology of his review of tapes relevant to Watergate and his attempts to produce evidence subpoenaed by the prosecution.

Nixon said that since he had been in office he had maintained a "personal diary file" of notes taken during meetings and

dictation belts "on which I record recollections." The materials were placed in the file by his secretary and "sealed under specific instructions that they may not be transcribed." Checking the file for April 15 during the weekend of Nov. 4–5, Nixon continued, he had found "personal notes" of the conversation with Dean, but no dictation belt. He said the notes made during the meeting would be submitted to the court.

A belt made June 20, 1972, on which he "referred to a telephone call with John Mitchell" had been located, Nixon said, and would be turned over to Sirica.

Nixon said he had made a "diligent search for other evidentiary materials that might shed light on the substance" of his conversation with Dean but had found "no such evidence." As a substitute, he offered tapes of two April 16 meetings with Dean, which he said covered "much the same subject matter" as the disputed meeting the previous day.

Regarding other conversations with Dean, Nixon said he had on June 4 listened to tapes of "a number of conversations" in order to "refresh my memory of those discussions." All the tapes reviewed that day, he added, covered meetings prior to March 21.

(Secret Service logs cited during Judge Sirica's hearings on the nonexistent tapes showed that tapes taken from storage June 4 included all recordings at Nixon's Executive Office Building office during the period Feb. 28–April 20.)

The March 21 cutoff applied, Nixon said, because he wanted to "confirm [his] recollection" that Dean had not reported "certain facts" before that date.

"There had been rumors and reports to the contrary," Nixon added, "one of them suggesting that John Dean and I had met 30 or 40 times to discuss Watergate—and I wanted to refresh my recollection as to what was the precise and entire truth."

The next review of tapes began Sept. 29, Nixon related, and covered the material subpoenaed by the special prosecutor and the Senate Watergate Committee. The reason, he said, was his "deliberate intention" to litigate the issue of presidential confidentiality "up to the Supreme Court, if necessary." But by late September, he had "come to the conclusion that the national interest would be better served by a reasonable compromise." This conclusion, Nixon said, led to the "Stennis Compromise" of releasing summaries of the tapes.

During this process of review, Nixon said, he first became aware of the "possibility" that two of the tapes might not exist. He ordered a further investigation "into the circumstances which caused the conversations not to be recorded," which was not "finally completed" until Oct. 27.

In addition to the April 16 tapes not covered by the subpoena, Nixon said he would release to the court further material to buttress his contention that the Dean and Mitchell conversations had not been recorded, including the full reel of telephone tapes for June 20, 1972 and the two reels made April 15 before the Dean meeting.

In a memorandum released Nov. 14, Judge Sirica rejected Nixon's offer of the April 16 tapes, saying that acceptance of the tapes would make the court a "depository" of extraneous material. Sirica said that if Nixon wanted to provide the grand jury with materials "that do not relate to the present hearing or materials that have not been subpoenaed, he should go through the . . . special prosecutor and not through the court."

Sirica said, however, that if Nixon felt it "advisable to waive any privilege and make tapes or other material public, he is of course free to do so at any time."

Sirica had announced Nov. 12 an agreement between the White House and the prosecution to speed transmittal of evidence to the grand jury. Under the accord, a panel of technical experts would examine the tapes and other material for "any evidence of tampering or alterations." All the tapes would be copied and all originals sealed and stored in a White House vault until delivery to Sirica. The White House was to submit an analysis and index of all subpoenaed material along with the original tapes. Prosecutors and presidential lawyers would hold a closed conference with Sirica to discuss claims of executive privilege.

In testimony before Judge Sirica on the question of the nonexistent tapes Nov. 12, Assistant Attorney General Henry E. Petersen recounted an April 18 telephone conversation with Nixon about the April 15 Nixon-Dean meeting. Petersen quoted Nixon as saying "I have it on tape if you want to hear it." Petersen said he had declined since he only wanted "what we are getting from John Dean directly." But on June 11 Archibald Cox, then special prosecutor, requested the tape and was told by letter from presidential counsel J. Fred Buzhardt Jr. that "the tape to which the President referred in his discussion with Mr. Petersen was a tape on which Mr. Nixon dictated his recollections of that conversation after it was finished. It would, of course, not be appropriate to produce that tape."

Cox firing ruled illegal. The dismissal of Archibald Cox as special Watergate prosecutor was declared illegal Nov. 14 by U.S. District Court Judge Gerhard A. Gesell in the District of Columbia.

Gesell said a Justice Department regulation, issued in establishing the office of the special prosecutor, stipulated that the special prosecutor could not be removed except "for extraordinary improprieties," a charge that had not been brought against Cox. The regulation also provided that the special prosecutor would continue to carry out his duties until he consented to termination of his assignment, Gesell noted. "This clause can only be read as a bar to the total abolition of the office of Watergate special prosecutor without the special prosecutor's consent," he said.

Gesell did not order reinstatement of Cox or declare illegal the appointment of his successor, Leon Jaworski. His ruling, he said, was designed to "declare a rule of law that will give guidance for future conduct with regard to the Watergate inquiry."

The regulation "has the force and effect of Law," Gesell declared, and was not diminished in this instance by the Nixon Administration's rescission of it three days after Cox was fired. Since it was reinstated less than three weeks later for Jaworski, Gesell noted, "it is clear that this turnabout was simply a ruse to permit the discharge of Mr. Cox."

The ruling was issued in a lawsuit brought by Sen. Frank E. Moss (D, Utah) and Reps. Bella S. Abzug (D, N.Y.) and Jerome R. Waldie (D, Calif.). Consumer advocate Ralph Nader had been a plaintiff but was dropped by the court on the ground he had no standing to sue on the issue.

Cox, whose reappointment to a position on the Harvard Law School faculty was announced Nov. 9, said later Nov. 14 he would not attempt to regain the post of special prosecutor. "For me to make any legal claims" under the ruling, he said, "would only divert attention from getting the real job done" of prosecuting the Watergate matter.

Rep. Abzug said Nov. 14 the decision established that President Nixon had been guilty of obstruction of justice in dismissing Cox and strengthened the basis for impeachment.

Gesell also commented in his ruling on the matter of a court-appointed Watergate prosecutor currently pending before Congress. He considered such an approach "most unfortunate," he said, since "the courts must remain neutral. Their duties are not prosecutorial."

"If Congress feels that laws should be enacted to prevent executive interference with the Watergate special prosecutor," he said, "the solution lies in legislation enhancing and protecting that office as it is now established and not by following a course that places incompatible duties upon this particular court."

He stressed that "Congress has it within its own power to enact appropriate and legally enforceable protections against any effort to thwart the Watergate inquiry."

Cox also agreed with this portion of Gesell's ruling. In a New York speech Nov. 12, Cox said while a court-appointed prosecutor would provide "much the best reassurance" for his independence, the procedure would evoke a partisan dispute and the loss of bipartisan support for the probe would be an "excessive" cost. He recommended presidential appointment of a prosecutor with guarantees of independence built in by legislation and the appointment subject to confirmation by the Senate.

House panel OKs prosecutor bill—A bill authorizing court appointment of a Watergate prosecutor was passed by the House Judiciary Committee by voice vote Nov. 13. The appointment would be made by three members of the U.S. district court in the District of Columbia, the three selected by the entire 15-member court.

The bill carried an amendment requiring the prosecutor to report monthly to the committee "such information pertinent to the question of whether impeachable offenses have been committed by the President." The amendment, proposed by Rep. Tom Railsback (R, Ill.), was approved by a 26–12 vote.

The committee rejected a Republican proposal that the attorney general make the appointment under the proviso the prosecutor could only be fired for gross impropriety. The vote was 21–17.

Jaworski to get access to documents—Special Watergate prosecutor Leon Jaworski informed U.S. District Court Judge Gerhard A. Gesell Nov. 14 that the White House had assured him he would have access to tapes and other documents relating to the work of the White House "plumbers" squad.

Stephen N. Shulman, attorney for former White House aide Egil Krogh Jr., had filed a motion with Gesell seeking access to a series of tapes of President Nixon's conversations concerning the work of the plumbers squad, which Krogh had headed. Krogh was indicted Oct. 11 on two counts of making false declarations to a federal prosecutor in connection with the 1971 break-in at the office of the psychiatrist treating Pentagon Papers defendant Daniel Ellsberg.

The affidavit from Jaworski to Gesell indicated that the special prosecutor's office would have access to the material in question and would give Krogh any information of an exculpatory nature.

Bars national security defense—In his first act as special prosecutor, Jaworski Nov. 12 filed a legal brief in U.S. district court in Washington, rejecting arguments that Krogh's action was justified by reason of national security when he lied under oath.

Nixon offensive goes public. President Nixon actively campaigned to mute his Watergate and credibility problems with a four-day round of public appearances in the South Nov. 17–20.

Nixon answers editors' questions—The President answered 17 Watergate questions in his appearance Nov. 17 before the Associated Press Managing Editors Association at the Disney World Hotel near Orlando, Fla.

Neither party was "without fault" in the 1972 campaign, Nixon said. "Quite a bit of violence on the other side. I never spoke any place without getting a pretty good working over. Neither party was without fault with regard to the financing. They raised $36 million, and some of that, like some of ours, came from corporate sources and was illegal because the law had been changed and apparently people didn't know it. . . ."

At another point in the one-hour session, Nixon said: "I made my mistakes, but in all of my years of public life I have never profited, never profited from public service. I've earned every cent. And in all of my years in public life I have never obstructed justice. . . . People have got to know whether or not their President is a crook. Well I'm not a crook. I've earned everything I've got."

The President made the declaration in discussing his personal finances. When he had left office as vice president in 1961, he said, his net worth was $47,000, but he "made a lot of money" in the next eight years: $250,000 from his book, Six Crises; between $100,000 and $250,000 a year practicing law; selling all his stock in 1968 for about $300,000; his New York apartment for $300,000; and another $100,000 due him from his law firm.

The President was asked about a press report he paid $792 in federal income tax in 1970 and $878 in 1971 and whether public officials should disclose their personal finances. Nixon said he had disclosed his personal finances and would make another report available "because, obviously, you're all so busy that when these things come across your desk maybe you don't see them."

In reply to the query, he said he paid $79,000 in income tax in 1969 and "nominal amounts" in the next two years. Why the nominal amounts? he asked. "It wasn't because of the deductions for shall we say a cattle ranch or interest or you know all these gimmicks that you've got where you can deduct from." But because his predecessor Lyndon Johnson "came in to see me shortly after I became President" and suggested he take the legal deduction from his income tax for his vice presidential papers, as Johnson had with most of his Presidential papers. He did this, Nixon said, his papers being appraised at $500,000, "many believe conservatively, at that amount," he added. He would be glad to have the papers back, he said, and pay the tax "because I think they're worth more than that."

Queries about the tapes—Nixon discussed at length, in response to queries, his White House tapes of Watergate conversations. Concerning the belated admission that two of the tapes sought by the court did not exist, Nixon said he was informed on Sept. 29 or 30 that the two tapes "might not exist" and that it was not "finally determined" until about Oct. 27. He referred, in the context of whether the two tapes in question were important, to the fact that they had not been subpoenaed by the Senate Watergate committee, only the court. He also stressed that "I have done everything that I possibly can to provide the evidence that would have existed had we found the tapes."

He said he had listened to some of the other tapes sought by the court and they would prove "without question" that "I had no knowledge whatever of the Watergate break-in before it occurred," that "I never authorized the offer of clemency to anybody and as a matter of fact turned it down whenever it was suggested," and that the first time he heard of the payment of blackmail money to a Watergate defendant was on March 21 from his former counsel John W. Dean 3rd.

He said his personal reaction to the discovery that the two tapes did not exist "was one of very great disappointment because I wanted the evidence out."

The non-existent tapes involved concerned a conversation with Dean on April 15 and a telephone talk on June 20, 1972 with his former campaign director John N. Mitchell. On the Mitchell call, Nixon said, he "happened to have dictated a Dictabelt" on that day "which I found" and also "found that I had referred" to the Mitchell phone call. "It said," Nixon disclosed, "first, that I called John Mitchell to cheer him up because I knew he was terribly disheartened by what had happened in the so-called Watergate matter. Second, he expressed chagrin to me that the organization over which he had control could have gotten out of hand in this way. That was what was on that tape."

Asked later why he had never inquired of Mitchell what he knew, Nixon replied that, "Looking back, maybe I should have asked him but the reason I didn't is that I expected him to tell me and he had every opportunity to and decided that he wouldn't, apparently."

Nixon said he thought he also might have a Dictabelt of the April 15 Dean conversation but "what I found was not a Dictabelt" but "my handwritten notes made at the time of the conversation," which he had turned over to the court. Nixon said he had a conversation with Dean on April 16 which was recorded and contained repeated references to their disputed conversation the day before and he would make that information available to the court even though the court had not subpoenaed it.

The President discussed the White House taping system. "This is no Apollo system," he said, it "was not a sophisticated system." It cost $2,500 and was "a little Sony" with "these little lapel mikes in my desks." Johnson had had "much better equipment," he noted.

Cox and the federal prosecution—Nixon was asked whether he had told former Watergate prosecutor Archibald Cox "to stay out of the Ellsberg case" or if he thought the new prosecutor should be kept from the Ellsberg probe. "I have never spoken to Mr. Cox at all," Nixon replied. He had talked with Assistant Attorney General Henry E. Petersen about it before Cox took over from him as prosecutor, and had told Petersen "that the job that he had—and I would have said the same thing to Mr. Cox—was to investigate the Watergate matter, that national security matters were not matters that should be investigated" because of their "highly sensitive" status. "I don't mean by that that we're going to throw the cloak of national security over something because we're guilty of something," Nixon said. "I'm simply saying that where the national security would be disserved by having an investigation, the President has the responsibility to protect it and I'm going to do so."

The President was asked if there had been "any discussion of legality or illegality" at the time he gave his former aide Egil Krogh Jr. approval for the "Ellsberg project." Nixon said neither Krogh nor others had testified to such "an assumption," namely, "that I specifically approved or ordered the entrance into Dr. Ellsberg's psychiatrist's office." He first learned of the break-in, Nixon said, on March 17, and he personally "thought it was a stupid thing to do, apart from being an illegal thing to do." He pointed out that at the time the Administration was concerned about news leaks "which were seriously damaging to the national security."

The President recalled Petersen's testimony that at the time he was supplanted by Cox "the case was 90% ready" and pointed out that for six months under Cox the case "has not been brought to a conclusion." He thought that "now, after six months of delay, it's time that the case be brought to a conclusion."

As for the new special prosecutor, Nixon said "he cannot be removed unless there is a consensus of the top leadership" of both houses of Congress, which, he said, included "a very substantial majority" for the Democrats.

The Jefferson Rule—Nixon again cited his version of "the Jefferson Rule," as he phrased it. In response to a query whether he felt the executive privilege was "absolute," he said he did not, that he had waived executive privilege for members of his staff who had any knowledge of or charges against them in the Watergate matter and had voluntarily waived privilege in turning over the tapes. He said he had not carried the tapes case to the Supreme Court because that would have been "a confrontation" between the two branches and "would have established very possibly a precedent . . . breaking down constitutionality that would plague future presidencies."

Referring "to what I call the Jefferson Rule," Nixon said President Thomas Jefferson had refused a court order to turn over correspondence in the White House files, turning over instead a summary of the correspondence. Then John Marshall, "sitting as chief justice, ruled for the President," Nixon said.

Queries on Haldeman, Ehrlichman—In reply to a query about his former top aides H.R. Haldeman and John D. Ehrlichman, Nixon said he held "that both men and others who have been charged are guilty until I have evidence that they are not guilty" (a misstatement, acknowledged by Nixon later in the conference; he meant the reverse). He still considered Haldeman and Ehrlichman "dedicated fine public servants" and believed that "when these proceedings are completed that they will come out all right." He added that, "unfortunately, they've already been convicted in the minds of millions of Americans by what happened before a Senate committee."

Brother's phone tapped—Asked if he had ordered the Secret Service to tap the telephone of his brother F. Donald Nixon, a California businessman, the President said the Secret Service "did maintain a surveillance" and "for security reasons" and his brother "was aware of it." Asked if his brother was aware "before or after the fact of the surveillance," Nixon said "during the fact because he asked about it and he was told about it and he approved of it." Asked if it made any sense to conduct surveillance when somebody knew about it, Nixon said "the surveillance involved what others who were trying to get him perhaps to use improper influence and so forth might be doing, and particularly anybody who might be in a foreign country."

Raising the milk prices—Nixon himself raised the issue of the 1971 increase in federal milk price supports.

"I want the fact out because the facts will prove that the President is telling the truth," he told the editors. Charges that his Administration raised the price support for milk in 1971 "as a quid pro quo" for a promise by milk producers of substantial contributions, he said, was "just not true." He said "Democrats in Congress put a gun to our head" by demanding a price-support increase, so his Administration put a lower increase into effect.

Nixon also appeared before Republican governors meeting in Memphis Nov. 20, where he created a favorable impression. He had traveled to Georgia Nov. 18 and encountered cheers at one place and jeers at another.

Nixon meets more congressmen, disputes Cox. Continuing his effort to counteract the damage to his credibility caused by the Watergate scandal, President Nixon Nov. 16 had held the last of a series of meetings with members of Congress.

In an 80-minute session with 28 House Republicans, Nixon touched on several issues, some not directly related to Watergate. In one of the few public comments recorded after the meeting, Rep. Charles W. Whalen Jr. (Ohio) called it an exercise in frustration, much like "fingering the piano" without hitting the keys. There were "contradictions," Whalen said, which could be "harmful in the long run" compared with the short-term gains of the current Nixon offensive.

According to Whalen, who said his notes included verbatim quotes, Nixon accused former special prosecutor Archibald Cox of backing out at the last minute on Nixon's proposed compromise to release summaries of White House tapes. As Whalen quoted Nixon: "Cox changed his mind on Friday night [Oct. 19] because of lack of confidence in [Senator John C.] Stennis. We did not know until Saturday he had changed his mind."

(Nixon's statement was denied by Cox and conflicted with other known material concerning the incident. [See below])

Asked about public disclosure of the Watergate tapes, Nixon reportedly responded that he hoped to do so, but would not release "those involving irrele-vant material and national security and third parties—innocent third parties that might be hurt."

According to Whalen, Nixon also referred to the $100,000 gift from billionaire Howard Hughes to Nixon's close friend Charles G. Rebozo, saying that when Rebozo returned the money to Hughes he was accompanied by an agent from the Federal Bureau of Investigation, who had recorded serial numbers and dusted the bills for fingerprints. Rebozo had said he deposited the money in a safe deposit box and later returned the same bills to Hughes.

(The New York Times reported Nov. 20 that the FBI agent referred to by Nixon, Kenneth Whitaker, told Justice Department superiors that Rebozo, a personal friend, had asked him to verify that the money returned to Hughes was the same money he had been given. Whitaker said he could not, and he indicated that the serial numbers on the bills he saw were not consecutive nor were the bills themselves new, the Times reported.)

Version of Cox incident disputed—Informed of Nixon's reported assertion that former special prosecutor Cox had reneged on the compromise tapes plan, Cox said Nov. 17 that "if the President said that, he either fell into a slip of the tongue or was misinformed." Cox said the written record made it clear "that I was opposed to the Stennis proposal," but had never questioned Stennis' integrity.

Documents made public by Cox shortly before his dismissal Oct. 20 also apparently conflicted with Nixon's statement. In a memorandum dated Oct. 18 to then-Attorney General Elliot L. Richardson, Cox had detailed a series of objections to the compromise plan, including its "narrow scope" which would have denied him access to other tapes and documents. Cox also contended that it might be difficult for "any one man [Stennis] operating in secrecy, consulting only with the White House" to inspire public confidence in the authenticity of a summary of the tapes.

A letter to White House legal consultant Charles Alan Wright dated Oct. 19 (which Cox said was delivered by mid-morning the same day) objected that the actual tapes would be withheld even if it meant dismissal of charges against former government officials who had "betrayed the public trust." In the same letter, Cox again decried the directive that access to other tapes "bearing upon criminal wrongdoing" would be left to White House discretion.

Wright replied in a letter also dated Oct. 19 (which Cox said was delivered at 5:23 p.m. that day), saying that "the differences between us remain so great" that further discussion of the compromise plan "would be futile."

A further contradiction had come in an Oct. 21 statement by presidential chief of staff Alexander M. Haig Jr., who acknowledged that Cox's refusal to accept the compromise proposal had been known in the White House three days earlier.

Richardson role debated—Further details emerged Nov. 16 on Nixon's charge that former Attorney General Elliot L. Richardson had been untruthful in relating his role in the formation of the compromise plan on the tapes and his subsequent resignation.

According to senators who had attended meetings with Nixon Nov. 13–14, Nixon had said Richardson "was not telling the truth. I have not said this publicly because I did not want to hurt him." At issue were Richardson's public statements and his sworn testimony before the Senate Judiciary Committee.

While Richardson had said he resigned partly because he disagreed with Nixon's order that Cox refrain from using the courts in trying to obtain presidential tapes and documents, Nixon and his chief of staff Alexander M. Haig Jr. reportedly asserted that Richardson had originated the order and had approved the firing of Cox.

Despite challenges from some senators, Haig and Nixon reiterated the charges, Haig having said "I have read Elliot's testimony and it is not true." Nixon then reportedly interjected in a joking tone: 'Well, who's going to get him on perjury?"

According to a Washington Post report Nov. 18, Richardson had submitted documents to the Senate Judiciary Committee in early November supporting his statements. Among them was his own draft of the compromise proposal, dated Oct. 17, which did not mention a ban on Cox's access to White House tapes and documents. Another document—titled "Summary of Reasons Why I Must Resign"—reportedly made no reference to the issue of future access to White House material and, according to the Post, indicated that the question had never arisen.

Jaworski affirms scope of Cox probe. Special Watergate prosecutor Leon Jaworski told the Senate Judiciary Committee Nov. 20 that "nothing has been dropped from our agenda of activities" and said the investigation was progressing "without undue delay."

Jaworski said "excellent ground work was laid" by the special office's staff, which he lauded as "professional" and "objective" and "dedicated." (This view was not shared at the White House. According to Press Secretary Ronald L. Ziegler Nov. 29, the staff of the special Watergate prosecutor held an "ingrained suspicion and visceral dislike for this President and this Administration." The charge did not apply to Jaworski; Ziegler described him as "a very respected man, a very fair man.")

Jaworski told the panel he considered the Presidential properties at San Clemente, Calif. and Key Biscayne, Fla. within the jurisidction of his probe, and the wiretapping of the President's brother, F. Donald Nixon, "could be" another possible area of investigation as well as the $100,000 cash contribution from Howard R. Hughes to the President's friend, Charles G. Rebozo.

Jaworski said he had sent four letters requesting Presidential documents and was prepared to go to court if necessary to obtain material vital to the prosecution. Reminded by Sen. Birch Bayh (D, Ind.) of Nixon's statement Oct. 26 he would not turn over presidential papers to the new special prosecutor, Jaworski replied: "Then we're going to be in a lawsuit, sir, if that's the case."

If national security were brought into the issue, Jaworski said, he had an arrangement with the White House to listen to the tape recordings and read the papers involved and then judge for himself the merit of the national security claim.

Jaworski status clarified—A regulation issued Nov. 20 by Acting Attorney General Robert H. Bork stipulated that Jaworski's jurisdiction, as well as his tenure, would not be abridged by the President without the consensus of eight Congressional leaders—the majority and minority leaders of the House and Senate and the chairmen and ranking minority members of the judiciary committees of both houses.

Jaworski's job charter was amended, Bork said, to correct inadvertent ambiguous wording in the original text and thus "safeguard . . . your independence."

Sen. Edward M. Kennedy (D, Mass.) objected to the revision Nov. 21; he said it permitted the President and the attorney general, in consultation "with a few members of Congress, to limit or remove entire areas of the special prosecutor's investigation." Kennedy did not consider this strengthening the independence of the prosecutor, whose sole restriction in the charter heretofore concerned only removal from office. Kennedy condemned the change as "a massive new loophole which might serve to aid and abet the continuing Watergate coverup."

(Bork's own tenure as acting attorney general was challenged Nov. 23 by Sen. William Proxmire [D, Wis.], who cited a federal law requiring his confirmation by the Senate after 30 days in office, which expired Nov. 19. His actions since then, Proxmire said, were subject to challenge and nullification.)

Senate gets 2 prosecutor bills—Two bills for a Watergate special prosecutor were reported to the Senate Nov. 21 from the Judiciary Committee. A Democratic-supported bill called for court appointment of the prosecutor and dismissal only by the court for gross impropriety. A White House-supported bill put the appointment and dismissal in the hands of the attorney general with the prosecutor having access to court challenge on an ouster.

Tape erasure disclosed. The usefulness of presidential tape recordings as evidence in the Watergate case, as well as President Nixon's credibility, suffered further damage Nov. 21 when the White House revealed that a key segment of one of the subpoenaed tapes was blank. In subsequent testimony before U.S. District Court Judge John J. Sirica, Nixon's personal secretary Rose Mary Woods said she had made the "terrible mistake" of accidentally erasing a portion of a June 20, 1972 conversation between Nixon and H. R. Haldeman, then his chief of staff.

Special White House counsel J. Fred Buzhardt Jr. told Sirica Nov. 21 that an 18-minute portion of the tape contained an "audible tone" but no conversation. Buzhardt said he had learned of "the phenomenon" Nov. 14 in the process of preparing an analysis and index of the tapes for the court, and Nixon had been told "shortly thereafter." Buzhardt attributed the delay in informing the court to "ambiguity" in the original prosecution subpoena, which he said was thought by White House lawyers to have covered only one Nixon meeting that day, while in fact there were two meetings, the first with John D. Ehrlichman, then domestic affairs adviser, the second with Haldeman.

(A memorandum submitted to the court by the prosecution Aug. 13 had said: "Ehrlichman and then Haldeman went to see the President. The inference that they reported on Watergate and may well have received instructions, is almost irresistible.")

Buzhardt said "a large number of technical tests" had been conducted with the problem tape Nov. 20 but had not provided an explanation for the unrecorded portion. "All other tapes are audible," Buzhardt added.

After Buzhardt's announcement, Sirica ordered the original tapes submitted to him for safekeeping, saying "this is just another instance that convinces the court that it has to take some steps, not because the court doesn't trust the White House or the President," but "in the interest of seeing that nothing else happens."

The White House Nov. 26 turned over to the court the subpoenaed tapes, along with a document analyzing the tapes and outlining claims of executive privilege for some of the material.

The document also contained the White House explanation for the blank space in the June 20, 1972 tape, which it said occurred approximately three minutes and 40 seconds after the beginning of Nixon's conversation with Haldeman. The erasure was caused, the document stated, "by the depression of a record button during the process of reviewing the tape, possibly while the recorder was in the proximity of an electric typewriter and a high intensity lamp."

Haldeman's handwritten notes of the meeting (also submitted into evidence by the White House) reflected, according to the document, "that the President gave instructions to Mr. Haldeman to take certain actions of a public relations character which related to the Watergate incident."

(In his notes, Haldeman wrote: "Be sure EOB [Executive Office Building] is thoroughly checked re bugs at all times." "What is our counterattack?" "Hit the opposition w/their activities. Point out libertarians have created public callousness. Do they justify this less than stealing Pentagon Papers, [columnist Jack] Anderson file, etc? We should be on the attack for diversion.")

When the prosecution contended in court that the Haldeman notes indicated the "obliterated portions" must have related to Watergate, presidential counsel Leonard Garment objected to the characterization.

"The exhibit will speak for itself," Sirica replied.

Miss Woods gave her own account of the tape "accident" Nov. 26-28. She related that she had been in her White House office Oct. 1 transcribing the Ehrlichman meeting, with instructions to stop there, she said, because presidential chief of staff Alexander M. Haig Jr. had told her the Haldeman conversation which followed was not covered by the subpoena.

The Haldeman portion had just begun, she said, when her telephone rang. In reaching for the phone, "through some error on my part," she pressed the "record" button rather than the "stop" button. At the same time, Miss Woods continued, she must have pressed on the foot pedal of the machine, which could have erased a part of the tape.

After her phone conversation (which she described at various points in her testimony as lasting four, five or six minutes), she discovered the "record" button still depressed, replayed the tape and discovered the "gap." She immediately informed Nixon, who, she said, told her "don't worry about it." There was "no problem because that's not one of the subpoenaed tapes."

Miss Woods testified later that it was not until the White House was making copies of the tapes in preparation for complying with the subpoena that the full 18-minute length of the gap was discovered. She said she did not think she could have been responsible for the entire erasure.

Sirica interrupted her testimony at one point to ask why she had not told the court of the erasure in her Nov. 8 testimony. Miss Woods replied that she had "understood we were talking only about the subpoenaed tapes. All I can say is that I am dreadfully sorry."

Sirica then asked that the portion of her Nov. 8 testimony concerning "precautions" against erasure be read.

Using the same recorder she had operated while transcribing the tapes earlier, Miss Woods Nov. 27 replayed in court a copy of the disputed tape. According to courtroom observers, only isolated words or phrases could be understood during the portion before the "gap": while with Ehrlichman Nixon asked for "a little of that consomme," complained about the press being "violently pro-Humphrey" in 1968, said something about the Supreme Court and told Ehrlichman that "presidential speeches are dull." After Haldeman entered, there was small talk about a trip to the West, then the 18-minute buzzing segment, varying in tone and intensity and described as something like the noise made by an electric shaver.

After Miss Woods had described the layout of her White House office (the

A recorder had been on a typing table, the phone on a side desk at right angles to the typing table), she was asked to reconstruct the Oct. 1 incident. Assistant prosecutor Jill Volner quickly noted that, when Miss Woods reached around to "answer" the phone, she immediately lifted her foot from the recorder pedal.

After the demonstration, two prosecutors inspected Miss Woods' White House office. A prosecution spokesman said later only that "our purpose was to view," and that technical experts would inspect the office and the typewriter and lamp cited by the White House as possible causes for the humming noise on the tape.

B Miss Woods was represented by "a lawyer of her own," Charles S. Rhyne. She testified that after she had received a subpoena to appear, Haig had told her that "none of the White House lawyers would come down with me."

C *Privilege claims outlined*—In an "index and analysis" of Watergate tapes and documents submitted to Judge Sirica Nov. 26, the White House said some of the subpoenaed material would be subjected to claims of executive privilege. Sirica was to rule on the claims before relaying evidence to the grand jury. The document made the following assertions:

June 20, 1972 meetings: The session with John D. Ehrlichman contained nothing relating to Watergate and was "subject in its entirety" to a claim of privilege to "protect the confidentiality of advice given to the President." The portion of the Haldeman tape remaining after the erasure was not related to Watergate; privilege was claimed.

D June 20, 1972 phone call to John N. Mitchell: not recorded, Nixon's dictation belt of "recollections" submitted.

June 30, 1972 meeting with Haldeman and Mitchell: Related to Mitchell's pending resignation from the Committee to Re-Elect the President, with "a few passing and collateral references to Watergate which are not substantive." The conversation related to matters which had "a direct bearing on the President's ability to operate his office" and included "discussions of highly personal matters." The tape was subject "in its entirety" to a claim of privilege.

E Sept. 15, 1972 meeting with counsel John W. Dean: Approximately 33 minutes and nine seconds of tape related to Watergate and would be released; the remainder was subject to privilege.

F March 13 meeting with Dean and Haldeman: "No particularized claim of executive privilege," since—although the tape contained advice "from his counsel on official responsibilities"—the subject matter related so often to Watergate that other material could not be separated.

G March 21–22 meetings: Related to Watergate and not subject to privilege. In addition, a cassette recording of Nixon's "recollections" was submitted.

April 15 meeting with Dean: Not recorded; Nixon's handwritten notes submitted.

Governors irked at tape 'bomb'—Republican governors who a few days earlier had praised President Nixon's candor during their meeting in Memphis reacted with demands for new explanations Nov. 23–24 to the disclosure of a "gap" in one of the subpoenaed Watergate tapes.

Gov. Tom McCall (Ore.), who had been assured that Nixon knew of no further Watergate "bombs" to be dropped, said Nov. 23 that Nixon's "insensitivity to what is a bombshell" made it almost impossible to help him politically. "You're already in a morass of problems and here disaster stares you in the face in the form of this tape, and you don't even recognize it. I just don't see how they're ever going to crawl out."

Gov. Daniel J. Evans (Wash.) said Nov. 24 "it would have been infinitely better if he [Nixon] had just let us know." Despite having "probably the most representative and sympathetic audience of any group in the country," Evans said, Nixon "just didn't square with us."

(According to Gov. James E. Holshouser Jr. (N.C.), Nixon during their meeting had stressed the "very important" point that "the key tapes for the key dates are there in audible language.")

While disclaiming the suggestion that there might have been intentional tampering with the tapes, Gov. Winfield Dunn (Tenn.) said Nov. 23 that the incident nevertheless was a "terrible blow" to the "confidence of the people." This "revelation," Dunn said "does call for some further explanation."

Gov. Robert D. Ray (Iowa), a sometime critic of Nixon who had felt "much better" after the Memphis meeting, said Nov. 23 that the latest tape incident "once again raises serious doubts in the minds of people as to whether or not a full disclosure" of Watergate would be made as Nixon had promised.

Panel of tape experts named—Judge Sirica Nov. 21 announced an advisory panel of technical experts to "study the authenticity and integrity" of the Watergate tapes. The group was chosen by the prosecutor's office and the White House.

Sirica said the panel had already held its first meeting, at which a draft proposal had been developed for a "series of pilot tests to explore possible ways to validate the recordings." The tests were to be completed in January 1974. Members of the panel:

Richard H. Bolt, chairman of Bolt, Beranek and Newman Inc.; Franklin Cooper, president of Haskins Laboratories; James L. Flanagan of Bell Telephone Laboratories Inc.; John G. McKnight, an audio consultant; Thomas G. Stockham Jr. of the University of Utah; and Mark R. Weiss, vice president for acoustics research of Federal Scientific Corp.

Law firm cites impeachable offenses. A public interest law firm contended Nov. 24 there was "ample" evidence that President Nixon could be held accountable for 28 "indictable common crimes." In releasing a study of the criminal law involved in the allegations of wrongdoing against the White House, William A. Dobrovir, head of the law firm, specified:

"What we're saying is that the President could properly be indicted and made to stand trial on all these charges—on the basis of probable cause"; "we're also saying that the House of Representatives could, today, impeach Richard Nixon for these same offenses."

The "indictable common crimes" listed in the study involved conspiracy, illegal wiretapping, burglary, obstruction of justice, perjury, conspiracy to defraud the U.S., bribery, fraud, embezzlement and tax evasion. The activities cited included the Watergate scandal, campaign financing, violation of civil liberties and use of federal funds for personal enrichment.

Others press for impeachment—The AFL-CIO continued its drive for the President's impeachment with a statement Nov. 22 charging that Nixon "has committed an impeachable offense by creating a special and personal secret police, by hiding its illegal activities behind 'national security,' and by obstructing justice in the name of 'national security.'"

(Labor Secretary Peter Brennan said Nov. 22 "labor should not lead these attacks." While the President "could make mistakes like anyone else," he said, until "that is proven in the proper way we have to work with this Administration.")

The International Executive Board of the AFL-CIO Newspaper Guild adopted a resolution Nov. 15 calling for initiation of impeachment proceedings against Nixon "without further delay." Wire service groups dissociated themselves from the resolution, and there was some dissent within the guild that the action would compromise editorial objectivity. The resolution itself passed by a 15–1 vote.

(White House aide Bruce Herschensohn criticized the national media in its Watergate reporting Nov. 24 as "a kangaroo court" whose "verdict is very clear from the outset." The media, he said, "should be subject to the same scrutiny as they give their target, the President." Herschensohn was addressing a "Support the President" rally in Albuquerque attended by about 600 persons.)

Chesterfield Smith, president of the American Bar Association, giving his personal position, spoke out Nov. 27 against "continuation of this political never-never land" of public doubt and suspicion against the President. Nixon's "continued right to the Presidency" he said, should be decided in a Congressional impeachment investigation. Smith opposed a forced resignation because it could be construed as "nothing more than a political assassination."

CBS restores 'instant analysis.' The Columbia Broadcasting System (CBS) announced Nov. 12 that after a five-month trial it was rescinding its ban on analyses of presidential speeches immediately after their delivery.

News Council unable to get data. The National News Council said the White House had failed to respond to numerous requests for documentation of President Nixon's Oct. 27 criticism of television network newscasts, it was reported Nov. 24.

In his press conference Oct. 27, Nixon accused the network newscasters of "vicious" and "distorted" reporting. Ken W. Clawson, director of the White House Office of Communications, later confirmed to the New York Times that an Administration list of press "sins" committed against the President had been compiled.

William Arthur, director of the council, said he had asked White House Press Secretary Ronald L. Ziegler to enumerate instances of "hysterical" or "distorted" reporting, but there had been no response.

GSA concedes political hiring. The General Services Administration (GSA) conceded that it had sometimes given preferential treatment to politically-referred applicants for civil service jobs in violation of Civil Service Commission personnel regulations, it was reported Nov. 24. The GSA said in a report to the commission (filed Nov. 10 but not made public) that it had abolished its "special referral unit."

The GSA was responding to charges made by the commission after an investigation of hiring practices in one of the GSA's East Coast regions. According to a commission spokesman, "improprieties" had been found in 16 of a sample of 20 hirings checked. Preferential treatment had been given to applicants referred by "nominally political or clearly partisan sources," reportedly including the Republican National Committee and the Committee to Re-Elect the President. The commission charged that "unmistakable pressure" had been placed on GSA personnel officials "to take extraordinary steps to find jobs and assure placement" for political referrals.

GSA Administrator Arthur F. Sampson, a Nixon appointee, said his agency had "some problems" in hiring, but added that "personal injustices and system breakdowns" might have been caused by the attempt to bring in "fresh blood and new ideas."

Halperin suit affidavit released. Morton H. Halperin, a former National Security Council (NSC) official, asserted in a sworn statement made public Nov. 27 that three days after NSC member Henry A. Kissinger had orally agreed to limit Halperin's access to sensitive national security data, Halperin's telephone was tapped as part of a White House effort to stop leaks of such information.

The statement was part of an affidavit given by Halperin in connection with his civil suit against Kissinger and others, whom he held responsible for illegal wiretaps that were placed on him for 21 months beginning in May 1969.

Kissinger reported certain of wiretap— Henry A. Kissinger told a former White House associate that he was "virtually certain" his telephone had been tapped at some point since he had joined the

Administration in 1969, according to the New York Times Nov. 25.

According to the Times source, identified only as a "former White House official," Kissinger remarked on the wiretap shortly before his confirmation as secretary of state Sept. 21. When the former official pursued the remark, the Times said, Kissinger replied, "At least you know the plumbers don't work for me."

Tape gap still a puzzle. Unexplained "gaps" in President Nixon's Watergate tapes continued as the center of attention in the courtroom of Judge John J. Sirica Nov. 28–Dec. 6. Amid contradictory explanations from White House aides and lawyers for the 18-minute blank space in one tape and the disclosure of additional gaps in others, Sirica reacted skeptically to White House testimony, at one point asking Rose Mary Woods, Nixon's personal secretary, if there had been efforts to "cover up" information that should have been given to the court.

Presidential counsel J. Fred Buzhardt Jr. revealed Nov. 28 that there were a "number" of spaces on the subpoenaed tapes without "identifiable sound." Buzhardt said the gaps were discovered in the process of copying the tapes Nov. 14, the same day he determined the full extent of the 18-minute gap in the June 20, 1972 conversation between Nixon and chief of staff H. R. Haldeman.

Buzhardt and presidential lawyer Leonard Garment attempted to dismiss the new gaps as an inconsequential and "collateral" issue, the significance of which would have to be determined by technical experts. Assistant prosecutor Richard Ben-Veniste noted, however, that some of the spaces lasted "several minutes." Buzhardt said the gaps could have occurred when the "sound-actuated" taping system was set off by extraneous noises besides conversation.

(Alexander P. Butterfield, the former White House aide who revealed the existence of the system, had said the recorders were activated by voices.)

(A White House spokesman said later Nov. 28 that the seven subpoenaed conversations were "intact," except for the disputed 18-minute gap in the Haldeman tape.)

Sirica and the prosecutors returned to the question of the White House delay in telling the court of the gap in the Haldeman tape. When Buzhardt said it took a "close reading" of the prosecution memorandum (which stated "Ehrlichman and then Haldeman went to see the President") to determine that the Haldeman conversation was covered by the subpoena, Sirica asked if such a "careful reading" was really necessary. "It takes a very careful reading," Buzhardt replied, "because it calls for two meetings, not one."

Ben-Veniste noted that the memo had been given to the White House Aug. 13 and that the U.S. Court of Appeals opinion upholding Sirica's access to the tapes had included the memo.

"And of course you studied that opinion?" Ben-Veniste asked.

"I read it, yes," Buzhardt replied.

Buzhardt conceded in testimony Nov. 29 that he had at one point concluded there was no explanation of how the gap in the Haldeman tape "could have been done accidentally." But then he conducted tests of his own, he said, and managed to create a buzzing sound similar to that on the tape by recording on a machine near an electric typewriter and high-intensity lamp. Although he had never "interrogated" Miss Woods, he said he had come to believe she could have caused the entire erasure by accidental misuse of the recorder. This had been presented as the official White House explanation as a "logical belief," not a "real certainty."

In another development Nov. 29, Ben-Veniste introduced evidence that Miss Woods had custody of originals of nine additional tapes from Nov. 19 to Nov. 26. Although the tapes were not covered by the subpoena, they had been requested by special prosecutor Leon Jaworski and involved former presidential counsel John Dean's allegations that in early January there had been White House discussions of executive clemency for Watergate defendant E. Howard Hunt.

Buzhardt maintained that he had not been "aware" that Miss Woods had nine tapes but said he knew she had reviewed one tape of "some telephone conversations." He later conceded that at the same time Miss Woods was reviewing the tapes, he was corresponding with Jaworski on the availability of them. Asked again whether he knew Miss Woods was reviewing the tapes with which he was concerned, Buzhardt replied, "I may well have been advised. I don't know."

Butterfield also testified Nov. 29, expressing surprise at the poor quality of some of the recordings. Butterfield said he had understood that the Secret Service had installed "the best equipment to do the job." He added that the machines were checked daily, even on weekends, when Nixon was working in Washington.

In testimony Dec. 4, Lawrence M. Higby—Haldeman's former assistant and currently in the Office of Management and Budget—said Haldeman had instructed him by telephone Nov. 14 or Nov. 15 to retrieve from Haldeman's files the notes of the June 20 1972 meeting. According to Higby, Haldeman already knew of the gap in the tape and was turning over the notes at White House request.

The question of the "ambiguous" prosecution subpoena surfaced again Dec. 4. Samuel J. Powers, a Florida lawyer who joined Nixon's legal staff in November, said that when he was shown the subpoena Nov. 14, he had no trouble seeing that the Nixon-Haldeman meeting was covered. White House chief of staff Alexander M. Haig Jr., appearing Dec. 5, related that after he had been told of Powers' assessment by Buzhardt, he replied "this is a pretty late date to be telling me something like that."

Haig said he reported the problem to Nixon the next day and Nixon was "almost incredulous that such a mistake could have been made." Haig said Nixon's reaction was to suggest that "we have to do whatever is technically feasible to re-constitute the tape, if that can be done."

Haig explained that he had delayed telling Nixon for one day so the President could give a speech without "worrisome" new information.

Haig said he was further disturbed by a Nov. 20 call from Buzhardt, who said there was no explanation for the 18 minutes of hum on the Haldeman tape. Haig said he relayed the message to Nixon after the President's meeting with Republican governors. Nixon was "very concerned," Haig said.

In earlier testimony Dec. 5, Miss Woods was recalled when contradictions arose concerning the gap in the Haldeman tape. Powers had told the court that shortly after he and Buzhardt had discovered the length of the gap, Miss Woods entered the room and was "shocked" that the gap could have been so long when she had been on the telephone for only a few minutes. Powers said she then left the room, came back with her tape recorder and demonstrated how the "accident" had happened.

Recalled to the witness stand, Miss Woods denied that she had re-enacted the incident for the lawyers. "I was in there only two or three minutes," she said. "I did not even sit down . . . all they told me" was that "some sort of meter" had shown the gap.

Questioned further about her relationship with White House lawyers, Miss Woods said she thought she had been represented by them as late as Nov. 22. She related a Nov. 8 meeting with Buzhardt, Powers and Garment, during which she was told "not to volunteer anything" and "to answer questions 'yes' or 'no'" and not to "get into a lot of discussion on anything."

Sirica urged Miss Woods to try to recall anything that might help explain the tape gap. "Was it by accident?" he asked, "or was it by some action taken by somebody to erase something that the court should hear, to cover up something, if that is the expression, to prevent justice from being done?"

Miss Woods replied that she knew no more than what had already been told.

Haig returned as a witness Dec. 6 with what he felt was an innocent explanation for the disputed gap—that Miss Woods might have spoken on the phone, while the recorder was erasing, longer than she had testified. Haig said Nixon had told him that she had been "somewhat imprecise" in telling Nixon of the incident. One of the "theories developed," Haig continued, was that Miss Woods was "tired and couldn't remember how long she had been on the phone."

(Haig told newsmen after the court session, "I've known women that think they've talked for five minutes and then have talked for an hour.")

Haig related that until White House lawyers had settled upon the "accidental" explanation, there had been speculation on "devil theories"—that "perhaps some sinister force had come in and applied the other energy source and taken care of the information on the tape." He said the idea was discarded.

Sirica recessed the hearing pending technical examination of the tape.

4 tapes cleared for jury—Responding to a request by special prosecutor Jaworski that the Watergate grand jury's hearing of the subpoenaed Watergate tapes should not be delayed, Judge Sirica said Nov. 30 that the four tapes not subject to claims of executive privilege could be turned over immediately.

(Jaworski had suggested Nov. 29 that all of Nixon's tapes be turned over to the court for safekeeping. White House Press Secretary Ronald L. Ziegler called the suggestion "nonsense.")

Grand jury extended. President Nixon Nov. 30 signed a bill providing for extension of the original Watergate grand jury six months to June 4, 1974. The bill also provided that a further six-month extension could be granted by the U.S. District Court for the District of Columbia if the grand jury requested.

The House had passed the bill Nov. 6 by a vote of 378–1. The Senate concurred by a voice vote Nov. 19.

In an order made public Dec. 4, Judge Sirica formalized the six-month extension "unless earlier discharged in accordance with law."

Stennis denies consent to tape plan. Sen. John C. Stennis (D, Miss.) said Dec. 4 that he had not agreed to the final White House version of the abortive compromise plan to release summaries of the subpoenaed Watergate tapes. Failure of the compromise had resulted in the dismissal of special prosecutor Archibald Cox and the resignation of Attorney General Elliot L. Richardson.

Stennis told the Washington Post he "had no idea" that the White House wanted him to authenticate a transcript of the tapes to be given to Judge John J. Sirica. According to Stennis, he was to have prepared two copies, one for the White House and one for the Senate Watergate Committee. "There was never any mention about the court," Stennis said. "I wouldn't have done it if there was. . . . I was once a judge and the courts can ask for what they want."

The Post quoted a Stennis associate as saying that Stennis had been "surprised and somewhat flabbergasted" when President Nixon announced that a copy of the Stennis-authenticated summary would be turned over to the court. The associate said Stennis had understood the final agreement as providing for verbatim transcripts of all the subpoenaed conversations, not simply the summaries announced by the White House.

Samuel Dash, chief counsel for the Senate committee, said Dec. 4 that Nixon's offer of an authenticated version "was presented as a separate offer to the committee and was not tied to Cox." According to Dash, Committee Chairman Sam J. Ervin Jr. (D, N.C.) "had no impression that the offer involved Cox at all."

Stock market erratic. The stock market continued to reflect the nation's economic and political uncertainty. Since Oct. 26, the Dow Jones industrial average of New York Stock Exchange shares had fallen 169 points. According to a brokerage partner Nov. 28, "This is going to be a very volatile market—up and down—until we get clarification on the energy question and on our leadership in Washington."

FBI campaign against left disclosed. J. Edgar Hoover, the late director of the Federal Bureau of Investigation (FBI), ordered a campaign in May 1968 to "expose, disrupt and otherwise neutralize" the "New Left" movement, according to internal FBI memoranda released Dec. 6 by the Justice Department.

A second memo, issued April 28, 1971, ordered that the campaign be discontinued immediately.

White House criticized on tax ruling. Judge Charles R. Richey of federal district court in Washington Dec. 11 ordered the Internal Revenue Service (IRS) to grant tax-exempt status to the Center for Corporate Responsibility. Richey said the IRS had acted improperly in delaying for more than two years action on the group's request for determination of its status and eventually denying tax-free standing to the nonprofit organization. [See p. 122]

Experts rebut White House on tape gap. U.S. District Court Judge John J. Sirica announced Dec. 13 that a panel of technical experts did not believe the electric typewriter or the high-intensity lamp used in the office of President Nixon's personal secretary Rose Mary Woods was the "likely cause" of an 18-minute gap of buzzing sounds in one of the subpoenaed Watergate tapes.

The panel's preliminary findings rebutted an explanation that presidential counsel J. Fred Buzhardt Jr. had offered as a "logical belief." The tape involved a June 20, 1972 conversation between Nixon and H. R. Haldeman, then White House chief of staff.

Sirica said the panel had conducted tests with "advanced equipment" in "several facilities" and had found "indications" that the recorder used by Miss Woods "could have produced the buzz." However, further tests would be needed to confirm this. Sirica also said the experts doubted that any conversation recorded "under the buzz" could be retrieved.

Sirica noted that in addition to the question of the gap, the panel had been asked to determine whether the entire .tape was the original one or a copy that had been edited by such operations as cutting and splicing. Sirica said the group would present a conclusive report in January 1974.

Buzhardt told newsmen later that he still believed his own explanation and had been able to reproduce the buzzing tone. But, he said, "we'll accept whatever they find."

Jaworski gets access to files. Special Watergate prosecutor Leon Jaworski announced Dec. 12 that the White House had agreed to allow prosecution investigators to search White House files for documents relevant to the Watergate case.

Jaworski said the arrangement provided that his investigators would work from a prepared list and search the files with the assistance of White House counsel, in the presence of the Secret Service. He added that if new documents turned up during the search he would ask that they also be released.

In effect, Jaworski said, the White House had "opened the safe." But Deputy Press Secretary Gerald L. Warren—while praising the arrangement as "another example of the degree of cooperation" with the prosecutor—cautioned that the search would be restricted to "particularized areas."

An earlier instance of voluntary compliance by the White House had been disclosed by Jaworski Dec. 10. A "substantial number" of tapes and documents, he said, were turned over Dec. 8. Neither Jaworski nor the White House would reveal the content of the material, which had not been subpoenaed.

3rd grand jury OKd—Judge Sirica Dec. 12 approved special prosecutor Jaworski's request that a third Watergate grand jury be convened.

Jaworski said the new jury, to be sworn in Jan. 7, 1974, was needed to aid in the investigation of illegal campaign contributions.

Senate shelves prosecutor bill. The Senate Democratic leadership decided Dec. 11 to defer floor action on a bill providing for court appointment of a special Watergate prosecutor.

Majority Leader Mike Mansfield (D, Mont.) said part of the reason for the decision was "the outstanding job" being done by special prosecutor Jaworski. Other spokesmen said the strategy would be to hold the bill on the calendar as leverage against the White House should Jaworski's position be threatened. The leaders were also reportedly concerned over doubts of the bill's constitutionality.

Also set aside provisionally were substitute measures giving Jaworski other forms of protection against dismissal or restrictions on his jurisdiction.

Saxbe confirmed as attorney general. The Senate voted 75-10 Dec. 17 to confirm one of its members, Sen. William B. Saxbe (R, Ohio), as attorney general. The opposition vote was generally based on constitutional grounds that prohibited a member of Congress from taking a post whose salary was increased by legislation while the member served in Congress. Congress sought to nullify this by passing a bill reverting the attorney general's salary from the $60,000 a year set when Saxbe was in the Senate to $35,000. The salary bill was approved in final form by the Senate Dec. 6 and House Dec. 7 and was signed by President Nixon Dec. 10. After signing it, the President formally submitted the Saxbe nomination to the Senate.

Another barrier to the nomination was removed when the Senate dropped from the salary bill an unrelated provision attached by the House to reform the Congressional franking privilege.

At a confirmation hearing before the Senate Judiciary Committee Dec. 12, Saxbe had assured his colleagues he would "vigorously support" the special Watergate prosecutor in his probe to determine whether "high crimes and misdemeanors" were committed by the White House. "I'll fight for his right to proceed as he sees fit," Saxbe said of prosecutor Leon Jaworski. "It's a covenant I made with myself that the chips were going to have to fall as they may," he told the committee.

Jaworski, who was called by the committee to the hearing, pledged to inform Congress of any attempt to block his investigation.

Saxbe told the committee he would "excuse" himself from the Justice Department's reopened inquiry into the fatal 1970 shootings by National Guardsmen at Kent State University in his home state of Ohio.

Lawyer plays White House tape. William A. Dobrovir, an attorney for Ralph Nader in the milk fund lawsuit, admitted Dec. 18 that he had played a White House tape recording of a conversation between President Nixon and dairy industry leaders at a Washington cocktail party the night before. [See p. 123]

Early impeachment vote urged. Melvin R. Laird, who announced Dec. 19 his resignation as presidential counselor, effective Feb. 1, 1974, said he believed a vote on impeaching President Nixon "would be a healthy thing" in resolving the issue. He thought the House should take the vote by March 15, 1974 because of the Congressional elections later in the year.

Vice President Gerald R. Ford told reporters Dec. 12 if the impeachment question were not voted by the end of April 1974, "then you can say it's partisan."

House Judiciary Committee Chairman Peter Rodino (D, N.J.), after meeting with a bipartisan leadership group of his committee, announced Dec. 19 that the panel had agreed on an April target date for reporting to the House on its impeachment inquiry.

Rodino Dec 20 announced the selection of John M. Doar, 52, a Republican who was a member of the Johnson and Kennedy administrations in the Justice Department, as special counsel to the committee to head the impeachment probe.

Graham critical. The Rev. Billy Graham expressed criticism Dec. 22 of President Nixon's judgment and isolation. In an interview published in the evangelical publication Christianity Today, Graham, a personal friend of the President, said, "Until there is more proof to the contrary I have confidence in the President's integrity—but some of his judgments have been wrong and I just don't agree with them."

The President, he said, "has made mistakes, and this is one of them: you cannot, as President, isolate yourself."

Privilege claims on tapes upheld. U.S. District Court Judge John J. Sirica Dec. 19 upheld, with minor exceptions, President Nixon's claims of executive privilege on portions of three of the Watergate tapes subpoenaed by the special prosecutor.

Sirica ruled that the parts of Nixon's June 20, 1972 meetings with advisers John D. Ehrlichman and H. R. Haldeman which remained on tape after the disputed 18-minute obliteration of a conversation with Haldeman on Watergate were irrelevant to the prosecutor's investigation.

While the White House had claimed privilege on all of a June 30, 1972 meeting with Haldeman and former Attorney General John N. Mitchell, Sirica said that passing references to Watergate—reportedly lasting about five minutes—could be heard by the prosecutor, but that the remainder of the tape would be withheld.

Sirica also sustained the privilege claim on part of a Sept. 15, 1972 meeting with counsel John W. Dean 3rd.

Court gets jurisdiction on committee suits. A bill giving the U.S. District Court for the District of Columbia jurisdiction over any civil suit filed by the Senate Watergate committee to enforce its subpoenas against the President became law Dec. 17 when President Nixon declined to either sign or veto it within 10 working days after final passage. The Senate had approved the bill by voice vote Nov. 9, and the House concurred Dec. 3, also by voice vote. The measure was a response to Judge John J. Sirica's Oct. 17 dismissal of the committee's suit on the ground that a statutory basis for jurisdiction was lacking.

The bill, which applied only to the Watergate committee, gave the court original jurisdiction, "without regard to the sum or value of the matter in controversy, of any civil action heretofore or hereafter brought by [the committee] to enforce or to secure a declaration concerning the validity of any subpoena or order" issued to the President or any other executive branch official to obtain tapes or documents relevant to the committee's investigation.

The measure also stated that the committee could litigate a suit not only in its own name but in the name of the United States, a function normally reserved to the Justice Department.

A
B
C
D
E
F
G

In a statement released Dec. 17, Nixon said he "strongly" disagreed with the "ill-advised" legislation because the "control of litigation" was the "proper function of the executive branch, relinquished only in limited and specific circumstances." The reason for appointment of a special prosecutor, Nixon said, was to avoid the "constitutional anomaly" created by such a bill.

While he could not "sanction" the bill, Nixon added, he could not veto it "in the present circumstances," since "Congress and the public would place an interpretation upon a veto . . . entirely contrary" to his reasons for doing so.

Committee sends subpoenas—Lawyers for the Senate Watergate committee Dec. 19 served subpoenas covering nearly 500 presidential tape recordings and documents. White House counsel accepted the subpoenas, but did not indicate whether Nixon would comply. The committee had unanimously approved the subpoenas Dec. 18.

In addition to tapes and documents directly related to the Watergate case, the subpoenas sought information on the $100,000 contribution made by industrialist Howard R. Hughes through Nixon's friend C. G. Rebozo, and information on alleged Administration favors to the dairy industry in return for campaign contributions.

The subpoenas also sought Nixon's daily appointment log from Jan. 1, 1970 through Dec. 19, 1973.

Meanwhile, the committee pressed for enforcement of its original subpoena, asking the U.S. Court of Appeals Dec. 18 to either retain jurisdiction and rule on the subpoena, or return the case to Judge Sirica for a ruling under the new law on jurisdiction.

2nd 'enemies' list revealed. The Joint Committee on Internal Revenue Taxation disclosed in a report Dec. 20 that the White House gave the Internal Revenue Service (IRS) in September 1972 a list of 575 persons "to see what type of information could be developed concerning the people on the list." The report was based on testimony from Johnnie Walters, then IRS commissioner, who said he received the list from former White House counsel John W. Dean 3rd as an intermediary for former Nixon aide John D. Ehrlichman.

Walters told the panel he apprised Treasury Secretary George P. Shultz of the matter and was directed to "do nothing" about it. The panel's own investigation concluded that there was "no evidence" that the IRS had acted on the matter and that, in fact, there was evidence some persons on the list should have received closer scrutiny by the IRS.

The list, composed primarily of contributors to Sen. George McGovern's Democratic presidential campaign and of McGovern staffers, was separate from the first White House "enemies" list previously disclosed by Dean to the Senate Watergate committee.

CBS charges reprisal in suits. In a brief filed in response to federal antitrust suits against the three television networks, CBS charged Dec. 21 that the government had embarked on "an unlawful plan" to "restrain, intimidate and inhibit criticism of the President of the United States and his appointees."

The CBS brief argued that "as early as October 1969" the Nixon Administration had prepared plans to "use the power and machinery of the federal government" to stifle television news coverage. The purpose of the suits, CBS contended, was not to enforce antitrust law, but to threaten or punish news organizations.

Credibility loss large. The President's loss of credibility extended to almost three-quarters of the American public, according to a Louis Harris survey published Dec. 24. By 73%–21%, it found, the public agreed that Nixon "has lost so much credibility that it will be hard for him to be accepted as President again."

However, the survey query that "he has reached the point where he can no longer be an effective President and should resign for the good of the country," was rejected 45%–44% (11% undecided).

A Gallup sampling Nov. 30–Dec. 3 (results published Dec. 16) found the public 54% against (35% for) compelling Nixon to leave office. The 35% in favor included 5%, or an estimated seven million persons, who had taken action in support of their opinion, such as a petition or message to Congress. The finding a month earlier was 54%–37%.

Louis Harris pollsters asked this question of a cross section of households Nov. 13–16: "Would you respect President Nixon more or less if he resigned from the office of President to allow Gerald Ford to take over as President in an act of national unity?" The results, published Dec. 17: more respect 45%; less respect 31%; not sure 24%.

Public release of tapes doubtful. Deputy White House Press Secretary Gerald L. Warren acknowledged Dec. 28 that President Nixon's decision to make public either summaries or transcripts of Watergate tapes and documents was being "re-evaluated."

Warren said release of the material was still under review largely because of two recent events connected with presidential tapes: the "indiscretion" by an attorney involved in the dairy producers campaign funds case in playing a tape at a Washington cocktail party, and the broad scope of the Senate Watergate Committee's subpoenas of presidential material.

Warren denied a Dec. 28 Washington Post report that two unnamed senior White House aides were no longer convinced of Nixon's innocence in the Watergate cover-up. Warren conceded, however, that there were ambiguities in the tapes—the publication of which "could lead to confusion in the minds of the American public and further distortion in this matter."

Citing "senior presidential aides," the Post said Nixon and his advisers had decided that the content of some of the tapes, if released, might convince the public that Nixon was involved in the cover-up conspiracy, although his involvement or awareness might not be direct enough to constitute obstruction of justice.

Two of the aides "who had consistently maintained" that Nixon was innocent, the Post said, now believed the tapes showed that Nixon knew of the cover-up at least several days before March 21, the date the President had cited as his first awareness of it.

According to the aides, it was still unclear whether Nixon actually knew of offers of executive clemency and payoffs to the original defendants or was simply trying to "contain" the case for political purposes. The legal distinction, the aides said, would not be apparent to the public.

The Post said that instead of public disclosure, Nixon and his advisers had decided to release material in the future only to the House Judiciary Committee, which had begun an inquiry into possible impeachment proceedings. Any sign of non-cooperation with that panel, White House aides said, would only increase the chances of impeachment. The Senate Watergate Committee's subpoenas, however, would be resisted.

Dow closes at 850.86. The Dow Jones industrial average closed Dec. 31 at 850.86, a sharp contrast to the 1972 closing of 1,020.02. The index had reached a record high in early January of 1,051.70 but had fallen gradually, finally staging a strong recovery in October when the index rallied at 987.06.

Editorial Reaction to
the Watergate Affair

Cooperating Newspapers

Akron (Ohio) Beacon Journal (174,000)
Albany (N.Y.) Knickerbocker News (71,000)
Albuquerque (N.M.) Journal (66,000)
Anchorage (Alaska) Daily Times (13,000)
Ann Arbor (Mich.) News (37,000)
Atlanta Constitution (209,000)
Baltimore News American (201,000)
Baltimore Sun (165,000)
Biloxi (Miss.) Daily Herald (37,000)
Birmingham (Ala.) News (76,000)
Boston Globe (261,000)
Boston Herald American (211,000)
Buffalo Evening News (284,000)
Burlington (Vt.) Free Press (45,000)
Charleston (S.C.) News & Courier (66,000)
Charleston (W.Va.) Gazette (60,000)
Charlotte (N.C.) Observer (170,000)
Chattanooga (Tenn.) Times (64,000)
Chicago Daily Defender (21,000)
Chicago Daily News (435,000)
Chicago Sun-Times (536,000)
Chicago Tribune (768,000)
Christian Science Monitor (Mass.) (216,000)
Cincinnati Enquirer (195,000)
Cincinnati Post & Times-Star (234,000)
Cleveland Plain Dealer (403,000)
Cleveland Press (374,000)
Columbia (S.C.) State (107,000)
Columbus (Ohio) Dispatch (222,000)
Dallas Morning News (243,000)
Dallas Times Herald (232,000)
Dayton (Ohio) Daily News (113,000)
Denver Post (255,000)
Denver Rocky Mountain News (205,000)
Des Moines (Iowa) Register (246,000)
Des Moines (Iowa) Tribune (109,000)
Detroit Free Press (593,000)
Detroit News (640,000)
Emporia (Kans.) Gazette (10,000)
Fall River (Mass.) Herald-News (42,000)

Fort Worth (Tex.) Star-Telegram (98,000)
Gary (Ind.) Post-Tribune (72,000)
Hartford (Conn.) Courant (160,000)
Honolulu (Hawaii) Advertiser (74,000)
Honolulu (Hawaii) Star-Bulletin (124,000)
Houston Chronicle (303,000)
Indianapolis News (183,000)
Indianapolis Star (225,000)
Kansas City (Mo.) Star (310,000)
Kansas City (Mo.) Times (324,000)
Lincoln (Neb.) Star (27,000)
Little Rock Arkansas Democrat (74,000)
Little Rock Arkansas Gazette (108,000)
Long Island (N.Y.) Press (418,000)
Los Angeles Herald Examiner (513,000)
Los Angeles Times (966,000)
Louisville Courier-Journal (233,000)
Louisville Times (172,000)
Memphis Commercial Appeal (214,000)
Miami Herald (383,000)
Miami News (86,000)
Milwaukee Journal (347,000)
Minneapolis (Minn.) Tribune (238,000)
Nashville Tennessean (139,000)
Newark (N.J.) Star-Ledger (246,000)
New Bedford (Mass.) Standard-Times (73,000)
New Orleans States-Item (128,000)
Newsday (L.I., N.Y.) (459,000)
New York Amsterdam News (83,000)
New York Daily News (2,130,000)
New York Post (623,000)
New York Times (846,000)
Norfolk (Va.) Ledger-Star (105,000)
Norfolk (Va.) Virginian-Pilot (129,000)
Oakland (Calif.) Tribune (208,000)
Oklahoma City Daily Oklahoman (181,000)
Oklahoma City (Okla.) Times (103,000)
Orlando (Fla.) Sentinel (129,000)
Philadelphia Evening Bulletin (634,000)
Philadelphia Inquirer (464,000)

Phoenix Arizona Republic (170,000)
Pittsburgh Post-Gazette (236,000)
Pittsburgh Press (344,000)
Portland (Me.) Press Herald (56,000)
Portland (Me.) Sunday Telegram (112,000)
Portland (Ore.) Journal (135,000)
Portland Oregonian (244,000)
Providence (R.I.) Journal (67,000)
Richmond (Va.) News-Leader (121,000)
Richmond (Va.) Times-Dispatch (144,000)
Roanoke (Va.) Times (63,000)
Rochester (N.Y.) Democrat & Chronicle (143,000)
Rockford (Ill.) Register-Republic (35,000)
Sacramento (Calif.) Bee (167,000)
Saginaw (Mich.) News (61,000)
St. Louis Globe-Democrat (293,000)
St. Louis Post-Dispatch (326,000)
St. Petersburg (Fla.) Times (163,000)
Salt Lake City (Utah) Tribune (108,000)
San Diego Union (152,000)
San Francisco (Calif.) Sun Reporter (9,000)
San Juan (P.R.) Star (48,000)
Seattle Times (245,000)
Springfield (Mass.) Union (79,000)
Syracuse (N.Y.) Herald-Journal (126,000)
Toledo (Ohio) Blade (175,000)
Toronto (Ont.) Globe & Mail (264,000)
Toronto (Ont.) Star (375,000)
Tulsa (Okla.) Daily World (110,000)
Vancouver (B.C.) Province (104,000)
Wall Street Journal (497,000)
Washington Post (500,000)
Washington Star-News (302,000)
Wichita (Kans.) Beacon (125,000)
Wichita (Kans.) Eagle (60,000)
Winston-Salem (N.C.) Journal (78,000)
Winston-Salem (N.C.) Twin City Sentinel
  (46,000)
Worcester (Mass.) Telegram (63,000)

MITCHELL TELLS ERVIN COMMITTEE HE SHIELDED NIXON FROM TRUTH

After a holiday recess, the hearings of the Senate committee investigating Watergate and other campaign irregularities resumed July 10–12 with the appearance of former Attorney General John N. Mitchell.

In three days of testimony, Mitchell maintained that Nixon had not been involved in the Watergate break-in scheme or the subsequent cover-up. Mitchell said July 10 that he had withheld information from Nixon to prevent damage to the re-election campaign and the presidency. He said he was concerned not so much about Nixon's ability to withstand exposure of the Watergate case as the fact that an inquiry might lead to the exposure of other "White House horror stories," such as the break-in at the office of Daniel Ellsberg's psychiatrist, the proposed fire-bombing of the Brookings Institution and the falsification of cables relating to the 1963 death of South Vietnamese President Ngo Dinh Diem. Mitchell sought, however, to blunt earlier charges of his own involvement in the Watergate affair. He said July 10 that he "had to violently disagree" with the testimony of former campaign aide Jeb Stuart Magruder that Mitchell approved the break-in plan and gave instructions to destroy related documents. Mitchell also disputed the testimony of former presidential counsel John W. Dean 3rd concerning discussions of payments to the Watergate defendants.

At the July 11 session, Mitchell conceded that he had failed in his obligations to Nixon by not informing him of the ramifications of the Watergate affair, but he also implicated former presidential advisers John D. Ehrlichman and H. R. Haldeman in participating in a "design not to have the stories come out." Mitchell insisted that Nixon had not asked him for a complete account of Watergate.

Sens. Daniel K. Inouye (D, Hawaii) and Howard H. Baker Jr. (R, Tenn.) questioned Mitchell's credibility before the committee, pressing him on how far he might go to shield Nixon. Mitchell maintained that he had never needed to fabricate stories about Watergate; he simply withheld information. He insisted that "the good name of the President is going to be protected by the facts and by the President himself," thus, Mitchell said, it was no longer necessary for him to conceal his own role in the cover-up. Mitchell defended his involvement in the various Watergate-related episodes by insisting that in June 1972 "the most important thing to this country was the re-election of Richard Nixon. And I was not about to countenance anything that would stand in the way of that re-election."

Under intense questioning July 12 by the committee's chief counsel, Samuel Dash, Mitchell conceded that some of his testimony during the hearings differed from earlier statements. Mitchell attributed this to memory lapses and the fact that he was not "volunteering" information to earlier Watergate investigators —including the FBI—in the months following the break-in.

The New York Times

New York, N.Y., July 13, 1973

Out of John N. Mitchell's testimony has come the useful and all-purpose phrase: "White House horrors." It is a most appropriate label, not merely for the Watergate break-in and cover-up, but for the entire list of White House-sponsored illegal acts of political espionage and even broader violations of constitutionally guaranteed rights and liberties.

Even if it is ultimately established that Mr. Nixon had no personal knowledge of any or all of the horrors, or of their cover-up, he is the responsible authority at the White House. At the heart of the matter is the fact that the horrors have been committed, and that they emanated from the White House. Mr. Mitchell's defense of his alleged decision not to inform the President about the White House horrors has been that he considered Mr. Nixon's re-election of paramount importance and that, had the President been told of the "plumbers'" dirty work, he would have had to take actions and authorize disclosures that might have led to his defeat at the polls.

Such judgment as to what the President might have done or how the American people might have reacted is of course pure conjecture. What is truly alarming is that a palace guard could believe it was its right and duty to prevent the President from knowing what "horrors" had been committed in his name, in the fear that his action to halt the wrongdoing might hurt him in the hustings.

The question must ultimately be asked what might have happened had not the bungling of the White House horror crew, and subsequent pressure by courts and press, led to public exposure. Is there the slightest indication that those who claimed that they kept matters hushed up for the good of Mr. Nixon and his re-election would have come forward with the truth later on? The evidence so far is to the contrary. The cover-up continued and was intensified after the election; and the facts were not permitted to see the light of day until they either were forced into the open or were exposed by various participants in the affair as part of their personal defense.

There is increasingly persuasive evidence that, except for the Watergate bungle, the White House horrors would have continued to haunt the nation. Telephones would have continued to be tapped illegally. "Enemy" offices would have continued to be broken into. Political opponents would have continued to be sabotaged. The integrity of the F.B.I., the C.I.A., the Internal Revenue Service and other Government agencies would have continued to be undermined. Factions within the White House would have continued to spy on each other, with a view to enhancing their own secret powers.

These things are not figments of anybody's imagination. The White House horrors had come to pass; and the country was within an inch of not knowing that they might become the established routine of governmental power. In some measure, moreover, these horrors were spawned by the doctrine implied by the internal security plan of 1970 about which President Nixon did indeed know everything and which—after the late J. Edgar Hoover's refusal to cooperate—was superseded by the White House plumbers, again with the President's knowledge and approval.

Viewed in this perspective, the story of the White House horrors can no longer be treated as a tale of bungling political spies who happened to work in the White House. It contains instead all the elements of a horror story about a narrow escape from the kind of governmental power that must never again be allowed to emanate from the White House.

The Evening Star and The Washington Daily News

Washington, D.C., July 13, 1973

In several respects the three-day probing of John N. Mitchell's role in Watergate produced the most depressing and frustrating testimony yet to emerge from the Ervin Committee. It was hardly enlightening, for the former attorney general added virtually nothing in the way of conclusive factual answers to two critical questions: Who authorized the Watergate break-in of June 17, 1972? And, more importantly, what was the President's role in the instigation and cover-up of a whole raft of sordid related events?

The problem is not that Mitchell ignored either question. He quite simply dismissed the first as an insanity beyond his comprehension. As to the second, Mitchell's sworn assertion is that he tried to shield the President from involvement by deliberately and *successfully* avoiding any discussion with him on the subject of "White House horrors"—in order first to avoid jeopardizing the 1972 re-election campaign, and later to ease Mr. Nixon's path in the second term.

Can that testimony, in the first place, be believed? Well, given Mitchell's pre-eminent role as political adviser, the intimate relationship between the two men and what is known of their personal characteristics, believing it strains our credulity, as quite clearly it did that of nearly every member of the Senate panel.

But credibility is one thing and hard evidence is another. If Mitchell was backed occasionally into a corner this week, he proved to be more than a match for his interrogators most of the time in the art of legal skirmishing. His account of his own motives and conduct was essentially unshaken. And the consequence of that is that what President Nixon actually knew or didn't know from all the sources available to him, what he actually did or didn't do, will have to become clear from other sources—if indeed it is to become clear at all.

One consequence of the testimony is incontrovertible. By his own admission, repeated time after time, Mitchell placed political expediency above everything else. In the words of Senator Ervin, he "exalted the politics of the presidency" above the constitutional responsibilities of the office. At times, as attorney general, he countenanced silence on violations of law. These are awesome confessions from one who served as the chief law enforcement officer of the land. And they suggest, if nothing else, the necessity in the future to divorce the office of attorney general as thoroughly and irrevocably as possible from partisan political activity of any kind. Mitchell is by no means the first attorney general to try to serve both politics and the law. He should be the last.

The Washington Post

Times Herald

Washington, D.C., July 12, 1973

"We had to destroy the village to save it." If you read "Nixon presidency" for "village," you will see how the nightmare logic that was given voice in the course of the Vietnam war applies to the Watergate confessions of John Mitchell. Again and again during his two days of public testimony before the Ervin committee, the former Attorney General and Nixon campaign director defended the proposition that somehow the Nixon presidency and its value to the nation could only have been "saved" by—in effect—perverting its integrity and making it an accomplice to the commission of common crimes and wholesale violations of the Constitution it was sworn to uphold. Taking Mr. Mitchell's account of events at face value, along with his explanation of his own motives in participating in the Watergate cover-up, one can only be astounded by its arrogance, by the paraphrase that springs to mind: We had to destroy the President to save him.

The "we" in this case includes Mr. Mitchell and those other high (and medium high) officials of the President's government and campaign who, according to the former Attorney General, failed to inform the President of the crimes that had been committed in his behalf and sought to prevent those crimes from coming to public attention by—what else?—committing further crimes. Had the President found out about it all, Mr. Mitchell explained, he would have "lowered the boom" on the malefactors and then the public would have got wind of it and then the President himself might have been harmed in his re-election campaign. Looking about him at the political wreckage now, Mr. Mitchell curiously enough still seems to harbor some confusion as to whether he might not actually have been right in his thinking at the time. "Probably"—he concedes—he was wrong, but he doesn't seem to be sure.

And yet even that much concession is more than John Mitchell seemed capable of offering in terms of the legal and moral questions involved. His Senate interrogators were able to draw from him, in strictly practical, expedient terms, an opinion that the attempt to cover-up these things had certainly led to a messy situation. But, except for the concession Senator Weicker finally extracted from him concerning his silence on the doctor's office burglary, when they approached him on the legal and moral aspects of what he had done they generally ran into a blank wall. That was one of the strangest and most discomfiting aspects of his testimony overall. The former chief law officer of the land did not seem *quite able* to *understand* the questions concerning the propriety of entertaining (at the Justice Department, no less) recommendations for criminal activities to be undertaken with his help. And the same easy amorality and obtuseness prevailed when he was questioned on the propriety of acquiescing in a strategy which called for perjury in court on the part of high campaign officials or of failing to report to the President—let alone to law enforcement officials—that some of the most powerful men around Mr. Nixon had been breaking the law systematically. The President had to get re-elected, Mr. Mitchell explained. Wasn't that explanation enough? No? Well, he had no actual obligation himself to report these things. Would that do? No? Well, actually some of the wrongdoers would be shuffled out of the White House after the election . . . and anyway, look what the Democrats would have done with an admission of White House involvement . . . and besides that the President had more important things to do than clean the criminals out of his White House—he was after all *President*. The irony turns back and devours its own tail, but Mr. Mitchell didn't seem to notice.

The former Attorney General's wistful imagery—Gordon Liddy should have been "thrown . . . out of the window"; the implicated White House aides might have been exposed, but "it would have been simpler to have shot them all"—underlined the burden of his cynical, lawless message. There was a kind of ostentatious bravado to it, a lot of sarcasm, a lot of roughneck stuff. As with previous witnesses before the Ervin committee, we will withhold any judgment concerning the veracity of Mr. Mitchell's account of the facts—particularly those that are in dispute. But taken at his word, the former Attorney General did not seem to us to present a very savory version of the facts, and—like some of the President's other defenders—he seemed to us to present, perhaps inadvertently or of necessity, a highly damaging picture of the presidential role so far as keenness and competence are concerned. We have in mind not only the default of presidential control over the White House that Mr. Mitchell suggested and invoked, but also the fact that Mr. Nixon kept an Attorney General for three years who could be as blind to the claims of a government of laws as Mr. Mitchell—by his own account—appears to be.

Accepting Mitchell's testimony, one can speculate endlessly on the validity of his political premise of the dire consequences that may have befallen the 1972 Republican campaign if he had acted differently. Assuming that Mr. Nixon was unaware of what was going on, what would have happened if he had been told? Suppose that a clean breast had been made of the whole affair, that the President had frankly and firmly "lowered the boom" which Mitchell says he so feared. Would that, either before or after the election, have proved to be politically devastating? We are by no means sure.

But whatever the facts as to that, the great irony of Mitchell's asserted strategy of silence is that the President's position today could hardly be worse. And it is becoming more obvious with each passing day that the chief responsibility for dispelling the confusion, and for getting at the truth, rests with the President himself.

CHICAGO DAILY NEWS

Chicago, Ill., July 12, 1973

John Mitchell brought the Watergate mess into its sharpest focus Tuesday. Senate committee member Herman Talmadge asked the former attorney general if he had not put "the expediency of the election" above his responsibility to the President in his confessed Watergate cover-up, and Mitchell answered:

"In my mind the re-election of Richard Nixon, compared to what was available on the other side, was so much more important that, yes, I would put it just that way."

The committee-room audience was startled, and it had a right to be. For here, from the man who had been the principal law-enforcement officer of the United States, was the flat assertion that the end easily justified the dirty, unlawful means, even though those means involved trying to cheat the opposition presidential candidate out of his chance for election, and the voters out of their free choice.

Mitchell added that in hindsight, he thought his judgment might have been faulty. But the implication was that he wasn't sure even now.

There were other remarkable aspects of Mitchell's testimony — the instances where he contradicted his own prior statements as well as the testimony of those other two self-contradictors, John W. Dean III and Jeb Stuart Magruder. Sorting out the truth from the vast fabric of lies and counter-lies in this miserable case is getting to look like a hopeless task.

But at least the American people have now been brought into close range with the evil core of Watergate, and we hope they won't avert their eyes because of its ugliness.

Historian Daniel J. Boorstin sheds useful light on this core in pointing out that the Watergate scandal indicates the rise of a "cult of personality" — a phrase most familiarly applied to the apparatuses created around Soviet and Chinese dictators.

In the group around President Nixon — as in those around Stalin and Mao — Boorstin notes the exuberant dedication to the leader and a growing ruthlessness in his behalf: "the desire to kill off the enemy, the desire to follow the leader wherever he leads, the refusal to compromise with others, the lack of liberal charity toward your electoral opponent." The whole Watergate affair has suited that characterization perfectly, and Mitchell's matter-of-fact assertion summed it up.

Boorstin also noted some more positive aspects of Watergate — for example, that "the separation of powers concept of American government is proving itself in some interesting new ways. . . .

"I think this episode has probably had the effect abroad of dramatizing our concern with certain standards of public morality. . . . And it has dramatized the power of Congress. It has dramatized the integrity of our courts, and it will probably have the effect of making anybody who sits in the presidential chair be more scrupulous of his use of the government — of the powers of the Presidency."

We agree with Boorstin that while Watergate has posed a challenge to American institutions, those institutions are proving equal to the challenge. What we hope the public perceives however, is the need for the institutions to press their counterattack to the end, and for the free press to continue reciting the details, however embarrassing they may be to the principals and to the nation. Only the truth can keep a democracy operating.

ARKANSAS DEMOCRAT

Little Rock, Ark., July 12, 1973

There were only two parts of John Mitchell's first five hours of testimony that we found convincing.

One came when he said it was vital to re-elect Richard Nixon "compared to what was available on the other side." Despite the scattered boos heard in the committee room, the public agrees with Mitchell. The Gallup Poll last week showed that if the election were held today, Richard Nixon would get 53 per cent of the vote and George McGovern would get only 47 per cent. This is a pretty sad comment upon poor McGovern, in view of the revelations of Watergate and the number of people who are getting on TV and blaming the President for them.

John Mitchell, in fact, is the first witness not to point the finger at the President, and this is the only other time we found him believable. We do not think the President ordered anyone to break the law in order to re-elect him or to protect him.

We can not be that positive about John Mitchell, especially after his opening day's testimony. His explanations strain rational thinking and his recantations have a hollow ring. Here was a smart lawyer, one of the heads of a firm employing 800 persons, a man who has spent his life judging people, making tough decisions and giving advice so highly regarded that he was one of the most prosperous lawyers in the nation. Now why would a man like that even listen, much less associate or hire, perjurers, burglars, and conspirators? If someone else hired them, why didn't he get rid of them the first time they exposed their shabbiness? And, as Sen. Herman Talmadge asked, if he hadn't been able to stop what was going on, why, as the chief law enforcement officer of the nation and Mr. Nixon's closest adviser, didn't he at least tell the President about the mess they were in?

Could it be that Mitchell was responsible for the mess? Or, if not responsible for starting it, could he be the one who planned to cover it up? Although they may have larceny in their hearts, we have been unable to believe that hired-hands like Dean, Magruder and Liddy would have gone so far for so long without someone in a high place giving the okay.

John Mitchell may not be that man. But he is also not the indecisive, uninformed pushover he made himself appear to be in his testimony.

THE TENNESSEAN

Nashville, Tenn., July 15, 1973

"These rights robbers (have) a monstrous idea . . . Their leaders have misled them into believing their cause is so right they can commit any wrong." —Atty. Gen. John N. Mitchell, May 10, 1971

MR. John N. Mitchell, former Attorney General of the United States and a man who once said a society "must encourage the best and discourage the worst" in human behavior, admitted that in the case of Watergate, he did neither.

Mr. Mitchell, with hands shaking perceptibly whenever he lifted them from the witness table, stolidly denied he had authorized the political intelligence gathering schemes, and the allegations made by previous witnesses.

Although he frequently professed an absence of recollection about key events described in previous testimony, Mr. Mitchell stuck to his story that he had minimal involvement in the coverup and that he deliberately withheld information from President Nixon about the bugging, the cover-up and "White House horror stories" to prevent any damage to the President's bid for re-election.

Sen. Herman Talmadge asked: "Am I to understand from your response that you placed the expediency of the next election above your responsibilities as an intimate to advise the President of the peril that surrounds him? Here was the deputy campaign director involved, here were his two closest associates in his office involved, all around him were people involved in crime, perjury, accessory after the fact, and you deliberately refused to tell him that? Would you state that the expediency of the election was more important than that?"

Mr. Mitchell: 'Senator. I think you have put it exactly correct. In my mind, the re-election of Richard Nixon, compared with what was available on the other side, was so much more important that I put it in just that context."

In sum, the election of Mr. Nixon was more important than the laws of the land, more important than the ideals of a free society, and more important than the principles of justice which Mr. Mitchell, at an earlier time, had sworn to uphold.

There is a rare irony in the fact that in the years previous to Watergate, both Mr. Nixon and his attorney general spoke of the necessity to cease the granting of special immunities and moral sanctions to those who deliberately violate the public laws.

Mr. Nixon once put it this way: "Let us now lay to rest the deleterious doctrine that those who speak for popular or favored 'causes' are entitled to favored considerations before the bar of justice. We must re-establish again the principle that men are accountable for what they do. . ."

The President's re-election was a popular "cause for which men high in government committed crimes. And John Newton Mitchell admitted he was interested in withholding the truth from the grand jury and the American people although he knew the public laws had been broken. "Yes," he said, "we wanted to keep the lid on. We were not volunteering anything."

As he sat testifying before the Senate committee, it was easy to remember Mr. Mitchell's most famous line during his part in the Nixon administration: "Don't judge us by what we say, but by what we do."

*   *   *

Sadly, that has become the standard of judgment for the men responsible for Watergate and its coverup, including the man who was once the chief law enforcement officer of the land.

THE RICHMOND NEWS LEADER
Richmond, Va., July 16, 1973

John Mitchell and Richard Moore appeared before the Senate Watergate Committee last week, and the treatment they received was dissimilar to the treatment dished out to practically every other prior witness. Indeed, the performance of the committee last week erased any vagrant hope that equanimity and even-handedness might still lie at the heart of its deliberations. The committee's intention now is clear: It is not so much to get at the truth, as it is to hoist Richard Nixon by his thumbs.

Let it not be said that in connection with Watergate there were not many mischievous deeds carried out by persons in the Nixon administration. Almost everyone acknowledges that those deeds occurred, and deplores them. The effort now is supposed to be directed at determining who was responsible for them. Yet the goal of the committee and its enthusiasts in the press seems to be to discredit those who deny any complicity on the part of Richard Nixon, and to laud those who say that he pulled all the strings.

John Mitchell was the first witness who did not bow before the committee with the goodie-two-shoes deference of the teacher's pet. Mitchell was sardonic, categorical. He countered countless "do you-mean-to-tell-me" questions with unperturbed responses that yes, that was precisely what he meant to tell them. And he was plausible: He did not tell the President about the Watergate cover-up, he said, because to have done so would have elicited the wrath of the President — and brought consequent harm to his re-election campaign. Yes, said Mitchell: Keeping the cover-up from Mr. Nixon was imperative, given the prospect of, say, a President McGovern.

The committee fell back in disarray. But soon it was on the attack again, ripping into Richard Moore. Poor Moore. He is reminiscent of one's sixth-grade arithmetic teacher — kindly, somewhat absent-minded, eminently good. And his testimony was sensational. John Dean had suggested that Moore could confirm much of what Dean had said. On the contrary, Moore flatly contradicted the essential Dean charge — *i.e.*, that Mr. Nixon knew of the cover-up prior to March 21. Not so, said Moore; what's more, he said, on March 20 Dean told Moore that the President did not know. Senator Ervin, whose impartiality is suspect, objected to a question from Senator Gurney intended to ascertain Moore's impression of what Dean knew. Any answer to such a question, said Senator Ervin, would have to be based on surmise. Never mind that Dean's own surmises about the President knowing of the cover-up on September 15 were accepted by most of the committee members as gospel truth.

The treatment of the Mitchell and Moore testimony by the anti-Nixon press has been as unfair as their treatment by the committee. The Mitchell testimony was accompanied by newspaper accounts suggesting he was lying. And the astonishing Moore testimony, the first by anyone not implicated in the whole Watergate mess, was played very low. Said *The Washington Post* report: "In a prepared account differing from Dean's far more in tone and interpretation than in fact, Moore said that on the basis of his conversations with both Dean and Mr. Nixon earlier this year it is his 'deep conviction... that the critical facts about the Watergate' did not reach the President until Dean supplied them to him last March 21." *The New York Times* placed its account under a two-column headline at the fold. Other headlines of the same size on the same page read: "Podell Indicted on Charge of Taking Airline Bribes," and "Slaying to Avenge Holdups Charged to Sonny Carson."

The anti-Nixon people on the committee and in the press know that most of the public believes the last person it hears. They do not want the public to believe Mitchell and Moore. So the public has been implicitly told that Mitchell was not appropriately servile, and probably lied; that Moore is loyal to the President and consequently not credible. This is the impression left by the committee's incivility in its handling of these two witnesses, and by the press's reporting of their testimony. It is too bad. And it is yet another reason why the investigation of Watergate-related matters should be conducted not before TV cameras, but before a grand jury. What we have now is a political hanging party.

Los Angeles Times
Los Angeles, Calif., July 13, 1973

John N. Mitchell's testimony is a self-portrait of a trusted Cabinet member, a confidant of the President, who betrayed that trust with irresponsibility.

Mitchell's extraordinary irresponsibility is nowhere better illustrated than in his testimony that he concealed the Watergate break-in and the "White House horrors" from Mr. Nixon because he thought that to do otherwise might somehow hurt the President's reelection campaign. Mitchell said he was convinced that the President would have acted against the conspirators and criminals, forcing public disclosure and thereby embarrassing the prospects for reelection.

That was not the only alarming admission by Mitchell. In his three days of testimony before the Senate committee, he acknowledged that he had maintained in a position of authority and trust a man who had proposed a campaign of criminal activities to the reelection committee, that he had accepted without protest and permitted without objection the commission of perjury by a man who had been his principal assistant in the committee, that he had suppressed information pertinent to a federal trial.

And yet this man, so close to the President, so trusted, saw these not as flagrant breaches of that trust but as ultimate acts of loyalty to Mr. Nixon.

If Mitchell's testimony is to be believed, President Nixon must also be judged a man of extraordinary irresponsibility. For Mitchell now has told us that the President, despite their long and close friendship and association, never, in those critical days, turned to Mitchell to find out what was going on, not even at the peak of confusion that the President so dramatically described in his memorandum of May 22. Never once, the committee was told, did the President's curiosity lead him to pick up the phone and call one of the few men who might have had the answer. It is a portrayal of splendid isolation that strains belief.

But is Mitchell's testimony to be believed? That, at this moment, is for each senator, each citizen to decide. Mitchell has sought to challenge the fundamental assertions of Jeb Stuart Magruder that tied Mitchell to the break-in plot and attributed to Mitchell the go-ahead on G. Gordon Liddy's plan for "dirty tricks." He has sought to challenge the fundamental assertions of John W. Dean III that linked the President with the coverup.

We can only say that Mitchell's testimony has not, as we see it, lifted the heavy burden of suspicion placed on the White House by Dean's testimony. The detailed web of events that Dean so convincingly wove has not been torn, not yet. Dean's testimony, like Magruder's before him, benefited from an appearance of determined revelation. Mitchell's testimony, like Maurice H. Stans' before him, suffered from an appearance of guarded reluctance.

So it is that a response by the President, when he recovers from the unfortunate viral pneumonia that has hospitalized him, emerges as more important than ever.

We have already said that Mr. Nixon's response to the committee last Saturday, particularly his refusal to make available White House documents, was unsatisfactory. And we now have been told that he has taken further steps to deny documentation. This is an abuse of executive privilege, a false interpretation of those elements of the Constitution designed to protect the division of federal power. Nothing in the tradition of executive privilege, nothing in the Constitution is intended to conceal criminal activity.

This makes of enormous importance the forthcoming meeting between Mr. Nixon and Sen. Sam J. Ervin Jr. (D-N.C.), chairman of the Senate Watergate committee. The committee has shown restraint and wisdom in trying to avoid a constitutional confrontation that would be inherent should it try to subpoena executive documents. We agree with the claim of the committee for access to those materials touching on criminal activities.

What the committee seeks here is not an intrusion into the President's business, his function as national leader. The committee seeks only materials made relevant to a criminal investigation by sworn testimony, materials also germane to the work of the special investigator in the Department of Justice. To make these available violates no constitutional principle. On the contrary, it satisfies the necessity of the law, not to weaken the Presidency but to strengthen it by separating from it those things that are criminal.

NIXON CITES CONSTITUTIONAL DUTY IN REFUSING TO HAND OVER PAPERS

President Nixon formally notified the Senate Watergate committee July 7 that he would not testify before the committee or permit it access to presidential papers. The President stated his own position in a letter to the committee chairman, Sen. Sam Ervin (D, N.C.). Nixon emphasized in his letter that his action was "based on my constitutional obligation to preserve intact the powers and prerogatives of the presidency and not upon any desire to withhold information relevant to your inquiry."

"At an appropriate time during your hearings," he wrote, "I intend to address publicly the subjects you are considering." He also said his staff was under instructions to cooperate fully with the committee in furnishing "information pertinent to your inquiry." Elsewhere in the President's statement, however, he said "the White House will continue to cooperate fully with the committee in furnishing information relevant to its investigation except in those instances where I determine that meeting the committee's demands would violate my constitutional responsibility to defend the office of the presidency against encroachment by other branches." As for his refusal to provide presidential papers, Nixon said: "No president could function if the private papers of his office, prepared by his personal staff, were open to public scrutiny. Formulation of sound public policy requires that the President and his personal staff be able to communicate among themselves in complete candor, and that their tentative judgments, their exploration of alternatives, and their frank comments on issues and personalities at home and abroad remain confidential." He concluded "that if I were to testify before the committee irreparable damage would be done to the constitutional principle of separation of powers."

Sen. Ervin's reaction to the Nixon letter was critical. He said later July 7 he believed that the committee had authority to subpoena presidential testimony and papers but that he opposed such action. Ervin cited precedents going back to an 1807 Supreme Court ruling requiring that presidential documents relating to a treason trial be produced. Committee vice chairman Howard H. Baker Jr. (R, Tenn.) said July 8 the separation of powers doctrine barred the committee from subpoenaing the President, but he expressed hope "some other means can be worked out" to obtain Nixon's account of events. Sen. Daniel K. Inouye (D, Hawaii) said testimony from Nixon was "vital to his future." While "silence does not necessarily indicate guilt," he said, "unfortunately many people do interpret silence in that manner."

While steadfastly refusing to testify or provide White House documents to the Senate Watergate committee, President Nixon consented July 12 to meet privately with Ervin. A White House spokesman later emphasized that Nixon's acquiescence to a meeting was merely a "courtesy" to Ervin and did not constitute any retreat from the President's position regarding presidential testimony or executive privilege.

White House Press Secretary Ronald L. Ziegler had said July 2 that President Nixon would speak out on charges made against him in the Watergate case after the select Senate committee completed the first phase of its investigative hearings. That phase, focusing on the Watergate break-in and subsequent cover-up, was not expected to be finished before August.

The New York Times
New York, N.Y., July 10, 1973

President Nixon has a strong constitutional case in refusing to testify before the Senate Watergate investigation. The committee has indeed been mindful of the separation-of-powers doctrine from the start, and has never made any serious move to subpoena the President.

But in politics and the practice of leadership, as opposed to constitutional law, Mr. Nixon's problem remains serious, and all the evidence suggests that he still cannot bring himself to see this problem for what it is. It is simply that allegations of serious wrongdoing have been made, though not proven, against the President and his most trusted lieutenants.

Instead of acknowledging that he understands the gravity of these charges and moving promptly to refute them in a convincing form, Mr. Nixon has only taken refuge in constitutional abstractions, in a Constitution, moreover, which he showed little reluctance to bend to his own purposes when he has felt it necessary to continue war in Indochina or hold back public funds which the Congress had duly appropriated.

* * *

It is at least arguable that the President may have the legal right to act in this way; but is it right for him to do so if he has the slightest awareness of the need to restore public trust in himself and his Presidency? It is demonstrably true that a very large number of Americans, irrespective of party, believe that Mr. Nixon has behaved dishonestly about the Watergate conspiracy. Under such circumstances, it is hardly effective leadership to wreathe oneself in flag and Constitution and trust that all bad feeling will go away.

In his letter to Senator Ervin over the weekend, the President said that he would publicly address the Watergate accusations "at an appropriate time." That promise is certainly to be welcomed, but Mr. Nixon must realize that he has no great reserves of either time or credibility to draw upon. Normally a forthright Presidential statement would clear the air, as Americans are naturally disposed to believe the President of the United States when he says something. But what is one to think of Presidential testimony that changes to adapt to each new disclosure; of the attempt to disown an officially prepared document (the memorandum submitted for the Senate's interrogation of John W. Dean 3d) as a "White House statement" but not a "White House position"; or even of the President's own reluctant admission that he had approved a plan for clearly illegal activity, though it was presumably never put into effect?

* * *

Because he is President, Mr. Nixon finds it inappropriate to appear before a Congressional committee. But because he is President, he should have an interest in convincing the public that he is not implicated in any criminal conspiracies. The surest way of refuting his accusers before he is convicted in the public mind by default is to submit to the same test of veracity that the accusers went through: testimony under oath, in public, with full opportunity for interrogation and cross-examination. In his own political interest, Mr. Nixon would do well to volunteer to be interrogated, perhaps by the special Watergate prosecutors or by representatives of the Congress, or both, under special conditions that all could agree upon and that would leave the constitutional prerogatives intact.

At this late stage in the Watergate crisis, it is hard to see any other way in which Americans could once again be encouraged to believe in the President.

The Courier-Journal

Louisville, Ky., July 14, 1973

PRESIDENT NIXON'S hospitalization with an unfortunate attack of viral pneumonia doubtless will delay his meeting with Senator Ervin, chairman of the select committee, in order to sort out the White House position on documentary evidence about Watergate. That could be all to the good, in giving Mr. Nixon more time to reflect on the wisdom of provoking a historic legislative-executive confrontation over matters having directly to do with his responsibilities as president.

The repeated changes of course by the White House on the issue of testimony by aides or ex-aides and on their files have been an unwarranted obstruction to the Watergate inquiries from the start, and have hurt Mr. Nixon's claim to be interested only in seeing that all the facts come out. It has been difficult, in fact, to avoid regarding the twists and turns of administration strategy not as concern for the Constitution but as fear of implication in unforgiveable abuses of official responsibility.

Clearly, no President should be compelled to accept a subpoena requiring his personal appearance before a congressional inquiry. The independence of the executive branch would indeed be compromised if Congress were to get into the habit of calling presidents up to Capitol Hill for grillings on every matter.

But while the concept lawyers and historians know as "executive privilege" is firm in this sense, it can be pushed too far. That is what Mr. Nixon has been doing. If there is no constitutional or legal case for denying John Dean a copy of documents from his former White House files, and there is no case for refusing to give the committee certified copies of documents on which it has second-hand reports, what is the President's motivation?

The same question could be raised with respect to Mr. Nixon's use of "executive privilege" to refuse a subpoena for Agriculture Department memoranda on the milk-price decisions of 1971, when enormous donations from the dairy co-ops allegedly influenced the White House to shift gears on the price-support level. Again, as in his assertion last spring (soon reversed) that executive privilege extended to every single employe of the federal government because the President is their boss, Mr. Nixon has been busy converting a legitimate constitutional protection into a farce.

Only an administration with something to hide could quibble with the Ervin Committee as the President's spokesmen, and Mr. Nixon himself, have done over the John Dean papers. Last May 22, the President promised the Ervin Committee full cooperation, specifically mentioning Mr. Dean's right to copy information needed to anchor his testimony before the Senate panel. The next day, "White House lawyers" contradicted that decision; they prepared guidelines that specifically forbade Mr. Dean's making notes on his former White House files. But the guidelines were kept secret.

Then, in his July 6 letter to Senator Ervin, President Nixon stressed two refusals: He would make no appearance under committee subpoena, and he would refuse to transmit White House documents under a subpoena. Clear enough, but this recent version of the ground rules made no mention of the committee's standing request for aid to Mr. Dean, who is supplementing the record of his testimony before the committee. Then, four days later, a White House spokesman at last made public the May 23 decision (contradicting the President's promise of the previous day) to refuse Mr. Dean any help, or even the right to make copies or notes.

The performance reminded Senator Ervin of an ordinary rule of evidence which he stated in his questioning of former Attorney General Mitchell Wednesday: "When a person refuses to produce evidence . . . an inference may be drawn that the reason he does not produce it is because he knows it to be unfavorable to him." Mr. Mitchell disagreed, once more citing the tortured "separation of powers." But Mr. Mitchell already had so clearly established that he believes the ends justify the means—in his testimony that he would have overlooked almost anything to get Mr. Nixon re-elected—that his credentials for fair interpretation of the law or the Constitution are in grave doubt.

Senator Ervin's aren't. His experience as a lawyer, judge and chairman of congressional committees that have studied the Constitution and the relations of the branches of the federal government have given him a firm understanding of how far "executive privilege" can be extended. He conceded, again while questioning Mr. Mitchell, that when the President is engaged in performing "in a lawful manner one of his constitutional or legal duties" he is entitled to keep secret the confidential discussions he and his aides exchange. That is the exact historic meaning of executive privilege.

But note the words, "in a lawful manner." Because of them, executive privilege cannot cover whatever information a president or presidential aides might possess about criminal activities. The White House is not a royal court; there is none of the untouchability or unerring correctness of monarchy about the presidency. Just as soon as he recovers his health, President Nixon should come forward with the information the committee seeks, especially if he wishes, as his daughter and other spokesmen have said, "to get on with the business at hand" in his foreign and domestic responsibilities.

If all is as the President says it is, then the Watergate case is history—but a very important history of an institutional illness whose remedy Congress is exploring. The separate, but related, issue — ably pursued in Senator Baker's questions—of how the committee can obtain the President's own account of his knowledge of the Watergate incidents and the cover-up, could be resolved rather easily once the issue of the documents is cleared up.

The constitutional separation of the presidency and Congress must be protected. But it would not be impaired by the President's voluntary submission of evidence that is crucial to the work of the select committee, without casually pushing the disagreement to the level of a constitutional confrontation. It is time—and we hope the Ervin-Nixon talks will be the occasion for it—for the President to stop using the cloak of executive privilege to cover not only the legitimate concerns of the presidency but also the possible crimes and other "horrors" buried in those White House files.

The Hartford Courant

Hartford, Conn., July 8, 1973

President Nixon has now refused to testify before the Senate Select Watergate Committee "under any circumstance," and the reason he gives finds him in good company.

His remarks are made in a letter to committee chairman, Senator Ervin, and state he has concluded that if he were to testify, "irreparable damage would be done to the constitutional principal of separation of powers."

"The constitutional doctrine of separation of powers is fundamental to our structure of government," he said. "Its preservation is vital. In this respect, the duty of every President to protect and defend the constitutional rights and powers of his office is an obligation that runs directly to the people of the country."

Mr. Nixon is following a long line of precedents, commencing with George Washington himself, and extending to the late President Truman. Indeed, Mr. Truman named others who have declined to respond to subpoenas or demands for information of various kinds by Congress, including Presidents Jefferson, Monroe, Jackson, Tyler, Polk, Fillmore, Buchanan, Lincoln, Grant, Hayes, Cleveland, Theodore Roosevelt, Coolidge, Hoover, and Franklin Roosevelt.

This cannot fail to be an impressive array for supporting President Nixon's refusal, coming as it does from all varieties of political opinion. The underlying contention is that every branch of government is designed to be "a coordinative representative of the will of the people—that in maintaining his rights against any trespass of Congress, a President defends not himself but the people."

It is interesting and important that even a House Judiciary Committee of the Forty-Fifth Congress declared "The Executive is as independent of either house of Congress as either house of Congress is independent of him, and they cannot call for the records of his actions, or the action of his officers against his consent, any more than he can call for journal or records of House or Senate . . . Otherwise the President would become a mere arm of the legislative branch."

To those who would suggest this is only a legalistic dodge to avoid speaking out on Watergate, Mr. Nixon gives a pointed answer. In his letter to Senator Ervin he emphasizes his decision is based on Constitutional obligation and not on any desire to withhold information relevant to the Watergate inquiry.

Indeed, with all the investigations going on into the Watergate incident, it seems almost impossible that the facts will not come out. And Mr. Nixon stresses again his statement of May 22 when he directed that the right of executive privilege "as to any testimony concerning possible criminal conduct" no longer be invoked for present or former members of the White House Staff. In the case of his former counsel, John Dean, he also has waived the attorney-client privilege.

This certainly leaves wide avenues of probing completely open to the Select Committee. In addition, Mr. Nixon himself has said that when the hearings are concluded, he will address publicly the subjects the committee is considering.

We feel sure he will do this. And as The Courant has emphasized before, we hope he will do so at a conference of the news media, answering such questions and issues as may be raised there. We still believe this way he can best make plain the whole truth about Watergate and the White House to the satisfaction of the country, and dispel the fogs of confusion, allegation and innuendo that have troubled the nation so long. But as for going before the Senate Select Committee, we do not believe he should do so.

The Boston Globe

Boston, Mass., July 10, 1973

As the Senate Watergate hearings go on and on, two things have become clear. President Richard Nixon must answer all questions that have arisen in the scandal, both for his own and the nation's sake, and the sands of time are running out for him to do this with success.

The problem is no longer when, for it must be soon. The problem for the President is how, and in what forum. According to the White House, his statements will come in a forum that is "appropriate." Since its precise nature has not been disclosed, the possibilities seem worth exploring.

It should be stated at the outset that although conservatives on the Right and radicals on the Left have been calling for Mr. Nixon's resignation or impeachment, neither step at present is either viable or called for. Serious though the charges undoubtedly are, all of the evidence is simply not in. This is in part because the President himself has not spoken out since May 22 as he should have. But in any case, both prudence and fairness dictate that the call for such an action or judgment not be made at this time.

Yet the question remains of the President's speaking out, and it must be answered soon.

Eight days ago in a letter to Chairman Sam J. Ervin (D-N.C.) Mr. Nixon declared that under no circumstances would he testify before the Senate committee or for that matter respond to a subpoena for presidential papers. He said that to do otherwise would violate his constitutional duty to preserve the independence of the Presidency and the principle of separation of powers.

Last Thursday President Nixon agreed to meet privately with Chairman Ervin at an unnamed date. The same day, he was hospitalized, and there has been no agreement reached to avoid what the committee has called a "fundamental constitutional confrontation."

It could involve, eventually, not only presidential papers but a presidential appearance.

Two points in this controversy, incidentally, show how circumstances can alter cases and give rise to irony. Mr. Nixon's letter cited a communication from the late President Truman, after he had left office, refusing to respond to a subpoena to testify before the old House Committee on Un-american Activities. Mr. Nixon, as a Congressman and critic of Truman, had launched his national career as a member of that committee.

The other point concerns a precedent Mr. Nixon did not cite, for it went in the other direction. Supreme Court Chief Justice John Marshall ruled that a subpoena could constitutionally be served on President Thomas Jefferson after counsel for Aaron Burr, on trial for treason, called for a presidential document concerning a Gen. Wilkinson that would be helpful to Burr's defense. The irony here is that last year a US Supreme Court majority, most of them Mr. Nixon's appointees, cited in a footnote Chief Justice Marshall's ruling to show in the newsmen's privilege case that no one, not even the President, was exempt from a subpoena. But more of this later.

A part of the present problem is that we are far beyond legalisms and even constitutionality. For it is now all too clear that much of what the administration has done has been unconstitutional. And this must explain why Prof. James MacGregor Burns, the noted historian, has called this the "worst crisis of the Presidency that the United States has ever seen."

Perhaps that is why the US Supreme Court's official historian, Prof. Paul Freund of Harvard Law School, tells us that today, "Everybody is his own constitutional lawyer, and it is frankly bigger than a legal question." It is in this sense like the Vietnam war, which transcended, and in our view violated, the Constitution.

If the law could be relied upon to predict what the courts will do, it might say, or at least used to say, that the President need not respond to a Senate subpoena. But this does not answer the entire question either for Mr. Nixon or for the country. He must, in some way, answer the charges.

What is an "appropriate forum"? Surely not a press conference, where the format and the awe and respect for the high office inhibit the necessary follow-up of questions and where, in any event, the testimony is unsworn. And for the President to make a statement without any questions asked, or in answer to questions written in advance, or asked in the privacy of the White House, would be less than satisfactory, too.

It is impossible, as Sen. Ervin has said, to cross-examine a written statement.

Let us assume, as seems likely, that the courts would not compel the President to appear before the Senate committee. In this case Mr. Nixon's problem is still the same. He still has to answer. And the Senate, legally, is in a weaker position than a federal grand jury investigating a crime. This was the Jefferson-Burr-Marshall situation, and Jefferson avoided having to appear in court by sending over a paraphrase of the sought document which then helped to clear Burr.

The Ervin committee is concerned, legalistically speaking, with the need for new legislation, not with a man's alleged guilt or innocence. But a grand jury would be directly concerned with the latter. And there is now no question that the Watergate hearings will lead inexorably to such court proceedings, for it is now clear that perjury and obstruction of justice and other crimes have been committed.

This means that the question of a presidential subpoena might in any case have to be decided by special prosecutor Archibald Cox and the courts. And that can only happen, it appears, after considerable delay, well into next year possibly. Meanwhile the American nation, its economy disorganized and its fundamental beliefs and traditions corroding, must suffer through a prolonged constitutional crisis. This our nation does not need at all.

The question, then, is really not legal or constitutional, but practical and political. President Nixon has an overwhelming political obligation to answer questions. Regardless of whether he has a legal obligation to do so, he should want to appear voluntarily before the committee. And he should be willing to tell not only all he knows or does not know about Watergate and its cover-up, but about such other matters as his meeting at San Clemente with US District Judge Matt Byrne, who was called there not once but twice during the Ellsberg trial.

It could be, and we hope it will be the smartest thing Mr. Nixon has ever done. He would have the odds in his favor, unless the truth is not in his favor.

In any case, Mr. Nixon should act like a President. He should not appear to hide. He should speak out. And he should answer the questions.

ALBUQUERQUE JOURNAL

Albuquerque, N.M., July 14, 1973

President Nixon's sudden and fanatic devotion to the fictional principle of executive privilege reminds one of the drinking driver who flees the scene of an accident because he'd rather face the penalty for a hit-and-run charge than betray the evidence of his drinking.

A careful reading of the constitution of the United States — would that New Mexico's constitution were nearly so concise — fails to turn up even a remote hint of executive privilege. The document is most explicit in its delineation of legislative privilege, and it offers strong implications supporting the doctrine of judicial privilege which has flourished for decades.

Article II, which sets up the nation's executive power, however, is preponderant in the enumeration of the duties and responsibilities of the executive. Among such responsibilities are the mandates that "he shall, from time to time, give the Congress information of the state of the union" and "shall take care that the laws be faithfully executed"

Nor does the constitution provide that the legislative, executive and judicial divisions of government function each in its own vacuum. Many of the executive's powers, for example, are to be exercised only "by and with the advice and consent of the Senate."

Nor does the durable constitution abrogate the executive's rights, privileges, responsibilities or liabilities as a citizen of the United States.

In an atmosphere of widespread distrust, flagging confidence, deteriorating dollar values, spiraling inflation, immunity and special privilege for friends, surveillance and harassment for "enemies" and a general breakdown of official credibility, the state of the union today is "sick abed and dying."

And, in such a state, it is the President's clear-cut duty, both as executive and citizen, to make his report to Congress — under oath, if necessary — and submit all relevant documentation in his custody.

Otherwise, the only alternative is a legislative authority as uninformed or misinformed, as crippled and ineffective, as void of credibility as the executive branch finds itself today.

THE CINCINNATI ENQUIRER

Cincinnati, Ohio, July 14, 1973

PRESIDENT NIXON is pursuing what he must recognize as a risky course in declining (1) to testify personally before the Senate committee inquiring into the Watergate matter or (2) to volunteer a series of White House documents of interest to committee members.

The most obvious risk is that the American people, who tend to adhere to the sometimes-valid notion that an honest man has nothing to fear from interrogation (or, for that matter, from wiretapping), will interpret his position to be an admission of guilt. It would be so easy, the reasoning runs, for Mr. Nixon to dispose of his accusers' allegations once and for all by the simple expedient of subjecting himself to the committee's cross-examination.

Those who are convinced of the logic of that simplistic view probably will not be moved by Mr. Nixon's contention that, by choosing his own time and his own forum for an elaboration of his views on the Watergate matter, he is in reality defending the prerogatives — indeed the constitutional mission — of the high office he holds.

Those who have delved into the history of the presidency, however, recognize the soundness of Mr. Nixon's position. They also recognize his as the course not of cowardice, but of courage. The easy way, after all, is rarely the courageous way.

For Mr. Nixon to subject himself to the interrogation of a congressional committee would be to establish the committee as an agency representing the American people with credentials superior to his. A Congress, one of whose committees had wrested such as acknowledgment of power from the White House, would be extremely reluctant to hand it back intact. A more likely consequence would be that Mr. Nixon and his immediate successors would find themselves bedeviled by a Congress intent upon seizing the initiative from the White House on a whole range of issues from government spending to foreign policy.

There is an instructive example of how perniciously presidential authority can be eroded by the troubled White House years of Andrew Johnson, the nation's 17th President and the only President to be impeached.

At issue, basically, was how the defeated South should be treated in the days that followed the Civil War. Mr. Johnson, an antisecessionist Southerner himself, was committed to a policy of amicable reconstruction as defined by President Lincoln before his assassination. But congressional leadership was in the hands of a cabal determined to treat the South as occupied enemy territory indefinitely.

Emboldened by what they perceived as Mr. Johnson's reluctance to assert the prerogatives of his office, the leaders in Congress ulitmately produced the Tenure in Office Act, which declared that no President could dismiss a member of his Cabinet without congressional consent.

It was his determination to challenge the constitutionality of that statute that became ammunition for his impeachment.

It is probably true that every new President ultimately undergoes a struggle with Congress to determine whether the executive or the legislative branch is going to have the upper hand. The Presidents who lost that struggle — or else didn't bother to wage it — are the Presidents history has forgotten. Those who grasped the nettle are those who have emerged as significant, if not great, Presidents.

The framers of the Constitution, in all likelihood, intended the executive and the legislative branches to be roughly equal in power — each a check against the other. The system works best when each asserts its power, when neither simply acquiesces in the assertions of the other.

Mr. Nixon may be more sensitive than many of his predecessors about the powers of his office for the obvious reason that he has served one full term with a hostile Congress and faces the prospect of serving a second in the same circumstances. But even if Congress were controlled by Mr. Nixon's own party, there would still be a struggle: that is the nature of the system — a system that Mr. Nixon is determined to defend, even at the price of his personal discomfort and embarrassment.

The San Diego Union

San Diego, Calif., July 6, 1973

Front page headlines erupted across the United States of America when President Nixon said recently that he would speak again to the Watergate issue when the time was right. His statement should not have come as a surprise to anyone. Nobody indicted for a crime for week after week in front of millions of television viewers without having the chance to exercise his most fundamental legal protections could remain silent on so grave an issue, either for personal reasons or for the sake of the office that he holds.

Altogether, the need for additional presidential discussion on Watergate is a grim testimonial to the political impact of the Senate committee hearings. Of equal importance, it is a reminder of the corrosive effect that those hearings can have on the confidence of Americans.

Only six weeks ago, on May 22, the President said plainly: "I had no prior knowledge of the Watergate operation . . . I took no part in, nor was I aware of any subsequent efforts that may have been made to cover up Watergate."

There is something wrong in placing such categorial assertions by the nation's highest elected official on the same plane as those of such persons as John Dean—a man who by his own admission had a major role in the break-in at the Democratic National Headquarters and who conspired afterwards to protect the guilty from punishment for the crime.

Nevertheless this is what happened in no small degree last week. This melancholy fact underlines the ability of the Senate committee investigating Watergate and other campaign activities to manipulate public opinion through the theatrics of the video screen and to politicize what should be essentially a legal process.

While all of us may applaud the zeal with which the truth about Watergate is being sought, we also must realize that ends do not justify means. It is plain in this case that an extra-legal political trial can have implications far beyond what happens to the present cast of Watergate characters.

Nor is there any danger that the development of the whole truth about Watergate is dependent solely on the Ervin Committee and its televised proceedings. Right now there are five congressional committees busy investigating the break-in. There are four parallel administrative criminal investigations and four civil suits. When all is said and done, all of the facts have to come out. Unless the system is upset, the issue will be settled by the courts in the fashion contemplated by the Constitution.

This is another way of saying that the dangers of the Senate Watergate committee, proceeding as it now is, outweigh its potential for good. Under the guise of public morality it can erode many of the civil rights that belong to the innocent as well as the guilty by convicting without permitting the accused to face and cross examine the accuser, by passing off opinion as fact, through acceptance of hearsay evidence and by developing the subtle psychology that public servants do not have the same legal protections as ordinary citizens.

We believe the whole matter belongs in the courts and the sooner Senator Ervin's hearings are ended the more likely it will be that the guilty will be punished.

AMERICAN AIRLINES CHAIRMAN SPATER REVEALS ILLEGAL CONTRIBUTION TO GOP

George A. Spater, chairman of American Airlines, revealed July 6 that he arranged for the illegal contribution of $55,000 in corporate funds to the Finance Committee to Re-elect the President in early 1972. Spater said the money, with another $20,000 from individual contributors, had been given after he was approached in late 1971 by Herbert W. Kalmbach, former personal counsel to President Nixon. At the time of the contribution, Kalmbach was attorney for United Airlines, the largest U.S. carrier. Further, the Civil Aeronautics Board (CAB) then had before it a plan for American's merger with Western Airlines, a move strongly opposed by United. (The CAB rejected the merger July 28, 1972.)

"I knew Mr. Kalmbach to be both the President's personal counsel and counsel for our major competitor. I concluded that a substantial response was called for," Spater said in a statement issued by the airline. "Under existing laws a large part of the money raised from the business community for political purposes is given in fear of what would happen if it were not given. A fair and honest law is one that would remove the need of any candidate to exert such pressures, as well as the need for any businessman to respond," Spater said.

American acknowledged July 9 it had asked the Nixon re-election committee to return the $55,000. The finance committee said July 11 it had sent American a check for $55,000. In an accompanying cover letter, the finance committee denied being aware of the illegal nature of the gift. Federal laws prohibit corporate campaign contributions and state that corporations and their officers, as well as campaign committees and their officials, are liable to criminal prosecution.

The American Airlines contribution was initially revealed by special Watergate prosecutor Archibald Cox. Cox said if other corporate officers came forward with admissions of illegal gifts, "their voluntary acknowledgement will be considered as a mitigating circumstance in deciding what charges to bring." Cox praised Spater's forthrightness, but declined to rule out action against American and its officials.

(Eastern Airlines said July 6 that Kalmbach had approached the company for a contribution but had been turned down).

ST. LOUIS POST-DISPATCH

St. Louis, Mo., July 10, 1973

The crude snakedown of American Airlines to obtain money for President Nixon's re-election campaign adds another turn to the viper's tangle of wrongdoing that falls under the heading of Watergate. The special Watergate prosecutor, Archibald Cox, announced the airline's admission that it had made illegal corporate contributions under "pressure" from the White House.

The shocking story was confirmed by George A. Spater, chairman of American Airlines, who agreed to co-operate fully with Mr. Cox's office. Mr. Spater said the contributions were solicited by Herbert W. Kalmbach, then Mr. Nixon's personal attorney, during a period in which an American Airlines merger case was before the Civil Aeronautics Board. Mr. Spater said Mr. Kalmbach told him $100,000 was expected from his firm.

At Mr. Spater's direction, American officials paid out $75,000 in cash in five installments from November 1971 through March 1972 to the Committee for the Re-election of the President. Of this sum, $55,000 came illegally from corporate sources; federal law forbids corporate contributions to political campaigns.

Without excusing the airline, one can sympathize with Mr. Spater's position. "I knew Mr. Kalmbach to be both the President's personal counsel and counsel for our major competitor; I concluded that a substantial response was called for," he explained. What Mr. Spater described amounts to about as crass a piece of political extortion as one could imagine.

Mr. Cox, who is investigating reports that Nixon fund-raisers used such tactics to obtain campaign donations, emphasized that American Airlines volunteered its acknowledgement of the illegal contributions and indicated the action will be considered in deciding what charges to bring. This is fair enough, particularly as a tactic to encourage voluntary disclosure by others. Mr. Cox should be offered all the co-operation possible as he seeks to bring charges against those who may have tried to undermine the foundations of the nation's governmental system.

The New York Times

New York, N.Y., July 11, 1973

Like a major earthquake, the Watergate scandal has transformed the political scene. But politicians, like other human beings, prefer to look backward and cling to old ways. The members of the Senate Rules Committee, in particular, seem unable to comprehend how much the ground has moved under their feet.

While tens of millions of Americans have sat transfixed for hours before their television screens listening to testimony about secret political contributions, attaché cases stuffed with hundred dollar bills, and dirty political tricks financed by cash from concealed sources, the Rules Committee has quietly been meeting to draft amendments to weaken the Federal Election Campaign Act.

When that law went into effect on April 7 last year, it established reporting procedures that were intended to take some of the mystery out of how political campaigns are financed. Each new revelation about the financing of last year's campaign—mostly before April 7 —has brought fresh proof of the need to strengthen rather than weaken the new law and extend the reforms.

American Airlines, for example, has disclosed to Watergate Special Prosecutor Archibald Cox that it contributed $55,000 in corporate funds to the Nixon campaign. Such contributions are illegal under the new law, as indeed they were under the old but unenforced Corrupt Practices Act of 1925. Eastern Airlines has announced that it refused a similar solicitation from the Nixon campaign, but Mr. Cox reportedly has in his possession a secret list compiled for the White House of other corporations that did contribute.

A stockholder's suit against International Telephone and Telegraph Corporation has brought to public attention a memorandum from a former I.T.T. official detailing how he was pressured by his corporate superiors to contribute to Lyndon B. Johnson's Vice-Presidential campaign in 1968 with the understanding that he would be reimbursed out of corporate funds if he filed a fake expense account. Political observers agree that I.T.T. is hardly unique in this devious practice.

Another lawsuit is pending in an effort to uncover the whole story of the substantial contributions made by the dairy lobby immediately before and after President Nixon ordered an increase in dairy price supports. Investigation is also under way into the contributions to the Nixon campaign by the Teamsters Union after a Presidential commutation unexpectedly released former Teamsters president James R. Hoffa from prison.

* * *

Against the background of these developments it is astounding that the Senate Rules Committee has the temerity to report out two amendments to the new law that would narrow its scope. The first would remove the requirement that each contributor list his name, address and occupation. Instead, only his name would be reported. Undoubtedly, the existing requirement is now somewhat burdensome to campaign treasurers, but once it is widely known, it will become a matter of simple routine. It is no more onerous for the contributor than providing identification to get a check cashed. If addresses and occupations are not listed, the reports on contributions become much less meaningful.

Another amendment would repeal a section of the law forbidding any individual member of a corporation or union which holds a Government contract—as some unions do under the manpower training program—from making donations to a company-controlled political fund. These funds too easily become vehicles for some of the abuses which the Watergate investigations are bringing into view.

There is need for a strengthening of the existing law and combining it with provision for new sources of campaign financing from public funds. The objective is to achieve a balance between many modest contributions from individual citizens and limited public subsidy for some campaign expenses. There is no need for a return to the mystification and corruption-breeding practices permitted by the old weak law.

Members of the Senate who think they can slip back to the bad old days are misreading the public's post-Watergate sophistication. They run the risk of being retired from public life altogether.

The Virginian-Pilot

Norfolk, Va., July 9, 1973

By now, everyone is familiar with the fact that $100 bills were being tossed around the Watergate like confetti last year. The Committee for the Re-election of the President (CREEP) seemed to have money to burn (if not to shred), and there was enough left over to finance honeymoons and such.

Even after the arrest and conviction of Gordon Liddy and Company, when the conspirators started to put the heat on the White House for hush money, the President of the United States said that there would be no problem raising a million dollars for the purpose — or so John W. Dean III testified to Senator Sam Ervin's Select Committee investigating Watergate.

Where did all the money come from?

A lot of it was extorted from businesses that deal with the government, it is safe to say. The dictionary defines the act of extortion as "the crime of obtaining money or some other thing of value under color of office, when none or not so much is due, or before it is due." That appears to an accurate description of some of the fund-raising that filled the coffers of CREEP — and Maury Stans' safe — in 1971 and 1972.

The raw transactions that involved the dairy industry, which contributed more than $400,000 in exchange for an increase in milk price supports that cost consumers millions, and the International Telephone and Telegraph Corporation have been chronicled extensively in the past year.

Now we have the admission by American Airlines of a corporate gift to President Nixon's re-election campaign last year. It is illegal for a corporation to make political contributions. (Corporate executives sidestep the law sometimes by making contributions in their own names, for which they are later reimbursed with company funds. According to documents that have been filed in U. S. District Court in New York, that was the ITT practice starting as early as 1960.)

The American Airlines admission came in a statement by chairman George A. Spater, who said that the gift was solicited by Herbert W. Kalmbach, who was Mr. Nixon's personal attorney and one of the chief fund-raisers for the Republicans. Mr. Kalmbach "said that we were among those from whom $100,000 was expected," Mr. Spater said.

At the time Mr. Kalmbach put the bite on Mr. Spater, American Airlines was seeking to merge with Western Airlines, necessitating the approval of the Civil Aeronautics Board. (The merger was rejected by the CAB last July.) United Airlines, a client of Mr. Kalmbach and a competitor of American Airlines, was opposing the merger strongly.

"I knew Mr. Kalmbach to be both the President's personal counsel and counsel for our major competitor," Mr. Spater said. "I concluded that a major response was called for."

It amounted to the gift of $75,000 in five installments, starting in November 1971. The first four installments, totaling $20,000, came from "non-corporate sources." The last $55,000, paid to the Committee for the Re-election of the President in March 1972, came from corporate sources. Some of the American Airlines money is said to have been "laundered" by a broker in Lebanon to conceal its source.

Campaign funding is the soft underbelly of American politics. "Under existing laws," Mr. Spater said in his statement, "a large part of the money raised from the business community for political purposes - is given in fear of what would happen if it were not given. A fair and honest law is one that would remove the need of any candidate to exert such pressures, as well as the need for any businessman to respond."

Special prosecutor Archibald Cox is investigating the funding of Watergate. What he discovers — and the indignation it provokes among the American public — should lead to "a fair and honest law." And that might be the public funding of our politics.

The Philadelphia Inquirer

Philadelphia, Pa., July 11, 1973

Last Friday, the board chairman of American Airlines confessed his company gave $55,000 to President Nixon's 1972 campaign in direct violation of U. S. criminal law. The admission tended to depict the crime as business as usual, with the implication that unnumbered other American businesses are equally guilty.

Americans who do not believe it should be business as usual should watch carefully in the next few weeks, as Congress considers amendments to campaign financing laws. A major movement is building to emasculate existing regulations — laws that every day's new disclosures demonstrate are in need of emphatic strengthening.

The request in the American Airlines case was made by Herbert W. Kalmbach, according to American chairman, George A. Spater.

"I knew Mr. Kalmbach to be both the President's personal counsel and counsel for our major competitor," Mr. Spater said. "I concluded that a substantial response was called for . . . Under existing laws a large part of the money raised from the business community for politcial purposes is given in fear of what would happen if it were not given."

Mr. Spater's charges amount to extortion and blackmail. And they add up to perversion and subversion of the foundations of the electoral process.

Credibility is added by conventional wsidom. Ask any businessman you know. Our own unscientific, off-the-record poll produced a predominance of answers that sound like "everybody does it — except me."

★   ★   ★

But more impressive substantiation came recently in an affidavit by John T. Naylor, a former vice president of International Telephone and Telegraph Corporation, the mammoth conglomerate whose chairman, Harold S. Geneen, made something of a reputation not long ago for his interest in Chilean domestic politics.

In a deposition filed in connection with a civil suit against ITT's management, Mr. Naylor told of being pressured into contributing $1,200 to the vice presidential campaign of Lyndon B. Johnson in 1960 — 13 long years ago. Mr. Naylor swore that his corporate bosses told him to pay the money with a personal check and then recover it by lying on his expense accounts — which he said he refused to do.

Mr. Naylor swore that he confronted Mr. Geneen with his objection to this criminal policy and was told:

"Jack, that subject should never be mentioned. Everybody does it and the board wanted it this way. It is paying off big in Washington . . . You can't afford that kind of money personally, and I think the board and I were fair in making it good."

Archibald Cox, the special prosecutor, and his staff are pursuing the criminal aspects of the most recent Presidential campaign, and give every indication they will do so vigorously. Mr. Cox now has access to a list involving some $19 million in pre-April 7, 1972, contributions to Mr. Nixon's campaign — a list previously so secret as to have been retained only by Mr. Nixon's private secretary, Rose Mary Woods. Thus anyone who made any questionable—or palpably illegal — contributions would do well to let Mr. Cox and the Senate Select Committee know about it quickly and directly, before someone turns up at their door with handcuffs.

★   ★   ★

But while all that was going on, word was leaked that the Senate Rules Committee, in secret on June 27, had voted to remove from the Federal Election Campaign Act of 1971 the requirement that contributors' addresses and occupations be reported, and to kill a prohibition designed to prevent sandbagging government contractors.

David Cohen, operations director of Common Cause, the citizens' lobby which has been commendably active in the campaign reform movement, vowed his group would fight against the watering-down effort expected this month.

Speaking of the Rules Committee proposal, Mr. Cohen said: "They've decided to make legitimate the political funds that are the main sources of political corruption."

We agree, and believe members of both houses of Congress must be judged sternly and with a maximum of public attention on their stands.

The Washington Post
Times Herald

Washington, D.C., July 13, 1973

Washington has been buzzing for at least a year with stories about how the incredible amounts of money for the re-election of Richard Nixon were raised. The titillation quotient of the stories rose with each additional effort on the part of Mr. Nixon's re-election apparatus to shield its donor lists from public view and with each enticing behind-the-scenes glimpse the public was able to get. There have been reports about the money laundered through Mexico, the money in Bernard Barker's bank account, the milk money which began to flow just before the milk price support decision was reversed in favor of the dairymen, the Vesco cash in a briefcase and much more. Some of these reports remain murkier than others. But now comes American Airlines' disclosures and, in one blinding flash, we can see a lot more clearly just how this sleazy business really works.

Special Watergate Prosecutor Archibald Cox announced last Friday that American Airlines had voluntarily disclosed that it had made an illegal cash contribution of $55,000 from corporate funds to the effort to re-elect Mr. Nixon. George A. Spater, the airline's board chairman, elaborated in a formal statement which revealed that company officials, acting at his direction, had delivered a total of $75,000 in cash to the Nixon effort, but that $20,000 of that sum came from "non-corporate sources."

Mr. Spater's rather poignant statement tells us a great deal in general about the confluence of money, politics and American business, and quite a lot in particular about how those forces came into play in the Nixon campaign in 1972. Mr. Spater said, "I was solicited by Mr. Herbert Kalmbach, who said that we were among those from whom $100,000 was expected . . . I knew Mr. Kalmbach to be both the President's personal counsel and counsel for our major competitor. I concluded that a substantial response was called for."

Well, we'd say that is roughneck politics by any standard. Now it is true that Mr. Kalmbach issued his own statement indicating that he had neither cash nor a corporate contribution on his mind when he made the solicitation, and the Finance Committee to Re-elect the President rushed into print denying that it had "used extortion methods" to raise campaign funds. What they couldn't deny was that Kalmbach had two roles—one as Mr. Nixon's personal lawyer and the other as attorney for United Airlines. Nor can it be denied that $100,000 is a whale of a lot of money and that American Airlines is in an industry regulated by the government. More to the point, American then had a merger pending before the government and its chief competitor, United, was opposing it. The proposal was later turned down, so both of Mr. Kalmbach's clients won while American lost.

In any case, Mr. Spater and Mr. Kalmbach are grownups. Mr. Kalmbach knew whom he represented — the President *and* United Airlines—and he knew that Mr. Spater also knew. Mr. Spater had available to him sufficient legal talent to find out that campaign contributions from corporate funds were illegal, even if he didn't

know it when he talked to Mr. Kalmbach. So, there was a need not only for a "substantial response" but for one that would be difficult to trace. Thus, according to reports, there was a Lebanese "laundering" operation for American's $55,000 so that the money would come through as untraceable cash. Moreover, it was all delivered before the more stringent campaign financing law went into effect in April 1972.

It just happens that the records for some of those pre-April contributions have been lost or destroyed by Mr. Nixon's finance committee. Maurice Stans, Mr. Nixon's finance chairman, testified before the Ervin committee that there was nothing illegal about destroying those records. He justified his insistence on maintaining the confidentiality of his donor lists on grounds of high principle. "The committee's position all along," he said, "was that non-disclosure created no advantage to it, but that privacy was a right of the contributor which the committee could not properly waive. The right to live without undue intrusion is a long-respected benefit of the American system."

But it turns out that, indeed, there was an "advantage to it"—the advantage of a shelter behind which to hide violations by the donor, and possibly by the committee, of the criminal code of the United States. Mr. Spater gave a little different and, under the circumstances, probably a more candid view of the operation of the system. "Under the existing laws," he said, "a large part of the money raised from the business community for political purposes is given in fear of what would happen if it were not given."

So there was fear and there was secrecy and, with fellows like Mr. Kalmbach and Mr. Stans stalking through the corporate jungle, not even a wink or a nod was needed to get the message across. Mr. Cox says he hopes that other corporations will follow American's admirable example and make the tough, but in our view, correct decision to disclose voluntarily any illegal contributions. And so do we. Perhaps if enough corporations come forward and confess, before the government has to go through the arduous and costly process of investigating and prosecuting them, the public will see this shakedown for what it is and bring pressure for tough and sweeping reform of the campaign financing process.

Incredibly, the Senate Rules Committee hasn't yet gotten that message; it recently reported out two amendments to the campaign financing law which would weaken, rather than strengthen, it. More voluntary disclosure by corporations and greater public revulsion might well reverse this astonishing move by the Rules Committee and encourage a trend the other way—toward real reform. The big donors would benefit from this. But the general public would benefit far more. For the result would be cleaner, better government. If we've learned nothing else in this Watergate year, we've learned that dirty money, no matter how thoroughly it's laundered, makes for dirty politics and corrupt government.

St. Louis Globe-Democrat
St. Louis, Mo., July 8, 1973

The more that comes out of the Watergate investigation pertaining to the donation of funds to President Nixon's re-election campaign last year, the more it becomes apparent that there is a critical need for a thorough probe of all campaign contributions — whether they were made to the Republican or Democratic parties.

As it is now proceeding, the inquiry is totally one-sided. The spotlight is fixed on the Republicans. Any abuses of campaign finance laws by GOP supporters last year or any other year certainly should be brought out into the open, but by the same token so should any breaking of the rules by Democratic followers be investigated. This is the only fair way. The ludicrous assumption of some now is that the Democrats are clean while the Republicans have been dirtied.

American Airlines has admitted that, contrary to election statutes, it donated $55,000 in company funds to the President's re-election campaign in 1972. Under federal law, anyone who gives or receives campaign gifts from the coffers of corporations, labor unions or banks may be imprisoned up to two years and fined up to $10,000.

While American Airlines is to be commended for voluntarily giving this information to special Watergate prosecutor Archibald Cox, the action of making the illegal contribution cannot be condoned. It only serves to underscore the need for reform of campaign finance laws.

American Chairman George A. Spater, who disclosed the donation, laid the blame for such practices on existing laws under which, he said, "a large part of the money raised from the business community for political purposes is given in fear of what would happen if it were not given."

It is significant to point out that Spater did not make any claims that this was the situation with American. He did not say that the Administration threatened any adverse action on a pending merger of American with Western Airlines, a merger which ultimately was rejected by the Civil Aeronautics Board, nor was there any indication the White House was in any way involved in the decision.

Spater's generalization of "pressures" on the business community ignores the fact that the majority of contributions by either management or labor are made more on the basis of political philosophy than for fear of reprisal. People donate to the party they think will serve their interests best. Charges that have been made of "extortion" in last year's campaign don't wash. They only distort the picture.

If the investigators of campaign contributions want to have a real field day they should take a close look at some of the money that has been dumped into Democratic coffers by organized labor over the years. What about the legality of some of these political donations?

The law applies to Democrats and Republicans alike. It is a mockery of justice and fair play to scrutinize the finances of one party without checking just as thoroughly on those of the other. The lopsided investigation is badly in need of being brought into balance. To arrive at any genuine reform of campaign finance laws, it is mandatory that the finances of both major parties be probed in depth.

U.S. AGENCY ADMITS SPENDING $1.9 MILLION ON NIXON HOMES

The General Services Administration (GSA) announced June 21 that it had spent almost $1.9 million on President Nixon's homes in Key Biscayne, Fla. and San Clemente, Calif. The White House attributed all of the costs to security. The total included $1,180,522.64 for improvements and maintenance at Key Biscayne and $703,387.30 for San Clemente. The San Clemente total was an upward revision of a $460,312 estimate released by the GSA and White House aides June 14 as the amount spent on security at the California estate. The figure also contrasted sharply with the $39,525 figure listed by the White House May 26 as the amount for the same purpose.

A breakdown of the costs released by the GSA June 22 showed, among other items, expenditures at San Clemente of $184,174 for electrical work, $13,850 for landscaping, $12,315 for roof tile and repairing walls and a gazebo, $13,500 for a heating system, $2,800 for a swimming pool heater, $11,561 for a redwood fence, $3,800 for a sewer line, $4,834 for furniture in the President's den, $1,853 for installation of a flagpole and $476 for painting the flagpole. Among the items at Key Biscayne were $122,708 for bullet-resistant glass doors and windows, $122,714 for constructing a Secret Service command post, $995 for a septic tank and lid, $587 for a flagpole, $3,030 for golf carts for Secret Service patrol, $6,321 for an ice maker for Secret Service men and $475 for swimming pool cleaner. Funds were also spent to clean the beach at San Clemente and to correct beach erosion at Key Biscayne.

At a hearing by a House Appropriations Committee subcommittee, headed by Rep. Tom Steed (D, Okla.), Secret Service Director James J. Rowley said June 27 most of the public funds spent on the two Nixon homes had been requested by his agency for security reasons. Steed defended the federal expenditures as "not excessive." He said his panel, which approved the overall budget for the projects, had urged that decisions on presidential security "always be made on the side of too much rather than too little." GSA administrator Arthur F. Sampson also testified and said all of the funds were expended in relation to presidential business or to save additional federal expense. Both officials told the subcommittee the spending was done by the GSA at the request of the Secret Service and not on orders of the President.

In a related development, White House Press Secretary Ronald L. Ziegler July 3 angrily denounced newspaper articles that he said suggested wrongdoing in the purchase of the San Clemente estate. The outburst was sparked by a *Los Angeles Times* story that day saying special Watergate prosecutor Archibald Cox had begun a preliminary inquiry into the San Clemente purchase and improvements. Ziegler's denial was described as vehement.

The Courier-Journal

Louisville, Ky., June 18, 1973

THE MURKY DETAILS about who spent how much for what in buying and fixing up President Nixon's California and Florida estates seem as difficult to unearth as the secrets of Watergate. And as the facts slowly emerge, bit by bit, a similar justification is heard for practices that appear on the surface to be both shady and exploitive of the public interest. All of it, we are told once more, has been done in the interest of security.

The General Services Administration now admits government expenditures of roughly $456,000 to make the President's San Clemente estate safe to live in. And although some of the improvements clearly are warranted by considerations of Mr. Nixon's safety and privacy, and by the large government staff that invariably accompanies a President even on "vacation," some of the items raise questions. Why should $2,800 of taxpayers' money, for instance, have been used for work on Mr. Nixon's swimming pool? Why should a six-inch water line, installed at a cost of $6,260, have been paid for entirely from federal funds when it is used not only for fire protection but to fill the swimming pool?

Nobody can quarrel with spending whatever public money it takes to provide adequate protection for the President. But the expenditure lavished on the California estate and—though few hard figures have emerged—presumably on the Florida estate, too, goes beyond the line of what can be considered reasonably necessary. After all, these estates are privately owned; and though the doubling in value of Mr. Nixon's California property since he purchased it in 1969 has been due partly to a general rise in real estate prices in Southern California, the federally financed fencing, landscaping, new furnaces and other improvements obviously have made a tidy contribution.

What is more disturbing, however, is that so much of this spending has been done in secret, coming to light only because of the persistent digging of some newsmen. As recently as last month, for instance, the White House was suggesting that Mr. Nixon has spent $123,514 of his own money on improvements, compared with only $39,525 in federal funds. Now it turns out—if *these* figures can be believed as final—that the federal expenditure was 11½ times as great as that figure, and that California records indicate spending of only $10,950 by the President.

The same kind of secrecy has shrouded Mr. Nixon's purchase of the San Clemente estate (now valued at $1.6 million), in an intricate deal which leaves his millionaire friend Robert Abplanalp owning most of the property; just as it has concealed details of his $253,000 purchase in 1969 of the property on Key Biscayne with the help of that other mystery man, Bebe Rebozo. Throughout his 4 1/2 years in office, in fact, the President has volunteered information about his real estate holdings only when it has been forced from him.

This is, of course, his private property; and if that were the extent of the matter, little harm would be done by Mr. Nixon's lifelong penchant for secrecy. But two factors bring the matter into the realm of legitimate public concern. One is what appears to be extravagant use of government funds for purposes that seem to go considerably beyond the needs of presidential security. The other, even more troublesome to a good many Americans, is the financial arrangements that put the President in debt to private individuals who stand to profit greatly from being known as Mr. Nixon's closest friends.

Given those circumstances, the American public deserves and should demand a complete White House explanation of the financial details of the San Clemente and Key Biscayne transactions and the subsequent improvements. If Watergate is any guide, however, such an explanation will have to be dragged out piecemeal because it will never be offered voluntarily.

The Salt Lake Tribune

Salt Lake City, Utah, June 30, 1973

In days when traveling was more of a chore, Presidents lived in the White House though most of them also maintained homes in their native states. By contrast, President Nixon has residences in California and Florida in addition to making frequent use of government owned Camp David in nearby Maryland. All recent Presidents have had at least one favorite retreat where they spent considerable time.

The presidency is a demanding position and a chief executive cannot be blamed for wanting to get out of Washington to more relaxed surroundings. But when a modern president establishes a home away from the White House a number of special precautions must be taken for his safety. And the precautions are expensive.

For instance, latest figures from the General Services Administration show that $423,000 has been spent on Mr. Nixon's San Clemente, Calif., property alone.

As government spending goes, the cost of providing security requested by the Secret Service is a pittance. Still, the government's footing the bill for such security measures as landscaping and new roofing raises questions of propriety.

Obviously landscaping is a major factor in protecting the occupants of a house. But the same landscaping also enhances the value of the property which will accrue to the Presi-

dent after he leaves office and no longer needs the full scale protection. And who is to say which improvements are truly needed and which are frills?

The same observations apply, to a lesser degree, to the vice president. Friday, Vice President Agnew moved his family into a new $190,000 house in Maryland because his Washington apartment did not provide sufficient privacy. Nothing wrong with that. But the Secret Service ordered $125,000 in "protective" improvements on the new house and its grounds.

The trouble is that there is apparently no limit to how many times a president or vice president can move while in office, or how many houses he might buy or rent. And each of them would have to be made secure at considerable cost.

So far, the problem is more potential than real though President Nixon has taken the extra house thing about as far as it can logically go.

A solution might be for the government to purchase or build several presidential and vice presidential residences in different parts of the country. These could be made secure once and for all. Assuming that future presidents were satisfied with the permenant out-of-Washington lodgings, they could dispense with private holdings and the continuing expense of protecting them.

THE SUN

Baltimore, Md., July 6, 1973

Ronald L. Ziegler's intemperate reaction to the latest newspaper story suggesting possible impropriety in the matter of President Nixon's San Clemente hacienda hardly serves to quiet down some of the questions that have been raised. The target of Mr. Ziegler's ire on this occasion was the Los Angeles *Times*, which had reported that Archibald Cox, special prosecutor on Watergate and other affairs, was making a "preliminary inquiry" about San Clemente. Mr. Cox quickly denied it, saying that an aide had only asked for press releases and newspaper clippings so he could answer questions that come up on the subject. But Mr. Ziegler was not content with that. The story, he said, was "a smear," "innuendo," "unjust" and "unfair," and he added: "Statements that suggest any impropriety, in any way whatsoever, in the purchase of this home, are malicious, ill-founded and scurrilous in nature."

Mr. Ziegler further complained about stories concerning $703,367 in public funds for improvements on the President's house, charging that by innuendo they implied "ill-spending," when in fact, he said, the money went for security purposes, which is what the General Services Administration says too.

One trouble with all this lies in the cloud of obfuscation the White House has consistently maintained over San Clemente, listing as recently as May 29 improvements of less than $40,000, and still today declaring that the real estate deal under which the property was originally handled is a private matter, none of the public's business. This last might in ordinary circumstances be strictly so; and as for heavy expenditures on security that is unquestionably necessary, though some of the items may to the ordinary citizen seem rather odd.

What, then, makes these circumstances extraordinary, and why need the ordinary citizen be so suspicious? The answer seems to us to lie in a general attitude of the Nixon administration, covering San Clemente and Watergate and the Committee for the Re-election and the organization of the White House staff; an attitude that none of this is the public's business. It lies too, as we see it, in the administration's viewing of large sums of money, whether at San Clemente or in CRP, as somehow not real money, in common terms, but a sort of play money. Ordinary people simply do not understand, and Mr. Ziegler is not the best guide toward understanding.

The Star-Ledger

Newark, N.J., July 14, 1973

Attorney General Richardson has wisely decided that the controversy over the President's home in California and Florida should be reviewed by Special Watergate Prosecutor Archibald Cox. This would remove any suggestion of White House influence in another instance of official secrecy that has proved embarrassing for Mr. Nixon.

Mr. Nixon has been described as "appalled" by the "malicious, ill-founded and scurrilous" articles which he feels suggest wrongdoing in the purchase of his estate at San Clemente, Calif., and the use of government funds to improve his personal homes.

His anger may well be justified. But it is difficult to know because what should be public information is shielded by incomplete reports and continually revised figures.

There are two separate issues — the financing of the San Clemente purchase, and government expenditures to improve the California and Key Biscayne, Fla., homes.

It is common, and proper, practice for government to pay for improvements needed to protect the chief executive. Quarters for Secret Service agents, guardhouses, television scanners, shark nets, communications equipment and protective fencing would certainly fall in this category.

Other expenses, however, are questionable. These include furniture for Mr. Nixon's San Clemente den ($4,834), a swimming pool heater ($2,800), a new heating system ($13,500), a sprinkler system ($23,000), landscape maintenance ($25,524), a flagpole ($1,853) and $476 to paint the pole.

The total bill at San Clemente ran to $703,367. That's a far cry from the first figure the White House gave, $39,000, or even the General Services Administration's first estimate of $462,000.

The way Mr. Nixon acquired the San Clemente property is also shrouded in mystery. Until last May, there were no indications that anyone but Mr. Nixon had been involved in the $1.4 million purchase. Then the White House said the President had borrowed $625,000 from a millionaire friend, Robert M. Abplanalp, to help pay for the home and 29 acres of property. But that debt wasn't listed in Mr. Nixon's pre-election financial statement.

Later, the White House said, Mr. Abplanalp — who also has a home in the presidential complex on Key Biscayne — created an investment company that bought back all but five acres. But the White House refused to name the investment company or its officers. And property records in Orange County, Calif., do not indicate any division of the estate.

Ron Ziegler, Mr. Nixon's press secretary, says, "We have cited precisely what the transactions were and we have stated clearly what the transactions were." Hardly.

The public is entitled to know all about the President's financial dealings. Until it does, the White House's lack of candor can only arouse suspicion.

ST. LOUIS POST-DISPATCH

St. Louis, Mo., July 11, 1973

As a *Post-Dispatch* correspondent reported the other day from Washington, in any other year the revelations that nearly $2,000,000 in Government funds have been spent on two personal homes for President Nixon away from the White House would have stirred a major controversy. As it is, Mr. Nixon's housing situation should be scrutinized by the special Watergate prosecutor, Archibald Cox, and it is to be hoped that all the facts will be brought out.

A related aspect of Mr. Nixon's presidency is also of public interest though hardly susceptible of investigation. The federal money poured into the development of the properties at San Clemente, Cal., and Key Biscayne, Fla., is one thing; but the questions raised about the personality of a Chief Executive who seems to find it impossible to stay in one spot and work is quite another.

It is said that he works at San Clemente and Key Biscayne, and also at Camp David, the official presidential retreat not far from Washington, and perhaps he labors as he flies to and ro at the taxpayers' expense, but the work thic he espouses is hardly enhanced by this restless motion which of necessity must result in a slipping of the wheels.

It goes without saying that certain security precautions are needed and acceptable at a presidential residence, but like the elastic interstate commerce clause, security is stretched to cover such items as a septic tank, a flagpole, an ice maker, a swimming pool cleaner, a new furnace, tree trimming and weed removal and "security lighting and landscaping." What to do about it? It could be understood that once the President had left office the Federal Government would remove the "security" improvements from his place insofar as possible. Or the President might be limited by law to one private vacation residence.

As it is now, Mr. Nixon could establish other residences, say in New England and the Southwest, which could be developed at the taxpayers' expense. And we note the Vice President is following the Chief's lead and having all sorts of "security" improvements made at his new home in Maryland. We have an uneasy feeling all this ought to stop somewhere if we are to have a president and not a monarch.

The TENNESSEAN

Nashville, Tenn., July 28, 1973

WHITE House aides claim that President Nixon was unaware of the details of more than $700,000 in government spending for improvements to his San Clemente home.

The White House also maintains that most of the improvements were requested by the Secret Service for security purposes. However, government records show that many are of the type usually intended to improve the ease and convenience of the occupant rather than his safety—such as a $4,800 expenditure to furnish the President's study. The records also show that $1,800 in tax funds was spent to put up a flagpole at Mr. Nixon's private home.

The spending of more than $700,000 to fix up a home is bound to entail a good bit of hammering and sawing and the switching around of furniture. It will be a mystery to most people how the owner of the home could walk around in the midst of all this commotion and not ask some questions about how much it was costing him—or how much it was costing somebody.

Some will contend it was possible for Mr. Nixon to have been unaware that tax money was being spent for his private benefit. For the most part they are the ones who contend it was possible for a major political espionage operation to be planned and carried out —and then covered up—in the executive offices of the White House without the President knowing anything about it.

But what these apologists for Mr. Nixon do not explain is how a President can hope to run the country when he is unaware of so much that is going on around him.

THE SACRAMENTO BEE

Sacramento, Calif., June 29, 1973

The latest report that out of $703,367 in taxpayers' money spent on President Richard Nixon's private residence at San Clemente overlooking the Pacific Ocean, $132,852 was spent for landscaping and landscaping maintenance alone, betrays an inordinate extravagance by the General Services Administration and the Secret Service.

In explaining the outrageous expenditures the GSA and Secret Service have come up with an intriguing new term —"security landscaping." This was pulled out of the hat to describe one $25,524 item for landscape maintenance Oct. 18, 1969.

Other thousand dollar items revealed for the first time this week are: $3,320 spent July 22, 1969, to remove damaged plantings and another $1,454 to replace them. Why it would cost more to remove the plants than it would to replace them is puzzling to anyone who has wielded a trowel in his back yard.

Then there was $1,125 to replace damaged shrubs in November of the same year; another $1,496.08 to replace more damaged plantings in January 1970 and $1,658.35 for plantings in February. The cost of removing dry weeds staggers the imagination. A Nov.

3, 1970, item shows an $8,810 expenditure for this. Then another $1,100 was spent in government funds to remove dry weeds just four months later — March 17, 1971.

It is true presidents need much more security than other people, but if the expenditures were thought to be prudent and in the interest of the public at the time, why were the exact figures kept secret so long? Why were newsmen seeking a breakdown of the costs shunted among the General Services Administration, the Secret Service and the White House?

The most recent statement from San Clemente that President Nixon was "unaware" of any of the details of the $703,367 spent for improvements on his property is hard to believe. He must have noticed all the new landscaping, the beach cabana and the new furnishings in his study, among other things.

Nobody is charging the President with ordering these improvements at government expense, but now that he knows how much public money has been spent to enhance the value of his private property, Nixon should pay the bill out of his own pocket.

Until he does there will be a cloud over the Western White House at San Clemente.

NIXON REJECTS REQUESTS FOR TAPES

President Nixon July 23 rejected the Senate Watergate committee's request that he release tape recordings of his conversations about the Watergate case. (The existence of a recording system installed to secretly tape Nixon's White House conversations for "historical purposes" was revealed July 16 by Alexander P. Butterfield, a former presidential aide now serving as administrator of the Federal Aviation Administration, in testimony before the committee. A Secret Service spokesman acknowledged that the agency had installed the recording system but said it had never done similar work for any other administration.)

The disclosure of the secret recording system, confirmed by the White House, brought a request by the committee's chairman, Sen. Sam J. Ervin Jr. (D, N.C.), for access to the tape recordings of the President's conversations with persons involved in the Watergate case. The request—in a letter from Ervin—followed Nixon's rejection of a committee attempt to interrogate Secret Service agents on the White House recording operations. In his July 23 letter to Ervin, Nixon cited his earlier refusal to allow committee access to confidential presidential papers. Committee chairman Ervin had suggested July 13 that "some representative of the White House and some representative of the committee go through" the presidential documents and separate those pertinent to the panel's investigation. Nixon said the principle of confidentiality applied "with even greater force," because the tapes could be "understood or interpreted only by reference to an enormous number of other documents and tapes." Accordingly, Nixon said, the tapes would remain under his "sole personal control." Nixon said he had listened to "a number" of the tapes before their existence became publicly known. He maintained they were "entirely consistent with what I know to be the truth and what I have stated to be the truth." He conceded, however, that they contained "comments that persons with different perspectives and motivations would inevitably interpret in different ways."

After receiving the Nixon letter, the committee voted unanimously in executive session to issue two subpoenas to Nixon—one for recordings of five of his meetings with former counsel John W. Dean 3rd, the second for other documents related to Watergage. Announcing the subpoenas July 23 at the televised hearings, Ervin asserted that if "such a thing as executive privilege is created by the doctrine of separation of powers," it exists "only in connection with official duties." He said it could not be invoked for "either alleged illegal activities or political campaign activities."

The White House July 23 also rejected a request from special prosecutor Archibald Cox for tapes relating to Watergate. Cox had pointed out in his letter that his request for tapes "in aid of an investigation of charges of criminal conspiracy plainly raises none of the separation-of-powers issues you believe to be involved in furnishing so-called 'presidential papers' to the select committee." He also said it would "set no damaging precedents."

In reply, White House consultant Charles Alan Wright told Cox that "if you are an ordinary prosecutor and thus part of the Executive Branch . . . you are subject to the instructions of your superiors, up to and including the President, and can have access to presidential papers only as and if the President sees fit to make them available to you." Further, Wright said, the separation-of-powers argument did apply, since the tapes sought by Cox were to be used before grand juries and in criminal trials, thus creating a conflict with the Judicial Branch.

In a statement released after receipt of the Wright letter, Cox said he remained convinced "that any blanket claim of privilege to withhold this evidence from a grand jury is without legal foundation." Cox later July 23 issued a subpoena for the material he had requested.

In a letter to Ervin July 26, Nixon said he "must respectfully refuse" to produce the tapes called for in the subpoena. In reply to Cox' subpoena, Nixon said in a letter to U.S. District Court Judge John J. Sirica, dated July 25, that the "independence of the three branches of our government" was at issue and that the President was "not subject to compulsory process from the courts." Nixon agreed, however, to release several memoranda sent among his aides.

At a public session of the hearings July 26, the Ervin committee voted unanimously—on a motion by Vice Chairman Howard H. Baker Jr. (R, Tenn.)—to take the issue of Nixon's refusal to comply with the tapes subpoena to the courts.

After notification of Nixon's refusal to comply with his subpoena, Cox petitioned Judge Sirica July 26 for an order to release the tapes. Cox contended that Nixon had already at least partially waived executive privilege by allowing present and former aides to testify before the Ervin committee and the grand jury. After a 28-minute hearing, Sirica directed the White House to show cause by Aug. 7 why the tapes should not be produced.

Acknowledging that the issue would probably reach the U.S. Supreme Court, White House spokesman Gerald L. Warren said July 26 that Nixon "would abide by a definitive decision of the highest court."

The San Diego Union

San Diego, Calif., July 18, 1973

While the subject is serious, there is an element of incongruous humor in the sight of the Senate Watergate committee raising its voice in horror at the process of electronic surveillance on the one hand and demanding that the White House produce exactly such evidence on the other.

Humor aside, there can be no doubt that the matter of taping presidential conversations in Washington and at Camp David has become a major public issue over which American people are asked to pass judgment. Like so many of the other problems raised by Watergate, it is not an easy issue to define — to say nothing of reaching a judgment. Undoubtedly all modern presidents have engaged in the habit in some manner and to some extent, but always for the same purpose — to maintain a record.

Considering his bent for history and his philosophical respect for the office of the presidency, it is plausible that President Nixon ordered conversations in his offices to be recorded in order to preserve them for the future academicians. After all, he is presiding over a momentous upheaval of history. Future historians would be handsomely rewarded if they could hear a president's conversations as well as read the more carefully polished papers and books. Indeed, the Watergate affair, already assured of a place in American history, adds immensely to the value of presidential tapes, to the extent that they exist.

Nevertheless, the question is not in the future. It is in the here and now. Sen. Ervin wants the tapes for use of the committee on presidential campaign activities. The White House is declining to supply them, citing the need to separate legislative and executive affairs or executive privilege.

Executive privilege by itself is probably reason enough to keep the tapes for later study by historians, but there also are other compelling considerations.

For example, the foreign reaction to the disclosure of presidential tapes has been calm, along the thought that "everybody does it." Undoubtedly the discussions that President Nixon had in the Great Palace of the Kremlin or at his guest house in Peking also are electronically preserved. The point is that Communist China and the Soviet Union in a larger national interest are not broadcasting these tapes even to their own populace. It is a thought that the Senate committee should consider.

By the same token, and of greater immediate importance, the committee insists that it will not deliberately do anything to endanger the course of justice in Watergate. If it is sincere, the committee cannot now insist that it play the tapes which would undoubtedly jeopardize the right that those accused of crimes against self incrimination.

It very well may be that the tapes of the chief executive's conversations as they apply to Watergate eventually will be played before the Senate hearings.

In the larger interests of the United States of America this should occur only at the initiative of the President. In taking such initiative, the President should be guided by the same disciplines that must guide the Senate committee: nothing in the tapes should be made public if it endangers the course of justice, or protects any person from trial and punishment.

The Wichita Beacon

Wichita, Kans., July 20, 1973

How candidly, one wonders, will visiting foreign diplomats or heads of state ever again discuss delicate international policy with a United States president in the "sanctuary" of the Oval Office— or anywhere else for that matter ——now that secretly recorded tapes of such meetings by one president and the illicit telephone tappings of another have been brought to light?

Is no confidence to be honored?

However much historians and the news media would like to have access to every word uttered in the consummation of big domestic or international political deals there is a greater need for uninhibited honesty between leaders upon whose decisions the fate of the human race so often depends. To surreptitiously record conversations believed to be private impugns the integrity of the guest or the caller. To say the least, such conduct is not conducive to good will or improved relations.

Secret diplomacy has been a common and effective political tool throughout the history of nations. Individual privacy is not only a social courtesy, but a guaranteed right in this nation. Both diplomacy and privacy are violated by unannounced intrusions of electronic recording devices upon meetings and conversations.

In any case, truth will be served only by men, not machines. The existence of tape recordings does not insure that the truth will be known—machines are easily manipulated.

Integrity would perhaps best be served if all known tapes of secretly recorded calls and meetings involving any president were forthwith destroyed without disclosure of their contents, and future presidents restrained from engaging in such deceptions.

The Des Moines Register

Des Moines, Iowa, July 21, 1973

When the Ervin committee tried to get Secret Service officials to testify about the White House's program of recording presidential conversations, the committee ran into an order blocking their appearance. President Nixon directed that no Secret Service agent "shall give testimony to congressional committees concerning matters observed or learned while performing protective functions for the President or in their duties at the White House."

The President gave no reason for the order. He invoked neither executive privilege, separation of powers nor any other constitutional doctrine. By referring to the performance of "protective functions for the President," however, he left the impression that questioning of Secret Service agents might somehow compromise the President's security.

Of course it would be improper for a congressional committee to force the Secret Service to reveal measures taken to protect the President against physical harm. But the committee isn't the least bit interested in learning about security measures. The committee's sole interest is in learning details about the taping operation as they relate to testimony given the committee. The committee wants to find out if conversations with the President described by witnesses were recorded.

A former White House aide told the committee he believed the taping of presidential conversations was for historical purposes. Whatever the purpose, it's inconceivable that it related to national security. The taping apparatus was installed at public expense. The public is entitled to whatever light the Secret Service, which installed the recording system, can shed on the White House's recording operation.

The Ervin committee is a duly authorized committee of Congress conducting an investigation it is legally empowered to conduct. The President's action in denying the committee access to witnesses borders on obstruction of Congress.

The President has promised a statement explaining the White House bugging. Congress, a co-equal branch of government, should not have to be dependent for information solely on statements the President decides to issue. If Congress is denied the opportunity to elicit information from the sources it selects, its powers of investigation are effectively crippled.

The President's refusal to allow the Secret Service agents to testify shows a contempt for Congress and a contempt for the system of checks and balances. His action can only make Americans wonder what he is trying to hide.

The New York Times

New York, N.Y., July 24, 1973

President Nixon has written bad law and disastrous politics in his decision to withhold White House evidence affecting the Watergate affair not just from the Congress but also from the special prosecutor and, by extension, the nation's courts of law.

His action yesterday can only heighten the increasing suspicion of direct Presidential participation in Watergate—a concern based not on abundance of proven facts, but on unproven allegations and circumstantial evidence, alongside a series of deceptions, evasions and now suppression of evidence by the principal in the suspected conspiracy. The basic political problem posed by the President's own actions, far transcending any question of tape recordings or written memoranda, is how any elected leader can expect to govern under this rapidly growing mushroom cloud of doubt and suspicion.

Mr. Nixon spoke in near-monarchical tones in his written replies to Senator Ervin, chairman of the Senate Watergate investigation committee, and Archibald Cox, the special prosecutor for the Watergate scandal. Material evidence involving an alleged criminal conspiracy is to be held "under my sole personal control," Mr. Nixon said. He arrogated to himself the unique judgment of what would best serve "the interest not just of the Congress or of the President, but of the people." These are claims of a ruler who harbors the illusion that he commands the personal trust of the populace, whatever whims he chooses to follow.

Mr. Nixon's assertions of fidelity to a lofty constitutional doctrine, the separation of powers, sound hollow and hypocritical against actions which show contempt for the spirit of the Constitution, for the responsibilities of a citizen—all citizens—under the law and the expectations of moral leadership from the President of the United States. This new Nixon Doctrine virtually sets the person of the President above law and public ethics.

The legal counter-moves launched by the Senate committee and Prosecutor Cox immediately upon notice of the President's decision will lead to a court test on the subpoenas issued by both investigations. These will involve complex issues of great moment; but a voluntary submission of evidence by Mr. Nixon would have shown far more sensitivity to the immediate problem of popular confidence in Presidential integrity.

Perhaps there is still the slimmest chance of a reversal or compromise by Mr. Nixon if the political gravity of his situation can be brought home to him. Legal and court battles are ill-suited for such lessons, which can best be conveyed by influential members of the President's own party and political family.

Senator Baker, vice-chairman of the Watergate committee, could sound a highly significant voice, backed both by his present position and his potential to the Republican party of the future. Other leading Republicans might be able to get through to the President, men like Senators Goldwater, Scott and Aiken, certain key Governors and national committeemen, perhaps old political friends like Herbert Brownell or William P. Rogers. All else seeming to fail, these are influences which stand the best remaining chance of penetrating the wall against reality which Mr. Nixon has erected around himself.

Just as the Watergate scandal has advanced far beyond the burglary of the Democratic National Committee, so is the current constitutional clash far more profound than any question about tape recordings of months-old White House conversations. Mr. Nixon may well be right—he, after all, is the only person who admits to having heard the tapes—in saying that they would not settle the central questions about Watergate. Our own guess is that they will neither prove nor disprove his innocence or guilt.

The real issue which Mr. Nixon has posed is whether a President of the United States, once elected, can succeed in holding himself answerable to no one but himself.

THE RICHMOND NEWS LEADER

Richmond, Va., July 18, 1973

And so, there are tapes. About them, some thoughts:

(1) Their existence implies the non-involvement of Richard Nixon in the Watergate cover-up. Mr. Nixon knew the tapes were running; he knew that one day they would be made public. Surely he is not so dumb — nor so unconcerned about his historical reputation — that he would allow his own tapes to implicate him in Watergate. And let us suppose that on September 15, as John Dean has testified, Mr. Nixon congratulated Dean for Dean's role in the cover-up: Even if Mr. Nixon did know about the cover-up, he had ample time to say things for the taped record — subsequent to September 15 — that would contradict whatever he might have said on September 15 in the Oval Office. The logical assumption, then, is that the tapes exonerate the President, or at least do him no damage.

(2) Mr. Nixon very likely has been relying on the existence of the tapes as his bombshell revelation that would bail him out of the entire Watergate Thing. He has a penchant for the dramatic, for the long pass that connects when all seems lost. Yet the President could have been hung up on the problem as to how to explain to the public that every conversation in the Oval Office, in his office in the Executive Office Building, and over the phone at the President's Aspen Cottage at Camp David, were recorded. Now such concerns have been rendered beside the point by the decision of the Senate Watergate Committee to publicize the tapes' existence.

(3) The legality and ethics of the tapes are now under public debate. As to their legality, there seems little doubt that they were — and are — legal. Even if they were not legal on the basis of present law, blanket permission from the Attorney General can be presumed to exist. As to the ethics of the taping, that issue will be decided on the basis of the biases of the individuals doing the deciding. Pro-Nixon people will argue, as Barry Goldwater and Spiro Agnew have argued, that there was nothing unethical about them; indeed, that many politicians tape many conversations. Anti-Nixonites will argue that the revelation about the tapes simply verifies what they have been saying all along about the presence of a Gestapo-like mentality in the White House.

(4) If the tapes suggest an inherent irresponsibility on the part of Mr. Nixon, as many now are contending, then surely the manner of the revelation of the tapes' existence confirms an abiding irresponsibility on the part of the Watergate Committee itself. We now have categorical evidence that the Committee is not so interested in discerning The Truth about Watergate, as it is determined to destroy the President of the United States. The Committee learned of the existence of the tapes on Friday. On Monday, it trotted Alexander Butterfield before the TV cameras and put the questions to him. The Committee-members must have known the degree to which such a revelation would compromise presidential activity in the future, and would discredit many presidential decisions of the past. Would the Committee not have been more prudent if it had gotten in touch with the President privately, and said, "Look, we have executive testimony about some tapes. Can we discuss that testimony?" But no. The Committee bulled ahead, determined to put the President between a rock and a hard place — to put political pressure on him to release the tapes.

(The irresponsibility of the Committee merits a good deal of contemplation. The Committee-members regard themselves as judges. Senator Daniel Inouye has said he wants "to give the White House its day in court." He said yesterday the decision to put Butterfield in the witness chair was "judicious." Senator Sam Ervin said yesterday to witness Herbert Kalmbach, "My information is that you have co-operated fully with the prosecution." Very well. But responsible judges do not permit themselves — nor do they allow counsel — to chit-chat about recent testimony outside their courtrooms, as the Senators and counsel for the Committee chit-chat about testimony outside the Senate hearing room. And responsible judges do not leak — or allow leaks — of executive testimony given to counsel. Almost every day, executive testimony appears in *The New York Times* or *The Washington Post*.)

(5) Should the President release the tapes? Politically, perhaps one day he will have to; in its effort to sandbag him, the Committee may have given him no choice but to do so. Yet other questions are involved. Moral questions: Should he release the tapes simply to answer an accomplished liar? Separation-of-power questions: Should he establish the precedent of acquiescing in congressional demands that Congress be given the right to review tapes of Oval Office conversations? Selectivity questions: Once he releases some tapes, how can he refuse to release others? Suppose the Committee wants to "get to the bottom" of testimony from H.R. Haldeman. The President talked with Haldeman probably every day. Must the President therefore release every tape? And timing questions: The President should not release any tape before the Committee concludes its hearings into the matter of possible presidential involvement. If the President was involved, the nation shall find that out soon enough. If the President was not involved, he should wait out the hearings, reaffirm his innocence, and offer the public, or the Committee — or the pertinent grand jury — sufficient information to support his claim.

The Washington Post

Washington, D.C., July 24, 1973

President Nixon's refusal to accede to the request of the Senate Watergate Committee to make some presidential papers and certain tapes of his conversations available to the committee and his parallel refusal of Special Watergate Prosecutor Cox's request to make some specific tapes available to that office have precipitated a Constitutional crisis for no real Constitutional or legal reason. In his most recent letter to Sen. Sam Ervin denying access to the tapes, the President refers to his earlier letter of July 6 denying the committee access to presidential papers.

Mr. Nixon's letter of July 6 contains not only the essence of his reason for refusing the requests by Senator Ervin and Mr. Cox but also a passage which effectively refutes his argument. The heart of the July 6 letter was that to turn over the requested papers "would inevitably result in the attrition, and the eventual destruction of the *indispensable principle of confidentiality of presidential papers.*" Later in the same letter, in discussing his reasons for refusing to testify before the committee, he put his constitutional duty rather succinctly and, in our view, destroyed all his lesser arguments when he spoke of "the duty of every President to protect and defend the constitutional rights and powers of his office [as] an obligation that runs directly to the people of this country." This latter obligation is far larger than any "principle" concerning the confidentiality of presidential papers.

What is at issue here is not a question which may be resolved by legal needlework as, for example, it would be if the issue concerned how far the legislative branch can inquire into the thought processes and confidential exchanges within the executive as it administers, under the Constitution, the laws of the United States. Senator Ervin and Mr. Cox are not asking whether criminal activity has in fact, touched and tarnished the office of the President. We know it has because we have heard about it from Messrs. Mitchell, Dean, Magruder, et al. What is at issue is only to what extent those crimes we already know about have corroded and compromised that high office.

In other words, the Presidency—and with it the country—already have been badly damaged. The question now becomes, how that office—and thereby the country—can best be served by all who are involved, including the President. It is the integrity of the office—not the sanctity of presidential papers or tapes or conversations—which the confessed actions of the Deans, Mitchells and Magruders have put at issue, and it is that integrity that the various governmental processes now at play must salvage. Mr. Nixon, more than either Senator Ervin or Mr. Cox, is in a unique position to do this. And he was right, we think, when he argued that his duty to protect and enhance that office ran "directly to the people of this country."

The narrow considerations of separation of powers and executive privilege—whatever their applicability in other contexts may be—simply do not apply where the actions under investigation relate not to papers or conversations having to do with the execution of the laws under the Constitution, but rather with criminal activities at the core of government which erode both the moral and the political authority of the presidency. A one-time waiver of these principles in the effort to clean up the presidency can in no sense be deemed a permanent waiver, nor indeed can it be deemed to diminish the office or to prejudice future claims to executive privilege.

On the contrary, opening up the papers at this time would be an act of courage born of confidence on Mr. Nixon's part which would immeasurably enhance the people's trust in him—as distinct from those who have served him and the country so badly in his name. This is particularly so if the tapes, as he says, are consistent "with what I know to be the truth and what I have stated to be the truth." The country is prepared to accept, we would suppose, the reasonable amount of ambiguity that the tapes would necessarily contain. But it is not prepared for the President of the United States to allege, on the one hand, that he has it within his power to produce evidence which could help clear up one of the most dismal episodes in American history and then to refuse, on the other hand, to do so.

Mr. Nixon can still uphold his duty to his office and to the public by reversing himself and producing his evidence. That it might not "settle" anything, as he contends, does not distinguish it from most of the other evidence that has been presented in this case so far. That it would help us get to the bottom of the Watergate affair—which the President earnestly insists is what he wants most to do—seems undisputable. The alternative would seem to us to serve nobody's purpose—not even the President's. For if there is something in this evidence which conceivably might be misconstrued by the public to his disadvantage, there is something in withholding it which is certain in the end to be far more damaging. His choice, in short, is between a risk which is marginal by his own estimate, and the certainty that by suppressing his evidence he will inflict upon himself the incriminating inference suggested by Senator Ervin that he has something to hide—something so harmful to his case that he is determined to hide it indefinitely.

THE ROANOKE TIMES

Roanoke, Va., July 25, 1973

President Nixon's willingness to accept a constitutional crisis rather than release evidence he says will vindicate him in the Watergate affair is a terrible disappointment. The national government is suffering from creeping paralysis at a time when important decisions and actions are needed. Mr. Nixon stands at the center of the crisis. He can blame his friends for creating it, but not his enemies—whoever they are.

The great majority of the American people, we are convinced, want to believe the President guiltless either in the bugging or the cover-up. He started out with an overwhelming presumption of innocence by that majority. But public opinion polls indicate that as the weeks slip by, more and more of the people consider him to be in some way culpable: 70 per cent in the latest Gallup Poll. This is appalling, and the blame for the unprecedented slide in presidential popularity belongs largely to the President. His evasions and defenses have invited widespread disbelief.

His latest action, refusing to turn over tape recordings and other relevant documents to either the Senate investigators or the Justice Department's special prosecutor, can only have the same effect. Especially as the President says the tapes support his own version of the facts, yet might be interpreted otherwise by "persons with different perspectives and motivations." He will be judge and jury on this one, and rule them inadmissable.

Mr. Nixon obviously has his foes in mind when he refers to "persons with different perspectives and motivations." But what counts most is the American people. If they knew what was on the tapes, surely they could make a sound and mature judgment on their meaning—and not a prejudiced one, as Mr. Nixon feels his detractors would make.

If the President has his way, the public will not have that chance. He is denying them the means to rally their belief and support at the hour when he most needs them. Instead he is saying, in effect: Admire my toughness, and trust me. It is late in the day for that.

Chicago Tribune

Chicago, Ill., July 24, 1973

The Watergate investigation moved yesterday from the peaceful field of reason and persuasion to the battleground of the courts. Subpenas demanding the tape recordings of conversations between President Nixon and his aides regarding Watergate were ordered issued not only by the Ervin Committee of the Senate, but also by Special Prosecutor Archibald Cox.

Given the President's repeated refusal to provide the tapes which may provide the answers which so many people are seeking, there was probably no alternative. But the resort to subpenas is a shame nonetheless, because it leaves little room for flexibility and turns the confrontation into one of win or lose.

The shame is all the greater because Mr. Nixon's letter declining to provide the tapes was not all that unreasonable. He said, first, that while the tapes supported his own statements on the issue, they were subject to misinterpretation; and second, that they were interspersed with frank personal comments often wholly extraneous to Watergate.

This is not an implausible explanation. Had it been made earlier, it might have averted or postponed the confrontation. But coming so late—and this despite the President's illness last week—it prompted Sen. Ervin to scorn and to the suggestion that the President's idea of the separation of powers was "to separate a congressional committee from access to the truth."

Had the tapes—or even just the pertinent parts of them—been transcribed and submitted voluntarily—or had disinterested outsiders been asked to listen to the tapes and judge them, as Sen. Hugh Scott, the minority leader, suggested—there would have been no question of the separation of powers. The President would have been acting voluntarily.

Now he has taken to the trenches on two fronts. With respect to Congress, his claim of Presidential privilege is a well-established one. But in refusing to provide the tapes to his own Justice Department's special prosecutor on the ground that they would then be turned over to the courts and that this would violate the separation of powers between the Executive and Judicial branches, he is on shakier ground.

Perhaps reason can still be appealed to to produce a compromise that may save the country from this tragically unnecessary battle. Perhaps, as all three sides contemplate the dangers of the battlefield—and the effect the battle will have on the country, they will decide that reason is the better course. We hope so.

Newsday

Long Island, N.Y., July 24, 1973

We have come at last, on that long, long trail that started at the Watergate, to the moment of truth, as they say, to the ultimate question that now has to be answered: Does Richard M. Nixon recognize any lawful authority higher than his own?

If we are to judge by the President's messages yesterday to the Ervin Committee and to Special Prosecutor Archibald Cox, the answer would appear to be no. For Nixon is arguing that the national interest will be better served by withholding the tapes of his Watergate conversations; the tapes will therefore be withheld, and to hell with the reasonable requests of the legislative and judicial branches. And so the issue is clearly joined.

Mr. Nixon's arrogance vis-a-vis the Congress should come as no surprise, for there are numerous precedents: impoundment of funds, the continued bombing of Cambodia, the decision to constitute a "plumbers" unit to operate in defiance of the law. But if his arrogance is not unexpected, his lack of vision is. Does Nixon really think that legalistic rhetoric about separation of powers, executive privilege and the public interest will dispel the people's doubt—or halt the further revelation of his administration's involvement?

Now the issue goes to the courts. Both the Ervin Committee and the special prosecutor are issuing subpenas for the President's tapes. From the relatively gentle arena of the Senate investigating committee where there are, as Senator Ervin has said, no defendants, the argument moves to an adversary proceeding governed by the criminal law. Does Nixon for a minute believe that the national security, the dignity of the presidency or his own image will be enhanced by wrestling this historic issue through the courts?

To our way of thinking, the most surprising aspect of the President's decision on the tapes is his willingness to repudiate the promise he made two months ago about furnishing evidence. Given that commitment of May 22, it's hard to avoid speculating that the tapes—which were still a secret at that point—must indeed be highly prejudicial. The President's words on that occasion are worth recalling:

"It now appears that there were persons who may have gone beyond my directives, and sought to expand on my efforts to protect the national security operations in order to cover up any involvement they or certain others might have had in Watergate. The extent to which this is true, and who may have participated and to what degree, are questions that it would not be proper to address here. The proper forum for settling these matters is in the courts.

"Accordingly, executive privilege will not be invoked as to any testimony concerning possible criminal conduct or discussions of possible criminal conduct, in the matters presently under investigation, including the Watergate affair and the alleged cover-up."

Since that commitment is apparently now inoperative, to use a White House phrase, we hope the courts act firmly and swiftly to bring an end to what is clearly a deliberately contrived and continuing attempt to conceal the truth from the American people.

The Boston Globe

Boston, Mass., July 25, 1973

Two days prior to President Nixon's refusal to surrender White House tapes pertaining to the Watergate investigation by the Select Committee of the US Senate, Committee Chairman Sam J. Ervin Jr. (D-N.C.) declared that "it is becoming an intellectual feat to continue presuming that the President wasn't aware of the Watergate coverup."

Mr. Nixon's explanation of his refusal to surrender the tapes makes the intellectual feat no easier. The President stands on executive privilege and asserts the doctrine of the separation of powers. But, as Chairman Ervin and other authorities on the Constitution, including Special Prosecutor Archibald Cox, have pointed out, executive privilege covers only those matters relating to the proper exercise of the President's proper responsibilities. Emphasis is on the word "proper." The separation of powers likewise is in no way intended to block proper judicial or congressional inquiry into allegations of wrongdoing in the executive branch. The White House is not a royal court.

What the President demands for himself in his letters to the committee and to Mr. Cox is not merely that the executive branch be viewed as separate from and coequal to the congressional and judicial branches. He seeks to be considered as sitting a notch above the other two and in no way bound by their exercise of their own proper responsibilities.

John Ehrlichman, the President's former aide, yesterday set forth a similarly curious view of the President's powers, as currently conceived in the White House. In a kind of lesson in new civics, Mr. Ehrlichman lectured an obviously incredulous committee on the duties and responsibilities of the President and his staff. He pictured the burden as so heavy and so urgent as to outdate all the constitutional limits of the President's powers and the powers of his administrative staff as well. It is of course true that the responsibilities of the President are far heavier in the modern world than they were at the nation's birth. But the Constitution of the United States cannot be amended by the President's fiat, let alone by a President's John Ehrlichmans. Mr. Ehrlichman's delineation of the President's powers, as the Nixon White House conceives them, account in large measure for Mr. Nixon's current problems.

Mr. Nixon has interpreted the tapes as substantiating his assertion that he knew nothing about and did not participate in the conspiracy to obstruct justice after the Watergate burglary. But he acknowledges that "they contain comments that persons with different perspectives and motivations would inevitably interpret in different ways." What is it, then, which the President knows the committee or a Federal court would hear in the tapes that he does not want either of them or the American people to know?

The President in effect is "taking the Fifth." This is an entirely proper procedure for one whose testimony might tend to incriminate him in a criminal offense. It surely is not proper for a President of the United States to withhold information relating to allegations that he lent his high office to the subversion of a presidential election.

Chairman Ervin has said that Mr. Nixon's obduracy has converted Watergate into "the greatest tragedy this country has ever suffered."

The President reportedly will make the tapes public in his own chosen time in his own defense. But, as Committee Vice Chairman Howard H. Baker Jr. (R-Tenn.), has said, the committee is not trying to prosecute anyone or to protect anyone. It is trying to dig out the truth.

Mr. Nixon is not helping in that search. Moreover, if Mr. Nixon releases the tapes at his own convenience on some future day, he will be hard put to justify the claim of executive privilege which he asserts now.

But this is not all. Mr. Nixon has stated that the tapes "are under my sole control," and that "I personally listened to a number of them." This indeed, seems to be truly his executive privilege, but it is not now a privilege of his high office that he be the only one ever to hear them even if he so wished.

With the serving of subpoenas on the White House, a great constitutional issue has been raised, and it will be for the third branch of the government, the judiciary, to settle it. The question is whether the President can be compelled to surrender the tapes to the Ervin Committee or special prosecutor Cox, or both.

Our view is that this most important question can go for decision quite quickly to the US Supreme Court, just as the less important question of the Pentagon Papers case went there in a matter of a few weeks only two years ago.

That court can, and should, order the tapes turned over to the committee, with proper qualifications to eliminate extraneous, irrelevant material. This should not be beyond the wit of man to work out. And special prosecutor Cox has an even easier case before that court. He operates under the Executive branch, in which the separation of powers cannot apply, and the court will be up against its dictum a year ago in Caldwell, citing the Jefferson-Burr case, that the President is not exempt from giving evidence.

The White House has complained that Watergate is making it difficult almost to the point of impossibility for the President to administer his office. If this is so, the fault is the President's own.

"Our structure of values depends on mutual faith, and faith depends on truth ... Unless we find a way to speak plainly, truly unselfconsciously, about the facts of public life, we may find that our grip on the forces of history is too loose to control our own destiny."

It was President Nixon who once said that.

The Courier-Journal

Louisville, Ky., July 18, 1973

THE PRESIDENT'S passion for keeping a historical record of his administration can hardly be challenged on that ground alone if he was willing to record all the 'ers' and 'ahs,' the mistakes and the wild guesses of his private deliberations for eventual transcription in some sunkist presidential library, as the testimony of former Cabinet Secretary Butterfield has indicated to the Ervin committee.

It could be a mark of self-confidence that a Chief Executive would want historical access to all of his "business phone" conversations and all words uttered in any of four offices in or near Washington. But it also could be a deceitful venture in play-acting, both in the opportunity to guide conversations so they build a case (as John Dean says he believes happened in their final meeting), and in the chance to use another, unbugged phone or office for matters that might prove embarrassing in the archives.

In any event, the practice may turn out to be the salvation of the Nixon presidency, if he can now produce evidence that Mr. Dean and others misunderstood or deliberately misstated their post-Watergate conversations with the President.

But the callous and disturbing aspect of the Nixon administration's tap and tape mentality, with its overtones of "Big Brother," is that no one ever bothered to think of the other end of those high-level conversations. So far as Mr. Butterfield or the public record show, no one told the diplomats, Cabinet members, confidential advisers and elected officials that their words were being preserved. How much of what was said in the Oval Office, the Cabinet Room, Camp David or the "hideaway" office next door to the White House would have been changed? It's impossible to say. And, in fact, Mr. Nixon's reputation as a closed-off, private man indicates that not too many actually gained access to the four offices.

So, if the outcry against the unilateral tapping of all comments seems restrained, perhaps it was only because so few people had seen Mr. Nixon privately in the two years in question, and so few could recall embarrassing words or weak moments in the presence of a demanding leader.

It's reported that many governments elsewhere have taken it for granted that the White House records conversations with their diplomats and others. This is the kind of assumption an insider well might make. Similarly, Mr. Nixon's overseas chats with Dr. Kissinger and the wartime military and intelligence traffic between Washington and Saigon are examples of the valid national-security use of microphones and tape recorders. But they have nothing to do with the routine recording of phone conversations at the White House.

Thus, if all those loops of tape were so innocently archival, so dedicated to the documentary record as we are supposed to believe, why couldn't *everyone* have been told about the White House tapes and taps? It's difficult to think of an answer that does credit to an administration already infamous for its deviousness and lack of candor.

Nevertheless, the tapes are real, they are presumably in the custody of the Secret Service, and the question that now occurs is what use can be made of them to settle — once and for all — the most damaging series of accusations ever made against any president.

Not the least of the problems posed by existence of the presidential tapes, however, is that it now seems possible that a refutation, if that is what it is, of Mr. Dean's charges, has been available to Mr. Nixon all along, and that he was only awaiting the right dramatic moment to refute his accusers. So the challenge, since Mr. Butterfield supports the notion that this is exactly what the President and his lawyers have in mind, may be to convince people that the tapes haven't been edited to make Mr. Nixon look good. The months of delay in revealing existence of the tapes — and then seemingly only because of an after-thought question to Mr. Butterfield— do little to support the President's assertions that he, too, wants to get to the truth as quickly as possible.

The same sense of delay and obstruction is conveyed by the President's intervention yesterday to protect Secret Service agents from having to discuss White House procedures with the Senate committee staff. So this becomes still another item to add to the agenda of the Nixon-Ervin summit conference. Until the Senator and the President come to grips with the issue of documentary evidence, the danger of a major constitutional confrontation—even in the courts—appears real.

As matters now stand, the President will only hurt his case and abuse public trust by further refusal to make available to the federal prosecutor and the Ervin Committee the documentary evidence—now including the tapes—that they are asking for. While these materials are being assembled, he can start repairing some of the more ominous portents of the latest revelation by apologizing to those who may wonder whether their words were recorded for the ages or for some more subtle and self-serving purpose.

CHICAGO Sun-Times

Chicago, Ill., July 24, 1973

President Nixon's refusal to deliver recordings of White House conversations to Watergate investigators and his astounding decision to sit in judgment himself on the worth of the tapes as evidence seriously impede efforts to get at the truth of the Watergate conspiracy. In addition, he has certainly aggravated the already abrasive relationship between himself and Congress and invited possibly historic court tests of his power. Worst of all, he has skirted his own responsibility to clear the Presidency itself of any taint of Watergate complicity.

The President predictably invoked the doctrine of separation of powers in refusing to make the recordings available. A letter to Special Watergate Prosecutor Archibald Cox said disclosure of the material would do lasting harm to the "confidentiality that is imperative to the effective functioning of the Presidency." It added that the President "has concluded that it would not serve the public interest to make the tapes available."

What certainly was not predicted was that the President would consider it his executive privilege to pass without any form of rebuttal on the evidentiary substance of the tapes. Yet, in a letter to Sen. Sam J. Ervin Jr. (D-N.C.), chairman of the Senate Watergate committee, the President said, "If release of the tapes would settle the central questions at issue in the Watergate inquiries, then their disclosure might serve a substantial pub-lic interest that would have to be weighed very heavily against the negatives of disclosure. The fact is that the tapes would not finally settle the central issues before your committee."

The President said he had listened to a number of the tapes himself. He said they confirmed his previous statements on Watergate, in which he denied involvement, but he said also that they "contain comments that persons with different perspective and motivation would inevitably interpret in different ways." In other words, Mr. Nixon decided to substitute his own judgment for that of anyone else, on the ground he could not trust anyone else to interpret the tapes as he has interpreted them. He thus has confused the public interest with the White House interest — a confusion of viewpoints which, in fact, appears to have been central to the Watergate episode.

The President might be on firm ground if the subject matter of the tapes concerned foreign policy or national security. The tapes were requested by the Ervin committee, however, in order to check the accuracy of testimony given by central Watergate witness John W. Dean III. Dean had said he met with President Nixon on a number of occasions and indicated that a record of the conversations would show the President to have been involved in the Watergate cover-up. The Dean conversations, if they in fact did take place, surely would not en-compass matters either of foreign policy or national security, and the President's stubbornness can only result in placing his own motivation in doubt.

It is significant that the existence of the tapes became known only when it was disclosed in Watergate testimony that the President's office was bugged with voice-activated recording devices. The President since has decided to remove the recording equipment, thus acknowledging it was wrong to secretly record every word of public or private business uttered in his office. Why does he not now see that it is equally wrong to virtually insist that the tapes are his property, that "the tapes, which have been under my sole personal control will remain so?"

The tapes are in fact public property. Information on them may be needed to determine the credibility of Watergate witnesses, or the culpability of individuals under investigation, including former White House aides and a former attorney general. Mr. Nixon last week made the shockingly insensitive statement that he would do his job and let others "wallow in Watergate." The obstinacy of his position, then and now, places him on a collision course with Congress. The subpenas authorized by the Senate Committee and Cox for the tapes are certainly in order, for, as Cox said, "the effort to obtain these tapes and other documentary evidence is the impartial pursuit of justice according to the law."

THE DAILY HERALD
Biloxi, Miss., July 24, 1973

President Nixon's decision not to provide the special Watergate prosecutor or the Ervin Committee with tapes of his telephone conversations comes as a disappointment.

It is difficult to see how executive privilege bars the release of the tapes. They are not being sought in connection with White House executive decisions. They are needed, to put it bluntly, to prove beyond a doubt that the President was not involved as a witness, an accessory or a participant in the Watergate cover-up. They are needed to prove or disprove the allegations of President Nixon's lawyer, John W. Dean 3rd.

It is difficult to find a question of separation of powers between the executive and the legislative branch in this particular case. A Washington lawyer, Nathan Lewin, writing in the Washington Post, cites a Supreme Court decision that says a U. S. senator may be called by a grand jury and asked about activities "casually or incidentally related to legislative affairs, but not a part of the legislative process itself."

The analogy is reasonable. Prosecutor Archibald Cox doesn't want information on executive decisions. Neither does the Ervin Committee. They want only to obtain from the White House information unrelated to specific executive branch functionings to clear up charges that are a legitimate part of their investigations.

President Nixon campaigned on a firm law and order stance. Now his former attorney general, John Mitchell, has been indicted on a charge of obstructing justice. In a campaign speech on October 15, President Nixon praised Mr. Mitchell for demonstrating "his determination to see justice done to the overwhelming majority of law-abiding citizens, as well as to those who break the law." If Mr. Nixon approved so thoroughly of Mitchell's alleged determination to see justice done, he could demonstrate that by cooperating with Prosecutor Cox and the Ervin Committee.

Again on Nov. 5th, shortly before the elections, the President said in a radio address, "We need to recognize, first, that politics is not merely a game to be played hard and for keeps, with everyone defending his own interests as best he can... It is not an auction in which the prize of office is awarded to the highest bidder for the favor of the voters."

Thus far, two big corporations have admitted making illegal contributions to Mr. Nixon's campaign; and other charges put his re-election committee in a very bad light. Here again, the President is challenged with making his actions comply with his statements of principle.

He promises to make a statement at a later date. But it is difficult to see how another television appearance can clear up the charges, made under oath, of presidential involvement in the Watergate cover-up. The issue CAN be cleared up, however, by making the tapes available. There is indeed a separation of powers between the two branches of government under our Constitution. But there is also the constitutional requirement that they check and balance each other. One is just as important as the other. And it is that check and balance, -- the need to keep each other honest -- not the separation of powers, that is at issue in the matter of the White House tapes.

LEDGER-STAR
Norfolk, Va., July 26, 1973

The worst fears of many thoughtful Americans may be dispelled by White House statements accepting court rulings as binding on the executive in the historic confrontation over the presidential tapes. But only the worst fears; serious misgivings remain despite the responses of Gerald Warren, the deputy press secretary, to newsmen's questions about the first subpoenas served on an American president since Aaron Burr was tried for treason during the administration of Thomas Jefferson.

What, Mr. Warren was asked, will happen in the event the courts require Mr. Nixon to hand over the tape recordings of certain Oval Office conversations to Sen. Ervin's Watergate investigating committee, or to Special Prosecutor Archibald Cox?

Mr. Warren was not happy to comment on such a hypothetical situation, but his answer was positive: "There's no question that he would abide by court rulings . . . The President abides by the law."

This assurance suggests that the constitutional collision will not be as shattering as it conceivably could be. But for the head-butting by the executive and legislative branches even to be pushed into the courts at all, let alone all the way to a precedent-setting decision, is cause for foreboding. One branch or the other is likely to be weakened more than is good for the country. And there is the risk the other will come out stronger than it ought to be in a governmental system which gave real meaning to the phrase "balance of powers."

The problem with showdowns, no matter how entertaining they are in movie Westerns and James Bond fantasies, is that there must be a winner and a loser, just the opposite of a balance. It's a lot easier to savor the drama of a fight to the finish than to appreciate the harmful potential and the desirability of "settling out of court."

Speculation as to what might happen should a president refuse to comply with a subpoena is truly frightening, and it is to Mr. Nixon's credit that he has let it be known he would not precipitate such a crisis, even though he apparently does intend to press on toward a judicial determination of the issue that President Jefferson avoided in 1807. When Chief Justice John Marshall ordered him to hand over certain papers for use in the Burr trial, he did so.

Mr. Nixon's position of course is more difficult than Jefferson's, for the Watergate "overzealousness" and the Senate hearings have placed the President himself, fairly or unfairly, on trial before the public. Which is all the more reason he should have sought a compromise by which whatever information the tapes contain would have been made available without being subpoenaed. Particularly so, inasmuch as this is a fight he stands to lose by winning, for withholding the tapes will tend to be taken as an admission of complicity in the Watergate cover-up.

That personal consideration aside, the system of government that has served this country so well for almost two centuries is ill served by this collision. No doubt the vehicle is not going to fly to pieces. But it may not run as well afterward.

THE SUN
Baltimore, Md., July 25, 1973

In his letter to Senator Ervin in which he declined to release any White House tapes, President Nixon said, approximately repeating an earlier statement, that "at an appropriate time during the hearings I intend to address publicly the subjects you are considering." It has also been said previously, by Mr. Ronald Ziegler as we recall, that a presidential response would come before an "appropriate forum."

Deciding what an appropriate time may be could be difficult for the President, with the climate around him worsening as it is. Perhaps he hopes that the testimony of other witnesses, for example John D. Ehrlichman and H. R. Haldeman, will improve his case sufficiently to prepare the ground for a presentation of his own. Considering Mr. Ehrlichman's appearance yesterday, with its discourse on how hard a job the presidency is in the world of today, along with an assurance that Mr. Nixon is not paranoid, this would seem a less than solid hope.

Even harder will be the selection of an appropriate forum. Another television performance like that of April 30, when the departure of Mr. Ehrlichman and Mr. Haldeman and the firing of John W. Dean 3d were announced, would hardly suffice. That effort was almost a fiasco, and stood as such until the real fiasco of the long statement of May 22, when Mr. Nixon invoked national security beyond the bounds of credibility except for the dwindling band of the inveterately gullible.

Nor will it do for him to try the seemingly-casual approach of last week's little pep-and-resolution talk to the White House staff, with its suggestion that he and all similarly responsible persons were working in the perspective of "the ages," while others "wallowed" in Watergate. Tricks such as this have sometimes worked for Mr. Nixon in the past. We do not believe they will work any longer.

It has been proposed more than once, sometimes by people who ought to know better, that the proper forum would be a major extra-special press conference, a "free-swinging" press conference, on the sole subject of Watergate and its ramifications. Such a conference, in our opinion, would be a mess, serving neither the President nor the public. It would be overblown in advance, and overdone in the event both by President and press, and would almost certainly but increase the confusion.

It is too late now for Mr. Nixon to use a press conference to his advantage. Had he held regular press conferences—the last was on March 15—instead of huddling isolated in the virtual bunkers of his various places of residence, he could have established a line of normal communication with the country, and could have explained himself as events progressed. But that opportunity he has thrown away; and all we can do now is await his judgment, or guess, on the appropriateness of time and place for defending himself.

The Evening Bulletin

Philadelphia, Pa., July 25, 1973

With President Nixon at loggerheads both with the Senate Watergate committee and Special Watergate Prosecutor Archibald Cox over his refusal to release White House tape recordings and other documents bearing on the scandal, it is late, but perhaps not too late, to urge moderation.

Only moderation can avert a Constitutional crisis shattering to the American people's faith in the workings of their government.

The conflict is being presented as an abstruse one involving the Constitutional separation of powers among the executive, legislative and judicial branches of government. But can it be resolved on that basis? As the lawyers push their arguments to the extremes, the public may still be left frustrated as to the truth about Watergate.

Mr. Nixon may be constitutionally correct when he denies the right of the senators to have access to tapes of his private conversations with his aides. But who is to decide, the courts? The separation of powers also applies to them, as a White House letter reminds Special Prosecutor Cox.

If the courts upheld Mr. Nixon, would that satisfy the public? If the courts decided that Mr. Nixon had no right to withhold information relating, not to his official duties, but to political activities or possibly criminal activities, how could this be enforced if the President held firm? Such a showdown is frightening to contemplate.

This is not the way out of the Watergate dilemma. The great strength of the American system of government lies in the capacity of the three coequal branches of government to function without pressing their respective powers to an extreme.

They accommodate, they compromise. The structure is not rigid and inflexible. There is a mutual tolerance in it that allows it to bend to avoid breaking.

It would only compound the tragedy of Watergate if a struggle over disclosure of all the facts about unsavory, indeed, criminal political activity resulted in a constitutional deadlock that no one could really win and that might do irreparable harm to the functioning of our government.

In this situation, there are leaders in both great political parties who do not despair of a solution, who do not insist that the President surrender his position on separation of powers, but who hope and believe that he will find a way to release the pertinent information in his possession to the public.

It has to be conceded that, constitutional powers aside, there are great difficulties in making this information public without at the same time disclosing confidential presidential business that has nothing to do with Watergate.

Surely, however, it is not beyond the ingenuity of man to devise a method that would be respectful of the powers of the Presidency and its privacy and still disclose the essentials about Watergate.

Surely, there are persons of integrity, now no longer directly involved in public life, whom the President, the Congress and the public could trust to screen these White House tapes for what is relevant? Such names occur as former Senator John Williams of Delaware and former Governor William Scranton of Pennsylvania.

This, admittedly, might be no solution so far as settling the conflict between the President and the special Watergate prosecutor is concerned. But while the prosecution of wrongdoers is important, it is far more important from the viewpoint of public confidence that the impasse between the President and the Senate be resolved. Disclosure of the truth, rather than punishment of individuals is the critical issue.

Men of goodwill, men of fairness, leaders of both parties should join now to urge some such solution to the deadlock. The nation cannot afford long to continue in the present state of dreadful unease that comes from uncertainty over Watergate and that deprives it of effective national leadership.

Economic problems at home, the debacle of the dollar and the growing intensity of economic competition abroad, the energy crisis, the vitally needed reform of the Federal Government structure and of its relations with state and local government — all cry for strong and direct leadership from the President.

The White House tapes and documents that the President now withholds may not end the debate, but the refusal to disclose them and let the public judge — whether constitutionally correct or not—deepens the present crisis of confidence.

Beyond tapes and papers, and more important than their disclosure if they settle nothing, will be the President's own promised statement to the public on the subjects being considered by the Senate Watergate committee.

Even though Mr. Nixon declines himself to appear before that committee—and his right to so decline is not challenged—Mr. Nixon will be the final and most crucial witness in whatever forum at whatever time he deems it appropriate to speak.

Here again, he might consider announcing one course of action that would be conciliatory to Congress and perhaps help to inspire public confidence.

The Constitution which President Nixon has hitherto cited as a protective barrier against some forms of disclosure opens a door for him to come forth positively in presenting his case.

It says that the President shall "from time to time" give Congress information on the State of the Union. It says that on "extraordinary occasions" he may convene both Houses, or either of them.

The State of the Union is now the State of the Presidency. The occasion is truly extraordinary. And no press conference, no White House television spectacular, no formal written statement could present a forum so solemn, so proper, so eminently suitable as a presidential address to Congress and the nation.

Can Mr. Nixon not now find it in himself to so move to open the doors of the Constitution and lower the barricades between himself and the people and their representatives?

The Dallas Morning News

Dallas, Tex., July 28, 1973

THE COUNTRY is now having a dramatic political science lesson, acted out before the background of the Watergate hearings and the subpoenas for presidential tapes.

The subject is the principle of separation of powers, one of the most fundamental ideas underlying our constitutional system. This is the principle of allotting the various powers of government to separate branches in order to keep a single branch from concentrating total power, thereby becoming a threat to our liberty.

The doctrine itself is older than the country. It was drawn from Montesquieu's theory, recognized in 1774 by the First Continental Congress in the Declaration of Rights of the colonists. It was also incorporated into several state constitutions during the Revolutionary War.

The architects of the U.S. Constitution put the separation of powers doctrine in harness alongside their design for checks and balances, the goal of both being to keep power decentralized as much as possible without making government hopelessly ineffective.

THE DOCTRINE is not absolute. The separation is not airtight. There are points of access between the separate branches, and at times in our history strong individuals in one branch or the other have overstretched the powers of that branch.

Nevertheless, the general goal of the Founding Fathers has so far been achieved. Never has the leadership in one branch succeeded in completely subordinating the other two branches to its will.

The most aggressive president, Franklin Roosevelt, at first turned Congress into a rubber stamp but his New Deal ran into fierce resistance in the Supreme Court. And this resistance was upheld by Congress when he tried to override it with the court-packing plan.

The Radical Republican Congress, in an earlier attempt, tried to break the presidency immediately following the Civil War. But the impeachment of President Andrew Johnson failed by one vote.

PRESIDENT Nixon's refusal to hand over his tapes and papers to Congress now is an action which is probably viewed by most of the public in a way that is colored by each voter's opinion of the personalities involved. But there is also a principle involved, one that is probably more important than all the politics.

The gravity of what Congress is asking can perhaps best be outlined by reversing the situation: What would be the reaction of the Congress and the public if the President sent a battalion of troops over to the Capitol to seize the records and papers of the senators and representatives?

In refusing Congress' demands for inside White House information, Nixon is not setting a precedent. Jefferson did that, and it has been followed by Monroe, Jackson, Tyler, Polk, Fillmore, Lincoln, Grant, Hayes, Cleveland, Theodore Roosevelt, Coolidge and Franklin D. Roosevelt—by FDR on six different occasions.

The doctrine of separation of powers means that the two great elective branches of our federal government are answerable primarily to the people who elected them and not directly to each other. It is on that ground that President Nixon is making his stand and basing his refusal to surrender to Congress' demands.

KALMBACH, EHRLICHMAN TESTIFY AT HEARINGS

Herbert W. Kalmbach, former personal attorney and fund raiser for the President, testified before the Senate Watergate committee July 16–17 and detailed how he had raised and channeled $220,000 to the original seven defendants in the Watergate break-in for legal fees and support of their families. Kalmbach maintained throughout the questioning that he had acted with the approval of John Ehrlichman and under the specific instructions of John Dean. He testified that Ehrlichman stressed the payoffs must be kept secret to prevent "misinterpretation" of White House motives in paying the Watergate defendants. But Kalmbach insisted he had thought the funds were "humanitarian" and only for the defendants' legal fees and family support.

In his statement, Kalmbach denied having any prior knowledge of the Watergate break-in or of participating in a conspiracy to cover-up the burglary or other acts of campaign sabotage. In retrospect, Kalmbach told the committee, he felt "used" by Nixon's chief aides: Haldeman, Ehrlichman, Mitchell and Dean. "It is just as if I have been kicked in the stomach," he said. Kalmbach cited his "implicit trust" in Dean and Ehrlichman as justification for his actions. "It is incomprehensible to me, and was at that time, I just didn't think about it that these men would ask me to do an illegal act," he said.

Anthony T. Ulasewicz, who had testified May 23, returned July 18 to detail how, acting for Kalmbach, he clandestinely disbursed the payoffs —sometimes unsuccessfully—to Watergate conspirator G. Gordon Liddy; Dorothy Hunt, the late wife of conspirator E. Howard Hunt Jr.; Hunt himself; lawyers for the conspirators; and Frederick C. LaRue, former campaign strategist for Nixon.

One of the two men closest to President Nixon, John D. Ehrlichman, until April 30 Nixon's assistant for domestic affairs, appeared before the committee July 24. In testimony described as confident and aggressive and at times quarrelsome, Ehrlichman defended every aspect of his and the President's actions before, during and after the Watergate break-in and wiretapping. Declaring that his testimony would "refute every charge of illegal conduct on my part," he singled out former White House counsel John Dean as the principal source of information implicating him and the President in the case. He challenged Dean's contention that the Watergate issue was a major preoccupation of the Nixon Administration during the three months following the June 17 break-in. Under questioning, Ehrlichman explained his role in the Labor Day 1971 burglary of the office of Daniel Ellsberg's psychiatrist and in the events surrounding it. Despite the committee's disbelief, Ehrlichman insisted that the President had statutory authority to order the break-in in the name of national security.

Countering Dean's statement that the White House was engaged by the events of the campaign, Ehrlichman said, "in 1972 with the foreign situation as it was, the President decided quite early that he simply could not and would not involve himself in the day-to-day details of the presidential primaries, the convention and the campaign. He made a very deliberate effort to detach himself from the day-to-day strategic and tactical problems."

In other testimony, Ehrlichman reiterated his denial that he had sought CIA aid for E. Howard Hunt Jr. He disclaimed any part in asking the CIA to formulate an excuse to block FBI investigation of financial links between the Watergate conspirators and the Committee to Re-elect the President. He took issue with a statement made by former Acting FBI Director L. Patrick Gray 3rd. Gray had told government investigators that at a June 28, 1972 meeting with Ehrlichman and Dean, Ehrlichman had told him the Hunt documents should "never see the light of day." Consequently he burned them, Gray had said.

DAYTON DAILY NEWS
Dayton, Ohio, July 20, 1973

The merciless eye of the television camera has revealed much about the personalities of the Senate Watergate committee. Millions of viewers now know Chairman Sam Ervin (D-N.C.) as "an old country lawyer" who can roll words like "fiduciary" and "eleemosynary" on his tongue like Demosthenes shifting stones from one cheek to the other.

Vice Chairman Howard Baker's (R-Tenn.) political star is rising as the result of his careful manner and intelligent questioning. Sen. Edward Gurney (R-Fla.) has been exposed as a White House apologist who does not have the White House's respect. Sen. Joseph Montoya's (D-N.M.) mediocrity is as obvious as dandruff.

The hearings have told the public important things about the men on the Ervin committee — things they would never have learned in the 30-second doorside interviews that generally constitute televised reports about congressional hearings. Must there be an event of Watergate magnitude before the people get a direct look at the action?

Many congressional hearings are about as interesting as watching a log rot back to its elements. Live coverage is expensive. But it may be politically expensive for Americans to know as little about the men who run their government as they know now. There is much discussion about the isolation of the President. Perhaps the deeper issue is the isolation of the people.

Confirmation hearings would commend themselves to the cameras. Those appointed to head the huge Cabinet bureaucracies are often private individuals, unknown to the public at large. Even if viewers observed nothing more about a new Secretary than his tendency to smile at curious moments, that information could form a bridge of interest to questions of substance later on.

Supreme court justices make decisions that affect our lives profoundly, yet how many people, given nine names and nine photographs, could match them successfully?

Hearings, like soap operas, are plotted ahead of time. Unlike soap operas, they often take on a life of their own, heading in directions that can explore a man's character. Congress should offer public television at least, the opportunity to give extensive coverage to important confirmation hearings.

THE ANN ARBOR NEWS

Ann Arbor, Mich., July 25, 1973

WHEN Martha Mitchell said last week that she is "sick of Watergate," she probably echoed the sentiments of many Americans, but there may be as many or more who are fascinated by the televised hearings of the Senate investigating committee.

Former Attorney General John Mitchell's wife isn't exactly an unbiased observer of the hearings, and that raises a question or two. It has been suggested that most of those who say they are bored with the proceedings are Republicans, and that the ones who are enjoying the hearing are Democrats.

We doubt that such a generalization is accurate. There must be Democrats who are unhappy that it is n e c e s s a r y to air this country's dirty linen in such a manner, and t h e r e m u s t be Republicans who while unhappy over Watergate see some benefits to be gained in a thorough expo-

sure. And there must be thousands of persons with one or more courtroom experiences w h o- are relishing the s i g h t of lawyers squirming in their unaccustomed role as witnesses.

Mrs. Mitchell is r i g h t, of course, that the hearings are "rehearsed." Almost everything that is being said by witnesses has been said previously to the senators or to committee counsel. It has become commonplace for a witness to reply wearily to a ques- t i o n e r at t h e public hearings: "Well as I testified earlier . . . "

THERE ARE other aspects of the hearings that bother some viewers. The senators appear so sensitive to the criticism that the hearings may be infringing on the legal rights of witnesses who have been or may be subject to criminal charges that they almost ooze sympathy at times for people they have subpenaed. They fall over themselves voicing their gratitude

for the testimony. They praise each other, laud their bipartisanship, and Senator Baker is ever r e a d y to agree — in fulsome phrases — with the sage observations of the committee chairman, Senator Sam Ervin.

One catches himself nodding in agreement with the elder statesman's biblical analogies and gentle lectures to the transgressors among the witnesses. And when Senator Ervin is reminded (and reminds listeners) of southern justice and morality so out of tune with Watergate one is tempted to put away thoughts of the notorious political machines that have sent many lesser men than Ervin to Congress.

THE political exposure the committee members are g e t t i n g couldn't be bought, but it would be easier on audience and witnesses if each did not have to have his turn at asking questions and so often the same questions.

But Connecticut is w a t c h i n g W e i c k e r , or so he assumes; Hawaii is watching Inouye; Florida is watching Gurney; New Mexico is watching Montoya; Georgia is watching Talmadge. And Senator Baker may be thinking the whole country is watching him. Such hearings present a great platform for launching national political careers.

At 76, San Ervin can't be nursing any political ambitions, and his career is already marked by achievements that would satisfy m o s t men. He has performed well, in our view, in the task given him, and if we had any criticism it would be that he has tolerated too m u c h repetitious questioning and is not above a little grandstanding himself. It may be wrong to criticize this latter tactic, however. Watergate without a leavening factor such as Ervin's puckishness might be dreary indeed.

THE WALL STREET JOURNAL

New York, N.Y., July 17, 1973

Presidential aide Richard A. Moore has been an exceedingly effective witness on the President's behalf at the Watergate hearings. In our minds, in fact, he has, at least for the time being, offset John Dean's damaging testimony on the central question of whether Mr. Nixon knew of the elaborate cover-up, and therefore presumably condoned it.

Mr. Moore is one of the few Watergate witnesses who inspires personal faith. He comes with the recommendation both of Mr. Dean and Mr. Nixon. He has a long and distinguished personal career, and no shady blotches have been uncovered. Unlike most witnesses on all sides, he has no need to justify his own actions in the Watergate case either to the public or to himself. It seems, indeed, that he has been a persistent advocate of getting the facts out. His conduct before the committee, finally, carries the ring of a man who is not telling a contrived story but merely relating the truth as he sees it.

Mr. Moore testified that as late as March 20, Mr. Dean said he did not believe the President knew of the cover-up. Mr. Dean also said, Mr. Moore testified, that the President exhibited surprise when Mr. Dean spelled out the criminal involvement of White House aides on March 21. This account of Mr. Dean's state of mind in March seems to be generally corroborated by the committee's exhibit 39, the uncompleted report Mr. Dean worked on at Camp David. Mr. Moore's personal impression after meetings with Mr. Nixon and Mr. Dean was also that the President did not know. All of this contradicts Mr. Dean's present story of consistent presidential involvement, and instead supports the President's statement that he learned of the cover-up on March 21.

After Mr. Dean's testimony, we said our judgment was that he told a

credible story, establishing a prima facie case of presidential involvement. But, especially given the character and presumed motivation of the two witnesses, Mr. Moore has moved us back into the pre-Dean inconclusiveness. If you listen carefully to what the President's critics are saying, indeed, you will find it made up of surmises, must-have-beens and should-have-knowns, or in other words, the same sort of circumstantial evidence that has been discussed for months.

This morass of circumstance, of course, certainly does create suspicions about presidential involvement. The suspicions are enhanced by the continued failure of the President to give us a complete and detailed account of his view of what happened, especially so after yesterday's disclosure that tapes of Oval Office conversations are available to him. Yet none of this is quite the same as the direct evidence Mr. Dean offered and Mr. Moore has now disputed.

Mr. Moore's appearance also shed some light on the question of a proper forum for a presidential explanation. The committee is of course trying to get President Nixon to agree to be examined personally, and Mr. Moore provided a neat test of how the committee, which really did not effectively cross-examine Mr. Dean, behaves toward a witness whose testimony disturbs the preconceptions of Mr. Nixon's guilt.

There is by now general agreement, we take it, that the name-the-date questioning by assistant counsel Terry F. Lenzner befits the dignity of an insurance claims court in Brooklyn. Senator Weicker got his chance to play bully. Senator Ervin, for all his famed knowledge of the Constitution, was scarcely better, hectoring the witness to prove nothing more than that the newspapers covered the Watergate arrest, and having the effrontery to ob-

ject when Senator Gurney asked Mr. Moore for the same kind of speculation taken with relish from Mr. Dean. Let the President make an explanation, but perhaps he could find a more dignified forum.

The committee's lapse from its initial even-handedness is part of a broader mood, understandable but not especially constructive. Probing into Watergate has turned up plenty of reasons—the break-in, the attempts to turn the IRS to political ends, the Ellsberg burglary, the planning of illegal tactics in dealing with domestic subversion—to feel revulsion at what went on in and around the White House. But this revulsion does not prove that the President's critics are always right, that whatever is charged has been proved.

The best antidote for this mood, it seems to us, is to try to sort out precisely what the President is accused of at any particular time. Is it the charge that he engineered the cover-up? Is it that he should have known about the illegalities? Is it that he erred in his choice of men? Is it that he failed to relay John Dean's reports to the FBI? These are far different charges, with far different implications for Mr. Nixon's presidency. And while we think some have been amply proved, that does not prove the rest.

The important question, it seems to us, is whether Mr. Nixon has been deliberately lying to the American people. Have his explanations so far been patent contrivances, or essentially the truth as he sees it? Mr. Dean's testimony was in effect one answer to this question, but now Mr. Moore's surprisingly effective rebuttal suggests that all of the points will not be scored by the same side, and that final judgment must wait until the available evidence is in.

DAYTON DAILY NEWS

Dayton, Ohio, July 26, 1973

John Ehrlichman's testimony to the Senate Watergate committee has been interesting not for any revealed truths. He has revealed none and even seems to be trying to put a few back. The testimony has been interesting for the attitudes radiated by a man who was one of President Nixon's closest advisors.

Mr. Ehrlichman has shown himself to be a man of blithe amorality concerned almost exclusively with the expediency of any matter, a man incapable of perceiving even the gross distinctions between events that are only superficially similar. Take the matter of the money paid to the Watergate burglars.

It is well established that while some of the $400,000-plus was for legal fees, some of it also was paid to assure the guilty pleas and subsequent silence of the defendants. The money was secretely raised and secretly paid out, through a spy-like system of money drops, code names and elaborate cross-country sneaking.

Yet Mr. Ehrlichman said he could see nothing to worry about in that. Weren't defense funds set up, he asked, for black militant Angela Davis and for Daniel Ellsberg, the Pentagon papers revelator?

Yes, they were, but those were public campaigns for money. Persons who donated to them knew what they were giving their money for, while much of the money for the Watergate defendants was diverted from contributions made for Mr. Nixon's re-election.

Additionally, the funds for Miss Davis and Mr. Ellsberg were established at least in part to make sure that the judicial process would work fairly, while the fund for the Watergate burglars was used at least in part to subvert the judicial process by buying the defendants' silence.

Neither does Mr. Ehrlichman seem to have worried about, or even noticed, the question of propriety involved when the executive branch — for Ehrlichman, Dean, Kalmbach and the others were de facto the administration — took to covertly bankrolling persons against whom the government itself has brought criminal charges.

The picture that comes through from Mr. Ehrlichman, as it has from testimony of some other former presidential aides, is of an administration actually incapable of understanding that in the subtle accounting of rights and responsibilities between citizens and their government, it is the citizens who have the strongest claim to the rights, the government that bears the most responsibility. If it is ever otherwise, we simply will no longer be a free people.

The Burlington Free Press

Burlington, Vt., July 19, 1973

HERE WE ARE at the Watergate circus, folks, and do we ever have a biggie today! I mean, like wow, this is really super. The Watergate persecutors — pardon me, prosecutors — have just discovered that President Nixon has had virtually all of his conversations secretly recorded since early 1971. Isn't this shocking, folks? Gad, how shocking!

What's that? President John Kennedy also made secret tape recordings of both telephone conversations and staff meetings?! But Arthur Schlesinger, that great Kennedy worshipper and author of hysterical — pardon me again, historical — prose says it was "inconceivable" that Kennedy would ever have approved of such an "incredible" system as Nixon's. Oh, the director of the Kennedy Library reports there are at least 60 Dictabelts of Kennedy conversations and 125 magnetic tapes of Presidential meetings?

But the Kennedy tapes can be kept secret, can't they? I mean, they have to be screened and reviewed thoroughly. Sure, that was nearly a dozen years ago, but those tapes contain "sensitive" talks. Now, the Nixon tapes are different — they are pretty current and maybe they can hurt Nixon. I mean, what's the purpose of this Watergate circus anyway? Get Nixon, nothing more and nothing less! Right on!

Just had a horrifying thought, folks. If Daniel Ellsberg really wanted to get the facts about our involvement in Vietnam, why didn't he steal—pardon me again, secure — the Kennedy tapes rather than the Pentagon Papers? Oh, that would have embarrassed Kennedy who started the war rather than Nixon who ended it? Oh yes, of course. Get Nixon!

Well, anyway, we've really got Nixon where we want him with Herbert Kalmbach's testimony about all that secret campaign cash. What's that? Joe Kennedy bought the Presidential election of 1960? Big Labor funneled massive amounts of secret cash into the 1968 campaign against Nixon? But all that was justifiable. After all, it was spent AGAINST Nixon, and that makes all the difference.

It's really sad, though, that Nixon doesn't have a mistress in the White House like good old Franklin D. Roosevelt. I mean, could we ever get him on that one! Like wow, outasight. It's all right for a progressive President to have a mistress, of course, but Nixon is such a reactionary.

Say, what about Nixon's ties with Joe McCarthy? Oh, spare me the thought, is it really true that McCarthy was a great good friend of the Kennedys who spent many a weekend at Hyannisport? And that Bobby Kennedy began and nurtured his political career at McCarthy's knees? Gad, let's forget that one. We mustn't lose sight of the purpose of this Watergate circus. Get Nixon!

Well, folks, the circus is just about over for today. But we'll be back tomorrow, and tomorrow and tomorrow, until we can tear down this President. And while we're doing that we'll continue to promote the fortunes of the most solid and honest candidate around for the Presidency — Teddy Kennedy himself. You know, the chap who was kicked out of Harvard for cheating — pardon me again, chatting — at examinations. The Chappaquiddick Kid himself. How progressive can you get?

Now don't forget: In this circus the elephants are the bad guys and the jackasses — gracious, I mean donkeys — are the good guys. And to hell with compassion and truth and perspective. I mean, like wow, this IS a circus, right?! — F.B. Smith

The Washington Post

Washington, D.C., August 1, 1973

It had the quality of a daytime TV show—an excessively rollicking, over-hearty, "suspense-filled" contest: all right, John Ehrlichman, you have just quadrupled your winnings on "Can You Explain This Away?" Do you want to go on for more? Invariably Mr. Ehrlichman did. And his answers, which were consistently more clever than plausible, suggested that he must be quite a whiz at riddles, conundrums and other word-and-meaning plays designed to astonish and outwit. Of these, our favorite after five days remains the distinction Mr. Ehrlichman made between E. Howard Hunt's briefcase and its contents. Thus, Mr. Ehrlichman instructed the committee's counsel that John Dean had testified, "I told him to get rid of the briefcase, not the contents." The light flashes on and the scoreboard shows another "win." But it is a game.

And what a game. Ever on the offensive, ever unwilling to concede the slightest error in his behavior (although eager to address himself to the moral failings he perceives in others), Mr. Ehrlichman has constructed a novel theory of the Watergate scandals. It is that those who sponsored them (with a few exceptions) are blameless and that those to whom the damage was done were at fault. As cockeyed as it is audacious, Mr. Ehrlichman's theory of the case seems to absolve its author personally of responsibility for anything questionable he did. Indeed, even his tape-recording of telephone calls appears to have proceeded from nothing more complicated than the fact that his White House telephone came equipped with a knob that you could turn and thus record your calls. So it was probably the telephone's fault. Or the dictaphone's fault. Or something.

Finally one had to admire the sheer brilliance, the virtuosity of the performance-as such. But its burden of meaning and its message were something else again. We will leave aside for the time being the stark conflicts between Mr. Ehrlichman's version of events and the versions rendered by half-a-dozen or more previous witnesses. What we find noteworthy are the attitudes and assumptions that informed Mr. Ehrlichman's testimony. There was, first, the smoldering volcano of resentments—against the committee, against all political opposition, against some local "culture" which he supposes to exist that is bereft of all feeling for family, country or moral goodness.

If you saw the world that way—which is to say, if you saw those who differed from or disagreed with you in that light—it would be a short step to the conclusion that democracy simply can't be trusted. And Mr. Ehrlichman seems to have had rather little trouble in taking that step. Thus there is evidently no criminal or autocratic act that he would deny Mr. Nixon and the Nixon entourage the right to commit on the theory that they know what is best and are only doing whatever it is—spying, housebreaking—for our own good. The generic name for this justification, of course, is "national security," a consideration which Mr. Ehrlichman believes is not only paramount, but also peculiarly and exclusively understood by Mr. Nixon and the men who have served him.

But is it? Surely there is something wrong with a theory which asks us to believe that (1) the President and his fallen confidants were uniquely qualified to perceive in the behavior of foreign governments and individuals both here and abroad those tendencies and intentions that constituted a threat to our well-being, while (2) the same President and his same confidants were incapable of perceiving for a full year what was going on in their own inner councils, in the White House and administration over which they presided—and, indeed, in the very meetings they attended. That irreconcilable dilemma of logic is a large part of the legacy of Mr. Ehrlichman's five days before the Senate Committee.

The Star-Ledger
Newark, N.J., July 19, 1973

There was a pathetic, poignant quality about the witness before the Senate Watergate Committee, even though he was well-groomed, was attired in an expensive, softly shaped suit and spoke in firm, even tones.

He did not look like a man who had been taken, a patsy, a fall guy. But that's what he finally conceded he was to the Senate probers; there was a sad, unbelieving expression as he purged himself of the bitter memory of men high in the White House who had set him up, men in whom he had complete trust.

For Herbert W. Kalmbach that was the ultimate demeaning ignominy, the degrading experience of a prominent, highly respected attorney being used as a messenger boy and then betrayed by the man to whom he had loaned $20,000, the man who tape recorded a phone conversation without his knowledge, in a crude attempt to absolve himself of complicity in the Watergate payoff scheme.

* * *

KALMBACH'S appearance before the committee did not add much in a material manner to these hearings; the only testimony of any significant impact was the disclosure that former Presidential aide John D. Ehrlichman had taped a phone conversation with Kalmbach the day before the latter's appearance before a federal grand jury.

There is a possibility that Ehrlichman may have committed a criminal lapse by trying to suborn a witness to commit perjury by suggesting to Kalmbach that he should tell the jury that their only previous meeting was some time before in California, the last time they purportedly had spoken to each other.

But this is a matter for the criminal process, a matter that no doubt will be ultimately determined by a grand jury. The irony of this situation is inescapable, the possibility that Ehrlichman's own recording device may provide the evidence for these charges, which obviously was not the intent of the self-serving taping.

* * *

IN A NUMBER of other ways, the Kalmbach recital, delivered in a flat monotone, was dramatically revealing. It lifted the curtain on a grim, shoddy atmosphere in the Nixon White House, a chilling repository of unrelieved suspicion and distrust among highly placed, influential men in the Administration who arrogantly abused the pervasive power of their office to impose their will on subordinates in shadowy, sinister operations to manipulate a Presidential election.

This is what Watergate is all about; it is not merely a cheap burglary committed by paid hirelings; it was an insidious attempt to misuse government institutions in a criminal manner by men who professed to exalt the law but actually subverted it.

If the Kalmbach experience is typical, along with the other instances of unquestioning subservience to higher ups that came to light during these hearings, then it can be seen that these men had been used ruthlessly and callously for ulterior — and possibly criminal — motives.

The recording device was an indispensable instrument for these men with a passion for secrecy and unlimited power, men who subverted the democratic process for their own purpose, or, worse still, ostensibly in the name of the President. Mr. Nixon himself resorted to an extensive use of sophisticated recording equipment to tape conversations and phone calls. We are now told that this was done for historical purpose, the electronic documentation of the Nixon era.

* * *

BUT THIS SAME material, surreptitiously gathered, has far more useful purpose in a contemporary dimension. It has the awesome potential of determining the truth in an unequivocal manner. These tapes may well hold the decisive element in establishing the full responsibility for the Watergate affair — the planning, the bungled execution of the break-in at the Democratic national headquarters, and the covert attempt to conceal involvement of White House aides and officials of the President's campaign committee, including former Attorney General John N. Mitchell.

There are reports that the President may resist attempts by the Senate Select Committee to obtain tapes and documents directly relevant to the investigation of the Watergate affair. It would be done on the constitutional doctrine of separation of powers.

That premise, if exercised under executive order, has constitutional soundness. But it lacks soundness in other even more significant areas, the most important being the far more demanding test of public opinion — and the potential historical damage to the Nixon incumbency.

The President would be doing himself and his Administration the gravest disservice if he pursues this self-serving course, if that is what it actually is. It would have the poisonous effect of casting suspicion on Mr. Nixon, even if the facts and circumstances are in fact extenuating. The truth, in the end, is the President's best, if not his only, defense in this sordid affair.

Orlando Sentinel
Orlando, Fla., July 27, 1973

UP UNTIL now, there has been one ingredient missing to make the daily Watergate show a smash hit: namely, an applause meter.

And, as a careful earful of the weighted audience reaction would indicate, the antiadministration witnesses would win hands down, while those trying to imply innocence on the part of President Nixon or his associates would be greeted with audible sneers.

Sen. Sam Ervin finally felt compelled to admonish those in the meeting room during fellow Democratic Sen. Herman E. Talmadge's questioning of John D. Ehrlichman Wednesday.

Ervin asked that the audience "refrain from expressing approval or disapproval of the testimony of the witness." His chastisement was seconded by Sen. Talmadge and amplified by the Republican vice chairman, Sen. Howard H. Baker.

We agree with Baker that the job of the committee will be even more difficult if it is "cast in the role of conducting a circus or entertainment."

☆ ☆ ☆

THE ONLY trouble is that Ervin's concern is rather belated. Recently a newsman who attended the hearings on a visit to Washington told us that the senators obviously preened as they came before the TV cameras and how they obviously played to the audience during their turns at questioning.

The attitude of the audience is shared by the press corps situated at the long table behind the witness chair. Unfortunately it is permeating some of the reports carried on the major wire services from the hearings and in editors' judgments of what to transmit on those wires.

Applause or disapproving sounds from the audience, slanted stories reading like reviews which make a folk hero out of Ervin, and even the senator's twitching of his ample eyebrows to express his opinions of testimony he disagrees with, all have one thing in common; viz. a show biz approach to a very serious subject.

DURING THE examination of John Dean by Republican Sen. Ed Gurney, Dean became confused as to the location of a meeting in a hotel. A writer for a national newsmagazine passed a note to Dean's attorney to help the former White House counsel in his testimony. This was done by a writer supposedly objectively reporting the proceedings.

The committee has nothing to be proud of in the carnival atmosphere of the Watergate hearings and it is time Ervin did something about it. But the Washington press corps (one of whose brightest hours was the uncovering of Watergate) wins no laurels for objectivity in its behavior.

Richmond Times-Dispatch

Richmond, Va., July 15, 1973

While testimony on the Watergate scandal has continued to gush from the televised hearings of the Sam Ervin committee, historian Daniel J. Boorstin has attempted, in an interview with *Congressional Quarterly* to put the affair into some kind of long-range perspective. Eventually, after the clamor has died down and verdicts on individual guilt have been rendered, this is an exercise the nation as a whole will need to undertake if future such gross abuses of power are to be avoided.

Dr. Boorstin, who is director of the Smithsonian Institution's National Museum of History and Technology, makes a good point. What makes the Watergate schemes so different from past misdeeds at high levels of government is not that men have suddenly become more avaricious than in the past, but that the *opportunities for misuse of power* have grown vastly.

The natural tendency when one hears the terms "White House" or "Executive Office of the President" is to think of the President and just a few of his well-known close advisers. But Dr. Boorstin observes:

"Why there are hundreds of people who write on White House stationery. This is a new phenomenon. In fact, it's a phenomenon which has astonished and properly astonished, some senators who asked the counsellor of the President if he ever saw the President and he said he didn't. And I think there are something like 40 persons who bear some title such as counsellor to the President or assistant to the President or something of that sort. Now this is a relatively new phenomenon: the opportunity for the President to get out of touch with the people who speak in his name."

◄ ►

Not only has the proliferation of White House jobs made it possible for persons to use or seem to use the prestige of the President without his knowledge, the growth has made it possible, Boorstin notes, for a President to say with some credibility that he wasn't informed of the involvement of his own employes in the scandal which has enveloped the office of the presidency.

Whether the President was aware of the covert illegal activities of those on his staff before last March is still an open question. A measure of encouragement may be drawn from this week's assertions by former Atty. Gen. John N. Mitchell and White House special counsel Richard A. Moore that, in contradiction to the Dean testimony, the President was uninformed by his staffers of the illegal attempts—such as raising of "hush money" for break-in defendants—to cover up the Watergate affair.

So assuming for now that the President did not have guilty knowledge, the fact would remain that men employed in the White House or in the President's re-election campaign were able, without the President knowing, to hatch such despicable plots as: hiring agents to break into the headquarters of the opposition political party and into private homes and offices; eavesdropping electronically in violation of the law; distributing bogus political flyers aimed at destroying political opponents by depicting them as sexually immoral or deviant persons; intercepting private mail without a court order; manufacturing expressions of public support for the President's policies to be published in major newspapers; diverting hundreds of thousands of dollars in campaign funds to support illegal acts; and conspiring to obstruct justice.

◄ ►

If the growth of a large, anonymous White House bureaucracy did contribute to a climate in which presidential power could be abused, the phenomenon did not wholly originate with Mr. Nixon. Franklin D. Roosevelt, an activist President, was one of the first chief executives to rely heavily on a large staff. It is interesting to note that an FDR committee, in recommending in 1939 the addition of a number of executive assistants to the president, said such aides "should remain in the background, issue no orders, make no decisions, emit no public statements. . .They should be possessed of high competence, great physical vigor and a passion for anonymity." In recent years, some presidential aides have tended to be more influential than cabinet members.

Mr. Nixon, of course, cannot evade responsibility for the characters of the men he appointed to these high posts. Moreover, despite his reputation as a "conservative" president, he increased the number of White House employes by 21 per cent and the cost of the White House bureaucracy by 105 per cent during his first term. One reason given for this increment was the President's desire to create a new layer of control in order to master the teeming federal bureaucracy, but in light of his inability—by his own accounting—to retain mastery over what his own aides were doing, this rationale seems awfully lame today.

If there is a lesson from Watergate, it may have to do with the corrupting nature of unguarded power. The people elect only one President and they expect him to be accountable. But when hundreds upon hundreds of anonymous men can use the enormous prestige of the White House for their own devices, their power—which is not derived directly from the will of the people—is increased and the President's—which is—is diminished. It is not a healthy situation for a democracy.

THE DENVER POST

Denver, Colo., July 27, 1973

THE CONCEPT of executive power which John Ehrlichman and his attorney offered the Senate Watergate Committee this week would be appropriate for the dictator of a totalitarian society. It is totally inappropriate for the president of the United States.

Under that concept, the president may lawfully order his agents to break into the homes and offices of American citizens and seize their possessions, if the president decides the breakin is necessary to protect national security information against foreign espionage activities.

In ordering such a breakin, according to Mr. Ehrlichman, the president may ignore the requirement of the Fourth Amendment to the Constitution that he seek a warrant from a court so that "the right of the people to be secure in their persons, houses, papers and effects against unreasonable searches and seizures shall not be violated . . ."

The president may also ignore, in the Ehrlichman view, the principle of separation of powers, which requires that the judicial branch pass in advance on the reasonableness of an intended search by the executive branch and that the executive branch not be the judge in its own case.

Implicit in Mr. Ehrlichman's testimony was the assumption that the president may act in this matter, not through the authorized agencies of government such as the FBI, but through a secret force of presidential agents who are responsive to his orders rather than to the law.

THE OPPORTUNITIES for abuses under this concept are terrifying and innumerable. Justifications related to national security have been used time and again to cover the worst transgressions of dictators against their citizens. The Ellsberg breakin itself is an indication of where this concept can lead.

"In questions of power," wrote Thomas Jefferson, "let no more be heard of confidence in man, but bind him down from mischief by the chains of the Constitution." If Mr. Nixon and his associates had been less restive in their constitutional chains, the Watergate tragedy might never have taken place.

What is most disturbing about the Ehrlichman concept is that Ehrlichman has testified it reflects the thinking of President Nixon himself. The Ervin Committee has performed a valuable service by bringing this concept to light and allowing it to be debated before a national television audience.

If the White House was convinced that the Ellsberg breakin was necessary to protect national security information against foreign espionage activities, its proper course was to try to convince a court of that necessity and obtain a search warrant.

The Fourth Amendment does not prohibit the government from using searches and seizures to protect the national security. It only provides that the government must first convince a court that the search or seizure is reasonable.

OBVIOUSLY, THE White House must have believed its chances in court were poor. It would have taken an imaginative judge indeed to see sufficient relationship between the files of Ellsberg's psychiatrist and the national security to justify the issuance of a warrant.

So the President's secret agents acted without authority of the courts in a simple burglary, which the White House apparently thought it could not expect from the FBI.

It is bad enough for the perpetrators of such a burglary to believe it was authorized by the President. It is even worse, as reflected in Ehrlichman's testimony for the President himself to believe that the burglary was justified.

ST. LOUIS POST-DISPATCH

St. Louis, Mo., July 22, 1973

President Nixon touched on a paramount aspect of the Watergate disaster in some impromptu remarks as he left the Bethesda Naval Hospital. He termed "poppycock" any suggestion that he might resign, and declared with emotion: "Let others wallow in Watergate; we are going to do the job we were elected to do." The question, of course, is not the President's resolve but his ability.

Under present circumstances, Mr. Nixon cannot govern effectively. Only he knows the full extent of his involvement in the Watergate crimes, but as time and testimony pass and he continues to refuse to deal candidly with the issues the country must conclude he has something to conceal. Each day the witnesses before Senator Ervin's investigating committee add threads to the web that is being spun around the President's person.

The disclosure that Mr. Nixon surreptitiously taped conversations with some of those who have been testifying at the Capitol offers the President an ideal way to clear himself of suspicion. It seems quite simple: if he is not guilty let him prove it by giving the tapes to the Senate committee. The implications of a refusal cannot be overlooked.

In this particular case there is no merit in the argument over executive privilege, the right of the President to preserve the privacy of his office. Under constitutional provisions for separation of powers a president does have certain executive privileges, and whether Congress has the right to subpena him or his papers is a matter that must be judged by individual circumstances.

There is nothing in the separation-of-powers doctrine, however, having to do with *voluntary* testimony. Mr. Nixon has perfect freedom to testify if he so desires; the argument over forced testimony may be useful to the President as an excuse for not testifying, but to invoke it is close to an admission of guilt.

If one takes the President at his word, he intends to try to weather the crisis and he obviously believes he can govern. But the evidence, in the loss of morale and momentum that permeates the executive agencies, is to the contrary.

The Congress is in rebellion. The reorganization of the White House staff under Gen. Haig is said to be along the same lines as the secretive operation that helped bring on the scandal. Former Secretary of Defense Melvin Laird, who could give Mr. Nixon excellent political counsel, has been trying to re-establish liaison between the White House and the agencies, without notable success. Although he drafted him as a special assistant, Mr. Nixon has not been taking Mr. Laird's advice on Watergate.

So there is really nothing going on in the Government to indicate Mr. Nixon has a grip on events; one sad example of disarray is the inadequate Phase 4 anti-inflation program. It may be true, as is sometimes postulated, that Mr. Nixon feels he can deal with foreign affairs of great moment and produce a generation of peace, in which event his domestic failures and even the crimes of Watergate will be reduced in history to relative insignificance.

There is no way for this to occur. Watergate represents a massive effort by the highest officials of the Government to subvert the two-party system and the democratic processes through which the country functions. Nothing remotely resembling it ever happened before. For better or worse, Mr. Nixon will be known in history as the Watergate President, and how he deals with the crisis of his presidency will be a major part of that story.

This is the historic issue that now confronts Mr. Nixon. Whether he is deeply involved or not, the disclosures have been so sensational and his own reaction so abysmally lacking, that his prestige may be irretrievably lost. If it cannot be regained and the country set back on the road to decency and normality, then it is Mr Nixon's patriotic duty to resign.

TWIN CITY SENTINEL

Winston-Salem, N.C., July 23, 1973

There are now more investigations into the Nixon administration and the Committee to Re-Elect the President than we can keep track of, and we suspect that some of our readers may be having the same trouble in following the headlines and sorting out who's investigating what.

Herewith an abbreviated list of the major investigations that are underway this summer:

—The Senate Select Committee on Presidential Campaign Activities is investigating the Watergate burglaries and bugging, the subsequent coverup, related political sabotage, illegal handling of campaign money, and other campaign practices.

—Two federal grand juries have been convened in Washington, D. C., to hear evidence presented by Special Prosecutor Archibald Cox. One hears Watergate-related evidence, the other hears evidence on fund-raising, illegal contributions, the ITT antitrust settlement, campaign sabotage, and violations of the election laws.

—The House Armed Services subcommittee on intelligence matters is questioning the use of the CIA by the White House "plumbers unit" for its clandestine and illegal espionage work. A Senate Armed Services committee has held hearings on the same matter.

—A House Government Operations subcommittee is probing the use of $1.9 million for "security" improvements at the President's homes in San Clemente and Key Biscayne. The investigation may include the means by which Mr. Nixon purchased the San Clemente residence.

—The Agriculture Department's failure to tell farmers about the size of the 1972 Russian wheat deal is under scrutiny by the Senate's Permanent Investigations subcommittee. A similar inquiry was made by the House Agriculture Committee.

—A Florida grand jury is investigating illegal campaign activity during the 1972 presidential primary, and has indicted Donald Segretti, a campaign aide in the pay of the White House.

—A federal grand jury in Houston is investigating corporate contributions to the Nixon campaign, and the "laundering" of such money in Mexican banks.

—A Los Angeles grand jury is hearing evidence on the break-in of the office of Daniel Ellsberg's psychiatrist by members of the White House "plumbers unit."

—Four federal grand juries, in Los Angeles, Detroit, Chicago and Las Vegas, are investigating links between organized crime and the Teamsters Union, whose president, Frank Fitzsimmons, is a political ally of President Nixon. The Justice Department is reported to have quashed an FBI investigation that focused on Fitzsimmons' dealings with alleged leaders of organized crime.

—The U. S. Attorney's office in Newark, N. J., has begun an investigation into the President's commutation of the prison sentence of Angelo (Gyp) DeCarlo, reputed Mafia leader who served less than two years of a 12-year term.

—A New York grand jury has returned indictments in the Vesco case against Maurice Stans, finance chairman of the Nixon campaign, and John Mitchell, campaign director.

—A Maryland grand jury is looking into the source of funds pumped into Republican fundraising events and the election campaign of former Rep. William Mills, who apparently committed suicide on May 23 after it was disclosed that he had received $25,000 from the Nixon campaign.

—A House Commerce subcommittee has probed the efforts of Charles Colson, former White House counsel, to influence the appointment of an official of the Securities and Exchange Commission, and the handling of the ITT antitrust suit.

All these exclude some other notable matters such as the milk deal, the IBM antitrust suit, and last week's discovery that the Pentagon was giving Congress phony reports on the bombing of Cambodia. And we may well be ignorant of or overlooking some other investigations. Plainly there is enough here for even the strongest of stomachs.

PANEL RECESSES AFTER HALDEMAN TESTIFIES

The Senate Watergate Committee heard testimony July 30–Aug. 1 from President Nixon's former chief adviser, H. R. Haldeman, who surprised the committee with the revelation that he had recently listened to White House tapes of meetings involving former counsel to the President John W. Dean 3rd. After what Committee Chairman Sam J. Ervin Jr. (D, N.C.) later called a "powder puff" objection from Haldeman on the ground of executive privilege, Haldeman read a prepared addition to his lengthy opening statement, contending that his review of the tapes refuted Dean's assertion that Nixon had been involved in the Watergate cover-up as early as Sept. 15, 1972. Haldeman continued with allegations that Dean was a central figure in the cover-up and had "badly misled" his superiors in the White House.

The committee returned to the issue of the tapes July 31 with expressions of outrage that Haldeman, a private citizen, had been given access to evidence the White House had denied the committee and had even been allowed to take the tapes home with him. Sen. Ervin denounced Haldeman's testimony on the tapes as "counterfeit" and asserted that the testimony was part of a "planned action" by the White House.

Questioned later on his own involvement in the Watergate affair, Haldeman for the most part replied he had no recollection of meetings at which earlier witnesses had said he had been told of break-in plans or cover-up activities. Haldeman acknowledged Aug. 1 that as a counteroffensive against Administration opponents he had suggested Feb. 10 that a story be leaked blaming anti-Nixon demonstrations in 1972 on Democratic presidential candiate Sen. George S. Mc-Govern (S.D.) and Communist party financial support for the demonstrations. The Aug. 1 session was also highlighted by disclosure of a March 30, 1972 memorandum to Haldeman from Charles W. Colson, then a White House counsel, warning that Richard G. Kleindienst's confirmation hearings, which were delayed in the Senate Judiciary Committee, could directly link the President and other high Administration officials to a controversial government antitrust ruling involving the International Telephone and Telegraph Corp. (ITT). In the memo, Colson argued that Kleindienst's nomination as attorney general should be withdrawn in order to prevent disclosure of other White House memos which could "lay this case on the President's doorstep."

Before adjourning its hearings Aug. 7 for a scheduled one-month recess, the Senate committee took further testimony Aug. 3 from Acting FBI Director L. Patrick Gray 3rd and Aug. 7 from former Attorney General Richard G. Kleindienst and Assistant Attorney General Henry E. Petersen, among others.

Gray termed his already acknowledged destruction of documents taken from the safe of one of the Watergate conspirators "a grievous misjudgment." He also related his warning to President Nixon July 6, 1972 that "people on your staff are trying to mortally wound you by using the CIA and FBI and by confusing the question of CIA interest in or not in people the FBI wishes to interview."

Kleindienst testified that while he ordered a thorough investigation of Watergate immediately on learning of the break-in June 17, 1972, he did not have "credible evidence" implicating high Administration officials until April 15. Petersen, who headed the Justice Department's Watergate investigation before appointment of a special Watergate prosecutor, told the Senate panel that he had advised the President to dismiss Haldeman and Ehrlichman. He expressed anger that a special prosecutor had been appointed for the Watergate case.

The Watergate panel recessed having taken sworn testimony from 33 witnesses and compiled 7,573 pages of testimony in 37 daily sessions since May 17.

Meanwhile, there were these developments relating to the disposition of the Watergate tapes:

■ Lawyers for President Nixon filed a brief in U.S. district court in Washington Aug. 7 claiming that the courts had no power to compel release of presidential documents if the President believed such a disclosure was "contrary to the public interest." The White House was responding to a show cause order obtained July 26 by special prosecutor Archibald Cox in the dispute over tape recordings of Nixon's conversations with figures in the Watergate case.

■ The Senate Watergate committee filed suit in U.S. district court Aug. 9 to compel President Nixon to release tapes and other documents related to Watergate. The committee's complaint stated that even if the President had the authority to withhold certain confidential material, the authority did "not extend to the protection of materials relating to alleged criminal acts." The committee also argued that Nixon had already waived executive privilege, especially regarding possible criminal matters, in his statement of May 22, by allowing present and former aides to testify before the committee, and by allowing H. R. Haldeman to listen to some of the tapes after leaving the White House staff.

■ In a brief filed Aug. 13 in U.S. district court, Cox argued that President Nixon had "no constitutional power to withhold the evidence" in the tape recordings of presidential conversations "merely by his own declaration of the public interest." Cox reaffirmed his argument that Nixon had already waived privilege on the tapes by his selective disclosures of some of the material.

Richmond Times-Dispatch
Richmond, Va., August 3, 1973

In politics as in economics, there is a point of diminishing returns, a time when results become too insignificant to justify the efforts made to obtain them. And the Senate Watergate committee is rapidly approaching that point, if indeed it has not reached it already.

What, after all, is the committee's objective? It is not to investigate the life of Richard M. Nixon from the moment of his birth, not to convict those who broke into the office of Daniel Ellsberg's psychiatrist, not to examine the expenditures on President Nixon's California and Florida homes, not to massage the ego of Chairman Sam J. Ervin Jr. and not to promote the presidential ambitions of Vice Chairman Howard H. Baker Jr. No, the committee has one assignment, and one assignment only: To investigate the campaign practices followed in the 1972 presidential election and determine "the necessity or desirability of the enactment of new congressional legislation to safeguard the electoral process by which the President of the United States is chosen."

If the committee ended its investigation today, it would have enough evidence to support the need for "new congressional legislation" to regulate political campaigns more effectively and more stringently. This fact has been recognized by the Senate itself, which decided Monday that it had learned enough to know that campaign reforms are necessary. On that day, the Senate overwhelmingly approved and sent to the House of Representatives a bill that would severely restrict campaign spending and establish more rigid rules for certain other campaign activities. With the Senate having concluded, in effect, that it does not need the Watergate committee's recommendations, what would the committee accomplish by continuing its inquiry *ad nauseam* ?

— — —

Some people argue, masochistically, that a prolonged and exhaustive investigation is needed to shock the American people into an awareness that political leaders can, and sometimes do, abuse their power and infringe on the rights and dignity of citizens; and that it is necessary to continue the investigation until Mr. Nixon's guilt or innocence has been determined. But these arguments collapse under the onslaught of reason and reality.

For one thing, the American people have been shocked to the depths of their souls already. There is no need to continue to pound them incessantly with memos, letters, testimony and tapes that simply confirm what they already know: that some high officials engaged in dubious, disgusting, unethical and illegal acts during the 1972 campaigns.

For another, it is becoming increasingly unlikely that the committee will resolve the question of the President's guilt or innocence. His chief accuser is former White House Counsel John W. Dean III, whose charges rest not upon his direct, personal knowledge of Mr. Nixon's complicity in Watergate but upon impressions Dean formed from conversations with the President and upon certain assumptions that he made as a result of his understanding of White House procedures. Moreover, his testimony is suspect because he is a confessed wrong-doer, a man who has admitted that he participated in perjury and other illegal activities associated with Watergate. Former White House aides H. R. Haldeman and John D. Ehrlichman, who were closer than anyone else to Mr. Nixon, have contradicted Dean, but most members of the committee have indicated that they do not believe all that these two men have said.

And what about those presidential tapes on which are recorded Watergate conversations that Mr. Nixon held with some members of his staff? By themselves, they almost certainly would not constitute satisfactory, conclusive evidence of the President's guilt or innocence. The very authenticity of the tapes would be open to challenge, and some of the conversations would be subject to varying interpretations.

So conclusive proof of the President's guilt or innocence may be beyond the Watergate committee's reach. Anyway, it has neither the power nor the duty to acquit or convict, in a legal sense, any accused person. In the case of lesser officials, this task must be left to the judicial system. Grand juries and Special Prosecutor Archibald Cox are active in this area, and they should continue their efforts until they have accomplished all that they can accomplish. In the case of an officially accused President, guilt or innocence can be established, legally, only through impeachment proceedings, a congressional responsibility. If such extreme action against Mr. Nixon is ever deemed justified, the House of Representatives will have to place formal charges and the Senate will have to conduct a formal trial.

— — —

Our point, it must be emphasized, is not that the Senate Watergate committee has performed no useful service in exposing the scandals of 1972 but that it has, for all practical purposes, completed its mission. It has determined the need for campaign reforms. There is no necessity for it to continue to pile pebbles on top of the mountain. Indeed, prolonging the investigation will only deepen the gloom that has demoralized the nation and weakened its government.

But if the committee persists, it should, in all fairness, broaden the scope of its inquiry. If it is going to analyze the attitudes, the code of conduct and the pre-1972 political activities of Richard Nixon to determine whether he has followed a pattern of behavior that could have contributed to last year's corruption, it should analyze the attitudes, the codes of conduct and the pre-1972 political activities of Democratic leaders whose behavior also might have helped create a climate conducive to corruption. If it is going to read confidential Republican political memos, it also should read confidential Democratic political memos. If it is going to investigate Republican espionage activities, it also should investigate Democratic espionage activities. In other words, if the Watergate committee really believes that it has the duty to open the dark closets of the past to show how dirty politics can be, it should open all of the closets—not just those in the Republican house.

OKLAHOMA CITY TIMES
Oklahoma City, Okla., July 31, 1973

THROUGHOUT the Watergate hearings, members of the Ervin Committee, from the chairman to lawyers on the staff, have maintained that the sole purpose of the hearings was to gather information on what transpired last year which might be of interest in framing new election laws.

To all protests that the hearings are being conducted as if the President and some witnesses were on trial, Ervin and others have responded indignantly that this is no trial. But the impression persists that they do, in fact, regard it as one.

FRIDAY, not long before time for the television cameras to shut down, Sam Ervin donned his country lawyer expression and decided to favor the television audience with some more of his rustic observations. But before he was well into the act, John Ehrlichman's attorney, a Mr. Wilson, interrupted to take exception to a point.

"Senator, may I say something?" he began.

"No, sir, you may not!" Ervin shot back, "You're not a defendant here. . ." From that point the discussion became rather heated. Wilson was trying to steal some of the precious remaining moments on camera, and Ervin was not about to let him get away with that. The senator seemed outraged.

BUT IN that room full of lawyers, not one grasped the point the senator made with his inadvertent use of the word "defendant." Sam Ervin does regard this inquisition as a trial, after all his protestations to the contrary. Someone should have asked him immediately who is the defendant.

The Senate, of course, has no authority to bring an impeachment against anyone, including the President. In the Watkins decision of 1957, the Supreme Court ruled that committees of Congress must remember that they have no legal right to expose merely for the sake of exposure. The high court told Congress — in what was assumed then to be a landmark decision— that any witness before a congressional committee may ask that the relevance of any question to pending legislation be stated. The court said that if there is none, the question may not be put.

THE ERVIN Committee is asking the kinds of questions which could be relevant to an impeachment —if they were being asked by a committee of the House of Representatives. The committee lawyers have asked questions about how policies are shaped, decisions taken, and personnel matters discussed, within the presidential offices. These questions have not yet been challenged, so their relevance to pending legislation has not been stated.

The hearings have been a trial in all but name and rules. The rules of any trial court would bar most of the stuff discussed in these televised proceedings. Few judges would permit the amateur theatrics that have marked almost every day's show.

But at least the chairman has now dropped his pretenses that this is not, in fact, an adversary proceeding, with defendants under attack by prosecutors as if on trial for their lives.

THE DENVER POST

Denver, Colo., August 12, 1973

DURING THIS SUMMER of national discontent over Watergate, Sen. Howard Baker of Tennessee has proclaimed repeatedly and correctly that a key question in the inquiry is "what did the President know and when did he know it?" At the end of the first phase of the inquiry, the hearings have produced no satisfactory answer. The testimony is contradictory, and the President himself refuses to shed more light by releasing tape recordings of important conversations.

Whether the courts will force the President to supply the tapes no one can yet say. If they do not, Senator Baker's question may never be answered satisfactorily.

On the other hand, the question itself is not the only important one arising from the hearings. It is a limited question, in that it is directed primarily at the Watergate affair and not at the other information the hearings have brought to light about Mr. Nixon's conduct of the presidency.

The nation is now confronted with a broader question:

Whatever he did or did not know about Watergate, was Mr. Nixon's behavior in office during the period covered by the Senate inquiry consistent with the standards the American people have a right to associate with the president of the United States?

Some of the facts are in controversy; but this much, at least, has been established firmly by the Senate hearings and by the President's own public statements:

FIRST, President Nixon authorized the FBI in mid-1969 to tap the telephones of staff members of the National Security Council and of four newsmen. The wiretaps made without customary authorization from the courts, were designed to detect leaks of "national security" information. Whether they were constitutional under those circumstances has not been resolved; but the Supreme Court has held that similar taps for "internal security" purposes are unconstitutional.

SECOND, President Nixon approved in 1970 a secret intelligence plan providing for burglary, electronic surveillance and "covert coverage" of mail by government agents in the interest of national security.

The plan contains specific warnings that the burglary and covert mail coverage proposed are illegal. Mr. Nixon has said his approval was rescinded after five days in the light of objections by the late J. Edgar Hoover of the FBI; but testimony before the Senate committee suggested that some form of the plan may have been carried out.

THIRD, President Nixon established in 1971 a secret investigating unit within the White House to look into sensitive security matters and stop security leaks. This unit, "the plumbers", was a means of by-passing the regular investigating units of the government and of opening the way for techniques the regular agencies would probably not have used.

FOURTH, President Nixon personally issued the general authorization, although perhaps not the specific instructions, that led to the burglary of the office of the psychiatrist of Daniel Ellsberg in Los Angeles.

John Dean, the White House counsel, has testified that Egil Krogh, head of the plumbers, told him the authority came from "the oval office." It is not clear, however, how specific the President's grant of authority was. John Ehrlichman, who was present, has said the President used broad and strong language to instruct Krogh to get to the bottom of the Pentagon Papers case. Ehrlichman testified, "one in Mr. Krogh's situation might well believe that he had been charged with taking extraordinary measures."

Mr. Nixon himself has said that "because of the emphasis I put on the crucial importance of protecting the national security, I can understand how highly motivated individuals could have felt justified in engaging in specific activities that I would have disapproved had they been brought to my attention."

FIFTH, President Nixon instructed H. R. Haldemen to make sure that the investigation of the Watergate breakin was limited so as not to touch upon the activities of the plumbers unit or the covert operations of the CIA.

The President's tapes would establish exactly how the instructions were put. But, in response to the President's words, Haldeman sent the deputy director of the CIA to tell the acting director of the FBI that five arrests should be sufficient and that it was not advantageous to have the Watergate inquiry pushed, especially in Mexico.

Although CIA officials insisted then—as they do now—that CIA was not involved in Watergate and that they knew of no CIA operation that would be hurt by an FBI investigation in Mexico, the FBI was asked to curtail its investigation and did curtail it for a time.

SIXTH, President Nixon delayed for at least a week — and probably longer — before authorizing the Justice Department to pass on to Judge W. Matthew Byrne Jr. in the Ellsberg trial information about the burglary of Ellsberg's psychiatrist's office.

When Henry Peterson of the Justice Department mentioned a report on the burglary to the President on April 18, Peterson said the President told him to stay out of it because it was a national security matter.

On April 25, Peterson and Atty. Gen. Kleindeinst convinced the President that information about the burglary had to be given to the judge. Peterson said he and Kleindeinst had agreed in advance that they would resign if the President did not agree.

SEVENTH, President Nixon authorized a discussion between Ehrlichman and Judge Byrne about a job as FBI director for the judge, while the Ellsberg trial was still in progress.

EIGHTH, President Nixon authorized the "bugging" of his White House offices and the recording of his telephone conversations without the knowledge or consent of the people whose words he captured on tape.

NINTH, President Nixon withheld from the Watergate prosecutor tapes and other material that could help to establish the guilt or innocence of persons under investigation for criminal activities. By withholding the same tapes and material from the Senate Watergate Committee, he handicapped an important effort to establish the truth before the American people.

TENTH, President Nixon presided over a staff that brought moral shabbiness into the conduct of White House affairs and into the running of his 1972 reelection campaign.

The President may not have known of the White House "enemies" list, of the use of Internal Revenue Service audits and FBI investigations to harrass the "enemies," of the hiring of private investigators to dig up political dirt, of the fabrication of State Department cables to discredit the late President Kennedy and of the "dirty tricks" of Donald Segretti.

But the people responsible for gross misconduct at the White House and crimes at the Committee to Reelect the President were his staff and his supporters, and they sought to do what they thought the President would want them to do, whether he issued specific orders or not. Mr. Nixon has acknowledged that he must bear some responsibility for the consequences of their acts.

WITHIN THE next few weeks, President Nixon is expected to issue another major pronouncement on these matters. He may be able to place his conduct of the presidency in a far more favorable light. But he has a massive task.

The points listed above perhaps do not add up to "high crimes and misdemeanors" that would constitutionally justify the launching of impeachment proceedings in the House of Representatives. But they clearly have not added to the prestige of the presidency or the confidence of the people in their chief executive. They have brought the Nixon presidency under a cloud, and the nation will continue to suffer as long as that cloud remains.

Americans may prove willing to give Mr. Nixon the benefit of the doubt on the Watergate charges themselves as far as his personal and direct involvement goes.

None of the Senate testimony so far proves conclusively that the President understood the nature of the breakin or the coverup. And no testimony or evidence has thus far been conclusive enough to convince a majority of Americans that Mr. Nixon should not be allowed to finish out his term.

What keeps the cloud over the Nixon presidency is not therefore, only the unproved suspicion relating to Watergate. It is also the strong indication that the President has been using his powers and allowing others to use his powers in ways that evade the law, bypass the regular law enforcement agencies, jeopardize the individual's right to privacy and threaten to deprive citizens of the equal protection of the laws.

What the Watergate hearings have shown about the President's handling of his constitutional obligation to "take care that the laws be faithfully executed" is not inconsistent with information that has come to light in other forums.

Another congressional committee has learned that the President authorized a 14-month campaign of secret bombing attacks against Cambodia without authority from Congress and without telling Congress. Courts throughout the country have been reviewing his impoundment of funds lawfully appropriated by Congress and ruling that he acted improperly.

AT THE HEART of the President's problem is his attitude toward the restrictions imposed upon him by the laws and the Constitution. That is the point on which the American people need reassurance far more than on his role in Watergate.

We hope Mr. Nixon can provide that reassurance in the pronouncement he makes within the next few weeks. If he cannot, his continued tenure in the White House will remain a source of national discontent.

The Star-Ledger

Newark, N.J., August 1, 1973

The names and the faces have changed, but it is clear that the testimony before the Senate Watergate Committee this week will not vary in the slightest from the hearing record of the past several days.

The continuity in the White House recital of Watergate became immediately apparent in the opening statement of the latest witness, crew-cut H.R. (Bob) Haldeman, the President's former No. 1 man. He wasted no time in trying to establish the innocence of himself and Mr. Nixon of any involvement, both the planning and the cover-up of the political scandal.

The presentation was matter-of-fact and orderly, almost dry in context. And then Haldeman, the former advertising executive turned politician, dropped the bombshell: He had listened recently to the secret White House recordings of two of the President's meetings with John W. Dean 3d, the dismissed White House counsel and the star witness against Mr. Nixon, Haldeman and Ehrlichman & Co.

These are the same tapes that the President is prepared to engage in a constitutional confrontation with Congress on the murky premise of executive privilege; these tapes are being withheld from the committee, an arm of Congress, and the government's own special prosecutor, Archibald Cox.

MR. NIXON had no compunction in turning over the tapes to Haldeman in July, when he was a private citizen, but insists he cannot permit them to be used in a private audition, attended by two ranking members of the Senate Select Committee — Chairman Sam Ervin Jr. and Sen. Howard H. Baker Jr., the Republican vice chairman, and Prosecutor Cox.

We suggest that the President may have gravely weakened his case on constitutional protection by permitting Haldeman to listen to the tapes, even letting him take them to his home overnight. It should be apparent, even to Mr. Nixon, that his former chief deputy had no privileged or official status in July, when he got the tapes to review for the President.

But it should be remembered, too, that at the time that Mr. Nixon turned the secret recordings to Haldeman for a private evaluation their existence was not known. This dramatic disclosure was made later, when the Senate Committee staff interviewed another former White House aide who unwittingly revealed that the President's offices had an elaborate recording system.

It was entirely possible, as one well-informed Washington columnist suggests, that the recorded conversations may contain some gamey political discussion that the President understandably does not want divulged. A private audition confined to responsible legislators and the prosecutor could still maintain the confidentiality of any portions that might prove embarrassing to Mr. Nixon. The only importance of these recordings is material directly relevant to the Watergate affair.

The Haldeman version of the now famous tapes is distinctly different than the one given by Dean, who said that the conversation with Mr. Nixon indicated that he was aware of the Watergate affair and had volunteered the information that he had assured executive clemency to Watergate defendants.

Haldeman places an entirely different interpretation on the conversations, on the basis of his intimate association with the President and his personal knowledge of the Nixon personality and approach. One does not have to stretch credulity to suggest that Haldeman's version could suffer from the same close association with the President and his still unswerving loyalty to his former chief.

IF ONE WERE to accept the version of Haldeman and the witness who preceded him, John D. Ehrlichman, the former No. 2 man in the Nixon White House, the only culprit from the inner council was John Dean. It was the latter who misled the President and his aides, Haldeman and Ehrlichman, by not keeping them posted on the true state of affairs.

This may or may not be so, but it should be clear that the fundamental conflicts in testimony that have emerged, not only involving Dean but other principals in this sordid affair cannot be resolved unless there is conclusive corroboration.

And that could be provided by the secret White House tapes, reviewed in private by Senate committee members and the special prosecutor. At this stage, it is the only possible practical approach to resolve the sharp variances in the testimony presented to the Senate committee. It is the only way that the President can remove the dark shadow of suspicion that has been cast on the White House by the political conspiracy.

Getting to the bottom of Watergate is a matter that involves the national welfare as well as Mr. Nixon's incumbency. It is not being helped by frustrating efforts to release the White House tapes; the contention of executive privilege no longer has substance in the light of the disclosure that the President made them available to his former chief aide, Haldeman.

The Charlotte Observer

Charlotte, N.C., August 2, 1973

The lid has been lifted a little and the country can begin to see how the Nixon organization managed the hoax. We refer to the maneuvering during the 1972 campaign, and for a year before, to make it appear that violent forces were threatening the President's safety at public appearances — and then use that picture to remove those who might dissent.

President Nixon visited Charlotte on Oct. 15, 1971, for a massive rally at the Coliseum. It was Billy Graham Day, and although the President was here to honor Mr. Graham it also was obvious to all but the most politically naive observers that he was here for political purposes: to associate himself with a popular evangelist and to win gusty applause.

The Coliseum rally was hardly a private affair, a t t e n d e d by selected guests. It was big and public, and consequently the exclusion of those who might not admire Mr. Nixon amounted to a denial of their constitutional rights. But there was that exclusion, and some people — including some who went there with tickets to applaud the President and Mr. Graham — were manhandled and ejected for spurious reasons.

The Secret Service, certainly, must act aggressively at times to protect the President. But that was not what we had in Charlotte, and it is not even clear that the Secret Service was allowed by the White House to perform that legitimate function. Instead, the Nixon political organization appears to have been in charge. If so, what we had was political hooliganism, under auspices of the President of the United States.

We had been willing to believe the manhandling of law-abiding Charlotte people was based, at least, upon excessive fears or hysteria on the part of those in charge; in other words, that although they were trampling on the Constitution they at least were motivated as much by their own irrational fears as by their tendency toward totalitarian methods.

That, it turns out, was giving them too much credit. H. R. Haldeman was monitoring security plans for Mr. Nixon's appearances. Sen. Lowell Weicker, a Republican who feels outrage over the lawlessness of the Nixon organization, disclosed a memorandum Wednesday at the W a t e r g a t e hearings that he said showed the White House welcomed demonstrations against Mr. Nixon because of the backlash they could inspire.

And more: The memo showed that Mr. Haldeman had written "good" next to a notation that some demonstrators at the Charlotte rally "will be violent" and "great" next to the memo's report that demonstrations would be directed toward Mr. Graham as well as toward Mr. Nixon.

The Nixon group's idea, apparently, was that it could make the most, politically, from such developments. But it also apparently moved to use those possible demonstrations as a pretext for suppressing orderly dissenters. It is not extreme to compare this approach with the one employed by the Nazis in their use of Communist opposition as an excuse to suppress other dissenters at Nazi rallies.

In Charlotte, as U. S. District Judge James B. McMillan concluded in an order Tuesday, there was "an utter lack of evidence" that 14 excluded young people who later filed a damage suit had threatened Mr. Nixon's safety. In ordering the Secret Service to stop barring people from presidential appearances because they are dissenters, the judge said that in Charlotte there was "a wholesale assault upon the civil rights and liberties of numerous citizens."

But was the Secret Service, which has been politicized by the White House at least to some extent, really running the show? One person who seemed to be in charge at the Coliseum, giving Charlotte's police orders at times, was Ernie Helms, who was not a police officer and not a Secret Service agent. There have been reports that he and others were recruited for the task.

It is important for the public to know whether Mr. Helms was working for the Secret Service, or perhaps for the White House's political operatives. Whatever answers are immediately offered, they should be treated with skepticism until the proof is in. Were private citizens— such as the Charlotte mother forced out of the Coliseum with her fourth-grade son because she had chatted with two long-haired students inside — being manhandled not because of official Secret Service judgments but because of the judgments of the Nixon political strategists?

If so, Charlotte may not have been the first instance. After the government misconduct here, we pointed out that very similar episodes had taken place a month before when Mr. Nixon was in Dayton, Ohio; a month before that when he was in Springfield, Ohio; and a week before that when he was in Bangor, Me. In each case law-abiding people were set upon by men who may have been Secret Service agents or may have been privately paid hoodlums answering to the White House.

The shadow of White House lawlessness grows longer. We repeat what we said immediately a f t e r the Charlotte episode: "We strongly object . . . This is not a banana republic."

ARKANSAS DEMOCRAT
Little Rock, Ark., August 4, 1973

It seemed to us that some sympathy for President Nixon was beginning to develop — a sort of backlash — until he refused to turn the tapes over to the committee. The tide turned then because, if the tapes proved him innocent, as he said they did, why not release them?

Then, this week, we had the bombshell dropped by H. R. Haldeman, which was that he had listened to the tapes and, in fact, had taken one home for 48 hours. As Sen. Sam Ervin, D-N.C., was quick to point out, the President blotted out his own excuse for not furnishing the tapes to the Committee. Executive privilege, which was the excuse, would hardly extend to ex-Presidential aides, who, after all, make up a not insignificant slice of the population of Washington, D.C.

To those of us who still don't believe the President is guilty of any criminal acts, Haldeman's testimony was reassuring. He said that the tape proved that neither he nor the President had done anything wrong, that they refuted John Dean's incriminating testimony and, furthermore, that he thought anyone listening to them would come to the same conclusion. But this probably is not the general reaction, which takes the form of more anger, more suspicion directed toward the President.

It bothers us that Haldeman listened to the tapes alone even in the privacy of his home. The White House had maintained that the tapes were in the custody of the Secret Service, but obviously the custody is more that of a check-out girl than a security guard. Now, if the tapes are ever made available to the public and they prove Mr. Nixon innocent, the charge will be made that the tapes were altered by some of those Watergate electronic experts who are out on bail.

But, regardless of that, the tapes have become such a major issue in the investigation of this scandal that we do not see how the President can afford not to make them available to the committee. Perhaps his strategy is to let some witnesses like Haldeman have the benefit of hearing the tapes before they testify in order to blunt some of the sharp, accusatory questioning by the committee. In the case of Haldeman, for example, his testimony about what the tapes contained really diverted the committee. Then, at the strategic time, the President will come to some accommodation with the committee.

Indeed, at week's end, some Washington reporters were saying that Republican leaders fully expected Mr. Nixon to find some way to let the committee hear the tapes. This could come in the form of a private listening party in the White House for Ervin, the Democratic chairman of the Watergate Committee, and Sen. Howard Baker, the Republican vice chairman. The two men made the suggestion in a television interview the other day. We would add, as others have, that to make the session more meaningful, Prosecutor Archibald Cox ought to be invited, too.

A private, informal meeting like this would head off a constitutional crisis. It probably would satisfy the public, too. And it would also allow the President to save face. It's our opinion that Mr. Nixon is going to have to do something like this just to save his job.

THE SACRAMENTO BEE
Sacramento, Calif., August 2, 1973

It is hard to escape the conclusion President Richard Nixon attempted to use his former chief of staff, H. R. Haldeman, to give the American people and the Senate Watergate Committee a self-serving version of secretly recorded presidential conversations concerning the Watergate scandal.

Haldeman's testimony that the contents of the tapes he listened to clear the President of involvement in wrongdoing can only be taken as the interpretation of a self-interested witness and viewed, as several committee members put it, with suspicion.

There is an old doctrine of law that the best evidence is the actual document or recorded information, not an involved party's version of it.

———

Why did the President, knowing Haldeman was to testify before the committee, ask him to listen to a number of tapes which the President himself insists are utterly confidential personal possessions? Haldeman says he heard at least one tape after leaving his White House post and was a private citizen.

The fact raises strong suspicion the President, while refusing to release the tapes themselves, wanted Haldeman to be in a position to give a version of their contents which would support the President's claim of no complicity in Watergate or its coverup. This is bolstered by the fact the President offered only the most feeble objection — committee chairman Sen. Sam Ervin of North Carolina rightly termed it a "powder puff" objection — to Haldeman's being questioned about the contents of the tapes he heard. Further, it was Haldeman who volunteered the knowledge he had listened to them at all, thus practically inviting committee interrogation.

———

The whole matter of Haldeman's testimony about the tapes smacks of careful staging which would permit Nixon to stay in the background like a tight-lipped ventriloquist using Haldeman's mouth.

It simply will not wash. Only the most gullible would be persuaded by this dumb-show.

Legally, having thus permitted this Pandora's box of suspicion to be opened, it appears imperative the President should be compelled to give the committee and the American people the tapes themselves, and let interpretations fall as they may.

HERALD-JOURNAL
Syracuse, N.Y.
August 5, 1973

The unfair standards employed in the Watergate investigation are highlighted in the recent "name-calling" by John J. Wilson, attorney for former White House aides H. R. Haldeman and John Ehrlichman.

News media seeking President Nixon's scalp were outraged at the use by Wilson of the words "the little Jap" when angered by tactics by Sen. Daniel Inouye, a member of the Senate Watergate committee. Wilson made the remark while chatting with two reporters and said later that he did not think the quote would be used. The reporters gleefully used it.

Yet no one appears outraged when the press, itself, refers to Haldeman and Ehrlichman as "Hans and Fritz", "the two Nazis", the "White House Gestapo," or call Haldeman "Himmler."

These names, used freely by some of the press in news stories, and reportedly by senators in cloakroom conversations, are more vicious than the words that Wilson let slip out.

These references to Haldeman and Ehrlichman are more brutal because they are calculated spleen, not a name uttered in frustrated anger, as Wilson's remark was made.

And they are more terrifying because they refer to the infamous brutality of the Nazi movement in Germany before and during World War II. Anyone with any soul at all would hesitate to call a man "Himmler" but columnists like Joseph Kraft appear to delight in doing so.

Yet no one is outraged at this. Why not?

DAILY NEWS
New York, N.Y., August 1, 1973

Former top White House aide H.R. Haldeman testified to the Senate Watergate probers on Tuesday that he not only had heard two of the "presidential tapes" dealing with disputed points in that sordid affair but actually took one home after he departed his official post.

The tapes may, as Haldeman said, support President Richard M. Nixon's claim to innocence on all counts with regard to the bugging and cover-up. But it seems to our lay minds that the President also undermined his claim that the recordings are privileged papers by giving his onetime chief of staff access to them.

If Mr. Nixon is letting friendly witnesses refresh their recollections of key meetings by referring to the tapes, he will find it hard to convince the courts—if it comes to that—or the American people that they should not be heard by committee members or at least by an objective, unbiased outsider.

CHICAGO Sun-Times

Chicago, Ill., August 12, 1973

There is perhaps nothing so embarrassing in all the Watergate testimony as L. Patrick Gray's confession that he burned secret documents along with his family's Christmas trash because that's what he thought the President's men wanted him to do. Gray, the acting head of the Federal Bureau of Investigation, showed himself to have been so in reverence of the office of the President, so in awe of its executive magnificence, that his sense of right and wrong became distorted. It is this, the confusion of reverence with respect, of awe with loyalty, that characterizes the first phase of the Senate Watergate hearings. And one of the results of the hearings certainly ought to be a fresh awareness that democracy is not nourished by awe and reverence. It doesn't thrive on unquestioning worship. Democratic government is a comparatively simple mechanism that works best when its participants temper their respect with an insistence on rational decisions made in the public interest by fully accountable individuals.

Gray just seems to have served his country without understanding it, and if there is a single tragedy to be identified as a common bond among Watergate witnesses, that is the one. Gray, the quintessential Decent Man, shared his misunderstanding of the limits of authority with the arrogant power brokers, John D. Ehrlichman and H. R. Haldeman. He shared it with John W. Dean III, the young man on the make, suddenly scrambling to survive the muck. The full Watergate cast of characters, in fact, with the singular exception of the outspoken Henry E. Petersen, seems to have come to government prepared only to manipulate it or to be manipulated by it.

Petersen, assistant attorney general in charge of the Justice Department's criminal division and the man to whom the Watergate investigation was entrusted prior to the appointment of a special prosecutor, seemed to hold both the government and President in respect, but he did not equate the two. Petersen indicated that he believed he was a co-equal citizen with any of those with whom he came in contact in the course of his duties, and, by his own account, he said to the President on April 15: "If I reach the point where I think you are involved, I've got to resign. If I come up with evidence on you, I am going to waltz it over to the House of Representatives."

That is an infinitely healthier attitude than was exhibited in Gray's admission that he held the Presidency to be "above and beyond reproach." There are echoes of Nuernberg in that phrase, however uncomfortable the knowledge may be. If a dormant American strain of authoritarianism is not to become active and virulent, private citizens and public servants are going to have to be able to question the actions of a President as quickly as they would the actions of a governor or a village trustee. The power of each one derives from the same source.

There is a recent report from the Department of Health, Education and Welfare entitled, "Records, Computers and the Rights of Citizens." The report has no connection with the Watergate scandal but is germane to the study of what occurred. The report is, fundamentally, an assault on authoritarianism. It insists that there must be limits to a government's power to gather data about its citizens because "it is becoming much easier for r e c o r d-keeping systems to affect people than for people to affect record keeping systems."

The Watergate episode is crowded with individuals who have adopted the view that it is the purpose of government to affect people, rather than the contrary. It is not surprising that Watergate involved illegal entry and bugging and taping. Nor is it surprising that some of the principals in the sorry drama have reacted to authority with bent knees and genuflection. But it's time for a reversal. Watergate has underscored the need for democratic decision making, and the need for holding the decision-makers' feet to the fire whenever they forget that they represent a democratic nation and its people.

THE KANSAS CITY STAR

Kansas City, Mo., August 2, 1973

Public men sometimes react in strange and wondrous ways to public events. And not always, it seems to us, with a logic that we mere mortals can understand.

Watergate offers three recent cases in point. Our sense of proportion and balance has been offended by recent comments by the President of the United States and the senior senator from North Carolina. Our sense of justice, of the American imperative of avoiding prejudicial prejudgment of any man, has been equally outraged by the action of a congressman from Massachusetts.

And since Watergate has added words and phrases to the vernacular, we would like to haul out an old word for immediate application. President Nixon, Senator Ervin and Representative Drinan stand guilty of obfuscation. And that, for the leaders of any society, can be a grave offense.

To begin with, let us consider Rep. Robert F. Drinan (D-Mass.), who has obviously leaped to his own conclusions and introduced a resolution to impeach the President. It is an act that defies rational explanation. To be sure, Drinan's background as one of the most bitter of Nixon haters makes his motives rather transparent, and equally suspect.

It is time, he suggests, "to think the unthinkable." So the representative has charged ahead full speed, but we trust the charge will be slowed by the House Judiciary Committee, now the somewhat uneasy custodian of his resolution. Even so, the mere fact that it has been introduced may undercut the continuing investigation of both the Ervin committee and of Archibald Cox, special prosecutor. No one could interpret the resolution as the result of any thoughtful and objective weighing of the evidence to date. And certainly most Democrats would regard it as an open embarrassment to their party.

But if that was one extreme of obfuscation, Mr. Nixon has gone to the other. In a toast at a dinner for the prime minister of Japan, he said, "Let others spend their time dealing with the small, murky, unimportant, vicious things." Really, Mr. President.

Of course the chief executive is entitled to make his case and we trust that he will, in time. The sooner the better, for the nation's peace of mind. But we fail to see that such a putdown of Watergate and its implications is in any way an effective defense. It is, rather, an ostrich-like stance that is risky for the President himself.

Certainly the American leader must spend time, as he said he would, developing "a better world." But a nation shocked by Watergate, whatever the ultimate revelation of presidential involvement may be, must assume that building a better nation is a priority part of building a better world. We need to know the truth of Watergate, in so far as it is knowable, and to find, s o m e h o w, ways to protect ourselves against such things in the future.

We fail to accept the possible conclusion that Mr. Nixon, by his words, was countenancing the activities now lumped under the general heading of Watergate. To do so would also be to think the unthinkable. We must assume that the President, too, wants the facts to be known. For if we are to accept other presidential statements at face value, his defense must lie in those facts.

To sort them out, and to serve the cause of justice, there is a special prosecutor. Mr. Nixon may disagree with the purpose and the methods of the Senate committee, and within the context of the adversary relationship, that is understandable enough. But surely he does not intend to downgrade the importance of the Cox investigation or to suggest that its purview is no greater than the small, the murky, the unimportant and the vicious.

We have one more individual on our list of extremists and obfuscaters: The honorable chairman himself. Indeed, Mr. Nixon's words seemed almost to be cut from the same cloth as the senator's at one of the committee sessions last week. But the President minimized, so to speak, and the senator maximized.

The chairman did so by classifying Watergate as "the greatest tragedy this country has ever suffered." And that, we submit, was one of the silliest things said to date about Watergate. Conscious or unconscious hyperbole is a device that does not always serve the purpose of politicians. Even folksy and, in general, admirable politicians like Senator Ervin.

But as we say, public men are often inclined to strange reactions and the rest of us, we suppose, must grin (which is sometimes very difficult) and bear it.

Representative Drinan has jumped an irrational mile to an as yet unacceptable conclusion.

President Nixon has left the impression that certain sordid events of the 1972 campaign were of minimal importance and ought not to concern those working for a better world.

Senator Ervin, by so overstating his case, has worn for the moment the headgear of the oratorical clown, thus adding a touch of the ridiculous to the serious business of his committee.

None of the three has contributed wisdom to the debate. On the contrary. Each, in his way, has laid rude hands on the overriding purpose of the moment, which is to discover the truth and then, thoughtfully and fairly, to take such actions as may best serve the cause of a better nation.

TWIN CITY SENTINEL
Winston-Salem, N.C., August 3, 1973

We are beginning to understand more of why the Nixon administration was so jumpy about "leaks."

As everyone knows it was leaks that led to formation of the now-famous White House "plumbers," and their job in turn was to sandbag the dikes of "national security."

But keeping state secrets intact is one thing. Protecting officials who have been saying one thing and doing another is something else. Events of recent days put the worries about leaks in a different light.

One of the l e a k s that has been much cited and denounced was a 1969 report that U.S. warplanes were dropping bombs in Cambodia. It was a rather routine report, but it was hotly and thoroughly denied at the time.

Now, from recent discoveries of the Senate Armed S e r v i c e s Committee, we can see why the story caused so much unrest in the White House.

At the time the administration was claiming that Cambodia was a neutral nation. Actually it was at t h e beginning of a secret 14-month war during which 100,000 tons of bombs were dropped on the ''n e u t r a l'' nation's territory. Not even t h e civilian head of the Air Force knew it was happening. Senior members of military committees in Congress were equally ignorant.

The secret war in Cambodia at least had some claim to national security, even if the war was illegal — as a federal court recently ruled. But this was not true of a lot of other information lying around the White House. If ever released, some of these documents might show that certain administration statements about the ITT antitrust settlement were, to borrow a phrase from John Mitchell, nothing less than a ''p a l p a b l e, damnable lie.''

Take, for example, the claim that the settlement, highly favorable to ITT, was handled "exclusively" by the Justice Department's leading trust-buster, and that politics had nothing to do with it. In one memo that came to light last week, Charles Colson, a presidential counsel, wrote to H.R. Haldeman that:

"There is a Klein to Haldeman memo, date June 30, 1971, which of course precedes the date of the ITT settlement, setting forth the $400,000 arrangement with ITT. Copies were addressed to Magruder, Mitchell and Timmons. This memo put the A.G. (Attorney General Mitchell) o n constructive notice at least of the ITT commitment at that time and before the settlement, facts which he has denied under oath. We don't know whether we have recovered all the copies . . . despite a search this memo could be lying around anything at 1701 (re-election headquarters)."

At the time Colson wrote that memo, in March 1972, a parade of administration witnesses were before a Senate committee, denying that anyone knew that ITT had pledged $400,000 to the Republican 1 9 7 2 convention before ITT won its case in an out-of-court settlement.

As the Colson memo indicates, quite a few people knew about it, but they were saying otherwise. N o wonder that the administration had such a demand for "plumbers," paper shredders and burn bags.

THE WALL STREET JOURNAL.
New York, N.Y., August 3, 1973

At this stage in the Watergate proceedings the most helpful question to keep in mind is: What is the issue, anyway?

Despite its surface simplicity, the question keeps slipping out of focus. Every time the attention of the Watergate committee and the nation starts to zero in on a definable issue, a dozen distractions erupt someplace else. Some of the upcropping issues, in particular the question of executive privilege for the Oval Office tapes, are in fact central to the matter at hand. Others, in particular the campaign indiscretions being dredged up by some Senators and reliable sources, strike us chiefly as efforts to find new ways to embarrass the administration when it seems the central question falters in that purpose.

Senator Baker's formulation of the central question—what did the President know and when did he know it—serves well enough as a one-sentence summary, but leaves the true importance unexplored. The answer to Senator Baker's question is important not merely as a historical curiosity, but as the answer to further questions: How much importance should we really attach to Watergate? Can we as a nation pretty much put the matter behind us, or is it still an issue demanding momentous decisions?

Regardless of the President's direct involvement, of course, the Watergate affair renders a severe judgment on his governance. As we have been saying from the moment last year's political campaign opened, that Watergate could occur at all indicts the kind of men the President has chosen and the kind of atmosphere he allowed to grow in the White House. But if that is the whole of the matter it is largely behind us. Presidents do make mistakes, which must be balanced against their successes. There has been a change of guard at the White House. The details of precisely who is guilty of what will be decided by competent courts. There should be more discussion of whether the lesson has been truly learned, but that can and probably must wait until headier questions have been resolved.

For the matter can scarcely be put aside if the President was deeply involved, as John Dean has charged and many Americans believe. That would mean that the cover-up is still going on today, every day, as the White House issues denial after denial. Such a total breach of faith with the American people could not be simply ignored for the next three years, and what to do about it would remain very much on the national agenda.

This, it seems to us, is what the televised Watergate hearings are all about, or should be. Which is essentially the truth, John Dean's testimony or President Nixon's May 22 explanation? For our part, we feel that no satisfying answer has yet emerged, and we doubt that any will unless or until key portions of the Oval Office tapes are released. As we have said previously, we thought that John Dean did make a prima facie case, but that it was eroded by presidential aide Richard Moore. Now, if you focus not on various embarrassments but the central issue, Mr. Dean's case has been further eroded by John Ehrlichman and H. R. Haldeman.

In the case of Mr. Ehrlichman it's especially hard to focus this narrowly. His doctrine of implied powers of the presidency screams for attention. Perhaps there are extreme circumstances when a President would be morally justified in breaking the law, but Mr. Ehrlichman was talking about the break-in attempting to steal Daniel Ellsberg's psychiatric records. A man who would stretch implied powers to cover that would stretch it to cover anything.

Yet that tells us next-to-nothing about presidential involvement. The other strong impression left by Mr. Ehrlichman's testimony was that regardless of whether he was telling the truth, the committee was no match for him. Certainly the questioning did not succeed in exposing inconsistencies or otherwise seriously denting his story that the cover-up resulted from a weak link in the chain of delegation, namely, John Dean

Mr. Haldeman was even more effective in rebutting Mr. Dean. The heart of the allegations against the President revolve around a handful of meetings with Mr. Dean, and Mr. Haldeman was the first witness to offer a contradictory direct account of some of them. He was present at one and much of another, and his account is plausible and internally consistent. His contention that Mr. Dean is confusing the March 13 meeting with the March 21 meeting would in itself explain away much that would incriminate the President, for at the later date the remarks in question are entirely consistent with the President's official explanation.

And of course, Mr. Haldeman's account was based on a recent rehearing of the Oval Office tapes of the two meetings, which is both a strength and a weakness. It is difficult to believe anyone would directly lie about the content of the tapes so long as a possibility remains that a court may order them released. But if the tapes say what Mr. Haldeman says they do, it is more difficult than ever to understand why the President refuses to release them. It's baffling to imagine that the same President who would order the tapes made, and we now learn, the same President who turned some of them over to Mr. Haldeman even after he left the White House, would simply from principle turn so fastidious about their release.

In our judgment John Dean's testimony on the central question has so far received no important corroboration, and has been at least balanced by contrary witnesses. There may be still further developments, but at the moment two things continue to raise suspicions about the President. One is a general though questionable assumption that inevitably he would know everything important going on in the White House. The other is the natural inference of complicity to be drawn from his refusing to release the tapes even if procedures can be designed to meet the legitimate demands of executive privilege.

If we were confined simply to weighing the direct evidence the Watergate hearings have produced so far, we could believe that the President has been telling the truth, or at least is entitled to a presumption of innocence, and that the matter can be put behind us. But if so, we cannot understand why he doesn't take the action within his power to dispel the chief current reason to believe otherwise.

VICE PRESIDENT'S FINANCES PROBED; AGNEW CALLS KICKBACK CHARGES LIES

Vice President Spiro T. Agnew announced Aug. 6 he was under investigation for possible violations of criminal law. The investigation was being conducted by George Beall, U.S. attorney for Maryland, concerning allegations of kickbacks by contractors, architects and engineers to officials of Baltimore County. Agnew was Baltimore County executive from 1962 to 1967 before his election as governor of Maryland.

In his brief statement Aug. 6, Agnew had said he would make no further comment on the investigation until it was completed, "other than to say that I am innocent of any wrong-doing, that I have confidence in the criminal justice system of the United States and that I am equally confident my innocence will be affirmed." After Agnew's statement of innocence was published, Knight Newspapers carried a report that the government was investigating allegations that Agnew received $1,000 a week from contractors while county executive and governor and a lump sum payment of $50,000 after he became vice president. There were further reports Aug. 8 that Agnew had retained a New York law firm and had met with President Nixon to discuss the case. The reports indicated that the probe was focusing on state contracts awarded during Agnew's tenure as governor in 1967–68 and on federal contracts by the General Services Administration in Maryland since Agnew became vice president in 1969.

Agnew held a televised press conference Aug. 8 to deny wrongdoing. He said reports that he received payoffs from contractors were "false, scurrilous and malicious." He denounced as "damned lies" reports he took kickbacks of $1,000 a week from contractors. Asked if he ever had "a political slush fund financed by Baltimore County contractors," Agnew said "never." Had he ever received money from contractors or businessmen for his personal use? "Absolutely not." Had anyone "threatened to drag you into this unless you helped to kill the Baltimore County investigation?" "I'm not going to foreclose the possibility that such things may have happened," he said. "Neither am I going to assert at this moment that they did." But no one had directly asked him to kill the probe, Agnew said. "Defamatory" statements were "being leaked to the news media," he said, and he could not "remain silent." Whatever their source, he asserted, "I have no intention to be skewered in this fashion." Agnew suggested that the allegations against him be "looked at as accusations that are coming from those who have found themselves in very deep trouble and are looking to extricate themselves from this trouble and are flirting with the idea that they can obtain immunity or reduced charges, perhaps, by doing so."

Agnew made his personal finance records available Aug. 14 to the U.S. attorney's office in Baltimore, Md. He also volunteered to answer questions in the investigation. In volunteering to open his records for inspection, which Beall had invited him to do, Agnew made several constitutional reservations. "I do not acknowledge that you or any grand jury have any right to the records of the vice president," he said. "Nor do I acknowledge the propriety of any grand jury investigation of possible wrongdoing on the part of the vice president so long as he occupies that office." The records of Agnew's two-year administration as governor of Maryland and "any and all" financial records of his campaign for the governorship were subpoenaed by federal investigators Aug. 10.

The New York Times

New York, N.Y., August 11, 1973

Vice President Agnew's first response to disclosure that he was under investigation for possible criminal violations in the letting of Maryland public contracts was a declaration of innocence, coupled with the statement: "I have confidence in the criminal justice system of the United States."

The flood of rumors published in the wake of the first stories then prompted the Vice President to hold a free-swinging news conference in which he denounced as "damned lies" allegations that he had taken kickbacks from contractors. "I have nothing to hide," he repeatedly told reporters.

That is an admirable posture, especially by contrast with the reticence of President Nixon in supplying information needed to illuminate key aspects of the Watergate scandals. But the Agnew stance of full willingness to be judged by the American system of criminal justice is hardly advanced by the hesitancy he is now showing in making himself subject to the processes of that system.

*   *   *

The original formal notice from United States Attorney George Beall of Baltimore said his office was looking into allegations involving such crimes as bribery, extortion, conspiracy and tax fraud. The Beall letter solicited Mr. Agnew's voluntary cooperation in turning over copies of his personal financial records and income tax returns. Instead of meeting the deadline set in that notice, the Vice President, through his lawyers, has obtained an extension of at least one week to give him time to decide whether he will cooperate in the investigation. Without waiting for him to make up his mind, Federal investigators have subpoenaed Maryland records covering Mr. Agnew's term as Governor and his campaign finances in that period.

In his news conference Mr. Agnew kept open the possibility that his ultimate decision might be to contend that his position as Vice President made him immune from indictment, prosecution or even testimony. That would be an extension of the argument made by legal representatives of Mr. Nixon earlier this week that a President can be tried in the courts for crimes he committed only after he has been impeached, convicted and removed from office.

Whatever merit that still untested doctrine may have for the President, with the fateful responsibilities he must discharge, it has much less when applied to the Vice President whose executive duties have always been so minimal as to defy definition. It becomes more dubious still when the grand jury inquiry in which he is involved focuses largely on events before Mr. Agnew became Vice President—the period in which he served as county executive of Baltimore County and Governor of Maryland.

*   *   *

Mr. Agnew has said that he wants to get the advice of his own lawyers and of constitutional authorities before making up his mind on his future course. In the end, however, the decision must be his, and he has said that he will make it independently of the President or anyone else.

We hope Mr. Agnew will make it in the spirit of the answer he gave when asked whether he would make any attempt to obtain F.B.I. or Justice Department files in connection with the Baltimore investigation. His response was that he "would not encourage the use of any kind of approach to this case that would allow me privileges not readily available to any person under investigation."

That response is precisely in line with Mr. Agnew's original expression of faith in his ability to prove his innocence under the system of criminal justice that applies to all other Americans. It is the course to which he will be well advised to return, whatever detours may be concocted for him by the researchers to whom he has turned.

The American people have had since Watergate a surfeit of doubletalk from officials who promised candor and delivered obfuscation. The best way for Mr. Agnew to maintain the credibility of his assurance that "I have nothing to hide" is to cooperate unreservedly in the grand jury inquiry and whatever legal proceedings may grow out of it.

The San Diego Union

San Diego, Calif.,
August 10, 1973

A nation worried by the hurricanes of Watergate, which mercifully has been pushed into the background for a month, has received another jolt to its sensibilities by the news that federal investigators are looking into the background of Vice President Spiro Agnew.

Little more is known to the public at the present time except that the stories of kickbacks from persons doing business with government, as well as reports of bribery and conspiracy, are supposed to go back about five years to the period when Mr. Agnew was governor of Maryland.

It does seem strange that something of the magnitude alleged in press reports could remain a secret for five years. Certainly, we could not presume to reach any conclusions in the matter. Indeed, we don't see how anybody can on the basis of what is known. At this time Mr. Agnew must be taken at his word that the accusations are falsehoods.

On the whole, we thought that Mr. Agnew's decision quickly to face the press rather than to remain silent until the proper legal time was sound. He conducted himself forthrightly and well, and gave the American people much to think about.

Most troublesome were his observations that the secrecy that must necessarily surround some of the investigative and legal process was not one of the protections that apparently is accorded to vice presidents. He made it clear that the leaks involved came from "sources close to the federal investigators."

This is a melancholy commentary on our times. In the last three or four months, we have seen leaks from the National Security Council, the White House, the Senate investigating committee, law enforcement agencies, federal grand juries where raw hearsay evidence is offered and even from federal investigators under oath to respect security. A senator on the Watergate committee has admitted that he leaked information, and there is now a concerted effort to strip the cloak of secrecy from the discussions of the President and his closest advisers.

It can be said that the entire Watergate disclosure is the result of leaks from sources close to the sources. That is correct. It can be said that some good will come from Watergate and perhaps even the Maryland investigation, and that is correct.

But it also is true that there is a point at which the bad of such tactics far outweighs the good. If Vice President Agnew is correct in his emphatic and forthright assertions that he is innocent, we may well have reached that point.

The Washington Post

Washington, D.C., August 8, 1973

Vice President Agnew has made a dignified and proper response to the disclosure that he is under federal investigation for possible criminal conduct. The United States Attorney for Maryland, Mr. George Beall, is pursuing broad allegations of kickbacks by contractors to Maryland politicians. It is necessary to emphasize that the prosecutors have not yet presented evidence to a grand jury, let alone obtained an indictment. Mr. Beall has only notified the Vice President that the inquiry is under way, and that it reaches his activities. Mr. Agnew has replied by declaring his innocence of any misbehavior, and asserting his confidence in the American system of justice.

By this statement of faith in the courts and their ability to bring out the truth, Mr. Agnew suggests that he does not intend to hide behind his high office. It appears that he does not choose to wrap himself in dubious interpretations of the Constitution, or in privileges questionably extracted from it. His words indicate that he is prepared to undergo the unpleasant necessity of this investigation as he would if he were still Governor of Maryland, or Executive of Baltimore County, or indeed a common citizen like any other. As a citizen, and a very prominent one, he is now entitled to have the rest of the country remember that many a man has come into court under the gravest charges and proceeded to clear himself completely.

The motive of the investigator is a question that sometimes crosses the mind when a leading politician comes under criminal investigation. In this case, the circumstances are reassuring. There is no reason to suspect any motive but the prosecutor's sworn duty to enforce the law. Mr. Beall was appointed by President Nixon. He is a Republican, and the son of an old and distinguished Maryland Republican family; his late father sat in the United States Senate, and his older brother sits there now. The current kickback investigation has also reached Dale W. Anderson, the Democrat who is the current Baltimore County Executive. It is a nonpartisan inquiry into allegations of bipartisan misconduct.

This investigation into the possibility of kickbacks in Maryland is not connected with the series of scandals revolving around the Watergate incident and the financing of the 1972 national election. The kickbacks, if any actually took place, fall into a familiar if deplorable pattern of corruption. Unlike the issues being raised by the Watergate revelations, kickbacks are a kind of crime with which the American courts have had a great deal of experience.

But while the investigation of the Vice President is entirely separate from the Watergate scandals, it can only reinforce the sense of loss that many Americans feel as they regard their national government. It can only increase the sense of being adrift, as lawyers debate how to handle serious charges against men in very high offices—charges for which there is no precedent in our history as a nation. Our political and legal system is coming into a time of severe and unanticipated testing. The test, in the case of Mr. Agnew, is whether the U.S. Department of Justice and the federal courts, if it comes to that, can proceed as they would proceed with any other public official—rigorously, impartially and promptly. That is the tradition to which Mr. Agnew, in his brief statement, entrusts himself, and that is the hope to which most Americans will now turn.

Chicago Tribune

Chicago, Ill., August 8, 1973

As the old saying goes, it never rains but it pours. To add to the troubles already facing the Nixon administration, we now learn that Vice President Agnew is under investigation for possible violations of criminal law in Maryland, apparently while chief executive of Baltimore County and later while governor of the state. It is reported that the charges involve kickbacks, bribery, and income tax evasion.

If this investigation had been undertaken and publicized by the enemies of Mr. Nixon and Mr. Agnew, of whom there are many, it might have been looked upon skeptically as part of an already well orchestrated plan to get rid of both of them and install somebody else, presumably a Democrat, as President.

But it wasn't. The investigation is being conducted by the Republican U. S. attorney for Maryland, George Beall. Mr. Beall's brother, J. Glenn Beall, was elected senator from Maryland in 1970 with the strong backing of the White House. The backing was so strong, indeed, that it included a reported $140,000 in cash provided by Herbert Kalmbach, the Nixon lawyer whose name has popped up as a dispenser of cash in the Watergate affair. Sen. Beall reported no such contribution, and has said that he doesn't remember it. However these confusing jigsaw pieces are laid out, they don't create a picture of a political conspiracy.

The story was first published in yesterday's edition of the Wall Street Journal, a paper which by no stretch of the imagination can be accused of baiting the Nixon administration. As soon as it appeared, Mr. Agnew issued a statement acknowledging that he had been advised by letter of the investigation and that he was innocent of any wrong-doing. The letter had been approved by Atty. Gen. Elliot Richardson.

And so we confront the astonishing spectacle of a Justice Department conducting two simultaneous investigations of possible criminal activity, one involving the President of the United States and the other the Vice President. It will be a long time before all the facts are in and historians can sort out this phenomenon. In the meanwhile the administration will have to labor under a new cloud and the whole country will have to suffer.

But it is already possible to offer two words of caution and one of consolation.

First, Mr. Agnew's eager critics had better restrain their ebullience until more of the facts are in. They will no doubt be tempted to talk about resignation and impeachment; but what they say is not going to affect Mr. Agnew's decision. All it will do is create more confusion, hurting the dollar abroad and the stock market at home. After all, the charges are not brand new. Some of them surfaced during the 1968 campaign, especially in the New York Times, and then subsided without substantiation.

Second, Mr. Agnew himself should resist any temptation to invoke executive privilege and the separation of powers. The charges involving him have even less to do with the duties of the executive branch than Watergate does. Both the separation of powers and executive privilege are essential ingredients in our system of government—last resorts to protect one branch from being devoured by another. It would be a shame to invoke them, and thus risk having them destroyed, in a matter where they have no business. Especially one involving things alleged to have happened largely before Mr. Agnew became Vice President.

Finally, the consolation. There is something almost awe-inspiring about seeing the judicial arm of government pursuing possible criminal charges against the two top officials of that government. Dismaying as it all is, this is something which has never happened, and probably could never have happened, in any other country at any time in history.

THE CHRISTIAN SCIENCE MONITOR
Boston, Mass., August 11, 1973

One of the wondrous things about the American political system is its unpredictability. You think you know who is going to be running for what job next time around — and then something happens: Edmund Muskie losing his cool and weeping, or George Romney saying he was brainwashed, or a Republican Department of Justice attorney from a long line of distinguished Maryland Republicans putting the former Republican governor of Maryland, the now Republican Vice-President of the United States, in his investigatorial sights.

It's like a child tapping a kaleidoscope. Every piece moves and changes its relationship to every other. The pattern is new and different. Old calculations are out the window. Everyone affected has to sit down and do his sums all over again.

Only last week Spiro Agnew was rated in the polls as the Republican who could run strongest against Edward Kennedy. But that was last week. How would he run against a Kennedy candidacy now, even if he is cleared of all impropriety? Only last week Mr. Agnew was the big-name Republican in most demand for party rallies and candidate launchings. Any Republican getting ready to run in 1974 was already trying to line up an Agnew speech. Today, if you were getting ready to run for the Senate — or City Hall — what big-name Republican would you most want to come to your town and speak on your platform?

As of today you, a prospective 1974 or 1976 candidate, would probably want Nelson Rockefeller, Ronald Reagan, Howard Baker, or Charles Percy. Those four names are the obvious beneficiaries of any slippage in a potential Agnew candidacy.

Was Mr. Agnew going to run anyway? He had never declared that he would be a candidate in 1976. There has been a consistent thread of hesitancy from the beginning of his national career. He never quite sounded like a man who really wanted to go higher than the vice-presidency. Yet his popularity in the party and his own freedom from taint of Watergate had made him the favorite candidate of many of the party's local leaders.

What happens should Mr. Agnew be indicted? The possibility must certainly be considered by his party, and by all politicians. Does Mr. Agnew resign? If that should happen the United States would have its first experience under the new amendment to the Constitution covering the succession. The President would nominate a new vice-president to take office on confirmation by a majority vote in both houses of Congress. Who would Mr. Nixon nominate? And what would that do to the hopes of the hopefuls for 1976?

And then there are the Democrats, watching in dazed fascination from the sidelines. Four months ago was the 1976 Democratic nomination worth having? It didn't seem like it. Today — spring freshets of money are refilling the almost empty Democratic coffers. The Republicans are the ones suffering from shortages.

It's the great American game — because it's still — an open game.

The Des Moines Register
Des Moines, Iowa, August 9, 1973

Now it is the Vice-President under investigation. The Justice Department's probe of Spiro Agnew's conduct as governor of Maryland and U.S. Vice-President covers possible bribery, extortion and tax fraud.

This is not another Watergate in the sense that a reluctant government was pushed into investigating Agnew by the media. The initiative for the probe came from the U.S. attorney's office in Baltimore. The U.S. attorney is an employe of the Justice Department, which approved the investigation.

T h e d e p a r t m e n t deserves commendation for tackling this politically explosive situation. The apparently forthright way it is going about the Agnew probe is in contrast to its gingerly handling of the Watergate case, which resulted in near-success for the cover-up.

But the fact remains that the Justice Department investigation is a case of the administration investigating itself. The administration has an enormous stake in Agnew's establishing his innocence. If the federal grand jury refuses to indict him, the public will naturally wonder how effectively the Justice Department pursued the case.

Agnew is entitled to the same treatment as any other person suspected of criminal conduct. The Watergate case has created a situation that makes it difficult, if not impossible, for the Justice Department to approach the Agnew case in a normal manner. Watergate has cast a cloud over the department's integrity that can be dispelled only by a demonstration that the department is not mired in politics. Over-eager officials might be anxious to indict Agnew, though an indictment might not be warranted, as proof of the department's rehabilitation.

In fairness to the public, and to Agnew, the investigation of Agnew's conduct is best handled by the Justice Department. The special office established to prosecute the Watergate case is ideally suited to take on the Agnew probe. At the very least, the Justice Department's moves in connection with Agnew ought to be taken in consultation with the special prosecutor and with his concurrence.

Atty. Gen. Elliot Richardson has decided to keep the investigation inside the Justice Department, though he apparently did notify Special Prosecutor Archibald Cox about the case initially. Richardson evidently is convinced that the Justice Department is capable of handling the matter properly. We doubt that the public shares the conviction. Confidence that justice is being done is as important as justice being done.

ARKANSAS DEMOCRAT
Little Rock, Ark., August 10, 1973

Just when it appeared that the Nixon administration and the Republican Party might get a breather from the damaging blows dealt them by the Watergate scandals, along comes one of the sharpest arrows of all aimed at the GOP's Mr. Clean himself, Vice President Spiro T. Agnew.

According to reports from both Washington and Baltimore, the vice president has been on the take. One source has him accepting kick-backs from contractors to the tune of $1,000 per week and another says he took a bribe of $50,000.

Unlike his boss, President Nixon, who is a bit slower to respond to personal attacks, Agnew immediately called a press conference and branded as "damned lies" the rumored charges against him and declared that he would be fully vindicated.

Perhaps so. Perhaps not.

Whether Agnew is guilty of all of the rumored charges, time alone will tell. What is clear at this point is that he is under investigation by the United States attorney for Maryland for possible violations of the criminal statutes as well as by a grand jury that has been looking into his activities since January.

"Where there's smoke . . ."

And that's but part of the continuing political nightmare in this heated summer of our discontent. If Agnew is found guilty it will be a further eroding of the people's faith in their system and the men they have elected to run it.

Many persons, with reluctance, have accepted the idea that Nixon might have to resign or face impeachment and with equal reluctance they had begun to think of Agnew for the presidency.

Not any more.

Now in all probability he is finished. His hopes for succeeding Nixon either by impeachment or at the polls in 1976, are shattered. Agnew himself may face removal by Congress if found guilty. So long as the criminal shadow hangs over him, his effectiveness as the nation's number two man is zero, and even if all of the charges are proved false, by their very nature they will have stained him like tatoos that can never be erased.

The rumors about Agnew are cause for lament far outside the councils of the GOP. All citizens, regardless of political persuasion, should share the sorrow and fright that this new crisis in leadership has forced upon the country. First Nixon, weakened and humiliated by Watergate, and now Agnew openly suspect of using his high office for personal enrichment at the public's expense.

Leadership without followers is a mockery and yet that is the political vacuum this dynamic duo has created for America. Their actions have drowned out their oft-spoken words about "law 'n order" and have left the people wondering who they should follow and why.

Can chaos be far behind?

THE BLADE

Toledo, Ohio, August 12, 1973

VICE President Spiro Agnew handled himself adroitly and cooly in fielding questions at a hastily arranged press conference held to answer allegations of kickbacks and bribery in which he may have been involved. He labeled such accusations—and they are not yet formal charges—as "damned lies" and emphasized that he has nothing to hide from the federal investigation now under way.

In that regard, his openness and candidness stand in sharp contrast to the blanket of secretiveness and isolation in which President Nixon has wrapped himself while refusing to lay the facts of Watergate on the table or to turn over to investigators any type of evidence that would help clear up a confused picture.

There is no doubt a natural temptation for Mr. Agnew's staunchest supporters to label any investigation into some of his activities as vice president and a former governor of Maryland as politically inspired, triggered if not quarterbacked by Democratic opposition in hopes of fatally wounding him in the public eye. That does not appear to be the case in this instance.

This investigation into suggestions that Mr. Agnew received kickbacks of $1,000 a week from Maryland contractors and a $50,000 lump sum after he became vice president was launched, and is being pursued, by a Justice Department that is very much a part of a Republican administration. It is also reasonable to infer that no federal prosecutor starts an investigation of the vice president without the knowledge of the President.

The prosecutor of this case is a young Republican attorney appointed by Mr. Nixon and whose brother was elected U.S. senator from Maryland in 1970 with strong White House support. (So strong, in fact, that it included a "donation" of $140,000 funneled to him through Herbert Kalmbach, Mr. Nixon's former personal attorney—a sum which, for some reason, the senator neither reported nor remembers.)

And the letter that went from the prosecutor to Mr. Agnew informing him that he is a target in the wide-ranging investigation had the personal approval of Attorney General Elliott Richardson, a respected member of the Nixon administration. So it is rather obvious that this Agnew investigation is pretty much of a Republican show at the moment—a fascinating chapter in American history in which the Government is pressing separate inquiries into possible illegalities by both the President and vice president of this nation.

There is wondering, of course, at Mr. Nixon's true feelings about Mr. Agnew's new crisis. Obviously, it will hurt the Republican party; but there is strong evidence from 1972, when the White House virtually ignored other party candidates, that Richard Nixon is willing to put his own survival above that of anyone else, the GOP included.

The President has been badly burned by Watergate revelations. He knows only too well that there has been talk of his resigning and a resolution introduced in the House calling for impeachment even though that seems a highly unlikely turn of events today. So if perchance some of the sheen is rubbed off Mr. Agnew, he would look far less attractive as the salvation of the GOP and any latent Republican support for impeachment of Mr. Nixon could be thus greatly eroded.

This would represent some Machiavelian thinking by Mr. Nixon and his tight-knit crew, to be sure. But after what has already been learned of their attitude toward former stalwarts in the Administration who got caught in the Watergate scandal, who can say that it has not been given more than a fleeting moment of reflection in the Oval Office?

THE ☼ SUN

Baltimore, Md., August 8, 1973

Great care must be exercised at this point in any consideration of the news that Vice President Agnew is under investigation, along with others, on allegations that include bribery, extortion and tax fraud; allegations reportedly having to do with the awarding of state contracts while he was Governor of Maryland in 1967 and 1968, and of federal contracts in Maryland let by the General Services Administration since he became Vice President.

These are allegations only, and the prosecutors of the United States attorney's office in Baltimore have not yet even presented to a grand jury any evidence on which the charges are based. Much less has Mr. Agnew been indicted, nor does the announcement of the investigation mean that he necessarily will be indicted. He himself, properly declining comment until the investigation has been completed, expresses confidence in the criminal justice system and confidence that his innocence will be affirmed. There, at this moment, the matter should be permitted to rest, while the investigation proceeds.

It has to be recognized, however, as a matter of considerable political moment, in view of questions about Mr. Nixon's future in office. According to the careful report of *The Wall Street Journal*, it is so recognized in Washington. The formal notice to Mr. Agnew from U.S. Attorney George Beall was, the *Journal* reports, first cleared by Attorney General Richardson before its hand-delivery to the Vice President, and Mr. Richardson further notified Archibald Cox, special prosecutor for Watergate and its ramifications.

Again, great care must be exercised against any jumping at conclusions. The notification to Mr. Cox did not connote, so far as anyone knows or has so much as intimated, any Agnew involvement in Watergate, and it should be pointed out that in the rather exhaustive probing of the Ervin committee, with all its lurid revelations, Mr. Agnew's name has not figured. This aspect is now emphasized in Mr. Richardson's subsequent decision to keep the Agnew investigation strictly within the Justice Department, not giving it to the special prosecutor.

A fair, dispassionate and orderly pursuit of the processes of the law is the requirement in this case now.

Baltimore, Md., August 10, 1973

The current federal investigation of Vice President Agnew, whatever the outcome, could hold residual benefits for Maryland politics. It may reveal at long last the extent to which high elected officials seem to lean favorably to some private consultants bidding for state business, while ignoring other competitors in the field. For years less than a handful of consultant firms has dominated public works projects in Maryland. And now federal investigators, who have subpoenaed state Department of Transportation records, are about to make a microscopic examination of their favored status and of allegations involving bribery, extortion and tax frauds.

For Marylanders who have concerned themselves over such matters, the inquiry could not have come at a better time. Two massive bridge projects have already cost the state extra millions of dollars because of time delays and cost overruns. The Chesapeake Bay bridge was completed 15 months behind schedule and cost $30 million more than anticipated. The outer harbor bridge crossing is already 44 months off schedule and $33 million over its initial estimated price. As noted in these columns earlier this week, the consultant fees for both bridge projects have risen by an even higher percentage than the costs of construction.

Critics have long charged the overruns are part of a unique political system, which finds consultant firms or their officers contributing or collecting campaign funds for officeholders at election time. The allegations reportedly lodged against Mr. Agnew go far beyond political kickback, however, and in any case are still only allegations. It may be, as state officeholders often claim, that private consultants are chosen solely on their present standing and past performance in the field. It may even prove—who can be sure?—that the consultant's interest in politics is no more than that of your average, concerned citizen.

HERALD☒EXAMINER

Los Angeles, Calif., August 9, 1973

Vice President Spiro Agnew went before the nation's press Wednesday and subjected himself to a barrage of questions concerning accusations of misconduct when he held public office in Maryland.

The charges were perpetrated by the same gang of Nixon-haters who specialize in innuendos, vague "official sources," and who care nothing of what happens to the country as long as they can get the President.

Agnew told the reporters the allegations against him were "false, scurrilous and malicious ... damned lies." He will fight to prove his innocence under the laws of this nation which presumes a person to be innocent until proven guilty.

Agnew told it like it was. His self-assurance, his concise answers, and his command of the English language added to the excellent impression he made on the national television audience as well as those who were present at the press conference.

We believe Agnew will prove his innocence — just as we believe President Nixon will be cleared of wrongdoing in the Watergate case.

Both questions will be decided, however, in the Courts — and not by those who snipe at the President and Vice President from the gutter.

SENATE PASSES ELECTION REFORM BILL LIMITING FEDERAL CAMPAIGN FUNDING

A campaign fund reform bill that would set the strictest controls yet on political campaign funding was approved by the Senate July 30 by an 82–8 vote. The bill would impose ceilings on the amount of single contributions and on spending by candidates. It would also establish a new federal agency to monitor and enforce the bill's provisions.

Among those provisions:

■ Individual contributions to candidates for president or Congress would be limited to $3,000 per election, applying separately to a primary election, a general election or a runoff. The same limit would apply to gifts from special interest fund-raising organizations.

■ Donations of more than $50 would have to be made by a traceable check.

■ The total annual contributions by an individual, including his or her spouse and children, would be limited to $25,000 for all federal candidates and fund-raising committees.

■ Donor identification, as in the current law, would be required by occupation and place of business as well as by name and address.

■ Total campaign expenses for a seat in Congress would be limited to an equivalent of 10¢ a voter in the district or state represented in the primary contest and 15¢ a voter in the general election. A presidential candidates' limit would be the same as a senator's in each state.

■ The Congressional franking privilege for free mailing would be suspended for mass mailings 30 days prior to elections.

■ The current law's provision requiring equal broadcast time for all candidates for president and Congress would be repealed.

■ Another current restriction against contributions by fund-raising groups organized by corporations or unions with government contracts would be repealed, on the ground that it was discriminatory in permitting contributions by non-contractors.

■ During debate on the bill, a proposal for public financing of federal elections was tabled by a 53–40 vote July 26 after assurance was given the issue would be taken up later in the year in separate legislation.

The New York Times
New York, N.Y., August 10, 1973

Whether or not Vice President Agnew is drawn further into the burgeoning scandal in his home state of Maryland, the Federal investigation of alleged kickbacks and bribery there will put the spotlight more fiercely than ever on the shocking way in which political campaigns are financed. With the country still trying to digest the massive revelations of the Senate Watergate committee, no further illustration of corruption in the electoral system is needed to establish the case for drastic reform. The danger is, rather, that Congress will be panicked into adopting legislation that will mollify a rightly aroused country without providing genuine and lasting change.

The bill hastily passed by the Senate in July is a fair indication of what may happen. In the emotions aroused by recent events—indignation, shock, perhaps political fearfulness—amendments were, in the words of Senator Cannon of Nevada, "offered and accepted simply as a result of the pressures of Watergate rather than as a result of study and hearings in committee. . . ." Though the measure passed in the Senate is reasonably good on the whole, it has glaring weaknesses which should be remedied when the House takes up the measure next month.

Foremost among these is the astonishing repeal of a provision in the present law which forbids corporations and trade unions holding Government contracts to contribute through their own political action funds. Another loophole would enable these national organized entities not only to give money but to evade the contributor limits by making multiple gifts through state and local committees across the country. At the same time, small "cause" organizations, which serve the public interest, would be severely limited and perhaps driven out of existence. In this blatant favoring of special interests, the bill, as Senator Baker of Tennessee blandly put it, "does not reflect the kind of thorough examination of the electoral process" that Watergate should stimulate. In addition, it is clearly an incumbents' bill, with spending limits so low that challengers would have little chance against better-known opponents in office.

The endless complexities of campaign finance legislation, exemplified anew, point more and more decisively to some form of public financing as the answer to this knotty problem. The idea is picking up surprising support. The Senate Finance and Rules Committees are scheduled to hold hearings on some form of public financing in the fall, with such Senators as Baker and Russell Long of Louisiana apparently moving in this direction. The House will have to debate the question in framing its own bill next month; the Udall-Anderson version, calling for Federal contributions in proportion to privately raised funds, already has 125 co-sponsors.

The public funding of campaigns involves problems of its own which are not to be belittled—particularly in the case of primaries. But it might be far more profitable for Congress to concentrate on these problems than to continue the vain and interminable search for formulas to protect the country against the known, extensive and inescapable evils of mixing private money and public politics.

The MIAMI NEWS
Miami, Fla., August 11, 1973

Not even waiting for the Ervin Committee to complete the Watergate hearings, much less propose reforms in the federal election laws, the Senate passed a whole series of amendments to the campaign act, then went home to tell a cynical public of a new political climate in Washington.

Two points stand out: The Senate didn't lack for rhetoric on the horrors of Watergate during five days of debate, nor will the election system be repaired overnight from the "dirty tricks" of the last two years.

And yet the bill, which limits to a degree the contributions to a political campaign, contains features which should be enacted in advance of the 1974 elections. One is the repeal of the Federal Communications Act's "equal time" provisions so that major candidates can debate on TV and radio without the handicap of minor candidates muscling in.

The second important provision creates an independent, non-partisan elections commission to enforce all campaign spending and disclosure laws. The commission would have the ability to prosecute violations without having to turn to or wait upon the Department of Justice, which works under much political handicap itself.

The Senate took care of the fat cats, who finance many campaigns, by ending the flow of anonymous cash, like that which poured into the Nixon campaign and provided payoff money for the Watergate wiretappers. An amendment by Florida's Lawton Chiles would require that any contribution of more than $50 be made by check, traceable to the giver. The Senate limited to $3,000 the amount any one person could contribute to a candidate's campaign and would limit to $25,000 the amount a person could give to all candidates in an election year.

Most serious flaw is a failure of the Senate to reduce effectively the political clout of special interest contributors, such as labor's COPE and the medical profession's AMPAC, and individual business executives with interests to promote or protect. Direct contributions of corporate or union funds remain unlawful but the Senate opened the way to many more "voluntary" political funds.

The reform amendments now go to the House, which has never shown itself to be in a hurry about political cleanups. But mounting public criticism, in the wake of Watergate, may shame the representatives into early action.

THE LOUISVILLE TIMES
Louisville, Ky., August 9, 1973

Now that both major political parties have achieved the necessary publicity with proposals for campaign-spending limits in this fall's races, they should immediately get together and agree on a formula to follow. The dollar ceilings proposed by the Republicans and the Democrats are not so far apart as to cause any major difficulty.

The Republican position, first advanced July 3, calls for a ceiling of $150,000 on over-all spending by each major party. The Democratic plan, belatedly unveiled this week, would allow each party headquarters $25,000 for over-all expenses, limit the mayoral candidates to $62,000 each and restrict spending in the county judge's race to approximately $35,000 per candidate. That adds up to $122,-000, plus what is spent by the candidates for other city and county offices and the General Assembly.

In 1969, when the Burke-Hollenbach Campaign Fund reported spending $122,435 and the Jefferson County Republican Campaign had outlays of $235,633, the total reported general election expenses of candidates for offices other than mayor and county judge were $93,673. These races involved a total of 114 aspirants for 20 General Assembly and 12 aldermanic seats, the city police court judge and prosecutor and nine countywide offices. Among these were the commonwealth's attorney, sheriff, county and circuit clerks and county attorney.

The Republican proposal then is the more restrictive of the two. Its danger lies in the leverage it would give party headquarters over the candidates for the lower offices. Anyone showing some independence or incurring the displeasure of the people at the top might find himself overlooked when his allotment within the $150,000 ceiling was being determined.

The Democratic idea of allowing seekers of independent offices to raise and spend their own money thus seems the fairer of the two. It certainly would encourage ticket splitting by letting candidates achieve an identity of their own and not tying their fates tightly to how the top of the ticket fares.

This suggests a compromise. Why not request the rival candidates for each office to reach agreements on individual spending ceilings? Such a method would provide for an over-all spending limit, certainly higher than that proposed by either party headquarters, but one reached by all the candidates.

Otherwise, the parties are not too far apart. In principle, they support financial disclosure, complete reporting of campaign contributions and outlays and the establishment of a bipartisan oversight or ethics committee, although the Republicans would make their body a permanent one.

Where there is likely to be a breakdown is in the Democrats' call for restrictions on the use of paid advertising. This would be linked to an agreement by radio and television stations and newspapers to provide an agreed-upon amount of time and space.

The idea has much to commend it. Joint radio and television appearances by the candidates and "Meet the Press" type interview shows during prime time promise to ventilate the issues better than would 30-second radio and TV spot announcements. Nor would the lack of newspaper advertising hinder the public in reaching a decision.

But as radio, TV and newspaper executives have emphasized, the complete Democratic package is unacceptable, for various reasons.

Fortunately, neither party has put forward a set of non-negotiable demands. Both have indicated a willingness to compromise. If they can reach some sort of reasonable spending limitation, agree to disclose fully all campaign gifts and expenditures, lay the groundwork for a permanent "oversight" committee and establish a format for joint radio and television appearances, then other things will fall into place. The visual and verbal pollution that usually accompanies political campaigns in the form of garish billboards and ads aimed at building an image rather than disseminating the truth would automatically be limited by the spending curbs.

Candidates would be freed of the necessity to try gimmicks. They could strive for real communication with the voters, hearing them out and being heard, in return.

Watergate has shown the need for such a style of campaigning as a result of public revulsion with the things that went on in 1972 simply because so much money was available with which to attempt to corrupt the political process. Louisville and Jefferson County can pioneer this new way this fall. The opportunity should not be lost.

THE MILWAUKEE JOURNAL
Milwaukee, Wis., July 28, 1973

One way to cut the cost of America's long election campaigns is simply to shorten them. Thus a Senate passed bill would trim federal election campaigns by providing that:

— No congressional or senatorial primary could be held before the first Tuesday in August.

— No presidential nominating convention could begin before the third Monday of that month.

Some critics worry that this would be unfair to a candidate challenging an incumbent representative, president or senator who has had two years, four years or six years to gain name recognition, propagandize his constituents and organize his re-election campaign. Yet in the age of TV and jet travel, a good case can be made for shorter campaigns.

A presidential challenger usually has been campaigning for months prior to the convention and is a familiar figure. Once nominated, he's on the cover of Time and Newsweek and on the network news nightly. His every move and word in public is covered by an army of newsmen as he jets from place to place.

Even an obscure George McGovern was a household word by the time his 1972 campaign got rolling. His trouble was rejection, not recognition. Thus, limiting presidential campaigns essentially to September and October seems reasonable. While a challenger might lose some organizational time, he now doesn't make much of a public push until Labor Day anyway.

A congressional challenger, of course, may have more trouble offsetting an incumbent's natural advantages. A challenger could, however, start campaigning long before the primary, as many already do. Then his face is known and views are exposed before the runoff. Besides, a primary early in August would still give candidates about 12 weeks for electioneering. That is more than they have now in Wisconsin, where the primary is in September and challengers seem to have a fair shake.

The Senate reform is a moderate step toward diminishing lengthy campaigns that tend to exhaust candidates, issues, voters and funds. It deserves support.

THE INDIANAPOLIS NEWS
Indianapolis, Ind., August 6, 1973

Election reform is in the air. Congress is striving to curb the practice of political candidates accepting large campaign contributions from corporations, influential lobbies and individuals. Most of these attempts appear doomed to fail.

They are unlikely to have an effect because they consist chiefly of reporting requirements which are easily circumvented, and limits on the amounts of the contributions. One campaign reform already in force is the income tax checkoff which invites the individual taxpayer to kick in toward the campaign expenses of national candidates. This money is administered by the government rather than being given directly to the candidate cited by a contributor. It is the germ of tax-paid campaigns much sought after by liberal spokesmen and legislators which would have the effect of breaking the link between a candidate's appeal to the people and his ability to raise funds.

What is missing from these various schemes is the recognition that the real cause of excessive campaign contributions is the excessive power government holds over the contributors. If the price of milk, for example, were not established by government fiat there would be no reason for the milk industry to contribute so heavily to both parties. If the power of OSHA and the Environmental Protection Agency to interfere with the operations of business were less awesome businesses would not feel impelled to placate the government with generous donations to office-holders.

If the complaint is that large corporations and powerful lobbies are attempting to purchase favors from the government, the most beneficial solution would be to remove the government from the position of being able to bestow favors. This would not only help to reform campaign practices, it would go a long way toward restoring productivity to the economy and freedom to the people.

Detroit Free Press

Detroit, Mich., August 1, 1973

THE U.S. SENATE, far more than the House, has caught the mood of the nation in its drive for election reforms.

With an ear tuned to the Watergate hearings and public reaction, the Senate just passed, 82-8, a tough reform bill. The response from the other side of Capitol Hill was a hearty ho-hum. For example, Rep. Wayne L. Hays, D-Ohio, said the Senate bill will be assigned to the elections subcommittee and "we'll probably be able to have some hearings in September."

Unless the representatives get a clear message from the electorate, the chances are very good that the reform bill will die in committee or be so gutted that it will be beyond repair by a joint conference committee. Many congressmen will spend part of their August vacations back in their home districts, and if they get the message from constituents that it is time for reform, they will carry that message back to Washington.

Since they run every two years, representatives are understandably reluctant to change the rules that they've won by. They are, from experience, the real experts on campaigning.

They should apply that experience to coming up with genuine reforms in federal election procedures — for the presidency, the Senate and the House.

The Senate has given the House a good bill to work with. It sets up a non-partisan seven-member commission outside the administration to monitor elections. It provides stiff fines and prison sentences for violators. The President would prefer to keep enforcement within the Justice Department. Obviously, there are compelling arguments for an independent agency.

The Senate bill still is very heavy on the "thou shalt nots" which limit campaign activities without much in the bill to permit greater public access to information on candidates. There is, however, essential modification of the equal time rules governing television.

Right now the equal time provision seriously limits public exposure of leading candidates by requiring equal television time for all the crackpots who see a chance to spout off for the price of a filing fee. Station managers react by limiting exposure of all candidates. A carefully drawn modification of equal time is essential to opening up television to an effective role in informing the public on major candidates. It should come in time for the Senate and House races of 1974 as a preparation for the 1976 presidential elections.

The Senate bill sets reasonable limits on the amount any individual can contribute to a single candidate and provides bookkeeping procedures that will guard against phantom committees and suitcases full of cash.

It is essentially a good bill, one that can be supported in the House and one that Sen. Howard Baker, R-Tenn., could easily have supported with a "yes" vote instead of merely voting "present." Sen. Baker argued that the legislation is premature, that Congress should wait until the Watergate hearings are over and the committee makes its recommendations. His argument will be repeated often by congressmen who are looking for any excuse to delay.

The Watergate hearings are bound to turn up additional areas where reforms are needed. That doesn't mean that obvious reforms shouldn't come right now. This round of reforms, after all, is an addition to the changes that became effective during the 1972 campaign and which resulted in some improved practices in the later stages of that campaign.

Any unnecessary delays, including those suggested by Sen. Baker, will only increase the electorate's cynicism. There is a mounting feeling that Congress will whip up a lot of talk through the Watergate hearings and then do nothing.

The something that can be done, and soon, is House support for the Senate bill. The people should send their congressmen back to Washington in September, ready and willing to deal effectively with election abuses.

Los Angeles Times

Los Angeles, Calif., July 30, 1973

Considering what we have learned about the abuses occurring under the present system of financing political campaigns in this country, it is not surprising that the idea of using public money to finance federal elections is picking up impressive support. Nonetheless, the U.S. Senate is wise in refusing to jump aboard this particular bandwagon without a long and careful look.

Several proposals for public financing of congressional and presidential elections were offered during Senate debate on a new campaign reform law. None has been adopted, but the Senate Rules Committee will hold exhaustive hearings on the subject in September.

The hearings should be useful, and may produce a workable plan deserving adoption. But we doubt it.

It is true, as disclosures arising from the Watergate investigations have made all too clear, that the existing system encourages candidates to have an unhealthy dependence on contributions from wealthy individuals or special interests.

In such a situation, the idea of going over to a system of public financing of campaigns has an undeniable appeal to the unwary. Closer examinations leaves no doubt, though, that public financing has serious shortcomings.

One objection that can be made to just about any public financing plan is the potential danger of manipulation by the party in power. If some people are capable of burglarizing the rival party's campaign headquarters, others may be capable of finding ways to funnel more public money to their own party's candidates than to those of the opposition.

Unless strict limitations could be imposed on acceptance of private campaign contributions after a public financing law went into effect, it is hard to see what good would be done. Total spending would merely go higher than ever, much of the spending might be frivolous, and the potential for influence buying and selling would still be present.

Yet, if strict spending limitations were imposed under a system of either private or public campaign financing, the net effect would be to make it more difficult for challengers to upset entrenched officeholders, who have all the advantages of incumbency. The House should give serious thought to this point before going along with the spending limitations voted by the Senate last week.

Similarly, it is obvious that any public financing law not covering primary election campaigns would deal with only half the problem. But any attempt to include primary candidates would open up a nightmarish nest of problems.

How would you decide who would be eligible for federal subsidy of his primary campaign? If the rules were too loose, the result would be a mob of candidates, some running merely for the exercise or to advertise their law practices at public expense. If the rules were too tight, the result would be to freeze out an incumbent's challengers within his own party.

Another problem would be to devise a formula for public financing of general elections that would neither pose unfair barriers to third and fourth parties nor be so generous as to encourage an unhealthy proliferation of parties.

Until persuasive answers to such objections are forthcoming—and so far they are not—Congress should concentrate on improving the present system by tougher enforcement, more generous tax breaks for small campaign donors and strict limitations on how much any person, no matter how wealthy, can contribute. Fortunately, it seems likely that some progress on the latter point will be made this year.

Congress should also give serious attention to proposals that would decrease dependence on private contributors by providing that a given amount of television time be made available, at government expense, to presidential and vice presidential candidates.

It could be that reform efforts will fail, that in the final analysis the only answer will be a system of broad federal financing of elections. But, as of now, it is by no means clear that this is the case.

NIXON ADDRESSES NATION; MEETS WITH NEWSMEN

President Nixon told the nation in a televised speech Aug. 15 that it should give up its "backward-looking obsession" with Watergate, turn the case over to the courts and start attending to "matters of far greater importance." The speech, and an accompanying written statement, comprised the President's fifth major statement on the Watergate scandal affecting his Administration.

In his speech, the President said it was clear that the Senate Watergate hearings and some of the commentary on them were directed toward implicating him personally in the illegalities that occurred. He accepted full responsibility for the abuses that occurred during his Administration and his re-election campaign and asserted it was his duty to defend the office of the presidency against false charges. He declined to offer a point-by-point rebuttal of charges in the case and restated his previous denials of complicity. Nixon explained his actions after the Watergate break-in occurred, much of it again a restatement of his previous stand that he pressed repeatedly for information and was repeatedly misled until mid-April of 1973. Then, he said, it became clear that the situation was "far more serious" than he had believed and that the investigation should be given to the Criminal Division of the Justice Department. At that time, Nixon said, he turned over all the information he had to that department with the instruction it should "pursue the matter thoroughly," and he ordered all members of his Administration "to testify fully before the grand jury." He pointed out that the case was now before a grand jury in the hands of a special prosecutor appointed with his concurrence. "Far from trying to hide the facts," the President emphasized, "my effort throughout has been to discover the facts—and to lay those facts before the appropriate law-enforcement authorities so that justice could be done and the guilty dealt with."

Nixon dealt at length with his refusal to turn over to the special prosecutor or the Senate committee his recordings of conversations he held in his office or on his telephone. There was "a much more important principle" involved in this, he said, "than what the tapes might prove about Watergate." That principle was the confidentiality of presidential discussions.

Nixon linked the Watergate abuses to an attitude arising during the 1960s "as individuals and groups increasingly asserted the right to take the law into their own hands, insisting that their purposes represented a higher morality." He said their attitude "was praised in the press and even from some of our pulpits as evidence of a new idealism. Those of us who insisted on the old restraints, who warned of the overriding importance of operating within the law and by the rules, were accused of being reactionaries." This new attitude, he said, "brought a rising spiral of violence and fear, of riots and arson and bombings," all in the name of peace and justice. Political discussion turned into "savage debate," he said. "Free speech was brutally suppressed, as hecklers shouted down or even physically assaulted those with whom they disagreed." "The notion that the end justifies the means proved contagious," the President said, and it was not surprising that some persons adopted the same morality in 1972.

President Nixon fielded an intense barrage of questions on Watergate during most of a 50-minute news conference Aug. 22 on the lawn of his San Clemente, Calif. home. It was Nixon's first news conference in five months and his first televised news conference in 14 months. In the course of the questioning, Nixon accepted all responsibility for the Watergate scandal, said he would not resign and pledged a strong term of office. He attacked his Watergate critics, said he would abide by a "definitive" Supreme Court decision to make public his taped recordings of conversations being withheld from Watergate investigators and strongly defended Vice President Spiro T. Agnew.

There were only three questions on non-Watergate matters—two relating to Agnew as the subject of a federal criminal investigation and another on the secret bombing of Cambodia in 1969. The questioning was intensely personal, even on the non-Watergate topics. The President was asked if he would expect Agnew to resign if the latter was indicted, and whether he (Nixon) owed the American people an apology on the secret Cambodia bombing in light of his public statement to the contrary. On Watergate, Nixon was asked how much blame he accepted for its abuses, whether an action represented the appearance of a lack of moral leadership, whether he ever considered resigning and why he had not informed prosecutors of information given him of criminal wrong-doing.

The President appeared nervous, but stumbled less over his words than during an appearance two days before in New Orleans, when his delivery and angry shoving of an aide drew press comment and subsequent White House reassurance that the President possessed a positive attitude and could govern. The President was in New Orleans to address the 74th national convention of the Veterans of Foreign Wars (VFW). The President's speech was dominated by his defense of the secret Cambodia bombing. Nixon denounced his war policy critics and the "unilateral disarmers" who would have the country "cop out from our responsibilities in the world."

The New York Times

New York, N.Y., August 17, 1973

President Nixon's speech on the Watergate scandals and the supplementary statement issued by the White House are as remarkable for what they omit as for what they contain. In essence, they constitute a concession by Mr. Nixon that he has no detailed defense to offer against the damaging testimony before the Senate Watergate committee. In place of a rebuttal, he offers an omnibus denial and a plea for the public to turn its attention to other pressing public issues. It is a sad, disappointing and wholly unconvincing performance.

Insofar as he ventures into specifics, Mr. Nixon makes statements that are highly questionable. This applies particularly to the President's repeated assertion that, beginning on March 21, "I launched an intensive effort of my own to get the facts and to get the facts out." The unhappy fact is that throughout this entire year of scandals and denials, the White House has volunteered only one material bit of information. That was the fact of the burglary of the office of Daniel Ellsberg's psychiatrist. And for this disclosure Mr. Nixon can take no credit. By his own statement, he knew of the break-in for more than a month before the judge in the Ellsberg trial was notified; and he made the reluctant disclosure only because it was plain that Attorney General Kleindienst and Assistant Attorney General Petersen would have resigned if he had not.

In urging that Americans leave Watergate to the courts and turn their attention elsewhere, Mr. Nixon seems still unaware that the issues involved far transcend the conviction of particular individuals. Watergate does not just refer to a bungled burglary in a Washington office building; it is a shorthand description of lawlessness and ruthlessness on the part of the White House, the Nixon campaign organization and certain members of the Nixon Cabinet. The vast powers of the Government were being used corruptly and irresponsibly to serve partisan and private ends.

Much of this wrongdoing has been concealed under a fog blanket of "national security" and "internal security." Despite his assurance that he can protect the nation's security "by constitutional means," the President even now has not really condemned this wrongdoing. He mitigates it as due to an excess of zeal when, in fact, some of the worst excesses resulted from settled policy which he defined and from calculated decisions which he or senior members of his staff approved. It was Mr. Nixon himself, after all, who set up the White House "plumbers" and who personally briefed Egil Krogh, the chief plumber, on the importance of his mission. Each current word of Presidential criticism is more than offset by a balancing comment: "It is essential that such mistakes not be repeated. But it is also essential that we do not overreact to particular mistakes by tying the President's hands in a way that would risk sacrificing our security."

Can the public really believe that the President has learned the lessons of Watergate when he displays so little recognition that his high-ranking aides gravely distorted traditional concepts of individual freedom and democratic process in the name of "security."

Perhaps the most extraordinary passage of President Nixon's speech was his bald assertion that it is Watergate that stops him from acting on the nation's urgent problems. "Legislation vital to your health and well-being sits unattended on the Congressional calendar," he declared. That is a strange remark from a Chief Executive who has vetoed three out of the last four Health, Education and Welfare appropriations bills, has impounded health funds and has blocked—even illegally pocket-vetoed—health bills passed by Congress.

It is equally astonishing to find the President blaming the concern over Watergate for his inability to grapple effectively with inflation or the decline in the value of the dollar. While there are worldwide factors that make it unfair to hold the Administration wholly responsible for these economic ills, it is incontestable that the Administration has all but run up the surrender flag in its efforts to contain the runaway rise in prices. As the calamitous advent of Phase 4 makes clear, the White House simply has no program for dealing with inflation —and Watergate is merely a stormcellar in which it now seeks to hide.

The proper and necessary role for the courts is to determine culpability for the specific crimes committed in this far-ranging series of scandals. But the President would be on sounder ground, even in that phase of the inquiry, if he stopped withholding the tapes needed to help establish the truth or falsity of disputed testimony.

Even if Mr. Nixon had not undercut his own claim of confidentiality for these records of White House conversations by permitting H. R. Haldeman to take one of them home after his resignation as a Presidential aide, there would be an easy way to make the tapes available as evidence without creating anxiety about the freedom with which insiders, outsiders or representatives of foreign countries could converse with the President.

The proper course for Mr. Nixon would be to turn the tapes over to a Federal judge or to an impartial screening panel for exclusion of secret military information and anything else that was irrelevant. The material would then be released to the Watergate special prosecutor and the grand jury, thus enabling the courts to get on with their task.

It would also be helpful for the President to make good on the point-by-point rebuttal of specific charges which was long promised by the White House but which was absent from Wednesday's supplementary statement. As long as Mr. Nixon withholds both the tapes and a factual reply, the public will have to conclude that he

The Burlington Free Press

Burlington, Vt., August 17, 1973

PRESIDENT NIXON showed remarkable restraint Wednesday night in his address to the nation on the Watergate affair. Any other leader, who had been subjected to the orchestrated hate and political abuses he has endured these many months, would not have reacted in such a forthright yet statesmanlike manner.

The President's political enemies, including a goodly number in the press, will continue to wallow in the muck of their vendetta, firmly grasping their "backward looking obsession" with Watergate, and continuing to play their wretched little game. But ALL Americans of conscience and decency will answer the President's call to "get on with the urgent business of our nation."

Despite the remarkable restraint of the President's remarks, he did make several telling points. One was the incontestable truth that the attitude which led to the Watergate affair was born in "the extremes of violence and discord in the 1960s." The criminal violence-prone activists and others of their ilk laid the groundwork. The "advocacy press" and the political punksters took it from there.

"No individual, no group and no political party has a corner on the market on morality in America," the President said, and a truer statement was never made. The Watergate affair itself is certainly no worse than many, many other political excesses over the long reach of American history. What is really different about Watergate is the contemptible conduct of a portion of the nation's press in "covering" it, and the grossly cheap showmanship of the political opposition in exploiting it.

Sadly, some observers are too obsessed to learn anything. There is the absolutely inane statement of one so-called "news analyst," for example, that the President's address didn't prove much because his views remain at variance with those of one other person, his fired counsel John Dean. What of the dozens of other witnesses who have defended his position? What if only Dean defended the President and the dozens of others didn't, would such credence then be given to Dean's position?

In any case, the President's address served the essential purpose of appealing to the better nature of the American people. There is still room for honest men to disagree, of course, but no longer is there room for small-minded men to visit more hate and recrimination upon the nation.

As for the controversy over the tapes, we applaud the President for refusing to buckle under to the demands of those who would destroy the separation of powers. As Charles L. Black Jr., the Luce Professor of Jurisprudence at Yale University, noted in the New York Times recently, it is "not only the President's lawful privilege but his duty as well" to protect his records of consultations.

President Nixon's address, in a word, was magnificent. He has done far more than was required of him in this most unfortunate situation, and now the public must join him in the constructive pursuit of national leadership. He is a very great President who deserves the enthusiastic support of those who truly care for America and all for which it stands. — F. B. Smith

Maine Sunday Telegram
Portland, Me., August 19, 1973

Did President Nixon in a 30 minute speech rebut 12 weeks and 2 million words of televised testimony about Watergate?

No. Of course Nixon did not. It is doubtful if the world's greatest theatrical genius and phrase maker, even with every iota of truth on his side, could turn tables so heavily stacked against him for so long. And Nixon, whatever his assets, is certainly no theatrical genius and no great phrase-maker.

So those who may have hoped that Nixon's Wednesday night speech — possibly the most important in his 27-year political career — would produce an overnight miracle of redemption for the President were foredoomed to disappointment.

The speech came far too late and said far too little that was new to change minds that were already made up either for or against Nixon.

Those who wholly disbelieve and distrust Nixon still do. Those who believe that the Senate Watergate Committee and the news media are out to "get Nixon" for personal or political spite, are likely to feel the same way. The President's speech changed little on these extremes.

However we think the President probably scored heavily with millions of less opinionated Americans when he said that "a continued backward looking obsession with Watergate is causing this nation to neglect matters of far greater importance to all of the American people... The time has come to turn Watergate over to the courts, where the questions of guilt and innocence belong."

In our judgment this was a political speech, not a legal defense.

Whether or not Nixon's speech succeeded or failed will be determined by whether or not the President is able to regain his long missing political power and leadership. Without that, he will be no more than a caretaker.

"The role of the President is to lead the nation, and the office must fill two functions" says George Reedy, longtime assistant to President Johnson and a wise student of the Presidency. "One function is to manage the affairs of the country and the other is to hold the nation together — to give the nation some unity, to set a moral tone, to inspire confidence among our citizens. During the last two years of the Johnson administration, as during the last two years of the Hoover and Truman administrations, the Presidency was unable to fill that role."

At this moment, it is gravely doubtful whether by the power of his own persuasion President Nixon will ever be able to fulfill this vital second role during his last three years in office.

But this second function of the Presidency is critically necessary to the well-being of Americans, more so than at any time. We as citizens must help therefore.

If we do not, the nation will suffer far more than Nixon or the Republicans will suffer.

It is not Nixon's money but the nation's money which is feverish and sick from inflation.

It is not Nixon's dollar, but the American dollar which is sagging the world over.

It is not Nixon's foreign policy which is hamstrung, but America's chances of future peace which are stalled.

This newspaper, like many citizens, was not greatly persuaded by Nixon's speech. We wish he had done it differently. We wish he had made it sooner. But nit-picking at his speech and its timing serves little worthwhile purpose now.

So, until we have far more solid reasons than the allegations of John Dean, we accept the President's statement in which he said; "I had no prior knowledge of the Watergate operation; I neither took part in nor knew about any subsequent coverup activities; I neither authorized nor encouraged subordinates to engage in illegal or improper campaign tactics. That was and is the simple truth."

We accept this statement without enthusiasm, even as we accept Nixon's apology for the conduct of his staff. "I accept full responsibility" he said.

This is not an attitude on our part of "forget and forgive". Far from it. Under Nixon, the repute of the Presidency has been blackened. He acknowledges this. He has no option to do otherwise. His duty now must be to redeem his office by immaculate performance.

But we as a nation must not now make the Presidency powerless in order to spite or reward or demean Nixon. To do so would cause more damage to the nation and to the world than to Richard Nixon.

Huge as he may loom today, Richard Nixon is a short-lived mortal. This nation and its Presidency are — pray heaven — worthy of far longer duration. Let us not damage them.

The Evening Star
The Washington Daily News
Washington, D.C., August 16, 1973

Essentially, what the President was saying last night was that he wants the great majority of Americans to help him cut his losses on Watergate so that he can get back to running the country.

It was a predictable appeal. And to a degree it was a very compelling appeal. It may well strike a responsive chord across the country, although probably not to the extent that Mr. Nixon would like to expect.

Overall, we find the President's performance curious, both for what he chose to say and what he chose not to say. He was forthright here, obfuscatory there. He was conciliatory, yet stubborn. He scored points and lost some. He stated his case well, and yet, in what seemed a deliberate way, he left it open to serious attack.

What have we learned from it? About Watergate and the specifics of the cover-up, we know almost nothing more than we knew before. Both in his speech and in a brief, somewhat repetitious accompanying paper, Mr. Nixon pretty much served up a rehash of his springtime statements on the scandal. Once again, he denied any complicity in the planning of the burglary or in the conspiracy to obstruct justice. He did acknowledge that questions remain about some of his actions in the long, tangled affair. Then, giving no good reason, he told the nation he would not enter a point-by-point rebuttal of even the key, challenging pieces of testimony from the Senate hearings.

The public, we believe, will find this disappointing. The total cynics aside, those people who have kept up with the subject and are willing to hear the President's side are as much in the dark as ever on a number of serious questions. To name but one, which should have been starkly obvious to the White House: Did former FBI Director Pat Gray, as early as last July, personally warn the President that his close aides were acting in such a way as to "mortally wound" him, and if Gray said that, why was the President so imprudent as to ignore it? We don't know, and because we don't know, the President's credibility will remain in doubt.

Similarly disappointing was Mr. Nixon's unyielding resistance to releasing relevant parts of his taped conversations. He was eloquent on the subject, and he put the best face on it he could. Boiled down, though, the thesis he presented last night was but an elaboration of what must come across to the public as a legalistically defensive maneuver. It offends common sense.

On the positive side, the President revealed a new and refreshing perspective on the whole affair. Specific details and the tapes aside, Mr. Nixon was perceptibly more candid and open in conceding the extent of wrongdoing in his administration, and in acknowledging that on both the national-security and political fronts, many of the men around him went off the moral deep end. "The notion that the end justifies the means proved contagious," he said. That was right on the mark.

The tone and deportment of the President also were reassuring. Gone was the gratuitously offensive manner, the cloying emotionalism of some of his earlier appeals. Blessedly absent was the caustic kissing off of Watergate as trivial. If Mr. Nixon was in anguish, as some speculated, it did not show. If he was angry, it showed only indirectly. He got some digs in, notably at the Ervin committee. The committee, though, had that coming.

Central to the President's address was the conviction that the worst is over, or should be over, that John Dean's damaging testimony now should be seen as flimsy and unsubstantiated, and that the courts should take it from here. He hopes the public not only will agree but, through pressure on Congress, will come to his aid on that point.

Public confidence, as Attorney General Richardson said recently, is a fragile commodity. Once eroded, it is not easily restored. And Mr. Nixon is kidding himself if he thinks that, on the basis of one speech, his critics will quiet down and the country will shove Watergate into the past.

And yet the speech was probably a net plus for the President. Perhaps he has turned the corner. The public, we dare say, is not only sick of Watergate but thoroughly in agreement with Mr. Nixon that the time has come for the President, Congress and everyone else to pay more attention to the vital business facing the country. The President, in his forthcoming press conference and other public actions, ought to go farther to reinforce that point, and at the same time to correct some of the flaws and omissions of last night's speech. We hope he does.

The Standard-Times

New Bedford, Mass., August 17, 1973

President Nixon, whose astonishing decline in popularity since last November is principally attributed to his refusal to seek the best possible advice from as many sources as possible, persists in this practice. Before his television broadcast to the nation Wednesday night, he would have done well to request a few words of counsel from Vice President Agnew.

Mr. Agnew, whose name was linked to wrongdoing by news reports, immediately seized the initiative, held a news conference without delay, and presented such an attitude of candor and cooperation that he won the plaudits of everyone, even those elements of the media normally hostile to him. Wednesday night was not Mr.

Nixon's first attempt to do this, and he still hasn't made it.

Admittedly, the President's televised speech and a "white paper" released simultaneously, which addressed itself to Watergate-related matters in greater detail, are apparently only the first steps in a program of response to criticism pertaining to his office and administration.

Frankly, because we do not anticipate Mr. Nixon's impeachment, we hope his effort to remove the clouds from the presidency and to get Congress and the nation back on the tracks will succeed. We think if he held a press conference and answered all questions asked until there were no more questions, it would help a great deal.

But the Wednesday night broadcast was a low-keyed start that did not answer the questions we believe to be in the minds of most of those listening.

First of all, the President persists in talking about Watergate, and all of the broader events now generally associated with the kind of thinking that produced it, as if it had happened in some administration other than his. Even if one assumes that Mr. Nixon was, in fact, misinformed, even lied to, and knew little or nothing of these events, he cannot remain so aloof for he is, in truth, involved.

—It was he who hand-picked the top-level aides whose bad works we are now hearing about. Over a period of months or years, it was he who

encouraged, probably trained, and directed them. It was by his decision, implicit or otherwise, that he eventually came to take their advice and no other;

—It was he who allowed himself to be isolated from his own party, from his friends in government, from leaders of Congress, and from the American public — starting as long ago as the day when he fired Interior Secretary Hickel for warning him publicly that he was not communicating with the people;

—It was he who rejected the several warnings reportedly made to him of impending disaster from those who had his well-being and that of the party and nation at heart, presumably because he could not bear to believe that he had chosen unwisely in selecting those closest to him;

—It was he, through years of tape recordings, who unilaterally violated the "confidentiality" of presidential conversations, of which he now makes so much. Surely dozens, perhaps hundreds of people who talked with him and believed the conversations inviolate, must now live in fear, knowing that the same administration that produced the "Watergate mentality" has a record of what was said. The shocking ruthlessness with which the White House staff treated its "friends," the fact that Mr. Nixon has already permitted a former White House aide to take some of these tapes home and listen to them, will not reassure those with apprehensions;

—It was he who named the men, assigned them to the highest levels of government, worked with them closely for years, called them his friends, whom he now charges with having misled him for months concerning a matter of the gravest importance. Surely this is a shocking failure of top-level communication by a system he established. One wonders in what other important areas the President might have been misled or deliberately misinformed.

Yet Mr. Nixon persists in holding the matter at arm's length, offers questionable argument for continuing to withhold evidence, relies on an unconvincing "national security" defense for illegal acts by government, and urges the nation to forget Watergate and go on to the country's goals and problems.

This kind of approach — too late, too general, too aloof — won't work. Meanwhile, the nation suffers from leaderlessness and dangerous drift.

The Washington Post

Times Herald

Washington, D.C., August 17, 1973

It was a speech of large silences and vague insinuations, hardly what the public had been led to expect from the accounts of presidential preparation for Wednesday night's television address. Perhaps the most interesting aspect of that address as a whole and its accompanying "white paper" was the curiously detached status—almost that of bemused spectator—which Mr. Nixon assumed for himself. "The time has come for the rest of us to get on with the urgent business of our nation," he said.

The "rest of us"? But surely this is Mr. Nixon's administration, and surely it was in his name and in his behalf that men who were his appointees and closest confidants committed the crimes and excesses that the President now "deplores." And surely he cannot expect us to regard him as just another outraged American registering his reactions from somewhere in the third balcony. Yet that was the attitude Mr. Nixon assumed the other evening, and it was, in our view, this studied sense of remoteness that vitiated his more straightforward statements concerning the nature of the wrongdoing that has been exposed. "In a free society," Mr. Nixon said, "the institutions of Government belong to the people. They must never be used against the people." And again: "No political campaign ever justifies obstructing justice, or harassing individuals, or compromising those great agencies of Government that should and must be above politics." What rendered these unexceptionable statements so lifeless, what made them seem so pro forma, was the context in which they were made. Mr. Nixon now acknowledges that plenty went wrong. But he will not seriously consider *why* it went wrong.

We are certainly not recommending here some lachrymose televised "confession" of guilt or even of fault. We have in mind nothing more demanding or dramatic than a candid and realistic appraisal by the President of Watergate cause and effect. Mr. Nixon's former attorney general and former commerce secretary have been indicted. Others of his most important appointees are under criminal investigation. The FBI, the CIA and the federal courts were all subjected to improper pressures in his behalf. Does he really believe—and does he expect us to believe—that all this can be explained as the consequence of some "contagious" virus of the 1960s? What is the President trying to tell us? That Abbie Hoffman set a bad example for John Mitchell and that the former chief law officer of the land was very impressionable? What kind of "explanation" is that?

Just as Mr. Nixon seemed to blame the upheavals of the 1960s for the wholly distinct misbehavior (and worse) that has marked his administration, so he also seemed the other evening to blame the law enforcement

agencies of government for failing to inform him of the dimensions of the Watergate disgrace—even though sworn testimony indicates that his own White House agents were trying in his name to stop those agencies from doing their job. Similarly, he tended to blame the Congress for the paralysis of his own White House and to blame the "critics" of the Watergate scandals—not the perpetrators of those scandals—for the ill effects of Watergate on government. It it undoubtedly true that there would be more faith in the U.S. government here and abroad if people were not talking so much about the Watergate scandals. But people wouldn't be talking about them at all if they hadn't happened—and that surely is the point.

This whole array of misplaced blame is what we found so disheartening about the President's speech and it was of a piece with his own assumed air of personal detachment. Both suggest to us that Mr. Nixon has yet to face up to the meaning of Watergate, has yet to acknowledge, even to himself, what went wrong. In a number of passages, the President made statements that conflict one way and another with sworn testimony of several Senate committee witnesses. But these passages, and the disputes they reflect, seem to us less important at the moment than the overall tenor of the President's speech. For it really will not do for Mr. Nixon to let it be known merely that he is bored with the show. And it will not do for him to suggest that he is being prevented from doing the nation's business by this tiresome affair or that the public's attention is being focused on these unprecedented squalors only because some people are trying to keep him from fulfilling his "mandate." None of the improper activities that are under consideration by the Ervin committee was "mandated" by the voters. Indeed, had they not been suppressed before the election, his "mandate" might have been somewhat more modest. And until people are satisfied that those activities—which are not such ancient history as Mr. Nixon implies—have been properly aired and dealt with, Mr. Nixon's administration will continue to operate under a cloud.

The President cannot have it both ways. He cannot disassociate himself from those acts of his administration that have appalled people and take credit for those of which they approve. He cannot say the uncertainties caused by the scandals are wrecking his opportunities to get on with a higher mission—and then blame the uncertainties on someone else. Mr. Nixon accuses the Senate committee and some commentators of "an effort to implicate the President personally in the illegal activities that took place." Well, the President *is* implicated: he is the President, these things took place under his roof, and he has yet to convey to the American people that he understands either his own responsibility or their justifiable dismay.

BUFFALO EVENING NEWS
Buffalo, N.Y., August 18, 1973

It is most unlikely that any development in the next few weeks will yield a surgically clean, wholly convincing answer about Watergate that will satisfy either President Nixon's severest critics or his warmest admirers. A clear-cut legal or historical judgment based on indisputable knowledge seems months off yet, if indeed it ever comes.

Meanwhile, we are all stuck with a political reality commanding that the business of the government go forward, and recognizing that some of the lessons of Watergate are already plain. The President in consequence has suffered a massive and roughly measurable erosion of public confidence in his conduct of this highest office in the land. This is a contemporary fact that the nation, and especially the President, must cope with.

We do not share the view that Watergate can yet be turned over to the courts alone. Congress has an obligation to continue to explore Watergate and its ramifications not only to learn the truth, if it is learnable, but to enlighten legislators about statutory remedies.

We do agree with the President, however, that Watergate should not be allowed to numb and paralyze the other activities of government. And on this it is only the President himself who can take the lead. Only he can reassert his leadership, as he now recognizes with a flurry of newly scheduled trips and public appearances, including a forthcoming diplomatic journey to Europe.

Any ideas that he has of getting out among the people, of speaking up on issues and answering questions, of making himself more open and accessible as he once insisted the presidency must be, definitely point in the right direction during what is an obviously severe crisis of presidential confidence and trust. One way for Mr. Nixon to look at this part of the problem is that he is in an unscheduled campaign where he must work to win back the mandate he had last November before the spreading Watergate stain clouded, confused and spoiled it. This new campaign will require him to circulate, discuss, debate and seek to persuade.

There is also a political, as distinct from the constitutional, aspect of the problems of the tapes. All the signs we see indicate that the public would welcome, whatever the outcome of the litigation, the release, on some basis, of at least the most important of the White House conversations bearing on Watergate. We have never assumed that the President could be forced by subpoena into yielding material he was determined to withhold. But there are ways in which the essence of whatever light the tapes will shed on the truth about Watergate can be put before the public without violating confidential relationships or disturbing the separation of powers if the will is there. We hope that, in the final analysis, it will be.

Beyond all the normal areas of presidential leadership mentioned by President Nixon in this week's address, moreover, is a special one for the White House. This nation needs strict laws, as Watergate has already proved beyond doubt, to prevent political campaign abuses and e s p e c i a l l y to safeguard fundamental personal liberties from indefensible governmental assault. It needs tougher laws against wiretapping, against military and civilian surveillance of citizens, against a multitude of encroachments on personal privacy such as burglary-breakins in the name of national security.

If Congress has an obligation to correct loopholes in these basic American safeguards, the President's obligation to lead the way is at least as great. And strong proposals in these policy fields are needed to back up his pledge to work for a "new level of decency and integrity" in politics and to ensure that national security is protected " by constitutional means, in ways that will not threaten freedom."

Such a bold reassertion of presidential leadership may or may not win back the public confidence the President has seen slip away during the Watergate drama. But it's an effort worth making, for the alternatives of remaining isolated or of vainly trying to ignore Watergate are unlikely to revive the sense of mandate he felt so clearly last January.

The San Juan Star
San Juan, P.R., August 17, 1973

President Nixon's long-awaited address on Watergate Wednesday night and the 3,000-word statement that came with it were, we regret to say, disappointing. We had hoped the President would do a more convincing and detailed job of refuting the key allegations made against him before the Ervin committee.

Instead, he repeated in very general terms his past denials that he had known about the White House cover-up of the Watergate scandal, while it went on for an incredible nine months from his outer office.

It would have been better for Nixon to announce dramatically that he was calling off his legal rearguard actions and was releasing tapes of his discussions on Watergate, so it could be determined whose version of the facts is correct. Unfortunately, he chose to argue long and unconvincingly that the very institution of the presidency would crumble if he turned the recordings, because then no adviser would ever speak frankly to a President. (This is aside from the point, but leaders who want candid advice should not wire their offices.)

Ironically, if Nixon had not secretly recorded conversations with aides and callers, he would be largely off the hook at this point in the Watergate hearings. Whether or not he took part in the cover-up would be his word against former White House Counsel John Dean's, and the public would tend to believe the President.

The country is unlikely to accept Nixon's argument that he is guarding the tapes because of "executive privilege" or "separation of powers." Every modern President has made public loads of sensitive and classified material when it was in his interest —and stamped Top Secret on utter trivia that was embarrassing.

There is a case to be made in Nixon's plea that he be allowed to put Watergate behind him so he can get on with the business of running the country. But Watergate cannot be neatly relegated to a corner before all the facts are known. And the President will not be granted the confidence he needs to lead effectively until suspicion is stilled that he was involved in obstructing the investigation of Watergate and other illegalities of his "plumbers."

The President and a platoon of lawyers, advisers and speechwriters spent almost two weeks preparing Wednesday night's Watergate defense. Our initial conclusion is that Nixon is making a grave mistake by clutching to his bosom the Watergate tapes, wrapped in a legistic mantle of confidentiality. In a practical country, the feeling is that people with nothing to hide do not hide things.

CHICAGO Daily Defender
Chicago, Ill., August 30, 1973

When it was announced that President Nixon was going to make public his latest defense of the executive privilege hypothesis and of his ignorance of the Watergate capers, there were those who had nurtured the wish that at last he had found an honest way out of the deepening quicksand. They turned their television sets on to a drab rehashing of the same old argument which lacked the substance of truth and the rationale to sustain it. There was much disappointment, even among his devoted disciples.

The trouble is that Mr. Nixon, with an unquenchable thirst for absolute power, has driven himself into a corner from which he can find no ladder of escape. A point of the whole scandal which has not been articulated enough, is that here is a great apostle of moral rectitude and civil obedience who went forth in proverbial sack cloth and ashes, with the Old Testament fervor preaching the hallowed doctrine of law and order as the only antidote to the militant social heresy which flared up in the late 60s under the name of the black revolution, and who now excuses burglary, wire tapping and other bold infractions of the law on the grounds of national security.

Mr. Nixon's apologia was followed by a press conference in his luxurious San Clemente retreat where once again he repeated the argument about not having contrived the excesses committed under his name. He sounded more like a broken phonograph disc than a repentant sinner at the confessional.

Even if he had been able to prove his case in the Watergate break-in or cover-up, his image in history has been permanently scarred.

THE KNICKERBOCKER NEWS
••• UNION-STAR •••
Albany, N.Y., August 16, 1973

After 37 days of Senate Watergate hearings and three months of presidential silence, President Nixon last night made his third — and what had been billed as his definitive — statement on the scandals that have enveloped and all but immobilized his administration.

He also issued a supplementary printed statement.

Both fell far short of the mark.

Although the President followed his pattern of admitting a little bit more in each new statement than he had admitted before (conceding, for instance, that some members of his staff may have committed crimes) and while he promised to be more vigilant, he really did not answer the major questions and did not attempt to explain the contradictions in the sworn testimony of his closest aides.

His generally rambling and defensive discourse was shot through with half truths, evasions and outright distortions unworthy of a President of the United States. He compounded this insult to the intelligence of his fellow citizens by urging them, in effect, to pressure the Senate Watergate committee into calling off its hearings and take Mr. Nixon off the hook.

Categorically denying any prior knowledge of or complicity in the Watergate break-in or subsequent coverup, Mr. Nixon continued to imply that he was so naive or ignorant of what was going on in his own White House that he didn't learn the extent of the Watergate scandal until last March — only five months ago and almost a year after the events.

If we are to believe this, the President is, at the very least, an incompetent executive.

But this very contention is in direct conflict with the sworn testimony of at least three of his own appointees — including former White House counsel John Dean, former acting FBI director L. Patrick Gray and assistant attorney general Henry E. Peterson — who said they repeatedly warned the President long before last March that the Watergate scandal was vast and involved some of his closest aides.

Mr. Nixon pointedly ignored this glaring contradiction in his speech last night. And he failed to explain why his continued insistence that national security was involved in some of the Watergate misdeeds was denied by his own CIA director and acting FBI director. He also failed to explain why neither Mr. Peterson nor former Attorney General Richard Kleindienst recalls receiving the orders the President says he gave for an "intensive investigation" of Watergate.

On the question of releasing the White House tapes of his conversations, Mr. Nixon argues that this would cripple the presidency because "this kind of discussion is only possible when those who take part in it know that what they say is in strict confidence."

Wrong on two counts: (1) Never before has such evidence been crucial in determining whether a President has committed a crime. (2) Since most of the individuals whose conversations with the President were secretly recorded were unaware of this fact, their confidentiality and trust in the President already were breached by the act of clandestine taping.

Mr. Nixon hit bottom when he attempted to link the Watergate crimes with the anti-war protests and civil rights demonstrations of the 1960s. "We must recognize," he said, "that the extremes of violence and discord in the 1960s contributed to the extremes of Watergate."

We must recognize no such thing. This is the sort of distortion that has won Mr. Nixon the sobriquet of "Tricky Dick" To equate public protests, however violent, with attempts within the White House to corrupt government agencies for political purposes, to subvert the Constitution and to sanction and cover up crimes ranging from burglary, bribery and forgery to obstruction of justice is the grossest kind of deception. To hear such dissembling from the nation's chief executive is sickening.

Finally, in a transparent attempt to throttle the Senate Watergate Committee (whose most searching questioners have been Mr. Nixon's fellow Republicans) the President indirectly but clearly suggested that Americans flood the Senate with protests in order to force the hearings to be cut short, so that, in his words, we will not stay "mired in Watergate" and he can get on with more important matters.

Nonsense. There is nothing more important to the future of this nation than getting to the bottom of this worst scandal in our history, so that we can make sure it never can happen again. Equally absurd is the president's assertion that he still possesses a "mandate" from the voters as of last November's election. He apparently hasn't been following the polls, which show that most Americans, including many who voted for him last November, don't believe him or have confidence in him, and that he is the most unpopular president in the last 20 years.

For the President's sake, as well as the sake of the country, we had expected and hoped for more from Mr. Nixon last night. We didn't get it. What we got was disappointing and inadequate. Both the country and Mr. Nixon will suffer for it.

ARKANSAS DEMOCRAT
Little Rock, Ark., August 16, 1973

Like much of the other summer TV fare, President Nixon's long awaited answer to the Watergate charges had a rerun quality about it.

Pre-empting the airwaves Wednesday night, Mr. Nixon spent 30 minutes rehashing his excuses for not knowing about Watergate and its massive cover-up. Much of what he said was a repeat of a previous statement on May 22 and what was not a repeat was cliche'. The President just about pulled out all of the stops in this department and at one point even resurrected the old, stained, "peace with honor" slogan of the Vietnam War.

For the man, who a few weeks ago was boasting that he would let others "wallow in Watergate," the President did little to shed new light on the scandal so the nation, could in fact, be done with it and "turn it over to the courts." If the public was confused before his speech about the full ramifications of Watergate, they were even more so after it. Mr. Nixon did not answer any of the gut questions about the mess but instead raised new questions. While admitting at the start of his speech that he had "full responsibility" for the scandal, he later placed the blame on "the extremes of the 60's" for creating the moral climate in which a Watergate was possible.

The President's rebuttal was disappointing in many other ways as well. He did not explain how it was possible that his top aides could be up to their necks in such a sink hole while he was unaware of it. He did not clarify how his FBI director could tell him of the spreading scandal and why he ignored the warning. Nor did he bother to answer the most important question of all, how he could allow one of his aides access to those secret tape recordings, while denying the same privilege to the Ervin committee.

On the subject of the tapes, Mr. Nixon did nothing to detour the head-on constitutional crisis they have precipitated. He said the tapes would not be released as a matter of principal. A principle that was more important than Watergate, because it embraced the very credibility of our government. Once again Mr. Nixon held up the boogyman of national security as an excuse to do just what he wants. It now appears this question will have to be resolved in the courts and it will be of interest to see whether the President ignores that branch of government just as he has the legislative arm.

At the time of his speech, Mr. Nixon's national popularity had sunk to a low of 31 per cent. This is in stark contrast to the overwhelming mandate given him at the polls less than a year ago. He was well aware of it. He spoke of that resounding victory and lectured his audience about turning away from Watergate and getting on with the task of America's greatness. Nice words. High sounding words. But they are asking too much. America can hardly forget Watergate. Especially when their President won't let them. For almost four months he has dodged the true issues. He has failed to answer the real questions. He has magnified his guilt by silence. His speech Wednesday night did little to clear his name.

In fact it only added to the growing mistrust that surrounds the presidency, and no one should take joy from that.

THE CHRISTIAN SCIENCE MONITOR

Boston, Mass., August 24, 1973

President Nixon strengthened his position in fielding all questions on Watergate shot at him by the press Wednesday in San Clemente.

It was the kind of performance his friends and critics have been urging. Apart from an early nervousness, he showed a resilience of spirit, an adroitness, that should be an answer to reports that the President's composure, as well as public support, had been weakened by the Watergate ordeal.

True, there were problems with the format the President chose for his first open press session in five months. The press were summoned almost by surprise. There was the usual lack of opportunity to follow up on questions. And a press conference, as Senator Ervin pointed out after listening to the President's performance, still fails to offer the kind of cross-examination needed to get an exact fix on Watergate.

But it was a press conference. And it does mark a significant turn toward conciliation and away from counterattack. A start toward resolving the Watergate tangle, and toward rebuilding the President's standing among the American people, could stem from it.

The President, in acceding to demands for a press conference, did not give ground on most of the key elements of his defense. While he was speaking in San Clemente, his lawyer Charles Alan Wright was defending before Judge Sirica in Washington the President's right to keep the Watergate tapes from Congress and the courts. On the issue of wiretaps and illegal entry, the President agreed the Ellsberg break-in was wrong specifically but did not back off from his right to do whatever he thought necessary under his "inherent power" as President to defend national security. He did not yield over the propriety of meeting the Ellsberg trial judge for the FBI chief vacancy.

Nor did the President close the door on his opportunities for counterattack. He still portrayed — here and in New Orleans — as out to get him all those who disagree with his policies on Vietnam, social reforms, and so forth. This is an unfortunate device of Mr. Nixon's. Indeed, there are many Americans who may disagree with the President on Southeast Asia, busing, aid to parochial schools, and yet wish him no political or personal harm. They want him to survive. They know that when the President is in trouble the country is in trouble.

The tendency to cast opponents as enemies has been one of the themes behind the Watergate revelations. But leaving Watergate aside, it is a principle of democracy that opposing views exist and have a right to be heard and weighed and ultimately voted upon.

The President availed himself of the right to present his case through the press Wednesday. How far he will have convinced doubters about Watergate remains to be seen — we expect that the polls will show a favorable public response. But by openly accepting tough leading Watergate questions he has brought himself back more in touch with the American people. He has made himself less remote.

THE TENNESSEAN

Nashville, Tenn., August 25, 1973

AT HIS news conference in San Clemente, President Nixon was almost his old combative self as he dealt with the press in barely controlled fury, fielding its questions on Watergate while criticizing the preoccupation with it.

★ ★ ★

He had at least stopped sitting behind a wall of silence. If the tension between him and the press corps skirted the breaking point a few times, he nevertheless answered its questions.

In the process, he managed to contradict the testimony of his former White House counsel, the acting FBI director, the attorney general, the former attorney general and the statements of his daughter.

It was clear enough he had opened the counterattack against his critics in a bid for public support to put Watergate behind and get on with other things. If the opening gun was in New Orleans, where he spoke to the VFW, his press conference was a salvo with the underlying thread of a persecuted president whom the press had never liked or supported and of many others who had never accepted his mandate of 1972.

Mr. Nixon's verbal self portrait is of a man surrrounded by enemies, even some on his own staff who played fast and loose with him while he was trying to get the truth out. Other unnamed people don't want him to give strong leadership and cut the size of bureaucracy.

The President's defense of his own actions and that of others is curious. He had tapes at the White House because he found the capability already there. He refuses to give them up because other presidents have so refused. If there is something wrong with wiretapping, well, the Kennedy administration had far more than his. And, the President opened a new can of worms by claiming that government-authorized burglaries took place on "a very large scale" during the Kennedy and Johnson administrations.

This is the kind of unsupported claims that Mr. Nixon deplores in others. But the point is, previous wrongs do not make something right. What another president did, if wrong, is not an excuse for Mr. Nixon's administration to do likewise.

Throughout his long political career, when he has found himself in a squeeze, Mr. Nixon has countered criticism of his excesses by saying that others do it too, by attacking imaginary enemies, persons or institutions, if vulnerable, and by deflecting the argument into another area.

In New Orleans, while defending the duplicity of secret bombings in Cambodia, Mr. Nixon said, "I find that some politicians and some members of the press who enthusiastically supported the administration which got us into Vietnam 10 years ago are now critical of what I did to get us out." That is a debaters' ploy, and it doesn't answer the problem about deceiving the American people.

★ ★ ★

It is an interesting counter-offensive, but what is sad is that Mr. Nixon does not yet seem to grasp what is at the heart of the nation's worst political scandal, which he thinks "is water under the bridge."

The Dallas Morning News

Dallas, Tex., August 24, 1973

THE PRESIDENT has now gone through his long-awaited grilling by the national press corps. His critics' disappointed reaction to this event, which they've been demanding for months, reminds us of an old World War II story.

It seems there was a draftee who spent all his time wandering around the barracks area, picking up every piece of paper he could find. He would look at each scrap of paper, mutter "that's not it," and throw it away. He would then go on to the next find, mutter, "that's not it," and continue the search. After days of this, he was finally taken to the post psychiatrist, who examined the searcher, ruled him psychologically incapacitated and presented him with a certificate of medical discharge.

The draftee seized this paper, read it and then joyously exclaimed, "THAT'S it!"

A SIMILAR single-mindedness seems to motivate the total behavior of the President's most dedicated critics. Saying that the truth must be served, first they demanded that he remove the shield of executive privilege from his aides, so that they could be questioned by the Senate panel. The President did. But then the critics declared that these were only underlings and, in the interest of finding the truth, the President himself should speak on the issue.

He did. But the critics declared that this speech was too vague and self-serving. In the interest of truth, they said, he should make a more detailed answer to the questions that were being raised during the TV hearings. He postponed meeting this demand until the hearings recessed, but he then spoke again to the nation, taking responsibility, deploring the incident and asking Americans to let him get on with his job.

The critics immediately branded this as mere window-dressing and issue-dodging. They declared that, in the interest of truth, the President should subject himself to some really probing questions from the professional interviewers of the Washington press corps.

He has now done that, fielding the toughest questions before live TV.

His critics' reaction? Need you ask? They've instantly ruled that he has not really faced up to the crucial questions and that something more will have to be done.

The big step that is demanded in the interest of truth at this point is a complete airing of the President's confidential tapes and papers. If only that were done, the critics say, the truth would out, the matter would be settled and the country could move on to other problems.

That, of course, is exactly what they have said about all the other steps that they have demanded the President take—all those other steps that, once taken, they have immediately dismissed as empty and meaningless.

We suspect that the tapes, too, will be similarly shrugged off if they are released and fail to serve the critics' true purpose. That purpose is not to bring out the truth, but to humiliate Richard Nixon completely, destroy his mandate from the voters and drive him out of the presidency.

THE ONLY way that President Nixon can really satisfy most of his critics is to grovel before the nation's voters, confess total guilt on every charge that his critics have thought up and announce his resignation.

Somehow we get the feeling that if the President took that unlikely action, a coast-to-coast chorus of critics would shout in harmony, "THAT'S it!"

The Dispatch

Columbus, Ohio, August 24, 1973

PRESIDENT Nixon put it succinctly in his press conference Wednesday —. we have been mesmerized by Watergate to the point where we are paying too little attention to the people's business.

Presidential press conferences traditionally last 30 minutes and when the minute hand moves to that point, a senior correspondent signals finis with "Thank you, Mr. President."

THAT POINT came Wednesday. But it was then that Mr. Nixon made his significant observation.

He noted that the first 30 minutes of questioning had been devoted exclusively to Watergate. This shows, he said very correctly, "how consumed we are" with scandal rather than the "business of the people."

THE CHIEF Executive then launched into an additional 20 minutes of commentary devoted to that higher priority, those matters which genuinely concern the people — a peaceful world scene and a domestic economy which is stablized.

The President was asked whether his capacity to govern had been damaged by the droning recitation of the Watergate case.

MR. NIXON'S reply carried significant implications.

He said that "to be under a constant barrage of 12 to 15 minutes a night, on each of three major (television) networks for four months, tends to raise some questions in people's minds with regard to the President and it may raise some questions with regard to the capacity to govern."

ANOTHER question is raised all too ominously.

It is whether this daily barrage of television commentary places undue power in the hands of three persons who have the opportunity to sway and mold public opinion regardless of whether their commentary is based on objective fact.

SOME YEARS ago, a representative of a nondemocratic totalitarian regime observed that if you din the people with a lie often enough and long enough the people will tend to believe it to be truth.

The people should recognize and appreciate Mr. Nixon's candor in saying that the Watergate caper is an episode which "I deeply deplore," that "I would have blown my stack" had he been aware of the facts of Watergate and that the wrongdoers must be brought to trial and punished.

MR. NIXON should be commended for his refusal to cut and run in the face of Watergate's deplorable excesses and for pledging to spend the balance of his term of office "trying to get the people of the U.S. to recognize, whatever mistakes we have made, in the long run this administration" deserves more high marks than low marks.

Most importantly, the people should recognize that their penchant to depend on a few minutes of capsulized "news" each evening can do them, their country and their governors more harm than good.

Truth seekers can indeed be victimized by truth twisters.

The Charleston Gazette

Charleston, W.Va., August 22, 1973

President Nixon, in his Aug. 15 speech and statement on Watergate, had this to say:

". . .I at no time authorized the use of illegal means by the special investigations unit, and I was not aware of the break-in of Dr. Fielding's office until March 17, 1973."

But in his May 22 statement on Watergate, the same President Nixon had this to say:

". . . The options initially approved had included resumption of certain intelligence operations which had been suspended in 1966. These in turn had included authorization of surreptitious entry — breaking and entering, in effect — on specified categories of targets in specified situations related to national security."

The President went on to explain in his May 22 statement that the intelligence operations he described were authorized for only five days. Their authorization was withdrawn, he said in that same statement, after FBI Director J. Edgar Hoover objected to the operations.

The Dr. Fielding mentioned in the President's Aug. 15 statement was Daniel Ellsberg's psychiatrist, and it was Dr. Fielding's office that was broken into and his files riffled by the special investigations unit — otherwise known as "The Plumbers" — also referred to by the President in his Aug. 15 statement.

In his Aug. 15 televised address, President Nixon defended his refusal to turn over tapes of White House conversations to the special Watergate prosecutor and the Senate Watergate committee on the grounds that such conversations must be kept in strictest confidence.

"The law has long recognized that there are kinds of conversations that are entitled to be kept confidential," he said, "even at the cost of doing without critical evidence in a legal proceeding. This rule applies, for example, to conversations between a lawyer and a client, between a priest and a penitent, and between a husband and wife."

Mr. Nixon did not touch upon the need for confidentiality between doctor and patient, nor did he mention the right of privacy between Ellsberg and his psychiatrist in his reference to the break-in of Dr. Fielding's office.

The President did concede on Aug. 15 that his May 22 statement was "not precisely accurate" when he said he learned of the break-in at the psychiatrist's office on April 18 and ordered the information given to the judge trying Ellsberg on April 25.

The latest information from the President is that he first learned of this break-in on March 17 — four days before he began his own investigation of Watergate and nearly a month before he authorized John Ehrlichman to feel out Judge Byrne on acceptance of the FBI directorship, a period in which the President saw the judge briefly during his talk with Ehrlichman.

So it is that the President has now admitted he knew something that could affect the Ellsberg trial three weeks before he saw the judge and five weeks before he told the judge about the break-in, a situation which led to dismissal of the Pentagon papers charges against Ellsberg.

There are other facets of Mr. Nixon's professed knowledge of the break-in of Dr. Fielding's office that call for more than casual reading.

One has to do with his "not precisely accurate" statement of May 22 in which he said "It was not until the time of my own investigation that I learned of the break-in at the office of Mr. Ellsberg's psychiatrist, and I sepcifically authorized the furnishing of this information to Judge Byrne."

But his corrective statement of Aug. 15 had to do only with dates, implying an insignificant four-day discrepancy — and apparently let stand, again by implication, an element of immediacy in his earlier statement that he had "specifically authorized" the furnishing of information to Judge Byrne.

Indeed, a closer reading discloses an admission that for 39 days he withheld from a trial then in progress evidence which the attorney general considered significant and the trial judge thought important enough to warrant dismissal of the charges.

The other discrepancy deals with the President's expressed interest in a prompt dispatch of the break-in information to the trial judge. Mr. Nixon reviewed the matter on Aug. 15 in these words:

"On April 25, Atty. Gen. Kleindienst came to me and urged that the fact of the break-in should be disclosed to the court, despite the fact that, since no evidence had been obtained, the law did not clearly require it. I concurred, and authorized him to report the break-in to Judge Byrne."

What he failed to mention in this explanation, however, was that Kleindienst had told the Senate Watergate committee that the President had been reluctant to provide the i n f o r m a t i o n and that he (Kleindienst) threatened to resign if Mr. Nixon persisted in an act which the attorney general considered an illegal suppression of evidence.

What story would the White House tapes tell?

The Oregonian

Portland, Ore., August 26, 1973

The flap that has developed over President Nixon's press conference comment that security-related "burglarizing" occurred in previous administrations as well as his has its amusing aspects. The White House, Justice Department and FBI decline to document Mr. Nixon's assertion. But one of his constant editorial critics, the New York Times, has done so in detail, in a story printed in The Oregonian Friday. So has the Associated Press and other news agencies quoting "former high FBI officials."

"I should also point out to you," the President said, "that in the three Kennedy years and the three Johnson years through 1966, when burglarizing of this type did take place, when it was authorized, on a very large scale, there was no talk of impeachment and it was quite well known."

Indeed, as the Times pointed out, surreptitious entry to install electronic eavesdropping devices, as well as outright burglaries, have been established practices of the super-secret spy and crime-busting agencies going back at least to the Administration of Franklin D. Roosevelt. Such practices were used not only in efforts to break codes and obtain other information from foreign embassies, but to nail criminals and to carry out surveillance of such domestic radical groups as the Black Panthers and the Weathermen, the AP reported.

The plan submitted by Tom Charles Huston, a security adviser to the President, to reinstate illegal entry and other such methods which generally had been de-authorized in 1966 was approved, at first, by President Nixon in 1970. A few days later it was canceled because of the objections of the late J. Edgar Hoover, FBI director, who rejected the use of his agency to get information for other agencies. Evidently, underlings Gordon Liddy and Howard Hunt, who made the bungling raid on the psychiatrist for Daniel Ellsberg, who made public the secret Pentagon Papers, got their authority and cash from someone other than President Nixon, as Watergate testimony has shown. This break-in was deplored by Nixon and was of questionable security relationship.

The reporting of 40 years of wiretapping and surreptitious entry, restricted in legality in recent years by Supreme Court decisions, does not, of course, enhance the prestige of the United States government among American citizens or foreign capitals, even though in many other countries such activities are even more commonplace. President Nixon said Wednesday that the bugs have been taken out of White House offices. It would help if he would also make a definitive statement soon as to the exact nature of such secret information-gathering practices which are authorized and legal. Big Brother should worry everyone.

WINSTON-SALEM JOURNAL
Winston-Salem, N.C., August 31, 1973

SIRICA ORDERS TAPES TURNED OVER FOR PRIVATE JUDICIAL EXAMINATION

U.S. District Court Judge John J. Sirica Aug. 29 ordered President Nixon to turn over to him for private examination the tape recordings of presidential conversations involving the Watergate case. The disputed tapes had been subpoenaed by special prosecutor Archibald Cox. While rejecting Nixon's claim of immunity from court processes, Sirica said in an opinion accompanying his order that he had "attempted to walk the middle ground between a failure to decide the question of privilege at one extreme, and a wholesale delivery of tapes to the grand jury at the other." Sirica said he was willing to recognize the validity of a privilege "based on the need to protect presidential privacy," but the courts must decide whether such a privilege had been properly claimed. He said he was "simply unable to decide the question of privilege without inspecting the tapes."

Sirica said he had found it necessary to decide only two questions "for the present": (1) whether the court had jurisdiction on the issue of executive privilege, and (2) whether the court had the authority to enforce the subpoena by ordering production of the material for private inspection. Both questions, he said, "must be answered in the affirmative." Sirica rejected as "unpersuasive" the White House argument that constitutional separation of powers gave the President immunity from compulsory court processes. Such a contention, Sirica said, "overlooks history." The framers of the Constitution, Sirica noted, had shown a "general disfavor of government privileges, or at least uncontrolled privileges." Nor had they intended to create a "watertight" division of functions among the branches of government.

Although Sirica decided that the proper procedure would be his examination of the tapes and a determination of portions not subject to privilege and thus available to the grand jury, he said he was "extremely reluctant to finally stand against a declaration of the President" that the taped conversations had occurred in the exercise of official duties and were subject to privilege in their entirety. He conceded that his inspection might indeed constitute a "compromise of privilege," but said it would be an "extremely limited infraction and in this case an unavoidable one." Sirica's compromise would be to excise portions he might deem privileged and send only the unprivileged parts to the grand jury. This procedure, he had said earlier in his opinion, would be "tantamount to fully enforcing the subpoena as to any unprivileged matter." But, if the evidence was so "inextricably intertwined" that separation became impossible, "the whole must be privileged and no disclosure made to the grand jury."

Sirica stayed enforcement of his order to allow Nixon to appeal and ruled that if the President appealed, the stay would be extended indefinitely pending completion of appeals.

In a statement released at San Clemente Aug. 30, the White House said Nixon would seek review of Judge Sirica's order to release the tapes in the U.S. Court of Appeals for the District of Columbia. Nixon had said Aug. 22 that he would abide by a "definitive" Supreme Court decision. A statement released Aug. 29 had said Nixon would not comply with Sirica's order.

Judge Sirica's order to President Nixon to produce the White House tapes puts one more strain on our constitutional system. After the "confrontations" between executive and legislative branches over the impoundment of funds and the bombing in Cambodia, we now have confrontation between the executive and the judiciary over the right of the executive to withhold evidence from the courts in a criminal proceeding.

The questions at issue are not simple, and reasonable men may differ in their answers.

Certainly, every reasonable man will agree that the president must always be entitled to discuss matters of state with his advisers in absolute confidence. President Nixon is as much entitled to that privilege of confidentiality as any other president back to the days of George Washington.

But what is involved here is apparently not matters of state, such as national security, but criminal acts and conspiracies. President Nixon himself and most of his former advisers who have testified now concede that some of his subordinates in the White House and re-election committee were involved in these acts and conspiracies. And John Dean, the former White House counsel, testified that Mr. Nixon was aware of some of these illegal acts and, in effect, condoned them by not taking action against the perpetrators.

Dean's assertions have been challenged by other witnesses. This conflict of testimony is what makes the tapes so crucial.

As for confidentiality, it has been argued that Mr. Nixon breached the principle when he let one of the prime suspects, H. R. Haldeman, listen to certain tapes and then give his own self-serving version to the Ervin committee.

Given all the circumstances, Judge Sirica, then, may have had little choice but to rule as he did, ordering the President to let him have the relevant tapes with the assurance that he would listen to them in private and exercise the utmost discretion in deciding whether any excerpts whatsoever might be pertinent to the grand jury's investigation.

This decison was received with joy by Archibald Cox and Sen. Sam Ervin. The special prosecutor and the chairman of the Senate investigating committee naturally hope that the tapes, if delivered to the judge, will clear up matters that are now in controversy.

Perhaps they will and perhaps they won't. The only thing that is certain is that we now have a new conflict between two of the co-equal branches of government. In the history books it will rank as another major achievement of the President who promised "to bring us together again."

In the circumstances we can only be thankful that our constitutional system has proved even sturdier than the wonderful one-hoss shay which, after all, lasted no more than a hundred years to a day.

Those White House tapes continue to haunt President Nixon, and well they might. As long as they remain locked away, they are an invisible barrier between him and the people who put him into office, a ghostly presence tantalizing with an offer of proof undelivered.

But proof of what? That is the question.

The legalistic case for sitting on the tapes is the one Mr. Nixon stressed again in his Watergate statement, and it has a plausible side. Certainly a President would be handicapped if his private conversations with aides, with congressmen or with foreign diplomats were thrown open to the public. The law should and does allow for confidences to be kept. The Oval Office of the President cannot be converted into a goldfish bowl.

But the fact is that the President himself demolished the privacy of his office and his telephone lines by ordering everything recorded on tape, and we're confronted by a puzzle. If the President regarded the talk in his office as too "candid" or too sensitive to bear repeating, why put it on tape where a touch of a button will replay it? Recordings are made to be replayed.

Presumably the tapes were for the historical record, to be filed away for posterity with presidential papers. Perhaps it wasn't intended that they be touched again until all the principal characters were gone. Yet we have it on Mr. Nixon's word that different interpretations can be put on what was said in the particular tapes at issue in the Watergate case, and we have another puzzle.

If contemporaries with all the circumstances fresh in mind couldn't agree on what the tapes mean, how can historians of the next century be expected to reach an accurate judgment?

Mr. Nixon made the point that if the presidential conversations were revealed, "persons talking with a President would never again be sure that recordings or notes of what they said would not at some future time be made public, and they would guard their words against that possibility."

But the fact seems to be that only the President knew the conversations were being taped; hence he could guard his own words as recorded for posterity while encouraging others to be "candid," not knowing.

Another puzzle. If the President was guarded and his visitors were candid, how could the tapes do other than show him in the best possible light? And if that is the case, is the principle of executive privilege so unbending, so fragile, that it can't permit an exception to clear him of blame in this most exceptional affair?

Defenders of government-sponsored wiretapping, including many of Mr. Nixon's supporters if not the President himself, are fond of saying that no one should mind being tapped unless he has something to hide. That too creates a puzzle now that the Presi-

CHICAGO DAILY NEWS
Chicago, Ill., August 18, 1973

dent is in the position of hiding the tapes while insisting that there's nothing to hide.

We have long thought, and still do, that a compromise could resolve the tape dilemma without destroying the principle of separation of powers. It would merely involve allowing a small delegated group of trusted citizens to hear the tapes in closed session and report its findings. By continuing to reject such a solution, Mr. Nixon further contributes to an erosion of confidence and adds new dimensions to the puzzle of the tapes.

Portland Press Herald
Portland, Me., August 31, 1973

Federal Judge John J. Sirica moved with due and deliberate caution to the right destination in his handling of the suit to force President Nixon to release the disputed tape conversations to the Watergate special prosecutor.

Judge Sirica's order to release the tapes moved directly to appeal as expected. The same course would have been followed had the decision favored the President's position. The appeals will continue until the highest court has passed on the issue.

The judge did not challenge Mr. Nixon's argument as to presidential privilege for the purpose of keeping executive discussion confidential. But he did declare, significantly, that the judiciary and not the executive must be the judge of proper use of that privilege when it is challenged.

Making it meticulously clear that he did not intend any suggestion as to Mr Nixon's trustworthiness in judging his own executive privilege, Judge Sirica wrote:

"For the courts to abdicate this role to presidents or anyone else, to make each officer the judge of his own privilege, would dishonor the genius of our constitutional system and breed unbearable abuse."

The judge moved in practical manner in asking that he be permitted to hear the tapes. Only in that manner could the court satisfy itself as to the nature of the recorded conversations.

"If privileged and unprivileged evidence are intermingled, privileged portions may be excised so that only unprivileged matter goes before the grand jury. If privileged and unprivileged evidence are so inextricably connected that separation becomes impossible, the whole must be privileged and no disclosure made to the grand jury."

That is a wholly sensible course. Since the supposedly secret federal grand jury proceedings in Washington are blabbed to a waiting keyhole columnist on a daily basis, we can understand the President's reluctance to have the tapes heard in that environment. But the procedure as set forth by Judge Sirica offers the assurance that only relevant portions of the tapes would be heard by the jurors. And there is the additional security in the provision that should it be impossible to segregate the appropriate portions of the dialogue, none of it would be disclosed.

Judge Sirica's action appears to be in the best tradition of judicial proceedings.

DAYTON DAILY NEWS
Dayton, Ohio, August 31, 1973

President Nixon has rarely looked more self-damagingly rigid than in his out-of-hand rejection of Judge John Sirica's order that he yield disputed tape recordings for private, confidential review by the court.

Special Prosecutor Archibald Cox won his point, but Judge Sirica allowed him only a severely limited victory. Not even a president can withhold evidence from a grand jury investigation of crimes, the judge said. Beyond that, however, the White House got what it wanted, or had said it hoped for, in Judge Sirica's ruling.

The decision recognizes — indeed reinforces — the legitimacy of Mr. Nixon's claim to executive privilege in the conduct of the presidency. It assures the President that any random irrelevancies on the tapes would be withheld from the grand jury by the judge, and the ruling even goes so far as to say that should judicial review find the relevant and the irrelevant materials inseparable, the claim of privilege would be spread over all the material.

What that means is simple. Only the specific utterances bearing on possible guilt or innocence in criminal issues could pass across the bench to grand jurors. The confidentiality that Mr. Nixon says he is seeking to preserve in the relations of the presidency would be upheld in general — to be breached only in exceptionally narrow and improbable circumstances and actually strengthened in all other situations.

As others have — the Watergate committee and Prosecutor Cox himself before he was forced to seek a remedy in court — Judge Sirica has tried in his ruling to offer the President a compromise that would acknowledge the necessary authority of grand jury proceedings yet leave the legitimate confidences of the executive branch unimpaired and free of any implied intimidation by the other branches of the federal government.

The judge wisely sought to forestall a grinding constitutional crash over the issue, choosing to decide the case to the greatest degree possible on its unique specifics and involving constitutional considerations only to the limited extent necessary for clarifying the circumstances of the case itself.

The decision is sound in its reasoning, sound in its conclusions and sound in its responsible attempt to clear a limited middle ground on which the prosecutor and the President could meet. By rejecting the chance to compromise on specifics without compromising on principle, Mr. Nixon has rejected the best chance he has had, and perhaps the last one he will have, to lead the Watergate affair to a crisis-free conclusion.

THE BLADE

Toledo, Ohio, August 20, 1973

THE key point on which Richard Nixon has struck his personal stance in the Watergate investigation is what he proclaims as his sacred duty to protect the institution of the presidency. He cannot release tapes of crucial conversations, he cannot turn over certain documents, he cannot respond to subpenas, he must hold himself above the reach of the Senate committee and the special prosecutor and the courts, he has no choice but to stand adamantly on the principles of executive privilege and confidentiality — all this because, as he put it in one representative statement in his speech last week, of his "constitutional responsibility to defend the integrity of this great office."

The validity of this line of premises as an applicable legal tenet is being argued in the courts of law. But in the court of public opinion, the President's most eloquent espousals of this lofty mandate have obviously left the huge majority of the American people simply unconvinced. And the reason,

of course, is that his argument is so transparently a distortion of the situation that the Watergate scandal actually represents.

As an institution, the office of the presidency does not belong to Mr. Nixon but to the American people. Their stake in its integrity and its future is far more substantial and profound than his. Citizens now living and generations to come will be looking to the office for leadership and governance within the democratic framework long after the incumbent has left the job and been given whatever place in posterity history deems him to deserve.

Thus, any preoccupation with the protection of the presidency should rest with the American public, and Mr. Nixon's attempt to make it otherwise reverses the true picture. He depicts himself as battling to defend the institution against assault and sabotage from external forces, but the fact is that the real attack on the prestige

and subversion of the integrity of the presidency has come from within. It was the Nixon administration, the Nixon executive staff, the Nixon re-election organization that were responsible for the scandal of Watergate and all its attendant evils. And it is that truth which has cast the shadow of suspicion over Richard Nixon himself.

The President cannot dispel that cloud by throwing up a smokescreen of lofty abstractions and pious platitudes about executive principles that have in effect lost their meaning by his very handling of them. So long as he engages in rhetorical feints, sets himself above the law that governs other citizens as well as other constitutional institutions of government, and refuses in the name of that stance to present any real evidence to support his protestations of innocence. Mr. Nixon cannot hope to persuade his constituents that his hallowed posture of preserving the presidency is anything but another phase of the cover-up.

THE DALLAS TIMES HERALD

Dallas, Tex., August 31, 1973

CHIEF U.S. District Judge John J. Sirica's historic order directing President Nixon to deliver the White House Watergate tape recordings for his private review is correct if there is to be proper pursuit of possible criminal law violations.

For the first time in modern history it, indeed, places the judicial branch over the executive level, but it need not be a precedent cast in the granite if his minutely defined procedure is followed by Judge Sirica.

He meticulously laid down the ground rules for inspection of the tapes and expressed extreme reluctance to "finally stand against a declaration of the United States on any but the strongest evidence. Need for the evidence requires that a claim not be rejected lightly. The court is simply unable to decide the question of privilege without inspecting the tapes."

Therein lies the crux of the Watergate matter. Were individuals guilty, or not guilty, of criminal misconduct and if so should they be moved through the established process of grand jury inquiry and possible court trial?

Judge Sirica carefully delineates his rights to examination of the evidence.

In his ruling he soundly states that if privileged and un-

privileged evidence are intermingled, privileged portions may be excised so that only unprivileged matter goes before a grand jury that also meets in secret proceedings.

If the unprivileged and privileged evidence are so inextricably connected that separation seems impossible, the whole must be considered privileged and no disclosure made to a grand jury.

The ultimate decision rests upon the wisdom, judgment and responsibility of Judge Sirica in the privacy of his chambers.

And the strictest commitment of secrecy must come from the grand jury . . . a commitment that has been flagrantly broken in recent weeks when grand jury and government leaks spilled into newspaper print.

President Nixon should make available those tapes that might have direct bearing on a criminal violation. He should retain those tapes that involve other highly confidential national security matters.

Judge Sirica has attempted to walk "the middle ground between a failure to decide the question of privilege at one extreme, and a wholesale delivery of tapes to the grand jury at the other."

As he concluded, the one would be a breach of duty; the other an inexcusable course of conduct.

Pittsburgh Post-Gazette

Pittsburgh, Pa., August 30, 1973

JUDGE SIRICA candidly said he sought a compromise in his ruling on the President's tapes in the Watergate matter. He ruled that the tapes be given him as a judge so that he could listen to them and then decide whether they should be handed to a grand jury.

The judge said that "the court has attempted to walk the middle ground between a failure to decide the question of privilege at one extreme, and a wholesale delivery of tapes to the grand jury at the other."

Mr. Sirica

But Judge Sirica's compromise, like most compromises, falls between two stools. It would have been appealed to the higher courts anyway, but now both sides may raise questions about its validity.

On the one hand it appears to override the assertion of President Nixon's attorneys that the tapes are covered by executive privilege and can't be turned over to anyone. The judge is saying they must be released to him. We approve that aspect of the decision since it agrees with our contention all along that the President should release the tapes, as they seemed to be a key piece in the jigsaw puzzle of just who was responsible for the Watergate coverup.

But, unfortunately, Judge Sirica sets such tight parameters that we are in danger of never knowing the contents of the tapes, even if they are pried out of the President's hands. He said that if privileged and unprivileged material are intermingled, only unprivileged material may be taken out and transmitted to the grand jury. Furthermore — and this could be the real joker — the judge said that "if privileged and unpriv-

ileged evidence are so inextricably connected that separation becomes impossible, the whole must be privileged and no disclosure made to the grand jury."

So no one should be easy about this ruling.

President Nixon's attorneys understandably could object to a procedure where a judge in effect said, "Let me listen to the tapes and decide whether or not the contents shall be released outside the executive branch." They might argue that the courts should decide the basic issue of privilege first, rather than following this "peek-a-boo" procedure.

But Special Prosecutor Cox perhaps should have qualms about accepting the precedent, too. Is it wise to allow one man to listen to the tapes and decide yea or nay, especially in an unprecedented situation where criminal implications touching the President himself are at stake?

If Judge Sirica were to decide "yes," then he could establish a procedure in which privileged and unprivileged material could be sorted out by, say, a panel of distinguished citizens.

But if he were to decide "No," under the procedure he chose yesterday, there would be no opinion about the tapes but his own. (That assumes, of course, that he was upheld on appeal.) The White House would have lost a privilege the President strongly defends, but the public would have ended up no wiser about the most critical issue in the Watergate matter — the President's own degree of responsibility.

In the long run it might have been better had Judge Sirica forthrightly made his decision on broad grounds, rather than trapping himself into basing a momentous ruling on one man's opinion gained from the internal evidence of the tapes themselves.

Arkansas Gazette.

Little Rock, Ark., August 31, 1973

THE STAGE is set for the dreaded constitutional confrontation but let the record show that Judge John J. Sirica of the United States District Court at Washington did everything that he could to avoid it, short of abdicating the role of the judiciary in the American system of government.

Indeed, Judge Sirica's decision in the case of President Nixon's secret tape recordings is a model of both resolution and restraint. He has ordered the President or a subordinate to present certain tapes — nine of them — that may be critically relevant, in whole or in part, to the processes of justice in the Watergate conspiracy. At the same time Sirica has stipulated that the tapes are to be screened, to determine relevancy and privilege, only by him, the presiding judge. Thus the vaunted confidentiality of the tapes would be guarded to the maximum degree consistent with the pursuit of justice, certainly to a greater degree than that exercised by the President himself in the celebrated loan-out of one or more tapes to H. R. Haldeman, private citizen.

No one can reasonably doubt that some of the information in the nine tapes —especially the ones involving dialogue between Richard Nixon and John Dean — go to the heart of the Watergate conspiracy and fixing of responsibility. Nevertheless, as Judge Sirica observed in his short, lucid opinion, the Court is "simply unable to decide the question of privilege without examining the tapes." In any case it is plain that the Court has accommodated the President to the maximum. Would that the President had reciprocated in kind!

* * *

WHAT Mr. Nixon has done, rather, is to make no concession at all but simply to reassert that the President stands constitutionally above compliance with the orders of any court: He continues on a collision course, when he might have followed the example of President Thomas Jefferson in a developing confrontation with Chief Justice John Marshall in 1807. Marshall ordered Jefferson to present a letter that was relevant in the trial of Aaron Burr. Jefferson, in his turn, disputed the authority of Marshall to command the letter *but he produced it anyway*, to avoid the crisis. Thomas Jefferson had nothing to hide.

Sirica would have set a potentially disastrous precedent if he had held that the President is above the requirements of the law, but even in making his choice the judge phrased his opinion in the most diplomatic of terms. He said that the court intended no suggestion that the "respondent" could not be trusted to be his own judge in matters of privilege, but that the Court was reluctant to set a precedent that might "encourage some *future* high executive officer to become a despot" (the italics are ours).

How could the judge have been more gentlemanly or tactful, in exempting the incumbent President from the tendencies that all of us know, or should know, he not only harbors but indulges! The entire story of Watergate and its related scandals is the story of a president and an administration turning to the practices of despotism.

* * *

JUDGE Sirica set aside five days for appeal and certainly an issue of such tremendous import cannot be settled at any level except that of the Supreme Court. The initial White House response left open the possibility of the White House refusing to obey or even to appeal, but it is hardly conceivable that Mr. Nixon could keep the issue from coming to rest finally in the Supreme Court. It is hard to believe, in turn, that the highest court, even a court with four Nixon appointees, would hold that the President, like a king, is above the law.

In his recent public appearances Richard Nixon called on the Senate and all of us to turn our attention from the Watergate and leave the issues there to be settled in the Courts. That is precisely what the district judge is calling upon Nixon himself now to do — leave the issues to the courts to determine.

No one can say what the Supreme Court will decide in the end, nor whether Nixon is prepared to stand in the White House door, as it were, defying the highest court in the land. But if it comes down to *that* kind of confrontation, there will be only one recourse left in the defense of the Constitution, and everyone knows what it is.

Los Angeles Times

Los Angeles, Calif., August 30, 1973

Judge John J. Sirica's request for private inspection of the Watergate tapes will commend itself to reasonable persons as the reasonable way to deal with the problems of criminal and constitutional law at issue.

The judge would have the opportunity to separate, if he could, matters covered by a legitimate claim of executive privilege from matters pertaining solely to the investigation of crimes. The judge in effect denied the President's claim to be the sole judge of executive privilege, while granting that the disputed tapes may be covered by the privilege.

The President says he will not comply. Yet we believe there is a way out of the impasse, a way that would satisfy the intentions of Judge Sirica's careful order while avoiding concessions of executive power by the President.

This way lies in the President's doing voluntarily what Judge Sirica has ordered him to do.

We believe that the President should take this voluntary approach because we see little if any good coming from the pressing of this case to a decision by the Supreme Court.

A Supreme Court ruling upholding the President would be the most damaging, for it would constitute an unprecedented formal grant of broad power to this and all future Chief Executives.

The President argues that a curb in the unlimited executive privilege he claims would set a precedent likely to do much harm; we believe that a court ruling in the President's favor would set a precedent potentially much more dangerous to liberty.

A Supreme Court ruling upholding special prosecutor Archibald Cox's request for release of all the taped material to the grand jury would be on balance less damaging to the structure of government. But we share Judge Sirica's reluctance to grant so sweeping a claim; we believe that the claim of executive privilege is legitimate and necessary when made to protect the confidentiality of the President's legitimate business. Common sense would give the President some discretion in defining the extent of his privilege.

A Supreme Court ruling that said, in effect, that the problem was too sensitive for the court to handle would avoid the setting of potentially damaging precedents, but would leave the current issue of the Watergate tapes unresolved.

The best foreseeable Supreme Court decision would be one upholding Judge Sirica's carefully circumscribed approach: that if the material is relevant, and separable from other material, the grand jury should have it. Yet even here we confess to a certain uneasiness, a nagging suspicion that a grant of such power to the judiciary by the Supreme Court could later be expanded into a claim of unwarranted judicial authority over the Presidency. The founding fathers did not attempt to define too closely the relationship of each branch of government to the other; the absence of absolute rules on the separation of powers leaves room for accommodation and compromise, as dictated by experience.

It is precisely that kind of accommodation and compromise the President would achieve if he would voluntarily do what Judge Sirica has ordered him to do. He could continue to stand on his claim of executive privilege while freely giving the tapes for inspection to Judge Sirica in the criminal prosecutions, and to another third party in the Senate investigations.

Such an accommodation would mitigate the constitutional confrontations and avoid erosion of the executive's legitimate powers while satisfying the nation's legitimate interest in having someone other than the President assess the contents of those tape recordings.

EHRLICHMAN INDICTED; TAPES RULING APPEALED

There were these developments in the Watergate case during the first half of September:

■Former White House domestic affairs adviser John D. Ehrlichman, "plumbers" group coordinators Egil Krogh Jr. and David R. Young Jr., and convicted Watergate conspirator G. Gordon Liddy were indicted Sept. 4 by a Los Ángeles County grand jury on charges stemming from the 1971 break-in at the office of Daniel Ellsberg's psychiatrist. The indictment detailed 16 overt acts in connection with the planning and execution of the burglary. Ehrlichman was also charged with perjury for his denial before the grand jury of prior knowledge of the break-in. Listed in the charges as unindicted co-conspirators were convicted Watergate conspirators E. Howard Hunt, Jr., Bernard L. Barker, and Eugenio Martinez; and Felipe DeDiego, a Cuban national from Miami.

■At his Sept. 5 news conference, President Nixon declined to elaborate on what he would consider a "definitive decision" by the Supreme Court on the issue of the Watergate tapes. He had said earlier that he would heed such a decision. Nixon said the matter would be discussed in court during the appeal procedure and comment before then would be "inappropriate." Nixon reiterated his position that absolute confidentiality of presidential conversations was essential to the "proper conduct" of the office. This principle, he said, was the justification for the "hard line" he had taken in regard to compliance with Judge John J. Sirica's ruling that he (Sirica) be allowed to privately examine the tapes.

■James W. McCord Jr. and Jeb Stuart Magruder were ordered by Judge Sirica Sept. 5 to refrain from offering public lectures or interviews. Both were free pending sentencing for their roles in the Watergate burglary. Asserting that criminals should not "profit by their wrongdoing," Sirica warned McCord and Magruder that such speeches might have an adverse effect on future trials growing out of the Watergate affair.

■The suit by the Senate Watergate committee to obtain its own access to the presidential tapes was dealt a potentially damaging blow Sept. 6 when Judge Sirica granted the White House a two-week delay—until Sept. 24—for responding to the committee's motion to force compliance with its subpoenas. Because of appeals which would follow Sirica's decision on the suit, the latest delay was seen as pushing a final resolution past the committee's projected adjournment date of Nov. 1.

■Lawyers for President Nixon Sept. 6 asked the U.S. Court of Appeals for the District of Columbia to overturn Sirica's order to Nixon to surrender the tapes. The White House action was technically not a routine appeal of Sirica's decision but a separate suit, naming Sirica as defendant and special prosecutor Archibald Cox as an interested party, asking the court to nullify Sirica's ruling. The court agreed to hear the case *en banc* and confirmed its speeded up schedule, announced Sept. 4, under which filing of briefs and oral arguments were to be completed by Sept. 14.

■In his own response to Sirica tape ruling, special Watergate prosecutor Cox took an approach similar to that taken by the White House: rather than appealing directly, Cox filed a separate action naming Sirica as respondent and asking that the court amend Sirica's order. Cox asked first that Nixon be ordered to surrender the tapes directly to the grand jury without judicial screening. If the court were to decide that Sirica's inspection of the tapes was proper, Cox asked the court to set standards for the screening. Cox added that he should be allowed to assist Sirica in the determination of relevant evidence, since Sirica, unlike the prosecutors, was "not in a position" to have complete knowledge of the possible relevance of all portions of the tapes. The White House was granted a delay until Sept. 19 to file its final reply.

■The Senate Watergate committee decided Sept. 12 to resume its Watergate hearings Sept. 24, to hold three public sessions a week and to try to conclude the sessions by Nov. 1. The need for more investigation on the panel's final two phases of its probe—campaign sabotage and contributions—was given as the cause of a later resumption date that was originally planned. Committee Chairman Sen. Sam J. Ervin Jr. (D, N.C.) said committee members hoped to expedite the hearings by concentrating on "salient points" from "key witnesses."

■In a surprise move Sept. 13 the Appeals Court for the District of Columbia issued a unanimous memorandum urging an out-of-court settlement under which Nixon (or his delegate), along with his counsel Charles Wright and prosecutor Cox, would examine the tapes to determine what material could go to the grand jury. The court noted that the settlement would require voluntary submission of the tapes by Nixon, but beyond that the court would not "presume to prescribe the details" of how Nixon should work with the two counsel.

Des Moines Tribune
Des Moines, Iowa, September 3, 1973

Senator Robert Dole (Rep., Kan.), a former Republican national chairman, said he is toying with proposing a halt to the Watergate hearings. A Dole spokesman later said the senator would be satisfied if the Ervin committee went behind closed doors so the press and public could not hear the testimony.

Dole said he is worried about the problems facing the country, particularly inflation. He wants the country to tackle these issues and not be diverted by Watergate.

Dole is an experienced enough legislator to know that nothing the Senate committee does about Watergate prevents attacks on other problems. The investigation occupies the time of seven senators. Other Americans have plenty of opportunity to observe the Ervin committee and fight inflation.

The mentality responsible for the Watergate cover-up was characterized by a conviction that embarrassing incidents should be hidden from view at all costs. The idea that the public has a right to the facts was foreign to those who engineered the cover-up conspiracy.

Dole's desire to put the Ervin committee probe of the Watergate break-in, "dirty tricks" and campaign contributions behind closed doors makes us wonder how much prominent Republicans have learned from the Watergate experience. The Ervin committee disclosures are embarrassing to the Nixon administration and the GOP, but the answer does not lie in more cover-up. The more the public learns about wrongdoing, the greater the likelihood the public will demand effective safeguards to prevent a repetition.

Dole is doing no more than following the lead of President Nixon when Dole calls for turning over the Watergate case to the courts. Much of what remains to be disclosed about campaign tactics and financing is not necessarily illegal and would not necessarily be disclosed if "left to the courts."

Talk about leaving Watergate to the courts is a thinly-disguised plea for more cover-up. The country has had enough of cover-up.

The Hartford Courant
Hartford, Conn., September 14, 1973

The vote of the Senate Watergate Committee to resume public hearings two weeks from now and to try to complete them by November 1 obviously is going to draw a mixed bag of public reaction.

There can be no doubt at all that it is the absolute duty, as well as the urgent public wish, that the several agencies entrusted with getting to the bottom of the Watergate affair, do so with unremitting vigor and thoroughness, no matter how gruelling the task may be.

This is the only way the truth can be arrived at and justice done, the guilty punished, the innocent cleared. This is the desire and demand of President Nixon. This is the way to the reassurance so agonizingly sought by every American on the probity of the democratic system.

For all that, there is bound to be suspicion in some quarters that the Senate Watergate committee vote — unanimous as it was — was the result of some kind of insidious pressure to call off the bloodhounds and let culprits escape.

However, it is Senator Ervin himself, chairman of the Senate probers, who asserts the committee is "not responding at all to pressure" to keep the hearings from public view. And anyone knowing how doggedly this Democrat kept his committee at work five days a week, endlessly chivying all kinds of witnesses on all kinds of subjects — germane or irrelevant — will not feel gulled at accepting this ipse dixitism.

The Senate panel itself feels the time has come to expedite the search for justice and truth. And presumably in the weeks up to now, the members have had an opportunity to evaluate the long and detailed examination of the type they have already conducted into the Watergate break-in and alleged White House cover-up, and now understand better how to push the inquiries forward more surely and cogently.

Senator Gurney is known to feel that the hearings have become destructive, serving more to vilify the Administration than to enlighten the public. Anyone skeptical of this opinion because the Senator is a Republican, can listen to Senator Weicker, also of the same camp. The Connecticut Senator, who has been the most persistent examiner, is said to believe the public might turn against the committee if the investigations drags on.

As for the public itself, there is plenty of evidence that it is beginning to turn its attention elsewhere from Watergate — toward the high cost of living, for example. And even the networks that have been covering the hearings live, now are not certain whether they will continue when the Senate panel resumes.

Then there are specific, legalistic situations to be taken into consideration. Some Senate committee members feel the special Watergate prosecutor's office appears to be doing its job well, and that the committee's hearings at this stage could interfere with the other probes, including the indictment of three "plumbers" in connection with the Ellsberg burglary.

All these things, as well as commonsense, make the Senate panel's vote to get on expeditiously with its investigations a move well taken.

However, let it be said first and last that getting out the truth, whole and nothing but, is the absolute duty of all the probing agencies, no matter how long it takes, or how fine the mills must grind. Justice and truth demand it, the public cries out for reassurance on American democratic principals. Let things be expedited where they can, but now above all times, never at the expense of honesty and fairness.

Chicago Tribune
Chicago, Ill., September 3, 1973

Judge John J. Sirica has commendably lowered the boom on convicted Watergate burglar James McCord and conspirator Jeb Magruder for their plans to strike it rich on the college lecture circuit. Both men claimed altruism as their motive, citing repertoires replete with penitent remorse and warnings of the dangers of overzealousness, but they didn't mind pocketing fat fees at the same time. Judge Sirica raised an angry protest and is expected to rule these personal appearances out of order this week.

It is distressing enough that men like McCord and Magruder have the gall for this kind of exploitation and that, in so many cases it is allowed. But what is most disturbing is that they have such ready audiences. Americans have a penchant for making celebrities—if not heroes—out of almost anyone who makes the headlines, no matter what vile act produced their fame. Thus convicted dope pushers pack them in at college lecture halls, and convicted murderers produce best sellers, and convicted swindlers appear on television talk shows.

This national trait cannot easily be eradicated, but we may at least be thankful for having men around like Judge Sirica, who are convinced that crime should not pay.

The Detroit News
Detroit, Mich., September 14, 1973

The members of the Senate Watergate committee got where they are today because they possess sensitive political feelers that tell them which direction to go and when to start and stop. Their feelers now tell them to bring the Watergate hearings quietly to a halt.

Thus, the members of the committee decided this week to delay and curtail their inquiry. Instead of resuming work next week, as previously planned, they will wait until Sept. 24; instead of grinding away on a daily schedule, they will limit their sessions to three a week; instead of dragging out the show until next year, they aim to close shop by Nov. 1.

Both Sen. Sam Ervin and Sen. Howard Baker say that the committee has caved in under pressure from the President and other Republican leaders. Perhaps those pressures indeed have exerted no influence on the committee. However, the pressure of public opinion obviously has. The committee's feelers tell it the public is weary of seeing the President horse-whipped five days a week on television.

Chairman Ervin himself has said: "You could carry this on forever, you know, until the last lingering echo of Gabriel's horn trembled into ultimate silence, if you want to go into all the campaign contributions." And of course Sen. Ervin would be quite happy to do just that if the public would sit still for it and the television networks would continue to broadcast it.

The fact remains that the public, Ervin and the TV networks all know when enough is enough. The committee has long since completed the work it set out to do and has begun to repeat itself; it has completed its function of emotional and moral catharsis for a nation shocked by Watergate; now, for all practical purposes, the battleground has shifted to the courts. So the horn has already blown on the committee; now it's just a question of getting gracefully out of business—which is what the committee began to do this week.

The Boston Globe
Boston, Mass., September 15, 1973

The out-of-court compromise suggested by the US Court of Appeals for the District of Columbia in the dispute over the Watergate tapes appears totally to disarm President Nixon.

We believe a resolution of the constitutional issue concerning a President's powers under a government of law, rather than a chief executive's fiat, transcends what may or may not be on the tapes which Mr. Nixon is so loath to surrender.

The court will, of course, "discharge its responsibility" on the constitutional issue when and if Mr. Nixon declines the suggested compromise. He has until Thursday to make his decision. And even if the constitutional issue is not decided in this case, which involves Special Prosecutor Archibald Cox's demand for the tapes, it almost certainly will arise again, as it should, as the Senate Watergate Committee's demand for the tapes works its way to the US Supreme Court.

But the pragmatism of the Appeals Court's suggested compromise should be recorded as a stroke of pure genius, which surprised both sides. It is akin to a dramatist's resolution of a conundrum that had baffled everybody until the last curtain. The President's claim that disclosure of what may or may not be on the tapes would wreck the confidentiality without which his office cannot function properly is negated by the Court's proposal that Mr. Cox and either the President or his lawyers review the tapes together to decide what may or may not be relevant to allegations of the possible obstruction of justice and other crimes.

The court notes that Mr. Cox "was selected for his position directly or indirectly by the chief executive himself." Thus, it did not even need to mention that Mr. Nixon did not consider his confidentiality wrecked when he, of his own volition, permitted others similarly appointed, including H. R. Haldeman after he had left the government, to review the tapes and even remove some of them from the White House. Mr. Cox, too, is part of the executive branch.

"If the President and the special prosecutor agree as to the material needed for the grand jury's functioning," said the court, "the national interest will be served. At the same time, neither the President nor the special prosecutor would in any way have surrendered or subverted the principles for which they have contended."

The court specifically denies that it intended sending the President a signal that there is no merit to his claim for special treatment under the laws by which the nation is governed. Nevertheless, he might be wise so to regard it. The court has given him an out. If he does not take it, he may be hard put to explain why, especially inasmuch as he disclosed at his last news conference that he eventually may surrender the tapes voluntarily.

Former Attorney General John N. Mitchell's demand that the tapes be surrendered to him for use in his defense against charges of obstruction of justice in the Vesco case, now going to trial in New York, awaits resolution. If he is denied "exculpatory evidence," the case against him could be dismissed for the same reasons that dismissal was ordered in the Ellsberg trial. The charges against most of Mr. Nixon's other one-time advisers and associates could be dismissed for the same reason, putting the President in what would be a very embarrassing position indeed. The decision in the Mitchell case will turn on relevancy, but it is hard to see how relevancy can be determined so long as the President embargoes the tapes.

In short, the compromise suggested by the Appeals Court would relieve Mr. Nixon of several embarrassments. He would do well to follow the court's suggestion.

The Virginian-Pilot
Norfolk, Va., September 4, 1973

In choosing to appeal rather than ignore Judge Sirica's order to deliver to his chambers nine White House tapes, President Nixon was consistent with his August 15 statement that "the time has come to turn Watergate over to the courts, where the questions of guilt or innocence belong." Had he elected to ignore the order on the contention that the Presidency is beyond the Judiciary's reach, he would have mocked not only the Constitution's concept of three-branch government but his own pronouncement as well. For he would have challenged as it never has been challenged the institution "where the questions of guilt or innocence belong"; moreover, in the withheld evidence he would have provided an escape ticket for principal Watergate figures.

The ticket may be issued yet. Mr. Nixon is relying on the Supreme Court, where the Sirica ruling now is headed, to sustain his position that the separation-of-powers doctrine and the Presidential need for confidentiality guarantee him immunity from any subpoena of his records. While he has said through a spokesman that he would honor a "definitive order" from the Supreme Court, he might resort to further strategy should it go against him. His counsel has made it clear enough that he sets greater store by safeguarding the tape recordings of his Watergate conversations than by "the extraction of the last ounce of flesh by the criminal process."

Even so, for the moment at least the criminal process is on track and moving. Immediately after ruling that he should screen the Nixon tapes for possible forwarding to the Watergate grand jury, thus favoring the Justice Department's special prosecutor, Archibald Cox, Judge Sirica refused to consolidate with the Cox suit against the President a parallel action brought by Senator Ervin's Watergate investigating committee. The White House lawyers as well as Mr. Cox had opposed the committee's move for consolidation. Mr. Cox argued that merging the two suits to obtain the tapes would delay a final decision on his case and thus impede the grand jury's work looking toward indictments.

If Mr. Nixon, then, by taking the appeal route supported his insistence that Watergate belongs in the courts, he did little to advance his underlying desire, which is to deemphasize the issue. The Ervin Committee has not made the last of its headlines. Meanwhile, Mr. Cox's legal task forces are poking into, besides the break-in and bugging of the Democratic National Headquarters in Watergate last year, illegal contributions by corporations to the Nixon reelection campaign, campaign "dirty tricks" by Republican and White House agents, the White House "plumbers" whose most infamous escapade was the break-in of Daniel Ellsberg's psychiatrist's office, and the I.T.T. bribery-extortion case. Faced with an extensive series of indictments, trials, and appeals, Mr. Cox and his entourage expect to remain in business through the Nation's bicentennial year of 1976.

The Wichita Eagle
Wichita, Kans., September 10, 1973

Much as everyone would like to see the Watergate investigations concluded and the truth brought to light, it is difficult to disagree with Judge John Sirica's decision not to turn over the presidential tapes to the Senate select committee out of hand.

Pressed by the chief counsel to the committee, Samuel Dash, to order the tapes be made available so the committee could finish its hearings before Congress adjourns the 1973 session, the judge ignored the plea and granted the President's attorney a two-week delay in filing response to the Senate committee's motion.

Sirica said, "The court believes this is a very important case, and it is determined not to be pushed into a half-baked job." He went on to say that the White House is not dragging its feet, that the request for the delay was a reasonable one, and that he had not himself had time to finish reading the 35-page committee motion filed last week.

Some very fundamental constitutional questions are involved in the whole matter of the Watergate investigation, and the judge is quite right to proceed with deliberation.

The companion question of whether Nixon must turn his tapes over to the Watergate grand jury is another matter, and will be acted upon in due course by the U.S. Court of Appeals in Washington. But surrendering the tapes to a grand jury, conducted in secrecy and designed only to determine whether there are grounds for indictment, is an entirely different thing than turning them over to the Ervin committee, which has become more sideshow than investigation.

Both the champions and the detractors of Nixon will, if they love America, hope that its system doesn't suffer from the Watergate investigations. And Judge Sirica's ruling will help to insure that it does not.

The New York Times

New York, N.Y., September 16, 1973

The Circuit Court of Appeals for the District of Columbia has provided President Nixon with an opportunity to back away from the constitutional confrontation toward which he appears headed in the battle of the White House tapes. If Mr. Nixon's overriding concern is to protect the separation of powers rather than defend the concept of executive confidentiality as such, then the court's ingenious proposal could lead to a compromise satisfactory to both sides.

The court's memorandum "contemplates a voluntary submission of such portions of the tapes to the two counsel as satisfies them." Professor Charles Alan Wright, the chief White House attorney in the case, would naturally accept as much or as little of the tapes as his client, the President, chose to submit. Mr. Cox, however, would presumably be satisfied only if he heard all of the disputed tapes and decided for himself what portions of them were necessary for his purposes.

With regard to confidentiality, the court states Mr. Nixon's position rather differently from the way in which he himself has stated it. According to the court's memorandum, "The President has maintained that he alone should decide what is necessarily privileged and should not be furnished the grand jury." But Mr. Nixon has sometimes asserted that all of his conversations are privileged and the tapes of none of them could ever be turned over to any grand jury without compromising the Presidency in the future. If he firmly adheres to this extravagant claim, he can find no basis for compromise in the court's proposal.

* * *

Insofar as the separation of powers is his controlling concern, the court neatly bypasses that problem by substituting an adversary procedure between Mr. Cox and Mr. Wright in place of an *in camera* inspection of the tapes by Chief District Judge John Sirica. The court points out that each of the opposing counsel "was selected for his position, directly or indirectly, by the Chief Executive himself." That is an argument that Mr. Cox has also made when pointing out that he, too, is a member of the executive branch, despite the high degree of independence with which he is charged.

If the tapes are incriminating to the President himself or to H. R. Haldeman and John Ehrlichman, his former aides, to whose fate he has linked himself by repeated endorsements, then it would scarcely be in Mr. Nixon's interest to yield the tapes to Mr. Cox. If, however, his concern for the tapes is wholly disinterested, it ought to be possible for his counsel, Mr. Wright, to reach agreement with Mr. Cox on what portions genuinely deal with national security or other irrelevant topics and should therefore be deleted from the transcript before it is read to the grand jury.

* * *

Beyond the nine tapes sought by Mr. Cox for his prosecutorial purposes, there are many other tapes of Presidential conversations that may be the best evidence available on disputed points in other criminal cases. The lawyers for former Attorney General John N. Mitchell and former Secretary of Commerce Maurice Stans have subpoenaed tapes, notes and other records of meetings of President Nixon or members of his staff with persons involved in their case. On behalf of the White House, the United States Attorney in New York has moved to quash the subpoena.

If the subpoena is quashed and Mr. Mitchell and Mr. Stans are subsequently convicted, they could appeal to a higher court on the ground that they had been denied evidence that might have exonerated them. If the subpoena is upheld but the President refuses to comply, the trial judge might feel compelled to dismiss the indictment. Either way, the defendants could go free.

The subpoena in the Mitchell-Stans case demonstrates the far-reaching significance of the battle over the tapes. That case is only one of several likely to emerge out of the Watergate scandals. It is extraordinarily rare that defendants in a criminal case can plausibly claim that they discussed the matters mentioned in the indictment with the President of the United States or his aides. But Mr. Mitchell and Mr. Stans are making that contention, and others in the near future in other cases are likely

to do so. That fact underscores the importance of President Nixon's yielding the tapes.

When serious crimes are alleged to have been committed, no claim of confidentiality can be allowed to prevail. Executive privilege was never intended to be a shield for wrongdoing.

Pittsburgh Post-Gazette

Pittsburgh, Pa., September 7, 1973

THE INDICTMENT of John Ehrlichman for the Ellsberg break-in shoves center stage the question of presidential crime and punishment. Although Mr. Ehrlichman denied any complicity, he said that if, in the name of the President, he had authorized the burglary, he would under the circumstances have been justified.

Before the Ervin committee, Ehrlichman attorney John Wilson argued that a piece of legislation, ironically titled the Safe Streets Act of 1968, empowered the President to break the law in order to protect national-security information against foreign intelligence activities.

Ehrlichman

Sen. Ervin gagged at that interpretation; so did we. It would allow a president's violation of the individual liberties of his political opponents to be neither criminal nor punishable so long as he claimed national-security immunity. Every dictator worth the title has jailed or murdered his political competitors in the name of national security.

* * *

One would be foolhardy to say that no president under any circumstances may authorize burglary or even more heinous acts, even when the nation and its liberties face a mortal danger which is clear and present.

If to find the code to defuse H-bombs planted in a dozen cities, the President has to authorize burglary or even murder, he commits a crime which by common agreement is justifiable and for which he is not punished but rather praised. The act remains punishable but rightly goes unpunished.

Neither Mr. Ehrlichman nor President Nixon has claimed that Dr. Ellsberg's leaking of the Pentagon Papers put or threatened to put the nation in mortal danger. All that reasonably could be claimed was that the leak would embarrass past administrations and weaken the government's ability to assure confidentiality in foreign-policy negotiations.

Mr. Nixon has obliquely defended the break-in by justifying a 1970 anti-news leak plan under which the burglary by the White House "plumbers unit" would have been permissible. In earlier administrations, Mr. Nixon claimed, similar authorized break-ins did take place. His implying that other presidents "did it" would not, however, justify his having done it.

And, in fact, on Aug. 15 he conceded that in some instances "a zeal for security did go too far and did interfere impermissibly with individual liberty."

The Wilson-Ehrlichman-Nixon defenses of presidential criminality fail, then, not simply because they depend for justification on national security. Rather, they fail because they attempt generally to justify presidential violations of law and the Constitution by wrapping a national-security blanket, with an "others did it, too" pin, around all such transgressions. With fatal shortsightedness, they would construe the law and the constitution to mean that the President is above the law.

* * *

These defenses suggest that Mr. Nixon and/or some of the men around him were so savagely partisan as to be insensitive to the need for placing individual liberty above all other considerations except in the face of the most dire threat to the nation.

We are thus left wondering if these men have the capacity to distinguish mere political embarrassment from potential national disaster. An inability to discriminate between monumental and lesser threats and these sweeping justifications for presidential criminality pose a threat to American liberties far greater than any which the Pentagon Papers leak could have or did pose.

The courts will determine if Mr. Ehrlichman is guilty of the crime which he defended in principle but denied in fact.

It must remain the task of the people to reject the notion, and anyone who espouses it, that American presidents are above the law.

The Des Moines Register
Des Moines, Iowa, September 12, 1973

The indictment of John Ehrlichman and three others on burglary and other charges in connection with the burglary of the office of Daniel Ellsberg's psychiatrist is another acute embarrassment for the White House. All four men worked for the White House at the time of the 1971 break-in.

President Nixon has denounced the burglary as "illegal, unauthorized—and completely deplorable." But the President admitted that when he learned of the episode last March he did his best to keep it hidden.

The President said he was first informed about the burglary Mar. 17, 1973, a month before the Justice Department learned of it. He admitted that he ordered Asst. Atty. Gen. Henry Petersen not to discuss the matter before a federal grand jury. The burglary was disclosed to the Ellsberg trial judge only at the insistence of Petersen and Atty. Gen. Richard Kleindienst, who said they would have resigned if Nixon blocked disclosure to the court.

It is hard to understand why the President sought to shield an incident he describes as illegal, unauthorized and deplorable. The President never has explained why he failed to notify the Justice Department about the break-in when he learned of it. If it had not been for Petersen's and Kleindienst's demand for disclosure, it is possible that those responsible for the burglary would have escaped detection and indictment.

The President has called for Watergate and related matters to be turned over to the courts. The indictment of the former White House aides in connection with the Ellsberg burglary assures that their part in the episode will be fully aired. But the trial is not likely to throw light on the peculiar behavior of the President in this case—behavior that at times came close to obstructing justice.

THE DAILY OKLAHOMAN
Oklahoma City, Okla., September 7, 1973

ONE of the less savory aspects of the Watergate affair is the continuing exposure of the ambitions of various public figures that is incidental to the hearings and investigations.

The latest such revelation comes in the wake of a California grand jury's indictment of several former White House and presidential campaign figures. John D. Erlichman and others have been charged with conspiracy and other crimes in the case of a break-in at the office of a psychiatrist who had treated Daniel Ellsberg.

This seems to be the normal, to be expected, outcome of a long investigation of that matter by the grand jury. It was surely no surprise to those indicted. But it was denounced by the special prosecutor named in Washington to deal with other allegations against the same men, among others.

Prof. Archibald Cox, a former Solicitor General of the U.S (in the Kennedy administration), and members of his staff see the action of the California jury as interference with their own prosecutions. Their irritation was unconcealed. But there is surely more to their protests than that. The Cox staff has shown no aversion to public notice. Seven of his key aides had worked for the Kennedy family in various capacities, and their sympathies were certainly not with Nixon and his administration. They have asserted a sort of autonomy which seldom appears in the federal government structure, and have made public statements which have irritated the Senate committee members as well as administration stalwarts.

Cox, in fact, seems to consider the Watergate post a golden opportunity to achieve a new fame as a lawyer and as a public servant. An ambitious man can take a national reputation like that and go as far as he likes in politics or his profession. The professor has never been known as a shrinking violet type. His first act on arrival in Washington for this special job was to assemble a staff that was large even for that city. Then he asked Congress to fund it to the tune of nearly $3 millions. The money was appropriated without a whimper from Congress.

Cox's plans for prosecutions have not been revealed in detail, but there is no doubt that he has envisioned some s e n s a t i o n a l trials, which should be front page news for weeks or months. But out in California there are other lawyers with similar visions of new fame, and they have been working with the grand jury which returned this week's indictments.

Ambitions in collision thus played a part in the indictments and denunciations. But there are other men of ambition involved in the various investigations and hearings, and they are not likely to stay their own hands to make way for rivals. On the Ervin Committee, there are conflicts among the Senators themselves, and between some Senators and chief counsel Sam Dash. There the argument seems to center on the televised hearings. Some want the cameras removed; some want them to stay. Dash wants all the sensational publicity possible, and makes no secret of the fact.

But there may be risk in pushing all such personal ambitions for publicity and glory too far. Many members of Congress, from various parts of the nation, returned from the August recess to report that their constitutents have had their fill of Watergate publicity, and are worried about the real business of government. Some of the lawmakers want to turn the rest of the Watergate affair over to the courts, now that it has had full enough exposure to alert the citizenry to the fact that there was skulduggery in the 1972 campaigns. That would probably please Cox and irritate Ervin.

But it would probably please most Americans.

The Standard-Times
New Bedford, Mass., September 8, 1973

The U.S. Court of Appeals out-of-court compromise solution to the dispute between President Nixon and the Watergate grand jury over the White House tape recordings will satisfy neither Mr. Nixon's supporters nor his opponents, but it may offer a clue as to what can be expected, even if the issue goes to the Supreme Court.

The seven judges of the appeals court, in an unusual move, urged the President and lawyers for both sides to avoid a constitutional confrontation by settling the issue themselves. Specifically, they recommended that Mr. Nixon voluntarily submit portions of the recordings to Archibald Cox, the Justice Department's special prosecutor, and Prof. Charles Alan Wright, the chief White House attorney, for their examination.

The two attorneys, together with the President himself or his delegate, would decide what parts of the tapes could properly go to the grand jury, according to the proposal.

There is an understandable reticence on the part of the judiciary, and among many members of Congress as well, to press this matter to the point where the highest courts in the land must define, to the last semicolon, the meaning of the U.S. Constitution in this vital area of separation of powers. Such inflexible definitions have a way of backfiring unexpectedly at later dates, in other circumstances. Moreover, the strength of the Constitution lies in the flexibility of interpretation it allows, thus enabling it to meet the changing needs of greatly differing eras.

Obviously, any ruling on the constitutional question, if it is to be for somebody — as the absolutists in this controversy urge — must then be against somebody, and neither the Executive nor the Legislative Branches is eager to risk a judicial diminution of its traditional prerogatives.

It is our view, however, that the appellate court's compromise proposal would be improved if, instead of calling for Messrs. Cox and Wright to examine the recordings, it provided for turning them over to a blue-ribbon commission acceptable to Congress and the nation generally. Surely we can still put together a panel of men and women above reproach and suspicion, whose judgment in this matter a majority of Americans would be willing to accept.

Finally, we are inclined to agree with Standard-Times columnist James Kilpatrick in his conclusion that this issue of the tapes is, in essence, more political than legal. Because it is, it is quite possible for Mr. Nixon to win the court battle and lose the country.

In other words, since it seems increasingly likely that a reticent court may not hand down the "definitive" ruling the President insists on if he is to release the tapes, we believe he should permit them to be examined anyway, in the interest of clearing the Watergate clouds, and restoring confidence in the office of the presidency.

Agnew Affair:

RESIGNATION RUMORED; GRAND JURY CONVENES

Speculation that Vice President Spiro T. Agnew was considering resignation from office mounted as the federal investigation of possible criminal violations involving the vice president continued.

According to a *Washington Post* report Sept. 20, a principal White House official had predicted Agnew's resignation in the "next few weeks." That report was said to have come from an "Eastern Republican" who was told by the official that Agnew's resignation "would give the President an opportunity to set a whole new tone for the Administration." However, Gerald L. Warren, deputy White House press secretary, denied the *Post* report Sept. 20 and said Nixon was not seeking to apply any pressure on Agnew to leave office. At a White House briefing Sept. 19, Warren had reaffirmed the President's Sept. 5 statement that he had "confidence in the vice president's integrity during the period that he had served as vice president." The investigation involving Agnew covered the period prior to his election as vice president in 1968.

The federal grand jury in Baltimore investigating political corruption began hearing evidence against Agnew Sept. 27 after Agnew had failed, at least temporarily, in an attempt to have the House investigate charges of violation of bribery, conspiracy and tax laws. In an atmosphere of rumors and denials involving his possible resignation and reports of "plea bargaining" with the Justice Department, Agnew Sept. 25 attempted to block the grand jury proceeding by requesting the House to begin an inquiry into the case, arguing that any criminal proceeding against a vice president holding office was unconstitutional and that the House was the only proper forum for the case. After a meeting with House Democratic leaders Sept. 26, Speaker Carl Albert (D, Okla.) said he would take no action "at this time" on Agnew's request. Agnew's approach to the House came after two private meetings with President Nixon, on Sept. 20 at Agnew's request and on Sept. 25 at Nixon's request.

As a precedent for his request of a Congressional inquiry, Agnew relied on the 1826–27 case of Vice President John C. Calhoun, who had asked the House to inquire into newspaper allegations of profiteering on military contracts while Calhoun was secretary of war. A report by a select House committee had exonerated Calhoun. The Calhoun case, it was noted, did not supply a complete parallel to the Agnew situation, since Calhoun was not the subject of a criminal investigation by a judicial body. Noting that he had been the subject of "public attacks" that might "assume the character of impeachable offenses," Agnew called on the House to "discharge its constitutional obligation" and follow the Calhoun precedent.

Lawyers for Agnew and House leaders concerned with impeachment precedents were reportedly studying the 1872–73 case of Vice President Schuyler Colfax, who had been charged with illegal activities, all of which took place before he became vice president in 1869. A House committee began hearings in December 1872 into charges of bribery against Colfax. During its probe, the committee discovered other incidents of possible bribery. Despite the evidence of misconduct, the committee concluded that impeachment was intended to remove a person from an office he had abused while occupying it. The committee decided not to impeach.

On the question of whether a vice president could be indicted while in office, some legal historians cited the 1804 indictment of Vice President Aaron Burr on state charges of murder in connection with the slaying of Alexander Hamilton in a duel in New Jersey. Both the crime and the indictment occurred while Burr was vice president. Burr was never arrested or prosecuted on the charge.

Lawyers for the vice president filed suit in federal district court in Baltimore Sept. 28 in an attempt to halt the grand jury investigation of possible criminal violations by Agnew. In a formal motion and accompanying affidavit, Agnew's lawyers launched a two-pronged attack on the investigation, citing constitutional restraints on the prosecution of a vice president in office, and charging the Justice Department with conducting "a deliberate campaign" of news leaks "calculated and intended to deprive [Agnew] of his basic rights to due process and fair hearing." The suit asked the court to prohibit the grand jury "from conducting any investigation looking to possible indictment" of Agnew and from "issuing any indictment, presentment or other charge or statement" pertaining to the vice president. The suit also petitioned the court "to enjoin the attorney general of the United States, the United States attorney for the District of Maryland and all officials of the United States Department of Justice from presenting to the grand jury any testimony, documents or other materials" that might be used to indict Agnew. It asked the court to bar the department from "discussing with or disclosing to any person any such testimony, documents or materials."

Rocky Mountain News

Denver, Colo., September 27, 1973

SPEAKER Carl Albert was quite right to turn down Vice President Spiro T. Agnew's move to get the House of Representatives to investigate charges that he took bribes from Maryland businessmen.

In his reply Albert noted that the Agnew matter was "before the courts"—where we believe it belongs—and that the House would not act "at this time."

Thus Albert (and the Democratic leadership) rejected Agnew's basic argument in asking for a House inquiry: that "the Constitution bars a criminal proceeding of any kind" against a sitting vice president.

The stage is now set for a proper judicial determination of the Agnew case. Atty. Gen. Elliot L. Richardson correctly has decided to present the evidence he has against Agnew to a federal grand jury in Baltimore.

For their part, Agnew's lawyers hope to block that step in the courts, claiming that the vice president is immune to any criminal proceeding short of impeachment and trial in Congress.

If both parties hold to their course, the question should proceed fairly promptly to the Supreme Court. That is of course the proper body to decide whether Agnew constitutionally can be indicted and tried in a court while he holds office.

Should the Supreme Court uphold his view of his immunity, then it would be the time for the House to face up to its duty and investigate Agnew with an eye to possible impeachment.

Impeachment is a fateful move, a last resort against unworthy officeholders. It should not be entered into lightly as a convenience to an individual's defense strategy, no matter how highly placed he may be.

If possible, the process should be avoided. It would consume much time, paralyze Congress' other work, polarize that body and lead to a trial with political overtones. In such a supercharged political atmosphere, a balanced verdict based solely on evidence may not be possible.

The best thing for the country and probably Agnew too would be a quick, fair trial in a federal court. The vice president thinks otherwise and is following another line of defense.

Though we disagree with his course, we repeat that during the coming court proceedings he is entitled to—as President Nixon put it the other day—"the same presumption of innocence which is the right of any citizen."

THE   SUN

Baltimore, Md., September 21, 1973

The rather obvious falling out between the Nixon and Agnew cliques in Washington is but the latest evidence of unseemly comportment by this administration. The Vice President, at least for the moment, is a lonely and embattled figure. Threatened with indictment or impeachment, charged with petty venality, humiliated by open speculation about a replacement, Mr. Agnew has gotten precious little support from President Nixon. Indeed, it seems to be the kind of support the rope gives the hanged man and it has impelled Victor Gold, Mr. Agnew's volatile former press secretary, to complain of a White House effort to force a resignation in the interest of propelling John Connally into the Vice Presidency.

This is back-alley stuff. Yet before the Vice President is depicted as a victim of political thuggery, it is well to remember that only a few months ago, Mr. Agnew was adroitly distancing himself from Mr. Nixon's Watergate mess. That a Vice President should come on television to assure the country with a straight face that he has confidence in the President was a put-down of breathtaking dimensions. It compares with Mr. Nixon's recent grave assurances of Mr. Agnew's integrity "during the period that he has served as Vice President."

The many failings of this administration have repeatedly shocked the American people. We have had to witness a President confessing his culpability for the political atmosphere that produced a Watergate yet squirming to absolve himself from personal responsibility for specific misdeeds. We have had to listen to a Vice President tell us he is under investigation for "bribery, tax fraud, extortion and conspiracy"—all "damned lies" resulting from allegations of receiving kickbacks while he was Baltimore county executive.

Of a more personal nature, we have had to contemplate a supposedly economy-minded President who was willing to spend $10 million in public funds on his private estates in San Clemente and Key Biscayne. And we have had to read reports that our Vice President has been willing to accept free food from Food Fair, free booze from a political contributor and "celebrity discounts" from the Sheraton Park Hotel, his Washington residence for more than four years.

Now, on top of all this, the President and the Vice President seem intent on "skewering" (Mr. Gold's word) one another. If the skewering were merely a game politicians play, it could provide welcome respite from more sordid revelations. But the relationship between a President and a Vice President is so delicate and a rift so dangerous that we are not amused. Rather, we view the open display of estrangement as further evidence that this administration does not know where its true public responsibilities lie.

Detroit Free Press

Detroit, Mich., September 26, 1973

THE JUSTICE DEPARTMENT'S decision to present the allegations of criminal acts against Vice President Agnew to a federal grand jury means that attempts to negotiate a way out of the long conflict ahead have failed. As a result, the welfare of the nation now depends to an extraordinary degree on whether the beleaguered vice president is willing, if he should be indicted, to sacrifice for the national good.

Attorney General Elliot Richardson said he had hoped, through negotiations with Agnew's lawyers, to avoid "problems which might . . . result in a constitutional dilemma of potentially serious consequence to the nation." But that effort had failed.

The information about those problems has been sketchy, but it would appear that the vice president would not come to terms with demands that he resign and, in return for his agreement to resign, agree to plead guilty to a lesser charge in the Maryland kickback case. Thus, apparently, the Justice Department and the administration believe they have enough of a case against the vice president that it must go to a grand jury, and he is unwilling to do anything that would seem to acknowledge any guilt.

Mr. Richardson's decision—and presumably it is one sanctioned by the President—forces the issue. The country now faces the prospect of a frontal assault by the Justice Department on a sitting vice president. If Mr. Agnew chooses to fight the case, it also faces the prospect of a prolonged trial and/or an impeachment procedure.

During the year or more that either procedure could take, the vice president would be living under a cloud, only a heartbeat away from the presidency. That situation is intolerable, placing the country in greater peril than even the Watergate paralysis of this summer.

If indeed the evidence against him is so great that the grand jury feels compelled

to indict him, Mr. Agnew's highest remaining service to his country would be to resign. It would be the only way to spare the nation from further harm while he pursues his effort to clear his name.

To call upon one of the two top officials of the United States to resign, even conditionally, is not something to be done lightly. The filling of the job of vice president on an interim basis will itself be an unsettling process.

But this is an extraordinary situation, and the vice president will have to put the good of his country before even his concern for his own reputation. Such a sacrifice would be the only thing left to him, the only hope of sparing the country another wrenching crisis when it has recently passed through so many other crises.

There is something in all of us that responds with admiration to a man's determination to stand and fight for his own good name. But if the evidence should prove strong enough for a Republican prosecutor to seek an indictment, and a Republican administration to sanction that decision, such a stand by the vice president would involve too great a risk for the country. Thus, we are left with merely the hope that the vice president's better instincts will prevail.

If the evidence is strong, and the vice president does not resign, the Congress will have no choice but to undertake impeachment proceedings. Congress alone can tell a vice president that he has to resign.

Far better it would be for the nation if his conscience, rather than the wracking processes of impeachment, brought an end to this unhappy chapter in American history.

The New York Times

New York, N.Y., September 27, 1973

In the search for personal vindication, Vice President Agnew has chosen a course of action that is constitutionally obscure and most likely to expose the nation to uncertainty and potential risk.

However much one may disagree with his legal position, Mr. Agnew is certainly within his rights to argue that the Constitution bars a criminal proceeding of any kind against him unless and until he is impeached and removed from office. But in seeking to use the House of Representatives as an alternative to the grand jury system and thereby opening up the prospect of a lengthy battle in the courts, he has made a serious misjudgment of where his responsibility lies.

*   *   *

The Constitution and the precedents are much less clear on the issue of criminal proceedings against a Vice President than Mr. Agnew suggests in his letter to Speaker Albert. Article I, Section 3, Clause 7, states: "Judgment in cases of impeachment shall not extend further than to removal from office, and disqualification to hold and enjoy any office of honor, trust or profit under the United States: but the party convicted shall nevertheless be liable and subject to indictment, trial, judgment and punishment according to the law."

That language suggests but does not expressly state that the authors of the Constitution envisaged that a President, Vice President or other "civil officers of the United States" would be removed from office by impeachment first and then subjected to indictment and trial. However, the clause could also reasonably be interpreted as simply stating that impeachment does not preclude other punishment. On its face, therefore, this language does not compel the House of Representatives to act on the impeachment issue in advance of criminal proceedings in the courts.

Constitutional experts disagree, and the only two precedents involving the Vice Presidency diverge. In 1826 Vice President John C. Calhoun called upon the House to investigate an allegation that he had profited from a contract while previously serving as Secretary of War in the Monroe Administration. A House select committee conducted an inquiry that exonerated Calhoun within a few weeks. Quite understandably, Mr. Agnew cites that precedent and quotes the eloquent language used by Calhoun.

*   *   *

Equally understandably, Mr. Agnew does not cite the other precedent involving Vice President Schuyler Colfax in the first Grant Administration. Colfax in 1872 was accused of taking a bribe a few years earlier when he had been Speaker of the House. The House Judiciary Committee decided that Colfax could not be impeached because the alleged act occurred before he became Vice President and therefore the matter should be left to the courts. Colfax was never indicted—but he left public life in disgrace. It is uncertain whether the House could adopt the same position now with regard to the Agnew case because it is uncertain whether the charges against him relate only to his period as Governor of Maryland or extend also into the period of his Vice Presidency and include involvement in Federal as well as state contracts.

It is significant that members of Congress and Federal judges are also "civil officers" within the Constitution's meaning but that Congressmen and, in recent decades, judges have been indicted and tried on criminal charges without being subjected to prior expulsion or impeachment.

When the news of possible criminal charges against him broke last month, Mr. Agnew responded with a brief statement expressing full confidence in the nation's criminal justice system. His reason for wishing now to bypass that system and throw his case into the political cockpit of the House is hardly persuasive. Referring in his letter to Speaker Albert to "a constant and ever-broadening stream of rumors, accusations and speculations," Mr. Agnew asserts, "the result has been so to foul the atmosphere that no grand or petit jury could fairly consider this matter on the merits."

But Mr. Agnew can scarcely assume that the members of the House and Senate, all of whom are elected politicians, are less aware of these rumors and less likely to be biased than are ordinary citizens called to serve on a jury. In reality, the public could have much more confidence that the charges against Mr. Agnew, presuming that any indictment is forthcoming, would be fairly and dispassionately weighed in a court of law than they would be by the House acting as a grand jury and the Senate sitting as a trial jury. For this reason, Speaker Albert is surely wise in taking the position that the House will not act on Mr. Agnew's request for an investigation into the allegations that he took kickbacks from Maryland contractors as long as his case is before the court.

If Vice President Agnew's attorneys go ahead with their constitutional challenge against any action by the Baltimore grand jury in his case, then the matter could ultimately be resolved only by a decision of the Supreme Court. That could well take many months. During those months Mr. Agnew would be effectively incapacitated from performing his sole important function—that of serving as a standby President in the event of the resignation, death or total disability of Richard M. Nixon.

As a citizen Mr. Agnew is unquestionably innocent until proven otherwise in a court of law. But as a potential President, Mr. Agnew should not only be presumed innocent but also should be perceived to be above suspicion. A prolonged procedural struggle in the courts concerning the priority to be given a possible impeachment as against a possible indictment would leave a cloud over Mr. Agnew's head and would pose the risk of an awkward and intolerable void in the transfer of Presidential power in the event of an emergency. From the standpoint of the nation, such a risk is unacceptable.

The Philadelphia Inquirer

Philadelphia, Pa., September 20, 1973

The now chronic crisis of the Watergate and its associated scandals and the more acute crisis of Vice President Agnew's tribulations have left participants and observers at a loss for hyperbole. Suffice it to say that the events, collectively, are without parallel or useful comparison in previous American history.

Unprecedented circumstances are perilous ones on which to deliver generalities or to flirt with simple answers. But it would be worse folly to ignore the one common thread: Over it all hangs the relatively simple question of whether the criminal justice system in the U. S. prevails over men in power or is prevailed over by them.

There is, and will be, no simple answer to that simple question. But as the next few months go on, for most of us there will emerge a preponderant impression favoring one extreme or the other. And we believe that that general impression will influence, for many years beyond, the behavior of public officials and private citizens.

★   ★   ★

Vice President Agnew, it seems increasingly apparent, has settled on a course of action for weathering his particular storm. Having recognized that his larger political ambitions are irreparably damaged, he is going to fight with every device available to exonerate himself.

Sen. Barry Goldwater, a gentleman of splendid candor, said of Mr. Agnew last Thursday: "I think this man has been framed. Every politician in the country could have this same thing pulled on us."

And Assistant Attorney General Henry E. Petersen, a man of impressive resoluteness and dispassion, was quoted by Fred P. Graham of the Columbia Broadcasting System five days before as saying of the still secret criminal case against Mr. Agnew: "We've got the evidence. We've got it cold."

In the clear choice those extremes represent, many people are making a choice on ideological preferences, which is natural enough. Our faith in — or hope for — the criminal justice system leaves us undisturbed by the fact that we are not tempted to make judgment today one way or the other.

★   ★   ★

But as the evidence against Mr. Agnew goes to the grand jury, and in due time when other evidence is brought to the bar against the men of enormous power who are implicated in the Watergate, there must be one ringing imperative: No deals.

The unprecedented crisis of credibility now trying America's institutions of justice was largely caused by dealing — by twisting and accommodating.

Mr. Agnew and those who will be charged as the Watergate prosecutions go forward are entitled to the most scrupulous protections that legal procedures allow. But the nation and the institution of the law itself are entitled to a scrupulous demonstration that justice can, and will, prevail without bargaining or manipulation.

THE CHRISTIAN SCIENCE MONITOR

Boston, Mass., September 27, 1973

We do not know (because the U.S. Supreme Court has never decided the issue) whether "the Constitution bars a criminal proceeding of any kind" against an incumbent vice-president. But our own sense of the American Constitution is that no man is above the law — whether he be a vice-president or even a president.

Taking then as our premise the doctrine that in the United States only the people are sovereign and that no man is above the law we agree with Speaker Albert that the House of Representatives in Washington should not at this stage agree to constitute itself as a court of inquiry into the charges lodged against Vice-President Spiro Agnew in Baltimore.

It might come to that in the end as it did in the case of Vice-President Calhoun which Mr. Agnew cited in his petition to the House. But the regular judicial process, it seems to us, provides a useful preliminary screen for the charges against Mr. Agnew. If those charges are unfounded or insubstantial the Grand Jury in Baltimore will so determine, and that is the end of the matter. If found substantial and serious enough to warrant an indictment then the court in Baltimore can consider whether to hand the matter over to the House of Representatives on the theory of constitutional immunity, or proceed in Baltimore as though the Vice-President were only another citizen.

It was, we think, perfectly proper for Mr. Agnew's lawyers to try to take the case out of the hands of the Grand Jury in Baltimore and put it into the House of Representatives in Washington because it is right and proper for the lawyers to do all they can for their client. But what is right and proper for them to try is not necessarily the best thing in the general interest to have done. Ideally the decision would be made on a forthright moral basis rather than on technicalities of the law.

If the House were to take the case the matter would be out of the courts and in the political arena. It might drag on for months and even years. In the meantime the proposition would have been accepted that a vice-president is different from other men and above the law which operates in the case of others.

No matter how honorable the motive may be, the fact is that the proposal by Mr. Agnew that the House take over his case does have the appearance of an attempt to avoid the regular operation of a judicial proceeding which is under way. It was made after the Attorney General had decided that the evidence would go to the Grand Jury. Indeed, it was made just two days before the scheduled presentation of the evidence. There is

every appearance of a maneuver designed to keep the matter out of the courts. Mr. Agnew's lawyers prefer to take their chances in the political arena of the House.

No ordinary citizen could keep his case out of the courts by such a device. That in itself seems to us to be a sufficient reason why the House should at this stage decline. It is true that under the Constitution only the House can deal with the high office of the vice-presidency. But as yet that office is not in question. The immediate question is only whether charges of improper conduct against a citizen are serious enough to warrant an indictment. Unless and until there is such a finding we do not think that there is a special case calling for the special and unusual resort to a House committee of inquiry.

The Washington Post

Washington, D.C., September 27, 1973

The one meaningful duty of the vice presidency is a contingent one which may not occur during the tenure of any one incumbent. But it is no less vital to the country on that account, because that one duty simply stated is to pick up the burdens of the presidency at a time of extraordinary national stress. This imposes upon a vice president a continuing obligation that is quite different from the requirement upon every citizen—including the vice president—to obey the law. It is the vice president's sworn duty to *uphold* the law.

Similarly, the obligations imposed upon a vice president demand more of him than simply that he be innocent of a crime. For the effective discharge of his responsibility as a stand-in to the presidency, he must not even appear to be guilty of wrongdoing—to hold himself free, in other words, of any taint which would rob his office and himself of public confidence. It is in this light that one must examine not the allegations which have been raised against Mr. Agnew in recent months— for no formal charges have been placed against him —but his response to original official notification that he was the target of an investigation and his subsequent twists and turns in his defense as it developed once it began to appear that this investigation might lead to his indictment on criminal charges.

From the beginning, Mr. Agnew embarked on a vigorous and skillful defense. As soon as it became known that he was formally the subject of a federal criminal investigation, he issued a statement in which he declared, "I am innocent of any wrongdoing . . . I have confidence in the criminal justice system of the United States and . . . I am equally confident my innocence will be affirmed."

Shortly thereafter, he summoned the press to a conference which was televised nationally. He told the nation, "I have nothing to hide." He also disclosed that as soon as he had heard rumors of the investigation and stories that he was trying to impede it, he sent his lawyer to George Beall, the United States Attorney in Baltimore, to make assurances that he, Mr. Agnew, had no intention of blocking the investigation. Although he did not rule out a resort to constitutional arguments, Mr. Agnew in early August gave every appearance that he was prepared to deal with his problems in the only acceptable way for a man in his office—that is to say, quickly, cleanly and openly.

Then, after several quiet weeks, came reports of private conversations between Mr. Agnew's lawyers and the Department of Justice. Attorney General Richardson has now confirmed that such conversations did take place. Though both parties attempted to keep the substance of the talks private, the essence of those discussions became public and it disclosed that the vice president's "confidence in the criminal justice system," had apparently collapsed. All the evidence suggests, in fact, that he was prepared to bargain away his high office in exchange for the dropping of all or most of the charges against him. When negotiations broke down, and the Department of Justice decided to present its evidence about Mr. Agnew to the Baltimore grand jury, the vice president then appealed to the House of Representatives. That body, he claimed, was the only one which could carry out the kind of investigation contem-

plated by the Constitution for civil officers of the government. The measure of his retreat from his professed faith in the criminal justice system—and from his earlier publicly-stated distrust of congressional investigatons—can best be seen in what he had to say about the Senate Watergate Committee only a few weeks ago. The congressional investigation, the vice president said, "tends to complicate the search for truth by making both witnesses and (the) committee players on a spotlighted national stage." He also said such investigations had a "Perry Masonish impact" which made the public the ultimate judges of facts which should be heard before the court.

The move to the House gives us a good notion of the desperate position at which Mr. Agnew has lately arrived. It is consistent with his lawyers' view that he has to be impeached by the House and removed by the Senate before he can be indicted for criminal conduct. It is, in short, a clever maneuver, because if the vice president's legal argument prevails and if, for whatever reason the Congress thereupon fails to remove him by impeachment, Mr. Agnew could not be convicted of a crime until his term of office expires and the statute of limitations has run out on many if not all of the charges that might be placed against him.

Now this, we would acknowledge, is an entirely proper legal strategy for any private citizen engaged in a fight to avoid indictment or conviction for criminal activity. It may well be precisely the right sort of maneuvering and the best possible course of action if the objective is nothing more than to spare the vice president from going to jail. But precisely what would be right and reasonable about this strategy for a private citizen is what is wrong about it for the vice president of the United States. For what the vice president has clearly conveyed in the course of his various shifts of position is that he is not, in the last analysis, prepared to place his confidence in the judicial process, that he does not want to allow his case to move through the grand jury proceedings toward a possible indictment or conviction, that he is in fact prepared to seize upon whatever legal device may come to hand in order to prevent any of these things from happening. On the contrary, it appears that his lawyers are poised to put their case for impeachment as a precondition to indictment to the test of the federal judiciary, now that the Speaker of the House has wisely and correctly refused to grant him the special inquiry he requested Tuesday afternoon.

And so, presumably, we are confronted with a protracted and quite possibly inconclusive battle in the courts—not over the vice president's innocence or guilt, not over anything, in fact, that would serve to clear his name or to satisfy public doubts, but over a procedural, constitutional issue which can only delay that quick, clear answer which a man in his high official position ought to wish to provide as a matter of course. For Spiro T. Agnew, as citizen of the United States and entitled to all its protections under law, it is a sensible and perhaps even a sound strategy. For Spiro T. Agnew, vice president of the United States, it is a strategy so contrived, evasive and insensitive to the real issues at stake as to raise serious questions, of and by itself, about his continuing fitness for the high office he holds.

AKRON BEACON JOURNAL
Akron, Ohio, September 27, 1973

Vice President Agnew is a shrewd politician. But he has never laid claim to being a constitutional expert.

Both that strength and that weakness were graphically demonstrated by Agnew's letter to House Speaker Carl Albert late Tuesday. It was a sound political stroke which displayed, in the process, a woeful ignorance of the origins and precedents of the Constitution.

★

Agnew said, essentially, that the Constitution bars "a criminal proceeding of any kind" against him while he is in office, and therefore the grand jury in Baltimore has no authority to indict him. The only way to clear his name, then, is for the House to investigate the charges against him as the first — and if he is cleared, the last — step in impeachment proceedings.

The House, he said, quoting John C. Calhoun, is the repository of "the sole power of impeachment." And the House, therefore, is the only body that can take legal action against him.

★

Agnew is right about only one thing: The House is indeed the sole body with the power to impeach. But there is nothing whatever in the Constitution t h a t bars a grand jury from investigating and, if warranted, indicting him for crimes committed within the span of the statute of limitations and the geographical scope of its authority.

A s t u d y of the discussions by the Founding Fathers, in fact, suggests that indictment is a far preferable course to impeachment. As Prof. Richard Wooddesson of Oxford wrote in 1792, only three years after the Constitution was ratified, "Impeachments are not formed to alter the law, but to carry it to more effectual execution, where it might be obstructed by the views of too powerful delinquents."

Or, as Constitutional scholar Irving Brant wrote last year, "impeachment is . . . designed to remove high-ranking offenders from the protection of the executive branch or of subservient courts." It is, then, a last resort if normal criminal procedures fail.

★

In his letter, Agnew cited as precedent the request for a hearing made in 1826 by Calhoun, and the fact that a House investigation cleared Calhoun. The difference is that Calhoun was under attack for war profiteering, but not under any legal cloud. No grand jury was investigating him.

A more accurate, but hardly more helpful, precedent was available to Agnew in the case of Aaron Burr, vice president under Thomas Jefferson. Burr was indicted while in office by two states, New Jersey and New York, in the former for murdering Alexander Hamilton, in the latter for challenging Hamilton to the fatal duel in the first place.

Burr wasn't tried in either state, but the indictments were not challenged.

And, of course, Federal Judge Otto Kerner was indicted, tried, convicted and jailed without ever being impeached.

★

Agnew, it seems obvious, is in no danger of being "protected" by the executive branch, which was why his attempt to get House intervention was a good political stroke. A man being pursued by wolves is eager to accept sanctuary wherever he can find it. And Agnew saw his best chance in the House.

The House has had the opportunity — and the duty under the Constitution — for the past several months to launch its own investigation if it chose to explore the impeachment route, and has declined.

If Agnew could have persuaded the leadership to accept the chore, he would have been assured of something less than vigor. And he might have persuaded the grand jury to lay off while the clock ticks on the statute of limitations.

★

This is not to presume his guilt. Certainly, though, Atty. Gen. Richardson would not let information go to the grand jury unless he thought he had something. No matter how innocent Agnew may be, this is a devastating political blow.

Now Speaker Albert has dealt him another one, though Albert's reasoning was as specious as Agnew's. The House won't touch it because it is "before the courts," Albert said.

Forgetting that as "the repository of 'the sole power of impeachment,'" the House also has a duty to investigate on its own charges of "high crimes and misdemeanors" by the vice president while in office.

The Courier-Journal
Louisville, Ky., September 27, 1973

BY REJECTING Vice President Agnew's appeal for a fair and open hearing, the body that John C. Calhoun in 1826 dignified with the title, "the Hall of the immediate representatives of the people," has rendered an essentially political decision. Because of it, the nation faces the dismaying prospect of further months of uncertainty and dwindling trust as both the President and Vice President fight court battles over the sort of immunity the Constitution may or may not throw over their persons and their official conduct.

House Speaker Carl Albert says the Agnew matter is before the courts, and therefore he will not act on the vice presidential letter. That is a flimsy excuse. It also is inconsistent with the Democratic pursuit of the Watergate affair on two parallel tracks, before both Congress and the courts.

Of course, Mr. Albert is not the House of Representatives, and it is possible that after the Vice President asks a court to freeze the grand jury proceeding at its present, tentative stage, the House could change its mind. But that's unlikely. The Speaker's party has the votes to turn aside any effort, by Minority Leader Gerald Ford or other Republicans, to give Mr. Agnew the hearing, "by the grand inquest of the nation," that he seeks.

Delay after delay

To leave the Maryland bribery charges up in the air while successive layers of federal courts deliberate the grave constitutional issues with only the slightest of precedents as guides is not only a slow, torturing process, but also not a sure process.

For example, it seems likely that Attorney General Richardson is prepared to appeal any lower-court freeze on grand jury action to the Supreme Court, since he surely anticipated such an eventuality in deciding that it was constitutionally permissible to let the grand jury hear the evidence gathered by Prosecutor Beall.

This would entail more delay, in a court which first must cope with the broader issue of President Nixon's refusal to release his tapes of White House conversations relating to Watergate and assorted scandals. And it also might pose a dilemma for Chief Justice Burger, who in the event of a successful impeachment of Mr. Agnew by the House would end up presiding as a trial judge—with the Senate as jury—in the same case in which he had ruled on the issue of immunity.

The difficulty of appeals to precedent, including even the parallel case in which Vice President Calhoun was cleared by a House committee after he asked it to investigate the charges of war-profiteering that had been brought against him, is that the power of impeachment has been so infrequently and inconsistently used. When Federal Judge Otto Kerner was indicted, tried and convicted, but not impeached, was that a precedent? When Associate Justice William Douglas' impeachment was sought, by the Republicans, but without any indictment or prospect of one, was that a precedent? The plain question is whether, if a vice president appeals directly to the people's branch of government, it can turn him away.

The House of Representatives has not been asked to impeach Mr. Agnew. It has been asked to give him a fair hearing. The House would be the fitting forum for that hearing, since its processes could permit the greatest degree of both openness and understanding tolerance on an issue from which Mr. Agnew says he has nothing to fear. Moreover, the actions of the House should not compromise constitutional immunity, if such exists, from other forms of prosecution after Mr. Agnew leaves office.

Perhaps Mr. Albert's reply is temporary. Perhaps it is designed to give each member of Congress time to consult his or her constituents. If so, the House can watch what happens in the Maryland courts, talk to its constituents, and then grant Mr. Agnew a hearing that would be swift, fair and open. Why should the Vice President, like another victim of a White House intrigue, be left there hanging, to twist slowly, slowly in the wind?

TAPES COMPROMISE FAILS; HUNT, BUCHANAN TESTIFY

There were these developments in the Watergate case during late September:

■Five of the original defendants in the Watergate case filed petitions with the federal court in the District of Columbia Sept. 14 and 17 seeking to have their pleas of guilty withdrawn. Four of the defendants—Bernard L. Barker, Frank A. Sturgis, Virgilio R. Gonzalez and Eugenio R. Martinez—filed a petition with the court Sept. 14 so they could be tried before a jury. A petition for E. Howard Hunt Jr., the fifth defendant, was filed Sept. 17 for dismissal of the charges against him.

The four told the court they were victims of "a cruel fraud initially perpetrated on them to obtain their participation in the Watergate activities" and their guilty pleas had been "false and involuntarily entered under the force and compulsion of a belief that the necessity to protect national security interests precluded them from asserting the defenses they had to the charges against them." They also contended that they had been directed to plead guilty "to avoid the exposure of secret, confidential and sensitive national security operations of which they were a part."

Hunt's petition claimed that he had been "coerced into abandoning" his defense because the government "unconstitutionally deprived him of evidence" to support his defense and, further, that "the investigation and prosecution of this case were contaminated by misconduct by many responsible White House and law enforcement officials." Even assuming that Hunt's acts were illegal, the petition said, Hunt "cannot be convicted for acts committed within the scope of his employment at the direction of high government officials."

■Former White House special counsel Charles W. Colson invoked his constitutional protection against self-incrimination under the Fifth Amendment in refusing to answer questions from the Senate Watergate committee Sept. 19. Colson's lawyer said his client would refuse to answer the committee's questions at this time because Colson was a "target" of the grand jury probing the burglary at the office of Daniel Ellsberg's psychiatrist, among other matters.

■Special prosecutor Archibald Cox and attorneys for President Nixon told the U.S. Court of Appeals for the District of Columbia Sept. 20 that they had failed in their efforts to reach an out-of-court compromise on access to tapes of Nixon's Watergate conversations. The court's Sept. 13 memorandum suggesting the compromise attempt had said that if the effort failed, the court would rule on the issue. Nixon's lawyers' final reply brief filed with the court Sept. 19 had argued that any order compelling release of the tapes would "tear down the office" of the presidency—"too high a price to pay, even for Watergate."

■The Senate Watergate committee resumed its televised hearings Sept. 24 with Hunt in the witness chair. Hunt, testifying under a grant of immunity from prosecution, gave his first public testimony on the case, although he had been questioned under oath by various judicial and Congressional panels behind closed doors on more than 25 occasions. Hunt revealed his close working relationship with Colson and gave details on the Watergate break-in itself and some of the "dirty tricks" he had performed for the White House. Hunt pleaded abandonment by the Administration, whose high officials had encouraged his participation in Watergate for legitimate national security reasons. Hunt denied seeking executive clemency or influencing other defendants to plead guilty.

■Following two days of testimony from Hunt, the committee opened the second phase of its probe Sept. 26, focusing on alleged political sabotage during the 1972 presidential campaign. The first witness was Nixon speechwriter Patrick J. Buchanan. Questioning Buchanan, the committee's majority set out to show that the policy groundwork for the campaign sabotage in 1972 had been firmly laid in early political strategy memorandums. Memos were released revealing Buchanan's urgings during the 1972 primaries to Nixon supporters to act to knock out one Democratic contender—Sen. Edmund S. Muskie (Me.)—considered a strong challenger to Nixon, and to elevate another Democratic contender—Sen. George S. McGovern (S.D.)—considered a weak challenger to the President. But Buchanan proved to be a superior witness for the Nixon Administration. He denied any illegal or unethical tactics. He asserted he had neither suggested nor participated in such activity. He portrayed his memo recommendations as within the bounds of political precedent. He declared that Nixon won his landslide re-election not because of Watergate and dirty tricks but in spite of them. Buchanan's performance was rated one of the strongest, and the committee's one of its weakest, of the probe.

Los Angeles Times
Los Angeles, Calif., September 30, 1973

The continued investigation into the Watergate affair will disclose additional facts, but the central issue raised by the scandal requires no further illumination. It is the question of power and its use, a problem as old as the history of government.

The basic charter under which we live, the Constitution, is essentially a device to limit and divide and contain authority. The founders were convinced that unchecked power intoxicates the wisest of men. James Madison said, "The truth is that all men having power ought to be mistrusted."

The petty players in the Watergate drama knew that what they did—burglary, bugging and wiretapping—were crimes, and yet they did not regard themselves as criminals. They thought they were acting under the "highest authority" and, more significantly, were confident that this authority could and ought to be able to set aside the law at will.

They were not alone in that view. They had heard two recent U.S. attorneys general argue in almost those same terms in behalf of presidential power. But after facing U.S. Dist. Judge John J. Sirica, the Watergate burglars must have had second thoughts.

As Times staff writer David Shaw pointed out (Sept. 22), they confronted not only a judge but a zealous judge, a judge indignant over the refusal of the conspirators to name the "higher-ups," a judge irritated by the defense counsel and impatient with the prosecution. They discovered that Sirica had his own notions about power and its uses. Sirica wanted to find out the whole truth about Watergate; in pursuit of this objective, which he regarded as more important than merely punishing the culprits before him, he wielded his authority with coercive effect. He sentenced one defendant to 20 years in prison and added a $40,000 fine. He sentenced five others to provisional terms of 35 to 40 years and fined each up to $50,000. Offering "no promises or hopes" if they talked, he promptly promised nevertheless "to weigh that factor" before imposing final sentence.

At the conclusion of the trial, it was clear that Sirica and the defendants were not far apart in their philosophy. A Los Angeles attorney told Shaw: "What Sirica did is the same thing all those Nixon people did in Watergate. He, in effect, said the ends justify the means."

Dean Murray Schwartz of the UCLA law school emphasized the "subtle, but nonetheless significant, difference between a judge who tells a defendant, 'My normal sentence for this offense is five years, but if you cooperate, I'll give you one year,' and a judge who tells a defendant, 'My normal sentence for this offense is five years, and if you don't cooperate, I'll give you 20 years.'"

Sirica did not shrink from the use of power that was intended to accomplish a result that actually had no bearing on the specific charges against the defendants in his court. But few in authority ever do, so the issue extends beyond Sirica and Watergate. It goes to the question of government power in any era from the authority of the President, Congress, the courts, and on down the scale.

The problem can never be resolved, but Madison was right. A wary eye must be kept always on the exercise of power, and never more so than when its arbitrary use—especially by the courts—is justified in the name of some noble objective.

WORCESTER TELEGRAM.
Worcester, Mass., September 25, 1973

President Nixon is insisting on an absolute right to keep his tape recordings confidential.

Special Prosecutor Archibald Cox and federal Judge John J. Sirica are just as insistent that no man, not even the President, is above the law and that President Nixon has no right to withhold evidence of possible criminal activity on the part of presidential aides or anyone else.

A Supreme Court decision on the question now seems unavoidable. President Nixon has found unacceptable Judge Sirica's compromise of letting the judge decide in the privacy of his chambers the relevancy of any evidence contained in the tapes and the question of whether it could be made public without endangering national security. Nor could the President's lawyers arrive at an out-of-court agreement with Prosecutor Cox, as suggested by the federal Court of Appeals. No matter what the Appeals Court now decides, its ruling seems certain to be appealed to the Supreme Court.

Yet even then, it is not clear what President Nixon would do should the Supreme Court rule against him. He has said he would abide by a "definitive" ruling of the high court, but he has refused to define what he means by that. A constitutional confrontation may be in the making.

It is far from clear why the President has felt compelled to take such a stand. Former aides testifying before the Senate Watergate committee have insisted that the nine tape recordings in question would clear President Nixon's name and help to rehabilitate the image of his administration. Yet the President's lawyers filed a brief with the Appeals Court last Wednesday that argued: "To allow a court, which has no jurisdiction, to indict or to try an incumbent President, to conclude that a President has committed a crime, merely as an incident to an evidentiary ruling, would be wholly intolerable."

Adding to the confusion, former associates of the President, now under indictment for Watergate-related crimes, have pleaded innocent and are themselves seeking access to the tapes in an apparent attempt to prove it. If the relevant portions of the tapes were never made available to the courts, the defendants might have to be freed on the grounds that possibly exculpatory evidence was being withheld.

Perhaps it is not yet too late to avoid a constitutional confrontation. The courts have indicated they would bend over backward to avoid a showdown with the President, so long as they can be convinced that no criminal evidence is being withheld.

For if it were to come to the point where the President defied the Supreme Court, several members of Congress, including both senators from Massachusetts, have said that Congress would have no option but to impeach him. The country does not need anything like that.

THE EMPORIA GAZETTE
Emporia, Kans., September 22, 1973

POLITICS makes strange bedfellows. But it is passing strange indeed to find Richard Nixon and the New York Times huddled together. And in the Watergate tapes issue that is precisely where they are.

The Times complained that in his ruling on the subpoena of the tapes Judge Sirica "avoids the elusive problem of defining the abstract limits of executive privilege." And Richard Nixon is still demanding a "definitive decision" from the Supreme Court.

Neither the Times nor President Nixon seems to see what Judge Sirica sees clearly: that there are two definitive decisions to be made, two issues. The judge knows that there are certain overlapping factors in these issues, and therefore conflicts between them. But he did a pretty good job of juggling the two.

Richard Nixon himself brought up one of the issues when he stressed his lieutenants' right to privacy in their conversations with him. He might have added that their right was enhanced because they did not know their words were being recorded. This right of privacy, a civil right, is indeed at issue in the courts. For if every man who talks with his executive — in government and out — knows that his conversation is public property, there will be precious little meaningful business conversation between executives and their lieutenants in this country.

But also at issue in the Watergate tape decision is the separation of powers under the United States constitution. Is this separation absolute and inviolable, or is it subject to the demands of criminal jurisprudence?

Judge Sirica ruled clearly that executive privilege is *not* inviolable. And he ruled that the right of the citizen to privacy *is* inviolable. He ruled that the court has a right to examine the Watergate tapes in chambers (without the presence of the news media, the Senate committee or even a grand jury). Then if he, the court, finds in the tapes any evidence of criminal activities which can be separated from the privileged conversations he will extract this evidence and send it to the grand jury.

That would seem to limit civil rights. *But* the judge further ruled that "if privileged and unprivileged evidence are so inextricably connected that separation becomes impossible, the whole must be privileged and no disclosure made to the grand jury."

In short, he ruled that executive privilege is limited but that the right of the citizen to privacy is inviolable, even at the expense of judicial procedure.

What more "definitive" ruling can the President or the New York Times ask?

THE DALLAS TIMES HERALD
Dallas, Tex., September 23, 1973

THE FAILURE of President Nixon and Special prosecutor Archibald Cox to reach a compromise which would have settled the question of release of the Watergate tapes makes a court decision on the momentous issue inevitable. And that decision could have portent far beyond the immediate issue of the White House tapes touching on Watergate.

If the Supreme Court, which now undoubtedly will make the final determination, rules that confidential information in the form of documents, including tapes, in the President's possession can be held inviolate from court use or scrutiny that will settle the matter.

But to get some bare inkling of what a decision adverse to the President would portend, one needs go no further than Dallas.

Former Atty. Gen. Waggoner Carr and John Osorio, defendants in criminal cases growing out of the Texas stock scandal, have filed suit in federal court here seeking White House taped conversations which they believe would bolster their defense.

The filing of the Carr and Osorio suits adds a whole new dimension — and one of almost infinite expanse — to the Watergate tapes question.

Suppose the Supreme Court rules that under the Constitution executive privilege does not extend to information needed in the prosecution of a criminal case and orders the tapes released. Would not the constitutional rights of defendants be at least equal to those of the prosecutors? Specifically would not Carr and Osorio be entitled to their tapes also?

Because the law cannot be discriminatory, apparently they would have the same legal right to White House tapes as would Cox. And beyond that, any defendant in a criminal action — and perhaps even in a civil action — during this or any past administration who believed that White House documents written or taped touched on his case could subpoena those documents.

We urged the President to join Cox in reaching a compromise on release of the tapes, as the Circuit Court of Appeals suggested to avoid further court action. We thought, and still think, that this action by the President would have been in his own best interest — assuming his avowed innocence of any Watergate complicity.

Certainly it would have been in the best interest of the nation in order to facilitate settlement of the whole Watergate affair as soon as possible.

But even had he done so, thus ending the legal argument concerning the tapes in the Watergate case, it is apparent now the action would not have settled the broader crucial question. The filing of the Carr and Osorio suits saw to that.

Presumably, even in the event of a Watergate tapes settlement out of court the two defendants here would carry their subpoena cases all the way to the Supreme Court. Thus now, irregardless of Watergate, the Supreme Court sooner or later would have had to rule on the Constitutional question of absolute executive privilege.

THE ARIZONA REPUBLIC
Phoenix, Ariz., September 20, 1973

The U.S. Supreme Court may rule for or against the President on the Watergate tapes, but it won't end the battle over whether a recorded conversation is personal property or whether it belongs in the public realm.

Consider, for instance, the hassle between the Ervin Committee and Watergate prosecutor Archibald Cox regarding the taped conversations that President Nixon claims he cannot be forced to let anyone hear.

Although Cox was appointed by a Nixon surrogate, and presumably represents the President, he is suing to get the President's tapes. But, he says, there is no reason James W. McCord, a member of the team that broke into the Watergate Democratic headquarters, should hear the tapes. To add to the confusion, the Ervin Committee, which wants the tapes, says it has presented "an even stronger case for the materials subpoened" than does Cox.

Another Senate committee, this one headed by Sen. Bill Fulbright, demanded some tapes of conversations in which Dr. Henry Kissinger took part before it would recommend his confirmation for secretary of State. It didn't get the tapes, but two of its members were allowed to hear them, and on their recommendation the committee voted for confirmation.

A little further down the list in the battle of tapes, some leaders of the dairy industry are demanding tapes made when they had a conference with President Nixon. Through White House counsel, President Nixon has declined this request so presumably the dairy people will go to some court or other.

Sooner or later, it seems the courts will have to consider bugging devices an extension of a written record. If President Nixon had written down what he said during the crucial Watergate conferences, or if he had dictated to a secretary what he recalled, no court would have even considered putting those records in the public domain.

However, the c a s e s involving the President also i n v o l v e the matter of executive privilege and the separation of powers. A person who puts a bug in his martini olive and gets a record of a conversation at a restaurant table can claim no such privilege. If his tape does in fact bear on a criminal charge and might put a person in jail (or keep him out of jail), it seems to us that he should not be shielded from producing such evidence in court. At least, the shield should be no bigger than the shield that might be invoked for his other records and papers.

Some authorities have come up with a proposal that seems more like a cop-out than a solution. A federal judge has ruled that he himself should hear the Nixon tapes and decide whether they should be made public. Fortunately, that ruling is on appeal And the Foreign Affairs Committee, has decided if the whole committee can't hear some tapes, it will be satisfied with a report from two members who were allowed to hear them.

T h i s half-solution won't work very well. If controversial tapes are r e l e a s e d to anyone, they should be released to everyone. Otherwise, the confusion regarding what's actually on the tapes will be even worse confounded.

Senator Fulbright's committee has voted to conduct "a full examination of the use of electronic and other means of surveillance of American citizens in connection with alleged intelligence gathering and other activities related to the foreign policy . . "

Maybe that will help clarify some, but certainly not all, of the issues r e g a r d i n g confidential tapes.

Pittsburgh Post-Gazette
Pittsburgh, Pa., September 22, 1973

ALAS, hopes have been dashed for a compromise on the Presidential tapes bearing on Watergate crimes. Even after three sessions President Nixon's attorneys a n d Archibald Cox, the special prosecutor in the Watergate case, could not agree on a plan proposed by the U.S. Court of Appeals.

So now we head for a "high noon" type of showdown in the courts over whether or not Mr. Nixon can be compelled to release them. It was precisely this head-on confrontation of the cowboy movie type which the court had sought to avoid by suggesting in a highly unusual memorandum that a way be found for Mr. Nixon, his attorney, and Mr. Cox to review the tapes in private to determine what should and what should not go to the grand jury.

Mr. Cox immediately assented. So apparently it was the White House which felt that the Appeals Court proposal still breached the "executive privilege" concept the President has felt it was so important to uphold.

The Appeals court now must write a decision. Its ruling almost certainly will be appealed to the U.S. Supreme Court either by Mr. Nixon or by Mr. Cox.

But even the Supreme Court may not be the final scene of the drama. For Mr. Nixon has said he will obey only a "definitive" Supreme Court ruling on the tapes, but has declined to define what he means by "definitive."

Sen. Edward Kennedy (D-Mass.) was prompted to assert that if the President did refuse a Supreme Court order to release the tapes, then that would be grounds for the start of impeachment proceedings.

That really would be "high noon."

We had hoped that sort of ultimate confrontation could be avoided and editorially had urged (Sept. 17) that Mr. Nixon accept the compromise. We noted: "The genius of the American system has been the ability of contending branches of government to find ways to avoid forcing rulings and precedents which might unduly strain the system."

It is regrettable that the White House disregarded this wisely pragmatic operational approach.

Richmond Times-Dispatch

Richmond, Va., September 30, 1973

Of all the witnesses who have appeared before the Senate Watergate committee, E. Howard Hunt probably is the most pathetic, not only because of the personal tragedies he has suffered but also because of the distortion of justice that his case seems to symbolize. It is difficult to consider Hunt's testimony without concluding that in his case, and probably in the cases of all the other men who have been found guilty on Watergate charges in the Washington court of Federal District Judge John Sirica, justice went wildly awry.

Hunt admits that he participated in the break-in at the Democratic party's Watergate headquarters, but he insists that he was motivated by a compelling sense of duty to his country and that he fully believed the operation to be legal. Ignorance of the law may excuse no man, but Hunt apparently considered the mission lawful not because he was ignorant but because he had been *assured* by his superiors that it was legal. There is a difference.

We cannot vouch for Hunt's veracity, of course, but his testimony did have the clarion ring of plausibility. A former officer for the Central Intelligence Agency, he devoted years of his life to spying—one way or another—for his country. His was a profession that stressed the importance of unwavering loyalty and obedience to superior authority. When he went to the White House, soon after his retirement from the CIA, he naturally carried his talents and his attitudes with him.

At the White House, Hunt was a member of the Special Investigations Unit, one of whose assignments was to find and plug the leaks of classified government information. Operation Watergate had been explained to him, he said, as a mission to determine whether the Cuban government was secretly pouring money into the Democratic campaign. He had been told, he testified, that the plan had the approval of such highly placed men as Jeb Stuart Magruder, a former White House aide and then deputy director of the Committee to Re-elect the President; former White House Counsel John W. Dean III; former White House Special Counsel Charles W. Colson; and former Attorney General John N. Mitchell.

Which of these men actually approved the Watergate escapade is, of course, a matter of dispute. Magruder has admitted that he did, and he has sought to implicate others. Certainly it stands to reason that *someone* in authority directed Hunt and the men who actually executed the break-in. And it is easy to understand how they could have been persuaded by the dignitaries above them that the operation was legal or, even if illegal, vital to the security of the country.

Still, it can be argued that Hunt and the others were grown men and that they should have known better. Now they must pay the price for their foolish loyalty and blind obedience to orders. But is the price they are being asked to pay fair? It will not be fair if they are the only ones to suffer the wrath of the law as a result of Watergate. It cannot be considered fair so long as the high officials who planned and authorized the whole thing remain unpunished.

Certainly the price being exacted from Hunt is exorbitant. Judge Sirica sentenced him provisionally to 35 years in prison, the maximum, with a promise to consider reducing the term if Hunt cooperated in the continuing Watergate investigation. Obviously this does not represent a judicious effort to fit the punishment to the crime but a blatant attempt to torture Hunt into total submission. Even now, after only a few months in prison, Hunt, who has suffered a stroke and been physically attacked and robbed by fellow prisoners, is a broken man.

He and his jailed Watergate colleagues may deserve to be punished, but they do not deserve to be treated as scapegoats. At the very least, Judge Sirica should release Hunt and the others on bond until the Watergate investigation has been completed and all the others involved in the crime can be brought to the bar of justice. Then, and only then, can the roles and responsibilities of all the participants be fairly assessed.

The Virginian-Pilot

Norfolk, Va., September 26, 1973

Among all the characters in the drama of Watergate, E. Howard Hunt and Charles Colson are a fascinating twosome.

Mr. Colson was responsible for the hiring of Mr. Hunt as a consultant to the White House, where he soon was part of the investigative team that was known as "the plumbers." As everybody knows now, Hunt and G. Gordon Liddy masterminded — if that's the word — the burglary of the Democratic headquarters in the Watergate as well as the break-in earlier at the office of Daniel Ellsberg's psychiatrist.

Mr. Hunt was a CIA agent was for 21 years before he retired in 1970 (he went to work at the White House in the summer of 1971) and he liked to think of himself as a professional spy. He also authored a number of thrillers under various pen-names. Former CIA Director Richard Helms has characterized him as "a bit of a romantic."

Mr. Colson is, or was, a genuine tough guy among all the synthetic tough guys in the White House. (He once was the youngest company commander in the Marines.) He joined the President's staff in 1969 with a reputation as a no-holds-barred political type and soon was known as everybody's favorite SOB in the White House — which, considering the competition at the time, was no small trick. He appeared to bask in the reputation. He not only delivered the famous line that he would walk over his grandmother to insure the President's re-election, he made a point of circulating a memo saying he wanted everybody on the staff to know he had made the statement. It is not surprising that Richard M. Nixon, who had something of a gut-fighter's reputation in days gone-by himself, appreciated Mr. Colson's dedication and talents. In his chronicle of the election last year Theodore H. White says that Mr. Nixon liked to talk politics with Mr. Colson and the two frequently huddled together in the White House. Any man who could get around Ehrlichman. Haldeman & Co. is a formidable operator.

The big difference in the faces of rare of Messrs. Colson and Hunt is of course, that was one was caught and the other wasn't.

While it is difficult to believe that a professional spy didn't know what he was doing when he burglarized the Democrats' offices, it is easy to sympathize with Howard Hunt in human terms. As he said in his testimony, "I find myself confined under a sentence which may keep me in prison for the rest of my life. I have been incarcerated for six months. For a time I was in solitary confinement. I have been physically attacked and robbed in jail. I have suffered a stroke. I have been transferred from place to place, manacled and chained, hand and foot. I am isolated from my four motherless children. The funds provided me and others who participated in the break-in have long since been exhausted. . . ."

If Mr Hunt's life is in ruins, his sponsor seems to have prospered. When he left the White House to enter private practice, he got a handsome retainer from the Teamsters. (By coincidence or not, that was just a year after he recommended clemency for Jimmy Hoffa, the former president of the Teamsters.) Although his name was mentioned often in connection with Watergate, Mr. Colson had led a charmed life until quite recently. He wasn't directly implicated and he maintained stoutly that he had done nothing wrong. He has not been charged or convicted, disgraced or fired, and he even took a much-publicized lie-detector test. But now he has been told that he is under investigation by one of the grand juries probing Watergate. He took the Fifth Amendment when he appeared before the Ervin Committee in closed session last week, and he will not be called as a public witness. And he was fingered by Howard Hunt in his testimony this week. Mr. Colson is learning what it's like to be among the walked-upon.

Tulsa Daily World

Tulsa, Okla., September 28, 1973

PATRICK BUCHANAN is one of the second-rank witnesses before the Senate Watergate Committee, but his testimony was memorable for several reasons.

For one, he took his audience to the firing line of Presidential politics where the picture is not entirely bright and wholesome. The "dirty tricks" part of campaigning points up the need for firmer ethical and moral standards in politics—before the public becomes even more convinced than it already is that everybody connected with political life is dishonest and will do almost anything to win.

Those standards will not be easy to establish—and will be even harder to enforce. But Watergate itself is the proof and result of ever-lower levels of conduct in campaigning that finally reached the anything-goes gutter and smeared our highest political institution, the PRESIDENCY.

In addition to adding to our education, so to speak, BUCHANAN proved to be an outspoken, candid man of strong conservative convictions who gave the ERVIN Committee as much as he took.

His opening statement was enough to make the entire Committee and its staff blush in chagrin. Not only did they fail even to give him the courtesy of telling him about his appearance before he read of it in the press, said BUCHANAN, but the stories that appeared in leading newspapers and on network television made him out to be an "architect" of sordid chapters in the 1972 campaign.

He charged the Committee staff with an unjustified "covert campaign of vilification" against him, although the top investigators repeatedly denied having any of the documents cited in the stories leaked to the press.

"So it seems fair to me to ask," said BUCHANAN, "*how can this Select Committee set itself up as the ultimate arbiter of American political ethics, if it cannot even control character assassins within its own ranks?*"

That central question drew only feeble answers from the staff and Senators on the Committee. BUCHANAN is not the first person to raise it, but the persistent undercover campaign against certain witnesses is a stain on the Committee's record that cannot be wiped off or forgiven.

THE DAILY OKLAHOMAN

Oklahoma City, Okla., September 29, 1973

TESTIMONY this week by Patrick J. Buchanan, a presidential speech writer, might help place the Watergate affair in perspective if his words could be as widely circulated as have been the more sensational revelations and allegations.

Watergate has been so minutely analyzed, rationalized and sermonized that it may be accorded a niche in history far out of proportion to its real importance. That will be for the historians to assess. The truth is, though, that the efforts of President Nixon's political enemies have been so prodigious they have succeeded in convincing many Americans that Watergate is a national tragedy.

Not only that, they have imputed to Watergate fundamental implications of an unseemly bloating of presidential power. They see it as intertwined with the issues of impoundment of federal funds and presidential war-making authority.

Restoring some sanity to the national debate was Buchanan's testimony before the Senate Watergate committee that the break-in at the Democratic national headquarters was "wrong, but not grievously wrong." He criticized the Democrats' double standard in deploring dirty campaign tricks when they have employed some of the same tactics.

Buchanan insisted that some campaign pranks are a normal part of politics and not necessarily wrong. He conceded that certain workers in the Nixon re-election committee went too far and violated the law. The fact this wasn't the first time it was done does not excuse their excesses, but it should caution people not to go overboard in their condemnation.

Obviously, there was an attempt by high committee officials, once the break-in was discovered, to avoid embarrassment in the middle of the 1972 election campaign. It was obvious, too, that they were equally anxious to keep the whole affair from Nixon. Of course, this is precisely the point on which friends and foes of the President disagree.

Fervent descriptions of the burglary and subsequent cover-up attempt as the "crime of the century" or the nation's "worst scandal ever" are hardly warranted, however. Nevertheless, because of their access to the communications media, Nixon's enemies have been able to build the Watergate affair into something far more serious than it really was.

The same lack of perspective is present in allegations against Vice President Spiro Agnew of political corruption while he was Baltimore County executive and later governor of Maryland. The public still doesn't know—nor, apparently, does Agnew himself—the full extent of what he's charged with. From the information that has leaked out, it seems to involve what has been common practice in Maryland—and other states, too, for that matter. That is, soliciting campaign funds from contractors and giving government contracts to contributors.

Just because someone else is doing something wrong does not excuse one's own wrongful actions. But it is manifestly unfair to single out an individual to be the means of condemning a whole system.

The general feeling is that Agnew is ruined politically, whether or not he is finally vindicated. Yet there is evidence that Watergate has become such a bore with the American public that for Republicans generally it won't have as much impact on the 1976 presidential election as economic issues. The condition of the consumer's pocketbook by then may put Watergate in perspective after all.

THE MILWAUKEE JOURNAL

Milwaukee, Wis., September 26, 1973

As E. Howard Hunt sees it, his life has been shattered because he did what was once praised — served the United States government as a clandestine agent. There is some troublesome truth in his lament.

Hunt notes that the Central Intelligence Agency trained him as a spy and gave him two commendations during 21 years of service. As for the Ellsberg and Watergate break-ins that he plotted as a White House employe, Hunt says that he believed he was carrying out legal missions authorized by the highest government officials.

Hunt gets carried away when he contends that "the country . . . which directed me to carry out the Watergate entry is punishing me for doing the very things it trained and directed me to do." The country and the Nixon administration zealots who hired Hunt are not one and the same. One must also wonder why Hunt did not perceive some moral or legal distinctions between espionage directed against foreign powers and burglarizing Democratic Party headquarters.

Nonetheless, after a lifetime as a dutiful secret agent in good standing, Hunt has more of an excuse for his unsavory entanglements than do most of the others who have been implicated. Indeed, he now has the mark of a fall guy. He faces perhaps a long prison stay. Already he has been knocked around in jail, suffered a sharp decline in health, lost his wife in a plane crash, exhausted the defense funds that had been provided him.

Some may say that Hunt should have known better. Probably so. Yet spying is always a dirty business and, given the blessings he received from on high, it seems unfair to come down crushingly on Hunt — particularly when it remains to be seen whether anyone in the upper reaches of the Nixon administration will ever see the inside of a jail cell.

DAYTON DAILY NEWS

Dayton, Ohio, September 28, 1973

Watergate witnesses are subject to frequent memory lapses but are seldom at a loss when it comes to theory. What motivated the incredible series of criminal actions that emanated from the White House and the Committee to Re-Elect the President? Pick your witness.

For John Mitchell it was dedication to a man. For Messrs. Haldeman and Ehrlichman it was that, plus the national security. Again and again the theme was sounded: if someone other than Richard Nixon had gained the presidency, some vague awfulness would have befallen the republic.

Jeb Stuart Magruder laid the Watergate misdeeds at the door of anti-war demonstrators. He indicated that their civil disobedience had left him morally confused, like a tenderfoot scout who has overheard the boys in the next tent making light of the Oath.

Now Patrick Buchanan, presidential speechwriter and tactician, has offered a new theory. He compares apples and oranges, points out that he is comparing apples and oranges, yet somehow leaves the impression that the comparison is valid anyway.

The Buchanan theory centers on Dick Tuck, a Democratic gadfly who has made an elaborate hobby out of bedeviling Richard Nixon. Mr. Tuck's pranks are legendary. He once donned an engineer's cap and signaled a campaign train to pull away from the station just as Mr. Nixon was beginning a major address from the train's rear platform. He hired a gaggle of obviously pregnant black women to parade around Miami Beach bearing signs that read "Nixon's The One." He posed laughing children around Mr. Nixon in San Francisco's Chinatown. The kids carried signs that referred, in Mandarin, to an embarrassing loan Howard Hughes had made Mr. Nixon's brother.

Buchanan suggests that the Tuck pranks so tickled funny-bones at the White House that it was decided that staffers would pull a few practical jokes of their own. If some of the tricks turned sour, it was only because the pranksters got a bit over-enthusiastic in their quest for new laughs.

Well, bunk. Burglary is not funny. Neither is character assassination. Both were staples of the Watergate repertory. Stories were leaked that suggested Sens. Humphrey and Jackson were sex perverts. Pro-war advertisements were taken in the names of non-existent citizens' groups. Campaign literature was faked illegally. A phony letter to a newspaper charged Sen. Muskie with a racial slur. Plans were made to firebomb a research institute.

These "tricks" did not depart from the essential innocence of the Dick Tuck pranks because they never shared it to begin with. Tuck's gags were obvious jokes the moment they occurred. The Watergate tricks worked only when they could be concealed. Mr. Tuck's jokes embarrassed but did no lasting damage to their target; the Watergate tricks tried to obliterate theirs.

The Nixon men often broke the law. They always lied. And they never, never indicated that they were anything but deadly earnest.

The Chattanooga Times
Chattanooga, Tenn., September 27, 1973

The Senate investigating committee has resumed its attempt to unravel the secrets of the Watergate scandal and concerned citizens are trying again to understand the motivations behind it all. For both, E. Howard Hunt Jr., a former CIA agent and a member of the White House special intelligence unit so deeply involved, spoke more than idle words in his self-serving statement as a witness.

In level tones he told of alleged mistreatment in prison, where he has been held since a guilty plea early this year, the misery of solitary confinement, the sense of degradation in being handcuffed and leg-shackled in public. Then he added:

"Beyond all this, I am crushed by the failure of my government to protect me and my family as in the past it has always done for its clandestine agents."

One can understand the reaction without condoning it in the least. As an intelligence operative, Mr. Hunt was no doubt keenly aware of the government's seemingly contradictory policies regarding an agent abroad — its readiness to deny his existence, if necessary, and its willingness to provide for his family, if needed.

But he knew, or should have known, he was engaged in no legitimate intelligence mission, clandestine though it certainly was, when he participated in the break-in at the Watergate headquarters of the Democratic party, or directed the burglary of the office of Dr. Daniel Ellsberg's psychiatrist, or made tentative plans to steal documents from an office in Reno. These were American citizens whose rights were being trampled, not enemies of the state to be accorded surveillance.

Why the confusion? He gives the answer in part: His belief that "my participation in the Watergate was an activity authorized within the power of the President of the United States . . . I considered my participation as a duty to my country. I thought it was an unwise operation but I viewed it as lawful."

It is a damning insight into the mental attitudes engendered and nurtured by persons at the very highest level of the White House.

THE SAGINAW NEWS
Saginaw, Mich., September 30, 1973

Patrick J. Buchanan, a political speechwriter of no small ability who served the President faithfully throughout the 1972 election campaign, spent as much time finger-waggling at the Senate Watergate Committee the other day as it did finger-waggling at him.

Along the way Mr. Buchanan made some points which we are not disposed to disagree with — namely that a dirty trick in politics is a dirty trick no matter who pulls it and that Democrats have no corner on ethics.

Buchanan cited examples of where others have strayed in past years. He went on to ask what is the difference between "this" and "that"? The answer, of course, is none where it obviously shows a lack of ethics. And it certainly is wrong to accept any double standard in this regard.

The difficulty arises in accepting the general thesis advanced by Mr. Buchanan that certain things are okay in politics as pranks. If we accept that, where is the line drawn and who draws it? Pat Buchanan sees ghost-written ads and undercover operatives as legitimate weapons in political campaigns. These, according to Mr. Buchanan, are pranks, not dirty tricks; all part of the game.

He loses us here for the simple reason that the 1972 presidential campaign demonstrated what is possible in the name of pranks without the application of ethics. It opens the door to sabotage upon the individual and upon the political process.

It deserves to be emphasized that Mr. Buchanan did not defend some of the practices engaged in during 1972. What disturbs is the underlying theme of his testimony. It fell back upon the now familiar line that others have done it and got away with it, we do it and we're being character-assassinated.

This oversimplifies greatly and evades the clear cut issue that has been drawn in the Watergate investigation. It is simply that too many individuals with too much money to spend and too little regard for ethics, much less the legal improprieties of what they were doing, indulged in the worst kinds of attempts at character assassination and unwarranted invasions of privacy.

These acts were hardly pranks. Even Mr. Buchanan would and did agree with that. But they amply demonstrate the dangers inherent when the pranks mentality is allowed to run wild. No line was drawn when it should have been. The result was a gross dirty trick on the free elective process.

If we are willing to accept this, then nothing shall have been learned by Republicans or Democrats — and we can lay aside all fair campaign practices laws and get on with ever more dirty politics as usual.

The disillusionment of the Americam people over what this produced in 1972 suggests they are not willing to accept that as the wave of the future from either party.

The New York Times
New York, N.Y., September 29, 1973

Patrick J. Buchanan charged the Senate Watergate committee with having conducted a "covert campaign of vilification" against him. But later in his testimony, the special consultant to President Nixon engaged in what can best be described as a classic example of the political smear.

As a veteran political strategist, Mr. Buchanan appears to have sensed that an attack on the philanthropic foundations could provide just the sort of diversion that would get the Senators' minds off the subject of political burglaries and dirty tricks.

Mr. Buchanan: "Well . . . the Ford Foundation, for example, provides funds for the Institute for Policy Studies. The I.P.S. holds, has held, it is my recollection . . . seminars with Congressmen, for staffers and the like, and they deal in trying to influence Congressmen and the like to vote in one direction. . . . The Institute of Policy Studies has in turn funded the Quicksilver Times which . . . is one of the radical, what they call underground newspapers, which has a political point of view which is sold for profit."

The significance of the Quicksilver Times not having been immediately grasped by the committee, Mr. Buchanan offered a compendium of other allegedly political foundation activities, including support of voter registration which, he suggested, led to the election of a black mayor in Cleveland, and the subsidy of the Southern Christian Leadership Conference which had sent him some "strictly political literature." He also complained of occasions when "as soon as a . . . Brookings study is done, you will see it on the front page of The New York Times and The Washington Post . . . and these things are moved into the political bloodstream, and one of my basic contentions is that there is an imbalance in resources with regard to these foundations."

The Watergate committee's chief counsel, Samuel Dash, subsequently informed the committee that the general counsel for the I.P.S. had telephoned to say that it had never funded the Quicksilver Times and that the only money the institute itself had ever received from the Ford Foundation was $6,000 in 1964. (The foundation subsequently said the amount was actually $7,800.) After Senator Gurney had characterized the radical, anti-Republican content of the Quicksilver Times as part of the "dirty tricks department," the committee inserted the publication in its record, even though, as Senator Ervin suggested, it had no relationship to the hearings.

Regrettably, the committee lacked either the will or the sophistication to challenge Mr. Buchanan's contemptible diversionary tactics. None of the members denounced the attempt to establish a non-existing link between an obscure, radical publication and a major foundation. The Senators appeared too enthralled by Mr. Buchanan's amoral political joviality to question his arrogant insistence that even the most outrageous election abuses perpetrated by the President's surrogates were nothing more than politics-as-usual.

AGNEW QUITS AS PART OF PLEA BARGAIN

After strenuously denying any improper or illegal behavior for more than two months, Spiro T. Agnew resigned the vice presidency and pleaded no contest (nolo contendere) to one count of evading income tax on $29,500 during 1967 in a dramatic courtroom hearing in Baltimore Oct. 10. In return for Agnew's resignation and no-contest plea, the Justice Department agreed to drop all other pending charges and request leniency on the tax evasion charge. (Agnew had faced federal indictment for violation of bribery, conspiracy and tax laws.) After Agnew entered his plea, U.S. District Court Judge Walter E. Hoffman asked Agnew if he understood that waiving indictment and pleading no contest was "the full equivalent of a plea of guilty." Agnew concurred and Hoffman sentenced him to a fine of $10,000 and three year's unsupervised probation. Hoffman said that without the recommendation for leniency by Attorney General Elliot L. Richardson, he would have been inclined to follow his usual procedure in tax evasion cases of imposing a fine and prison sentence of two to five months.

In a statement read to the court, Richardson said no agreement could have been reached without a provision that he appeal for leniency. Richardson emphasized that a central element of the agreement was that the department be allowed to present the details of its other evidence against Agnew while agreeing to waive prosecution based on it.

Richardson said that for the people to "fairly judge the outcome" of the Agnew case, he would offer an "exposition of evidence" which "establishes a pattern of substantial cash payments to the defendant during the period when he served as governor of Maryland in return for engineering contracts with the State of Maryland."

According to the "exposition of evidence," Agnew—shortly after becoming governor in 1967—established a system of taking payments from engineering firms. I. H. Hammerman 2d, a Baltimore investment banker, acted as "collector" from companies designated by Jerome B. Wolff, then chairman of the Maryland State Roads Commission. The three agreed—on Agnew's order—that the payments would be divided 50% for Agnew and 25% each for Hammerman and Wolff.

The evidence also detailed the relationship between Agnew and the presidents of two engineering firms who made direct cash payments. One, Lester Matz of Matz, Childs and Associates, continued making "corrupt payments" to Agnew after he became vice president.

As required by law, Agnew's formal instrument of resignation was a statement transmitted to Secretary of State Henry A. Kissinger. Agnew also formally notified President Nixon by letter, saying "the accusations against me cannot be resolved without a long, divisive and debilitating struggle in the Congress and in the courts." Agnew had concluded that it was "in the best interest of the nation" that he relinquish the office. In his reply, Nixon praised Agnew's "strong patriotism" and "all that you have contributed to the nation by your years of service as vice president."

Agnew's action touched off an immediate search by President Nixon for a successor. House Speaker Carl Albert (D, Okla.) became next in line for the presidency until the office of vice president was filled, for the first time, under the provisions of the 25th Amendment to the Constitution, ratified in 1967.

During the two weeks preceding the surprise hearing in Baltimore, there were the following major developments in the Agnew affair:

In a Los Angeles speech Sept. 29, Agnew declared to a cheering audience of Republican women, "I will not resign if indicted." He went on to bitterly denounce the Justice Department and, without specifically naming him, Assistant Attorney General Henry Petersen for leaking malicious information to the media. The Vice President claimed that "individuals in the upper professional echelons" of the department who had been "severely stung by their ineptness" in the Watergate case were "trying to recoup their reputation at my expense." "I'm a big trophy," Agnew declared.

President Nixon told a news conference Oct. 3 that Agnew's refusal to resign was "altogether proper," but took issue with Agnew's criticism of Petersen's handling of the investigation. Nixon said the charges against Agnew were "serious and not frivolous."

In an unusual action, Judge Hoffman Oct. 3 authorized Agnew's attorneys to investigate—with full powers of subpoena—the alleged news leaks by Justice Department officials. Under Hoffman's order, the lawyers could privately question under oath and take sworn depositions from any persons they deemed "appropriate and necessary." Some lawyers were quoted Oct. 4 as believing that Hoffman's order was unprecedented in that a person under criminal investigation but not yet under indictment was granted such broad authority to question prosecutors and others involved. The order was also seen as a potential source of further constitutional issues in the Agnew case if reporters questioned by his attorneys refused to reveal their sources.

In another action Oct. 3, Judge Hoffman summoned the grand jurors and delivered a special charge cautioning them to "disregard totally any comments you might have seen or heard from any source, save and except what you have heard or seen in your grand jury room while in official session." Hoffman called the press "integral and necessary," but added that "unfortunately, in the present-day grab for priority in getting news items, the news media frequently overlook the rights of others, especially where criminal matters are involved."

The Washington Post
Times Herald
Washington, D.C., October 7, 1973

Tulsa, Okla.
October 6, 1973

VICE PRESIDENT AGNEW through his attorneys, has declared war on the press in a move that can only obscure the central question that lies before the Grand Jury investigating him.

The subpoenas served on reporters and news media yesterday also set up what must surely become a landmark case before the U.S. SUPREME COURT. For only the highest Court in the land can resolve the essential issue in this conflict of Constitutional principles.

The confrontation is between the right of the free flow of information and the right to a fair trial. We are not ready to say that the VICE PRESIDENT has been denied a fair trial by the stories that have appeared about him—although undoubtedly he has been hurt politically.

But is it the "leaks" that have hurt him, or the fact he is under investigation by a Grand Jury? He has not been charged with any crime, but the mere fact that a man in so high an office is involved in such an investigation is bound to be sensational news. It cannot be kept a secret and it cannot be treated as a routine story.

AGNEW is understandably upset by some of the leaks and the speculation, which he believes to have come from the JUSTICE DEPARTMENT. But his subpoenas, authorized by the Federal Judge in charge of the Grand Jury at Baltimore, are not directed at the possible *sources* but at the *intermediary*— the press.

The newsmen and the media will have to fight this attack as a crippling abridgment of the FIRST AMENDMENT guarantee of free expression. If it is allowed to continue unchecked, the whole area of investigative reporting will be undermined, for no one would give confidential information if he knew the origin could be revealed by Court order.

It boils down to this: Should any Judge, at his own discretion, be the arbiter of what may be printed or broadcast—through the weapons of subpoena power, the threat of contempt citations and other leverage held by his Court? This is a direction in which our society already is moving, and no more serious threat to freedom of the press exists.

Meanwhile, what of AGNEW? If there is evidence against him to warrant a charge, that will be the central issue: Guilt or innocence. Who told what to a reporter must not be allowed to divert attention from that question. If the VICE PRESIDENT has done nothing wrong, as he states, he is entitled to be freed of suspicion and suspense. If there is serious evidence against him, then it should be presented in Court.

We have deplored irresponsible leaking of misinformation—and still believe it is wrong. But the harm here is in trampling one part of the Bill of Rights to try to preserve another.

The current administration has a genius for pushing the country into situations which place undue and unwelcome stress on our durable old Constitution. The latest in the line of a seemingly unending stream of sharp constitutional tests has been posed by Vice President Agnew's assertion that the Department of Justice has engaged in a systematic and deliberate campaign of leaking information to the press in an effort to destroy him politically, in the course of destroying any chance he may have of receiving a fair hearing before a grand or petit jury. This has led to issuance by Mr. Agnew's lawyers of subpoenas to reporters from The Washington Post, The Washington Star News, The New York Times, The New York Daily News, CBS News, NBC News, and Newsweek and Time magazines. All of this presages a monumental and, in our view, an entirely avoidable constitutional confrontation over the First Amendment.

Mr. Agnew revealed on Aug. 6 that he had been informed that he was the target of a federal grand jury investigation. There can be no doubt that since that time numerous stories based on information from sources close to the investigation have appeared concerning the nature of the charges being made against the Vice President, the names of the witnesses against him, his state of mind and the nature of the negotiations between his lawyers and the Department of Justice. From this, his lawyers have drawn the conclusion that "a number of officials in the prosecutorial arm of our government have misused their offices in an immoral and illegal attempt to drive the Vice President from the office to which he was elected, and to assure his conviction."

Since Judge Walter E. Hoffman issued no opinion on the motion in which this argument was made, one cannot know with certainty just how he reacted to that rather startling assertion. He gave two pretty clear indications of his thinking, however. First, he granted the Vice President's lawyers extraordinary authority to take depositions in a criminal proceeding prior to the conclusion of grand jury deliberations and he gave them subpoena power to make the taking of those depositions possible. The second hint came in his very strong admonition to the grand jury to consider only the evidence presented to it and to disregard press reports in the case. In the course of that statement, Judge Hoffman went on to say:

We are rapidly approaching the day when the perpetual conflict between the news media, operating as they do under freedom of speech and freedom of the press and the judicial system, charged with protecting the rights of persons under investigation for criminal acts must be resolved.

The first question is whether such a conflict really does exist. And the next question is whether this case offers the best occasion for resolving it. We believe that the answer to both questions is, no. The Constitution is full of useful ambiguity which through our history has permitted reasonable men to reconcile conflicting rights and interests in a spirit of accommodation which preserves the essence of the Constitution without placing unbearable stress on our nation's institutions. Constitutional clashes have generally been avoided, and wisely so, whenever possible. Such a clash could have been avoided here.

Mr. Agnew's argument is that he should not be indicted because, among other things, the prosecutors have fatally flawed their case by filling news pages and the airwaves with prejudicial information against him. While he has every right to assert that claim, we would doubt that it has much substance. The fact that the trials of Sirhan Sirhan, Angela Davis, Jack Ruby and Bobby Seale were successfully concluded indicates that American

judges know very well how to pick juries in highly publicized criminal cases and we do not see how Mr. Agnew's trial—if it ever comes to that—would be all that much more vulnerable to prejudicial pre-trial publicity, especially since the publicity has clearly cut both ways.

At the most, his assertions, if supported by the facts, might indicate that other prosecutors or another special prosecutor should be named to handle his case.

And that is the heart of the matter. Mr. Agnew's grievance is with the Department of Justice and not—as he himself has acknowledged—with the press. The press is peripheral to his argument. Attorney General Elliot L. Richardson has conducted an investigation into the leaks alleged to have come from his department. Mr. Agnew's lawyers can—as they may well have already done—subpoena the Attorney General and any officials working for him, including the FBI agents who have questioned federal prosecutors. It is hard to believe that Mr. Agnew's highly skilled defense team, building upon the information already developed within the department, cannot ferret out the information they need by means of interrogations conducted under oath.

To go beyond that by asking reporters to reveal the names of sources who gave information under a pledge of confidentiality is to jeopardize an extraordinarily important constitutional principle by use of a legal ploy that is not only premature but probably marginal in the case at hand. The First Amendment right of freedom of the press is not a right flowing to newsmen individually or collectively. It is, rather, grounded on the founding fathers' belief that only a people free to receive the greatest possible flow of information could govern themselves wisely. Thus, the right put into jeopardy here is the reader's right or the viewer's right to receive as much information as newsmen—by the exercise of their best judgment rather than that of some governmental instrumentality—can conscientiously gather and responsibly present to them.

The Agnew case illustrates the point. The professional obligation of the press is to question the veracity and probable accuracy of the information their sources have revealed. And a further mission of the press is to provide the public with as much information as possible about the fitness of elected officers to conduct the people's business; this is fundamental to public participation in the democratic process.

The ability to assure confidentiality to sources is vitally important to this mission. That ability was severely jeopardized in *Branzburg v. Hayes*, in which the Supreme Court decided that pledges of secrecy made by reporters did not outweigh the obligation to respond to a grand jury subpoena and to answer questions in a criminal investigation. If the press' ability to guarantee confidentiality is limited even more, the capacity to inform the public will be severely, if not irreparably, impaired.

This newspaper has long believed that the words of the First Amendment were sufficient unto themselves and that judicial or legislative efforts to define or codify these freedoms in precise and detailed terms are potentially damaging to the freest possible flow of information to the public. For years prior to the Branzburg decision, informal accommodations which served the interests of justice and preserved the principle of freedom of the press were possible. With the Branzburg decision on the books, each new situation presents yet another threat to the free functioning of the press. Lawyers like to say that hard cases make bad law. It can likewise be said that incautious challenges to broad constitutional principles can lead, not to greater clarity and precision, but to bad constitutional precedents—to the progressive erosion, in short, of fundamental rights which, by their very sweep and breadth, have served us well for almost two centuries.

The New York Times

New York, N.Y., October 11, 1973

The drama of Spiro Agnew has reached its appointed end. For him, the sad dénouement in a Baltimore courtroom concluded his sudden, steep descent from occupant of the second highest constitutional office to convicted criminal—a descent that began two months ago with the official warning from a Federal prosecutor that he was under investigation on grave charges.

For the public, his personal tragedy is part of the larger tragedy of the Nixon Administration. Overwhelmingly re-elected less than a year ago, the Administration is almost daily beset by fresh scandal. And the public can only look on in mingled shame and dismay.

The deal Mr. Agnew made with Attorney General Richardson to avoid full prosecution by pleading "no contest" to a single charge of income-tax evasion obviously made it beneficial for him to resign the Vice-Presidency instead of adhering to the aggressive battle plan he has followed in recent weeks. If he had clung to office through indictment, trial and possible protracted legal appeals, an intolerable shadow would have fallen across not only his own office but also the Presidency to which he might at any time have been called.

From the outset of his case, it has been imperative that all the facts be brought out and nothing hushed up. It has also been essential that the case be disposed of in reasonably swift fashion without compromising Mr. Agnew's rights or endangering the public interest. Both of these imperatives have been met by the settlement announced yesterday. Although it is beyond question that if Mr. Agnew were a private citizen, he would have been dealt with much more harshly, it is also true that for a public official who rose so high, disgrace and banishment from public life are severe punishment indeed.

Mr. Agnew's downfall spares the nation the danger that he might have become President, a strong political possibility if his corrupt dealings had not become known. Yet the unblinkable fact is that, even when Mr. Nixon chose him as his running-mate five years ago, he was plainly unqualified by the fundamental criteria of experience, character and demonstrated competence to be placed in immediate line of succession to the Presidency.

President Nixon bears a heavy moral responsibility for that choice. In the atomic age, the nation simply cannot afford a Vice President selected for the frivolous, selfish reason that he was a political cipher who offended no faction or interest group. When it turns out that the man chosen was lacking in probity as well, an undeserved honor is converted into a personal tragedy, and the nation becomes aware that it has been running a terrible risk these last five years.

Important though it is, the Agnew story is only one episode in the larger drama of the Nixon Administration. The President's own income-tax returns are the subject of dispute. Grave accusations of criminal misconduct by the President's former legal counsel remain unresolved. Indictments may soon be forthcoming against some of the President's closest former aides, while two of his former Cabinet members are about to go to trial on criminal charges. The courts have yet to make their final ruling on the President's desire to withhold from the grand jury the tapes of conversations dealing with many disputed points in the Watergate criminal conspiracy.

Mr. Agnew's resignation goes only part way toward resolving the crisis in national leadership. President Nixon has much to do if confidence in that leadership is to be restored.

© 1973 by The New York Times Company Reprinted by permission

THE DENVER POST

Denver, Colo., October 11, 1973

Spiro T. Agnew has served the public interest by his decision to resign Wednesday as vice president of the United States.

By leaving office and entering a plea of no contest to a charge of income tax evasion in 1967, he has brought about, as he said, a "swift disposition" of a matter that has troubled him and the nation for several months, and he has spared the American people the continuing agony and embarrassment of having in the second highest office of the United States a man who has broken the law and acted improperly in the carrying out of a public trust.

Agnew made this admission in a Maryland courtroom Wednesday:

"I admit that I did receive payments during the year 1967 which were not expended for political purposes, and that, therefore, these payments were income taxable to me in that year and that I so knew. I further acknowledge that contracts were awarded by state agencies in 1967 and other years to those who made payments, and that I was aware of such awards."

Atty. Gen. Elliot L. Richardson has put the matter in stronger terms. He said evidence obtained from several former associates of Agnew in Maryland "established a pattern of substantial cash payments" to Agnew, not only while he was governor of Maryland but continuing as late as December, 1972, while he was vice president of the United States.

Richardson said the government was ready to press for a bribery indictment against Agnew, but "to have done so would have been likely to inflict upon the nation serious and permanent scars."

While Agnew has said he is innocent of illegal acts, apart from income tax evasion, the other charges against him will not now be adjudicated.

The office of vice president now stands empty. The most pressing business of the nation is to fill it calmly and expeditiously with a person who could, hopefully, act as a unifying force in an era of discontent, and one who is unquestionably of the stature to serve as President if need be.

This country is in no mood for another partisan, divisive or obscure vice president. What it needs is a person acceptable to the Congress and a person who is respected by Americans who disagree with him. He should be a man of commanding public stature and background. The nation is tired of having to discover who the Eagletons and Agnews are, and then to be discouraged by flaws in their backgrounds.

We have no doubt that President Nixon can find such a person within the ranks of the Republican Party, where he is most likely to look, and that the Democrats who control Congress will be willing to approve him promptly.

The Charleston Gazette
Charleston, W.Va.
October 11, 1973

A sorry chronicle of immorality, deceit, and hypocrisy came to an inconclusive end Wednesday afternoon when the Vice President of the United States, exposed as a common criminal, left his office in disgrace.

►The nation's foremost champion of "law and order" offered no defense to a charge of income tax evasion.

►The nation's best known critic of "soft" judges gratefully acccepted a token sentence from a lenient court, obviously glad to concur in the kind of legal deal that would lessen the chances of prosecution on other charges.

It is difficult to contain surging contempt when one views Spiro Agnew's crushing humiliation. It is difficult because Spiro Agnew, since 1968, has had the damnable effrontery to instruct the United States on morality.

During his tenure, hardly a month has gone by without an Agnew lecture to the press, which, as it turned out, he had good reason to fear; an Agnew lecture to critics of the government, from whom he imperiously withheld constitutional guarantees; an Agnew lecture to the courts, which he held to be enemies of the state.

This man, who now must walk among the Americans he has hypocritically chastised, merits no compassion except for the circumstance that he played only a single role in a drama of corruption being played out in Washington.

Agnew willingly played the role of administration hatchet man, appealing to fascist mentalities and rousing the frightened and insecure to rebellion against the principles that distinguish democratic America from the totalitarian states.

Agnew's role, although well-defined, wasn't a leading role. We have seen more prominent players stride arrogantly across the stage in this incredible administration of Richard M. Nixon. Who knows what petty vices are hidden beneath their Agnewian bluster?

While more than half the governed mistrust the government, it isn't an unlikely prediction that before this infamous era has run its course there will be events as startling as Agnew's collapse—perhaps more so.

Democrat and Chronicle

Rochester, N.Y., October 11, 1973
It's better this way.

Tragic and shocking event though it is, the resignation of Spiro T. Agnew from the Vice Presidency puts an end to an ugly mess that was placing heavy strains on the nation.

And there would have been worse to come. In Agnew's own words, there could have been no resolution of the conflict "without a long, divisive and deliberating struggle."

Attorney General Elliot Richardson has said that the resignation should be perceived as a "just and honorable" decision. So it was, and so it will probably be received. Americans are not a vindictive people.

But it can also be seen now as an inevitable decision for Agnew, the tide was unstemmable. His reputation was gone and public esteem low. And it's now been confirmed that he had been involved in the past in wrong-doing.

Even a man who was never a quitter could not take that kind of knowledge into battle with him and have much real chance of coming out on top.

Agnew's plea of no contest to a charge of federal income tax evasion was, in the judge's opinion, tantamount to an admission of guilt.

Agnew has denied that the unreported payments received from contractors while he was Maryland governor affected his official actions, and has said further: "My acceptance of contributions was part of a long-established pattern of political fund raising in the state."

Agnew apparently did nothing more than others had done before him. But that didn't make the practice right even in those days. And what may have been considered normal behavior then is no longer acceptable in the wake of Watergate and heightened public demands for greater political morality.

If anything good can come out of this unhappy affair, it may be a much greater sensitivity, among politicians and public alike, to the need for integrity in the conduct of the public's affairs. The nation is tired of graft and dirty tricks.

And it is of course crucially important that the man who is chosen to follow Agnew be above all suspicions. America needs nothing so much as a shiny new knight. One man that the President will certainly want to consider is former Secretary of State William P. Rogers. The next Vice President must be first and foremost a person of unstained reputation.

The Sun Reporter

San Francisco, Calif., October 13, 1973
While the full terms of the negotiated deal achieved between the U. S. Department of Justice and former Vice President Spiro Agnew are not fully known, we find the punishment of resignation as fine for income tax evasion, with the promise of no further prosecution, another example which violates the concept that we are a nation of laws and not men.
Spiro Agnew began as a ward dealing politician who used his opportunities for political advancement to one heartbeat away from the most powerful politician position in the world. Along the way, he violated the nation's laws and used his high political position to ride herd on some of the nation's most honored principles: freedom of the press, the right to peacefully assemble, and, above, all, the concept of law and order without justice. He ignored the first dictum of politics: that Caesar's wife must be above reproach.
We have insisted that no individual in America is guilty until the verdict has been rendered in the court of law by a jury of his peers. Moreover, we do not believe that the president or the Vice President are men who are placed above the law. We cannot agree that Agnew's resignation from the Vice Presidency and his plea of nolo contendere, with the $10,000 fine and three years probation, equates itself on the scale of justice with penalties that have been levied against others who without fame or position, dare to cheat Uncle Sam and the Internal Revenue Service. If men in high places pay so little as a result of crimes against the state, how can we justify long prison terms for lesser mortals not provided with a position of trust from which to steal and rob the people?

The Charlotte Observer

Charlotte, N.C., October 12, 1973

The disgrace and fall of Spiro T. Agnew as vice president of the United States delivers yet another profound shock to the American political system. The second-ranking officer of the land, a man put forward by his President and his party as a righteous advocate of law, order and decency, is revealed to be personally corrupt. He is forced to plead no contest to a charge of income tax evasion in order to escape a certain prison term for even shabbier crimes.

It is enough to disillusion American voters, who have been disillusioned only too often in recent elections. The John Kennedy "Camelot" turns out to have been a land of mere mortals and grave compromises. The Lyndon Johnson campaign for peace was actually a declaration of war. The Richard Nixon pledge to "bring us together" has torn us apart and left us with a snarl of moral and legal issues known simply as "Watergate."

The hypocrisy of the country's overblown politics, in which appearance means more than substance, has caught up with us. It is an hypocrisy made worse by 20th century communications and advertising methods, in which symbols and images mean more than reality and dimension. The people are regarded as children who must be protected from the truth and spared the hard facts necessary to make intelligent decisions.

Hypocrisy's Toll

Even before the Agnew case reached crisis proportions, the hypocrisy was beginning to take its toll. Men of conscience in American political life, aroused by Watergate and its disgusting picture of what politics has become, announced they were washing their hands of it. Sen. Harold Hughes of Iowa has announced his retirement. Sen. William Saxbe of Ohio has announced his. Sen. Marlowe Cook of Kentucky is said to be on the brink of an announcement. In their private conversations, local and state political figures are expressing the same disgust.

Yet, so ingrained is the habit, the sham continues even in the wake of Agnew's exposure and resignation. Asked for their reactions, senators, congressmen, national and state political leaders dissemble before the cameras. They express sorrow for the fallen vice president's personal tragedy rather than outrage over his betrayal of the people's trust.

And at the White House, where Agnew's capitulation is a supreme embarrassment, President Nixon lights the stage for another distracting round of the politics of appearance. Limousines come and go in the night, bearing key advisors and political figures the President is said to be consulting. Congressmen and senators are asked to submit names of possible successors; governors are polled over the telephone.

More Theatrics

But the President has known since before July that his vice president was under serious investigation and since late summer that the investigation was building toward a crisis. He was kept abreast of the findings and participated in decisions regarding the plea bargaining, knowing full well what that would mean. Obviously, he has been deliberating over his choice of a new vice president for weeks; today's theatrics are simply a distraction aimed at lifting the sagging confidence of the American people.

The people have had too many distractions. If the President has a firm choice (and by now he probably has) he should bring him on for public examination, without the effort to pre-condition the people's response. It is reminiscent of President Johnson's coy indecision over whether to make Hubert Humphrey his running mate during the 1964 Democratic Convention.

The Choice In '68

The nation got into this situation because Mr. Nixon played to appearances in choosing Agnew as his running mate in 1968 and stubbornly stayed with him in 1972, when prudence suggested making another choice. He did not look for a man of stature and substance. He chose a man who would project the desired image: a suburbanite to appeal to the growing suburban constituency, a man reputed to be tough on dissenters and street demonstrators, a man knowledgeable in local (but not national) affairs, a man of ethnic appeal.

Elevated overnight to national prominence, Mr. Agnew gratefully carried out whatever dubious tasks the President found for him, though some of them demeaned him and his high public office.

In choosing his successor, Mr. Nixon will do the nation added disservice if his choice again is dictated by appearance rather than honesty and national need. The next vice president must be a man capable of governing in a nation and world rushing toward profound change. He must not be another of the President's political guided missiles.

Among the men said to be foremost in the President's favor are several who, at cursory glance, seem to be less than the national trust requires. Would John Connally restore confidence by dealing directly and candidly with the American people and the nation's problems? Would Gov. Nelson Rockefeller, whose political views are said to be undergoing basic change? Would Ronald Reagan?

No Caretaker

There are many political figures of conscience and honor available to the President, experienced men capable of standing up to the challenges of the nation and the world They need not be instantly recognizable to the electorate; they must be able to prove themselves under the glare of the congressional scrutiny that is ahead. We hope the President will look to such a person.

The Congress will play a major role in the outcome. The Senate and the House each must approve the President's nominee by majority vote. There is talk among Democrats of demanding a caretaker who will not seek the presidency in 1976. That talk should be disregarded. When the Congress wrote the succession amendment in 1965, it pledged that partisan considerations would not bear on the confirmation decision. That pledge should be honored today. The nation needs a man capable of leading. The President and the Congress must work to nominate and confirm him.

The Salt Lake Tribune
Salt Lake City, Utah, October 12, 1973

There is no minimizing the severe jolt suffered by this country with the sudden conviction and resignation of its vice president. The proper course is to somehow learn from and eventually rise above these awful events.

Foremost, President Nixon and congressional leaders must complete naming of Mr. Agnew's successor as swiftly as it is possible to find someone qualified and acceptable. Mr. Nixon has made an excellent start in this direction, immediately involving spokesmen from both houses of Congress in the nominating process. The worst development at this point would be a prolonged political clash over who should fill the vacancy.

Next, the nation might as well face the fact that it had a discreditable vice president for more than four years. At the very time he was loudly lecturing others for what he considered their unethical, disgraceful or disloyal behavior, Mr. Agnew, his court statement confirms, had accepted money on which he failed to declare federal income taxes. More than that, the manner of the court settlement entitles anyone to conclude that Mr. Agnew, while a Baltimore official and later Maryland governor, extorted kickbacks, among the lowest forms of government corruption.

His staunch denial of wrongdoing and outraged vow to achieve vindication, in the shadow of his agreement not to fight the felony tax charges, further destroys his credibility. He has dishonored the office of U.S. vice president. It was appropriate that he resign.

And it was fitting that he be allowed to step down with what appears a relatively light sentence. His plea was obviously bargained for by a Justice Department that was prepared to prosecute with strong evidence. But the case could have lasted months if the vice president, as was his right, decided to endure a trial. Then, the country and its central government would have suffered a lingering crisis, at a time when foreign and domestic affairs require, instead, public confidence and unity of purpose.

The President may, however, find it difficult to rally public support. Seldom has an administration been so thoroughly shaken. Two former cabinet members—John Mitchell and Maurice Stans—are still under indictment for perjury before a grand jury and it hardly seems necessary to list the White House resignations that accompanied Watergate disclosures. Mr. Nixon's ability for selecting advisers and administrators is, at this point, increasingly questioned.

Yet, in its historic context, the country's current embarrassment need not be fatal. Americans have demonstrated an extraordinary capacity for surviving deep divisions and political disaster with both their system of government and the principles that strengthen it substantially intact.

If a few office-holders, even at the highest levels, become ensnared in scandal, are all politicians crooked? We doubt it. And if the public generally accepts that rationalization, then the country is indeed in great peril.

There may be something in the electoral process that distorts an honest man's values or attracts a venal one's attention. But the answer is finding it and rooting it out, not tolerating it. The system and the principled people who serve it were responsible for uncovering the truth, unpleasant though it may be, and forcing Mr. Agnew to face his ultimate obligation to the American public. These strengths and such faith in ideals need stressing as Americans assess the future.

Mr. Agnew has lost his prestige as well as his office. His political career, once so bright, is a smoking ruin. His place in history will be heaped with reprehension. A term in federal prison could hardly add much more as punishment. Especially since to impose it would have required a long courtroom agony the country needs now to avoid.

Mr. Nixon and Congress must settle on a vice presidential replacement without awkward delay. American voters must pay closer attention to standards and methods for filling elective office. This has been a disillusioning period in U.S. political life, but it needn't be a dispairing one.

Anchorage Daily Times
Anchorage, Alaska, October 11, 1973

THE RESIGNATION of Spiro Agnew as vice president of the United States was a stunning event.

But it was one that the Republic will survive and perhaps that thought should be uppermost in the minds of all today as the choice of an appointed successor is awaited.

That the resignation is a shattering personal tragedy for Mr. Agnew and his family goes without saying. It would be so for any man, of high station or low.

In a sense, too, it is a political tragedy for the nation. For regardless of one's feelings for or against Mr. Agnew—and he prompted passions both ways—he was a man who had to be regarded as a future presidential possibility, until his sudden downfall began.

FOR A NATION of 200 million people, the United States has precious few men who stand near the top of the political pinnacle. Spiro Agnew, as vice president, was as close as a man could be to the very summit.

Now, of course, there is one less man who can be considered in line for the highest office in the land. Mr. Agnew has not simply been bumped aside, perhaps later to shoulder his way back to the forefront. He has been eliminated, eradicated, obliterated.

The easy thing to do, of course, is to say that he brought this upon himself by past actions which, from all anyone can judge at this distance, were truly illegal and deserving of punishment.

But it's human, too, to sympathize with the man, as one would do with any other human being whose life has collapsed in ruins.

TO A GREAT degree, however, Mr. Agnew's resignation, his sentencing by the court, and his ouster from public life—while unique in American politics—is largely a personal tragedy for the man and his family.

The government will go on. The Republican party smeared with another blemish in this year of the Watergate, will stagger but not fall. The Democratic party, while condemning the sin, is not likely to further assault the sinner.

Presidential politics—and the unknown future of the battle over the Nixon tapes—will go on, heading for the next campaign in 1976.

The question now becomes this: Will the man chosen for appointment to the vice presidency automatically loom as heir apparent to the Republican nomination in '76? If so, will the House and the Senate confirm him?

The Virginian-Pilot
Norfolk, Va., October 12, 1973

If there is any consolation in the ruin of ex-Vice President Spiro T. Agnew, it is the restoring of confidence in the Department of Justice.

Attorney General Elliot Richardson made the point yesterday in the course of an hour-long press conference in which he answered as best he could every question on the Department of Justice's role in the Agnew case. But perhaps the point should be made in blunter style — that is, in the Agnew case the fix did not go in.

It is necessary to say so in the wake of Watergate, when the cover-up reached right into the White House. For the good name of the Department of Justice was one of the casualties of the scandal, together with the good names of the Federal Bureau of Investigation and the Secret Service, which were also suborned to the greater glory of Mr. Nixon's re-election.

An Administration that prided itself upon its concern for "law 'n' order" has now seen the forced resignation of the Vice President, two Attorneys General of the United States, the acting director of the FBI, the two most trusted aides to the President, and a host of lesser officials in positions of power and trust. With the fall of the Vice President, who was free from the taint of Watergate, the Administration's disgrace is nearly total. Both Mr. Agnew and ex-Attorney General John Mitchell, who were the chief champions and symbols of the crusade for "law 'n' order," are now revealed to have been hypocritical, or worse. Mr. Nixon personally is not yet free of the shadow — and the threat — of Watergate. If the Supreme Court orders the President to surrender the famous secret tapes and he refuses, Mr. Nixon will be asking to be impeached. His authority is not enhanced by the ruin of the Vice President.

As for Mr. Agnew, few will want to defend him once the weight of the 40-page statement of evidence that was entered into the court record on Wednesday is generally understood. The document is a damning indictment of the ex-Vice President. Mr. Agnew entered into an arrangement whereby he regularly received 50 per cent of kickbacks from engineering fees on public work while he was Governor of Maryland. (The original proposal was to split the take three ways, but Mr. Agnew demanded half of the proceeds.) He accepted payoffs regularly from two other large engineering firms while he was Governor and after he became Vice President. He not only continued to accept money as recently as December of last year, he actively solicited the illicit payoffs. While he was serving as Vice President, he accepted cash payments in envelopes left on his desk, like any corrupt ward-heeler in local politics (which is just how and where he got his start).

In short, Mr. Agnew was a crook — a chiseler and a grafter, by habit and by instinct. If those are hard words, the evidence supports them. By copping a plea to evasion of Federal income taxes, Mr. Agnew kept out of jail, which now seems to be all that his lawyers wanted. But he is liable to a civil claim for back taxes on the kickbacks and payoffs that went unreported — and the amount appears to be in six figures. In the interests of justice the Internal Revenue Service must prosecute the claim vigorously.

CHICAGO DAILY NEWS
Chicago, Ill., October 11, 1973

All the boldness, the self-righteousness, the b r a v u r a of Spiro Agnew dissolved in a split-second on Wednesday as he resigned the vice presidency and then pleaded no contest to a charge of income tax evasion. But even in that moment of his personal ignominy, the paramount issue was not Agnew, but the nation. In a year of anguish and confusion, this was the lowest hour. The nation had lost its second-highest elective officer and the symbolic team at the top of the administration had fallen apart. Unless President Nixon can now rise above the political maelstrom and propose a man of unchallengeable honor and prestige and integrity, things will move from bad to worse.

That is the first and foremost job. There will be many men eager to do the honors. The vice presidency, in a term when the President cannot succeed himself, is a natural springboard to the Presidency. But the nation at this moment can hardly concern itself with events three years off — and neither in conscience can the President. The nation is in trouble, a malaise not less ominous because it is a sickness of the spirit. Unless confidence in leadership can be restored promptly, the trouble will worsen at home and abroad.

As to Agnew, several things need to be said, and the first is that, whatever may be chalked up on the credit side, he has let his country down in a manner few men have managed who have enjoyed such honor and acclaim.

In 1967, the year before he became Mr. Nixon's running mate for the vice presidency, the crime took place to which Agnew has now pleaded no contest (which Federal Judge Walter E. Hoffman promptly branded as the equivalent of guilty) and for which he was sentenced to three years' probation and a fine of $10,000.

The evidence presented to the court detailed payoffs to Agnew continuing into his vice presidential term and only ending in 1972.

Throughout that period Agnew maintained his stance as the exemplar and the voice of patriotic virtue. In particular he excoriated the communications media, doing his level best to convey the idea that his opponents in the press were corrupt and disloyal for presuming to challenge the views that he espoused.

Give him one thing: He played the role as expertly as any old Shakespearean stager who ever trod the boards. Millions of Americans believed him and trusted him. We can testify to this: We have been on the receiving end of hundreds of letters and phone calls demanding that we cease our vilification of Spiro Agnew and confess our error.

There is a lesson in this somewhere, and it is not that the press is infallible. It is that there is often a difference between what a man seems and what he is, and one assigned job of the press is to keep probing and testing and refusing to be put off by anybody, of whatever rank.

This nation will survive this jolt, as it has been surviving a year of shocks and setbacks. As Mr. Nixon himself said the other day, it would take a real genius to knock the U.S.A. off its foundations. But it does seem that in these past several months a lot of people have been trying, and we can hope that a bruised and buffeted nation will now be able to pick itself up, and with a little help from its leadership move out of the valley and on toward a happier destiny.

The News and Courier
Charleston, S.C., October 12, 1973

Shock, surprise and sorrow are the terms describing public response to the resignation of Vice President Spiro T. Agnew, sentiments which The News and Courier shares. Mr. Agnew's plea of no contest to charges of income tax evasion, and acceptance of a $10,000 fine and probation, amount to admission of guilt to avoid trial and possible conviction of broader charges of corruption before he came to Washington from public office in Maryland.

In a sense Mr. Agnew is the most prominent victim to date of a "new morality" in American politics. The Watergate scandal, which apparently had not touched Mr. Agnew, has sharpened public concern over campaign finances and other practices. In this field the press and other media of public information have adopted an aggressive role that Mr. Agnew had been especially vocal in denouncing. His personal fall from grace is all the more poignant on account of his previous stress on "law and order."

In defense of Mr. Agnew — if it is indeed a defense — is the old, loose standard of political ethics in American politics, said to be especially applicable to the State of Maryland. Payment for political favors is nothing new in the history of our country, or any other country of our acquaintance. The lines of personal integrity become blurred in political practices that have achieved a degree of acceptance either because they were not generally known or because they were ignored as "part of the game." Other qualities — such as courage, tenacity, popularity and the ability to "get things done" — have been important elements in political success, as in other fields.

Spiro Agnew had the misfortune to be exposed at "this point in time," to employ the Watergate cliche, when corruption is in the headlines. The same trend that brought his downfall has been working against President Nixon. Demands for Mr. Nixon's resignation or impeachment no doubt will continue even as he seeks a successor to Mr. Agnew as the stand-in for the President.

For the first time under the 25th Amendment, the President will be invoking the newly established power to name a possible successor without the formality of a popular election. His choice must be confirmed by Congress. Both the President and the Congress have a solemn duty to choose well, not only for the remainder of Mr. Nixon's term but for whatever may be the effect on the 1976 election.

Whether the next Vice President will or should be a contender for President already is the subject of argument. If the man or woman is to be judged fit for the top office in 1973, we see no reason why he or she should be barred for consideration in 1976 and thereafter.

In any event, we view the turn of events in the executive offices of our country with compassion as well as concern. The seats of the mighty are occupied now, as always, by human beings. They have faults as well as virtues common to all men. The qualities of leadership cannot include perfection, much as we may yearn for it. The future of this country, and of the world, depends on more than one person or group of persons in public life.

In a Republic, nobody is unexpendable. If Spiro Agnew's departure helps to improve the standard of government and the public's understanding of politics, it will serve a useful purpose in an unprecedented manner.

The Toronto Star
Toronto, Ont., October 11, 1973

The resignation of vice-president Spiro Agnew over a criminal charge to which he, in effect, has pleaded guilty, deals another staggering blow to American and international confidence in the Nixon administration.

The irony of that administration's law-and-order gospeller falling afoul of the law himself, and bargaining on his plea to escape punishment for worse offences, will escape nobody.

But the personal fate of Spiro Agnew is an insignificant thing compared to the further shock it has dealt to a government still reeling from the earthquake of Watergate.

The United States is still the most influential country in the world and when it has a government that cannot conduct its affairs competently, the whole world suffers.

The international monetary system is drifting dangerously, largely because of lack of U.S. leadership. This has not yet damaged trade, but it could do so, and undermine prosperity all over the world.

The Middle East war shows how fragile is the detente between the superpowers. The Soviet Union is re-supplying Egypt and Syria with weapons as the fighting goes on, and is egging on other Arab states to attack Israel. The United States is re-supplying the Israelis, and few people doubt that it would feel obliged to intervene militarily if Israel seemed about to go under—in which case the Soviets might easily be drawn in too. The U.S. needs a government that can work undistractedly at stopping the fighting and building a secure peace in the Middle East; otherwise the structure of world peace may collapse.

The looming scarcities of energy concern not just the U.S., but the whole Western world, and the problem will become manageable only if the American government faces up to it resolutely.

Instead of American leadership in these vital matters, there is a U.S. government nearly paralyzed by scandals.

How can confidence in the government, and its capacity for decision-making, be restored?

The obvious first step is to replace Agnew with an eminent, statesmanlike person whose honesty and integrity are credited by all. In the choice of a successor, the president proposes and the Congress disposes, a simple majority of both Houses being required for confirmation. The Democratic majorities in Congress will do their nation and the world a disservice if—as some reports suggest—they insist on a nonentity in order to avoid building up a strong Republican candidate for the presidency in 1976.

But it is doubtful whether the choice of the most ideal vice-president, overwhelmingly endorsed by Congress, could repair the ruined prestige of the Nixon administration. The Agnew fiasco puts another black mark on the president's record, for this is the man he chose and then re-chose to be his trusted deputy. Agnew, together with all the other discredited and departed high officers of the Nixon regime, impeaches the president's judgment if not his integrity. Can confidence be restored unless he also goes?

WINSTON-SALEM JOURNAL
Winston-Salem, N.C., October 12, 1973

What is there to say about Spiro Agnew now that the first shock is over?

Let us start with the good. Agnew's assaults on the news media were the best thing that has happened to the American press in this century.

Editors and publishers tend to be as smug about their craft as doctors, lawyers and morticians. Agnew shook them — the best of them, that is, — out of their complacency. Wherever newspaper people met — at their state and national conventions, in the seminars that now are held regularly on many campuses — they began to give themselves the kind of critical appraisal they had previously reserved for other crafts and professions. The professional publications, too, were enlivened by articles of self-examination and self-flagellation.

This healthy process continues, and all of us who have printer's ink in our hearts and veins must be grateful to Agnew for starting it.

And there is another reason for gratitude. In an administration made up almost entirely of card-carrying pallbearers, the vice president provided a touch of color and an occasional burst of excitement. Reporters and editors will forgive a public man almost anything if he gives them color for their copy; and in the Nixon mortuary, he was about all the press had to work with.

So much for the good. If we now turn to some less praiseworthy aspects of the Agnew career, it is not to kick a man who is down but to raise some questions about the Americans who cheered him while he was up.

What did so many Americans see to admire in a man whose character is now so starkly revealed.

In his forays north and south, east and west, Agnew established himself as the undisputed light-heavyweight champion of the upper dog. No man in the land was his equal in smiting the afflicted and comforting the comfortable. Wherever he went, upper dogs and fat cats paid $100, $500, $1,000 a plate to see their Spiro trample on welfare mothers, poverty workers, the young lawyers trying to help the urban poor, the fathers, mothers- and young people who thought that the Vietnam war was something less sublime than the quest of the Holy Grail.

Why?

There are certain kinds of people — insecure people — who love a bully and who will applaud his bullying. But we never thought America was teeming with people like that.

Americans in the past have given their warmest admiration to men of heart and vision. But here they were idolizing a man who, it must be said, had the heart of a pawnbroker and the vision of a proctologist.

It was never a secret that Spiro Agnew was the all-time Olympic freeloading champion. Even at the height of his recent trouble, with the spotlight on him, he could not resist freeloading off the likes of Frank Sinatra, so help us!

Yet millions of Americans hoped that he might be our next president. What a glorious concept of the presidency these people must have had!

And if we must wonder about their taste, what can we think of the leader who gave us Spiro Agnew not once but twice?

The American people put down Sen. George McGovern as a fool for picking a running mate with a flawed medical record. So what does that make President Nixon?

It was not that the President didn't have better advice. One day, well before the time to choose a running mate for 1972, he asked the late Dean Acheson what he should do about Agnew.

Acheson was used to being consulted on foreign policy, and he was probably surprised by the question. He rather liked Agnew — he found the vice president a refreshing contrast to most of the nonentities in the Nixon entourage. But after a moment's reflection he replied:

"I'd say you should bench Agnew — but not on the Supreme Court."

It was sound advice. And if it had been taken, how much pain and shame would have been spared the President, the nation and Spiro Agnew himself!

DAILY NEWS
New York, N.Y., October 11, 1973

The meteoric political career of Spiro T. Agnew has come to a shocking and tragic end.

Agnew resigned as Vice President yesterday, then went into a federal courtroom in Baltimore to enter a plea of no contest to one count of income tax evasion.

Spiro T. Agnew

There is no way to soften or prettify Agnew's case. He acted illegally, and what he did cannot be excused or condoned. The law is the law and all must live by it, be they powerful or obscure, rich or poor.

In his statement to the court, Agnew said he had decided against a protracted legal battle that would inevitably have distracted the public's attention from "important national problems." It was the proper decision, but one that came rather late in the day.

How swiftly the nation recovers from this latest shock will be determined largely by President Richard M. Nixon and the Congress. Under the Constitution, the President has the responsibility of nominating a new Vice President, who must be confirmed by a majority of the House and Senate.

We hope that both will measure up to the challenge at hand, rising above narrow political considerations so as to serve the interests of the nation.

The U.S., already awash in crises at home and abroad, can ill afford either a constitutional stalemate or an ugly partisan brawl.

The Topeka Daily Capital
Topeka, Kans., October 12, 1973

Vice President Spiro T. Agnew declared loudly and often that he was innocent of charges of political corruption. By his own admission, he was guilty.

On national television, he said stories reporting he had received kickbacks were "damned lies." It now is clear that Agnew characterized himself.

To his public, because he seemed untouched by Watergate and because of his lip service to law and order, he epitomized Mr. Clean. He was not clean. His hands were soiled by kickbacks paid to him, some even delivered to him in his White House office.

How the law would have treated any other citizen found to have been a participant in shakedowns over a 10-year period that involved hundreds of thousands of dollars can hardly be compared with what it administered to Agnew.

By plea-bargaining, he was able to obtain freedom from further investigation and prosecution simply by pleading no contest to one count of income tax evasion, a felony, in 1967. Part of the deal was that he must resign the vice presidency, pay a $10,000 fine and remain under probation for three years.

Atty. Gen. Elliot Richardson said he considered the resignation penalty enough without imprisonment for any period of time. That is his opinion. What the deal demonstrates most is the use of plea bargaining to extricate the second highest government official from the tangling tentacles of the law he swore to uphold.

Agnew had denied he had indulged in plea bargaining. He became serious when the legal noose tightened.

Perhaps Agnew's resignation should have been expected. he was not receiving backing from President Nixon, he had been denied an independent investigation by the House of Representatives, and a federal judge had refused to halt the grand jury investigation of him.

Then, too, there was a change in the tenor of Agnew's oratory. In a West Coast speech, he delivered a fighting defense that brought his followers to their feet, cheering. He was expected to continue his public defense effort in Chicago. Instead, he spoke only kind words about President Nixon.

Probably the reason President Nixon maintained so discrete a silence on Agnew was that he had all the information available to the Justice Dept. plus whatever Agnew chose to tell him in their face - to - face meetings.

This also could explain some of the backstage maneuvering that has been underway regarding the possible nomination of a new vice president. Those with inside information were aware that Agnew was about to resign, or that the case against him was of sufficient gravity to open impeachment proceedings.

But now that the resignation is an accomplished fact, the appointment of a vice president under terms of the new, and still unused, 25th Amendment to the U.S. Constitution is drawing the attention of Republican leaders over the nation as well as in Congress.

Under the 25th Amendment, President Nixon will nominate a vice presidential candidate. Before the appointment becomes official, it must be approved by majorities in the House and the Senate. Because the vice presidential nominee could later become the heir apparent to the presidency, and since both houses are controlled by Democratic majorities, the vice presidential nomination will be eyed most carefully from a political standpoint in addition to all others.

President Nixon has said he will nominate a new vice president within a week, and when he does, the spotlight will be turned away from sordid details of the Agnew case.

But before it does, there will be many second thoughts among future presidential aspirants as to how closely they will scrutinize their vice presidential choices at national conventions.

In retrospect it appears that Sen. Tom Eagleton of Missouri was spotless compared with Agnew. One day, conventions may decide to put aside their rubber stamps, flex their muscles and do their own picking of vice presidential nominees.

The best that can be said for Agnew is that he resigned when he sought to match his political fame with fortune through kickbacks — and got caught.

The worst is that he knowingly and wantonly dragged the nation's second highest public office through the muck and mire of political corruption. He failed a public trust.

SEGRETTI TESTIFIES; SIRICA'S TAPES RULING UPHELD

The Senate Watergate committee heard testimony Oct. 3 from Donald H. Segretti on the "dirty tricks" he played on Democratic candidates seeking the presidential nomination in 1972. Segretti appeared at the televised public hearing under a court grant of limited immunity from prosecution. Segretti, 32, had pleaded guilty Oct. 1 to three charges of conspiracy and illegal campaign activities, the case being handled by the special federal Watergate prosecution. Segretti, a lawyer, told the committee he had been recruited by and reported to a White House aide, Dwight L. Chapin, Nixon's appointments secretary until January when he resigned. He said he was told his work was secretive and was not to be traced to the White House.

Looking back, Segretti said he realized his activities were wrong and regretted any harm caused by them. He apologized for one "scurrilous letter" he faked accusing two Democratic candidates of sexual misconduct.

On Oct. 4 Martin Kelly, 24, and Robert M. Benz, 24, testified on their efforts to disrupt the Democrats in 1972. Both men said they had been hired by Segretti. Benz said he committed the political sabotage and espionage to give the Democrats "a little bit of a dose of their own type of activities."

Frank Mankiewicz, national political director of the McGovern campaign, testified Oct. 11 that the Republican "dirty tricks" in the 1972 campaign were successful in causing discord among the Democratic candidates and that this quite possibly changed the course of the campaign. He said the campaign sabotage and espionage conducted by the GOP agents were not "politics as usual." The apparently-concerted testimony of previous GOP witnesses that it was normal political practice might be the latest and most dangerous "dirty trick" of all, Mankiewicz said.

The U.S. Circuit Court of Appeals for the District of Columbia in a 5–2 decision Oct. 12, held that President Nixon must turn over his Watergate tape recordings to the U.S. district court and declared that the President was "not above the law's commands." The decision upheld in substance U.S. District Court Judge John J. Sirica's decision Aug. 29 for the President to turn over the tapes so that the court could determine whether they contained evidence that should be presented to the grand jury.

The appeals court ordered the President to turn over the complete tapes in question, specifying which parts should and should not be disclosed. The final decision to send any or all of the material to the grand jury would then be made by the district court. The judge would hold a closed hearing on the issue if either disputant desired. Then he could "order disclosure of all portions of the tapes relevant to matters within the proper scope of the grand jury's investigation," the appeals court held, unless he found in "particular" statements or information "that the public interest served by nondisclosure outweighed the grand jury's need for the information." The appeals court did not give up its earlier bid for an out-of-court compromise.

On the question of presidential immunity, the court said: "The Constitution makes no mention of special presidential immunities. Indeed, the executive branch generally is afforded none. This silence cannot be ascribed to oversight." "Though the President is elected by nationwide ballot, and is often said to represent all the people, he does not embody the nation's sovereignty. He is not above the law's commands..."

On the issue of executive privilege, the court said "the Constitution mentions no executive privilege, much less any absolute executive privilege." While there had been "longstanding judicial recognition" of executive privilege, it noted, it was the longstanding corollary opinion of the courts that "the applicability of the privilege is in the end for them and not the executive to decide."

Judge Sirica told five of the Watergate burglars Oct. 1 it was not his intention to impose maximum sentences in their cases. He said "such a disposition would not only be unwarranted but unjust." The five men—E. Howard Hunt Jr., Virgilio Gonzales, Eugenio Martinez, Frank Sturgis and Bernard Barker—had received provisional maximum sentences from Sirica in March. But Sirica, calling them into court, explained that a maximum term was mandatory under the law in any provisional sentencing announced while awaiting more information for final sentencing. The final sentence would be based on presentencing reports, on the law and on "fairness, compassion, understanding and justice," Sirica emphasized. He reminded the defendants that the degree of their cooperation with investigatory panels was one of his evaluating factors.

The American Civil Liberties Union called Oct. 4 for the impeachment of President Nixon. In a resolution adopted "overwhelmingly" by its board of directors, the organization said "there is now substantial public evidence of President Nixon's participation in high crimes and misdemeanors, and these acts have violated the civil liberties of the people of the United States and the rule by law." ACLU Chairman Edward J. Ennis said the impeachment was being sought on six grounds: "specific provoked violations of the rights of political dissent; usurpation of Congressional war-making powers; establishment of a personal secret police which committed crimes; attempted interference in the trial of Daniel Ellsberg; distortion of the system of justice; and perversion of other federal agencies."

Los Angeles Times

Los Angeles, Calif., October 14, 1973

The conflict between the President and the courts has moved up another notch. It is a conflict that could have been avoided and still could be avoided, if only the President were to take one of the several compromises open to him, compromises that would both serve the national interest and protect his legitimate privileges.

But once he opposed Judge John J. Sirica's solution to the dispute, and once he turned down the sensible compromise suggested by the U.S. Court of Appeals for the District of Columbia, he left the Court of Appeals no choice but to issue a ruling best avoided.

The court focused on the President's sweeping claim to absolute privileges as the central flaw in his position. The court majority argued against his contention that he, and only he, can decide what is privileged and what is not, what can be released to the public or to a former staff member, and what can be withheld from the grand jury. For in this case, as the court pointed out, special prosecutor Archibald Cox made a "uniquely powerful argument" that portions of the tapes contain evidence "peculiarly necessary" to the grand jury

investigating the Watergate burglary and its cover-up.

Sensibly enough, the court did not go as far as Cox wanted. Recognizing that the President has a legitimate executive privilege necessary to the conduct of his office, the court turned down Cox's request for all the tapes and supported instead Judge Sirica's finding that he should examine them, selecting those that are pertinent and withholding irrelevancies and national security matters.

For those who are uneasy, as indeed we are, about the power of judges to give commands to Presidents, the compromise suggested earlier by the Court of Appeals offered an even more sensible way out: the President and Cox would meet and jointly decide what to release to the grand jury and what to withhold, thus avoiding sacrifice of principle by either side.

The problem with the President's defense of the principle of executive privilege is that he has stretched it to absurdity.

He argues that disclosure of the tapes would inhibit the free and easy flow of confidential advice that a President has to have. But it was he, after all, who made the tapes, secretly, without the

knowledge of the persons he was talking to. It seems to us that disclosure of certain parts of certain tapes to a grand jury can scarcely have so chilling an effect on future conversations as the knowledge that he took down every word that came from the lips of his unsuspecting partners in conversation.

As we have said before, we see little if any good coming from the anticipated Supreme Court ruling. A decision upholding the President would constitute a dangerously broad formal grant of power to this and all future Presidents. A decision to avoid a decision would leave the issues of the tapes unresolved. A decision upholding the lower courts could set a precedent that later could be expanded into an unwarranted claim of judicial authority over the Presidency.

The definition of the separation of powers was left imprecise and inexact by the founding fathers because it cannot be precisely defined. Its resolution must be left to experience, to compromise born of the spirit of moderation. It is that spirit that is lacking in the President's position, and its absence does the country no good.

The Washington Post

Times Herald

Washington, D.C., October 14, 1973

THE ARIZONA REPUBLIC

Phoenix, Ariz.

October 15, 1973

A federal court of appeals has upheld Judge John Sirica's order telling President Nixon to submit the Watergate tapes to him. Judge Sirica was ordered to hear the tapes in secret and decide whether they will be revealed in the various Watergate trials.

The decision is not final. The U.S. Supreme Court will be the final arbiter. It should act on the matter promptly.

While we will not try to anticipate the highest court in the land, it is obvious that the decisions so far, if allowed to stand, will carve out a new relationship between the executive and the judicial branches of the government.

Instead of being co-equal, the judicial branch will be clearly held to supersede the executive branch. When a judge—any judge—has the right to decide whether a president's—any president's—private records should be made public, then the courts clearly are superior to the executive branch of the government.

The appellate c o u r t decision, going against the President, came just two days after the vice president (who stands on the same le gal legs as the President) withdrew his demand for records of reporters and television commentators.

It would be passing strange for the U.S. to end up in a position in which the President is forced to submit his confidential records to a judge for review, while the media is allowed to keep its own records safe from any review.

Another round in the historic constitutional battle between President Nixon and the Watergate grand jury, represented by Special Prosecutor Archibald Cox, is over. The U.S. Court of Appeals for the District of Columbia Circuit has held that portions of the disputed tapes relevant to the proper scope of the grand jury's inquiry may be made available to that body unless the President can demonstrate to Judge John J. Sirica an overriding public interest in withholding "particular statements or information." The appellate court then fashioned careful procedures which make it possible for the President and his lawyers to make full arguments on his claims to any item of evidence he deems privileged and for the district court to select any material on which the President's claim is upheld.

On its way to that careful conclusion, the court of appeals reached some powerful and extraordinarily constructive conclusions about the way in which the Constitution and the laws of the United States apply at the top of the American government. In reaching its decision, the court had to deal with two contentions pressed by the President's lawyers which, if allowed to stand, would have severely distorted our constitutional system. The arguments that the President is immune from compulsory process and that the claim of executive privilege, when made by the President, is absolute, were both rejected.

In asserting presidential immunity from compulsory judicial process the President had relied on the argument that the Constitution provides only one way to reach a sitting President — impeachment. His lawyers also suggested that the court's lack of physical power to enforce obedience to a subpoena on the President demonstrated his immunity. The court considered that argument no impediment whatsoever to following what it took to be the mandate of the law. The court could find nothing in the text of the Constitution justifying the President's claim of immunity and declined his lawyers' invitation to find it by inference, saying "These are invitations to refashion the Constitution and we reject them."

Then, addressing the core of the President's claim to immunity, the court said, "Though the President is elected by nationwide ballot, and is often said to represent all the people, he does not embody the nation's sovereignty. He is not above the law's commands: 'With

all its defects, delays and inconveniences men have discovered no technique for long preserving free government except that the Executive be under the law . . .' (quoting from the steel seizure case). Sovereignty remains at all times with the people, and they do not forfeit through elections the right to have the law construed against and applied to every citizen."

Passing then to the President's claim that his discretion to assert executive privilege is absolute, the court stated that assessing the validity of the claim of the privilege and its scope is a judicial, not an executive function. It then went to the heart of the mischief which would result if the President's argument were enshrined in law by saying, "Any claim to executive absolutism cannot override the duty of the court to assure that an official has not exceeded his charter or flouted the legislative will."

The court did recognize the existence of an executive privilege, but said that the interests that would be served by withholding information had to be balanced against those which would be served by disclosure. Because the President had permitted testimony regarding the taped conversations, the court concluded that the material was no longer confidential. It also noted that Special Prosecutor Cox had made a compelling showing of the grand jury's need for the material.

The only problem remaining was for the court to devise measures to protect material that did not relate to Watergate, that might deal with national defense or foreign affairs or that for some other reason might warrant protection. It devised a careful procedure, permitting segmentation of the tapes and secret *in camera* arguments on disputed items.

In our view, the court of appeals decision was correct and eminently wise. In no sense did the court hold that the President was powerless to protect material which for good reason should not be disclosed. It gave short shrift, however, to the notion that anything short of absolute privilege would cripple the presidency for all time. The measures it devised for culling the material seem both careful and fair. And most important, in our view, the court flatly and persuasively rejected the notion that, apart from impeachment and conviction, the President is above and beyond the reaches of the Constitution and the law of the United States.

The Salt Lake Tribune
Salt Lake City, Utah, October 6, 1973

When special prosecutor Archibald Cox went to court to force President Nixon to turn over the so-called Watergate tapes it was widely assumed that the issue would ultimately be decided by the Supreme Court. In fact, Mr. Nixon said he would only heed a "definitive" ruling by the top court.

Vice President Agnew's battle to prevent a federal grand jury from hearing evidence against him and possibly returning an indictment is also likely to find its way to the Supreme Court.

These are the most publicized tests of executive prerogatives now working their way through the lower courts. But there are others, chief among them a challenge to presidential impoundment of appropriated funds and to use of the pocket veto.

Most people probably believe, indeed they have been led to believe, that when these basic constitutional questions reach the nine justices a clear answer will be forthcoming. After all, isn't that what the Supreme Court is supposed to do, interpret the Constitution and tell the people how it applies?

The answer to the question may. be yes. Yet the likelihood is slight that the court will hand down sweeping dictates that will settle all the questions raised by President Nixon, Vice President Agnew and others.

In the first place, the court has not yet even agreed to rule on any of the constitutional questions headed its way. Thus the justices could dispose of some of them by refusing to hear the cases at all.

Assuming the Nixon and Agnew cases go all the way and the Supreme Court agrees to hear them, there still are any number of ways the justices might act. Louis Henkin, a constitutional-law professor at Columbia University, told The Wall Street Journal that what is likely to happen is that the Supreme Court "will be very cautious. It will decide as little as it has to, on very narrow grounds." Another constitutional law professor, Phillip B. Kurland of the University of Chicago, suggested that the court might refuse to accept the Nixon case on grounds it is a political controversy that the government's political branches, not its courts, should resolve.

The court's possible reluctance to face the issues squarely raises the question of whether a straight answer is what the country needs, whether candor might be more damaging than evasion. Is it better to hand down a narrow ruling which would not back the executive branch into a corner or come up with a broad opinion which would invite a grave crisis of government?

The public, we again submit, expects clearcut rulings that will settle the constitutional questions once and for all time. But the public of today and of the future may be better served by rulings tailored to the temper of the times, rulings which get their message across without inviting further confrontation and, at worst, outright defiance.

THE RICHMOND NEWS LEADER
Richmond, Va., October 4, 1973

Golly-gee-whizzing all the way, Federal District Judge John Sirica told five of the original seven Watergate defendants on Monday that "it was never my intention . . . that the maximum terms of the provisional sentences [given in March] should become the final sentences."

The five conspirators — E. Howard Hunt and the four Cuban-Americans caught inside the Watergate — were appearing before Sirica in an effort to withdraw the guilty pleas they had submitted in January at the Watergate trial. Sirica took the opportunity to clear up "what appears to be a widespread misunderstanding" of the provisional sentences (Hunt, for example, was given 35 years) that Sirica imposed on all five to pressure them into co-operating with authorities investigating Watergate. Such lengthy terms, said the judge, "would not only be unwarranted, but unjust." And if Sirica denies the defendants' request to have their guilty pleas changed, he said, then "it will be perfectly apparent at that time . . . that [final sentences are] predicated, as [they] should be, upon fairness, compassion, understanding, and justice."

Well, Sirica fooled a lot of people about his "intention" when he first put the screws to the Watergate defendants in March. Indeed, the only thing that Sirica made "perfectly apparent" about his exercise of the power to sentence was that either the defendants spilled their guts or Sirica would make sure that they served every wretched day in prison that he could milk out of their crimes. Not once — until Monday — did Sirica ever so much as hint that the decades-long provisional sentences were anything except exactly what he intended to hand out should the defendants not co-operate. Now Sirica would have the world believe that Hunt and the Cuban-Americans should have known Sirica was saying: "Gosh, fellas, I'm going to sock you with 35 or 40 years in jail, but I'm just fooling around in the hope that you might be a teensy-weensy bit helpful with the rest of the case. Don't worry — I'm not mad, and your final sentences will be sugar and spice."

Sirica now can afford to portray himself as a grievously misunderstood judge, because Sirica has succeeded in forcing the defendants to talk. Even Hunt, the once tight-lipped veteran of more than 20 years in the CIA, has been pressured into telling all to the Senate Watergate Committee. And seeing the victory that his judicial torture has produced, Sirica deftly tries to hide the whips and racks that await the next defendant who offends his strange concept of justice. If Sirica is permitted to use his inquisitorial devices again — which he should not be allowed to do — perhaps he will at least have the grace to admit that he understands the significance of each turn of the screw.

The New York Times
New York, N.Y., October 14, 1973

The powers of the Presidency have never been static or neatly defined. Support for a strong Chief Executive grows during times of uncertainty and crisis. The great Depression, World War II and the emergence in the last three decades of the United States as superpower in a world of uneasy nuclear balance have inevitably given enormous new responsibilities and prerogatives to the White House. The dimension of these changes makes it particularly important that the nation. remember it is literally founded on the rejection of absolute power in the hands of any man.

When President Nixon insists on the absolute right to withhold the White House tapes from the Federal grand jury investigating the Watergate scandals; he usurps precisely such absolute power. To that claim of unchecked Presidential power the Court of Appeals for the District of Columbia has now given an emphatic rebuff: "Though the President is elected by nationwide ballot, and is often said to represent all the people, he does not embody the nation's sovereignty. He is not above the law's commands. . . . Sovereignty remains at all times with the people and they do not forfeit through elections the right to have the law construed against and applied to every citizen."

The court, in upholding Chief District Judge John J. Sirica's order for surrender of the tapes, took great care to protect the legitimate prerogatives of an effective Presidency. It acknowledged that "wholesale public access" to executive deliberations would have a crippling effect. Once again, the judges pleaded with Mr. Nixon to settle the matter without confrontation by reconsidering the appeals court's earlier recommendation for an informal agreement with special prosecutor Archibald Cox "as to what portions of the subpoenaed evidence are necessary to the grand jury's tasks."

What the court clearly could not brook is Mr. Nixon's continued illusion that he is the law. Even the two judges who dissented from the majority's denial of executive privilege in the matter of the tapes concurred that the court did have jurisdiction over the issue— a position categorically denied by Mr. Nixon.

In narrow terms, the court held that the taped conversations are no longer confidential. Since testimony about these conversations has already been given by a number of persons, including Mr. Haldeman who had actually listened to the recordings, there no longer remains any reason for depriving the grand jury of the best available evidence—the tapes themselves.

The court pointedly reminded Mr. Nixon that he stated publicly on May 22, 1973: "Executive privilege will not be invoked as to any testimony concerning possible criminal conduct or discussions of possible criminal conduct, in the matters under investigation . . ." It is because the President subsequently claimed for himself alone precisely the privilege he considered inapplicable to all others that the collision course between him and the judiciary has become so inexorable.

Mr. Nixon has built his case in large measure on the image of himself as a guardian of the separation of powers as laid down in the Constitution. What he has conveniently overlooked, as the court put it, is that when the President declares himself sole judge in such matters as the tapes, the consequence is to mix—rather than to separate—executive and judicial functions. In even more basic terms, Mr. Nixon was reminded that "the courts in this country always assume that their orders will be obeyed, especially when addressed to responsible government officials."

There has never been justification for Mr. Nixon's extravagant claim that Judge Sirica's order threatens "the continued existence of the Presidency as a functioning institution." The true threat to the Presidency is the lingering suspicion that Presidential privilege is being abused in an effort to interfere with the processes of criminal justice. No threat to a democratic society is more serious than the creation of a sovereign power above the law.

The Cleveland Press

Cleveland, Ohio, October 13, 1973

At a time when many Americans are disgusted with politics and politicians, the record of the U.S. Justice Department, under Attorney General Elliot L. Richardson is proof that the system really can work if the right men are in charge.

Richardson, who took over the Justice Department six months ago, has three qualities the Nixon Administration badly needs — competence, personal integrity and political independence.

His insistence that all the damaging allegations be spelled out in the Agnew settlement showed a keen sensitivity to the public's right to know.

Credit also should go to Assistant Attorney General Henry E. Petersen and U.S. Attorney George Beall for pursuing the Agnew case despite loud protestations of innocence from the then vice president and his supporters.

Richardson's appointment of Democrat Archibald Cox as special prosecutor in the Watergate case showed a commendable willingness to let the chips fall where they may

And his contention that even influential crooks can be brought to justice is the kind of talk people are eager to hear from the nation's No. 1 law enforcement officer.

Under Richardson and his chief deputy, William D. Ruckelshaus, the Justice Department now has its strongest leadership in years, perhaps its strongest since the New Deal.

The tendency, under presidents of both parties, has been to appoint old cronies and political wheeler-dealers, rather than distinguished prosecutors, to the attorney generalship.

The opposite is true of Richardson, who rooted out corruption, without regard to party, while state attorney general in Massachusetts.

It's possible that he'll stub his toe on tough cases in the months ahead. But the new man at Justice looks now like he has the qualifications to do the job.

TULSA DAILY WORLD

Tulsa, Okla., October 2, 1973

U.S. DISTRICT Judge JOHN SIRICA says he will reduce the sentences he previously imposed on E. HOWARD HUNT and four other confessed Watergate burglars. It's high time.

One need not downgrade the seriousness of the Watergate burglary to say that prison terms ranging up to 40 years were obviously unreasonable. But punishment wasn't the motive for the heavy-handed sentences anyway. The idea was to force the defendants to cooperate in naming others involved in the crime.

In other words, the Judge's original sentence in each case was a threat.

"It was never my intention—and again I repeat with emphasis—that the maximum terms of the provisional sentences should become the terms of the final sentences," the Judge said. "In this case such a disposition would not only be unwarranted but unjust."

Judge Sirica said he hoped that would clear up "what appears to be a widespread misunderstanding" about

the temporary, maximum punishment he ordered for the five men. But we're still not sure we clearly understand.

SIRICA now appears to be trying to have it both ways. It was a threat. but again it wasn't because he planned to reduce the terms.

(The threat didn't produce much new evidence from the five men involved, but it may have been something of an inspiration to another defendant, JAMES McCORD. He stayed with his plea of innocence and began cooperating with authorities.)

If the original punishment was mere bluff, the Judge is party to a kind of legal deception. If not, it was a heavy-handed way to extract testimony.

It also seems to lower the credibility of the burglars' testimony in any future prosecution of higher-up defendants. Having been told they would go to prison for 40 years if they didn't incriminate someone, one's natural implication would be to incriminate.

St. Louis Globe-Democrat

St. Louis, Mo., October 15, 1973

The United States Court of Appeals has ruled fairly in upholding Judge John J. Sirica's order that President Nixon must turn over Watergate-related tapes for private review, so the judge may decide if a grand jury should hear them.

The ruling is fair because the appeals court has taken special pains to see that President Nixon may protect those portions of the tapes which deal with national security or foreign relations of a sensitive nature.

"The central question before us is, in essence, whether the President may, in his sole discretion, withhold from a grand jury evidence in his possession that is relevant to the grand jury's investigations," the court's 5 to 2 majority opinion said.

The court further observed that the President "is not above the law's commands."

Counsel for the President had argued that executive privilege gives Mr. Nixon unquestioned right to withhold the tapes. The court reacted in this way:

"The Constitution makes no mention of special presidential immunities . . . Counsel for the President nonetheless would have us infer immunity from the President's political mandate, or from his vulnerability to impeachment, or from his broad discretionary powers. These are invitations to refashion the Constitution and we reject them."

President Nixon assuredly is within his rights in taking his case to the Supreme Court, as he has indicated on several occasions he would do. The President has said he will obey "a definitive ruling" by the Supreme Court.

Such a pledge by Mr. Nixon would appear to preclude any possibility that he holds himself above the law. The President's claim thus far is that the confidentiality of his office will be destroyed if he is forced to surrender private papers or documents. He considers the tapes to be in this category.

Now it remains for the Supreme Court to decide if it agrees with the appeals court that the central question is whether the President may, in his sole discretion, withhold evidence from a grand jury.

Watergate is not a matter of state. It involves allegations of crookedness in the executive branch of our government.

There was no White House fervor to withhold evidence from the grand jury in the case of Spiro Agnew.

The Detroit News

Detroit, Mich., October 7, 1973

The American Civil Liberties Union, which didn't bat an eyelash when the political rumor-mongers were ripping President Nixon's good name to shreds at the peak of the Watergate hearings, has now launched a crusade to impeach the President for alleged violations of civil liberties.

This attack is hypocritical and a disservice to a nation which, having struggled through the worst of the Senate's Watergate maelstrom, can ill afford the turmoil and discord which a serious effort at impeachment would stir.

Strictly from a strategic point of view, the ACLU's effort is badly timed. At the depths of the Watergate hearings when the President's popularity had dropped to rock bottom, several members of the House of Representatives tried to initiate proceedings against Mr. Nixon. They failed. Now, when national calm has been restored and the President has regained some of his prestige and public support, such a movement would seem to have even less chance of success.

All this could change, of course, if the question of presidential tapes should go to the Supreme Court, if the Supreme Court should order the President to hand his tapes to Judge Sirica and if President Nixon should refuse to comply. This sequence of events would lead to the constitutional crisis which most Americans hope will be avoided; that crisis would furnish fertile ground for the seeds of the impeachment movement.

Once again, we urge the President to take the step by which he may forestall that grim showdown.

We understand and respect his determination to defend the principle of executive privilege and confidentiality against infringement by the other branches of American government. This principle is critical to the continuing vitality of the presidency.

In fact, even Samuel Dash, chief counsel for the Senate Watergate committee, has admitted in court that "we could probably agree with two-thirds of the President's brief" on executive privilege and confidentiality. And no doubt Judge John Sirica, Archibald Cox and many members of the House and Senate also acknowledge the essential merit of the President's position.

Nevertheless, the question of the tapes remains. The effort to get them will persist and may lead to the much-feared crisis unless the President does something to satisfy the prosecutors and his critics.

What can the President do? Without compromising his position, he can voluntarily offer to sit down with a couple of senators and the special prosecutor and listen with them to the tapes. These men could determine among themselves which portions, or whether any portions, of the tapes are pertinent to the Watergate investigation.

Unless the President takes such action, he will remain on a collision course with the judiciary and will continue to be the target of virulent political attack and impeachment efforts. He can, of course, survive all this but the cost to him personally and to the nation seems inordinately high, especially if there's an easier way out of the quandary.

Meanwhile, we do not think that Watergate, scandalous as it was, yet justifies the extreme redress of impeachment, which would rock the nation to its political foundations. The ACLU and others who advocate impeachment should pause and ask themselves whether they are seeking a desirable remedy or merely a political scalp—and whether the taking of a scalp is really worth that much.

DAYTON DAILY NEWS
Dayton, Ohio, October 9, 1973

After listening to the recitation of dirty tricks and sabotage against Democratic candidates in last year's Florida primary, Watergate committee member Sen. Edward Gurney (R-Fla.) dismissed the o p e r a t i o n as "rinky-dink" and said, "All of us in politics expect tactics like this from fringe elements."

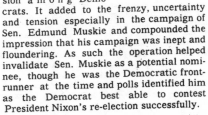

Gurney

Tawdry and improvisational the operation certainly was. But rinky-dink? Hardly.

The sabotage contributed to the dissension a m o n g Democrats. It added to the frenzy, uncertainty and tension especially in the campaign of Sen. Edmund Muskie and compounded the impression that his campaign was inept and floundering. As such the operation helped invalidate Sen. Muskie as a potential nominee, though he was the Democratic frontrunner at the time and polls identified him as the Democrat best able to contest President Nixon's re-election successfully.

If the operation itself was rinky-dink, the result to which it contributed was something much more. It was a distortion and perversion of the election process. It ended with the nomination of Sen. George McGovern, the Democratic party's weakest candidate. Maybe that would have happened in any case, but now on one ever can be sure.

As for Sen. Gurney's claim that all politicians expect such tactics from fringe elements, well, perhaps many do. Elections attract nuts and show-offs and not always as candidates. For the record, however, the sabotage in the Florida primary was initiated by the White House staff on behalf of the President of the United States and bankrolled with money contributed for his re-election.

Was Sen. Gurney saying more than he meant to when he indirectly suggested that the current administration is a fringe element?

The Register-Republic
Rockford, Ill., October 5, 1973

A sometimes contrite, sometimes accusing Donald H. Segretti has told the Senate Watergate Committee the "dirty-tricks" he perpetrated to help win President Nixon's re-election were, in his opinion, "similar to college pranks" which had occurred during his school days at the University of Southern California.

This is an alarming statement of naivete from a 33-year-old lawyer who was paid $45,000 by Nixon's personal lawyer for heading the so-called dirty tricks campaign in 1971 and 1972.

Dirty tricks is an oversimplified description of the slander, manipulation and dishonesty Segretti and his aides employed to insure the President's re-election.

Among other things, he admitted using what was supposed to be stationery of Sen. Edmund Muskie to distribute a letter charging Sens. Hubert Humphrey and Henry Jackson with sexual improprieties in an effort to shoot down Muskie's chances as a Democratic candidate.

This is no college prank. It's nothing less than the unlawful and unethical use of a distinguished senator's name in a dishonest slander.

Even without the letter Muskie probably couldn't have beaten Nixon. It's unlikely anyone could have. But it's sickening, and frightening, to think that a political contest among some of the best men in our government might be influenced by one of Segretti's collegiate pranks.

Although Segretti ended his testimony with a denunciation of his political trickery, he opened the session with an unbelievable blast at the press.

He complained he had been "abused by rumor, character assassination, innuendo and a complete disregard for the privacy of myself and my family."

It's an interesting complaint. We can't help but wonder what Sens. Muskie, Jackson and Humphrey would have to say about the Donald Segretti of 1971 and 1972.

The Charlotte Observer
Charlotte, N.C., October 9, 1973

The Nixon campaigners wanted for 1972, in the words of H. R. Haldeman, "a Dick Tuck capability." Instead, they got a tasteless and sometimes vicious array of dirty tricks that may or may not have had any material effect on the Democrats.

Elsewhere on this page Mr. Tuck himself comments on what a "Dick Tuck capability" means. Compared with Donald Segretti's testimony before the Ervin Committee, several crucial differences become obvious.

Mr. Tuck, however much he may annoy some, is a genuine prankster. His activities, mostly d i r e c t e d at Richard Nixon, are legion. There was the time during the 1968 campaign, for instance, when Mr. Tuck hired a group of pregnant black women to parade outside a hotel Mr. Nixon was staying at with signs saying, "Nixon's The One."

The activities of Mr. Segretti and his cohorts tended to be downright scurrilous; for e x a m p l e, the dispatch of a phony letter on Sen. Muskie's stationery that falsely accused Sens. Hubert Humphrey and Henry Jackson of conduct ranging from homosexuality to drunken driving with call girls.

Mr. Segretti has pleaded guilty in a Washington court to three misdemeanors and he faces a maximum sentence of three years.

Besides the q u a l i t y of activities, there is another distinction. Mr. Tuck for the most part operated on his own, sometimes in league with candidates, sometimes on a freelance basis. Mr. Segretti was directed and financed by members of the President's official family.

In this and other matters, the Nixon campaign partisans took an established p r a c t i c e and carried it beyond the bounds of decency. A remark by John Ehrlichman, made in another context, illustrates the attitude. Asked by Sen. Herman Talmadge whether a president, under the inherent powers d o c t r i n e, could, for instance, order a murder, Mr. Ehrlichman replied: "I don't know where you draw the line, senator." These men were never able to draw the line.

It is probable that Mr. Segretti's activities had little effect upon the Democrats' campaigns. But that his tricks were inept does not diminish their significance. They, along with enemies' lists and promiscuous wiretapping, marked a departure in American politics — an attempt by the party in power not just to defeat but to destroy the other party.

The real difference b e t w e e n Mr. Tuck and Mr. Segretti is that one was engaged in pranks and the other was e n g a g e d in reprehensible smears and political subversion.

The Courier-Journal
Louisville, Ky., October 13, 1973

THE SECOND ROUND of Watergate hearings so far has produced testimony laced with two self-serving themes which are largely irrelevant but nagging distractions: that last year's political espionage and sabotage had no appreciable effect on the outcome of the presidential race and that such dirty tricks have been a standard feature of previous campaigns by both parties.

While it would be foolhardy to claim that the malicious mischief of Donald Segretti, Louisville's Michael McMinoway and other agents cost Senator McGovern the election or decisively affected the outcome of the string of Democratic primaries, it would be equally foolish to reject the claim of Frank Mankiewicz, Senator McGovern's former political director, that these dirty tricks contributed to "an unparalleled atmosphere of rancor and discord within the Democratic Party." The political effectiveness of the spying and sabotage is, at best, a matter of conjecture. The morality most certainly is not.

Similarly, the defensive claim of some witnesses that the Democrats weren't simon-pure in 1972 and in earlier campaigns has not been accompanied by hard evidence and is irrelevant to the matters at hand. No one doubts there have been dirty tricks in the past, but to argue that mischief as highly organized and well-financed as last year's is part of America's political tradition is nonsense.

But there's no nonsense to fears that the suspicions generated by last year's tricks will haunt campaigns to come and may tragically curtail the use of political volunteers.

NIXON FIRES COX, THEN CONCEDES ON TAPES

President Nixon agreed Oct. 23 to submit tapes containing White House conversations about the Watergate case to Federal District Court Judge John J. Sirica. For three months, Nixon had insisted that the tapes remain in the White House under his absolute control. The President abruptly reversed himself in the midst of a mounting government crisis, laced with the threat of an impeachment effort, that resulted from his abrupt discharge Oct. 20 of special Watergate prosecutor Archibald Cox and return of the federal Watergate prosecution to Justice Department jurisdiction.

Cox had rejected a White House compromise plan to end the tapes dispute by furnishing investigators with a "summary" of the taped presidential conversations that would be verified by Sen. John Stennis (D, Miss.). Nixon's compromise plan was his response to an order Oct. 12 by the U.S. Circuit Court of Appeals for the District of Columbia that he turn over the tapes to Sirica. The President directed Attorney General Elliot L. Richardson to discharge Cox. Richardson refused and resigned Oct. 20. Deputy Attorney General William D. Ruckelshaus was then asked to fire Cox, and after refusing was in turn fired the same day. Solicitor General Robert H. Bork, who became acting attorney general after Ruckelshaus' discharge, dismissed Cox.

The crisis began Oct. 19 when Nixon announced his "compromise" plan. He said it had been drawn up by Richardson and agreed to by Senate Watergate committee Chairman Sam J. Ervin (D, N.C.) and Vice Chairman Howard H. Baker Jr. (R, Tenn.). Cox had rejected his compromise plan, Nixon said, but he had decided to take "decisive actions" anyway in order to avert a "constitutional crisis" and "lay the groundwork upon which we can assure unity of purpose at home and end the temptation abroad to test our resolve." He had decided, therefore, Nixon said, not to seek Supreme Court review of the appeals court decision Oct. 12 ordering him to surrender the tapes to the U.S. district court supervising the Watergate probe. It was not in the national interest, the President contended, "to leave this matter unresolved for the period that might be required for a review by the highest court." "Though," he continued, "I have not wished to intrude upon the independence of the special prosecutor, I have felt it necessary to direct him, as an employe of the executive branch, to make no further attempts by judicial process to obtain tapes, notes or memoranda of presidential conversations."

Cox rejected Nixon's "compromise" tapes plan later Oct. 19 and said he would take his objections to it before the court. In his judgment, Cox said, "the President is refusing to comply with the court decrees." Cox said the proposed summary would lack "the evidentiary value of the tapes themselves" and "no steps are being taken to turn over the important notes, memoranda and other documents that the court orders require."

The announcement that Cox had been fired came on Saturday evening Oct. 20. White House Press Secretary Ronald L. Ziegler said Richardson had resigned rather than discharge Cox. Ruckelshaus was then asked to carry out the President's order to discharge Cox. When he refused, according to Ziegler, Ruckelshaus was fired. Cox's dismissal was finally carried out by Solicitor General Bork, who was appointed acting attorney general.

The President also announced through Ziegler that he had abolished the special Watergate prosecutor's office as of 8 p.m. and transferred its duties back to the Justice Department where they would "be carried out with thoroughness and vigor." Ziegler said Cox had been discharged because he had "pressed for a confrontation at a time of serious world crisis."

FBI agents were sent later that evening to seal off the special prosecutor's offices. The next day, they were replaced by U.S. marshals. Nixon aide Alexander Haig conceded Oct. 23 he was "guilty" of ordering the FBI to seal off the offices. He said he acted to preserve the files after hearing reports that staffers were leaving with "huge bundles under their arms." Acting Attorney General Bork announced Oct. 22 that he had placed Henry E. Petersen in direct charge of the Watergate case "and all related matters previously being directed by the special prosecutor." Petersen would use the evidence and staff already assembled, as well as other department personnel, Bork said, "to see that these cases are pressed to a conclusion and that justice is done."

A flood of protest erupted over the abrupt ouster of Cox and resultant departures of Richardson and Ruckelshaus Oct. 20. Telegrams and letters of protest began arriving at the White House and at the Capitol. By Oct. 23, Western Union in Washington had been "inundated" with messages, according to a company official—more than 150,000 telegrams, "the heaviest concentrated volume on record." Even conservative members of Congress reported the preponderant tone of the messages was "negative" advocating impeachment.

American Bar Association (ABA) President Chesterfield Smith warned Oct. 22 that Nixon was attempting to "abort the established processes of justice." He urged the courts and Congress to take "appropriate action" to "repel" the "attacks" by the President. Delegates to the 10th biennial convention of the American Federation of Labor and Congress of Industrial Organizations (AFL-CIO), meeting in Bal Harbour, Fla. Oct. 18–23, passed a resolution by acclamation Oct. 22 calling on President Nixon to resign and the House to impeach him "forthwith" if he did not.

The threat of impeachment began to take shape in Congress Oct. 23. Eight impeachment resolutions, co-sponsored by a total of 31 Democrats, were offered in the House, where impeachment charges could be brought by majority vote. House Democratic leaders agreed unanimously Oct. 23 to have the Judiciary Committee begin an inquiry into possible impeachment. House Republican leaders, facing the Democratic move, endorsed the inquiry. The President's decision to yield the tapes to the court did not deter the move toward an opening of the impeachment process. House Judiciary Committee chairman Peter W. Rodino Jr. (D, N.J.) said Oct. 24, after conferring with 19 other Democrats on the panel, that its impeachment investigation would "proceed full steam ahead."

The President's reversal of position and consent to turn over the tapes to the court was revealed in a dramatic and brief announcement before Judge Sirica Oct. 23. At that time, the administration had been expected to present the response of the President to the court's decision insisting upon surrender of the tapes.

Sirica asked the President's attorneys if they were prepared to file "the response of the President" to his Aug. 29 order as modified by the appeals court. Charles Alan Wright, chief of the President's Watergate legal defense team, stepped forward and said "the President of the United States would comply in all respects" with Sirica's order as modified by the higher court. The announcement was totally unexpected. Wright explained that the President still maintained that his previous posture was correct and the "summary" would satisfy the court's needs, but the problem was that even if the court agreed with him "there would have been those who would have said the President is defying the law." "This President does not defy the law," Wright declared, "and he has authorized me to say he will comply in full with the orders of the court."

At a news conference later Oct. 23 with Nixon's chief of staff Alexander M. Haig, Wright said "we all miscalculated" the reaction to the President's recent course.

THE SPRINGFIELD UNION
Springfield, Mass., October 22, 1973

In the light of the sensational weekend developments in Washington, crucial days lie ahead for the stability of the federal government — and its image before the nation and the world.

Part of the dismal picture is the prospect of impeachment moves when Congress convenes tomorrow.

It is questionable whether President Nixon would ultimately be removed from office. If the House completes the impeachment, or indictment, stage, the Senate might not convict him.

Nevertheless, Nixon's firing of Archibald Cox and William Ruckelshaus, and his forcing of Elliot Richardson's resignation, for their insistence on doing their job, has fueled powerful support for impeachment, at least.

As Williams College Prof. James M. Burns has said, the course to be taken by Congress will depend in some degree on whether the court holds Nixon in contempt for his actions.

But the shocking display of willfulness by the President in turning his back on the judicial system, disposing of officials highly dedicated to its support, will also be a factor.

In this, Nixon has strengthened the belief of many Americans (perhaps most by now) that he is hiding an involvement of his own in all phases of the Watergate affair.

At one time, he declared he would abide by a "definitive" decision of the Supreme Court on the matter of turning over his Watergate tapes. Now he appears unwilling to risk any decision by that court.

Also, he turned down U.S. District Court Judge Sirica's ruling that the tapes should be examined privately by the judge himself, with Cox and presidential representatives.

The purpose of that would be to determine what parts of the tapes were pertinent to the Watergate prosecution, and what parts should be withheld for national security or other urgent reasons.

In his hard-handed preoccupation with "executive privilege," President Nixon has shaken the nation's confidence in him — and the world's, at a point when diplomacy could be vital to a peace in the Mideast.

This is a momentous time in American history. The wisdom of Congress will have to make up for the lack of it in the White House.

Detroit Free Press
Detroit, Mich., October 16, 1973

AS THE NATION struggles to define the limits of presidential power, it needs all the guideposts it can get. Surely one of the best guides yet offered is to be found in the opinion by the U.S. Circuit Court of Appeals on the President's attempt to withhold his Watergate tapes.

Those tapes, the court concluded in upholding Judge John Sirica's order, should be turned over to the courts to shed whatever light they can on possible criminal actions by members of the President's staff.

The appeals court's 5-2 decision was even more forceful and direct than Judge Sirica's carefully balanced original decision, which forbade the President to withhold the tapes. To the majority on the Court of Appeals, the positions taken by the President's lawyers "are invitations to refashion the Constitution, and we reject them."

Far from posing a threat to "the continued existence of the presidency as a functioning institution," as the President's lawyers argued it would be, Judge Sirica's decision was found to be based on sound doctrine. "The Constitution makes no mention of special presidential immunities," the court said. "Indeed, the executive branch is afforded none."

In ringing terms, the court reiterated the fundamental principle that no man, not even the President, is above the law. "Incumbency," said the court, "does not relieve the President of the routine legal obligations that confine all citizens."

If there is a single buttress that has been

strengthening the country as it has faced the Agnew and Watergate scandals, it has been the renewed demonstration that the laws do indeed apply to those in high places. Sometimes the processes seem to work with painful slowness, but in the end they have worked to force the vice president out of office and to punish many of the President's closest associates.

The complaint can be and is being made that former Vice President Agnew escaped with too light a punishment, and the point has some force to it. It can also be argued that the President has too often gotten by with arrogant assertions that the law does not restrict his actions — in impoundment of appropriated funds, in the illegal Cambodian bombing, in his refusal thus far to turn over the tapes.

Slowly, though, the nation's institutions —the courts, the federal prosecutors, the Justice Department—are calling the executive branch to account. The President is subject to the law. The lawful society can deal with its own evils.

All of us must hope that the President recognizes that he must obey the decisions of the courts, if ratified by the Supreme Court, and turn over the tapes of White House conversations where they are relevant. If he should fail to get the message, he will find an aroused electorate ready to demand that he be made to comply.

The rule of law is being restored, and the public official who tries to ignore its claim does so at his own peril. This includes especially the President of the United States.

The Washington Post
Times Herald
Washington, D.C., October 21, 1973

In particular, the Special Prosecutor shall have full authority . . . for . . . determining whether or not to contest the assertion of "Executive privilege" or any other testimonial privilege . . . The Attorney General will not countermand or interfere with the Special Prosecutor's decisions or actions . . . The Special Prosecutor will not be removed from his duties except for extraordinary improprieties on his part."

Those are the crucial provisions from the original order setting up the office of Special Prosecutor Archibald Cox—an order which also gave him full authority to investigate and prosecute offenses arising out of just about any aspect of the Watergate case, in its broadest sense, including specifically "allegations involving the President, members of the White House staff, or presidential appointees . . ." And these are also a part of the guidelines for Mr. Cox which were presented in advance to the Senate Judiciary Committee in its hearings on the appointment of Elliot Richardson as Attorney General. They formed the basis, in other words, of a solemn compact between the Nixon administration and the Senate, which was a condition for Mr. Richardson's confirmation for reasons which are all too familiar to all of us.

It was President Nixon's brutal violation of this compact which directly brought about the crisis in government which is now upon us, with the resignations of Attorney General Richardson and his deputy, William Ruckelshaus.

It is impossible at this stage to measure the full consequences of what has happened, or to predict how events will now unfold. What is important for now is to be very clear in our minds about the defaults and abuses of presidential power that brought us to this critical juncture.

Two successive "investigations" of Watergate by the President had been demonstrably incomplete if not criminally negligent. John W. Dean III, who allegedly conducted the first, pleaded guilty Friday to actual obstruction of justice; the second investigation was supposedly conducted by John Ehrlichman, who has conceded that he thought of it as no more than an "inquiry." Throughout, it appears from testimony before the Senate Watergate committee, there was a singular lack of cooperation with Justice Department investigators; access to White House officials and materials was systematically impeded. The President himself had conceded that there may have been a cover-up, while denying participation in it—or even knowledge of it—until early this year.

It was this stark and demoralizing record which caused the Senate Judiciary Committee to demand strict commitments from Mr. Richardson and from Mr. Cox that the latter would be given a totally free hand. And it is against this background that one must examine the extraordinary statement by President Nixon on Friday night recounting his failed effort to seek a compromise with Mr. Cox over the latter's demand for tapes of presidential conversations, memoranda, notes and other material which he deemed to be essential to his work. The U.S. Court of Appeals has held that this material should be turned over to Judge John Sirica of the federal district court here for a determination as to which parts, if any, should be presented to the grand jury as a part of Mr. Cox's evidence. In his statement, the President said he had decided against further appeal to the Supreme Court, but that he wouldn't abide by the appeals court ruling that he must submit the material in the absence of an out-of-court agreement with the special prosecutor. Instead, he described in great detail his efforts to work out a settlement with Mr. Cox—and then

announced that it had failed. Accordingly, the President said, he had "felt it necessary to direct (Mr. Cox), *as an employee of the executive branch,* to make no further attempts by judicial process to obtain tapes, notes or memoranda of presidential conversations."

In other words, faced with three choices, the President failed to adopt any of the three. Instead he, in effect, shredded the compact with the Senate which was a condition precedent to Mr. Richardson's confirmation for his job and to Mr. Cox's acceptance of his—a compact which plainly precluded interference in the special prosecutor's work and specifically authorized the special prosecutor to make any effort he saw fit to obtain precisely the material that the President finally sought, in defiance of the court, to place beyond his reach.

The proposed bargain, as described by the President's statement, was that he would prepare a summary of the relevant portions of the requested tapes and would have Sen. John Stennis authenticate it by listening to the tapes and comparing them with the summary. Along the way, the President elicited some kind of agreement—the extent and nature of that agreement is not yet clear—from Sen. Sam Ervin and Sen. Howard Baker of the Watergate committee to this arrangement. He also cited large questions of national interest as his reason for wanting to dispose of this matter now, without taking it to the Supreme Court.

In return for the summaries he was willing to provide, Mr. Nixon wanted Mr. Cox to agree that "there would be no further attempt by the special prosecutor to subpoena still more tapes or other presidential papers of a similar nature." After Mr. Cox turned the deal down, Mr. Nixon went ahead and announced that he was going to pursue the route suggested in his aborted bargain anyway and that the summaries, after having been duly authenticated by Senator Stennis, would then be made available to Judge Sirica and to the Senate Watergate committee.

What, in sum, did Mr. Nixon do? Having lost two rounds in court, he attempted to seize immediate control of the prosecution of a series of criminal cases in which he is at least potentially a defendant. He further sought to substitute his own judgment and enforcement power for that of the federal courts, whose jurisdiction he acknowledged by sending his lawyers to plead his case there in the first place. In recent days people have been heard to observe that Vice President Agnew got a very lenient deal in his tangle with federal prosecutors. But consider by comparison the arrangement Mr. Nixon contrived for himself: In matters in which he and many of his most important associates are under examination for possible misconduct in office, he proposes to define what the prosecutor may or may not do and what the grand jury may or may not hear and, in many important senses, to preside as judge, as well.

Mr. Nixon, in other words, has served notice to the world that, in one crucial aspect touching on his own conduct, the Watergate investigation had gone as far as he intends to permit it to go. For his part, Mr. Cox served notice that he would carry out his responsibilities for as long as he would be permitted to do so. He responded, in other words, as a man of honor and integrity, as did the two senior officials of the Justice Department. Honor has been a rarity in the long, dismal history of the Nixon administration's performance in this affair. To recall this history is to raise the most profound questions about Mr. Nixon's own honor—as well as his competence to conduct the affairs of government.

THE ATLANTA CONSTITUTION
Atlanta, Ga.
October 22, 1973

No man is above the law. That includes the President of the United States.

The U.S. House of Representatives should move promptly to begin impeachment proceedings against Richard M. Nixon, the 37th President of the United States.

We do not say such a thing lightly. This is a grave time in American history. The impeachment of a President is a frightening concept. It has occurred only once since the nation was founded. Yet President Nixon, with the near incredible arrogance of his action in firing Archibald Cox, has left the Congress and the American people little choice.

Cox, the special prosecutor for the Watergate investigation, was named to the sensitive position by U.S. Attorney General Elliot L. Richardson with the apparent approval of President Nixon. Cox, a distinguished attorney, was approved also by the U.S. Senate after a careful public hearing aimed at establishing that Cox would conduct an independent thorough investigation of the Watergate scandal.

Cox was fired by President Nixon because he persisted in doing just that, insisting that White House tapes of conversations and White House papers bearing directly on the criminal activities of Watergate were important to the investigation.

Attorney General Richardson, a man of courage and integrity, resigned his office rather than fire Cox. Richardson noted that in appointing the special prosecutor he had promised that such a prosecutor would be independent and "aware that his ultimate accountability is to the American people." That is still true, and this is also the measure of President Nixon's accountability. Deputy Attorney General William Ruckelshaus succeeded Richardson; he was fired by the President when he too refused to fire Cox.

President Nixon has made the beginnings of impeachment proceedings a near certainty. It is a measure of what has happened when a conservative South Georgia Congressman, W.S. "Bill" Stuckey of Eastman, can say as he did in the immediate aftermath: "The country and the House of Representatives will demand impeachment proceedings in order to get the facts out in the open." We agree with that. We think most Americans do.

In addition, President Nixon is now in open defiance of a direct federal court order to release the White House tapes.

Nixon's abrupt action has done another thing. It has scuttled any chance that Congress will act swiftly to approve Congressman Gerald Ford as the new Vice President. Not now. Not until the question of impeachment is settled.

The President of the United States is, in Richardson's phrase, ultimately accountable to the American people. President Nixon is no exception. The Watergate investigation will—and should—go on. President Nixon will not block it by firing one special prosecutor, nor can he long maintain a position of being above and beyond the law.

The Cincinnati Post
TIMES ☆ STAR
Cincinnati, Ohio, October 22, 1973

THE STATES-ITEM
New Orleans, La.
October 22, 1973

This nation faces the gravest constitutional crisis in its history. The President is acting in open defiance of Congress and the Courts.

By abolishing the office of special Watergate prosecutor and dismissing its head, Archibald Cox, the President has violated a solemn agreement with Congress. Establishment of the office and appointment of Mr. Cox were condition precedents to Senate approval of Elliot L. Richardson as attorney general.

The President has gone back on his word to Mr. Cox, Mr. Richardson, Congress and the American people. He said Mr. Cox would be given a free hand in his investigation of Watergate and related matters. Even before the stunning events of the past weekend, it was clear the White House had sought to thwart the investigation at every turn.

Mr. Richardson had no alternative but to resign.

The President has defied a U.S. Court of Appeals ruling ordering him to turn over the disputed White House tapes to U.S. District Judge John Sirica. Instead of appealing the ruling to the Supreme Court or complying with it, the President announced an arrangement of his own with Sen. John Stennis of Mississippi. Under this arrangement, the President will prepare a summary of the tapes and permit Sen. Stennis to listen to the recordings the President deems pertinent to verify his version of the facts.

The President obviously did not wish to risk having to defy a "definitive" ruling by the Supreme Court. It is clear he does not want to turn the tapes over to someone not of his own choosing.

We have reached the point where we no longer can believe our President. His actions seem motivated solely by expedience and self-interest. He consistently has sought to suppress the truth about Watergate and related matters, instead of trying to bring truth to light.

First, the President said this was a matter for the Courts, not Congress. Now, he says it is a matter for Congress, in the person of Sen. Stennis, and not the Courts. What next?

Mr. Nixon, who all along has based his position on the principle that all three branches of government are co-equal, has sought to place himself above the other two.

When we have a president who places himself above the law, we no longer have a president. We have a dictator.

We agree with Mr. Cox's statement of Saturday night:

"Whether ours shall continue to be a government of laws and not of men is now for Congress and ultimately the American people to decide."

The events of the past few days in Washington are ugly, shocking and ominous.

President Nixon, the professed champion of "law and order," on Friday night defied a Federal Court order to turn over certain Watergate tapes — recordings that may answer the question, "Was the President himself implicated in the Watergate coverup?" as former White House counsel John W. Dean III has charged.

Simultaneously President Nixon announced a dubious "compromise" by which he himself would write a summary of the tapes, have it "authenticated" by Sen. John C. Stennis, an acknowledged supporter of Mr. Nixon, then presented to the federal judge as "evidence."

Accompanying this self-serving and legally flimsy plan was the President's command that Archibald Cox, the special Watergate prosecutor, make no further attempt to supoena any tapes or papers.

As an honorable lawyer and indeed as a patriotic American, Cox could not swallow the President's evasive play. The honorable attorney-general, Elliot Richardson, stung by Mr. Nixon's breach of the pledge that Cox would have "absolute authority" to pursue the Watergate scandal to the fullest, turned in his resignation. When the honorable Deputy Atty. Gen. William Ruckelshaus refused a presidential order to fire Cox, he himself was fired, and a new, docile appointee, Robert Bork, took over the Department of Justice.

Abruptly the President ordered the special prosecutor's office closed, sealed off by FBI agents, and the Watergate investigation put back into the Department of Justice, now headed by Mr. Bork.

THIS IS NOT only breath-taking drama but an important national issue.

Clearly President Nixon broke a firm commitment to allow Cox a free investigative hand. Clearly President Nixon is disobeying the orders of two Federal Courts to turn over to U.S. Judge John J. Sirica the tape recordings relevant to the Watergate affair. Those nine tapes record conversations with key former members of the Nixon White House staff — Ehrlichman, Haldeman, Dean — and former Atty. Gen. Mitchell. Whether or not any of these men has committed perjury or conspired to obstruct justice, and whether or not the President has spoken truthfully about his professed non-involvement in the Watergate coverup, are mysteries apparently locked up in the subpoenaed tapes.

Why is President Nixon so reluctant to turn over the tapes?

His stated reasons are not convincing. He says the American people can't stand further "strain." He says the nation must avoid a "constitutional confrontation." He says some foreign power may be tempted to take advantage of America's seeming disunity in this moment of international crisis.

All of these strike us as preposterous and downright insulting. The growing suspicion is that the President won't release the tapes because he doesn't want a special prosecutor, or the federal courts, or the American people to know the words recorded on them.

As a politician, Mr. Nixon is entitled to try to duck embarrassing questions — but as an American citizen, indeed as the nation's leader, he is not entitled to disobey court orders and thus place himself above the law.

In America we enjoy the rule of law, not the rule of men. It is an ugly, shocking and ominous moment when the President defies such a basic American principle.

The Toronto Star
Toronto, Ont., October 22, 1973

President Richard Nixon has placed himself above the law and shown no higher motive than to cling to office—even if the cost is a paralysis of government in the United States.

His actions over the weekend, and the attitude they reveal, justify the moves for impeachment promised by members of the House of Reprentatives.

Nixon stepped over one of the lines that divide free societies from tyrannies by decreeing, in effect, that equal enforcement of the laws shall not apply to the president himself.

The president who preached respect for law placed himself above it by defying a court order to hand over tapes of his private conversations on the Watergate scandal. This can only strengthen the already widespread suspicion that the tapes contain material implicating him in that scandal or the attempt to conceal responsibility for it.

By firing special Watergate prosecutor Archibald Cox for persisting in his attempts to get the tapes released, Nixon reneged on a commitment to the Congress and the American people. When Cox was nominated, Attorney-General Elliot Richardson —obviously speaking as the president's agent—assured the Senate judiciary committee that the prosecutor would operate independently of the White House, and would be free to follow the trail of truth wherever it might lead. When it led to the president, Cox was sacked.

This, the protest resignations of Richardson and Deputy Attorney-General William Ruckelshaus, and the sealing of Richardson's and Cox's offices by presidential order, will extinguish any remaining hope of the administration's co-operating in the exposure and punishment of all the Watergate conspirators.

Nixon's action amounts to a massive gamble that he can get out from under the Watergate investigation once and for all by eliminating the man who was directly responsible for bringing the conspirators to justice.

Given the complicated procedures involved in impeachment, the lack of stomach in Congress for such a fight and external problems dramatized in the Middle East war, Nixon may very well get away with this gamble.

But even if he does it may paralyze the American government, a grave threat to a world that still relies economically, politically and morally on sound and effective American leadership.

American democracy rests on a division of powers between the executive, the legislature and the judiciary, and therefore on a faithful respect by each branch for the powers of the others. The Nixon administration has shown its contempt for judicial authority, and if the president stays on, there is a grave risk of stalemate between the executive and the Congress. When he nominates a successor to Richardson—the only strong symbol of integrity on the domestic side of his administration—how can the Senate be confident that his nominee will enforce the laws even-handedly? If he cannot get his choices for cabinet officers confirmed, he cannot really govern.

The president's conduct when the Watergate investigation came too close to him must, after this terrible year, fill the American people's cup of bitter disillusionment and cynicism about politics. If he is able to hang on to office, they may despair of the system itself. Now it is up to Congress to forestall that by defending the constitution from a president who is subverting it.

St. Petersburg Times

St. Petersburg, Fla., October 22, 1973

Like most people in this country, The Times until now has sought solutions to Watergate that did not include the extreme step of resignation or impeachment of President Nixon. But the President's unrestrained attempt to stop the independent prosecution of the Watergate crimes and his unreasonable purge of the Justice Department are so far outside the normal rules of constitutional government that the national interest now requires that Mr. Nixon resign, or if he refuses, that he be impeached.

FROM THE beginning of the confrontation over the tapes, the President has possessed the capacity to resolve it. He could maintain the principle of separation of powers and still obey the courts merely by voluntarily releasing the sections of the tapes adjudged to be evidence in the criminal cases as an act of his own.

Yet he refused. Now, having lost twice in court, his actions exceeded the bounds of reason when Mr. Nixon attempted to seize the prosecution in which he himself is a potential defendant, thereby violating both his own promise to Congress and the prerogatives of the judiciary.

By his own actions, the President has destroyed much of the public's trust in his judgment, an essential tool of leadership in a free society.

BY HIS OWN actions, the President has shown a contempt for public opinion that reveals how power has corrupted his ability to respond to the American people.

By his own actions, the President has brought into question his own respect for the rule of law, the cement of every law-abiding society.

By his own actions, the President has shown contempt for the good health of America's form of constitutional government, precipitating constitutional crises unnecessarily and for reasons in conflict with sound judgment.

If the tapes show the President is guilty of some wrongdoing, Mr. Nixon is covering up evidence out of self interest. If the tapes show he is innocent, Mr. Nixon is acting so capriciously as to call into question his own judgment.

Impeachment is an extraordinary remedy, but this is a grave time for American democracy. Mr. Nixon has been granted many chances to apply lesser remedies himself.

INSTEAD of compromise, Mr. Nixon has added another breach of trust. He has decided to continue the Watergate coverup, despite assertions in August of repentance for the original coverup.

WHAT HAS BEEN laid out before the public as the Watergate crimes demand more than superficial remedies. In no sense could the public merely forget that Mr. Nixon's deputies had attempted to bribe a federal judge during the Ellsberg trial. Nor can a nation governed by the ballot overlook enormous sums of private money appearing to influence Administration policy on milk prices and anti-trust decisions. Then there was more than $10-million in campaign funds accepted secretly in an attempt to evade federal election laws.

A nation respecting the right of personal privacy has been chagrined at the Administration's use of illegal phone taps on 17 reporters and government officials during its first two years in office. In defiance of the Constitution, the President approved a secret police plan authorizing break-ins.

The President's closest friend, Charles Rebozo, held in safety deposit for Mr. Nixon for three years $100,000 from billionaire Howard H. Hughes. Some $10-million in tax money has been used to enhance Mr. Nixon's two private estates.

Taken in one large lump, this extraordinary chain of irregularities has given the nation a government whose method is inimicable to the democratic process. In public policy it gave us the secret and illegal Cambodia bombings of 1969. It has shaped a presidency which ignores Congress by impounding duly appropriated funds for reasons of policy, rather than implementing the law.

An incredible climax of this record of deceit came in Friday night's White House statement on the tapes. It contained two falsehoods: It said Atty. Gen.

Elliot Richardson was the author of the proposal on the tapes. Richardson said the proposal described was not the one he offered. The statement claimed Sen. Sam Ervin agreed to accept summaries of the tapes. Ervin said he had agreed to accept verbatim transcripts.

This morass of broken laws and promises demands investigation, prosecution and a firm reassertion of the principle that high office does not relieve men of the obligations of law. Archibald Cox would have provided this reassertion of principle if Mr. Nixon had honored his promise of an independent investigation. Now the President has halted the investigation and broken his promise.

SOME CLAIM THAT in the firings there is no basis for impeachment, no "high crimes and misdemeanors." However, there are sufficient illegalities in the sorry record of Watergate to make a strong case. In addition, the President on Friday failed to comply with or appeal an order of the District Court of Appeals. It is possible, indeed likely, that the court will act against him shortly.

✔ ✔ ✔

By far the most disturbing aspect of the firings of Cox and Ruckelshaus was the taint of a grab for power.

The special prosecutor, an officer of the government created by the insistence of the Senate, was abolished by the President without consulting Congress. The prosecutor's office was quickly sealed by FBI agents. Even personal papers could not be removed by staffers. All this happened while the nation was distracted by a serious war in the Middle East and while Secretary of State Henry Kissinger is conferring in Moscow. It follows close on the heels of claims by the President's lawyers that he has the power to refuse to respond to court subpoenas to supply evidence in criminal prosecutions.

CERTAINLY the mood of these actions seems to suit a banana republic more than the American system of checks and balances and shared powers.

If Mr. Nixon is allowed to prevail in these methods that violate the fundamental traditions of American government, there is a grave danger to the system itself.

✔ ✔ ✔

The collapse of this Administration's ability to lead does not mean the collapse of our government. That should be kept always in mind.

Mr. Nixon's misuse of his powers indeed invites a constitutional crisis. Yet the Constitution remains a steady guide, its farsighted provisions unflinching even in the face of such governmental trauma as presidential resignation or impeachment.

Our Constitution has worked for 200 years because elected leaders made the accommodations necessary in a system of shared powers. Of that need for accommodation, Mr. Nixon seems to have no understanding whatsoever.

Although the nation still lacks a vice president, the Constitution's line of succession covers that contingency. If some in that line lack all the attributes Americans might desire, one strength of the federal system is its capacity to ensure great stability through the period of a temporary president until the people choose a new leader.

Equally important at a time like this, we believe, is the fundamental toughness of the American character.

FROM COAL MINERS in Kentucky and West Virginia to Kansas ranchers and Ohio farmers, from mill hands in Birmingham and Pittsburgh to executives in New York and Los Angeles, most Americans are impatient with gross corruption and ready if need be to fulfill their time-honored duty to throw the rascals out and then get back to normal.

There is no doubt that the days ahead offer political strife and emotional turmoil. Overriding that, however, is the urgent desire for renewed unity. The country has surmounted grave problems in the past. We are convinced it can do so again.

The Burlington Free Press

Burlington, Vt., October 22, 1973

THE ENTIRE WATERGATE affair finally has been fully exposed as vicious partisan politics at its very worst. The firing of Special Prosecutor Archibald Cox, and the hysterical reaction to it, demonstrates beyond the shadow of a doubt that this whole sorry mess boils down to a cheap underhanded attempt by President Nixon's opponents to overthrow the massive mandate given by the American people just last November.

So the opponents want to use the Democrat Congress to impeach the Republican President for firing the inept Cox, who after all was nothing more than a simple employe of the executive branch? Fine, just try it! If the attempt were to succeed, nothing less than a revolution will have occurred, and we can guarantee that a violent counter-revolution would soon follow. Then who would be held responsible for tearing this great nation apart?

President Nixon made only one mistake in this whole affair, and that was when he failed to fire Cox months ago before the vendetta got out of control. But the President wanted to be fair, he leaned over backwards to be fair, but his opponents do not know the meaning of fairness — or honesty and integrity, for that matter. The anti-Nixon people aren't interested in compromise, or meeting half way; they demand everything their way or else — and the nation and its democratic processes be damned!

The anti-Nixon people weren't honest enough to seek the President's impeachment a few weeks and months ago, and why not? Because then Spiro Agnew was next in line for the Presidency. So instead of working down from the top, they worked up from the bottom and succeeded in removing Agnew on a relatively minor income-tax-evasion charge. Now they can go after Nixon with gusto, gall, and ghastly malice!

WHY CANNOT THE PRESIDENT fire one of his own employes — or two or three, for that matter? Congress and the court have no more right to interfere in this matter than the President has to interfere with the internal affairs of the other branches of government.

Archibald Cox, of course, as well as the two fellows who departed the scene with him, is a Kennedy-Harvard type who always impressed us as one who was educated beyond his intelligence. He was out to "get" Nixon, but failed miserably, so now the ball is tossed to a wretched crew of other poor losers — Kennedy, Mondale, Tunney and their ilk. These people never forgave Richard Nixon for two sins of commission: Ending American involvement in the wider Vietnam war which President John Kennedy had started, and winning the greatest landslide election victory in the history of Presidential politics.

And thus there was the Watergate circus, and Archibald Cox, and all the rest now history. So let 'em try to impeach this President and stage a revolution overturning the verdict of the American people. Just let 'em try! — F.B. Smith

ALBUQUERQUE JOURNAL

Albuquerque, N.M., October 24, 1973

President Nixon's decision to surrender the tapes and other White House documents pertinent to the Watergate investigation averted — or at least tempered — the most serious domestic crisis facing the nation since the Civil War.

He is to be commended for placing national interest above his personal pride and his fierce loyalty to a nebulous set of principles, however questionable they may have been.

But the President should neither be commended nor readily forgiven for the arrogance, and selfish pride which precipitated the crisis. Numerous avenues had been left open for him to soothe the anxieties of a bewildered public and to satisfy the urgent needs of both Congress and the judiciary. There was a time when his final compromise would have satified the minimum requirements of Congress, the courts and even the special Watergate prosecutor.

The President's descent from the lofty tower of secrecy he had built around himself was, for him, an act of extreme humility. It is to be hoped that the experience will not prove to be unduly traumatic, for only by humility and mutual respect for Congress, the judiciary and the American people can his administration survive.

The Salt Lake Tribune

Salt Lake City, Utah, October 22, 1973

By defying the courts, by breaking promises and by firing or forcing the resignations of the dedicated men who opposed his violation of accepted legal procedures, President Nixon removed all doubt that he considers himself above the rule of law.

In so doing he forfeited confidence in his present ability to lead the nation, a confidence expressed many times over the years by this newspaper.

Mr. Nixon's frantic response to Special Watergate Prosecutor Archibald Cox's announced intention to resist a gerry-built, illegal plan for partial release of the Watergate tapes seems the reaction of a desperate man. It appears to be the reflex retaliation of a man determined to take things into his own unsteady hands.

When the events of the past few days are considered together with the recent shabby performance of former Vice President Agnew, the President's arrogant actions affirm, at least in the public mind, an admission of complicity in the Watergate scandal.

At a time when the faint breaking of a spark can start a worldwide conflagration, President Nixon exhibits himself as a power-blinded despot, willing to plunge the country into internal strife merely to prove a point which two lawfully instituted courts have overwhelmingly rejected.

In these perilous times the country requires a more stable person at its head than Mr. Nixon has shown himself to be in recent days.

In firing Mr. Cox and Deputy Attorney General William D. Ruckelshaus and forcing the resignation of Attorney General Elliot Richardson, the President broke, in full view of a startled nation, his promise to give the country an impartial investigation of the scandal that now has virtually consumed his administration.

Almost from the day that promise was made, if Mr. Cox is correct, the administration refused to live up to the spirit or the letter of its agreement. Further, Mr. Nixon aborted an orderly appeal of the tapes question to the Supreme Court by announcing Friday he would defy rather than appeal the latest court decision against him. When Mr. Cox insisted that the rule of law take precedence over the rule of Nixon, he was eliminated in a ruthless fashion almost unprecedented in the nearly 200 years of American nationhood.

The rapid-fire resignation and firing of Mr. Richardson and Mr. Ruckelshaus, who also refused to bow to presidential fiat, removes from government three of this failing administration's most conscientious public servants. Their forced departure raises questions whether there is any place left in this government for decent, forthright men.

In each of his three bids for the nation's highest office, The Tribune supported Richard Nixon because we believed he possessed those qualities of leadership which would best serve the country. But the Nixon performance, since the very beginning of the Watergate debacle, has eroded that support to the vanishing point.

Surely he has not, since Watergate broke, shown himself to be a leader devoted to the best interests of the people. It is apparent now he surrounded himself from the beginning with a palace guard contemptuous of the unique system of American democracy under which fair play and the rule of law, not men, dominate. The rare exceptions, such as Mr. Cox, Mr. Richardson and Mr. Ruckelshaus quit or invited firing in a futile, last-ditch effort to restore reason to an administration seemingly bent on self-destruction.

In consideration of his acknowledged accomplishments and in view of our years of support for the man and for many of his policies, it is with regret that we now find it necessary, for the good of the country, to call upon Richard M. Nixon to resign as President of the United States. If he fails to do so, Congress should move with alacrity to impeach him.

The New York Times

New York, N.Y., October 22, 1973

The desperation of President Nixon's moves this weekend to block the Watergate investigation makes it plain that neither law nor orderly governmental process now stand as obstacles to the exercise of his will.

In firing Special Prosecutor Archibald Cox, the President has broken his original pledge, transmitted to the Senate by Attorney General Richardson as a condition for the latter's own confirmation, that nothing would be allowed to interfere with Mr. Cox's search for the facts. Mr. Richardson's resignation, followed by the peremptory discharge of Deputy Attorney General Ruckelshaus for refusing to become Mr. Cox's executioner, provides eloquent testimony that the President has embarked on a course that honorable men in his Administration could not follow.

The constitutional confrontation, which the courts and the special prosecutor tried so hard to avoid, has been precipitated by a President who considers himself sole judge of the law and who uses the power of his office to purge independence from the executive branch and to supersede the mandate of the courts by arbitrary exercise of his will.

This espousal of absolute rule has thrown the country into a governmental crisis of fearful dimensions. The Justice Department is discredited and paralyzed. The far-flung Watergate prosecutions are in receivership under Acting Attorney General Robert H. Bork, a Nixon loyalist willing to carry out the President's imperious order for Mr. Cox's discharge. Under these circumstances, the pledge by White House Press Secretary Ronald Ziegler that the Justice Department will now pursue the investigations "with thoroughness and vigor" can only be treated as a sick joke.

*   *   *

The position of the Senate Watergate committee has been left in a cloudy never-never land by the on-again, off-again agreement between the White House and the committee's leaders, Senators Ervin and Baker, concerning the tapes. Whatever promises were made originally by the President and his lawyers were quickly rendered meaningless by a seemingly endless series of devious shifts in subsequent White House interpretations.

The weekend debacle has brought to light for the first time some indication of the multitude of ways in which the President has been seeking to obstruct the inquiry into the Watergate scandals. Mr. Cox disclosed that his efforts to get at the facts were frustrated on a much broader front than the disputed tapes of Presidential conversations. Documents of Presidential aides were placed beyond his reach by transfer to the shelter of "Presidential files." This cover of executive privilege was used after Mr. Nixon had personally assured the American people: "Executive privilege will not be invoked as to any testimony concerning possible criminal conduct in the matters under investigation."

These behind-the-scenes deceptions have now been followed by open defiance of Congress, the courts and the ousted special prosecutor. Using the Federal Bureau of Investigation in the manner of a totalitarian police force, the President directed its agents to swoop down on the special prosecutor's offices and to deny Mr. Cox and his staff access to their files or even to their personal papers. One Cox associate, confronted by this gross abuse of police power, commented aptly that "one thinks in a democracy this would not happen."

The road now to be taken must be considered in the grim context of Mr. Cox's parting message: "Whether we shall continue to be a government of laws and not of men is now for Congress and the people to decide."

The responsibility for carrying the investigations forward must be picked up without delay by Congress and the courts. No diversionary tactics by the White House can be allowed to deflect attention from that responsibility—not the President's self-serving claim that he is protecting the historic confidentiality of his office nor the familiar plea that the Presidency must not be weakened "at a time of serious world crisis."

No crisis transcends in seriousness contempt for the law by a President, charged under the Constitution with executive responsibility for insuring enforcement of the law. This domestic crisis is almost wholly of the President's own making. Chief District Judge John J. Sirica warned in his decision on the tapes that Mr. Nixon's intransigence would set the White House apart as "a fourth branch of government" and place the President entirely beyond the reach of the law. The Court of Appeals for the District of Columbia, in upholding the Sirica order for surrender of the tapes, reminded Mr. Nixon that "the courts in this country always assume that their orders will be obeyed, especially when addressed to responsible government officials."

The courts, having been rebuffed by Mr. Nixon in their plea for a reasonable compromise, cannot now accept the President's dictate that he will neither appeal their orders nor comply with them. While the clear normal recourse would be a contempt citation, enforcement of such an order against the President would present enormous difficulties. Indeed, the need for continued functioning of Government would all but rule out enforcement against an incumbent Chief Executive.

It becomes, therefore, the first business of Congress to take the necessary steps—and to stand ready to override a Presidential veto that might nullify them—to enable the courts and the grand jury to reconstitute the abolished office of special prosecutor. Given true independence from the executive branch and headed, if possible, by Mr. Cox, the office could then move this crucial unfinished investigation forward to prosecution and trial.

Perhaps the most tragic aspect of the President's course is that his studied defiance of law and of the courts is driving a lengthening list of responsible citizens, including many Congressional moderates of both parties, to the conviction that only the constitutional remedy of impeachment offers any hope of restoring the country to balanced government under the rule of law.

With a Vice President freshly resigned and no replacement yet confirmed, this would unquestionably have to be a move of last resort—one that can only be viewed with grave disquiet. The President still has the opportunity to turn back from the reckless path down which he is rushing. A good start would be for him to remember, and live by, his oath to execute and uphold the law.

The Seattle Times

Seattle, Wash., October 22, 1973

THE real challenge facing President Nixon today is not with Congress or the courts. It is to convince a bewildered public that he has not violated the American sense of fair play.

There appears to be no legal question about Mr. Nixon's right to fire Archibald Cox. The Cox arrangement — a member of the executive branch investigating that branch—was awkward from its beginnings.

But the administration had pledged to the Senate that Cox would have a completely free hand.

Instead, it appears, Mr. Nixon's concept of executive privilege is to take precedence over that pledge and over the orders of the federal courts.

IN short-circuiting the processes of justice that otherwise would have carried the Watergate-tapes issue to the United States Supreme Court, the President said he acted "with great reluctance, only to bring the issue of Watergate tapes to an end."

He said he "concluded . . . that it is not in the national interest to leave this matter unresolved for the period that might be required for a review by the highest court."

Mr. Nixon must be thoroughly aware today of how gravely he miscalculated. Instead of ending the tapes issue, he has magnified it. And if it was not in the national interest to have the issue pursued in the courts, what can be said of the national interest in view of the much greater dimensions the whole sorry controversy has now achieved?

The compromise solution proposed by the President — to have the highly respected Senator Stennis listen to the tapes and verify the accuracy of a summary prepared by Mr. Nixon — has much to recommend it. And it may yet be the key to resolving the narrow question of what is in the tapes.

But the larger questions of confidence and fair play challenge the President to do more than sit tight on his Friday-night statement.

Mr. Nixon cannot meet this challenge by firing people or by adroit legal maneuvering or by adopting a posture of defiance toward Congress and the courts.

DESPITE all the clamor about impeachment, we think the responsible leaders of Congress will — and should — approach that ultimate confrontation with great caution, particularly in view of the vice-presidential vacancy.

In his statement Friday, Mr. Nixon observed that "what matters most in this critical hour is our ability to act—and to act in a way that enables us to control events, not be paralyzed and overwhelmed by them."

All right, Mr. President. You're still at bat.

THE ■ PROVINCE

Vancouver, B.C.
October 22, 1973

There was an air of virtual madness in the convulsions of President Nixon over the weekend. His actions stunned his supporters, and lent credibility to the wildest charges of his enemies.

He has made it almost impossible not to believe that he is himself a guilty man prepared to destroy any man or institution that seems likely to expose his personal guilt in the Watergate conspiracy.

Through the murky months that have undermined the confidence of his country and the world in Richard Nixon's administration, only one bright spot has appeared.

That was the performance of Attorney-General Elliot Richardson, the man who tracked down and ousted Spiro Agnew. At last, it seemed, America had found a brave and honest man near Nixon. Now Nixon has forced him out.

After dark on Saturday the FBI seized the files built up over months by Special Prosecutor Archibald Cox, who was determined to uncover everything about Watergate, no matter who was brought down.

Now Cox is gone, and Richardson, and William Ruckelshaus, the second top man in the Justice Department. All are out because they would not go along with yet another slick and slimy tactic of Richard Nixon in his bid to keep the Watergate truth from coming out.

That tactic involved defying the courts and distorting the U.S. constitution. James Reston commented on it: "The tactical skill of this administration is admitted, but its self-complacent stupidity and moral squalor are monumental."

Nixon wanted Cox fired because in his view the country could not afford a great constitutional showdown during a time of world crisis, and in his judgment such a showdown would come if Cox carried on his court battles to get the Watergate tapes.

Instead Nixon himself has brought on a bigger battle. By being once more too smart but short of judgment he has destroyed all vestiges of credibility. Congress is now talking seriously of impeaching him. So it should. America would be better off without him, no matter who fills in the rest of his term.

DAYTON DAILY NEWS

Dayton, Ohio, October 22, 1973

President Nixon has placed himself above the law. If he does not return to the law, the President must be impeached. The vigor with which Mr. Nixon precipitated events over the week end and the elaborate planning that obviously had gone into his series of maneuvers indicate that the President does not contemplate moderating his claims.

If he does not retract his challenge, however, the basic civil institutions of the nation can be preserved only if Mr. Nixon is confronted and overcome with impeachment proceedings. We cannot have a nation of law if the premier elected official places himself aside from the law, and if we do not have a nation of law, we cannot have a republic. Mr. Nixon has compelled the country into its most dangerous domestic crisis since the Civil war.

The compromise Mr. Nixon announced for resolution of the court struggle over his secret tape recordings was not a compromise at all. It was a unilateral declaration by the President which, when Special Prosecutor Archibald Cox predictably declined the proposition, was used by Mr. Nixon to justify the firing of Mr. Cox and to put Attorney General Elliot Richardson and Mr. Richardson's deputy, William Ruckelshaus, in positions of untenability.

Contrary to the impression he has sought to create, the President has not arranged to spare the nation the constitutional showdown that could have come had he appealed his tapes case to the Supreme court and lost there. He instead has rushed the crisis on the nation in ways that fuzz the sharpness that would have been true with a Supreme court finding against him.

Mr. Nixon has contrived a maze of quasi-legal and merely lawful-seeming confusions, but once traced through them, this is where the issue emerges: Having chosen not to appeal to the Supreme court from an adverse ruling in the appellate court, the President is now bound, as any citizen would be, to abide by the standing, district-court order that he submit his tapes to Judge John Sirica. This Mr. Nixon has not done, though it is his duty. This Mr. Nixon has indicated he will not do, though to be lawful, he must.

Richard Nixon is not exercising executive prerogative. He has assumed executive privileges instead, taking for himself powers that the Constitution does not confer on him. There remain two ways in which Mr. Nixon yet could spare the country the trauma of impeachment proceedings. He still could appeal to the Supreme court or he could deliver the tapes to Judge Sirica as he must otherwise do. If he does neither, Congress, in order to preserve the democratic institutions of the nation, must unflinchingly initiate and conduct the President's removal from office.

Los Angeles Times

Los Angeles, Calif., October 22, 1973

President Nixon has forced a new and unnecessary crisis on the nation he leads by ignoring an order of the courts and by his dismissal of special prosecutor Archibald Cox.

The discharge of Cox is, in itself, a breach of the President's word. For Cox was dismissed for doing precisely what he was authorized to do. The guidelines for his office, which were a condition for the confirmation of the appointment of Elliot L. Richardson as attorney general, authorized the special prosecutor to "determine whether or not to contest the assertion of 'executive privilege' or any other testimonial privilege."

Mr. Nixon, in the name of avoiding a constitutional crisis, has pushed the nation in that very direction.

Mr. Nixon, in the name of compromise, has compromised only with the Senate Watergate committee.

And by his handling of this matter, Mr. Nixon has made it a crisis of men and integrity, forcing from his Administration two of its most competent, respected and trustworthy officials—Richardson, the attorney general, and William D. Ruckelshaus, the deputy attorney general. Their only honorable recourse was to leave office, something which says a great deal about what Mr. Nixon has done.

In sum, Mr. Nixon has said he was acting decisively to move the nation ahead to new unity at a time of international turmoil, but in fact he has pushed the nation back to the uncertainties and divisions of last April, when his closest White House advisers left in controversy. He has rejected reasonable compromise. He has also rejected the orderly procedure of appeal to the Supreme Court. He has resorted, instead, to a confrontation with both Congress and the courts, a confrontation with unpredictable consequences for the nation.

We do not know all the details of the negotiations that went on last week. It is well that a compromise was tried. We can understand the willingness of the Senate Watergate committee leaders to strike a bargain that will give them part of what they failed to get through the courts. But we think Cox was only fulfilling his basic responsibility when he rejected the same compromise. For it was a compromise that risked the obstruction of justice by denying to the courts the content of the tapes in a form likely to be judged acceptable. And it was a compromise that ignored an order of the U.S. Court of Appeals.

So the courts are exposed to an unprecedented possibility that they may be required to determine if the President is in contempt. Certainly the nation will not be satisfied with Mr. Nixon's substitution of his authority for that of the courts. The courts, in finding against Mr. Nixon in this matter, argued that no man, not even the President, may stand above the law. But it was a decision that invited compromise, not defiance.

And so Congress is required to respond to Mr. Nixon's breach of promise. Mr. Nixon committed himself, when he nominated Richardson last April 30, to give the new attorney general "total support" as Richardson coordinated all federal agencies "in uncovering the whole truth about this matter," the matter of Watergate. Subsequently, Mr. Nixon accepted the Senate demand for a special prosecutor, and on May 19 the guidelines for the special prosecutor became a part of the Senate decision to confirm the appointment of Richardson.

Mr. Nixon has made serious mistakes these last days, mistakes that discredit his leadership and peril the balance of federal power. The mistakes require correction.

DAILY NEWS

New York, N.Y., October 22, 1973

THE WATERGATE CASE

—was revived and escalated to new heights of fury and confusion over the weekend by a rapid sequence of events that climaxed in President Richard M. Nixon's unceremonious dismissal of Special Prosecutor Archibald Cox.

Attorney General Elliot Richardson thereupon resigned—as he felt he had to do in good conscience. His deputy, William Ruckelshaus, was fired for refusing to drop the ax on Cox.

Nixon   Cox

The issue that triggered this explosive new crisis was Cox's refusal to obey a presidential order to drop his efforts to obtain, through the courts, both the famous White House tapes touching on Watergate and certain other presidential notes, memos and documents.

Federal District Judge John Sirica had ruled that the President must turn over to him nine tapes to determine whether they contained information needed by a grand jury probing the Watergate scandal. A U.S. Circuit Court of Appeals affirmed that ruling.

Rather than take the case to the Supreme Court, Mr. Nixon put forth his own compromise solution, which Cox termed unacceptable. Exit Cox, and enter a host of furious liberals and partisans clamoring for the President's scalp, and damning him for high-handed, dictatorial methods.

The storm over Cox's ouster has overshadowed the substance of the President's proposal. It calls for release of partial transcripts of the disputed tapes to Judge Sirica and the Senate Watergate committee.

The White House script is to be checked against the original tapes by Sen. John Stennis (D-Miss.), a man of highest probity, to insure that no relevant material is omitted. For Mr. Nixon, this represents—

A CONSIDERABLE RETREAT

—from his previous position that any disclosures would do irreparable damage to the "confidentiality" of intimate White House communications. A few weeks ago, this concession would have been widely hailed as wise and statesmanlike even by many who now are most vocal in their condemnation of the President.

It is worth noting, too, that the compromise was not simply a presidential ukase. The plan for partial release, coupled with verification by Sen. Stennis, was deemed acceptable by Sen. Sam Ervin (D-N.C.), chairman of the Watergate committee, who has never been accused of being a Nixon puppet.

Still, the wolves are in full cry, accusing the President of flouting the constitutional principle of—

SEPARATION OF POWERS

—and defiance of the courts. The first charge is strictly a phony. Cox was a presidential appointee and there seems to be no legal question about Mr. Nixon's right to remove him.

If anyone violated the spirit of the Constitution it was the Senate when it forced the executive branch to accept Cox as a condition for confirming Richardson.

As to the second accusation, it might be well to reserve judgment until we hear whether the courts really feel affronted. It is conceivable they will hold that the President has complied substantially with the judicial directives and accept his course of action.

However the legal pros and cons are resolved, there can be no denying that this latest eruption over Watergate is a national misfortune.

Perhaps the fundamental differences between Cox and Mr. Nixon made an unseemly showdown inevitable. But the manner in which it came about has left many Americans baffled, uneasy, and anxious to hear from the President personally a clarification of the issues as he sees them.

THE MIAMI NEWS
Miami, Fla., October 22, 1973

The News does not think it is good for the country to push every controversial national issue to the last resort of law nor to force a final, definitive resolution of every conflict among our institutions. Like Prof. Archibald Cox, we feel that our system functions well in the absence of ultimate confrontations between the various institutions of our government.

But President Nixon has compelled precisely such a confrontation with his dismissal of Prof. Cox as special prosecutor in the Watergate affair and the accompanying resignations of the Attorney General and his deputy. Prof. Cox was carrying out Mr. Nixon's own mandate under a pledge, relayed through former Attorney General Elliott Richardson, that the President would keep hands off the case which, after all, involved the President's own personal integrity as its central theme.

As far as we can determine from reading the available information on the incidents of the past weekend, Mr. Nixon has committed no specific illegal act relative to the resignations in the Justice Department. He has gone back on what the nation thought was his own solemn word, a very important breach of honor when the President is concerned.

Judge Sirica put the Senate Select Committee (Sen. Sam Ervin) out of the White House tape matter. Judge Sirica did leave the door open for a compromise, recognizing Prof. Cox' legitimate interest in the tapes as prosecutor. The weekend's reports showed that several different people received several different versions of what that compromise was.

President Nixon has conceded court jurisdiction. But he wants the material on the tapes to get into court on his own terms, not the terms on which evidence in a criminal investigation is usually handled. His actions immediately intensify the questions that naturally arise about the content of the tapes. The people have a right to think, especially now, that there are statements on the tapes not involving national military security that could be very damaging to the President and-or his present and former staff members.

Mr. Nixon plays to multiple crises. He forces power issues. In forcing this one, he has attempted to compromise, and has thwarted, the processes of justice and government. The integrity of these processes is the soul of this nation. Because we have confidence in the flow of issues through the courts and because our history proves we are a nation of laws, we have surmounted many crises in our history. President Truman's seizure of the railroads and his obedience to the court's reversal of his position; President Eisenhower's support of the court in the Little Rock school crisis, are but two recent examples of Presidential recognition of the court on the one hand and of allegiance to it, however reluctant the President, on the other.

When we see that President Nixon interposes himself in this process, we sense a serious breakdown in our democratic procedures, the procedures that protect our freedom and assure us of a government responsive to the people.

The News has been most reluctant to join the current clamor for impeachment. If Mr. Nixon were impeached by the House and found guilty by the Senate, what would come next? Can we endure a hiatus in leadership elected by the people? Yet, can we endure the lack of confidence and the suspicion of present leadership? An impeachment process would have the heavy advantage, at this time, of bringing out all the issues and revealing all information. Impeachment would result in the open trial of Mr. Nixon himself that so far has been skirted. The Senate would become a courtroom if impeachment were voted by the House, and, as happens in a courtroom, witnesses could be examined and cross-examined and something a lot closer to the truth than is available to us now could be illuminated.

Mr. Nixon performs in strange and sudden ways, with a propensity for deals and accommodations, with assertions that he is protecting us from ourselves and from too great a knowledge of the mysteries of the inner sanctums of government. He does not seem to recognize the difference between leadership and power.

So disturbing are the events of this past weekend, piled onto the whole Watergate matter and the disclosure of his former Vice-President's corruption that the nation sorely needs a clearing of the air, a resolution of uncertainties. Mr. Nixon has not reacted forthrightly to the standard political challenges nor to the demands of the Congress nor the courts.

Impeachment proceedings would serve those purposes. And though The News' objections to many of Mr. Nixon's policies, practices and his style of governing are well known, we hope fervently impeachment would prove him to have conducted his office honorably and in the highest national interest. It is a lot more important that he be proved right rather than us.

Washington Star-News

Washington, D.C., October 22, 1973

As FBI agents swooped down on his office and took possession of the files, Archibald Cox said it is now up to Congress, and ultimately the American people, "whether ours shall continue to be a government of laws and not of men." We would add that the courts, too, still have a part to play. Otherwise, the ousted special prosecutor just about summed it up.

President Nixon has blundered catastrophically in his handling of the White House tapes issue, and has placed himself in an untenable position in relation to the courts. Unless he can find a way to back-track quickly— and he is not behaving like a man who has much idea of retreating—he is on a course which could lead to unimaginable difficulties.

For starters, it seems almost inevitable that hearings looking toward impeachment proceedings shortly will get under way in Congress.

Where did the President go so wrong?

His critical error was not the firing of Cox, which triggered the departure also of the attorney general and his deputy. Nixon should have let the special prosecutor do the job for which he was hired. But presidents, technically speaking, have a right to fire whole cabinets if they see fit. It may indeed be that by the time Cox ended his remarkably effective news conference Saturday afternoon, it was too late for Nixon. Perhaps as a chief executive whose direct order had been defied, he really had no choice by then but to order Cox removed.

Nor was it wrong for Mr. Nixon to try to work out a compromise solution to his dilemma, a solution whereby he could comply in spirit, as he saw it, with the courts' demand for information as to the content of the tapes, but a solution which at the same time would not involve surrender on the basic issue of executive privilege. There is such an issue. There is substance to the contention that an administration could not function if its private consultations might at any time be laid bare at the order of a judge.

The President's willingness to provide digests of the tapes in question, authenticated by Senator Stennis, did assure so far as we are concerned that nothing on those tapes which related to Watergate would escape the grand jury's and the public's attention. That is no small concession—what part, if any, Mr. Nixon played in the Watergate cover-up has been, after all, the central question plaguing us all.

It seems clear that the President made his crucial mistake when, having learned that Cox was opposed to the suggested compromise, he forbade him to pursue in court any further effort to secure the tapes themselves. It was here that Mr. Nixon irretrievably crossed his Rubicon, precipitating what the White House now recognizes as the "firestorm" events of Saturday. At that point, the President did two things. First, he broke the solemn word of his administration, offered at Elliot Richardson's confirmation hearings, as to the freedom of action that would be allowed the special Watergate prosecutor. Specifically, among other things, the senators were promised that the prosecutor would have full authority for "determining whether or not to contest the assertion of 'executive privilege.'" The prosecutor would be free to contest this issue. The courts would decide.

But the second thing Mr. Nixon did, in his Friday directive to Cox, was to make it cruelly plain that, so far as he was concerned, the courts would not decide between him and the prosecutor. He, the President, had done the deciding. The courts would not be permitted to hear from the prosecutor on this issue.

There would, moreover, be no appeal to the Supreme Court, such as might produce that definitive decision by which Mr. Nixon had once promised to abide. There would be no production of the tapes and other evidentiary material the District Court had ordered produced. There would be the digests described in the White House "proposal"—no longer a proposal, but a course of action proclaimed by the President. The courts, presumably, could like it or lump it. And Cox was forbidden to argue, on behalf of the grand jury, that the court was entitled to anything more.

Why? Why was it necessary to pursue this arbitrary course, flouting established institutions for the resolving of disputes? The office of special prosecutor had been set up to provide the courts with an officer who could argue the Watergate cases with no taint of White House influence, avoiding any suspicion that the administration might try to continue to cover up. Why at the crucial moment subject it, as just another twig on the executive branch, to precisely the sort of presidential control and interference from which it had been promised immunity?

Why should not the White House present its proposal to the court, while Cox stated his objections? Why should the court not decide?

Quite simply, because President Nixon has sought to adopt a position above the law. And that, to put it gently, has most serious implications for the future of government in the United States. There is a name for a system in which the executive assumes such a position. The name is dictatorship.

The Star-News hopes and believes that the courts and Congress will stand up to the challenge that has been thrown at them. We hope and believe, too, that Richard Nixon will turn back from a dark road which can lead only to tragedy for him and for the country.

OREGON Journal
AN INDEPENDENT NEWSPAPER

Portland, Ore., October 22, 1973

The United States has survived past perils of equal magnitude and undoubtedly its considerable strengths will see it through the alarming constitutional crisis that confronts it today.

But the nation has never faced a dilemma quite like the one that erupted over the President's White House tapes over the weekend.

In what can only be viewed as an act of desperation to keep his recorded conversations away from the courts, the Congress and the Watergate grand jury, President Nixon has ignored a court order and hurled a direct challenge at Congress.

The firing of Archibald Cox, the special prosecutor named with full assurance that he would have absolute independence in prosecuting those involved in Watergate-related crimes, defies the President's own pledge. In the process, he drove out of office two of the men who stood above the scandals of his administration—Atty. Gen. Elliot Richardson and deputy Atty. Gen. William Ruckelshaus. The dismantling of the special prosecutor's function and assigning the prosecution to the Justice Department, which itself is not untainted by Watergate, further diminishes public confidence in the administration's ability and willingness to clean up its mess.

What the courts will do after the President in effect placed himself beyond the reach of their order is uncertain. What is more certain is that the Congress is now forced to think the unthinkable—impeachment.

When the lawmakers return to duty —and it says something about the inadequacies of Congress that its members were taking a long weekend when the constitutional crisis hit—representatives will have to give serious consideration to impeachment as one of the few constitutional mechanisms available to resolving a showdown of this kind.

One cannot help but wonder what it is about those tapes that makes it worthwhile for the President to bring his government to the brink of catastrophe.

If he is to continue under these circumstances, he will preside over a government approaching paralysis. It is unlikely that he could get a new attorney general, or anyone else, confirmed now. The Watergate Committee's efforts are more likely to be extended, after the demise of the special prosecutor, than phased out. A standoff between congressional rejection of presidential prosposals and presidential vetoes of congressional desires is predictable.

Can the nation afford such paralysis, let alone the lack of confidence and growing bitterness toward its government? With the Middle East situation what it is, Southeast Asia still smoldering, and Secretary of State Henry Kissinger applying his considerable talents in pursuit of peace, the country can hardly tolerate stalemate and stagnation.

From the dismal vantage point the weekend's developments provide, that would seem to be our fate today and perhaps for the more than three years remaining of the second Nixon term. While Congress is forced against its sentiments to think of impeachment, Mr. Nixon also may have to ponder his own unthinkable—resignation.

In the meantime, a vacancy in the presidency has to be viewed as a greater possibility than it was a week ago. Consequently, Congress cannot allow the present turmoil to delay fulfillment of its responsibility to fill the office of vice president.

The Boston Globe

Boston, Mass., October 22, 1973

The grave constitutional crisis which nearly everybody had hoped could be avoided now confronts our nation. And this has come about because President Richard M. Nixon has defied the courts in refusing to surrender the Watergate tape recordings and has fired Special Prosecutor Archibald Cox.

Attorney General Elliot L. Richardson has resigned, honorably and with great integrity reminding President Nixon of his repeated promises to the Senate last April that his special prosecutor would have "all the independence, authority and staff support needed;" that he would have "full authority" for "determining whether or not to contest the assertion of 'Executive Privilege," and that Mr. Richardson would "not countermand or interfere" with Mr. Cox's "decisions or actions."

Mr. Richardson's Deputy Attorney General, William Ruckelshaus, has been dismissed by the President because he refused to fire Cox. The Justice Department is now headed by Acting Atty. Gen. Robert H. Bork, the Solicitor General, and will now take over the Watergate prosecutions — or what is left of them. Mr. Cox's office was for a time sealed off by agents of the Federal Bureau of Investigation.

President Nixon has stated that the prosecutions and investigations "will continue with full vigor." But in the process, great damage, and perhaps irreparable damage, has been done to that basic element in all court proceedings — integrity and the appearance of integrity.

Mr. Cox has put it another way: "Whether ours shall continue to be a government of laws and not of men is now for Congress and ultimately the American people" to decide.

He was fired for disobeying the President's order that he, "as an employee of the executive branch, . . . make no further attempt by judicial process to obtain tapes, notes or memoranda of presidential conversations."

All of this leaves standing a 5-to-2 decision of the US Court of Appeals upholding Cox, rejecting the President's claims of an absolute privilege, and ordering the President, if an out-of-court agreement could not be reached, to turn the tapes over to Judge John Sirica.

It is left standing because Mr. Nixon has chosen not to appeal it to the US Supreme Court. And in not surrendering the tapes, the President has placed himself above the laws that he swore faithfully to execute.

Mr. Nixon last Friday night said he had proposed to "submit to Judge Sirica, through a statement prepared by me personally from the subpoenaed tapes, a full disclosure of everything contained in those tapes that has any bearing on Watergate." The summary's "authenticity," he said, would be assured by letting Sen. John Stennis listen to the tapes and compare them with the summary.

This was unacceptable to Mr. Cox and, we think, with very good reason. As he pointed out, a summary of the tapes "lacks the evidentiary values of the tapes themselves," and other court-ordered material in the possession of the White House was not included in Mr. Nixon's proposal. Innocent men might be convicted, and guilty men might go free, because of the government's failure to produce all such pertinent evidence in court. There is the further point, though Mr. Cox did not mention it, that tapes can be doctored, and that such doctoring, in turn, can often be detected by experts.

(This latter aspect might not be within the purview of the Senate Watergate Committee, whose chairman, Sen. Sam Ervin (D-N.C.), said yesterday he expects the White House to furnish the tapes to Sen. Stennis and "furnish to the committee a verbatim statement of exactly what the tapes recorded.")

What we have now is a grave constitutional impasse between the executive and judicial branches of government, and understandably a movement is growing in the legislative branch to take the route of impeaching the President. Many of our respected legislators, who until now had wisely refrained from calling for such a step, have spoken out in favor of it.

But such a process would be agonizing for this nation. It would take much time, in a period when war is raging abroad and economic problems beset us at home.

Mr. Nixon has stated that under his proposal, "America will be spared the anguish of further indecision and litigation about tapes." We think his proposal defies a lawful court order and would obstruct justice. But we also think the impeachment process would bring anguish and perhaps indecision too.

And in such a period of turmoil, freedom of the press and the people's right to know could face even graver danger than they have faced in the past.

There is another way to spare the nation from all this. It was done tidily and quickly and in full accordance with the processes of law only recently, when Spiro T. Agnew resigned as Vice President.

With full respect for the high office he holds, and indeed because of that respect, we urge President Nixon to do the same.

Ledger-Star

Norfolk, Va., October 22, 1973

The President has gone too far—

This was undoubtedly the reaction of many an American to Mr. Nixon's firing of Special Prosecutor Archibald Cox, plus the simultaneous exit from office of Attorney General Elliot Richardson and his deputy, William P. Ruckelshaus.

However, the first thing that needs to be said about these extraordinary events of the weekend, stemming from the Watergate tapes dispute, is that the national dismay ought not to extend to the kind of overkill response which would heap up even greater public damage.

To seize almost blindly on impeachment proceedings as an answer to the President's peremptory actions, as some are urging, or to mount an effort to pressure him into resignation would simply replace one excess with another, one more dangerous and, at this juncture anyhow, too traumatic in proportion to the issues involved.

★　★　★　★

Impeachment, a last-resort device, should pivot on some gross illegality or dereliction and would always have to be weighed in the light of the harm the process itself might inflict on the country.

If Congress should abandon the caution this moment calls for and rush ahead on the impeachment route, the country would be plunged into desperate new agonies. One result of making the President a defendant would be a virtually leaderless situation, what with only an unconfirmed vice presidential nominee standing by.

But to warn against a destructive overreaction to the President's moves is not to minimize the distressing lapses in his judgment as he made these latest attempts to assert a privileged status for his office vis-a-vis the other two branches of government.

In the Cox firing and attendant happenings, the unhappy consequences have been at least threefold:

1. Mr. Nixon has affronted the nation and the Congress to a degree he may not even yet be aware of. This was in the repudiation of the independence which had been given Special Prosecutor Cox for getting to the bottom of the Watergate bugging and cover-up, wherever that inquiry might lead. Most Americans had certainly looked on Mr. Cox's conduct of that effort as both skilled and dispassionate, and upon his pursuit of the White House tapes in the face of Mr. Nixon's resistance as one impressive proof of the integrity of the investigation.

To be sure, Mr. Nixon did have the power to fire Mr. Cox, technically an employe of the executive branch. But this was an unusual arrangement, in which the special prosecutor had been deliberately vested with independence—from presidential control most of all.

To renege on this was a flagrant turnaround. And the assertion that Mr. Cox should have acceded to presidential orders not to pursue the tape matter in court, as a part of the compromise worked out with the Ervin Committee for releasing a summary of the tapes' contents, just won't wash.

Nor will the decision to fire Mr. Cox look any better if the courts should themselves be persuaded by Mr. Nixon's attorneys to accept the compromise agreed to for the parallel, but entirely separate Senate inquiry. Mr. Cox's independence is the crux of the disturbing issue raised over the weekend. That independence was arbitrarily overruled even though one condition of Mr. Richardson's confirmation by the Senate for attorney general was that Mr. Cox could not be removed except for unusual "improprieties."

2. The nation has lost the services not only of the able Mr. Cox, but of two of the most esteemed men in an already badly shattered administration. Ironically, in fact, Mr. Nixon may well have propelled one presidential possibility for 1976 well into the center ring of prospects owing to the way the public will surely respond to Mr. Richardson's demonstration of integrity.

3. The President has worked himself finally into an impossible corner, with his implied assertion of immunity from the laws and the courts. If a president can balk probes of wrongdoing when the evidence may be interspersed with his confidential materials, and can fire any federal employe who defies him on the point, who is to prosecute—since all the federal prosecutors are executive branch employes? Surely the Constitution contemplated no such general immunity from the law for anybody in this country.

Mr. Nixon, of course, won't necessarily have the final word on the point. There may well be more from the courts or from Congress; there is, for one thing that possibility raised by Sen. Ervin that Congress itself could now appoint a prosecutor, as in Teapot Dome, who could not be fired by the President.

★　★　★　★

From all the above-cited consequences, plus the general damage to the President's credibility and the apprehension he has generated over what some yet-to-come assertion of power may do to the fabric of American government, this seems plain:

Mr. Nixon has seriously erred, in his judgment of the public temper among other things, and if the error does not at this point justify the ultimate in reproof, it is he who must bear the responsibility for bringing such reproof to the point of active consideration in some quarters.

He has made an already dispiriting situation much worse.

Chicago Tribune

Chicago, Ill., October 22, 1973

President Nixon has perpetrated what may the worst blunder in the history of the Presidency.

In the name of national interest and security in the midst of a raging Mideast war and increasing international tensions, Mr. Nixon tried to put the entire Watergate mess behind him with an out-of-court deal on the release of the controversial White House Watergate tapes. Because the deal was more a political solution than a legal one— because Mr. Nixon failed to take into account the principles of the men who ran his Justice Department and the importance of his earlier commitment to the independence of the Watergate prosecution— the deal fell apart. He responded rashly and precipitously, with what portend to be disastrous consequences.

He broke no law and violated no constitutional provision in ordering the firing of special prosecutor Archibald Cox. All of his actions were well within the acknowledged powers of the Presidency. But because of the enormity of the Watergate scandal and the depth of the hostility towards him in Congress, Mr. Nixon has made the constitutional crisis he sought to avoid a looming reality.

His critics are denouncing him as "a dictator." His enemies in Congress— and not a few of his former friends —are demanding impeachment proceedings on the ground that the President's actions constitute obstruction of justice.

With the departure of Atty. Gen. Elliot Richardson and Deputy Atty. Gen. William Ruckleshaus, his administration lost two of its best men and stands condemned by their opposition to him. His party is being torn into pro and anti-Nixon factions, with the majority apparently in the latter.

Because of his earlier commitment to an independent prosecution, the President's credibility—or what remained of it—has been totally discredited.

His image as a statesman and his hopes of a lofty place in history have been shattered. Mr. Cox, the man he

sought to make the villain of this piece, has instead become a martyr. The Senate Watergate committee, which had at first seemed agreeable to his compromise, has now returned to the attack and will pursue its investigation more aggressively than before.

Could this have been avoided? Mr. Nixon should have realized when the Cox appointment was made that he was setting in motion legal machinery he could neither divert nor stop except thru the cataclysmic kind of confrontation the nation experienced this weekend. If he did not want the Cox probe, he should not have agreed to it. Having agreed to it, if he truly expected to be vindicated, he should have let the investigation run its course and let the dispute over the White House tapes be resolved by the courts.

Instead, he blundered, and now must pay the price. But neither he nor the nation should be subject to the price many of Mr. Nixon's critics and political enemies now seem to have in mind— a hysterical, inflammatory, and divisive political inquisition such as that which led to the purely political impeachment of President Andrew Johnson in 1868. We are, as Mr. Cox said, a nation of laws, not men. Personalities, personal hatreds, and partisan ambitions must not be allowed to intrude upon the resolution of this controversy.

The confirmation of Vice President-designate Gerald Ford should not in any way be impeded by this dispute. Talk of holding his appointment hostage for release of the Watergate tapes and the like cannot be countenanced. His appointment has nothing to do with the Watergate controversy and his qualifications for office have not been changed one whit by the events of the weekend.

It seems probable that there will be debate over impeachment resolutions. If so, it must be orderly, dispassionate, and concerned solely with the law. The nation can ill afford the kind of rupture that anything less impartial would produce. Under no circumstances should aspirants to the Presidency in either party be permitted to turn any such

discussion into a campaign forum.

As for Mr. Nixon, he must recognize that the course he has pursued and is pursuing is wrong and that he has brought this catastrophe upon himself thru his own actions. We don't know how he can rescue himself from this legal muddle and political shambles but he must try. He must seek reconciliation with the Congress, the courts, and the

American public. He made this colossal blunder. He must now do everything in his power, no matter how humbling, to undo it to whatever extent possible. As he noted, these are trying times in the world. But while the United States cannot afford a constitutional crisis, neither can it afford any more pugnacious obstinacy on the part of its chief executive.

Orlando Sentinel

Orlando, Fla., October 23, 1973

FOR WEEKS his political foes have been pressuring President Nixon, in every conceivable way, to accept a compromise in the White House tapes issue.

Friday such a compromise was reached and concurred in by Chairman Sam Ervin and Vice Chairman Howard Baker of the Senate Watergate committee.

Predictably, we now find the vultures of the left and the labor union monopolies demanding Nixon's impeachment.

✿ ✿ ✿

REVEALING the contents of the tapes, after scrutiny by Sen. Stennis, is not enough. Obviously that does not serve the purpose of this unsavory gang of power seekers whose single motivation since the election of 1968 has been to bring this government down.

They want power, and Archibald Cox, the fired special prosecutor, was their arrogant Trojan horse. Unfortunately, many otherwise responsible people have been fooled into thinking that the motives of these revolutionaries are wholesome.

Admittedly, a weakened administration was forced into the Cox appointment, and, to that

extent, helped bring the present crisis on itself.

Golda Meir filling her cabinet with Egyptians could be no more outlandish than Elliot Richardson's appointment of the former solicitor general in the Kennedy administration.

✿ ✿ ✿

NONE OF THIS is designed to defend the excesses of Watergate. Former administration officials unquestionably were involved in those scandals, and they should be punished.

Most importantly, however, nothing disclosed in the whole Watergate mess so far proves that the President was guilty of anything more than bad judgment in some of his personnel selections.

That is precisely why the tapes are important. We have been told that the way to prove or disprove John Dean's story of Nixon's personal knowledge of the Watergate coverup is to reveal the contents of the tapes.

So what happens? Nixon decides to reveal the tapes in a manner acceptable to the Senate committee's chairman and vice chairman, and Archie Cox threatens to have the President held in contempt of court.

Why shouldn't Nixon fire him? Cox and his ilk don't want the President found innocent. They want his dead body.

THE DALLAS TIMES HERALD

Dallas, Tex., October 23, 1973

THE VOICES of congressmen calling for impeachment of President Nixon grow louder but it is much too early to consider seriously the tortuous and traumatic experience which would be involved in any attempt to remove the President from office.

Although millions of Americans are deeply and properly disturbed at the President's firing of special prosecutor Archibald Cox and the dismantling of the top echelon of the Justice Department, they realize that the Watergate tape controversy must be played out in federal court before there are solid grounds for an impeachment attempt.

But these same Americans are dazed and irate at the pattern of arrogant disregard for the courts and the Congress which has marked the actions of President Nixon since the Watergate scandal broke last spring.

He agreed, albeit reluctantly, to the appointment of an independent prosecutor, but when Cox refused to accept an edited version of the tapes the President insisted Cox be fired. Mr. Nixon also turned his back on his promise to accept a "definitive" ruling of the Supreme Court in the tape controversy. Instead, he ducked a Supreme Court hearing, thus appearing to be attempting to set his own rules on what is right and legal.

If Federal Judge John Sirica accepts the tape transcript, as authenticated by U.S. Sen. John Stennis, the reaction resulting from the Cox dismissal will be somewhat quieted. But Cox has warned that cases against several high former officials of the Nixon administration may be untriable if the tapes themselves are not made available.

In any case, the nation should not have to wait "two or three weeks," as indicated by White House counselor Mel Laird, to learn more about the contents of the President's tapes.

It is possible that there will never be sufficient evidence to support the impeachment of the

President. But President Nixon is impeaching himself in the minds and hearts of his countrymen by his failure to press for a complete investigation of Watergate and the trial and punishment of those involved in the break-in and the cover-up.

His aides are mouthing tired phrases about "legality" and presidential privileges. What we need to hear now are honest comments about morality and presidential responsibilities. We shrink from the thought that a man elected in a landslide last November may not be fit or able to give needed leadership to this troubled land. Only Richard Nixon can save himself and the nation from further trauma.

THE INDIANAPOLIS STAR
Indianapolis, Ind., October 23, 1973

To strive for some understanding of President Nixon's dismissal of Archibald Cox, special Watergate prosecutor, it is necessary to try to put oneself into Mr. Nixon's shoes.

In assenting to the arrangement by which an independent prosecutor was to be given untrammeled authority to conduct a grand jury investigation without direction or limitation, Mr. Nixon must have realized that he was opening his whole administration to a probe of unknown scope. But apparently he did not perceive the possibility that his own office — the presidency itself — would become the target of an attempt to establish a precedent that the President is subject to court subpena to compel him to deliver documents he regards as confidential.

That attempt is the issue over which Cox was fired.

The question of whether Mr. Nixon has been seeking to protect himself, personally, against disclosure of information in the celebrated White House tapes seems to have been effectively put aside in the compromise agreement to make content of the tapes available to the Senate Watergate Committee. As we understand the agreement, any information in the tapes linking Mr. Nixon to the Watergate affair will become available to the Senate committee. So that is not now the object of his concern, whether or not it ever was.

What Mr. Nixon says he is trying to prevent is the further development of a confrontation — brought about by Cox — between the power of the presidency and the power of the courts.

The President offered to Cox a similar compromise, by which content of the tapes, verified by an outside observer who would listen to them, would be made available to Cox and the grand jury. Cox rejected the offer. He insisted on pursuing his effort to obtain the tapes themselves under compulsion of a court order.

Cox had obtained such an order from United states Disrict Judge John J. Sirica, who has been upheld by the Court of Appeals. The order directs the President to produce the tapes to Judge Sirica, who would listen to them and decide whether to make them, or parts of them, available to the grand jury.

Mr. Nixon insists that the tapes are confidential documents of the presidential office and that it is the prerogative of the President alone to determine whether they should be disclosed. His position is that the constitutional independence of the presidency is at stake, that the President cannot be compelled to yield documents either to Congress or to a court and that no other stance is reconcilable to the inherent powers and responsibilities of the office.

It must also be said that Mr. Nixon is fighting for his own political life. Involved in the relentless pursuit of the Watergate affair is an obvious endeavor of some of his enemies to oust him from office. One way to do that would be to destroy his ability to control the Executive Branch.

A step in that direction was the confirmation of Elliot L. Richardson as attorney general on condition that he appoint Cox as special prosecutor with full support and independence. Thus when President Nixon ordered Richardson to dismiss Cox his response was that he could not do so and must resign. Although a member of the President's Cabinet, Richardson actually was a prisoner of the Senate.

The President apparently concluded that acceptance of the Cox arrangement was a blunder. In retrospect it was. The President of the United States like anyone else makes mistakes and must take the blame for them. Nonetheless he must continue being President and he is entitled to loyal support from the Executive Branch. Without that kind of support, he cannot carry out the duties of the most difficult job in the world.

The Charleston Gazette
Charleston, W.Va., October 23, 1973

Before President Nixon took fateful action last Saturday, Sen. Robert C. Byrd observed that if Mr. Nixon were to fire Archibald Cox he would be firing a man for doing his duty.

Within hours after Byrd thus answered a reporter's question, the President had fired Cox, the special Watergate prosecutor. After Atty. Gen. Elliot Richardson resigned in protest, Mr. Nixon fired Deputy Atty. Gen. William Ruckelshaus, who also objected to Cox's removal.

Then, in a move not unlike those taken by the leaders of South American juntas, President Nixon dispatched FBI agents to the Justice Department, there to prevent access to evidence gathered by Cox and his assistants.

Before all this happened, the President had permitted the deadline for appeal to elapse, and thus stood in contempt of a federal district court which had upheld an earlier ruling that he should turn the White House tapes over to Judge John Sirica for a determination of their value, if any, to a grand jury.

For these incredible actions, the President's close supporters offer only one excuse: Cox had declined to accept a compromise on the tapes which would have permitted Sen. John Stennis to hear some of them and review a summary to be prepared by Mr. Nixon.

Because some members of the Senate Watergate committee had indicated approval of the compromise, these supporters seemed to be saying, Cox should have done so, also.

But the Senate committee is investigating Watergate with an eye to legislative reform. Cox was investigating Watergate with an eye to prosecuting those to whom the trail led. There is a considerable difference, and, as Sen. Byrd suggested might happen, the President fired Cox for doing his duty.

Congressmen now are beginning to utter the word "impeach" out loud and without the usual reservations. It is refreshing to see them discard some of the caution that has kept them silent while an American President set himself above the law.

The Nixon administration is a shambles. Several of its most prominent figures are under indictment. Congress is obliged, at this point, to prevent Mr. Nixon from seizing the government. It has come to that.

Post-Tribune
Gary, Ind., October 23, 1973

The President of the United States must understand the mood of the people. He must understand that his election on a law-abiding platform means that his obstruction of justice by stopping the Watergate probe — a legal move he dictated — is a complete contradiction of his mandate and promises.

Every pressure possible, including impeachment hearings conducted calmly and with no political overtones, must be placed on Richard M. Nixon so he will be forced to change his stance. He must make proper amends with the courts, with the staff appointments he made and unmade and with Americans. And they must be convinced the President is convinced he took the wrong steps. If he cannot accomplish that, he should resign. In the meantime the course of action on naming a vice president should continue. It will be hard with the President's self-made problems hanging over Congress but it must be done.

The resignation of Atty. Gen. Elliot Richardson and the firing of William P. Ruckelshaus makes both men stand high in the eyes of Americans. It also should have warned the President of the gravity of his actions. Two such dedicated public servants would have gone to any length to avoid their actions but — thank God — they saw the magnitude of the President's mistake and chose to follow their convictions. It is certain, in so doing, that they felt their convictions were those of most Americans. They did what they thought was right. We think they were right and that the President was wrong. He must be made to see he was wrong, to believe he was wrong and to right the mistake. If he cannot do that, then he should leave the office of the presidency.

The President chose the legal path for the Watergate probe. He chose the man to follow that path. Then he fired that man, Archibald Cox, for doing what he was instructed to do when the path seemed to get too hot under foot. No matter what the truth is, the general impression will be that President Nixon just has too much to hide and he will use any method to suppress the information.

It is difficult to believe this all took place less than a year after Nixon was re-elected. It is appalling the number of things that have happened to almost completely stall the governmental machinery. It should be a political 2 x 4 between the eyes of the President when he sees what has taken place, and much of it because of his own actions. He has destroyed his credibility and has assured himself of an unwanted place in history.

Cox did a classic job in simplicity when he said:

"Whether ours shall continue to be a government of laws and not of men is now for the Congress and ultimately the American people" to decide.

We believe Congress will decide. If it does not, we know the people will decide. And they will be pretty blunt with the office of the President and with the Congress:

America will be a government of laws!

Honolulu Star-Bulletin

Honolulu, Hawaii, October 23, 1973

To the extent that newspaper endorsements affect presidential elections, the Star-Bulletin has been a party to the present national anguish. Twice we endorsed Richard M. Nixon for the office of President.

Moreover, this newspaper had hoped until this past weekend that the President himself could survive the scandals of 1973 with his personal honor, for he is the custodian of our national honor, a stewardship he was elected to keep through 1976.

But the hopes that Richard Nixon could "bring us together" and our dreams of "peace with honor" have collapsed in disillusionment with an administration that is on its moral deathbed. Mr. Nixon should resign and let the nation come back to life.

There was still hope, even through his refusal to release the Watergate tapes, that the administration and the President's reputation could be salvaged by the two leaders in Justice, Elliot Richardson and William Ruckelshaus. They were the unsoiled ones, the men who could put fidelity to the Republic above loyalty to the politician who ran it. On Saturday, President Nixon required them to do exactly that, and they chose their self-respect over political allegiance.

In demanding this personal obeisance when it outraged their own convictions, Mr. Nixon has answered the horrible question. For it is now apparent that the Mitchells, the Haldemans, the Ehrlichmans, and all the other sad characters in this tragedy, had the choice between honor and their jobs, and they chose their jobs. The moral collapse within the White House was not possible without the head of the house knowing it or approving it or sponsoring it, or all three of these things. His present imperiousness in the firing of Archibald Cox and his subsequent dismantling of the Justice Department is condemning evidence that a staff member would not question the wishes of Richard Nixon and still remain a staff member. It is now clear that the executive branch of the national government has been corrupted by guile and lust and that this national pain should not be prolonged.

But if he resigns, or if he refuses to resign and is impeached, what then? What of his fabled skill at foreign policy and who will succeed him?

It is time to stop giving the President the credit for his subordinates' success but blaming them when he fails. Henry Kissinger has been the genius of our foreign policy, and any President with intelligence can execute it.

In terms of succession, the President, by choosing to resign rather than face impeachment, could work out in advance with Congress the selection of the strongest possible successor — a person who could restore our faith in government and each other.

Such an act would benefit Mr. Nixon's image when the history of these unhappy days is recorded.

Congress, in turn, ought to rise above its political podium and give us a leader, recognizing that self-government is too precious a commodity to be thought of this year in terms of future elections.

While we feel that Nelson Rockefeller is the best equipped to lead the nation at this time, such different men as Ronald Reagan or Hubert Humphrey might also bring us back together. So probably could Daniel Evans, or Walter Mondale, or Charles Percy, or Edmund Muskie, or Barry Goldwater, or Elliot Richardson.

The mechanics are simple. One of these men, or someone of similar stature, should be named vice-president, then the President must resign rather than put himself and the nation through the inevitable ordeal of impeachment. Then the Congress must name another vice-president, Gerald Ford, perhaps, or someone similarly qualified.

Then the new President and Vice President can get on with the task of healing our wounds, or restoring our faith in our leaders and in one another. We want to sing "God Bless America" again and believe that we're worthy of it.

THE ARIZONA REPUBLIC

Phoenix, Ariz., October 23, 1973

The Nixon-haters don't want the President's tapes; they want his head.

It all started when one of Nixon's own aides said conversations in the President's office had been t a p e d. Presumably they could throw some light on the Watergate break-in and cover-up.

But the President refused to give the tapes to either Sen. Sam Ervin of the Senate's Watergate investigating committee, or to Attorney Archibald Cox, who headed a Department of Justice team investigating Watergate.

The President's r e a s o n s for withholding the tapes ranged from confidentiality and national security through executive powers to separation of powers.

Neither Ervin nor Cox recognized the President's claims, and both went to court to get the tapes. U.S. District Judge John Sirica ordered the President to produce the tapes and said he would decide whether they should go to Cox for presentation to a grand jury. Judge Sirica refused to order the tapes turned over to Ervin, saying he lacked jurisdiction in the case.

A federal appellate court upheld the Sirica ruling in regard to Cox, but the 5-2 verdict also suggested a compromise be worked out if possible.

Last Friday such a compromise was a n n o u n c e d by the White House. It had been agreed, according to the announcement, that the President would have a summary of the tapes put on paper and would then allow Sen. John Stennis, D-Miss., to listen to the tapes and be sure that they were accurately reflected by the summaries. The summaries would then go the Ervin committee, Judge Sirica, and presumably anyone else who wanted them.

This deal was approved by Sen. Ervin, Democratic leader on the Watergate committee, and by Sen. Howard Baker, his Republican counterpart. But it was not acceptable to Cox, who opposed the compromise even before Judge Sirica had a chance to determine whether it was satisfactory.

This led to the dismissal of Cox, the dismissal of Deputy Attorney General William Ruckelshaus and the resignation of Attorney General Elliot L. Richardson.

The situation is unprecedented in American political history and shows the incredible rupture that has occurred among the three supposedly equal branches of the government.

But unless the c o u n t r y was ready to allow Cox to become the fourth branch of the government, able to do as he pleased without let or hindrance, the present crisis was unavoidable.

In simple parlance, Cox worked for the Department of Justice, which is part of the executive branch of the government and from which the line of command leads to the President.

It is true that when Cox was made investigator of the Watergate mess, he was told he would have a free hand. That probably was a mistake, but many clients have promised their lawyers a free hand.

But when the client becomes dissatisfied with his l a w y e r's work, the boss has the obvious right to fire the attorney. And when it was clear as could be that Cox had no intention of taking orders from the President, and in fact told reporters in a televised interview that he might try to get a court to hold Nixon in contempt, the President did what he had to do: he fired Cox, with the Richardson and Ruckelshaus reverberations following.

What Nixon did has many parallels in American political history. Probably the most celebrated was President Truman's firing of Gen. Douglas MacArthur. Truman said MacArthur refused to obey his orders. He r e m o v e d the general from command in Korea. The sequence of events between Nixon and Cox was the same.

To no one's surprise, the recently muted talk about impeaching President Nixon has been revived. The senators who apparently were ready to c o n f i r m Rep. Gerald Ford as vice president are now talking of holding his nomination in ransom.

This is, perhaps, the true tragedy of Watergate. It is purely a political issue, in which such long accepted presidential rights as the ability to fire a lawyer in the Department of Justice have been called into question.

If there is to be an impeachment, the sooner the House moves the better. But it should be clearly understood that the basis is simply a grab for political power. The hate-Nixon group is even willing to take Speaker Carl Albert for president if they can get rid of Nixon.

The tapes are no longer the issue. The way is clear for both the courts and C o n g r e s s to learn what's in the tapes, although the country may pay a terrific price in the years ahead for this violation of executive privilege.

The issue is Nixon h i m s e l f. Whether his opponents will seek to get rid of him, or will let him remain a prisoner in the White House, is the immediate question.

The Evening Bulletin
Philadelphia, Pa., October 24, 1973

The white-hot anger of the American public, goaded to the breaking point by presidential arrogance, finally penetrated the White House. It has put an abrupt end to one perilous piece of Watergate brinksmanship.

Mr. Nixon's sudden announcement that he will comply in full with court orders to deliver his secret Watergate tape recordings for scrutiny by U. S. District Judge Sirica is a display of elemental prudence. With a foot over the abyss, Mr. Nixon's instinct for political survival reasserted itself. He drew back.

"This President does not defy the law," his lawyer proclaimed.

What this President did not dare defy was the indignation of the people at his latest Watergate maneuvers.

It is true that he was not yet formally in contempt of court, and Congress was still warily approaching the subject of impeachment. But Congress ultimately responds to public opinion, and public endurance was all but exhausted.

Mr. Nixon exhausted it by first committing himself to an independent prosecution of Watergate crimes, and then reneging on his pledge; by committing his constitutional arguments for executive privacy to the courts, and then trying to play games with them.

But most of all, he cracked the shell of public restraint by a strategem that sacrificed the public services of three honorable men—Special Prosecutor Cox, Attorney General Richardson, and Deputy Attorney General Ruckelshaus.

With the public storm growing, with his "Stennis compromise" coming unstuck in the Senate, with impeachment moves afoot in the House, Mr. Nixon retreated.

• • •

Now the President will surrender the secret tapes, as he could have done long ago, under arrangement that will protect from disclosure all elements not pertinent to the Watergate scandal.

They may remove public suspicion as to Mr. Nixon's own complicity in the Watergate coverup, and so demonstrate that his only concern in withholding them was what he said it to be—protection of Presidential powers, privileges and privacy.

That would not, however, alter the fact that his extreme interpretation of his power has run counter to the opinions of two courts, and it has run counter to what most Americans perceived as his simply duty to cooperate fully in clearing up an ugly Administration scandal. He has put the country through a wringer.

Moreover, the President's surrender of the tapes still does not put things right. The course of the broad Watergate investigation is not what it was before he stirred the public storm.

No amount of explanation about the President's reasonable and statesmanly concessions in offering the so-called "Stennis compromise" on the tape recordings — about his desire to avert constitutional confrontation in the midst of international crisis—can obscure his action in ordering Mr. Cox not to press further in the courts for tapes and presidential papers.

Not only the firing of Mr. Cox as a disobedient subordinate, but Mr. Nixon's abolition of the independent investigation Mr. Cox headed remains an accomplished fact.

In the light of the events of recent days, as well as all the presidential foot-dragging of the past, how can the public have confidence in an investigation of Watergate under regular Department of Justice auspices?

As former Attorney General Richardson said, the investigations Mr. Cox was conducting need to go forward under someone who has the same kind of independence.

Congress owes it to the country to act now to insure beyond any doubt that the investigation of Watergate offenses goes forward under an independent special prosecutor.

OKLAHOMA CITY TIMES
Oklahoma City, Okla., October 24, 1973

PRESIDENT NIXON surrendered a matter of principle when he agreed to give the controversial tape recordings to Judge John Sirica. It has been evident for some time that the President does not consider the conversations on the tapes to be damaging to his case, but he was holding out on the basis that the confidentiality of presidential documents, especially of conversations in his official office, must be preserved.

In that, he had the support of some of the nation's leading constitutional lawyers and professors. Even some of Archibald Cox's Harvard associates warned that if it came to a showdown, Cox would lose that argument.

But the pressure to avert an impasse centered on the basic constitutional question overcame the sound objections to release of the tapes. Thus we avoid a slam-bang, shoot-out type showdown between two branches of government which must be equal if our system of checks and balances is to mean anything in the future.

THERE had been some objections, since Saturday, that Cox had not really asked for more than the Watergate evidence on certain tapes. Former Attorney General Elliot Richardson dispelled doubts on that score in his Tuesday press conference, telecast live to the nation. It was Cox's insistence that he not be foreclosed from asking for any document or recording covering any portion of the Nixon presidency which precipitated his dismissal, Richardson revealed. Richardson indicated that he himself was inclined to Cox's view, rather than the President's, on this matter.

Such a blanket grant of authority to fish in the White House files would be intolerable to any executive. But what the present actors on the Washington stage seem to forget is the importance of setting precedents in high offices of the federal establishment.

Future presidents would have been crippled in dealing with Congress, the press, and the subordinate departments of government if such special powers had been allowed one man.

CONSTITUTIONAL principles have been ignored before in recent days. The Agnew affair, related only in that it damaged the administration and removed Nixon's backup man from the line, should have been acted on first by the House of Representatives, before an indictment was sought and obtained in the courts. A Justice Department properly concerned with preserving the processes prescribed by the Constitution would h a v e secured an impeachment and conviction, and then gone to court against private citizen Agnew.

Some future crisis will tell us how much the cavalier attitudes toward our basic law which have shaped recent events will cost in the long term. But there will be a price to pay.

Des Moines Tribune
Des Moines, Iowa, October 23, 1973

The man President Nixon chose to listen to the Watergate tapes, Senator John Stennis (Dem., Miss.), has not been involved in the Watergate investigation and has no special knowledge of evidence in the case. The senator was hospitalized and recuperating from gunshot wounds during the time when many of the intricate details of the case became public.

President Nixon did not pick Stennis for his expertise about Watergate. Why did he choose him? The President clearly regards him as trustworthy. Stennis was one of a handful of congressmen who were told about the administration's secret bombing of Cambodia in 1969. The Mississippi Democrat rewarded that trust by keeping mum about the bombing, never telling his colleagues and never raising questions about it.

Under the President's plan, Stennis would listen to the tapes to determine whether summaries prepared by the White House fairly described their contents. Only someone who is intimately familiar with the details of the Watergate case could know the significance of passages and realize the importance of omissions. Even with the best of intentions, an auditor without the requisite background for understanding the tapes would be handicapped. The public never could be assured that his approval of the summaries meant that everything of significance had been revealed.

The President billed his plan to have Stennis listen to the tapes as a "compromise." But the selection of Stennis was not a joint decision; it was the President who chose Stennis.

If it does not offend the President's constitutional principles for a member of the Senate to listen to tapes of White House conversations, why should it be offensive for Senator Sam Ervin or Senator Howard Baker to listen? It would make far more sense for these men, who have been sifting Watergate evidence for months, to be given access to the tapes in preference to John Stennis. It would make more sense still for the special prosecutor or a judge such as John Sirica, who presided at the first Watergate trial, to hear the tapes and determine which segments should be presented to the grand jury.

The President's "compromise" has all the earmarks of an effort to have the tapes judged by the friendliest possible audience. This may be satisfactory to the President, but it will not satisfy an increasingly suspicious American public. Archibald Cox deserves the gratitude of Americans for sticking to his guns and refusing to be party to a sham compromise.

NIXON DEFENDS WATERGATE ACTIONS, ASSAILS MEDIA AT NEWS CONFERENCE

President Nixon defended his dismissal of special Watergate prosecutor Archibald Cox and assailed the media, particularly television, for "vicious, distorted" reporting during a televised White House press conference Oct. 26. Nixon began with an opening statement devoted largely to the situation in the Middle East and the recent U.S. military alert. He also announced that a new special prosecutor within the Justice Department would be appointed to replace Cox. He said the prosecutor would have "independence" and "total cooperation from the executive branch."

The question-and-answer session following Nixon's statement was concerned primarily with Watergate developments and their effects on the situation in the Middle East. Among the highlights:

■ Asked if the new prosecutor would "have your go-ahead to go to court if necessary to obtain evidence from your files if he felt it was vital," Nixon said he did not expect that to be necessary, that the events that led to Cox's dismissal were "matters that can be worked out and should be worked out in cooperation and not by having a suit filed by a special prosecutor within the executive branch against the President." Nixon stated firmly that "we will not provide presidential documents to a special prosecutor. We will provide, as we have in great numbers, all kinds of documents from the White House. But if it is a document involving a conversation with the President I would have to stand on the principle of confidentiality."

■ Asked if he thought America was at the point of rebellion over "too many shocks," Nixon said he was confident that the American people "can ride through the shocks that they have." He went on to blame the media for the shocks. "I have never heard or seen," he declared, "such outrageous, vicious, distorted reporting in 27 years of public life.... When people are pounded night after night with that kind of frantic, hysterical reporting, it naturally shakes their confidence."

■ As to how he was "bearing up emotionally under the stress of recent events," Nixon replied: "Well, those who saw me during the Middle East crisis thought I bore up rather well.... The tougher it gets the cooler I get . . . I have what it takes."

■ When asked what had "so aroused your anger" about the television coverage of recent events, Nixon replied: "Don't get the impression that you arouse my anger.... You see, one can only be angry with those he respects."

■ In response to a question about "what goes through your mind when you hear of people who love this country and people who believe in you say, reluctantly, that perhaps you should resign or be impeached," Nixon began by saying, "I'm glad we don't take the vote of this room." He added that at the time of the December 1972 bombing of North Vietnam "exactly the same words were used on the networks ... that were used now—tyrant, dictator, he's lost his senses, he should resign, he should be impeached. But I stuck it out and as a result of that ... we brought peace to Vietnam...." "As far as what goes through my mind," he said, "I will simply say that I intend to continue to carry out to the best of my ability the responsibilities I was elected to carry out last November. The events of this past week I know, for example, in your head office in New York [CBS-TV] some thought it was simply a blown-up exercise, there wasn't a real [Middle East] crisis. I wish it had been that. It was a real crisis. It was the most difficult crisis we've had since the Cuban confrontation of 1962."

THE BLADE
Toledo, Ohio, October 31, 1973

IN HIS ardent attempt to convince the country that he is not cracking under the strain, President Nixon resorted to an Agnewesque, sledgehammer attack on the broadcast media at his press conference last Friday. "I have never seen such outrageous, vicious, distorted reporting in 27 years of public life," he declared.

That may be Mr. Nixon's viewpoint as seen from the distant reaches of his various retreats. But what he overlooks in reacting in such dudgeon against continued coverage of Watergate and related matters is this:

Never in the nation's 197 years has it experienced an administration so steeped in corruption, immorality, and deception that we have reached the sorry point where the President himself hears loud talk of impeachment; his vice president resigns in disgrace, a confessed criminal; two of his former cabinet intimates—John Mitchell and Maurice Stans—await trial under criminal indictments; his former top White House legal adviser pleads guilty to obstructing justice; two former high presidential assistants—H. R. Haldeman and John Erlichman—face criminal trials; a host of others close to the President are exposed almost daily for participating in highly questionable acts or decisions, and a number of the most honorable members of this tainted Administration were either fired or have resigned in disgust.

That, Mr. President, is the other side of the coin.

OKLAHOMA CITY TIMES
Oklahoma City, Okla., October 29, 1973

IT has been a general rule for years that a politician cannot win a war with the news media. He may win a battle now and then, but the boys with the notebooks and microphones always get in the last licks.

The rule may still hold for the long run, but for now President Nixon has clearly won a round. His televised news conference last Friday was a service to the nation in many respects, not the least of which is that it exposed so clearly the basic antagonism between the President and some correspondents.

HIS cool and competent performance also revealed a seldom seen glimpse of Nixon the man — the flash of anger so long suppressed. Since we're all prone to blow our stack on occasion, it's good to see the President be human and let off a little steam.

Legitimate debate will continue on whether some TV commentators are guilty of what the President called "outrageous, vicious, distorted reporting." But his major point, namely that when people are pounded daily with "frantic, hysterical reporting it naturally shakes their confidence," is well taken.

HEALTHY skepticism is a necessary part of any good political reporter's makeup, but it needs to be balanced with at least an honest effort at objectivity. That some of the President's news conference targets have long since abandoned any pretense at impartiality is hardly debatable.

The American public has always liked a scrapper, and their embattled President has demonstrated he can dish it out as well as take it. His old enemies didn't lay a glove on him.

Some of Nixon's advisers have been urging him to hold more frequent news conferences. If he does, the real winners will be the American people.

THE WALL STREET JOURNAL.
New York, N.Y., October 29, 1973

President Nixon's critics now hold him at their mercy; there is very little he can do to avoid the total destruction of his administration if they fully exploit the advantages he has already handed them. We only hope that his opponents recognize that the awesome power to destroy a President carries with it grave responsibility to the nation and to the future of the political process.

It's hard to imagine anything the President can do in his own defense. He cannot offer to compromise, for no compromise short of total capitulation will end the present suspicion and distrust. He cannot "tough it out;" his opponents have too many options. He cannot even effectively offer arguments that ought to be heard.

Congress, for example, is about to create a special prosecutor responsible to Judge Sirica rather than to the Executive Branch. In effect, Judge Sirica would be made responsible for a vigorous prosecution even while he is sitting in judgment on the same case. At every turn, he would be weighing arguments made by a prosecutor he appointed. This flies in the face of centuries of judicial evolution, not to mention modern sensitivity about far less significant conflicts of interests. Surely arguments against such a step at least ought to be heard.

Yet we see little the President can do to avoid it. His appointment of a new special prosecutor within the Executive Branch could scarcely be expected to head off demands for an arms-length inquiry. If he raises arguments against a judicial prosecutor, he will only make matters worse. If, as is probably inevitable, the President vetoes a bill establishing such an office, he will only add to the mistrust and deepen the crisis.

Once a special prosecutor is appointed, in any branch, further, we see nothing the President can do to limit his access to information within the Executive Branch. Surely there is *something* to the matter of executive confidentiality, and it is up to Presidents to defend it. But if the President now tries to draw any line, hold out for any compromise, he is vulnerable to accusations of covering up.

Nor is there anything the President can do to limit the scope or procedures of such an investigation. If the President's critics abandon self-restraint, this would become a presidential destruction machine. For even if there are no more real crimes to be uncovered, the Nixon administration is in no shape to withstand a process that keeps rumor and innuendo in the headlines every day for the next three years.

Such considerations, indeed, seem to us at the heart of the dispute between the President and Archibald Cox. A special prosecutor's office inevitably will be loaded with political implications above and beyond guilt or innocence on any particular charge. But Mr. Cox and his supporters saw it as divorced from any political consideration. He made no nod toward bipartisanship in his appointments, for example, and in the natural course of events ended up with a staff loaded with supporters of the President's political opponents. Of course this encouraged political fears in the White House. But about the last thing President Nixon can now effectively argue is that the next prosecutor needs to be more of a politician than Mr. Cox was.

The President, in short, has become a pitiful, helpless giant. For the most part, he has no one to blame but himself. The Watergate burglary did after all occur, as did the attempted cover-up. Even assuming that the President carried only indirect responsibility for these crimes, his handling of the matter has been consistently horrible. His defenses have always been too stiff, his concessions too late.

The Stennis compromise on the tapes would have been helpful if it had been offered earlier, but its delay and its explanation meant that the President got no credit for it. Instead, the accompanying act of firing Mr. Cox totally dominated the weekend announcements, and while it was within the President's legal powers, the firing cost him the confidence of the people. To retain any position at all he was forced to capitulate to the courts on the tapes. If they implicate the President, that will inevitably become known. If they do not, he could have avoided most of his present predicament by releasing them voluntarily long ago, as these columns and others urged.

Even now the President is mishandling the slight prospects he has for a successful defense. He is lashing out at the television networks, which may or may not have something coming, but which have little to do with his present troubles. The thing they did that hurt him most was to broadcast Mr. Cox's press conference, which is no sort of media sin. And even today the President refuses to release the tapes to the public, though this would be the one thing that might help him—if they proved exculpatory his defenders would be in position to argue that public assumptions of his guilt were wrong once and may be wrong again.

By now, though, most of the initiative lies in the hands of the President's critics. They can destroy him, and probably even force him from office. Even so stubborn a man as Mr. Nixon has a breaking point beyond which he will feel impelled to resign, as he felt impelled to give up the tapes to Judge Sirica. If his critics press the battle without self-restraint he will be forced into evermore-desperate defenses, which may give rise to impeachment. By holding back on the confirmation of Gerald Ford as Vice President, the President's critics have within their grasp the chance to change from a Republican administration to a Democratic one without benefit of an election.

We are not predicting these dire events, but merely noting that the President himself does not have much power to avoid them. If they do not occur, tribute must be paid to the self-restraint and responsibility of his critics in Congress and elsewhere. We hope and trust they will rise to this occasion, for large things lie in the balance.

One, which important members of Congress have recognized in the recent Middle East crisis, is the danger of a crippled President in international affairs. It is not merely a matter of how the Russians and others judge their opportunity, but how a President must judge his response. It is plausible to speculate that in the recent crisis the President had to act more belligerently than otherwise to make his point with the Russians. In important negotiations, alternatively, he may be forced to give away more than necessary to preserve a spirit of detente for domestic political reasons.

But an even more important stake concerns loyalty to the political process. There are already those who believe Spiro Agnew was dumped by his political enemies. If Mr. Nixon is dumped from the presidency on the far murkier evidence now available, it will leave a bitter residue in the nation. It would change in vicious directions the way the political game is played in this nation.

None of this is to argue that Mr. Nixon's critics should stand silent. We certainly think the House inquiries on impeachment should go forward, if only to sort out plausible from implausible grounds for so drastic a step. Surely there must be some way to insure that reasonable suspicion of crime is investigated. But Mr. Nixon's critics do need an awareness of the need for self-restraint, of a need to be doubly sure of their evidence and aware of the possible pitfalls. With the President as defenseless as he now is, it falls on his opposition to assure the nation that whatever is done is done responsibly.

CHICAGO Daily Defender
Chicago, Ill., October 30, 1973

Not even the Delphic Oracle could predict how Mr. Nixon would be able to extricate himself out of the mud hole into which he has been relegated by curious events of his own making. Watergate and its auxiliary happenings put him in a perpetually uncomfortable defensive posture.

His explanation of the latest related incidents, namely, the unceremonious firing of special prosecutor Cox and deputy Attorney General Ruckelshaus and the reversal of the President's decision on the Watergate tapes, suffers from too apparent lack of candor and plausibility.

It seems hardly conceivable that Mr. Nixon would have gone to the lengths he did for the sake of a constitutional principle. Certainly after the sacking of Mr. Cox and the subsequent resignation of Attorney General Richardson, few people, even among faithful members of the GOP clan, can believe that Mr. Nixon did not have an enormous amount to hide, not in terms of national security but in personal political terms.

One begins to wonder if the Watergate saga as such is any longer relevant to the wider issue of Presidential credibility. President Nixon's surrender of the tapes does not shut off doubts about the legality of his whole thesis of confidentiality. The surrender increases the confusion among the American people and the anxieties of America's friends abroad.

Taken in its bizarre totality, the Watergate affair is sapping America's influence. The question of impeachment at the moment seems rather remote. It is doubtful that a resolution to that effect could muster the required majority to pass the House where it must originate. But the conviction is getting momentum in Congressional circles and among the people at large that Mr. Nixon can no longer govern the country effectively. He should resign to save further embarrassment to the country and to himself.

THE SAGINAW NEWS
Saginaw, Mich., October 30, 1973

In the aftermath of his latest televised news conference the President has put more distance, not less, between himself and the people, the Congress and the nation's mass media.

In common parlance, Mr. Nixon blew it Friday night with a shabby attack on the press and an unheeding response to the federal legislative branch of governnent.

While the nation was reassured about Mr. Nixon's apparent state of good health and the power of the President to deal effectively with international crisis, there was no assurance that Mr. Nixon can soon bring about a domestic reconciliation which his badly shaken administration so sorely needs.

Rather than projecting the image of a national leader who truly understands the width of the credibility gap that now confronts his administration, the President proceeded along old but familiar lines.

This was the old Richard M. Nixon we were seeing — the old Richard Nixon who has never made his peace with the press, the old-new Richard Nixon who wants Watergate cleaned up on his own terms, the old-new Richard Nixon who seemingly fails to comprehend the public's dismay as those he has chosen to draw closest to him disappear one after another into the jaws of probes.

Unfortunately the President did little the other night to restore public confidence in the present administration.

It was almost unreal.

Here is the nation and the Congress still reeling from the now infamous "Saturday night purge" of Archibald Cox, Elliot L. Richardson and William Ruckelshaus — and there is the President describing Mr. Cox as a troublemaker who had to go. But there is the promise of a new Watergate special prosecutor with not an iota of assurance that the new one will have any freer hand than the fired one. Incredible.

Here is an investigation building around the President's pal, C. G. (Bebe) Rebozo involving the sale of securities which threatens Mr. Rebozo's job as the head of a Key Biscayne, Fla. bank — and there is the President defending Mr. Rebozo as an honorable man who used sound judgment in returning a $100,000 campaign gift from the Hughes Corp. after sitting on it for three years.

And finally here is the President, who advised the press only a few weeks ago to "give us hell when you think we deserve it," giving the press hell for doing the job it is obligated to do.

As for Mr. Nixon's unbridled attack on the television networks —

which included some backtracking to include the printed media — the news gatherers can live with that. There is no law anywhere that declares the media immune from presidential criticism.

In Mr. Nixon's present situation, however, it came across as a desperate attempt to once again discredit the press when things are going badly. It's an old trick in politics. Slay the bearer of the message. Only this time it doesn't wash except among those prone to blame the media for the President's troubles. With them it wins the President some scattered applause. For the most part, however, it will only lower the President's standing in public esteem.

We really don't know what it is that Mr. Nixon expects from the press any more. But one thing he cannot expect is that it become part of a cover up. Moreover, in light of the fact that the press and the electronic media are vigorously pursuing leads which, up to now, have proved anything but false, it is distressing that Mr. Nixon has chosen to characterize Watergate coverage as "outrageous, vicious and distorted."

These problems the press did not create for Mr. Nixon. Its chief guilt up to now has been reporting the problems that have beset the President and exposing the scandals that have cast his administration in such bad light.

Yet even for Mr. Nixon such an attack as the one he unloaded the other night reached an uncharacteristic high.

The bad part of it is that turned a news conference into a confrontation — one of the worst confrontations the public has ever been privy to witnessing between a President and the press before the glaring eye of TV cameras. Worse, we may now wonder when, if ever, Mr. Nixon can again meet with the press under any other conditions but confrontation.

Whether that was the worst of the three tactical mistakes Mr. Nixon made the other night is, to be sure, debatable. While there can be no question that the President has further truncated his already strained relations with the media in this country, the public isn't going to get all upset over that.

The public's more legitimate concern is that he has also managed to harden the resolve of Congress to look into the possibility of impeachment proceedings and forced the Senate to reject out of hand an administration-appointed Watergate prosecutor investigating the administration.

Each of these things raises grave questions about Mr. Nixon's future

relationships with Congress and his ability to govern effectively.

Mr. Nixon has projected not the image of a President behind whom the people are ready to unite but rather the image of one whose actions and utterances simply cloud the air with still more doubt. The President did nothing to clear

away the heavy cloud the other night.

Investigation has become a way of life for the Nixon administration. That is truly tragic. The people have reached the point where they are wondering every day — what next? And eventually there is something. That is equally tragic.

THE NASHVILLE TENNESSEAN
Nashville, Tenn., October 28, 1973

THE TRAGEDY for the country is that President Nixon perceives his difficulties, but won't concede that absolute candor is his admit that absolute candor is his only route to rescue.

The chief executive can suggest that the doubts and suspicious and cynicism about his leadership arise from the impact of the television screens. But that is an irrational viewpoint, for television didn't bring on the Watergate avalanche, or Mr. Nixon's private housing arrangements, or the Agnew resignation.

* * *

The networks didn't fire Special Prosecutor Archibald Cox and wipe out, with a single stroke, two of the top men at the Justice Department who were trying to salvage some integrity for this administration.

Incredibly, Mr. Nixon now proposes to recreate the office of Special Prosecutor which he did away with in a fit of anger. Thus he not only ignores the destruction which he left at Justice, but suggests with a straight face that his administration will investigate itself up to, but not including the President.

Since Mr. Nixon has reiterated his authority to fire such a prosecutor at any time, what attorney in his right mind is going to accept such a post? If one did, where would there be any credibility of prosecution in a situation where the prosecutor is expected to be sweetly reasonable to White House suggestions?

If there is a Special Prosecutor, he must be independent of the White House with full authority, if necessary, to take the President into court. The Congress and the Courts cannot be a party to a whitewash of Watergate, or depend on Mr. Nixon's latest promise of full cooperation. He pledged that before, and he broke that pledge.

Mr. Nixon was right in saying that "Justice delayed is justice denied," but it has been the White House which has forced delay and confrontation. It was the White House which used every legal strategem, tactic and loophole to resist giving up the tapes and documents necessary for any court proceedings.

And, the President made clear, it will continue to resist further such demands. Therein lies the curious paradox of Mr. Nixon's words of wanting "an expeditious concluson" and his deeds of blocking just that.

Mr. Nixon moves to command headlines, influence events, and to try to project the image if the "cool" leader, statesman and peacemaker. Yet it comes off badly and with deepened suspicions, simply because he is devious when there is no need.

In his discussion of the Cox firing, Mr. Nixon said of his so-called compromise: "Atty. Gen. (Elliot) Richardson approved of this proposition." Mr. Richardson and his associates have both indicated he did not approve. Which are we to believe?

Mr. Nixon spoke of cooperation with a special prosecutor, yet Mr. Cox in his news conference told of an absolute lack of cooperation form the White House. Which are we to believe?

In commenting on the Middle East, Mr. Nixon said, ". . . I know for example in your head office in New York, some thought it was simply a blown-up exercise . . . It was a real crisis, the most difficult since the Cuban confrontation of 1962."

Communist leader Leonid Brezhnev suggested Friday that Washington had intensified the Middle East situation and reacted irresponsibly by circulating "fantastic rumors" about Soviet intentions. Mr. Nixon said it was a real crisis, and Mr. Brezhnev indicated it wasn't.

* * *

Well, one could go on and on itemizing Mr. Nixon's positions which seem in disagreement with the facts, or at least in a state of ambiguity. If there is a crisis of confidence in his leadership, it stems not from the television news or the printed pages, but from Mr. Nixon's inability to be direct and candid.

Mr. Nixon will not solve his problem by attacking his critics, or lead the nation out of the wilderness of Watergate by glossing over the gravity of damage he has done himself. Mr. Nixon boasted of his "coolness" at his news conference. Would that the nation could also boast of his candor.

THE PLAIN DEALER

Cleveland, Ohio, October 27, 1973

Congress should proceed with legislation to establish the office of Watergate special prosecutor under the authority of U.S. District Judge John J. Sirica.

It is apparent now that President Nixon has no intention of naming such a prosecutor to represent the government and give that person truly a free hand and the total cooperation of the executive branch.

Mr. Nixon tried to be convincing at his news conference last night when he revealed that Acting Atty. Gen. Robert H. Bork next week would announce a special prosecutor to replace Archibald Cox, who was fired a week ago by the President.

But it did not come off.

There was no specific assurance the new man would have a free hand. Rather, the President once again stated emphatically that he, personally, must defend the office of the president against disclosure of confidential material. He would supply information from presidential documents, but not the documents. Would the presidential files be available if the prosecutor wanted them? Mr. Nixon only could hope this confrontation would not be necessary. He would "cooperate."

All the national agony which the country suffered one week ago tonight when the President brought about two firings and one resignation of key persons in the Watergate prosecution seemingly has not touched Mr. Nixon.

He played the same old record last night even though it is highly unlikely now that anyone believes an administration-backed investigation into Watergate — so necessary to prosecute the guilty and clear the innocent as Mr. Nixon himself declares — could be thorough or impartial. The Justice Department did not establish an enviable record in its first efforts in the case.

Obviously, and despite his thin attempts at humor, the President is deeply resentful of television. His cutting remark that he was not angry with television people because he could get angry only with those persons he respected, stunned the assembled news reporters. So did his abrupt departure. He stalked off the podium suddenly with no closing words, no final arguments, no attempt to summarize, not even waiting for the traditional "Thank you, Mr. President" from the senior correspondent.

Contrary to his declaration, Mr. Nixon seemed a little shaken by the attacks made recently on his motives and character. But also contrary to his rhetoric last night, the impression is, he has no intention of giving one inch on the matters of the confidentiality and privileges of his office, come what may.

This leaves it up to Congress and Judge Sirica.

ST. LOUIS POST-DISPATCH

St. Louis, Mo., October 28, 1973

In dismissing Special Prosecutor Archibald Cox, President Nixon went so far in undermining public confidence in himself that he cannot now recoup his loss by appointing a new, ostensibly independent, special prosecutor. Indeed, Mr. Nixon's press conference assurances that a new prosecutor would be named this week and would be given "total co-operation" were hollowed almost immediately by a statement that the President would not give him presidential documents and would "stand on presidential confidentiality."

Nothing seems to have changed, except that the next special prosecutor will not even have the seeming assurances of Administration backing that Mr. Cox thought he had. So the public has no reason to expect that the prosecutor will be left alone by the White House, or might not be fired if he too pressed hard for evidence of Administration wrong doing.

What is needed now is a new independent special prosecutor, authorized and funded by Congress and appointed by a court having nothing to do with hearing the case. Congress has indisputable authority to provide for such an officer under Article 2 of the Constitution (Section 2, Subsection 2) giving it power to vest appointments in the courts.

The creation of an independent special prosecutor's office is necessary, even while the House of Representatives goes ahead with its own impeachment inquiry, since the House investigation would be aimed primarily at impeachable offenses, whereas evidence already gathered indicates the existence of widespread lower-level Administration crimes which impeachment would not cover but which should still be prosecuted by an agency not answerable to the Nixon Administration Justice Department.

The subservience of the Justice Department has already been demonstrated by the floundering responses of acting Attorney General Robert Bork and Assistant Attorney General Henry Petersen when they were asked by the press after the Cox dismissal whether they would be free to demand evidence even if the trail led into the White House. Moreover, Mr. Petersen, who headed the Watergate investigation before Mr. Cox took over and who again took charge when Mr. Cox was fired, has been compromised by his admission that he relayed secret grand jury testimony to the White House and by his initial failure to press the investigation into the highest levels of the Administration.

After Mr. Nixon's recent actions in attempting to dictate a compromise to the courts on the subpenaed White House tapes and his discharge of Mr. Cox when the special prosecutor would not go along, the country needed no further evidence that the President was determined to thwart a full investigation of Administration offenses and to resolve the matter by a whitewash. The roar of protest from the public led Congress to begin impeachment proceedings. And bills to provide for a new special prosecutor began moving in both houses.

Clearly, the need now is for quick action in establishing the new office so that it can take custody of the Cox files before evidence can be consigned to shredders, as it has been in the past by agents working in Mr. Nixon's behalf. A special prosecutor is also needed promptly to contend for White House tapes and other evidence so that the courts would not have to undertake this prosecutorial function on their own action.

Members of Congress should not allow themselves to be diverted from the objective by complaints from Administration spokesmen to the effect that an independent special prosecutor's office would be a free-wheeling fourth branch of government. Once such an office is set up, it would still be bound by the law and subject to the rulings of the courts. Having promised through his designated Attorney General, Elliot Richardson, that Mr. Cox would be independent and then having repudiated his pledge, Mr. Nixon is no longer in a position to object to a congressionally-established prosecutor. Such an officer is now essential to restore public faith in the integrity of government.

Long Island Press

New York, N.Y., October 27, 1973

President Nixon, trying to undo the damage he wrought last weekend, has announced plans to appoint a new special Watergate prosecutor to replace the fired Archibald Cox. The President's proposal is too little, too late and too incredible.

The words Mr. Nixon used last night were reminiscent of those he spoke several months ago when Mr. Cox was appointed. The special prosecutor would, Mr. Nixon said then and last night, have independence, full cooperation of the White House and the goal of bringing to light all the Watergate details, however sordid and whomever they affect.

We know too well what happened to Mr. Cox's independence. It vanished, along with his job, when he disagreed that a compromise offered by the President was reasonable. It might have suited the Senate Watergate Committee's legislative purposes, but it would not have served those of a prosecutor. Indeed, Mr. Nixon's compromise might have allowed some of those involved in Watergate or related political scandals, to escape punishment.

We know, too, what happened to the full cooperation Mr. Cox was promised. The White House refused to turn over several documents the special prosecutor requested, above and beyond the presidential tapes. And we know what happened to the full Watergate disclosure. It remains undisclosed.

We fail to see how another prosecutor, still under the thumb of the executive branch, will fare any better if he, as is likely, pursues the same trails Mr. Cox blazed.

A special prosecutor must, indeed, be appointed to replace Mr. Cox. But he must be one who cannot be fired by Mr. Nixon. Legislation has been introduced in the Senate to recreate the special prosecutor's office, but this time under the authority of U.S. District Court Judge John J. Sirica.

That is the only special prosecutor the public should accept. The Congress should approve the legislation quickly. We hope Mr. Nixon would not veto it, but if he does, Congress must approve it over his veto.

Only with the appointment of a truly independent prosecutor will the public have a chance to learn the real truth. Then Mr. Cox's groundwork, and the integrity displayed by Attorney General Elliot Richardson and his deputy, William Ruckelshaus, will not have been in vain.

* * *

We were particularly disturbed by Mr. Nixon's attitude toward the media. He began his discussion of the Watergate affair by jokingly referring to "our attempts to get a cease-fire on the home front." Then he went out of his way to declare war on the media.

Calling news reports vicious, distorted, frantic and hysterical is hardly our view of genuine truce efforts. Responding to a question about his anger at TV reports by saying, "I only get angry at those I respect" is no way to heal wounds.

Such tactics ill befit a president who ran on a slogan of "Bring Us Together." Mr. Nixon and former Vice President Agnew, at the height of their popularity, could not convince the public that the press was the cause of the nation's trouble. After the media's fine exposure of the Watergate scandal, and Mr. Nixon's and Mr. Agnew's own problems, we don't think the public will be fooled now, either.

TWO TAPES MISSING; NIXON URGED TO RESIGN

The political storm around the Nixon Administration and its involvement in the Watergate affair heightened with the disclosure Oct. 31 that secret recordings of two White House discussions on the case did not exist. The two were among the nine tapes that President Nixon had fought a bitter Constitutional battle to keep secret, relenting only after the Administration was rocked by the public reaction to the firing of his special Watergate prosecutor and the resignation and dismissal of the attorney general and his deputy. Many Congressional leaders expressed doubt at the White House's explanation for its failure to produce the tapes in court.

The tapes said to be nonexistent involved a telephone conversation on June 20, 1972, three days after the Watergate burglary, between President Nixon and his then campaign manager, John N. Mitchell, and an April 15, 1973 conversation Nixon had with his former counsel, John W. Dean 3rd. White House special counsel J. Fred Buzhardt said the Mitchell call had not been recorded because Nixon had made the call from the residential part of the White House on a phone that was not plugged into the White House recording system. The Dean conversation was not recorded, Buzhardt said, because of an apparent malfunction of a tape recorder in the Executive Office Building.

Among the other important developments in the Watergate case:

■ The House Judiciary Committee met Oct. 30 to consider impeachment proceedings and approved a grant of broad subpoena power to its chairman, Rep. Peter W. Rodino Jr. (D, N.J.)

■ Former Attorney General Richard G. Kleindienst told Watergate special prosecutor Archibald Cox two weeks before Cox was fired by President Nixon that the President had personally intervened in the Justice Department's antitrust case against International Telephone & Telegraph Corp. (ITT). Nixon had ordered him not to appeal a lawsuit against ITT to the Supreme Court, Kleindienst said. *The New York Times,* which broke the story Oct. 29, based its report on the incident on "sources close to the case," but Kleindienst issued a statement confirming the report Oct. 31 after controversy arose about the source of the leak of his "confidential" disclosure to Cox. The White House issued a statement Oct. 29 that did not deny but sought to explain President Nixon's order to halt the Justice Department's suit against ITT. The statement condemned the leak of the "confidential" information and blamed Cox's staff for making the disclosures public. Cox admitted Oct. 30 that he may have been an indirect source of the leak. Appearing before the Senate Judiciary Committee which was investigating the circumstances of his dismissal, Cox said he had told committee members Sen. Edward M. Kennedy (D, Mass.) and Sen. Philip A. Hart (D, Mich.) and two of their aides about Kleindienst's conversation

with him. "It is quite clear I broke the attorney general's confidence," Cox said, but he blamed the "inexcusable" incident on "carelessness, not malice."

■ In a brief appearance at the White House Nov. 1, President Nixon announced he would appoint Sen. William B. Saxbe (R, Ohio) to succeed Elliot L. Richardson as attorney general. Nixon then left the room without answering questions, and Acting Attorney General Robert H. Bork announced that with Nixon's approval he had appointed Houston lawyer Leon Jaworski, a Democrat, to succeed Cox as special Watergate prosecutor. In announcing Jaworski's appointment, Bork said Jaworski would have the same charter as Cox, with the additional commitment that Nixon would not exercise "his constitutional powers" to fire him without the consent of a "substantial majority" of eight Congressional leaders from both parties.

■ White House deputy press secretary Gerald L. Warren assured reporters Nov. 2 that Nixon was "not giving any thought to resigning" and "has no intention of resigning."

■ "A lot of discussion" of resignation was heard in the cloakrooms of Congress, according to Rep. Robert H. Michel (Ill.) Nov. 3. Michel was chairman of the GOP Congressional Campaign Committee. Rep. John H. Rousselot (R, Calif.) said "discussion of how effective he can be as a President is very much evident." Sen. Edward W. Brooke (Mass.) Nov. 4 became the first Republican senator to publicly call for Nixon's resignation. Sen. George D. Aiken (Vt.), dean of Congressional Republicans, told the Senate Nov. 7 Congress should move to impeach Nixon or "get off his back."

■ Despite demands for his resignation, Nixon said he had no intention of "walking away from the job" he was elected to do, in a national address Nov. 7 on the energy crisis.

■ President Nixon undertook a series of meetings with Republican members of Congress Nov. 9 to counteract the decline in public confidence in his leadership. In his closed meetings with the legislators, which included some friendly Democrats, Nixon sought their approval with assurances of his innocence of wrongdoing and his intentions to prove it by disclosure of Watergate documents in his possession, to the courts first and public next. The sessions were given a mixed review from those members of Congress who commented to reporters afterwards.

■ The issue of nonexistent White House Watergate evidence became further clouded Nov. 12 as President Nixon revealed that a previously-mentioned memorandum on his April 15 conversation with his counsel John Dean was not among his files for that date. A dictation belt of the memo was to have been released to Judge John Sirica of the U.S. District Court.

DAILY🔲NEWS

New York, N.Y., October 31, 1973

The Senate Judiciary Committee's attempts to canonize Archibald Cox suffered something of a setback yesterday when the ousted special prosecutor displayed some tarnish marks on his shining armor.

Archibald Cox

Cox appeared before the panel with a galloping case of guilty fidgets after a leaked account of a supposedly confidential conversation he had with former Attorney General Richard Kleindienst made morning newspaper headlines.

Amid profuse apologies and fervent acts of contrition, Cox told the senators he may have been, through "error or carelessness," the source of the story.

While the senators were digesting that morsel, Cox dropped another gem. He said he had mentioned the Kleindienst talk—which dealt with the famed (or is it fabled?) International Telephone and Telegraph anti-trust action—to Sens. Edward Kennedy and Philip Hart and two members of their staffs.

Now that is intriguing news indeed. Here is a man alleged to have no political axes to grind blabbing information to two of President Richard M. Nixon's most dedicated enemies.

At the least, it qualifies Cox for a boob rating in the judgment department. And it certainly raises questions about just how lofty and impartial Cox was in his pursuit of Watergate wrongdoers.

We trust the committee will not be too embarrassed to pursue those inquiries. In that same thought-provoking session yesterday, Cox also offered—

AN INTERESTING ASSESSMENT

—of the oft-rehashed, much-disputed settlement of the ITT case. The theory trumpeted by administration critics is that ITT got a sweetheart deal after pledging money for 1972 national convention expenses.

Cox, answering a direct question from Committee Chairman James Eastland (D-Miss.), took this position:

"I've always thought the terms of the ITT settlement were a perfectly good bargain from the point of view of the government. And that's the opinion I get from most anti-trust lawyers."

The financial community, which votes with its money, rendered the same verdict. ITT stock took an unmerciful drubbing when details of the agreement were announced in 1971.

That being the case, why the sweat to whip a dead horse? Too much time, money and energy have been spent already trying to find evidence of corruption in a case which, apparently, was handled wisely and properly.

HERALD🔲EXAMINER

Los Angeles, Calif., November 2, 1973

That surely was an ironic mishap which befell former Watergate prosecutor Archibald Cox this week. Because of what he admitted was an "inexcusable" lapse in personal probity, he slipped and dropped kerplunk from the white horse he had been riding as a martyred champion of political virtue.

His besmirching fall, significantly, had little disturbing effect on most members of the Senate Judiciary Committee probing his discharge by President Nixon. His embarrassed explanation, in fact, was generally hailed as further proof of noble character.

To his credit, it should be emphasized that Cox voluntarily and speedily confessed his impropriety. He opened the committee hearing on Tuesday by freely declaring he was the likely source of a Monday newspaper story depicting the President as having interfered in the Justice Department antitrust case against the International Telephone and Telegraph Corp.

He had obtained confirmation of this, he said, from former Attorney General Richard Kleindienst in the course of his Watergate investigation into suspected White House influence peddling. And he admitted passing on this explosive information to Democratic Sens. Edward Kennedy and Philip Hart, two of the President's most outspoken critics.

"I don't know how the story got out," he said, "but it is quite clear I broke Kleindienst's confidence. During the stress and strain of the last two weeks I spoke more freely than I intended with a few friends.

"It was an error of carelessness, and inexcusable, but not something I did deliberately. I hope you will be charitable enough to believe I did not intend the information to be leaked to the press."

This we cannot buy. Cox is a committed political adherent of the Kennedy family. In the 1960 campaign, Cox served as chief of John F. Kennedy's research staff, and after the election he was rewarded by appointment as solicitor general in Robert F. Kennedy's highly politicized Justice Department.

Upon being named Watergate prosecutor, Cox began recruiting his staff among Kennedy-connected lawyers and political operatives.

Of the 11 senior aides he recruited, seven were former Kennedy hands. Sen. Ted Kennedy, who used political pressure to abort the Chappaquiddick grand jury investigation, denied disclosure of the Cox bombshell to the press. That's as believable as Kennedy's explanation to the nation after the tragedy that snuffed out the life of a young woman. For all its smooth carpentry, Kennedy's television statement did not dispel most doubts and questions.

Enemies of Richard Nixon, on the Senate committee and elsewhere, clearly are still determined to persist in the drive to canonize their hero as some kind of latter-day saint. Less partisan observers will note that his halo has been bent.

𝔇𝔢𝔱𝔯𝔬𝔦𝔱 𝔉𝔯𝔢𝔢 𝔓𝔯𝔢𝔰𝔰

Detroit, Mich., November 1, 1973

CONTRITION IS SUCH A rare commodity in Washington these days that Archibald Cox has managed to take a little — but only a little — of the curse off his indiscretion in leaking information about the ITT case.

Nonetheless, it remains a most unfortunate indiscretion, and one that does tend to lend credence to the President's argument that he has been victim of a partisan plot. The President has not been victimized by a plot but by his own blundering, but it is unfortunate that Mr. Cox has done something that seems to support the plot theory.

And the former special prosecutor's probable leak is doubly regrettable because it occurred in conversations with Democratic senators and their staffs. Mr. Cox knew better, and he should have done better.

His indiscretion, however, and his honest acknowledgement of it do not solve the President's problem about the special prosecutor. Mr. Nixon's firing of Cox, and the loss of former Attorney General Elliot Richardson from his Cabinet, leave him with a credibility problem. There is no way he can appoint a new special prosecutor, after firing Mr. Cox,

and give the country much assurance that the man will have a free hand to deal with the assorted Watergate scandals.

That is why Congress ought to pursue its plan to create a new special prosecutor, independent of the President, and give him a mandate to deal with every last vestige of Watergate culpability. Only then is there likely to be much confidence that the mess has been cleaned up, and only then will we be able to "put Watergate behind us," as the President has so often urged that we do.

The Kansas City Times

Kansas City, Mo., November 2, 1973

The question of the White House tapes is fast turning from dramatic conflict to ludicrous farce.

What next?

The latest episode is being greeted by some citizens with an openmouthed wonder and cynical headshaking as if a rascality were abroad in the land that is amusing in its presumption that anyone would believe its protestations of innocence and coincidence.

Two of the essential tapes that have caused such furor and dissension and which brought the government to the edge of a constitutional showdown now are gone. Did they roll under the President's desk? Could they have been mixed up with the Mantovani cartridges? Did anyone look under the sofa cushions?

No, no. It now seems that the two tapes never existed at all. The tape that was supposed to be a telephone conversation between the President and former Attorney General John Mitchell on June 20, 1972, was never made because the recording system wasn't connected to the phone that was used. The other alleged tape of a conversation between the President and his then assistant, John Dean, April 15, 1973, never made it because the tape ran out before the conversation occurred. Now it is said that the tape was checked out and returned last July by a White House aide.

The question then is this: Why was the country put through the agony of a massive confrontation over an issue that could in no way be resolved over listening to tapes that didn't exist? Why was Archibald Cox fired over the matter and why was it necessary to put everybody through the wringer with the departure of Elliot Richardson and William D. Ruckelshaus from the Department of Justice? Why the monumental hassle?

The lame answer from J. Fred Buzhardt, lawyer for the President:

"It was not until several weeks ago when the President considered disclosure that review of the tapes by him was commenced. It was not definitely determined that the two conversations in question were not recorded until late last week."

If this is true, Mr. Nixon by this time must believe he is truly living in a nightmare, pursued by the cruelest of political furies. But true or not, the credulity of the most patient and loyal of the President's supporters is being tested severely. It is hard to believe that a building full of sharp, experienced lawyers wouldn't hurry to the tapes the instant they became a national issue.

But if the story is true, and if no one knew of the vacant spots in the White House sonic annals until very recently, then the competence of the executive operation is called into serious question. It is not unlike the Watergate burglary and other depredations of the 1972 campaign: If the President knew, he is implicated. If he didn't know, he should have.

Above all else this administration needs to reestablish credibility. The latest twist of the tapes makes that more difficult than ever and may have moved public belief beyond redemption. More to the point, a laughable government is an impotent government.

Herald News

Fall River, Mass., November 3, 1973

The latest White House maneuver in the battle of the tapes puts an even greater strain on the credulity of the American people. Judge Sirica is now asked to believe that two of the most crucial tapes of presidential conversations never existed, even though no doubt about their existence was expressed by the President or anyone else until now.

New York Senator Buckley, who is certainly conservative, accurately said that this latest maneuver "puts the burden of proof" on the President. Too much has already happened for the White House to suppose the public will accept an unsubstantiated claim of this kind. How Judge Sirica can is another matter, and it is hard to see how the judge can proceed to examine the claim except through an administration-dominated Justice Department.

The maneuver may therefore legally succeed, but if it does, it will leave a legacy of public suspicion which will haunt this administration as long as it remains in office. No one, including the President of the United States, can be convicted of anything on the grounds of suspicious conduct, but on the other hand, that the chief executive should avoid direct action by the courts in this fashion leaves at best grave doubts about his suitability for the office he holds.

The President is doing so much damage to the presidency that it is hard to see how he can possibly repair the harm already done. If the possibility does exist, it can only be by total candor, a policy that has certainly not been tried.

CHICAGO DAILY NEWS

Chicago, Ill., November 3, 1973

The disappearance of two of the most important Watergate tapes just about cuts it as far as public patience is concerned. Up to this point one could at least hope that the scandal — and especially the issue of President Nixon's involvement in the cover-up — was moving toward some kind of resolution. Now even that seems frustrated by the blunder of the malfunctioning tapes — if it was a blunder.

And that is a question the public is entitled to ponder. For if the loss of these particular tapes among the original nine was a coincidence, it was one to end all coincidences.

One of them would have disclosed the conversation between President Nixon and former Atty. Gen. John N. Mitchell, considered most likely to bear on whether the President was mixed up in the cover-up. The other presumably recorded the conversation between John W. Dean III and the President, in which Dean says he told Mr. Nixon he was ready to "end the cover-up." What the remaining seven tapes may disclose (or whether any of *them* is blank) we do not know. But certainly the two in question had been expected to be pivotal in disposing of the central Watergate issue.

Now, recorders do malfunction, of course. And it is wildly possible that the machine chose that particularly embarrassing moment to cut out.

But the sad part is that by now, the public is not going to accept the White House's word on a stack of Bibles. Too often the White House has made some solemn avowal that things were one way when it knew all the time they were a different way, and in the end the truth came out and the President's credibility dropped another notch.

This is just about the end of the line. Credibility is shot, public faith in the administration's integrity is shot, and the only question remaining is how the nation can get through the next three years until it can choose a new leader.

Congress should certainly proceed to determine whether grounds for impeachment exist. Even the new vice president-designate, Rep. Gerald Ford, says this is necessary in the circumstances. If in all the many scandals now under investigation a "high crime or misdemeanor" by the President has occurred, then impeachment is the designated remedy under the Constitution, with charges to be brought by the House of Representatives and tried by the Senate. Not only the public, but also the President himself stands to benefit from a clear determination of his culpability.

The House Judiciary Committee's prompt and angry party-line split as it launched its inquiry pointed up the high volatility of the issue, and the warning is clear that the whole subject of impeachment is explosive and must be approached with utmost care. The proposal that the House investigation be transferred to a select committee of representatives chosen for their balance and discretion is well worth considering.

Of course, the hope persists that somehow this prolonged sequence of jolting, humiliating disclosures can be resolved in some easier way.

It still seems barely possible for the President and Congress to reach an agreement on the powers and the freedom of action for a new special prosecutor that will permit rational movement toward a Watergate conclusion outside the impeachment route.

But the decision must be quick and explicit. Time and the public's endurance are running out.

THE DALLAS TIMES HERALD

Dallas, Tex.
November 2, 1973

TRUE OR FALSE, the latest Watergate revelation concerning the non-existence of primary White House tapes involving President Nixon lends to deeper erosion of rapidly waning public confidence.

Suspicion and doubt about who, and what, to believe is compounded by the latest of almost daily stunning developments. The American people are revolving in a whirlpool of uncertainty unprecedented in our history.

The White House, after months of wrangling over presidential tapes that had been resolved by agreement to turn them over to U.S. District Judge John J. Sirica, now throws in the bomb that two key conversations actually were never taped.

One was a telephone conversation between President Nixon and former Attorney General John Mitchell immediately following arrests in the Watergate break-in; the other was a presidential conversation with former White House aide John W. Dean III shortly before Nixon fired Dean in April.

The White House explanation is that Nixon's conversation with Mitchell "apparently was made from a telephone extension in the White House not hooked into the recording system."

And the famous Dean conversation with the President—testified to by Dean before the Senate Select Committee—was not recorded because of a malfunction, or basic inadequacy, in the recording system.

President Nixon once told Asst. Atty. Gen. Henry Petersen that he had the Dean tape, but later in the day reported that he was mistaken; that he had only a written memo of the discussion. The continuing episodes lead to the painful question rarely asked in American history:

Is the President of the United States telling the truth?

The burden of proof is upon him if there is to be restoration of White House credibility and public confidence. And the presidential critics and opposition party carry a similar burden of responsibility in establishing total validity of all charges made.

Los Angeles Times

Los Angeles, Calif., November 1, 1973

It is asking a great deal to expect people to believe that two of the most crucial conversations between President Nixon and Watergate principals were not recorded by the elaborate White House bugging apparatus.

A mechanical breakdown is possible. A telephone not connected to the system is understandable. But the delay in saying anything about such matters undermines the credibility of the story.

There have been many opportunities for the White House to indicate over recent months any gaps in its collection of tapes of the President's private conversations and telephone calls.

Mr. Nixon himself has told of listening to some of the tapes before the existence of the tapes became known to the public and having concluded "that the tapes would not finally settle the central issues" apparently because "they contain comments that persons with different perspectives and motivations would inevitably interpret in different ways." That was on July 23. Three days later Mr. Nixon referred to a request for "recordings of five meetings between Mr. John Dean and myself" and said: "I must respectfully refuse those recordings."

The revelation last July 16 of the secret taping procedure was confirmed immediately by the White House. From the moment the special prosecutor subpoenaed specific tapes, there was never a denial about the existence of the tapes, just a long and tangled legal fight about the appropriateness of handing them over. Only a week ago, when the President finally agreed to give the tapes to the U.S. District Court in Washington, his special counsel told the judge that "this President does not defy the law and has authorized me to say he will comply in full with the orders of the court." Those orders included a specific demand for the two tapes now reported missing.

Are we being asked to believe that in all these months no one in the White House, not even the President, had enough curiosity to want to listen again to that crucial conversation with John W. Dean III, the former White House counsel, or that crucial telephone call to John N. Mitchell, the former attorney general? Are we being asked to believe that only now, suddenly, out of the blue, it was discovered that these conversations were never recorded?

It is a story that brings to the lips of the nation two words: Incredible. Unbelievable.

The Virginian-Pilot

Norfolk, Va., November 2, 1973

Perhaps a technical expert can show conclusively, or at least satisfy himself, that the White House tape recorder for reasons of its own did not function during President Nixon's dialogue with John W. Dean III back in mid-April. It is possible that Mr. Nixon by purest chance used an extension phone that was not tied into the recording system when on June 20, 1972 he talked with John N. Mitchell about the Watergate break-in of three days earlier. But even with that resolved, the White House still would have some tall explaining to do about the tardiness of its report to Judge John J. Sirica that it cannot supply two vitally important tapes among nine that were subpoenaed by the Watergate prosecution team because they do not exist and never have.

It was three and a half months ago, on July 16, that Alexander P. Butterfield, a former Presidential aide, disclosed in testimony to the Ervin Committee the operation of an automatic White House taping apparatus. The Ervin Committee immediately undertook to obtain records of the much-disputed Dean and Mitchell conversations with the President, along with three other tapes. Mr. Nixon in a July 23 letter to Senator Ervin declined to yield the lot, saying: "The fact is that the tapes would not finally settle the central issues before your Commit-

tee. Before their existence became publicly known, I personally listened to a number of them. The tapes are entirely consistent with what I know to be the truth and what I have stated to be the truth. However, as in any verbatim recording of informal conversations, they contain comments that persons with different perspectives and motivations would inevitably interpret in different ways . . . " He made no mention of significant gaps in the tapes collection although he knew very well that the Committee was particularly interested in his talks with Mr. Dean, whom he had dismissed as Presidential counsel over the Watergate issue, and with former Attorney General Mitchell, who had left the Justice Department to direct the Nixon re-election campaign and subsequently come to Watergate grief. Nor did the President's former chief of staff, H.R. Haldeman, report tape voids when, a little later, he told the Ervin Committee that he had taken five tapes to his home and listened to two covering White House meetings of September 15, 1972 and March 21. Further, Special Watergate Prosecutor Archibald Cox in all his hassling with the President and the Justice Department over the nine tapes he wanted, which led to his being fired two weeks ago, received no hint that he was subpoenaing more than existed.

The entire business of the White

House tapes is incredible. But nothing in it seems more incredible than the idea that the White House legal staff did not learn until now, until after Mr. Nixon in capitulation had agreed to honor Judge Sirica's order for the tapes, and until the time to take them to court had arrived, that they did not have all the goods.

As ineptly as Mr. Nixon and his associates have handled the tapes issue, with all their legal backing and filling, including Mr. Nixon's reneging on assurances given to Mr. Cox of White House support and his own independence, their word that the Dean and Mitchell tapes never were cut deserves every consideration. It is impossible to forget, just the same, that all along many doubts have been expressed, on paper and on the air, of the reliability of any tapes the White House might deliver. One is bound to remember, too, those shredders at the Nixon campaign headquarters and the Haldeman orders for clean files and the suggestion that certain FBI papers should "never see the light of day" and the "deep-sixing" of folders taken from broken safes—and those park-bench meetings and code names and hundred-dollar bills hastily collected to buy silence . . .

Mr. Nixon's new Attorney General and Special Watergate Prosecutor couldn't have arrived at a nicer time.

The 🌳 State

Columbia, S.C., November 5, 1973

WILL THE incredible series of events involving the President and the Watergate affair never end?

We devoutly want to believe in the President and in what he says and does. But at every turn, after yielding to him the benefit of doubt, a subsequent event surfaces to wring out his credibility again.

That is the impact of the new revelation that two supposed tapes of secret Presidential conversations with principals in the Watergate affair do not exist.

One of the conversations was by telephone with former U.S. Atty. Gen. John Mitchell. He has said he never told Mr. Nixon about any cover-up, nor did Mr. Nixon ask him about it. The other conversation was with former Special Counsel John W. Dean III, who believes that the President knew of the cover-up which Mr. Dean thought he was assigned to engineer.

Mr. Nixon has steadfastly denied any knowledge of any White House activity to help the arrested conspirators who broke into and bugged the Democratic National Committee Headquarters at the Watergate complex in Washington.

It was widely anticipated that the tapes held the truth of the President's actions and attitudes. His initial position was that the tapes were protected by executive privilege. He declined to let them be heard by the court or by the Senate Watergate Committee.

The President reversed his position two weeks ago to avoid a confrontation with the U.S. District Court or to forestall a definitive decision by the U.S. Supreme Court on executive privilege. He agreed to provide the nine tapes sought by the government's prosecutors for Judge John J. Sirica to audition to determine what, if any, of the President's conversations should be heard by the grand jury.

The White House now says the telephone conversation with Mr. Mitchell was not recorded and that the tape reel ran out and was not replaced to record the conversation with Mr. Dean.

While we have criticized the President for ineptness in handling the White House responses to the investigation, and particularly his interference with the special prosecutor, we have to accept the account of the missing tapes as truth. The circumstances reported by the White House *are* possible, and we do not believe the President to be a liar. We can't help but wonder, though, why the discovery of the missing tapes wasn't made and announced weeks ago. That would have been more believable than this belated revelation.

Even before this latest flap, the President's credibility with the American public was powder dry. Even an innocently struck spark could ignite the fire that will destroy public confidence in Richard Nixon, his noble quest for peace in the world notwithstanding.

FORT WORTH STAR-TELEGRAM

Fort Worth, Tex., November 2, 1973

President Nixon's credibility has been further strained, whether rightly or wrongly, by his failure to deliver two of the nine White House tapes ordered by Federal Judge John J. Sirica.

There is no way to produce the missing tapes, White House lawyer J. Fred Buzhardt told Judge Sirica, because the subject conversations were never recorded.

It was another shock to a nation which has come in recent months to accept the bizarre as the norm.

In the running controversy over whether the President should release the tapes, Mr. Nixon finally dampened some doubts when he capitulated and said he would surrender the tapes. The new situation is one in which the President cannot erase new doubts. He doesn't have the eraser, the two tapes needed to satisfy the court's order.

Even assuming the White House explanation is true, there will be wide disbelief; for it has been months since the tapes became a focal issue in the Watergate investigation.

It is difficult to understand how a person whose activities are so deeply questioned could leave his best defense, the tapes, undisturbed, unlistened to, until it is suddenly discovered before they are to be surrendered to a federal court that they don't exist.

Missing is the first conversation following the Watergate break-in between the President and former Attorney General John Mitchell. The conversation was on a phone not equipped with a recording device, the White House said.

The other missing tape is a meeting between the President and former White House Counsel John Dean on April 15. In this case, the White House reported an extremely rare malfunction in the recording equipment.

Secret Service technician Raymond C. Zumwalt said he knew of no other instance when the automatic machine had failed to record, and didn't remember the April 15 malfunction until Mr. Buzhardt reminded him of it.

The President's latest problem may be his most indefensible; for how could he have gone through the months of controversy and not, as Deputy White House Press Secretary Gerald Warren reported, ever ask to listen personally to the nonexistent tapes? Or at least count them to see that he had nine.

It is another embarrassment for the administration. The nation's citizens must be asking themselves, "What next?"

The Globe and Mail

Toronto, Ont., November 2, 1973

One of the craftier theories that attached itself to the Watergate matter was that President Richard Nixon's strategy was to resist strenuously all efforts to obtain tapes of recorded conversations with aides and others—and then, capitulating, submit tapes that did not incriminate him at all. This masterstroke, it was reasoned, would confound and embarrass those who were certain he had something to hide.

If that was the plan, it did not work out quite as intended. After lengthy, heavy debate about nine tapes, about who might have said what to whom and about which, we learn that two tapes do not exist.

These are not omissions that can be made up by throwing in a couple of Oval Room philosophical dissertations recorded by Prime Minister Pierre Trudeau or a seven-inch reel of light chit-chat by Leonid Brezhnev. The missing tapes are—wouldn't you know it—the gems of the collection: conversations the President had with his campaign manager, John Mitchell, three days after the Watergate break-in; and with John Dean, at that time his counsel.

All of those who have tried, against daunting odds, to follow Watergate through its twists and turns—even to follow President Nixon through his—will have some difficulty understanding how it is possible to count tapes that aren't there. This is a special skill, perhaps, to be classed with the uncanny ability to hear a silent majority.

Has anyone thought to ask H. R. Haldeman whether he returned all of the tapes he took home one weekend at the invitation of Mr. Nixon? If the missing tapes were the result of a malfunction, why did it go unnoticed when Mr. Haldeman was giving a helping hand?

As Mr. Nixon was saying the other evening, "The tougher it gets, the cooler I get . . .", and you have to admit that he would have to be cool to the point of nonchalance, in the full fury of the debate on tapes, not even to bother to inform himself of what was on tape. According to Gerald Warren, no effort had been made to find the recordings until last weekend. Supercool!

Since the most plausible explanation seems to have escaped the attention of the senior people concerned with the production of the tapes, we call to their attention the modern technique in dealing with sensitive recordings. In the crisp language of Mission: Impossible, they "self-destruct".

The search for tapes should be called off, and a new one mounted for two small piles of ash.

BUFFALO EVENING NEWS
Buffalo, N.Y., November 2, 1973

It is an over-used phrase, but Sen. William Saxbe was unquestionably correct when he referred, moments after his nomination as U. S. attorney general Thursday by President Nixon, to a national "crisis of leadership."

The impact of that crisis on the nation has already radically altered fundamental conditions under which both Sen. Saxbe, the blunt-spoken Republican from Ohio, and the new special Watergate prosecutor, Texas Democrat Leon Jaworski, will operate from the way their predecessors did.

Both men, for one thing, will be operating in a highly polished goldfish bowl. The Senate no doubt will, and surely should, screen the Saxbe nomination closely. And while the Jaworski appointment is not subject to confirmation, Congress has been assured that its leaders would be closely consulted if the President felt it necessary to dismiss him — which was assuredly not the case with the dismissal of Archibald Cox.

Congress may also still press forward with creating a statutory office of special prosecutor, appointed by and answerable to the courts. Because this would assure complete independence of the executive branch, we had preferred that procedure. But it should be noted that the convulsive events of the Cox dismissal and the principled resignation of Elliot Richardson as attorney general have in themselves created a new set of conditions under which Mr. Jaworski has accepted his assignment — and that these actually do provide a more clear-cut line of independent authority, in some respects, than Mr. Cox enjoyed.

The President's promise not to dismiss him without congressional leaders' express consent is only one element. Another is his promise to take on members of the Cox staff, which strengthens confidence in his independence, provides continuity and should promote rapid prosecution of pending cases.

Beyond that, and perhaps most important, is the fact that any evidence or allegations of wrongdoing on the part of the President himself would now fall under the express jurisdiction of the House Judiciary Committee, since it has now undertaken a formal inquiry into the possibility of a presidential impeachment. But no such parallel inquiry was going on while Mr. Cox was special prosecutor, so he was necessarily in the ambiguous position of both nominally working for and investigating the chief executive himself — which gave rise to a White House feeling that Mr. Cox was "out to get" the President. Now, however, there is less reason for that kind of conflict, since it would be logical for Mr. Jaworski to refer anything that seems to point at the President directly to the Rodino Committee in the House, and to concentrate his own efforts on all other targets. Because the House investigation focuses on the President, other investigations don't need to.

THE SUN
Baltimore, Md., November 2, 1973

President Nixon's selection of Senator William Saxbe to be Attorney General and Leon Jaworski to be special prosecutor of political corruption will not quell the suspicions of the Senate, the legal profession or the nation. Not after the White House declaration of the nonexistence of two of the tapes that the last Attorney General and special prosecutor lost their jobs pursuing. Mr. Jaworski is a distinguished enough trial lawyer, and at an age, 68, most invulnerable to improper pressures, to qualify for the job. What's wrong with him is that Mr. Nixon chose him. This was not the case with Archibald Cox, which was what was right about Mr. Cox.

If the President could exercise his real choice for Attorney General, it would not be Mr. Saxbe, any more than it would have been Elliot Richardson before him. Each appears to value his own self-respect more than the boss's approbation. The nomination illuminates the extent to which Mr. Nixon's deceptions throughout the sordid Watergate affair have narrowed his options and limited his political power. The President can still win backing for a foreign policy initiative and have the veto of a money bill sustained. But he cannot convince anyone, least of all the Senate, of the honesty of his intentions over Watergate.

Mr. Saxbe was a veteran but uninspiring attorney general of Ohio, a downstate rural Republican possessing a certain folksy appeal but hardly a legal giant in the eyes of discerning Ohioans. He rode on Mr. Nixon's coattails to the Senate in 1968 and then did not make any notable legislative contribution. But his statesmanship did develop in the form of a gritty independence of mind. He did not hesitate to criticize Mr. Nixon's policies on Watergate, the Vietnam war and other matters. In fact, Mr. Nixon's complaint that networks had said "he's lost his senses" over the bombing of Hanoi last December really referred to Senator Saxbe's comment to the Cleveland *Plain Dealer* at the time that the President "appears to have lost his senses." Unlike others who have risen higher than they might have had reason to expect, Mr. Saxbe was never all that awed by either the Senate or the fact that he was a senator. Just before nomination to Mr. Nixon's cabinet he had decided that six years in the Senate in the service of Mr. Nixon's party was enough.

Like Mr. Richardson and like Gerald Ford for the vice presidency, Mr. Saxbe is chosen not as the man Mr. Nixon wants most, but as the Republican with the best chance of winning confirmation. Similarly, Mr. Jaworski appears to have been chosen because he is part of the nation's conservative legal establishment at a time when that establishment is up in arms over the President's handling of the Cox affair. Even so, and despite the respect that the Senate invariably shows to its own members and will show to one who has proved a willingness to step on presidential toes, this may not be enough. Mr. Richardson was confirmed only on the assurance that he would appoint a special prosecutor who would be truly independent. Mr. Nixon then welshed on Mr. Richardson's commitment. The commitment to Mr. Jaworski's independence and access, now made by the acting Attorney General, Robert Bork to the press, has little credibility. The Congress now has every reason to create the office of special counsel to the grand jury, leaving the selection to the courts.

THE RICHMOND NEWS LEADER
Richmond, Va., November 6, 1973

In appointing Senator William Saxbe to succeed Elliot Richardson as Attorney General, President Nixon once again has confounded his supporters by giving in to his critics.

Saxbe is hardly the prime choice for the post; no doubt the President could have found a candidate as qualified for the job among junior assistants at the Justice Department. His appointment clearly was not one calculated to get the best man for the job, but one designed to pacify the Senate. Saxbe has been a frequent critic of the Nixon administration, and his nomination probably will encounter little opposition when confirmation comes to a vote. Although nominally a Republican, Saxbe has commented that the President's stand on the Watergate issue makes him look like a piano player in a bawdy house who doesn't know what's going on upstairs. He also has said that President Nixon "must have taken leave of his senses" when he ordered the December, 1972, bombing in North Vietnam.

Saxbe supports gun control, and the union shop. He opposed the ABM proposal, the nomination of Clement Haynsworth to the Supreme Court, and the Nixon voting rights measure because it didn't go far enough. He also wants to withdraw U.S. troops from Europe. As recently as October 28, he said, "Nixon is through, finished, in terms of his effectiveness over the next few years." This is the man to whom the President has turned in his search for the nation's top lawyer.

The President's willingness to cave in to his critics also was evident in his agreement not to fire the new special prosecutor, Leon Jaworski, without first conferring with congressional leaders. These concessions do not typify the actions of a man known as a tough fighter. They represent a continuing erosion of presidential authority, conceded bit by precious bit to the legislative branch. When he fired Archibald Cox, the President showed his mettle, but that action now has been cancelled out by the Saxbe appointment and still more concessions to Congress. In such ways does Richard Nixon box himself in— first by saying that he will or will not do a certain thing and then beating a hasty retreat.

If Congress wants a special prosecutor, there is no reason that the executive branch must appoint one to investigate itself. Congress could set up its own special prosecutor's office, perhaps working out of the General Accounting Office, which would report only to Congress. That would be more in keeping with congressional objectives, anyway, instead of forcing the President through pressure politics to accede to congressional demands. Those same pressures now bring the nation an Attorney General-designate who is mediocre at best, merely to avoid a confirmation hassle with the Senate. The Justice Department deserves better, and so does the nation.

Chicago Tribune

Chicago, Ill., November 2, 1973

President Nixon has selected Sen. William Saxbe of Ohio and Texas attorney Leon Jaworski as replacements for former Atty. Gen. Elliot Richardson and special prosecutor Archibald Cox.

Considering the extent of Mr. Nixon's Watergate troubles, these are puzzling appointments. Rather than reversing the error he made in ousting Mr. Richardson and Mr. Cox, Mr. Nixon could be compounding it.

His choice of Mr. Saxbe for the attorney general's post is an obvious play for the support of Congress. Mr. Saxbe would certainly seem to be qualified for the job, having been attorney general of Ohio for eight years. His outspoken independence and criticism of Mr. Nixon in the past is also in his favor as far as Congressional confirmation is concerned.

But the tobacco-chewing Mr. Saxbe shows every indication of continuing his independence, if not his hostility to Mr. Nixon. While averting a confrontation with Congress now, Mr. Nixon may be inviting an even more cataclysmic one later.

With the selection of Mr. Jaworski as special prosecutor, Mr. Nixon has done nothing to alleviate the apprehensions of the American people. What was needed was a man of such towering stature as to command optimum public confidence in the justice department's prosecution of the Watergate case. For all his abilities as a lawyer and his record as a past president of the American Bar Association, Mr. Jaworski is little known thruout the nation. His association with Nixon-protege John Connally is not confidence inspiring either.

Mr. Nixon's selections may have some appeal on Capitol Hill, but they may well place an intolerable burden on the Department of Justice in its efforts to equitably resolve the Watergate crisis. The President cannot be content to deal solely with Congress in this controversy; he must deal with the public. Tho they may prove to be good men for their jobs, Mr. Saxbe and Mr. Jaworski are not really what the American people had in mind.

The Dallas Morning News

Dallas, Tex., November 3, 1973

Leon Jaworski of Houston, an authentic legal luminary of almost half a century's standing, says he was asked to take the job of special Watergate prosecutor as a duty to his country—and that he accepted it on that basis, though only on the absolute understanding that he would have a free hand.

The former president of the American Bar Association appears to have been Nixon's original choice, even before Cox. But it is only now, says Jaworski, that White House assurances of independence are absolute enough to convince him he can function as he must.

After Cox, Jaworski has his job of establishing trust and credibility

cut out for him. Sen. Sam Ervin is saying that he won't do—that nobody named by the White House will —but the nonpolitical Jaworski has a reputation and a repertory of achievement more than equal that of Ervin's and there should be a general disposition to let him show his stuff.

The people shouldn't have to wait forever for the Watergate answers, says Jaworski, and they're going to get them as soon as he can get them —especially the answers about the "missing" tapes.

Jaworski is noted for his warmth and ability to lead. If anyone can build a credibility from the ruins of the Watergate investigation, he is the man to do it.

Des Moines Tribune

Des Moines, Iowa, November 2, 1973

President Nixon ignored congressional and public sentiment in the selection of Leon Jaworski to replace Archibald Cox as special prosecutor. Jaworski, a Texas lawyer, was named by Acting Atty. Gen. Robert Bork, but there is no question that the choice was cleared with the White House and approved by the President.

Cox was fired because he was too aggressive to suit the President in his pursuit of presidential tapes and documents. The firing made it clear—to everyone except the White House—that it was essential to replace Cox with a prosecutor divorced from the Justice Department and the President. Numerous congressmen have co-sponsored legislation calling for establishing an independent prosecutor's office to be headed by a prosecutor named either by Congress or the courts.

By brushing aside this sentiment and naming Jaworski, the President has assured still more controversy about his conduct in office. It ought to have been obvious to the President that it is improper to be party to selecting an official to investigate his own conduct. His willingness to ignore the proprieties will be regarded by many Americans as still more evidence of the President's complicity in cover-up.

There can be no public confidence in an investigation of the President by a man hand-picked by the President, especially one with close ties to the President's ally, John Connally. Congress ought to let the President know this in no uncertain terms by pushing ahead with legislation to set up an independent prosecutor's office.

President Nixon's choice of Senator William Saxbe of Ohio to be attorney general is less subject to criticism. Saxbe is a maverick Republican who has not hesitated to criticize the administration.

It remains to be seen, however, whether Saxbe has the requisite stature to revive the shattered Justice Department. Saxbe has held mostly legislative posts in public life, serving only briefly as Ohio attorney general. The Justice Department at this point badly needs leadership from someone with impeccable credentials in law and public administration.

When the Justice Department was riddled with scandal in the wake of Teapot Dome, President Calvin Coolidge turned to Harlan Fiske Stone as his attorney general. Stone, then dean of the Columbia University Law School, went on to become a distinguished member of the U.S. Supreme Court. We wish President Nixon had been inspired by Coolidge's example.

Minneapolis Tribune

Minneapolis, Minn., November 2, 1973

Among Americans of all political views, yesterday's two appointments by the Nixon administration should strike a responsive chord. We use the adjective advisedly. "Responsiveness," locally and nationally, has become a theme more often talked about than observed. President Nixon's choice of Sen. William Saxbe as attorney general and his approval of Leon Jaworski as Watergate special prosecutor seem to us an illustration of what responsiveness is all about.

That conclusion is supported both by the appointees' qualifications and by the conditions under which they were asked to serve.

Jaworski lacks the national reputation for legal brilliance that Archibald Cox brought to the prosecutor's job and exhibited before Mr. Nixon fired him. But Jaworski also has a record of public service and is highly regarded as a lawyer. Nothing suggests that the Texas Democrat will take his assignment lightly.

As a senator from Ohio, Saxbe is better known. Aside from his qualifications to be attorney general, which appear adequate, he has something else in his background that makes his appointment significant. A Republican, Saxbe became one of the strongest critics of the president's conduct of the Vietnam War. During last December's bombing of Hanoi he raised questions about Mr. Nixon's motives and stability — the same kind of questions that the president last week accused broadcast commentators of raising irresponsibly. Saxbe's nomination is a welcome change from Mr. Nixon's tendency to surround himself with yes-men.

The most impressive demonstration of presidential responsiveness was the promise of independence for the special prosecutor. He would not be discharged, Mr. Nixon said, without the consent of House and Senate leaders from both parties and senior Republican and Democratic members of the two judiciary committees.

Moreover, the new prosecutor has been explicitly assured of independence in investigating Watergate and related matters. He has been promised full cooperation by the executive branch. Thus the barriers to investigation that Cox described the day before he was fired may have been lowered. But experience strongly suggests reserving judgment until Jaworski has had time to put his promised independence to the test.

For now, we think it fair to say that the president has shown — belatedly, under great public pressure — a responsiveness lacking before. Unfortunately, public confidence is harder to rebuild than to destroy. The loss of Cox, Elliot Richardson and William Ruckelshaus remains real. And applause for the president's new directions on independent investigation is muted by the regret that these steps were not taken earlier.

ST. LOUIS POST-DISPATCH
St. Louis, Mo., November 2, 1973

President Nixon's nomination of Republican Senator William Saxbe to be Attorney General and his approval of a Democratic Houston lawyer, Leon Jaworski, as a new Watergate special prosecutor were obviously designed to neutralize opposition. As a member of the Senate, Mr. Saxbe is no doubt visualized as a nominee whose confirmation fellow Senators would be reluctant to oppose.

As a former president of the American Bar Association and as a Democrat, Mr. Jaworski is no doubt seen as an appointee who would be less objectionable to Democrats and who would soften the opposition of the American Bar Association, which has urged the creation by legislation of a special prosecutor's office independent of the Executive Branch.

Neither clever political calculations nor new Administration promises of independence for the special prosecutor, however, should be allowed to deter or delay Congress in establishing a special prosecutor totally independent of the Nixon Administration. In dismissing Special Prosecutor Archibald Cox after pledging that he would be allowed to be independent, President Nixon has lost all claim to congressional or public faith in his promises.

It makes no difference now that he has nominated a respected Republican Senator to head the Justice Department and that he has said, through acting Attorney General Bork, that Mr. Jaworski will not be dismissed without the consent of the Senate and House leaders of both parties and of top members of the judiciary committees of the two houses.

No matter how respected Mr. Saxbe is, he should not be confirmed so long as he concurs in the Nixon Administration's obviously self-serving plan of giving its own Justice Department, of which Mr. Jaworski's office would be a part, the responsibility for investigating and prosecuting crimes committed by members of the Administration. No matter how upright Mr. Jaworski is, he will not make the scheme for a special prosecutor within the Executive Branch acceptable.

Beyond the matter of Mr. Jaworski's personal integrity, however, there is a question as to his suitability as special prosecutor. He is a friend of former Treasury Secretary John Connally, who has been linked to the questionable ITT antitrust settlement. And he is from Texas, where his legal associates could well have ties with big oil firms accused of making illegal contributions to the Nixon campaign.

There is only one acceptable way to approach the Watergate prosecution, and that is for Congress to speedily create a truly independent special prosecutor's office with ample funding and wide jurisdiction.

The Dispatch
Columbus, Ohio, November 2, 1973

NOMINATION of Ohio's William B. Saxbe by President Nixon to be his fourth attorney general may be just what the U.S. Department of Justice needs — a dose of earthy candor.

That Senator Saxbe can be candid or that he is a rare maverick on the Washington political scene cannot be questioned.

THAT THE Justice Department has been wounded by Watergate developments is apparent. Many of its conscientious career employes are disheartened and yearn for a champion.

Mr. Nixon's first attorney general, John Mitchell, stands accused of violating the laws he swore to enforce. The second, Richard Kleindienst, resigned as he felt he was too close to persons under investigation.

THE THIRD, Elliot Richardson, also resigned when he determined he could not carry out the orders of the President.

Now, the Senate is being asked to confirm the name of Bill Saxbe, a tobacco-chewing gentleman farmer from rural Ohio.

BUT BILL SAXBE is more. He has a built-in desire to return public confidence to the Department of Justice.

Mr. Saxbe's earthy candor has generated quite shocking statements about President Nixon's policies from time to time. It should be no surprise if this same candor evokes more of the same.

THROUGHOUT it all, Ohioans can remind the nation, Mr. Saxbe should be credited with a sort of native honesty, the kind that will initially please a few while astonishing the rest.

Such forthrightness may not be popular with most politicians. But it can be more productive than rhetoric and hedging.

OHIO Republican partisans are understandably upset by Mr. Nixon's nomination. In all probability, it means that Democrat Governor Gilligan will name someone from his own party to complete Mr. Saxbe's term in the Senate.

Yet there is logic in the Saxbe observation that a viable and forward-going Justice Department, holding the confidence of the American people, is more important.

MR. SAXBE reported he had been candid with the President when the appointment was discussed. He confessed, "I told him I had done some things in my life that I'm ashamed of, but I assured him I had done nothing criminal."

Mr. Saxbe also told the President that "he would have to take me warts and all."

Well, warts and all, Mr. Saxbe is offering himself as a needed catalyst to restore morale to the Justice Department and public confidence in that vital governmental agency.

If Mr. Saxbe is speedily confirmed by his Senate colleagues, the nation can count on one thing — Bill Saxbe will say what he thinks, right or wrong.

Amsterdam News
New York, N.Y., November 3, 1973

Labor leader George Meany said it all a few days ago when he said that the lack of confidence of the American people in President Nixon has made it impossible for him to continue as a viable leader of this nation.

What else is there to say.

The White House, which should represent the pinnacle of truth and honesty to the American people, has been caught in so many lies that even the most patriotic American can no longer believe what is said by anyone connected with it.

To put it another way, we have a crisis of credibility at the very top of our government which makes it impossible for that government to govern.

And the person most directly responsible for that crisis is Richard Milhouse Nixon.

Nothing more needs to be said at this time.

It's time to act.

And if there is any love or patriotism in Richard Nixon for his country and the American people, he should be the first one to act.

And he should act by resigning from the office he holds as a first step toward putting an end to the crisis he has created.

Finally, if Richard Nixon does not have the patriotism for his country to act in this crisis, the only remedy left is for the Congress to act.

Thus, if Nixon won't resign, the Congress should impeach him.

THE PLAIN DEALER
Cleveland, Ohio, November 1, 1973

Just how independent will Sen. William B. Saxbe be when he is named U.S. attorney general and is confirmed by his colleagues on Capitol Hill?

Saxbe had built a reputation as a maverick, a shoot-from-the-hip critic of President Nixon. He was a tobacco-chewing, unusual, tough man of the Midwest soil when he landed in Washington.

But not long after that he turned out to be a better than average Nixon supporter on his voting record.

Yesterday he came out of his personal conference with President Nixon sounding like a convert to the Nixon viewpoint. Whatever doubts he may have had — and some sharp Saxbe quotes recently put him on the opposite side — seemed to have disappeared.

"I'm satisfied that the President has acted honorably in the situations that have risen since Watergate," said Saxbe in the White House driveway as he left. "This is the thing I wanted to know."

In fact, Saxbe said Mr. Nixon had gone further than Saxbe would have recommended in releasing tapes of presidential conversations. Anyone expecting Saxbe to challenge the President would call that a letdown.

Saxbe has swerved from moderate to conservative and back fairly often in his career. He once declared that J. Edgar Hoover should retire while he still had the nation's respect — but then in a speech to Ohio Republicans said it was good to keep Hoover on as FBI chief after he had passed retirement age.

Saxbe had a good military record as a World War II bomber pilot, and became a lieutenant colonel in the Ohio National Guard. He often voted a hard military line.

Yet when President Nixon unleashed the massive bombing of North Vietnam last December, Saxbe dovishly commented that the President "appears to have taken leave of his senses."

Still, Saxbe has appeal to broad segments of the public, and his movement from a tough law-and-order stand to a more liberal one may have reflected the people's own pendulum swings.

Besides, he was state attorney general for eight years, longer than any other person and longer than he has been a senator. He could be an effective executive in the Justice Department. He could help to rebuild morale there. It was shaken to the roots by the resignation of Elliot L. Richardson, who was the Nixon administration's outstanding Mr. Clean.

Saxbe is more interesting, though hardly as august nor as brilliant a lawyer as the man he is to succeed. We are unsure whether Saxbe can help the President to recapture the public support he has lost, but he will add a wholesome downstate farm flavor to the cabinet, at least.

This high position, on one of the hottest spots in the government, could be a springboard for Saxbe if he has further ambitions. But that will depend on whether and how well he survives his coming ordeal as attorney general of the United States.

THE DENVER POST

Denver, Colo., November 4, 1973

The office of the presidency, as Richard Nixon realized in the concept of his campaign when he sought to "bring us together," is much more than just an office at the head of one branch of our government. The presidency must be the national focus of our ultimate loyalty and confidence. Ironically, it was just a year ago this Sunday that The Post wrote its final editorial supporting Mr. Nixon for the presidency because among other reasons we believed he was the better man to produce effective national unity.

The American people must have an instinctive trust in their president, strong enough to override in time of crisis the inevitable partisan feelings of difference on lesser issues. One can disagree with a president on issues such as impoundment of funds, on the structure of a welfare program, or a move in world politics. But in a time of national crisis, such as the recent alerting of our military forces in the Middle Eastern situation, the people must be able to trust automatically the President's integrity. And on simpler matters, it is intolerable that on a question of whether or not the tapes were really lost, a great number of people simply don't take the word of their President.

Whether or not President Nixon deserves this low image as to his trustworthiness is arguable. Partisans can give endless tit-for-tat on that score.

What is not arguable is that, right or wrong, the situation has now degenerated to where the trust of the people in the President's integrity is shattered. Halfway measures cannot restore that confidence, whether among our people or among our allies overseas.

How then can this intolerable situation be resolved?

First, the office of the vice presidency must be promptly filled by congressional action. If Mr. Ford is acceptable after thorough examination, fine. If not, then an alternate candidate must be nominated and confirmed by Constitutional processes. We will not solve our crisis of Constitutional confidence by departing from Constitutional means.

When the vice presidency is filled, the Republican Party must live up to its responsibilities. Even Senator Goldwater recognizes that the credibility of the President is at an intolerable low point. The Republican Party should try to persuade the President to resign.

Stepping aside from the office of the presidency when trust has been lost is not a new idea. Lyndon Johnson, although elected by a mandate nearly as large as that of Richard Nixon, realized that Vietnam had broken his relationship of trust with the people. He stepped aside by not running again, and history thinks well of him for it. Similarly history would think well of a Nixon decision to step down, not as admission of guilt, but as a recognition that the needed trust essential to the conduct of his office has been lost. Richard Nixon would gain stature by such a selfless move.

If, however, resignation is not in the cards, then this newspaper has come to the reluctant conclusion that only an impeachment proceeding will heal our hemorraghing of national confidence in the presidency.

Impeachment preparations which have started should be speeded in the Congress, since they take time, and if the vice presidency is filled and a resignation is not forthcoming, the bringing of the impeachment proceedings needs to be swift. The country mustn't dither about decision.

An impeachment process before the elected representatives of the people is the only method, short of resignation, that can now finally resolve the erosion of trust in the presidency. It would be a national decision in which all the evidence is brought out and a vote taken.

If the House of Representatives after mature deliberation decides there is not enough evidence to bring the President to trial before the Senate, that decision should finally quiet Washington. As we have said before, no one wants a president to stand trial on less than sound legal grounds, and the presence or absence of those grounds is for the House to decide.

If the matter goes to trial and the Senate decides the evidence does not justify the President's removal, well and good! The people will have spoken by the best Constitutional means available to them, and by the rules. That would put an end to it, and the President could go about his business vindicated by a reliable tribunal.

If the Senate should vote to remove the President, so be it! It would be the end of a regrettable chapter, not of the country.

If President Nixon chooses to resign after a qualified successor is in office, it would be easier for the country and better for him in the history books.

But if he must face impeachment proceedings, let's get on with them. From those proceedings, the people will get a decision on which some part of their basic trust in the presidency can be re-established.

The Detroit News

Detroit, Mich., November 4, 1973

After Rep. Gerald Ford has been confirmed as vice-president, President Richard Nixon should resign.

If he does not resign, serious consideration should be given to his impeachment.

We come to these conclusions with deep regret. This newspaper has been one of Mr. Nixon's strongest supporters. Watergate aside, we still agree with many of his basic policies and we believe that many of his successes will be recognized by historians of the U.S. presidency.

However, unless the present crisis of authority is resolved—through the installation of a new president or the acquittal of Mr. Nixon in impeachment proceedings—the country must endure 38 more months of the doubts, charges and recriminations which have destroyed the President's ability to lead.

True, Mr. Nixon has tried in recent days to resolve the crisis with conciliatory actions. He has agreed to surrender his tapes; appointed one of his strongest GOP critics, Sen. William Saxbe, to be his fourth attorney general; picked a widely respected lawyer and Democrat, Leon Jaworski, to be the new special Watergate prosecutor; pledged "complete freedom" to Jaworski and agreed that he will not be discharged without approval by a bipartisan panel of congressional leaders.

Unfortunately, these actions will not halt the rumbling anti-Nixon avalanche which this administration helped bring down upon itself. The momentum is now too great.

The White House's assertion that two key Watergate tapes never existed and can't be delivered sinks President Nixon's credibility to an all-time low. Someone in the White House is guilty either of unbelievable stupidity or outright lies. In either case, public confidence in this administration suffers the final shattering blow.

Since the missing tapes might prove or disprove whether Mr. Nixon took part in the Watergate cover-up, we find it hard to believe that the White House did not know until recently, as it now claims, that the tapes never existed. The stakes were too high for the White House to have taken so casual an attitude. Do intelligent and concerned persons make assumptions in matters so important without checking the physical evidence?

Along the tortuous course of the past months, we have criticized the President at some points and defended him at others but we find small basis for defense in the present case. The latest episode of the tapes is but one more in a series of ambiguous, contradictory and puzzling statements and deeds which have eroded the confidence of people who once believed in Mr. Nixon.

To repeat, this matter of the tapes is the final blow to public trust. That final disillusionment makes three more years of a Nixon administration too bleak, too dangerous a prospect.

Too many important decisions would remain in suspense. Issues of domestic policy would be decided less and less on their merits and more and more by the degree of presidential disarray.

America's status as a world leader would suffer. An administration which cannot maintain confidence at home cannot forever enjoy unshaken confidence abroad. President Nixon was able to avert a possible Soviet-American confrontation in the Middle East last month. But if public confidence and bipartisan support continue to dissipate, would he be able to exert the same influence in a foreign crisis six months hence?

We would prefer to see the nation avoid the stress and turmoil of impeachment. That stress and turmoil could be avoided, of course, if Mr. Nixon would, after Ford's confirmation, step down and let the new vice-president succeed to the presidency. Ford may not be the glamor boy of American politics but he is a competent man whom people trust, a man who could bring unity to a divided nation.

We hope Mr. Nixon will see this suggestion as a wise one for himself and as a necessary one for the national welfare. If he does not see it that way, the next step in the unfolding tragedy of Richard Nixon may be impeachment. Distressing as that procedure might be, it would be less distressing than three more years of political vendetta.

Enough is enough.

Washington Star-News

Washington, D.C., November 7, 1973

Some of President Nixon's erstwhile supporters have joined with many of his ancient foes in clamoring for his resignation. We have no intention of adding our voice to that chorus, which is unseemly, unfair and unwise, from the point of view not only of Mr. Nixon but of the nation.

Which is not to say that we are convinced of the pristine purity of the President. Far from it: We have the gravest doubts as to Mr. Nixon's fitness to occupy the highest office in the land.

The point is that resignation would resolve none of those doubts. Indeed, such an act would obscure, perhaps forever, the vital question of Mr. Nixon's innocence or guilt in the Watergate affair and its attendant scandals. There would be no catharsis in this. Indeed, resignation would leave a legacy of bitterness and suspicion in at least that 27 percent of the electorate which, by some mind-boggling leap of faith, continues to believe that Mr. Nixon is doing a good job as President and is innocent of complicity in Watergate.

Some of those who are asking Mr. Nixon to step down are doing so on the grounds that he has lost his capacity to govern, that he is politically "crippled." It is true that Mr. Nixon's power and prestige have been impaired and, given what we now know about Watergate, that is not altogether a bad thing. But "crippled"? That must come as news to the President's opponents on the Hill, who have been unable to override one of his eight vetoes (the most recent on October 30) this year. It must also come as news to both sides in the Mideast crisis.

When a tide of emotion is running high, it is easy to get swept away. So perhaps it is worth recalling that Mr. Nixon's popularity has not yet fallen to the 1951 level of a president now widely regarded as one of our near-great leaders — Harry S. Truman.

In any event, ours is not a parliamentary system under which a president is accountable to sudden gusts in the fickle wind of public opinion. No charges of criminality have been lodged against him and the President cannot be compelled to resign an office to which he was lawfully elected.

If he is to be required to step down, Mr. Nixon is first entitled to his day in court. If he has been guilty of "high crimes and misdemeanors," if he has violated his oath to see to it that the laws are justly enforced, then he — and the American people — are entitled to a bill of particulars.

There are those who draw back in fear from the trauma of impeachment proceedings. We have a greater faith in the toughness of the American people, the resiliency of our institutions and the genius of our Constitution.

In our view, the first order of business ought to be the confirmation by the Senate of Vice President-designate Gerald Ford. For if Mr. Nixon is to be swept aside, it is essential that the people's mandate of 1972 be assured. It is to the credit of House Majority Leader Carl Albert, at present the next in line for the presidency, that he realizes that a Democratic succession would destroy the legitimacy of the government.

Once Ford has been confirmed, the House Judiciary Committee ought to move with all deliberate speed in its investigation to establish whether a case for the impeachment of the President exists. Should it so find, it will be up to the House to act upon the committee's recommendation, either rejecting it or sending it forward to the Senate.

The national weal requires a speedy and definitive end to the Watergate scandal. But that end must be fair to the President and to the country, and it must be seen to be fair.

Article II of the Constitution provides for the removal of a president from office. It would be the final irony if a president charged by his opponents with abusing the Constitution were hounded from office by a constitutional short-cut which might poison the well of American politics for generations to come.

A forced resignation would leave an intolerable question mark on the political horizon and create more stresses than it would relieve. It ought not to be contemplated.

The Wichita Eagle

Wichita, Kans., November 7, 1973

It is becoming increasingly clear that the greatest service Richard M. Nixon can now render the country is to resign his presidency.

The only alternative to resignation should be what now appears an impossible task: an almost immediate return to some reasonable level of public confidence. Impeachment should not be a consideration. Indeed, to date no one has brought forth evidence of an impeachable offense and the President and the turmoil resulting from what now appears to become a long, drawn-out partisan squabble over this issue would be too much to ask of the nation.

This of course gives rise to the logical question: why then should he resign?

According to the polls 72 per cent of the people have said they have no confidence in his leadership, and their disenchantment is reflected in the Congress, where even such erstwhile stout defenders as Sen. Peter Dominick of Colorado are urging Republicans to dissociate themselves from Nixon. Such others of his former defenders as William S. Buckley Jr. and Joseph Alsop have called for resignation, too. Even so staunch a partisan as presidential aide Pat Buchanan has said: "There is no question the President's ability to govern and lead has diminished. Some people won't believe him whatever he says."

When the nation's leader is no longer able to lead, the country faces a crisis that is far graver than any of the matters that have led to that situation.

Shock has f o l l o w e d upon shock. The President has isolated himself, indulging his passion for secrecy and emerging only occasionally to offer an unconvincing explanation or address himself to some subject other than the primary national concern, which is the degree of his implication in Watergate and his fitness to continue in office.

He has repeatedly said one thing and done another — and this dates far beyond Watergate. He has at the very least surrounded himself with people who have subsequently been shown to be unworthy of his confidence or of the nation's trust. His remaining defenders point to his accomplishments in foreign affairs, and indeed this appears to be his strongest field, but unfortunately the proof of diplomacy is a long time coming, and only history can assess it accurately.

And surely the lack of confidence in him at home must have its effect, too, upon international relations. When each new day brings fresh rumors of resignation, and when the preliminary processes of impeachment already are begun, it is difficult to think that other countries can deal with this administration with any confidence.

At home the citizen awaits his newspaper every morning with apprehension to see whether any new enormity has developed overnight. The majority of people no longer feel that they can place credence in what Nixon says, and they mistrust what he does.

Nor has the nomination of a new prosecutor and a new attorney general done anything to assuage the uneasiness, for these men have been given approximately the same guarantees given to Archibald Cox and Elliot Richardson, and they are gone.

So far have matters progressed, and so long have they been permitted to be unresolved, that it seems unlikely the President ever can restore the confidence of the nation in him. Even if the new special prosecutor or the Ervin committee or both should absolve him of personal guilt in Watergate, it is unlikely at this point that the people would believe it. Three more years of such a presidency would be extremely damaging to the nation.

In s u c h circumstances, the Congress should move as swiftly as possible to confirm the appointment of Gerald Ford unless some grave fault in him is discovered, and already exhaustive examination of his background has as yet disclosed none. Once Ford is vice president, Nixon will be free to resign.

The President has insisted he will not give up his office, but many informed people believe that decision also is subject to change, once it becomes clear to him that he cannot effectively function as head of state any longer, and that the alternative to resignation is almost certainly impeachment.

For whether or not he was convicted, impeachment would be a long and a traumatic experience for the nation, during which the ability of the government to act would be further impaired and our powerful adversaries might be emboldened to undertake some dangerous adventure.

The nation should be spared that possibility. And it would appear that it can be spared only through Nixon's early resignation.

THE WALL STREET JOURNAL.
New York, N.Y., November 14, 1973

President Nixon is meeting with Republican Congressmen on Watergate this week, and his advisers now talk of releasing to the public some version of the famous Oval Office tapes. This is all to the good, but we are far from convinced that it represents a clear break with the White House's history of being no more forthcoming than absolutely necessary.

By now, of course, the impression that the White House is holding back is so deeply ingrained in most of us nothing the President could say or do could quickly reverse it. Even if every record in the White House were released, someone would charge that something is held back—and given the history of the case who could confidently say him nay? So even at best this legacy will haunt Mr. Nixon for the rest of his presidency; even though he can run the government he will be unable to move the nation.

It would help considerably, though, if only the President could communicate the message that, yes, he believes something went terribly wrong. Of course he has made statements to that effect, and taken pro forma responsibility for the actions of his subordinates. But none of this has carried any conviction. The statements that have carried conviction have been those suggesting that what went wrong was that the press distorted the story, that in the Watergate episode the President should not be offering apologies but receiving them.

This diagnosis has been adopted by the President's supporters around the country. Our mail makes it clear that even our own often-sympathetic criticism of the President is taken by some as evidence of an Eastern press cabal, though we would hope there are also readers who recognize that in these columns the press is no more immune to criticism than any other institution of American society. In the Watergate case the press has not been 100% perfect, and of course one can find sins to seize upon.

In general, though, the press coverage of Watergate has been repeatedly and massively vindicated by events. The press did not invent the burglary, nor did it imagine the cover-up. The press is not the origin of the legal troubles of so many former White House aides. What went wrong was something far more basic and fundamental, something in the White House itself.

The President has not in truth given us much of his thinking on this question, and trying to smoke it out might be a better objective for informal congressional questioners than trying to trip Mr. Nixon on the specifics of individual charges. In the absence of a White House explanation of how Watergate came to happen, the field is all the more open for outside speculations. The harsh theory, of course, is that the President himself is deeply implicated, at least in the cover-up. This does provide a logical explanation for the continuing hesitancy to lay his cards on the table, but we would prefer to withhold judgment so long as there is so little direct evidence of so portentous a charge.

The charitable theory is that the President made serious mistakes in his selection and use of men. Even before Watergate we felt that his selections put far too much emphasis on the test of personal loyalty, to the point where independence and stature were seen as disqualifications for White House service. And when the President's men were chosen, he apparently tended to rely on them in ways that isolated him from independent advice. Watergate was but the most dramatic symptom of this failing.

From this perspective, we find little comfort in the subsequent handling of the scandal. Surely the President would be in better shape today if he had given more weight to the counsel of Elliot Richardson. Even more disquieting was the treatment of Charles Alan Wright, who took his commanding legal reputation out on a limb for the President and was told only at the last hour that tapes essential to his case were nonexistent. It is almost as if Mr. Wright's stature and independence marked him within the White House as not quite worthy of full confidence.

Which leaves us wondering even more about the President's thinking on how Watergate came to pass. We wonder not only what went wrong, but whether anything has been learned.

Newsday
Long Island, N.Y., November 9, 1973

A consensus is emerging in the country that President Nixon's credibility, authority and ability to govern effectively have been damaged irreparably.

It has, after all, been four months since John Dean, under oath in nationally televised Senate hearings, accused the President of being implicated in an attempt to obstruct justice. Americans have waited patiently for the President's rebuttal. Each action he has taken since then to clear himself has only served to increase public suspicion that he is not telling the truth. The firing of Special Prosecutor Archibald Cox and the missing tapes were the last straws.

At the end of his televised address on the energy crisis Wednesday night, Nixon predicted once more that he would ultimately be cleared, and in response to calls to step down voluntarily he declared that he had no intention of resigning.

But while his tone was firm, even the President must have been aware that he has cashed his last blue chip of credibility. How can he continue to function under the present circumstances—with Congress overriding his vetoes, public confidence (as reflected in the polls) at an unbelievable low and a Democratic landslide apparently building up for 1974? Even when he has made positive moves that might otherwise reflect credit on his leadership —as in the Middle East and energy crises —he gave the impression of exaggerating. Even though he did not create these crises, he has left an uncomfortable feeling that they were exploited in such a way as to make him appear indispensable.

Clearly it would serve the national interest if the country were governed by someone other than Richard Nixon. Two weeks ago, after Cox was fired, we said that only three options remain: (1) handing over the tapes (2) resigning from office (3) facing removal. The President gave up the tapes, but stunned the nation with the claim that the crucial conversations had never been recorded. He says he will not resign. That leaves the final option: The impeachment process should be launched as soon as possible by the House of Representatives.

We emphasize that impeachment is only the first step in an orderly legal procedure defined by the Constitution. Impeachment itself is not conviction. It is an indictment brought by a majority vote of the House and the indictment then is tried before the Senate with the Chief Justice presiding. If the Senate finds the official guilty by a two-thirds vote, he is removed from office.

Impeachment would be a long, drawn-out business, and perhaps not ultimately conclusive. But it would be in accord with the Constitution, and the founding fathers never imagined that the impeachment of a President would be easy. They included it in the Constitution as the best way to deal with a President suspected of illegal acts. If they had considered it his duty to resign when he had lost the confidence of the people or the ability to govern (as in a parliamentary system), they would have said so. They opted instead for the more stable governmental structure that has served this nation for almost 200 years.

Of course, if impeachment proceedings are instituted, the President might then change his mind and decide to resign—as Spiro Agnew did when faced with overwhelming evidence of guilt. For this reason it is imperative that Gerald Ford be approved as vice president as soon as possible. Then the stage would be set for an orderly transition should the President be removed or decide to resign.

If 1974 is to be a year of new beginnings, as we all hope, the way to start is with the machinery of government moving as it was designed to do by the Constitution. As far as the President is concerned, he has nothing to fear from the impeachment process if his conduct, as he claims, has been above reproach. The Constitution was written to protect the rights of all American citizens. Today, 17 months after Watergate, it should be put to work to find out, once and for all, whether Richard Nixon is fit to be President.

TAPE ERASURE DISCLOSED; NIXON SEEKS SUPPORT

President Nixon's campaign to recover political and public support for his leadership in the wake of the Watergate scandal suffered a major setback Nov. 21 when the White House revealed that a key segment of one of the subpoenaed presidential tape recordings was blank. In subsequent testimony before U.S. District Court Judge John J. Sirica, Nixon's personal secretary Rose Mary Woods said she had made the "terrible mistake" of accidentally erasing a portion of a June 20, 1972 conversation between Nixon and H. R. Haldeman, then his chief of staff.

Special White House counsel J. Fred Buzhardt Jr. told Sirica Nov. 21 that an 18-minute portion of the tape contained an "audible tone" but no conversation. Buzhardt said he had learned of "the phenomenon" Nov. 14 in the process of preparing an analysis and index of the tapes for the court, and Nixon had been told "shortly thereafter." Buzhardt attributed the delay in informing the court to "ambiguity" in the original prosecution subpoena, which he said was thought by White House lawyers to have covered only one Nixon meeting that day, while in fact there were two meetings. After Buzhardt's announcement, Sirica ordered the original tapes submitted to him for safekeeping.

In testimony Nov. 26–28, Miss Woods said she had been transcribing the tape in her White House office Oct. 1 when her telephone rang. In reaching for the phone, "through some error on my part," she pressed the "record" button rather than the "stop" button. At the same time, Miss Woods continued, she must have pressed on the foot pedal of the machine, which could have erased a part of the tape. When she completed the phone conversation, which she said lasted no more than six minutes, she replayed the tape and discovered the gap. Miss Woods said she did not think she could have been responsible for the entire 18-minute erasure. After she had described the layout of her office, Miss Woods was asked to reconstruct the incident. Assistant prosecutor Jill Volner quickly noted that, when Miss Woods reached around to "answer" the phone, she immediately lifted her foot from the recorder pedal.

Among other Watergate developments during the second half of November:

■ The dismissal of Archibald Cox as special Watergate prosecutor was declared illegal Nov. 14 by U.S. District Court Judge Gerhard A. Gesell in the District of Columbia. Gesell said a Justice Department regulation, issued in establishing the office of the special prosecutor, stipulated that the special prosecutor could not be removed except "for extraordinary improprieties," a charge that had not been brought against Cox. Gesell did not order reinstatement of Cox or declare illegal the appointment of his successor, Leon Jaworski. His ruling, he said, was designed to "declare a rule of law that will give guidance for future conduct with regard to the Watergate inquiry."

■ Nixon Nov. 16 held the last of a series of meetings initiated Nov. 9 to take his case to Republicans in Congress. During the series Nixon had met 220 Republican members of Congress and 46 generally friendly Democratic members.

■ President Nixon appeared at a question-and-answer session before newspaper executives at Disney World, Fla. Nov. 17. During the nationally-televised meeting, Nixon answered 17 questions relating to the Watergate affair. At one point in the one-hour session, Nixon said: "I made my mistakes, but in all of my years of public life I have never profited, never profited from public service. I've earned every cent. And in all of my years in public life I have never obstructed justice.... People have got to know whether or not their President is a crook. Well I'm not a crook. I've earned everything I've got."

■ Nixon defended his record Nov. 20 in a private session with Republican governors meeting in Memphis, Tenn. During the meeting Nixon reportedly assured the governors that he knew of no further Watergate "bombs" to be dropped. After the disclosure of the gap on one tape, Gov. Tom McCall, who had attended the Nov. 20 meeting, said Nov. 23 that Nixon's "insensitivity to what is a bombshell" made it almost impossible to help him politically. "You're already in a morass of problems and here disaster stares you in the face in the form of this tape, and you don't even recognize it. I just don't see how they're ever going to crawl out."

■ The Senate Watergate Committee Nov. 27 suspended further public hearings until early 1974. It said the action was taken to allow more time for preliminary investigation of the two remaining items on its agenda—a contribution by milk producers to the Nixon re-election campaign and a cash payment of $100,000 accepted by Nixon's friend, Charles G. Rebozo, from aides of industrialist Howard R. Hughes. The money, purportedly intended for Nixon campaign use, was later returned.

Maine Sunday Telegram
Portland, Me., November 18, 1973

To be brief and blunt — we are appalled by the way possible impeachment of a President of the United States is turning into a tawdry Roman circus.

We think it is time to speak out loudly and clearly against the rancour, the spite, the plain hate that are too frequently the hallmarks of many current movements to impeach President Nixon.

Impeachment of any President of the United States is the most radical, massive, dangerous kind of surgery that can be performed upon the body politic of this nation.

If that kind of political surgery is needed then, it must be done.

But it must be recognized that it can kill the patient while cutting out the disease. Let us remember that the patient is the nation. The alleged disease is the man now in the White House.

Like radical and massive surgery upon the human body, impeachment of a President is a last resort, to be taken only in the direst circumstances after all other possible cures and remedies have been exhausted.

If and when impeachment of a President is the only course left, then it must be approached with extremely cool heads, with impartiality and with precise care for the process of law.

This is not the case today. The drives to get petitions signed, letters sent, coupons mailed is a phony circus, which is coming dangerously close to turning a majestic judicial process into a kind of popular blood-letting binge.

Stewart Alsop, in his column in Newsweek, described the impeachment atmosphere in Washington today. He writes: "There is a fever abroad in this city today, uncomfortably like the ferocious fever that sometimes seizes a fight crowd when the knees of a punch-drunk fighter begin to wobble. The danger is that when the punch-drunk President is brought down, the Presidency itself will be brought down."

But much of the crowd is so infected with the emotion of "getting Nixon," they don't realize they may destory the temple.

On the evidence so far exposed, we do not think there are legal grounds for impeachment of the President, let alone evidence for a conviction of him after a trial in the Senate.

Until damning new evidence is uncovered, documented so it can stand cross-examination in a court of law, we are opposed to massive and dangerous surgery upon the body politic of the United States — which is what impeachment of President Nixon will mean. That however is another consideration.

What we consider here today is the current approach toward possible impeachment of Nixon. It is grossly marred by those using impeachment talk as a way to vent their own personal hate of Nixon.

The antics of those "out to get Nixon", by those urging impeachment only to vent their personal feelings of hate and distrust of the man.

Let us all respect the impeachment process. It is a great and majestic instrument for bringing to trial the President of the United States. The House of Representatives must decide whether it will invoke that process, by deciding whether it has evidence to warrant bringing in such an indictment.

The number of letters drummed up or sent in, the number of petitions criculated or signed, the results of public opinion polls should have no influence whatever. Impeachment is a legal process.

The Oregonian
Portland, Ore., November 16, 1973

U. S. District Judge Gerhard A. Gesell's ruling in Washington, D.C., that the acting attorney general had no legal authority to fire Watergate Special Prosecutor Archibald Cox, on the order of President Nixon, but doesn't have to rehire him, is ridiculously illogical. Furthermore, and of greater consequence, it seeks to establish a kind of legislative control over the executive branch that should not be tolerated under the Constitution's separation of powers.

In the interest of sanity and future good government, the Department of Justice should appeal Judge Gesell's ruling to the U. S. Supreme Court, rather than let it stand because it does not seek to restore Cox to his job.

Judge Gesell's opinion that "Mr. Cox served subject to congressional rather than presidential control" is wildly irrational. Cox was appointed by then Attorney General Elliot Richardson and the appointment was not subject to confirmation by the Senate. With respect to his own confirmation as the new attorney general, however, Richardson assured the Senate Judiciary Committee that Cox would have authority to pursue his investigation of Watergate-related charges without hindrance from Richardson or the President.

Judge Gesell's extension of the "advise and consent" obligation of Congress from a Cabinet officer to one of his appointees would open unacceptable opportunities for Congress and its committees to control the executive departments, if allowed to stand. The Constitution does not give Congress such administrative power, nor should a representative of the judiciary seek to do so. If it had such authority Congress or any of its committees could paralyze the administration of any president, or reduce it to subservience to congressional politics and partisanship.

The foundation question here is not whether or not Cox should have been fired, or even the reason he was fired. Nor did the court have before it the question of whether Cox's successor, Leon Jaworski, will be allowed to function independently of the acting attorney general, who appointed him, or the President. The issue is the authority of the executive branch to administer. The Supreme Court should be asked to rule on what seems to be a clear invasion by Congress of the executive powers, as defined by a single judge.

St. Petersburg Times
St. Petersburg, Fla.
November 19, 1973

President Nixon's counteroffensive is working. It is clear after his performance at Disney World and his reception in Georgia that he will not be impeached.

THE POWER of the presidency is too great. The hesitation of Congress to embark on a course yielding no positive political points is too strong. The constitutional processes cannot be applied even to a President with Mr. Nixon's performance.

This has grave long-term possibilities for the nation. If Mr. Nixon can violate the Constitution and get away with it, will other presidents be tempted to risk even more serious violations? What will be the effect on the political climate when the man who picked the Watergate conspirators and coverup artists is not punished?

On the scorecard of credibility, the President's mastery of TV give-and-take still isn't enough:

✔ He lost points when Archibald Cox was accused of changing his mind. The written record fully supported Cox.

✔ Mr. Nixon lost again when he and Gen. Alexander Haig accused Elliot Richardson of lying when the record backs Richardson.

✔ Mr. Nixon appeared petty and self-serving when he tried to blame a dead Lyndon Johnson for Nixon's own failure to pay his fair share of federal income taxes.

✔ And nothing could have shown more clearly the depths to which Mr. Nixon has brought the presidency than when he said: "People have to know whether or not their president is a crook. Well, I am not a crook." When in memory has the head of a democratic nation been called upon to make such a statement?

The President's strategy is all too clear: Blame Democrat Lyndon Johnson for Mr. Nixon's tax troubles (and for White House taping). Blame congressional Democrats for the energy shortage and his milk deal.

OF COURSE, the jury is the American people. They will decide about Watergate in upcoming elections. The prospect should not be pleasing to the Republican Party. The public may tolerate a crippled President for three years, but Mr. Nixon will never restore his credibility. There is no way that this prospect can be considered good for the country.

Chicago Tribune

Chicago, Ill., November 19, 1973

There's one question that should have been asked of Mr. Nixon but wasn't when he appeared Friday evening before the Associated Press Managing Editors' convention in Florida. It is why he didn't make himself available for this sort of candid question-and-answer session long ago.

Mr. Nixon took the 17 questions in stride. He answered them confidently and even seemed to hanker for tougher ones, running overtime in order to answer an unasked question about the relationship between high milk prices and campaign contributions from milk producers [he said there was none].

Several of his responses, especially his explanation of the missing Watergate tapes, reflect atrocious carelessness on the part of the White House staff; but from Mr. Nixon's own position, they were plausible enough. His explanation of his low income taxes for 1970 and 1971—thanks to a $500,000 deduction representing the charitable contribution of his Vice Presidential papers—was certainly more reasonable than the earlier headlines implying that he had somehow received refunds exceeding the amount of his payments.

And so it went. He offered apparently candid and plausible accounts of where he got the money to buy his Florida and California real estate [mostly by selling stock and a New York apartment]; on the bugging of his brother's phone [his brother knew of it and the surveillance involved "what others might be doing"]; and on the burglary of Daniel Ellsberg's psychiatrist's office ["a stupid . . . illegal thing to do"]. His answers tend to support his emotional assurance that he is "not a crook," and they put the burden of proof more squarely than ever on his critics.

Mr. Nixon's cause would probably have been better served if the editors had stuck to the alleged scandals and asked tougher questions. Mr. Nixon

himself seemed to think so, and volunteered to talk about milk prices — a move which one NBC commentator promptly referred to as "manipulating" the news conference. To some people, it seems Mr. Nixon can do no right.

A public press conference such as this might have avoided much of the damage of Watergate if it had come months ago. The long delay is hard to understand. Friday's answers suggest that some of the questions in the editors' minds—and the public's—have been baseless, and that others have explanations that are at least superficially reasonable.

While it is true that a President must live up to standards higher than those that apply to lesser mortals; and while it is true that the whole Watergate saga has been distressing, it is still inappropriate for anyone to criticize unless his own record is clear. And in a day of generally sagging moral character, when corruption is found in both political parties; when the young people who have complained the loudest about Mr. Nixon can often be found signing up for food stamps at taxpayers' expense in order to prove their "independence" of society; when shoplifting is rampant; when it is widely regarded as acceptable to demand unreported wages in cash in order to get undeserved payments in Social Security, welfare, or unemployment compensation; and when otherwise intelligent employers acquiesce in this form of cheating, it is fair to ask whether Watergate is indeed the shocking aberration that some claim, or is simply the most conspicuous manifestation of an amorality that has been around for some time.

Mr. Nixon's conference has not removed all suspicion, but it has cleared the air, put things in fairer perspective, and above all paved the way for subsequent appearances which, in time, should reduce the credibility gap that has plagued his administration.

The News American

Baltimore. Md., November 20, 1973

AFTER several dramatic, abrasive and inconclusive confrontations with the White House press corps—each followed by extended retreats into a sort of brooding seclusion—President Nixon last week adopted a striking new strategy to meet the challenge of Watergate.

Abruptly ending his isolation, he first moved boldly to regain the political offensive by inviting Republican and conservative Democratic members of Congress to an extraordinary series of intimate discussions of the problem. Then he undertook a blitzkrieg of public speeches and question-answering forums which continue this week.

His theme remains constant. He admittedly is guilty of errors in judgment, and accepts blame for the deplorable results. But he personally is innocent of any wrongdoing, and positively will not resign despite the cries of critics he views as seeking to destroy his leadership.

The theme is the same as it always has been throughout the scandals. What is new is that it is being voiced with such loud and repeated insistence. It is being sounded, furthermore, with confident good humor, quick-witted aplomb and the self-possession of total conviction.

Mr. Nixon, in a word, seems to have grasped at last that one of his greatest Watergate problems has been psychological—and of his own making. Thanks to his normal secretiveness and tendency to take indefensible positions, he has created the appearance of evasion and guilt where none at all has been proven.

By coming out in the open and hammering away at the fact that the whole case against him is built on suppositions, guilt by association and the uncorroborated testimony of one discredited man, the President is taking the most effective psychological counter-action possible.

It may have come too late to be more than partially successful, and probably has. At the very least, however, if accompanied by a follow-through on promises to be more cooperative with the courts and Watergate probers, it should give some second thoughts to those who have been clamoring for resignation or impeachment.

The Hartford Courant

Hartford, Conn., November 18, 1973

It was a month ago that The Courant editorially opposed calls for the impeachment of President Nixon.

At that time such talk seemed premature in view of what was publicly known about the Watergate affair and the events that followed in its train.

And there were vexing legal questions concerning on what grounds impeachment proceedings could be based.

In the subsequent weeks, however, the whole situation has only become more muddled and confused, wracking and riving the country and the citizens to a point of complete distraction.

This has got to stop. The miasma enveloping the nation and the Presidency has got to be cleared up now without being allowed to drag its weary length any further.

If impeachment, or an attempt at impeachment, is the best way to do it, The Courant now believes Congress should get about it without further delay, and clear the air so the country can breathe again.

In James J. Kilpatrick's column on the opposite side of this page today, he too is calling for impeachment as a resolution of this problem. However, he looks at it principally as a solution for the Republican Party, while we regard an attempt at impeachment, or impeachment itself, as necessary to clear the air and get on with the nation's business.

There still remains, of course, the question of whether Congress has sufficient grounds, under the Constitution, to vote impeachment. The Constitution provides that the House of Representatives may impeach—that is to say, indict—a federal official on charges of treason, bribery, "or other high crimes and misdemeanors."

It is true that the President has repeatedly said

that members of his staff indulged in wrong doings through "overzealousness." Watergate plumbers have been jailed. There has been the hassle over withheld tapes and the firing of the Special Prosecutor. "Informed sources" have raised many allegations. Members of Congress, and even some of the Republican Party, have had harsh things to say about Mr. Nixon's conduct and policies.

But what actually constitutes "high crimes and misdemeanors" on the part of a President is a subject legal scholars have wrestled over for generations.

Nevertheless, let Congress go ahead and try to impeach. Even its very failure to find grounds would in its way help the situation. It would indicate that whatever Mr. Nixon's errors and failings have been, they have not been criminal.

No one can be unaware of some of the more depressing angles of impeachment. It has been said that "An impeachable offense is whatever a majority of the House considers it to be at a given moment in history." That House is heavily Democratic, and in some pockets, wildly liberal and emotionally very much opposed to President Nixon.

One way or another, the process of impeachment now seems, after all these dreary and wearying months, the best way of trying to get at a resolution of this muddle and of putting the nation back on the track. It might have been handled differently earlier, but now the situation is indeed as thick as mud and politicking won't clear it up.

Give due process the chance offered in the Constitution to render equal justice to Mr. Nixon and the nation, too. That due process at this point seems to be to get on with impeachment, and clear the air one way or another.

ST. LOUIS POST-DISPATCH

St. Louis, Mo., November 20, 1973

Toward the end of President Nixon's meeting with a newspaper editors convention in Orlando, Fla., it became apparent that the alloted time would run out before he could offer an explanation of the Administration's increase in milk support prices. It was an explanation that Mr. Nixon obviously wanted badly to give, for several times during the session he virtually begged to be asked about allegations that the rise in supports was the *quid pro quo* for heavy financial contributions from the dairy industry.

So as the program ended without the milk issue having been raised, Mr. Nixon gave an order: "Television keep me on." Whereupon the cameras were obediently kept trained on the Chief Executive who went on to give his side of the story. The significance of the incident ought not to be ignored. Every television viewer is familiar with the words "I'm sorry our time is up," which ushers off the air lesser politicians and celebrities. But a president's television time is never up; he can command as much or as little of it as he wishes, and he can order the cameras to keep rolling. Incidents such as this demonstrate the absurdity of the claim that Mr. Nixon is a helpless victim of the networks.

Arkansas Gazette.

Little Rock, Ark., November 26, 1973

President Nixon within the last few days has pulled out all the familiar old wheezing old stops, plus one new one, courtesy of the "energy crisis." Following is a kind of Whitman's Sampler, or, rather, a pull-out and throw-away of some, at least, of the maple-filled centers.

1. Mother On Deathbed. He revived the tale of his mother on her deathbed, saying that she wasn't going to "quit", and didn't want him ever to quit, either.

2. Waving The Flag. This was at Macon, Ga., on the occasion of the 90th birthday of Carl Vinson, a former chairman of the House Armed Services Committee. Mr. Vinson had helped set the stage a day or so before by saying we needed a flock more atomic-powered missile subs in order to stay still farther ahead of the Russians, and while Nixon didn't actually promise the old civilian warrior any in so many words, he did promise to name one of the ones we already had for Vinson. More generally, the C-in-C said he didn't think the Russians "want war" (surely not, now that they are full of all that cheap wheat and have joined the Pepsi generation into the bargain) and didn't think the Chinese did either, but that we had to remain "strong", lest either they or Mauritius might think that we are letting our guard down. So much for that enormous domestic lobby that wants America to remain *weak*.

3. Waving the *Confederate* Flag. We remarked before that he had been whistling Dixie on his latest campaign tour seeking to remain in office, though we must concede that the grand old air sounded just a little shrill, as if whistled by a graveyard. But he certainly gave it the old college try, literally. At Macon, again, he brought up a hitherto unheard of (by us at least) room-mate at Duke Law School, who had convinced the Yankee-descended Nixon in jig time that Grant wasn't the greatest American general, after all, (Nixon had not yet heard of Patton, a Virginian), but had to be ranked behind at least three great Confederate captains, in that order, Lee, Jackson and Joe Johnston. This is a good one, though not as good as the story, adequately vouched for, about Nixon, possibly with a leg up from the same roomie, shinnying through the dean's transom to find out about his finals grades a few hours in advance of posting, because he couldn't stand the suspense. Always was an ambitious lad.

4. Football. At Macon, yet again, Nixon described the Atlanta Falcons as "the comeback team of the year," and reportedly drew a few yocks from the crowd when he said he possibly should ring up Falcon coach Norm Van Brocklin ("the Dutchman," to Hard Cosell and the rest of us intimates) and find out how he had done it. The Falcs are coming, all right, as they demonstrated to the Vikes the next night, but they are not a comeback team because they haven't yet been anywhere to fall away from and then come back to.

5. Thanksgiving. Somewhere along the way said we ought to be thankful for the wheat we still have and for a turkey, even at golden goose prices, and, in kind of a virtuoso double, dedicated this year's observation to the memory of John F. Kennedy, on the anniversary of whose death the holiday falls, and whom Nixon was bedeviling up to the day of his death in Dallas.

6. The New One, the Missing Back-up Plane Gambit. Although the Defense Department was to fly two whole planeloads of congressman and assorted bureaucrats to Macon the next day, the President was careful to point out to the Associated Press Managing Editors at Disney World on Saturday night that, in the interests of energy conservation, he had not even brought his "back-up" plane with him, so "if this one [the one he did ride] goes down, they won't have to impeach." Here, one supposes, we are not only expected to feel pity for the man but also awe at his raw courage. That is, until we ask ourselves — which is soon enough — "What is this man saying." Not even the most elusive of high-wire-artist Presidents can change airplanes in mid jetstream. All a back-up plane is for is to ensure that if anything goes wrong between touchdown at one point and take-off again, the stand-by is there to be pressed into use.

The worst that could happen in the absence of the back-up plane would be that Mr. Nixon might have to spend a little extra time on the ground, like the rest of us, for nobody obviously is going to let him take off in the plane he has if there is the slightest hint of anything wrong—not after all that money we've all got invested in "security" blankets at San Clemente.

The Philadelphia Inquirer

Philadelphia, Pa., November 20, 1973

After months of seclusion, it is a welcome change to find President Nixon going public again. And though he is devoting much of this sudden new offensive to an exercise he once described as "wallowing in Watergate," that also is welcome.

For it is an unhappy fact, as one of those Republican senators invited to the White House last week — Oregon's Robert Packwood — told Mr. Nixon to his face, that Watergate has virtually destroyed his credibility. And with it, the young Oregonian bluntly warned, the President's "ability to inspire and lead this country" is also destroyed.

"The problem with the public," Sen. Packwood said, "is that they no longer believe you. They no longer trust the integrity of this administration."

It is encouraging, therefore, to find Mr. Nixon openly discussing Watergate in his meetings with senators and congressmen, in his speeches, and in that televised session with editors Saturday evening. But too many questions have been only partially answered, misleadingly answered or unanswered to make these disjointed appearances any satisfactory substitute for full disclosure.

The President himself, in his Saturday evening press conference, seemed to suggest that he was eager to get the full story out. Regarding those non-existent tapes, for example, he expressed his "very great disappointment" and said, "I wanted the evidence out." And in respect to the tapes which do exist, he commented: "I trust in some way we can find a way to get the substance to the American people."

Well, if Mr. Nixon really wants "the evidence out," we have three suggestions:

—First, simply release the tapes. The White House has been suggesting that this might present legal problems. Last week, however, Judge John Sirica issued a memo stipulating that "if the President thinks it advisable to waive any privilege and make tapes or other material public, he of course is free to do so at any time."

—Second, accept the Ervin Committee's request for an informal meeting, a transcript of which would later be publicly released.

"I think the only way out he has now," Sen. Barry Goldwater said recently with his characteristic forthrightness, "would be to show up some morning at the Ervin Committee and say, 'Here I am, Sam. What do you want to know?'"

The White House has hinted that Mr. Nixon might be willing to meet with the two ranking members of the committee — Sen. Ervin and Sen. Baker. That being so, why not meet with the full committee? The administration has been talking about "an appropriate forum" for the President. None would be more appropriate than the select committee created by Congress to investigate the scandals which have rocked his administration.

—Third, guarantee the independence of the special prosecutor and assure him of access to those "tapes, notes or memoranda of Presidential conversations" which Archibald Cox was fired for wanting to pursue.

In the final analysis, the best chance for getting at the full truth lies in the courts. That will take time, but by his very willingness to make available to the courts any information at his disposal, Mr. Nixon could dispel many of the doubts that he really wants "the evidence out."

"The repair of relations with the public," Sen. Packwood told Mr. Nixon, "... depends on what you are willing to reveal." If the President genuinely wants to reveal all, the opportunities are readily at hand.

WINSTON-SALEM JOURNAL

Winston-Salem, N.C., November 28, 1973

Our hearts go out today to Miss Rose Mary Woods. For 23 years, as the Girl Friday of Richard M. Nixon, she has enjoyed the reputation of a perfect secretary — smart, efficient, always right on the button. But now she has to admit in open court that she is just a big dumb cluck who pushed the wrong thing and, zippo, discovered that 18 minutes of prime tape were missing, just the 18 minutes Judge Sirica wanted most to hear.

In this embarrassing situation, we are glad to hear from Miss Woods, President Nixon proved to be the perfect boss. In freehand translation, he told her something like this:

"Don't worry, honey. It's just one of those inconsequential tapes I was preserving for posterity . . . just one of those tapes I fought to the death to keep from Ervin and Baker . . . just one of those tapes for which I fired Archibald Cox and lost the services of my attorney general and deputy attorney general . . . just one of those tapes that the federal district court and the court of appeals thought I ought to give to the grand jury. Don't give it a second thought, Rose Mary."

So perhaps Miss Woods doesn't need our sympathy. But what about Judge Sirica? Man, he needs all he can get.

A year or so ago, the judge looked like the Bengal tiger of the federal bench. G-r-r-r-r! But for the past few weeks, President Nixon and his lawyers have made him look like a caged monkey — a monkey to which they keep throwing peanuts that turn out to be all husk and no meat.

How long can the ex-tiger sustain life on such a diet? Tune in tomorrow for the next installment of our great national soap opera, "Rose Mary and the Tapeworm."

THE SACRAMENTO BEE

Sacramento, Calif., November 29, 1973

Even President Richard Nixon's most stalwart supporters must be shaken by the latest disclosure concerning the Watergate tapes—the assertion by Nixon's secretary, Rose Mary Woods, that she "accidentally" erased a critically significant, 18-minute segment of one of them.

Coming on the heels of White House admissions that two other important tapes are either missing or never were recorded, this new development plunges the nation into a deeper crisis of mistrust as to the President's role in Watergate and the unsavory mess of its attempted coverup.

Most dismaying at this juncture is the probability we will never know for sure just what happened to the tapes. To conclude this vital evidence has been lost through such freak mishaps of coincidence as is offered by White House explanations stretches credibility to the breaking point.

Indeed, public opinion surveys indicate ever growing numbers of Americans simply do not believe it all could have happened so conveniently by accident.

Expert technicians familiar with the kind of tape machine used by Miss Woods in her transcribing of the presidential tapes say flatly the erasure of the 18-minute segment could not have happened as Miss Woods says it did. Miss Woods, after all, assumes she accidentally erased the segment. It well may be the erasure occurred before she received the tapes for transcription. It is unlikely we shall ever know just how that portion was erased.

What is significant is that the missing tapes and the erased portion of the tape recorded June 20, 1972, three days after the Watergate break-in at Democratic national headquarters, bear directly upon the President's knowledge of the event, as might be revealed in conversations with his top aides and others.

It is precisely those conversations, from among scores of other tape-recorded presidential conversations, which now are revealed to be missing from the presidential tapes. How can the public possibly believe this is due to such a strange coincidence of accidents as the White House would have us believe? How long can government survive these lacerations of the people's confidence?

The Kansas City Times

Kansas City, Mo., November 28, 1973

Miss Rose Mary Woods, the superprofessional master secretary who hardly ever makes a mistake and who has served Richard Nixon faithfully for more than 20 years has finally made a mistake.

What did Miss Woods do? The mistake was not an uncorrectable typing error or even a misunderstanding in dictation or a bad translation from shorthand. It was not a wrong spelling of an addressee's name. It was not even a wrong address.

What Miss Woods did was to push the wrong button and erase a great bunch of the Watergate tapes. A full 18 minutes. Miss Woods says that is exactly what happened.

Thus the long hum was due to the human error of an overworked, loyal stenographer and anyone who says otherwise is not chivalrous.

Maybe it happened that way. Maybe the long arm of coincidence is longer than anyone had dreamed. But the latest tape erasure comes on top of the earlier findings that one tape had run off the spool at a crucial moment and that another was nonexistent because the conversation was over a phone without a tap.

It is hard to believe that conversations so vital to the historic analysis of the Nixon administration, 1969-1977 A.D., would be handled in such a careless manner. Or that Mr. Nixon's extremely efficient and completely loyal secretary would wipe out 18 minutes of history—the words of the boss—so thoughtlessly.

Should Miss Woods be fired? Should Mr. Nixon be fired? Has everything gone to pot since the efficiency of Haldeman and Ehrlichman has been taken from the White House? Does anyone believe anything any more?

The Courier-Journal

Louisville, Ky.
November 23, 1973

SOMETHING STRANGE has happened to the President's tape recorders since their existence was hinted at by his legal counsel in June 25 testimony and confirmed by another White House aide three weeks later. Their quality has taken a nose-dive, the price has been marked down and, of course, a few tapes are missing or contain blank spots.

Before the latest revelation of the long hum in an important presidential meeting of June 20, 1972, the main missing tapes were the telephone call the same day to former Attorney General Mitchell about the Watergate arrests two days earlier, and an April 15, 1973, talk with John Dean. It was in relating his version of that Executive Office Building talk that Mr. Dean (before the Ervin Committee) first referred to the possibility of White House tapes. In that Sunday evening discussion, Mr. Dean said, Mr. Nixon began "asking me a number of leading questions which made me think that the conversation was being taped and that a record was being made to protect himself."

Twenty-one days later, Alexander Butterfield told the Ervin committee of highly efficient recording devices that could pick up any and all conversations in the President's offices. The devices were the sophisticated kind which automatically turn on in response to any sound impulse. This sort of "voice-activated" equipment had been obtained, the former White House aide said he believed, purely to provide the historical archives with a unique record of presidential discussions and decision-making.

So much other testimony in the Ervin hearings or in court has covered the vital role of the Secret Service in reloading, monitoring, checking, marking and storing the presidential tapes that it came as a shock to learn last week, during Mr. Nixon's editors' conference, that all this technical expertise had been concentrated on a "little Sony . . . (and) these little lapel mikes in my desks." The President referred to the inadequacies of the system twice more in the Disney World press conference, saying ". . . The system itself was not a sophisticated system" and ". . . I just wish we had a better system." He also compared his own tape recorders unfavorably to President Johnson's "much better equipment."

Clearly, something has happened to the White House historical preservation system and its basement full of recording devices since it came to light last summer. Now, even the President's efficient secretary, Rose Mary Woods, has complained about the poor quality of the recordings which made it difficult to make out words in some of them. Yet, even in complaining that "this was no Apollo system," the President continues to claim that the seven other subpoenaed tapes are good enough to provide evidence sought by the court.

Perhaps so: given Mr. Nixon's latest pledge to lay all the facts before the public, we doubtless can expect to gather around our radios one night soon to hear what's left of the tapes for ourselves. In the meantime, we can chew on how it is that a fancy system installed in most of the President's offices to give historians such useful grist has suddenly become almost as junky a communications system as two paper cups connected by a string.

Long Island Press

New York, N.Y., November 28, 1973

The Watergate tapes controversy gets, in the words of Lewis Carroll, "curiouser and curiouser." As it does, the efforts of President Nixon to restore public confidence become more and more difficult.

The "non-existence" of two subpenaed tapes was a severe blow to White House credibility, and Mr. Nixon's explanations were not satisfactory. But through his counter-offensive, "Operation Candor," the President hoped to convince the public —and Republican politicians, who hold the key to his future—that all the bad news was behind him. Indeed, he told Republican governors only last week that he knew of no more Watergate bombshells.

But another bombshell quickly followed—the disclosure that 18 minutes of one of the most important tapes had been erased. Instead of bolstered credibility, Mr. Nixon has more unanswered—or unsatisfactorily answered—questions, and more public doubt.

The tape in question involved a conversation between Mr. Nixon and his chief of staff, H.R. Halderman, on June 20, three days after the Watergate break-in. White House lawyer J. Fred Buzhardt told U.S. District Court Judge John Sirica last week that the 18-minute gap was discovered on Nov. 14, and the President was notified soon after. Yet, the special prosecutors, Judge Sirica and the public were kept in the dark for another week.

Damaging as that sounds, Mr. Nixon's personal secretary compounded the problem when she told Judge Sirica she had accidentally wiped out the recording on Oct. 1, six weeks earlier than Mr. Buzhardt's admission—and told the President within five minutes.

She said Mr. Nixon told her "it was no problem because it was not a subpenaed tape." The White House contends that former special Watergate prosecutor Archibald Cox had subpenaed the tape of a meeting between the President, Mr. Haldeman and John D. Ehrlichman, the domestic affairs adviser. But the White House says there was no such meeting—only separate meetings with Mr. Ehrlichman and Mr. Haldeman.

Actually, Mr. Cox's subpena left little room for the contention by Mr. Buzhardt that "it was not understood by White House counsel . . . that this particular conversation was within the subpena." Mr. Cox's subpena memoradum seems clear that he was talking about two consecutive conversations, not one. In it, the prosecutor said the President "met with John D. Ehrlichman and H.R. Haldeman . . . on June 20, 1972 from 10:30 a.m. until approximately 12:45 p.m." He also said "Ehrlichman and then Haldeman went to see the President."

* * *

Miss Woods' explanation of how the erasure took place, and the discrepancies with her testimony on Nov. 8, also strain the public credulity. In her first court appearance, when asked whether she had taken precautions to avoid erasure, Miss Woods replied: "Everyone said to me, 'Be terribly careful.' I don't think I'm so stupid that they had to go over and over it. I used every possible precaution." Asked what precaution, she snapped, "I used my head, the only one I have."

Now we learn that this testimony took place five weeks after she accidentally erased the 18-minute Haldeman-Nixon conversation. The remaining portion of the tape contains no reference to Watergate. Mr. Haldeman's notes of the conversation indicate they discussed Watergate, and a White House "counter-attack," in their June 20 meeting.

The White House hopes the public will believe that Miss Woods accidentally pushed the record button, instead of the stop button, when she reached to answer a telephone call. It also wants the public to accept the contention that "no attempt had been made to reduce any of this (Haldeman) conversation to writing," though Miss Woods had testified she spent 30 hours typing a transcript of the tape.

Taken separately, the explanations could all be plausible, though there still would be some contradictions. Put together, Mr. Nixon's tapes nightmare seems to be still growing. We doubt that any substantial evidence will ever come from the tapes —even though they are finally in Judge Sirica's hands.

Symbolically, they are a weight Mr. Nixon will have difficulty getting off his back. Unless he does, the chances of his regaining public confidence remain dismal.

The Pittsburgh Press

Pittsburgh, Pa., November 28, 1973

The electronic misadventures of Rose Mary Woods have pretty well destroyed any public-relations benefit President Nixon might have derived from finally turning over his Watergate tape recordings to U.S. Judge John J. Sirica.

Miss Woods, who has been Mr. Nixon's personal secretary 22 years, told the judge she may mistakenly have caused an 18-minute "gap" in an important recording by pressing the wrong button while transcribing the raw tape nearly two months ago.

Unfortunately, the missing material was a private conversation between the President and his White House chief of staff, H. R. Haldeman, three days after the Republican-financed break-in at Democratic national headquarters in the Watergate office building June 17 of last year.

Even if Miss Woods' version of the incident ("I am just dreadfully sorry") is true, millions of skeptical citizens will have a hard time believing it.

After all, Rose Mary Woods is more than just a new girl at the office who isn't quite sure which buttons to push on the boss' tape recorder.

"Everyone said to me: 'Be terribly careful,' " she told the court Nov. 8. "I don't think I'm so stupid they had to go over and over it. I used every possible precaution."

Why the erasure — or "gap," as she calls it — was not reported to the judge until last Wednesday is a question open to conjecture.

Miss Woods said she was told by the President and others "not to worry" because that particular conversation with Mr. Haldeman was not under subpoena.

It seems obvious, however, that Rose Mary's boo-boo will be seen as just one more in a long string of errors and deceptions that have seriously impaired the President's credibility with the American people.

CHICAGO DAILY NEWS

Chicago, Ill., November 28, 1973

Rose Mary Woods' gargantuan bungle of the Watergate tape caps the climax of a story that has taxed human belief since the beginning.

It was only Nov. 8 when the President's personal secretary was testifying — rather primly — that she had, of course, taken every precaution in transcribing the tapes. "Everyone said to me, 'Be careful,' " she said. "I don't think I'm so stupid that they had to go over and over it."

And yet five weeks earlier (it now turns out) in transcribing what apparently was a particularly sensitive taped conversation between Mr. Nixon and his former aide, H. R. Haldeman, she had pushed the wrong button and erased several minutes of dialog.

How did she manage this? Well, she first testified that she did not know whether she had put her foot on the foot pedal or the record button stuck; later she decided that she "must have" kept her foot on the pedal.

And what had she done about it? She told the President. And what did he say? "He said, 'There's no problem because that's not one of the subpenaed tapes.' "

No problem? The credibility of the President of the United States hangs by a thin thread. . . . The Watergate tapes are expected to provide the most critical evidence bearing on Mr. Nixon's veracity. . . . Public opinion polls show that two-thirds of the citizens believe the tapes to have been doctored . . . . If they weren't, then the faithful transcription and delivery of relevant tapes could go far toward turning the tide in the President's favor.

And there was no problem? Good grief!

There is, of course, a grave problem, and Miss Woods has made her modest contribution toward worsening it. The problem is that the American people have begun to believe that the Executive Office has become so entangled in expediency that it has lost touch with the simple worth of truth.

You may recall that Alice told the Queen, "There's no use trying, one *can't* believe impossible things," and the Queen said, "I daresay you haven't had much practice. When I was your age I always did it for half-an-hour a day. Why sometimes I've believed as many as six impossible things before breakfast."

The people of this Wonderland have been told six times six times six impossible things, and are longing for some simple, homely facts that will hold till still tomorrow.

The San Diego Union

San Diego, Calif., November 28, 1973

When asked by newsmen recently why the Administration had not announced the "bombshell" that 18 minutes of a recording of White House conversations had been erased, presidential counsel J. Fred Buzhardt said because the erasure was not considered a bombshell.

Events just may prove him right. The testimony of Secretary Rose Mary Woods as to how she obliterated a portion of the tape is within the realm of possibility. The administration's position that it did not announce the act immediately because it did not believe that the tape had been subpoenaed by the court could have been an honest misjudgment. And the poor quality of the particular tape, as exhibited in open court this week, raises some doubt that the missing conversation was of transcendent importance.

Nevertheless, the erased portion of tape, whether or not it is of any value at all so far as getting to the bottom of Watergate is concerned, has added to the burdens of the Administration. It has given the President another credibility problem just at a time when there was evidence that he had taken the initiative in the courts to make the fullest possible disclosure of his knowledge concerning the Watergate affair. .

Even the courts accept Miss Woods' explanation there are un-doubtedly more Watergate bombshells—or duds—in the offing. The Senate investigating committee, for example, has recessed until mid-January. Plainly running out of steam and bickering openly, the committee will probably draw a second breath and fight for survival by covering the well-trod ground of political contributions of Howard Hughes and the dairy interests. On another front there could be some tension in the offing between the Administration and special Prosecutor Leon Jaworski, who also appears to be broadening and intensifying his efforts. Additionally, there is an impeachment study progressing in the House and numerous legal actions in various arenas that will serve to keep the Watergate issue alive. Inflation, a war in the Middle East and even the imminence of a major change in American life style because of an energy crisis have not diverted the public fascination from this footnote of American history.

Indeed, it appears that nothing will put the issue to rest short of full and frank disclosure by the Administration of all facts that bear on the legitimate congressional and court concerns. Considering the tenacity of Watergate and the damage it has already done to our unity even the loss of some executive confidentiality would be a small loss in comparison.

DAYTON DAILY NEWS

Dayton, Ohio, November 28, 1973

Rose Mary Woods, President Nixon's personal secretary, ought to be charged with destruction of evidence. Without prejudging the outcome of such a charge, it is clear that the circumstances not only warrant but virtually require that the issue be resolved in criminal proceedings.

Consider some of the points: Miss Woods testified before Judge John Sirica as recently as two weeks ago and, though such testimony would have been relevant, made no mention of having accidentally erased part of one tape. By her own testimony now, she knew the erasure had occurred Oct. 1.

Miss Woods says the 18-minute erasure—of a conversation Mr. Nixon had with aide H.R. Haldeman shortly after the Watergate break-in—occurred because she mistakenly pushed the "record" button on her tape machine while answering a phone call. The call, however, she has said, lasted only five or six minutes, meaning that Miss Woods had to keep her foot pressed on the machine's pedal not only through the phone call but for a n o t h e r 12 minutes as well.

The "erased" tape does not appear actually to have been erased. Instead, the critical 18-minute segment bears a buzzing sound. When tape is erased by the kind of rather elaborate mistake Miss Woods described to the court, the tape either should be silent or should carry no more noise than a mild tape "hiss."

It is impossible not to notice the incredible series of misadventures that has befallen evidence in President Nixon's care. Two tapes have been lost—and were known to have been lost weeks before Mr. Nixon's attorneys informed the court that had subpoenaed the tapes. A dictabelt Mr. Nixon promised to substitute for one missing tape is now said to be missing, too. The Nixon-Haldeman session shortly after Watergate has been obliterated. Documents that the President refused to give to Special Prosecutor Archibald Cox but promised to Mr. Cox's replacement, Leon Jaworski, still haven't been delivered to the new prosecutor, three weeks after they were asked for.

Any one of those b u m b l e s would be believable. Together, they achieve a wild statistical improbability. The President's much-heralded and much hoped-for campaign for coming clean with the Watergate and related evidence is turning out only to be a busy round of speeches in which Mr. Nixon proclaims his innocence while the evidence that he said would exonerate him is being lost, destroyed or withheld.

Detroit Free Press

Detroit, Mich., November 28, 1973

ALTHOUGH THE PRESIDENT'S attempts to avoid impeachment ought to be high drama, it all too often reads as if he were trying to bring back burlesque.

The continuing fiasco of the White House tapes is like nothing so much as a slapstick routine. The misadventures of Abbott and Costello could scarcely top any of what we are seeing now.

How was it they always managed to look so guilty when the friendly neighborhood beat patrolman sauntered by? How could Rose Mary Woods possibly permit the erasure of 18 minutes of one of the tapes that was going to help clear the president?

Indeed, the most credible aspect of the various explanations of what has happened in the tape story is that it is so incredible. Would anyone, setting out to clear the record, make up so many preposterous incidents? It is so absurd as to be almost believable.

The effect of this is that, however useful the remaining tapes may prove in court for nailing particular subordinates of the president, they are no longer of much value for clearing the record as a whole. We do not know whether the White House is guilty of duplicity on the tapes; no one can know.

The lost, unrecorded or erased portions of the White House conversations are too convenient for the rest of the record to be accepted as a faithful documentation of the president's relationships with the principals in the Watergate and related scandals. Mr. Nixon and his agents did this to themselves. They made it impossible to get to the bottom of the story.

Their handling of the tapes makes it all the more important that the special prosecutor pursue his independent inquiry and that the House of Representatives proceed in an orderly way with its inquiry into the grounds for impeachment. We think resignation would not resolve the country's dilemma about Mr. Nixon, and we do not think a consensus yet exists for impeachment.

But the House committee can proceed with its investigation, in a reasoned and careful way, sorting out the multitude of c h a r g e s that have been made, testing whether any of them can be made to stick in the extraordinary courtroom of an impeachment proceeding. That seems to us to be the best means, with the best regard for due process, to deal with the problems the president's performance raises.

And an orderly inquiry ought to be preferable to the president's own, absurd, do-it-yourself attempt to "make things perfectly clear." Surely it could not provide the country with any more disconcerting surprises.

Des Moines Tribune

Des Moines, Iowa, November 27, 1973

The disclosure that portions of the Watergate tapes are missing and erased shows why the "Stennis compromise" for hearing the tapes was unsatisfactory and why special prosecutor Archibald Cox was right in rejecting it.

Under the administration's plan, Senator John Stennis (Dem., Miss.) was to have been furnished a detailed summary of the tapes by the White House. Stennis would be given the tapes and instructed to compare the summary with the taped conversations. The senator then would certify to the court whether the summary was an accurate representation of the recordings.

The White House learned on Sept. 29 that portions of the tapes were missing. The "Stennis compromise" fell apart on Oct. 19. The White House capitulated on Oct. 23 and agreed to give the tapes to the court. The White House did not notify Judge John Sirica about the missing portions until Oct. 31.

The White House has not satisfactorily explained the month-long delay in publicly revealing that some of the subpoenaed conversations were unavailable. It is possible that Stennis would have been told everything that the White House subsequently disclosed to Judge Sirica.

But it is also possible that the effort to have Stennis verify the accuracy of a White House summary was an effort to get by with less than full disclosure of the condition of the White House tapes.

The disclosure that tapes are missing was followed by hearings in Judge Sirica's court, with witnesses sworn and subject to cross-examination. The custody of the tapes has been gone into in exhaustive detail. Even if Stennis had been told about the missing portions, or discovered it himself, he would have been unable to conduct the kind of judicial inquiry being undertaken by Judge Sirica.

These hearings should throw light on whether there has been tampering with the tapes. The question may never be settled with certainty, but the public at least has confidence that the court is attempting to arrive at the truth. The court, moreover, is operating in the open, with the public in a position to hear the testimony and form its own judgments.

The "Stennis compromise" called for Stennis to operate in secret without accountability to the public. Senator Stennis was hand picked by the White House. Judge Sirica is beholden in no way to the chief executive.

The more that comes out about the tapes, the more the country is indebted to Cox for rejecting the "Stennis compromise" and insisting that the tapes be turned over to Judge Sirica.

The Honolulu Advertiser

Honolulu, Hawaii, November 29, 1973

President Nixon is stepping up Operation Candor this week as the tangle of the Watergate tapes tightens around him.

Even those willing to give Nixon the benefit of every doubt should be dismayed at the confusion White House handling has contributed.

ON OPERATION CANDOR, his attempt to make everything perfectly clear, judgment is best withheld. The operation may be applauded, but there are good questions about the degree of candor.

On the tapes, the key question of what they say about Watergate is being overshadowed by the equally important matter of what they don't say at crucial points — and why.

And that has to be viewed against Nixon's previous statement that he listened to the tapes and they, in effect, clear him of involvement in Watergate and its coverup.

At this point, it may be the Watergate tapes will prove little except their unreliability as evidence.

IN THIS WEEK'S swirl of events there is the passing of the Senate Watergate committee hearings, not permanently, it is said, but until mid-January while its staff looks into the Nixon milk fund and Howard Hughes' $100,000 gift to Bebe Rebozo.

Those may or may not be important side issues in the general mess called Watergate. Both could contribute something to the drive for campaign reform.

The Senate committee has done much to make the nation aware of Watergate's importance, but an even greater contribution should be such reform legislation.

MEANWHILE, Nixon's Operation Candor, the proceedings in Judge Sirica's Federal court, and the work of the special prosecutor will keep the Watergate issues before the public in coming weeks.

So far there have been few indictments or guilty pleas in connection with Watergate. But the special prosecutor is reported looking into more than three dozen types of crimes that were either committed or proposed in connection with the scandal.

That list includes conspiracy, breaking and entering, arson, illegal wiretapping, perjury, bribery, lying to the FBI, bribing a witness, contempt of court, contempt of Congress, destruction of evidence, campaign finance violations, blackmail, falsifying government documents, income tax violations, embezzlement, extortion, slander, libel, intercepting mail, malicious campaign mischief, flight to avoid prosecution or testifying, and theft.

A REVIEW OF that list might be recommended for those who wonder why concern over the Watergate affair continues and grows with each revelation. Some of those charges could potentially be lodged against the President of the United States.

Indeed, the Watergate affair has come a long way since the days when President Nixon's press secretary described it as "a third-rate burglary."

When it will end is anybody's guess. There are many statements about the public having seen only the tip of the iceberg. We note Senator Howard Baker's remark last week: "It is entirely possible that Watergate will not be over any time soon."

The Birmingham News

Birmingham, Ala., November 30, 1973

Another clownish chapter has been added to the Watergate business that has had more clowns than Ringling in both the Senate and federal court versions.

And the public, which has shown positive signs long since that it is time to produce results and fold the tent, now is told that the performance will adjourn for a time and reconvene after the first of the year, to run its course by late February. Or so it is said.

Latest display of the ridiculous extent to which Watergate and its side performances have gone came a few days ago following appearance in U. S. District Judge John J. Sirica's court of President Nixon's longtime secretary, Miss Rose Mary Woods, who testified concerning her handling of some of the White House tapes.

There is little question but that the on-again, off-again reported existence of certain tapes and whether some did or did not exist is a strange episode in that portion of the Watergate inquiry.

But a member of the prosecutor's staff in Judge Sirica's court, Jill Volner, hied herself to the White House to have a first-hand look at Miss Woods' desk, where she sat when she took dictation, how she operated the tape machine, where she kept her pencils and, as far as we know, when she took coffee breaks and what she had for lunch.

After she was done with her White House visit she smilingly posed outside the White House, reportedly trying to hail a taxi.

This is not a children's game of cops and robbers. Or at least it shouldn't be. It is a serious business, consuming valuable government time at public cost.

The politics of the affair have been well milked and the clowns have done their acts and had several encores.

It's time to produce or bring the business to an end, including such childish vignettes as the one played to the galleries this week.

THE MIAMI NEWS

Miami, Fla., November 23, 1973

The newest missing chunk of White House tapes would defy belief if the whole fiasco had not already destroyed any trace of credulity on the part of the American people.

Less than 36 hours after President Nixon told a Republican governors' session in Memphis that he knew of no further embarrassing revelations to come out of the Watergate scandal, his lawyer, Fred Buzhardt, was in court to say to Federal Judge John J. Sirica, in effect:

"Oops, we forgot to mention that 18 minutes of conversation between Mr. Nixon and his chief aide, H.R. Halderman, has been blotted out of the third tape by a mysterious tone."

Aw, c'mon, fellas. This thing long ago got too ridiculous. The only reason left for believing the White House version is the fact that a four-year-old child could devise better lies.

Judge Sirica is dead right to try to get his hands on the tapes. If anything, he's still being much too polite about it. He ought to have subpenaed them immediately.

The remaining step — and it already is overdue — is to begin impeachment proceedings immediately in the House of Representatives. There is no other way to get to the bottom of this whole mess, with sufficient disclosure either to clear the President of any complicity or to get him out of there so we can get on with the serious business of this country.

NIXON DISCLOSES FINANCES; JUDGE REBUKES IRS

President Nixon disclosed data on his personal finances Dec. 8 to "remove doubts" that had arisen and "correct misinformation" about "what I have earned and what I own." The data included his income tax returns for 1969–72 and an audit of his private financial affairs since Jan. 1, 1969 conducted by the New York accounting firm of Coopers & Lybrand. According to the data, Nixon had become a millionaire during his presidency, his net worth having more than tripled (from $307,141 to $988,522). It also revealed that he had paid unusually low federal income tax payments for one with his income and no state income tax, although he maintained a residence and voted in California.

The President acknowledged the controversial nature of two major tax decisions which substantially reduced his federal income tax obligations. One involved his gift to the U.S. of his vice presidential papers, which enabled him to list huge continuing deductions. The other involved the sale of some California property in 1970 for which no capital gain was reported and no capital gain tax paid. The President offered to submit both matters for re-evaluation to a Congressional tax committee and to abide by its decision. This could amount to an additional claim of nearly $300,000 in taxes. The committee selected, which consented to Nixon's request, was the Congressional Joint Committee on Internal Revenue Taxation, composed of the five senior members of the House Ways and Means Committee and the five senior members of the Senate Finance Committee. The committee met Dec. 12 and chairman Wilbur D. Mills (D, Ark.) told reporters afterwards its members agreed to proceed as it customarily did in other cases with a full inspection of all aspects of the Nixon tax returns.

In his statement on his financial affairs, Nixon declared his intention to make a gift to the American people of his home at San Clemente, Calif. at the time of his death or the death of Mrs. Nixon, whichever was later.

Among other important developments in the political crisis besetting the Nixon Administration:

■ Egil Krogh Jr., former head of the special White House investigations unit dubbed the "plumbers," pleaded guilty Nov. 30 to a civil rights charge stemming from a Labor Day 1971 break-in at the Los Angeles office of the psychiatrist who had treated Pentagon Papers defendant Daniel Ellsberg. In return for Krogh's guilty plea, the special U.S. prosecutor's office agreed to dismiss charges of making false declarations in connection with the break-in. Krogh told U.S. District Court Judge Gerhard Gesell he would cooperate with the special Watergate prosecutors after he had been sentenced.

■ In testimony before Judge John Sirica on the gap in a subpoenaed tape recording, White House chief of staff Alexander Haig Jr. related that until White House lawyers had settled upon the "accidental" explanation, there had been speculation on "devil theories"—that "perhaps some sinister force had come in and applied the other energy source and taken care of the information on the tape."

■ The Senate Democratic leadership decided Dec. 11 to defer floor action on a bill providing for court appointment of a special Watergate prosecutor. Majority Leader Mike Mansfield (D, Mont.) said part of the reason for the decision was "the outstanding job" being done by special prosecutor Leon Jaworski.

■ Judge Charles R. Richey of the U.S. district court in Washington Dec. 11 ordered the Internal Revenue Service to grant tax-exempt status to the Center for Corporate Responsibility. Richey said the IRS had acted improperly in delaying for more than two years action on the group's request for determination of its status and eventually denying tax-free standing to the nonprofit organization. Because the White House had failed to comply with court orders regarding evidence in the case, Richey said, he regarded this as an admission that the White House had acted improperly in causing the center's request to be denied. Richey agreed with the center's charge that it had been "singled out for selective treatment for political, ideological and other improper reasons which have no basis in the statute and regulations." Richey also said the White House had improperly claimed executive privilege on four documents and one tape recorded conversation. The documents eventually were submitted to him privately. They "demonstrate that the White House staff did in fact consider using the IRS against their 'enemies.'"

In another controversial IRS ruling, the *Washington Post* reported Nov. 19 that the IRS had revoked the tax-exempt status of the Fair Campaign Practices Committee, a 19-year-old nonprofit, nonpartisan group.

Chicago Tribune
Chicago, Ill., December 11, 1973

President Nixon has made the most complete disclosure of his finances and income tax returns ever made by a Chief Executive. He has also invited the Joint Congressional Committee on Internal Revenue Taxation to examine the two most controversial items and to determine whether he still owes additional taxes which could amount to about $250,000.

Mr. Nixon has chosen the best—and perhaps the only satisfactory—way to answer the many charges which have been made with respect to his personal finances. And unlike many of his belated Watergate "explanations," he has done it soon enough to seize the offensive and put his critics on the defensive, at least for the time being.

The decision to produce 50 documents relating to his personal finances was, of course, a calculated risk. It meant disclosing that a wealthy drug manufacturer had settled a $25,000 trust on Tricia Nixon back in 1958, at a time when she was 8 years old, her father was Vice President, and drug prices were under attack. It meant confirming that he has paid only token taxes for three years, that he has paid no state taxes in California or anywhere else, and that he paid no capital gains tax on the sale of part of his estate at San Clemente, one of the two items the joint committee is asked to review. The other is the $576,000 deduction which he will have taken over a five-year period for the donation of his Vice Presidential papers to the National Archives.

This deduction is the biggest issue in terms of money, but also the hardest to attack. From the dates given in Mr. Nixon's statement, one can only conclude that he was scrambling to get the gift made before the deadline which Congress was about to impose—and at a time when he was urging tax reform to make the rich bear a fairer burden of income taxes.

Consider the dates: On March 25, 1969, Mr. Nixon had about 1,000 crates of his Vice Presidential papers shipped over to the National Archives. On April 8, an appraiser, summoned from Chicago, began appraising the papers. On April 21, 1969, Mr. Nixon called for a number of changes in the tax laws, including one that would tighten the restrictions on charitable contributions. During the summer Congress shaped a law which ruled out deductions for the donation of personal papers; a cut-off date of July 25, 1969, was inserted, and Mr. Nixon finally signed the bill on Dec. 30, 1969, calling the tax reforms good.

One may raise eyebrows over what Mr. Nixon was doing while asking for tighter restrictions, but it seems silly to argue—as many are doing now—that Mr. Nixon didn't intend to make the contribution. The only reasonable questions involve the dating of certain papers. These are matters involving Treasury Department regulations rather than statutes.

On the capital gains and the California taxes, Mr. Nixon would seem more vulnerable. But here again, the federal laws are so complex and the state laws vary so widely that it would be rash, at this juncture, to try to judge the validity of the President's position.

The point is that Mr. Nixon should be treated just as any other taxpayer would be treated under the same circumstances. His critics have been eager to assume that he is wrong even before knowing all of the details. His worst proved offense has been poor judgment; the whole story of Watergate has been marked by bad judgment and abominable handling in the White House. But when it comes to tax liability—and talk of impeachment—Mr. Nixon's critics will have to be more specific than they have been so far.

OKLAHOMA CITY TIMES
Oklahoma City, Okla., December 5, 1973

NOT that the closed mind crowd will ever believe it, but the valuation of President Nixon's vice presidential papers has been substantiated by the country's premier authority on valuable documents. Ralph Newman, the expert who made the appraisal, says the papers actually are worth even more than the $500,000 Nixon claimed for tax deduction purposes when he donated them to the government.

By taking advantage of existing tax law at the time, as did his predecessor, Nixon was able to reduce his income tax to nominal amounts in 1970 and 1971. For this he is now being criticized in some quarters, even though he has made available more detailed information regarding his personal finances and tax returns than any president in history.

NEWMAN is the Chicago library official and owner of the Abraham Lincoln Book Shop who has helped every president since Herbert Hoover assess his confidential papers for posterity. Nixon sought his services after the 1968 election on the recommendation of President Lyndon Johnson.

There was no criticism leveled at Johnson when he used the completely legal donation of documents for tax purposes. Yet somehow a different standard is being applied to Richard Nixon.

THE thought occurs that it would be most interesting to learn as much about the personal financial and tax records of John F. Kennedy and Lyndon B. Johnson as we already know about those of Richard M. Nixon. For that matter, the tax returns of Nixon's congressional critics would make some lively reading.

Much has been made of the proposition that no president of the United States ought to be above the law. Well and good, but no president ought to be held below the law, either.

The Birmingham News
Birmingham, Ala., December 14, 1973

One of the most highly professional staffs in the Congress, that of the Joint Committee on Internal Revenue, will soon begin to audit President Nixon's 1969-72 income tax returns.

The joint committee agreed to the action following the President's disclosure of his financial affairs since taking office in 1969 and his request that his tax returns be examined by the committee.

In his request to the committee, the President asked that two items be given especially close scrutiny: These were the validity of the $576,000 deduction for his gift of papers to the National Archives and a possible capital gains liability resulting from sale of some of the San Clemente real estate.

In an unprecedented move, the President made the request for the committee audit and disclosed his financial affairs in order to answer criticism which raised questions as to the legality of the deductions and as to whether the President paid the taxes he was legally required to pay.

All of which is well and good—if the committee staff settles quietly to work and comes up with an unemotional evaluation free of bias.

But statements Wednesday from Committee Chairman Wilbur D. Mills contained darker overtones, and raised some questions.

Why does the committee staff, described as one of the most professional in the capital, require extra manpower?

Are five individual income tax returns so complicated that more than a battery of experts are needed to audit them?

And why should the time required by the audit be described as "months?" Shouldn't a few weeks be all that is necessary to give the closest kind of scrutiny?

Another disturbing statement by Mills was that the committee may require public hearings.

After the public, televised Watergate hearings which went their undisciplined, capricious way for agonizing months, the prospect of seeing the President's tax lawyers and accountants on the witness stand is appalling.

God forbid that we have another televised political circus. It is doubtful, however hard he might try, that Mills can upstage the sainted jowly senator from North Carolina.

Surely Mills has a higher regard for the process he is heading up and for the American people than to subject the nation to another televised political blood-letting.

Obviously the President made his request to the committee in good faith, with the avowed purpose of putting his tax matters in the committee's hands for judgment. The motivation was also to get the matter before the American people in its proper legal context rather than to have it examined under the warped lens of political bias.

Mills said that the staff probably will give the committee interim reports and information from these may be made public. This procedure is all well and good, if the partial information in these reports does not lend itself to distorted and erroneous judgments.

The end result, Mills said, will be a "factual report to . . . Congress and the public."

Such a report is certainly desirable in the highest degree, but Mills should be forewarned that factual reports have a way of being completely invalidated by distortion, rumor and innuendo which are dramatized in a highly charged atmosphere for public consumption.

The American people deserve the truth about the President's tax matters, since he has surrendered all personal privilege in making them available through the committee.

To give less than an unemotional and factual report is to betray both the good intentions of the President and the American people.

OREGON Journal
AN INDEPENDENT NEWSPAPER
Portland, Ore., December 11, 1973

When a millionaire with an annual salary of $200,000 pays the same amount of taxes as a family making $8,000 a year, something is badly out of balance in our "progressive" income tax.

President Nixon's greatest contribution to his country's domestic condition may be inadvertent—dramatizing the inequity of the tax structure to the point that pressures for reform cannot be ignored.

It is probably unfair for the beleaguered President to be kicked around on his income taxes. He—and his accountants and tax lawyers—did what the law would seem to expect. That is to take advantage of an assortment of legal loopholes and gimmicks that allows the rich to pay comparatively less in taxes than their earnings would justify in a progressive tax system.

The only question about the legality of the Nixon taxes so far raised has to do with the donation of his vice presidential papers to the national archives. And even that is only a question about whether he complied with all the procedures prior to the 1969 repeal of the law that legitimitized the tax write-off for that type of donation.

Whether he should have profited so heavily from the vice presidential papers is another matter. They were acquired at public expense while he held a public office that gave them whatever value they had. It would seem, therefore, that they should have been public property anyway. But that is a moral concern, not a legal one.

It is well that the law that allowed that escape from taxation has been repealed. It is obvious, however, that a lot more ought to be done to build fairness into a tax system that was supposed to be based on a taxpayer's ability to pay.

Mr. Nixon's disclosure of his tax returns helps to show how wealthy persons can avoid taxes. The laws were written one by one to allow them to do just that.

Perhaps the Nixon disclosure will help to inspire Congress to get serious about tax reform.

New York Post

New York, N.Y., December 10, 1973

Whatever legal judgments may finally be rendered about some aspects of President Nixon's financial files, the statement accompanying their release once again dramatized the moral bankruptcy of his leadership.

His words were clearly unresponsive to the underlying questions previously raised—and now confirmed and multiplied—about his tangled financial affairs. In effect he seemed to be presenting a technical lawyer's brief to prove—in his earlier infelicitous phrase —that "I'm not a crook." But even if that position can be sustained, the heart of the indictment stands.

Thus, by his own report, it is established beyond dispute that for three of the four years of his first term, Mr. Nixon paid a total of less than $6000 in taxes, and that for two of those years, 1970 and 1971, he paid less than $1000 annually. The key device employed to achieve this tax immunity was the "gift" of his Vice Presidential papers (many of them government documents) to the National Archives. This was assertedly made before repeal of the loophole provision in July, 1969. In addition—a disclosure apparently at variance with an earlier statement—he deducted $250,000 in interest payments on his real estate taxes.

Meanwhile, as a result of his tax maneuvers and a series of realty transactions, his net worth has risen from $307,141 on Jan. 20, 1969—inauguration day—to $988,522 on last March 31.

Even if there were no troublesome questions about whether Mr. Nixon used and abused the powers of his office for private financial advantage, the overall portrait of his operations would express gross insensitivity to the appearance of things. Millions of ordinary Americans were meeting heavy tax burdens amid the stress of inflation while he was escaping taxation.

And others were dying in Vietnam. "I have proceeded in a manner I thought both prudent and in the best interest of my family," Mr. Nixon said. Did it never occur to him that his acquisitive life-style and tax gimmickry caricatured all his solemn appeals to the nation for sacrifice and self-discipline? Was he so arrogantly confident that the truth would remain hidden—at least for the duration of his Presidency—that he could live by the credo of "the public be damned?"

Obviously Mr. Nixon recognizes that his belated exercise in "full disclosure" will not "lay to rest" many of the issues created by his report. He felt obliged to propose, for example that the conservative-dominated Joint Congressional Committee on Internal Revenue Taxation review the deductions he took on his private papers and on the sale of land adjacent to his San Clemente estate. It is hardly the President's prerogative to determine what body of Congress should explore these matters.

Moreover, as Sen. Weicker (R-Conn.) pointed out yesterday, this is essentially the business of the Internal Revenue Service. Is the President admitting that the IRS can no longer command public confidence because of the unusual eight-day audit that approved his negligible tax payments in 1971 and 1972—an exercise so hasty that it inevitably invites suspicion of heavy urgent White House pressure?

Innumerable details of the Presidential accounting will stir unease and debate. This is the acknowledgment that he retained for himself unspent portions of his $50,000 annual expense account, supplementing his $200,000 salary—and these added sums were protected by his tax refuges. There is the extraordinary confession at the White House briefing that he was unaware that he had not been paying any California income tax, again a disputed legal point but one on which his avowal of ignorance must be considered astonishing.

There is the revelation that his own auditors disputed the view of his tax accountant that no capital gain should be declared on the San Clemente property sale. There is the saga of the trust fund set up by pharmaceutical magnate Elmer Bobst for Tricia Nixon.

In short, Mr. Nixon was understating the matter when he conceded that "questions and controversies may continue as a consequence of these disclosures." They surely will; not the least will concern the absence of evidence in the latest documents that his papers were actually donated to the Archives before Congress nullified that provision.

* * *

Amid all the ramifications that remain to be explored, the incontestable and unforgettable image is that of a President who almost totally eluded taxation for two years and paid a minor fraction in a third while his assets were expanding—and while he presided over a nation hurt by war and inflation.

The moral shallowness and cynicism unfolded in that portrait transcends legal arguments. It is consistent with the insolvency of spirit that was to emerge on so many levels of the Administration which has given us Watergate, the White House horrors, the Saturday night massacre, the tales of the missing tapes, and so many other shabby scenes.

The Providence Journal

Providence, R.I., December 11, 1973

Friends and critics alike can welcome President Nixon's disclosure of his personal finances during his first term as one necessary step toward restoring confidence in himself personally and in his administration, although that one step by no means clears the a··

We suspect we are not alone in finding the Pre·· ident's action not enough. Doubtless he is right·that no previous president ever has made so comprehensive a disclosure of personal finances while in office. But neither has any president in memory ever incurred more public doubt about his personal probity. Certainly, none has ever felt compelled to stand before an audience and ·publicly declaim "I am no crook." In this context of pervasive suspicion, Mr. Nixon's action may be too little, too late.

Indeed, Mr. Nixon allowed that "questions and controversies may continue as a consequence of these disclosures"—and so they do. They arise both from facts of substance disclosed, and from the framework of circumstances in which those facts became public.

The two key questions of fact are whether Mr. Nixon actually realized a capital gain from the sale of land in San Clemente, which he did not report as income; and whether the donation of his vice presidential papers actually was made before the legal expiration date allowing such deductions. These questions have been submitted by Mr. Nixon to a joint congressional committee on internal revenue. While some question may be raised why a congressional committee should perform a task normally submitted to a tax court, the public may expect the committee to weigh the technicalities and come up with a reasonably acceptable finding. But whether the committee finds Mr. Nixon to be on the right or wrong side of the technical tax questions is really not the crux of the problem.

Mr. Nixon's least problem is how much money he owes the Treasury. The real rub is to what degree he can restore public confidence in him as a man having the moral stature to exercise leadership of a great nation. At this point, such restoration of confidence can be built only on a foundation of self-evident probity. But here is where Mr. Nixon's latest action falls unhappily short.

Like so many of his actions in response to other crises of confidence, most of them under the general heading of Watergate, this one comes too late to be perceived as the spontaneous reaction of an innocent man wrongly accused. It comes too grudgingly to avoid the appearance of one more twist in a long course of maneuverings to get off the hook.

Moreover, the new questions that release of the documents raises are even tougher ones—questions of ethics and of equity which cannot be answered with facts and figures. For example, was there a potential conflict of interest in Mr. Nixon's involved land deals with close millionaire friends, Abplanalp and Rebozo, which add up in final analysis to a gift of tens of thousands of dollars from those friends? What of Mr. Nixon's accepting a 25,000 dollar trust fund from the president of a major pharmaceutical concern for his daughter Tricia in 1958, when he was vice president, at a time when federal regulation of the drug industry was under fire? Do the social-benefit arguments for tax loopholes, designed to encourage philanthropy, really apply to Mr. Nixon's deductions of $576,000 for donating his vice presidential papers to the same government which paid his salary and paid the costs of amassing those papers? Or does this presidential deduction spotlight a pattern of abuse, repeated in hundreds of less-famous citizens' tax returns, which allows men of great wealth to pay less income tax than persons of humble means?

Public response to these larger questions will weigh heavily on Congress in its pondering of impeachment proceedings against the President. That response may be muted now, but we are certain that when Congress adjourns for Christmas recess and its members return to the grassroots, they will be getting answers loud and clear. What they hear at home in the next few weeks may well determine who will lead this country for the next three years.

The New York Times

New York, N.Y., December 11, 1973

President Nixon has at last made what appears to be a complete disclosure of his financial affairs. Only a team of qualified accountants can fully understand all of the financial data that Mr. Nixon has released and determine whether they are complete and accurate. Similarly, experienced tax lawyers have to examine the deductions he has taken and the decisions about tax liability he has made. If the proposed review by the Joint Committee on Internal Revenue Taxation is to be more than an empty political gesture, the committee has to make a thorough audit of these financial records.

For his own sake and to avoid debilitating doubt about his financial integrity, it is unfortunate that Mr. Nixon did not adopt a policy of complete candor long ago. Whatever is embarrassing in the information he released over the weekend could not damage him half so much as the untruths, half truths, and evasiveness of his prior "explanations" that usually obscured more than they explained and helped to spawn unpleasant rumors. Better yet, if the President had conducted all of his financial affairs since taking office on the assumption that each decision would soon become public knowledge he might well have avoided some serious failures of judgment. In the half light of secrecy, he failed to perceive controlling truths that would have been evident to him if he had realized—as all public officials should realize—that he was living in a glass house.

One such truth is that persons in public office ought not to accept large financial favors from wealthy individuals. Since officials usually do not have the private resources to reciprocate such favors, the suspicion inevitably arises that they may pay them back through government favoritism. Mr. Nixon permitted Elmer H. Bobst of the Warner-Lambert Pharmaceutical Corporation to establish a trust fund for one of his daughters. How can the public ever be certain that this gift did not subsequently influence the Nixon Administration's enforcement of drug and antitrust laws affecting Warner-Lambert? Mr. Nixon likewise accepted huge loans from Robert Abplanalp and C. G. Rebozo, both of whom also have extensive business interests.

When the President sold much of the land in his San Clemente estate to Messrs. Abplanalp and Rebozo on favorable terms, he was guilty of poor judgment in treating the transaction for tax purposes as one in which he made no profit.

Mr. Nixon has likewise shown poor judgment in failing to pay income tax either to California or to the District of Columbia. Federal law exempts members of Congress and Federal officials from paying income tax to the District where they are presumably only temporarily domiciled. But that is no excuse for failing to pay income tax to the state which an official claims as his permanent legal residence. That is particularly true of Mr. Nixon, inasmuch as he not only votes in California and owns a home there but also described his San Clemente estate as his "primary residence" in order to obtain favorable tax treatment on the sale of his New York cooperative apartment. California is either Mr. Nixon's legal residence or it is not; he cannot have it both ways depending upon which saves him more money in a given situation.

Most serious of all, there is the obscurity that still shrouds Mr. Nixon's deduction of $570,000 for the gift of some of his public papers to the National Archives. Were the papers actually transferred before the deadline established by a change in the tax law? Was a proper deed for the papers ever executed and accepted by the Archives? If so, was it signed by Mr. Nixon or someone holding power of attorney in his behalf? Nothing in the statement released by the President over the weekend clears up these and other questions.

There is something unseemly about high public officials taking huge tax deductions for the gift of papers which they accumulated while being paid by the public. That is why Congress changed the law to bar such deductions. If Mr. Nixon met the deadline, he is legally entitled to claim this deduction. But it is a matter that cannot be left hanging in doubt.

A tax system that depends upon the cooperation of millions of private citizens cannot long survive if it is shown that those who should set an example are instead taking advantage of loopholes and walking a narrow line between the legal and the illegal

The Courier-Journal

Louisville, Ky., December 11, 1973

THE RISK in President Nixon's "full disclosure" of his financial affairs is that while it may help persuade some more Americans that he is not a crook, it also emphasizes the tardiness of his conversion to candor while further dramatizing his stake in tax laws loaded with benefits for the very wealthy.

The further risk is that new revelations, such as the $80,000 gift of pre-presidential papers to the government in 1968, will surface like so many Haldemans or Kalmbachs — both of whom supposedly severed all White House connections months ago — to make people wonder anew whether the President truly has told all.

Is there a citizen today who isn't thinking about writing off at least some of his Christmas-card expenses as a tax deduction, the way Mr. Nixon does, or perhaps even willing his modest bungalow to the government so as to gain a San Clemente-type tax writeoff while still alive to enjoy it? One does not have to question the legality of any of the President's financial activities to wonder about an internal revenue code that taxes a $15,000 wage-earner at about the same rate as a President with a $200,000 salary and $50,000 expense account.

Is this, in truth, the fruit of self-reliance and frugality and honest toil that President Nixon has been talking about since the 1968 campaign? Or is it the way the rich grow richer by hiring accountants who search for shelters in the law? Is this the great American dream? Or do a lot of Americans suddenly realize that Senator McGovern might have been on the right track last year—and not talking some kind of fiscal lunacy—when he assailed the vast inequities in how our national income is distributed?

Why no state taxes?

At any rate, we're now well launched on Operation Candor, only seven months after the White House responded to press questioning by listing total federal expenditures at San Clemente at $39,525. How far we have come in such a short time! But how far we still have to go if the President really hopes to restore "the confidence of the American people in the integrity of the President."

What are we really to think, for example, of a man who states that his voting residence is California, and thus avoids having to pay taxes in the District of Columbia, but also omits paying income taxes in California? Of a man who takes advantage of a terrible law (he knew in 1969 that Congress was about to repeal it) to effectively sell his vice presidential papers to the public for $576,000? Of a man who indignantly insists that the government spent only $68,000 on his home at San Clemente, while somehow finding it possible to ignore nearly $140,000 in landscaping (some of which surely enhanced the property's value), and the work (including installation of a swimming pool cleaner) done at Key Biscayne?

What we *are* to think, presumably, is the same thing President Nixon obviously thought when newsmen first began asking questions last year about who really paid for the San Clemente residence and all the renovation of that property: that everything was legal but the public might not *understand*. It might not understand the news that he had borrowed more than half a million dollars from wealthy friend Robert Abplanalp, since some critics might compare this kind of moral example with the $18,000 "friendship" fund that almost got him thrown off President Eisenhower's ticket in 1952. It might not understand how it is that the nation's elected leader could preach about self-sacrifice while living like a king. It might not understand why a President who ducked the tax-reform issue in his 1968 and 1972 campaigns, and has pushed only for such cosmetic changes as the minimum tax, could take advantage of a discriminatory tax code rather than fight to change it.

Or maybe the public *would* understand, only too well. Perhaps it would demand that the Joint Congressional Committee on Internal Revenue Taxation, which is to consider the questions of the vice presidential papers and capital gains at San Clemente, hold open hearings so the nation can learn more about these fancy tax shelters. Perhaps it would insist that the promised further revelations in Operation Candor include not only such issues as the ITT affair and the milk deal, but good-faith compliance with requests for tapes and other White House documentation.

Perhaps the public would even begin to wonder why it is that only the peril of impeachment began to pry from this President the kind of documentation that any other citizen might be ordered by Internal Revenue to tote down to the federal building next week.

THE STATES-ITEM

New Orleans., La., December 11, 1973

In an action without precedent, President Nixon has released more than 50 documents with his personal income tax returns from 1969 through last year.

These disclosures should be detailed enough to answer any fair-minded demand for information. As well, they appear to toe the line on legal tax requirements.

Yet it was easy to anticipate before the disclosure that however complete the data many of the carpers would overlook the unusual concession of privacy by Mr. Nixon to carry on their attacks.

Going beyond the opening of his private financial records, the President says he will leave it up to the House-Senate Committee on Internal Revenue Taxation to determine whether his tax deductions were legal and whether he made a gain in the sale of part of his California estate.

Mr. Nixon has leaned backward so far on allowing trespass into his private life it is almost frightening, realizing that many of his critics who originally called for disclosures are not actually interested in them but in tumbling him from the presidency at whatever cost to the nation.

The Cincinnati Post
TIMES ➤ STAR
Cincinnati, Ohio, December 10, 1973

"In conducting my private affairs in public office, I have proceeded in a manner I thought both prudent and in the best interests of my family.

"And even though both American law and tradition protect the privacy of the papers I am releasing today, these documents are being made public because the confidentiality of my private finances is far less important to me than the confidence of the American people in the integrity of the President. "—Richard M. Nixon in releasing 50 documents concerning his personal finances and taxes since he became president.

About the best that can be said of what the President revealed is that he certainly gets an "A" for disclosure. Nothing comparable has ever been seen before from a president of the United States.

But we part company with his judgment that what was revealed will help restore confidence in the integrity of the President. In fact we feel the result likely will be the reverse.

We are well aware that it is the law that nobody owes any public duty to pay more taxes than the law demands. And we assume that every deduction claimed by the President is legally correct (although he has asked a congressional committee to rule on two items on which he might have to pay an additional $267,-000 in federal income taxes).

But the picture that comes through from his financial disclosures is that of the leader of this nation who permitted his tax lawyers and accountants to cut every corner and take every advantage to keep his federal income taxes down to near zero—in full awareness that the Internal Revenue Service was headed by his appointees.

We submit that the President of the United States had much more than the interests of his family and being prudent to think of in the handling of his personal finances while in public office.

He should have been conscious of the necessity of setting a good example as the leader of this country in paying his income taxes.

Some of the things his documents showed:

In the last three years, he paid federal income taxes of slightly less than $2000 per year on adjusted gross income averaging $264,000 per year.

He paid no state income taxes.

In the past four and a half years, his net worth rose from $307,000 to close to a million, yet his tax payments have tended to go down instead of up.

He claimed business and entertainment deductions on his homes in Key Biscayne and San Clemente.

He claimed depreciation of personally owned White House office furniture.

Etc. Etc. And, of course, the big reason for the low taxes was the $576,000 in deductions he claimed for the gift of his vice presidential papers to the government.

Take the first item listed above alone —the fact he averaged paying less than $2000 a year in federal income taxes the past three years.

Just about the poorest wage-earner pays that much.

If that sort of fact helps restore faith in the President, then we need complete re-education on the human beings around us.

What he did reveal was a lack of the ethical leadership that should be an integral part of the President of the United States.

ST. LOUIS POST-DISPATCH
St. Louis, Mo., December 12, 1973

Instead of refuting the so-called "false rumors" about President Nixon's personal finances and restoring public confidence in "the integrity of the President," the data released by the White House over the weekend serves only to confirm much of what the news media had reported and to leave still unanswered numerous questions casting doubt on the moral example set by the President as a taxpayer.

In the first place, the Nixon financial data was not made public in a high-minded gesture of candor, as the White House implied, but was issued in a desperate attempt to rescue Mr. Nixon's sagging reputation and to stem the mounting pressure for his impeachment or resignation.

Rather than showing that the President provided a model for the honest taxpayer, as the Chief Executive might be expected to do, the White House data shows that Mr. Nixon invoked every conceivable gimmick to avoid paying taxes and succeeded to an extent that no ordinary taxpayer could have hoped for. His newly expressed willingness to pay back taxes, if they should be adjudged due, represents no demonstration of magnanimity but appears rather as the frantic effort of a financial manipulator to make amends after he has been caught.

If the press, congressional and other investigators had not dug into Mr. Nixon's questionable dealings, there is no reason to think that the White House would ever have come forth with its financial disclosures. Those disclosures confirm that: for his presidential years, 1969-72, Mr. Nixon paid only $78,650 in federal income taxes on an adjusted gross income of $1,122,264 (for each of two years the amounts were less $900, or the equivalent of the tax for a family with an income of $7500); that he paid no California income tax, although he maintains a residence there; that his net worth more than tripled in four years, from $307,141 to $988,522, partly by the use of tax avoidance schemes which probably would have been challenged by the Internal Revenue Service if the taxpayer

had been any other than the President of the United States, who appoints the head of the IRS and holds great power over all federal employes.

Despite the belated avowals of candor, the newly released Nixon financial documents still leave many questions unresolved. Why, for example, did Mr. Nixon himself not sign a deed donating his vice presidential papers to the National Archives, a gift that was supposed to entitle him to a $576,000 tax deduction? Was the lawyer who did sign legally authorized to do so? Were the deed and the transfer of papers dated in time to justify a deduction before the legal deadline of July, 1969?

Independent investigative data indicate the President not only did not follow the requirements of the law but that his tax lawyers and accountants persisted in trying to evade the law on Mr. Nixon's capital gains and on his vice presidential papers after timely advice to the contrary from some of his advisers.

Now that Mr. Nixon's shabby record of pennypinching and tax evasion has been forced into the open, the President has proposed to resolve the matter by turning his tax affairs over to the Congressional Joint Committee on Internal Revenue Taxation and to abide by its judgment. Even if this group, chaired by Representative Wilbur Mills and dominated by a conservative majority, should rule against him, Mr. Nixon obviously hopes to end the criticism by paying some $267,-000 in back federal taxes.

But no other citizen could get off so simply, with a political forum to decide his case and Government-paid lawyers to argue it. Nor would the congressional device resolve the questions of a possible obligation of $64,000 in California income taxes and the undervaluation for property tax purposes of his California estate.

The new Nixon financial disclosures underscore the need for an independent special prosecutor, empowered to delve into the President's financial affairs, and for further financial inquiries in the impeachment proceedings already in progress in the House.

Boston Herald American
Combining the best features of the Herald Traveler and Record American
Boston, Mass., December 12, 1973

In keeping with his public promise, President Nixon last weekend issued one of the most extraordinary documents ever to come from the White House. Its more than 150 pages of figures and complicated records were intended to counter months of suspicious speculation on the propriety of his personal finances.

Let it be noted, immediately, that the disclosure of this mass of information is encouraging proof that Mr. Nixon truly believes he has nothing to hide in the Watergate swamp. Unfortunately, as always in that mess, his frankness has come too belatedly and too reluctantly to restore the credibility he has lost.

A non-expert perusal of the presidential finance accounting would indicate that there is nothing obviously illegal about any of the intricate and profitable matters involved. Like the average citizen, Mr. Nixon simply gave himself the benefit of any and all doubts and loopholes in existing tax laws.

Few persons are in a moral position to cast stones at that. Providing financial security for

one's family is the name of the game in the United States. Unless some of the President's actions are ruled counter to law — a possibility he asks Congress to decide — he stands frankly on the record he has submitted.

Once again we commend Mr. Nixon for making that record public. It was a move totally contrary to his self-damaging ordinary zeal for protecting his privacy and the prerogatives of his office. One can only hope that he will now continue to respond openly to other challenges of Watergate.

Unhappily, we think, this is about the best that can be said about the President's financial disclosures. Rightly or wrongly, the public is not likely to accept that fact that a man with an income of $250,000 a year can sometimes legitimately pay less taxes than the average office worker.

Or that the same man, while serving as their national leader, could by reason of association with millionaire friends, increase his net worth in only four years from $307,000 to $988,000. It just doesn't seem right, no matter how legal the means may have been.

THE COMMERCIAL APPEAL
Memphis, Tenn., December 11, 1973

WITH THE 50 documents on his personal finances which President Nixon has released, with the $25,000 audit he paid for himself, and the $313,582 General Services Administration examination of its records pertaining to Nixon property, the Chief Executive has set a record for public disclosure.

Never before has a president been so candid about his private finances.

His purpose has been to get allegations of illegal deals, misuse of campaign funds, secret portfolios of stock and a Howard Hughes bonanza off his back. Answers to such allegations and other rumors have been given in detail.

BUT ONE OF Nixon's principal reasons for such disclosures was to boost the nation's confidence in himself and his presidency. It's hard to see how the financial picture he has given us can do that.

An American president is more than just a chief administrative official. He is a symbol. He must be able to lead. He should be able to instill hope and patience in trying times. He is the only one who can speak out in a national crisis and persuade the people to face up to their problems.

In short, the person in the White House must be able, in clear conscience and without a trace of hypocrisy, to call on all segments of our society to take difficult steps in trying times, to live with problems, and to try to whip them.

For all the trouble he's gone to, for all his candor, Nixon's income and tax revelations are not going to add confidence in the President or respect for the office he holds.

It is just not possible when a man whose net worth has increased from $307,141 on Jan. 1, 1969, to $988,522 on May 31, 1973, a man whose salary and expense allowances in office in that period have totaled $1,090,635, reveals that his entire income tax for three of four years was less than $6,000. In one year, 1970, it was only $793.

However legal it may have been, it's not going to impress a working stiff who makes just enough to get by each year and pays a lot more to the Internal Revenue Service.

That is the heart of the matter. Most Americans gripe about taxes. But generally speaking they regard the federal income tax as fair. They look on it as something they have to pay to keep the country going. It provides services and security, while asking that each individual pay his fair share in meeting common needs.

But something is wrong when a wealthy person pays less in income tax than ordinary working people.

Nor does it make much sense to call on a joint congressional committee to decide whether the rich taxpayer owes more than his expensive attorneys told him he did. That could only lead to a political decision — worthless in court which is where tax claims are tried.

Also, while it is interesting to learn at this point that the Nixons plan to donate their San Clemente estate to the government upon death, there is no guarantee that the government would want a permanent California White House.

IT WAS A NICE try, and it's good to know Nixon can prove he doesn't have a million dollars stashed away in secret. But we're afraid the average taxpayer won't buy the idea that the President owes less because of a loophole. Instead, many of us would think that this calls for reforms in the tax system itself and that the President should be setting a higher example for the country.

President Nixon's personal tax disclosures should do little to elevate public confidence in his sense of propriety. For even if all of his positions are legally acceptable, ethical questions would remain.

THREE AREAS are in dispute:

One involves his claimed deduction of $576,000 for donating some of his vice presidential papers to the National Archives. The legal uncertainty is whether the gift was made before the 1969 cut-off date abolishing such deductions.

Although the documents were delivered to the Archives in time, the deed transferring ownership was not turned over until April 1970.

And to this day, neither the Archives nor the General Services Administration has signed the deed and thereby formally accepted the papers and the conditions Nixon stipulated for donating them.

Yet aside from such technicalities, it would appear unseemly for the President to have even tried to beat the deadline on a loophole Congress had decided to close.

THE SECOND disputed area involves the San Clemente transactions. The President's regular tax lawyers and accountants insist he realized no taxable gains.

But the firm of Coopers and Lybrand, hired by Nixon to prepare an independent audit, concludes he should have paid taxes on a capital gain of $117,370 for selling land surrounding his home.

The House-Senate joint committee on taxation has agreed to rule on the President's returns, and he has promised to abide by its decision.

Even so, if the verdict favors Nixon, it might be viewed suspiciously unless the committee members are willing to disclose their own returns to erase any doubts that they might be protecting themselves in gray areas.

THE THIRD POINT in dispute concerns Nixon's non-payment of state taxes. The law exempts elected Federal officials from District of Columbia taxes — but not from taxes in their home states.

Nixon, of course, maintains his San Clemente home and votes in California. Yet he has not paid taxes there, claiming to be exempt because he resides primarily in Washington, D.C.

The California tax board is expected to review the case. But even if the board sustains Nixon, there would be the ethical question of whether he should take advantage of state-tax shelter unavailable to ordinary citizens.

THE PRESIDENT'S tax problems, of course, are not his worst. If the rulings are unfavorable, he could simply pay up. Congress would be highly unlikely to impeach on such grounds.

Still, the tax disclosures do suggest dubious discretion, and that can hardly strengthen President Nixon's leadership.

Los Angeles Times
Los Angeles, Calif., December 11, 1973

According to the tax returns which he released over the weekend, President Nixon paid only $78,650 in federal income taxes on an adjusted gross income of more than $1.2 million during the period 1969 through 1972. In two of those four years, though earning $250,000 a year just from his job as President, Mr. Nixon's federal tax bill actually came to less than $1,000—about what an average citizen making $7,500 or $8,500 a year would pay.

It isn't right that a man can make that much money and fall so far short of paying his fair share of the tax burden. And because it isn't right, President Nixon's unprecedented action in opening the books on his private financial affairs will not succeed in its purpose of alleviating the criticism which has been directed at him.

It appears that Mr. Nixon has tripled his wealth since becoming President. He says he did nothing dishonest, and as far as tax payments are concerned there is no indication that he did. All he did was take advantage of a big presidential expense account and make what he called "prudent" use of provisions of the tax code.

As the President recognized in his statement accompanying release of his financial records, the tax handling of two important transactions—donation of his vice presidential papers to the National Archives and sale of some property at San Clemente—is open to challenge. But these, like the issue of whether he should have paid state income taxes to California, are technical questions of the sort which arise routinely with the tax returns of high-income Americans.

Mr. Nixon's request that the Joint Congressional Committee on Taxation review these two transactions, and his promise to abide by the bipartisan group's findings, are unusual. But this is an unusual case.

The late Judge Learned Hand once wrote that "There is nothing sinister in so arranging one's affairs to keep taxes as low as possible . . . for nobody owes any public duty to pay more than the law demands."

The people are inclined to expect a higher standard from the President of the United States; they don't like to see him grubbing around, like your ordinary millionaire, for ways to minimize his taxes. This is especially true of a President who has glorified the Puritan ethic in his political oratory.

Expecting Presidents to pay higher taxes than the law requires is, nonetheless, a misdirected exercise. It is much more important to reform the tax laws so that no high-income American—President or not—can escape paying taxes commensurate with his income.

The provision allowing huge deductions for gifts of private papers has already been changed, but many other questionable opportunities for avoiding taxes are still in the law.

The reform applicable to Mr. Nixon's case involves the minimum tax. Congress passed a bill in 1970 to make wealthy persons pay at least some federal income tax no matter how many deductions and tax shelters they have, but the minimum tax provision itself has too many loopholes. Whatever else Congress may do about tax reform, a rougher minimum tax would at least end the kind of gross inequity that surfaced in Mr. Nixon's case.

THE SUN

Baltimore, Md., December 2, 1973

Early in the Ervin committee hearings a former White House aide said he had warned Mr. Nixon of a "cancer" on his presidency, in regard to Watergate and closely related matters. The aide chose an apter word than perhaps even he knew at the time. There was a cancer, and is a cancer, and in the manner of metastasizing cancer it has spread through the entire body of the Nixon presidency. It has gone far beyond the Watergate affair and other aspects of the 1972 political campaign that the committee was specifically, and we now know narrowly, charged wih investigating.

Each week, each day, each hour of most days, the deterioration becomes more shockingly apparent. Word of its spread comes now from this source, now from that. The reading today cannot but be that Mr. Nixon is in more serious trouble than his most skeptical critics would have predicted earlier. His very capacity to govern at all is brought under severe question.

There are three ways of dealing with this condition. One is to let it go on and on, to permit the mess to develop piecemeal in courts and committees to its end, which is hard to conceive of as other than a bitter end. This would mean further clouded and disputed charges and revelations. It would mean an indefinite continuation of the Nixon "counteroffensive" which so far has fared miserably. It would mean a President concentrated first of all, no matter what might be claimed to the contrary, on his personal political survival, while his little band of spokesmen grew shriller and more evasive in efforts to help achieve that end.

A second way would be for Mr. Nixon to resign after Mr. Ford becomes Vice President. Mr. Nixon repeatedly says he has no intention of resigning, but others have said that before, and then resigned. In the interests of the country we do not think he should, by which we mean that a precipitant resignation would leave unanswered questions that must be answered if the nation is to come in the most decent shape through this tremendous crisis: and of course it will come through in one way or another, for it is not the fate of the republic, but of one man, that is at issue.

It seems to us that the best way is the third way, by the orderly impeachment process as provided in the Constitution. We are not advocating impeachment, or conviction. We are advocating the process. Impeachment, let it be repeated, is not conviction. It is indictment, after a scrupulous consideration of serious charges as to whether they are false charges or not; whether or not they can be drawn into a bill of particulars pointing to the Constitution's "high crimes and misdemeanors."

The process of impeachment is now under way in the Judiciary Committee of the House of Representatives. It should go forward, scrupulously and as free as possible from partisan taint, to determine whether a bill of particulars can be drawn, and presented to the House and then, should we come so far, to the Senate for final determination.

As has often been said, this is a long, slow process, and for the country would be a "traumatic" experience. But it is a strictly constitutional way, and it is the only way, as we now discern the case, in which the many skeins of the tangle may be brought together in one proper place, and the questions answered. As for trauma, will this way be more traumatic than an endless prolongation of the present state of affairs, or than the sudden resignation of a President under a storm of doubt that would never be dispelled?

The Chattanooga Times

Chattanooga, Tenn., December 4, 1973

One by one, the "foot soldiers" of the Watergate scandal are being overcome by the weight of evidence uncovered by intensive investigations: Donald Segretti is in jail for his campaign sabotage antics; Dwight Chapin, President Nixon's former appointments secretary, has been indicted on perjury charges growing out of the incidents for which Mr. Segretti pleaded guilty.

And now, Egil Krogh Jr., former White House aide and head of the "plumbers" — actually a form of secret police — has pleaded guilty to a civil rights charge relating to the burglary of the office of Dr. Daniel Ellsberg's psychiatrist — in search of material on the former's psychological background.

It is instructive that in making his plea, Mr. Krough abandoned the specious defense that "national security" was the overriding concern when it was decided to go outside the boundaries of the law in search of material that would have had no bearing at all on national security.

Said Mr. Krogh: ". . . Upon serious and lengthy reflection, I now feel that the sincerity of my motivation cannot justify what was done and that I cannot in conscience assert national security as a defense."

"I simply feel that what was done in the Ellsberg operation was in violation of what I perceive to be a fundamental idea in the character of this country — the paramount importance of the rights of the individual. I don't want to be associated with that violation any longer by attempting to defend it."

Quite obviously, opinions vary as to whether Dr. Ellsberg was right in releasing the so-called Pentagon Papers.

But just as obviously, that did not justify authorization by the Administration (which authorization the President disclaimed, although accepting responsibility) of a wholly illegal operation.

One can admire Mr. Krogh's forthrightness in shucking off this absurd rationalization while at the same time condemning his activities, which included lying to the Watergate grand jury. And one can only speculate about what information he will present when some of the "generals" in the affair go on trial.

So, despite his plea, Mr. Krogh's career lies in ruins. It illustrates, sadly, just one result of blind allegiance to those whose scruples are of the "ends justifies the means" variety.

The Washington Post

Washington, D.C., December 21, 1973

THE SHOCK and dismay that attended President Nixon's firing of Archibald Cox on October 20, quite naturally—and admirably—led many members of Congress to consider ways in which they might guarantee the independence and professional longevity of whoever succeeded him as Special Watergate Prosecutor. It is worth recalling that those were the days before Leon Jaworski had come upon the scene and before it was evident that the Special Watergate Prosecution Force was not destined to go the way of the dodo bird. So, in the aftermath of the October 20 "massacre," as it was known, a certain number of bills were introduced in the House and Senate seeking to create a pressure-and intimidation-free prosecutor's office. Now they are coming to a vote in each chamber, and the question is whether intervening events have not rendered them at best obsolete and at worst positively harmful to the prospects of Mr. Jaworski's success. We think the answer is that this legislation has in fact been made both unnecessary and undesirable by what has occurred in the past several weeks.

In an article elsewhere on this page, Rep. William Cohen, a Republican from Maine, argues the case against what is apparently the most popular of these bills: a measure authorizing the U.S. District Court to name a Special Watergate Prosecutor who is wholly insulated from Executive Branch manipulation and answerable only to itself. We think Mr. Cohen is right. From the point of view of those who are genuinely committed to the vitality and effectiveness of the Special Watergate Prosecutor's office, it is probable that the best thing that could happen to this legislation—if it is passed—is that it be vetoed. That is because it has such an enormous potential for mischief, deliberate and inadvertent.

At a minimum, and in the best and most innocent of worlds, the mere creation of a wholly new prosecutor's office would be bound to delay and complicate the present prosecutor's job, to generate obstructive legal challenges and otherwise to dissipate the momentum Mr. Jaworski has gathered. In a less innocent world, which seems to be the one we live in, enactment of such legislation could be taken by the White House as a pretext to get rid of Mr. Jaworski, or at least to hamper and undermine his work. A President so inclined would not veto the legislation—he would welcome it.

Mr. Jaworski's record in his brief time in office is a crucial element in this calculation. He has by all accounts demonstrated himself to be determined, independent and, generally speaking, equal to the job. The White House has already begun to put out stories concerning its dissatisfaction with some of his activities. In the House, an alternative measure to the court-appointed prosecutor bill which is known as the "Dennis substitute" and would merely strengthen Mr. Jaworski's tenure and independence is being supported by Representative Cohen and others. While this approach sounds preferable to us, it is our general view that the best result would be enactment of no legislation at all at this time —including legislation which we have previously supported making the prosecutor's appointment subject to Senate confirmation and strengthening the statutory basis of his independence.

We think Mr. Jaworski is doing just fine. We think the enactment of legislation affecting his office, even that mandating relatively modest changes in his charter, puts his continuance in office and his effectiveness at risk. And we think that very large body of congressmen and senators who have committed themselves to the creation of a court-appointed prosecutor, along with those who are committed to the passage of less drastic measures, should be seeking ways to leave these votes in abeyance for the moment. Traditionally, after all, Congress is known for a certain skill at putting off and putting over what it does not wish to bring to a final vote. Finding ways to do just that in this matter should not strain its inventiveness.

AKRON BEACON JOURNAL
Akron, Ohio, December 2, 1973

A YEAR AGO, impeachment of a president was unthinkable. Today, it is not only thinkable, it is discussed openly by serious men. Unfortunately, Richard Nixon has given us good reason to think and talk seriously of impeachment.

Impeachment is not conviction; it is indictment by the House of Representatives. And it serves a dual purpose. The impeachment process is not only the constitutionally prescribed method of removing a president from office; it is also a way — perhaps the only way — a president in the situation Mr. Nixon now finds himself can be cleared.

A full-blown House investigation and Senate trial would do much to clear the air around the President or to remove him from office. In either case, the nation would have more confidence in its president than it does now.

Mr. Nixon's credibility was somewhere close to zero when it was revealed that 18 minutes of a taped conversation between the President and his former aide, H. R. Haldeman, had been erased. The conversation three days after the Watergate break-in was the first between the President and his chief of staff after the burglary.

The story of the erasure was followed by a farfetched tale told by the President's personal secretary, Rose Mary Woods, of how she "accidentally" erased the tape during a telephone conversation. Her loyalty to her boss may be laudable, but her story defied belief.

The question of what was erased remains. Was it the weather that Nixon and Haldeman were talking about? Maybe some off-season trade by the Washington Redskins? Haldeman's notes say the subject under discussion was Watergate.

Mr. Nixon was in full swing with what he called "Operation Candor" at the time the latest disclosure was made. He was rushing around the country, much as a candidate on a campaign trip, trying to rally support. He was making public appearances, which we welcomed, and he seemed to be gaining a little.

In Memphis, he told Republican governors that if there were any more Watergate-related bombs he was not aware of them. Then came the missing 18 minutes, prompting Oregon Gov. Tom McCall to remark that it "shows a lack of comprehension of what a bombshell is."

We suspect that Mr. Nixon has now slipped to a new low. Under examination, Operation Candor appears to have been nothing more than undelivered promises. We hope that Mr. Nixon can and does deliver on his promises; that he can and will prove that he is "not a crook."

But we cannot wait forever, or even until January 1977, when his present term expires. And we have had too much evasiveness from the White House to rest our hopes on voluntary resolution by the President of any of the nagging questions about his integrity.

At the time of the furor over the missing tapes of conversations between the President and John Dean and between the President and John Mitchell, we said the President should be given one more chance to prove himself. He has had that chance, and has used it to produce 18 minutes of blank tape, undelivered promises and continued obfuscation.

It would be foolish to suggest that the United States could not stand another 38 months of the kind of constantly battered non-leadership it has had for the past eight months. The strength of this country is such that it can stand almost anything. But why should the nation subject itself to an administration that is distrusted, disbelieved and suspected of being morally bankrupt when there is a constitutionally viable alternative?

It is now considered possible that the Senate Watergate committee will not resume its hearings. That would cause no great damage to the cause of justice. The committee has served its purpose, but there may be little more of use it can contribute.

The case now belongs in the House, where Rep. Peter Rodino's Judiciary Committee is moving at a painfully slow pace with its investigation to determine if impeachment is warranted.

We believe it is.

The House has more than enough to justify indictment: Watergate, bombing of Cambodia, illegal impoundment of funds appropriated by Congress, the secret police unit known as the plumbers, the milk deal and others. Perhaps none warrants conviction, but any or all warrant a full hearing in which all sides are presented. And while the President might now for some not-yet-explained reason refuse to admit evidence in his own defense, if he has any he would surely present it to the Senate if his continuation as President depended on it.

It is difficult for anyone to admit making a mistake, and more than 61 pct. of the American voting public cast their ballots for Richard Nixon little more than a year ago. There is no doubt that an overwhelming majority of Americans preferred Mr. Nixon to Sen. George McGovern. The Beacon Journal joined with most other newspapers in endorsing Mr. Nixon.

But the Richard Nixon we endorsed, and the Richard Nixon most Americans voted for, is not the Richard Nixon we now know.

The choice is no longer Nixon or McGovern. The Senate moved swiftly in approving the nomination of House Minority Leader Gerald Ford as vice president. The House should do the same. Rep. Ford is no standout; he may, in fact, stand as a monument to mediocrity. But by all accounts he is honest, and that counts a great deal these days.

Mr. Ford appears to represent basically the same views the country understood Mr. Nixon to hold on election day 1972. And he is, of course, a Republican, the same as Mr. Nixon. His approval as vice president would remove a major barrier now standing between Mr. Nixon and impeachment: The man next in line for the presidency is a Democrat, House Speaker Carl Albert.

For a Democratic Congress to impeach and convict a Republican president — especially one elected in a landslide — so that a Democrat could assume the nation's highest office would be unspeakable; with Mr. Ford no such problem exists.

The fear has been expressed that impeachment would tear the country apart. That was a convincing line until it became apparent that the Watergate scandal was not about to go away. The continuing scandal is at least as divisive as an impeachment proceeding would be, and impeachment would have an end in sight. Republican insiders are worried that Watergate is likely to be around through the 1974 elections; an orderly, fair impeachment proceeding could easily be over well before next November.

Three things should be remembered about impeachment:

It is only an indictment, not a conviction;

It could clear the President; force him to submit evidence that he would not, for whatever reason, submit voluntarily;

It is a process approved by our founding fathers in the Constitution and meant to be used when necessary.

We hope that in any impeachment proceeding the President can clear himself. But we would be willing to abide by whatever verdict the Senate returned. If the Senate cleared the President from any involvement in "high crimes and misdemeanors" it would be far better than another Operation Candor, possibly followed by another blank tape.

It is now up to the House. It must proceed with the confirmation of Gerald Ford as vice president. And, distasteful as it surely must be, the House must proceed to impeach President Richard Nixon.

THE LINCOLN STAR

Lincoln, Neb., December 8, 1973

"Operation Candor," President Nixon's late-blooming effort to restore public confidence, has taken a nosedive.

Now offered to the court and the public, after all the other unbelievable explanations about what happened to the missing tapes and parts of pertinent conversations, is Gen. Alexander Haig's "devil theory" which assumes that "some sinister source" may have caused 13 minutes of the 18-minute buzz that drowns out a Nixon-Haldeman conversation about Watergate.

Gen. Haig, the President's top aide, told Judge Sirica Thursday that such talk was circulating among White House staff members. The President's legal staff told him, Haig said, that tests they made Nov. 20th convinced them at that time "that the machine used by Miss Woods could not have made the tones . . . That therefore suggested that some sort of outside energy force had been applied to the tape. I refer to that as the devil theory today."

He might as well have told the judge that the devil made her do it.

The White House, apparently having exhausted its meager supply of credible explanations, is threatening the public with the specter of black magic, as if we Americans were an isolated tribe of simple innocents who would believe anything the agents of the god in Washington told them.

How long can an otherwise trusting people put up with it?

Pittsburgh Post-Gazette

Pittsburgh, Pa., December 8, 1973

PRESIDENT Nixon's top aide, Alexander M. Haig Jr., may have discarded too quickly the "devil theory" which he considered briefly as an explanation for the foul-up that ruined a key tape in the Watergate investigation. It is as plausible to believe that the devil made Rose Mary Woods wipe out a crucial conversation taped in the White House as to believe other reasons that have been advanced for the various Watergate misadventures.

According to the devil theory that Mr. Haig put forward at hearings before Federal Judge John J. Sirica, it was reasoned in the absence of "finite explanation" for the tape's erasure that "some sort of outside energy force" had been applied to the tape.

This is just as believable as much of the testimony adduced in months of Watergate hearings. It reinforces our suspicion that the chief of the fallen angels — the supreme spirit of evil — has long lurked in the White House, missing no opportunity to work his will upon the vulnerable mortals therein.

It was perhaps inevitable that, having exhausted all natural explanations for the Watergate scandals, an explicator would fall back upon the supernatural as an excuse for misconduct.

Wittingly or not, Mr. Haig has cast his boss in the role of a Faust tormented by Mephistopheles, with a timely assist from Rose Mary Woods. As Flip Wilson would say, the devil made her do it, just as he had a diabolic hand in the Watergate and Ellsberg burglaries, the tidal wave of corrupt and corrupting campaign funds, the cynical attempts to impede justice and, in sum, all of the "White House horrors" which could not be more aptly attributed.

The Kansas City Times

Kansas City, Mo., December 8, 1973

The White House tapes hearings have been adjourned temporarily by Judge John J. Sirica, presumably to serve subpoenas on unknown demons. No one knows what caused the 18-minute lapse and buzzing on the spool handled by Miss Rose Mary Woods, the President's secretary. But Gen. Alexander Haig, White House adviser, says there may be "no finite explanation."

General Haig said there had been discussion of what he refers to as "devil theories." He said that the President's counsels were very much concerned "because tests they made convinced them at that time that Miss Woods could not have made the tones. . . That, therefore, suggested some sort of outside energy force had been applied to the tape. . ."

Truly, the tapes seem to have been cursed from the beginning. First there was the spool that ran out before a significant conversation could be recorded. Then there was the tape that didn't exist because no recorder was attached to a particular telephone. Now there is the conversation that seems to have been blasted from human ken by an unhuman power. The general referred to a "sinister source," but said he did not believe Miss Woods was sinister.

But that does not mean that the presidency isn't pursued by hostile spirits or that Miss Woods was not possessed. Nor can zapping rays by a hovering flying saucer be ruled out, or muffling ectoplasm. Oh, the possibilities are endless for mischief perpetrated by beings from other worlds or by bad elves from the forest around Camp David.

There may be other questions to be asked before exorcists and advisers in demonology or space creatures are summoned. General Haig has put the matter on a metaphysical plane with his reference to "finite explanations." And indeed, what is the ultimate reality of the tapes? Do they exist because we perceive them or do we perceive them because they exist? Can we believe in a real, objective existence of the tapes and does Watergate have universal essence? Or are they subjective perceptions written on the blank tablet by observance?

Did the Devil make them do it?

The Salt Lake Tribune

Salt Lake City, Utah, December 13, 1973

U.S. District Judge Charles R. Richey, sitting in Washington, says he is "concerned not only with direct political intervention, but also with the creation of a political atmosphere generated by the White House in the Internal Revenue Service which may have affected the objectivity of those participating in the IRS ruling . . ."

Judge Richey's concern accompanied his decision that the Center of Corporate Responsibility, Inc., was improperly denied exemption from federal income taxes as a nonprofit organization.

Whether or not the White House generated the "political atmosphere" Judge Richey alludes to is beside the point at the moment. The important consideration is that there is in the Internal Revenue Service a situation that permits generation of a "political atmosphere" regardless of which party occupies the White House. Too many of the people on the policy making and adjudication levels are political appointees, rather than civil service employes.

Political appointees get their jobs because they are of the same political ilk as the man making the appointment. Their tenure depends on how long they and their benefactors remain in political tune. The natural progression is that appointee listens very closely to what tune his boss is singing. He tends to harmonize with the boss, even when the chief sings off key.

But there is an advantage to having political persons sitting at high levels. They can control the way an agency is run and if they fail to exercise control in the best interest of the nation, a new man can take over quickly without having to resort to lengthy dismissal procedures as in the case of civil service workers.

But, those same civil service workers are not dependent upon which way political winds blow for their job security. They are positioned to execute their jobs objectively, letting their conscience and the law guide them. Yet, that same conscience can be, and has been, a roadblock. The record is replete with examples of officious, nit-picking bureaucrats who have inordinately delayed routine decisions.

Finding a middle course between total political control and total civil service employment depends on many factors. But, in determining who pays taxes and how they are collected, the ultimate goal must be to create an agency that is as fair to all citizens as is humanly possible.

A starting place in seeking the level of objectivity in the Internal Revenue Service that Judge Richey finds desirable might be to appoint the internal revenue commissioner for a seven-year term. This would carry him across at least one presidential term and, probably, beyond the tenure of his immediate political superior the secretary of the treasury.

This would leave the Internal Revenue Service with some political control, but reduce, even minimize, the chances for the White House, or other source, to create the "political atmosphere" Judge Richey finds deplorable.

SAXBE NOMINATION IS CONFIRMED; IMPEACHMENT INQUIRY PROGRESSES

There were these developments in the Watergate affair during late December:

■ The Senate voted 75–10 Dec. 17 to confirm one of its members, Sen. William B. Saxbe (R, Ohio), as attorney general. The opposition vote was generally based on constitutional grounds that prohibited a member of Congress from taking a post whose salary was increased by legislation while the member served in Congress. Congress sought to nullify this by passing a bill reverting the attorney general's salary from the $60,000 a year set when Saxbe was in the Senate to $35,000. The salary bill was approved in final form by the Senate Dec. 6 and House Dec. 7 and was signed by President Nixon Dec. 10. After signing it, the President formally submitted the Saxbe nomination to the Senate.

■ A bill giving the U.S. District Court for the District of Columbia jurisdiction over any civil suit filed by the Senate Watergate committee to enforce its subpoenas against the President became law Dec. 17 when President Nixon declined to either sign or veto it within 10 working days after final passage. The Senate had approved the bill by voice vote Nov. 9, and the House concurred Dec. 3, also by voice vote. The measure was a response to Judge John J. Sirica's Oct. 17 dismissal of the committee's suit on the ground that a statutory basis for jurisdiction was lacking.

■ William A. Dobrovir, an attorney for Ralph Nader in the milk fund lawsuit, admitted Dec. 18 that he had played a White House tape recording of a conversation between President Nixon and dairy industry leaders at a Washington cocktail party the night before. Dobrovir said he was "extremely sorry." The disclosure prompted federal District Court Judge William B. Jones Dec. 19 to order all subpoenaed documents sealed at the Justice Department's request.

■ Sen. Sam J. Ervin Jr. (D, N.C.), chairman of the Senate Watergate committee, announced Dec. 19 that he would not seek re-election at the end of his fourth term in 1974. Ervin, 77, said it was unreasonable to assume that his "natural force" would "stay unabated" through another six-year term.

■ Melvin R. Laird, who announced Dec. 19 his resignation as presidential counselor, effective Feb. 1, 1974, said he believed a vote on impeaching President Nixon "would be a healthy thing" in resolving the issue. He thought the House should take the vote by March 15, 1974 because of the Congressional elections later in the year.

■ House Judiciary Committee Chairman Peter Rodino (D, N.J.), after meeting with a bipartisan leadership group of his committee, announced Dec. 19 that the panel had agreed on an April target date for reporting to the House on its impeachment inquiry. Rodino Dec. 20 announced the selection of John M. Doar, 52, a Republican who was a member of the Johnson and Kennedy administrations in the Justice Department, as special counsel to the committee to head the impeachment probe.

■ Lawyers for the Senate Watergate committee Dec. 19 served subpoenas covering nearly 500 presidential tape recordings and documents. White House counsel accepted the subpoenas, but did not indicate whether Nixon would comply. The committee had unanimously approved the subpoenas Dec. 18.

Detroit Free Press
Detroit, Mich., November 24, 1973

"No senator or representative shall, during the time for which he was elected, be appointed to any civil office under the authority of the United States, which shall have been created, or the emoluments whereof shall have been increased during such time." (Article I, Section 6.2 of U.S. Constitution).

SINCE ITS ADOPTION in 1789, the U.S. Constitution has been amended 26 times by procedures clearly outlined within that document. It is a process which the Founding Fathers thoughtfully made both simple to understand and reasonably difficult to achieve.

Deliberate amendment has enabled the basic document to evolve in a manner which has served us well in the past.

The President requests that we now bypass that basic document and its amendment procedure so as to permit Sen. William Saxbe, R-Ohio, to serve as attorney general.

Mr. Nixon would have Congress pass a law rolling back the salary of the attorney general to $35,000 a year. That's where it was before Mr. Saxbe, during his current term, joined in the vote which raised the salary to $60,000 a year.

The Senate Judiciary Committee is understandably reserved on that request, and has sent the bill to the floor without recommendation. That step stresses the importance of the issue but permits the full Senate to resolve it.

The trouble is, the Constitution doesn't qualify its disqualification article.

This isn't the first time the nation has been asked to sacrifice the stability of the Constitution for the expediency of the moment. But usually when that has been done in the past, the nation has regretted the departure from founding principles.

The President's current request has some appeal. Mr. Saxbe has the qualities this nation could use right now in an attorney general. He has the knowledge and the political skills needed for the job. He can work with the President and with Congress. He has shown some ability to act independently from the President.

But the Saxbe selection already has caused a serious legal problem. Sen. William Proxmire argues that Acting Attorney General Robert H. Bork is serving illegally, since such interim appointments are good for only 30 days. The administration wants to "tough it out" on this one, too, but that will only increase opposition to the proposed legislation and to Mr. Saxbe if and when the nomination finally comes.

Mr. Nixon has played too long with this appointment and with the Constitution. It is time to accept the idea that Mr. Saxbe is a good man for the job but that the Constitution makes him ineligible. Mr. Nixon should be quick about finding an alternate selection for attorney general, a man with Mr. Saxbe's qualifications (and he is no unique political animal) but without the constitutional disqualifications.

Washington Star-News

Washington, D.C., November 27, 1973

It is clear that the framers of the Constitution intended only to prevent members of Congress from deliberately cashing in on their votes when they put in a restriction against senators and representatives serving in any federal civil office after having voted to raise the salary for that office.

It would seem, therefore, that legislation rolling back the salary for the office of attorney general would be sufficient to clear the way for confirmation of Senator Saxbe of Ohio to head the Department of Justice.

During the first year of Saxbe's Senate term, he voted in 1969 for legislation that raised the salary of cabinet officers from $35,000 to $60,000. According to those who question his nomination, that makes him ineligible to serve as attorney general because of a prohibition in Article 1, Section 6 of the Constitution, which says that no member of Congress shall be appointed to any civil office for which the "emolument . . . shall have been increased" during his term in the Congress.

The Nixon administration has proposed to clear the way for Saxbe's confirmation by cutting the attorney general's salary back to $35,000. But critics claim this is not enough to overcome the Constitutional barrier.

There is a precedent for this, however. It was done in 1909 so that Senator Philander Chase Knox could be confirmed as Secretary of State. In 1876, the Senate confirmed Senator Lot M. Morill as secretary of Treasury even though cabinet salaries were increased in 1873 while he was in the Senate. And Senator Hugo L. Black was named to the Supreme Court in 1937 although he had voted to increase the retirement benefits of Supreme Court justices, which certainly seems to fall into the "emolument" category.

In the present Watergate atmosphere, it is not unusual that nitpickers have been going over the Saxbe nomination looking for flaws and threatening to challenge the nomination in the courts if he is confirmed. It has become the style these days to question every move and motive of the Nixon administration.

It should be obvious to anyone that Saxbe did not vote for the pay increase for cabinet officers because he expected some day to become one. Given his strong criticism of several Nixon policies, it was a sure bet until Watergate came along that he would never be asked to serve in the cabinet. We believe that cutting the salary back to $35,000 while Saxbe serves as attorney general sufficiently cures whatever constitutional defect the nomination may have had.

ARKANSAS DEMOCRAT

Little Rock, Ark., December 3, 1973

It is regrettable that at a time of deep national distress when the very fabric of our government is being tested that the Congress should be called upon to circumvent the Constitution.

The matter involves the appointment of Sen. William B. Saxbe as attorney general. The problem is that while a senator, Saxbe voted to raise the salary of the attorney general and the Constitution clearly states that such action now prohibits him from serving in that office. To side-step this constitutional conflict-of-interest barrier, Congress has been asked to pass a special law lowering the attorney general's salary from the new $60,000 figure to $35,000, which was where it was when Saxbe cast his vote. On Wednesday, the Senate approved this legalistic maneuver, 75-16, and it appears that the House will do likewise. So Saxbe will take the post if the ruse is upheld by the Supreme Court, where opponents say it will land.

Sen. Robert Byrd, D-W.Va., is leading the fight against the measure by arguing that it is an underhanded way to amend the Constitution. "The constitutional provision against the appointment of Mr. Saxbe is complete, final, absolute and beyond remedy by legislation," Byrd said. We agree and are happy to note that both Arkansas senators, McClellan and Fulbright, concur. They voted against it.

The issue is not Saxbe himself. He Is qualified by training, experience and dedication for the job. Nor is the issue President Nixon, who nominated him. If the President is to be faulted at all, it is only for the reason that once again his aides have let him down by not checking-out Saxbe before Mr. Nixon sent his name to the Congress. This provision in the Constitution is not widely-known among the public, but you would think someone in the White House would be familiar with it.

No, the only issue is the Constitution and the cavalier zeal that some members of Congress display when it comes to tinkering with it. The Constitution is the supreme law of our land. As it is played with, ignored or twisted to fit any and all new situations, it is weakened and ceases to be the bulwark all of our laws must have. Law and order becomes farcial when the makers of laws pull end-runs around the foundation of all of our laws.

It should not be allowed to happen. The precedent could be too costly. The nation is full of other fine lawyers who could fill this post just as well as Saxbe and with no shadow hanging over him. The President should recognize this fact, and pull down his name and put forward another.

Chicago Tribune

Chicago, Ill., December 8, 1973

Now that Congress has managed to confirm Gerald Ford's nomination as Vice President [after nearly two months], maybe it can concentrate on Sen. William B. Saxbe's nomination as attorney general, which it has been bouncing around since Nov. 1.

There is a real problem with Mr. Saxbe, of course, in that the Constitution prohibits the appointment of a member of Congress to a federal job the pay of which was raised during his current term in Congress. The administration and its supporters seek to remedy this by passing a special bill reducing the attorney general's pay to $35,000, where it was before being raised to $60,000 in 1969. This was finally approved by Congress yesterday, clearing the way for the nomination to be made officially.

But Congress hasn't confined itself to legitimate obstacles. In the House, the Saxbe bill was amended so as to provide for a reform of congressional franking privileges [true, House rules provide that amendments must be germane — but what are rules for, after all, except to be broken?]. Sen. Gale McGee, the Wyoming Democrat who heads the Senate Civil Service Committee, waxed righteously indignant over this tomfoolery in the House—but his solution was a curious one. He said he would hold up Senate action on the Saxbe-franking privilege bill until the House acted on a bill of his own providing for voter registration by postcard.

Fortunately this impasse was settled and the Saxbe measure was disentangled from franking privileges. But in the meanwhile another Democrat, Sen. William Proxmire of Wisconsin, dipped his paddle in the puddle by suing to have Acting Atty. Gen. Bork thrown out on the ground that it is illegal for the cabinet post to be held in an acting capacity for more than 30 days.

So here we have Congress dilly-dallying over the Saxbe nomination and at the same time accusing Mr. Bork of holding office too long. It's as if a policeman were to rip off a man's clothing and then arrest him for indecent exposure.

It's high time to get this business settled. There is a real question whether reducing Mr. Saxbe's pay will meet the constitutional objection. Prof. Philip B. Kurland of the University of Chicago, a constitutional authority whose initials appropriately stand for Phi Beta Kappa, is among several experts who say that the pay-cut bill simply compounds the violation because it is special legislation for the benefit of a member of Congress—which is also illegal.

One sensible addition to the Saxbe bill therefore would provide for a judicial test of its legality as soon as possible. This is necessary in order to prevent lasting uncertainty as to the legality of actions taken by Mr. Saxbe in office. While the courts are at it, they should be asked to determine the legality of what Mr. Bork has done since Nov. 19, when his 30 days expired. These legal obstacles—inconvenient as they may be — must not simply be brushed aside like mosquitoes.

The Des Moines Register

Des Moines, Iowa, December 21, 1973

The U.S. Senate voted 75 to 10 to confirm Senator William Saxbe (Rep., Ohio) as attorney general. Saxbe is an undistinguished choice, and the Justice Department badly needs prestigious leadership, but the Senate followed the tradition of allowing the President broad latitude in selecting his Cabinet members.

The Senate's willingness to rubber stamp nominees for attorney general is one of the reasons the post has been held so often by politicians. Presidents have not hesitated to n a m e m e n such as J. Howard McGrath, Herbert Brownell, Robert Kennedy, John Mitchell a n d Richard Kleindienst, confident that they would be confirmed even though they had been deeply involved in partisan politics.

The dangers of a politicized Department of Justice have become blatantly obvious with Watergate, but the Senate still cannot bring itself to insist on non-political management — especially when the nominee comes from Senate ranks.

The unwillingness of the Senate to use its power of confirmation to safeguard the Justice Department makes it evident that if justice is to be insulated from politics, reform will have to be achieved by other means.

Senator Sam Ervin (Dem., N.C.) has advanced one possible method with the introduction of a bill calling for the Justice Department to be made into an independent agency of government.

The attorney general under the Ervin bill would not be a member of the President's Cabinet. He would be appointed by the President, subject to Senate confirmation, for a six-year term.

The attorney general, rather than the President, would name the assistant attorneys general, U.S. attorneys and the FBI director, and these officials would be answerable to the attorney general.

A drawback to the proposal is that anti-trust and other government legal policies would be made by officials who are not answerable even indirectly to voters at the polls.

It is more of a drawback, however, to have the administration of justice determined by political favoritism and payoffs in the form of campaign contributions. As Senator Ervin declared when he introduced his bill, "A cornerstone of our system of justice is the faith of the American people in that system and their belief in its fairness. Even the appearance of impropriety or unfairness undermines faith in that system.

"For this reason, Congress should now thoroughly review the duties and function of the Department of Justice and take action to ensure that it is independent of political influence. The Department of Justice should be insulated from the direct political control of the executive branch of government to preserve the independence essential to the proper administration of justice."

Even under the Ervin bill, the attorney general would be the President's choice. It still would be up to the Senate to insist on a man of probity, ability and independence. With a six-year term, he would be less subject to political replacement.

The Ervin proposal looks like a good compromise between total separation from the administration and total political subservience to it.

The TENNESSEAN

Nashville, Tenn., December 22, 1973

A BILL giving the Senate Watergate committee power to subpoena presidential tapes and documents related to the Watergate investigation has become law without the President's signature.

★ ★ ★

As a result the committee has voted to subpoena a large number of documents hitherto withheld from the committee's investigators. The tapes and documents the committee wants cover the President's meetings and conversations with an estimated 30 persons whose names have been linked to the Watergate scandal.

The new laws opens up the possibility that the public will receive deeper insight into the abuses of the nation's political process by members of the President's campaign organization than has heretofore been possible.

The committee has been hampered considerably in its investigation by the inability to obtain vital documents from the White House. The committee has received much first-hand testimony from witnesses such as Mr. John Dean, former presidential attorney, Mr. John Mitchell and Mr. Maurice Stans, former cabinet members and campaign leaders. But the testimony of these men needs to be checked against available documents to find out to the greatest extent possible who has been telling the truth and who has not been.

The committee has also received much second-hand or "hearsay" testimony which may either be verified or refuted by tapes and documents which may now be subpoenaed from the White House. The tapes and documents may also contain much new material which would throw light on matters the committee is empowered to investigate—such as the ITT case, political contributions to the Nixon campaign from the dairy industry and other matters pertinent to the 1972 campaign.

The committee has been hampered in its efforts to learn the facts by the President's refusal to hand over essential tapes and documents. Although the White House was required to surrender relevant Watergate material to the federal courts, Mr. Nixon continued to stand on executive privilege when similar material was sought by Congress. And federal district court ruled Oct. 17 that the committee lacked authority under existing law to subpoena the tapes and documents. So a bill authorizing the subpoena power was quickly introduced in Congress and was readily passed and sent to the White House.

Mr. Nixon strongly criticized the bill, and refused to sign it on grounds it would harm the American political system. But he didn't veto it, either, saying he recognized that "Congress and the public would place an interpretation upon a veto which would be entirely contrary to my reason for vetoing it."

★ ★ ★

Whatever his reason might have been, the President no doubt foresaw a certain overriding of his veto in Congress—and Mr. Nixon was not misinterpreting the effect this would have on his sagging political fortunes.

The Oregonian

Portland, Ore., December 23, 1973

The Democratic Congress, without a formal declaration of war, has launched a full-scale attack of unmitigated ferocity on the executive branch and its Republican head, Richard M. Nixon. If not stopped in the courts on constitutional grounds, a prolonged assault of this nature would leave the office of the presidency, whoever occupied it, a hollow shell, completely subservient to the legislative branch, a ribbon-cutting front for Congress which has no administrative skills of its own and has demonstrated its inability to govern.

This is not what the framers of the American Constitution sought when they created three separate and equal branches of government, each to perform its functions and to checkmate the others.

A federal judge, John Sirica, ruled last summer that the Senate's Watergate Committee chairmaned by Sen. Sam Ervin did not have statutory authority to subpoena voice recordings and other confidential documents of the President. Thereupon, Congress whipped through a law, which went into effect Monday, granting the courts jurisdiction to enforce such congressional subpoenas. The Ervin committee now has issued 60 pages of subpoenas demanding that the President deliver, by Jan. 4, 481 tapes and documents on a wide variety of subjects related, presumably, to the Select Committee's investigation of 1972 campaign practices.

This action constitutes exactly the massive fishing expedition President Nixon said he anticipated should the committees of Congress or the courts be given the right to so invade the administrative, diplomatic, security and military functions assigned to a president. In a somewhat comparable tour de force by subpoena by the Watergate special prosecutor, Judge Sirica ruled the other day, after listening to presidential tapes in chambers, that only small portions could be heard by a federal grand jury. Major portions included matters relating to security or other affairs having nothing to do with the Watergate investigation. Yet the Ervin committee seeks to obtain and audit 481 documents, willy-nilly, in its so far futile search for evidence that the President committed crimes in getting re-elected by a landslide of votes in 1972.

The statute under which the Ervin committee issued these subpoenas is only the beginning gun in Congress' war on the presidency. On Tuesday, the Senate rushed through without debate and on voice votes a packet of bills to give the Senate and the House and all its committees authority to establish procedures to abrogate a president's right to claim executive privilege—confidentiality—in resisting congressional demands for documents.

A White House attorney said of the Ervin committee's subpoenas that to comply "would almost shut down the executive branch," due to the mass of information sought. If the Senate's new package is adopted, the multiplicity and range of demands for executive papers from all the committees of Congress can only be imagined. The burden on the courts as the executive branch sought to protect its vital documents from such raids would be intolerable.

Congress has managed to function, despite its archaic rules, for almost 200 years without such powers of subpoena of executive documents. The present custodian of presidential powers has no valid choice except to fight the Ervin committee's guerrilla war through the Supreme Court and to veto any new legislation destructive of the presidency. The constitutional principle involved is far more important to the nation than any Watergate-related information which might be gleaned from the Ervin committee's massive assault on the White House.

The San Diego Union

San Diego, Calif., December 21, 1973

The Senate Watergate committee has decided to subpoena at least 200 tapes and documents from President Nixon just as a lawyer for the Ralph Nader organization offered a startling example of where a breach of executive confidentiality can lead.

William Dobrovir, who got a White House tape as evidence in a Nader-directed suit against the Administration, decided it would be "fun" to play it at a party. Then he had the effrontery to question the ethics of a network which reported this flagrant abuse of legal propriety.

Mr. Dobrovir entertained his guests with a casette copy of an original tape of a conversation in the President's office. Is anyone keeping track of what happens to sensitive tapes and documents after they are surrendered by the White House? It is depressing to consider what lies ahead if tapes by the dozen are turned over to the 80 lawyers and lesser sleuths and clerks on the staff of Sen. Ervin's committee.

President Nixon resisted parting with any of this material from his office files on grounds that confidentiality was essential to the conduct of affairs in the executive office. That very sound principle has been breached in the interests of helping grand juries and the courts get to the bottom of the Watergate case and related matters. If justice is the aim, the first step is to assure that this confidential material will be used for legitimate investigative work — and nothing more.

THE DAILY OKLAHOMAN

Oklahoma City, Okla., December 20, 1973

FOR many months, the controversy over the confidential nature of the White House tape recordings has raged unabated. Each time that a particular demand seemed to be satisfied — one way or another — a new demand has arisen. Now some of these records have been made available, on court orders, to either judges or opposing lawyers. And as many predicted, the recipients of some of them have already violated the terms under which they received them.

The most flagrant abuse of ethical standards was the playing of one tape at a Washington cocktail party by one of the lawyers to whom it had been entrusted. If the episode had taken place in any state with an active bar association standards committee, the perpetrator of this act would face disbarment proceedings promptly. Such is the climate of Washington, though, that his action will produce little more than sniggers from the delighted admirers who find the very existence of such records unethical.

The Washington "hate Nixon" crowd is large, and it dominates almost every federal agency and bureau. Some of its leaders have been promoted by the Nixon administration, perhaps in a vain effort to create a government of national unity. But many more have held on to their posts through one administration after another, drawing ever-higher pay but doing less and less useful work for the nation. They now have the time to play parlor politics in a big way, and devising daily ways to "get him out" has become the biggest parlor game in town.

The depth of the hatred these dedicated liberals feel for Nixon must be understood. It does not stem from what he has done, but from what they fear he might do. When they accuse him of reaching for enough power to change the very nature of our government, they are really saying that he might one day become powerful enough to weed the whole lot of them out of the federal bureaus. When they charge that he is not adequately concerned with the welfare of the people, they mean quite literally that he does not share their view of how that welfare is best served.

And when they insist that there be no men in any of the offices dealing with the energy crisis who have ever worked in the energy businesses of the nation, they are really demanding that only career federal bureaucrats be allowed to make the rules. After all, they reason, making regulations is a career, and they do not welcome outsiders who are rank amateurs at it. To such minds, the form of a regulation is more important than its effects.

But it was not a bureaucrat who committed the worst faux pas in the tapes affair. It was a lawyer associated with gadfly Ralph Nader, William Dobrovir, who amused party guests by playing a tape recording of a discussion in the Oval Office. This is an abuse of confidence which should surely not go unnoticed by the court which obtained and supplied the tape.

Meanwhile, the Watergate committee of the Senate has asked for a fresh supply of White House records, in which to fish for possible evidence of improprieties.

THE RICHMOND NEWS LEADER

Richmond, Va., December 20, 1973

So it has come to this:

A very low-grade human being by the name of William Dobrovir, who represents Ralph Nader in the milk fund case, played a tape recording of Oval Office conversations for guests attending a weekend cocktail party. Surely it is the desire of the William Dobrovirs of this nation to reduce the President to a quivering hulk of protoplasm. And those who are aghast at what Dobrovir has done, are left to wonder what it must be like to cultivate such detestation for one man.

For the William Dobrovirs, it is not enough simply to disagree with Richard Nixon. Rather, the President must be totally humiliated; he must be held up to the nation as a living mockery of the ideas he espouses. What Dobrovir did does not derive from abysmal stupidity. It derives from a cynicism intended to debilitate President Nixon. What better way to cripple a man's reputation than, in a liquored atmosphere, to play tape recordings of his privileged conversations? How they must have laughed! How they must have agreed that their President is hopelessly inane!

Dobrovir's deed provides yet another appalling example of the corrosion of decency throughout the land. In this particular instance Dobrovir has diminished still more the confidentiality and the dignity of the presidency of the United States. There was little point in recording all Oval Office conversations. It was a presidential mistake. When the existence of the tapes became public knowledge, through Alexander Butterfield's compelled disclosure before the Watergate Committee last summer, Mr. Nixon should have ordered the Secret Service to destroy every tape that it possessed. The loss to history would have been minimal. The gain to Mr. Nixon, to the presidency, and to the stability of the nation would have been vast.

Now it is too late for that. And we have such spectacles as William Dobrovir playing a tape for boozy guests, and the Watergate Committee subpoenaing 200 tapes. Next month, who knows? The Watergate Committee may decide it needs 2,000 tapes. Transcripts of tapes may begin appearing in newspapers and books; 33 rpm records of the tapes, perhaps narrated by Daniel Ellsberg or William Dobrovir or Ralph Nader, may be sold in record stores throughout the country. And the President, and the presidency, will be consequently reduced to near nothingness. Dobrovir's deed offers but the latest abject occasion for the nation to lament the lost idea of fair play.

The Miami Herald
Miami, Fla., December 22, 1973

THE CHOICE of an Eisenhower Republican to handle the business of impeachment for the House Judiciary Committee enhances the chances of a reasonable conclusion to this vital matter. John M. Doar is called a man of courage with a cool head. It will take plenty of both qualities in the months ahead to assure that the fate of Richard Nixon and the nation itself does not hang on party-line politics.

It seems to us that the nation cannot and will not accept a vote of impeachment under such circumstances.

President Nixon last year carried 49 of the 50 states, a considerable mandate to govern. We don't agree with George Meany of the AFL-CIO that "Mr. Nixon's mandate has been washed away. His presidency is no longer viable."

This is no banana republic. Presidents of the United States should not be dismissed from office or be told to resign because somebody out of the street feels a mandate has been washed away.

The Constitution says a President shall be removed from office on impeachment for, and conviction of, treason, bribery and other high crimes and misdemeanors. Mr. Meany saw no crime in Mr. Nixon's handling of the Asian war he had promised to end and no misdemeanor in the bombing of Cambodia without the approval of Congress.

There are others who think impeachment by the House and conviction by the Senate are justified by the bombing of Cambodia alone.

What we have, in the words of historian Arthur Schlesinger Jr., is a "long list of potential criminal charges against the Nixon administration" and the probability that men appointed to high position by the President had engaged in a multitude of indictable activities.

Sen. Howard Baker, the Tennessee Republican on the Watergate committee, thought it most important in the beginning to determine how much the President knew and when he knew it. Yet James Madison, who helped author the Constitution, thought it absolutely necessary "that the President should have the power of removing assistants from office; it will make him, in a peculiar manner, responsible for their conduct, and subject him to impeachment himself if he suffers them to perpetrate with impunity high crimes and misdemeanors against the United States, or neglects to superintend their conduct, so as to check their excesses."

It will have to be decided by Republicans as well as Democrats in the House whether Richard Nixon has raised sufficient doubt as to his conduct of his office to justify impeachment. Democrats alone cannot make that judgment.

HOUSTON CHRONICLE
Houston, Tex., December 16, 1973

We are cautiously hopeful that investigation of the Watergate and related scandal allegations may finally be settling down to a coherent and sensible situation where the true facts can be brought out in the proper forum and the guilty punished.

For months there has been an inordinate amount of running around in circles and loudmouthed jabbering from all quarters, none of which seemed to be getting to the point.

Now there appears to be some order coming out of the chaos. Special prosecutor Leon Jaworski says the White House has agreed to open up its secret files so his office can search them for documents relevant to all his investigations. In fact, he says the search has already begun.

The pace of the special prosecutor's work has stepped up since Jaworski took over. He asked for and got a third grand jury to consider Watergate matters and indicated all three would be kept working steadily. The White House has been cooperating with him in what Jaworski said is a gratifying manner.

Now this is more like things should have been all along. The traditional judicial agencies are handling criminal allegations in the traditional manner, before a grand jury and in the courts, and with the cooperation of the rest of the executive branch. These are time-tested procedures of institutions which the people understand and respect.

The Chronicle is pleased that President Nixon has apparently seen fit to open White House files to the special prosecutor's office. This type of action seems a necessity if there is to be a restoration of public confidence. We assume the White House is now willing to do this because an atmosphere of trust has been established now that Jaworski is heading the prosecutor's office. It is another obvious advantage to having a man of Jaworski's stature handling this serious matter.

With this type of situation emerging, it is plainly time for everyone to let the normal agencies for criminal investigation and prosecution—the Department of Justice through its special prosecutor's office—proceed unhindered to uncover all the facts and initiate punishment for those who have committed crimes.

The nation finally appears to be on the right track in the Watergate probes and we would hope that the self-serving politicians will tone down their propagandizing and let the course of justice run.

BUFFALO EVENING NEWS
Buffalo, N.Y., December 18, 1973

"The President . . . shall be removed from office on impeachment for, and conviction of, treason, bribery, or other high crimes and misdemeanors."
—U. S. Constitution, Art. II, Sec. 4.

By our reading of the Constitution's impeachment clause, there is no way a President of the United States can legitimately be impeached for anything less than criminal misconduct of a serious nature. Thus far, in all of the investigating of the Watergate scandal and related matters, we have seen no proof of such serious misconduct by the President himself as would justify an impeachment. Until or unless we do see such evidence, we will not be among those advocating it.

The House Judiciary Committee, however, has been charged with the responsibility of considering whether impeachment charges should be brought, and after a good deal of hemming and hawing, it is beginning to consider how to proceed. We think it is high time—not only for it to get its inquiry in motion, but to set itself a reasonably expeditious deadline to complete its work and make a concrete recommendation, one way or the other, to the House.

Among the urgent matters on which the committee and its chairman, Rep. Peter W. Rodino, Jr. (D., N. J.) are still apparently undecided are: (1) selection of a special counsel and an advisory group of constitutional scholars; (2) the composition of a small and workable subcommittee to conduct an actual impeachment inquiry; (3) what kind of timetable, if any, can be agreed upon to reach a final committee judgment; and (4) whether all investigating sessions should be conducted in secret, as a grand jury would conduct an investigation of ordinary criminal charges.

Our own view on all these matters is governed by the belief that an impeachment is in fact closely analagous to an indictment, and that any pre-impeachment proceeding in the House should be conducted as much like a grand jury proceeding as circumstances permit. That is, the committee having that responsibility should take its evidence secretly, inquire as expeditiously and as thoroughly as possible into all aspects of the case, and then bring out either a definite "bill of impeachment" or the equivalent of an exonerating "no bill."

The matter is far too serious for Congress to permit, or the public to tolerate, any needless filibustering. Obviously, no impeachment case growing out of the various Watergate-related investigations can be brought to a head immediately, with so many loose ends still dangling. But very soon, now, the Senate's Ervin Committee should be bringing in its report, Federal Judge John Sirica presumably will have made his own findings as to the White House tapes, the two Watergate grand juries will be nearing completion of their work, will be nearing completion of their work the data concerning the President's finances will have been combed by congressional tax experts, and various other documents relating to the "plumbers," the ITT, milk price supports and other issues will have been made available.

It will then be squarely up to the Rodino Committee to sift through all this mass of data, to seek out whatever other evidence it thinks it needs, and conclude that it either does or does not have grounds for going any further with an impeachment action. Barring any startling new developments along the way, it should certainly be able to reach such a conclusion by no later than mid-spring. And the public, we think, will grow rightly impatient with any disposition to let the matter drift inconclusively any longer than that.

THE PLAIN DEALER
Cleveland, Ohio, December 21, 1973

Melvin R. Laird, the departing White House domestic adviser, and Vice President Gerald R. Ford want the House of Representatives to vote on impeaching President Nixon by Mar. 15 or so.

We agree with them, although not necessarily for the same reasons that motivate the two Republican leaders.

Both Laird and Ford served many terms in the House and regard themselves as good vote counters. They are convinced that if the question of impeaching the President comes to a vote fairly soon, it will fail. Then the GOP would be able to claim Nixon has been "vindicated" or "absolved of charges and the party might avert disaster in the 1974 elections.

Our reason for favoring a prompt vote has less to do with partisan politics than with the good of the country. With impeachment proceedings hanging over his head, the President, the White House and the executive branch of Government are near-paralyzed and unable to give the nation the leadership it needs.

Better to bring the impeachment matter to a head and get it over with one way or the other.

So far the House Judiciary Committee, which is to report whether or not there are grounds for impeachment, has been proceeding with the slowness of a congressman reaching for a luncheon check.

Thursday, however, the committee appointed John M. Doar, a liberal Republican and former assistant attorney general, as general counsel for its impeachment inquiry. Thus there is hope that the Democratic-controlled committee will get moving.

Some Democrats are suspected of not wanting the committee to resolve the question of Nixon's fitness to remain in office They would prefer to keep him as a weakened, suspect president so their party could score huge gains in 1974 and 1976.

That would be grossly unfair to the country, which is entitled to an effective president, whether it be Nixon or his successor. Nor would it be good politics, for the public would certainly see through any such shabby scheme.

The Detroit News
Detroit, Mich., December 23, 1973

If President Nixon does not intend to resign, impeachment remains the next best device for clearing away the suspicion and mistrust that surround the President and prevent him from functioning as an effective national leader.

Despite their unrelenting attacks on the President, however, many Democratic politicians in Congress are secretly glad to see Watergate remain an unresolved and continuing issue. Far from wanting to clear the air, they would just as soon have a scandal-ridden Nixon administration to kick around until 1976.

This helps explain why a Congress controlled by Democrats keeps talking about the possibility of impeachment but barely inches along in its deliberations on that topic. The Democrats don't want to destroy the issue on which they pin their hopes for congressional victories in 1974 and for conquest of the presidency two years after that.

Such an attitude rivals Watergate in its cynicism and could create a backlash of public opinion. Americans don't regard Watergate as some kind of political game between the two major parties but as a tragedy shared equally by the entire population.

Therefore, congressional Democrats should heed the warning of Republican Sen. Barry Goldwater, a severe Nixon critic who remarked with characteristic bluntness and cogency in an interview published in Boston this week: "I think it's incumbent on the Democratic leadership of the House to get off its tail end and move on this (impeachment inquiry). We have a nation of 210 million people who need leadership and need it badly."

Assuming that President Nixon will not resign and let Vice-President Ford take over, Americans can't get—at least, not until the 1976 elections—the kind of leadership they need and deserve unless Congress removes or lets fall the sword now hanging over President Nixon's head. Three years is too long to wait for a resolution of this crisis of leadership.

Congress should face up to its responsibility—now.

The Cleveland Press
Cleveland, Ohio, December 22, 1973

We disagree with departing White House counselor Melvin R. Laird's recommendation that the House of Representatives set a March deadline for a vote on the impeachment of President Nixon.

Though impeachment has been hotly discussed for many months, the House Judiciary Committee began its inquiry only in the most tentative way in late October. Hearings on the nomination of Vice President Gerald R. Ford have taken up much of the committee's time and attention since.

It was not until yesterday that the committee named its chief counsel for the impeachment inquiry.

Naturally Laird is urging what would be most beneficial to the White House. Understandably the President and his staff would like to know when they can stop holding their breath.

Rep. Peter W. Rodino, D-N.J., judiciary committee chairman, already has set a goal of April for the committee to report to the House. A goal is a more flexible proposition than a deadline and more suitable to this kind of developing study. Nevertheless, it is evidence that Rodino and committee members do not intend to let the impeachment inquiry drag on interminably. We believe that the committee should be counted on to act expeditiously, but on its own timetable.

Oakland Tribune
Oakland, Calif., December 26, 1973

Now that the House Judiciary Committee has at last hired the special counsel (Republican John Doar) to direct the impeachment investigation of President Nixon, there is cause to believe work will begin in earnest on this most momentous project. Certainly there has been more than enough delay.

Whether or not one agrees the House should make a formal, full-scale investigation of the impeachment question, the issue was joined when the Judiciary Committee undertook to make the study at the direction of the full House membership. But that was nearly two months ago (Oct. 24), and precious little has happened since.

Thus as time drags on, the question of presidential culpability remains in limbo, with the public genuinely confused as to what really may be the merits of the case against Mr. Nixon.

If the President did indeed commit "high crimes and misdemeanors" of a nature to cause the House of Representatives to bring a bill of impeachment and his trial by the U.S. Senate, then the public is entitled to have such accusations resolved without undue delay.

To keep the issue churning about in the public prints and on the airwaves without final determination certainly is not conducive to effective government, and the erosion of the President's leadership base has been increasingly evident as the days, weeks and months roll by without any concerted committee effort to move ahead with the investigation.

Mel Laird, himself a former congressman, was telling it like it truly is when, during announcement of his resignation as Mr. Nixon's chief domestic counsellor, he urged speedy House action on the impeachment resolution.

Noting that the continuing controversy over Watergate and other issues is hurting America's foreign and domestic policies, he suggested that "there's no reason why they can't pass judgment in the next 60 days."

Any committee delay appreciably beyond that date will surely give substance to suspicions, so far largely dormant, that the impeachment business is truly a narrow partisan political matter.

Republicans like Laird (indeed, even Vice President Ford voted in favor of the investigation when he was still a member of the House) want specific action, a yea or a nay, however uncomfortable may prove to be the ultimate route to a vote as all manner of misbehavior is publicly alleged against the President.

So if there are delays beyond the logical, 60-day deadline Laird offered, we can only conclude that the Democratic leadership is more interested in gaining some partisan political advantage over their GOP opposites than in firmly resolving one of the most historically important questions ever to confront the United States Congress.

Index

This index includes references both to the news digest and the editorial section. Those index entries printed in a roman typeface refer to the news digest. They: (1) Describe the event; (2) Note the date of the event, e.g. 10-10; (3) Indicate the page, the marginal letter parallel to the item on the page, and the column in which the item appears in that order, e.g. 80B1. Index entries referring to editorials are printed in *italic type* after the news digest entries under the **boldface alphabetical headings**. Editorial entries refer only to the page number.

FREIDIN, Seymour K.
Chotiner confirms hiring 8-28, 70A2
FULBRIGHT, Sen. J. William (D, Ark.)
Wiretapping report given 9-10, 46F2

G

GAGE, Nicholas
Subpoena issued 10-5, 81E1
GAGLIARDI, Judge Lee P.
Mitchell, Stans dismissal plea rejected 8-15, 30E3
Mitchell, Stans win trial delay 9-11, 32E3
Quashes tapes subpoena 10-18, 111G2
Mitchell-Stans trial delayed 10-23, 111C2
To get tape 12-6, 120E1
GALLUP Poll
Nixon popularity down 7-22, 36G1
Nixon popularity down to 31% 8-15, 37G3
Nixon popularity rises after speech 8-21 43D1
Agnew rating drops 8-29, 76F2
On Watergate committee investigation 9-2, 66C2
On Nixon & tapes 9-23, 95C2
Nixon rating dips 10-4, 95G1
Nixon rating down 11-3, 106C1
On Nixon 11-10, 12, 127C2
On Nixon resignation 12-16, 136D2
GARDNER, John W.
GOP Finance Committee to disclose funds 7-24, 28B3
GARMENT, Leonard
Nixon claims privilege on milk fund data 7-11, 27E1
Moore testifies 7-12, 16G3
Tape erasure disclosed 11-21, 131A3
Tape gap still puzzle 11-28, 133E2
GAUDREAU, Paul
Agnew office urged contract awards 10-10, 83G1
GEMMELL, Kenneth
Audit on Nixon homes issued 8-27, 31E3
GENEEN, Harold
Named in ITT memo 8-1, 62D2
GENERAL Accounting Office (GAO)
Dairy contribution memo revealed 6-27, 33F2
Md GOP violations charged 7-13, 28B1
Cites campaign violation 7-28, 29A1
Haldeman testifies 7-30, 58G2
McGovern unit cited 10-17, 110C2
Details 1972 campaign spending 8-23, 31D2
Nixon re-election committee reports 9-10, 32D3
Cites Wallace, Humphrey campaigns 10-30, 113E3
Chisholm fund violations alleged 11-16, 117A1
SBA probed 12-4, 118E1
Violations alleged 12-11, 123D3
Rpts Agnew office costs 12-17, 84C3
Rpts on Nixon homes 12-18, 123G1
GENERAL Motors Corp.
GOP gift pressure rptd 7-13, 27C3
GENERAL Services Administration (GSA)
$1.9 spent on Nixon homes 6-21, 25F1
House probe of Nixon homes spending ordered 7-12, 25G3
Eisenhower tapes revealed 7-17, 20D1

$10 million spent on Nixon homes 8-6, 29E2
Nixon discusses homes spending 10-3, 41D3
Agnew office urged contract awards 10-10, 83F1
U.S. costs at Nixon homes probed 10-11, 109G1
Concedes political hiring 11-24, 133B1
Nixon discloses finances 12-8, 120G3
GAO rpts on Nixon homes 12-18, 123E2
Admits spending $1.7 million on Nixon homes—150-152
GERRITY, Ned
Named in ITT 8-1, 62D2
GESELL, Judge Gerhard A.
Segretti pleads guilty 10-1, 71F2
Segretti given 6 months 11-5, 72E2
Jaworski granted access to documents 11-14, 72E3
Cox firing ruled illegal 11-14, 128F1
Krogh pleads guilty 11-30, 73C2
Rule Cox firing illegal—252
GIBBONS, Rep. Sam M. (D, Fla.)
Segretti cooperating with Cox 9-17, 70G3
GLANZER, Seymour
Kleindienst testifies 8-7, 65A1
GLEASON, Jack A.
Weicker concedes White House aid 7-11, 27B2
Named in Colson memo 8-1, 62F3
GOLDBERG, Lucianne C.
McGovern camp spy unmasked 8-18, 70F1
Chotiner confirms story 8-28, 70A2
GOLDWATER, Sen. Barry M. (R, Ariz.)
Reaction to secret recordings 7-16, 19D3
Reacts to Nixon speech 8-15, 39D3
Urges Watergate resolution 9-11–13, 87D3
Denies Agnew resignation story 9-18, 76F3
Named Agnew fund trustee 9-28, 79E3
On Agnew resignation 10-10, 82F2
Two tapes 'nonexistent' 11-1, 103A1
Opposes Nixon resignation 11-5, 106G3
On Nixon 11-14, 127F1
GONZALEZ, Virgilio R.
Ulasewicz testifies 7-18, 50D2
Seeks plea change 9-14, 71B1
Sirica rules out maximum sentences 10-1, 71C2
Refused bail 10-16, 72A1
Sentenced 11-9, 72B3
GOODELL, Charles
W.H. campaign vs Senate critics rptd 11-7, 108A3
GOODYEAR Tire & Rubber Co.
Campaign contribution disclosed 8-10, 30B1
Cox files charges 10-17, 109D3
DeYoung testifies 11-15, 116C3
GRAHAM, Rev. Billy
Haldeman testifies 8-1, 60F3
Criticizes Nixon 12-22, 135A3
GRAHAM, Fred. P.
On alleged Peterson remark 10-1, 79C2
Subpoena issued 10-5, 81F1
GRAHAM, Katharine
White House plan rptd 11-5, 104E2
GRAY 3rd, L. Patrick
Moore testifies 7-12, 17D1
Ehrlichman testifies 7-25, 54E3

Haldeman testifies 7-30–8-1, 58E1–61
Helms testifies 8-2, 63C1
Testifies 8-2, 63G2
Walters testifies 8-3, 63G3
Nixon releases Watergate statement 8-15, 39B2
Nixon discusses 8-22, 43G3
Dean pleads guilty 10-19, 71G3
CIA duped 10-30, 72D1
New ITT inquiry sought 10-31, 114C2
MacGregor testifies 11-1, 94C1
Testifies before Ervin committee—172
GREEN, Allen
Agnew resigns 10-10, 80E3
GRIFFIN, Sen. Robert (R, Mich.)
Named top campaign spender 9-13, 33D1
New special prosecutor urged 10-24, 99B3
On Nixon news conference 10-26, 101G2
GRINNELL Corp.
Nixon role in ITT case disclosed 12-29, 112E2
GRISWOLD, Erwin N.
Named in Colson memo 8-1, 61E3
Nixon role in ITT case disclosed 12-29, 112G1
GROOT, Jim
Gurney concedes wrongdoing 12-6, 119C3
GULF Oil Corp.
Campaign contribution disclosed 8-10, 30B1
Fined for gift 11-13, 116C1
Wild testifies 11-14, 116G2
GULF & Western Industries Inc.
Approached for GOP gift 8-1, 30G1
GURNEY, Sen. Edward J. (R, Fla.)
Contribution rptd 7-2, 27D2
Reacts to Nixon move 7-8, 11C3
Questions Moore 7-12, 17G2
Interrogates Butterfield 7-16, 18A3
Interrogates Ehrlichman 7-25, 54B3
Haldeman testifies 7-31, 60A1
Reacts to Nixon speech 8-15, 40A1
Hunt testifies 9-24, 67E1
Segretti aides testify 10-4, 92G2
New special prosecutor urged 10-25, 99A3
Nixon role in ITT case disclosed 12-29, 113F1
U.S. probing finances 10-31, 113G3
Dissents on resolution 11-13, 126G1
Bellino cleared 11-27, 118C2
Concedes wrongdoing 12-6, 119B3
Watergate committee role viewed—161
Belittles campaign mischief—220

H

HAAG, John
GOP aided party 7-1, 69F3
HAIG Jr., Gen. Alexander M.
Nixon & Watergate 7-31, 36G3
Haldeman testifies 8-1, 61G2
Agnew meets 8-7, 74G2
Nixon meets Ervin, Baker 10-19, 97C1
Ordered FBI to seal Cox' offices 10-23, 97D2
Nixon reverses on tapes 10-23, 99G1
Jaworski independence affirmed 11-5, 107B2
Nixon Cox irritation cited 11-6, 107G2
Nixon won't resign 11-7, 105G2
Cox disputes Nixon 11-17, 130G2

Tape erasure disclosed 11-21, 131B3
Testifies 12-5, 133G3
Offers 'devil theory' on missing tapes—266
HALDEMAN, H. R.
$1.9 million spent on Nixon homes 6-27, 25G2
Dairy contribution memo revealed 6-27, 33E2
Mitchell testifies 7-10-12, 12B1–16
Moore testifies 7-12, 17B1
Nixon cooperation urged 7-15, 48D1
Butterfield testifies 7-16, 17E3
Kalmbach testifies 7-16, 48G2–50E1
Strachan testifies 7-20, 23, 51D2–52F1
Nixon limits aides' testimony 7-21, 57E1
Ehrlichman testifies 7-24–30, 52A3–57D2
Testifies 7-30–8-1, 57D2–61A3
White House firm on tapes 7-31, 22D1
Probes ordered 8-1, 36D3
Named in Colson memo 8-1, 61E3
Helms testifies 8-2, 63B1
Walters testifies 8-2, 63F2
Petersen testifies 8-7, 65C3
Ervin panel sues for tapes 8-9, 22D3
Nixon speaks on Watergate 8-15, 42B2
Nixon discusses tapes session 8-22, 24C2
Nixon discusses 8-22, 43G2, 44A3
Mitchell story rptd 8-25, 33E1
Amends testimony 8-28, 66G1
Amends testimony re tapes 8-28, 85C1
Memo released 9-26, 91A1
Nixon campaign figures revealed 9-28, 34A2
Mankiewicz testifies 10-11, 93G3
Subpoenaed tapes listed 10-19, 95E3
Milk fund case widens 10-23, 111C1
CIA duped 10-30, 72F1
Anti-media plans revealed 10-31, 102G1
White House compiles press 'sins' 11-5, 104E2
Campaign vs Senate critics rpts 11-7, 107G3
Kalmbach got $ in '69 11-7, 123B3
Continued confusion on tapes 11-8, 105G1
Nixon comments 11-17, 129G3
Tape erasure disclosed 11-21, 131A2
Tape gap still puzzle 11-28, 133D2
Chapin indicted 11-29, 73D1
Chapin pleads innocent 12-7, 73C3
Experts rebut W. H. on tape gap 12-13, 123F3
Testifies before Ervin panel—168, 170, 172, 173
HALL, Gus
GAO details 1972 campaign spending 8-23, 31F2
HALPERIN, Morton H.
Suit affidavit released 11-27, 133F1
HAMILTON, Alexander
Precedent cited 9-25, 77G3
HAMILTON, James
Interrogates Mardian 7-19, 50G3
HAMMER, Armand
GOP gift listed 9-28, 34F2
HAMMERMAN 2d, I. H.
Agnew resigns 10-10, 80D3
Agnew obstruction rptd 11-2, 84F2

Chronology

Sept. 4, 1971: Hunt and Liddy burglarize Ellsberg's psychiatrist's office.

*Jan. 27, 1972: Dean, Liddy and Magruder meet with Mitchell at Justice Department, Liddy presents plan for electronic surveillance, mugging squads, kidnaping teams and prostitutes to compromise the opposition at a cost of $1 million.

*Feb. 4, 1972: Same participants meet to discuss electronic surveillance of DNC headquarters.

*March 30, 1972: Mitchell, Magruder, Liddy and LaRue meet at Key Biscayne. Mitchell allegedly approves $250,000 plan including entry into DNC offices.

*May 27, 1972: First break-in at DNC headquarters.

June 17, 1972: Democratic headquarters raided; 5 arrested.

*June 19, 1972: Dean speaks with Colson and Ehrlichman; decision made for Dean to take custody of contents of Hunt's safe. Strachan tells Dean Haldeman instructed him to "remove and destroy damaging materials" from files.

June 20, 1972: Nixon, Haldeman and Ehrlichman discuss Watergate public relations offensive. Tape of meeting later subpoenaed and turned over to Sirica, but with an 18-minute gap. Later, Nixon and Mitchell discuss Watergate in telephone conversation. Recording later subpoenaed, but White House claims tape never existed.

*June 21, 1972: Dean meets with Gray regarding FBI's Watergate investigation.

June 22, 1972: Nixon denies White House involvement.

*June 23, 1972: Haldeman, Ehrlichman, CIA Director Helms and Deputy Director Walters meet. Walters later warns Gray that CIA operations in Mexico might be jeopardized by FBI investigators.

*June 26 & 28, 1972: Dean meets Walters to request CIA money for Watergate conspirators.

*June 28, 1972: Dean meets Mitchell about need for support money to obtain defendants' silence.

*June 28, 1972: Hunt files handed to Gray at White House meeting with Ehrlichman and Dean present; Dean describes papers as "political dynamite."

*June 29, 1972: Stans meets with Kalmbach on raising and distributing money to Watergate defendants.

June 30, 1972: Nixon, Haldeman and Mitchell meet to discuss Watergate. Tape of conversation subpoenaed and surrendered to Sirica.

July 1, 1972: Mitchell resigns as campaign manager.

*July 3, 1972: Gray destroys Hunt files.

July 6, 1972: Gray expresses concern to Nixon on White House interference with Watergate probe.

July 31, 1972: Washington Post reports campaign contribution was deposited in Barker account.

Sept. 15, 1972: Nixon, Dean and Haldeman meet. Nixon compliments Dean on doing a "good job" on Watergate case. Tape subpoenaed and turned over to Sirica.

Sept. 19, 1972: Seven men plead not guilty; released on bond.

Oct. 10, 1972: Washington Post reports break-up part of larger spying and sabotage effort against Democrats.

Oct. 23, 1972: Time magazine report links GOP spying by Segretti to White House.

Jan. 11, 1973: Hunt pleads guilty to all six charges against him; freed on bail. Justice Department charges Finance Committee of CRP with 8 criminal violations of election-financing law.

Jan. 15, 1973: Four Watergate defendants plead guilty; deny pressure from "higher-ups."

Jan. 22, 1973: Hugh Sloan discloses espionage funds paid to Liddy approved by Mitchell and Stans.

Jan. 30, 1973: Liddy, McCord convicted.

Feb. 7, 1973: Senate votes to establish committee to probe Watergate bugging and other espionage.

*Feb. 14, 1973: Colson warns President he must force Mitchell to admit role in Watergate planning.

Feb. 27, 1973: Nixon-Dean meeting; Nixon tells Dean to report directly to him on all Watergate matters.

March 13, 1973: Dean, Haldeman and Nixon meet and, according to Dean's testimony, discuss the possibility of payoffs to Watergate defendants. Tape of meeting later subpoenaed and eventually turned over to Sirica.

March 21, 1973: Dean meets with Nixon and, he later testified, tells him case may break open and that he would tell the truth to grand jury. Haldeman participates in part of the meeting. Later, Nixon meets with Haldeman, Ehrlichman, Ziegler and Dean, allegedly to discuss possibility of White House aides testifying before the grand jury. Tapes of both meetings later subpoenaed and turned over to Sirica.

March 22, 1973: Nixon meets with Haldeman, Ehrlichman, Mitchell and Dean to discuss, according to Dean's testimony, strategy to deal with Ervin committee. Tape subpoenaed and surrendered to Sirica.

March 23, 1973: Provisional sentences handed down on 5 defendants. McCord meets counsel to Ervin panel.

March 26, 1973: McCord asks for private meeting with Judge Sirica in letter. Los Angeles Times reports that McCord had implicated Dean and Magruder. Watergate grand jury reconvenes.

*March 28 or 29, 1973: Dean returns to D.C. Egil Krogh tells Dean Nixon personally ordered Ellsberg burglary.

March 30, 1973: Ziegler states no White House involvement in Watergate "event."

April 5, 1973: Nixon withdraws Gray nomination.

April 6, 1973: Dean secretly meets with federal Watergate prosecutors with information concerning the raid and subsequent developments.

April 5–7, 1973: Ellsberg trial Judge William M. Byrne offered government position by Ehrlichman.

April 15, 1973: Federal investigators learn of break-in at Ellsberg's psychiatrist's office. *Gray tells Ehrlichman he destroyed "politically sensitive" documents found in Hunt's safe. Dean meets with Nixon who, Dean later testified, said he had been joking when he discussed payoffs. Tape of meeting subpoenaed, but White House later claimed it never existed because of a mechanical malfunction.

April 17, 1973: Nixon announces "major developments" from a "new inquiry" on Watergate; agrees to testimony by his aides with conditions. Ziegler declares "inoperative" previous statements on Watergate.

April 19, 1973: John Dean warns he would "not become a scapegoat in the Watergate case." Kleindienst removes himself from Watergate case.

April 30, 1973: Haldeman, Ehrlichman, Kleindienst and Dean resign. Nixon accepts responsibility, denies involvement in cover-up. Attorney General Richardson given "absolute authority" on Watergate prosecutions. Strachan's resignation from USIA post announced.

May 2, 1973: White House aide David Young resigns; Egil Krogh Jr. takes leave of absence from undersecretary of transportation post. Hunt discloses CIA involved in break-in at Ellsberg's psychiatrist's office.

May 9, 1973: FBI wire-tap on Ellsberg revealed. New York Times reports McCord was pressured to blame CIA on Watergate break-in. Krogh resigns.

May 10, 1973: Nixon announces major staff reorganization. Dean charges effort to curb truth. Mitchell, Stans, 2 others indicted in Vesco case.

May 11, 1973: Charges against Ellsberg, Russo dismissed.

May 17, 1973: Senate Select Committee on Presidential Campaign Activities begins hearings.

May 18, 1973: Richardson appoints Archibald Cox special prosecutor for Watergate case.

May 22, 1973: Nixon explains White House role; concedes probable involvement of close aides in cover-up.

* Asterisks indicate that the event was alleged in testimony and may or may not be true.